T3-BNO-382

THE ENCYCLOPEDIA OF JEWISH INSTITUTIONS

UNITED STATES & CANADA

THE ENCYCLOPEDIA OF JEWISH INSTITUTIONS

UNITED STATES & CANADA

Edited by

ODED ROSEN

MOSADOT PUBLICATIONS, INC.

Ref
E
184
.J5
E53
1983

Published by Mosadot Publications, Inc.
6 Ben Zion Blvd, Tel Aviv 64285, Israel
Israel Mailing Address: P.O. Box 4435, Tel Aviv 61043, Israel
U.S. Mailing Address: 45 John St, Room 908, NYC, NY 10038
Telex: 341118 BXTV IL, Ext 1235

Copyright © 1983 by Mosadot Publications, Inc.

All rights, including translation into other languages, reserved. Reproduction of this book, in whole or in part, without written permission of the publisher is prohibited, except for brief passages or quotations embodied in reviews, magazine or newspaper articles.

Mosadot takes the utmost care in proofing & editing. Errors in publication, while rare, may occur. Such errors will be corrected in future editions. However, Mosadot Publications does not assume any liability to any party for any loss or damage caused by errors or omissions.

Published in Israel.

ISBN 0 913185 00 0

Contents

Preface

The first edition of The Encyclopedia of Jewish Institutions of the United States and Canada is published to fill the growing need for a readily available source of information. In compiling this Encyclopedia it has been our intention to appeal to those who want to find, with the least possible delay, vital and various information about Jewish institutions.

This book serves as a standard reference guide to: Synagogues, Congregations, Temples, Community Centers, Schools, Colleges, Universities, Women's Organizations, Service Agencies, National Organizations, Lodges, Fraternal Associations, Museums, Libraries, Hospitals, Nursing Homes & Senior Citizen Residences, among others, throughout the United States and Canada. Entries contain appropriate information on the institution's affiliations, accreditations, goals, services, activities, programs, members, employees, history, publications, facilities, achievements, names of current officers and staff, full address and telephone number.

In a number of cases, due to a lack of information supplied by the institutions or organizations, it has not been possible to include as much data as we would have preferred. However, the names, addresses and telephone numbers of all institutions lacking full data are included as a reference aid. We expect that fuller information will be included in the second edition which is already in the planning stage.

Arranged geographically, the entries are alphabetized by state or province, then by the local community and by name of institution. The sample entry, which follows this preface, illustrates the types of information included. On the following page is a list of abbreviations. Also included in this volume is an index listing all the institutions in alphabetical order.

An enormous amount of time and effort has been invested in this publication. All the information in this edition was supplied to us by the institutions. Needless to say, the length of each entry is by no means any indication of the relative importance or size of the institution. Every effort has been made to make this edition as up-to-date as possible. It is our hope that this book will also serve as a useful tool to the many who wish to know and learn about the North American Jewish Community.

The editor would like to thank the many people who contributed to this work, and to give special thanks to Jill Anolik and Aliza Kopman for their assistance in the preparation of this edition.

In a continuing effort to improve this encyclopedia and to insure that all information is current, we invite your comments, suggestions for improvement, and names and addresses of additional institutions, as well as information on omissions and errors. These should be addressed to: Editor, Mosadot Publications, Inc., 45 John St., Room 908, New York City, NY 10038 United States.

Mailing lists of Jewish institutions, including not only those in the encyclopedia, but also those stored on the database, are available. Requests should be directed to the above address.

The editor appreciates the cooperation of all those individuals who have provided information.

ODED ROSEN, Editor.

Sample Entry

[1] **Yeshiva of Flatbush Joel Braverman High School & Elementary School.**[2] A private rel day sch. [3] To dev in its stu a positive attitude to J values & an identification with the Torah way of life; to imbue its stu with a love for the Torah, the J people & the land of Is; to train stu in the highest standards of secular studies in order for the stu to function successfully in Am soc. [4] Secular & J studies with all Judaic content courses taught in Heb; Mishmar prog; advanced placement courses; seminars; stu govt org; sports; art; sewing; music; dance; eurythmics; choir; marching band. [5] Over 2,200 stu fr nursery through 12th grade; over 800 stu in the HS div & 1,400 stu in the elementary div. [6] 120 faculty mems in the elementary sch. [7] The elementary sch was est in 1927. The sch's F conceived and executed a new concept of total edu: a mixture of J heritage, modern Heb language & culture, & the gen culture of Western civilization to produce a modern Torah true J. In 1950 the HS was est. [8] Pub Kol Hatalmid – a literary journal in Heb; Pegasus – a literary journal in English; Phoenix – the sch newspaper. [9] HS facilites in the Joel Braverman Bldg, a fully air-conditioned four story structure above ground & three levels underground, include a swimming pool, gymnasium, auditorium with seating for 700, Beth Hamedrash, four sci labs, two demonstration rms, library with over 21,000 vols.[10] Pres Bd of Trustees: Allen Bodner; Adm: G. Eisenberg; Prin Gen Studies: Dr Abraham Zamichow; HS Prin: Rabbi David Eliach; Head Elementary Sch: Yeshayahu Ephraim Greenfeld.[11]**1609 Ave J, Bklyn NY 11230**[12] **(212) 377-4466.**

Key

[1] Name in full
[2] Classification/Definition
[3] Goal
[4] Services/Activities/Programs
[5] Members
[6] Employees/Volunteers
[7] History
[8] Publications
[9] Facilities/Achievements/Special Characteristics
[10] Titles/Positions – Names
[11] Address
[12] Phone Number

Key to Abbreviations

AB — Alberta
Add — Address
ADL — Anti-Defamation League
Adm(s) — Administration(s), Administrator(s)
Adv(s) — Advisor(s), Advisory
Agy — Agency, Agencies
AJL — Association of Jewish Libraries
AK — Alaska
AL — Alabama
Am — America, American, Americans
Apr — April
Apt(s) — Apartment(s)
AR — Arkansas
Assc — Associate(s)
Assn(s) — Association(s)
Asst(s) — Assistant(s)
Aug — August
Ave — Avenue
AZ — Arizona
AZA — Aleph Zadik Aleph
AZF — American Zionist Federation
AZYF — American Zionist Youth Foundation
BBG — B'nai B'rith Girls
BBYO — B'nai B'rith Youth Organization
BC — British Columbia
Bd(s) — Board(s)
Bdwy — Broadway
Bk(s) — Book(s)
Bklyn — Brooklyn
Bldg — Building
Blvd — Boulevard
Bus — Business
CA — California
Chem — Chemistry
Chil — Child, Children, Children's
Chr — Chairman, Chairmen, Chairwoman, Chairwomen, Chairperson
CJF — Council of Jewish Federations
Clin(s) — Clinic(s), Clinical
CO — Colorado
Co — Company, Companies
Col(s) — College(s)
Com(s) — Community, Communities
Commis — Commission(s)
Conf(s) — Conference(s)
Cong(s) — Congregation(s)
Coord(s) — Coordinate(s), Coordinator(s)
Corp(s) — Corporation(s)
Corsp — Corresponding
CT — Connecticut
Ct(s) — Court(s)
Ctr(s) — Center(s)
Cttee — Committee(s)
Cty(s) — County, Counties
DC — District of Columbia
DE — Delaware
Dec — December
Dept(s) — Department(s)
Dev(s) — Develop(s), Development(s)
DHL — Doctor of Hebrew Letters
Dir(s) — Director(s)
Dist(s) — District(s)
Div(s) — Division(s)
Dr(s) — Doctor(s), Drive
E — East
Edu — Education, Educational, Educator(s)
Est — Establish, Established, Establishment
Exec — Executive(s)
Ext — Extension
F — Founder(s), Founded
Feb — February
Fed(s) — Federation(s)
Fin — Financial
FL — Florida
Foun(s) — Foundation(s)
Fr — From
Fri — Friday
GA — Georgia
Gen — General
Gov(s) — Governor(s)
Govt — Government(s)
Grad(s) — Graduate(s)
Heb — Hebrew
HI — Hawaii
Hist — History
Hon(s) — Honor(s), Honorary, Honorable
Hosp(s) — Hospital(s)
HS — High School(s)
Hq — Headquarters
IA — Iowa
ID — Idaho
IL — Illinois
IN — Indiana
Inc — Incorporated
Ind — Industry, Industries
Ins — Institute(s), Institution(s)
Instr(s) — Instructor(s)
Intl — International
Is — Israel
J — Jews, Jewish, Jewry, Judaic, Judaica, Judaism
Jan — January
JCC — Jewish Community Center
Jr — Junior
JTS — Jewish Theological Seminary
Jul — July
Jun — June
JWB — Jewish Welfare Board
K — Kindergarten
KS — Kansas
KY — Kentucky
LA — Louisiana
Lab(s) — Laboratory, Laboratories

Key to Abbreviations

LI — Long Island
Ltd — Limited
MA — Massachusetts
Mar — March
MB — Manitoba
MD — Maryland, Doctor of Medicine
ME — Maine
Med — Medical, Medicine
Mem(s) — Member(s)
Met — Metropolitan
Mgmnt — Management
Mgr(s) — Manager(s)
MI — Michigan
MN — Minnesota
MO — Missouri
Mo — Month(s)
Mon — Monday
MS — Mississippi
MT — Montana
Mt(s) — Mountain(s)
Mus — Museum(s)
N — North
Natl — National
NB — New Brunswick
NC — North Carolina
NCSY — National Council of Synagogue Youth
ND — North Dakota
NE — Nebraska, Northeast
NH — New Hampshire
NJ — New Jersey
NM — New Mexico
Nov — November
NS — Nova Scotia
Num — Number
NV — Nevada
NW — Northwest
NY — New York
NYC — New York City
Oct — October
Off(s) — Office(s), Officer(s)
OH — Ohio
OK — Oklahoma
ON — Ontario
OR — Oregon
Org(s) — Organization(s)
PA — Pennsylvania
PhD — Doctor of Philosophy
Phila — Philadelphia
Pkwy — Parkway
Pl — Place
Pol — Political
PQ — Quebec
PR — Public Relations
Prep — Preparatory
Pres — President(s)
Prin(s) — Principal(s)
Prof(s) — Professor(s)
Prog(s) — Program(s)
Proj(s) — Project(s)
PTA — Parent Teacher Association
PTO — Parent Teacher Organization
Pub(s) — Publication(s), Publishing, Publish, Publishes, Published
QC — Queen's Counsel
Rd(s) — Road(s)
Rec — Recording
Rel — Religion, Religious
Rep(s) — Representative(s)
Rev — Reverend
RI — Rhode Island
Rm(s) — Room(s)
S — South
Sat — Saturday
SC — South Carolina
Sch(s) — School(s)
Sci — Science(s), Scientific
SD — South Dakota
SE — Southeast
Sec(s) — Secretary, Secretaries
Sept — September
Serv(s) — Service(s)
SK — Saskatchewan
Soc — Society, Societies
Sr — Senior(s)
St(s) — Saint, Street(s)
Stu — Student(s)
Sun — Sunday
SW — Southwest
Syn(s) — Synagogue(s)
Tech — Technology
Terr — Terrace
Thurs — Thursday
TN — Tennessee
Treas — Treasurer
Tues — Tuesday
TV — Television
Twp — Township
TX — Texas
UAHC — Union of American Hebrew Congregations
UIA — United Israel Appeal
UJA — United Jewish Appeal
Univ — University, Universities
US — United States
USY — United Synagogue Youth
UT — Utah
V — Vice
VA — Virginia
Vets — Veterans
Vol(s) — Volume(s)
VP(s) — Vice President(s)
VT — Vermont
W — West
WA — Washington
Wed — Wednesday
WI — Wisconsin
WV — West Virginia
WW I — World War I
WW II — World War II
WY — Wyoming
YMHA — Young Men's Hebrew Association
Yr(s) — Year(s)
YWHA — Young Women's Hebrew Association

INSTITUTIONS IN THE UNITED STATES

ALABAMA

Anniston

Temple Beth El. Affiliated with UAHC. 50 mems. Rabbi Mark A. Peilen; Pres: Jack Wallach; Edu: Allen Bodner; Sisterhood Pres: Shelma Gordon. **PO Box 1364, Annniston AL 36202 (205) 236–9249.**

Birmingham

Birmingham Jewish Day School. Com sch. To provide an intensive elementary edu in both Judaic & gen studies. Edu progs in K through grade 7; full J & gen studies prog; library containing 3,500 vols (juvenile & elementary Judaica & gen). 65 stu in grades K–7. 11 employees. F 1973 with one grade; has grown to include K–7. Pub PTA Newsletter. Located in Dr Miles Edu Bldg adjacent to J Com Ctr. Pres: Dr David Morrison; Dir: Rabbi Zev Silber. **3690–A Montclair Rd, PO Box 9206, Birmingham AL 35213 (205) 879–1068.**

Birmingham Jewish Day School, Library. Library contains 3500 vols (Juvenile & elementary Judaica & gen). For information on the Sch, see – Birmingham Jewish Day School, Birmingham, AL. **3960–A Montclair Rd, PO Box 9206, Birmingham AL 35213 (205) 879–1068.**

The Birmingham Jewish Federation. Mem of CJF. Organized 1935. Pres: Fred Berman; Exec Dir: Seymour Marcus; Exec Dir Designate: Richard Freidman. **PO Box 9175, Birmingham AL 35213 (205) 879–0416.**

Jewish Community Council. PO Box 7377, 3960–A Montclair Rd, Birmingham AL 35223 (205) 879–0411.

Knesseth Israel Congregation. Orthodox Cong affiliated with Union of Orthodox J Congs of Am. To promote Orthodox J life (syn & communal) in Birmingham; to increase awareness & observance through example, edu & providing social servs (2 kosher bakeries in town under supervision, take out pizza from Syn). Morning & Evening Servs: daily & Shabbat; Adult Edu; Conversational Heb Beginners Reading; Parashat Hashavua, Men's Talmud Class; Sisterhood; NCSY youth groups; Kiddy Craft Prog; Bar/Bat Mitzvah instruction; Chevra Kadisha; mikvah on premises; library containing 600 vols (Judaica, Heb, English, Yiddish). 150 families. 3 employees. F 1891 as Orthodox Cong by Russian (Lithuanian) immigrants; originally located in N Birmingham (1st Ave & 17th St N); moved to Mountain Brook Suburb in 1956; today the only Orthodox J cong in AL. Pub Knesseth Israel Bulletin. Facilities include social hall with 2 separte kitchens, main sanctuary seating 350, chapel, library, classrms, youth lounge, mikvah, gift shop, off. Rabbi Harry Rosen; Pres: Mark Paris; 1st VP: Martin Aaron; 2nd VP: Aubrey Lurie; 3rd VP: Floyd Berman; Treas: Avraham Grant; Sec: Shirley Aaron. **3225 Montevallo Rd, Birmingham AL 35223 (205) 879–1664.**

Temple Beth El. Affiliated with United Syn of Am. Rabbi Steven M. Glazer; Cantor Marshall Wolkenstein; Pres: Morton W. Stern; Edu Dir: Mark B. Levy; Youth Dir: Gloriann Levy. **2179 Highland Ave S, Birmingham AL 35256 (205) 933–2740.**

Temple Emanu-El. Affiliated with UAHC. 670 mems. Rabbis: David J. Zucker, Milton Grafman; Pres: Abe Kaplan; Sisterhood Pres: Loretta Newfield. **2100 Highland Ave, PO Box 3303–A, Birmingham AL 35205 (205) 933–8037.**

Temple Emanu-El Library. 2100 Highland Ave, PO Box 3303–A, Birmingham AL 35205 (205) 933–8037.

Demopolis

Congregation B'nai Jeshurun. Affiliated with UAHC. 12 mems. Rabbi Jerome M. Levy; Pres: Nathan Levy. **PO Box 340, Demopolis AL36732 (205) 289–2378.**

Dothan

Temple Emanu-El. Affiliated with UAHC. 80 mems. Rabbi Paul L. Tuchman; Pres: Jack Blumenfeld; Sisterhood Pres: Susan Blumberg. **PO Box 37, Dothan AL36302 (205) 792–5001.**

Florence

Temple B'nai Israel. Affiliated with UAHC. 58 mems. Rabbi Bernard Honan; Pres: Adolph Abroms. **201 Hawthrone St, Florence AL 35630 (205) 764–9242.**

Tri-Cities Jewish Federation Charities. Route 7, Florence AL 35632.

Gadsden

Congregation Beth Israel. Affiliated with UAHC. 57 mems. Rabbi Mark A. Peilen; Pres: Ferd C. Harwood; Sisterhood Pres: Susan Harwood. **PO Box 1616, 761 Chestnut St, Gadsden AL 35902 (205) 546–3223.**

Huntsville

Etz Chayim – Huntsville Conservative Synagogue. Affiliated with United Syn of Am. Pres: William Greenbaum. **7705 Bailey Cove Rd SE, Huntsville AL 35802 (205) 881–6260.**

Temple B'nai Sholom. Affiliated with UAHC. 120 mems. Rabbi Robert M. Scott; Pres: Barry Berman; Sisterhood Pres: Cecily Hovanes; Brotherhood Pres: Victor van Leevwen. **103 Lincoln St SE, Huntsville AL 35801 (205) 536–4771.**

Jasper

Temple Emanuel. Affiliated with UAHC. 27 mems. Pres: Abraham Cooperman; Edu: David E. Ostrich; Sisterhood Pres: W. Lewis. **1501 Fifth Ave, PO Box 1627, Jasper AL 35501 (205) 221–4000.**

Mobile

Ahavas Chesed Congregation – Dauphin Street Synqagogue. Affiliated with United Syn of Am. Rabbi Irwin Cutler; Pres: Mihcael Feinman; Edu Dir: Irvin Grodsky. **1717 Dauphin St, Mobile AL 36604 (205) 476–6010.**

Mobile Jewish Welfare Fund, Inc. Mem of CJF. Inc 1966. Pres: Herbert A. Meisler. **404 COne Office Park, Mobile AL 36609 (205) 343–7197.**

Spring Hill Avenue Temple, Congregation Sha'arai Shomayim. Reform Temple affiliated with UAHC, Natl Fed of Temple Sisterhoods, Natl Fed of Temple Brotherhoods, J Chautauqua Soc, N Am Fed of Temple Youth, Central Conf of Am Rabbis. To be a Beth Ha-Tefilla, a Beth Ha-Midrash & a Beth Ha-Knesset. Rel Servs; edu progs; Sisterhood; Brotherhood; youth group activities; library containing 500 vols (gen & specialized Judaica). 260 mems; 100 stu in grades pre-K through 10. 3 employees. F 1844; oldest J Cong (cemetery inc 1841) in the State of AL. Pub Bulletin (bi-weekly). Facilities include kitchen, sanctuary seating 220, offs, classrms, large auditorium with stage, more than adequate parking facilities. Pioneer in Jewish-Christian Dialogue Prog; 22 yr Ministerial Ins for clergy of area. Rabbi Steven L. Jacobs; Pres: Herbert Feibelman Jr; 1st VP: David Gardberg; 2nd VP: Jack Friedlander; Sec: Reita Franco; Treas: Richard Frank Jr; Exec Sec: June Baker; Dir Rel Ed; Barbara Paper. **1769 Spring Hill Ave, PO Box 7295, Mobile AL 36607 (205) 478–0415.**

Montgomery

Agudath Israel Synagogue. Affiliated with United Syn of Am. Rabbi Raphael Gold; Pres: Allan Nathanson; Edu Dir: Mrs Mitchell Allen. **3525 Cloverdale Rd, Montgomery AL 36111 (205) 281–7394.**

Jewish Federation of Montgomery, Inc. Mem of CJF. Organized 1930. Pres: Adolph Weil Jr; Sec: Barbara Marcus. **PO Box 1150, Montgomery AL 36102 (205) 263–7674.**

Temple Beth Or. Affiliated with UAHC. 276 mems. Rabbi David A Baylinson; Pres: Irvin Gassenheimer Jr; Edu: Jack Koch; Adm: Jane B. Kyle. **PO Box 6180, 2246 Narrow Lane Rd, Montgomery AL 36106 (205) 272–3314.**

Northport

Temple Emanuel. 14A Northwood Lake, Northport AL 35476.

Temple Emanuel Memorial Library. 14A Northwood Lake, Northport AL 35476.

Selma

Mishkan Israel Congregation. Affiliated with UAHC. 35 mems. Pres: Rubin Bernstein. **c/o Seymour Cohn, Houston Park, Selma AL 36701 (205) 874–9811.**

Sheffield

Jewish Monitor. Periodical pub. **PO Box 396, Sheffield AL 35660 (205) 766–0508.**

Tuscaloosa

B'nai B'rith Hillel Foundation, University of Alabama. Campus org. To support J life among the stu body; to edu the J stu & the public concerning Is, J culture, rel; to act as a social base for J stu; to recruit J stu for the Univ. Fri night servs, speakers, films, trips, dances, meals, etc. 150 mems. 4 employees. F late 40's. Facilities include kosher kitchen, sanctuary, auditorium, library, meeting rms. Exec Dir: Sheldon L. Rosenzweig; Exec Asst: Pam Gerstein; House Advs: Esti Applebaum, Hal Applebaum. **728 10th Ave, Tuscaloosa AL 35401 (205) 758–3280.**

Temple Emanuel. Affiliated with UAHC. 64 mems. Rabbi Leon J. Weinberger; Pres: Bennett Berman; Edu: Crystal Cooper; Adm: Toby Whitman; Sisterhood Pres: Beatrice B. Shulman. **PO Box 5607, Tuscaloosa AL 35405 (205) 553–3286.**

ALASKA

Anchorage

Beth Sholom. 1810 Cleveland Ave, Anchorage AK 99510 (907) 278–3807.

Congregation Beth Sholom. Affiliated with UAHC. 80 mems. Rabbi Lester Polonsky; Pres: Crysta Ellis. **1000 W 20th Ave, Anchorage AK 99510 (907) 272–8874.**

Fairbanks

Jewish Congregation of Fairbanks, Inc. 2100 Cushman St, Fairbanks AK 99701 (907) 452–1981.

ARIZONA

Flagstaff

Heichal Baoranim. 'Temple in the Pines.' To maintain a syn with J ideals & traditions for mems & their chil. Fri Evening Servs, the first & third Fri of the mo, meeting in mem's homes; High Holiday & Holiday Servs. 80 mems throughout Northern AZ. F in 1973 by Dr & Mrs Merrill Abeshaus, Dr & Mrs Len Ritt, & Dr & Mrs Ray Berman. The closest syn is located in Phoenix, 140 miles away. The Cong has no rabbi; mems take turns conducting the servs. Pres: Dr Merrill M. Abeshaus; VP: Judy Feldstein; Treas: Rory Madden; Sec: Len Ritt; Mem at Large: Ray Berman. **1801 E Hereford, Flagstaff AZ 86001.**

Mesa

Temple Beth Sholom. Affiliated with United Syn of Am. Rabbi Joseph Schonwald; Pres: Sid Lachter. **104 W First St, Mesa AZ 85201 (602) 964–1981.**

Phoenix

Arizona Torah High School for Boys & Arizona Torah High School for Girls. All-day Orthodox HS affiliated with N Central Assn of Cols & Schs, Torah Umesorah, Rabbinical Seminary of Am; accredited by N Central Assn. To provide the perfect blend of edu excellence in both Torah & secular studies & to reach out to our youth who seek the true meaning of their J heritage. Separate boys & girls accredited HS prog in Torah & secular subjects; Adult Edu; Mishmar prog; sports prog; art prog; Rel Servs; outreach prog for youth; library containing 2,500 vols (Judaica & gen); dormitory facilities. 50 stu in grade 9–12. 18 employees; 20 volunteers. F 1979 with freshman class; added new grade each year – at present have full 4 yr HS. Pub AZ Torah Highlights (3 times a yr); Hamayon (annual). Facilities include air-conditioned modern Beth Hamedrash in scenic location in N Phoenix, dormitory facilities on campus, kosher cafeteria, swimming pools, basketball cts, tennis ct. Boys' Div Prin: Rabbi Abraham Semmel; Girls' Div Prin: Rabbi Moshe Kamin; Dean of Stu: Rabbi Samuel Jacobs; Bd of Trustees Pres: Dennis Silvers; Secular Studies Prin: Norman Saunders. **400 W Pasadena St, Phoenix AZ 85013 (602) 277–3389.**

Arizona Torah High School for Boys & Girls Library. Library contains 2,500 vols (Judaica & gen). For information on the HS, see – Arizona Torah High School for Boys & Arizona Torah High School for Girls, Phoenix, AZ. **400 W Pasadena St, Phoenix AZ 85013 (602) 277–3389.**

Beth El Congregation. Affiliated with United Syn of Am. Rabbi Herbert Silberman; Cantor Reuven Taff; Pres: Sherman Minkoff MD; Exec Dir: Melvin Weisblatt; Edu Dir: Reuven Taff; Youth Dir: Judi Saperstein; Pre-Sch Dir: Judy Taff. **1118 W Glendale Ave, Phoenix AZ 85021 (602) 944–3359.**

Beth El Congregation Library. For information on the Cong, see – Beth El Cong, Phoenix, AZ. **1118 W Glendale Ave, Phoenix AZ 85021 (602) 955–3359.**

Greater Phoenix Jewish Federation. Mem of CJF. Includes surrounding communities. Organized 1940. Pres: Shyrle Schaffer; Exec Dir: Lawrence M. Cohen. **1718 W Maryland Ave, Phoenix AZ 85015 (602) 249–1845.**

Hebrew High School of Phoenix. To promote in J youth an appreciation of their Torah heritage & their eternal bond to Is. Curriculum includes the study of Torah, Talmud, Bible, Prophets & their traditional commentaries; Hist, Culture, Language & Geography of Is; secular prog includes Computer Programming, Typing, Sci, English & Hist. F in 1976. The sch consists of a Boys & Girls Div. Dirs: Rabbi Aaron Winter, Rabbi Avrom Semmel; Dir Secular Dept: Norman F. Saunders. **Girls Div: 5750 N Central,**

Phoenix AZ 85012; Boys Div Adm Off: 400 W Pasadena, Phoenix AZ 85013 (602) 277–3389.

Hebrew Institute of Arizona. Syn & day sch. The Day Sch is affiliated with Torah Umesorah. Rel Servs; Adult Classes: Talmud, Mishna, Heb & Torah. Est in 1977. Dir: Rabbi Moshe Metzger; Assc Dir: Rabbi Moshe Freedman. **935 W Maryland Ave, Phoenix AZ 85013 (602) 249–6338.**

Hebrew Institute of Arizona, Library. For information on the Ins, see – Hebrew Institute of Arizona, Phoenix, AZ. **935 W Maryland Ave, Phoenix AZ 85013 (602) 249–6338.**

Jewish Community Center of Greater Phoenix. JCC serving Phoenix, Scottsdale, Paradise Valley & Tri City. To enhance J life in Phoenix. Physical & cultural activities for all ages. 5,500 mems. The JCC dates back to a ctr operating in an old converted house at N 4th St in 1947. By 1951 the J population had grown to 1,200 families & the Ctr moved to N Central Ave on the old Heard estate. Continued growth caused the ctr to relocate again in 1953 to 1510 E Camelback Rd. Since 1962 the Ctr has been located at its present site. Facilities on the 12½ acre site include a health club, olympic size pool, univ sized gymnasium (practice home of the Phoenix Suns, professional basketball team) & meeting rms. The ctr operates a summer camp in Phoenix & a resident camp in Prescott. Pres: Leonard Miller; VPs: Michael Folb, Elaine Kort, Richard Raskin, Barry Schneider, Martin Shultz, Irv Shuman, Meyer Turken; Sec: Don Shifris; Treas: Allan Bulman; Exec Dir: Leonard Robinson; Asst Exec Dir: Robert Gottschalk; Bd of Dirs: Claire Bickel, Murray Cohen, Paula Dubnow, Al Fann, Joel Gereboff, Joan Goldfarb, Gerald Hart, Lenora Hausman, Robert Klein, Yetta Leibovitz, Karen Levinson, Iris Machiz, James McLain, Robert Mallin, David Marks, Karen Mehlman, Joel Miller, Seymour Rife, Marjorie Roth, Irv Saattler, Robert Shcolnik, Steve Shluker, Herbert Sperber, James Strassels, Beryl Sweet, Gerald Webner; Hon Bd Mem: Al Frelich. **1718 W Maryland Ave, Phoenix AZ 85015 (602) 249–1832.**

Phoenix Jewish Free Loan Association. To help people who find themselves temporarily in financially embarrassing situations. Loans money interest free; repayment is expected over a period of time. The usual clients are people who are unable to borrow fr financial ins, but still appear to be honest, hardworking & able to repay these loans if given an opportunity. The money is raised almost entirely fr the local J com. However, the Assn helps people of all races, creeds & rel preference. Clients come fr throughout Maricopa Cty. The Assn does not loan to people outside the cty. Pres: Mathis Becker; 1st VP: Harry Adler; 2nd VP: Ben Sonkin; Treas: Maurice J. Roth; Fin & Rec Sec: Harry Scholnik; Corsp Sec: Lee Kazan; Bd of Dirs – Chr: Harry Kipnis; Bd of Dirs: Harry Adler, Mathis Becker, Lee Kazan, Maurice J. Roth, Ben Sonkin, Harry Scholnik; Hon Bd Mems: Rabbi Barton Lee, Rabbi Albert Plotkin, Rabbi David Rebibo, Harry Rosenzweig, Newton Rosenzweig, Phil Taxman; Hon Life Pres: Leon Francis. **1718 W Maryland Ave, Phoenix AZ 85015 (602) 249–1832.**

Phoenix Jewish News. Com newspaper affiliated with Am J Press Assn, Natl Newspaper Assn, AZ Newspapers Assn, J Telegraphic Agy. As a bi-weekly com newspaper, to bring news of local, natl & intl interest to J families, readers in the Greater Phoenix area. 12 employees. F 1947. M.B. Goldman, publisher 1947–1961; Cecil Newmark, publisher 1961–1981. Publisher: Flo Eckstein; Managing Editor: Leni Reiss. **1536 W Thomas Rd, Phoenix AZ 85015 (602) 264–0536.**

Temple Beth Israel. Affiliated with UAHC. 1410 mems. Rabbis: Albert Plotkin, B. Charles Herring; Cantors: Maurice P. Chesler, Stephen Richards; Pres: Lawrence N. Frazin; Edu: Hannaa B. Adelman; Adm: Robert Shwedick; Sisterhood Pres: Betty Hoffman; Brotherhood Pres: Bernard F. Pollack. **3310 N 10th Ave, Phoenix AZ 85013 (602) 264–4428.**

Temple Beth Israel Library. For information on the Temple, see – Temple Beth Israel, Phoenix, AZ. **3310 N 10th Ave, Phoenix AZ 85013 (602) 264–4428.**

Temple Chai. Affiliated with UAHC. 74 mems. Pres: Michael Horewitch. **16026 N 32nd St, Phoenix AZ 85032 (602) 971–1234.**

Scottsdale

Ahavat Torah. Affiliated with United Syn of Am. Rabbi Leon Rosenberg; Pres: Dr Jay Le Grand. **10427 N Scottsdale Rd, Scottsdale AZ 85258.**

Har Zion Congregation. Affiliated with United Syn of Am. Rabbi Elliott M. Marmon; Cantor & Edu Dir: Barry M. Caplan; Pres: Marilyn K. Seplow. **5929 E Lincoln Dr, Scottsdale AZ 85253 (602) 991–0720.**

Temple Solel. Affiliated with UAHC. 305 mems. Rabbi Maynard W. Bell; Pres: Steve Gubin; Edu: Teri Berman. **6805 E McDonald Dr, Scottsdale AZ 85253 (602) 991–7414.**

Sun City

Temple Beth Shalom. Affiliated with UAHC. 550 mems. Rabbi Albert A. Michels; Pres: Himan B. Parks; Edu: Abraham Meth; Sisterhood Pres: Melva Simon; Brotherhood Pres: Irving M. Pallin. **12202 101st Ave, Sun City AZ 85351 (602) 977–3240.**

Tempe

Hillel at Arizona State University – Union of Jewish Students. Supported by the Phoenix J Fed & the Hillel Adv Council. To provide stu with information, guidance & positive J models at a time when youth are questioning all ins. Referral servs for Phoenix area stu who will be attending other cols; Hillel Adv Council city wide edu progs; seminars aimed at preparing J HS youth for col; pre-marital, intermarriage, rel & personal counseling to com young people; Scholar-in-Residence Prog which brings Is scholars to the area & makes them available both on campus & to com orgs; recruitment of stu to serve as staff in area rel schs & youth groups; resource assistance to J rel sch teachers; public information responses to Arab propaganda; counseling with & for parents of col age stu; library; social progs: Israeli dancing, film nights, Tues lunches, Sun brunches, weekday trips, cultural progs; High Holiday Servs; Passover Seder; Sabbath dinners; edu progs: classes ranging fr Heb to J hist; workshops. F as a full time unit in 1971. ASU Hillel is responsible for the creation of the J Faculty Assn & for a J Chataugua Soc grant being given to the univ library. ASU Hillel was one of the sponsoring orgs of the AZ Conf on the Holocaust. The Org has served as the Eastside Valley screening ctr to Tay Sachs disease. Hillel is responsible for Alpha Beta stores providing Passover items for the J com in Tempe. Rabbi Barton G. Lee; Sec: Betty Blitz. **1012 S Mill Ave, Tempe AZ 85281 (602) 967–7563.**

Lubavitch Center. Lubavitch com servs ctr. Blends Chassidic fervor & warmth with tradition & learning, to show that every J, fr whatever background he or she comes fr, is an integral part of the body of Is. Anti-missionary work; adult edu; Sabbath seminars; holiday progs; day camp; youth groups; syns; kosher kitchen; counseling; chaplaincy; Mitzvah Campaigns; hosp & prison visitations; sr citizens encounters; speakers bureau. Rabbi Z. Levertov. **915 W 14th St, Tempe AZ 85281 (602) 966–4649.**

Temple Emanuel of Tempe. Affiliated with UAHC. 175 mems. Rabbi David C. Pinkwasser; Pres: Michael Geyser; Sisterhood Pres: Ronnie Taxin. **5801 S Rural Rd, Tempe AZ 85283 (602) 838–1414.**

Tucson

Congregation Anshei Israel. Affiliated with United Syn of Am. Rabbi Arthur R. Oleisky; Cantor Maurice Falkow; Pres: Dr Daniel N. Karsch; Exec Dir: Louis Haber; Edu & Youth Dir: Clifford P. Schwartz. **5550 E 5th St, Tucson AZ 85711 (602) 745–5550.**

Congregation Anshei Israel, Alleyne Weisman Library. For information on the Cong, see – Cong Anshei Israel, Tucson, AZ. **5550 E 5th St, Tucson AZ 85711 (602) 745–5550.**

Congregation Chaverim. Affiliated with UAHC. 75 mems. Pres: Robert Friedman. **c/o Mr E. C. Kaplan, 6121 E 30th St, Tucson AZ 85711 (602) 790–9541.**

Jewish Community Council. Mem of CJF. Organized 1942. Pres: Dr Jack Cole; Exec Dir: Charles Plotkin. **102 N Plumer, Tucson AZ 85719 (602) 884–8921.**

Jewish Family Service of the Tucson Jewish Community Council. To provide individuals & families with skilled casework group work servs; to provide a well rounded family life edu prog to enrich & strengthen family life; to provide supportive servs needed because of particular family circumstances; to offer diagnostic servs to determine special needs of chil & adults. Individual, couple, family & group therapy to deal with problems in daily living as well as emotional growth – for youth in conflict with family or soc; for young adult searching for identity & career resolution; for adults, married or single, working on emotional growth, intimacy, or other problems of daily living; for the aged making sense of a lifetime of experiences; for sr citizens, J Family Servs social workers, counselors & volunteer aides extend understanding help & serve as a bridge between them & the com. Adoption – couples are led through adjustment periods, & whenever possible, chil are offered for adoption; counseling continues assisting the couple in adjusting to its new role as a family. Supporting servs – resettlement o refugees & newcomers; life supportive servs for the elderly, the homebound & the teenage parent which include homemaker servs, socialization, friendly visitors, volunteers & other special needs; Edu for Family Loving for people with similar concerns & common life situations; discussion series & single meetings for groups which are concered with parenting, marriage, sexuality, divorce, the middle yrs & aging. Est in 1949. With the combined efforts of lay leaders & professional guidance, the J Welfare Soc became the J Social Servs Dept of the Council. The J Social

Servs was accepted into the Conncil of Social Agy, now the Tucson Com Council, United Way, & became a recipient of the Combined J Appeal. The Drs Panel was org in 1951. It became an integral part of the J Social Servs, treating patients without a fee. In 1953 the J Social Servs was licensed as a chil placing agy. In 1958, with the expansion of servs to the aged, chil & involved family problems, the Attorneys Panel was formed to aid the Agy & clients. The request for casework & related servs increased. To reflect the knowledge that the family is the crucible in which healthy personalities are developed, the Agy changed its name to the J Family Serv. In 1959 a psychiatric consultant joined the professional staff. In 1959 a fee schedule was est. In 1963 the J Family Serv was awarded a natl award for superior initiative & achievment in the advancement of social welfare for the aged by the Council of J Fed & Welfare Funds. The Tucson Com Council recognized J Family Agy servs to the aged & it received the Council's meritorious award. The Agy had been housed in the Tucson Com Ctr since the bldg was opened in 1955; In 1964 the J Family Serv moved into the J Com House which is adjacent to the present Ctr. In 1980 an eastside off was opened to serve that segment of the com. The J Family Servs has undertaken various studies & projs that have resulted in the creation of new facilities & servs for the com – The Shanhouse Nursery Sch & K, the Day Camp, & the Golden Age Recreational Prog. The Agy's intensive study of the Aged led to the est of a wide range of non-institutional servs for the older person, & to the bldg of the Hanmaker J Nursing Home for the Aged. Pres: Michael W. Krause; Pres Elect: Ruth Kolker; VPs: Dr Michael Cohen, Nathan Miller, Mark Raven; Sec: Lawrence Subrin; Treas: Walter Sampson; Bd of Trustees: Linda Alpert, Joyce Becker, John Davis, Elayne Feder, Bette Gardner, Ann Goldberg, Donna Grant, Arthur Hirsch, Sally Kranitz, Dr Robert Levitin, Dr Martin Levy, Fern Marmis, Betejoy Oleisky, Donna Rabin, Fay Roos, Martha Rothman, Irene Sarver, Dr Jeffrey Selwyn, Molly Senor, Stephen Spitzer, Sharon Weich, Dr Kenneth Wortzel; Acting Exec Dir: Betty Orman. **102 N Plumer Ave, Tucson AZ 85719 (602) 792–3641.**

Temple Emanu-El. Affiliated with UAHC. 816 mems. Rabbi Joseph S. Weizenbaum; Pres: Nestor Roos; Edu: Mitchell C. Dorson; Adm: Catherine Kagan; Sisterhood Pres: Merle Schoolman; Brotherhood Pres: Morris Gross. **225 N Country Club Rd, PO Box 42887, Tucson AZ 85733 (602) 327–4501.**

Temple Emanu-El Library. For information on the Temple, see – Temple Emanu-El, Tucson, AZ. **225 N Country Club Rd, PO Box 42887, Tucson AZ 85733 (602) 327–4501.**

ARKANSAS

Blytheville

Temple Israel. Affiliated with UAHC. 34 mems. Pres: Elvin Greene; Sisterhood Pres: Sarah Nickol. **1500 W Chickasawba, Blytheville AR 72315 (501) 763–4148.**

Fort Smith

United Hebrew Congregation. Affiliated with UAHC. 29 mems. Pres: Nicol L. Wintory; Edu: Cynthia Wolf; Adm: Morton B. Marks Jr; Sisterhood: Dorothy Miller. **PO Box 785, Fort Smith AR 72902 (501) 452–1468.**

Helena

Temple Beth El. Affiliated with UAHC. 46 mems. Pres: A.F. Miller; Sisterhood Pres: Jane Galyean. **406 Perry St, Helena AR 72342 (501) 338–6654.**

Hot Springs

Congregation House of Israel. Affiliated with UAHC. 64 mems. Rabbi Selvin Goldberg; Pres: Howard Sellesinger; Adm: Rudi Wetzler; Sisterhood Pres: Lois Ginsburg. **300 Quapaw Ave, Hot Springs AR 71901 (501) 623–5821.**

Leo N. Levi National Arthritis Hospital. Hosp specializing in the treatment of arthritis & related diseases; sponsored by B'nai B'rith. Treatment includes hydrotherapy, physical therapy, diathermy & ultra sound; prosthesis-corrective shoes, hand splints, walking aids; medication & confs. In addition, the Hosp provides regular Sabbath Eve Servs, library, kosher kitchen, beauty salon, 8 guest rms which are available to relatives or spouses of patients. The Hosp opened on Nov 1, 1914. It is named for Leo N. Levi, a past intl pres of B'nai B'rith, who died during his term of off. At the end of the 19th century, many poor J suffering fr arthritis came to Hot Springs to bathe in the famous thermal waters. Often they had no money & asked the local Rabbi for help. The problem became too great for the small J com & the help of Dist 7 B'nai B'rith was sought. A cttee of investigation recommended that a free hosp be created to aid all people suffering fr arthritis. Originally, admission was free but with the changes in med costs & conditions, fees are charged to those who are able to pay. Pres: Harry H. Levitch; VP: Noland Blass Jr; Hon Pres: David M. Blumberg, Emile Grossbart, Sara J. Bagen; Adm: Dale Wagoner; Med Dir: Dr Fred Roberston; Chaplain & Social Servs Dir: Rabbi Dr P. Selvin Goldberg. **300 Prospect, Hot Springs Park AR 71901 (501) 321–9496.**

Jonesboro

Temple Israel. Affiliated with UAHC. 23 mems. Pres: Simon Nisenbaum; Sisterhood Pres: Elaine Young. **203 W Oak, PO Box 293, Jonesboro AR 72401 (501) 932–9333.**

Little Rock

Congregation B'nai Israel. One of the leading Reform Syn in the SW. To think of the J people as an extended family & to model for all the world the affection, concern, solicitude & help that can be present in a loving family; to welcome those who marry into the J faith; to adopt those who, not born J, choose us to be their family; to respect without rivalry those who choose other ways to approach God & to become decent people. Rel Servs; Rel Sch; Sisterhood; Adult Edu. Over 400 families. Cong B'nai Is was officially organized on Nov 11, 1866 by a group of J Civil War vets. The first 66 mems owned little more than a Sefer Torah, Shofar & a will to worship God together. The first sanctuary, a small rm in the Ditter Bldg between Rock & Cumberland Sts on E Markham, was dedicated on Aug 13, 1867. The Ladies Benevolent Soc, the forerunner of today's Sisterhood was organized in 1867. In 1868 a soc was est to aid the sick & to attend to the burial rites for the dead. By 1875 the Cong had purchased the land that is now Oakland Cemetery. In 1872 a second bldg was dedicated; soon after, a Sabbath Sch Talmud Yelodim Ins was begun with an average attendance the first yr of 55 chil. B'nai Is was one of 32 charter congs of UAHC. The Cong was represented at the first UAHC Assembly held in Cincinnati OH in 1873. In 1966 the Cong celebrated its 100 anniversary in its sanctuary at Capitol & Broadway. Since May 1975 the Cong has been housed at its present location. Rabbi E.E. Planick; Rabbi Emeritus Ira E. Sanders; Pres: Arthur J. Pfeifer; Adm: Mae Gardner; Sisterhood Pres: Dale Ronnel; Brotherhood Pres: Richard Lewis. **3700 Rodney Parham Rd, Little Rock AR 72212 (501) 225–9700.**

Jewish Federation of Little Rock. Mem of CJF. Organized 1911. Pres: Lee Ronnel; Exec Dir: Nanci Goldman. **Donaghey Bldg, Little Rock AR 72201 (501) 372–3571.**

McGehee

Meir Chayim Temple. Affiliated with UAHC. 25 mems. Pres: Barry Brunner; Sisterhood Pres: Rose B. Dreyfus. **210 N 4th, McGehee AR71654 (501) 222–4399.**

Pine Bluff

Temple Anshe Emeth. Affiliated with UAHC. 72 mems. Rabbi Leslie E. Sirtes; Pres: Paul Greenberg; Sisterhood Pres: Carolyn Greenberg. **PO Box 6022, Pine Bluff AR 71611 (501) 534–3853.**

CALIFORNIA

Alhambra

Temple Beth Torah. Affiliated with United Syn of Am. Rabbi Charles J. Shoulson; Cantor Morris Firestone; Pres: Burton R. Margulis; Exec Dir: Samuel Schiffman; Edu Dir: Ruth Slater; Youth Dir: Paula Svonkin. **225 S Atlantic Blvd, Alhambra CA 91801 (213) 283–2035.**

Anaheim

Temple Beth Emet. Affiliated with United Syn of Am. Rabbi George Schlesinger; Rabbi Emeritus: Aaron J. Tofield; Cantor Philip Moddel; Pres: Shirley Berko; Exec Adm: Shirley Glowalla; Edu Dir: Samuel Nissan. **1770 W Cerritos Ave, Anaheim CA 92804 (714) 772–4720.**

Arcadia

Temple Shaarei Tikvah. Affiliated with United Syn of Am. Rabbi Dr Joseph Hirsch; Cantor Salomon Edelman; Pres: Marvin F. Donner; Edu Dir: Betsy Tyree; Youth Dir: Jeff Ronald. **550 S Second Ave, Arcadia CA 91006 (213) 445–0810.**

Arleta

Temple Beth Solomon of the Deaf. Reform Temple affiliated with UAHC, CJF of Greater Los Angeles, Greater Los Angeles Council on Deafness. To promote Judaism among the deaf. Rel Servs; Rel Sch; Youth Group; Sisterhood; Men's Club; Sr Citizens Group; Young Adults Havurah; Com Prog Off. 197 mems; 60 families; 30 individuals. 5 employees, 40 volunteers. TBSD was f in 1960 by deaf people themsevles. In 1965 TBSD purchased its facility from Temple Beth Torah. TBSD is the first & oldest syn of the deaf, & the only one to own & operate its own facilities. Pub TBSD Congregation News (monthly). Facilities include sanctuary bldg with off, classrms & storage rms; social hall with off, stage & kitchen (non-kosher). Rabbi Alan Henkin; Pres: Alvin Klugman; VP: David Balacaier; Prog Coord: Marla Petal; Corsp Sec: Adele Podolsky; Treas: Bess Hyman; Pub Editor: Marge Klugman. **13580 Osborne St, Arleta CA 91331 (213) 899–2202.**

Artesia

New Jewish Singles – Orange County. Social club for J singles. Meets about 4 times a mo in mems homes. Mailing list of 200. **PO Box 631, Artesia CA 90701 (714) 761–1870, (213) 421–1539.**

Bakersfield

Congregation B'nai Jacob. Affiliated with United Syn of Am. Rabbi Pincus Goodblatt; Cantor Jacob Panski; Pres: Rhoda Moss. **600 17th St, Bakersfield CA 93301 (805) 325–8017.**

Temple Beth El. Affiliated with UAHC. 140 mems. Rabbi Steven Peskind; Pres: Arthur Rockoff; Edu: Miriam Beam; Sisterhood Pres: Barbara Asher. **2906 Loma Linda Rd, Bakersfield CA 93305 (805) 322–7607.**

Barstow

Congregation Beth Israel. Affiliated with UAHC. 12 mems. Pres: Samuel Sochis; Edu: Lorraine Sochis. **c/o Samuel Sochis, 2009 Barcelona Ave, Barstow CA 92311 (714) 256–7693.**

Belmont

Jewish Family & Children's Services. To provide edu, counsel, therapy, support & outreach to strengthen family life within the J com & to assist chil, youth & adults in developing & maintaining their maximum human potential. For additional information, see – Jewish Family & Children's Services – San Francisco, CA. **490 El Camino Real, Belmont CA 94002 (415) 591–8991.**

Berkeley

The Aquarian Minyan. Egalitarian J spiritual com. Shabbat, Holyday & Festival celebrations combine traditional prayers & songs with innovative liturgies, dance, storytelling & personal sharing to provide an experience of the essence of the observance. Sponsors workshops, particularly in J mysticism & related topics; Shabbat Servs weekly, meeting at people's homes; retreats; hall rented for holidays when a large turn-out is expected. 100 mems; attendance at weekly Shabbatot between 10–40; at High Holiday celebrations, 300–400 persons. F in 1974 by people who attended a mo-long series of workshops & seminars on Kabbalah with Rabbi Zalman Schachter, a former Lubavitcher Chasid who was then Prof of J Studies at the Univ of Manitoba in Winnipeg. The Minyan evolved their own way of celebration, innovative & spontaneous, with emphasis on singing, movement, chanting, storytelling & sharing. Gradually, an awareness of the need for additional structure was expressed such as dues, membership, leadership, classes & workshops. Newsletter with mailing list of 500. **PO Box 7224, Berkeley CA 94707 (415) 848–0965.**

Chabad House. Lubavitch com serv ctr. Blends Chassidic fervor & warmth with tradition & learning, to show that every J, fr whatever background he or she comes fr, is an integral part of the body of Is. Anti-missionary work; adult edu; Sabbath seminars; holiday progs; day camp; youth groups; syns; kosher kitchen; counseling; chaplaincy; Mitzvah Campaigns; hosp & prison visitations; sr citizens encounters; speakers bureau. Rabbi Chaim Drizin. **2340 Piedmont Ave, Berkeley CA 94704 (415) 845–7791.**

Congregation Beth El. Affiliated with UAHC. 330 mems. Rabbi Arnold L. Levine; Cantor Benjamin Roth; Pres: Robert Katz; Edu: Phyllis Mintzer. **2301 Vine St, Berkeley CA 94708 (415) 848–3988.**

Congregation Beth Israel. Traditional Syn. Dedicated to personal intellectual growth. Rel Servs; Heb Sch classes range fr nursery sch through 12th grade; youth groups; Summer Day Camp; Toddler Nursery Sch Prog; Edu Prog: Heb, Confrontation with J, Mishna, Prayer, & Women in J. Rabbi Joseph Leibowitz; Pres: Marvin Winer; 1st VP: Mordy Rosen; 2nd VP: Linda Blum; Sec: Naomi Stamper; Treas: Archie Greenberg; Sisterhood Pres: Irene Resnikoff; Trustees: Judi Bloom, Don Cervantes, Jonathan Francis, Ezra Hendon, Aaron Marcus, John Meyers, Barbara Rothblatt, Mark Schickman, Irene Resnikoff, Joan Sopher, Fried Wittman, Marti Zedeck; Prin of the Heb Sch: Rena Rosen. **1630 Bancroft Way, Berkeley CA 94703 (415) 843–5246.**

Judah L. Magnes Memorial Museum. The J Mus of the W. To collect & exhibit artistic, historical & literary materials of J interest. Changing exhibitions of contemporary J artists & historical themes of contemporary interest; displays of J ceremonial art fr around the world, graphic & fine art illustrating the Bible, J customs, people, coins & medals, & a Holocaust collection recording the Nazi era; Library of Judaica containing 7,500 bks & periodicals in English, Yiddish & Heb, & a collection of liturgical & Yiddish theater music scores; noted for its collection of documents & artifacts on the J of India, & its collection of textiles & customs fr the N African & European J coms; sponsors the Ins for Righteous Acts which conducts research into incidents where non-J saved J lives; Western J Hist Ctr collects documents memorabilia of J hist in the Western US including Anglo-J newspapers pub in the W since 1960, diaries & photographs; maintains other servs including traveling exhibitions prog; tours led by trained docents; gift shop. 1200 mems. Est in 1962. The ins is named after Judah L. Magnus born in the Bay Area & f of the Hebrew Univ in Jerusalem, the Am Civil Liberties Union, Am J Cttee, & Hadassah. As of 1966, the mus has been located at its present location in an historic Berkeley mansion. Bks & pamphlets available on J life in San Francisco, CA & Europe; catalogues on exhibitions. Under the direction of the mus, several J cemeteries have been preserved. Restoration is planned for the acquired oldest standing syn in CA. Pres: Jacques Reutlinger; VPs: Mathilda Albers, Prof William Brinner; Treas: Harry Blumenthal; Rec Sec: Prof Sheldon Rothblatt; Corporate Sec: Seymour Fromer; Bd of Trustees: Beth Burstein, Norman Coliver, Walter Frank, Marianne Friedman, Stanley R. Harris, Florence Helzel, Morton Lieberman, Bernard Osher, Jeremy Potash, Raine Rude, George Rynecki, Gary Shapiro, Henri Korb, Steven Swig, Dr Marvin S. Weinreb, Stephen Zellerbach, Arthur Zimmerman; Women's Guild Pres: Raine Rude; Dir: Seymour Fromer; Curator: Ruth Eis; Curatorial Asst: Alice Perlman; Register: Ted A. Greenberg; Exhibits Designer: William Chayes; Librarian: Jane Levy; Order Dept: Arlene Sarver; PR: Malka Weitman. **2911 Russell St, Berkeley CA 94705 (415) 849–2710.**

Midrasha, East Bay Community High School. Inter-congregational HS affiliated with Cong Beth El, Cong Beth Israel, Berkeley; Temple Beth Hillel, Richmond; Temple Beth Abraham, Oakland. To serve as an inter-congregational, one day a week, supplementary sch. Edu curriculum for 8th–12th graders. 100 8th–12th grade stu. 10 employees. Sch in 13th yr. Meets in 2-mem congregation sch. Adm: Diane Bernbaum; **2301 Vine St, Berkeley CA 94708 (415) 848–3988.**

National Council of Jewish Women. Women's volunteer org. Dedicated in the Spirit of J to advancing human welfare & the democratic way of life. Activities are organized around five prog priorities: women's issues, chil & youth, aging, J life, & Is. Women's Issues – major concerns are: ratification of the Equal Rights Amendment, protection of the right of every women to have access to safe & legal abortion, removal of gender related discrimination in all areas of life; provision of edu progs on the prevention of domestic violence & treatment for its victims, sponsoring of widow to widow counseling & progs for single parents. Chil & Youth – primarily concerned with: the rights, needs & quality of life of the nation's chil & youth; juvenile justice, especially the treatment of adolescent girls; & foster care; variety of projs that support servs to the young people in their coms (the Council is deeply committed to advocacy efforts needed to effectively change the way chil are treated under the law). Is – carries out numerous edu & social welfare progs in Is; has long been a strong advocate for the State of Is; furthers current major proj in Is, the Research Ins for Innovation in Edu, which is part of The Hebrew Univ Sch of Edu. J Life – places emphasis on: J edu & the problems of Soviet J; J edu progs for individuals of various ages & interests designed to assist people in exploring their understanding of & attitudes toward J, & rekindling their interest in their rel; involvement in the resettlement of Soviet J immigrants & in advocacy on behalf of those J who are refused permission to leave the USSR. Aging – major focus is on dev & support of legislation on behalf of older adults, day ctrs, housing for the elderly, adult edu, enrichment progs, volunteer placement progs, sheltered employment projs, nutrition & transportation servs, multipurpose ctrs, nursing homes, ombudsman progs, & self training for & by the elderly. **3165 Adeline St, Berkeley CA 94703 (415) 549–0788.**

Rabbi Morris Goldstein Library at Judah L. Magnes Memorial Museum. For information on the Ins, see – Western Jewish History Center of The Judah L. Magnus Memorial Museum, Berkeley, CA. **2911 Russell St, Berkeley CA 94705.**

Western Jewish History Center of the Judah L. Magnus Memorial Museum. Manuscript & archival research library concentrating on the contributions of J & their ins to the Am W. To collect & exhibit manuscripts that show the intellectual, social, business & cultural influence of the J. Library contains 50 bks & bound periodicals, 30 vols of bound oral hist, 287 archival collections, 10 files drawers of vertical file, 40 titles of microfilm, 35 titles of periodicals, 134 oral hist tapes, 76 other tapes, 500–1,000 photographs, diaries, notebks, business papers letters, legal documents & pamphlets; newspaper collection including: The Hebrew fr Jan 1864 to Jun 1876, Emanu-El – a San Francisco newspaper that began in 1895, current J newspapers, special interest papers; bk collection; special collections: Western J Americana, Judah L. Magnes Archives, David Lubin-Harris Weinstock Archives, Western J Periodicals, Western J Imprints, Western Syns & J Ins; Oral Hist Prog; manuscript collection; Rabbi Morris Goldstein Library: 7000 vols, special collection including Haggadah & Siddur fr all over world, rare bk collection of 250 vols & manuseriats dating fr medieval times. Glimpses of Jewish Life in San Francisco; Family History Guide (a pamphlet); The Family of Isaac & Rebecca Harris (a genealogical pamphlet); oral hist projs: San Francisco Jews of Eastern Origin 1880–1940; Marshall Kuhn – Catalyst and Teacher, formerly the Northern California Jewish Community Series; San Francisco J of Eastern European Origin – interviews currently available to the public include Eugene Block, Lilan Cherney, Jean Braverman LaPove, Yehudi Menuhin, Reuben Waxman, Vivian Dudune Solomon, Jesse Levin, Art Rosenbaum, Rabbi Saul White, Daniel Goldberg, Philip Bibel, Bassya Bibel, Celia Alperth, Zena Druckman, Thelma Rosenberg & Rose Ets Hokin; Persecution, Migration, & Intergration: From Germany to the Bay Area, 1933–1947, a video cassette proj; Look Back with Love; The Jews of the West: The Metropolitan Years; Abe Haas: Portrait of a Proud Businessman. Chr: Norman Coliver; Dir: Dr Moses Rischin; Archivist: Ruth Rafael; Asst Archivist: Lauren Lassleben. **2911 Russel St, Berkeley CA 94705 (415) 849–2710.**

Beverly Hills

American Committee for Shaare Zedek in Jerusalem – Western Region. To help future generations meet the health needs of Jerusalem and Israel. Continuing support of century old hospital which moved in 1979 fr old quarters to new $55 million ultra modern medical complex overlooking Jerusalem. Offers total patient & community care. University affiliated teaching hospital contains main hospital building planned for more than 500 beds, emergency shelter, outpatient clinics, school of nursing, clinical labs, research ins, central library, facilities. Ensures the full observance of J tradition. Open to all irrespective of rel, race or national origin. **265 S Robertson Blvd, Rm 5, Beverly Hills CA 90211 (213) 659–6800.**

The American Friends of Haifa University. 9301 Wilshire Blvd, Suite 510, Beverly Hills CA 90210 (213) 273–4707.

American Friends of the Hebrew University. 8665 Wilshire Blvd, Beverly Hills CA 90221 (213) 657–6511.

Beth Jacob Congregation. Orthodox Syn. **9030 W Olympic Blvd, Beverly Hills CA 90211 (213) 278–1911, 272–1922.**

Maccabee Athletic Club. 239 E La Cienega Blvd, Beverly Hills CA 90211.

New Shul Singles. To provide an atmosphere where single people can interact on a social & cultural basis. Diners Club meets mo for private dinner at a restaurant; Gallery Visits meets quarterly at art galleries for viewing & discussion with the artist; concert evenings at the Hollywod Bowl preceded by picnic dinner, & at Los Angeles Philharmonic Orchestra at the Music Ctr; Little Theater nights six times a yr in conjunction with Los Angeles Theater Alliance. **9454 Wilshire Blvd, Beverly Hills CA 90212 (213) 276–9838.**

Sun Air Federation & Home for Asthmatic Children. 221 N Robertson Blvd, Beverly Hills CA 90212 (213) 272–4371.

Temple Emanuel of Beverly Hills. To serve the spiritual, rel & edu needs of its cong & the com. To combine the richness of rel heritage with the practicalities of modern day life. Rel Servs, Fri evening & Sat morning, Sun morning Minyan; Rel Sch for K–12th grade including an audio lingual Heb teaching prog for upper grades; Emanuel Com Day Sch for pre-K–6th grade; Sisterhood; Brotherhood; Temple Fellowship; K'hillat Emanuel; Temple Youth Group; social action progs; Adult Edu; creative arts; Adult & Jr Choir; Young Adults; Single Parents; 40's Plus; Emanuelites, Golden Age Group. F in 1939. Sanctuary located at 300 N Clark Dr. The Clark Dr structure encompasses the Rabbi Harrison Chapel, nursery sch, bridal rm, auditorium, Bd rm & rabbinical offs. The sch bldg at 8844 Burton Way houses classrms, auditorium, J library, J shop, meeting halls, exec offs & underground parking. Rabbi Meyer Heller; Rabbi Stephen M. Robbins; Cantors: Baruch Cohon, Edward Krawll; Pres: Gerald Factor; Edu: Theodore Sharfman, Judith Bin-Nun, Joyce Seglin, Nancy Cooper; Adms: Ralph A. Feinstein, Evelyne Levy; Sisterhood Pres: Thiel Meisenberg; Brotherhood Pres: Ted Wolfe. **8844 Burton Way, Beverly Hills CA 90211 (213) 274–6388.**

Temple Emanuel of Beverly Hills, Library. For information on the Temple, see – Temple Emanuel of Beverly Hills, Beverly Hills, CA. **8844 Burton Way, Beverly Hills CA 90211 (213) 274–6388.**

Union of Orthodox Congregations. 150 N Almont Dr, Beverly Hills CA 90211 (213) 278–4805.

Brandeis

The Brandeis-Bardin Institute. Located on 3,200 acres of secluded countryside in the Simi Valley of Southern CA. To make committed J out of the uncommitted & J leaders out of the committed; to demonstrate that J constitutes the most effective way to achieve universal moral ends & that Judaism is a viable rel/moral option to the non-J as well as to the contemporary J world. BCI summer leadership prog – for men & women 19 to 25 – includes visiting lecturers & scholars, musicians, artists, dancers; physical labor; study; sports activities including swimming, horseback riding, tennis & other sports. Camp Alonim (for chil between 8 & 15) offers swimming, horseback riding, drama, music, folk dancing, Heb instruction & observance of the Sabbath. Other progs include Counselor-in-Training prog (for 16 yr olds) & Jr Counselor-in-Training prog (for 15 yr olds), three sessions, each three weeks long during Jul & Aug, adult prog including Introductory Weekend Ins for married couples, Introductory Weekend for young singles, Weekend Ins for mems of the House of the Bk Assn people who have become mems of the Ins after participating in an Introductory Weekend, with Mem Weekends featuring Scholars-in-Residence sessions, folk dancing & singing; Brandeis-Bardin Forum on Contemporary Values held in Los Angeles. F by the late Dr Shlomo Bardin with the support of the late Supreme Court Justice Louis D. Brandeis. After a start with col youth at Amherst, NH, the ins moved to its present location in 1947. The ins is not affiliated with either the Reform, Conservative or Orthodox denominations. It is J. There are over 7,500 BCI alumni. Dir: Dennis Prager; Asst Dir: Bettie Rifkind; Edu Dir: Joseph Telushkin; Pres: Jack I. Saltzberg; Chr: Willard Chotiner; V Chr: Richard Gunther, Ira Weiner; VPs: Eli Boyer, Mel Fingerman, Louis Hasson, Robert Gore Rifkind, Lawrence Weinberg; Treas: Orrin Kabaker; Sec: Irwin Field; Chr Emeritus: Steve Broidy; Bd of Dirs: Matt Appelman, Dr Ellis Berkowitz, Michael Blankfort, Carl Brown, Rita Chotiner, Gilbert Dreyfuss, Ruben Finkelstein, Gerald Goldberg, David Gould, Frank Horny, Aaron Kotler, Edward Landa, Paul Lehmann, Steve Needleman, Naomi Paul, Seymour Rosenberg, Robert Shafton,

Barbi Weinberg, Robert Wittenberg, Dr Robert Barnhard, Ronald Blanc, Sol Bojarsky, Dr Robert Carroll, Alvin Dick, Lawrence Field, David Gill, Paul Goldman, Lois Gunther, Dr Leo Kaplan, Max Laemmie, Norman Lee, Stanley Michelson, Gerald Novorr, Bettie Rifkind, Dr Wilbur Schwartz, Herbert Solomon, Betty Weiner, David Zerner. **1101 Peppertree Lane, Brandeis CA 93064 (213) 348–7201, (805) 526–1131.**

The Brandeis-Bardin Young Adults. Sponsored by Brandeis-Bardin Ins for age range 25-35. Educates & deepens J committment. Monthly lectures on J topics, traditional Shabbat dinners, workshops, holiday celebrations & havdalah experiences. F late 70's. 300 young adult mems. **1101 Peppertree Lane, Brandeis CA 93064 (213) 348–7201, (805) 526–11**

Camp Alonim of the Brandeis-Brandin Institute. For additional information, see – The Brandeis Brandin Institute, Brandeis, CA. **1101 Peppertree Lane, Brandeis CA 93064 (213) 348–7201, (805) 526–11**

House of the Book Association, Brandeis-Bardin Institute. For information on the Ins, see – Brandeis-Bardin Institute, Brandeis, CA. **1101 Peppertree Lane, Brandeis CA 93064 (213) 348–7201, (805) 526–1131.**

Burbank

Burbank Temple Emanu-El. Affiliated with United Syn of Am. Rabbi Mervin B. Tomsky; Cantor Samuel Fordis; Pres: Louis Bernstein; Nursery Sch Dir: Helen Rieder. **1302 N Glenoaks Blvd, Burbank CA 91504 (213) 845–1734.**

Burlingame

American Committee for the Weizmann Institute of Science. 1801 Murchison Dr, Contour Level, Burlingame CA 94010 (415) 697–3253.

Canoga Park

Congregation Beth Kodesh. Affiliated with United Syn of Am. Rabbi Elijah Schochet; Cantor Avrum Schwartz; Pres: Judith Springer; Adm: Nancy Lachman; Edu Dir: Michael Dinin; Youth Dir: Merrill Alpert. **7401 Shoup Ave, Canoga Park CA 91307 (312) 346–0811.**

Kadima Hebrew Academy. Affiliated with Solomon Schechter Day Schs Assn. Prin: Rabbi Phillip Field; Chr: Albert Lusen. **22600 Sherman Way, Canoga Park CA 91307 (213) 346–0849.**

Temple Solael. Affiliated with UAHC. 506 mems. Rabbi Bernard M. Cohen; Cantor Bernard D. Gutcheon; Pres: Martin Solomon; Edu: Lynda S.K. Rocklin; Adm: Louis Kotzen; Sisterhood Pres: Charlotte Shore; Brotherhood Pres: Mort Saperstein, Burt Fischler. **6601 Valley Cir Blvd, Canoga Park CA 91307 (213) 348–3885.**

West Valley Jewish Community Center. 22622 Vanowen St, Canoga Park CA 91307 (213) 346–3003.

Castro Valley

Congregation Shir Ami. Affiliated with UAHC. 39 mems. Pres: Karl Hand. **4529 Malabar Ave, Castro Valley CA 94546 (415) 538–9660.**

China Lake

All-Faith Chapel, Hebrew Congregation. Affiliated with UAHC. 22 mems. Pres: Pat Siegal. **Naval Weapons Center, China Lake CA 93555 (714) 939–3506.**

Chula Vista

Temple Beth Sholom. Conservative Syn with Col of Judaism – Adult Ins; affiliated with United Syn of Am, Women's League for Conservative Judaism. Rel Servs; adult classes; Sisterhood; Sr Group; Men's Club; cultural breakfasts; socials; family servs; periodical Shabbat dinners; cong Seders; Hanukkah dinners; Purim Carnivals; Lag-BaOmer picnics; Presch; Afternoon Sch; library (Heb, Yiddish, English, Spanish). F 1958. Pub Shabbaton (weekly), Kol Y'fay Nof (monthly). Facilities include sanctuary seating 200+, kosher kitchen, social hall, library, classrms, presch & baby-sitting facilities, Judaica shop, branch of San Diego Col of J. Hosts activities of ORT; B'nai B'rith Women, Hadassah, War Vets; WIZO. Pres: Aaron A. Mannis; Rel VP: Alan M. Anzarouth; Men's Club Pres: Jack Katzman; Sisterhood Pres: Ann Worchel; Youth Leader: Kathryn Paul; Librarian: Edith Lerch. **208 Madrona St, Chula Vista CA 92010 (619) 420–6040; mail add: PO Box 385, Chula Vista CA 92012.**

Claremont

Hillel Council Claremont College. Claremont CA 91722 (213) 621–8000.

Corona

Temple Beth Sholom. Affiliated with United Syn of Am. Pres: Dennis J. Brandt. **823 S Sheridan, Corona CA 91720 (714) 737–9322.**

Costa Mesa

American Association for Ethiopian Jews. To aid Ethiopian J & to preserve their culture; to inform world J about their plight so that action may be taken. Conducts charitable progs to support absorption of Ethiopian J in Is; maintains speakers bureau & files of articles, correspondence, records & photographs of Ethiopian J. About 12 chapters throughout the US; affiliates in Canada, Australia, France & Is; 50 bd mems. F in 1975. The org is a merger of Am Pro-Falasha Cttee & the Friends of Beta-Is (Falasha) Com in Ethiopia. Annual information paper, The Falasha Update; selected literature & reprints. **304 Robin Hood Lane, Costa Mesa CA 92627 (714) 642–8613.**

Temple Isaiah of Newport Beach/Irvine. Affiliated with United Syn of Am. Rabbi Robert Jeremiah Bergman; Pres: Mitchell B. Russakow; Edu Dir: Shoshana Adler. **PO Box 10414, 2401 Irvine Ave, Costa Mesa CA 92627 (714) 540–1310.**

Temple Sharon. Affiliated with United Syn of Am. Rabbi Hershel Brooks; Cantor Meyer Liss; Pres: Edythe Zwickler; Edu Dir: Pnina Stein. **617 W Hamilton, Costa Mesa CA 92627 (714) 631–3262.**

Covina

Jewish Federation Council – Eastern Region. 801 W San Bernardino Rd, Covina CA 91722 (213) 444–4584.

Culver City

National Jewish Hospitality Committee & Information Centers. NJC is an outreach prog for couples in mixed marriages, non-J interested in Judaism, & J who have left Judaism. To serve non-J & J interested in Judaism; to improve the welcome that converts to Judaism receive in the J com. Autobiographies of converts who encourage others to become J are publicized. Rabbinic Bd made up of Conservative & Reform Rabbis. F in 1974. Pres: Rabbi Allen Maller; Exec Dir: Steven Jacobs; Rabbinic Bd: Rabbi A. Abramowitz, Rabbi Mayer Abramowitz, Rabbi Charles Agin, Rabbi Jacob Agus, Rabbi Robert Alper, Rabbi Philip Aronson, Rabbi Stanley Asekoff, Rabbi Marvin Bash, Rabbi Bernard Baskin, Rabbi Jerome Bass, Rabbi Kenneth Berger, Rabbi Abner Bergman, Rabbi Donald Berlin, Rabbi David Bial, Rabbi Murray Blackman, Rabbi Irving Bloom, Rabbi Aaron Blumenthal, Rabbi Ben Zion Bokser, Rabbi Joseph Brandriss, Rabbi Robert Bronstein, Rabbi Leonard Cahan, Rabbi Bernard Cohen, Rabbi Martin Cohen, Rabbi Hillel Cohn, Rabbi Beryl Cohon, Rabbi Lawrence Colton, Rabbi Matthew Derby, Rabbi David Eichhorn, Rabbi Jonathan Eichhorn, Rabbi Ira Eisenstein, Rabbi Sheldon Elster, Rabbi Seymour Essrog, Rabbi Arnold Fink, Rabbi Oscar Fleishaker, Rabbi Allen Freehling, Rabbi Theodore Friedman, Rabbi Joseph Gallinger, Rabbi Jerrold Goldstein, Rabbi Noah Golinkin, Rabbi Morris Goodblatt, Rabbi David Gordis, Rabbi Robert Gordis, Rabbi Morris Gordon, Rabbi Earl Grollman, Rabbi Joshua Haberman, Rabbi Martin Halpern, Rabbi Meyer Heller, Rabbi Lester Hering, Rabbi Richard Hertz, Rabbi Harris Hirschberg, Rabbi Steven Jacobs, Rabbi Arnold Kalman, Rabbi Gerald Kaplan, Rabbi Reuben Katz, Rabbi Joel Klein, Rabbi Bernard Kligfeld, Rabbi Gilbert Kollin, Rabbi Jossef Kratzenstein, Rabbi Michael LeBurkien, Rabbi Barton Lee, Rabbi William Leffler, Rabbi Arthur Lelyveld, Rabbi Samuel Lerer, Rabbi Stephen Lerner, Rabbi Martin Levin, Rabbi Jonathan Levine, Rabbi Reuben Levine, Rabbi Norman Lipson, Rabbi Alvin Leiberman, Rabbi David Lincoln, Rabbi Allen Maller, Rabbi Richard Marcovitz, Rabbi Amos Miller, Rabbi Judah Nadich, Rabbi Hiroshi Okamoto, Rabbi Shimon Paskow, Rabbi Fishel Pearlmutter, Rabbi Jerome Pine, Rabbi Gunther Plaut, Rabbi Albert Plotkin, Rabbi Tzvi Porath, Rabbi Seymour Prystowsky, Rabbi Stanley Rabinowitz, Rabbi Simon Resnikoff, Rabbi Barry Rosen, Rabbi Robert Seigel, Rabbi Sanford Shapero, Rabbi Jacob Shtull, Rabbi Hillel Silverman, Rabbi Abraham Simon, Rabbi Ralph Simon, Rabbi Bernard Spielman, Rabbi Jordan Taxon, Rabbi Saul Teplitz, Rabbi Noach Valley, Rabbi Max Vorspan, Rabbi Frank Waldorf, Rabbi Lewis Weintraub, Rabbi Alton Winters, Rabbi Aaron Wise, Rabbi Barry Woolf, Rabbi Herbert Yoskowitz, Rabbi Sheldon Zimmerman, Rabbi Martin Zion. **Temple Akiba, 5249 S Sepulveda Blvd, Culver City CA 90230 (213) 398–5783.**

Temple Akiba. Reform Temple affiliated with UAHC. To enhance J life & strengthen the J people. Rel Servs; J edu from nursery sch to post-confirmation; Adult Edu; JME – summer day camp & resident camp; weekend retreats; youth groups; outreach prog to welcome non-J into the J com; Sisterhood; Havurot; the Mordechai Soloff Library contains 1,500 vols (Judaica). 425 families; 1000 individuals; 22 in nursery sch; 200 in primary sch; 95 in Jr HS; 26 confirmation. 20 employees, 50 volunteers. F 1953. Monthly bulletin. Facilities include sanctuary seating 450; social hall seating 250; 10 classrms; library; youth off. Welcomes converts warmly into Cong. Rabbi Allen Maller. **5249 S Sepulveda Blvd, Culver City CA 90230.**

Temple Akiba Library. Library contains 1500 vols (Judaica). For information on the Temple, see – Temple Akiba, Culver City, CA. **5249 S Sepulveda Blvd, Culver City CA 90230 (213) 870–6575.**

Daly City

B'nai B'rith Women Central Pacific Region. Regional Dir: Roberta Steiner. **Westlake Med Bldg 201, 48 Park Plaza Dr, Daly City CA 94015 (415) 994–3400.**

Downey

Temple Ner Tamid. Affiliated with UAHC. 145 mems. Rabbi Stuart Lasher; Cantor Sidney Bloom; Pres: Leo Taslit; Sisterhood Pres: Marcia Levin; Brotherhood Pres: Don Jacobs. **10629 Lakewood Blvd, Downey CA 90241 (213) 861–9276.**

El Toro

Temple Eilat. Affiliated with United Syn of Am. Rabbi Steven D. Schatz; Cantor Joseph Chazan; Pres: Phyllis Lee. **24432 Muirlands Blvd, El Toro CA 92630 (714) 770–9606.**

Encinitas

Temple Sinai. Affiliated with United Syn of Am. Rabbi Gerald B. Weiss; Pres: Ed Carrol. **677 Santa Fe Dr, Encinitas CA 92024.**

Temple Solel. Affiliated with UAHC. 76 mems. Rabbi Bernard B. Goldsmith; Pres: Stephen Cohen. **890 Balour Dr, PO Box 786, Encinitas CA 92024.**

Encino

Chabad of the Valley. Orthodox Syn; Gan Israel Day Camp of the Valley; affiliated with Friends of Lubavitch Inc, World Wide Chabad Movement. To educate & to assist; to promote J identity. Daily & Shabbath Servs; Presch; K; Afternoon Schs; summer camps; counseling; Adult Edu; hosp holiday visitation; com outreach; library containing 800 vols (Traditional J). 120 presch stu; 160 afternoon sch stu; summer camp 330. 40 employees. A branch of West Coast Chabad Lubavitch, serving the San Francisco Valley. Pub Newsletter (quarterly); Annual Journal. Facilities include four ctrs & syns in Hollywood, Tarzana, Westlake & Encino. Exec Dir: Rabbi Joshua B. Gordon; Assc Dir: Rabbi Mordy Einbinder; Edu Dir: Rabbi Aaron Abend; Presch Dir: Renee Hutchings; CONEJO Regional Dir: Rabbi Mendel Goldman; Youth Dir: Menachem Bryski; Adm: Gladys Husman. **4915 Hayvenhurst Ave, Encino CA 91436 (213) 784–9985.**

Maarev Temple. Affiliated with United Syn of Am. Rabbi Jack Riemer; Cantor Uri Frenkel; Asst Rabbi Gerald Weiss; Rabbi Emeritus Dr Kalman Freidman; Pres: Al Resnick; Exec Dir: Art Williams. **5180 Yarmouth Ave, Encino CA 91396 (213) 345–7833.**

Valley Beth Shalom. Affiliated with United Syn of Am. Rabbi Harold M. Schulweis; Cantor Herschel Fox; Asst Rabbi Frederic J. Margulies; Pres: Darwin Miller; Exec Dir: Leonard H. Smith; Edu Dir: Dr David Elcott; Day Sch Prin: Barry Rich; Youth Dir: Sue Shrell. **15739 Ventura Blvd, Encino CA 91436 (213) 788–6000.**

Valley Beth Shalom Library. For information on the Syn, see – Vally Beth Shalom, Encino, CA. **15739 Ventura Blvd, Encino CA 91436 (213) 788–6000.**

Eureka

Temple Beth El. Affiliated with UAHC. 38 mems. Rabbi Leo Trepp; Pres: Arnold Hrskovic. **Hodgson & T Sts, PO Box 442, Eureka CA 95501 (707) 422–9686.**

Fremont

Temple Beth Torah. Affiliated with UAHC. 161 mems. Rabbi Steven B. Kaplan; Pres: Florence Silver; Sisterhood Pres: Suzanne Harrosh. **42000 Paseo Padre Pkwy, PO Box 6017, Fremont CA 94538 (415) 656–7141.**

Temple Beth Torah Library. For information on the Temple, see – Temple Beth Torah, Fremont, CA. **42000 Paseo Padre Pkwy, PO Box 6017, Fremont CA 94538 (415) 656–7141.**

Fresno

Congregation Beth Jacob. Affiliated with United Syn of Am. Rabbi Samuel Schwartz; Pres: Ben M. Lubic; Edu Dir: Roslyn Bloom. **406 W Shields Ave, Fresno CA 93705 (209) 222–0664.**

Temple Beth Israel. Affiliated with UAHC. 248 mems. Rabbis: Joseph Melamed, David L. Greenberg; Cantor Michael Loring; Pres: Stanley M. Ziegler; Edu: Joseph Melamed; Sisterhood Pres: Alexis Stacy; Brotherhood Pres: Leonard Albert. **PO Box 1328, Fresno CA 93715 (209) 264–2929.**

Fullerton

Temple Beth Tikvah of North Orange County. Reform Temple affiliated with UAHC. To help the young & old to make full use of the great heritage of the J people by beautifying their lives & making them more meaningful through our traditions & customs, & to enhance J living in keeping with the Reform Movement. Dedicated to the worship of God & the study of Torah. Rel Servs, Sabbath & Holidays; Rel Sch for K through Confirmation; Heb Sch; Bar/Bat Mitzvah preparation; Heb HS; library; Adult Choir – Kol Tikvah; Jr Choir; Jr Chavereem for chil ages 8 to 13; Adult Edu; Early Childhood Learning Ctr; Jr Youth Group for 7th through 9th graders; Sr Youth Group for 10th through 12th graders; Sisterhood; Brotherhood; Friendship Club for Sr Adults; Chugim for youth ages 9 to 12; Havurah; summer progs: Camp Tikvah, Tikvah Teens for 9th to 12th graders. 350 families. F in 1964. Located on 5 acres. Temple facilities include a sanctuary & social hall. Rabbi Haim Asa; Cantor Eli Cohn; Pres: Edith Goodman; Edu: Daniel A. Bender; Sisterhood Pres: Charlotte Salkin; Brotherhood Pres: Jack Hack. **1600 N Acacia Ave, Fullerton CA 92631 (714) 871–3535.**

Garden Grove

Jewish Federation of Orange County. Mem of CJF. Sponsors: United Jewish Welfare Fund. Organized 1964; inc 1965. Pres: Dr Daniel Ninburg; Exec Dir: Donald L. Gartner. **12181 Buaro, Garden Grove CA 92640 (714) 530–6636.**

Jewish Studies Institute Day School. Affiliated with Solomon Schechter Day Schs Assn. Prin: Frank Salkoff; Chr: Dr Hal Kravitz. **12181 Buaro St, Garden Grove CA 92640 (714) 636–3361.**

Gardena

Southwest Temple Beth Torah. 14725 S Gramercy Pl, Gardena CA 90249 (213) 327–8734.

Gilroy

South Santa Clara-San Benito County Jewish Community. Gen meeting held first Thurs of each mo. Pres: Jack Fisher; Sec: Stuart Blumberg. **PO Box 143, Gilroy CA 95020 (408) 779–6456, 842–2308.**

Glendale

Temple Sinai. Affiliated with UAHC. 182 mems. Rabbi Marvin M. Gross; Cantor Harvey L. Block; Pres: Jack Spillman; Edu: Martin Zinkow; Sisterhood Pres: Lois Samson. **1212 N Pacific Ave, Glendale CA 91202 (213) 246–8101.**

Hollywood

Ahavath Israel Congregation. Orthodox Syn. Daily Servs morning & evening; Adult Edu courses, Shabbat classes; com servs: charity, hosp visits & com Seder. The oldest & presently the only Orthodox cong in Hollywood. Rabbi Teitelbaum; Cantor Y.M. Weberman; Pres: Jack Azoff; VPs: Hyman Adler, A. Aaron Goldenberg, Jack Haffner; Treas: Samuel Gazin; Sec: Henry Lewis. **5454 Virginia Ave, Hollywood CA 90029 (213) 464–3885.**

Huntington Park

Huntington Park Hebrew Congregation. Affiliated with United Syn of Am. Cantor Irving Jacobs; Pres: Marie Mills. **PO Box 867, 2877 E Florence Ave, Huntington Park CA 90255 (213) 585–4436.**

La Jolla

Congregation Beth El. Affiliated with United Syn of Am. Pres: Charles T. Rosen; Exec Dir: Harold H. Benowitz; Edu Dir: Zelda Goodman. **8745 La Jolla Scenic Dr, La Jolla CA 90237 (714) 452–1734.**

La Mirada

Temple Beth Ohr. Affiliated with UAHC. 250 mems. Rabbi Lawrence J. Goldmark; Cantor Steven Showstack; Pres: Irwin Berman; Edu: Dottie Abel; Sisterhood Pres: Carol Scher; Brotherhood Pres: Mickey Skolnick. **15721 E Rosecrans Blvd, La Mirada CA 90638 (714) 521–6765.**

Lafayette

Cotler Memorial Library, Temple Isaiah. For information on the Temple, see – Temple Isaiah, Lafayette, CA. **3800 Mt Diablo Blvd, Lafayette CA 94549 (415) 283–8575.**

Temple Isaiah. Affiliated with UAHC. 680 mems. Rabbi Shelley Waldenberg; Cantor Richard B. Silverman; Pres: Diane Portnoff; Adms: Terry Bloom, Harriet Bloom; Sisterhood Pres: Catherine Sherman. **3800 Mt Diablo Blvd, Lafayette CA 94549 (415) 283–8575.**

Lakewood

Temple Beth Zion-Sinai. Conservative Syn affiliated with United Syn of Am. To provide for the edu, rel, social & cultural needs of the com. Daily, Sabbath & Holiday Servs; Family Sabbath first Fri of the mo; Rel Sch K through HS with Biblical Heb

Language Prog which enables stu to read & understand the Bible & prayer bk; Sun morning special interest groups; Confirmation Dept; library; Family Edu Prog – an award winning prog involving the entire family; Adult Edu Prog with discussions, guest speakers, classes; Sisterhood; Men's Club; Boy Scouts; weekly Bingo Night. 320 families. Est in 1952 in temporary quarters. On Apr 11, 1954 the Syn, then called the Lakewood J Com Cong, was dedicated. After merging with the Woodruff Com Ctr in 1962, the Cong changed its name to Temple Beth Zion. Because of growth in membership, plans were made for a new, larger bldg. In Oct of 1970 the new bldg was dedicated. In 1974, after another merger, the name of the Temple was changed to its present one. The Shofar (monthly newsletter). Facilities include a social hall seating 200, a sanctuary seating 160, a small sanctuary seating 20, a youth lounge, a kosher kitchen with separate meat & dairy areas, gift shop, edu bldg housing with seven classrms & two offs, & temple offs. Rabbi Wayne Allen; Cantor Yehuda Keller; Edu Dir: Steven Schatz; Pres: Leon Shalom; VP: Ben Alhadeff. **6440 Del Amo Blvd, Lakewood CA 90713 (213) 429–0715, 1014.**

Temple Beth Zion-Sinai Library. 6440 Del Amo Blvd, Lakewood CA 90713 (213) 429–0715.

Lancaster

Beth Knesset Bamidbar. Affiliated with UAHC. 75 mems. Rabbi E.R. Kraus; Pres: H.J. Schissell; Edu: Lawrence Greatman; Sisterhood Pres: Della Carmona. **PO Box 1008, 1611 E Ave J, Lancaster CA 93534 (805) 942–4415.**

Larkspur

Kol Shofar. Affiliated with United Syn of Am. Rabbi David White; Pres: Fred B. Cherniss. **20 Magnolia Ave, Larkspur CA 94939 (415) 924–6081.**

Livermore

Congregation Beth Emek. Affiliated with UAHC. 78 mems. Rabbi Gary A. Schoenberg; Pres: Gary Kerbel; Edu: Leonard Cooper. **1886 College Ave, PO Box 722, Livermore CA 94550 (415) 443–1689.**

Long Beach

Jewish Community Center of Long Beach, College Student Services. Col stu servs serving stu attending sch in the Long Beach/W Orange Cty area of CA, as well as stu attending sch elsewhere but whose parents reside in the area. To provide cultural & intellectual enrichment as well as a place to meet for J col stu. Discussions; cultural arts & social events including dances, parties, sports activities, art progs, com forums, special celebrations, communal Shabbat pot luck dairy dinners, creative worship servs, Is awareness, social servs & social action projs. The JCC of Long Beach began this serv in 1980. Events are open to undergrad & grad stu, full & part-time. Dir: Hildy Sheinman. **3801 E Willow, Long Beach CA 90815 (213) 426–7601.**

Jewish Community Federation of Greater Long Beach & West Orange County. Mem of CJF. Sponsors: United Jewish Welfare Fund. Inc 1937. Pres: Roselle Sommer; Exec Dir: Oliver B. Winkler. **3801 E Willow Ave, Long Beach CA 90815 (213) 426–7601.**

Long Beach Hebrew Academy. Rabbi E. Piekarski. **3981 Atlantic Ave, Long Beach CA 90807 (213) 424–9787.**

Long Beach Jewish Connection. Sponsored by Long Beach/W Orange Cty J Com Fed. To bring singles together to learn more about their J heritage & local & overseas J coms. Field trips to places of J interest in area; speakers; movies; Sunday brunches; Shabbat dinners. **3801 E Willow, Long Beach CA 90815 (213) 426–7601, 636–5970, 439–7334.**

Society of Israel Philatelists. 1125 E Carson St #2, Long Beach CA 90807 (213) 595–9224.

Temple Beth Shalom. Affiliated with United Syn of Am. Rabbi Shalom Podwol; Cantor David J. Kane; Pres: Ida Z. Bobrow; Edu Dir: Frank Salkoff. **3635 Elm Ave, Long Beach CA 90807 (213) 426–6413.**

Temple Israel. Affiliated with UAHC. 530 mems. Rabbis: Jonathan M. Brown, Wolli Kaelter; Cantor Alan Weiner; Pres: Lynne Rosenstein; Edu: Sherry Bissell; Adm: Helena S. Medoff; Sisterhood Pres: Polly Alevy. **3538 E 3rd St, PO Box 14406, Long Beach CA 90814 (213) 434–0996.**

Los Altos Hills

Congregation Beth Am. Affiliated with UAHC. Reform Temple. Meetings held once a mo; Sisterhood; library. 582 mems. Rabbis: Sidney Akselrad, William C. Berk; Cantor David Unterman; Pres: Mark Levi; Sisterhood Pres: Sherry Mehl. **26790 Arastradero Rd, Los Altos Hills CA 94022 (415) 493–4661.**

Congregation Beth Am Library. For information on the Cong, see – Congregation Beth

Am, Los Altos Hills, CA. **26790 Arastradero Rd, Los Altos Hills CA 94022 (415) 493–4661.**

Los Angeles

Adat Shalom. Affiliated with United Syn of Am. Rabbi Morton A. Wallack; Cantor Leon G. Bennet; Pres: S. Zachary Samuels; Exec Dir: Jule Rivlin; Edu Dir: Frances Wilkotz. **3030 Westwood Blvd, Los Angeles CA 90034 (213) 475–4985.**

Akiba Academy. J Day Sch under the auspices of the Conservative movement & affiliated with Solomon Schechter Day Schs Assn. Accredited by the CA Assn of Independent Schs, the Western Assn of Schs & Cols, & the Bureau of J Edu of Los Angeles. To provide an outstanding edu in all subjects. Gen & J studies for chil in grades K through eighth grade; The J prog emphasizes contemporary Heb, the study of traditional texts, customs, ceremonies, hist, tradition & other aspects of J life. Est in 1967. Headmaster: Rabbi Laurence Scheindlin; Asst Prin: Judith Koenig; Pres: Dr Emanuel Abrams; Exec VP: Ben Kukoff; VPs: Judith Eber, Elia Weinbach; Sec: Ellen Jacobs; Treas: Errol Fine; Edu Cttee Chr: Rabbi Robert Wexler; Rep to the Exec Cttee: Dianne Zimnavoda; PTA Pres: Anne Rosenblatt. **10400 Wilshire Blvd, Los Angeles CA 90024 (213) 475–6401. Middle Sch Site: 3030 Westwood Blvd, Los Angeles CA 90034.**

American Association for Ethiopian Jews. To aid Ethiopian J & to preserve their culture; to inform world J about their plight so that action may be taken. Conducts charitable progs to support absorption of Ethiopian J in Is; maintains speakers bureau & files of articles, correspondence, records & photographs of Ethiopian J. About 12 chapters throughout the US; affiliates in Canada, Australia, France & Is; 50 Bd mems. F in 1975. The org is a merger of Am Pro-Falasha Cttee & the Friends of Beta-Is (Falasha) Com in Ethiopia. Annual information paper – The Falasha Update; selected literature & reprints. Pres: Prof Howard M. Lenhoff; F Pres, Exec VP: Dr Grenum Berger; Treas: Dr Theodore Norman; VPs: Nathan Shapiro, Edith Everett; Sec: Jeffrey Stone. **Natl Materials Ctr, 6505 Wilshire Blvd, Rm 802, Los Angeles CA 90048 (213) 852–1234 Ext 276.**

American Friends of the Tel Aviv University. 1900 Ave of the Stars, Los Angeles CA 90067 (213) 556–3141.

American Jewish Committee. 6505 Wilshire Blvd #319, Los Angeles CA 90048 (213) 655–7071.

American Technion Society. 8170 Beverly Blvd, Los Angeles CA 90048 (213) 651–3321.

American Zionist Federation – Western Region. Coordinating agy of the Am Zionist Movement encompassing 16 natl mem orgs. Constituent orgs: Am J League for Is, Am Mizrachi Women, Am for Progressive Is-Hashomer Hatzair, Am Sephardi Fed, Assn of Parents of Am Israelis, Assn of Reform Zionists of Am-ARZA, B'nai Zion, Emunah, Hadassah, Labor Zionists Alliance, N Am Aliyah Movement, Pioneer Women, Rel Zionists of Am, Telem-Movement for Zionist Fulfillment, United Zionists-Revisionists of Am, Zionist Org of Am. Corporate orgs: Bd of Rabbis of Southern CA, Am Congress of J fr Poland & Survivors of Concentration Camps; Sephardic Assn; Max Nordau Shelters for Is. Syn affiliates: Stephen S. Wise Temple, Temple Is of Hollywood, Temple Solael. Zionist Youth Movements: Betar, Bnei Akiva, Habonim, Hashachar, Hashomer Hatzair, Masada. To motivate Am J to accept the Zionist principles that all the J in the world are one people with Is as the ctr of J life. Provides a Speakers' Bureau which keeps the com at large informed with up-to-date information on the Middle E & Is; supports agy assisting J who need or want to settle in Is; encourages the est of ins & data for edu in J, Heb & culture of the J people; furthers the efforts of fund raising orgs supporting J edu, youth progs & advancing J welfare; supports progs encouraging Am J youth to participate in Zionist work & activities nationally & locally; promotes research, study & discussion of Zionist ideals & aims. Close to one million Am J. F in 1970. Pres: Frank Horny; Exec Dir: Charlotte P. Abramson; Adm: Elaine Solomon. **6505 Wilshire Blvd, Los Angeles CA 90048 (213) 655–4636.**

American Zionist Youth Foundation – University Service Department. A proj of the col div of Am Zionist Youth Foun in consultation with the Is Aliyah Ctr. To promote Zionist activities & awareness on campus. Sponsors lectures & seminars in the US & Is; provides assistance for the est & maintenance of Zionist stu groups, garinim & batim (houses) on campus; sponsors leadership training seminars; provides Is shlichim for campuses; serves as a clearing house & distributing agy for brochures, pamphlets, posters, bks, exhibits, films & slide shows; provides materials & information about aliyah, summer, six mo & yr long progs in Is; distributes information on rel & Torah study progs in yeshivot, kibbutzim & special progs for rel men & women in Is; maintains follow up prog for Is prog returnees; offers special stu discounts for Is oriented magazines & journals; maintains a network of over 70 campus reps. Zionist Activist – a newspaper,

Zionist Organizing Manual & Sourcebook; Zionist Comments; Zionist Press Serv. SW Regional Coord: Lisa Huppin. **6505 Wilshire Blvd, Los Angeles CA 90048 (213) 655–9828.**

American Zionist Youth Foundation, Inc – West Coast Region. A nation wide Zionist org affiliated with HS & cols. To instill in young J a strong sense of J identity & a deep devotion to Is. Provides support & back-up servs for Israeli emissaries (shlichim) & leaders of the Zionist youth movements; coords inter-movement activities; produces, amasses & disseminates edu material used by the various Am Zionist youth movements & orgs, camps, schs & com ctrs; devs audio-visual materials on Is, holidays & matters of gen J concern; organizes edu activities & special seminars for youth leaders; offers records & bks to the gen public in the area of Is folk dancing; advises & assists rel Zionist movements & orgs; initiates & maintains long & short term progs in Is for young people; encourages Zionist progs in Yeshivot, day schs & rel camps; stu activities dept divides its work between HS & col activities & servs; devs edu, cultural & prog materials for training seminars & confs; Is Prog Ctr sponsors progs bringing young people to Is for a summer, progs offering experiences in dance, music, archaeology, nature study, kibbutz life & extensive touring; offers Sherut La'am (serv to the people), a six mo to a one yr prog combining Heb language study with work in a kibbutz or a dev town with other progs including a semester at an Is univ, rel kibbutz work study prog & a J studies prog. HORA – newsletter pub three times a yr by the Is Folk Dance Ins. W Coast Regional Dir: Yoni Rochell. **6505 Wilshire Blvd, Los Angeles CA 90048 (213) 655–9828.**

Ampal (Israel Development). 6505 Wilshire Blvd #203, Los Angeles CA 90048 (213) 653–5633.

Anti-Defamation League of B'nai B'rith – Pacific SW Regional Office. Dedicated in purpose & prog to translating the Am heritage of democratic ideals into a way of life for all Am; works to counter assaults on the safety, status, rights & image of J. For additional information, see – Anti-Defamation League of B'nai B'rith, New York City, NY. **6505 Wilshire Blvd, Suite 814, Los Angeles CA 90048.**

B'nai B'rith Messenger. Periodical pub. **2510 W 7th St, Los Angeles CA 90057 (213) 380–5000.**

B'nai B'rith Women. 6399 Wilshire Blvd, Los Angeles CA 90048 (213) 651–4924.

B'nai David-Judea Congregation. Orthodox Syn. **8906 W Pico Blvd, Los Angeles CA 90035 (213) 272–7223, 276–9269.**

B'nai Tikvah Congregation. Affiliated with United Syn of Am. Rabbi Marvin Bornstein; Cantor William B. Nussen; Pres: Edith Hanff. **5820 W Manchester Blvd, Los Angeles CA 90045 (213) 776–5933.**

Bet Tzedek Legal Services. Offers free legal assistance to low-income persons. **7966 Beverly Blvd 210, Los Angeles CA 90048 (213) 658–8930.**

Beverly Fairfax Neighborhood Organization. 163 S Fairfax Ave, Los Angeles CA 90036 (213) 931–1511.

Blumenthal Library, Sinai Temple. 10400 Wilshire Blvd, Los Angeles CA 90024 (213) 474–1518.

Board of Rabbis. 6505 Wilshire Blvd, Los Angeles CA 90048 (213) 852–1234.

Bonds for Israel. 6380 Wilshire Blvd, Los Angeles CA 90048 (213) 653–8400.

Bureau of Jewish Education. 6505 Wilshire Blvd, Los Angeles CA 90048 (213) 852–1234.

California Jewish Press. A California Press Bureau Pub. **6399 Wilshire Blvd #511, Los Angeles CA 90048 (213) 651–2230.**

Camp JCA of Jewish Center Association. 6505 Wilshire Blvd #209, Los Angeles CA 90048 (213) 653–4260.

Camp Max Strauss. 6505 Wilshire Blvd, Los Angeles CA 90048 (213) 852–1234.

Chabad House, Mid-City. Lubavitch Com Servs Ctr. Blends Chassidic fervor & warmth with tradition & learning, to show that every J, fr whatever background he or she comes fr, is an integral part of the body of Is. Anti-missionary work; adult edu; Sabbath seminars; holiday progs; day camp; youth groups; syns; kosher kitchen; Russian Immigrant Aid Soc; counseling; chaplaincy; Mitzvah Campaigns; hosp & prison visitations; sr citizens encounters; speakers bureau. **420 N Fairfax, Los Angeles CA 90036 (213) 655–4739.**

Chabad House, West Coast Headquarters. Lubavitch com servs ctr. Blends Chassidic fervor &

warmth with tradition & learning, to show that every J, fr whatever background he or she comes fr, is an integral part of the body of Is. Anti-missionary work; adult edu; Sabbath seminars; holiday progs; day camp; youth groups; syns; kosher kitchen; Russian Immigrant Aid Soc; counseling; chaplaincy; Mitzvah Campaigns; hosp & prison visitations; sr citizens encounters; speakers bureau. Rabbi Shlomo Cunin. **741 Gayley Ave, Los Angeles CA 90024 (213) 272–7113.**

Children's Asthma Res Ins & Hospital. CARIH. **1060 W Pico Blvd, Los Angeles CA 90048 (213) 558–0014.**

Coalition for Alternatives in Jewish Education. 8512 Whitworth Dr, Suite 1, Los Angeles CA 90035 (213) 659–0325.

Community Relations Committee. 6505 Wilshire Blvd #802, Los Angeles CA 90048 (213) 852–1234.

Congregation Ahavath Israel. Orthodox Syn. **5454 Virginia Ave, Los Angeles CA 90029 (213) 464–3885.**

Congregation Beth Israel. Orthodox Syn. **8056 Beverly Blvd, Los Angeles CA 90048 (213) 651–4022.**

Congregation Magen David. Orthodox Syn. **9717 W Pico Blvd, Los Angeles CA 90035 (213) 879–3681.**

Conservative Synagogue Information. 15600 Mulholland Dr, Los Angeles CA 90024 (213) 476–9777.

Department of Single Adults, Jewish Federation Council of Greater Los Angeles. Serv org comprised of reps of many Los Angeles J single groups & unaffiliated mems of the single com. Sponsors outreach progs; sponsors J Assn of Singles Servs, age range 21–35, & JASS II for singles 35 plus; offers leadership dev seminar & leadership weekend; responsible for the operation of JASSLine & JASSLine II, a weekly recorded tape of events of interest to J single adults, operated 24 hours a day by volunteers; maintains a master calendar of major progs offered by single adult orgs. Dir of the Dept is available for consultation & resources to professionals & leadership of existing progs & to those who are developing new progs. JASSLine sponsored by the Dept of Single Adults went into operation Oct 15, 1979. The Jewish Singles Guide To Los Angeles. Dir: Rosalind Lawson. **6505 Wilshire Blvd, Suite 501, Los Angeles CA 90048 (213) 852–1234, 990–8640.**

Dor Chapter. Sponsored by B'nai Zion. Young adults fraternal & Zionist org. Offers both social & cultural activities. Sponsors two projects in Israel: a home for retarded chil & a vet rehabilitation ctr; social & cultural events; monthly meetings; study sessions. **6351 Wilshire Blvd, Suite 211, Los Angeles CA 90048 (213) 655–9128.**

Emissary of the Rebbe for the West Coast. Rabbi S.D. Raichik. **101 N Edinburgh Ave, Los Angeles CA 90048 (213) 931–0913.**

Frances-Henry Library, Hebrew Union College – Jewish Institute of Religion. Contains almost 60,000 vols as well as periodicals, microfilms, records & tapes covering every aspect of J intellectual endeavor. Annual journal of HUC-JIR Libraries – Studies in Bibliography & Booklore, appearing since 1953, is only learned journal devoted to J bibliography pub in US. **3077 Univ Ave, Los Angeles CA 90007 (213) 749–3424.**

Freda Mohr Multiservice Center. Sponsored by: J Fam Serv, J Fed Council. Provides information & referrals to all relevant sources. **351 N Fairfax Ave, Los Angeles CA 90036 (213) 655–5141.**

Gateways Mental Health Center. 1891 Effie St, Los Angeles CA 90026 (213) 666–0171.

Government of Israel Trade Center. Dev of trade relations between US & Is. For additional information, see – Government of Israel Trade Center, New York City, NY. **6380 Wilshire Blvd, Los Angeles CA 90048 (213) 658–7924.**

Guardians of Jewish Home for the Aged. 6505 Wilshire Blvd #503, Los Angeles CA 90048 (213) 651–3640.

HA'AM. Univ of CA, Los Angeles J newsmagazine pub once a mo during the academic yr. To inform & edu stu on issues relevant to the com; to present the stu viewpoint on pol, economic & social issues to the com-at-large. Local news, natl & intl affairs, special coverage on Is in each issue. 15,000 copies distributed throughout the Los Angeles met area. Staff of 25. In addition, many stu contribute articles on specific topics. F about 10 yrs ago by stu. The paper has remained strictly in stu hands & is pub by the ASUCLA Communications Bd. The paper encourages stu of all backgrounds, beliefs & opinions to write, thus becoming a forum for critical debate & analysis of contemporary problems & issues. Editor-in-Chief: Natalie Gluck; Bus Mgr: Cindy Rogoway. **112E Kerckhoff Hall, 308 Westwood Plaza, Los Angeles CA 90024.**

Habonim – Camp Gilboa. Labor Zionist summer camp affiliated with Haboim-Dror Labor Zionist Youth, Habonim Camping Assn, Am Camping Assn. To educate young J towards a strong J & Labor Zionist identity. Seven-week summer prog for chil aged 10–16 with regular camp prog & strong emphasis on Heb study. 120 campers of the ages 10–16 years old per session. 25 employed councellors. 40 years of camping experience. Kosher kitchen; sports facilities. Registrar: Dori Orenstein. **8339 W 3rd St, Los Angeles CA 90048 (213) 655–1868.**

Hadassah – Pacific Coast Region. For additional information, see – Hadassah, New York City, NY. **6505 Wilshire Blvd #404, Los Angeles CA 90048 (213) 653–9727.**

Hadassah Zionist Youth Commission. 6505 Wilshire Blvd #404, Los Angeles CA 90048 (213) 653–9727.

Hamburger Home for Girls. A professionally staffed, psychiatrically oriented residence providing a semi-protective, home-like atmosphere for young women between 16-24. **7357 Hollywood Blvd, Los Angeles CA 90046 (213) 876–0550.**

Hebrew Union College – Jewish Institute of Religion. Ins of higher learning in Am Reform J. Accredited by the Middle States Assn of Cols & Secondary Schs, the N Central Assn of Cols & Secondary Schs, the Western Assn of Schs & Cols; affiliated with the Univ of Cincinnati, the Greater Cincinnati Consortium of Cols & Univs, the Univ of Southern CA, Washington Univ, NY Univ & the Hebrew Univ. Dedicated to the study of J in the spirit of free inquiry. The Rabbinic Sch: two yr prog of study leading to the Master of Arts degree, following the successful completion of the Yr in Is prog with an additional one yr prog is available for rabbinic stu to specialize in J communal studies, J edu or social ethics; upon receiving the Master of Arts degree, the stu transfers to the HUC-JIR in Cincinnati or NY for the remaining two yrs of the prog leading to ordination. Edgar F. Magnin Sch of Grad Studies: progs leading to the degree of Masters of Arts, Dr of Heb Letters, Dr of Heb Studies & Dr of Philosophy; the sch participates in a variety of progs in cooperation with the Univ of Southern CA & with depts of rel of other univs & theological schs. The Sacred Music Prog: courses are offered for syn professionals, organists & choir dirs dealing with the various literatures & backgrounds of syn music. Rhea Hirsch Sch of Edu: undergrad courses & full time grad training in J edu leading to Bachelor of Sci in Heb Edu, Bachelor of Sci in J Edu, Masters of Arts in J Edu, Master of Arts in Heb Edu with stu in the masters degree prog required to spend their first yr at the Sch of J Studies in Jerusalem & during the course of study, each stu receives formal placement which includes both teaching & supervision in a sch setting, research & dev progs; special progs include Confluent Edu, Early Edu, Library Sci, Summer Ins. The Jerome H. Louchheim Sch of J Studies: degrees offered include Master of Arts in J Studies, Bachelor of Sci in J Studies, Bachelor of Arts with a Major in Rel & a Specialty in J Studies offered by the Univ of Southern CA in cooperation with the Col; Assc in Arts in J Studies; offers courses as part of the undergrad prog at the Univ of Southern CA. Sch of Communal Servs: degrees offered include Master of Arts in J Communal Serv, Double Master of Arts in J Communal Serv & Social Work, Master of Arts in J Communal Serv & J Edu, Certificate in J Communal Serv; faculty offers lectures & seminars in J identity, com org, the J component of social servs & J thought to professional & laymen active in J communal servs. The Ins of Contemporary J of Hebrew Univ & the Sch of J Communal Servs of HUC co-sponsor the World Seminar for J Servs in Jerusalem, with the Edu & Culture Dept of the World Zionist Org & the Ins of Leadership Dev of the J Agy. Frances-Henry Library contains 60,000 vols as well as periodicals, microfilms, records & tapes. Skirball Mus houses 12,000 objects reflecting 4,000 yrs of J hist, culture & art. College offers guidance & counseling; stu orgs; stu activities: lectures; concerts; films & other public events which enrich the cultural & intellectual life of the com. Est in 1954. Classes first met at the Wilshire Blvd Temple. Within three yrs the sch acquired a bldg in Hollywood Hills. The Sch is now located on a five acre site adjacent to the campus of Univ of Southern CA. Pub The Hebrew Union College Annual; Chronicle; Heb Union Col Press pub scholarly bks by mems of the faculty & alumni. Facilities include the Mae Swig Edu Ctr, the Anna Grancell Stu Ctr, the Joseph Periodical Reading Rm, The Walter S. Hilborn Chapel, the Joseph H. Rosenberg Branch of the Am J Archives, the Edu Lab & Learning Ctr, the Jacob Sonderling Conf Rm, faculty ctr & an audio-visual ctr & adm offs. Dean: Rabbi Uri D. Herscher DHL; Dir Edgar F. Magnin Sch of Grad Studies: Rabbi Stanley Chyet PhD; Dir of Sch of Communal Serv: Gerald B. Bubis; Dir Rhea Hirsch Sch of Edu: Rabbi William Cutter PhD; Bd of Overseers – Chr: Howard I. Friedman; Hon Chr: Martin Gang, Jack H. Skirball; V Chr: Herbert R. Bloch Jr, Sherrill C. Corwin, William S. Louchheim, Dr Edgar F. Magnin, Lester Ziffren; Hon

V Chr: Mrs B. Joseph Hammond; Treas: John R. Adler; Asst Treas: Mrs Jack H. Skirball; Dir of Skirball Mus: Nancy Berman. **3077 University Ave, Los Angeles CA 90007 (213) 749–3424.**

Heritage Southwest Jewish Press. Four separate J newspapers serving San Diego Cty, Orange Cty, Greater Los Angeles & Central CA. The four editions have a total of over 44,000 paid subscribers. Est in 1914. Heritage has won awards for excellence in J journalism including three Smolar Awards. Editor: Dan Brin; Publisher: Herb Brin. **Heritage Plaza, 2130 S Vermont Ave, Los Angeles CA 90007 (213) 737–2122.**

Herzl Day School. Conservative day sch. Accredited by The Western Assn of Schs & Cols, Los Angeles Bureau of J Edu, The Solomon Schechter Day Schs Assn. To provide an environment which will help prepare its stu for life in contemporary soc, both as Am & J; to meet the individual needs of its stu; to bring immigrant stu into the mainstream of Am soc; to encourage family involvement so that the values of the home are similar to the values of the sch. Secular & J studies, electives, trips, retreats. Est in 1972 as a jr/sr HS. In 1980 it changed to just grades 7–9 & in 1982 again to grades 7–12. Pres of the Corp: Harry Blank; Chr of the Bd: Amnon P. Feffer; V Chr: Bruce Rudich; Sec: Marianne Hecht; Headmaster: Rabbi Jacob Pressman; Dir/Prin: Sonia Berman; Judaica Coord: Rabbi Neil Comess-Daniels. **1039 S La Cienega Blvd, Los Angeles CA 90035 (213) 652–1854.**

Hillel Council. 900 Hilgard Ave, Los Angeles CA 90024 (213) 474–1531.

Hillel Extension. 900 Hilgard Ave, Los Angeles CA 90036 (213) 475–0427.

Hillel Jewish Center – University of Southern California. Non-denominational Ctr affiliated with B'nai B'rith Hillel Foun, J Fed Council of LA. To serve the J com on campus. Rel servs during the sch yr; variety of social progs; Israeli folk dancing; non-credited informal classes; rel, career & personal counseling; social action. 2000 stu; 400 faculty & staff. 3 full-time employees, 4 part-time employees; several volunteers. F 1942. Prior to that it was the 'Menorah Society' for ten yrs. Pub Schemesh (monthly, Sept–Apr). Facilities include kosher kitchen, sanctuary, library, studio rms, lounge. Dir: Rabbi Laura Geller; Prog Dir: David Gotfrid; Off Mgr: Gage Levy. **3300 S Hoover St, Los Angeles CA 90007 (213) 747–9135.**

Hillel, Los Angeles Administration. 900 Hilgard Ave, Los Angeles CA 90024 (213) 474–1531.

Histadrut Israel Campaign. 8455 Beverly Blvd #308, Los Angeles CA 90048 (213) 651–4892.

Hollywood Temple Beth El. Affiliated with United Syn of Am. Rabbi Martin N. Levin; Cantor Nathan D. Katzman; Pres: Stan Seiden; Exec Dir: Dr Bert Gerard; Edu Dir: Isadore A. Rubinstein. **1317 N Crescent Heights Blvd, Los Angeles CA 90046 (213) 474–1518.**

Israel Aliyah Center. 6505 Wilshire Blvd, Los Angeles CA 90048 (213) 655–7881.

Israel Consulate. 6380 Wilshire Blvd, Los Angeles CA 90048 (213) 651–5700.

Israel Government Tourist Office. 6380 Wilshire Blvd, Los Angeles CA 90048 (213) 658–7462.

Israel-American Chamber of Commerce. Offers assistance to mem US firms interested in economic activity in & with Is. Provides extensive trade assistance; pub market research reports; aids in dev of trade & investment between US & Is. For additional information, see – American-Israel Chamber of Commerce & Industry, Inc, New York City, NY. **6399 Wilshire Blvd, Los Angeles CA 90048 (213) 658–7910.**

Jewish Association of Singles Services. JASS for age range 21-35; JASS II for age range 35 plus. Outreach progs of Dept of Single Adults of J Fed Council – serv org comprised of reps of many Los Angeles J singles groups & unaffilliated mems of singles com. Resource org & liaison with individuals. Participants given practical leadership skills which enables them to serve the needs of their constituents more effectively; offers leadership dev seminars, leadership weekend; responsible for operation of JASSLine & JASSLine II: Weekly recorded tape of events of interest to J single adults in Los Angeles area operated 24 hours by volunteers. JASSLine (213) 852–0909 fr Los Angeles, (213) 907–8858 fr San Fernando Valley; JASSLine II (213) 651–4420; JASSLine Orange Cty (714) 537–JASS. **6505 Wilshire Blvd, Los Angeles CA 90048 (213) 852–1234 ext 2500, 990–8640 ext 2500.**

Jewish Big Brothers Association. Offers a variety of servs for single parent families including parent-child counseling, volunteer "Big Brothers" to serve as role models; summer camp prog for boys with special needs. **6505 Wilshire Blvd, Los Angeles CA 90048 (213) 852–1234.**

Jewish Committee for Personal Service. 1891 Effie St, Los Angeles CA 90026 (213) 666–0171.

Jewish Community Bulletin. 6505 Wilshire Blvd, Los Angeles CA 90048 (213) 852–1234.

Jewish Community Foundation. 6505 Wilshire Blvd, Los Angeles CA 90048 (213) 852–1234.

Jewish Community Library. 6505 Wilshire Blvd, Los Angeles CA 90048 (213) 852–1234.

Jewish Community Service Center. 163 S Fairfax Ave, Los Angeles CA 90046 (213) 938–6271.

Jewish Conciliation Board. 163 S Fairfax Ave, Los Angeles CA 90036 (213) 938–6271.

Jewish Daily Forward. West Coast edition in Yiddish a Sunday Supplement in English. **1161 N Ogden Dr, Los Angeles CA 90046 (213) 659–0861.**

Jewish Family Service. 11646 W Pico Blvd, Los Angeles CA 90064 (213) 879–0910.

Jewish Family Service. Freda Mohr-Multiservice Center, 351 N Fairfax Ave, Los Angeles CA 90036 (213) 655–5141.

Jewish Family Service of Los Angeles. Multiservice org for individuals & families consisting of non-med servs. To strengthen & preserve J family & com life; to provide continuity of identity & to strengthen the effective ties of com that prevent alienation. Counseling: individual personality adjustment, marital, parent chil or other family relationships, problems of transiency, retirement (individual, group or family counseling); Cult Clin; J Family Life Dev: preventive prog & an enrichment prog providing a variety of outreach, supplementary & supportive servs; Servs for the Elderly: counseling, information & referral, filling out forms & applying for benefits, therapy groups, rap sessions, social action groups, activity groups, volunteer visiting aides & a telephone reassurance prog, help to srs in finding work & locating available housing, special servs to a limited num of frail elderly clients as part of the State of CA Dept of Health which includes in-home care, day care, protective servs, transportation & other servs as part of a three yr research proj; Aides to the Elderly: aides trained to do light housekeeping, shopping, meal preparation, bathing, dressing, provide transportation for med appointments & socialization; crime prevention prog – edu & security devices for the elderly in apts; Kosher Meals Prog: five sites serving 100 kosher meals a day at each site (also attempts to provide edu, socialization & some recreation programming), a home delivered meals prog for about 160 people each day; Protective Servs Prog: for the isolated & impaired elderly who, with an intensive casework relationship, can remain in the com; Immigration & Resettlement Servs: progs which extend fr premigration planning to resettlement activities; J com free burial prog; volunteer servs. Serves over 15,000 people in Los Angeles Cty. Serves individuals & families in which at least one mem identifies as J; non-sectarian servs are also provided in progs funded by govt grants. Over 150 paid employees; 700 volunteers. In 1854 the Hebrew Benevolent Soc was incorporated as the com's first organized charitable org. This org later developed into the J Family Serv of Los Angeles. Whenever needs arose, mems of the Hebrew Benevolent Soc, joined later by the Ladies Hebrew Benevolent Soc, took it upon themselves to meet those needs. The benevolent socs in Los Angeles began to dev cooperative arrangements with other welfare agy to try to avoid duplication of efforts & to set limits on needy people who were arriving in Los Angeles fr other cities. The J family agy in Los Angeles began the 1930's with a new name, J Social Serv Bureau. The change in name reflected a beginning change in function to social servs rather than financial aid. Pres: Ilene Olansky; Exec Dir: Arnold R. Saltzman. **6505 Wilshire Blvd, Suite 614, Los Angeles CA 90048 (213) 852–1234.**

Jewish Federation Council of Greater Los Angeles. Mem of CJF. Sponsors United Jewish Welfare Fund. Organized 1912; Recognized 1959. Pres: Osias Goren; Exec VP: Ted Kanner; Exec Dir: Mervin Lemmerman. **6505 Wilshire Blvd, Los Angeles CA 90048 (213) 852–1234.**

Jewish Free Loan Association. Administers interest-free loans for purposes which will help individuals who are unable to secure funds elsewhere to become or remain self-supporting. **6505 Wilshire Blvd, Los Angeles CA 90048 (213) 655–6922.**

Jewish Home for the Aged. 6505 Wilshire Blvd, Los Angeles CA 90048 (213) 658–7145.

Jewish Labor Committee. 6505 Wilshire Blvd, Los Angeles CA 90048 (213) 653–3501.

Jewish National Fund. Land reclamation & afforestation in Is. For additional information, see – Jewish National Fund of Am, New York City, NY. **6420 Wilshire Blvd, Los Angeles CA 90048 (213) 655–8100.**

Jewish National Hospital at Denver. 4929 Wilshire Blvd, Los Angeles CA 90010 (213) 938–7263.

Jewish Singles Connection. Sponsored by Com Serv Div of J Centers Assn for age range 21-59. Consortium of singles progs & activities co-sponsored with synagogues & com agys in Western Region of Los Angeles. Provides information about, & referrals to, affiliated progs including wide variety of social-cultural, support, serv, & J heritage progs, relationship progs, fin progs, & recreational activities. Connector – a co-ordinating calendar/newsletter of activities in W Los Angeles & adjacent coms. **5870 W Olympic Blvd S 206, Los Angeles CA 90036 (213) 272–1073.**

Jewish Theological Seminary of America. Conservative rabbinical seminary accredited by Middle States Assn of Cols & Secondary Schs; chartered Bd of Regents NY State. Establishing & maintaining a theological seminary for the prepetuation of the tenets of the J religion; the cultivation of Hebrew literature; the pursuit of biblical, rabbinic, theological & archaeological research; the intergation of J & gen philosophy & learning; the advancement of J scholarship; the est of a library; the fostering of the study of J sacred music; the edu & training of J rabbis & teachers; the ordination of rabbis; the promotion of better understanding among people of different rel & ethnic backgrounds & the fostering of deeper insights into the philosophy & thought of rel; the est & maintenance of a col of liberal arts. For additional information, see – Jewish Theological Seminary of America, New York City, NY. **15600 Mulholland Dr, Los Angeles CA 90024 (213) 879–4114.**

Jewish Vocational Service. 6505 Wilshire Blvd, Los Angeles CA 90048 (213) 655–8910.

Jewish War Veterans. 6505 Wilshire Blvd, Los Angeles CA 90048 (213) 655–4752.

Jewish Youth Dept. 6505 Wilshire Blvd, Los Angeles CA 90048 (213) 852–1234.

Julia Singer Pre-School Psychiatric Center. 8730 Alden Dr, Los Angeles CA 90048 (213) 855–5000.

Knessest Israel of Hollywood. Orthodox Syn. **1260 N Vermont Ave, Los Angeles CA 90029 (213) 665–5171.**

Kol Echad Chorale. Vocal ensemble that performs the full range of J music, fr folk songs to classical & sacred works. Ongoing auditions for new voices in all sections to fill vacancies as they arise; singers attend weekly rehearsals; performances about once a mo. Age range fr 20 plus. **1620 Corning St, Los Angeles CA 90035 (213) 859–1057.**

Kosher Overseers Association of America, Inc. To promote Kashruth. Kosher supervision; certification; Pub of articles, booklets, bks of kashruth & general J themes of historical, religio-legal & philosophical nature; serving food firms nationally & internationally. F 1957, Inc 1963. Pub include Jews on the Frontier (hardcover); The Frontier Jews (paperback). Facilities include offs & library (private) with 2,500 vols (Rabbinic, historical, kashruth, homiletical). Pres: Sam Kalb; Chr Bd of Govs: Dr H. Robert Weiner; Rabbinic Adm: Dr I. Harold Sharfman. **9415 Kramerwood Pl, Los Angeles CA 90034; PO Box 1321, Beverly Hills CA 90213 (213) 870–0011.**

Labor Zionist Organization. 8339 W 3rd St, Los Angeles CA 90048 (213) 655–2842.

Legal Aid Society of Los Angeles. 1550 W 8th St, Los Angeles CA 90015 (213) 487–3320.

Leo Baeck Temple. Affiliated with UAHC. 600 mems. Rabbis: Leonard I. Beerman, Sanford Ragins; Cantor William Sharlin; Pres: Theodore Williams; Edu: Linda Thal; Adm: Nancy Lachman. **1300 N Sepulveda Blvd, Los Angeles CA 90049 (213) 476–2861.**

Levy Sephardic Library, Sephardic Temple Tifereth Israel. For information on the Temple, see – Sephardic Temple Tifereth Israel, Los Angeles, CA. **10500 Wilshire Blvd, Los Angeles CA 90024 (213) 475–7311.**

Los Angeles Council of Mizrachi Women. 6505 Wilshire Blvd, Los Angeles CA 90048 (213) 653–6606.

Los Angeles Zionist Federation. 6505 Wilshire Blvd, Los Angeles CA 90048.

Marina Del Rey Young Singles. Sponsored by American Jewish Cong Dedicated to creative survival of J Life, effective support of Is, freedom of Soviet J, religious freedom, social justice. Meetings, lectures, social events, social interchange for J singles. **6505 Wilshire Blvd, Los Angeles CA 90048 (213) 651–4602.**

Martyrs Memorial. 6505 Wilshire Blvd, Los Angeles CA 90048 (213) 852–1234.

National Conference of Christians & Jews. 3580 Wilshire Blvd, Los Angeles CA 90010 (213) 385–0491.

National Council of Jewish Women. Women's volunteer org. Dedicated in spirit of J to advancing human welfare & the democratic way of life. For information, see – National Council of Jewish Women, Washington DC. **543 N Fairfax Ave, Los Angeles CA 90036 (213) 651–2780.**

National Jewish Information Service for the Propagation of Judaism, Inc. A J missionary org chartered by the State of CA. To convert non J to Judaism; to serve as a J defense agy to combat those who are anti-J, anti-Judaism or anti-Is. Private classes at the org's Hq in Los Angeles; Correspondence Academy of Judaism sends bks & other materials free of charge upon request; Col for J Ambassadors trains ambassadors who visit stu all over the world & est branches of the org in their locales. F Mar 24, 1960. Pres: Rabbi Moshe M. Maggal; 1st VP: Dr Lawrence J. Epstein; Sec & PR Dir: Rachel D. Maggal. **5174 W 8th St, Los Angeles CA 90036 (213) 936–6033.**

New Jewish High School. 1317 N Crescent Heights Blvd, Los Angeles CA 90046.

New Jewish High School Library. 1317 N Crescent Heights Blvd, Los Angeles CA 90046.

Nitzan Chapter for Young Career Women. Sponsored by Beverly Hills Council of Pioneer Women. Interested in elevating the quality of life for women and youth in Is. Offers unique progs & seminars geared toward the young career woman within the ages 21-35. **1494 S Robertson Blvd, Los Angeles CA 90035 (213) 275–5345.**

North Valley Jewish Community Center of the Jewish Ctrs Assn of Los Angeles. J com ctr affiliated with the Natl J Welfare Bd, CJF. Informal recreation, edu & socialization within a J context. Early childhood edu servs; youth servs; chil servs; day-camp servs; family prog servs; adult prog servs; sr adult prog servs; singles servs; cultural arts servs. 1500 mems (300 families). 18 full-time employees, 50 part-time employees. F 1955. Pub Centerlife (bi-monthly), Prog Update (monthly). 15,000 sq foot facility. Pres: Mark Frazin; Exec Dir: Mark W. Zalkin; VPs: Len Rabinowitz, Carol Haaz, Ruth Warzez; Sec: Ellen Shapiro; Treas: Marom Gelfand. **16601 Rinaldi St, Los Angeles (Granada Hills) CA 91344 (213) 360–2211.**

Ohev Shalom Congregation. Orthodox Cong. Rel Servs; kosher meals for elderly; Talmud class (in Yiddish). F 1959 at 8301 W 3rd st, Los Angeles (moved in 1965 to present add). At one time had afternoon Talmud Torah with over 100 stu. Facilities include kosher kitchen, sanctuary seating, social hall. Rabbi Samuel Katz; Pres: Harry Garr; Gabbaim: A. Bob Judah, Carl Weiser. **525 S Fairfax Ave, Los Angeles CA 90036 (213) 653–7190.**

One Parent Information Network. Sponsored by Cedars Sinai Thalians Mental Health Center. Provides a resource & referral serv for single parent in W Hollywood-Westside areas; provides information on: single parent support groups, housing, day care, child care, schools, camps, physicians & dentists; maintains listing of current J & secular com activities; MSW available for counseling; educ & informative workshops on financial, legal servs, child dev, dating & relationships; grandparent prog matches older persons with single parent families. **8857 Saturn St, Los Angeles CA 90035 (213) 556–1687.**

Patrons Art Society. Devoted to the support of cultural & edu endeavors. Sponsors lectures, discussions, attendance at cultural activities held in conjunction with cocktails & dinner; donates money to support cultural progs. **4455 Los Feliz Blvd, Suite 804, Los Angeles CA 90027 (213) 664–7703.**

Pioneer Women – Na'amat. The training & edu of the Is woman & her family so that each can be best equipped to lead productive lives. For additional information, see – Pioneer Women Na'amat, New York City, NY. **1494 S Robertson Blvd, Los Angeles CA 90035 (213) 275–5345; 5820 Wilshire Blvd, Los Angeles CA 90036 (213) 938–9149.**

Research Service Bureau. 6505 Wilshire Blvd #902, Los Angeles CA 90048 (213) 852–1234.

Saul H. Curtis Library, Temple Beth Am. 1039 S La Cienega Blvd, Los Angeles CA 90035 (213) 652–5872.

Sephardic Congregation Kehal Yoseph. Traditional Sephardic Syn (Nusach Baghdad). To perpetuate the historic spiritual, cultural, & intellectual values of the Sephardic tradition; to maintain the euphonious pronunciation of Heb, & ancient chants & cantillations of the Babylonian minhag. Daily Rel Servs; Heb edu for chil; classes for adults; consultation on rel matters by Rabbi. Substantial sums of money are collected on a regular basis & distributed directly to orphanges, yeshivoth, & cultural & edu ins in Is; Sisterhood provides for dances, social events & chil parties; library contains more than 5,000 vols (rabbinics, kabbala). 360 mems. 3 employees. F June 1959, & represents Sephardim of numerous countries of origin: Iraq, Iran, India, Burma, Singapore, Indonesia, China, Morocco, Is, & a sprinkling of Ashkenazim. Pub The Shophar (quarterly). Facilities include sanctuary seating 400; social hall; a rabbi's study; kosher kitchen; offs & eight classrms. Possesses largest treasury of Siphre Torah in the entire city of Los Angeles; each Sepher Torah of Hebrew calligraphy encased in silver & gold containers for reading in upright position. Rabbi Elias H. Levi. **10505 Santa Monica Blvd, Los Angeles CA 90025 (213) 474–0559.**

Sephardic Congregation Kehal Yoseph, Rabbi Elias Levi Library. Library contains more than 5,000 vols (rabbinics, kabbala). For information on the Cong, see – Sephardic Congregation Kehal Yoseph, Los Angeles, CA. **10505 Santa Monica Blvd, Los Angeles CA 90025 (213) 474–0559.**

Sephardic Hebrew Center. 4911 W 59th St, Los Angeles CA 90056 (213) 295–5541.

Sephardic Magen David Congregation. 7454 Melrose Ave, Los Angeles CA 90046 (213) 655–3441.

Sephardic Temple Tifereth Israel. Rel Servs; library. 650 families. Organized in 1919 by young Sephardic J, mostly fr Turkey & Greece, who called the new cong the Sephardic Com of Los Angeles. In 1960 the Sephardic Com merged with another cong, the Sephardic Com & Brotherhood of Los Angeles, which had been f in 1930. The Cong has had several homes fr the time of its incorporation. In 1932 it constructed a beautiful temple in the mode of a pre-Inquisition Spanish syn. In 1973 Tifereth Is began construction of a new syn. The Syn maintains a garden with a fountain & a mus. The Cong is considered to be the second largest Sephardic cong in the US. The membership consists mainly of Sephardic J fr Turkey, Greece, Asia Minor, Morocco, Cuba, the Balkans, Is & Iran. Rabbi Jacob M. Ott; Hazzan Rev Isaac Behar; Gabbai: Aron Cohen; Pres: Hyman Jebb Levy; VPs: Max Candiotty, Raquel Bensimon, Theodore M. Cohen, Ralph Amado; Hon VP: Aron Cohen; Treas: Isaac Caston; Fin Sec: Samuel Tobey; Corsp Sec: Dr Seymour Eisman; Rec Sec: Regina Levy; Dirs: Victor Abrevaya, Louis Alcalay, Milton S. Amado, Richard J. Amado, Joseph Amega, Joseph V. Amira, Morris Angel, Joseph Arditti, Nat Barocas, Victor Behar, Benjamin B. Cherney, Joseph Block, Nathan Esquenazi, Maurice Hattem, Willy Leon, Vickie Levin, Raymond Mallel, Theodore Negrin, Leon D. Saul, Jacop Segura, Jack Seror; Exec Sec: Susan Halfon; Prin of Talmud Torah: Eliyahu Roussos. **10500 Wilshire Blvd, Los Angeles CA 90024 (213) 475–7311.**

Simon Wiesenthal Center for Holocaust Studies. On the Campus of Yeshiva University of Los Angeles. Non-profit org affiliated with the Yeshiva Univ of Los Angeles. Dedicated to the belief & hope that through edu & awareness, mankind will never allow an atrocity such as the Holocaust to reoccur. Permanent & traveling exhibits; library; outreach progs where survivors travel to schs; lectures; seminars; social action progs; Holocaust Mus: video monitor presenting recent news stories concerning human rights, a map showing the num of victims lost in the Holocaust, a mechanized information ctr providing answers to frequently asked questions, photos & artifacts fr the Holocaust, & a display of profiles of the 92 leaders most responsible for the Holocaust; Outdoor Memorial Plaza: features six black commemorative columns, each symbolically shattered at the top; Archives: original documents, periodicals, photographs, artifacts & important files & documents fr Simon Wiesenthal's private collection. F in 1979, the ctr is the only ins in N Am to bear the name & endorsement of Simon Wiesenthal, the famous humanitarian & hunter of war criminals. The ctr produced the first multi-media presentation of the Holocaust: Genocide. The org is supported by memberships, donations & grants. The Ctr also has offs in NY & Washington DC. Dean: Rabbi Marvin Hier; Dir: Alex Grobman; Asst to the Dean & Dir of the Outreach Prog: Rabbi Abraham Cooper; Dir of Research Projs: Rabbi Daniel Landes; Dir of PR: Lydia C. Triantopoulos; Dir of Membership Dev: Marlene Hier; Dir of Adm: Marilyn Goldetsky; Dir of Holocaust Stuies: Dr Alex Grobman; Dir of Media Prog: Marvin Segelman; Dir of Library Servs: Dr Gerald Margolis. **9760 W Pico Blvd, Los Angeles CA 90035 (213) 553–9035.**

Sinai Medical Center. CEDARS. **8720 Beverly Blvd, Los Angeles CA 90048 (213) 652–5000.**

Sinai Temple. Affiliated with United Syn of Am. Rabbi Solomon Rothstein; Cantor Joseph D. Gole; Asst Rabbi Zvi Dershowitz; Cantor Emeritus: Carl Urstein; Pres: Max Astrachan; Edu Dir: Rabbi Paul Schneider. **10400 Wilshire Blvd, Los Angeles CA 90024 (213) 474–1518.**

Skirball Museum – Hebrew Union College – Jewish Institute of Religion. Contains collections of J ceremonial art, rare textiles, paintings, etchings & archaeological artifacts. Collection of 12,000 objects. New permanent exhibition 'The Realm of Torah' exemplifying the centrality of the Torah in J life. Dir: Nancy Berman. **3077 Univ Ave, Los Angeles CA 90007 (213) 749–3424.**

Stephen S. Wise Temple. Reform Temple affiliated with UAHC. To provide rel, edu, cultural & athletic progs. Parenting; counseling; edu; sr citizens; women's group; singles group; rel, edu, cultural & athletic progs; Presch; library containing 1,200 vols, 700 audiovisual software; Afternoon Sch; Day Sch. 2,200 mems; 9,000 individuals; 400 infants-toddlers, 300 nursery, 600 stu day grades K–9, 400 stu Afternoon Sch, 300 post Bar Mitzva. 260 employees. F 1964. Pub Amarim (monthly); Bulletin (bi-weekly). Facilities include 2 large kitchens, 4 small kitchens, olympic swimming pool, wading pool, terraces, gift shop, 7 bldgs, sanctuary seating 2,000 when opened. Has sch orchestra, swim team, drama groups, performing chil choirs, dance groups. Rabbis: Isaiah Zeldin, Eli Herscher, Leah Kroll, Jonathan Miller; Cantor Nathan Lam; Edu Dir: Metuka Benjamin. **15500 Stephen Wise Dr, Los Angeles CA 90077 (213) 476–8561.**

Stephen S. Wise Temple Library. Library contains 1,200 vols, 700 audiovisual software, Judaica, chil & adult bks, Day Sch collection, teacher resourse ctr, Bible & Talmudic. **15500 Stephen S. Wise Dr, Los Angeles CA 90024 (213) 476–8561.**

Temple Beth Am. Affiliated with United Syn of Am. Rabbi Jacob Pressman; Cantor Samuel Kelemer; Asst Rabbi Harry A. Silverstein; Pres: Jack Colker; Exec Dir: William Strick; Edu & Youth Dir: Nadya Gross. **1039 S La Cienega Blvd, Los Angeles CA 90035 (213) 652–7353.**

Temple Beth Chayim Chadashim. Affiliated with UAHC. 132 mems. Rabbi Margaret Halub; Cantor Elliot Pilshaw; Pres: Gary Vogel. **6000 W Pico Blvd, Los Angeles CA 90035 (213) 931–7023.**

Temple Beth Israel of Highland Park – Eagle Rock. Affiliated with United Syn of Am. Rabbi Bernard Kimmel; Cantor Julian Wright; Pres: Charles Blauner. **5711 Monte Vista St, Los Angeles CA 90042 (213) 255–5416.**

Temple Beth Torah. Affiliated with United Syn of Am. Rabbi Ben Zion Bergman; Cantor Samuel Cohon; Pres: Henry Greenberger. **11827 Venice Blvd, Los Angeles CA 90066 (213) 398–4536.**

Temple Beth Zion. Affiliated with United Syn of Am. Cantor Linda Rich; Pres: Louis W. Barrat; Exec Dir: Raye Cowan. **5555 W Olympic Blvd, Los Angeles CA 90036 (213) 933–9136.**

Temple Isaiah. Affiliated with UAHC. 550 mems. Rabbis: Robert T. Gan, Albert M. Lewis; Cantor Robert Nadell; Pres: Dee Helfgott; Edu: Jack Horowitz; Adm: Lee Gleicher; Brotherhood Pres: Abram Kleinman. **10345 W Pico Blvd, Los Angeles CA 90064 (213) 277–2772.**

Temple Israel. Affiliated with UAHC. 735 mems. Rabbis: Daniel Polish, Nahum Ward; Cantor Aviva K. Rosenbloom; Pres: Bruce Rauch; Adm: Howard B. Lazar; Sisterhoood Pres: Eva Shulker; Brotherhood Pres: George J. Meyer. **7300 Hollywood Blvd, Los Angeles CA 90046 (213) 876–8330.**

United Jewish Appeal, Western Region Office. For additional information, see – United Jewish Appeal, New York City, NY. Dir: David Paikin. **6505 Wilshire Blvd, Suite 1104, Los Angeles CA 90048 (213) 651–3944.**

United Synagogue of America. 15600 Mulholland Dr, Los Angeles CA 90024 (213) 476–9777.

The University of Judaism. W Coast affiliate of the J Theological Seminary of Am. Accredited by the Accrediting Commis for Sr Cols & Univs of the Western Assn of Schs & Cols; Univ Col is accredited by the Assn of Hebrew Teachers Cols. To provide a ctr for original scholarly research in all areas of J life & thought; to train the professional leadership which the J com requires for its rel, edu, recreational & philanthropic ins; to train a Jewishly informed lay leadership for the com; to provide ongoing progs for both col stu & adults of all race & rel to deepen their knowledge of & appreciation for the J heritage, its tradition & values; to nurture the creative arts so that J life may be enriched through the efforts of the artist, the writer, the musician, the dramatist & the dancer; to perform a consultative & supervisory role for various edu, cultural & rel ins in the com. The David Lieber Grad Sch of J Studies: courses & degrees in the areas of Biblical Literature, J Edu, J Hist, J Philosophy, Heb Literature & Rabbinic Literature leading to a Masters degree in J Studies, Masters degree in Public Mgmnt & Adm, two degrees in edu, a Masters in Teaching, & in Teaching in J Day Sch Edu; The Grad Sch of Judaica: intensive work in classical J texts; The Univ Col of J Studies (undergrad degrees in J Studies) offers a joint prog with UCLA; The Adult Col of J Studies: provides a prog for adults who wish to pursue J studies on the col level; The Summer Ins: provides undergrad & grad courses; The Dept of Continuing Edu; The Jack M. & Bel Ostrow Library: houses 125,000 vols, 5,000 bound periodicals, 600 current periodicals, 30,000 pamphlets & an archive collection; The Max &

Pauline Zimmer Conf Grounds Camp Ramah; The Ctr for Contemporary J Life; The Earl Warren Ins of Ethics & Human Relations; placement servs; independent study; social activities; cultural progs. The idea of a Univ of J was first articulated by Dr Mordecai Kaplan in a speech given on Feb 4, 1945 at a public meeting. When the J Theological Seminary of Am announced its readiness in 1947 to open a univ of J with a sch of edu, the Los Angeles Bureau of J Edu endorsed the proj. The first classes of the Univ were held at Sinai Temple. Through a generous gift, the Univ was able to relocate in its own quarters. Since 1977 the Univ has been housed on its permanent site. Chr: Jack M. Ostrow; V Chr: Jack E. Gindi, Nathan Krems, Arthur Whizin; Treas: Max Zimmer; Sec: Cyrus Levinthal. **15600 Mulholland Dr, Los Angeles CA 90024 (213) 879–4114.**

University Synagogue. Reform Cong affiliated with UAHC. To strengthen & further personal growth & security while championing the causes of justice, brotherhood & peace for the J people & for all of humanity. Rel Servs; Cong Seder on the 2nd night of Passover; Confirmation Servs for 12th graders; Rel Sch for grades K through 12; Bar/Bat Mitzvah training; Sr HS Youth Group; Jr HS Youth Group; Shabbat weekend retreats; youth choirs; Early Childhood Learning Ctr; Edu Prog with forums, periodic study groups plus several classes that meet regularly during the week; Annual Adult Shabbat Weekend; Scholar in Residence Weekend; Family Shabbat Dinners; Family Shabbat Servs; Family Holiday Celebrations; Family Shabbat Weekend. 725 mem units. F in the mid 1940's. The syn was built in 1955. Facilities include a sanctuary seating 600 people; the Klein Hall which is used for meetings, banquets & receptions; the Seigel Lounge; the Chanock Memorial Rotunda, classrooms, offs; the Kleiner Library & Youth Lounge; a 130 seat chapel under construction. Rabbi Allen I. Freehling; Cantor Jay I. Frailich; Exec Dir: Joseph B. Joyce; Pres: Howard Banchik; Exec VP: Richard Goldstein. **11960 Sunset Blvd, Los Angeles CA 90049 (213) 472–1255, 272–3650.**

University Women of the University of Judaism. 15600 Mulholland Dr, Los Angeles CA 90024 (213) 476–9777, 879–4114.

Vista Del Mar Child-Care Services. A non-profit chil welfare org. Accredited by the Council on Accreditation of Servs for Families & Chil; mem agy of the United Way of Los Angeles, the J Fed Council, & the Chil Welfare League of Am. Provides residential treatment for emotionally disturbed chil ages 6 to 18, foster family care for chil to age 18, adoption servs & post adoption counseling, servs to unmarried parents, group home for adolescent boys, day treatment/day sch for pre-adolescents who are in danger of being placed in foster homes or ins care. Two affiliated social agy: Reiss-Davis Chil Study Ctr provides psychoanalytically oriented treatment of chil & their families, the training of psychotherapists, com edu & research; Home-Safe Chil Care provides family day care servs for pre-sch chil of single parent families. Exec Dir: Samuel P. Berman; Pres: George Konheim; VPs: Nathan Kates, Mrs Lionel Bell, Felix Juda, Dr Simon A. Wile, Percy Solotoy, Herbert R. Bloch Jr; Treas: Julius R. Wolf; Asst Treas: Harold M. Berlfein; Sec: Bernard M. Silbert; Asst Secs: Charles I. Schneider, Mrs Jacob A. Shuken; Bd of Dirs: Sheldon Appel, Mrs Henry Bamberger, Mrs Tom Bartman, Harold D. Berkowitz, Ira E. Bilson, Stanley Black, Paul Blackman, Stephen Chrystie, Davre J. Davidson, Mrs Lester Deutsch, Robert P. Dubin, Robert L. Feldman, William M. Fenning, Mrs James Feuerstein, Robert A. Finkelstein, Ben Franklin, Ernest J. Friedman, Mrs Howard Fuhrman, Mrs Sy Fuhrman, Bernard Gelson, Mrs Myer Gensburg, Albert H. Gersten Jr, Dr Eugene Gettelman, Donald T. Gillin, Mrs Edgar L. Gold, Marvin Goodson, Sam Greenbaum, Mrs Dixon Harwin, Marvin Hoffenberg, Stuart Jaffe, Donald B. Kaufman, John Lear, Maurie Liff, Mrs Sidney Lushing, Mrs I. Lew Mintz, Richard M. Mosk, Jack Paul, Mrs Dennis Rose, Hugo Rosenstein, Judge Frances Rothschild, Mrs Rudolph Schaefer, Mrs Walter R. Schoenfeld, Sidney W. Schuman, Larry Schwimmer, Perry Steiner, Bruce Stiglitz, David M. Stromberg, Mrs David M. Stromberg, Mrs William Teller, Mrs Jerry Weintraub, Ted Zuckerman. **3200 Motor Ave, Los Angeles CA 90034 (213) 836–1223.**

West Coast Talmudical Seminary (Yeshiva Ohr Elchonon Chabad). 7215 Warring St, Los Angeles CA 90046 (213) 937–3763.

Westside Jewish Community Center. 5870 W Olympic Blvd, Los Angeles CA 90036 (213) 938–2531.

Westwood Bayit. A kosher J stu living cooperative near the campus of the Univ of CA at Los Angeles. A ctr for rel, cultural & socially oriented J both on the campus & com level; Shabbat & Holiday Servs; kosher Shabbat meals; observes all holidays with appropriate activities. 21 young men & women stu. The stu share the responsibility of cooking & maintaining the house. Est in 1974. **619 Landfair Ave, Los Angeles CA 90035 (213) 478–9326.**

Wilshire Boulevard Temple. Dedicated to the ideal of perpetuating & enhancing J life in Am. Rel

Servs; Rel Sch; Adult Edu; Temple Srs; Sisterhood; Brotherhood; temple camps: Camp Hess Kramer & Gindling Hilltop Camp – spiritual, edu, cultural & social progs for every age group. 2,400 families; 300 col stu. Chartered in 1862. Servs were first held in Arcadia Hall. They then moved to Leck's Hall. Later, the Cong used Los Angeles' single courtroom for their servs. On Aug 18, 1872 the cornerstone for the first temple was laid. Almost a yr later, the temple was dedicated. Following the dedication, the Cong flourished. In Mar of 1896 a new temple was dedicated. The growth of the membership made the old temple inadequate. As a result, the Cong decided to purchase a lot on Wilshire Blvd for the purpose of bldg a new temple. On Oct 7, 1928 the first Sun Sch classes were conducted in the new bldg. On Feb 15, 1929 servs were held in the Temple Auditorium. The sanctuary was completed in Jun 1929. The Edgar F. Magnin Rel Sch facility was added in 1963. Pub Bulletin of the Wilshire Boulevard Temple (weekly). The Temple maintains the Home of Peace Memorial Park. Rabbi Edgar F. Magnin; Rabbi Alfred Wolf; Pres: Sheldon Belousoff; VP: Dr Ralph Bookman; Sec: Gordon Gelfond; Treas: Donald Glabman; Trustees: J. Robert Arkush, Alan L. Belinkoff, Frank Feder, Fred A. Fern, Eugene S. Goodwin, Felix Juda, Mrs Harry A. Mier, Bernard Roth, Frank Schiller, Sidney W. Schuman; Hon Pres: Edward Lee Kozberg; Hon Trustees: Max Firestein, George M. Thompson; Adm: Stephen E. Breuer; Dir of Music: Charles Feldman; Gen Mgr Home of Peace: Mark Greenstein; Sisterhood Pres: Sheila Bernstein; Brotherhood Pres: J. Lampert Levy; Sr Pres: Gertrude Kallin. **3663 Wilshire Blvd, Los Angeles CA 90010 (213) 388–2401.**

Women's American ORT – Pacific Southwest District XI. Autonomous membership affiliate of the Am ORT Fed composed primarily of Am J men. To build the ORT prog overseas, promote quality edu in the US & to rejuvenate vocational edu in the US. For additional information, see – Women's American ORT, New York City, NY. Pres: Sybil Semar; Chr Exec Cttee: Rona Newman; VPs: Barbara Adler, Eva Bluestein, Sally Goodman, Phyllis Levin, Fran Sanoff, Anne Spiegel, Lynn Suffin, Lia Warman; Treas: Sheila Beller; Fin Sec: Frances Greenberg; Rec Sec: Chelle Friedman; Corsp Sec: Sherri Lipman; Parliamentarian: Lucille Brotman; Exec Dir: Terry Burns. **6505 Wilshire Blvd, Suite 512, Los Angeles CA 90048 (213) 655–2911.**

Women's Conference. 6505 Wilshire Blvd #1002, Los Angeles CA 90048 (213) 852–1234.

Women's League for Conservative Judiasm. 15600 Mulholland Dr, Los Angeles CA 90024 (213) 476–9777.

Workmen's Circle. 1619 S Robertson Blvd, Los Angeles CA 90035 (213) 552–2007.

Yeshiva University of Los Angeles Library. 9760 W Pico Blvd, Los Angeles CA 90035 (213) 553–4478.

Yeshiva University of Los Angeles. Affiliate Yeshiva University NYC. Includes Menachem Begin Sch of J Studies, Yeshiva Prog, Beit Midrash Prog, Kollel. Stu pursue BA degree at col of their choice. Incorporates Simon Wiesental Ctr for Holocaust Studies. F 1977. **9760 W Pico Blvd, Los Angeles CA 90035 (213) 553–4478.**

Young Judea – Camp Judea. 6505 Wilshire Blvd #201, Los Angeles CA 90048 (213) 653–4771.

Zionist Orgnization of America. Promote the philosophy of Zionism on local, natl & intl levels. To solidify world J coms with the Is com through cultural, edu, & historical doctrines. For additional information, see – Zionist Org of Am, New York City, NY. **5225 Wilshire Blvd, Los Angeles CA 90036 (213) 938–9183.**

Los Gatos

Congregation Shir Hadash. Reform Temple. Rel Sch, presch through col age programming including Jr Choir, Heb Sch, Conversational Heb & Rabbi's Seminar for Bar/Bat Mitzvah; Adult Edu. Rabbi Jerold Levy; Pres: Mel Jacobs; Membership Chr: Nesta Buechler. **PO Box 1635, Los Gatos CA 95030 (408) 227–8880, 356–1153.**

Malibu

Malibu Singles Havurah. Sponsored by Malibu J Ctr & Syn. To discuss contemporary J issues or explore other aspects of Judaism. 30 mems. In existence since 1980. Rabbi Neal Weinberg. **PO Box 4063, Malibu CA 90265 (213) 457–2979.**

Marin

Jewish Family & Children's Services. To provide edu, counseling, therapy, support & outreach to strengthen family life within the J com & to assist chil, youth & adults in developing & maintaining their maximum human potential. For additional information, see – Jewish Family & Children's Services – San Francisco, CA. **1330 Lincoln Ave, Rm 204, San Rafael, Marin CA 94901 (415) 456–7554.**

Merced

Jewish Community Center of Merced Co. Affiliated with UAHC. 49 mems. Pres: Ethel Brodie. **PO Box 2531, Merced CA 95344 (209) 722–0530.**

Mill Valley

The New Israel Fund. Philanthropic org set up in Am to help worthy Is causes. A truly joint involvement of Am J & Israelis, & not just a financial relationship. Specifically dedicated to helping new, self-help citizens groups working to create a better & more just Is soc. Meets social needs that are not being met by govt or conventional social welfare progs; assists the integration of the mentally ill into their own coms; est battered women's shelters & a rape crisis ctr; provides a framework for Arab J dialogue; sponsors progs for youth & the dev of youth leadership in underprivileged areas. An article published in English in the late 1970's by Prof Eliezer Jaffe of the Hebrew Univ Sch of Social Work caught the eye of Jonathan Cohen & Eleanor Friedman. Contact was made between the Am & Dr Jaffe, & in 1979 the fund was est. The agy limits its assistance to two yrs & not more than $10,000 for any single proj. More than $220,000 in grants have been given to some 50 projs. The fund does not provide money for equipment or bldgs, but 'only for content'. An Am & Is cttee works to formulate policy, evaluate funding requests & make grants, & coord outreach & edu efforts to involve others. Pub The New Israel Fund Bulletin (quarterly). Pres: Jonathan J. Cohen; Chr of Bd: Eleanor F. Friedman; Adm Dir: Jonathan Jacoby. **22 Miller Ave, Mill Valley CA 94941 (415) 388–8820.**

Modesto

Congregation Beth Sholom of Modesto. Affiliated with United Syn of Am. Rabbi Samuel Graudenz; Pres: Allen Greenberg; Edu Dir: Mary Drabkin. **1705 Sherwood Ave, PO Box 4082, Modesto CA 95353 (209) 522–5613.**

Roger S. Drabkin Memorial Children's Library, Congregation Beth Shalom. For information on the Cong, see – Congregation Beth Shalom, Modesto, CA. **1705 Sherwood Ave, PO Box 4082, Modesto CA 95352 (209) 522–5613.**

Montebello

Temple B'nai Emet. Affiliated with United Syn of Am. Rabbi Samuel Stone; Cantor Joel Stern; Pres: Abe Baron; Edu Dir: Abe Michlin. **482 N Garfield Ave, Montebello CA 90640 (213) 721–7064, 723–2978.**

Monterey

Congregation Beth Israel. Reform Cong affiliated with UAHC, Natl Fed of Temple Sisterhoods, UJA (operates chapter). To further rel edu, worship & social life; to be a clearing-house for J activities in S Monterey Bay as the only syn in the area & only J ins on the Monterey Peninsula. Rel Servs; edu progs; workshops & seminars; Sisterhood & Men's Club progs; Presch; Afternoon Sch; Sun morning edu prog; home to local ARMDI & Hadassah & UJA chapters; representation of J tradition & State of Is in the gen com & especially in the face of the large Arab com at the US Defense Language Ins; library containing 1,000 vols (J reference, literature, liturgy, chil books, documentary, biography & hist). 173 mems (120 families, 53 individuals); 64 stu in grades K–9, plus 16 presch stu. 6 employees. Chartered 1956 as a CA non-profit corp, the Monterey Peninsula J Ctr was a homeless coalition of committed J lay people until the 1976 aquisition of a sch & bldgs & hiring of Rabbi in 1977; scheduled to move to new Carmel Valley site by spring 1984. Pub Shofar (monthly newsletter). Facilities include sanctuary seating 235, 4 classrms, kitchen, library, Judaica gift shop, off, atrium garden area on 7/8 acre of land near downtown Monterey. By Apr of 1984 a move will be made to a new property in Carmel Valley, which is at present only in planning stages. Rabbi Mark Wm Gross. **151 Park Ave, Monterey CA 93940 (408) 675–2759.**

Newall

Congregation Beth Shalom of the Santa Clarita Valley. Affiliated with United Syn of Am. Rabbi Kenneth Leitner; Pres: Susan Reed; Youth Dir: Bonnie Horwitz. **PO Box 39, Newall CA 91321 (805) 259–4975.**

Newport Beach

Shir Hama'alot. Affiliated with UAHC. 310 mems. Rabbi Bernard P. King; Cantor Arie Shikler; Pres: David Sandor; Edu: Nancy Levin; Sisterhood Pres: Barbara Segal; Brotherhood Pres: Ronald Speyer. **2100 A Mar Vista, Newport Beach CA 92660 (714) 644–7203.**

Temple Bat Yahm. Reform Cong affiliated with UAHC. To provide rel inspiration & quality edu; to perpetuate the precious J heritage, & strengthen J in the com now & for future generations. Rel Servs; Adult Edu Classes; Adult Bnai Mitzvah Class; pre K through confirmation classes held on Sun morning & weekday afternoons; Jr Choir; Sisterhood; Jr & Sr Youth Groups; Singles Group; social activities. 244

mems. Rabbi, Cantor & a part time staff of 20 teachers & aides; two youth leaders; sec; bookkeeper; gardener & maintenance help. F in 1973. Construction of the permanent bldg began in Feb of 1981. Scribe & Scribeleh. Rabbi Mark S. Miller; Pres: Winnie Ross; Exec VP: Steve Edwards; VP Edu: Donna Van Slyke; VP Mems: Marcia Dunn; VP Ritual: Jerry Gould; VP Ways & Means: Larry Levenstone; Rec Sec: Dollie Brill; Corsp Sec: Carole Freedman; Treas: Ted Hankin; Trustees: Helen Levinson, Joel Moskowitz, Ben Helphand, Bernie Rome, Lane Serman, Micki Sholkoff, Joyce Tachner. **1011 Camelback St, Newport Beach CA 92660 (714) 644–1999.**

North Hollywood

Adat Ari El. Affiliated with United Syn of Am. Rabbi Moshe J. Rothblum; Cantor Allan Michelson; Rabbi Emeritus Aaron M. Wise; Asst Rabbi Brad Gartenberg; Pres: Leo Dozoretz; Exec Dir: Irma Lee Ettinger; Youth Dir: Kenneth Gross. **5540 Laurel Canyon Blvd, North Hollywood CA 91607 (213) 766–9426.**

Adat Ari El Congregation, Harold Singer Memorial Library. For information on the Cong, see – Adat Ari El Congregation, North Hollywood, CA. **5540 Laurel Canyon Blvd, North Hollywood CA 91607 (213) 766–9426.**

Adat Ari El Day School. Affiliated with Solomon Schechter Day Schs Assn. Prin: Dr Gene Stromberg; Chr: Jeffrey Bleaman. **5540 Laurel Canyon Blvd, North Hollywood CA 91607 (213) 766–3506.**

Congregation Mishkan Israel. Orthodox Syn. **6450 Bellingham, North Hollywood CA 91606 (213) 769–8043.**

Reform Synagogue Information. 13107 Ventura Blvd, North Hollywood CA 91604 (213) 872–3550.

Temple Beth Hillel. Affiliated with UAHC. 903 mems. Rabbis: James Kaufman, Morton Bauman; Cantor: Samuel W. Brown; Pres: Burton S. Rosky; Edu: Richard Feifer; Adm: Sandra B. Fine; Sisterhood Pres: Carolyn Salzer; Brotherhood Pres: Samuel Weise. **12326 Riverside Rd, San Fernando Valley, North Hollywood CA 91670 (213) 763–9148.**

Temple Beth Hillel Library. For information on the Temple, see – Temple Beth Hillel, North Hollywood, CA. **12326 Riverside Rd, San Fernando Valley, North Hollywood CA 91607 (213) 763–9148.**

UAHC Pacific Southwest Council. Rel & edu org serving J congs throughout the US & Canada. To encourage & aid the org & dev of J congs; to promote J edu, & enrich & intensify J life; to foster other activities for the perpetuation & advancement of J. For additional information, see – UAHC – Union of American Hebrew Congregations, New York City, NY. Pres: Allan B. Goldman; Dir: Rabbi Lennard R. Thal. **13107 Ventura Blvd, North Hollywood CA 91604 (213) 872–3550.**

Union Hebrew High School. Two com schs offering a four yr J edu prog available to all youngsters 12½ yrs of age or older. The Union Hebrew HS is a proj of the UAHC, Pacific SW Council, & is co-sponsored by the Los Angeles Bureau of J Edu. The S Bay Hebrew HS is co-sponsored by the Los Angeles Bureau of J Edu, the Pacific SW Councils of the UAHC & United Syn of Am. To enable youngsters to continue their J edu & strengthen their Heb skills while providing a meaningful & social experience. Courses of study: Bible, Heb Language, J Hist, Literature, Contemporary J Life, Israeli Culture, Vocabulary of J Life. Union Hebrew HS est in 1954; S Bay Hebrew HS est in 1976. Dir: Rabbi Erwin L. Herman; Prin: Rivka Dori; Registrar: Helen Rosenbaum. **13107 Ventura Blvd, North Hollywood CA 91604 (213) 872–3550, 986–5720.**

Valley Storefront of the Jewish Federation Council. Sponsored by J Fed Council of Greater Los Angeles. Drop-in information & referral serv for all ages, serving San Fernando Valley area without fee. **12821 Victory Blvd, North Hollywood CA 91606 (213) 984–1380, 877–1882.**

Western Federation of Temple Sisterhoods. 13107 Ventura Blvd, North Hollywood CA 91607 (213) 872–3550.

Northridge

Israel Today Media Group. Multi-media foun. Is Today TV: weekly prog on four channels in three cities includes local & intl newsfeatures, prog fr Is & a weekly Heb language segment; Is Today Radio prog: includes Yiddish & Is folk music & humor, cantorial music, com news, natl & intl news, live broadcasts fr Washigton DC & Jerusalem; Is Today: natl newsmagazine features articles & local news items on social issues, politics, rel, sports, the arts, edu, businesses, travel with special supplements giveing in-depth coverage to orgs, bus, travel & fashion (monthly language supplements include Heb & Russian). News magazine f in 1973. Is Today radio prog has been on the air since 1966; now serving a natl J com of 2,000,000 in NY, Los Angeles, San Francisco, San Diego, Las Vegas, Chicago. Editor/Publisher: Phil Blazer; Staff: Yehuda Lev, Ami Goldfarb, Barbara Dekovner Mayer, Alon Ben-Méir, Shirley Krims, Mark Lavie, Aaron Ostash, Bert Prelutsky, Merrill Simon, Myra Taylor. **10340 Roseda Blvd, Northridge CA 91326 (213) 786–4000.**

Temple Ahavat Shalom. Affiliated with UAHC. 335 mems. Rabbi Solomon F. Kleinman; Cantor Ray Roberts; Pres: Frances Krimston; Edu: Marvin Gottlieb; Sisterhood Pres: Sharon Brooks; Brotherhood Pres: Buddy Bregman. **18200 Rinaldi Pl, Northridge CA 91326 (213) 360–2258.**

Temple Ahavat Shalom, Library. For information on the Temple, see – Temple Ahavat Shalom, Northridge, CA. **18200 Rinaldi Pl, Northridge CA 91326 (213) 360–2258.**

Temple Ramat Zion. Affiliated with United Syn of Am. Rabbi Alexander Graubart; Pres: Dr Gordon L. Cooper; Exec Dir: Ronald Sandler; Prin: Joseph Rabinor. **17655 Devonshire St, Northridge CA 91325 (213) 360–1881.**

Temple Ramat Zion Library. For information on the Temple, see – Temple Ramat Zion, Northridge, CA. **17655 Devonshire St, Northridge CA 91325 (213) 360–1881.**

Oakland

Camp Arazim. To provide the northern CA J com with a quality edu J summer experience. Prog fr mid Jun through Aug divided into two or three week sessions includes J classes, daily prayers, Shabbat observance, archery, swimming, sports, drama, horseback riding, music, dance, games, crafts. Since 1972, Camp Arazim has served 2,700 chil fr over 20 different coms. Pres: Royston Lee; VP: Mark Abelson; Treas: Sander Stadtler; Sec: Pearl Schub; Exec Offs: Rabbi Marvin Goodman, Herbert Abrams; Exec Dir: Eugene LeVee. **1419 Bdwy Suite 612, Oakland CA 94612 (415) 839–6044.**

Camp Young Judea. Camp of Hashachar Zionist Movement; Sponsored by Hadassah. **1419 Bdwy, Suite 308, Oakland CA 94612 (415) 832–8448.**

Home for Jewish Parents. 115 bed non-profit nursing home; agy of the J Fed of the Greater E Bay. Nursing & psychosocial care; Live Oak Proj; outreach servs including nursing home visitation to those J elders in non-J nursing facilities; telephone reassurance; proposed shared housing prog; home delivered meal prog; congregate meal prog serving over 60 clients. 24-hour skilled nursing care to 57 clients; com care & residential servs to 58 residents. Est in 1952. The Home has a volunteer prog. Exec Dir: Ben Laub; Pres: Diane Rosenberg; VPs: Martin R. Aufhauser, Edward Blum, Morris Ginsburg; Sec: Cyril L. Weiss; Treas: Donal B. Rude; Exec Dir: Ben Laub; Bd Mems: Dr Stephen H. Abel, Dr Ronald P. Bachman, Rose Belzer, Lorin Blum, Max Brown, Roslyn Edelstone, Sidney H. Edelstone, Reba Ginsburg, Herbert Grutman, Shirley Grutman, Philip Harris, Harvey C. Levy, Elizabeth Lifschiz, Herman Lifschiz, Michael J. Lohnberg, Michael A. Olden, Donald Rosenberg, Harriet Rotner, Raine Rude, Faye Selinger, Ruth Smith, Audrey Wagman, Susan Wallach, Leo Wasserman, Sanford Wechsler, Ben J. Weiss. **2780 26th Ave, Oakland CA 94601 (415) 536–4604.**

Jewish Family Service of the Greater East Bay. To strengthen J families & individuals. Individual, family & group counseling; help to J immigrants in resettlement & adjustment to Am life; guidance to young J people who are victims of cults & need assistance in finding their way back to the J heritage; information & referral; outreach, advocacy & counseling & emergency assistance to srs. J Family Serv offers servs at three locations. Pres: Barry Gilbert; Co-Chr: Dr R. Lichtenstein; VPs: Norbert Nemon, Arthur Weil; Sec & Treas: Toby Berger; Bd of Dirs: Dr Daniel Adelson, Rabbi Ira Book, Audery Contante, Max Eis, Yehudit Goldfarb, Phil Gorman, Sarah Kriegel, Dorothy Lindheim, Ragina Mendel, Herbert Simon; Hon Mems: Marilyn Taplow, Helen Wasserman, Irene Gregory; Exec Dir: Marcia Fisch. **3245 Sheffield Ave, Oakland CA 94602 (415) 532–6314.**

Jewish Federation of the Greater East Bay. Mem of CJF. Organized 1918. Pres: Dr Marvin Weinreb; Exec VP: Dr Melvin Mogulof. **3245 Sheffield Ave, Oakland CA 94602 (415) 533–7462.**

Temple Beth Abraham. Affiliated with United Syn of Am. Rabbi Aaron Kriegel; Cantor Joseph Germaine; Pres: Herman A. Pencovic. **327 MacArthur Blvd, Oakland CA 94610 (415) 832–0936.**

Temple Sinai. Affiliated with UAHC. 609 mems. Rabbi Samuel Broude; Cantor: Bruce M. Benson; Pres: Stanley Lichtenstein; Edu: Judith Podolsky; Adm: Susan Kirschenbaum; Sisterhood Pres: Elaine Bachrach; Brotherhood Pres: Jerry Jackson. **2808 Summit St, Oakland CA 94609 (415) 451–3263.**

Ojai

Camp Ramah in California. On the Max & Pauline Zimmer Conf Grounds of the Univ of Judaism. J resident camp operating under the supervision of the Univ of Judaism in Los Angeles & located in Ojai, approximately eighty miles fr Los Angeles. 3 summer sessions & a winter session. Sessions I & II, plus the Winter Encampment, are for youngsters entering 4th through 10th grades. Session II is for youngsters entering 3rd through 11th grades. Ramah Academy conducts a series of six weekend confs during the academic yr for the leadership of the Los Angeles J com. A Scholar-in-Residence for the Ramah Academy is chosen fr outstanding personalities. Each camp session can accommodate up to 400 campers. Approximately seventy to eighty people participate in the Ramah Academy weekend confs. Pres: Maynard Bernstein; Dir: Dr Alvin Mars; Asst Dir: Rabbi Glenn Karonsky. **15600 Mulholland Dr, Los Angeles CA 90077 (213) 879–4114; Summer add: 385 Fairview Rd, Ojai CA 93023 (805) 646–4301.**

Ontario

Temple Sholom of Ontario. A conservative syn affiliated with United Syn of Am. Sabbath & Holiday Servs; Sun Sch for K to confirmation; Heb Sch; Pre Sch; Adult Edu; Sisterhood, Sr Citizens Group; youth groups: Ariel Bet ages 9 to 12, Ariel Gimel ages 13 to 16. F in 1955. Servs were held in a house for two yrs. In 1956 a one acre site was purchased & the present syn was erected. The Cong affiliated with the United Syn of Am on Jan 7, 1957. The first Rabbi was hired in 1957 & during the same yr, the Sisterhood was organized. The Temple owns four Torahs, all brought fr Europe. One Torah has been willed to the Temple by an Auschwitz survivor who kept three Torahs safe during the Holocaust & had them pieced together into one perfect scroll. Rabbi Moshe Pitchon; Pres: Dr Robert J. Postman; Prin: Marcialee Gans: Edu Cttee Chr: Zecharia Hovav; Sisterhood Pres: Sherrie Heller. **963 W 6th St, Ontario CA 91762 (714) 983–9661.**

Pacific Palisades

Jewish Congregation of Pacific Palisades. 16019 Sunset Blvd, Pacific Palisades CA 90272 (213) 459–2328.

Jewish Congregation of Pacific Palisades, Berrie Library. 16019 Sunset Blvd, Pacific Palisades CA 90272 (213) 459–2328.

Kehillath Israel. 16019 Sunset Blvd, Pacific Palisades CA 92072 (213) 454–9130, 2328.

Palm Springs

Jewish Welfare Federation of Palm Springs – Desert Area. Mem of CJF. Organized 1971. Pres: Jim Greenbaum; Exec Dir: Samuel J. Rosenthal. **611 S Palm Canyon Dr, Palm Springs CA 92262 (714) 325–7281.**

Temple Isaiah. Affiliated with UAHC. 742 mems. Rabbi Joseph Hurwitz; Cantor Joseph Cycowski; Pres: Henry Freund; Edu: Carolyin Winer, Leora Baron; Adm: Ethel Fischer; Sisterhood Pres: Louise Olenick. **Palm Springs Jewish Community Center, 332 W Alejo Rd, Palm Springs CA 92662 (714) 325–2281.**

Palo Alto

Congregation Kol Emeth. Conservative Syn affiliated with United Syn of Am. Sisterhood; bd meeting monthly; regular meeting monthly. Rabbi Sheldon Lewish; Pres: Michael Miller; Membership Chr: Michael Chessman; Sisterhood Pres: Donna Silverberg. **4175 Manuela Ave, Palo Alto CA 94306 (415) 948–7498.**

Jewish Family & Children's Services. To provide edu, counseling, therapy, support & outreach to strengthen family life within the J com & to assist chil, youth & adults in developing & maintaining their maximum human potential. For additional information, see – Jewish Family & Children's Services – San Francisco, CA. **299 California St, Palo Alto CA 94306 (415) 326–6696.**

Palo Alto School for Jewish Education. Secular J Sun Sch grades K through 8. To give the stu a feeling of identity & pride in their J heritage; to impart to the chil the joyful experience of learning. J studies; celebrating the J holidays; music prog; elective prog, cooking, Heb instruction, Yiddish drama, literature & ethics. Est in 1964 as a non-profit org offering a different, exciting approach to educating youngsters in J. Facilities include an auditorium, classrms & a playground. Dir: Leah Bernstein; Chr: Bob Moss; Sec: Norman Berger; Treas: Howard Cohen, Vicki Burnett; Membership: Janet & Eric Emanuel; Publicity: Shirley Gilbert; Com Relations: Harvey Ziff, Susan Weisberg; Hospitality: Jeanette Ringold; Teacher Selection: Susan Rinsky; Curriculum: Judy Lurie, Julian Davidson; Aide Coord: Ruth Lyell; Supplies: Joyce Shefren; Rm Parent Coord: Ellen Wallace. **830 E Meadow, Palo Alto CA 94303 (415) 494–2511.**

Pasadena

Pasadena Jewish Temple. Affiliated with United Syn of Am. Rabbi Maurice T. Galpert; Cantor &

Youth Dir: David Julian; Pres: Barry Segal; Edu Dir: Betty Fishman. **1434 N Altadena Dr, Pasadena CA 91107 (213) 798–1161.**

Pomona

Temple Beth Israel. Affiliated with UAHC. 240 mems. Rabbi Earl L. Kaplan; Cantor Herbert Isaacson; Pres: Henry Krieger; Edu: Marilyn Lubarsky; Sisterhood Pres: Isabel Louis. **3033 N Towne Ave, Pomona CA 91767 (714) 626–1277.**

Poway

Temple Adat Shalom. Affiliated with UAHC. 261 mems. Rabbi Sheldon W. Moss; Pres: Joyce Belk; Sisterhood Pres: Marlene Heller. **15847 Pomerado Rd, Poway CA 92064 (714) 489–1918.**

Rancho Palos Verdes

Congregation Ner Tamid of South Bay. Affiliated with United Syn of Am. Rabbi Daniel Pressman; Cantor Gadi Fishman; Rabbi Emeritus Bernard Wechsberg; Pres: Norman Lefkowich; Edu Dir: Dr Carol Berkowitz; Youth Dir: Sheila Poncher; Sec: Beverly Adler. **5721 Crestridge Rd, Rancho Palos Verdes CA 90274 (213) 377–6986.**

Redding

Congregation Beth Israel. Affiliated with UAHC. 25 mems. Pres: Todd Fineberg. **PO Box 201, Redding CA 96001 (916) 243–4159.**

Redondo Beach

Temple Menora. Affiliated with UAHC. 350 mems. Rabbi Leon M. Kahane; Cantor Avshalom Cohen; Pres: Stephen Fierberg; Edu: Moshe Halfon; Adm: Albert Welland; Sisterhood Pres: Ruth Cohen, Muriel Freed. **1101 Camino Real, Redondo Beach CA 90277 (213) 316–8444.**

Redwood City

Temple Beth Jacob. Conservative Syn affiliated with United Syn of Am. To transmit J to the chil in such a way as to enable them to be knowledgeable & responsible participants in J life, sensitive & ethical human beings & reliable custodians of an enduring heritage; to provide the opportunity for the mems & friends to experience J life to the fullest & to advance it in the most creative & joyful way possible; to find strength & inspiration in worship & study, in the sharing of life cycle events, in acts of caring, in reaching out to the wider J & non J coms, in concern & support for Is & in other expressions of J consciousness. Rel Servs; Family Servs held on the first Fri of the mo followed by a Shabbat dinner; Adult Studies, lecture series, Scholar in Residence prog & weekend kallot; Tallit & Tefillin – a Sun morning meeting for servs, discussion & breakfast; Rel Sch for grades K through 12; toddlers meet prior to each J holiday with their parents for holiday creativity & fun; Youth Groups for grades 7 through 12; Bar/Bat Mitzvah Training; Beth Jacob Srs – a social & cultural group for sr citizens that meets weekly. Torah Readers – individuals trained by the cantor to read the Torah in the syn; Beth Jacob Women involved in a broad spectrum of activities designed to meet the needs of today's J woman; Temple Choir; Havurot – groups of families that meet regularly in homes in an effort to pursue J & other interests in a more intimate setting. F in 1930, Temple Beth Jacob is the oldest syn on the San Francisco Peninsula. The first structure was erected in 1933. The Cong moved to the present site in 1953, & in 1960 the facilities were completed. Most of the syn was destroyed by fire in 1979. A new enlarged facility was dedicated in 1981. Facilities include a sanctuary seating 357 people, with additional seating for the choir, an auditorium seating 700 people, kosher kitchen, memorial garden where the Torah scrolls destroyed in the fire are buried, 10 classrooms, prin off, multi purpose rm, library, chapel seating 124 people, offs, gift shop, & a play area for chil. Rabbi H. David Teitelbaum; Cantor Hans Cohn; Pres: Dr Norman Stone; Exec Dir: Birdie Zelver. **1550 Alameda de las Pulgas, Redwood City CA 94061 (415) 366–8481.**

Reseda

Jewish Homes for the Aging of Greater Los Angeles. An independent ins. To fulfill the Mitzvah of the Fifth Commandment: honor thy father & thy mother. Cluster housing provides semi-independent living combined with servs offered at the Menorah Village campus. Some two dozen srs live in ranch homes adjacent to the Village. Outreach Ctr at Menorah Village: nearly 100 srs are transported to & fr the campus to socialize & enjoy a wide variety of progs & activities that increase their physical & mental well being. The skilled nursing facility provides 24 hour extended nursing servs. Over 700 srs on two campuses. Staff of nurses, aides, therapists, social workers & med dir. Est in the early 1900's when mems of the J com obtained a small cottage to enable elderly J to live in a traditional J environment. Subsequently, the num grew to 350 residents at the five acre site which came to be known as the Los Angeles J Home for the Aged. During the Depression, some J leaders purchased seven acres of farmland in Reseda for the Industrial Ctr for the Aged, a sheltered workshop plan for the prematurely elderly. After WWII, the Industrial Ctr was converted to a traditional licensed protective care & limited nursing facility called The CA Home for the Aged at Reseda. With the shift of the J population, a site was obtained in Reseda for the construction of the new J Home for Aged. In 1974 the residents were moved to the new facility. At the same time, the CA Home for the Aged began to adapt, innovate & create new approaches to serve the elderly – it became known as Menorah Village. In 1979 the two facilities merged & became known as the J Homes for Aging of Greater Los Angeles. On Oct 11 1981 ground was broken for a new nursing bldg at the Home. The Homes have been chosen by UCLA Sch of Med as the site for a new grad fellowship prog in geriatric med. Pres: Alfred S. Gainsley; VPs: Harry Berrin, Dr E. Raymond Borun, Sunny Caine, Marjory Gandelman, Dan Goodstein, Herbert Kaufman, Walter Maier, Dorothy Solom, Joe Weisman; Treas: Norman Ginsburg; Rec Sec: Harry B. Seelig; Fin Sec: Sam Engelman; Corsp Sec: William Maltz; Asst Rec Sec: Evelyn Gold; Asst Treas: Howard Goodman; Asst Fin Sec: Morey Berck; Asst Corsp Sec: Dr J. Salem Rubin; Hon Life Pres: H. L. Zuckerman; Hon Life Treas: Mischa Berg; Hon Life Asst Treas: Alvin Levine; Hon Life VP: Mrs Sam Hoffman; Hon Life Treas: Aaron Libitz; Bd of Dirs: Zucky Altman, Herb Aronson, Joe Batteiger, Jack Bayer, Alexander Berg, Mickey Brock, Edward Buzin, David Cohen, Ann Dinnerstein, Marsh Dozar, Ben Dwoskin, May Finkel, David Fox, Eugene Fisher, Solomon Friedman, Louis M. Gandelman, Sam Gelman, Irving Gertler, Florence Ginsburg, Leo Goldberg, David Goldman, Ann Gosenfeld, Sherman Grancell, Marcie Greenberg, Dr Seymour Greenstone, Harold Hammerman, Stanley Hirsh, Marvin Hoffenberg, William B. Horne, Harold A. Held, Louis Horwitz, Ernest Jacobs, Nat Jolton, Don Kahn, Maxwell Kaufer, Lee Kaufman, Walter Kaye, Bernardo Kracer, Ben Kroot, Solly Laub, Fred Laybhen, Martin Lee, John N. Levi Jr, Edward D. Marks, Mel Masirow, Estelle Nadler, Beverly Nathan, Helen Naythons, Rose Poe, Herbert Rosenkranz, Mace Rosenthal, Marvin D. Rowen, Martin Sacoder, Mae Schiff, Muriel Seelig, Lillian Shapiro, Nathan Shapiro, Fanny Shechtman, Sally Shulman, Tillie Silas, Sam Siberkraus, Morton Silverman, Matthew Solomon, William Stagen, Jerry Tishkoff, Mrs Bob Weinberg, Hella Weiner, Arthur Whizin, Max Zimmer. **18855 Victory Blvd, Reseda CA 91335 (213) 881–4411; Menorah Village, 7150 Tamapa Ave, Reseda CA 91335 (213) 345–1746.**

Menorah Village. For additional information, see – Jewish Homes for the Aged of Greater Los Angles, Los Angles, CA. **7150 Tampa Ave, Reseda CA 91335 (213) 345–1746.**

Temple Beth Ami. Conservative Syn affiliated with United Syn of Am. To transmit the teachings of the J heritage through the joyous observance of its rituals & ceremonies. To provide opportunities for mems to become acquainted with the beautiful customs through rel servs, adult edu & lively discussion. Rel Servs Fri evening, Sat morning & holidays. Fri Night Servs are followed by Israeli dancing & Oneg Shabbat, Sat Morning Servs by a Kiddush; Nursery & Pre-Sch; Heb Mechinah for chil ages 5 to 7; Five Yr Heb Dept, Bar/Bat Mitzvah; confirmation (three yr prog); Adult Edu; Havurah – a small grouping of temple families who gather at least once a mo; Sisterhood; Men's Club; Married Couple's Club; Sr Citizens Club; youth groups: Kadimah for 4th through 6th graders, Jr USY for 7th through 9th graders & Sr USY for 10th through 12th graders. Est in 1949, the Temple has the longest hist of any J ins in the W Valley. The sanctuaries were dedicated in 1962. Bldg facilities include: two sanctuaries capable of holding 1,000 people, library, 8 classrooms, kosher kitchen, two interior patios & Temple adm offs. Rabbi David Eli Vorspan; Cantor Tibor Moses; Exec Dir: Frank Locascio; Nursery Dir: Naomi Soroky; Youth Dir: Jeffrey Berns; Pres: Herbert Frankel; Exec VP: Alan Siebler; Edu: Irwin Koransky; Ways & Means: Ellen Fremed; Membership: Shirley Barsky; Rel: Edwin Cherney; Youth: Joyce Drogy; Publicity: Cheryl Dollins; Social Action: Erica Schwartz; House & Grounds: Norman Shapiro; Fin Sec: Richard Fremed; Treas: Marvin Esko; Rec Sec: Clara Rosenbluth; Corsp Sec: Sadye Kahanowitz; Sergeant at Arms: Ronald Katz; Protocol: Sam Hochberg; Bd of Dirs: Manny Berrenson, Hy Burstein, Seymour Chevlin, Philip Cooperman, Frances Friedman, Myrna Gold, Meyer Gottlieb, Allen Greenwald, Marvin Handel, Bernard Hellinger, Marshall Jacobson, Martin Katz, Paul Miller, Harvey Renner, Bernard Robinson, Wolf Schulesinger, Sima Schuster, Gladys Sturman, Robert Zacuto. **18449 Kittridge St, Reseda CA 91335 (213) 343–4624.**

Richmond

Temple Beth Hillel. Affiliated with UAHC. 99 mems. Rabbi Robert Kaiser; Pres: Allan Sagle; Edu: Walter J. Flexo, Robert Kaiser; Adm: Arlene Lisby; Sisterhood Pres: Zelda Holland. **801 Park Central, Richmond CA 94803 (415) 223–2560.**

Riverside

Temple Beth El. Reform Cong affiliated with UAHC. To meet the varying needs of the J com in the

Riverside area. Sabbath Servs, monthly Family Servs; Rel Sch for K through 10th grade confirmation, including 4 yr Heb Sch & preparation for Bar/Bat Mitzvah; Adult Edu; library; Sisterhood; Young Couples Club; Nursery Sch; Sr Youth Group for com J youth of HS age, Jr Youth Group for jr HS age; gift shop; interfaith Thanksgiving servs; com Seder; sponsor of Russian J & Vietnamese immigrant families; servs for col youth away fr home, servs to military persons at March Air Force Base. 200 mems. Temple Beth El grew out of the Riverside JCC f in 1944 by 21 mems. The Cong met for many yrs in a small bldg on 12th St. In 1964 the Cong moved to its present site. Monthly Bulletin; Directory of Mems pub by Sisterhood. Rabbi Philip M. Posner; Cantor Robert Sirotnik; Pres: Sidney Lerner; VP: William Becker; Treas: Maurice Atkin; Sec: Rosalie Silverglate; Parliamentarian: Irwin Feiles; Dirs – Fin: David Goldware; Membership: Charles Berliner; Properties: Larry Presser; Edu: Erv Kardos; Rel Practices: Harris Kanel; Youth Cttee: Harry Freedman; Sisterhood Pres: Jennie Greenberg; Chavarim: John Ruhren; Activites & Progs: Lou Fithian; Nursery Sch Pres: Robin Greenberg; Adm Liaison: Beverly Berliner; Bulletin Editor: Bob Berman. **2675 Central Ave, Riverside CA 92506 (714) 684–4511.**

Sacramento

Bureau of Jewish Education. Central agy for J edu serving Sacramento & the surrounding area; consulting agy for small J coms throughout Northern CA & NV. Operates the only Heb day sch in central CA – the Shalom Sch, Com afternoon elementary Heb Sch, & Com Jr/Sr Heb HS. The Bureau is also involved in edu projs such as the est of a J studies curriculum at CA State Univ, Sacramento. 32 full & part-time staff. Est in 1975. Pres: Bert Walters; VP: Michael Opper; Sec: Judy Salomon; Treas: Martin London; Exec Dir: Dr Stanley D. Halpern; Asst to the Dir: Iris Bachman. **2351 Wyda Way, Sacramento CA 95825 (916) 485–4151.**

Congregation Beth Shalom. 525 Fulton Ave, Sacramento CA 95825.

Congregation Beth Shalom Library. 525 Fulton Ave, Sacramento CA 95825.

Jewish Federation of Sacramento. Mem of CJF. Organized 1948. Pres: Alex Fahn; Exec Dir: Arnold Feder. **2351 Wyda Way, Sacramento CA 95825 (916) 486–0906.**

Mosaic Law Congregation. Affiliated with United Syn of Am. Rabbi Joseph J. Goldman; Cantor Martin London; Pres: Kenneth Gore. **2300 Sierra Blvd, Sacramento CA 95825 (916) 488–1122.**

Temple B'nai Israel. Affiliated with UAHC. 480 mems. Rabbi Lester A. Frazin; Cantor Michael S. Weisser; Pres: Irwin Weintraub; Edu: Michael S. Weisser; Sisterhood Pres: Ann Singerman. **3600 Riverside Blvd, Sacramento CA 95818 (916) 446–4861.**

Salinas

Temple Beth El. Reform Cong. Affiliated with UAHC. 128 mems. Rabbis: Allen Krause, Abraham Haselkorn; Pres: Marcella Schumacher; Sisterhood Pres: Francine Johansen. **1212 Riker St, Salinas CA 93901 (408) 424–9151.**

San Bernardino

Congregation Emanu-El. Affiliated with UAHC. 548 mems. Rabbis: Hillel Cohn, Jeffry Schein, Norman F. Feldheym; Cantor Gregory Yaroslow; Pres: Gloria Cutler; Edu: Jeffrey Schein, Hillel Cohn; Sisterhood Pres: Leslie Soltz. **3512 N 'E' St, San Bernardino CA 92405 (714) 886–4818.**

San Bernadino United Jewish Welfare Fund, Inc. Organized 1936; inc 1957. Pres: William Russler. **Cong Emanu-El, 3512 N 'E' St, San Bernardino CA 92405 (714) 886–4818.**

San Diego

Anti-Defamation League of B'nai B'rith – San Deigo-Arizona Regional Office. Dedicated in purpose & prog to translating the Am heritage of democratic ideals into a way of life for all Am, & to countering assaults on the safety, status, rights & image of J. For additional information, see – Anti-Defamation League of B'nai B'rith, New York City, NY. **7850 Mission Center Ct #207, San Diego CA 92108.**

Bureau of Jewish Education of San Diego, Inc. Coords J edu in San Diego. Beneficiary agy of the United J Fed, affiliated with the Am Assn for J Edu. To encourage intelligent planning & creative effort in the field of J edu calculated to promote the rel, cultural & spiritual growth of the individual & the com, & to make the com more aware of the prog & needs of J edu. Renders pedagogic servs; trains teachers for weekly rel & Heb schs, & grants appropriate credentials; advises schs regarding curriculum, methods & material; sponsors special events to raise the level of J culture. The bureau maintains the HS of J Studies, Col Credit Progs, Col of Judaism – Adult Ins, & J Affairs Council. Affiliated schs: Adat Shalom, Beth El, Beth Is, Beth Jacob, Beth Shalom, Beth Tefilah, Emanu El, Heb Day Sch, J Academy, Judea, Sinai, Solel, Tifereth Is. Pres: Dr Burton Jay; VPs: Dr Milton Lincoff, Dr Cortland Richmond; Sec: Marlene Zawatsky; Treas: Alvin Cushman; Exec Cttee Offs: Ed Caroll, Clare Greenwald, Dr Walter Ornstein, Dr Raulf Polichar, Dr Robert Rubenstien, Maedelle Weissman; Hon Bd Mem: Dr A.P. Nasatir; Exec Dir: Dr Yehuda Shabatay; Prog Dir: Pearl K. Solomon; HS Prin: Dr Laurence B. Kutler. **5511 El Cajon Blvd, San Diego CA 92115 (714) 583–8532.**

Chabad House. Lubavitch com servs ctr. Blends Chassidic fervor & warmth with tradition & learning, to show that every J, fr whatever background he or she comes fr, is an integral part of the body of Is. Anti-missionary work; adult edu; Sabbath seminars; holiday progs; day camp; youth groups; syns; kosher kitchen; Russian Immigrant Aid Soc; counseling; chaplaincy; Mitzvah Campaigns; hosp & prison visitations; sr citizens encounters; speakers bureau. Rabbi Y. Fradkin. **6115 Montezuma Rd, San Diego CA 92115 (714) 286–4747.**

Congregation Beth Tefilah. Affiliated with United Syn of Am. Rabbi Samuel Penner DD; Pres: Gerald Kahl; Exec Dir: Michael Menzer; Edu Dir: Annette Segal. **4967 69th St, San Diego CA 92115 (714) 463–0391,2.**

Council of Jewish Federations – Western Region. Dir: Mark Berger. **2831 Camino Del Rio S, Suite 217, San Diego CA 92108 (714) 296–6106.**

High School of Jewish Studies, San Diego, Library. Library contains 3000 vols (Bible, post-biblical literature, J philosophy, hist, reference, Zionism, ethics). For information on the HS, see – High School of Jewish Studies, San Diego, CA. **5511 El Cajon Blvd, San Diego CA 92115 (619) 583–8532.**

Jewish Campus Centers of San Diego. Com agy which serves the campuses in the San Diego area affiliated with B'nai B'rith Hillel Foun & the United J Fed of San Diego Cty. Provides financial, prog & professional resources; serves as the link between the campus & the J com. Est in 1977 by the United J Fed of San Diego Cty to meet the needs of individual stu, the existing J stu orgs & the gen campus com. Dir: Rabbi Jay N. Miller; Coord: Jackie Tolley. **5742 Montezuma Rd, San Diego CA 92115 (714) 583–6080.**

Jewish Community Center. Nursery Sch & Day Care Ctr; Camp JAYCEE; Sr Citizens Prog; Sr Nutrition which prepares l,250 meals each week; 72 special interest classes & activities; J Big Brother Prog; adm & operation of a com camping prog with 14 com wide encampments during the yr; Astor Judaic Library; The Source Travel Dept; Health & Physical Edu Prog; specialized progs for women, singles, col stu & new Am. 185 chil in the Nursery Sch & Day Care Ctr; 1,005 in Camp JAYCEE during the summer; 875 sr citizens. Full time exec dir; staff & trained volunteers. In 1945 the San Diego JCC Assn was incorporated. In 1947 the United J Fund Youth Cttee was requested to dev a JCC prog. In the summer of 1947 Camp JAYCEE was launched. Fr 1947 to 1949 other progs were est. In 1949 a full time youth activities dir was hired. In 1952 a full time exec dir was hired, facilities were rented & a varied prog was est. In 1958 the Ctr moved to its new facility. 14,000 individuals walk through the JCC doors each mo. Future plans include bldg on a 12 acre site in the N city area. N Cty off opened in 1981 with its first priority being progs for sr citizens. Pres: Stuart Hurwitz; VPs: Sheldon Peller, Susan Davis, Sonny Novidor; Sec: Susie Meltzer; Treas: Ted Bank; Bd Mems: William Bandes, Gene Berkenstadt, Steve Berkowitz, Lois Berson, Susan Channick, Philip Dyson, Al Eisman, Richard Engelberg, Sid Feintech, Phil Ginsburg, Joe Gotkowitz, Hank Gotthelf, David Hazan, Beverly Hecker, Hal Helfand, Eleanor Hoffman, Al Hutler, Dennis Jacobs, Ken Jacobs, Trina Kaplan, Rowan Klein, Lila Kramer, Helene Kutnik, Linda Luttbeg, Eli Meltzer, Harry Nadler, Gary Naiman, Robert Nathan, Nathan Rakov, Donna Rosen, Robert Rubenstein, Abe Salmanson, Stephen Shuchter, Robert Siegal, Irving Silverman, Al Slayen, Louis Vener, Eileen Wingard, Woody Woodaman. **4079 54th St, San Diego CA 92105 (714) 583–3300.**

Jewish Community Center, Samuel & Rebecca Astor Judaica Library. For information on the Ins, see – Jewish Community Center, San Diego, CA. **4079 54th St, San Diego CA 92105 (714) 583–3300.**

Jewish Public Affairs Committee. Chr: Gordon Gerson; Legislative Consultant: Jerome Sampson. **5511 El Cajon Blvd, San Diego CA 92115 (714) 582–2483.**

Pioneer Women – Na'amat. The training & edu of the Is woman & her family so that each can be best equipped to lead productive lives. For additional information, see – Pioneer Women Na'amat, New York City, NY. **5511 El Cajon Blvd, UJF Building, San Diego CA 92115 (714) 265–1325.**

San Diego Hebrew Home for the Aged. Non-profit residential & care facility for the aged. To provide high quality med & nursing care in meaningful, hygienic & homelike surroundings. Skilled nursing care; dietary servs; observance of kashruth; rehabilitative servs; social & recreation progs; beautician/barber; banking servs; personal laundry; transportation; podiatry; optical; dental; pharmaceutical; psychiatric servs. 102 employees; 65 volunteers. in 1945. The original bldg, located on Fourth Ave, housed ten elderly. To meet the demand of the growing J aged population, the Home, in 1945, built a 29 bed residential facility on a 2.5 acre site at its present location. In time, the J com recognized two problems. Firstly, when the resident could no longer care for his/her personal needs, he would have to leave the home for a higher level of care leaving behind the J atmosphere. Secondly, people were living longer & thus there was not enough rm in the existing residence. The Bd of Dirs of the Home raised funds, & a 27 bed skilled nursing unit was added in 1961. In 1969 an additional 15 beds were added. In 1978 a 29 skilled nursing unit, arts & crafts rm/adm wing, expanded kitchen, physical therapy dept, gift shop & beauty salon, third dining rm, & a major refurbishing of the existing facility were completed. All facilities have been built through private donations. Long range goals for the J aged of San Diego include: a broadening of servs to the homebound aged, day care, short-term rehabilitation/convalescent ctr, residential apt complex, & an increase of com awareness. Pres: Myron Sachs Shelley; 1st VP: Sonya Weinman; 2nd VP: Frank Goldberg; Treas: Edward Kahn; Sec: George Zeidell; Bd Mems: Dr Lester Blumenthal, Howard Brotman, Dr Arthur Cummins, Alvin Cushman, Philip Dreifuss, Morey Feldman, Sigrid Fischer, David Garfield, William Gerelick, Agnes Gibson, Robert Kohn, Pearl Cutler, Bert Epsten, Dorothea Garfield, Michael Naiman, Shearn Platt, Paul Rabb, Mark Steinberg, Dr Michael Stotsky, Herbert Weiss, Allan Ziman, Genesse Levin, Gary Naiman, Seymour Rabin, Arthur Rivkin, Irv Roston, Jeannette Rubin, Dorothy Sampson, Nadine Savitch, Victor Schulman, Dr Robert Siegel, Bruce Steinberg, Leonard Tessler, Jean Weissman, Leonard Zanville, Jim Zien; Exec Dir: Michael Ellentuck. **4075 54th St, San Diego CA 92105 (714) 582–5168.**

San Diego High School of Jewish Studies. A beneficiary agy of the United J Fed of San Diego Cty; affiliated with the Am Assn for J Edu & maintained by the Bureau of J Edu in cooperation with area congs. To inspire young people with a positive & abiding commitment to J & the State of Is; to prepare & encourage them to utilize the rel faith, ethical & moral standards & traditional insights of Judaism; to guide them in self identification with the values & ideals of the J people of all ages & in devotion to the task of transmitting these values & ideals to future generations; to inspire an ongoing interest & desire to be Jewishly informed & therefore engage in reading & study in areas of J interest. 8th through 12th grade; 10th grade confirmation class; col credit courses for HS jrs & srs; Shabbaton, camp weekend; Trip to Los Angeles; Summer Teen Tour in Is; preparation class for the Intl Bible Contest; Heb language classes at five different levels; Comparative Rel; J Law; Study of the Bible & Five Megillot; Modern J Hist; Study of the Holocaust & State of Is. 235 stu in two branches. Est in Sept of 1977 with a stu body of 150 at one location. Chr: Dr Raulf Policher; Prin: Dr Laurence B. Kutler; Pres: Dr Burton Jay; Exec Dir: Yehuda Shabatay. **5511 El Cajon Blvd, San Diego CA 92115 (714) 583–8532.**

Temple Beth Israel. Affiliated with UAHC. 1100 mems. Rabbi Michael P. Sternfield; Cantor Sheldon F. Merel; Pres: Eugene Heikoff; Edu: Helene Schlafman; Adm: Stephen Makoff; Sisterhood Pres: Lynne Lurie; Brotherhood Pres: Irv Weiner. **2512 Third Ave at Laurel St, San Diego CA 92103 (714) 239–0149.**

Temple Emanu-El. Affiliated with UAHC. 260 mems. Rabbis: Martin S. Lawson, Morton J. Cohn; Pres: Betsy Keller; Sisterhood Pres: Florence Somerman; Brotherhood Pres: Jerrold B. Gittelman. **6299 Capri Dr, San Diego CA 92120 (714) 286–2555.**

Tifereth Israel Synagogue. Affiliated with United Syn of Am. Rabbi Dr Aaron S. God; Cantor Joseph Lutman; Pres: Chuck Schwartz; Exec Dir: Susan Beer; Edu Dir: Chana Pelled; Youth Dir: Robert Svonkin. **6660 Cowles Mountain Blvd, San Diego CA 92119 (714) 697–6001.**

United Jewish Federation of San Diego County. Mem of CJF. Organized 1935. Pres: Pauline Foster; Exec Dir: Stephen M. Abramson. **5511 EL Cajon Blvd, San Diego CA 92115 (714) 582–2483.**

San Francisco

Adath Israel. 1851 Noriega St, San Francisco CA 94122 (515) 564–5665.

American Committee for Shaare Zedek in Jerusalem – Northwest Region. To help future generations meet the health needs of Jerusalem and Israel. Continuing support of century old hospital which moved in 1979 fr old quarters to new $55 million ultra modern medical complex overlooking Jerusalem. Offers total patient & community care. University affiliated teaching hospital contains main hospital building planned for more than 500 beds, emergency shelter, outpatient clinics, school of nursing, clinical labs, research ins, central library, facilities. Ensures the full observance of J tradition. Open to all irrespective of their rel, race, or national origin. **1654 33rd Ave, San Francisco CA 94122 (415) 661–2160.**

American Friends of the Hebrew University of Jerusalem. Pacific NW Dir: C. Roy Calder. **717 Market St, Suite 323, San Francisco CA 94103 (415) 391–9056.**

American Jewish Committee. Exec Dir: Ernest H. Weiner. **703 Market St, Suite 1500, San Francisco CA 94103 (415) 392–1892.**

American Jewish Congress. For additional information, see – American Jewish Congress, New York City, NY. Dir: Joel Brooks. **942 Market St, Suite 501, San Francisco CA 94102 (415) 391–6590.**

American Technion Society. Dir NW Region: John Hyams. **870 Market St, Suite 542, San Francisco CA 94102 (415) 392–1032.**

Anti-Defamation League of B'nai B'rith – Central Pacific Regional Office. Dedicated in purpose & prog to translating the Am heritage of democratic ideals into a way of life for all Am, & to countering assaults on the safety, status, rights & image of J. For additional information, see – Anti-Defamation League of B'nai B'rith, New York City, NY. Exec Dir: Rhonda Abrams; San Jose Chapter Pres: Nat Kalman. **760 Market St, Suite 837, San Francisco CA 94102.**

B'nai B'rith District Four. Central Area Regional Dir: Leonard Bernstein. **5 3rd St, Hearst Bldg, Suite 1220, San Francisco CA 94103 (415) 421–4505.**

Bais Hamedrash Keter Torah, School for Torah & Musar. 1898 Meridian Ave #2, San Jose San Francisco CA 94110 (515) 267–2591.

Bay Area Council on Soviet Jewry. Exec Dir: Regina Waldman. **106 Baden St, San Francisco CA 94131 (415) 585–1400.**

Beth Din, Jewish Court & Arbitration Committee. Rabbi Michael Schick (Orthodox). **1850 Ortega St, San Francisco CA 94122 (415) 661–4055.**

Beth Israel-Judea. Affiliated with UAHC. 364 mems. Rabbi Herbert Morris; Cantor Henry Greenberg; Pres: Francis E. Cappel; Adm: Bernice Wiener; Sisterhood Pres: Kaye Reinhertz. **625 Brotherhood Way, San Francisco CA 94132 (415) 586–8833.**

Beth Sholom. Affiliated with United Syn of Am. Rabbi Saul E. White; Cantor Israel Reich; Asst Rabbi Jonathan Slater; Pres: Harold Zimmeman; Exec Dir: Sheldon W. Lessem; Edu Dir: Janice C. Dalin. **14th Ave & Clement St, San Francisco CA 94118.**

Bureau of Jewish Education Library. For information on the Ins, see – Bureau of Jewish Education, San Francisco, CA. **639 14th Ave, San Francisco CA 94118 (415) 751–6983.**

Bureau of Jewish Education of San Francisco, Marin County & the Peninsula. Central coordinating, facilitating, & consulting agy for the various edu ins & progs operating within the greater San Francisco area served by the J Welfare Fed. To make J experiences as meaningful & rewarding as possible; to see that all of the com edu ins & progs provide quality edu, staffed by competent edu, in proper settings. Assists J learning in a variety of settings including: clubs, ctrs, camps, syns, chavurot, in travel to Is & other J coms around the world; allocates yearly grants-in-aid to stu wishing to attend a J summer camp or travel to Is, schs exhibiting a prescribed level of performance, com orgs desiring tc initiate new edu progs, educators & teachers for professional growth; conducts annual campaign to help stu of all ages enroll in a J sch or edu prog. The Bureau consists of six specialized edu depts: J Studies, Heb Studies, Youth Edu, Is Progs, Library Resources, & Media Servs. Each dept is staffed by pedagogic specialists. The specialists conduct demonstration lessons, workshops & seminars for teachers & prins in J schs, review & evaluate instructional & curricular materials, organize experimental approaches to J teaching & learning, & produce new edu materials including textbooks, workbooks, games, multi-media progs, study aids & teachers guides. F in 1897. The Bureau receives an allocation fr the J Welfare Fed; a membership org, the Ha-Maor Soc, also raises funds. Pres: Laurence E. Myers; VPs: Dr Raphael Reider, James Sammet, Fred Schalit, Vivian Solomon; Treas: John Rothmann; Sec: Edie Culiner; Exec Dir: Larry S. Moses; Adm: Kerin Lieberman. **639 14th Ave, San Francisco CA 94118 (415) 751–6983.**

Camp Arazim. Prog for N CA youth endorsed by United Syn of Am of Northern CA. **944 Market St, Suite 604, San Francisco CA 94102 (415) 397–1730.**

Camp Tawonga. Located in Stanislaus Natl Forest. Resident camp of United J Com Ctrs. **3195 California St, San Francisco CA 94115 (415) 929–1986.**

Congregation Anshey Sfard. 1500 Clement St, San Francisco CA 94118 (515) 752–4979.

Congregation B'nai David. 3535 19th St, San Francisco CA 94110 (515) 826–2595.

Congregation B'nai Emunah. Affiliated with United Syn of Am. Rabbi Theodore R. Alexander; Cantor Henry Drejer; Pres: Gary J. Neumann; Exec Dir: Ursula Landsberg; Edu Dir: George Ehrlich; Youth Dir: Flora Green. **3595 Taravel St, San Francisco CA 94116 (415) 664–7373.**

Congregation B'nai Israel. 590 Washington, San Francisco CA 94111 (515) 756–5430.

Congregation Beth Israel. Affiliated with United Syn of Am. Rabbi Herbert Morris; Cantor Henry Greenberg; Pres: Francis E. Cappel; Exec Dir: Bernice Wiener. **625 Brotherhood Way, San Francisco CA 94132 (415) 586–8833.**

Congregation Chevra Thilim. 751 25th Ave, San Francisco CA 94121 (515) 752–2866.

Congregation Emanu-El. Affiliated with UAHC. 1207 mems. Rabbis: Joseph Asher, Robert S. Kirschner; Cantor Joseph L. Portnoy; Pres: Nadine Rushakoff; Adm: G. Marvin Schoenberg; Sisterhood Pres: Joanne M. Levy; Brotherhood Pres: Bernard Goldberg. **PO Box 18247, Arquello Blvd & Lake St, San Francisco CA 94118 (415) 751–2535.**

Congregation Emanu-El Library. PO Box 18247, Arguello Blvd & Lake St, San Francisco CA 94118 (415) 751–2535.

Congregation Keneseth Israel. 1255 Post, San Francisco CA 94109 (515) 771–3420.

Congregation Magain David Sephardim. 351 4th Ave, San Francisco CA 94118 (515) 752–9095.

Congregation Ner Tamid. Affiliated with United Sun of Am. Rabbi Jack Frankel; Cantor Itzhak Emanuel; Pres: Ira B. Poretsky. **1250 Quintara St, San Francisco CA 94116 (415) 661–3383.**

Congregation Shaar Zahav. Affiliated with UAHC. 164 mems. Rabbi Allen B. Bennett; Pres: Paul J. Cohen. **PO Box 5640, San Francisco CA 94101 (415) 621–2871.**

Congregation Sherith Israel. Affiliated with UAHC. 806 mems. Rabbis: Martin S. Weiner, John L. Rosove, Morris Goldstein; Cantor Martin Feldman; Pres: Lee Bart Jr; Edu: John L. Rosove; Adm: Ernest Abbit; Sisterhood Pres: Sharon Silverman. **2266 California St, San Francisco CA 94115 (415) 346–1720.**

Consulate General of Israel. Consul Gen: Mordekhai Artzieli. **693 Sutter St, San Francisco CA 94102 (415) 775–5535.**

Hillel Foundation. 190 Denslowe Dr, San Francisco CA 94132 (515) 333–4922.

Israel Aliyah Center. 870 Market St, San Francisco CA 94102.

Israel Histadrut Council. 209 Golden Gate Ave, San Francisco CA 94102 (415) 431–6484.

Jewish Community Federation of San Francisco, Marin County & Peninsula. Mem of CJF. Organized 1910; Reorganized 1955. Pres: Richard Goldman; Exec Dir: Rabbi Brian Lurie. **254 Sutter St, San Francisco CA 94108 (415) 781–3082.**

Jewish Community Relations Council of San Francisco, Marin & Peninsula. Exec Dir: Earl Raab. **870 Market St, Suite 920, San Francisco CA 94102 (415) 391–4655.**

Jewish Family & Children's Services. Nationally accredited by the Council on Accreditation; mem of the Chil Welfare League of Am & the Assn of J Family & Chil Agy. The Agy is organized into three depts in San Francisco, branch offs in Marin & on the Peninsula, & a sheltered workshop. To provide edu, counseling, therapy, support & outreach to strengthen family life within the J com, & to assist chil, youth & adults in developing & maintaining their maximum human potential. J Family Life Edu:

provides preventive & edu progs at JCCs, temples, syns & other J ins; Emigre Prog: pre-migration, initial absorption, & post migration servs; family servs: counseling to individual & families, group counseling, family life edu, special servs to the aged & handicapped; Sr Outreach Prog: congs, youth groups & J orgs visit the J elderly & disabled on major J holidays & on a yr round basis; consultation servs to J nursery & day schs; shared sr housing; counseling servs to J prisoners at San Quentin & their families; research; scholarship & financial aid; Residential Treatment Prog for adolescent chil in four group homes; Sheltered Workshop; New Parenthood Prog: Post Natal Edu Support Group for new mothers, Mother-Infant, & Mother Toddler groups, Working Mothers Group, Fathers Group, & Going To Work Workshop; Telephone Talk Line for parents of chil under six yrs old. Full time staff of 67, including 32 professionals & 17 agy trained chil care workers. In addition to the regular agy staff, 250 individual volunteers & over 50 volunteer groups assist in reaching parents, the aged, & the bereaved. The agy, corporately known as the Eureka Benevolent Soc, was f in 1850. The Pacific Hebrew Orphan Asylum & Home Soc, later known as Homewood Terrace was est in 1872. These two agy merged in Nov of 1977 to form the present org. Offspring, a quarterly newsletter put out by parent volunteers, concerns issues of interest to parents of young chil. Exec Dir: Werner Gottlieb; Business Mgr: Paula Barta; Dir Dept Residential Prog: Jack Maslow; Branch Dir Peninsula: Alan C. Rass; Dir Dept Family Servs: Muriel Brotsky; Branch Dir Marin: Irving Kermish; Dir Emigre Dept: Anita Friedman; Dir Utility Workshop: Norbert Friedman. **160 Scott St, San Francisco CA 94115 (415) 567–8860.**

Jewish Home for the Aged. Exec Dir: Jerry A. Levine. **302 Silver Ave, San Francisco CA 94112 (415) 334–2500.**

Jewish National Fund. Exec Dir: Charles Steiner. **2266 Geary Blvd, San Francisco CA 94115 (415) 567–3440.**

Jewish Star. Periodical pub. **693 Mission St, San Francisco CA 94105 (415) 421–4874.**

Jewish Vocational & Career Counseling Service. Exec Dir: Larry Lucks. **870 Market St, Rm 872, San Francisco CA 94102 (415) 391–3595.**

Mount Zion Hospital & Medical Center. A voluntary non-profit, teaching hosp & med ctr; J sponsored ins. To take care of not only the J com but also the non J com; to dev progs which place a high value on edu & training, & on excellence of prog; to est a highly visible ins which would be the J com's contribution to the gen com – an ins in which the entire J com could take pride & which was & still is seen as a bulwark against the problems of anti-Semitism. Major heart & cancer ctr with resources for diagnostic servs includes the Maimonides Rehabilitation Ins, Pain Ctr, & the Claire Zellerbach Saroni Tumor Ins; major psychiatric prog with inpatient, outpatient & walk in crisis clin servs; comprehensive maternal & chil health servs; Perinatal Ctr; renal dialysis; Geriatric Servs Dept providing day care progs, & a teaching fellowship in geriatric med; special progs for the economically disadvantaged. Supports a house staff prog; trains dental interns, grad stu in periodentology, dental hygiene stu, med social workers, physical therapy & occupational therapy stu, pharmacy stu, X-ray technicians, radiation therapy tech stu & med technologists; provides clin training facilities for nursing stu; radiology. Facilities & other progs include respiratory therapy/pulmonary lab; social servs; speech pathology; physical therapy; nuclear med; nursery; neurosciences; med library; home care maternity servs; clin labs; dental; research; cardiology labs; outpatient dept; ambulatory servs prog. 439 beds; 18 bassinets; admits 12,000 patients annually; 170,000 ambulatory visits; 10,000 home care visits. On Nov 3, 1887, 43 San Franciscans met to talk about f a hosp which would provide free care for needy J patients in San Francisco. On Dec 15, 1896, 11 dirs of the Mount Zion Hosp Assn signed a document of purpose. The Hosp undertook, early in its hist, the training of young physicians. A Ladies Auxiliary Soc was formed the same yr the Hosp was chartered. In 1905 the Hosp merged with the Emanuel Sisterhood Polyclinic. A yr later, the San Francisco earthquake & fire destroyed the Clin. The hosp was only partially damaged. The city had hardly been restored when a cttee was appointed to solicit funds for the old wooden bldg which could no longer be repaired or expanded. The new brick bldg was ready for occupancy in 1913 as a 134 bed hosp. The bldg is still in use today as the Post Scott Bldg. The same yr, money was contributed for a Free Clin of Mount Zion Hosp. The new OPD Bldg was completed in 1917 & with it was organized a new social servs dept & dental clin. The Hosp evolved the first insurance plan to help private patients meet their hosp bills. Mount Zion was the first hosp in the area to start a psychiatric serv. In the 1940's Mount Zion treated thousands of J refugees. A new modern hosp was ready for use in 1951. In 1960 needs created by the new demands of med tech caused the com to raise funds which enabled the Hosp to add a sixth floor on its Post St wing, three floors on its Divisadero St bldg, & a new outpatient bldg. In the 1950's & 1960's the Hosp responded to changing socio-med needs with innovations such as the first hosp based home care prog, the first US funded chil & youth proj on the W Coast, the dev of the W Side Com Health Mental Ctr consortium & many other devs. Com Relation Dept: Irene Dobbins. **1600 Divisadero St, San Francisco CA (415) 567–6600, mailing add: PO Box 7921, San Francisco CA 94120.**

Pioneer Women Bracha Club. Is oriented membership org. Pres: Rose Lieber. **3240 Geary Blvd, San Francisco CA 94118 (415) 387–3077.**

San Francisco Jewish Community Publications. 870 Market St, San Francisco CA 94102 (415) 391–9444.

Sha'ar Zahav. 519 Castro St, San Francisco CA 94114 (515) 626–3131.

Sinai Memorial Chapel. The only J Mortuary in the Bay Area. **1501 Divisadero St, San Francisco CA 94115 (415) 921–3636.**

State of Israel Bonds Development Corp for Israel. Area Mgr: Louis Stein. **47 Kearny St, Suite 705, San Francisco CA 94108 (415) 781–3212.**

Tay Sachs Disease Prevention Program. Dir, Northern CA Tay Sachs Disease Prevention Prog: Dr. Mitchell S. Golbus. **Univ of CA Med Ctr, Health Sci West, HSW 1475, San Francisco CA 94143 (415) 666–4157.**

UAHC Northern California Council – Pacific Northwest Council. Rel & edu org serving J congs throughout the US & Canada. To encourage & aid the org & dev of J congs; to promote J edu, & enrich & intensify J life; to foster other activities for the perpetuation & advancement of J. For additional information, see – UAHC – Union of American Hebrew Congregations, New York City, NY. Pres: Joseph L. Podolsky, Arthur Guttman; Dir: Rabbi Morris M. Hershman. **703 Market St, Suite 1300, San Francisco CA 94103 (415) 392–7080.**

United Synagogue of America. 944 Market St, San Francisco CA 94102 (515) 397–1342.

Zionist Organization of America. Promote the philosophy of Zionism on local, natl & intl levels. To solidify world J coms with the Is com through cultural, edu, & historical doctrines. For additional information, see – Zionist Org of America, New York City, NY. **46 Kearny St, San Francisco CA 94108 (415) 391–7741.**

San Jose

Beth Midrash Keter Torah. Sch for Torah & Musar; independent edu facility for adult study of Bible, Talmud, J ethics, philosophy, hist & codes of law. Introductory, intermediate & advanced level classes. Dean: Rav A.H. Lapin; Pres: Herbert Turk. **1898 Meridian Ave, Apt 42, San Jose CA 95125.**

Camp Shalom. Day camp prog of JCC servicing pre-sch through seventh grade in Santa Clara Cty. **2300 Canoas Garden Rd, San Jose CA 95125 (408) 266–6317.**

Congregation Am Echad. Orthodox Syn. Adult Edu Prog: shiurim, study & discussion groups on Bible, Talmud, J philosophy, hist, laws & codes; social gatherings; Women's Study Group; Ladies Guild. Rabbi A.H. Lapin; Pres: David Bergman; Membership Chr: Joe Rinde; Pres Ladies Guild: Maisie Lapin. **1537 A Meridian Ave, San Jose CA 95125 (408) 267–2591.**

Congregation Shir Hadash. Affiliated with UAHC. 212 mems. Rabbi Jerold B. Levy; Pres: Melvin Jacobs; Edu: Irwin Maloff. **13500 Quito Rd, San Jose CA 95130 (408) 379–7522.**

Congregation Sinai. Traditional Syn. Heb Sch, Rel Sch, Jr Cong; Adult Edu; Young Couples Group; NCSY Youth Group. Rabbi Yakov Yellin; Pres: Eli Reinhard; Membership Chr: Rita Jacobson. **1532 Willowbrae Ave, San Jose CA 95125 (408) 264–8542.**

The Jewish Community Center. Mem agy of the Fed & the United Way. To provide a complete prog of activities – cultural, social, edu & recreational for all age groups. Chil, jr & sr high, adult classes; older adult social, recreation & volunteer servs prog; Summer Day Camp for K through 7th grade; Sr Adult Kosher Lunch Prog daily. Facilities include outdoor swimming pool, wading pool, barbecue & picnic table facilities; seating for 1,000 on a five acre site. Pres: Arnie A. Addison; Exec Dir: Al Friedman; Adm Asst: Fagie Rosen. **2300 Canoas Garden Rd, San Jose CA 95125 (408) 266–6317.**

Jewish Family Service of Santa Clara County. Constituent agy of the J Fed of Greater San Jose & United Way of Santa Clara Cty. Counseling & casework on family & individual adjustment problems; counseling & referral for the aged; J Family Resettlement Prog; information & referral. Fees are determined on a sliding scale according to income. Exec Dir: Arthur Goldberg; Pres: Burton Epstein. **2075 Lincoln Ave, Suite C, San Jose CA 95125 (408) 264–7140.**

The Jewish Federation of Greater San Jose. Central agy of the organized J com in Santa Clara Cty. To provide needed social servs in the com, Is & abroad. J Com Relations Cttee: promotes understanding between the J & the gen com; J Edu Cttee: implements progs for up grading the quality of J edu, promotes summer in Is experience for teenagers & devs com progs for adults; J Resettlement Prog: vocational guidance, edu & total servs prog for the absorption of Soviet J refugees; Hillel: provides edu & cultural progs for stu at San Jose State Univ & Santa Clara Univ; Young Leadership Dev: prog for couples between the ages of 25 & 40; Women's Div: coords the Pres' Cttee of women's J orgs in the com; Shalom Wagon: a proj to integrate newcomers; Rediscovery: a prog offered to public schs to advance the study of J life & hist; raises & allocates funds. Serves 15,000 J people in the cty. Est 1930. Jewish Community News (monthly newspaper). Pres: Ron Sosnick; VPs: Larry Berman, William Bloomfield, Marsha Dryan, Allen Guggenheim; Treas: Joan Fox; Corporate Sec: Alvin Frank; Women's Div Offs – Pres: Beverly Hirsch; VPs: Miriam Bent, Eileen Shapiro, Gail Joseph; Corsp Sec: Rosalie Gitin; Rec Sec: Merna Brein; Exec Dir: Nat Bent; Asst Dir: Janet Berg; Campaign Dir: Howard Sobel; Hillel Coord: Lisa Sinizer. **1777 Hamilton Ave, Suite 210, San Jose CA 95125 (408) 267–2770.**

National Conference of Christians & Jews. Exec Dir: Lillian Silberstein. **777 N First St, Suite 620, San Jose CA 95112 (408) 286–9663.**

Shalom Gardens. Jewish Cemetery. Complete Servs. **2255 Los Gatos-Almaden Rd, San Jose CA 95124 (408) 356–4151.**

Temple Beth Sholom. Reform Temple. Heb sch, Rel Sch, adult classes; jr & sr youth groups; pre-sch holiday progs; Sisterhood. Rabbi Arthur Kolatch; Pres: Laurence Krasno; Membership Chr: Elizabeth Dietz; Sisterhood Pres: Elaine Sager. **325 Cheynoweth Ave, San Jose CA 95136 (408) 224–1009.**

Temple Emanu-El. Reform Cong. Affiliated with UAHC. Brotherhood; Sisterhood; Evening Sisterhood; Sr Youth Group; Jr Youth Group; Rel Sch for pre-K through grade 12; Heb Sch for grade 4 through post Bar/Bat Mitzvah; Havurot; Singles Group; XYZ Sr Citizens Group; Adult Heb & continuing edu progs. Cong owns a cemetery. Mems: 850. Rabbis: David Robins, Michael Berk; Rabbi Emeritus Joseph Gitin; Cantor Bertram Berns; Pres: Dr Michael Cahn; Membership Chr: Howard Levine; Edu: Fred Marcus; Adm: Elaine Flynn; Youth Adv: Robert Michels. **1010 University Ave, San Jose CA 95126 (408) 292–0939.**

San Leandro

Temple Beth Sholom. 642 Dolores Ave, San Leandro CA 94577.

Temple Beth Sholom, Slater Memorial Library. 642 Dolores Ave, San Leandro CA 94577.

San Luis Obispo

Congregation Beth David. Reform Cong affiliated with UAHC & serving San Luis Obispo Cty. Dedicated to the spiritual, social & edu needs of the J com. Rel Servs Fri evening, Sat morning & holidays; monthly Family Servs; Shabbatons; Purim Carnival; library; J shop; Adult Edu; Torah Sch for pre-sch through 10th grade; Bar/Bat Mitzvah; out-reach classes – a Heb teacher is sent to Paso Robles, Los Osos & So Cty (as needed); provisions are made for youngsters with special edu needs; confirmation; two youth groups: Ruach for 7th–9th graders & TYG Temple Youth Group for 10th–12th graders; social & cultural activities. Over 100 families. F in 1959 with a meeting of five couples. In 1981 the Cong employed a full-time rabbi. The Cong has its own area in the local cemetery. Rabbi Harry A. Manhoff; Pres: Fred Russell; 1st VP: Emily McGinn; 2nd VP: Tibor Kalman; Corsp Sec: Kathy Saphir; Rec Sec: Ellen Weinstein; Treas: Harvey Blatter; Parliamentarian: Esther Silber; Rel Dir: Meyer Fein; Sch Cttee Rep: Herb Kabat; Bd Mems at Large: Richard Carsel, Daniel Kilikant, Sid Salinger, Jeff Eidelman; Publicity & Bulletin: Marlene Goldman. **2932 Augusta St, San Luis Obispo CA 93401 (805) 544–0760.**

San Mateo

B'nai B'rith Youth Organization – Central Region. For HS ages. Regional Dir: Pam DeGroot. **112 W 25th Ave, San Mateo CA 94403 (415) 349–0901.**

Peninsula Temple Beth El. Affiliated with UAHC. 580 mems. Rabbi Sanford E. Rosen; Cantor Herbert I. Epstein; Pres: Joyce Share; Edu: Dorothy Auerbach; Adm: William B. Nemoyten; Sisterhood Pres: Barbara Schefsky; Brotherhood Pres: Philip

Schneider. **1700 Alameda de las Pulgas, San Mateo CA 94403 (415) 341–7701.**

San Pedro

Temple Beth El & Center. Affiliated with UAHC. 280 mems. Rabbi David Lieb; Pres: Jerry Sorkin; Sisterhood Pres: Gabriella Savitt. **1435 W 7th St, San Pedro CA 90732 (213) 833–2467.**

San Rafael

Congregation Rodef Sholom. Affiliated with UAHC. 670 mems. Rabbis: Michael A. Barenbaum, Lee Bycel; Pres: Carole G. Friedlander; Sisterhood Pres: Suzanne Greenspan. **170 N San Pedro Rd, San Rafael CA 94903 (415) 479–3441.**

Congregation Rodef Sholom Library. For information on the Cong, see – Congregation Rodef Sholom, San Rafael, CA. **170 N San Pedro Rd, San Rafael CA 94903 (415) 479–3441.**

Santa Ana

Temple Beth Sholom Library. For information on the Temple, see – Temple Beth Sholom, Santa Ana, CA. **13031 Tustin Ave, Santa Ana CA 92705 (714) 532–6724.**

Temple Beth Sholom, Orange County. Affiliated with UAHC. 540 mems. Rabbi Frank E. Stern; Cantor Irving Green; Pres: Leonard Goodman; Edu: Lawrence Meyers; Adm: Sheldon Edwards; Sisterhood Pres: Michele Shugarman. **13031 Tustin Ave, Santa Ana CA 92705 (714) 532–6724.**

Santa Barbara

Congregation B'nai B'rith. Affiliated with UAHC. 400 mems. Rabbi Jonathan P. Kendall; Cantor Sharon Currier; Pres: Burt Bernstein; Edu: Beverly Abrams; Adm: Nora Noldon; Sisterhood Pres: Cynthia Janklow; Brotherhood Pres: Morris Herman. **900 San Antonio Creek Rd, Santa Barbara CA 93111 (805) 964–7869.**

The Santa Barbara Jewish Federation. Pres: Martin Bernstein. **PO Box 6782, Santa Barbara CA 93111.**

Santa Clara

Yeshivat & Midrasha Kerem. Comprehensive J edu facility. J studies fr the HS level through col with post-grad courses carried out in conjunction with nearby univs; separate schs for boys & girls. Rosh Yeshiva: Rabbi Matis Weinberg; Dean of Academic Affairs: Dr Gerald Margolis; Exec Dir: Rabbi Yankie Dinovitz. **250 Howard Dr, Santa Clara CA 95051 (408) 247–1722.**

Santa Cruz

Temple Beth El. Reform Cong. Affiliated with UAHC. Rel Sch – pre-sch through HS prog including Heb instruction; Youth Group; Lehrhaus J Adult Edu Prog; mini courses; Sisterhood. 212 mems. Rabbi Richard Litvak; Prin: Jacqueline Tuttle; Pres: Leo Greenberg; Membership Chr: Steve Karon; Sisterhood Pres: Carol Berman. **920 Bay St, Santa Cruz CA 95060 (408) 423–3012.**

Santa Maria

Temple Beth El. Affiliated with UAHC. 64 mems. Rabbi Irving A. Mandel; Cantor Aaron Rogoff; Pres: Sidney Weiser; Edu: Lorraine Pregozen; Sisterhood Pres: Errin V. Harmelen. **1501 E Alvin, Santa Maria CA 93454 (805) 925–9028.**

Santa Monica

Chabad House. Lubavitch com servs ctr. Blends Chassidic fervor & warmth with tradition & learning, to show that every J, fr whatever background he or she comes fr, is an integral part of the body of Is. Anti-missionary work; adult edu; Sabbath seminars; holiday progs; day camp; youth groups; syns; kosher kitchen; Russian Immigrant Aid Soc; counseling; chaplaincy; Mitzvah Campaigns; hosp & prison visitations; sr citizens encounters; speakers bureau. Rabbi A. Levitansky. **1247 Lincoln Blvd, Santa Monica CA 90403 (213) 395–4470.**

Jewish Family Service of Santa Monica. To create & promote personal growth; to enhance the conditions conducive to this growth, & enable the individual to lead a personally satisfying & socially useful life. Individual, relationship, marital & family counseling; information & referral servs; parent-chil, adolescent counseling; progs for srs; group counseling; outreach, family life enrichment progs; advocacy; volunteer servs; stu field work internships. The J Family Servs of Santa Monica began as the Santa Monica J Charities & Welfare, Inc organized by Julius Hoffman, Leo Rose & Harry Cohen in 1928. Donations were contributed & distributed when the need arose. In 1942 a part time J professionally trained social worker was employed. In 1953 a full time casework serv was est. In 1960, due to rising caseloads, an additional part time caseworker was employed. In 1963 the off moved to larger quarters in the downtown area of Santa Monica. Fees for servs are based on a sliding scale depending on the client's ability to pay. No one is denied servs because of inability to pay. Pres: Ruth Levine; VPs: Col Adolph Solomon, Larry Rosenstein; Treas: Dr Richard Levy; Sec: Dr Norton Stern; Bd: Florence Binder, Deborah Brenner, David Cohen, Vivian Ershoff, Nancy Freedman, Robert S. Goldsmith, Richard A. Heller, Nancy Lynn Highiet, Vira M. Lawton, Barbara F. London, Bunnie J. Sachs, Robert Schnider, Mrs Harice L. Seeds, Nancy Stein, Dr April Teitelbaum, Maurice Zusser; Exec Dir: Marvin R. Savlov. **1424 4th St, Santa Monica CA 90401 (213) 393–0732.**

Jewish Federation Council of Greater Los Angeles – Western Region. 2811 Wilshire Blvd #510, Santa Monica CA 90403 (213) 828–9521.

Jewish Spectator. Periodical pub. **PO Box 2016, Santa Monica CA 90406 (213) 829–2484.**

Pacific Jewish Center. Orthodox Syn. To restore a J neighborhood & make it a home for a vibrant & thriving com of Torah observing young J, all its intensive social & edu prog being geared to this end. Daily Syn Servs; Adult Edu; J all-day elementary sch; kosher food supplies; J outdoor leadership training (teenage adventure & Torah edu prog); Beit Midrash; Torah ins for adults; library with 1000 vols (Biblical & Talmudic, Heb only). 200 families, 100 individuals, 100 students. 18 employees, 30 volunteers. F 1977 in the Venice/Santa Monica neighborhood of S CA. Pub Context (quarterly). Facilities include syn (with kosher kitchen). 505 Ocean Front Walk, Venice CA 90291; Sch – 1515 Maple St, Santa Monica CA 90405. Rabbi Daniel Lapin; Pres: Michael Medved; VPs: Sol Genuth, David Altschuler; Sec: Sue Berry; Treas: Chalres Kaufman; Adm: Wendy Lapidus. **3115 6th St, Santa Monica CA 90405 (213) 392–8512.**

Temple Beth Sholom. Affiliated with UAHC. 265 mems. Rabbi Michael Oblath; Cantor Perryne Aisenman; Pres: Michael Hackman; Sisterhood Pres: Jean Lustig. **1827 California Ave, Santa Monica CA 90403 (213) 453–3361.**

Santa Rosa

Congregation Beth Ami. Affiliated with United Syn of Am. Pres: Saul A. Rosenthal. **4676 Mayette Ave, Santa Rosa CA 95405.**

Congregation Shomrei Torah. Affiliated with UAHC. 72 mems. Rabbi David Davis; Pres: Florence Brown; Edu: Ann van Soelen. **1717 Yulupa Ave, Santa Rosa CA 95405 (707) 539–6127.**

Saratoga

Beth David Hebrew High School. Conservative Syn affiliated with United Syn of Am. To provide edu progs that: challenge our teenagers with a sophisticated view of Judaism; help prepare them for the transition to adult life as committed J; give them the knowledge, skills & values to live a J life proudly. 40 different courses, in four study areas, on J sources (texts), J lifestyle (mityvol, halacha, T'fillah, values), J social studies (hist, Is, current events), Heb; electives (e.g. peer counseling). 80 students of the 8th–10th grades. 8 teachers (including rabbi). F 1973; originally part of the J Com HS of the S Peninsula. Facilities include kosher kitchen; sanctuary seating. Hebrew HS Adm: Steven Chevrin. **19700 Prospect Ave, Saratoga CA 95070 (408) 257–3333.**

Congregation Beth David. Conservative Syn affilieted with United Syn of Am. Sisterhood; Jr Kadima, Sr Kadima & USY youth groups; Heb Sch; Havurot – a system of social groups within the Cong which celebrate J life through study & observance of holidays together; library contains 1000 vols. 450 families. 26 employees. F 1963. Pub Beth David Star (monthly). Rabbi Daniel Pressman; Pres: Chalos Taubman; Sisterhood Pres: Barbara Taubman. **19700 Prospect Ave, Saratoga CA 95070 (408) 257–3333.**

Southern Campus Jewish Community High School. Four-yr curriculum presenting the rich sources of J hist, theology, culture & Heb. Jr high & HS age stu. Adm: Sandy Mayer. **19700 Prospect Ave, Saratoga CA 95070 (408) 257–3333.**

UAHC Swig Camp Institute. Dir: Harvey Shapiro. **24500 Big Basin Way, Saratoga CA 95070 (415) 392–7080; 703 Market St, San Francisco CA 94103 (415) 982–9886.**

Seal Beach

Congregation Sholom of Leisure World. Affiliated with United Syn of Am. Rabbi Sidney S. Guthman; Cantor William B. Mussen; Pres: Robert Grenrock. **13044 Del Monte Dr # 34A, Seal Beach CA 90740 (213) 596–3188.**

Sepulveda

Temple Beth Torah. Affiliated with UAHC. 155 mems. Rabbi Jerry Fisher; Cantor Michael Russ; Pres: Sherman Lenske; Edu: Jerry Fisher; Sisterhood Pres: Barbara Kessler. **8756 Woodley Ave, Sepulveda CA 91343 (213) 893–3756.**

Sherman Oaks

San Fernando Valley Region. 15477 Ventura Blvd #300, Sherman Oaks CA 91403 (213) 873–6811.

Temple B'nai Hayim. Affiliated with United Syn of Am. Rabbi Mika M. Weiss; Cantor Mark S. Gomberg; Pres: Montie P. Mazo; Exec Sec: Esther R. Bronner; Edu Chr: Marti Edelstein; Youth Dir: Gil Robbins. **4302 Van Nuys Blvd, Sherman Oaks CA 91403 (213) 788–4664.**

Temple B'nai Hayim Library. For information on the Temple, see – Temple B'nai Hayim, Sherman Oaks, CA. **4302 Van Nuys Blvd, Sherman Oaks CA 91403 (213) 788–4664.**

Simi Valley

Congregation B'nai Emet. Affiliated with UAHC. 40 mems. Pres: Tami Finkbeiner; Sisterhood Pres: Lynne Goodman. **PO Box 878, Simi Valley CA 93065.**

Temple Ner Tamid. Affiliated with United Syn of Am. Rabbi Gary E. Johnson; Cantor Steve Weiss; Pres: Lou Waxman; Edu Dir: Darlene Alworth; Youth Dir: Maxine Silverberg. **3050 Los Angeles Ave, Simi Valley CA 93065 (805) 522–4747.**

Stanford

B'nai B'rith Hillel Foundation at Stanford University. Umbrella org for all J activities on campus. Shabbat Servs; Traditional Egalitarian Servs; Liberal Servs followed once a mo with a Shabbat dinner; Orthodox Servs; High Holiday Servs; festival observances; Is progs; chug ivri; Is Information Desk; Is stu org; Is folk dancing; J studies; library of 1,500 bks & 100 current periodicals. Organized in 1959. HaKol (monthly newspaper with information, news & notices for the Stanford J com). Exec Dir: Rabbi Mark Cartun; Prog Coord: Karen Smith; Adm: Marina Bertelli; Sec: Sylvia Bates; Librarian: Sally Wieder; Publicity Coord: Cheryl Velick; Adv Cttee: Philip Barkan, Herbert L. Berman, Lawrence V. Berman, Daniel Bershader, Arthur Cohn, David Dorosin, John Felstiner, Lawrence Friedman, Victor R. Fuchs, Frederick Gillman, Renee Goldberg, Leah Kaplan, Sunny Kaplan, Marion Lewenstein, Seymour Martin Lipset, Raquel Newman, Richard Popp, Narman Robinson, David Rosehan, Robert Rosenzweig, Myra H. Strober. **Old Union Clubhouse Basement, PO Box 3034, Stanford CA 94305 (415) 497–1602.**

B'nai B'rith Hillel Foundation at Stanford University, Library. Library contains 1,500 bks & 100 current periodicals. For information on the Foun, see – B'nai B'rith Hillel Foundation at Stanford University, Stanford, CA. **Old Union Clubhouse Basement, PO Box 3034, Stanford CA 94305 (415) 497–1602.**

Stockton

Stockton Jewish Welfare Fund. Organized 1972. Pres: Tasha Stadtner. **5105 N El Dorado St, Stockton CA 95207 (209) 477–9306.**

Temple Israel. Reform Cong affiliated with the UAHC. Fri Evening Servs; Rel Sch – two day a week after sch Heb prog; Three Score Yrs Plus group for Sr Citizens; Adult Heb; Adult Edu classes; Sisterhood; Jr Youth Group; Sr Youth Group; library. 340 mems. Rabbi Steven A. Chester; Rabbi Emeritus Bernard D. Rosenberg; Pres: James M. Morris; Sisterhood Pres: Arlene Barr. **5105 N El Dorado St, Stockton CA 95207 (209) 477–9306.**

Temple Israel Library. For information on the Temple, see – Temple Israel, Stockton, CA. **5105 N El Dorado St, Stockton CA 95207 (209) 477–9306.**

Sun Valley

Valley Beth Israel. Affiliated with United Syn of Am. Rabbi Morris L. Rubinstein; Cantor Alan Lefkowitz; Pres: Abe Gelfand. **13060 Roscoe Blvd, Sun Valley CA 91352 (213) 782–2281.**

Sunnyvale

South Peninsula Hebrew Day School. To provide a comprehensive quality edu prog in gen & J studies. Pres: Dr Saul Weingarden; VPs: Dr Howard Rosenberg, Carol Saal; Dean: Rabbi Eli Lazar; Asst Dean: Malki Lazar; Nursery Dir: Joyce Wertman. **1030 Astoria Dr, Sunnyvale CA 94087 (408) 738–3060.**

South Peninsula Hebrew Day School Library. 1030 Astoria Dr, Sunnyvale CA 94087 (408) 738–3060.

Tarzana

Temple Judea. Reform Cong affiliated with UAHC. To provide a means of rel expression in the spirit of reform or liberal J; to provide a place of public worship in the Cty of Los Angeles; to est; maintain, & conduct a rel sch for the young; to further other rel, charitable, edu, social & social servs endeavors. Rel Servs; Sisterhood; Brotherhood; Youth Groups; Rel Sch; library. 850 mems. Temple Judea was f in 1952 by a handful of couples who felt the need for a temple in the valley. In Oct of that yr, the group, now numbering 22 people, began renting The Com Methodist Church on Amigo & Gault Sts in Reseda. In Mar 1953 the Cong was formally accepted into the UAHC with 31 paid up mems. In 1954 the first full time Rabbi was hired. The church was purchased by the Cong. Since hiring people was costly, the mems undertook to do most of the restoration work on the bldg themselves. By 1956 membership had grown to 175 families with 294 chil in the Rel Sch. The present site was purchased in 1958. The property on Amigo & Gault was sold to the Mormon Church. The Cong relocated to Lindley Ave using the existing houses for classrooms & offs. St Paul's Methodist Church allowed the Cong to rent its facilities. It was decided to first construct a social hall which would be multi-purpose. The opening of the social hall took place on Dec 10, 1960. The temple continued to use St Paul's for classes & occasional servs. By 1963 there were 314 families & 540 chil in the Rel Sch. Ground was broken for new classrooms in 1964. The existing houses were demolished. In Dec 1966 the new bldg was dedicated, consisting of a sanctuary with seating for 280, lobby, lounge, robing rms, kitchen & additional bathroom facilities. In 1969 Cong Kol Odom merged with Temple Judea. Rabbis: Steven B. Jacobs, Steven M. Reuben; Cantor Gerald L. Miller; Pres: Saul Leonard; VP Finance: Al Rosenbloom; VP Edu: Myron Dembo; VP Membership: Marcia Cayne; VP Personnel: Irv Klasky; Fin Sec: Herbert Eiseman; Treas: Gloria Grossblatt; Sec: Barbara Diamond; Long Range: Herb Lewis; Social Action: Saundra Mandel; Special Activities: Frances Saslow; Ritual: Mike Linsk; Adult Edu: Marietta Bernthol; Youth Activites: Jack Ben-Porat; Havurah: Carolyn Rothberg; House: Mort Denker; At Large: Howard Sibelman, Doris Cole, Larry Latt, Ray Silver; Brotherhood Pres: Don Biggard; Sisterhood Pres: Marlene Wallach; Sr Citizen Rep: Adolph De Jong; Rabbi Steven B. Jacobs, Rabbi Steven M. Reuben; Cantor Gerald Miller; Adm: Betty Sheiner; Edu Dir: Judy Aronson. **5429 Lindley Ave, Tarzana CA 91356 (213) 987–2616.**

Temple Judea, Paul M. Rubenstein Library. For information on the Temple, see – Temple Judea, Tarzana, CA. **5429 Lindley Ave, Tarzana CA 91356 (213) 987–2616.**

Temple City

Temple Beth David of the San Gabriel Valley. Affiliated with UAH 174 mems. Rabbi Alan R. Lachtman; Pres: Gerald M. Segal; Edu: Alan R. Lachtman; Sisterhood Pres: Laurie Kleinberg; Brotherhood Pres: Howard Gilford. **9677 E Longden Ave, Temple City CA 91780 (213) 287–9994.**

Thousand Oaks

Temple Adat Elohim. Affiliated with UAHC. 280 mems. Rabbi Elliot J. Holin; Cantor Michael Anatole; Pres: Marilyn Rosenthal; Edu: Janice Tytell; Sisterhood Pres: Sandra E. Taradash; Brotherhood Pres: Harry Pomeranz. **2420 E Hillcrest Dr, Thousand Oaks CA 91360 (805) 497–7101.**

Temple Etz Chaim. Affiliated with United Syn of Am. Rabbi Shimon Paskow; Pres: Dr Ira Goldberg; Edu Dir: Lana Kideckel. **1080 E Janss Rd, Thousand Oaks CA 91360 (805) 497–6891.**

Torrance

Chabad House. Lubavitch com servs ctr. Blends Chassidic fervor & warmth with tradition & learning, to show that every J, fr whatever background he or she comes fr, is an integral part of the body of Is. Anti-missionary work; adult edu; Sabbath seminars; holiday progs; day camp; youth groups; syns; kosher kitchen; Russian Immigrant Aid Soc; counseling; chaplaincy; Mitzvah Campaigns; hosp & prison visitations; sr citizens encounters; speakers bureau. Rabbi Eli Hecht. **24248 Crenshaw, Torrance CA 90506 (213) 326–8234.**

Jewish Federation of Greater Los Angeles – Southern Region. 3848 Carson St, Torrance CA 91503 (213) 540–2631.

Tujunga

Verdugo Hills Hebrew Center. Conservative Syn affiliated with United Syn of Am. Serving residents of Sunland, Tujunga, La Crescenta, La Canada, Montrose, Lake View Terrace, & Shadow Hills. Rel Servs, Sabbath & Holidays; Family Servs; Rel Sch: Bar/Bat Mitzvah preparation, Confirmation, Sun Sch, nursery/day care; Youth Group; Adult Edu; Sisterhood; Young Marrieds; Sr Citizens Group; social progs. F in 1941. The Verdugo Hills Hebrew Ctr is a founding mem cong of the E Valley Com Council, a div of the San Fernando Valley J Fed Council. Through this affiliation, Cong mems participate in rel & cultural progs with other syns in the E Valley, & with other rel groups in the Verdugo Hills. Rabbi David Mayer Baron; Cantor Mark Zalkin; Pres: Frank H. Wind. **10275 Tujunga Canyon Blvd, Tujunga CA 91042 (213) 352–3171.**

Tustin

Congregation B'nai Israel. Affiliated with United Syn of Am. Rabbi Rabbi Lewy; Pres: Robert Sklar. **13112 Newport Ave, Suite H, Tustin CA 92680.**

Van Nuys

Emet Jewish Young Professionals. Self-supporting, grass roots org; one of the largest singles orgs in Southern CA. Creative Shabbats, meetings, Is & disco dancing; trips; parties; game nights; sports outings. 300 mems; mailing list of 2,000; average age of participants is 27. **6467 Van Nuys Blvd #300, Van Nuys CA 91401 (213) 988–7278.**

Hillel Council. 13164 Burbank Blvd, Van Nuys CA 91405 (213) 994–7443.

Jewish Family Center. San Fernando Valley, 6851 Lennox, Van Nuys CA 91405 (213) 873–1520.

Pioneer Women – Na'amat. The training & edu of the Is woman & her family so that each can be best equipped to lead productive lives. For additional information, see – Pioneer Women Na'amat, New York City, NY. **13609 Victory Blvd, Van Nuys CA 91401 (213) 780–4165.**

Temple Ner Tamid. Affiliated with United Syn of Am. Rabbi Paul M. Katz; Cantor Maurice Glick; Rabbi Emeritus Bert A. Woythaler; Pres: Adrian Harris; Youth Dirs: Fred & Nora Rothstein. **15339 Saticoy St, Van Nuys CA 91406 (213) 782–9010.**

Temple Ner Tamid Library. For information on the Temple, See – Temple Ner Tamid, Van Nuys, CA. **15339 Saticoy St, Van Nuys CA 91406 (213) 782–9010.**

Valley Cities Jewish Community Center. 13164 Burbank Blvd, Van Nuys CA 91401 (213) 873–4620.

Venice

Bay Cities Synagogue. Orthodox. **505 Ocean Front Walk, Venice CA 90291 (213) 390–8868.**

Ventura

Temple Beth Torah. Affiliated with UAHC. 315 mems. Rabbi Bruce S. Block; Cantor: Patti Holin; Pres: Ira Goldenring; Edu: George Rubin; Sisterhood Pres: Mary R. Silverman; Brotherhood Pres: Mike Winagura. **Ventura Cty Jewish Council, 7620 Foothill Rd, Ventura CA 93004 (805) 647–4181.**

Ventura County Jewish Council – Temple Beth Torah. Organized 1938. Pres: Gerald Mechanick. **7620 Foothill Rd, Ventura CA 93003 (805) 647–4181.**

Visalia

Congregation B'nai David. Affiliated with UAHC. 70 mems. Pres: Louis Blechman. **PO Box 3822, Visalia CA 93278 (209) 732–7196.**

Vista

Temple Judea. Affiliated with United Syn of Am. Pres: Eitan M. Aharoni. **1930 Sunset Dr, Vista CA 92083.**

Walnut Creek

Congregation B'nai Sholom. Affiliated with United Syn of Am. Rabbi Gordon Freeman; Pres: Jim Solomon; Edu Dir: Sandy Kuttler; Youth Dirs: Evelyn Feldman, Lily Schneider. **74 Eckley Lane, Walnut Creek CA 94598 (415) 934–9446.**

West Covina

Temple Beth Ami. Affiliated with United Syn of Am. Rabbi Dr Henry E. Kraus; Cantor Mark Rosen; Pres: Mark F. Anapoell MD; Youth Dir: Jeffrey Ronald. **3508 E Temple Way, West Covina CA 91791 (213) 331–0515.**

Westminster

Hebrew Academy – Lubavitch, Library. 14401 Willow Lane, Westminster CA 92683 (714) 898–0051.

The Hebrew Academy Lubavitch. Traditional Heb day sch serving Long Beach & Orange Cty. Accredited by the Western Assn of Schs & Cols; authorized by the Col Entrance Examination Bd for matriculation to cols & univs. Half day rel studies & half day secular subjects; field trips; extracurricular activities including: scouting, stamp club, chess club, choir, dance troupe, music; Lubavitch Youth Club & B'nos Chabad offering social & recreational progs; PTO; Mommie & Me class involving mothers & chil fr 14 mo to 2 yrs 9 mo; library. 450 chil grades Nursery-HS; separate facilities for boys & girls at the upper sch level. 55 teachers. The Academy opened in 1968 with an enrollment of twelve chil. Rel Dean: Rabbi Yitzchok Newman; Prin: Dr Ivan Lerner; Dir: Rabbi Gershon Schusterman; V Prin: Cynthia M. Gould; Adult Edu, Camp Gan Is: Rabbi Moishe Engel; Special Progs: Rabbi Zev Kurtzman; Youth

Dir: Rabbi Moshe B. Rodman. **1401 Willow Lane, Westminster CA 92683 (714) 898–0051.**

Temple Beth David of Orange County. Reform Temple. Rel Servs; social action progs; Rel Sch for grades K through 10th grade; Heb HS; Bar & Bat Mitzvah training; Presch for chil fr 2½ to 5 yrs of age; Adult Edu; Choir; Sr Youth Group for grades 9–12; Jr Youth Group for grades 7–9; Kadima Group for grades 5 & 6; Sisterhood; Brotherhood; Couples Club; Sr Citizens Group; Singles Group; Bingo; Non-sectarian Presch; library. 277 mems. F in 1961 by a few families in the Rossmoor com. In the beginning, servs were conducted at the Com Congregational Church. In 1972 the first bldg of a three phase bldg prog was completed. In 1973 Temple Hillel of Huntington Beach & Temple Beth David merged to strengthen the com. A rel sch bldg was built & completed in 1975. The third phase of the sanctuary was completed in 1981. Facilities include a sanctuary, the rabbi's study, cantor's off, Judaica shop, adm off & a social hall; library. Rabbi Henri E. Front; Cantor Harry Newman; Pres: Gordon Kramer; 1st VP: Steve Chase; 2nd VP: Jackie Cordary; 3rd VP: Marilyn Elkins; Sec: Renee Blitstein; Treas: Helen Levin; Bldg & Grounds: Steve Hemlay; Youth Trustee: Larry Schultz; Ways & Means: Andy Peiter; Social Action: Annabelle Sandler; Publicity: Lorrayne Salvin; Rel Practices: Mickey Gubman; Sisterhood Pres: Florence Sudakow; Brotherhood Pres: Marc Sternshein; Couples Club Pres & Treas: Alan & Laurel Jarrick; Dir of Edu: Helene Holley; Presch Dir: Belleclaire Abel; Music Dir: Fay Newman; Off Mgr: Bette Banick. **6100 Hefley St, Westminster CA 92683 (714) 892–6623.**

Temple Beth David, Wendy Schedkman Memorial Library. For information on the Temple, see – Temple Beth David of Orange County, Westminster, CA. **6100 Hefley St, Westminster CA 92683 (714) 892–6623.**

Whittier

Beth Shalom of Whittier. Affiliated with United Syn of Am. Rabbi Norbert Weinberg; Cantor Walter Flexo; Rabbi Emeritus Joseph Smith; Pres: Richard Rothenberg; Edu Dir: Ofra Weinberg; Youth Dir: Donald Lorton. **14564 E Hawes St, Whittier CA 90604 (213) 941–8744.**

Woodland Hills

Temple Aliyah. Affiliated with United Syn of Am. Rabbi Melvin L. Goldstine; Cantor David Silverstein; Pres: Neil Markman; Adm: Ronnie Greenberg; Edu Dir: Judy Benes; Youth Dir: Lynn Cohen. **6025 Valley Circle Blvd, Woodland Hills CA 91367 (213) 346–3545.**

Temple Emet. Affiliated with UAHC. 220 mems. Rabbi John M. Sherwood; Cantor Larry Ellis; Pres: Stephen Shaw; Edu: Marshall Goldman; Sisterhood Pres: Marlene Schube; Brotherhood Pres: Phil Oberman. **20400 Ventura Blvd, Woodland Hills CA 91364 (213) 348–0670.**

COLORADO

Boulder

Congregation Har Hashem. Rel Servs; Rel Sch for ages 3–15; Adult Edu – Heb classes & lectures; Women's Group – monthly seminars; Shalom Circle – cultural & social activities; The Old & the Young – activities for sr citizens. Est in the mid 1960's. Rabbi Steven J. Steinberg; Pres: Robert Klutznick; VP: Norton Steuben; Treas: Filip Yeskel; Sec: Marian Safran. **3950 Baseline Rd, Boulder CO 80303 (303) 499–7077.**

Colorado Springs

Temple Shalom. J Cong of Colorado Springs & Pikes Peak Region affiliated with United Syn of Am & UAHC. Rel Servs; Rel Sch; Heb Sch; Heb Instruction; Adult Edu; Sisterhood; Men's Club; BBYO, Youth Group; Sr Guild; Singles Group; social functions. F in the spring of 1971 & started operations on Jul 1, 1971. It is the successor cong to the previous two J congs in Colorado Springs – B'nai Is Syn (Conservative) & Temple Beth El (Reform). Rabbi David L. Kline; Pres: Sidney Gritz; 1st VP: Alvin Blumberg; 2nd VP: Paulette Greenberg; Treas: Martin Emeson; Fin Sec: Ed Alyn; Rec Sec: Dolores Gross; 3 Yr Bd Mem: Daniel Winograd; 2 Yr Bd Mem: Sam Gordon; 1 Yr Bd Mem: Edwin Weissler; Sisterhood Pres: Ruth Goldman; Sisterhood Rep: Barbara Strauss; Men's Club Pres: Ron Solomon; Men's Club Rep: Werner Heim; Youth Group Pres: Craig Berman; Cttee Chr – Adult Edu: Walter Saunders; Bldg Fundraising: Alvin Blumberg; Bldg & Grounds: Sam Gordon; Bulletin: Dolores Gross; Cemetery: Michael Bram; Einstein Library: Gail O'Bryant; Fundraising: Larry Gross; Interior Decorating: Barbara Strauss, Jo'Ann Supperstein; Kiddush Fund: Zita Bram; L'Chaim Tree: Gloria Duitch; Mems: Paulette Greenberg; Rel Practices: Victor Goodstein; Rel Sch Prin: Jon Picker; Social Action: Art Lewittes; Youth Group Advs: Marc Stine, Ilene Lubin; Adm: Myrna Retsky. **1523 E Monument, Colorado Springs CO 80909 (303) 634–5311.**

Denver

Allied Jewish Federation of Denver. Mem of CJF. Sponsors Allied Jewish Campaign. Organized 1936. Pres: Ralph Auerbach; Exec Dir: Harold Cohen. **300 S Dahlia St, Denver CO 80222 (303) 321–3399.**

Alternatives in Religious Education. The pub & distribution of creative learning materials & teacher manuals for J edu settings. Pub each yr approximately 10 new products of various kinds including bks, mini courses, games, ditto paks & workbooks Catalog is mailed out in the spring to schs, camps, bureaus of J edu, JCCs & other ins which conduct J edu programming. F in 1974. Pres: Rabbi Raymond A. Zwerin; VP: Audrey Friedman Marcus. **3945 S Oneida St, Denver CO 80237 (303) 758–0954.**

Anti-Defamation League of B'nai B'rith – Mountain States Regional Office. Dedicated in purpose & prog to translating the Am heritage of democratic ideals into a way of life for all Am; to countering assaults on the safety, status, rights & image of J. For additional information, see – Anti-Defamation League of B'nai B'rith, New York City, NY. **300 S Dahlia St, Suite 202, Denver CO 80222.**

Beth Joseph Congregation. Traditional Syn. Monthly Father & Daughter Breakfast, monthly Father & Son Breakfast; Singles Prog; Chavura for young couples; Bk Review Series; weekly classes for women; monthly business persons lunch; Rel Sch for pre-sch through HS; library with 5000 vols (Judaica). Est in the 1920's. Rabbi Jerome Lipsitz; Cantor Isaac Koll. **825 Ivanhoe St, Denver CO 80220 (303) 355–7341.**

BMH-BJ Hebrew School. Afternoon rel sch housed at BMH & Beth Joseph Congs, & at a SE branch. To further J edu; to help J youth dev a feeling for their rel & culture; to encourage the continuation of J traditions in the home. Sch curriculum includes Heb, Bible, Prayer, J Hist, Customs & Music; Shabbat Prog with meaningful youth Servs & Kiddush; youth prog. The sch is close to 85 yrs old. Prin: Rabbi Samuel Biber; Edu Chr: Barbara Burry; Rabbi Dr Stanley Wagner, Rabbi Jerome Lipstiz. **560 S Monaco Pkwy, Denver CO 80224 (303) 388–4203; 825 Ivanhoe St, Denver CO 80220 (303) 355–7321.**

The Center for Judaic Studies, University of Denver. Most extensive academic prog in J studies in the Rocky Mt Region. To provide stu with a deeper understanding of the J component of western civilization within the context of academic scholarship. offers advanced placement col credit courses for HS stu; offers credit courses in J Studies at the Iliff Sch of Theology, St Thomas Seminary, & the Conservative Baptist Theological Seminary; participates in the PhD prog in Rel Studies jointly offered by the Univ of Denver & the Iliff Sch of Theology; sponsors annual Interfaith Conf; sponsors & houses The Rocky Mt J Historical Soc which is concerned with documenting J hist in the states of CO, MT, WY, ID & NM with progs including: exhibits, papers based on original research, field trips; & The Ira M. Beck Memorial Archives of Rocky Mt J Hist containing newspapers, manuscripts, private papers, pictorial & oral hist & memorabilia; sponsors the J Culture Ins which assists com orgs in the dev of progs of cultural interest, & pubs prog materials & guides. Other servs include: Denver J Information Bureau: directory of speakers & lecture-discussion topics available for progs at syns, churches, univs & com groups; Is Scholar-in-Residence: brings an Israeli scholar each yr to Denver & the servs of the scholar are offered free of charge to all interested groups; The Denver J Forum: brings leading J scholars to the com; Proj Outreach: assists small coms to dev J cultural & leadership progs with Proj Outreach staff serving as consultants; Colloquium on Contemporary J Thought: brings together Am J scholars representing diverse academic disciplines & ideological perspectives for a three-day colloquium to discuss issues of contemporary J relevance. Est in 1976. Great Confrontations in Jewish History; Traditions of the American Jew; Targum Onkelos to Genesis; Great Schisms in Jewish History; A Guide to the Jewish Rockies; Questions of Jewish Survival: The Denver Jewish Forum; Go & Study: Essays & Studies in Honor of Alfred Jospe; A Piece of My Mind. Dir & Prof of J Studies: Dr Stanley M. Wagner; Coord & Asst Prof of J Studies: Dr Raphael Jospe; Dir of Ecumenic Progs & Asst Prof: Dr Frederick Greenspahn; Dir & Archivist Historical Soc: Belle Marcus; Chr & Assc Prof of Hist, & Research Dir & Editor Historical Soc: Dr John Livingston; Dir of the J Culture Ctr: Saundra Heller; Instrs in Heb: Reuben Miller, Dr Uri Neil; Instr in J Studies: Rabbi Bernard Eisenman; Sec: Sheelagh Dytri. **Univ of Denver, Univ Park, Denver CO 80208.**

Central Agency for Jewish Education. 300 S Dahlia St, Suite #207, Denver CO 80222 (303) 321–3191.

Central Agency for Jewish Education, Library. 300 S Dahlia St, Suite #207, Denver CO 80222 (303) 321–3191.

Congregation Emanuel. Affiliated with UAHC. 1523 mems. Rabbis: Steven E. Foster, Richard J. Shapiro, Earl S. Stone; Pres: Arthur Frazin; Edu: Max Frankel; Adm: Mandell S. Winter; Sisterhood Pres: Ruth Goodman; Brotherhood Pres: Harvey Friedentag. **51 Grape St, Denver CO 80220 (303) 388–4013.**

Congregation Emanuel Library. For information on the Cong, see – Congregation Emanuel, Denver, CO. **51 Grape St, Denver CO 80220 (303) 388–4013.**

Congregation Hebrew Educational Alliance. Traditional Cong affiliated with the Union of Orthodox J Congs of Am. Rel Servs; Sisterhood – monthly luncheons, social progs & edu activities; Men's Club – monthly Bk Review & Breakfast; Young Couples Club; Young Singles Club; Downtown Luncheon Group; Rel Sch. 550 full mem families; 160 assc mems In the fall of 1926 the Beth David Sisterhood was formed for the purpose of creating new facilities for chil who were not receiving J edu. In 1928 the Beth David Brotherhood was formed, which soon merged with the Denver Hebrew Ins & took the name of the Denver Hebrew Edu Alliance. The growth of the Cong began in 1932 with the arrival of Rabbi Manuel Laderman. The Cong moved to its present location in 1953. Highlights (a monthly newsletter). Rabbi Daniel Goldberger; Rabbi Emeritus: Dr Manuel Laderman; Exec Dir: Neal S. Price; Pres: Arnold H. Cook; VPs: Sam Barter, Hyman I. Waldbaum, Dr S. Phillip Cohen, Goldie Smith, Richard Saliman, Ben Goldstein; Rec Sec: Bess Kaplan; Corsp Sec: Charlene Sachter; Fin Assc Sec: Leland Rudofsky; Treas: Label Gordon; Assc Treas: Albert Radetsky; Sisterhood Pres: Jane Sachs; Men's Club Pres: Dave Shafer; Edu Dir of the Rel Sch: Linda Siegal-Richman. **1555 Stuart St, Denver CO 80204 (303) 629–0410.**

Congregation Micah. Affiliated with UAHC. 39 mems. Cantor Uri Neil; Pres: Louis Wolfe; Edu: Uri

Neil. **2600 Leyden St, Denver CO 80207 (303) 388–4239.**

Congregation Rodeph Shalom. Affiliated with United Syn of Am. Rabbi Bernard Eisenman; Pres: Marvin Shamon; Exec & Edu Dir: Jerrold Leeson. **450 S Kearney St, Denver CO 80224 (303) 399–0035.**

Hope Center for the Retarded. 3601 E 32nd Ave, Denver CO 80205 (303) 388–4801.

Intermountain Jewish News. Weekly pub serving the Rocky Mountain J com. Provides natl & intl news, intensive local coverage & exclusive features fr Is. Circulation of 47,000 paid subscribers, 95% of whom live in the Denver met area. Average age of readership is male 46 & female 43 yrs. Est in 1913. Publisher: Miriam Harris Goldberg. **1275 Sherman St, Denver CO 80203 (303) 861–2234, 8333.**

National Jewish Hospital & Research Center – National Asthma Center. Non-sectarian med ctr for treating & studying respiratory diseases & disorders of the immune system; independent teaching hosp affiliated with the Univ of CO Med Ctr. Through patient care, basic biomedical & clin research & edu progs, NJH/NAC is dedicated to advancing health & to achieving an understanding of human biology. Clin emphasis is placed on asthma, emphysema, TB, chronic bronchitis, interstitial lung disease, occupational lung diseases & cystic fibrosis, immune system disorders, juvenile rheumatoid arthritis, systemic lupus erythematosus & immune deficiency diseases; immune system research, food allergy studies. Facilities include Cytogenetics Lab, Sleep Lab. Conducts basic research in the fields of biochemistry, microbiology & cellular & molecular biology; provides patient with supportive & rehabilitiation servs in assessing & meeting the psychological needs of adult & pediatric patients; conducts clin research relating to the social & emotional aspects of chronic respiratory diseases; sponsors edu progs with professional confs, grad & post grad training & a prog to re-educate teachers nationwide in the physical & emotional needs & rights of asthmatic chil; maintains social & psychological servs; provides recreational progs; provides kosher meals. Admission of 1,000 patients; 7,600 outpatient visits. More than 1,000 physicians, biomedical scientists, behavioral scientists, nurses, lab technicians, therapists, edu & support staff. On Nov 3, 1889 Denver's most prominent J met at a temple to discuss establishing a hosp for the homeless sick. On Nov 14 a hosp charter was adopted. On Apr 8, 1890 articles of incorporation were filed with the CO Sec of State for the J Hosp Assn of CO. Construction of the bldg took nearly two yrs. While working on the original bldg, Frances Jacobs passed away. Her charitable work among Christian & J groups spurred her friends to contribute toward the new ins. The Assn named the ins the Frances Jacobs Hosp. The bldg remained empty for seven yrs. All efforts to raise money for the Hosp were fruitless. The J citizens realized the proj of bldg was too great to be handled solely by the small com. In 1895 the rabbi proposed the possibility that B'nai B'rith open the Hosp under its auspices. In May 1899 the proj was approved. The name of the Hosp was changed to the Natl J Hosp for Consumptives. The Hosp was officially opened on Dec 10, 1899. In the autumn of 1901 the first addition was completed. Money was donated for a two story pavilion. The pavilion was dedicated in Jan 1903, increasing the hosp patient capacity by 50 beds. In 1907 the W campus was f as the Denver Sheltering Home which housed chil of TB victims. In 1912 NJH opened a new bldg which housed the first prog in the country for educating & rehabilitating TB patients. Seven yrs later, NJH pioneered in the field of pure sci research. In 1925 NJH became the training ctr in TB & chest med for stu at the Univ of CO, & the name was changed to Natl J Hosp at Denver. In 1940 a new prog of instruction in TB nursing was begun in affiliation with the Univ of CO Sch of Nursing. The Hosp broadened its chest med prog to include cardiology in the late 1940's. Its cardiopulmonary lab, set up in 1946, was the first in the country in a chest hosp. An adm ctr was completed in 1951 & a new med facility was completed in 1953. In Jul 1953 part of the Hosp was flooded. Through donations, the damage was quickly repaired. A seven floor basic research lab was completed in 1959. Hosp trustees formalized a name change in 1965 which had been in effect for several yrs. They registered the words 'and Research Center' as part of the NJH name. In 1974 a new 11 story health care & research bldg was dedicated. In 1978 the Natl J Hosp & Research Ctr & the Natl Asthma Ctr merged. Staff pubs sci papers & abstracts in sci journals. NJH/NAC is a two story campus complex of 22 bldgs on 30 acres, providing every modern facility for patient treatment & rehabilitation, basic & clin research, & the training of med professionals in its specialities. A nondenominational chapel is located in the May Bldg. NJH/NAC trains physicians, research scientists, nurses & public health personnel. Two & three yr clin, research & postdoctoral fellowships are offered in immunology, allergy & chest diseases in affiliation with the Univ of CO Health Sci Ctr.Bd of Trustees Chr: Andrew Goodman; Assc Chr: Jack Galter; Chr of the Resident Bd: Richard B. Tucker; Assc Chr of the Resident Bd: Charles M. Schayer; Pres: Richard N. Bluestein; Exec VP: Michael K. Schonbrun; V

Chr: Harold Krensky, Myron M. Miller, Robert B. Moch, Leonard M. Perlmutter, Joseph S. Schapiro, Jack J. Spitzer; Sec: Florian Barth; Asst Sec: Sidney A. Wolff; Treas: J. Peter Grace. **3800 E Colfax Ave, Denver CO 80206 (303) 388–4461.**

The Ranch Camp. To provide positive opportunities for youngsters to have fun in a safe, constructive environment; to structure experiences which should help campers feel comfortable in the out-of-doors; to provide opportunities to help campers dev an understanding of & a positive relationship with the rich J culture; to help campers understand the delicate nature of ecology & the necessity of conservation of the natural environment; to provide intimate group & individual experiences based on the precepts of a J heritage & a democratic soc. Instructional swim at least three times a week & free swim every day; horseback riding instruction a minimum of three times a week with options for additional riding experiences; observance of Shabbat by spending the day relaxing, discussing, hiking, swimming & participating in rel & cultural experiences; athletics including soccer, lacrosse, softball, volleyball, basketball, technical rock climbing, back packing, crafts, river rafting, camping; J edu combining worship, arts & crafts, music, dance, drama & folklore. Est in 1953 as a serv of the Denver JCC. Campers who are attracted to one particular specialty area have opportunities to pursue this interest. Every camper, with his/her cabin group, has the opportunity to plan at least one J experience to be shared with the entire camp. JCC Pres: Jim Judd; JCC Exec Dir: David Eskenazi; Camp Dir: Alby Segall; Adm Asst: Laurie Headley; Caretaker: Don Bornman; Ranch Cttee Co-Chr: Dan Grunfeld, Harold Lane; Ranch Cttee Mems: Jim Judd, Morey Cohen, Myrna Leibman, Paul Marcus, Mark Miller, Dena Schneider, Steve Greenholz, Jeanette Bernstein, Dell Bernstein, David Ravitch, Joel Kluger, Don Skupsky, Michael Towbin, Lisa Fine, David Tennenbaum. **PO Box 6196, Denver CO 80206 (303) 399–2660.**

Rocky Mountain Hebrew Academy. Coeducational sch for grades 7–12. To prepare its stu for meaningful J living in accordance with the ideals & values of the Torah, & provide them with a secular edu of the highest caliber. Complete curriculum of J & gen studies. J studies include Bible, Heb, Talmud, Hist & Customs; gen studies include Language Arts, Mathematics, Sci, Hist, Music, Art & Physical Edu. In addition, stu learn to prog a computer, participate in field trips, drama & writing for the sch newspaper. Est in 1979 in response to the needs of Denver's growing J com. Prin: Rabbi Samuel Biber; Pres: Marvin Z. Kark; VPs: Mourene Tesler, Nadene Kline; Sec: Barbara Zimmerman; Treas: Burton G. Kaplan. **560 S Monaco Pkwy, Denver CO 80224 (303) 355–7642.**

Temple Sinai. Affiliated with UAHC. 460 mems. Rabbi Raymond A. Zwerin; Pres: Jerry M. Gotlieb; Edu: Anita A. Fricklas; Adm: Oscar Sladek; Brotherhood Pres: Larry Kane. **8050 E Dartmouth Ave, Denver CO 80231 (303) 750–3006.**

Temple Sinai Library. For information on the Temple, see – Temple Sinai, Denver, CO. **8050 E Dartmouth Ave, Denver CO 80231 (303) 750–3006.**

Lakewood

Cancer Research Center & Hospital. 6401 W Colfax Ave, Lakewood CO 80214 (303) 233–6501.

Littleton

Congregation Beth Shalom. Affiliated with United Syn of Am. Pres: Harvey Goldstein; Edu Dir: Tamar Stitleman. **2280 E Noble Pl, Littleton CO 80120 (303) 794–6643.**

Pueblo

Temple Emanuel. Affiliated with UAHC. 45 mems. Rabbis: Jay R. David, Albert Yanow; Pres: William Berg; Edu: Lil Ryals. **1325 N Grand Ave, Pueblo CO 81003 (303) 544–6448.**

United Hebrew Center. Affiliated with United Syn of Am. Pres: Irvin C. Greenberg. **106 W 15th St, Pueblo CO 81003 (303) 544–9897.**

Trinidad

Congregation Aaron. Affiliated with UAHC. 10 mems. Pres: Beatrice Sanders; Sisterhood Pres: Kathryn Rubin. **Third & Maple, Trinidad CO 81082 (303) 846–3193.**

CONNECTICUT

Bloomfield

Beth Hillel Synagogue. Affiliated with United Syn of Am. Rabbi Philip Lazowski; Cantor Larry Fader; Pres: Joel Neuwirth; Edu Dir: Philip Lazowski. **160 Wintonbury Ave, Bloomfield CT 04002.**

Congregation Teferes Israel. To promote traditional Yiddishkeit; to uphold the sacred bond that exists between God & the J people; to foster & cement a close relationship between the J people wherever they are. Daily Minyonim, Sabbath & Holiday Servs; late Fri evening Oneg Shabbat Forum; Adult Edu; Talmud, Mishnayes classes; Rel Sch; Bar Mitzvah & Bas Torah classes; Sisterhood; Men's Club; Social Club; Youth Group. The Cong was formed in 1912. In 1926 Teferes Is joined with Chevre Kadishe & was recorded in the State of CT as Cong Chevre Kadishe Teferes Is. In 1956 a new bldg was dedicated with a membership of 39 families, & Rabbi Haskel Lindenthal became the spiritual leader. Due to an increase in mems, an addition was dedicated in 1960. The Rabbi received life tenure in 1964. The present bldg was constructed in 1969. Syn facilities include a sanctuary of 280 permanent seats expandable to 900, social hall accommodating 300 for dinner & dance, all purpose rm, small chapel, separate meat & dairy kitchens. Rabbi Haskel Lindenthal; Pres: Gerald Okrant; 1st VP: Dr Robert Rudnicki; 2nd VP: Ludwig Rosenberg; Treas: Goldie Goldstein; Rec Sec: Ruth Rudnick. **27 Brown St, PO Box 606, Bloomfield CT 06002 (203) 243–1719.**

Congregation Tikvoh Chadoshoh. Affiliated with United Syn of Am. Rabbi Hans S. Bodenheimer; Pres: Miriam Fleishman. **180 Still Rd, Bloomfield CT 06002 (203) 236–2010.**

Bramford

Temple Beth Tikvah. Reform Cong. Fri Night Servs, celebration of festivals; Nursery Sch; Rel Sch for pre-K through 7th grade, Confirmation Prog; youth group activities for stu in grades 5–12; Adult Edu courses; Bar/Bat Mitzvah. 200 families. Part-time sch prin, 11 teachers, nursery sch dir & 4 teachers, part-time music dir. F in 1976 as an outgrowth of a J com org. First syn locted on this part of the CT shoreline in 200 yrs. Pres: Myra Josephson; VP: Myron Cohen; Sec: Sandra Brand; Treas: Alan Lemkin; Dir of Rel Activities: Elaine Blechman; Dir of Edu: Sandra Walker; Dir of Progs: Irwin Siegelman; Dir of Facility & Grounds: George Hauer; Mem's at Large: Edward Gleich, Michael Price; Pres of Sisterhood: Anne Kahrimanis; Pres of Brotherhood: Les Auerbach. **64 Meadow Wood Rd, Bramford CT 06405.**

Bridgeport

Congregation Agudas Achim. Orthodox Cong affiliated with Union of Orthodox Heb Cong of Am. Rel Servs; Heb classes for Russian immigrants; Sisterhood; Men's Club; blood pressure screening for sr citizens; The Esther Goldberg Sr Citizen Ctr; congregate meals prog (luncheon) for elderly. 105 families; 60 sr citizens daily for luncheon (Mon – Fri) including shut-ins. 3 employees; 10 volunteers (RSVP). F 1900. Rabbi Mosha Epstein; Pres: Alfred Lowy; VPs: W. Rosenberg, Harry Kanner; VP Cong & Pres The Esther Goldberg Ctr: Joseph Goldberg; Treas: Herman Levine. **85 Arlington St, Bridgeport CT 06606 (203) 335–6353.**

Congregation B'nai Israel. Affiliated with UAHC. 650 mems. Rabbi Arnold I. Sher; Cantor Ramon E. Gilbert; Pres: Arnold Kaplan; Edu: Robert H. Gillette; Sisterhood Pres: Nila Breiner; Brotherhood Pres: Howard Rubinstein. **2710 Park Ave, Bridgeport CT 06604 (203) 336–1858.**

Congregation B'nai Israel Library. For information on the Cong, see – Congregation B'nai Israel, Bridgeport, CT. **2710 Park Ave, Bridgeport CT 06604 (203) 336–1858.**

Congregation Rodeph Sholom. Affiliated with United Syn of Am. Rabbi Israel C. Stein; Cantor Isaiah M. Grama; Pres: Albert Indenbaum; Exec Dir: Esther Kelman; Edu Dir: Gilah H. Amitai; Youth Dir: Stuart Gordon. **Park & Capitol Ave, Bridgeport CT 06604 (203) 334–0159.**

Congregation Rodeph Sholom Library. For information on the Cong, see – Cong Rodeph Sholom, Bridgeport, CT. **Park & Capital Ave, Bridgeport CT 06604 (203) 334–0159.**

Jewish Community Center of Bridgeport. 4200 Park Ave, Bridgeport CT 06604 (203) 372–6567.

Jewish Community Center of Bridgeport Library. 4200 Park Ave, Bridgeport CT 06604 (203) 372–6567.

Jewish Digest. Periodical pub. **1363 Fairfield Ave, Bridgeport CT 06605 (203) 384–2284.**

Jewish Federation of Greater Bridgeport, Inc. Mem of CJF. Sponsors United Jewish Campaign. Organized 1936. Pres: Jack Zaluda; Exec Dir: Gerald A. Kleinman. **4200 Park Ave, Bridgeport CT 06604 (203) 372–6504.**

Bristol

Beth Israel Synagogue. Affiliated with United Syn of Am. Rabbi Dr Henry Lieberman; Pres: Saul Roth. **339 W St, Bristol CT 06010 (203) 583–6293.**

Cheshire

Temple Beth David. Affiliated with UAHC. 127 mems. Rabbi Robert L. Rozenberg; Pres: Honey Davis. **3 Main St, PO Box 274, Cheshire CT 06410 (203) 272–0037.**

Colchester

Ahavath Achim Synagogue. Affiliated with United Syn of Am. Rabbi M. Leifer; Pres: David Flom. **Lebanon Ave C, Colchester CT 06415 (203) 537–2809.**

Danbury

The Clapboard Ridge Synagogue – Congregation B'nai Israel. Conservative Cong affiliated with United Syn of Am. To provide the full range of rel, edu, cultural & social opportunities to the local J com in a context of Conservative J & egalitarianism; to represent the mems to the com at large in matters of social concern & rel life; to work with other local & natl J groups to strengthen J unity & support the State of Is. Rel Servs; Afternoon Sch for grades K-11; Adult Edu; Youth Group; Sisterhood; Men's Club; family social events; first Shabbat of the mo – Family Kabbalat Shabbat geared to chil; third Shabbat of the mo – Shabbat Discussion geared to adults; monthly Shabbat Lunch Prog; kosher meat co-op; Judaica shop; J art display; CPR & first aid training; monthly Sun Morning Tallit & Tefillen Club; counseling & support groups as needed. 100 mem families. F in 1895 as an Orthodox syn, it provided a meeting place for observant J, a rel sch for the chil, & cemetery facilities. In the late 1950's the Cong liberalized & affiliated with United Syn. After a series of relocations, the Syn settled into its present facility in 1976 with its new name. Rabbi Jack Moline; Pres: Dennis Adler; VPs: Edward Samuels, Michael Braun; Corsp Sec: Susan Brooks; Rec Sec: Miriam Stein; Treas: Arlene Domue; Fin Sec: Jacqueline Levine; Sisterhood Pres: Nada Adler; Men's Club Pres: Dan Domue; Sch Prin: Sara Chester; Youth Dir: Jay Scheuer. **PO Box 1060, 193 Clapboard Ridge Rd, Danbury CT 06810 (203) 792–6161.**

Jewish Federation of Greater Danbury. Mem of CJF. Organized 1945. Pres: Pearl Turk; Exec Dir: Carol Effrat. **54 Main St, Suite E, Danbury CT 06810 (203) 792–6353.**

United Jewish Center. Affiliated with UAHC. 418 mems. Rabbis: Robert N. Levine, Jerome Malino; Cantor Samuel Radwine; Pres: Myrna H. Jacobs; Edu: Robert N. Levine; Sisterhood Pres: Vickie Kaplan; Brotherhood Pres: Laurence Sibrack. **141 Deer Hill Ave, Danbury CT 06810 (203) 748–3355.**

United Jewish Center of Danbury Library. For information on the Ins, see – United Jewish Center of Danbury, Danbury, CT. **141 Deer Hill Ave, Danbury CT 06810 (203) 748–3355.**

Danielson

Temple Beth Israel. Affiliated with United Syn of Am. Pres: Benjamin Goldstein. **Killingly Dr, Danielson CT 06239 (203) 774–9874.**

Derby

Beth Israel Synagogue Center. Serves the J com in the Lower Nagatuck Valley & nearby coms. Rel Servs; Edu Prog. 130 families. F in 1958. Pub Bulletins (monthly). Rabbi Aryeh Wineman. **300 Elizabeth St, Derby CT 06418 (203) 734–3361.**

East Haddam

Congregation Rodfe Zedek. Affiliated with United Syn of Am. Rabbi Henry O. Bernstein; Pres: Marvin Baron. **Orchard Rd, East Haddam CT 06423; Mailing add: Box 38A, Sillimanville Rd, Moodus CT 06469 (203) 873–8061.**

East Hartford

Temple Beth Tefilah. Affiliated with United Syn of Am. Rabbi Myer Asper; Pres: Fred Balet; Exec Dir: Gordon Katz; Youth Dir: Herb Flink. **465 Oak St, East Hartford CT 06118 (203) 569–0670.**

East Norwalk

Jewish Federation of Greater Norwalk, Inc. Mem of CJF. Organized 1946; reorganized 1964. Pres: Gary Oberst; Exec Dir: Charles Vogel. **Shorehaven Rd, East Norwalk CT 06855 (203) 853–3440.**

Norwalk Jewish Community Center. To enhance J life in the com; to provide chil & youth progs for families, & complete yr-round recreational & edu facilities. Pre-Sch Nursery Prog; After-Sch Ctr; Teen Lounge; Adult Edu; Sr Citizen Prog; Physical Edu Prog; J Summer Day Camp; Adopt-a-Bubba Prog; J Holiday Series. Mems fr Greater Norwalk com. Exec Dir: Les Cohen; Prog Philip Goldberg; Pres: Cliff Adlerblum; VPs: Linda Lander, Gerald Rabin, Irwin Weinstein, Brina Widlansky; Treas: Charles Mittel; Sec: Nancy Oberst; Bd of Dirs: Paul Ackert, Vicki Adlerblum, Barry Bernheim, Mark Brachman, Sherwin Coplin, Ellen Donen, Mel Feldman, Andrew Glickson, Norman Greenberger, Fred Heilbrunn, Daniel Kaplan, Frances Kaplan, Jerome Klein, Ronald Kupferberg, Bruce Lynn, Joel Miller, Charles Mittel, Dr Jeff Pivor, Neil Plain, Joseph Podrat, Dr Jack Rice, Howard Rosenbluth, Stephen Schaffer, Gerald Snider, Dr David Tesser, Albert Tishler, Bert Wollkind; Hon: Mayor William Collins, Rabbi Barry Freundel, Rabbi Jonas Goldberg, Rabbi Jacob Lantz, Florence Spaulding, Nora Tomasulo, Senator Alfred Santaniello Jr. **Box 483, Shorehaven Rd, East Norwalk CT 06856 (203) 838–7504.**

Fairfield

Congregation Beth El. Affiliated with United Syn of Am. Rabbi Leon Waldman; Cantor Charles Feld; Pres: Noel R. Newman; Adm: Lisa Schindler; Edu Dir: Esta Gross; Youth Dir: Stuart Gordon. **1200 Fairfield Woods Rd, Fairfield CT 06430 (203) 374–5544.**

List Residence of the Jewish Home for the Elderly of Fairfield County. Modern geriatric ctr serving J frail elderly fr Fairfield Cty. Accredited by the Joint Commis on Accreditation of Hosps; mem of Am Assn of Homes for the Aging, CT Assn of Non-Profit Facilities for the Aged, & Natl Assn of J Homes for the Aged. Diagnostic & therapeutic servs; dental & podiatry & eye, ear, nose & throat rms equipped & manned by qualified specialists; Physical Therapy Suite containing three hydro-therapy tanks, steps, parallel bars & other related equipment; recreational, spritual & social activities; library; Work Activity Ctr; Adult Day Care Prog; Outpatient Physical Therapy Dept; kosher Meals-on-Wheels to a local syn cong. The Ctr serves as a teaching ctr for four univs & three hosps. Residence has a total bed capacity of 240. Residents average 85 yrs of age (four-fifths are women). Day Care Ctr serves 25 clients a day. Approximately 300 full-time & part-time staff. Two pavilions comprise the List Residence: the Tan Pavilion & the Bennett Pavilion. Construction of the Tandet Pavilion began in Oct 1971 following several yrs of planning & fund raising. The 120 bed facility opened on Oct 15, 1973. Construction on the 120 bed addition, Bennett Pavilion, began in Jan 1979 & was completed Jul 1980. A Women's Auxiliary provides volunteers, educates its mems in gerontology & organizes fund raising for the residence. The Auxiliary pubs a bulletin – Chai Lights. The Home functions according to Orthodox rituals & precepts. All food is strictly kosher. Servs are conducted in Heb & English in the syn &, for those unable to attend, in the nursing units. Exec Dir: Dennis J. Magid; Hon Chr: Albert A. List; Hon Pres: David Goldstein; Hon Dirs for Life: Hon Samuel Mellitz, Michael Steinberg, William H. Tandet, Hon Archibald H. Tunick, Irving Weitz; Pres: Jerome S. Siebert; VPs: Sissy Bershad, Samuel J. Heyman, Harold E. Hoffman, Anne Kaufman, Jerome Klein, Mary Young; Treas: Earl J. Wofsey; Asst Treas: Saul Kwartin, Robert L. Levy, Robert H. Temkin; Corsp Sec: Alan H. Nevas; Rec Sec: William E. Kanter; Pres Women's Auxiliary: Marcia Lipton. **175 Jefferson St, Fairfield CT 06432 (203) 374–9461.**

Greenwich

Temple Sholom. Affiliated with United Syn of Am. Cantor Eliot Vogel; Pres: Stephen Brecher; Exec Dir: Norman Perlstein; Edu Dir: Marilyn Schlachter Schwartz. **300 E Putnam Ave, Greenwich CT 06830 (203) 869–7191.**

Hamden

Congregation Mishkan Israel. Affiliated with UAHC. 677 mems. Rabbis: Robert E. Goldburg, Mark

J. Panoff; Cantor Jonathan Gordon; Pres: Harry J. Wexler; Edu: Ronald Heiferman; Adm: Valentine Tuckell; Sisterhood Pres: Lois Sachs; Brotherhood Pres: Alan Postman. **785 Ridge Rd, Hamden CT 06517 (203) 288–3877.**

Temple Beth Sholom. Conservative Cong affiliated with United Syn of Am. To transform the ideas of our tradition into a progressive & modern prog of intelligent J living. Rel Servs, Fri evening, Sat morning, weekday mornings & festivals; Rel Sch comprising 1 yr weekly Pre-Heb Prog, 5 yr 3 day a wk Elementary Prog, & 3 yr Confirmation Prog; Jr Cong on Sat mornings; Adult Edu; Sisterhood; Men's Club; Mr & Mrs Club; sr progs; youth groups affiliated with USY. Temple Beth Sholom began in 1946 as the Hamden JCC. Facilities are available for weddings, Bar & Bat Mitzvahs. The Temple owns & maintains a cemetery in Hamden. Rabbi Alvin K. Berkun; Cantor Charles Gelman; Pres: Mrs Philip Lear. **1809 Whitney Ave, Hamden CT 06517 (203) 288–7748.**

Temple Beth Sholom, Esther Swinkin Memorial Library. For information on the Temple, see – Temple Beth Sholom, Hamden, CT **1809 Whitneg Ave, Hamden CT 06517 (203) 288–7748.**

Hartford

Connecticut Jewish Ledger. Periodical pub. **PO Box 1688, Hartford CT 06101 (203) 233–2148.**

Mount Sinai Hospital. Non-profit full serv com teaching hosp. To provide increasingly better health care for the com by supplying more qualified staff, newer instruments & better methods of treatment. Numerous branches of med including specialties: Ambulatory & Com Med, Anesthesiology Med, Internal Med, Allergy, Cardiology, Dermatology, Endocrinology, Geriatrics, Hematology-Oncology, Infectious Disease, Nephrology, Neurology, Pulmonary Disease, Rehabilitation Med, Family Med, Obstetrics & Gynecology, Pathology & Clin Labs, Pediatrics & Chil Behavior, Psychiatry, Radiology, Surgery, Dentistry & Oral Surgery, Gen Surgery, Neurosurgery, Ophthalmology, Orthopedics, Otolaryngology, Plastic Surgery, Thoracic & Cardiovascular Surgery & Urology. Mount Sinai Hosp provides med servs at Bradley Intl Airport, Hartford Civic Ctr, Smith Towers Geriatric Clin, Burgdorf Health Ctr, TBScreening Clin, Starkel Rd Geriatric Clin W Hartford, Communicable Disease Clin, Combined Hosps Alcoholism Prog, Hartford JCC, Help Heart Exercise Learning Prog, Receiving Home at Warehouse Point. Bed capacity of 379. 299 attending med staff, 56 house staff; serves as a teaching hosp with 34 full time med staff, 9 chiefs of servs; 371 full & part-time registered nurses, 50 full & part-time licensed practical nurses, nursing assts, clerical staff & adm staff, 4 nurse midwives, 25 certified physician assts. Mount Sinai Hosp began as a 39 bed gen hosp in the renovated Brainard Mansion on Capitol Ave in 1923. Construction of the Blue Hills Ave site began in 1948. In 1952 a fourth floor was added to the bldg. In 1967 the Hosp embarked on a construction prog enabling the Hosp to expand & improve facilities. During the 1970's the committment to dev a major teaching Hosp with full-time chiefs of servs in major clin depts was realized. Teaching progs include: Obstetrics/Gynecology Residency Prog, Surgical Residency Prog, Grad Physician Asst Training in Pediatrics, Sch of Radiologic Tech, Chil Life Servs, Social Work, Physical Therapy Prog, Pharmacy, Certified Occupational Therapist Assts, Am Dietetic Assn Prog, Home Care Servs, Hosp PR, Adm Residency Prog, Emergency Med Technician, Anatomical Pathology, Med Resident in Nuclear Med, Clin Psychology Internship Prog, Residency Prog in Nursing Adm. Pres & Exec Dir: Robert B. Bruner; Dir Personnel Servs: Louis Abbey; VP Div of Planning & Com Servs: Richard D'Aguila; Asst Exec Dir: J. Al Deag; VP Div of Professional Servs: Robert Frazier; VP Div of Med Care Servs: Dr Charles W. Parton; VP Div of Public Affairs & Dev: Douglas J. Rubinstein; VP Div of Patient Care Servs: Ronald Waack; VP & Treas Div of Adm & Fin Servs: Larry Wilder. **500 Blue Hills Ave, Hartford CT 06112 (203) 243–1441.**

Madison

Temple Beth Tikvah. Affiliated with UAHC. 206 mems. Rabbi David Wortman; Cantor Judy Koch; Pres: Myra Josephson; Edu: Margaret Lerner. **196 Durham Rd, PO Box 523, Madison CT 06443 (203) 245–7028.**

Manchester

Temple Beth Sholom. Conservative Syn affiliated with United Syn of Am. To foster J life & observance. Rel Servs – Fri evening & Sat morning; Minyan every evening; rel sch (Rabbi Leon Wing Rel Sch) for grades K–12; Sisterhood; Adult Edu Prog; youth groups – USY, Kadima. 350 families; 225 stu in grades K–12. 25 employees. Pub Bulletin (monthly). Facilities include kosher kitchen, sanctuary & chapel, library, gift & bk shop, classrms. Largest Syn in Hartford CT East-of-the-River area. Pres: Efrem Jaffe; Exec VP: Elliott Zimmerman. **400 E Middle Turnpike, Manchester CT 06040 (203) 643–9563.**

Meriden

Jewish Federation of Meriden – Meriden Jewish Welfare Fund, Inc. Organized 1944. Pres: Joseph Barker; Sec: Marcia Cheikin. **127 E Main St, Meriden CT 06450 (203) 235–2581.**

Temple B'nai Abraham. Conservative Syn affiliated with United Syn of Am. Rel Servs; Men's Club; USY; Kadimah; Afternoon Sch; library containing 500 vols (Judaica). 360 mems; 93 stu in grades K–9. 19 employees. F 1895. Pub The Scribe (bi-weekly). Rabbi Richard Plavin; Cantor Israel Tabatsky; Pres: Ruth Kahn; 1st VP: Isaac Rouinksy; Editor: Marcia Chenkin. **127 E Main St, Meriden CT 06450 (203) 235–2581.**

Middletown

Congregation Adath Israel. Affiliated with United Syn of Am. Rabbi Nathan Levenson DD; Pres: Irwin Zagoren; Edu Dir: Allen Marks; Youth Dir: Dr Joseph Zaientz. **PO Box 337, Middletown CT 06457 (203) 346–8780.**

New Britain

Temple B'nai Israel. Affiliated with United Syn of Am. Rabbi Harry Z. Zwelling; Pres: Leon Croll. **265 W Main St, New Britain CT 06052 (203) 224–0479.**

New Haven

Anti-Defamation League of B'nai B'rith – Connecticut Regional Office. Dedicated in purpose & prog to translating the Am heritage of democratic ideals into a way of life for all Am; to countering assaults on the safety, status, rights & image of J. For additional information, see – Anti-Defamation League of B'nai B'rith, New York City, NY. **1162 Chapel St, New Haven CT 06511.**

Congregation Beth El – Keser Israel. Conservative Cong affiliated with United Syn of Am. Daily & Sabbath Servs; Adult Edu; Afternoon Sch; library containing several hundred bks (Judaica). 247 mems. Beth El – Keser Israel merged 1968; Beth El broke away fr B'nai Israel (f 1891) in 1959; Keser Israel f 1909. Pub Beki Newsletter (monthly). Facilities include kosher kitchen, 2 halls, sanctuary seating 356, gift shop, offs rented to J orgs (such as B'nai Brith, Hadassah). Rabbi Elliot B. Gertel; Pres: Herbert Etkind; Ritual Dir: Louis Friedman; Musical Dir: Herbert Richmann. **85 Harrison St, New Haven CT 06515 (203) 389–2108.**

Jewish Family Service of New Haven. Mental health & social serv org affiliated with Family Serv Assn of Am; Assn of J Family & Chil Servs; United Ways of Branford, Milford, New Haven & the Valley; New Haven J Fed; Council on Accreditation. Professional counseling: individual, marital, family, group; auxiliary social serv; emergency assistance; outreach; information & referral; adoption; consultation to schs; preventive seminars & workshops on family life; immigration; volunteer; professional social work library containing 200 vols. 600 mems (500 families, 100 individuals). 8 employees; 10 volunteers. Facilities include offs for social workers, rm for volunteers, large group meeting rm. Pres: Carol Robbins; VPs: Marvin Teplitzky, Beverly Levy; Treas: Hannah Malkin; Asst Treas: Ivan Katz; Sec: Sidney Sussman; Exec Dir: Stephen G. Donshik. **152 Temple St, New Haven CT 06510 (203) 777–6641.**

The Jewish Historical Society of New Haven, Inc. J resource ctr. To promote the hist of the J com of the City of New Haven & surrounding towns. Historical documents about local hist; speakers on aspects of local J hist; records of the volunteer orgs of the com starting fr the 1840's to the present; several hundred photographs. F in 1977. Jews in New Haven (Vol I, II, III). The Soc is located in the J Home for the Aged in New Haven. Archivist: Edith F. Hurwitz; Curator of the Archives: Harvey Ladin; Pres: Werner S. Hirsch; 1st VP: Joel Wasserman; Treas: Jane Silverman. **169 Davenport Ave, New Haven CT 06519.**

Jewish Home for the Aged. To dev new levels of health & convalescent care & edu. Therapeutic, recreational & social activities; daily Rel Servs; dietary laws are observed. JHA provides meals for those in nursing homes or at home who can't cook for themselves & require kosher food, & for the Nutrition Prog at the JCC. Goodwin-Levine Adult Day Ctr provides therapeutic & preventive care during the day for the frail & disabled who then return to their homes. The Sisters of Zion, formed in 1908, promoted the est of the Home. The women's social serv org, realizing the special needs of the aged poor, formed a corp, developed local com support & acquired a bldg. During the yrs 1963–1970, an organized med staff was dev. In 1972 a study recommended the dev of a geriatric ctr with a broadening of care for the aged. This led to the bldg of the Cohn-Ginsberg Bldg & the dev of the Home's social servs prog & adult day ctr. In 1979 the Home was listed in the Natl Register of Historic Places in recognition of the architectural value of the Home, its role in the com & its hist of voluntary servs. The New Haven J Historical Soc is housed at JHA &

maintains historical material associated with the J Com of New Haven. Asst Dir: Stephen Casner; Dir of Nursing: Kathryn Robison. **167–169 Davenport Ave, New Haven CT 06519 (203) 789–1650.**

Lubavitch Youth Organization. An outreach org that familiarizes J men & women & chil with J practices & philosophy. Affiliated with the Chabad Lubavitch Movement. To bring the Light of Torah & J tradition to all corners of the world; to battle against assimilation, apathy & indifference to J living. In gen, this ins offers: Operation Helping Hand – provides aid to Russian immigrants; on campus progs – provide kosher foods, Fri night to Sun retreats, lectures, Shabbat servs & counseling; celebrations of holidays – sponsors seminars on Passover laws, Purim Party, Toys for Tots for chil in the hosp at Chanukah, helps with bldg of succas, distributes prayers bks for holidays; marriage & family counseling; Adult Edu Prog; helps est kosher kitchens in private homes; Mitzvah Mobile – introduces J men to the wearing of Tefillin, distributes rel articles, maintains traveling J library & audio visual ctr; Succamobile; & Summer Day Camp. Rabbi Zalman Morsow. **152 Goffe Terr, New Haven CT 06511 (203) 865–3649.**

New Haven Jewish Federation. Mem of CJF. Sponsors Combined Jewish Appeal. Organized 1928. Pres: Marvin Lender; Exec Dir: Arthur Spiegel. **1162 Chapel St, New Haven CT 06511 (203) 562–2137.**

New Haven Jewish Federation, Department of Jewish Education Library. 1162 Chapel St, New Haven CT 06511 (203) 789–0886.

Torah Academy of Connecticut. Orthodox HS. Branch of the Rabbinical Seminary of Am; accredited by AARTS & recognized by Torah Umesorah. To educate young men & women according to J tradition while at the same time offering an intensive gen studies prog. Gen studies; J studies; post HS Prog; Judaica & gen studies; Rel Servs; Post HS – Bais Medrash Prog; library with 3,000 vols (Judaica). 80 families; 55 stu grades 9–12. 5 employees full time, 12 part time. F 1976 by Torah Umesorah as a regional HS with dormatory facility. Pub Torah Academy Women (quarterly); TA Times (monthly). Facilities include kosher kitchen, dining rm, sch facilities, bais-medrash, dormatory. Dean Rabbi Yoel Adelman; J Studies Prin: Rabbi Nisson Fromowitz; Gen Studies Prin: Marc Blosveren; Dean of Stu: Rabbi Naftali Kalter. **330 Blake St, New Haven CT 06515; 570 Whalley Ave, New Haven CT 06515 (203) 397–3243.**

Torah Academy of Connecticut, Library. Library contains 3000 vols (Judaica). For information on the Academy, see – Torah Academy of Connecticut, New Haven, CT. **330 Blake St, New Haven CT 06515 (203) 397–3243.**

Yale Hillel Foundation. Rel, cultural, edu & resource ctr for J stu & faculty. To create J communal life at Yale. Rel Servs (Reform, Orthodox, Conservative); classes in Heb, Yiddish, Ethics, Bible, Midrasha, Demography, Am J Literature, Women's Issues; counseling; meals; celebrating; library containing 3,000 vols (Judaica). 3,000 mems. 3 employees; 10 volunteers. F 1943 as Yale Hillel; previously known as Kohut Forum. Facilities include off, rabbi's residence, kosher kitchen. Dir: Rabbi James Ponet; Asst Adm: Caryl Kligfeld; Prog Asst: Janina Frankel. **1904–A Yale Station, New Haven CT 06520 (203) 432–4174.**

Yale Hillel Foundation Library. Library contains 3,000 vols (Judaica). For information on the Foundation, see – Yale Hillel Foundation, New Haven, CT. **1904–A Yale Station, New Haven CT 06520 (203) 432–4174.**

New London

Beth El. Affiliated with United Syn of Am. Rabbi Carl Astor; Edu Dir: Marcia Barnestein; Pres: Seymour S. Hendel. **660 Ocean Ave, New London CT 06320 (203) 442–0418.**

Connecticut College Chavurah Hillel. Promotes J activities for area col stu; conducts col UJA campaign. Pres: Sloan Schickler; Advs: Dr Jerry Winter, Dr Ernest Schlesinger. **B'nai B'rith Hillel J Com Council of Greater New London, 302 State St, New London CT 06320 (203) 442–8062.**

Jewish Federation of Eastern Connecticut. Conducts comprehensive J activities in various areas including cultural, edu, youth, teen, pro-Is & resettlement progs; sponsors local UJA campaign. Reorganized in 1970. Pres: Gary Motin; Exec Dir: Eugene F. Elander. **J Com Council of Greater New London, 302 State St, New London CT 06320 (203) 442–8062.**

Solomon Schechter Academy of New London Cty. Affiliated with Solomon Schechter Day Schs Assn. Chr: Dr Burton Edelstein. **660 Ocean Ave, New London CT 06320 (203) 443–5589.**

New Milford

Temple Sholom. Affiliated with UAHC. 139 mems. Rabbi Norman D. Koch; Pres: Fred Golub; Edu:

Rochelle Golub; Sisterhood Pres: Judy Moskowitz; Brotherhood Pres: Barry Aronstam. **PO Box 509, New Milford CT 06776 (203) 354–0273.**

Newington

B'nai Sholom. Affiliated with United Syn of Am. Rabbi Kenneth Greene; Cantor Wilford Birnbaum; Pres: Aaron Friedman; Edu Dir: Robert Gerrol; Youth Dir: Sheila Schwartz. **26 Church St, Newington CT 06111 (203) 667–0826.**

Temple Sinai. Affiliated with UAHC. 311 mems. Rabbi Marc Brownstein; Cantor Samuel Katz; Pres: Elinor Reinor; Edu: Marc Brownstein; Sisterhood Pres: Shirley R. Gersten, Babs Liverant; Brotherhood Pres: Sheldon Wishnick. **41 W Hartford Rd, Newington CT 06111 (203) 561–1055.**

Norwalk

Beth Israel Synagogue. Orthodox Syn. Beth Is Adult Ins; Cave Coffee House– a prog for singles ages 17–27 which has been awarded the Natl Col Activities Award by the Union of Orthodox Congs of Am; Couples Club; Sisterhood; Heb Sch; Morning Minyan. F in 1906 to serve the needs of the J com. The oldest J house of worship in Norwalk & the only Orthodox syn. The Cong has the first com Eiruv in CT. A day sch is in the planning. Rabbi Barry Freundel; Cantor Jonathan Horowitz; Pres: Martin Weinberg; Chr of the Bd: A.J. Kurtz; Pres of Sisterhood: Mildred Schwartz. **40 King St, Norwalk CT 06851 (203) 866–0534.**

Congregation Beth El. Affiliated with United Syn of Am. Rabbi Jonas Goldberg; Cantor Debra Katchko Zimmerman; Pres: Alvin Schub; Edu Dir: Al Treidel. **109 E Ave, Norwalk CT 06851 (203) 838–2710.**

Temple Shalom. Affiliated with UAHC. 295 mems. Rabbi Jacob Lantz; Cantor Mark J. Lipson; Pres: Jack Rice; Sisterhood Pres: Ellen Hattenbach; Brotherhood Pres: Stanley Lieberstein. **259 Richards Ave, Norwalk CT 06850 (203) 866–0148.**

Norwich

Beth Jacob Synagogue. Affiliated with United Syn of Am. Rabbi Stuart G. Altshuler; Cantor Irving Poll; Pres: Simie Beit. **400 New London Turnpike, Norwich CT 06360.**

Orange

Lubavitch Yeshivah. Rabbi M. Hecht. **261 Derby Ave, Orange CT 06477 (203) 795–5261.**

Orange Synagogue Center Library. 205 Old Grassy Hill Rd, Orange CT 06477 (203) 795–2341.

Temple B'nai Shalom – Orange Synagogue Center. Affiliated with United Syn of Am. Rabbi Alvin Wainhaus; Pres: Lita A. Cooper; **205 Old Grassy Hill Rd, Orange CT 06477 (203) 795–2341.**

Temple Emanuel. Affiliated with UAHC. 178 mems. Rabbi Gerald S. Brieger; Pres: Margaret Cohen; Sisterhood Pres: Eleanor Feldman. **PO Box 897, 150 Derby Ave, Orange CT 06477 (203) 397–3000.**

Temple Emanuel Library. For information on the Temple, see – Temple Emanuel, Orange, CT. **150 Derby Ave, Orange CT 06477 (203) 397–3000.**

Ridgefield

Temple Shearith Israel. Affiliated with UAHC. 200 mems. Rabbi Elizabeth Rolle; Cantor Emil Hager; Pres: Sidney Weinstein; Edu: Elizabeth Rolle. **46 Peaceable St, Ridgefield CT 06877 (203) 438–6589.**

Rockville

B'nai Israel. Affiliated with United Syn of Am. Rabbi Marshall Press; Pres: Harold M. Levy; Edu Dir: Michael Turk; Youth Dir: Thomas Mastronarde. **54 Talcott Ave, Rockville CT 06066 (203) 875–5685.**

Simsbury

Farmington Valley Jewish Congregation. Affiliated with UAHC. 160 mems. Rabbi Howard S. Herman; Cantor Herman Shemonsky; Pres: Robert B. Fishberg; Edu: Thelma Shenkman; Adm: Thelma Shenkman. **55 Bushy Hill Rd, PO Box 261, Simsbury CT 06070 (203) 658–1075.**

South Windsor

Temple Beth Hillel. Affiliated with UAHC. 128 mems. Rabbi Neil Kominsky; Pres: Herbert Shook. **PO Box 403, 1001 Foster St, South Windsor CT 06074 (203) 644–8466.**

Stamford

The Center of the Jewish Community Library. PO Box 3326, Stamford CT 06905 (203) 329–8616.

Jewish Family Service. Agy serving Stamford, New Canaan, Greenwich & Darien. Dedicated to meeting the social serv needs of the com. Information & referral; short-term counseling covering emotional problems, marital crisis, interpersonal difficulties, parent-chil conflict, vocational confusion, mid-life melancholy & aging; Outreach to the Elderly: volunteer visiting of the elderly in their homes; J Family Life Edu; Russian & Indochinese refugee resettlement; client advocacy; legal servs; group servs including groups for widows & widowers, divorced women, newly arrived Iranian J & J identity group for newly arrived Russian refugees; training ctr for grad & undergrad stu in human servs & social work. Est in 1975 by the United J Fed. J Family Serv is unique in that many of its servs are delivered by volunteers – professional social workers, lawyers, Drs & retired persons who give of their free time. Exec Dir: Benjamin Greenspan; Clin Supervisor: Dr Howard Benditsky; Social Worker: Carol Cederbaum; Bd of Dirs – Pres: Dr Sidney Stern; Bd Mems: Cynthia Bitton, Ina Blumenthal, Frances Brenner, M. Cohen, Marilyn Dale, Vivian Feldman, Lila Feller, Dr Yakira Frank, Merna Gelband, Dr Samuel Kahn, Marjorie Laff, Dr Arthur Mostel, Ruth Reed, Susan Rubenstein, Arnold Spitalny, Dr Robert A. Fischl, Howard Halpern, Martin Manaly, Dr Harry Romanowitz, Frieda Knopf. **Newfield Ave & Vine Rd, PO Box 3038, Stamford CT 06905 (203) 322–6938.**

Temple Beth El. Affiliated with United Syn of Am. Rabbi Alex J. Goldman; Cantor Sidney G. Rabinowitz; Pres: Gordon J. Brown; Edu Dir: Larry Bloch; Youth Dir: Mel Rothstein. **350 Roxbury Rd, Stamford CT 06902 (203) 322–6901.**

Temple Sinai. Affiliated with UAHC. 319 mems. Rabbis: Stephen S. Pearce, Samuel M. Silver; Cantor Robert Borman; Pres: Herbert Gabriel; Edu: Robert Borman, Steve Rosman; Adm: Dorothy Fields; Sisterhood Pres: Majorie Bernstein; Brotherhood Pres: Robert Weiss. **Lakeside Dr, Stamford CT 06903 (203) 322–1649.**

United Jewish Federation. Mem of CJF. Inc 1973. Pres: Dr Charles Rosenberg; Exec VP: Stephen Schreier. **1035 Newfield Ave, Stamford CT 06905 (203) 322–6935.**

Stratford

Temple Beth Sholom. Affiliated with United Syn of Am. Pres: Jerome S. Arnold; Edu Dir: Andee Busker. **275 Huntington Rd, Stratford CT 06497 (203) 378–6175.**

Torrington

Beth El Synagogue. Affiliated with United Syn of Am. Pres: Bernard Polinsky; Edu Dir: Joan Libby. **124 Litchfield St, Torrington CT 06790 (203) 482–8263.**

Trumbull

Congregation B'nai Torah. Affiliated with United Syn of Am. Rabbi S. Jerome Wallin; Pres: Dr Sidney B. Cohen; Edu Dir: Jane Hillman; Youth Dirs: Mr & Mrs Robert Shulman. **5700 Main St, Trumbull CT 06611 (203) 268–6940.**

Wallingford

Congregation Beth Israel. Affiliated with United Syn of Am. Rabbi Michael Manson; Cantor & Pres: Dr Robert Couillard; Edu Dir: Herman Robbins. **22 N Orchard St, Wallingford CT 06492 (203) 269–5983.**

Waterbury

B'nai Shalom Synagogue. Orthodox Syn. Rel Servs; Sisterhood; Adult Edu; J com sch affiliated with J Fed of Waterbury. 213 mem families; 9 stu 1–6th grade. Syn is 11 yrs old; merged with Beth Is of Waterbury, Beth Is of Naugatuck. Facilities include sanctuary, chapel, kosher kitchen, social hall, gift shop. Rabbi Moshe Yeres; Pres: Joseph Weisman; Exec VP: Dr Michael Blumenthal; 1st VP: Ray Schain; 2nd VP: Albert Engel; Treas: Israel Goldstein; Fin Sec: Alvin Rosenbaum. **135 Roseland Ave, Waterbury CT 06710 (203) 754–4159**

Beth El Synagogue. Affiliated with United Syn of Am. Rabbi Charles Freundlich; Cantor & Edu Dir: Dr Irving Pinsky; Pres: Allen R. Traurug MD. **359 Cooke St, Waterbury CT 06710 (203) 759–4659.**

Jewish Federation of Waterbury, Inc. Mem of CJF. Organized 1938. Pres: Gloria Bogen; Exec Dir: Albert G. Effrat. **1020 Country Club Rd, Waterbury CT 06708 (203) 758–2441.**

Temple Israel. Affiliated with UAHC. 194 mems. Rabbi Arnold H. Miller; Pres: Jerome Summit; Sisterhood Pres: Liz Greengold, Roz Infeld, Rebecca Rearson; Brotherhood Pres: Julian Greengold. **100 Williamson Dr, Waterbury CT 06710 (203) 754–0187.**

Waterford

Temple Emanu-El. Affiliated with UAHC. 158 mems. Rabbi Aaron Rosenberg; Pres: Ken Webman;

Edu: Susan Goldstein; Sisterhood Pres: Barbara Weiss. **29 Dayton Rd, PO Box 288, Waterford CT 06385 (203) 443–3069.**

West Hartford

Beth El Temple of West Hartford. Affiliated with United Syn of Am. Rabbi Stanley M. Kessler; Cantor Moshe Lanxner; Pres: Bernie Selig; Edu & Youth Dir: David Ruran. **2626 Albany Ave, West Hartford CT 06117 (203) 233–9696.**

Emanuel Synagogue. Affiliated with United Syn of Am. Rabbi Howard Singer; Cantor Arthur Koret; Pres: Jerome E. Caplan; Exec Dir: Zana Baruch; Edu Dir: Alfred Weisel. **160 Mohegan Dr, West Hartford CT 06117 (203) 236–1275.**

Emanuel Synagogue Library. For information on the Syn, see – Emanuel Syn, West Hartford, CT. **160 Mohegan Dr, West Hartford CT 06117 (203) 236–1275.**

Greater Hartford Jewish Federation. Mem of CJF. Organized 1945. Pres: Daniel M. Neiditz; Exec Dir: Don Cooper. **333 Bloomfield Ave, PO Box 17–277, West Hartford CT 06117 (203) 236–3278.**

The Jewish Historical Society of Greater Hartford. To collect, & preserve in its archives, historical documents, pictures & memorabilia; to create a library of oral hist through taped interviews with significant personalties; to encourage study & research of the J com. Collection consists of 500 photocopies of documents; some 800 photographs; 250 tapes of interviews; press clippings & bks; 290 slides; film: Hartford Jews, 1900–1925; & 60 tape transcriptions. The Historical Soc also sponsors exhibits, bus trips, speakers & slide shows of J interest. F in 1971. Monthly Newsletter; annual brochure. Archives rm open to the public. Written inquiries handled without charge. Librarian & Adm Sec: Mrs Harry Cooper; Pres: Dr M. Delott Garber; VPs: Rabbi Howard A. Berman, Harry Cooper, David R. Harris, Doris Kashmann; Rec Sec: Mrs Ely Shor; Corsp Sec: Mrs Irving Bein; Treas: Mrs Charles Gershman; Asst Treas: Alexander Wasserman; Fin Sec: Mrs James Hurwit; Bd Mems: Rabbi Isaac C. Avigdor, Paul Basch, Sarah Buchstane, Mrs David Burman, Henry Cohn, Bernard Gilman, Martin D. Gold, Mrs Victor Harris, Morgan Himmelstein, James Hurwit, Joseph D. Hurwitz, Dane Kostin, Neil Macy, Mrs Ezra Melrose, Michael A. Peck, Mrs Edward Raphael, Harriet Samuels, Sidney Schulman, Mrs David Sheketoff, Mrs Lewis Sheketoff, Mrs Joseph Sherman, Joseph Soifer, Dr Irving Waltman, Mrs Irving Waltman, Harry Wolkoff, Mrs Harry Wolkoff; Hon Pres: Mrs Morris N. Cohen. **24 Cliffmore Rd, West Hartford CT 06117 (203) 236–4571.**

Sephardic Congregation of Greater Hartford. Syn affiliated with World Sephardic Fed & Am Sephardic Fed in NY. To retain the flavor of the Sephardic Culture with its social & rel traditions. Rel Servs held on the High Holidays; Sick Visiting Cttee; funds raised for needy families in Is; a prog of assistance to other Sephardic immigrants fr the Middle E in Is. 60 mem families. F in 19((& was known as the Oriental Brotherhood Hebrew Soc. The purpose was to provide for sick benefits, act as burial soc & hold High Holiday servs for its Sephardic mems. The Soc was f by seven families who had migrated fr Turkey in the early part of the century. Servs were first held in their own homes. In later yrs, space was rented in the lower level of an Ashkenazi Syn. At present, the Cong rents the Chapel of the Emanuel Syn. Pres: Henry Levy; VP: Moise Lasry; Treas: Max Levy; Sec: Abraham Sasportas. **21 Tumblebrook Lane, West Hartford CT 06117 (203) 233–1466, 1888.**

Solomon Schechter Academy of Greater Hartford. Affiliated with Solomon Schechter Day Schs Assn. Prin: Moshe Zwang; Chr: Dr Janis Abrahams. **160 Mohegan Dr, West Hartford CT 06117 (203) 233–1418.**

Temple Beth Israel. Affiliated with UAHC. 1359 mems. Rabbis: Harold S. Silver, Kerry Olitzky; Pres: Theodore B. Jacobs; Adm: Sylvia Oppenheimer; Sisterhood Pres: Devida Botwick; Brotherhood Pres: Bernard Gilman. **701 Farmington Ave, West Hartford CT 06119 (203) 233–8215.**

Westport

Temple Israel. Affiliated with UAHC. 513 mems. Rabbi Byron T. Rubenstein; Cantor Harold Brienes; Pres: Dorothy Freedman; Edu: Ruth Gruber. **14 Coleytown Rd, Westport CT 06880 (203) 227–1293.**

Wethersfield

Temple Beth Torah. Affiliated with United Syn of Am. Rabbi Dr George Rosenthal; Cantor Stuart Beckerman; Pres: Barry Goldberg; Youth Dir: Mark Azoff. **130 Main St, Wethersfield CT 06109 (203) 529–2410.**

Willimantic

Temple B'nai Israel. Conservative Cong affiliated with United Syn of Am. Rel Servs; Adult Edu; Heb Sch which meets three times a week; cultural & social activities. 150 families, Rel Sch of 50 stu. Est as an Orthodox syn under the name Cong Sons of Is on Jul 10, 1909. The Cong was first located on Main St, later moved to Bank St, & then in May 1965 to its present location. Pub The Bulletin (once a month). Rabbi Marc E. Samuels; Pres: Sheila B. Amdur; 1st VP: Morton Brown; 2nd VP: Paul Brody; 3rd VP: Dr Steve Kenton; Treas: Edward Schupack; Fin Sec: Dr Joseph Narotsky; Sec: Dr Jacob Duker. **345 Jackson St, Willimantic CT 06226 (203) 423–3743.**

Wilton

Temple B'nai Chaim. Affiliated with UAHC. 50 mems. Rabbi Charles D. Lippman; Pres: John Paul; Edu: Marilyn van Raalte. **c/o John D. Paul, PO Box 764, Wilton CT 06897 (203) 762–8852.**

Windsor

Congregation Beth Ahm. Affiliated with United Syn of Am. Rabbi Mark Raphael; Pres: Michael Rice; Edu Chr: Rhea Levin; Youth Chr: Salley Abbey. **362 Palisado Ave, Windsor CT 06095 (203) 688–9989.**

Woodbridge

Congregation B'nai Jacob. Affiliated with United Syn of Am. Rabbi Dr Arthur A. Chiel; Cantor Joshua Konigsberg; Pres: Robert S. Goodman; Exec Dir: Rhoda F. Myers; Edu Dir: Samuel Sloan. **75 Rimmon Rd, Woodbridge CT 06525 (203) 389–2111.**

Ezra Academy. Affiliated with Solomon Schechter Day Schs Assn. Prin: Rabbi Kopi Saltman; Chr: Dr Barr Forman. **75 Rimmon Rd, Woodbridge CT 06525 (203) 389–5500.**

DELAWARE

Dover

Congregation Beth Sholom. Affiliated with United Syn of Am. Rabbi Samuel R. Stone; Pres: Lawrence Klepner. **N Queen & Clara Sts, Box 223, Dover DE 19901.**

Wilmington

Adas Kodesch Shel Emeth Congregation. Orthodox Syn. To raise a generation of J that will be dedicated to the J people, Torah & the land of Is. Daily Minyan; Talmud Torah Rel Sch; Tallit & Tefillin Club; Adult Edu classes; yearly Yom Kippur Is Bond Appeal; Yeshiva Univ Annual Brunch; annual Bond purchase. 150 chil in the Talmud Torah. F as Ados Kodesch Cong in 1885. The first servs took place on King St. In 1900 the Lutheran Church on 6th & Franc Sts was purchased & the Talmud Torah was est. In 1907 a new syn was built. In 1961 land was purchased for a new bldg. In 1963 1,300 people gathered to pray on Kol Nidre night in the new syn. The Rabbi's fund disburses $1,500 annually to yeshivot, hosps & orphanages. **Washington Blvd & Torah Dr, Wilmington DE 19802 (302) 762–2705.**

Adas Kodesch Shel Emeth Congregation, Eleanor Bell Kursh Library. For information on the Cong, see – Adas Kodesh Shel Emeth Congregation, Wilmington, DE. **Washington Blvd & Torah Dr, Wilmington DE 19802 (302) 762–2705.**

Beth Shalom. Affiliated with United Syn of Am. Rabbi Kenneth Cohen; Cantor Andrew Salzer; Pres: Robert Jacobs; Exec Dir: Frances A. Stein; Edu Dir: Arlene Davis. **18th & Baynard Blvd, Wilmington DE 19802 (302) 654–4462.**

Congregation Beth Emeth. Affiliated with UAHC. 584 mems. Rabbis: Herbert E. Drooz, Peter H. Grumbacher; Pres: Richard D. Karfunkle; Edu: Peter H. Grumbacher; Sisterhood Pres: Diane Shuman; Brotherhood Pres: Henry Beckler. **300 West Lea Blvd, Wilmington DE 19802 (302) 764–2393.**

Jewish Family Service. 3717 Silverside Rd, Wilmington DE 19803 (302) 478–9411.

Jewish Federation of Delaware, Inc. Mem of CJF. Organized 1935. Pres: Paul R. Fine; Exec VP: Morris Lapidos. **101 Garden of Eden Rd, Wilmington DE 19803 (302) 478–6200.**

The Milton & Hattie Kutz Home, Inc. Nursing Home affiliated with N Am Assn of J Homes & Housing for the Aging, Am Assn of Homes for the Aging, DE Health Care Facilities Assn, J Fed of DE. To care for the J aged. Med & nursing servs; various therapies; social & recreational activities; social servs. 82 residents. 90 employees; 50 volunteers. Est 1960; predecessor group was Ladies Bichor Cholem, formed approx 80 yrs ago. Facilities include kosher kitchen, syn, facilities for nursing care of 82 residents. Pres: Steven J. Rothschild; VPs: Carl Cobin, Dorothy Goberman, Myra Kay; Exec Dir: D.G. Thurman; Treas: Norman J. Shuman; Sec: Sheldon A. Weinstein. **704 River Rd, Wilmington DE 19809 (302) 764–7000.**

DISTRICT OF COLUMBIA

Washington

Adas Israel Hebrew Congregation. Affiliated with United Syn of Am. Rabbi Stanley Rabinowitz; Cantor Arnold Saltzman; Asst Rabbi Stephen Listfield; Pres: Max M. Goldberg; Exec Dir: Sanford S. Cohen; Edu Dir: Marshall Kupchan; Youth Dir: Brenda Schlossberg. **2850 Quebec St NW, Washington DC 20008 (202) 362–4433.**

American Friends of Religious Freedom in Israel. PO Box 5888, Washington DC 20014 (301) 530–1737.

American Israel Public Affairs Committee. An umbrella org of the singular J org mandated to lobby the legislative & exec branches of the US Govt on behalf of close & consistently strong US-Is relations. 20,000 mems. Formerly known as the Am Zionist Council Public Affairs Cttee. Pres: Lawrence Weinberg; Exec Dir: Thomas A. Dine; Legislative Dir: Douglas Bloomfield; Information & Research Dir: Leonard Davis; Com Issues Dir: Arthur Chotin. **444 N Capitol St NW, Suite 412, Washington DC 20001 (202) 638–2256.**

Anti-Defamation League of B'nai B'rith – DC-MD Regional Office. Dedicated in purpose & prog to translating the Am heritage of democratic ideals into a way of life for all Am; to countering assaults on the safety, status, rights & image of J. For additional information, see – Anti-Defamation League of B'nai B'rith, New York City, NY. **1640 Rhode Island Ave NW, Washington DC 20036.**

B'nai B'rith Career & Counseling Services. Counseling servs to meet the needs of the entire J family from childhood through young adult to pre & post-retirement. 20 field offs throughout US serv approximately 40,000 people annually. Servs include: specialized workshops in scholarship selection; a Speakers Bureau; outreach servs; Edu & Career Library; masters & doctoral internships for grad stud in counseling; second career counseling for specialized groups such as widows, divorcees; job seeking skills & value clarification workshops; individual & group counseling servs; psych testing. Provides edu & occupational research which is pub in bk or career brief form including: Eight Years Later; in cooperation with B'nai B'rith Women, Seven Steps to A Job, Careers in Jewish Communal Service, College Guide for Jewish Youth. Est career advisor prog which allows clients to spend time on the job with advisors who supplement the work of the professional counselor. Libraries maintained with the large repository of information on careers, post-secondary edu, alternate ways of gaining further training & edu. Professional personnel with minimum of two degrees, mems of professional personnel assns. Est 1938. **1640 Rhode Island Ave NW, Washington DC 20036 (202) 857–6600.**

B'nai B'rith Hillel Foundations. Teaching, counseling & providing for the rel needs of J stu on col campuses. To make J rel & cultural values vital & relevant to the col generation. Activities include: classes, lectures, seminars, rel servs, holiday observances, free Univ of J Studies, intercollegiate Shabbatonim, leadership training, student ins, political action & social serv projs, struggle for J freedom in Soviet Union & Arab lands, support for the State of Is. Servs to hundreds of thousands of J univ stu & faculty in US & abroad. F in 1924 with the est of first Hillel Foun at Univ of ILwith Rabbi Frankel the first Dir, to be succeeded by Dr Sachar. **1640 Rhode Island Ave NW, Washington DC 20036 (202) 857–6600.**

B'nai B'rith International. World's largest J serv org. To promote J continuity, assuring J defense, enhancing J culture, providing voluntary servs to the local, natl & world coms, & advancing the contributions of the J to all humanity. BBYO for teenagers & Hillel Founs serving col stu & faculty & providing cultural, social, rel & edu programming for J youth; Intl Council of B'nai B'rith – policy-formulating arm on issues affecting B'nai B'rith & world J; maintenance of a global network of 15 cooperating offs around the world; B'nai B'rith Women; Anti-Defamation League of B'nai B'rith – monitoring of anti-Semitism & bigotry, fighting of J defamation through edu, legislation & vigilance; Career & Counseling Servs offs in various cities across the US – counseling to youth & adults; com servs; Com Volunteer Servs Commis; annual Hons Lodges – honoring of individuals who have done the most outstanding work in the field of citizenship, civic affairs, com serv & social action in their local coms; Sr Citizens Housing Prog; adult J edu – Ins of J, Living Rm Learning Groups, B'nai B'rith Great Bks & J Heritage Classics, Lecture Bureau, Bk Servs, Cultural-Edu Progs available for local meetings, regional & dist conventions; est of ties between J in the Diaspora & Is through such projs as the B'nai B'rith World Ctr in Jerusalem, Martyrs' Forest, Forest of Peace, Liberty Bell Plaza, Intl Is Lodge, & Is Investment Clubs; philanthropic projs; Leadership Dev Prog; Lodge Adv Prog; Young Leadership Prog; tours; mems insurance prog; Bowling Assn; Klutnick Mus – houses one of the largest collections of J ceremonial & folk art in N Am, & the only mus devoted to the J contribution to democracy & the world located in Washington DC (films, tours, lectures, four galleries, public theater, gift shop & bk store). 500,000 mems in 45 countries around the world, including 120,000 mems of B'nai B'rith Women & the tens of thousands of mems in BBYO & Hillel Founs. F in NYC in 1843 by 12 German J immigrants as an instrument of J unity. The f, all coming fr Germany, chose a German name, Bundes-Breuder (League of Brothers), & an alternate name, The Independent Order of B'nai B'rith (Sons of the Covenant). The first meeting of the first lodge was called to order on Nov 12, 1843. The name Brundes-Brueder was discarded in favor of B'nai B'rith. By 1855 the org had twenty lodges & 2,218 mems. In 1882 the first lodge abroad was f in Berlin. In 1913 the Anti-Defamation League was f. Women's groups began to function in 1897 as auxiliaries of B'nai B'rith. In 1923 the first B'nai B'rith Hillel Foun was est at the Univ of IL. BBYO was created in 1949 with AZA & BBG as its major components. The B'nai B'rith Vocational Servs Bureau, now the Career & Counseling Servs, opened in 1938. By 1947 membership had increased to 190,000; B'nai B'rith Women had 450 chapters with 103,000 mems & the num of Hillel Founs had grown to 180. In 1954 Camp B'nai B'rith (now known as B'nai B'rith Perlman Camp) was est in PA. In 1976 a second camp, B'nai B'rith Beber Camp, was est in WI. The Intl Ctr, doubling the space of B'nai B'rith Hq, was dedicated in 1976. The National Jewish Monthly; handbks for lodge offs & cttee mems; guide to energy progs; bklets, pamphlets & newsletters on aspects of com volunteer servs. Pres: Jack J. Spitzer; Exec VP: Dr Daniel Thursz; Sr VPs: Ricardo Holzer, Gerald Kraft, Alan B. Larkin, Murray Shusterman; Treas: Harry Babush; VPs: Seymour D. Reich, Ted Schneiderman, Henry J. Satsky, Milton Jacobs, Malcolm H. Fromberg, Jack Faber, Harry Levitch, Shlomo L. Gross, Harry Kingsley, Georges M. Bloch, Isaac Frenkel, Harold Fisher, Murray Ehrlick, Leon Krajmalnik, Stan Saacks, Jacob Prist; Pres B'nai B'rith Women: Dorothy Binstock; Asst to the Dir: David Levenfeld; Dir Div of Communications: M. Hirsh Goldberg. **1640 Rhode Island Ave NW, Washington DC 20036 (202) 857–6600.**

B'nai B'rith Klutznick Museum. Mus devoted to J contribution to democracy & the world. Includes four galleries, a public theatre, gift shop, bk store. Houses one of largest collections of J ceremonial & folk art in N Am composed of more than 1,000 objects dating fr antiquity to 19th century; maintains gallery devoted to hist & current serv projs of B'nai B'rith. Est in 1957. **1640 Rhode Island Ave NW, Washington DC 20036 (202) 857–6600.**

B'nai B'rith Women. Dedicated to the improvement of the quality of J life through voluntary servs. Mems work in clins, counseling & testing ctrs, schs, homes for the aged, hosps & wherever there is a need; BBW maintains the BBW Chil's Hom in Is (a residential treatment ctr for emotionally disturbed boys); BBW of Canada gives moral & material support to Is, & sponsors the BBW Group House in Jerusalem Is (a halfway house for 14 to 18 yr olds who need additional support in becoming secure, responsible adults); BBW-Hillel Human Relations Edu Prog brings J & Arab univ stu together to conduct social serv projs & promote mutual understanding, provides volunteer servs to border settlement & military outposts in Is; BBW provides progs directed toward the special needs of women on their own, career women, older women & young family women; sponsors workshops; supports BBYO & B'nai B'rith Hillel Foun & advises & co-sponsors their activities; help sponsor Operation Stork (joint effort with Natl Foun March of Dimes to help prevent birth defects through edu); BBW volunteers help conduct Tay-Sachs screening, work in prenatal care clins & help counsel teenage parents to give them the information they need to raise healthy chil; BBW volunteers visit Vets Hosps, nursing homes & ctrs for the elderly to help celebrate holidays, to read to patients, to assist the staff in giving patients & residents the attention they need; BBW takes progs designed to combat anti-Semitism & prejudice into elementary schs, shopping ctrs & com meeting places; in cooperation with the ADL, BBW informs its mems on the status of human rights around the world & works to promote human understanding; BBW speaks for its mems at the United Nations, White House, Congress & other governmental bodies; BBW maintains Public Affairs Prog which works to increase public awareness of the plight of Soviet J & J in Arab lands, & supports adult J edu. 125,000 women in the US & Canada; 200 chapters in Is, Latin Am, Australia, Europe & S Africa. F in 1897 as a women's social auxiliary of B'nai B'rith. In 1940 BBW organized a natl coordinating body. By the end of WWII BBW had grown into an org of more than 70,000 mems. The BBW Chil Home was created to care for Nazi-terrorized chil in Is. In 1956 the name BBW was adopted & BBW assumed full jurisdiction over its dists & chapters. Pres: Dorothy Binstok; Pres Elect: Beverly Davis; VPs: Ida Ruben, Irma Gretler; Treas: Hyla Lipsky; Asst to the Dir: Susan L. Brown. **1640 Rhode Island Ave NW, Washington DC 20036 (202) 857–6600.**

B'nai B'rith Youth Organization. Youth org for all J youth – Orthodox, Conservative, Reform, Reconstructionist & non-affiliated. To stimulate & preserve J values & to build a strengthened commitment to Is. Aleph Zadik Aleph (AZA) for young men & B'nai B'rith Girls (BBG) for young women provide: leadership training seminars; Living Ins of J; Is Summer Ins; Israeli sports tournaments; Is cultural parties; combatting of anti-Is propaganda in local HS; fundraising & support for Is; social activities; prog of sports; servs to the com; J cultural & rel progs; social action; natl & regional conventions; summer camps. 40,000 HS youth in 1,500 chapters throughout the world. Volunteer chapter advs – many fr B'nai B'rith lodges & women's chapters; professional staff mems at the Intl Hq, dist dirs, regional dirs, asst dirs & field supervisors. AZA was first organized in Omaha NE in May 1924. Within two mo of the first meeting, branches were opening up in other cities. In 1925 AZA became a natl org. Sponsored by B'nai B'rith Women's chapters, the first girls group was formed in San Francisco in 1927. By 1940 there were enough chapters to warrant a natl org. In 1944 BBG became a natl org federated with AZA in BBYO. In 1955 the first Leadership Training Ins was planned. In 1956 the first BBYO Is Summer Ins was held. In the 1960's BBYO adopted Noar Lenoar as their counterpart org in Is. Pub The Shofar (official newspaper); Program Calendar Workbook (pub every spring); Judaism Pamphlet Series. Dir: Dr Sidney M. Clearfield; Chr: Aaron Grossman. **1640 Rhode Island Ave NW, Washington DC 20036 (202) 857–6600.**

Coordinating Board of Jewish Organizations. 1640 Rhode Island Ave NW, Washington DC 20036 (202) 857–6500.

Economic Minister, Embassy of Israel. 3514 International Dr NW, Washington DC 20008 (202) 364–5500.

Fabragen Havurah. 1747 Connecticut Ave NW, Washington DC 20009 (202) 667–7829.

The Gallaudet College Hillel Club. J stu group at Gallaudet Col, the only liberal arts col for the deaf in the world; affiliated with the Natl Congress of the J Deaf. To serve the hearing impaired J stu. Shabbat Servs with sign language, interpreters; Passover Seder; social, cultural, edu & rel activities. 100 stu. F in 1951. Adv: Rosalie Callman. **Hillel Club, c/o Off of Campus Ministeries, Gallaudet Col, Washington DC 20002.**

Jewish Activist Front – Israel Information Center. George Washington University Center. Zionist stu group on campus. To promote a positive image of Is on campus. Provides information to those interested in living, working, or studying in Is; sponsors Is related progs with speakers & films; serves as a campus clearing house for information & explanation; JAF is also active in combatting Arab propaganda on the George Washington Campus. The group has its origins in the early 1960's & was at that time a very radical org. Leaders of the Groups: Missy Kahn, Nancy Jacobson, Doug Black. **800 21st St NW, Rm 417, Washington DC 20006 (202) 686–7574.**

Jewish War Veterans of the United States of America. Natl vets soc serv org. Mem agy of Conf of Pres of Major Am J Orgs; mem agy of Natl J Com Relations Adv Council. To uphold Am democratic tradition; to combat bigotry, discrimination & injustice in Am & world wide. Participates in natl vets lobby; maintains 11 local vets serv offs, & natl off in Washington DC; provides scholarships for chil of deceased & disabled vets; conducts volunteer prog at Vets Adm hosps; educates vets groups on issues relating to Is & the Middle E; supports & raises funds for Is Soldiers Rest & Rehabilitation Home in Beersheba; adopted 40 Soviet J refuseniks; confronts activities of anti-Semitic groups; sponsors low cost housing proj for sr adults; sponsors J boy scout troops; participates in J Fed campaigns & com relations agy; supports & promotes tourism to Is; provides summer camp scholarships; provides JWV complete insurance & travel prog for mems. F in 1896 by a group of J Civil War vets. The org was first named the Hebrew Union Vets. The JWV is the oldest active vets org in the US. Pub The Jewish Veteran (pub five times a yr). Natl Commander: Stanley Zwaik; Natl Exec Dir: Harris B. Stone; Asst Natl Exec Dir: Steve Shaw. Harris B. Stone; Natl Dir of PR: Joan Alpert. **1712 New Hampshire Ave NW, Washington DC 20009 (202) 265–6280.**

Jewish Week. Periodical pub. **774 National Press Bldg, Washington DC 20045 (202) 783–7200.**

Leadership Conference on Civil Rights. 2027 Massachusetts Ave NW, Washington DC 20036 (202) 667–1780.

National Christian Leadership Conference for Israel. 1629 K St NW, Suite 700, Washington DC 20006 (202) 223–4016.

National Conference on Soviet Jewry. Coordinating agy for major natl J orgs & local com groups in the US which are acting on behalf of Soviet J through public edu & social action. Seeks to: aid Soviet J who seek their right to leave for Is & elsewhere; combat rising anti-Semitism in the USSR; help J live in the Soviet Union with the rights, privileges & freedoms accorded other rel & natl minority groups; help protect the civil & personal rights of J within the USSR. Sponsors special progs & projs; organizes public meetings & forums; monitors trends in emigration as well as accumulates, evaluates & processes information concerning Soviet J. Est in 1964 as the Am J Conf on Soviet J & reorganized as NCSJ in 1971. The NCSJ has rallied support for the Jackson-Vanik amendment which has given tens of thousands of Soviet J a new life; sponsors the Washington based Congressional Wives for Soviet J; maintains a Washington off in close communication with the current Adm, Congress & Washington based experts; conducts private briefings; implemented the Adopt A Prisoner of Conscience proj; & administers the Soviet J Research Bureau. **2027 Massachusetts Ave NW, Washington DC20036 (202) 265–8114.**

National Council of Jewish Women. Women's volunteer org. Dedicated in the spirit of J to advancing human welfare & the democratic way of life. Activities are organized around five prog priorities: women's issues, chil & youth, aging, J life, & Is. Women's Issues – major concerns are: ratification of the Equal Rights Amendment, protection of the right of every women to have access to safe & legal abortion, removal of gender related discrimination in all areas of life, provision of edu progs on the prevention of domestic violence & treatment for its victims, widow to widow counseling & progs for single parents. Chil & Youth – primarily concerned with: the rights, needs & quality of life of the nation's chil & youth; juvenile justice, especially the treatment of adolescent girls; foster care; variety of projs that support servs to the young people in their coms; (the council is deeply committed to advocacy efforts needed to effectively change the way chil are treated under the law). Is – carries out numerous edu & social welfare progs in Is; has long been a strong advocate for the State of Is; furthers major proj in Is which is the Research Ins for Innovation in Edu (part of The Heb Univ Sch of Edu). J Life – places emphasis on: J edu & the problems of Soviet J; J edu progs for individuals of various ages & interests designed to assist people in exploring their understanding of & attitudes toward J & rekindling their interest in their rel; involvement in the resettlement of Soviet J immigrants & in advocacy on behalf of those J who are refused permission to leave the USSR. Aging – primary focus is on: dev & support of: legislation on behalf of older adults, day ctrs, housing for the elderly, adult edu, enrichment progs, volunteer placement progs, sheltered employment projs, nutrition & transportation servs, multipurpose ctrs, nursing homes, ombudsman progs & self training for & by the elderly. **1346 Connecticut Ave NW, Suite 924, Washington DC 20036 (202) 296–2588.**

National Ladies Auxiliary Jewish War Veterans of the USA, Inc. To encourage the doctrine of universal liberty, equal rights & full justice to all people everywhere; to combat the powers of bigotry wherever originating or whatever their target, & fight the battle of the J wherever assailed; to teach loyalty to & love of our country to our youth. Preserves the records of patriotic servs performed by the men & women of the J faith & shields fr neglect the graves of the heroic dead; provides extensive social servs & rehabilitative projs for active mems of the armed forces & to vets & their families which include assistance in emergencies, counseling on vet benefits, monitoring federal & state legislation, finding jobs for the disabled & doing all types of volunteer work in the Vets Adm hosps; donates many thousands of dollars for the purchase of med & surgical equipment for the Dr Chaim Sheba Med Ctr in Is, & supports the State of Is through the sale of Is Bonds; dev local JWVA com relation projs & natl campaigns which aid the physical & psychological welfare of all; provides insurance plans benefiting all mems; supports women's status in soc; provides chil welfare, edu & recreational progs for the handicapped & less fortunate chil while in hosps, homes & special schs; provides scholarships for the youth of Am to univs & cols; dev comprehensive day-to-day projs for the elderly in nursing homes or at home, & monitors legislation for better health plans. Many thousands of mems; hundreds of auxiliaries located in 25 states. Pub JWVA Bulletin (quartery). Natl Pres: Jeanette Shapiro; Sr VP: Florence Goldberg; Jr VP: Jeanette Schneider; Exec Dir: Ina Halperin. **1712 New Hampshire Ave NW, Washington DC 20009 (202) 667–9061.**

Near East Report. Newsletter that covers events & issues dealing with Am policy in the Middle E. To give up-to-date information on the Middle E & rebut anti-Is propaganda. Publishes: Analysis – in depth analysis which explains the who, what, where & how of events in the Middle E; Heard in Washington DC – an overview of congressional activity & comments on Middle E issues; Media Monitor – analysis & critique of media coverage of Middle E issues; Viewing the News – timely coverage of critical events frequently unreported in the Am press; Propaganda Pressures – investigative reports of Arab propaganda activities. Staff of four. F by I. L. Kenen in 1957. Myths & Facts – a concise record of the Arab/Is conflict. The newsletter is pub weekly (subscriptions are available natl & overseas). Editor: Moshe Decter; Asst Editors: Lori S. Bierman, David Silverberg; Editorial Asst: Lisa B. Schneider; Editor Emeritus: I. L. Kenen. **444 N Capitol St NW, Washington DC 20001 (202) 638–1225.**

Ohev Sholom Talmud Torah Congregation. Orthodox Cong. Daily Rel Servs; study groups; edu progs to which the com is invited. F in 1866, the Cong is a merger of Ohev Sholom & Talmud Torah. It is the oldest Orthodox Cong in Washington DC. Rabbi Hillel Klavan; Pres: Isidore Katz; 1st VP: Paul Rozof; 2nd VP: Harry Goldberg; 3rd VP: Samuel Bernstein; Treas: Benjamin Munitz; Fin Sec: Edward Karl; Sec: Zev Teichman; Exec Dir: Jack M. Spiro; Sexton: Ernest Friedman. **1600 Jonquil St NW, Washington DC 20012 (202) 882–7225.**

Secretariat for Catholic-Jewish Relations. 1312 Massachusetts Ave NW, Washington DC 20005 (202) 659–6857.

Temple Micah. Reform Cong affiliated with UAHC. To observe the beautiful tradition of J heritage in ways that are meaningful to modern men & women. Rel Servs; Oneg Shabbat; Adult Edu Prog; monthly Study Group; weekly Morning Study Group; Luncheon Discussion Circle; periodic workshops on the holidays; J Experiential Workshop; Spring Weekend Kallah in the Shenandoah Mts; One-day Winter Kallah; Rel Sch, K–HS; Youth Group; Choir. 234 mems F in 1963 as the SW Hebrew Cong. The Cong shares a bldg with St Augustine's Episcopal Church. Pub Vine (monthly newsletter). Rabbi Robert K. Baruch; Pres: Nancy Elisburg; Edu: Barbara Klestzick. **600 M St SW, Washington DC 20024 (202) 554–3099.**

Temple Micah Religious School Library. For information on the Temple, see – Temple Micah Religious School, Washington DC. **600 M St SW, Washington DC 20024 (202) 554–3099.**

Temple Sinai. Affiliated with UAHC. 680 mems. Rabbi Eugene Lipman; Pres: D.S. Mayer; Edu: Marlene G. Solomon; Adm: Marcus H. Laster; Sisterhood Pres: Alice Rabin; Brotherhood Pres: Theodore Bleecker. **3100 Military Rd NW, Washington DC 20015 (202) 363–6394.**

Temple Sinai Library. 3100 Military Rd NW, Washington DC 20015 (202) 363–6394.

Tifereth Israel Congregation. Affiliated with United Syn of Am. Rabbi A. Nathan Abromowitz; Pres: Lionel Kestenbaum; Exec Dir: Beth E. Cohen; Edu Dir: Mollie Berch. **7701 26th St NW, Washington DC 20012 (202) 882–1605.**

UAHC Mid-Atlantic Council. Rel & edu org serving J congs throughout the US & Canada. To encourage & aid the org & dev of J congs; to promote J edu & enrich & intensify J life; to foster other activities for the perpetuation & advancement of J. For additional information, see – UAHC – Union of American Hebrew Congregations, New York City, NY. Pres: Walter J. Klein; Dir: Rabbi Richard S. Sternberger. **2027 Massachusetts Ave NW, Washington DC 20036 (202) 232–4242.**

Union of Councils for Soviet Jews. 1522 K St NW , Suite 1110, Washington DC 20005.

Washington Hebrew Congregation. Affiliated with UAHC. 2180 mems. Rabbis: Joshua O. Haberman, Joseph P. Weinberg, Steven S. Mason; Cantor Roy Garber; Pres: Paul J. Mason; Edu: Ilana Rappaport; Adm: Julian Feldman; Sisterhood Pres: Jane R. Burka; Brotherhood Pres: Samuel L. Hack. **3935 Macomb St NW, Washington DC 20016 (202) 362–7100.**

Washington Hebrew Congregation Library, Hurston-Selinger-Tauber Libraries. 3935 Macomb St NW, Washington DC 20016 (202) 362–7100.

FLORIDA

Boca Raton

B'nai Torah Congregation. Affiliated with United Syn of Am. Rabbi Nathan Zelizer; Pres: Saul Glueckman; Exec Sec: Jan Braff. **1401 NW 4th Ave, Boca Raton FL 33432 (305) 392–8566.**

South County Jewish Federation. Pres: James B. Baer; Exec Dir: Rabbi Bruce S. Warshal. **2200 N Federal Highway, Suite 206, Boca Raton FL 33432 (305) 368–2737.**

Temple Beth El. Affiliated with UAHC. 880 mems. Rabbi Merle E. Singer; Cantor Martin B. Rosen; Pres: Ida B. Herst; Edu: Robin Eisenberg; Adm: Samuel P. Goldstein; Sisterhood Pres: Eleanor Marcus; Brotherhood Pres: Mortimer Heutlinger. **333 SW 4th Ave, Boca Raton FL 33432 (305) 391–8900.**

Brandenton

Temple Beth El. Affiliated with United Syn of Am. Rabbi Michael Klayman; Pres: Richard Hersh; Edu Dir: Delle Mintz; Youth Dir: Paulette Markowitz. **2209 75th St W, Brandenton FL 33529 (813) 792–0870.**

Clearwater

Beth Shalom. Affiliated with United Syn of Am. Rabbi Peter J. Mehler; Cantor Jonah Binder; Pres: David Baker; Exec Dir: Roberta Frankel; Edu Dir: Marian Paikowsky; Youth Dir: Paul Applefield. **1325 S Belcher Rd, Clearwater FL 33516 (813) 531-1418.**

Gulf Coast Jewish Family Service, Inc. Confidential individual, family & group counseling by a highly trained & qualified professional staff; psycho-social residential care & day treatment progs for older adults with emotional problems; emergency homemaker servs for disabled & elderly; preventive servs through Family Life Edu Progs designed to prevent everyday problems fr becoming serious; interest free loans to col stu for families experiencing financial difficulties; social servs programming for Kosher Sr Congregate Lunch Sites; social work outreach & referral counseling for the elderly; weekly loving contact fr a dedicated volunteer for problem chil. Pres: Murray M. Jacobs; 1st VP: Gertrude Clark; 2nd VP: Pauline Korman; Sec: Sidney Mitchell; Treas: William Israel; Bd of Dirs: Leonard Apter, Dr Louis Belinson, Dr Robert Davis, Lee Dorian, Henry Elkind, Dr Mortimer Elkind, Florence Fayer, Ellen Glassman, William Golson, Harry Green, Jacqueline Jacobs, Anne Kahana, Morris Kahana, Jenny Kleinfeld, Mickey Korman, Gladys Neumayer, Lenore Pearl, Sam Perlin, Harold Rivkino, Frieda Sohon; Exec Dir: Michael A. Bernstein. **304 S Jupiter Ave, Clearwater FL 33515 (813) 446–1005.**

Jewish Federation of Pinellas County, Inc. Mem of CJF. Includes Clearwater & St Petersburg. Organized 1950; reincorporated 1974. Pres: Reva Kent; Exec Dir: Gerald Rubin. **302 S Jupiter Ave, Clearwater FL 33515 (813) 446–1033.**

Temple B'nai Israel. Affiliated with UAHC. 509 mems. Rabbi Arthur Baseman; Pres: Saul Fein; Edu: Zena W. Sulkes; Adm: Belle Appelbaum; Sisterhood Pres: Jule Kroll; Brotherhood Pres: Robert Ederr. **1685 S Belcher Rd, Clearwater FL 33516 (813) 531–5829.**

Cocoa Beach

Brevard County Jewish Community Council. Pres: Sheldon Smith; Exec Sec: Frances Singer. **PO Box 126, Cocoa Beach FL 32931 (305) 453–4695.**

Coral Gables

Chabad House. Lubavitch com servs ctr. Blends Chassidic fervor & warmth with tradition & learning, to show that every J, fr whatever background he or she comes fr, is an integral part of the body of Is. Anti-missionary work; adult edu; Sabbath seminars; holiday progs; day camp; youth groups; syns; kosher kitchen; counseling; chaplaincy; Mitzvah Campaigns; hosp & prison visitations; sr citizens encounters; speakers bureau. Rabbi D. Eliezrie. **1540 Albenga Ave, Coral Gables FL 33146 (305) 661–7642.**

Temple Judea. Affiliated with UAHC. 450 mems. Rabbi Michael B. Eisenstat; Pres: Barry Hesser; Edu: Ray Berman; Adm: Lee Jubelirer; Sisterhood Pres: Barbara W. Goodman; Brotherhood Pres: Sorrel S. Resnik. **5500 Granada Blvd, Coral Gables FL 33146 (305) 667–5657.**

Coral Springs

Temple Beth Orr. Reform Cong affiliated with UAHC. To live up to its name & be truly a 'House of Light' in its com. Rel Servs; Nursery Sch for ages two through four; Sun Sch for grades K through three; Heb Sch for grades 4 through 7 which meets twice a week, during which studies in J & Heb in preparation for Bar & Bat Mitzvah are stressed, & Grades 8 & 9 which meet once each week; Jr & Sr Youth Group; Sisterhood; Bowling League; dances & theater parties; Adult Edu; J HS; Bd & Bd Social Club for sr citizens; bingo; Havurah. 480 families. Est in 1972 when a group of 12 dedicated J families, all newcomers to the city of Coral Springs, banded together to form what was then called Coral Springs Hebrew Cong. The Westinghouse auditorium was used by the Cong for the first five yrs of its existence. An all purpose bldg was erected & dedicated in 1977 as Temple Beth Orr. Facilities include a sanctuary, classrooms, meeting rms & a social hall. Pres: Joel Levenston; VPs: Dr Stephen Geller, Bert Steiner, Carol Wasserman, Joel Zeiger; Corsp Sec: Joel Klaits; Rec Sec: Barbara Weinstein; Fin Sec: Diane Berwick; Treas: Bruce Syrop; Three Yr Trustees: Jerry Brenman, Millie Friedman, David Greenspan, Charles Love, Janet Oppenheimer, Sid Rosenberg; Two Yr Trustees: Carl Berman, Stan Bernstein, Norman Green, Larry Johnson, Joel Latman, Dorothy Sands; One Yr Trustees: Judy Averbuch, Stephen Beyer, Sy Domnitch, Sid Gutsin, Irving Hirsch, Ellie Tomberg; Hon Trustee: Clarence Silver; Brotherhood: Jeff Askenas; Sisterhood: Toby Kantrowitz; Rabbi Donald Gerber. **PO Box 8242, 2151 Riverside Dr, Coral Springs FL 33065 (305) 753–3232,3.**

Dade City

Gulf Coast Jewish Family Service, Inc. Confidential individual, family & group counseling by a highly trained & qualified professional staff; psycho-social residential care & day treatment progs for older adults with emotional problems; emergency homemaker servs for disabled & elderly; preventive servs through Family Life Edu progs designed to prevent everyday problems fr becoming serious; interest free loans to col stu for families experiencing financial difficulties; social servs programming for Kosher Sr Congregate Lunch Sites; social work outreach & referral counseling for the elderly; weekly loving contact fr a dedicated volunteer for problem chil. **Dade City Hall, 612 E Meridian Ave, Dade City FL 33525 (904) 567–7657.**

Daytona Beach

Jewish Federation of Volusia & Flagler Counties, Inc. Mem of CJF. Pres: Dr Clifford R. Josephson; Exec Sec: Iris E. Gardener. **PO Box 5434, 504 Main St, Daytona Beach FL 32018 (904) 255–6260.**

Temple Beth El. Affiliated with UAHC. 254 mems. Rabbi Barry M. Altman; Pres: Howard Greisdorf; Sisterhood Pres: Irma Sacks; Brotherhood Pres: Stephen Ober. **507 Fifth Ave, Daytona Beach FL 32018 (904) 252–1248.**

Temple Israel of Daytona Beach. Affiliated with United Syn of Am. Rabbi Dr Mordecai HaLevi Genn; Pres: Bob Freedman. **1400 S Pennisula Dr, Daytona Beach FL 32018 (904) 252–3097.**

Temple Israel, Marvin Roth Memorial Library. For information on the Temple, see – Temple Israel, Daytona Beach, FL. **1400 S Peninsula Dr, Daytona Beach FL 32018 (904) 252–3097.**

Deerfield Beach

Temple Beth Israel. Affiliated with United Syn of Am. Rabbi Leon Mirsky; Pres: Joseph Lovy. **200 Century Blvd, Deerfield Beach FL 33441 (305) 421–7060.**

Delray Beach

Temple Emeth. Affiliated with United Syn of Am. Rabbi Bernard Silver; Cantor Banjamin Adler; Pres: Edward Rosenthal. **5780 W Atlantic Ave, Delray Beach FL 33445 (305) 498–3536.**

Temple Sinai. Affiliated with UAHC. 160 mems. Rabbi Samuel M. Silver; Pres: Bernard Etish. **PO Box 1901, Delray Beach FL33446.**

Deltona

Temple Shalom. Affiliated with UAHC. 65 mems. Cantor Michael Goodman; Pres: Marston L. Becker; Edu: Alvin Gamson. **PO Box 132, 1785 Elkcam Blvd, Deltona FL 32725 (904) 789–2202.**

Dunedin

Temple Ahavat Sholom. Affiliated with UAHC. 125 mems. Rabbi Jan Bresky; Pres: Elliot S. Kahana; Edu: Peggy Gerson; Sisterhood Pres: Clara S. Graff; Brotherhood Pres: Richard Kess. **2000 Main St, Dunedin FL 33528 (813) 734–9428.**

Fort Lauderdale

Jewish Federation of Greater Fort Lauderdale. Mem of CJF. Organized 1967. Pres: Victor Gruman; Exec Dir: Leslie S. Gottlieb. **8360 W Oakland Park Blvd, Fort Lauderdale FL33321 (305) 748–8200.**

Temple Emanu-El. Affiliated with UAHC. 425 mems. Rabbi Jeffrey Ballon; Cantor Jerome Klement; Pres: Frances L. Smith; Edu: Gladys Schlechter; Adm: Morris Watkins; Sisterhood Pres: Hilda Ivers; Brotherhood Pres: Nathan P. Baker, Milton Sperber. **3245 W Oakland Park Blvd, Fort Lauderdale FL 33311 (305) 731–2310.**

Fort Pierce

Temple Beth El. Affiliated with UAHC. 165 mems. Rabbi Joel C. Dobin; Cantor Bernard Selkin; Pres: Peggy Berg; Edu: Maxine Graber; Adm: Tydfil K. Schelin; Sisterhood Pres: Cecelia Pinkowitz. **4600 Oleander Ave, Fort Pierce FL 33450 (305) 461–7428.**

Gainesville

B'nai B'rith Hillel Foundation, University of Florida. The campus center for J students & faculty. To serve as a com ctr for J stu & faculty in Gainesville. Cultural & edu events; Sabbath & Holiday Rel Servs; social & recreational activities; volunteer & social action projs on behalf of J worldwide; active in gen com betterment & social causes; regular progs: Lox & Bagels Brunch, Sports, Bike Corner, Grads & Faculty, Study Group on Mishna, Spaghetti Dinner, Minyan & Breakfast, Happy Hour, Deli Dinner, Israeli Folk Dance Party, Young Couples Club; library; leisure courses: Aerobic Dancing, Heb, J Thought, Yiddish, & J Expression in Song. Facilities include a lounge, gift shop, & kosher meat store. Pres: Dr Todd Savitt; VP: Susan Jungries; Secs: Nancy Jacobs, Toby Hunter; Treas: Frank Brown; Dir: Gerald Friedman. **16 NW 18th St, Gainesville FL 32603 (904) 372–2900.**

B'nai Israel. Affiliated with United Syn of Am. Rabbi Allan Lehman; Pres: Dr Alan C. Levin; Edu Dir: Phyllis Warren; Youth Dir: Dr Harry Krop. **3830 NW 16th Blvd, Gainesville FL 32605 (904) 376–1508.**

The Isser & Rae Price Library of Judaica, University of Florida. The finest assemblage of Judaica in the Southeastern US. Not only to provide the materials necessay for intellectual dev but to act as a ctr for the exchange of ideas, aspirations, & the products of scholarship. Over 50,000 vols in all languages; major research collection in the broad areas of J hist, Judaism, rabbinics, Zionism & creative writing in Heb & Yiddish; current journals & magazines on the following subjects: Bible & Biblical archaeology, bibliography & booklore, edu, genealogy, gen interest, Heb literature & linguistics, J art, J-Christian relations, J hist, J & Israeli law, J med, J music, rabbinics, scholarly Judaica, Sephardic studies, Yiddish, Zionism. Est in 1977 when the Univ of FLacquired the Rabbi Leonard C. Mishkin collection, the largest private J library in the US. Two other additions have made the Price Library the largest & finest collection in the SE US: the private library of Dr Shlomo Marenof & the inventory of Bernard Morgenstern's NY bkstore. The library was dedicated on Mar 8, 1981. Pub Report, newsletter. Librarian: Robert Singerman. **Rm 18, Library E, Univ of FL, Gainesville FL 32611.**

Hollywood

Jewish Federation of South Broward, Inc. Mem of CJF. Organized 1943. Pres: Dr Robert S. Pittell; Exec Dir: Sumner G. Kaye. **2719 Hollywood Blvd, Hollywood FL 33020 (305) 921–8810.**

Temple Beth El. Affiliated with UAHC. 948 mems. Rabbis; Samuel Jaffe, Ben A. Romer; Pres: Owen L. Wyman; Adm: Ralph Birnberg; Sisterhood Pres: Elvia Tober; Brotherhood Pres: Sheldon Dickstein. **1351 S 14th Ave, Hollywood FL 33020 (305) 920–8225.**

Temple Beth El Library. For information on the Temple, see – Temple Beth El, Hollywood, FL. **1351 S 14th Ave, Hollywood FL 33020 (305) 920–8225.**

Temple Beth Shalom Day School. 4601 Arthur St, Hollywood FL 33021.

Temple Beth Shalom Day School, Meyerhoff Library. 4601 Arthur St, Hollywood FL33021.

Temple Sinai. Affiliated with United Syn of Am. Rabbi Seymour Friedman; Cantor Robert Unger; Rabbi Emeritus David Shapiro; Pres: A. Rosenthal MD; Exec Dir: Steven J. Kaplan PhD; Edu Dir: Rosalyn Z. Seidel; Youth Dir: Sharon Horowitz. **1201 Johnson St, Hollywood FL 33019 (315) 920–1577.**

Temple Sinai, Hyman Hornstein Library. For information on the Temple, see – Temple Sinai, Hollywood, FL. **1201 Johnson St, Hollywood FL 33019 (305) 920–1577.**

Temple Solel. Affiliated with UAHC. 569 mems. Rabbi Robert P. Frazin; Cantor Michael Kyrr; Pres: Alan N. Roaman; Edu: Karen L. Kaminsky; Adm: Sylvia Greenberg; Sisterhood Pres: Delly Weinberg; Brotherhood Pres: Robert Ankeles. **5100 Sheridan St, Hollywood FL 33021 (305) 989–0205.**

Jacksonville

Beth Shalom. Affiliated with United Syn of Am. Rabbi Gary G. Perras; Pres: A. Ira Foster; Edu & Youth Dir: Zvi Naveh; Sec: Rose Tincher. **4072 Sunbeam Rd, Jacksonville FL 32217 (904) 268–0404.**

Congregation Ahavath Chesed. Affiliated with UAHC. 596 mems. Rabbis: Howard R. Greenstein, Sidney M. Lefkowitz; Pres: Harvey Schlesinger; Edu: Harvey Leven; Adm: Charlotte D. Jacobs; Sisterhood Pres: Lois Schlesinger; Brotherhood Pres: Richard Miller. **8727 San Jose Blvd, Jacksonville FL 32217 (904) 733–7078.**

Jacksonville Jewish Center. Affiliated with United Syn of Am. Rabbi David Gaffney; Cantor Emeritus Abraham Marton; Pres: Nathan Krestul; Activities Dir: Blanche Slott; Edu & Youth Dir: Rabbi Dov Kentof. Solomon Schechter Day Sch Prin: Marilyn Sandler. **PO Box 23886, 10101 San Jose Blvd, Jacksonville FL 32217 (904) 268–6736.**

Jacksonville Jewish Center, Henry Kramer Library. For information on the Ctr, see – Jacksonville Jewish Ctr, Jacksonville, FL. **10101 San Jose Blvd, PO Box 23886, Jacksonville FL 32217 (904) 268–6736.**

The Jacksonville Jewish Federation. Mem of CJF. Organized 1935. Pres: Dr Ronald Elinoff; Exec Dir: Gerald L. Goldsmith. **5846 Mt Carmel Terr, Jacksonville FL 32216 (904) 733–7613.**

Solomon Schechter Day School – Jacksonville Jewish Center. Affiliated with Solomon Schechter Day Schs Assn. Prin: Marilyn Sandler; Chr: Judy Mizrahi. **10101 San Jose Blvd, Jacksonville FL 32217 (904) 268–6736.**

Southern Jewish Weekly. Periodical pub. **PO Box 3297, Jacksonville FL 32206 (904) 355–3459.**

Lakeland

Temple Emanuel. Affiliated with United Syn of Am. Rabbi Mordecai Levy; Pres: Dr Allen Weinstein; Youth Dir: Spencer Levin. **730 Lake Hollingsworth Dr, Lakeland FL 33803 (813) 682–8616.**

Margate

Pioneer Women – Na'amat. The training & edu of the Is woman & her family so that each can be best equipped to lead productive lives. For additional information, see – Pioneer Women Na'amat, New York City, NY. **1303 N State Rd 7, Margate FL 33063 (305) 979–3311.**

Temple Beth Am. Affiliated with United Syn of Am. Rabbi Dr Solomon Geld; Cantor Mario Botoshansky; Pres: Harry Hirsch; Edu Dir: Joy Kahn-Evron. **7205 Royal Palm Blvd, Margate FL 33063 (305) 974–8650.**

Melbourne

Congregation Ner Tamid. Affiliated with United Syn of Am. Cantor Abe Zendle; Pres: Dr Robert Mandel; Edu Dir: Jeanette Goldberg. **820 E Strawbridge Ave, Melbourne FL 32901 (305) 723–9112.**

Merritt Island

Temple Israel. Affiliated with UAHC. 127 mems. Rabbi David M. Eichhorn; Pres: Harvey Marron; Edu: Arleen Barton; Sisterhood Pres: Doris Edinger. **PO Box 592, Merritt Island FL 32952 (305) 636–4920.**

Miami

America-Israel Chamber of Commerce – Southeast Region. Offers assistance to mem US firms interested in economic activity in & with Is. Provides extensive trade assistance; pub market research reports; aid in dev of trade & investment between US & Is. For additional information, see – American-Israel Chamber of Commerce & Industry, Inc, New York City, NY. **3950 Biscayne Blvd, Miami FL 33137 (305) 573–0668.**

Anti-Defamation League of B'nai B'rith – Florida Regional Office. Dedicated in purpose & prog to translating the Am heritage of democratic ideals into a way of life for all Am; to countering assaults on the safety, status, rights & image of J. For additional information, see – Anti-Defamation League of B'nai B'rith, New York City, NY. **150 SE 2nd Ave, Suite 800, Miami FL 33131.**

Aventura Jewish Center. Affiliated with United Syn of Am. Rabbi David B. Saltzman; Cantor Lawrence Tuchinsky; Pres: Roy Sager. **2972 Aventura Blvd, Miami FL 33180 (305) 932–0666.**

Beth David Congregation. Affiliated with United Syn of Am. Daily Sabbath & Holiday Servs; Solomon Schechter Day School for grades K–6; Rel Sch with instruction three times a wk; HS with confirmation in 10th grade; Adult Edu classes & lectures; Sisterhood; Men's Club; USY prog; annual Fine Arts Cultural Series which brings outstanding artists to the com. F in 1912. The Syn is the oldest in the greater Miami area. Rabbi David H. Auerbach; Rabbi Emeritus Dr Sol Landau; Cantor William W. Lipson; Exec Dir: Sheldon G. Mills; Edu Dir: M. Kaspi-Silverman; Day Sch Prin: Audrey Dillaman; Pres: Donald R. Tescher; Exec VP: Philip Bergman; VPs: Jerome H. Shevin, Dr Jules G. Minkes, Mrs Norman Sholk, Martin Hellman, Jose Portnoy, Elayne Tendrich, Morris Cohen; Treas: Dr Stanley Zakarin; Asst Treas: Dr Abraham Benyunes; Fin Sec: Robert W. Spiegelman; Rec Sec: Myron Stayman. **2625 SW Third Ave, Miami FL 33129 (305) 854–3911; 7500 SW 120th St, Miami FL 33156 (305) 238–2601.**

Beth David Solomon Schechter Day School. Affiliated with Solomon Schechter Day Schs Assn. Prin: Audrey Dillaman; Chr: Donald Tescher. **7500 SW 120th St, Miami FL 33156 (305) 238–2601.**

Central Agency for Jewish Education. Affiliated with the Am Assn for J Edu. To perceive, learn, teach, observe & fulfill the teachings of the Torah. J HS: maintains intensive Heb Dept, jr & sr HS edu progs in cooperation with the local syns, Col Credit Prog in cooperation with Miami-Dade Com Col, joint progs with youth dirs & youth groups of the com, Outreach Prog for stu in public HS; Akiva Leadership Prog: devs within young people a strong J identity based on knowledge & commitment to the J com, & trains these young people to serve as future leaders of the Am J com; Ins for J Studies: offers preparation & professional dev of teachers on all levels of the J edu process, serves to enhance adult edu in the com, sponsors progs for lay & professional leadership of the Greater Miami J Fed & its constituent agy, provides counsel & guidance for J studies on an adult level throughout the com; Com Heb Ulpan: provides an intensive learning experience in modern Heb, emphasizing oral language skills taught with a specific Ulpan methodology which includes elements of J traditions & the culture of Is; Teacher Licensing & Placement; Teacher Fringe Benefits Prog: provides security for teachers in J schs through the partial payment of health insurance & retirement premiums & has become the major incentive for teachers to continue their professional growth & dev; Day Sch Dept: works to enhance the edu in the day schs, serves as a vehicle through which Feds allocate their funds to the schs & is instrumental in encouraging inter-sch cooperation & activities; Edu Resource Ctr Library: contains a circulating & reference library (English, Heb & Yiddish bks), library of tapes, records, filmstrips & cassettes, vertical file reference section, library of pedagogic references, & small gift & card shop; J Film Library: contains 143 films of varied subjects of J interest which enhance traditional class study, informal edu progs & serve as entertainment for the old & young; Com Servs Dept; J Special Edu: implements progs for chil with learning disabilities with classes held in Sun sch/Heb sch syn classes, com classes, & in a day sch. N Broward Fed CAJE: maintains or sponsors J HS, Teacher Professional Growth Progs, N Broward Midrasha-Ins for Adult J Studies, fed & communal J Agy progs, Is Scholarship Prog, Council of Edu Dirs & Rabbis, Council of Early Childhood Edu Dirs of N Broward, CAJE exec staff support for N Broward, edu consultation for the N Broward com, Home Start designed to involve parents of young chil in enhancing J holiday observances in the home. So Broward Fed CAJE: maintains or sponsors J HS, J Studies Prog, Col Credit Prog, Akiva Leadership Prog, Teen Tour to Is, Ins for J Studies, Com Heb Ulpan, J Special Edu, day schs, Yom Haatzmaut Celebration, S Broward Council of Rabbis & Edu Dirs, CAJE Progs for the J Fed of S Broward including Women's Div, leadership dev, campaign, mission orientation. Servs in other coms include teacher licensing & teacher placement, distribution of all CAJE pubs to the rel schs, making available the resources of the Edu Resources Ctr/Library, distribution of films fr the film library, consultation with prins, coordination & sponsorship of professional edu groups, inter-sch activities. Provides servs to the S Dade area & the J Fed of Greater Orlando. Over 1,500 teenagers in the J HS. The Greater Miami Bureau of J Edu was est in 1945. The Bureau played an important role in the growth of the J edu agy in the Miami com. During the 1950's & 1960's the Bureau expanded in many areas to meet the J com's edu needs. In 1972 the Bureau was reconstituted as the Central Agy for J Edu. The J HS

Prog was est & the Akiva Leadership Prog began in 1974. A com wide adult Heb Ulpan prog was begun, a new Day Sch Dept was est, & New cooperative adult edu progs were inaugurated. The J Special Edu Proj was approved in 1978. Pub The Fall Festivals; Chanukah Rappings; The Taming of Haman; Why Is This Season Different?; Touring Israel; Shabbat – The Fourth Commandment; Ten Lesson Plans on Jerusalem; Tzedakah – Not Charity But Justice!; The Holocaust – Return to the Homeland; The American Jewish Experience; The Influence of the Bible on American Colonists; Inter-disciplinary Integration in the Jewish Day School; Experiential Methodology in Teacher Training; Get Ready, Get Set, Play!; Playing for Keeps; Hava Na'Shira; Birkat Hamazon; Survey of Day Schools; Greater Miami Day School Survey; Judaica High School; A Biblical Sourcebook for Teacher & Layman; Whither Thou Goest; A College Guidance Handbook for the Observant Jewish Student.Pres: Alfred Golden; VPs: David M. Dobin, Arleen Rosenthal, Roberta Shevin; Sec: Judge Steven D. Robinson; Treas: Richard Levy; Nominating Cttee Chr: Gwen Weinberger; Dirs at Large: Richard Bloom, Nanci Goldstein, Leo Hack, Kenneth S. Hoffman, David Mesnekoff, Nan Rich; Exec Dir: Gene Greenzweig. **4200 Biscayne Blvd, Miami FL 33137 (305) 576–4030.**

Central Agency for Jewish Education, Library. For information on the Library & on Ins, see – Central Agency for Jewish Education, Miami, FL. **4200 Biscayne Blvd, Miami FL 33137 (305) 576–4030.**

Congregation Bet Breira. Reform Syn affiliated with UAHC. To be an innovative & involved cong. Heb Sch, Shabbat Sch, J Sch leading to confirmation; adult Heb classes. 400 families. F in 1976. Rabbi Barry Tabachnikoff; Cantor Stuart Pittle; Dir of Edu: Erwin Marshall; Pres: Naomi Olster; Fin VP: Benjamin Feinswog; VPs: Judie Brown, Marilyn Herskowitz, Allan Tavss; Sec: Tom Weidenfeld; Treas: Michael Wechter; Bd of Trustees: Dr Irwin Becker, Marvin Braun, Bert Brown, Howard Cantor, Steven Falk, Susan Gold, Jim Green, Stephanie Hauser, Lisa Kaplan, Theodore Klein, Marilyn Krick, Richard Levy, Nina Meyer, Israel Saferstein, Dr Lawrence E. Stein; Sisterhood Pres: Diane Meyer; Men's Group Pres: Leonard Nabutovsky. **9075 SW 87th Ave, Miami FL 33176 (305) 595–1500.**

Congregation Bet Breira Library. For information on the Cong, see – Congregation Bet Breira, Miami, FL. **9075 SW 87th Ave, Miami FL 33176 (305) 595–1500.**

Government of Israel Trade Center. Dev of trade relations between US & Is. For additional information, see – Government of Israel Trade Center, New York City, NY. **330 Biscayne Blvd, Suite 510, Miami FL 33132 (305) 358–8140.**

Greater Miami Jewish Federation, Inc. Mem of CJF. Organized 1938. Pres: Harry A. Levy; Exec VP: Myron J. Brodie. **4200 Biscayne Blvd, Miami FL 33137 (305) 576–4000.**

Israel Aliyah Center. 4200 Biscayne Blvd, Miami FL 33137 (305) 573–2556.

Israel Programs Office. Dept of the Greater Miami J Fed. To disseminate information about Is throughout the com with emphasis on promoting the participation of young people in progs that will enable them to experience Is. Conducts interviews & processes of applications to various Is progs; tries to generate interest in Is & more specifically in Is progs by organizing events such as Is prog fairs, rallies & stu activities. The first com shaliah opened the first Is Progs Off in 1970. Chr: Emanuel Berlatsky; Dir: Rena Genn. **4200 Biscayne Blvd, Miami FL 33137 (305) 576–4000.**

Jewish Family & Children's Service. To better family life in the com. Personal counseling; marital counseling; divorce counseling; parent-chil counseling; teenage counseling; family counseling; group counseling; family life edu; servs to the aging; consultation servs. Est in 1920. **1790 SW 27th Ave, Miami FL 33145 (305) 445–0555.**

Jewish Floridian. Periodical pub. **PO Box 2973, Miami FL 33101 (305) 373–4605.**

Miami Jewish Home & Hospital for the Aged, Inc. Non-sectarian, non-profit ins whose major function is to provide a comprehensive range of institutional & com based servs within the spectrum of long-term care. Accredited by the Joint Commis on the Accreditation of Hosps as both a nursing home & a specialty geriatric hosp. To maintain the highest level of activity for an individual to preserve the quality of life & the individual's self respect, & enable a individual to remain in his home for as long as possible. Long term nursing home beds with limited acute hosp intervention; short term convalescent beds; respite care; home delivered servs; training; clin & applied research; consultation & technical assistance. The Douglas Gardens Outpatient Mental Health Ctr, located on the Home & Hosp campus, serves people aged 50 & over. The Douglas Gardens Com Mental Health Ctr, located in S Miami Beach, serves individuals of all ages with both Ctrs providing treatment & rehabilitative servs to the deinstitutionalized population to insure resocialization & adaption to the com life style; provides servs which include: psychosocial evaluations, psychiatric evaluation, crisis intervention, individual & group psychotherapy, & telephone reassurance. The Com Care Adult Day Ctr, located on the Home's campus, & Douglas Gardens City of Miami Sr Adult Day Ctr, located at Legion Pk, provide a cost efficient alternative in long term care servs in a com based setting, with servs which include a complete range of med, mental, health, recreational, edu, transportati & social servs. The Ambulatory Health Servs Dept provides primary health care to those elderly in Dade Cty who do not have a primary physician. The Irving Cypen Towers, a 102 unit adult congregate living facility located on the Home's campus, permits the tenent use of the outpatient med servs. The Sr Com Servs Employment Prog provides training & skill dev to people over 55 whose income is below the federal poverty level guidelines. The Stein Gerontological Ins provides a div of research, planning & training. A staff of 500 physicians, nurses, social workers, physical & occupational therapists, group workers & critical support staff. Est in 1945 as a 23 bed home for the aged. In 1976 the Stein Gerontological Ins was organized. In 1979 the Home & Hosp was awarded a three yr com care system demonstration proj grant to implement a Serv Workers Action Team. In 1981 the Home & Hosp was one of 12 sites selected nationally to implement a Natl Long Term Care Channeling Demonstration Proj to test alternatives in care for the frail elderly. Located on an 11 acre site, the pavilions for ambulatory residents have 50 people in single rms & 20 more in twin rms. The nursing home has accommodations for 373 residents. Chr of the Bd, Hon Pres: Irving Cypen; Pres: Harold Beck; Hon VPs: Fay Ablin Stein, David B. Fleeman, Stanley M. Beckerman, Polly deHirsch Meyer, Etta Ruby, M. J. Kopelowitz, Lilyan Beckerman, Harry Chernin, Edward C. Levy, Mollie Silverman, Louis Stein; VPs: Marshall Wise, Harry A. Levy, Edward Shapiro, Arthur Pearlman, Solomon Garazi, Martin Margulies, Arthur P. Mark; Treas: Stephen H. Cypen; Fin Sec: Helen Rechtschaffer; Corsp Sec: Melvin H. Baer; Rec Sec: A. Jeffrey Barash; Assc Rec Sec: Gladys Israel; Exec Dir: Fred D. Hirt; Assc Dirs: Marc Lichtman, Olga Cenal; Med Dir: Dr Charles Beber. **151 NE 52 St, Miami FL 33137 (305) 751–8626.**

National Council of Jewish Women. Women's volunteer org. Dedicated in the spirit of J to advancing human welfare & the democratic way of life. Activities are organized around five prog priorities: women's issues, chil & youth, aging, J life, & Is. Women's Issues – major concerns are: ratification of the Equal Rights Amendment, protection of the right of every women to have access to safe & legal abortion, removal of gender related discrimination in all areas of life, provision of edu progs on the prevention of domestic violence & treatment for its victims, widow to widow counseling & progs for single parents. Chil & Youth – primarily concerned with: the rights, needs & quality of life of the nation's chil & youth; juvenile justice, especially the treatment of adolescent girls; foster care; variety of projs that support servs to the young people in their coms (the Council is deeply committed to advocacy efforts needed to effectively change the way chil are treated under the law). Is – carries out numerous edu & social welfare progs in Is; has long been a strong advocate for the State of Is; furthers major proj in Is which is the Research Ins for Innovation in Edu (part of The Heb Univ Sch of Edu). J Life – places emphasis on: J edu & the problems of Soviet J; J edu progs for individuals of various ages & interests designed to assist people in exploring their understanding of & attitudes toward J & rekindling their interest in their rel; involvement in the resettlement of Soviet J immigrants & in advocacy on behalf of those J who are refused permission to leave the USSR. Aging – primary focus is on dev & support of legislation on behalf of older adults, day ctrs, housing for the elderly, adult edu, enrichment progs, volunteer placement progs, sheltered employment projs, nutrition & transportation servs, multipurpose ctrs, nursing homes, ombudsman progs & self training for & by the elderly. **5220 Biscayne Blvd 202, Miami FL 33137 (305) 757–1305.**

South Dade Hebrew Academy. Early childhood, elementary sch & Jr HS for 3 yr olds through 9th grade. To provide every stu with the pride of J via the learning of tradition, modern Heb & the love of the nation of Is so that they will continue to maintain the unbroken chain of their heritage; to est a positive climate for learning in each classroom. Gen & J studies (all J classes conducted in Heb); complete bilingual prog; rel servs; optional speech & hearing screenings by a certified speech pathologist; library; field trips; after sch prog; reading & math labs which give not only instruction in basic skills but stress a free environment which allows stu to move laterally as well vertically; physical edu for grades 1 through 9; day care; enrichment progs in art & music. Faculty of 27. Est in 1969 by a group of far sighted com leaders who realized the importance & need for the perpetuation & dedication to J edu. During the first two yrs, the Academy rented classroom space fr Temple Or Olom. In 1971 they moved to the YMHA. Five yrs after the est of the Academy, the present facility was purchased. Magillah (quarterly magazine). Facilities include four bldgs, air conditioned classrooms, cafeteria, auditorium, sch

Ins; special classes for divorcees; hospital visitation prog; interfaith progs; Sisterhood; Brotherhood; two singles groups; three youth groups; Sr Citizens group; Rel Servs; basketball league; summer camp; library containing 8,000 vols (Judaica & J content hist, J writers fiction, non-fiction). 1700 families; 450 stu (grades 1 – 6); 200 presch stu; 900 stu Weekend Sch K–12. 200 employees. F 1955; formerly S Dade J Ctr. Pub Commentator (weekly). Facilities include sanctuary, two social halls, gym, library, gift shop, chapel, 38 classrms, two kichens. Sr Rabbi Herbert M. Baumgard; Asst Rabbi Morton Hoffman, Asst Rabbi Robert Goldsetin; Exec Dir: David Stuart; Assc Dir: Joan Schwartzman; Day Sch Dir: Ceil Coonin; Pres: Al Leibert; Exec VP: Barry Goldstein; VPs: Evelyn Goodman, Edgar Lewis, Ira Pozen, Edie Spiegel, Michael Weisberg; Fin Sec: Michael Brown; Treas: Jerold Schwarz; Corsp Sec: Robert Sandler; Rec Sec: Teddi Segal; Bd of Trustees Chr: Samuel Steen; Sisterhood Pres: Selma Rappaport; Brotherhood Pres: Ralph Cohen. **5950 N Kendall Dr, Miami FL 33156 (305) 667–6667.**

Temple Beth Am Library. Library contains 8,000 vols Judaica & J content – hist, J writers, fiction, non-fiction. For information on the Temple, see – Temple Beth Am, Miami, FL. **5950 N Kendall Dr, Miami FL 33156 (305) 667–6667.**

Temple Israel of Greater Miami. Affiliated with UAHC. 1691 mems. Rabbis: Haskell M. Bernat, Jeffrey K. Salkin; Cantor Jacob G. Bornstein; Pres: Bermont; Edu: Jacob G. Bornstein; Adm: Philip S. Goldin; Sisterhood Pres: Gloria Gilbert; Brotherhood Pres: Joel Pachino. **137 NE 19th St, Miami FL 33132 (305) 573–5900.**

Temple Israel of Greater Miami Library. For information on the Temple, see – Temple Israel of Greater Miami, Miami, FL. **137 NE 19th St, Miami FL 33132 (305) 573–5900.**

Temple Or Olam. Affiliated with United Syn of Am. Rabbi Samuel Rudy; Cantor P. Hillel Brummer; Pres: Linda Hornick; Edu Dir: Beth Schulberg; Youth Dir: Michael Mirello. **8755 SW 16th St, Miami FL 33165 (305) 221–9131.**

Temple Samu-El. Affiliated with United Syn of Am. Rabbi Edwin Farber; Pres: Dr Stephen Fain; Youth Dirs: Bram & Esthe Bottfeld. **9353 SW 152nd Ave, Miami FL33196 (305) 382–3668.**

Temple Zion. Affiliated with United Syn of Am. Rabbi Dr Norman N. Shapiro; Cantor Benjamin Dickson; Pres: Joseph S. Zipper; Exec Dir: Dorothy H. Grant. **8000 Miller Rd, Miami FL 33155 (305) 271–2311.**

Temple Zion, Ben Serkin Library. For information on the Temple, see – Temple Zion, Miami, FL. **8000 Miller Rd, Miami FL 33155 (305) 271–2311.**

UAHC Southeast Council – South Florida Federation. Rel & edu org serving J congs throughout the US & Canada. To encourage & aid the org & dev of J congs; to promote J edu & enrich & intensify J life; to foster other activities for the perpetuation & advancement of J. For additional information, see – UAHC – Union of American Hebrew Congregations, New York City, NY. Pres: Robert T. Benjamin Jr, Iris Franco; Dir: Rabbi Lewis Littman. **119 E Flagler St, Suite 238, Miami FL 33131 (305) 379–4553.**

Miami Beach

American Committee for Shaare Zedek in Jerusalem – Southeast Region. To help future generations meet the health needs of Jerusalem and Israel. Continuing support of century old hospital which moved in 1979 fr old quarters to new $55 million ultra modern medical complex overlooking Jerusalem. Offers total patient & community care. University affiliated teaching hospital contains main hospital building planned for more than 500 beds, emergency shelter, outpatient clinics, school of nursing, clinical labs, research ins, central library, facilities. Ensures the full observance of J tradition. Open to all, irrespective of rel, race or nationality. **605 Lincoln Rd, Suite 211, Miami Beach FL 33139 (305) 531–8329.**

The American Friends of Haifa University. 420 Lincoln Rd, Miami Beach FL 33139 (305) 531–1174.

Chabad House. Lubavitch com servs ctr. Blends Chassidic fervor & warmth with tradition & learning, to show that every J, fr whatever background he or she comes fr, is an integral part of the body of Is. Anti-missionary work; adult edu; Sabbath seminars; holiday progs; day camp; youth groups; syns; kosher kitchen; counseling; chaplaincy; Mitzvah Campaigns; hosp & prison visitations; sr citizens encounters; speakers bureau. Rabbi Abraham Korf. **1401 Alton Ave, Miami Beach FL 33139 (305) 672–8947.**

Congregation Lubavitch – South Beach Chabad. Orthodox Cong affiliated with World Lubavitch Org, Orthodox Rabbinical Council of S FL. To provide prayer, edu & social servs for the J population of Maimi Beach with special emphasis on Chassidic philosophy & warmth. Daily Rel Servs (throughout yr – 1120 Collins Ave, winter season –

3601 Collins Ave, Shabbos only - 1220 Ocean Dr); five daily classes (Chumash, Bible) Tanya (Chassidic Philosophy, Intermediate Talmud, Advanced Talmud, J Law); active Sisterhood; Mazusahs & Tefillin checked; counseling & reference serv; library of 250 vols (Talmud–Medrash–Mishnaios). 400 mems. 2 employees; 8 volunteers. F 1961 by Rabbi Abraham Korf; the first Lubavitch ins in SE US. Facilities include sanctuaries (3601 Collins Ave – 125 persons, 1220 Ocean Dr – 149 persons, 3601 Collins Ave – 70 persons). Est Kollel for sr citizens. Rabbi Sholom Blank; Rabbi Yoseph Kessler; Rabbi Yehuda Chitrik; Rabbi Eliahu Friedman; Pres: Max Lang; VP: Jack Katz; Treas: Karl Moskowitz. **1120 Collins Ave, Miami Beach FL 33139 (305) 673–5755.**

Farband Labor Zionist Alliance. The betterment of all Is. Active in all phases of J culture. 800 mems. There are four branches: David Bliss Branch 322, Lebidiker Branch, Chaim Weitzman Branch, Ben Gurion Branch. The Alliance works together on all projs in unison with the UJA, Histradrut, State of Is Bonds & the JNF. Dir & Chr David Bliss Branch: Josef Bernhaut; Chr Lebidiker Branch: Joseph Zuckerman; Chr Chaim Weitzman Branch: Moe Levine; Chr Ben Gurion Branch: Philip Kahn. **1 Lincoln Rd, Suite 320, Miami Beach FL 33139 (305) 532–1887.**

The Greater Miami Hebrew Free Loan Association. To loan money without interest or charges to those in need who are J & residents of Dade Cty, FL. Maintains a small fund fr which to provide Passover baskets to truly needed persons, provides loans to local residents. 130–150 individuals & families In 1950 a group of people met to form a Hebrew free loan assn to help people in need. The Assn was incorporated on Apr 13, 1950. The amount of an individual loan has escalated with the times, & the current maximum is $750.00 as opposed to the $25.00 maximum allowed in 1950. The Assn contributed $5,000 in State of Is bonds to est a branch of the Ezras Torah Fund in Is, to aid young couples & families, & to assist improverished Torah scholars. Pres: Joseph A. Nevel; VPs: Sue Berkowitz, Isaac Weis, Nathan Zeichner, Yolande Bernstein, Rabbi Phineas Weberman, Ben Clueck; Treas: Joseph Curtis; Fin Sec: Clara Eckhaus; Adm Asst: Norma M. Locke; Bd of Dirs: Abe Barkan, Sue Berkowitz, Fred Bernstein, Yolande Bernstein, Anna Green, Zelda Kunst, Joseph A. Nevel, Rose Siegal, Morris Luck, Joshua Galitzer, Abe & Rosalin Meisels. **1545 Alton Rd, Miami Beach FL 33139 (305) 532–1392.**

Hebrew Academy. 2400 Pine Tree Dr, Miami Beach FL 33140 (305) 532–6421.

Hebrew Academy – Elementary Media Center. 2400 Pine Tree Dr, Miami Beach FL 33140 (305) 532–6421.

Hebrew Academy Jr-Sr Library. 2425 Pine Tree Dr, Miami Beach FL 33140.

The Jewish Historical Society of South Florida, Inc. J resource ctr. To preserve the records of the foun & dev of J coms fr Key West to Tampa FL by all appropriate means, including the creation of oral hist; to dev the hist of all J natl & local ins, secular & rel; to pub historical papers; to stimulate col & univ stu in J local hist; to sponsor prizes in univs for the best theses & dissertations on facets of local J hist. Oral Hist Prog; tapes; files; archival materials. F in 1972. Pub The Jewish Frontiersmen: Historical Highlights of Early South Florida Jewish Communities; Man of the Frontier: Biography of Sol Schwartz. All servs are available to stu & researchers. Pres: Harriet Green; VPs: Abraham Lavender, Malvina W. Liebman; Hon Life Pres: Seymour B. Liebman. **605 Lincoln Rd, Suite 600, Miami Beach FL 33139 (305) 538–6213.**

Lehrman Day School of Temple Emanu-El. Affiliated with Solomon Schechter Day Schs Assn. Prin: Rowena Kovler; Chr: Laurence Schantz. **727 77th St, Miami Beach FL 33141 (305) 866–2771.**

Ohev Shalom Congregation. 7055 Bonita Dr, Miami Beach FL 33141 (305) 865–9851.

Pioneer Women – Na'amat. Cooperates with Na'amat, its sister org in Is, in the support of edu, vocational & chil care servs which imp the quality of life for Is through a broad network of 1,500 installations. In the US, Pioneer Women supports all progs for the advancement of human rights & is an authorized agy for Youth Aliyah. Pres: Harriet Green. **605 Lincoln Rd, Suite 600, Miami Beach FL 33139 (305) 538–6213.**

Temple Beth Sholom. Affiliated with UAHC. 1250 mems. Rabbis: Leon Kronish, Harry Jolt; Cantor David Conviser; Pres: Harold Vinik; Adm: Dennis J. Rice; Sisterhood Pres: Ronne Kaplan; Brotherhood Pres: Perry M. Fabian. **4144 Chase Ave, Miami Beach FL 33140 (305) 538–7231.**

Temple Beth Sholom Library. 4144 Chase Ave, Miami Beach FL 33140 (305) 538–7231.

Temple Emanu-El. Affiliated with United Syn of Am. Rabbi Irving Lehrman; Cantor Zvi Adler; Asst Rabbi Maxwell Berger; Pres: Carol Greenberg; Exec Dir: Vivian Becker; Dir: Dr Amir Baron; Youth Dir:

Jack Rosenbaum. **1701 Washington Ave, Miami Beach FL 33139 (305) 538–2503.**

Temple Emanu-El Library. For information on the Temple, see – Temple Emanu-El, Miami Beach, FL. **1701 Washington Ave, Miami Beach FL 33139 (305) 538–2503.**

Temple Menorah. Affiliated with United Syn of Am. Rabbi Mayer Abramowitz; Cantor Murray B. Yavneh; Pres: Joel Gray; Exec Dir: Marcia Levy; Edu Dir: Bryna Berman. **620 75th St, Miami Beach FL 33141 (305) 866–0221.**

Temple Ner Tamid. Affiliated with United Syn of Am. Rabbi Dr Eugene Labovitz; Pres: Morry Nathanson. **7902 Carlyle Ave, Miami Beach FL 33141 (305) 866–9833.**

Yad V'Kidush Hashem, House of Martyrs. Ins devoted to the Holocaust, search for facts. To commemorate Nazi victims; to reveal crimes; to determine who did or did not help survivors. Rel Servs; research progs, lecturing, counseling servs – all in regard to the Holocaust; Holocaust library. 100 members. F 1948 by Grand Rabbi Menachem M. Rubin – survivor of Aushwitz concentration camp & Rabbinical leader, an authority in Hassidic teachings. Pub Word & Opinion (periodically). F by Grand Rabbi Menachem M. Rubin. **4200 Sheridan Ave, Miami Beach FL 33140 (305) 532–0363.**

Young Israel of Sunny Isles. Orthodox Syn mem Natl Council of Young Is Syns. To be an Orthodox J ctr for worship, study & social activity. Rel Servs; classes in J studies; Holiday functions; J com information serv; Sisterhood; Heb Sch; active in secular com activities. 100 mems. 30 volunteers. F 1982. Pub Shalom Newsletter (before every Holiday). Facilities include kitchen, hall available for various com events that are consonent with the Young Is spirit. Brought many local residents back to an awareness of their J identity. Rabbi Rubin R. Dobin; Pres: Charles Skupsky; VPs: Sol Suszyn, Emanuel Lassar; Treas: Shlomo Hacohen; Sec: Rabbi Baruch Sufrin; Gabbai: Harry Gartner. **17480 Collins Ave, Miami Beach FL 33160 (305) 932–4433.**

North Miami

B'nai Sephardim Congregation of Greater Miami. To provide a focal meeting place for Moroccan families scattered throughout the greater Miami area. Rel Servs. 30 to 40 families. Lay Rabbinical Stu: Dr Leon Suissa. **44 NW 150th St, North Miami FL 33168.**

Temple Beth Moshe. Conservative Cong affiliated with United Syn of Am. Daily Rel Servs; Oneg Shabbat Servs followed by a refreshment hour sponsored by various individuals; Jr Cong which is a more advanced serv for boys & girls 11–1 yrs of age in which the skills of participants are dev to enable them to lead in chanting the servs; Adult Edu courses; lecture series; Pre Confirmation & Confirmation courses; USY Youth Group; Sisterhood; Men's Club; Cong Choir; catering servs; Rel Sch; Nursery Sch. 400 families; 150 chil in the Rel Sch; 60 chil in the Nursery Sch. Est in 1950 under the name of Beth Ameth in N Miami. The Cong moved to its present add in 1970 & changed the name of the Temple to the present one. The Temple is the only temple in the area of Sans Souci in N Miami. Bulletin (printed monthly); Newsletter (distributed every Fri night) provides a compilation of week's activities & a listing of honors of the week. The Temple maintains a gift shop. Rabbi Louis M. Lederman; Rabbi Emeritus Dr Joseph A. Gorfinkel; Cantor Moshe Friedler; Exec Dir: Irving Jaret; Prin: Anita R. Lederman; Nursery Dir: Barbara Shulman; Pres: Elliot Eiseman; VPs: Harvey Friedman, Samuel J. Jaffe, Seymour Smoller, Ruth Strehan; Treas: Abraham Baumgarten; Fin Sec: Melvyn Trute; Rec Sec: Marilyn Mandel; Corsp Sec: Pearl Levan; Chr of the Bd: Herbert S. Lelchuk; V Chr of the Bd: Harvey Friedman; Bd of Dirs: Sherman Baumrind, Dr Clarence Bayles, Saby Behar, Bonnie Brooks, Jack Carmel, Howard Cohen, Harold L. Fein, Lawrence Fein, Dr Robert Freedman, Barney Grossman, Dr Leonard L. Heimoff, Ricki Igra, Alvin Korfin, Joseph Krevolin, Harriet Margolin, Barnet Selby, Sandra Shapiro, Robert Shellow, Clara Smoller, David Stone, Dr Paul Swaye, Jay M. Tischenkel, Myles Tralins, Judith Trubin, Rita Weissman; Sisterhood Co-Pres: Vivian Lelchuk, Pearl Levan, Eileen Rand; Men's Club Pres: Samuel Golland; Bd of Govs: Irving Brown, Bernard Chaney, Danny Gordon, Selma Herzog, Vivian Lelchuk, Florence Linden, Frances Miller, Milton Pepper, Elaine Richman, Dr Goerge Segal, Dr Bertram P. Shapiro, Etta Thayer, Maxwell Weisblatt, Charles Weissman. **2225 NE 121st St, North Miami FL 33181 (305) 891–5508.**

North Miami Beach

Beth Torah Congregation. Affiliated with United Syn of Am. Rabbi Dr Max A. Lipshitz; Cantor Zvee Aroni; Pres: Marshall P. Baltuch; Exec Dir: Harvey L. Brown; Youth Dir: Peter Kadish. **1051 N Miami Beach Blvd, North Miami Beach FL 33162 (305) 947–7528.**

Congregation Etz Chaim, Metro Community Synagogue of Greater Miami. Affiliated with

UAHC. 60 mems. Pres: Doree Benson. **19094 W Dixie Highway, North Miami Beach FL33180.**

Hillel Community Day School. 19000 NE 25th Ave, North Miami Beach FL 33180 (305) 931–2831.

Hillel Community Day School, Rosenthal Library. 19000 NE 25th Ave, North Miami Beach FL 33180 (305) 931–2831.

The Metropolitan Community Synagogue of Greater Miami, Congregation Etz Chaim. Mems of the UAHC. To serve the gay & J com, as no other FL cong can. Rel Servs; Oneg Shabbat which follows Fri Night Servs; Passover Seder; Purim & anniversary parties; auctions; picnics; open houses; promotion of an understanding of homosexuality within the larger J com; MCS speakers bureau. Est by seven J parishioners of the met com church who preferred the faith of their parents. At first, MCS mems met at each others homes. Later, they used a Lutheran church, the downtown YWCA & a N Miami Beach art studio. In 1980 the Syn was formally inducted into the Union. Orthodox, Reform, Conservative & unaffiliated J openly worship as gays with other gay sisters & brothers, without discomfort, hostility or embarrassment. Mems take turns giving Torah lessons. Pres: Doree Benson; Sec: Sylvi Milton; Treas: Jay Schapps. **19094 W Dixie Highway, North Miami Beach FL 33180 (305) 931–9318.**

Temple Sinai of North Dade. Reform Temple affiliated with UAHC. To further J life; to educate our young; to meet rel needs of our Cong family. Full prog of syn activities including Rel Servs; Adult Edu; child edu in Nursery Sch, day sch (Sinai Academy – a liberal J day sch) Syn Sch; summer day camp; Brotherhood; Sisterhood; youth groups; choirs: Hollander– Rachleff Library contains 6000 vols (Judaica – adult & chil). 625 families; 100 individuals; 150 stu in Nursery, 500 stu in Sun Sch; 42 stu in Day Sch; 300 in summer day camp. F 1956; moved to present location in 1969; sanctuary dedicated 1969; sch bldg dedicated 1973. Pub Temple Sinai Bulletin (bi-weekly). Facilities include sanctuary seating 400 – expands to total of 1200 with social hall; social hall seating 200 for parties, swimming pool, outdoor patio, gift shop. Syn has full campaign for UJA – achieved almost 100% participation in 1981–82 campaign. Rabbi Ralph P. Kingsley; Assc Rabbi for Ed & Youth: Rabbi Julian I. Cook; Cantor Irvine Shukles; Adm Barbara Ramsey; Pres: Norman S. Klein; Nursery Sch Dir: Trudy Zaden; **18801 NE 22nd Ave, North Miami Beach FL 33180 (305) 932–9010.**

Temple Sinai of North Dade, Hollander-Rachleff Library. Library contains 6,000 vols (Judaica – adult & chil bks). For information on the Temple, see – Temple Sinai of North Dade, North Miami Beach, FL. **18801 NE 22nd Ave, North Miami Beach FL 33180 (305) 932–9010.**

United Synagogue of America – South-East Region. 1110 NE 163rd St, North Miami Beach FL 33162 (305) 947–6094.

North Palm Beach

Temple Beth David of Northern Palm Beach County. Affiliated with United Syn of Am. Rabbi William Marder; Pres: Jack Lee Kaplan. **321 Northlake Blvd, North Palm Beach FL 33408 (305) 845–1134.**

Orlando

The Jewish Federation of Greater Orlando. Mem of CJF. Organized 1949. Pres: Sonia Mandel; Exec Dir: Paul Jeser. **851 N Maitland Ave, PO Box 1508, Maitland FL 32751 (305) 645–5933.**

Liberal Judaism Congregation. Affiliated with UAHC. 465 mems. Rabbis: Larry J. Halpern, Andrew R. Hillman; Pres: Sidney R. Geist Jr; Rabbis: Larry J. Halpern, Andrew R. Hillman; Adm: Harriet Corey; Sisterhood Pres: Mary L. Goss; Brotherhood Pres: Larry Sloan. **928 Malone Dr, Orlando FL 32810 (305) 645–0444.**

Ohev Shalom. Affiliated with United Syn of Am. Rabbi Dr Rudolph J. Adler; Pres: Robert Gamson; Edu Dir: Moshe Elbanz. **5015 Goddard Ave, Orlando FL 32810 (305) 298–4650.**

Temple Israel. Conservative Cong affiliated with United Syn of Am. To est & maintain a syn & additional rel, social, edu & recreational activities; to strengthen Conservative J. Rel Servs; rel, social, edu & recreational activities; Sisterhood; Men's Club. Rabbi Chaim Z. Rozwaski; Cantor Leon Radzik; Edu Dir: Etty Baru; Youth Dir: Harold Wolf; Gabbai: Jacob Frank; Shamash: Roy Scheinberg; Pres: Dr Jes Baru; Exec VP: Julian Meitin; VP Rel: Dr Abe Tenzer; VP Edu: Dr Lawrence Richman; VP Fund Raising: Richard Katz; VP Mems: Stuart Farb; Treas: Jack Oppenheimer; Sec: Ellen Morrell; Men's Club Pres: Hyman Kaplan; Sisterhood Pres: Alma Kerben; Rabbi's Sec: Joan Wagner; Adm Secs: Faye Davis, Rachael Johnson. **4917 Eli St, Orlando FL 32804 (305) 647–3055.**

Palm Beach

Temple Emanu-El of Palm Beach. Affiliated with United Syn of Am. Rabbi Joel Chazin; Cantor David Dardashti; Pres: Alan H. Cummings; Edu Dir: Morrie Cohen. **190 N Cty Rd, Palm Beach FL 33480 (305) 832–0804.**

Pembroke Pines

Temple Beth Emet. Affiliated with UAHC. 125 mems. Rabbi Bennett H. Greenspon; Pres: Alan J. Kan; Sisterhood Pres: Maureen Eisenberg. **PO Box 8842, Pembroke Pines FL 33024 (305) 431–3638.**

Temple in the Pines. Affiliated with United Syn of Am. Rabbi Bernard P. Shorter; Cantor Bernard Engel; Pres: Robert Sims; Edu Dir: Dr Richard Corseri. **9730 Stirling Rd, Pembroke Pines FL 33024 (305) 431–5100.**

Pensacola

B'nai Israel Synagogue. Affiliated with United Syn of Am. Rabbi Maurice Schwartz; Pres: Franklin Kay; Edu Dir: Marsha Fish; Youth Dir: David Kaiman. **PO Box 9002, 1909 N 9th Ave, Pensacola FL 32503 (904) 433–7311.**

Pensacola Federated Jewish Charities. Organized 1942. Pres: Joe Rosenbaum; Sec: Mrs Harry Saffe **1320 E Lee St, Pensacola FL 32503 (904) 438–1464.**

Temple Beth El. Affiliated with UAHC. 158 mems. Rabbi N. William Schwartz; Pres: Fred K. Seligman; Edu: Rosann Mann; Sisterhood Pres: Pat Marcus. **800 N Palafox St, Pensacola FL 32501 (904) 438–3321.**

Plantation

Temple Kol Ami, Plantation Jewish Congregation. Affiliated with 575 mems. Rabbi Sheldon J. Harr; Cantor Nathan Corburn; Pres: Philip Fagelson; Edu: Morris Ezry; Adm: Frances Lee; Sisterhood Pres: Linda Smith; Brotherhood Pres: Allan Gross. **8200 Peters Rd, Plantation FL 33324 (305) 472–1988.**

Temple Kol Ami, Plantation Jewish Congregation Library. For information on the Temple, see – Temple Kol Ami, Plantation, FL. **8200 Peters Rd, Plantation FL 33324 (305) 472–1988.**

Pompano Beach

Temple Sholom. Affiliated with United Syn of Am. Rabbi Samuel April; Cantor Jacob J. Renzer; Pres: Dr Milton Isaacson; Edu Dirs: Fran Parnass & Gail Ehrlich; Youth Dir: Joanne Zipper. **132 SE 11th Ave, Pompano Beach FL 33060 (305) 942–6410.**

Port Charlotte

Temple Shalom. Affiliated with UAHC. 242 mems. Rabbi Samuel Kligfeld; Pres: David Abell. **Utica Ave & Sherwood Rd, Port Charlotte FL 33592 (813) 625–2116.**

Port Richey

Gulf Coast Jewish Family Service, Inc. Confidential individual, family & group counseling by a highly trained & qualified professional staff; psycho-social residential care & day treatment progs for older adults with emotional problems; emergency homemaker servs for disabled & elderly; preventive servs through Family Life Edu progs designed to prevent everyday problems fr becoming serious; interest free loans to col stu for families experiencing financial difficulties; social servs programming for Kosher Sr Congregate Lunch Sites; social work outreach & referral counseling for the elderly; weekly loving contact fr a dedicated volunteer for problem chil. **1718 W Kennedy Blvd, Port Richey FL 33568 (813) 848–5174.**

Sarasota

Sarasota Hebrew Day School. Affiliated with Solomon Schechter Day Schs Assn. Prin: Judy Kayser. **1050 S Tuttle Ave, Sarasota FL 33577 (813) 955–8121.**

Sarasota Jewish Federation, Inc. Mem of CJF. Inc 1959. Pres: Jerome Kapner; Exec Dir: Jack Weintraub. **2197 Ringling Blvd, Sarasota FL 33577 (813) 365–4410.**

Temple Beth Sholom. Affiliated with United Syn of Am. Rabbi Max Roth; Cantor Victor Jacoby; Pres: Audrey Watson. **1050 S Tuttle Ave, Sarasota FL 33577 (813) 955–8121.**

Temple Emanu-El. Affiliated with UAHC. 574 mems. Rabbis: Ahron Opher, Peter E. Hyman; Pres: Al E. Schaar; Edu: Peter E. Hyman; Sisterhood Pres: Lucille Gerber; Brotherhood Pres: Charles Steiner. **151 S McIntosh Rd, Sarasota FL 33582 (813) 371–2788.**

Sattelite

Temple Beth Sholom. Affiliated with United Syn of Am. Rabbi David Jessel; Pres: Elliot Kornberg MD. **NE Third St, PO Box 2253, Sattelite FL 32937.**

Seminole

Beth Chai. Affiliated with United Syn of Am. Rabbi Sherman P. Kirschner; Cantor Reuben Sabin; Pres: Sidney Werner; Edu Dir: Linda Kreps; Youth Dir: Harry Rubenstein. **PO Box 3235, Seminole FL 33542 (813) 393–5525.**

St. Petersburg

B'nai Israel. Affiliated with United Syn of Am. Rabbi Jacob Luski; Cantor Josef Schroder; Pres: Adele Morris. **301 59th St N, St Petersburg FL 33710 (813) 381–4900.**

Congregation B'nai Israel Library. For information on the Cong, see – Cong B'nai Israel, St Petersburg, FL. **301 59th St N, St Petersburg FL 33710 (813) 381–4900.**

Gulf Coast Jewish Family Service, Inc. Confidential individual, family & group counseling by a highly trained & qualified professional staff; psycho-social residential care & day treatment progs for older adults with emotional problems; emergency homemaker servs for disabled & elderly; preventive servs through Family Life Edu progs designed to prevent everyday problems fr becoming serious; interest free loans to col stu for families experiencing financial difficulties; social servs programming for Kosher Sr Congregate Lunch Sites; social work outreach & referral counseling for the elderly; weekly loving contact fr a dedicated volunteer for problem chil. **8167 Elbow Lane N, St Petersburg FL 33710 (813) 381–2373.**

Jewish Community Center of Pinellas County. Activities & classes in the creative & performing arts; early childhood playgroup; mother/toddler classes; health & physical edu; Camp Kadima providing a summer day camp for ages 2½ to 15 yrs; after sch prog for chil of all ages; teen activities; adult progs; social activities for singles; progs & activities for sr adults; social activities; Sr Friendship Club; holiday progs & activities. Est in the middle 1950's as the only social J communal agy in the area. It gave the com adults & chil an opportunity to meet & interact in the above mentioned progs. Facilities include meeting rms, a swimming pool, tennis court, basketball & soccer facilities. Most J orgs meet at the JCC. Exec Dir: Fred Margolis; Pres: Charles W. Ehrlich; VPs: Joseph Charles, Dr Bruce Lynn, Lee Smalley; Sec: Myra Gross; Treas: Dr Gordon Saskin; Bd Mems: Maxine Buchholtz, Ben Bush, Mel Fergenbaum, Florence Ganz, Victor Greenberg, Leonard Greenberg, Meni Kanner, Bonnie Kuperman, Drew Lucido, Bernard Panush, Nory Pearl, Jerry Phillips, Hy Phillips, Renee Raimi, Beth Resnick, Irving Silverman, Richard Weinberger. **8167 Elbow Lane N, St Petersburg FL 33710 (813) 344–5795.**

Pinellas County Jewish Day School. Affiliated with Solomon Schechter Day Schs Assn. Prin: Edwin Frankel; Chr: Dr Michael Phillips. **301 59th St N, St Petersburg FL 33710 (813) 381–8111.**

Temple Beth El. Affiliated with UAHC. 510 mems. Rabbis: David J. Susskind, Robert P. Kirzner; Cantor Miriam Berger; Pres: Sol Markman; Edu: Susan Burnett; Sisterhood Pres: Arzena Ginsberg; Brotherhood Pres: Irving Kramer. **400 S Pasadena Ave, St Petersburg FL 33707 (813) 347–6136.**

Sunrise

Temple Beth Israel. Affiliated with United Syn of Am. Rabbi Phillip A. Labowitz; Cantor Maurice A. Neu; Pres: Al Lang; Edu & Youth Dir: Stanley L. Cohen. **7100 W Oakland Park Blvd, Sunrise FL 33313.**

Women's League for Israel, Inc. Projs for the social, economic & edu welfare of Is youth. Homes in Jerusalem, Tel Aviv, Haifa & Nathanya where young people can find a place to live & receive vocational training, guidance & placement, & instruction in Heb; Com ctr in Haifa: prog includes clubs, ceramics, dramatics & various other hobbies; Com ctr in Hatzor: culture & recreational ctr for 7,000 chil & adults; Natl Rehabilitation & Vocational Training Ctr at Nathanya: includes a dormitory, evaluation ctr, classrms & workshops, progs for physically & emotionally handicapped & normal girls to dev their aptitudes, & nonresidents can use the ctr's evaluation & vocational training facilities; Weaving Workshop for the Blind: sightless men & women can gain economic & social independence; Ins for Edu & Social Workers: col level courses for men & women who will work with alienated youth, retarded chil, & parents of these chil; at Hebrew Univ, the bldg of three women's dormatory wings, cafeteria accommodating 600 stu at each of at least three lunch sessions: provides subsidized nutritious meals, stu ctr comprised of a gymnasium bldg, activities bldg & a hq bldg for the stu org; Rose Isaacs Chair in Sociology at Hebrew Univ: provides for teaching & research; Scholarship Endowment Fund: gives priority to disabled vets; Bk Endowment Fund: provides text bks & reference materials in the library of the Sch of Social Work; pilot prog for minimally brain damaged teenagers in the Jerusalem Home. 5,000 Am women. F in 1928 for girls coming to build a J State. The first Home, in Haifa, was completed in 1932. **5975 W Sunrise Blvd, Sunrise FL 33313 (305) 791–4840.**

Surfside

Jews for Jews Organization. Affiliated with Natl Anti-Cult & Missionary Task Forces of J Feds. To save J from cults & missionaries; to strengthen J identity; to make the J com aware of the dangers of cult & missionary recruitment; to help cult-impacted families rescue their chil fr the cult & missionary entrapment. Edu progs, audio-visual aids; research progs; counseling & therapy sessions; curriculum preparation; speakers bureau; resource library on cults & missionaries. 51 groups. 50 volunteers. F 1975. Pub Newsletter (monthly); Anti-Cult & Missionary Kit; The Challenge of Cults. Natl Chr: Rabbi Rubin R. Dobin; Exec Bd: Rabbi Emanuel Rackman, Rabbi Walter Wurzburger, Dr Stanley Wagner, Alex Scheinzeit, Robert Billig, Dr Abraham Dubin. **PO Box 6194, Surfside FL 33154 (305) 931–0001.**

Tallahassee

Temple Israel. Affiliated with UAHC. 200 mems. Rabbi Stanley J. Garfein; Pres: Sam Brooks; Edu: Wendy Brezin; Sisterhood Pres: Judy Winn; Brotherhood Pres: Jeffrey Jacques. **PO Box 3343, Tallahassee FL 32303 (904) 877–3517.**

Tamarac

Temple Beth Torah – Tamarac Jewish Center. Affiliated with United Syn of Am. Rabbi Israel Zimmerman; Cantor Henry Belasco; Pres: Jack Weiner; Edu Dir: Laura Zimmerman. **9101–15 NW 57th St, Tamarac FL 33321.**

Tampa

Chabad House. J stu ctr at the Univ of S FL. Beneficiary agy of Tampa J Fed; affiliated with the Central Org for J Edu, the Natl Edu Branch of the Lubavitcher Movement. To meet the different needs of today's stu. Lectures, Sabbath meals, holiday progs. Initiated in Feb of 1976. Ctr facilities include a lounge, library, syn & dining hall. Rabbi Lazar Rivkin. **CTR217, UC Box 2463, Univ of S FL, Tampa FL 33617; 13104 N 50th St, Tampa FL 33617 (813) 985–7926.**

Congregation Kol Ami. Conservative Syn affiliated with United Syn of Am. To further the ideals of J in the com. Rel Servs; Heb & Sun Sch; Men's Club; Sisterhood; Jr & Sr Young Judea youth groups. Rabbi Leonard Rosenthal; Pres: Allen L. Fox. **PO Box 270444, Tampa FL 33688 (813) 885–3356.**

Congregation Rodeph Sholom. Conservative Syn affiliated with United Syn of Am. Daily Morning Minyan; Men's Club; Sisterhood; Rel Sch; Youth Dept. 500 families. Organized in 1903. Pres: Howard Sinsley; Edu Dir: Rabbi I. Brod. **2713 Bayshore, Tampa FL 33609 (813) 837–1911.**

Hillel. Ctr for J edu, cultural, rel, pol & social expression in an academic atmosphere. Beneficiary of the Tampa J Fed & the State Hillel Fund. To provide a means for J identity geared to the interest & needs of a cohesive Univ of S FL J com, & to provide a formal outlet for contemporary J expression. Speakers, films, class & discussion groups, social events, rel servs, rallies & collections for Is. Open to any USF stu, & any J col stu in the Tampa Bay area. The entire com is welcome to all Hillel functions. **CTR 217, UC Box 2382, Univ of S FL, Tampa FL33620; 13422 Village Circle #121, Tampa FL 33617 (813) 988–7076.**

Hillel School. Day sch. To enable the stu to function as intelligent Am citizens & as knowledgeable, compassionate human beings; to nurture identification with the J people, its hist & with Is; to meet the individual academic & emotional needs of each chil. Edu of a superior quality in both gen & J studies; small classes; innovative teaching; flexible prog. **2713 Bayshore Blvd, Tampa FL 33609 (813) 839–7047.**

Jewish Community Center of Tampa. J ins open to all who wish to participate regardless of race, rel or creed. Dedicated to the preservation & strengthening of the J people & the J way of life. A variety of progs & activities for all ages. Pre-sch Pre-Sch, Early Childhood classes, extended day prog, Camp K'Ton Ton. Chil & Youth grades 1–12: Camp Chai; Music Sch; various classes including cooking, baton, photography, drama; gameroom activities; Youth Council; Heb; Is dancing; scouts; dances; overnights; plays. Adult Progs: Singles Group, Couples Club, bk reviews, numerous classes, Heb, Is dancing, Yiddish. Sr Adults: classes, counseling, food co-op, health screening & clins, Kosher Hot Lunch Prog, bingo, Chai Dial-A-Bus, outreach progs, a communications system for the deaf. Sch sponsors special events which include film series, com bk fair, Is Independence Day celebration, flea market, art exhibits, concerts, plays, ballet; health & physical edu for all ages: gymnastics, tennis classes, soccer league, softball league, basketball, football league, volleyball, aerobic dance, yoga, toddler gym, chil fitness classes, swim lessons, fencing, weight training. F in the 1920's in downtown Tampa, & then moved to Ross Ave & Nebraska. In 1935 the JCC moved to Hyde Park Ave. In 1961 the Ctr relocated to Manhattan Ave until 1962 when they moved into their present facility. Housed at the Ctr are the Tampa J Fed, Tampa J Social Servs, Chai Dial-A-Bus, various J orgs, Tampa Players, BBYO off, Sr Citizen Nutrition & Activities Prog. Ctr facilities include an auditorium, gym, outdoor pool, playground, ball field, picnic area, meeting rms, classrms, tennis courts, shuffleboard, gameroom, exercise rm & arts & crafts rm. Pres: Sharon Mock; VPs: Leslie Osterweil, Glenn Tobin, Sara Cohen, Marsha Levine, Leah Davidson; Sec: Alice Rosenthal; Treas: David Boggs; Memebership Coord: Muriel Feldman. **2808 Horatio, Tampa FL 33609 (813) 872–4451.**

Jewish Towers. Govt funded high rise housing for the elderly. One-bedrm & efficiency apts at modest rates. **3001 De Leon St, Tampa FL 33609 (813) 870–1830.**

State of Israel Bonds. Sold to individuals, institutions & orgs for purpose of maintaining & developing the State of Israel. To provide a central source of investment capital for Is historic progs of econ dev & immigrant absorption. Sells stock of govt owned Is corporations through its affiliate, Capital for Israel, Inc. **4601 W Kennedy Blvd, Suite 118, Tampa FL 33609 (813) 978–8850.**

The Tampa Jewish Federation. Coordinating body of all the J orgs. To help fellow J live as J with pride, in safety & without want, wherever they may be. Plans, budgets & does fund raising for the com; conducts an annual campaign on behalf of social welfare, com relations & cultural ins in Tampa, the US, Is & around the world; sponsors progs of edu, training & volunteer servs; Women's Div promotes the philanthropic & humanitarian efforts of the Fed through progs of edu, volunteer activity in local servs, & participation in the annual fund raising campaign; Young Leadership promotes an opportunity to dev an understanding of the J communal structure & their role in the com; Com Relation Cttee promotes understanding between the J & the gen com & strives to insure equal opportunities for all people; Pres Roundtable acts as a clearing house & coordinating instrument for inter-organizational concerns. The J Welfare Fed of Tampa, first incorporated in 1956, then reincorporated as the J Com Council of Tampa in 1969 & now as the Tampa J Fed, has served the com in many concrete & humanitarian ways. The Tampa Jewish Federation – a Directory of Jewish Organizations & Service. Pres: Hope Barnett; Exec Dir: Gary S. Alter. **2808 Horatio St, Tampa FL 33609 (813) 872–4451.**

Tampa Jewish Social Service. To provide direct servs to the entire com; to coord servs to meet the needs of the J com; to become a permanent & vital agy in the J com. Counseling to individuals & families; long & short term treatment; crisis intervention dealing with a specific & immediate problem, providing reassurance, & taking care of both the person in crisis & those directly effected, with the aim of helping the individual to function again; vocational & career counseling; counseling to all age groups in regard to all environmental problems; information & referral servs; volunteer servs; family life edu offering a wide range of information & skills to teach family mems to interact most effectively with one another; on going edu of the Bd of Dirs; edu of the J com in the areas of unmet needs within the com; edu of the gen com toward the enhancement of the quality of gen mental health care & social servs; edu of the J & gen com on the servs of Tampa J Social Serv: intra-agy planning – budgeting, prog, staff & faculty use; plannin within the J com – identification of needs, allocation of resources, consultation to other orgs; planning within the gen com – resources dev & com relations dev. Other progs include Therapy Group – providing a meeting of individuals with the goal of changing mems behavior & attitudes; Sr Prog – developed for the sr citizens to provide answers to questions & to problems such as housing, health, transportation, fin & employment concerns, problems with retirement & change & aging. The Tampa J Social Serv also provides help through career planning & help concerning problems special to young people who are considering careers & further formal edu, job placement, financial assistance, Dial-a-Bus, Russian resettlement, consultation to River Gardens, JCC & Camp Scholar, presch scholar evaluation, programming for singles. The Tampa J Social Serv also provides enrichment through the Golden Age Club, Job Corps, recreational activities, field trips, edu classes, & the Food Co-op. In 1936 a cttee was formed at Rodef Sholom Syn to help those J people who needed aid during the dark yrs of the Depression. A small group of women quietly & anonymously helped many Tampa families through those hard times. Eventually, the cttee broke away fr the Syn & began an agy housed in the JCC. It incorporated in 1954. Until 1973 Tampa J Social Servs aided in all types of social welfare, as well as forming the J Com Blood Bank & providing the nucleus that conceived of the J Towers & developed the professional agy Tampa J Social Servs has recently become. In 1973 the Agy began to be reconstructed along professional lines with the Bd expanded to take on administrative duties & the casework being handled by a professionally trained social worker. These plans became a reality in 1974. Pres: Paula Zielonka; VP: Steve Segall; Sec: Nancy Linsky; Treas: Dr Donald Mellman; Parliamentarian:

Joyce Swarzman; Bd of Dirs: B. Terry Aidman, Trudy Brinen, Jacob Buchman, Lucile Falk, Tanya Feldman, Dr Art Forman, Maril Jacobs, Jeremy Gluckman, Barbara Goldstein, Leonard Gotler, Audrey Haubenstock, Blossom Leibowitz, Debby Levinson, Dr J. Justin Older, John Osterweil, Ruth Polur, Sam Reiber, Irene Rubenstein, Richard Rudolph, Goldie Shear, Abe Silber, Dr Gerald Sokol, Dr Barry Verkauf, Nancy Verkauf, Mimi Weiss; Exec Dir: Anne Thal. **2808 Horatio, Tampa FL 33609 (813) 872–4451.**

Temple David. Conservative Syn. To preserve, emulate & perpetuate traditional J via the media of a modern intellectual interpretation of the Torah. Daily Rel Servs. Organized in Jul 1971. **2001 Swann, Tampa FL 33609 (813) 251–4215.**

Temple Shaarai Zedek. Reform Temple affiliated with UAHC. Reform Rel Servs on Fri evening & holidays; Sisterhood; Brotherhood; Jr Youth Group for 7th & 8th graders & SCHZFTY youth group for 9th–12th graders; Rel Sch prog of Pre-K through confirmation (10th grade). 540 families; 300 chil in the rel sch. F in 1894. The cong moved to its present location in 1956. Rabbi Frank N. Sundheim; Pres: Stanley W. Rosenkranz; Edu: Joan Altshuler; Adm: Dolores Curphey; Sisterhood Pres: Bobbie Taub; Brotherhood Pres: Bruce S. Goldstein. **3303 Swann Ave, Tampa FL 33609 (813) 876–2377.**

Trilby

Gulf Coast Jewish Family Service, Inc. Confidential individual, family & group counseling by a highly trained & qualified professional staff; psycho-social residential care & day treatment progs for older adults with emotional problems; emergency homemaker servs for disabled & elderly; preventive servs through Family Life Edu progs designed to prevent everyday problems fr becoming serious; interest free loans to col stu for families experiencing financial difficulties; social servs programming for Kosher Sr Congregate Lunch Sites; social work outreach & referral counseling for the elderly; weekly loving contact fr a dedicated volunteer for problem chil. **Trilby Adult & Community School, Old Trilby Rd, Trilby FL 33593 (904) 583–3421.**

Vero Beach

Temple Beth Shalom. Affiliated with UAHC. 65 mems. Rabbi Richard Agler; Pres: Harlod A. Sommer. **PO Box 2113, Vero Beach FL32960 (305) 569–1082.**

West Palm Beach

Anti-Defamation League of B'nai B'rith – Palm Beach County Regional Office. Dedicated in purpose & prog to translating the Am heritage of democratic ideals into a way of life for all Am; to countering assaults on the safety, status, rights & image of J. For additional information, see – Anti-Defamation League of B'nai B'rith, New York City, NY. **120 S Olive Ave, Suite 614, West Palm Beach FL33401.**

Jewish Federation of Palm Beach County, Inc. Mem of CJF. Organized 1938. Pres: Jeanne Levy; Exec Dir: Norman J. Schimelman. **501 S Flagler Dr, Suite 305, West Palm Beach FL 33401 (305) 832–2120.**

Temple Beth El. Affiliated with United Syn of Am. Rabbi Howard J. Hirsch; Cantor Elaine Shapiro; Pres: Sam Wadler; Edu Dir: Ruth Levow; Youth Dir: Larry Goldberg. **2815 N Flagler Dr, West Palm Beach FL 33407 (305) 833–0339.**

Temple Beth Torah. Affiliated with UAHC. 70 mems. Pres: Ronnie Kramer. **1125 Jackpine St, West Palm Beach FL33411.**

Temple Israel. Affiliated with UAHC. 450 mems. Rabbi Irving B. Cohen; Pres: Richard Shugarman; Edu: Ceceil Tishman; Adm: Stephen J. Goldstein; Sisterhood Pres: Ann Small; Brotherhood Pres: Alfred Fink. **1901 N Flagler Dr, West Palm Beach FL 33407 (305) 833–8421.**

Temple Israel Library. For information on the Temple, see – Temple Israel, West Palm Beach, FL. **1901 N Flagler Dr, West Palm Beach FL 33407 (305) 833–8421.**

GEORGIA

Albany

Albany Hebrew Congregation. Affiliated with UAHC. 132 mems. Rabbis: David M. Zielonka, Charles B. Lesser; Pres: Ed Farkas Jr; Sisterhood Pres: A. Kraselsky. **PO Box 3288, Albany GA 31706 (912) 432–6536.**

Athens

Children of Israel. Affiliated with UAHC. 100 mems Rabbi Fred M. Raskind; Pres: Sanford Schwartz; Sisterhood Pres: Marsha Tesser. **Dudley Dr, PO Box 5694, Athens GA 30604 (404) 549–4192.**

Atlanta

Ahavath Achim Congregation. Affiliated with United Syn of Am. Rabbi Harry H. Epstein; Cantor Isaac Goodfriend; Pres: Dr Herbert R. Karp; Edu Dir: Dr Philip D. Wendkos; Prog Dir: Alan Teperow. **600 Peachtree Battle Ave NW, Atlanta GA 30327.**

American Jewish Press Association. 390 Courtland St NE, Atlanta GA 30308 (404) TR6–8249.

Anti-Defamation League of B'nai B'rith – SE Regional Office. Dedicated in purpose & prog to translating the Am heritage of democratic ideals into a way of life for all Am; to countering assaults on the safety, status, rights & image of J. For additional information, see – Anti-Defamation League of B'nai B'rith, New York City, NY. **805 Peachtree Rd NE, Suite 633, Atlanta GA 30308.**

Atlanta Bureau of Jewish Education. 1745 Peachtree Rd NE, Atlanta GA 30309 (404) 873–1248.

Atlanta Bureau of Jewish Education, Library. For information on the Ins, see – Atlanta Bureau of Jewish Education, Atlanta, GA. **1745 Peachtree Rd NE, Atlanta GA 30309 (404) 873–1248.**

Atlanta Hillel. Col youth activity ctr affiliated with Atlanta J Fed, B'nai B'rith Hillel Foun. To create a J col com on the various univ campuses within the Atlanta com; to serve as a pluralistic base for J stu activity. 6,500 mems. 3 employees. F 1971 by Atlanta J Fed on the Emory Univ campus; currently includes beyond Emory, GA State, GA Tech, Oglthorpe & various small schs within Atlanta. Facilties include small programming facility with kosher kitchen, sanctuary & meeting rm. Chr: Perry Brickman; Co-Chr: Robert Wilensky; Treas: Jay Kessler; Dir: Rabbi Daniel Allen; Prog Dir: Miriam Rosenbaum. **Drawer A, Emory Univ, Atlanta GA 30322 (404) 329–6490.**

Atlanta Jewish Federation, Inc. Mem of CJF. Organized 1905; reorganized 1967. Pres: Max Rittenbaum; Exec Dir: David I. Sarnat. **1753 Peachtree Rd NE, Atlanta GA 30309 (404) 873–1661.**

Beth Jacob Synagogue. Orthodox Syn affiliated with Union of Orthodox Syns of Am. To enhance Torah life & to further observance of classical Judaism by worship, study & cultural activities. Daily & Shabbath Servs; daily adult edu progs in Mishnah, Talmud, Bible, Heb language; summer day camp prog for chil; teen & preteen groups; Sr Citizen Group; counseling servs; Sisterhood; Brotherhood; volunteer Chevra Kadisha Society; presch; afternoon sch; library containing 5,000 vols (Judaica). 500 families; 1800 individuals. 8 employees. F 1948. Pub monthly mimeo bulletin, periodic magazine in conjunction with holidays. Facilities include two kosher kitchens, sanctuary seating 1000, chapel seating 250, gift shop, youth lounge, 8 classrms, presch facility rms, outdoor play area, succah area. First Chebra Kadisha Society volunteer group; first presch syn group; home hospitality for strangers in shul provided every Shabbath. Rabbi E. Feldman; Pres: Dr Michael Feinerman. **1855 Lavista Rd NE, Atlanta GA 30329.**

Beth Jacob Synagogue Library. Library contains 5,000 vols (Judaica). For information on Syn, see – Beth Jacob Synagogue, Atlanta, GA. **1855 Lavista Rd NE, Atlanta GA 30329.**

Congregation Or VeShalom. Rel Servs; Rel Sch fr K-10th grad Adult Edu courses range fr contemporary issues to philisophical/theological subjects; Sisterhood; OVS Social Club (plans functions & affairs on a social level); Youth Group for 18 yrs & older. 350 families. F in 1913 with a membership of less than 20 families. The present bldg, the third to be occupied by the Cong, was dedicated in 1971. The Sephardic Cooks (a cookbook); Bulletin. Facilities include a stained glass window sanctuary that seats 750, chapel, social hall, kosher kitchen, library, gift shop, classrooms. The Cong holds an annual Bond Dinner. Rabbi S. Robert Ichay; Pres: Joseph Cohen; Sisterhood Pres: Fran Landau; Sec: Mrs C. Rafshoon. **1681 N Druid Hills Rd NE, Atlanta GA 30319 (404) 633–1737.**

Harry Epstein School. Affiliated with Solomon Schechter Day Schs Assn. Prin: Rabbi Zvi Shapiro; Chr: Martin Kogon. **600 Peachtree Battle Ave NW, Atlanta GA 30327 (404) 351–7623.**

The Jewish Home of Atlanta. Nursing Home; mem of Am Assn of Home for the Aged, Am Health Care Assn, Natl Assn of J Home & Housing for the Aging; affiliated with Augusta, Charleston, Macon & Columbus J Feds. Routine nursing care; regular visits scheduled with family physician, podiatrist, dentist; physical & occupational therapists who work with individual residents to maintain level of functioning; Rel Servs every Fri evening & Sat morning, all High Holy Days. 1700 mems; 200 families; 120 individuals; Nursing Home 120 residents. 115 employees; approx 80 volunteers. F 1951 as 30 bed facility; expanded in 1957; moved to new 120 bed facility in 1971. Pub The Jewish Home News (quarterly). Facilities include kosher kitchen, sanctuary, gift shop, hobby shop, auditorium, physcial & occupational therapy, dental off, beauty shop. Exec Dir: Deborah Beards; Bd Pres: Sidney Feldman; Nursing Dir: Jean Allwood; Bkkeeper: Nancy Chastain; Asst Exec Dir: Lee Olitzsky. **3150 Howell Mill Rd NW, Atlanta GA 30327 (404) 351–8410.**

Jewish Vocational Service of the Atlanta Jewish Federation. Job-placement servs. To prepare clients for job placement through the teaching of effective job search. Referrals for placement; career search planning, including job market research techniques, dev of resumes & effective interviewing skills; edu & vocational counseling & testing for HS stu & adults. This prog enables clients to evaluate their interests, abilities & values in order to determine vocational objectives. For HS stu, this prog includes col selection & relevant topics associated with post HS planning, including financial aid. For adults, this prog is valuable for those persons seeking a career change, re-entering the world of work or in search of a career. Early in the 1970's the Gate City B'nai B'rith Lodge of Atlanta est a job placement serv staffed by volunteers. The Serv outgrew its volunteer status. As Soviet refugees moved to Atlanta, it became obvious that a professional off was needed. The Atlanta J Fed assumed responsibility for the prog which opened its doors on Dec 4, 1975. Chr: Herman Lischkoff; V Chr: Albert Beerman; Exec Dir: Dr Mark L. Fisher. **1745 Peachtree Rd NE, Atlanta GA 30309 (404) 876–5872.**

Southern Israelite. Periodical pub. **188 15th St NW, Atlanta GA 30357 (404) 876–8248.**

Temple Emanu-El. Affiliated with UAHC. 450 mems. Rabbi Donald Tam; Pres: Stephen L. Zisser; Edu: Barbara Schaffer; Sisterhood Pres: Jacki Granath. **120 Copeland Rd, Suite 254, Atlanta GA 30342 (404) 257–0633.**

Temple Sinai. Affiliated with UAHC. 463 mems. Rabbi Philip N. Kranz; Cantor Sidney Gottler; Pres: Arthur Heyman; Edu: Ben Walker; Adm: Enid Kam. **5645 NW Dupree Dr, Atlanta GA 30327 (404) 252–3073.**

Temple Sinai, Library. For information on the Temple, see – Temple Sinai, Atlanta, GA. **5645 Dupree Dr NW, Atlanta GA 30327 (404) 252–3073.**

The Temple, Hebrew Benevolent Congregation. Affiliated with UAHC. 1439 mems. Rabbis: Alvin M. Sugarman, Fred V. Davidow; Pres: William A. Frankel; Edu: Richard Becker; Adm: Mark R. Jacobson; Sisterhood Pres: Thelma Wolf; Brotherhood Pres: Nathan Radin. **1589 NE Peachtree Rd, Atlanta GA 30367 (404) 873–1731.**

Yeshiva High School of Atlanta GA. Five yr col prep HS, grades 8–12. To be a ctr for J living as well as for J learning a place where young J become knowledgeable about who they are & where they are going Jewishly. Gen & J studies; Kollel Talmud Prog;

Chess Club; Yeshiva Hi-Lites Girls Chorale; Stu Council which oversees special activities & social events; Natl Hon Soc; sports; How To Study seminar for stu in grade 8; field trips; holiday celebrations. Teaching staff of 13; guidance counselor; librarian. In 1969 a small group of people met to est a J day sch on the HS level. Concerned with the rise of intermarriage, J ignorance, assimilation among the young people, & the need to provide a follow up to elementary edu, this group started a new J edu venture in the Atlanta J com. In memory of the hundreds of European yeshivot destoyed in the Holocaust, the sch was named Yeshiva HS of Atlanta. In 1970 the Sch opened in a remodeled mansion & was the only yeshiva HS between Washington DC & Miami. In 1976 the Yeshiva moved to the Atlanta JCC. In 1980 the sch received accreditation fr the Southern Assn of Cols & Schs. Yearbook; newspaper. Facilities include two gymnasiums, racquetball ct, swimming pool, tennis cts & ball fields. Pres: Charles Lowenstein. **1745 Peachtree Rd NE, Atlanta GA 30309 (404) 873–1492.**

Augusta

Congregation Children of Israel, Walton Way Temple. Affiliated with UAHC. 140 mems. Rabbis: Chaim J. Wender, Norman M. Goldburg; Pres: Joseph Goldberg; Sisterhood Pres: Sandra Lewis. **3005 Walton Way, Augusta GA 30909 (404) 736–3140.**

Federation of Jewish Charities. Mem of CJF. Organized 1937. Pres: Jack Steinberg; Exec Dir: Jay Rubin. **PO Box 3251, Sibley Rd, Augusta GA 30904 (404) 736–1818.**

Bainbridge

Temple Beth El. Affiliated with UAHC. 11 mems. Pres: Melvin H. Nussbaum. **PO Box 476, Bainbridge GA 31717 (912) 432–6536.**

Brunswick

Temple Beth Tefillot. Affiliated with UAHC. 22 mems. Pres: Robert M. MIller; Sisterhood Pres: Haila Nathan. **PO Box 602, Brunskick GA 31521 (912) 265–7575.**

Cleveland

UAHC Coleman Camp Institute. Dir: Allan Solomon. **Route #3, Cleveland GA 30528 (404) 865–4111, 3521; 119 E Flagler St, Miami FL 33131 (305) 379–4553.**

Columbus

Jewish Welfare Federation of Columbus, Inc. Mem of CJF. Organized 1941. Pres: Maurice Kravtin; Sec: David Helman. **PO Box 1303, Columbus GA 31902 (404) 561–3953.**

Shearith Israel Synagogue. Affiliated with United Syn of Am. Rabbi Theodore Feldman; Pres: Kenneth Goldman MD. **2550 Wynnton Rd, PO Box 5515, Columbus GA 31906 (404) 323–1443.**

Temple Israel. Affiliated with UAHC. 182 mems. Rabbi Alfred L. Goodman; Pres: Franklin Star; Edu: Marlene Garnett; Sisterhood Pres: Lorraine Williams. **PO Box 5086, Columbus GA 31906 (404) 323–1617.**

Dalton

Temple Beth El. Affiliated with United Syn of Am. Rabbi Zvi Ettinger; Pres: Lester Goldberg. **Valley Dr, Dalton GA 30720 (404) 278–6798.**

Macon

Sherah Israel. Affiliated with United Syn of Am. Pres: David Frolich. **611 First St, Macon GA 31201 (912) 745–4571.**

Temple Beth Israel. Affiliated with UAHC. 98 mems. Rabbis: Ronald M. Goldstein, Harold L. Gelfman; Pres: Joyce O. Harp; Sisterhood Pres: Claire B. Sigal. **892 Cherry St, Macon GA 31201 (912) 745–6727.**

Marietta

Congregation Etz Chaim. Conservative Cong. To offer a J way of life to those in the suburbs N of Atlanta. Daily Rel Servs; Sisterhood; Men's Club; Youth Group; Adult Edu; Sun Sch Prog; Rel Sch; Heb Sch; Confirmation Class; Chanukah parties; Purim parties; Passover Seders; Art Auction; social events. Over 200 chil in the Rel Sch. A group of people sharing a common need joined hands to help each other. This was the beginning of Cong Etz Chaim. The first Shabbat Serv was held on Sept 26, 1975 in a small crowded rm. Fri Evening Servs were lead by lay mems of the Cong. In Oct of 1975 a meeting was held, a nominating cttee was selected, & a name for the Cong was chosen. The first priority for many of the mems was J edu. In Jan of 1976, 35 stu were registered in the Sun Sch which met by grade levels in various stu homes. Land for the syn was purchased in 1979 & arrangements were made to enter into a sharing arrangement with a Lutheran church. In Sept of 1981 the Cong moved into its permanent bldg. Voice of Chaim. The Cong has participated in rallies for Soviet J & solidarity marches for Is. Rabbi Shalom Lewis; Pres: David Tinkelman; 1st VP: Richard Smith; 2nd VP: George Pristach; Treas: Robert Schwartz; Fin Sec: Steven Berman; Corsp Sec: Gail Vexler; Rec Sec: Carol Weissman; Bd of Trustees: Stanley Fineman, Barry Forrest, Howard Gordon, Neil Leser, Harvey Olitsky, Herb Schwartz. **1190 Indian Hills Pkwy, Marietta GA 30067 (404) 973–0137.**

Rome

Temple Rodeph Sholom. Affiliated with UAHC. 23 mems. Pres: Murray Stein; Sisterhood Pres: L.J. Heyman; Brotherhood Pres: H. Wachstetter. **406 E First St, Rome GA 30161 (404) 291–6315.**

Savannah

Agudath Achim. Affiliated with United Syn of Am. Rabbi Richard S. Fagan; Pres: Paul Cranman; Exec Dir: Ellen Waldman; Youth Dir: Debra Shelton. **PO Box 14317, 9 Lee Blvd, Savannah GA 31406 (912) 352–4737.**

The Hebrew Community School of Savannah. Playschool for 3 yr olds; Nursery for 4 yr olds; K for 5 yr olds; Afternoon Heb Sch Prog – major subjects offered are Bible, Prayer, Heb Language, Customs & Ceremonies, Is & J Hist. Prior to 1954 J edu in Savannah administered by three congs – Reform, Conservative & Orthodox. In 1954, following a study of J edu facilities in Savannah by the Am Assn for J Edu, a Bureau of J Edu was est in Savannah. Under the direction of the Bureau, the Orthodox Savannah Hebrew Sch & the Conservative Agudas Achim Rel Sch were consolidated into one sch which became known as the Hebrew Com Sch of Savannah. Prin: Rabbi Lewis Koplowitz; Past Prin: Rabbi Moshe Pavlov, Rabbi Yehuda Silver, Rabbi Shalom Streicher, Rabbi Zev Silber, Rabbi Aaron Levin, Samuel Rosenberg. **5111 Abercorn St, Savannah GA 31405 (912) 355–8111.**

Savannah Jewish Council. Mem of CJF. Sponsors UJF Campaign. Organized 1943. Pres: Barnard Portman; Exec Dir: Stan Ramati. **5111 Abercorn St, Savannah GA 31405 (912) 355–8111.**

Temple Mickve Israel. Reform Temple affiliated with UAHC. To promote Reform J teachings. Goal of Archives Mus is to preserve & display hist of the J in Savannah & GA. Rel Servs – Fri evening & Sat mornings; Life Cycle Events; Sisterhood; Brotherhood; Youth Group; study groups & 9 Havurot groups; Rel Sch – Sun mornings; Archives Mus; library containing 5,000 vols (gen Judaica – collections of 3 rabbis). 275 families; 74 stu in grades K–9. 5 employees plus 10 mems of Rel Sch faculty; 6 volunteers. Pub Contact (9 per yr); Third to None (bk). Facilities include kitchen, social hall, gift shop, library, classrms, offs, sanctuary seating aprox 400. Listed in Natl Register of Historical Places. Rabbi Saul Rubin; Adm: Joan Schwartz. **20 E Gordon St, Savannah GA 31405 (912) 233–1547.**

Temple Mickve Israel Library. Library contains 5,000 vols (gen Judaica – collections of 3 rabbis). For information on the Temple, see – Temple Mickve Israel, Savannah, GA. **20 E Gordon St, Savannah GA 31405 (912) 233–1547.**

Valdosta

Valdosta Hebrew Congregation – Temple Israel. Affiliated with United Syn of Am. Rabbi Israel Dvorkin QC; Pres: Sidney Hartnig. **600 W Park, Valdosta GA 31601 (912) 242–2590.**

HAWAII

Honolulu

Congregation Sof Ma'arav. Affiliated with United Syn of Am. Pres: Gertrude Serata. **PO Box 11154, Honolulu HI 96828 (808) 923–5563.**

Hawaii Jewish Welfare Fund. 817 Cooke St, Honolulu HI 96813 (808) 536–7228.

Temple Emanu-El. Affiliated with UAHC. 380 mems. Rabbis: Arnold J. Magid, Julius J. Nodel; Pres: Leonard M. Rand; Edu: Shlomo Benderly; Sisterhood Pres: Elizabeth Solk. **2550 Pali Highway, Honolulu HI 96817 (808) 595–7521.**

IDAHO

Boise

Ahavath Israel Synagogue. Rel Servs; Com Seder; Purim, Chanukah, Is Independence Day, Tu B'Shevat, Yom HaShoah observances; Sun Sch. Est in 1948. Pres: Gayle Speizer; VP: Irv Littman; Sec: Pam Heuman; Treas: Ed Heuman; Elders: Martin Heuman, Joel Stone; Layman: Eddie Heuman. **2620 Bannock St, Boise ID 83702 (208) 343–6601.**

Congregation Beth Israel. Affiliated with UAHC. 48 mems. Pres: Howard Kinslinger; Edu: Daniel Stern. **PO Box 353, Boise ID 83701.**

Southern Idaho Jewish Welfare Fund. 1776 Commerce Ave, Boise ID 83705 (208) 344–3574.

Pocatello

Temple Emanuel, Pocatello Jewish Community Center. Reform Temple affiliated with UAHC. Temple for rel servs, cultural center for J People of SE Idaho; Rel Sch for various age groups weekly. 25 families. F 1947. Before 1947, in the 1920s, a tight group of citizens worked together & conducted High Holiday Servs but had no bldg; in 1923 B'nai B'rith Lodge #920 est. Pub Temple Topics (bi-monthly). Facilities include sanctuary, small library, kitchen, dining rm used for monthly dinners for membership, com Seder & other activities. Pres: Sy Block; VP: Eli Oboler; Sec/Treas: Myron Borges; Dir: Noah Klein. **PO Box 1175, Pocatello ID 83204 (208) 232–4785.**

ILLINOIS

Belleville

Jewish Federation of Southern Illinois. Mem of CJF. Includes Southeastern Missouri & Northwestern Kentucky. Organized 1941. Pres: Leonard Linkon; Exec Dir: Bruce J. Samborn. **6464 W Main, Suite 7A, Belleville IL 62223 (618) 398–6100.**

Bloomington

Moses Montefiore. Affiliated with UAHC. 73 mems. Rabbi Gershon Blackmore; Pres: J.P. Osnowitz; Sisterhood Pres: Cathy Bergman, Arlene Slan. **102 Robin Hood Lane, Bloomington IL 61701 (309) 662–3182.**

Buffalo Grove

Congregation Beth Judea. Conservative syn affiliated with United Syn of Am, rel sch participates with Chicago Bd of J Edu. Rel Servs; youth progs; rel edu for chil & adults; social action; support for Is; library containing 500 vols (Judaica). 300 families; 300 stu. 3 full-time employees; 10 part-time employees. F 1969. Pub The Word (monthly). Facilities include kosher kitchen, sanctuary seating 300, 8 classrms, gift shop. Rabbi Howard Lifshitz; Cantor Jay Wm Corn; Pres: Stephen Gold. **PO Box 763, Buffalo Grove IL 60090 (312) 634–0777.**

Centralia

Temple Solomon. Affiliated with UAHC. 26 mems. Rabbi Howard M. Folb; Pres: Richard Rudman. **c/o Mr L. Linkon, Route 161 E, Centralia IL 62801 (618) 532–8749.**

Champaign

Champaign-Urbana Jewish Federation. Mem of CJF. Mem Central Illinois Jewish Federation. Organized 1929. Pres: Ira Wachtel. **807 Haines Blvd, Champaign IL 61820 (217) 356–5907.**

Sinai Congregation. Affiliated with UAHC. 260 mems. Rabbi Isaac Neuman; Pres: Miles V. Klein; Edu: Nancy Tepper; Sisterhood Pres: Nancy Tepper. **3104 W Windsor Rd, Champaign IL 61820 (217) 352–8140.**

Sinai Congregation Library. For information on the Cong, see – Sinai Congregation, Champaign, IL. **3104 W Windsor Rd, Champaign IL 61820 (217) 352–8140.**

Chicago

Akiba-Schechter Jewish Day School. Affiliated with Solomon Schechter Day Schs Assn. Prin: Isador Levy; Chr: Dr Haim Reingold. **5200 S Hyde Park Blvd, Chicago IL 60615 (312) 493–8880.**

American Committee for Shaare Zedek in Jerusalem – MidWest Region. To help future generations meet the health needs of Jerusalem and Israel. Continuing support of century old hospital which moved in 1979 fr old quarters to new $55 million ultra modern medical complex overlooking Jerusalem. Offers total patient & community care. University affiliated teaching hospital contains main hospital building planned for more than 500 beds, emergency shelter, outpatient clinics, school of nursing, clinical labs, research ins, central library, facilities. Ensures the full observance of J tradition. Open to all irrespective of their rel, race or natl origin. **79 Monroe St, Chicago IL 60603 (312) 236–5778.**

American Friends of Hebrew University. To disseminate information regarding the Hebrew University in Jerusalem. **4001 West Devon Ave, Suite 208, Chicago IL 60646.**

American Jewish Congress. A J com relations agy; a democratic & rep instrument of the Am J com. To help build a J homeland, fight anti-Semitism & all forms of racism, foster a positive sense of J identity,

& work toward full equality in a free soc for all Am. Defends the rights of the J poor & provides them with free legal counsel; supports the Equal Rights Amendment & the Women's Agenda; provides adult J edu: exhib Heb & Yiddish language records, J bk fairs & study guides for chapter discussions on great J bks; encourages greater funding for J edu; works to secure free emigration, rel & cultural rights for Soviet J; maintains Overseas Travel Prog which offers 250 departures on person-to-person group tours to J coms in 40 countries; concentrates its efforts on bldg public understanding of Is needs for security, dignity & peace; fights the Arab boycott; est the Louise Waterman Wise Youth Hostel in Jerusalem which draws thousands of young people fr all over the world, & holds citizenship prog for immigrant chil, conducts pilot projs which bring Moslem, Christ & Druze youth in Is into contact with young J, & sponsors a special prog for the widows & chil of fallen Is soldiers (recent additions to the hostel include a garden pavilion & Steinberg Cultural Bldg); maintains Martin Steinberg Cultural Ctr in NY which serv as a meeting place for young J people engaged in J music & dance, painti & sculpture, poetry, fiction & film making. F in 1918 by Rabbi Stephen Wise, Justice Louis Brandeis & other distinguished Am J. The Council of Greater Chicago was formed in 1934. The Palestinians: What is Real & What is Politics; Boycott Report – periodic review of current devs affecting the boycott; Congress Monthly (a journal free to all mems); Judaism (quarterly). Pres: David V. Kahn; Chr Exec Cttee: Lia Green; VPs: Elaine Fox, Fred Glick, Helen Gould, Harry G. Hershenson, David Lerner; Treas: Melynda Lopin-Erlich; Rec Sec: Sol Brandzel; Corsp Sec: David Grossberg; Fin Sec: Lionel Brazen; Prog Sec: Gail Winston; Pres Women's Div: Helen Gould; Natl VPs: Hon Paul Annes, Hon Max A. Kopstein, Walter Roth; Governing Council: Irene Amstadter, Dr Howard Aronson, Lily Baum, Ruth Brandzel, Shaina Cohen, Jane Favish, Asher Feren, Marjorie Feren, Sarah Field, Elmer Gertz, Marvell Ginsburg, Marilyn Golden, Carol Green, Anita Hershenson, Milton Herst, Ernest Katzenstein, Marlise Katzenstein, Hope Keefe, Abe Kogan, Bertha Levine, Arnold S. Levy, Rabbi Ernest M. Lorge, Bertha Marks, Harry Miller, Oscar Miller, Lottie Minkus, Joseph Minsky, Ida Mutter, Mary Nesselson, Rose Newman, Rosalie Oberman, Irving Paley, Esther Perlowsky, Rabbi David Polish, Louis Rocah, Lillian Rochlin, Frieda Rosenblum, Molly Schiff, Alice Schimberg, Greta Schruber, Hugh J. Schwartzberg, Ethel Shapiro, Sara Shapiro, Florence Sherman, Saul Silverstein, Sarah Singer, Dr Klara Tulsky, Irving L. Wein, Evelyn Wigodner, Daris Wineberg, Julian Wineberg, Bernice Zlatin; Exec Dir: Shirley Sachs; Legal Counsel: Sylvia Neil; Exec Sec: Rivian Flack. **22 W Monroe, Chicago IL 60603 (312) 332–7355.**

American-Israel Chamber of Commerce & Industry, Inc – MidWest. A non-profit business org with chapters in Am cities & Is. To est close contact between business people in the US & business people in Is; to encourage investments in new & existing industries in Is; to serve as a clearing house for business, commerical & industrial information about the US & Is for the mutual benefit of both nations; to promote the exchange of servs & ideas on a mutually profitable basis. Periodic luncheon meetings on topics of interest; information & active assistance to those individuals interested in business opportunities including benefits for encouraging capital investment; subscription to Is Business; priority assistance for business trips in Is through Midwest off & the Is-Am Chamber of Commerce off in Tel Aviv. Mems include business & professional people including patent attorneys, mgmnt consultants, manufacturers, wholesalers, retailers, & civic leaders. Midwest chapter est in 1958. Chamber Newsletter. Pres: Lloyd Shefsky; VPs: Burton Benjamin, Irving Footlik, Seymour Mandel, Walter Roth, Ernest Shapiro, Ray Silverstein, Howard Wolf; Sec: Richard Laner; Treas: David Schwartz; Exec VP: Roberta Lipman; Bd of Dirs: Eric Baum, Marc Berkman, Sidney Boyar, Morris Braun, Jack Chizewer, Sanford Cohn, Lester Crown, Isaac Dekalo, Milton Diller, Haim Duvshani, Calvin Eisenberg, Raymond Epstein, Alvin Friedman, I.C. Friedman, Herbert Giblichman, Howard Gilbert, Gerald Goldberger, Melvin Gore, Alfred Gruen, Philip Kaplan, Bernard Katz, Abe Kogan, Ted Krasnow, Richard Laner, Elain Leibovitz, Fred Lev, Myron Levy, Maurice Lewis, Jack Mallon, Charles Meyerson, Casimir Mikrut, Byron Pollock, Maurice Raizes, Sorrel Rosin, William Samuels, Martin Sandler, Steve Schneider, Bernard Schwartz, David Schwartz, Howard Silverman, John Sinsheimer, Morton Skolnik, Philip Spertus, Arthur Stark, Manfred Steinfeld, Nicole Terry, Maynard Wishner, Howard Wittenberg, Marvin Wolfe, Ihor Wyslotsky, Simon Zunamon. **180 N Michigan Ave, Chicago IL 60601 (312) 641–2937.**

Anshe Emet Synagogue. Affiliated with United Syn of Am. Rabbi Seymour J. Cohen PhD; Cantor Moses J. Silverman; Asst Rabbi Lawrence M. Pinsker; Pres: Sidney J. Goldstein; Exec Dir: Ida Altman. **3760 Pine Grove Ave, Chicago IL 60613 (312) 281–1423.**

Anti-Defamation League of B'nai B'rith – Midwest Regional Office. Dedicated in purpose & prog to translating the Am heritage of democratic ideals into a way of life for all Am; to countering assaults on the safety, status, rights & image of J. For additional information, see – Anti-Defamation League of B'nai B'rith, New York City, NY. **222 W Adams St, Chicago IL 60606.**

The Ark. A multi serv com based agy; beneficiary of the Fed of Met Chicago. To take care of both the physical & spiritual needs of its clients; to give volunteers a chance to act out their concern for humanity within the framework of Torah J. Legal counseling & representation through a corps of 14 attorneys; emergency financial aid; temporary housing; Meals-on-Wheels; transportation; assistance in completing govt forms; assistance in moving; weekly Shabbat food basket delivery; client advocacy; short term counseling; circumcision servs; camp scholarships; the arrangement of a J divorce; funeral arrangements; psychiatric counseling; med/dental servs in which volunteer dentists offer servs ranging fr cleaning to orthodontia & bridge work, volunteer Drs give routine examinations & tests & make referrals to med specialists, volunteer pharmacists dispense drugs at the on-premise pharmacy, nurses visit home bound persons & assist Drs on a volunteer basis; social servs which include home & phone visitors, home shoppers, home aids, drivers on call; J cultural & edu activities including weekly class in Bible or Pirke Avot & a weekly Kiddush; rel servs; com wide Chanukah party; distribution of food packages & presents on Purim & Passover; social events, Sun progs, picnics, tickets to professional baseball games, luncheons hosted by area syns. Approximately 2,100 people are serviced annually. Six full time workers & two part time staff workers; 225 volunteers. Est in 1971 by a J Dr, a rabbi, & a young woman involved in research on the J poor. The org began as a free clin in a small med suite. In 1973 it moved to its present site. The present facility contains a reception area, offs, a social rm for a drop in ctr & other progs, three med examining rms, a dental off, a lab, a pharmacy, a conf rm & a food pantry. The Ark sponsors a thrift shop. Exec Dir: Arden J. Geldman. **3509 W Lawrence Ave, Chicago IL 60625 (312) 478–9600.**

B'nai B'rith Hillel Foundation at the University of Chicago. J com on campus. To create a pluralistic J com for stu & faculty at Univ of Chicago engaged in living J tradition & culture in all its manifold variety. Lectures; films; study groups; rel servs; social recreation progs; Is folk dancing; Shabbat dinners; Pesach meals; holiday celebrations; counseling servs; research assistance; employment assistance; Is progs; hosp visitation; library containing 6,000 vols (Judaica & Hebraica). 1600 J stu at Univ of Chicago. 2 full-time employees, 1 part-time employee; volunteers. F 1938. In 1943 occupied present bldg. Pub Program Notes (3 times a yr). Facilities include library, meeting rms, classes, kosher kitchen, offs. Dir: Rabbi Daniel I. Leifer; Chr: Prof Harold Wechsler. **5715 S Woodlawn Ave, Chicago IL 60637 (312) 752–1127.**

B'nai B'rith Hillel Foundation at the University of Chicago Library. Library contains 6,000 vols (Judaica & Hebraica). For information on the Ins, see – B'nai B'rith Hillel Foundation at the University of Chicago, Chicago IL. **5715 S Woodlawn Ave, Chicago IL 60637 (312) 752–1127.**

The Bet Din. The rel law legislative authority of Conservative J in the midwestern US, & of the Rabbinical Assembly. Grants rel divorces, conducts conversions, renders decisions on J legal matters. The Bet Din is at the disposal of unaffiliated J who require its servs; consulted by the Midwest media concerning J law. F in 1948. The presiding Rabbi is solely responsible for all the activities & decisions of the Bet Din although he consults with his colleagues. Presiding Rabbi: Dr David Graubart; Exec Sec: Rabbi Dr Ephraim H. Prombaum; Exec VP: Rabbi Dr Morris Fishman. **5718 N Drake Ave, Chicago IL 60659 (312) 588–4252.**

Bet Yoatz Library Services. 6247 N Francisco, Chicago IL 60659.

Board of Jewish Education of Metropolitan Chicago. The central agy for J edu in the Chicago met area. To provide J schs of all types with a variety of special servs. Music; Early Childhood Ctrs; family edu; Heb language; curricula & pedagogic resources; teachers training; J & Heb studies; com BJE HS of J studies; Shabbatonim; Midrashet Kayitz Summer Sch (Summer Prog in Is); Ins for the Training of Master Teachers; Ins for Training of Lay Leadership in J Schs; Ins for Post Confirmands; Media Prog, Multi Media Ctr & Media Coord Training Seminar. Created new series of computer validated Heb language tests distributed nationally by the Am Assn for J Edu; recruits & places teachers & principals; sets standards for teacher & principal certification & licensing; provides pensions, life insurance & med coverage for principals & full-time teachers; pub instructional materials & textbooks; library with 19000 vols. Serves 16,000 J sch chil in 71 sch units. Est in 1923; BJE changed location in Mar of 1982. Kivunim; Family Education Newsletter; Early Childhood Newsletter; pub Zemer which is a music edu newsletter & Or V'Kol, a media edu newsletter. The BJE pioneered a new concept in the delivery of servs to J schs – the Servs Agreement approach. Pres: Sherwin B. Pomerantz; Exec VP: Rachel Greenbaum; VPs: Sima Browne, Jean Comar, Harold Levine, Dr Curtis C. Melnick, Phyllis Neiman. **618 S Michigan Ave, Chicago IL 60605.**

Bureau of Jewish Employment Problems. 220 S State St, Chicago IL 60604 (312) 663–9470.

Camp Ramah. Eight week camp under supervision of JTS. Emphasizes a complete J living situation. Dir: Rabbi David Soloff. **72 E 11th St, Chicago IL 60605 (312) 939–2393.**

Central Synagogue of the South Side Hebrew Congregation. Affiliated with United Syn of Am. Rabbi Dr Irving A. Weingart; Cantor Moses Schwimmer; Pres: Sydney H. Slone; Exec Dir: Sylvia Wippman. **30 E Cedar St, Chicago IL 60611 (312) 787–0450.**

The Chicago Board of Rabbis. Rabbinic group of Conservative, Orthodox, Reconstructionist & Reform rabbis. To interpret positive J in all its phases. Acts as the central agy for the production & broadcasting of all local J rel radio & TV progs. A Chaplaincy Cttee gives comfort, spiritual guidance & direction to J patients, residents & inmates of hosps, mental ins, homes for the aged, prisons & training schs throughout the state of IL. F in 1893 as the Chicago Rabbinical Assn. The prog of the Bd is made possible through the support of the J Fed of Met Chicago, by congregational allocations & by contributions made through the Friends of the Bd of Rabbis. The Chicago Bd of Rabbis participates in civic & com affairs together with reps of other faiths, & is recognized as the rel spokesman for the J com. Pres: Rabbi Joseph Tabachnik; VPs: Rabbi Harold P. Smith, Rabbi Karl Weiner, Rabbi Lawrence H. Charney; Sec: Rabbi Elliot H. Einhorn; Treas: Rabbi Joseph Strauss; Exec VP: Rabbi Mordecai Simon. **618 S Michigan Ave, Chicago IL 60605 (312) 427–5863.**

The Chicago Jewish Historical Society. To collect, preserve & exhibit memorabilia & materials of every kind pertaining to the settlement, hist & life of J & the J com of met Chicago IL; to conduct edu progs, encourage study & research & disseminate information pertaining to the settlement, hist & life of Jews & the J com of met Chicago IL. Maintaining archives collection; taping & transcribing oral hists; preparing exhibits; operating narrated bus tours of historic areas of Chicago; presenting speakers, panels, progs to the gen public on pertinent topics; holding workshops related to local J hist. 500 mems; 1 local group. F 1977 in the aftermath of the nation's Bicentennial celebration which included a major exhibit on the Am J experience, My Brother's Keeper, at the Mus of Sci & Ind. Some of the founders of the CJHS were docents at that exhibit. Pub Society News (quarterly); The German-Jewish Emigration of the 1930s & its Impact on Chicago (bk). Pres: Rachel B. Heimovics; VP: Doris Minsky; F Pres: Muriel Robin; Treas: Norman Schwartz; Sec: Ruth Brandzel. **618 S Michigan Ave, Chicago IL 60635 (312) 663–5634.**

Chicago Jewish Post & Opinion. Periodical pub. **6350 N Albany, Chicago IL60659.**

Chicago Rabbinical Council. An org of Orthodox Am trained & ordained rabbis. To promote the tenets of Torah J; to effect disciplined & organized J communal responsibility in all phases of the observances & practices of J. Serves as an assn for the clearance of ideas, problems & suggestions that may aid each rabbi in the performance of his rabbinical functions, & a clearing agy for the dissemination of authoritative information on the various problems of J rel living; reps the rel J com in the civic & social sense. Col Youth Servs est & endows a kosher kitchen on the campus of the Univ of IL at Champaign, serves J youth on various col campuses in Chicago & IL; Orthodox Ecclesiastical Ct issues J divorces, conversions, hears & resolves questions on J law & disputes; the Council certifies & supervises products as to their kashruth & Passover permissibility; endorses various caterers, hotels & bakeries. Thy People Shall Be My People; Parting of the Ways; At Thirteen – Religious Responsibilities; The Soul Returns To God Who Gave It; Kiddushin – Holy Matrimony; A Little Sanctuary; The Covenant of Abraham; Righteousness & Good Works; In The Priest's Office; Right Before The King; The Appointed Seasons of the Lord; An Everlasting Covenant; Passover in the Jewish Home. Pres: Rabbi Jack D. Frank; VPs: Rabbi Joseph Dietcher, Rabbi Irwin R. Pollock, Rabbi Solomon Rockove; Rec Sec: Rabbi Don Rosenbaum; Fin Sec: Rabbi Victor Amster; Treas: Rabbi David Montrose; Chr of Exec: Rabbi Isaac Mayefsky; Exec Sec: Rabbi Nathan I. Weiss; Kashruth Adm: Rabbi Benjamin Shandalov. **3525 W Peterson Ave, Chicago IL 60659 (312) 588–1600.**

Chicago Region Maccabi Association. 6326–28 N California Ave, Chicago IL 60659.

Chicago Sinai Congregation. Affiliated with UAHC. 750 mems. Pres: Howard A. Sulkin; Edu: Susan H. Shapiro; Adm: Carol Kallish; Sisterhood Pres: Dorothy Heyman, Elinore Klein; Brotherhood Pres: Joseph H. Woolf III. **5350 S Shore Dr, Chicago IL 60615 (312) 288–1600.**

Chicago Zionist Federation. Umbrella org of all Chicago com Zionist orgs; also serves as the regional off for the Midwestern US. Affiliated with Am Zionist Fed. Specializes in edu & aliyah related activities; sponsors a Scholar-in-Residence Prog; maintians Zionist Midrasha, Aliyah Council. Est in 1970. Sponsors annual Yom Haatzmaut & Yom Yerushalayim festivals. Pres: Rabbi William Frankel; Chr of the Bd: Miriam Soboroff; VPs: Martha Binn,

Jack Gilron, Leon Goldwater, Sidney Letush, Oscar Miller, Judy Telman; Fin Sec: Israel Steiger; Treas: Nathan Shapiro; Sec: Phyllis Sutker; Exec Dir: Dr Judith Rae Ross. **220 S State St, Chicago IL 60604 (312) 922–5282.**

Congregation B'nai David-Shaare Zedek. Conservative Syn. This house of worship is a merger of Budlong Conservative J Cong & Humboldt Blvd Cong in 1959, & Logan Square Syn which became affiliated in 1977. Pres: Allen Schecher; Co-Chr Bd: Norman Gottlieb, Lawrence Guysenir, Leonard Rotblat; VP: Mrs Henry Newman; Treas: Morris Wadro; Rec Sec: Allan Schechter; Corsp Sec: Hy Kutchin; Cantor Moses Rontal. **2508 W Fitch Ave, Chicago IL 60625 (312) 764–8825.**

Congregation B'nai Zion. Affiliated with United Syn of Am. Rabbi Haim Kemelman; Pres: Wilbur Millard. **6759 N Greenview Ave, Chicago IL 60626 (312) 465–2161.**

Congregation Beth Sholom Ahavas Achim. Orthodox Syn. To maintain & provide a place of worship; to be a ctr for J edu; to devote itself to Torah, work & charity. Daily, Shabbat & Holiday Servs; daily & Shabbat Gemorah classes; Sisterhood. When the Chicago J com moved N, two W Side syns, the Crozer Beth Sholom & the Ahavas Achim, merged, & in 1958 est the present Cong on Chicago's N Side. The only cong in the area that has three daily servs. Since 1962 the Syn has held yearly Is Bond Dinners. The Syn has housed the Girls Branch of the Ida Crown J Academy & the Brisk Yeshsiva. At present, the Yeshiva Migdal Torah meets at the syn. Rabbi Victor Amster; Pres: Seymour Pollack; VP: Rabbi Abraham DeKoven; Fin Sec: Norman Radloff; Treas: Rabbi Rueben Dietz; Rec Sec: Paul Brombreg. **5665 N Jersey Ave, Chicago IL 60659 (312) CO7–9055.**

Congregation Ezra-Habonim. Affiliated with United Syn of Am. Rabbi Dr Shlomo D. Levine; Cantor Henry H. Danziger; Pres: Fred W. Sinay. **2620 W Touhy Ave, Chicago IL60645 (312) 743–0154.**

Congregation Kol Ami. Affiliated with UAHC. 300 mems. Rabbi Arnold Kaiman; Pres: Manuel J. Robbins; Adm: Rickie Jacobs. **233 E Erie St, Chicago IL 60611 (312) 644–6900.**

Congregation Rodfei Zedek. Affiliated with United Syn of Am. Sr Rabbi Ralph Simon; Rabbi Vernon Kurtz; Cantor Abraham Lubin; Pres: Irving Paley; Exec Dir: Sandra Freedkin; Youth Dir: Ruth Stern. **5200 Hyde Park Blvd, Chicago IL 60615 (312) 752–2770.**

Congregation Rodfei Zedek Library. 5200 Hyde Park Blvd, Chicago IL 60615 (312) 752–2770.

Congregation Shaare Tikvah. Conservative Syn affiliated with United Syn of Am. To foster the observance of traditional Conservative J. Adult & Family Edu; communal activities catering to all persons of the J faith fr K to Sr; Ctr for Heb Edu, for chil 3–7, Heb Rel Sch for chil 8–12 yrs; Chug Tefillah for day sch stu; Rel Servs 3 times daily; David Sher Library; Men's Club which is affiliated with Natl Foun of J Men's Clubs; Sisterhood. 135 in Men's Club; 335 in Sisterhood. Est in 1942. The main sanctuary seats 1,300 people. The sanctuary stained glass windows are show-places in the city of Chicago. Lissner Hall has a fully equipped stage. Facilities include dairy & meat kosher kitchens. Rabbi Howard A. Addison; Rabbi Emeritus Dr Morris A. Gutstein; Hazzan: Donald N. Roberts; Sch Prin: Jeffrey Winter; Pres: Neil Handelman; VPs: Alvin I. Greenberg, Solomon Gutstein, Larry Prentiss, Marvin Rudnick, Russell Weinberg, Pinchas Zaid; Treas: Harry Kudesh; Fin Sec: Esther Kaplan; Corsp Sec: Dorothy Dreyfus; Rec Sec: Terrie Ship-Horowitz; Co-Chr of Bd: Paul R. Chapman, Eli Friedlander; V Chr of Bd: Jerome Sklansky; Sisterhood Pres: Ruth Appel; Men's Club Pres: Leo Sokol; Chever Pres: Daniel Seltzer; Efsharut Pres: Terrie Ship-Horowitz. **5800 N Kimball Ave, Chicago IL 60659 (312) KE9–2202.**

Drexel Home Temple. Affiliated with UAHC. 130 mems. Rabbi Israel Zoberman; Pres: Batya Dubovik; Adm: Bernard S. Pomerantz. **6140 S Drexel Ave, Chicago IL 60637 (312) 643–2384.**

Emanuel Congregation. Affiliated with UAHC. 886 mems. Rabbis: Herman E. Schaalman, Michael A. Weinberg; Cantor Robert Handwerger; Pres: Lawrence I. Falstein; Adm: Cecile Rose; Sisterhood Pres: Lucille Kartun; Brotherhood Pres: Gerald I. Bauman. **5959 N Sheridan Rd, Chicago IL 60660 (312) 561–5173.**

Free Friends of Refugees of Eastern Europe. An edu & social serv agy that serves Russian J Immigrants; grant recipient of the J Fed funded through the J United Fund. To re-introduce J to the recently arrived Russian J immigrants. Sponsors Summer in Is Prog; for Russian immigrants sponsors J content Russian language radio prog which provides music, information & edu; places of chil in J day schs & HS; provides bilingual counselors who act as interpreters between the parents & sch to smooth out problems; provides tutors & teachers to J schs without charge; maintains library of 2,000 bks in the FREE Ctr; conducts mass holiday celebrations including com Passover seders conducted by

Russian speaking rabbis with Russian language hagadas, Chanukah & Purim celebrations with gifts & holiday kits; sends Russian chil to J day & overnight camps; arranges Bar Mitzvah preparation in syns & prepares a celebration with food & music; performs circumcisions in the hosp with mass party held yearly for boys, parents & relatives; arranges funerals; provides brides & grooms with a chupah, rabbi & wedding celebration with food & music, & the bride is given Sabbath candlesticks; maintains Missionary Alert (FREE sends staff mems to confront the missionaries); provides summer jobs for young immigrants; distributes Passover food; gives talis, tefilin & prayerbk upon request; holds social gatherings, lectures & concerts; helps sponsor Shabbatons with syn & individual Am families; maintains Distribution Ctr where immigrants can get clothing & household needs; provides social servs; welcomes new immigrants with Sabbath candlesticks & a hand written Mezuza; holds sr citizen rap sessions; provides counseling servs, interest free loans & emergency financial aid; holds daily TESL English classes; acts as a furniture referral serv; finds jobs for the elderly; provides Outreach Prog to the sick & elderly in homes & hosps. Est about 1973. Shalom (Russian language, J content newspaper). FREE maintains a re-sale shop. Exec Dir: Rabbi Shmuel Notik; Pres: Mrs Yitzchok Kosofsky; Dir of Finance & Com Relation: Martha Binn; Bd of Dirs: Saul Binder, Mr & Mrs George Bornstein, Mr & Mrs Morris Futorian, Mr & Mrs Lawrence M. Friedman, Rabbi & Mrs Colman Ginsparg, Mr & Mrs Sy Handwerker, Dr & Mrs Chaim Hecht, Mr & Mrs Marvin Hoffen, Mr & Mrs Marvin Holland, Mr & Mrs Gerald Kaufman, Dr Leonard Kranzler, Rabbi & Mrs Joel Lehrfield, Mr & Mrs Abe Matthew, Dr & Mrs Stanton Polin, Dr & Mrs Semyon Meerkov, Mr & Mrs Sidney Meystel, Mr & Mrs Irving Reichstein, Mr & Mrs Lawrence Schwartz, Mr & Mrs Menard Schwartz, Mr & Mrs Nathan Shapiro, Rabbi & Mrs Harold Shusterman, Cantor & Mrs Wilhelm Silber, Dr & Mrs Vladimir Tzesis, Mr & Mrs Fred P. Tasner, Rev & Mrs Noah Wolff; Moes Chittim Liaison: Zvi Kurs. **Off & Social Ctr: 6418 N Greenview, Chicago IL (312) 274–5123; mailing add: 3756 W Devon Ave, Lincolnwood IL 60645.**

Government of Israel Trade Center. Dev of trade relations between US & Is. For additional information, see – Government of Israel Trade Center, New York City, NY. **174 N Michigan Ave, Chicago IL 60601 (312) 332–2160.**

Hadassah. Chicago Chapter of The Women's Zionist Org of Am. Conducts edu progs in US; provides health, edu & com servs; provides basic J edu as a background for intelligent & creative J living in Am; built & maintains in Jerusalem the Hadassah-Hebrew Univ Med Ctr with campuses at Kiryat Hadassah for healin teaching & research including Med Sch, Henrietta Szold Sch of Nursing, Sch of Dentistry; & an occupational therapy ctr, rehabilitation ctr & gen hosp on Mt Scopus; maintains a network of clins & com health ctrs; operates the Hadassah Com Col, Seligsberg / Brandeis Comprehensive Co-edu HS & Vocational Guidance Ins in Jerusalem; serves as principal agy in US for support of youth aliyah villages & day-care ctrs for immigrants & deprived youth; participates in J Natl Fund land purchase & reclamation progs; sponsors Hashachar – Zionist movement for Am youth fr ages 9–25; provides a residence for Am youth who come to Is for work & study. Over 9,000 women mems; has the same natl status as a region. F in 1913. Hadassah Magazine; Hadassah Headlines; study guides. Pres: Leah Stern Reicin; VPs: Lillian Feirstein, Arlene Freedman, Ada Rabinowitz Pearl Begun, Helen Gore, Gertrude Wexler. **111 N Wabash Ave, Chicago IL 60602 (312) 263–7473.**

Ida Crown Jewish Academy. Orthodox co-ed HS; mem State of IL, N Central Assn. Excellent col prep sch for both gen & J edu. Full curriculum & J observance; full counseling servs; diagnostic testing; ongoing edu research; special experiential learning prog for srs; intensive mesifta prog for boys; intensive medrasha progs for girls; J studies prog; preparatory progs; athletic progs; library containing 7000 vols (J & gen). 310 stu grades 9–12. 45 employees. F 1942. Pub sch paper (quarterly); annual yearbook. Facilities include kosher kitchen, shul, gym, woodshop, home economics rm, typing rm, labs (for chemistry, biology, physics). Prin: Rabbi Tsvi Blanchard PhD; Asst Prin: Rabbi Norman Goldberg; Adm: Abraham Buckman; Head of Counseling: Aryeh Merzel; Counselor: Judy Jackson; Registrar: Isa Mouscher. **2828 W Pratt Ave, Chicago IL 60645 (312) 973–1450.**

Ida Crown Jewish Academy, Library. Library contains 7000 vols (J & gen). For information on the Academy, see – Ida Crown Jewish Academy, Chicago IL. **2828 W Pratt Ave, Chicago IL 60645 (312) 973–1450.**

Israel Aliyah Center. 75 E. Wacker Dr, Rm 2104, Chicago IL 60601 (312) 332–2709.

Israel Government Tourist Office. 5 S Wabash Ave, Chicago IL 60603 (312) 782–4306.

Jewish Federation of Metropolitan Chicago. Mem of CJF. Organized 1900. Pres: Herbert S.

Wander; Exec Dir: Dr Steven B. Nasatir. **One S Franklin St, Chicago IL 60606 (312) 346–6700.**

Jewish United Fund of Metropolitan Chicago. Mem of CJF. Organized 1968. Pres: Herbert S. Wander; Exec Dir: Dr Steven B. Nasatir. **One S Franklin St, Chicago IL 60606 (312) 346–6700.**

Kam Isaiah Israel Congregation. Dual commitment to a dynamic living J & to social justice for all. Sabbath, Holiday Servs & celebrations; Rel Sch; Heb Sch; Confirmation Dept; Adult Edu, Bible & Talmudic literature classes, Heb instruction, lectures, Scholar-in-Residence Weekends; Sisterhood; Brotherhood; Chavurat Prog – a group of friends who gather together for a variety of purposes including J study & celebration; Youth Group; Social Action Prog which raises money & supports natl & intl protest groups on pol & social issues which affect J & other groups oppressed by injustice & intolerance. 700 mem families; 200 stu in Rel Sch & Heb Sch. 17 Heb & Rel Sch teachers. The oldest J cong in the Midwest, the Syn is a merger of several congs – K.A.M. f in 1847 by the first J settlers in Chicago, & Isaiah Is, a descendent of Beth Sholom, f in 1852. The Byzantine style sanctuary, built in 1924, was designated a Chicago landmark in 1977 & a natl landmark in 1978. A thirft shop is operated & supported by temple volunteers. The Sisterhood operates a gift shop, organizes guest speakers progs, a camp scholarship prog & a leadership workshop. The Brotherhood organizes various charitable & communal activities including the Cong blood drive. Rabbi Arnold Jacob Wolf; Rabbis Emeriti: Hayim Goren Perelmuter, Morton M. Berman; Cantor, Music Dir: Max Janowski; Temple Adm: Ilene H. Herst; Dir of Edu: Dr Alan Gorr; Pres: Howard Siegal; VPs: Marlene Richman, Mae Simon, Michael Schneiderman; Sec: Stephen Rubin; Treas: Frances Grossman. **1100 E Hyde Park Blvd, Chicago IL 60615 (312) 924–1234.**

Menorah Temple. Affiliated with UAHC. 250 mems. Rabbi Joseph M. Strauss; Cantor David Politzer; Pres: Irving Pearlman; Edu: Harry Hershman; Sisterhood Pres: Mollie Motch; Brotherhood Pres: Richard Jaffe. **2800 W Sherwin Ave, Chicago IL 60645 (312) 761–5700.**

Michael Reese Hospital & Medical Center. Affiliated with Pritzker Sch of Med of the Univ of Chicago, & with the J Fed of Met Chicago. To provide progressive med care to all patients regardless of rel, race or natl origin. Cora B. & L.E. Block Diagnostic Radiology Dept possesses most advanced x-ray, ultrasound & computerized axial tomographic equipment; Cardiac Surgery Prog is staffed by highly trained surgical teams & a Cardiac Surgery Intensive Care Unit equipped with computerized bedside monitoring; Cardiovascular Ins provides facilities for the diagnosis & therapy of cardiac disease; Dysfunctioning Chil Ctr evaluates & treats chil with multiple handicaps. Major divs, clinics & servs include: Diabetes Teachi Servs; Div of Endocrinology & Metabolism; Fertility Unit; Div of Gastroenterology; Div of Hematology-Oncology; Hemoglobin Clin; Hemophilia Ctr; Infections Control Prog; Infectious Diseases Div; Nerve Block Servs; Neural-Muscular Disabilities Prog; Dept of Neurology; Nuclear Med Div; Dept of Obstetrics & Gynecology; Dept of Ophthalmology; Oral Surgery Section; Dept of Orthopedic Surgery; Pediatric Endocrinology Prog; Pediatric Kidney Disease Prog; Perinatal Ctr; Peripheral Vascular Surgery Prog; Div of Plastic Surgery; Prenatal Screening Prog; Pritzker Chil Psychiatric Unit; Psychosomatic & Psychiatric Ins; Div of Pulmonary Med; Dept of Radiation Oncology; Dept of Rehabilitation Med; Renal Div; Rheumatology Prog; David T. Siegal Ins for Communicative Disorders est as a state ctr for the evaluation of deaf/blind chil & for psychiatric servs to deaf adults & chil & their families; Dept of Social Work; Dept of Special Servs for Patients at Reese; Spinal Deformities Prog; edu progs in the Michael Reese Sch of Health Sci including progs in undergrad & grad med edu, nursing, allied health professions, continuing physician edu, patient edu, research & sci training; clin & basic research which makes the Ins the natl ctr for the study of kidney stones diabetes & sickle cell disease; Babette & Emanuel Mandel Clin est as an outpatient diagnostic & treatment ctr; Wexler Clin; Psychiatric Clin; Dental Clin; Acute Care Area; Blood Ctr. Support & com programs include: free med care given for Russian J immigrants; Health Plan which offers comprehensive med care; health care resource & consultancy for the Council for J Elderly; outpatient & ambulatory servs for residents of the Drexel Home in Hyde Park; recreation prog for chil with renal disorders; joint prog between Michael Reese & the Hyde Park JCC which offers a variety of progs for Michael Reese staff, patients & residents of the com; med servs to adjacent coms. 32,000 patients are admitted to the 1,000 bed hosp each yr; 266,000 visits are made to the outpatient specialty progs; 74,000 visits are made to the emergency rm. Staff of 5,000 including: 600 med staff; 300 interns, residents & fellows; 1,500 nurses & nursing personnel; 450 volunteers. The hosp opened in 1881 with 60 beds & five staff physicians. The Nursing Sch opened in 1890. In 1907 the hosp was rebuilt to accommodate increasing patient loads. In 1913 Nelson Morris Research Ins & the Sarah Morris Chil Hosp were built & dedicated. During the 1920's & 1930's Mandel Clin, Florsheim

Library, & Meyer House were added. After WWII a major expansion of facilities & servs was undertaken. The Women's Bd sponsors the volunteer prog in which 450 volunteers serve in 40 various areas, operates the Gift Shop & Green Spot flower shop; the Servs League operates the Thrift Shop; the Med Research Ins Council raises funds for research progs; the Council of Contributing Orgs, an assn of com orgs, supports the work of the Med Ctr. 27 bldgs & four parks cover the Hosp's 45 acre campus. Offs of the Med Staff – Pres: Dr J. Robert Buchanan; Sr VP for Professional & Academic Affairs: Dr Richard H. Kessler; Sr VP for Corporate & Administrative Affairs: Morris Spector; VP Nursing: Heidi Beck; VP for Information Systems: Burnell Furstenau; VP for Dev: Charles H. Gold; VP for Finance: John R. Gunn; VP for Human Resources: Dean L. Kimmerly; VP for Professional Affairs: Dr Charles H. Lawrence; VP for Facilities & Support Servs: William R. Miller; VP for Academic Affairs: Dr Martin A. Swerdlow; Offs of the Professional Staff – Pres: Dr Gerald W. Sobel; VP: Dr James Sheinin; Sec-Treas: Dr Richard Evans; Bd of Trustees – Chr: Frank D. Mayer Jr; V Chr: Sidney Epstein; Treas: Lee Jennings; Sec & Gen Counsel: Samuel R. Rosenthal; Asst Sec: Daniel R. Swett. **2929 S Ellis Ave, Chicago IL 60616 (312) 791–2330.**

National Council of Jewish Women. Women's volunteer org. Dedicated in the spirit of J to advancing human welfare & the democratic way of life. Activities are organized around five prog priorities: women's issues, chil & youth, aging, J life, & Is. Women's Issues – major concerns are: ratification of the Equal Rights Amendment, protection of the right of every women to have access to safe & legal abortion, removal of gender related discrimination in all areas of life, provision of edu progs on the prevention of domestic violence & treatment for its victims, widow to widow counseling & progs for single parents. Chil & Youth – primarily concerned with: the rights, needs & quality of life of the nation's chil & youth; juvenile justice, especially the treatment of adolescent girls; foster care; variety of projs that support servs to the young people in their coms; (the Council is deeply committed to advocacy efforts needed to effectively change the way chil are treated under the law). Is – carries out numerous edu & social welfare progs in Is; has long been a strong advocate for the State of Is; furthers major proj in Is which is the Research Ins for Innovation in Edu (part of The Heb Univ Sch of Edu). J Life – places emphasis on: J edu & the problems of Soviet J; J edu progs for individuals of various ages & interests designed to assist people in exploring their understanding of & attitudes toward J & rekindling their interest in their rel; involvement in the resettlement of Soviet J immigrants & in advocacy on behalf of those J who are refused permission to leave the USSR. Aging – primary focus is on dev & support of legislation on behalf of older adults, day ctrs, housing for the elderly, adult edu, enrichment progs, volunteer placement progs, sheltered employment projs, nutrition & transportation servs, multipurpose ctrs, nursing homes, ombudsman progs & self training for & by the elderly. **53 W Jackson, Chicago IL 60604 (312) 663–9400.**

Ner Tamid Congregation. Affiliated with United Syn of Am. Rabbi Samuel Klein; Cantor David Brandhandler; Pres: Sydney H. Shapiro; Youth Dir: Thema Freidner. **2754 W Rosemont Ave, Chicago IL 60659 (312) 465–6090.**

Norman Asher & Helen Asher Library – Spertus College of Judaica. To provide information & bks on Judaica & Hebraica for Col's stu & gen com. Reference; lending; photocopying; library containing 72,000 vols (Judaica & Hebraica). F 1925; formerly called Leaf Library. Dir: Richard W. Marcus; Librarians: Dan Sharon, Robbin Saltzman; Periodicals Asst: Chava Feferman; **618 S Michigan Ave, Chicago IL 60605 (312) 922–9012.**

Park View Home. Affiliated with United Syn of Am. Rabbi David Graubart; Pres: Max Mendelson. **1401 S California Ave, Chicago IL 60622 (317) 278–6420.**

Pioneer Women – Na'amat. The training & edu of the Is woman & her family so that each can be best equipped to lead productive lives. For additional information, see – Pioneer Women Na'amat, New York City, NY. **220 S State St, Chicago IL 60604 (312) 922–3736.**

Schwab Rehabilitation Hospital. Affiliated with Mount Sinai Med Ctr of Chicago & Rush Presbyterian Med Ctr. To enable the patient to reach a maximum level of health & independence, & return to a productive life. Occupational therapy; physical therapy; vocational servs; communicative disorder therapy; psychological therapy & counseling; Social Work & Therapeutic Recreaction Depts; pediatric rehabilitation; outreach servs; Inpatient & Outpatient Clins; Rheumatology, Prosthetic, Pediatric, Orthotic, Cerebral Palsy Clins. Rehabilitation teams led by physiatrists (physicians specializing in physical med & rehabilitation), & including specialists in physical, occupational, speech & language therapy; nurses; psychologists & social workers; staff of consulting physicians specializing in cardiology, dermatology, neurosurgery, ophthalmology, orthopedics, otolaryngology, peripheral vascular disease, plastic surgery, psychiatry, radiology, rheumatology & urology. F in 1912 as a ten bed convalescent home. In 1956 the hosp, then called Rest Haven, became the first fully licensed & accredited physical med & rehabilitation hosp in the Midwest. PR: Sheila Atlas. **1401 S California Blvd, Chicago IL 60608 (312) 522–2010.**

Sentinel. Periodical pub. **323 S Franklin St, Chicago IL 60606 (312) 663–1163.**

Spertus College of Judaica. Four yr Liberal arts col offering a BA in J studies in a cooperative plan involving several cols & univs in the Chicago area; a beneficiary of the J Fed of Met Chicago. Undergrad courses in Heb Language, Modern Heb Literature, Biblical Studies, J Hist, J Thought & Talmud, Yiddish & Arabic; grad courses in J Edu & J Communal Servs. 12 permanent faculty mems. Est in 1925 as the Col of J Studies in assn with the Bd of J Edu. In the mid 1960's the sch separated fr the Bd of J Edu & began evolving into a four yr liberal arts col. In 1969 the Ins was given its present name & a few yrs later moved to its present site. In 1970 the Col was fully accredited by the N Central Assn of Cols & Secondary Schs. Also, in 1970 a consortium plan was conceived. In effect, Spertus became the Dept of J Studies in various cols & univs in the northern IL area. Courses were offered both at Spertus Col & the host ins. The Col's main academic affiliation is with the Univ of IL at Chicago Circle; Roosevelt, De Paul, & Northeastern IL Univs & Mundelein Col also participate in the consortium agreement. Chancellor: Dr David Weinstein; Dean: Dr Warren Bargad. **618 S Michigan Ave, Chicago IL 60605 (312) 922–9012.**

Temple Beth El of Chicago. Reform Temple affiliated with UAHC. To aid our congregants & the surrounding J com in the practice of Reform J; to install in our students positive attitude towards J & a love of Torah. Rel Servs; Sisterhood; Brotherhood; edu progs (chil, adults); library containing 10,000 vols (chil bks, Holocaust, gen reference, adult fiction). 850 mems; 200 stu pre K–10th grade. 5 employees. F 1872. Pub Beth El Bulletin (semi-monthly). Facilities include sanctuary, kitchen, sch rms, gift shop, library, social hall. Rabbi Victor H. Weissberg; Edu Dir: Tamar Weissberg; Assc Rabbi Bruce D. Aft; Exec Dir: Shari Bauer; Pres: Roger Hirsch. **3050 W Touhy St, Chicago IL 60645 (312) 274–0341.**

Temple Beth El of Chicago Library. Library contains 10,000 vols (chil bks, Holocaust, gen reference, adult fiction). For information on the Temple see – Temple Beth El of Chicago, Chicago IL. **3050 W Touhy St, Chicago IL 60645 (312) 274–0341.**

Temple Sholom. Affiliated with UAHC. 1815 mems. Rabbis: Frederick C. Schwartz, Donald B. Rossoff, David W. Weiss, Eric Friedland; Pres: Donald Kaufman; Edu: Barbara Gross; Adm: Robert Mills; Sisterhood Pres: Natalie Ferber; Brotherhood Pres: Tom Bornstein. **3480 Lake Shore Dr, Chicago IL 60657 (312) 525–4707.**

UAHC Great Lakes Council – Chicago Federation. Rel & edu org serving J congs throughout the US & Canada. To encourage & aid the org & dev of J congs; to promote J edu & enrich & intensify J life; to foster other activities for the perpetuation & advancement of J. For additional information, see – UAHC – Union of American Hebrew Congregations, New York City, NY. Pres: David Lebowitz, Richard Rhodes; Dir: Rabbi Alan D. Bregman. **100 W Monroe St, Rm 312, Chicago IL 60603 (312) 782–1477.**

Young Men's Jewish Council. Youth servs agy; mem of the Natl JWB. To provide the highest quality progs for chil in the com. Operates yr round prog for chil in Chicago & suburbs including gymnastics, puppetry, dramatics, sports, sci clubs, special events & skill dev classes; maintains yr round prog for retarded chil, teens & young adults; teaches independent living skill courses that move handicapped young people within the mainstream of the com; sponsors Day Care Ctr which was est to meet the needs of working parents; sponsors summer day camps, summer & yr round overnite camp, Camp Henry Horner (yr around overnite camp) which serves as the site for outdoor family camping & youth confs. Estin 1907. Camp Henry Horner started in 1914. Pres:Ken Solomon; 1st VP: Steven P. Gomberg; 2nd VP:E. Ronald Field; 3rd VP: Allan J. Reich; Treas: MarkR. Goodman; Sec: Jeffrey D. Crane; Bd of Dirs:Steven Anixter, Frederick D. Arkin, Barry L. Axelrod, Richard K. Berkowitz, Jeffrey D. Cane, Robert G. Davidson, Edie Eisenberg, E. Ronald Field, James H. Freehling, David G. Futransky, Robert Gecht, Richard Glabman, Ronald L. Goldsmith, Steven P. Gomberg, Mark R. Goodman, Raymond P. Gordon, Vance Johnson, Dennis M. Kleper, Ben Kugler, John Levy, Michael Lustig, David G. Miller, S. James Perlow, Allan J. Reich, Ben M. Roth, Edward A. Rowe, Lawrence C. Rubin, Joseph J. Schwartz, Ralph M. Segall, Randall Server, Michael H. Shulkin, Daniel B. Shure, Steven Sider, Jerold N. Siegan, Harvey J. Silverstone, Kenneth I. Solomon, Alan Solow, Jeffrey W. Taylor, Jonathan Vegosen, Robert Vihon, Robert Washlow. **30 W Washington, Chicago IL 60602 (312) 726–8891.**

Zionist Organization of Chicago. Chicago region of the Zionist Org of Am (the voice of Zionism in the Midwest). The ZOC is committed to the survival of the J people & enrichment of J life, & the living bridge linking the J of Is & Am. F & chartered in Chicago IL on Oct 25, 1898, the org is the first & oldest Zionist dist in the US. The Zionist movement began in Chicago & spread to other parts of the US. Pres: Harry Turner; Hon Pres: David S. Bern, Dr Paul Hurwitz; Exec Dir: Frank Issacs; Chr Exec Cttee: Ira D. Schultz; Chr Zionist Council: Judge Nathan M. Cohen; Co-Chr: Hon Marshall Korshak; V Chr: Morris Swibel; Hon VP for Life: Myron Weinstein; VPs: Gerald Freedman, Judge Jacob S. Guthman, Morton Koch, Dr Fred Levin, Nicholas Reisman, Hon Ivan M. Rittenberg; Hon VPs: Mrs Simon Chinn, Solomon Dinner, Edward Lewison, Dr Bernard Spiro, Mendel Wilkow; Pres Womens Div: Ruth Schultz; Treas: Albert H. Jacobson. **6326–28 N California Ave, Chicago IL 60659 (312) 973–3232.**

Danville

Congregation Israel Synagogue. Affiliated with United Syn of Am. Rabbi J. Rosenbaum; Pres: Gary Coopersmith. **949 N Walnut St, Danville IL 61832 (217) 442–6643.**

Decatur

Decatur Jewish Federation. Mem of CJF; mem Central Illinois Jewish Federation. Organized 1942. Pres: Jerry Gliner. **c/o Temple B'nei Abraham, 1326 W Eldorado, Decatur IL 62522 (217) 429–5740.**

Temple B'nai Abraham. Affiliated with UAHC. 106 mems. Rabbi J. Jerome Pine; Pres: Jay Brodsky; Sisterhood Pres: Natalie Cole. **1326 W Eldorado St, Decatur IL 62522 (217) 429–5740.**

Deerfield

Congregation B'nai Tikvah. Syn affiliated with United Syn of Am. To promote J rel, soc & cultural activities in the com. Rel Servs; activities for adults, youth, chil; Heb Sch for stu ranging in age fr K – Jr HS; two youth groups; Jr Choir; Youth Orchestra; dance troupe. 300 mem families; 380 stu in Heb Sch. Est in 1976. Holds a series of Shabbat family dinners. Pub Happenings (monthly). Rabbi Reuven Frankel; Dir of Edu: Dr Shlomo Moskovits; Pres: Herbert J. Linn; VPs: Stephen Marcus, Steven Waxman; Treas: Charles Shulkin; Sisterhood Pres: Judith Gillis; Youth Dir: Alon Redlich. **795 Wilmont Rd, Deerfield IL 60015 (312) 945–0470.**

Moriah Congregation. Affiliated with United Syn of Am. Rabbi Samuel H. Dresner; Pres: Roslyn Lettvin. **200 Hyacinth Lane, Deerfield IL 60015 (312) 948–5340.**

Dekalb

Northern Illinois Jewish Community Center, Inc. Communal org. Rel Sch; Syn; youth groups for HS stu; Hillel org for stu at Northern ILUniv; Sisterhood. **820 Russell Rd, Dekalb IL 60115 (815) 756–1010.**

Des Plaines

Maine Township Jewish Congregation. Affiliated with United Syn of Am. Rabbi Jay Karzen; Cantor Harry Solowinchik; Pres: Jeffrey Buckman MD; Exec Dir: Howard Blau; Edu Dir & Kadima: Larry Braun; USY: Hollis Kaplan. **8800 Ballard Rd, Des Plaines IL 60016 (312) 297–2006.**

Elgin

Congregation Kneseth Israel. Conservative Cong. B'nai B'rith Men & Women; Elgin area Hadassah; CKI Sisterhood; Elgin area J Welfare Chest; library. 100 stu grades K–9. 3 employees. F 1930s. Pub Bulletins to Congregants (monthly). Facilities include kosher kitchen, sanctuary, social hall, gift shop, Passover kitchen, library, lounge, Rel Sch classrms. Pres: Stuart Hanfling; VPs: Alan Lieberman, Blossom Wohl; Treas: Tobie Ida Raff; Sec: Fred Heinemann; Fin Sec: Al Miller. **330 Division St, Elgin IL 60120 (312) 741–5656.**

Elgin Area Jewish Welfare Chest. Mem of CJF. Organized 1938. Pres: Fred Heinemann; Treas: Stuart Hanfling. **330 Division St, Elgin IL 60120 (312) 741–5656.**

Evanston

Beth Emeth, the Free Synagogue. Affiliated with UAHC. 630 mems. Rabbis: Peter S. Knobel, David Polish; Cantor Sidney Medintz; Pres: Edward Yalowitz; Edu: Debbie Schwartz; Adm: Stanley May; Brotherhood Pres: Donald Draznin. **1224 Dempster, Evanston IL60202 (312) 869–4230.**

Mikdosh El Hagro Hebrew Center. Affiliated with United Syn of Am. Rabbi Mayer Gruber; Cantor Milton Foreman; Pres: Herman Moldavan; Edu Dir: Bernard Meer. **303 Dodge Ave, Evanston IL 60202 (312) 328–9677.**

Flossmor

Temple Anshe Sholom. 707 Elm St, Flossmor IL 60422.

Temple Anshe Sholom Library. 707 Elm St, Flossmor IL 60422.

Galesburg

Temple Sholom. Affiliated with UAHC. 59 mems. Pres: N. Al Halpern. **Corner North & Monroe Sts, PO Box 501, Galesburg IL 61401 (309) 343–3323.**

Glencoe

Am Shalom. Reform Cong. Dedicated to a quest for holiness, support of Is, & to local appeals for those in need. Heb Sch; Rel Sch; Sabbath & Holiday Servs; Adult Edu progs; nationally & internationally known speakers; music & other cultural events. 370 mem families. F in 1972. Facilities include library. Offs & Heb classrooms are housed in a large home in Glencoe IL. Rel Sch classes are held in a local public sch. Rabbi Harold L. Kudan; Cantor Joel Shapiro; Dir of Rel Sch: Sharon Morton; Pres: Dr David Benjamin Littman; Exec Dir: Ruth Rosenfeld; VPs: Robert Ury, Dr Arthur Dechovitz; Treas: William L. Gould; Sec: Marianne Mayer; Sec to the Rabbi: Ruth Bernard. **614 Sheridan Rd, Glencoe IL 60022 (312) 835–4800.**

Am Shalom Library. For information on the Ins, see – Am Shalom, Glencoe, IL. **614 Sheidan Rd, Glencoe IL 60022 (312) 835–4800.**

North Shore Congregation Israel. Affiliated with UAHC. 1499 mems. Rabbis: Herbert Bronstein, Michael Levenson, Edgar E. Siskin; Cantor Jeanne Diamond; Pres: Edward S. Ex; Edu: Leonard Kramish; Adm: Alvin Platt; Sisterhood Pres: J. Greenebaum; Brotherhood Pres: Myles A. Jarrow. **1185 Sheridan Rd, Glencoe IL 60022 (312) 835–0724.**

North Shore Congregation Israel, Oscar Hillel Plotkin Library. For information on the Cong, see – North Shore Congregation Israel, Glencoe, IL. **1185 Sheridan Rd, Glencoe IL 60022 (312) 835–0724.**

Glendale Heights

Congregation Am Chai. Affiliated with United Syn of Am. Rabbi Morris Fishman; Pres: Joseph Rotstein; Edu Dir: Art Reisman. **292 N Brandon, Glendale Heights IL 60137 (312) 980–6699.**

Glenview

B'nai Jehoshua Beth Elohim. Affiliated with UAHC. 720 mems. Rabbi Mark S. Shapiro; Cantor Steven S. Sher; Pres: Marshall D. Krolick; Edu: Susan Gordon; Adm: Miriam S. Goone; Sisterhood Pres: Sandra Boyar; Brotherhood Pres: Fred Babsin. **901 MIlwaukee Ave, Glenview IL 60025 (312) 729–7575.**

Congregation B'nai Jehoshua Beth Elohim, Tommy Schwartzkopf Library. For information on the Cong, see – Congregation B'nai Jehoshua Beth Elohim, Glenview, IL. **901 Milwaukee Ave, Glenview IL 60025 (312) 729–7575.**

Godfrey

Temple Israel. Affiliated with UAHC. 36 mems. Rabbi Robert P. Jacobs; Pres: John Gilbert. **1414 W Delmar; Godfrey IL 62035 (618) 466–4641.**

Herrin

United Hebrew Temple of Benton. Affiliated with UAHC. 46 mems. Pres: Melvin Baldinger. Sisterhood Pres: L. Zwick. **c/o Mr Jim Storch, 120 N Park Ave, Herrin IL 62948 (618) 439–3521.**

Highland Park

Congregation Solel. Affiliated with UAHC. 525 mems. Rabbi Robert J. Marx; Pres: Stanton W. Brody; Edu: Fran Cohen; Adm: Carol E. Marshall. **1301 Clavey Rd, Highland Park IL 60035 (312) 433–3555.**

Congregation Solel Library. For information on the Cong, see – Congregation Solel, Highland Park, IL. **1301 Clavey Rd, Highland Park .IL 60035 (312) 433–3555.**

Lakeside Congregation for Reform Judaism. Syn affiliated with the UAHC. Weekly Worship Servs; Sun & Heb Sch; Adult Edu; social activities; celebrations for J holidays. Est in 1955. Rabbi Harold S. Jaye; Rabbi Emeritus Joseph L. Ginsberg; Pres: Hugo Nevard; VPs: Joel M. Dalkin, Oran Naefach; Sec: Robert L. Benton; Treas: Lee J. Loventhal II; Dirs: Mrs Martin P. Abramson, George P. Amberg, Mrs Robert E. Axelrod, Clarence L. Coleman Jr, John E. Deimel, Mrs Jeffrey A. Finkle, Merrill A. Freed, Mitchell L. Hollins, Harvey C. Kaplan, Charles F. Kellner, Robert P. Keno, Herbert W. Kirchheimer, Mrs Henry Kohn Jr, Paul H. Leffmann, Mrs Alan J. Levin, Philip H. Magnus, Allan H. Marx, Louis E. Pepperberg, Mrs James S. Rosenbaum, James L.

Salzenstein, John L. Shapin, Edward S. Solomon, Jerry M. Suttin, Mrs Miller H. Ullmann, Michael J. Zidman; Pres Women's Assn: Mrs Philip Schwimmer. **1221 Cty Line Rd, Highland Park IL 60035 (312) 432–7950.**

Mid-East Information Resource. Independent grassroots org which offers its resources to all. To counteract with truth, facts & edu the myths, lies & ignorance which permeate our culture. Organized 90 seminars & workshops since 1976 with the leaders being rabbis, profs & com leaders with expertise in areas of the Middle E. Bureau of Speakers: MEIR sends discussion group leaders with audio visual presentations to J & secular com orgs. One of the films the Bureau uses is The Dhimmi produced by World Org of J fr Arab Countries. The speakers are lay spokespersons who have been trained in seminars. Information Kit: are compiled of literature fr the consulate, J orgs, clippings & articles. MEIR is creating a Seminar-in-Writing on Everything You Need to Know About The Middle E to Fight Arab Propaganda: bks, pamphlets, news clippings, articles to provide a basic immersion in such central topics as Arab Psychology & Islam, PLO & the Palestinians, J fr Arab Countries, Soviet J, Soviet Domination in the Mid E – all focusing on the realities of seeking peace & a strong Is. Est in 1975 in reaction to the UN resolution equating Zionism with racism. Educational Columns. Meir gives progs to youth & Christian orgs free as a public serv. Exec Dir: Gail Winston. **871 Marion Ave, Highland Park IL 60035 (312) 432–1735.**

North Suburban Synagogue Beth El. Conservative Syn affiliated with United Syn of Am. To further the goals of Conservative Judaism & to provide edu & worship facilities. Rel Servs, edu progs, Sisterhood, Men's Club, chorale group, counseling; food servs; Presch; HS; Afternoon Sch; library containing 17,000 vols (Judaica & related subjects). 1750 mems; 925 families; 3600 individuals. 50 employees. Est June 1948. Facilities include sanctuary, kosher kitchen, gift shop. Rabbi William Lebeau; Cantor Aryeh Finkelstein; Edu Dir: Dorothy Wexler; Ritual Dir: Harry Halbkram; Exec Dir: Samuel Rade; Prog Dir: Judy L. Yaillen. **1175 Sheridan Rd, Highland Park IL 60035 (312) 432–8900.**

North Suburban Synagogue Beth El, Maxwell Abbell Library. Library with 17,000 vols – Judaica & related subjects. For information on the Syn, see – North Suburban Syn Beth El, Highland Park, IL. **1175 Sheridan Rd, Highland Park IL 60035 (312) 432–8900.**

Hoffman Estates

Beth Tikva Congregation. Affiliated with UAHC. 350 mems. Rabbi Hillel Gamoran; Cantor Seymour Roth; Pres: Michael D. Firsel; Adm: Ruth Ziegler; Sisterhood Pres: Eileen Schur. **300 Hillcrest Blvd, Hoffman Estates IL 60195 (312) 885–4545.**

Homewood

Temple B'nai Yehuda. Affiliated with UAHC. Memberes: 307. Rabbi Leo R. Wolkow; Cantor Henry Altman; Pres: Charles Dreyfuss; Edu: Susan Bayer; Adm: Barbara Riffer; Sisterhood Pres: Eve Colbert. **1424 W 183rd St, Homewood IL 60430 (312) 799–4110.**

Joliet

Joliet Jewish Welfare Chest. Mem of CJF. Organized 1938. Pres: Dr Bernard Kliska; Sec: Rabbi Morris M. Hershman. **250 N Midland Ave, Joliet IL 60435 (815) 725–7078.**

Lincolnwood

Congregation Yehuda Moshe. Orthodox Syn affiliated with Union of Orthodox J Congs, Council of Traditional Syns (Chicago). To develop rel, edu, cultural & civic progs in Orthodox tradition. Daily Servs; Sisterhood; D'var Torah; Talmud classes; charitable campaign; mikvah; library containing 600 vols (Bible, Talmud, Judaica). 95 families. 4 employees. F 1964; original name Beth Torah Cong. Pub Yehuda Moshe Bulletin (monthly). Facilities include kosher kitchen, sanctuary seating 340. Rabbi Dr Oscar Z. Fasman; Pres: Dr Gilbert Lanoff; Hon Pres: Jack Reiss, Bernard Cohen; VPs: Dr Oscar Novick, Jack Shapira, Dr Manuel Silverblatt; Gabbai: Shalom Knobloch; Mikvah Dir: Rose Knobloch; Superintendent: Michael Stern. **4721 Touhy Ave, Lincolnwood IL 60466 (312) 673–5870.**

Lombard

Congregation Etz Chaim. Affiliated with UAHC. 233 mems. Rabbi Steven M. Bob; Pres: David Stahl; Edu: Merle Erlich; Sisterhood Pres: Bette Stahl; Brotherhood Pres: Ted Booden. **1710 S Highland Ave, Lombard IL 60148 (312) 627–3912.**

Long Grove

Temple Chai. Affiliated with UAHC. 235 mems. Pres: David Rosenfeldt; Edu: Eliezer Berkman; Sisterhood Pres: Beverly Schreiber. **RT 6, PO Box 423, Long Grove IL 60047 (312) 537–1771.**

Mattoon

Mattoon Jewish Center. Affiliated with UAHC. 12 mems. Pres: Aaron Steinberg; Edu: James Lively; Adm: Carl Lebovitz. **PO Box 881, Mattoon IL 61938 (217) 234–2245.**

Morton Grove

Northwest Suburban Jewish Congregation. Affiliated with United Syn of Am. Rabbi Lawrence Charney; Cantor Joel Roznick; Pres: Robert Tecktiel; Exec Dir: Ronald Summer; Edu Dir: Aaron Klein; Youth Dir: Mark Magiers. **7800 W Lyons, Morton Grove IL 60053 (312) 965–0900.**

Northbrook

Beth Shalom. Affiliated with United Syn of Am. Rabbi Carl Wolkin; Cantor Charles Segelbaum; Pres: Jerry Stanton; Exec Dir: Harvey R. Gold; Edu Dir: Sander J. Mussman. **3433 Walters Ave, Northbrook IL 60062 (312) 498–4100.**

Sager Solomon Schechter Day School. Affiliated with Solomon Schechter Day Schs Assn. Prin: Dr Howard Rosenblatt; Chr: David Hoffman. **350 Lee Rd, Northbrook IL60062 (312) 498–2100.**

Northfield

Am Yisrael Library. Four Happ Rd, Northfield IL 60093.

Pioneer Women – Na'amat. The training & edu of the Is woman & her family so that each can be best equipped to lead productive lives. For additional information, see – Pioneer Women Na'amat, New York City, NY. **466 Central Ave, Northfield IL 60093 (312) 446–7275.**

Temple Jeremiah. Affiliated with UAHC. 510 mems. Rabbis: Robert D. Schreibman, Alan Tarshish; Cantor Sharona Feller; Pres: James Foster; Edu: Anne M. Lidsky; Adm: Fern Kamen. **PO Box N 193, 937 Happ Rd, Northfield IL 60093 (312) 441–5760.**

Oak Park

Oak Park Temple. Affiliated with UAHC. 304 mems. Rabbis: Gary S. Gerson, Leonard J. Mervis; Pres: Sam Helfer; Edu: Jeffry Kondritzer; Adm: Jean Felix; Sisterhood Pres: Joan Dicker; Brotherhood Pres: Harris Dicker. **1235 N Harlem Ave, Oak Park IL 60302 (312) 386–3937.**

Oak Park Temple, B'nai Abraham Zion Library. For information on the Temple, see – Oak Park Temple, Oak Park, IL. **1235 N Harlem Ave, Oak Park IL 60302 (312) 386–3937.**

Olympia Fields

Temple Anshe Sholom, Beth Torah. Affiliated with UAHC. 629 mems. Rabbi Donald N. Gluckman; Cantor Mark Elson; Pres: Stephen D. Gabelnick; Edu: Mark Elson; Adm: Selma Lillienfeld; Sisterhood Pres: Ruth Holzman; Brotherhood Pres: Hal Rogoff. **20820 Western Ave, Olympia Fields IL 60461 (312) 748–6010.**

Park Forest

Congregation Am Echad. Affiliated with United Syn of Am. Rabbi Roy D. Tenenbaum; Pres: Max Adler; Edu Dir: Esther Weiss; Sec: Ellen Kahn. **160 Westwood, Park Forest IL 60466 (312) 747–9513.**

Congregation Beth Sholom. Affiliated with UAHC. 208 mems. Rabbi Minard Klein; Pres: Joseph H. Singer; Sisterhood Pres: Thelma Kollman; Brotherhood Pres: Daniel Rosenfeldt. **1 Dogwood, Park Forest IL 60466 (312) 747–3040.**

Congregation Beth Sholom Library. 1 Dogwood, Park Forest IL60466 (312) 747–3040.

Peoria

Congregation Anshai Emeth. Reform Cong affiliated with UAHC, NFTS, NFTY, CCAR. Rel, edu, social, cultural enrichment of the J com. Rel Servs; Rel & Heb Schs; Adult Edu prog; Jr & Sr high youth group; 'College Connection' (col outreach prog); library (gen Judaica). 262 families; 130 stu in Rel Sch; 31 stu in Heb Sch. Pub Bulletin of Congregation Anshai Emeth (bi-weekly), Congregation Anshai Emeth Yearbook (annual). Facilities include sanctuary seating 600, 12 classrms, rabbi's study, kitchen, social hall, lounge, gift shop. Rabbi Jerald Brown; Pres: Bernard Rubin; VP: Sue Pritzker; Treas: Elaine Rhodes; Sec: Mark Moses. **5614 N Univ St, Peoria IL61614 (309) 691–3323.**

Jewish Federation of Peoria. Social serv agy affiliated with UJA, CJF, Natl J Com Relations Advisory Council. To engage in philantropic, cultural or other communal activities which will contribute to the welfare of the J com. Fund raising; budgeting & allocations; cultrual & edu progs; com relations activities; information & referral serv; serv to specific groups (e.g. sr citizens, single adults, young leadership); transient relief prog; fostering of cooperation among local J orgs. 600 families; 1900 individuals. 2 employees. Org 1933; inc 1947; formerly the J Com Council & Welfare Fund. Pub The Jewish View (quarterly newsletter), Annual Report. Pres: Marilyn Weigensberg; Exec Dir: Peretz A. Katz; VPs: Morey Slodki, Mark Moses; Sec: Irwin Zeisel; Treas: Dr Charles Enda. **3100 N Knoxville, Suite 17, Peoria IL 61603 (309) 686–0611.**

Peoria Hebrew Day School. To educate the whole chil; to imbue stu with Torah values & gen edu that will prepare them to become valuable mems of the Am J com; to cultivate love for the land of Is. K–8th grade; gen & J studies; basketball teams; Is dance group; Fire & Police Safety Prog; participation in Peoria Cty spelling bee; after-sch bowling; Sci Fair; dramatics; Choir; Arts & Crafts Club. Faculty of licensed, experienced, progressive teachers. F & incorporated in 1971. The first complete day sch in central IL. Embraces all elements of the J com by conducting its rel classes in a manner non prejudical to any of these elements. The OPT, an org for parents & teachers, produces close cooperation between parents & teachers, fosters the pursuit of excellence in academic & cultural endeavors among the stu, has a prog of activities for parents, & plans fund raising activities in order to purchase edu equipment for the sch. Prin: Robert A. Scott; Pres: Harriet Margolies; VP: Dr Thomas E. Halperin; Treas: Ethel Kahn; Sec: Eunice Galsky. **3616 N Sheridan Rd, Peoria IL 61604 (309) 688–2821.**

River Forest

West Suburban Temple Har Zion. Affiliated with United Syn of Am. Rabbi Joseph Tabachnik; Cantor Howard Brindell; Pres: Judith Loevy; Exec Dir: Doris Levin; Edu Dir: Sara Eisen; Youth Dir: Debbie Markman, Mark Katz. **1040 N Harlem Ave, River Forest IL 60305 (312) 366–9000.**

West Suburban Temple Har Zion Library. For information on the Temple, see – West Suburban Temple, River Forest, IL. **1040 N Harlem Ave, River Forest IL 60305 (312) 366–9000.**

Rock Island

Jewish Federation of the Quad Cities. Serv org. To further the welfare & quality of life of the J com. Raises & disburses funds; plans for the charitable, social, cultural, rel & edu advancement of the J com; fosters cooperation among local J orgs. Pres: Samuel Gilman; VP Campaign: Norman Rich; VP Allocations: Marvin Schrager; VP Com Relations: Lawrence Satin; VP Cash Mobilization: Kenneth Freeman; Sec: Herman Segal; Treas: Paul Halpern; Bd of Trustees: Dr William Abel, Jerome Altheimer, Mac Barkan, Rabbi Robert Benjamin, Jeanne Davis, Jerome Dockterman, Jeffrey Eirinberg, Cantor Abraham Ezring, Kenneth Freeman, Martin Galex, Morris M. Geifman, Jay Gellerman, Samuel Gilman, Lewis Glick, Bruce Goldberg, Bernard Goldstein, Jerald Greenblatt, Sidney Greenswag, Paul Halpern, Kasse Handelman, Rabbi Stanley Herman, Morton Kaplan, David Learner, David Levin, Vicki Levin, Paul Light, Robert Markman, David Messro, Trudy Moses, Jack Moskowitz, Martin Rich, Norman Rich, Samuel Sable, Lawrence Satin, Marvin Schrager, Herman Segal, Lawrence Siegel, Louis Siegel, Michael Siegel, Judi Stroud, Steven Strulowitz, A. L. Tunick, Robert Versman, Julian Weigle, Bernard Weindruch, Ira Weindruch; William Zessar; Exec Dir: Judah Segal. **224 18th St, Suite 511, Rock Island IL 61201 (309) 793–1300.**

Tri-City Jewish Center. Affiliated with United Syn of Am. Cantor & Exec Dir: Abraham J. Ezring; Pres: Jay M. Gellerman; Edu & Youth Dir: David Mayer. **2715 30th St, Rock Island IL 61201 (309) 788–3426.**

Rockford

Ohave Sholom Synagoge. Affiliated with United Syn of Am. Rabbi Jacob Chinitz; Pres: Meyer Abarbanel; Edu Dir: Sol Burstein; Youth Dir: Ruby Lash. **3730 Guilford Rd, Rockford IL 61107 (815) 226–4900.**

Rockford Jewish Community Council. Mem of CJF. Organized 1937. Pres: Eugene Levin; Exec Dir: Daniel Tannenbaum. **1500 Parkview Ave, Rockford IL 61107 (815) 399–5497.**

Temple Beth El. Affiliated with UAHC. 190 mems. Rabbi Robert J. Orkand; Pres: Judith Picus; Sisterhood Pres: Gloria Dermer. **1203 Comanche Dr, Rockford IL 61107 (815) 398–5020.**

Skokie

Camp Young Judea. Affiliated with Hadassah. To give J campers a positive edu experience with their J & Zionism. Summer camp; experiential edu; Shabbat observant; kashrut observant; swimming; boating; arts & crafts; sports; Is singing & dancing. 265 stu. 65 employees; 40 volunteers. F 1969.

Facilities include kosher kitchen, sports facilities, waterfront, arts & crafts. Camp Dir: Bini W. Silver; Chr: Sue Kaufman. **4155 W Main St, Skokie IL 60076 (312) 676–9790.**

Congregation B'nai Emunah. Affiliated with United Syn of Am. Rabbi Harold J. Stern; Cantor Allen Stearns; Pres: Harold Tannenbaum; Edu Dir: Henry Sokolow; Youth Dir: Les Strauss. **9131 Niles Center Rd, PO Box 272, Skokie IL 60076 (312) 674–9292.**

Congregation Bene Shalom, Hebrew Association for Deaf. Affiliate with UAHC. 167 mems. Rabbi Douglas Goldhamer; Pres: Yetta Abarbanell. **4435 Oakton, Skokie IL 60076 (312) 677–3330.**

Congregation Kol Emeth Library. For information on the Cong, see – Cong Kol Emeth, Skokie, IL. **5130 W Touhy Aye, Skokie IL60076 (312) 673–3370.**

Congregation Or Torah. Orthodox Cong affiliated with Council of Traditional Orthodox Syns. To provide an atmosphere for J worship & a base for formation of an Orthodox J com interested in serving the J com at large. Daily Servs; weekly classes in Talmud, Mishna, Torah, prophets, special lectures; Women's Group; hosp visiting serv; youth progs – Syn & B'nai Akiva. 133 mems. F 1969 by a group that wished to form an independent Ahskenazi syn in Skokie. Pub Bulletin (quarterly). Facilities include sanctuary, social hall, kitchen, meeting rms. Rabbi Irwin R. Pollock; Pres: Allan Ray; VPs: Seymour Greenfeld, Allan Zahtz; Women's Group Pres: Judy Gorell. **3740 W Dempster, Skokie IL 60076 (312) 674–3695.**

Hebrew Theological College. Orthodox cong afflilated with US Dept of Edu. To train rabbis for leadership roles in J world. HS; Col of Adv Hebrew Studies; Sch of Liberal Arts & Sciences; Teachers Ins for Women; Rabbanic Sch; Graduate Sch; library containing 57,000 vols (Judaica, Heb). 65 stu 9–12, 160 stu col. 100 employees, 50 volunteers. Pub Scholarly Works (quarterly). Facilities include kosher kitchen, dormitory, sports fields. Pres: Don Well; Asst Dean: Jerold Isenberg; HS Prin: Irvin Pollock. **7135 N Carpenter Rd, Skokie IL 60077 (312) 267–9800.**

Hebrew Theological College, Saul Silber Memorial Library. 7135 N Carpenter Rd, Skokie IL 60077 (312) 267–9800.

Hillel Torah N Suburban Day School.7120 N Laramie Ave, Skokie IL 60077 (312) 674–6533.

Kol Emeth. Affiliated with United Syn of Am. Rabbi Nathan Levinson; Cantor Barry Schechter; Pres: Norman Engelberg; Edu Dir: Zev Rogalin. **5130 W Touhy Ave, Skokie IL 60077 (312) 673–3370.**

Mayer Kaplan Jewish Community Center. 5050 W Church St, Skokie IL 60077 (312) 761–2304.

Mayer Kaplan Jewish Community Center, Gollay Memorial Library. 5050 W Church St, Skokie IL60077 (312) 761–2304.

The Niles Township Jewish Congregation. Affiliated with United Syn of Am. Rabbi Neil Brief; Cantor Shlomo Shuster; Pres: Jack G. Stein; Exec Dir: Cyril G. Oldham; Edu Dir: Rabbi David Brusin; Youth Dir: Hollis F. Kaplan. **4500 Dempster St, Skokie IL 60076 (312) OR5–4141.**

Philip A. Newberger Memorial Library of Judaica. Hillel Torah N Suburban Day School, 7120 N Laramie Ave, Skokie IL 60077 (312) 674–6533.

Skokie Valley Traditional Synagoge. 8825 E Prairie Rd, Skokie IL 60076 (312) 674–3473.

Skokie Valley Traditional Synagoge Library. 8825 E Prairie Rd, Skokie IL 60076 (312) 674–3473.

Solomon Schechter Day School of Skokie. Affiliated with Solomon Schechter Day Schs Assn. Prin: Charlotte Glass; Chr: David Hoffman. **9301 Gross Point Rd, Skokie IL 60076 (312) 679–6270.**

Temple Beth Israel. Affiliated with UAHC. 520 mems. Rabbis: Ernst M. Lorge, Samuel N. Gordon; Pres: Sheldon Cantor; Adm: Sylvia Kaplan; Sisterhood Pres: Mary Horelick; Brotherhood Pres: Ben Glitman. **3939 W Howard St, Skokie IL 60076 (312) 675–0951.**

Temple Judea Mizpah. Affiliated with UAHC. 514 mems. Rabbi Marc E. Berkson; Cantor Richard Green; Pres: Edwin Blitz; Edu: Esther Sultz; Adm: Beverly Smolensky; Sisterhood Pres: Karen Franks; Brotherhood Pres: Melvin Kramer. **8610 Niles Center Rd, Skokie IL 60077 (312) 676–1566.**

Yeshivas Brisk. HS combining rel & gen studies; advanced Talmudic studies; Rabbinic Ordination Prog; Grad Sch of Talmudic Studies. Rosh HaYeshiva: Rabbi Aaron Soloveichik; Prin HS Div of Rel Studies: Rabbi Erwin Giffin. **9000 Forestview Rd, Skokie IL 60203 (312) 674–4652.**

Springfield

Springfield Jewish Federation. Mem of CJF. Organized 1941. Pres: Dr Stephen P. Stone; Exec Dir: Leonore Loeb. **730 E Vine St, Springfield IL 62703 (217) 528–3446.**

Temple B'rith Shalom. Affiliated with UAHC. Rel Servs; Sisterhood; Rel Sch. Springfield Hebrew Cong, the first J cong in Springfield, was est on Apr 2, 1858 with 19 mems. In 1866 a plot of land in the Oak Ridge Cemetery was purchased. A charter was granted in 1867. In 1874 the first Rel Sch was organized with a membership of 12 chil, & a plot of ground for a temple was purchased. In 1876 the temple was dedicated. The Cong affiliated with the UAHC in 1877. In 1915 the women's org, Mite Soc, affiiated with the Natl Fed of Temple Sisterhoods. In 1916 a new charter was procured. Though for the past 40 yrs the Cong had been known as B'rith Sholom, the change became official with the new charter. Construction of a new temple began on May 18, 1916. The bldg on the present site was dedicated Sept 9, 1917. In 1957 the cornerstone of the Memorial Bldg was dedicated. In 1958 a centennial dinner was held. In Nov 1958 the Memorial Bldg was dedicated. In 1959 the Temple was honored for a century of serv to Reform J at the 45th Biennial Gen Assembly of the UAHC. A 105th Anniversary Dinner Meeting honoring the Sisterhood was held on May 19, 1963. In 1964 sanctuary improvements were completed. In 1980 the Rel Sch merged with the local Conservative Temple. Rabbi Joshua Goldstein; Rabbi Emeritus Meyer M. Abramowitz; Offs: Robert Weiner, Mrs Milton D. Friedland, David E. Goldman, Mrs Max Parienti. **1004 S 4th St, Springfield IL 62703 (217) 525–1360.**

Sterling

Temple Sholom. Affiliated with UAHC. 20 mems. Pres: Dolf Jakobs; Sisterhood Pres: Sonny Jakobs. **c/o Mr Dolf Jakobs, 21956 Ridge Rd, Rt #2, Sterling IL61081 (815) 625–2599.**

Urbana

HaKesher. Ctr for reform J programming on Univ of IL campus in Urbana; affiliated with UAHC off in Chicago. Progs & materials on rel & cultural topics; clearing house for Is oriented programming. 6 to 7 mem stu cooperative. HaKesher began in 1975 as an alternative to the then mostly Orthodox Hillel facility on campus. It was originally called HaBayit & was the forerunner of several Reform Baytim located on campuses across the US. Operating funds & prog support are obtained fr UAHC. **1004 W Nevada #1, Urbana IL 61801 (217) 344–7842.**

Waukegan

Am Echod. Affiliated with United Syn of Am. Rabbi William Fertig; Cantor Leo Grad; Pres: Murray Brown; Youth Dirs: Mr & Mrs Joseph Black. **1500 Sunset Ave, Waukegan IL 60085 (312) 336–9110.**

Wilmette

Beth Hillel Congregation. Affiliated with United Syn of Am. Rabbi David Lincoln; Cantor Raphael Edgar; Pres: Robert Stempel; Edu Dir: Theodore Z. Weiss; Youth Dir: Randy Sostock. **3220 Big Tree Lane, Wilmette IL 60091 (312) 256–1213.**

INDIANA

Bloomington

B'nai B'rith Hillel Foundation. 730 E 3rd St, Bloomington IN 47401 (812) 336–3824.

B'nai B'rith Hillel Foundation Library. 730 E 3rd St, Bloomington IN 47401 (812) 336–3824.

Evansville

Adath B'nai Israel. Affiliated with UAHC. 280 mems. Rabbis: Michael B. Herzbrun, Bernard H. Lavine; Cantor Regina Y. Heit; Pres: Alan Shovers; Sisterhood Pres: Phyllis Present. **3600 Washington Ave, Evansville IN 47715 (812) 425–8222.**

Evansville Jewish Community Council, Inc. Mem of CJF. Organized 1936; Inc 1964. Pres: Joel Lasker; Exec Sec: Maxine P. Fink. **PO Box 5026, Evansville IN 47715 (812) 477–7050.**

Temple Adath Israel. Affiliated with United Syn of Am. Rabbi Joseph Topel; Pres: Alan Shovers; Edu Dir: Rabbi Joseph Topel; Exec Sec: Ann Diamond. **3600 Washington Ave, Evansville IN 47715 (812) 477–1577.**

Fort Wayne

B'nai B'rith Emek Beracha Lodge 61. Serv org focusing on human needs & com concerns. Supports ADL & attempts to secure justice & fair treatment for all citizens. Hillel Foun has dev intensive campus com progs. B'nai B'rith Career & Counseling Servs include pre-retirement counseling. The Lodge sponsors B'nai B'rith youth orgs BBG & AZA. Fort Wayne Lodge est 1865. Pres: Ron Miller. **c/o Fort Wayne J Fed, 227 E Washington Blvd, Fort Wayne IN 46802.**

Congregation Achduth Vesholom. Affiliated with UAHC. 267 mems. Rabbi Richard B . Safran; Pres: Stanley Lipp; Sisterhood Pres: Maureen Grinsfelder, Carole Krainess, W. Monroe. **5200 Old Mill Rd, Fort Wayne IN 46807 (219) 744–4245.**

Fort Wayne Jewish Federation. Mem of CJF. Organized 1921. Pres: Marvin Crell; Exec Dir: Eli J. Skora. **227 E Washington Blvd, Fort Wayne IN 46802 (219) 422–8566.**

Jewish War Veterans of the USA, Larry Ress Post 368. Works to fight bigotry & anti-Semitism, to remember those who died in the serv of their country, & to be the patriotic voice of J. F 1946 by Abe Latker who became first commander. Participates in Memorial Day & Veteran's Day parades; provides entertainment once a month for all patients at VA Hosp; sponsors used book sale to raise money for servicemen in Is. Membership open to anyone who has served in US Military. Pres: Cal Kalstein. **c/o Fort Wayne J Fed, 227 E Washington Blvd, Fort Wayne IN 46802.**

Orthodox Jewish Cemetery Association. To allow any J person in Fort Wayne the opportunity to purchase & be buried in the Assn's land located on the Decatur Rd. F early 1900's. Pres: Irving Brateman. **c/o Fort Wayne J Fed, 227 E Washington Blvd, Fort Wayne IN 46802.**

Gary

Temple Israel. Affiliated with UAHC. 130 mems. Rabbis: Albert Yanow, Garry J. August, Carl I. Miller; Pres: Robert Rottenberg; Sisterhood Pres: Dorothy Koplow. **601 N Montgomery St, Gary IN 46403 (219) 938–5232.**

Hammond

Congregation Beth Israel. Affiliated with United Syn of Am. Rabbi Raphael Ostrovsky; Cantor Andrew Rustein; Pres: Harry Nelson. **7105 Hohman Ave, Hammond IN 46321 (219) 931–1312.**

Temple Beth El. Affiliated with UAHC. 240 mems. Rabbi David M. Horowitz; Pres: Warren Yalowitz; Sisterhood Pres: Frances Gerson. **6947 Hohman Ave, Hammond IN 46324 (219) 932–3754.**

Highland

The Jewish Federation, Inc. Mem of CJF. Organized 1941; reorganized 1959. Pres: Sam Gray; Exec Dir: Barnett Labowitz. **2939 Jewett St, Highland IN 46322 (219) 972–2251.**

Indianapolis

Bureau of Jewish Education. Central agy for J edu affiliated with the J Welfare Fed of Indianapolis. To provide servs to the J com at large, as well as to selected groups in the gen com. In addition to early chil & supplementary edu, it provides servs to the whole State of Indiana. Media Ctr; Teacher Ctr; Computer Ctr; promotion of Heb studies in public schs & in ins of higher edu; Home Start Prog; Cadet Prog; library containing 8,000 vols (Judaica, Heb). 50 stu (early childhood); 220 stu (elementary); 50 stu (HS); 160 stu (adult edu). 26 employees. Est 1911; formerly J Edu Assn. Pub Mivzak (quarterly), Darkon Laivrit (Textbook for Heb stu). Facilities include kosher kitchen, auditorium, classrms, introduction of Heb at local Uni, est of the Edu Directors Council – for Teacher Inservs & com wide edu progs. Exec Dir: Dr Uri Korin; Pres: Donald Katz; VPs: Myrna Fang, Dr S. Edwin Fineberg, Lawrence Reuben; Treas: Benjamin Goldfarb; Sec: L. Steven Miller. **6711 Hoover Rd, Indianapolis IN 46260 (317) 255–3124.**

Bureau of Jewish Education Library. Library contains 8,000 vols (Judaica, Heb). For information on the Ins, see – Bureau of Jewish Edu, Indianapolis, IN. **6711 Hoover Rd, Indianapolis IN 46260 (317) 255–3124.**

Congregation Beth El Zedek. Affiliated with United Syn of Am. Rabbis: Sandy Eisenberg Sasso, Dennis C. Sasso; Cantor Robert Zalkin; Pres: Fredrick L. Resnick; Exec Dir: Mrs Louis Bursky; Edu & Youth Dir: Mrs Serane Blatt. **600 W 70th St, Indianapolis IN 46260 (317) 253–3441.**

Hebrew Academy of Indianapolis. Independent sch serving the entire com. An orthodox, traditional day sch dedicated to promoting the ideals of J, love of Torah, Is & God; & to educating chil to become creative, intelligent persons. Presch; day sch; Midrasha prog for HS stu, for post jr HS; J edu; Adult Edu; Ulpan. 170 stu grades presch – 8. 35 employees. F 1970. Facilities include independent structure, gym, soccer field, kosher kitchen. Pres: March Hasten; Dir: Raymond Stern; Adm: Sylvia Blain. **6602 Hoover Rd, Indianapolis IN 46260 (317) 251–1261.**

Hebrew Academy of Indianapolis Library. 6602 Hoover Rd, Indianapolis IN 46260 (317) 251–1261.

Indiana Jewish Post & Opinion. Periodical pub. **611 N Park Ave, Indianapolis IN 46204 (317) 634–1307.**

Indianapolis Hebrew Congregation. Affiliated with UAHC. 1060 mems. Rabbis: Jonathan A. Stein, Peter H. Schweitzer; Cantor Janice L. Roger; Pres: June Herman; Edu: Elaine Arffa; Adm: Muriel Romer; Sisterhood Pres: Ruth Smith; Brotherhood Pres: Joe Mehlman. **6501 N Meridian St, Indianapolis IN 46260 (317) 255–6647.**

Indianapolis Hebrew Congregation Library. For information on the Cong, see – Indianapolis Hebrew Congregation, Indianapolis, IN. **6501 N Meridian St, Indianapolis IN 46260 (317) 255–6647.**

Jewish Educational Association. 6711 Hoover Rd, Indianapolis IN 46260 (317) 255–3124.

Jewish Educational Association Auxiliary Library. 6711 Hoover Rd, Indianapolis IN 46260 (317) 255–3124.
(317) 634–1307.

Jewish Welfare Federation, Inc. J Fed affiliated with CJF. The central org for budgeting, social planning & fund raising primarily for J health, welfare & edu servs. The JWF initiates, plans & coordinates the Indianapolis J com social serv prog; responsible for the supervision of the fiscal & administrative operations of the J agy. The Fed is the J com arm in determining its health & welfare needs; helping the various constituent agy to cooperate in providing com servs. 12 employees; 500 volunteers. F 1904. Pub JWF Report (monthly). Pres: David H. Kleiman; Exec VP: Louis Solomon; VPs: Sigmund Beck, Mrs Leonard Berkowitz, Gerald Kraft, Robert Rose; Sec: Dr Edward Gabovitch; Treas: Irwin Rose. **615 N Alabama St, Rm 412, Indianapolis IN 46204 (317) 637–2473.**

National Jewish Post, Inc. Chain of six weekly J newspapers with offs in Indianapolis, St Louis, Chicago & NYC. 35 employees. Started in 1932; originally KY J Chronicle, then added a natl edition, & changed to the J Post; absorbed Opinion & became J Post & Opinion; added IN J Post & Opinion, MO J

Post & Opinion, Chicago J Post & Opinion & the J Post of NY. Editor & Publisher: Gabriel Cohen. **611 N Park Ave, Indianapolis IN 46204.**

Kokomo

Temple B'nai Israel. Affiliated with UAHC. 28 mems. Pres: Jerry Kopelov; Edu: Stuart Green; Sisterhood Pres: Bette Anderson. **618 W Superior St, PO Box 1290, Kokomo IN 46901 (317) 452–0383.**

Lafayette

Federated Jewish Charities. Mem of CJF. Organized 1924. Pres: Francine Jacoby; Fin Sec: Louis Pearlman Jr. **PO Box 676, Lafayette IN 47902 (317) 742–9081.**

Marion

Sinai Temple. Affiliated with UAHC. 43 mems. Pres: Jack Young; Sisterhood Pres: Nancy Young. **c/o Mr Jack Young, 1001 Euclid Ave, Marion IN 46952 (317) 664–4453.**

Michigan City

Michigan City United Jewish Welfare Fund. Mem of CJF. Pres: Nate Winski; Treas: Harold Leinwand. **2800 Franklin St, Michigan City IN 46360 (219) 874–4477.**

Sinai Temple. Affiliated with UAHC. 165 mems. Rabbis: Joseph A. Edelheit, Karl Richter; Pres: Iris Ourach; Edu: Joseph A. Edelheit; Sisterhood Pres: Vicki Leinwand. **2800 Franklin St, Michigan City IN 46360 (219) 874–4477.**

Sinai Temple Library. For information on the Temple, see – Sinai Temple, Michigan City, IN. **2800 Franklin St, Michigan City IN 46360 (219) 874–4477.**

Muncie

Beth El Temple. Affiliated with UAHC. 50 mems. Pres: Helen B. Schwartz; Sisterhood Pres: Bertha Bugauer. **PO Box 2395, 525 W Jackson St, Muncie IN 47302 (317) 288–4662.**

Muncie Jewish Welfare Fund. c/o Beth El Temple, PO Box 2792, Muncie IN 47302 (317) 284–1497.

Richmond

Beth Boruk Temple. Affiliated with UAHC. 65 mems. Pres: Kenneth Woodman; Edu: H. Leventhal. **c/o Dr Kenneth Woodman, 3040 Parkwood Dr, Richmond IN 47374 (317) 962–6501.**

South Bend

Jewish Federation of St Joseph Valley. Mem of CJF. Organized 1946. Pres: Isidore Rosenfeld; Exec VP: Bernard Natkow. **804 Sherland Bldg, South Bend IN 46601 (219) 233–1164.**

Temple Beth El. Affiliated with UAHC. 318 mems. Rabbis: Elliot Rosenstock, Albert M. Shulman; Pres: Eugene Abrams; Edu: Babette Maza; Sisterhood Pres: Patricia Schlossberg; Brotherhood Pres: Eugene Oppenheim. **305 W Madison St, South Bend IN 46601 (219) 234–4402.**

Terre Haute

United Hebrew Congregation. Reform Cong affiliated with UAHC. To promote & preserve the J com of W-Central In Shabbat Worship; Rel Sch; afternoon Heb schs; Youth Group; Sisterhood; Adult Edu; social activities; com resource; library. 150 families. A merger in 1935 of the two original Terre Haute syns, B'nai Abraham (Orthodox) f 1889, & Temple Israel (Reform), f 1858 as 'Terre Haute Zion Gemeinde'. Pub United Hebrew Congregation Bulletin (monthly – except July & Aug). Facilities include kitchen, rabbi's study, sanctuary, com hall. Rabbi Joseph P. Klein; Pres: Jerry Einstandig. **540 S 6th St, Terre Haute IN 47807 (812) 232–5988.**

West Lafayette

B'nai B'rith Hillel Foundation at Purdue. 912 W State St, West Lafayette IN 47906 (317) 743–1293.

B'nai B'rith Hillel Foundation at Purdue, Library. 912 W State St, West Lafayette IN 47906 (317) 743–1293.

Temple Israel. Affiliated with UAHC. 120 mems. Rabbi Burton E. Levinson; Pres: Henry Weiner; Sisterhood Pres: Harriet Morrison. **620 Cumberland, West Lafayette IN 47906 (317) 463–3455.**

Zionsville

UAHC Myron S. Goldman Camp Institute. Dir: Rabbi Ronald Klotz. **9349 Moore Rd, Zionsville IN 46077 (317) 873–3361.**

IOWA

Ames

Ames Jewish Congregation. Affiliated with UAHC. 39 mems. Pres: Robert Gitchell. **6712 Calhoun, Ames IA 50010 (515) 233–1347.**

Burlington

Temple Israel. Affiliated with UAHC. 8 mems. Pres: Irvin Stein; Sisterhood Pres: Sue Waples. **830 Division, Burlington IA 52601 (319) 752–1138.**

Cedar Rapids

Jewish Welfare Fund of Linn County, Iowa. Mem of CJF. Organized 1941. Treas: Jay Beecher. **3227 Parkview Ct SE, Cedar Rapids IA 52401 (319) 365–5100.**

Temple Judah. Affiliated with UAHC. 89 mems. Rabbi Robert E. Ourach; Pres: Ron Feder; Sisterhood Pres: Ethel Berg. **3221 SE Lindsay Lane, Cedar Rapids IA 52403 (319) 362–1261.**

Temple Judah Library. For information on the Temple, see – Temple Judah, Cedar Rapids, IA. **3221 Lindsay Lane SE, Cedar Rapids IA 52403 (319) 362–1261.**

Davenport

Temple Emanuel. Affiliated with UAHC. 225 mems. Rabbi Robert M. Benjamin; Pres: Victor A. Rothbardt; Adm: Betty Cottrell; Sisterhood Pres: Myra Kipperman. **1115 Mississippi Ave, Davenport IA 52803 (319) 326–4419.**

Des Moines

Bureau for Jewish Living. Affiliated with JESNA, JWB. To provide edu & social activities for com & col. Edu progs; athletic progs; presch. 700 families; 1400 individuals; 180 stu 20 employees. F 1915 by Rabbi Zeichik (Orthodox) & Rabbi Mannheimer (Reform). Facilities includes gym, sch, kosher kitchen. Exec Dir: Rabbi Robert Addison; Presch Dir: Esther Bergh; Day Sch Prin: Kathy Ricker; JCC Dir: Myra Shindler; Hillel Dir: Debbie Entine. **924 Polk Blvd, Des Moines IA 50312 (515) 277–5566.**

Jewish Federation of Greater Des Moines. Mem of CJF. Organized 1914. Pres: Marvin Winick; Acting Exec Dir: Elaine Steinger. **910 Polk Blvd, Des Moines IA 50312 (515) 277–6321.**

Temple B'nai Jeshurun. Affiliated with UAHC. 268 mems. Rabbi Jay Goldburg; Cantor H. R. Brown; Pres: Jay S. Daniels; Edu: H.R. Brown; Sisterhood Pres: Sandi Stamp. **5101 Grand, Des Moines IA 50312 (515) 274–4679.**

Tifereth Israel. Affiliated with United Syn of Am. Rabbi Barry D. Cytron; Cantor Pinchas Spiro; Pres: Harlan Hockenberg. **924 Polk Blvd, Des Moines IA 50312 (515) 255–1137.**

Dubuque

Congregation Beth El. Affiliated with UAHC. 39 mems. Pres: Sol Tabak; Sisterhood Pres: Ruth Silverberg. **475 W Locust St, PO Box 185, Dubuque IA 52001 (319) 583–3473.**

Fort Dodge

Congregation Beth El. Affiliated with United Syn of Am. Rabbi Sam Levi; Pres: Dr Herb Jonas; Exec Dirs: Dr Herb Jonas, Jonathan Rutstein; Edu Dir: Lora Levi. **507 N 12th St, Fort Dodge IA 50501 (515) 576–2024.**

Iowa City

Agudas Achim. Affiliated with United Syn of Am. Rabbi Jeffrey R. Portman; Pres: David M. Lubaroff; Edu Dir: Alan Widiss; Youth Dir: Nancee Blum. **602**

E Washington St, Iowa City IA 52240 (319) 337–3813.

Marshalltown

Sons of Israel. Affiliated with United Syn of Am. Pres: Barry S. Kaplan. **211 W Church St, Marshalltown IA 50158 (515) 753–7870.**

Ottumwa

B'nai Jacob. Affiliated with United Syn of Am. Pres: Arnold Sigel. **529 E Main St, Ottumwa IA 52501 (515) 684–7456.**

Sioux City

Jewish Federation. Mem of CJF. Organized 1921. Pres: Henry B. Tygar; Exec Dir: Doris Rosenthal. **525 14th St, Sioux City IA 51105 (712) 258–0618.**

Mount Sinai Temple. Affiliated with UAHC. 122 mems. Rabbi Albert A. Gordon; Pres: Milton Glazer; Sisterhood Pres: Frances S. Kline; Brotherhood Pres: Don Slotsky. **PO Box 2128 NS Station, Sioux City IA 51104 (712) 252–4265.**

Shaare Zion Synagogue. Conservative Syn affiliated with the United Syn of Am. Rel Servs; Women's League. 175 mem families. F in 1925. Rabbi Shawn Zell; Cantor Harry Sterling; Pres: Dr Aaron Katz; VP: Larry Shapiro. **1522 Douglas St, Sioux City IA 51105 (712) 252–4057.**

Waterloo

Sons of Jacob Synagogue. Affiliated with United Syn of Am. Rabbi Sol Serber; Pres: Joseph Weissman. **411 Mitchell Ave, Waterloo IA 50702 (319) 233–9448.**

Waterloo Jewish Federation. c/o Congregation Sons of Jacob, 411 Mitchell Ave, Waterloo IA 50702.

KANSAS

Manhattan

Manhattan Jewish Congregation. Affiliated with UAHC. 24 mems. Pres: Don Roufa. **1509 Wreath, Manhattan KS 66502 (913) 539–8462.**

Overland Park

Hyman Brand Hebrew Acadamy. 5901 College Blvd, Overland Park KS 66211.

Hyman Brand Hebrew Acadamy Library. 5901 College Blvd, Overland Park KS 66211.

Temple Beth El. Affiliated with UAHC. 160 mems. Cantor Eugene Naron; Pres: Arthur Berger; Sisterhood Pres: Darline Berger. **9400 Nall Ave, Overland Park KS 66207 (913) 642–8707.**

Topeka

Temple Beth Sholom. Reform Cong affiliated with UAHC. To meet the spiritual & rel needs of all J in Topeka. Rel Servs; Rel Sch for grades nursery – 10; Presch; Adult Edu; Sisterhood; library; Youth Group; Learning Ctr; Chevrah Group; Campership Prog which helps to support summer camp attendance at J camps; sponsorship of a Blintze Brunch that serves as a fund raiser & an introduction to J foods & culture. 145 families; 60 stu in the Rel Sch; 100 women in the Sisterhood. Temple Beth Sholom grew out of the merger of two earlier congs which were f in 1905 & 1915. They merged, eventually changed their name, & built the first syn in Topeka. In 1928 the Syn became Reform but made provisions for its Orthodox mems. In 1964 the Cong moved fr the original syn to the current syn. In 1979 the Cong completed a major addition to the bldg. Semi-Monthly Bulletin. Facilities include a sanctuary with 78 permanent seats which is expandable to 400; classrms; rabbi's study & an off. Beth Sholom is the only syn in the city. Rabbi Fred N. Reiner. **4200 Munson, Topeka KS 66604 (913) 272–6040.**

Temple Beth Sholom Library. For information on the Temple, see – Temple Beth Sholom, Topeka, KS. **4200 Munson, Topeka KS 66604 (913) 272–6040.**

Topeka-Lawrence Jewish Federation. Mem of CJF. Organized 1939. Pres: Irving Sheffel. **323 SW Greenwood, Topeka KS 66606 (913) 354–1818.**

Wichita

Hebrew Congregation. 1850 Woodlawn, Wichita KS 67208.

Hebrew Congregation Library. 1850 Woodlawn, Wichita KS 67208.

Mid-Kansas Jewish Federation, Inc. Mem of CJF. Organized 1935. Pres: Nancy Matassarin. **400 N Woodlawn, Suite 8, Wichita KS 67208 (316) 686–4741.**

Temple Emanu-El. Affiliated with UAHC. 202 mems. Rabbi Arthur J. Abrams; Pres: Reta C. Kamen; Sisterhood Pres: Jene Fisher; Brotherhood Pres: George Matassarin. **7011 E Central, Wichita KS 67206 (316) 684–5148.**

Temple Emanu-El Library. For information on the Temple, see – Temple Emanu-El, Wichita, KS. **7011 E Central, Wichita KS 67206 (316) 684–5148.**

KENTUCKY

Ashland

Temple Agudat Achim. Affiliated with UAHC. 24 mems. Pres: Don Korros; Sisterhood Pres: Bernice Gehringer. **c/o Robert Simons, 805 Clara, Ashland KY 41101 (606) 329–1840.**

Lexington

Central Kentucky Jewish Association. Mem of CJF. Pres: Judith R. Levine. **258 Plaza Dr, Suite 208, Lexington KY 40503 (606) 277–8048.**

Lexington Havurah. Affiliated with United Syn of Am. Pres: David R. Wekstein; Rel Dir: Irwin G. Cohen; Treas: Avram Levine; Edu Dir: Jeremy Popkin. **3379 Sutherland Dr, Lexington KY 40502 (606) 272–1459.**

Temple Adath Israel. Reform Cong affiliated with UAHC. Rel Servs; Rel Sch; Sisterhood; Youth Group. F in 1904. Rabbi William J. Leffler; Pres: Dr Charles Gorodetzky; 1st VP: Joseph H. Miller; 2nd VP: Mrs Morris A. Brazin; Sec: Dr Ira P. Mersack; Treas: Dr Nat H. Sandler. **124 N Ashland Ave, Lexington KY 40502 (606) 266–3251.**

Louisville

Adath Israel – Brith Sholom. 1649 Cowling Ave, Louisville KY 40205 (502) 451–4050.

Adath Israel – Brith Sholom Library. 1649 Cowling Ave, Louisville KY 40205 (502) 451–4050.

Bureau of Jewish Education. 3600 Dutchmans Lane, Louisville KY 40205 (502) 454–5416.

Congregation Adath Jeshurun. Affiliated with United Syn of Am. Rabbi Simcha Kling; Asst Rabbi: Robert B. Slosberg; Cantor & Edu Dir: Marshall A. Portnoy; Pres: David M. Carney. **2401 Woodbourne Ave, Louisville KY 40205 (502) 458–5359.**

Congregation Adath Jeshurun Library. For information on the Cong, see – Cong Adath Jeshurun, Louisville KY. **2401 Woodbourne Ave, Louisville KY 40205 (502) 458–5359.**

Congregation Anshei Sfard. Orthodox Syn. Rel Servs. Rabbi Solomon Roodman; Pres: Stanley Sosowsky; Pres Emeritus: Herman Wasserman; Chr of the Bd of Dirs: Myron L. Horvitz; VP: Harold Frankel; Fin Sec: Isadore Ignatow; Rec Sec: George Gibson; Treas: Alvin Borowick; Cemetery Warden: Rebecca B. Krupp; Assc Cemetery Warden: Sadie Baer. **3700 Dutchmans Lane, Louisville KY 40205.**

Jewish Community Federation of Louisville. Affiliated with CJF. Fund raising for local, natl & overseas J needs; coordination of com relations, leadership dev, planning & budgeting. Full gamut of agy servs including hosp, family vocational servs, JCC, etc (these are autonomous agy but the Fed is responsible for fund raising & long-range planning); library containing 6438 vols, 669 audiovisual items (J literature & reference). 9200 mems; 2800 families. 5 full-time employees; 500 volunteers. F 1934 as Conf of J Orgs. Pub Community (bi-weekly); Adath Louisville: the Story of a Jewish Community, by Herman Landau (bk, 1981). Facilities include 13 story Shalom Tower with 150 apartments for sr citizens. Award-winning newspapers, Council of J Fed, 1981 & 1982. Pres: Toni G. Goldman; VPs: Howard Markus, Allan B. Solomon, Dr Gerald Temes, Charles Weisberg; Treas: David Goldstein; Sec: Mickey Baron; Assc Dir: David M. Epstein; Asst Dir: Jan M. Rothschild; Controller: William H. Matheny; Endowment Fund Dir: Clarence F. Judah. **3630 Dutchmans Lane, Louisville KY 40205 (502) 451–8840.**

Jewish Community Federation of Louisville, Library. Library contains 6438 vols, 669 audiovisual items (J literature & reference). For information on the Fed, see – Jewish Community

Federation of Louisville, Louisville, KY. **3630 Dutchmans Lane, Louisville KY 40205 (502) 451–8840.**

Kentucky Jewish Post & Opinion. Periodical pub. **1551 Bardstown Rd, Louisville KY 40205 (502) 459–1914.**

The Temple. Affiliated with UAHC. 880 mems. Rabbis: Lenoard H. Devine, Chester B. Diamond, Herbert S. Waller; Pres: James Hertzman; Edu: Irvin Goldstein; Adm: Jack Benjamin; Sisterhood Pres: Lynn Goddy, N. Schwartz; Brotherhood Pres: Gerald Ehrlich. **5101 Brownsbord Rd, Louisville KY 40222 (502) 423–1818.**

Temple Shalom. Affiliated with UAHC. 74 mems. Rabbi Stanley Miles; Pres: Joe Wolf; Edu: Yvonne Wenger. **4220 Taylorsville Rd, Louisville KY 40220 (502) 458–4739.**

Owensboro

Temple Adath Israel. Affiliated with UAHC. 15 mems. Pres: Joel High. **429 Daviess St, Owensboro KY 42301 (502) 683–9723.**

Paducah

Temple Israel. Affiliated with UAHC. 59 mems. Rabbi Howard M. Folb; Pres: Ted Hirsch; Sisterhood Pres: Laurie Ballew; Brotherhood Pres: Michael Resnick. **330 Joe Clifton Dr, PO Box 1141, Paducah KY 42001 (502) 442–4104.**

LOUISIANA

Alexandria

B'nai Israel Synagogue. Conservative Syn affiliated with United Syn of Am. Rel Servs. 40 families. F 1913. Facilities include kosher kitchen, sanctuary seating 250. Pres: Bernard Kaplan MD. **PO Box 5086, Vance & Hickory Sts, Alexandria LA 71301 (318) 445–4586, 9367.**

Gemiluth Chassodim. Affiliated with UAHC. 174 mems. Rabbi Martin Hinchin; Pres: David C. Caplan; Edu: Martin Hinchin; Sisterhood Pres: N. Marks. **PO Box 863, 2021 Turner St, Alexandria LA 71301 (318) 445–3655.**

The Jewish Welfare Federation & Community Council of Central LA. Mem of CJF. Organized 1938. Pres: Harold Katz; Sec/Treas: Mrs George Kuplesky. **1261 Heyman Lane, Alexandria LA 71301 (318) 442–1264.**

Baton Rouge

Jewish Federation of Greater Baton Rouge. Mem of CJF. Organized 1971. Pres: Justine Herzog. **PO Box 80827, Baton Rouge LA 70898 (504) 769–0561, 0504.**

Liberal Synagogue. Affiliated with UAHC. 158 mems. Rabbi Ronald N. Brown; Cantor David Haas; Pres: Mose Wander; Adm: Elinor Goldberg. **9111 Jefferson Highway, Baton Rouge LA 70800 (504) 924–6773.**

Temple B'nai Israel. Affiliated with UAHC. 226 mems. Rabbis: Jan M. Brahms, Walter G. Peiser, Lester W. Roubey; Pres: Albert Fraenkol II; Sisterhood Pres: Lynn Weill; Brotherhood Pres: William Schwartz. **3354 Kleinert Ave, Baton Rouge LA 70806 (504) 343–0111.**

Lafayette

Temple Rodeph Sholom. Affiliated with UAHC. 54 mems. Rabbi Henry Sandman; Pres: Theodore J. Dreyfus; Sisterhood Pres: Blondy Kaplan. **603 Lee Ave, PO Box 2564, Lafayette LA 70501 (318) 234–3760.**

Yeshurun Synagogue. Affiliated with UAHC. 25 mems. Rabbi Selwyn Geller; Pres: Mark Konikoff; Edu: Edye Mayers; Sisterhood Pres: Cathy Cold. **PO Box 53711 OCS, 1520 Kaliste Saloom Rd, Lafayette LA 70505 (318) 984–1775.**

Lake Charles

Temple Sinai. Affiliated with UAHC. 95 mems. Rabbi Sherman Stein; Pres: Shirley Reinauer; Sisterhood Pres: Corene Davidson. **713 Hodges St, Lake Charles LA 70601 (318) 439–2866.**

Metairie

Gates of Prayer. Affiliated with UAHC. 576 mems. Rabbi Kenneth Segel; Cantor David Goldstein; Pres: E. Burt Harris; Edu: Betty B. Lazarus; Adm: Eric G. Reiter; Sisterhood Pres: Marcia Wolfson; Brotherhood Pres: Henry Rynski. **4000 W Esplanade Ave, Metairie LA 70002 (504) 885–2600.**

Lakeshore Hebrew Day School. Orthodox unaffiliated day sch. To guide the stu fr nursery through the early teenage yrs, encompassing every phase of J dev while emphasizing the importance of high academic excellence. Gen & J studies fr presch–8th grade; PTA. The only Heb day sch in LA, it was est in 1970 to provide the J com of New Orleans with an environment in which the chil could obtain a secular edu along with a J edu. The sch moved to their present bldg in 1978. Facilities include a gymnasium-cafetorium, library, sci lab, art rm & classrooms. Heb Studies Dirs: Rabbi Moshe Deitsch, Rabbi Abraham Muken; Secular Prin: Barbara Boling. **5210 W Esplanade Ave, Metairie LA 70002 (504) 885–4532.**

Tikvat Shalom Conservative Congregation. Mem of United Syn of Am. Rel Servs; Sat morning family Shabbat progs; Sisterhood; Men's Club; USY youth group; Adult Edu Ins; Rel Sch. F in 1960. Rabbi Eric Cytryn; Pres: Abraham Gerber; Exec Dir: Ashiyn Bevis; Edu Dir: Betty Kupersmit. **3737 W Esplanade Ave, Metairie LA 70002 (504) 899–1144.**

Monroe

Congregation B'nai Israel. Affiliated with UAHC. 161 mems. Rabbi Alan L. Ponn; Pres: Mortimer Raphael; Edu: Alan L. Ponn; Adm: Helen W. Luckett; Sisterhood Pres: S.J. Shlosman. **2400 Orell Pl, Monroe LA 71201 (318) 387–0730.**

Congregation B'nai Israel Library. For information on the Cong, see – Congregation B'nai Israel, Monroe, LA. **2400 Orell Pl, Monroe LA 71201 (318) 387–0730.**

United Jewish Charities of Northeast Louisiana. Mem of CJF. Organized 1938. Pres: Morris Blumenthal; Sec/Treas: Ruth Zipkes. **2400 Orell Pl, Monroe LA 71201 (318) 387–0730.**

Morgan City

Temple Shaare Zedek. Affiliated with UAHC. 20 mems. Pres: Leonard H. Roes. **PO Box 329, Morgan City LA 70380 (318) 385–2552.**

New Iberia

Congregation Gates of Prayer. Affiliated with UAHC. 35 mems. Pres: Bernard Lahasky; Sisterhood Pres: Shayne Wormser. **PO Box 488, New Iberia LA 70560 (318) 364–1218.**

New Orleans

American Red Magen David for Israel – David Ben Gurion Chapter. Official Is Red Cross serv. Raises funds for serv in Is. F in 1922. **1701 Dryades St, New Orleans LA 70113 (504) 525–2971.**

Anti-Defamation League of B'nai B'rith. To translate the promise of democracy into the reality of daily living. Works to project a positive image of J, & to secure justice & fair treatment for all citizens. **535 Gravier St, New Orleans LA 70130 (504) 522–9534.**

B'nai B'rith Council, City of New Orleans. Communication & organizing arm of B'nai B'rith. Serving on the council are reps fr the Anti-Defamation League, the Lodges, BBYO, & Adult Edu of the B'nai B'rith. **535 Gravier St, New Orleans LA 70130 (504) 525–2755.**

B'nai B'rith Hillel Foundation. Edu, recreational & spiritual prog for the stu at Tulane, Loyola, & Univ of New Orleans. Informal classes, social functions & rel servs. **912 Bdwy, New Orleans LA 70118 (504) 866–7060.**

Chabad House. Lubavitch com servs ctr. Blends Chassidic fervor & warmth with tradition & learning, to show that every J, fr whatever background he or she comes fr, is an integral part of the body of Is. Anti-missionary work; adult edu; Sabbath seminars; holiday progs; day camp; youth groups; syns; kosher kitchen; counseling; chaplaincy; Mitzvah Campaigns; hosp & prison visitations; sr citizens encounters; speakers bureau. Rabbi Zelig Rivkin. **7037 Freret St, New Orleans LA 70118 (504) 866–5164.**

Commission on Jewish Education – Communal Hebrew School. Est in response to need to enhance J Edu. Communal Heb Sch offers classes for stu fr Nursery Sch to HS. Special one-day a week prog for chil fr Reform cong. Sponsors Is Pilgrimage for teenagers (6 weeks in Is); in-serv training & consultation for local J educators; Lakeshore Hebrew Day Sch which has an enrollment of over 100 stu, many of whom are chil of recently arrived Soviet J refugees; scholarships. **1631 Calhoun St, New Orleans LA 70118 (504) 861–7508.**

Congregation A.A. Anshe Sfard. Orthodox Syn. To promote traditional modern Orthodox J while maintaining a warm family atmosphere. Rel Servs; Sisterhood; Adult Edu, Sun Breakfast. F in 1896 by Polish & Russian immigrants. **2230 Carondelet St, New Orleans LA 70130 (504) 522–4714.**

Congregation Beth Israel. Orthodox Syn. To promote & teach the principles & practices of traditional J & to fulfill the needs of young modern J in an Orthodox setting. Rel Servs; Shabbas family dinners, Shabbaton retreats; Fri onegs; Sisterhood; Brotherhood; Sun Sch, youth progs; Adult Edu; Bar/Bat Mitzvah training. Over 400 mems. F in 1904 with 4 charter mems. **7000 Canal Blvd, New Orleans LA 70124 (504) 283–4366.**

Congregation Chevra Thilim. Orthodox Syn. Committed to an active edu prog emphasizing the role of young people in the framework of Orthodox J. Daily Rel Servs; Sisterhood; Brotherhood. F in 1876. **4429 S Claiborne Ave, New Orleans LA 70125 (504) 895–7987.**

Congregation Gates of Prayer. Reform Temple. Nursery Sch; Rel Sch; Sisterhood; Brotherhood; Youth Group; Jr Youth Group; Adult Edu. F in 1850. The Cong began as Orthodox with German ritual. The Cong is the first J ins in Jefferson Parish. A cemetery is maintained. **4000 W Esplanade Ave, New Orleans LA 70119 (504) 885–2600.**

Israel Bonds. Sold to individuals, institutions & orgs for purpose of maintaining & developing the State of Israel. To provide a central source of investment capital for Is historic progs of econ dev & immigrant absorption. Sells stock of govt-owned Is corporations through its affiliate, Capital for Israel, Inc. **604 Baronne Bldg, New Orleans LA 70112 (504) 524–8756.**

Jewish Children's Regional Service of Jewish Children's Home. J chil caring agy serving 7 southern states: AL, AR, LA, MS, OK, TN, TX. To protect, care for & edu J chil. Camp scholarship; edu aid; placement of chil without homes in foster homes; placement of emotionally or behaviorally disturbed chil in special facilities; counseling; servs to chil at home; adoption; consultation; information & referral. Organized in 1854 & then known as the Assn for the Relief of J Widows & Orphans. The Assn was formed because of the yellow fever epidemic which left many chil orphaned & many women widowed. In 1946 the facility that housed the chil closed, & the present prog was formed. Exec Dir: Viola Weiss; Pres: J.M. Cohn; VPs: Jacques L. Weiner Jr, Mrs Louis Stern; Treas: Bernard S. Jacobs; Sec: Saul Stone; Hon Offs: Marx J. Borod, Carol B. Hart, Harris Hyman Jr, Edith Deutsch Lashman, Benjamin F. Lewis, Henry Mastlansky, M. E. Polson, Daniel L. Scharff, David R. Schwarz, Solis Seiferth, Judge Louis H. Yarrut. **5342 Charles Ave, PO Box 15225, New Orleans LA 70175 (504) 899–1595.**

The Jewish Civic Press. Monthly newspaper. To pub a tabloid on a monthly schedule disseminating world & regional news to New Orleans & the rest of the state of LA, & to AR. Est in 1965. Publisher: Abner L. Tritt. **PO Box 15500, New Orleans LA 70175 (504) 895–8784.**

Jewish Community Center. Com ctr serving the New Orleans com. Physical edu; public affairs; pol forums; lectures; J edu; library containing 1,000 vols. The JCC dates back to 1855 when The Young Men's Hebrew & Literary Soc was formed. This org ceased to exist in the 1880's. In 1891 The Young Men's Hebrew Assn was organized by the Harmony Club. A bldg was erected in 1895 & was used by all citizens of New Orleans for debates, musical activities & Mardi Gras ceremonies. In 1939 a new bldg was erected to replace the original which was destoyed by fire. This bldg opened its doors as The Young Men's & Young Women's Hebrew Assn. A second fire in 1947 destroyed the bldg, & the agy then relocated in the J Chil Home in 1948. At that time, it changed its name to the JCC of New Orleans. In 1966 the JCC moved to its present facility. Facilities include kosher kitchen, swimming pool, health club, weight rm, auditorium, small meeting rms, gymnasium, dance studio, library, large field. Pres: Michael Berenson; VPs: Hartwig Moss, Alan Rosenbloom, Robbie Rubenstein; Sec: Linda Zoller; Treas: Max Fuksman; Exec Dir: Bernard Vrona; Prog Dir: Ann Eisen. **PO Box 15950, New Orleans LA 70175 (504) 897–0143.**

Jewish Endowment Foundation. Funding for the Future. Provides seed money for innovative programming, other future needs of J com. Funding is accomplished through encouragement of bequests & specialized lifetime deferred giving progs. **211 Camp St, New Orleans LA 70130 (504) 525–0673.**

Jewish Family & Children's Service. Family, individual & group counseling for chil, youth & their families; adoption, foster care, & placement servs; aid to sr citizens; Family Life Edu Prog; yearly Family Life Ins; resettlement of Soviet J refugees. **107 Camp St, New Orleans LA 70130 (504) 524–8476.**

Jewish Federation of Greater New Orleans. Central coordinating fundr org for all the J social serv agy in the com. J Welfare Fund: secures the funds necessary to provide servs to the J com in New Orleans & throughout the world; Women in Fed: provides a continuing prog of edu & involvement for the women in the com; Com Relations Cttee: fosters positive com relations & takes action on behalf of the Fed, specifically in the areas of Is & Soviet J; Lemman-Stern Young Leadership: dev prog for young men & women which creates a fuller understanding of J communal life. Each yr, mems of the prog participate in a mission to Is & attend innovative & informative sessions. Constituent Agy: JCC, J Chil Regional Servs, J Family & Chil Servs, B'nai B'rith Hillel Foun, Touro Infrimary, New Orleans Home for J Aged; Affiliates: Com Endowment Foun, The J Times; Beneficiary Agy: Lakeshore Hebrew Day Sch; Divs: Commis on J Edu. In 1913 The J Charitable & Edu Fed was formed to serve the New Orleans J population. In 1936 a separate org, the J Welfare Fund, was est. The two bodies merged in 1960 to form the J Welfare Fed. This was reorganized in 1977 as the J Fed of Greater New Orleans. The primary beneficiary of the Fed is the UJA. Through the J Agy in Is, these funds support resettlement & absorption of new immigrants, day care ctrs, progs for youths & sr citizens homes. Through the Joint Distribution Cttee, progs are est for the aged, the physically & mentally ill, & the handicapped throughout the world. Other natl, overseas & local agy also receive allocations fr the Fed. Pres: Joan Berenson; Exec Dir: Gerald Lasensky. **211 Camp St, Suite 500, New Orleans LA 70130 (504) 525–0673.**

The Jewish Times. Private newspaper (pub every other week, 26 issues annually). Disseminates news of the organized J com served by the J Fed of Greater New Orleans; coverage of local, natl & intl news which is not presented either in depth or in analysis by any other media in the area. Readership in excess of 12,000. The Fed pledges a paid subscription for each one of its mems. **211 Camp St, Suite 500, New Orleans LA 70130 (504) 524–3147.**

National Council of Jewish Women – Greater New Orleans Section. Volunteer org. To advance human welfare & the democratic way of life locally, nationally & internationally. Prog priorities include: volunteerism, Is, quality of J life, justice for chil, servs for the aging, individual rights & responsibilities. New Orleans section has a membership of 1,500, including an evening branch known as Moonlighters. F in 1893, NCJW is the oldest natl J women's volunteer org. The New Orleans section was begun in 1897. For additional information, see – National Council of Jewish Women, New York City, NY. **4747 Earhart Blvd, New Orleans LA 70125 (504) 488–5388.**

New Orleans Home for Jewish Aged. Intermediate care facility commonly referred to as Willow Wood. 24 hour restorative nursing care, med servs, social servs, nutritional programming, a planned prog of activities, physical therapy, housekeeping/maintenance servs. 99 beds. Est in 1962 as a home for the well aged, the Home has developed into a full serv facility. **3701 Behrman Place, New Orleans LA 70114 (504) 367–5640.**

Temple Sinai. Reform Cong. Affiliated with UAHC. Rel Servs; J Edu progs for adults & chil; cultural & social activities; burial ground; Youth Group; Sisterhood; Brotherhood. Est in 1870, the Temple is the oldest Reform J Cong in New Orleans. Rabbis: Murray Blackman, Myra Soifer; Pres: Julius L. Levy Jr; Edu: Myra Soifer; Adm: Herbert Barton; Sisterhood Pres: Waynette Cohen; Brotherhood Pres: Charles L. Stern. **6227 St Charles Ave, New Orleans LA 70118 (504) 861–3693.**

Temple Sinai Library. For information on the Temple, see – Temple Sinai, New Orleans, LA. **6227 St Charles Ave, New Orleans LA 70118 (504) 861–3693.**

Touro Infirmary. Non-profit non-sectarian gen teaching & research hosp. Provides med servs for patients in New Orleans area; accepts medically indigent patients for diagnosis on both an out-patient & in-patient basis. F mid 19th century by Judah Touro. **1401 Foucher St, New Orleans LA 70115 (504) 897–3311.**

Touro Synagogue. Reform Cong affiliated with UAHC. To combine the advantage of a large major syn with personal small group interaction. Rel Servs; Rel Sch; Adult Edu; Youth Group; Sisterhood; Brotherhood; adult retreats. F in 1828, the Cong is the oldest in the Mississippi Valley. Rabbi David S. Goldstein; Cantor Ralph Slifkin; Pres: Donald Mintz; Edu: Jennie Schneider; Adm: Dorothy K. Portnoy; Sisterhood Pres: Susan Mintz; Brotherhood Pres: Oscar Z. Levy Jr. **St Charles at General Pershing, New Orleans LA 70115 (504) 895–4843.**

Women in Federation of the Jewish Federation of Greater New Orleans. A permanent adjunct to the total J Fed of Greater New Orleans. To provide a yr round prog of edu & involvement for the women of the com. Com calendar; Lemann-Stern Young Leadership Dev; Shalom Corps which greets newcomers; Shabbaton for sharing the Sabbath experience; Campaign Women's Div. Shalom – a directory of J ins & other helpful facts. Membership in the orgs is open to any woman who makes a pledge to the J Welfare Fund Campaign. The org is structured with a Bd of elected mems & the pres of all women's orgs & sisterhoods. Pres: Florette G. Margolis; Proj Chr: Sylvia Gerson, Nancy Jacoves; Chr, Women's Campaign: Marilyn Katz; Adm Asst: Margot Garon. **211 Camp St, Suite 500, New Orleans LA 70130 (504) 525–0673.**

Shreveport

B'nai Zion Congregation. Reform Cong affiliated with UAHC. Worship, study & benevolence according to the essential ideals & principles of Reform J. Sisterhood; Brotherhood; Youth Group; Rel Sch for chil between the ages 4–16; Rel Servs; library of Judaica; Rabbi's Luncheon Discussion Group. Est in 1857 as Har El Cong & later chartered as Hebrew Zion Cong in 1866. In 1915 the name was officially changed to Bnai Zion. Rabbi Richard A. Zionts; Pres: Abry S. Cahn; VP: Mrs Everett Rubenstein; Treas: Raymond S. Morris. **175 Southfield Rd, Shreveport LA 71105 (318) 861–2122.**

Congregation Agudath Achim. Affiliated with United Syn of Am, & Natl Org of Conservative Syns. To maintain & strengthen Traditional J; to dev a stronger J com; to encourage J fellowship. Rel Servs; Heb Sch; Sun Sch; youth activities; USY; Young Adult Group; Sisterhood; Men's Club. Est in 1901 by a group of men & women dedicated to an enriched J life. Facilities include a sanctuary, edu & activities bldg & social hall. Rabbi H. D. Uriel Smith. **9401 Village Green Dr, Shreveport LA 71115 (318) 797–6401.**

Shreveport Jewish Family & Childrens Services. Counseling & welfare agy affiliated with Council of J Feds, Assn of J Family Servs Agy, Natl Assn of Social Work, Conf of J Communal Serv. Professional therapeutic counseling servs for families & individuals. Therapeutic counseling for disturbed youth, marital conflict, emotional problems, parent-child relationships, drug abuse, problem pregnancies; fin assitance; servs for the elderly; emergency referrals. Help is given in private confidential interviews by professionally trained, experienced, licensed counselors who can assist a troubled person in understanding his problem &, when necessary, intervening in its resolution; when dealing with teenagers, intervention with the cts & law officials is usually a necessity. 4 employees; 50 volunteers. F as part of the Shreveport J Fed in 1966. Pub Highlights (monthly). Resettled 30 new Am (Russian) families. Exec Dir: David Abrams; Social Work Clin Consultant: Rabbi Emanuel Kumin. **2030 Line Ave, Shreveport LA 71104 (318) 221–4129.**

Shreveport Jewish Federation. Mem of CJF. Organized 1941; Inc 1967. Pres: Arnold Lincove; Exec Dir: David S. Abrams. **2030 Line Ave, Shreveport LA 71104 (318) 221–4129.**

MAINE

Auburn

Beth Abraham. Affiliated with United Syn of Am. Rabbi Norman Geller; Pres: Allen Bean. **Main St & Laurel Ave, Auburn ME 04210 (207) 783–1302.**

Bangor

Jewish Community Council. Mem of CJF. Organized 1949. Pres: George Z. Singal; Exec Dir: Sanfred Pasternack. **28 Somerset St, Bangor ME 04401 (207) 945–5631.**

Lewiston

Lewiston-Auburn Jewish Federation. Mem of CJF. Sponsors United Jewish Appeal. Organized 1947. Pres: Bertha Allen; Exec Dir: Howard G. Joress. **134 College St, Lewiston ME 04240 (207) 786–4201.**

Orono

University of Maine at Orono Hillel. Univ stu group affiliated with B'nai B'rith Hillel Foun. Shabbat Servs with Kiddush; monthly bagel & lox brunches; discussions of J rel & culture such as "Have Am J 'Sold Out' on Progressive Social Values?"; Celebration of all J holidays as a community; speakers & films of J interest brought to campus; library containing 300 vols (J hist, Is, prayer, anti-Semitism, culture). 125 mems. F 1945. Co-Advs: Lianne Harris, Avis Smith; Pres: Bob Gordon; VPs: Vivienne Joffe, Jeff Goulsten; Rel Coords: Peter Brown, Jason Goodfriend. **Hillel University of Maine at Orono, Orono ME 04469 (207) 773–9631.**

Portland

Jewish Community Center of Portland. To provide for the mental, moral, spiritual & physical welfare of its mems & the entire com; to promote literary, charitable, edu, social, moral, rel & benevolent endeavors in the City of Portland; to help in every way possible the J com of Portland ME; to endeavor to bring the J com into harmony & union, & to foster & dev the highest ideals of Am citizenship in all the J in the com. Est in 1939. Pres: Saul A. Goldberg; VP Programming: William Cohen; VP Mems: Alan Zimmerman; VP House: David Small; VP Athletics: Marshall Mack; VP Camping: Irwin Novak; VP Fin: Samuel Novick; VP PR: David Lieberman; Treas: James Baker; Asst Treas: Bradley Kaplan; Sec: Joan Hirsch. **66 Pearl St, Portland ME 04101 (207) 772–1959.**

Jewish Federation Community Council of Southern Maine. Mem of CJF. Sponsors United Jewish Appeal. Organized 1942. Pres: Richard D. Aronson; Adm: Cecelia E. Levine. **66 Pearl St, Portland ME 04101 (207) 773–7254.**

Jewish Home for Aged. 158 North St, Portland ME 04112 (207) 772–5456.

Temple Beth El. Affiliated with United Syn of Am. Rabbi Harry Z. Sky; Cantor Kurt Messerschmidt; Pres: Jerome Goldberg; Adm: Daniel Epstein; Youth Dir: Yisroel Serik. **400 Deering Ave, Portland ME 04103 (207) 774–2649.**

MARYLAND

Aberdeen

Harford Jewish Center. Reform Temple affiliated with UAHC. As the only syn in the cty, to represent J to Jews & non-Jews. Rel Servs; edu progs; Sisterhood; Brotherhood; Presch; Sun & mid-week Heb Sch; library containing 500 vols (J interest). 132 families; 100 stu pre-K through 10th grade. 1 employee. F 1955. Facilities include kosher kitchen, sanctuary seating 136, gift shop. Rabbi Kenneth Block; Pres: W. Weintraub; 1st VP: Barry Trager; 2nd VP: Paul Oxenberg; 3rd VP: Richard Salmonsohn; Treas: David Samuels; Sec: David Schneck; Pres Ladies Auxiliary: Sue Weinstein. **402 Paradise Rd, Aberdeen MD 21001 (301) 272–8316.**

Annapolis

Annapolis Jewish Welfare Fund. 601 Ridgley Ave, Annapolis MD 21401.

Arnold

Kol Ami. Affiliated with United Syn of Am. Pres: Ira L. Snyder; Edu Dir: Sheila Litzky. **517 Mystic Lane, Arnold MD 21012 (301) 268–9254.**

Temple Beth Sholom. Affiliated with UAHC. 133 mems. Rabbi Robert Klensin; Pres: Glen Jackson; Sisterhood Pres: Beverly Handwerger. **PO Box 59, 1461 Old Annapolis Rd, Arnold MD 21012 (301) 974–0900.**

Baltimore

Associated Jewish Charities & Welfare Fund. Fund raising agy affiliated with many Baltimore orgs. Raises funds for 37 local, natl & overseas J agy; operates as social planning & budgeting agy to coord progs of local agy; introduces new servs to meet com needs; works with other private & public agy for com welfare. Pres: Willard Hackerman; 1st VP: Shoshana S. Cardin; VP Adm: Manuel Dupkin; VP Social Planning & Budgeting: Jonathan W. Kolker; Treas: Richard Davidson; Asst Treas: Linda C. Miller; Sec: Samuel S. Kahan; Asst Sec: Herschel L. Langenthal; Exec VP: Stephen D. Solender. **101 W Mount Royal Ave, Baltimore MD 21201 (301) 727–4828.**

Baltimore Hebrew College. 6800 Williamson Ave, Baltimore MD 21215.

Baltimore Hebrew College, Meyerhoff Library. 6800 Williamson Ave, Baltimore MD 21215.

Baltimore Hebrew Congregation. Reform Cong affiliated with UAHC. To interpret the moral & spiritual legacy of the past into an affirmation of the present & future life. Prayer Servs; Rel Sch; Special Edu; Adult Edu; retreat & camping prog; arts & crafts; Stu Choir; dancing; Sisterhood; Brotherhood; Mixed Bowling League; Sr Men's Fellowship; Parents Assn; Havurah; Jews by Choice; Young Marrieds; Over 35 Singles; youth groups. 1700 mems. Chartered in 1830 as MD's first J Cong. In 1892 the Cong joined UAHC. The Cong moved to its present bldg in 1951. The bldg complex includes the Straus Social Hall, Dalsheimer Auditorium, Hoffberger Chapel & Gallery, Solomon Rothschild Ctr, Sylvia & Joseph Rosenfeld Music & Media Ctr, Eisenberg Art Rm, meeting halls, library, kitchen, 42 classrms, youth activities ctr. On the High Holydays there are special Servs for chil, col stu & the deaf. Two cemeteries are owned & maintained by the Cong. Rabbi Murray Salzman; Rabbi Harvey J. Winokur; Rabbi Sheila C. Russian; Cantor Gail P. Hirschenfang; Cantor Emeritus Joseph Rosenfeld; Exec Dir: Malcolm Hellman; Sec to the Cong: Louise M. Glazer; Adm of Rel Sch: Samuel Sharrow. **7401 Park Heights Ave, Baltimore MD 21208.**

Baltimore Jewish Times. Periodical pub. **2104 N Charles St, Baltimore MD 21218 (301) 752–3504.**

Beth El. Affiliated with United Syn of Am. Rabbi Mark G. Loeb; Rabbi Emeritus Jacob B. Agus; Cantor Saul Z. Hammerman; Pres: Mildred Miller; Exec Dir: Rose Pollack; Edu Dir: Joseph Lipawsky. **8101 Park Heights Ave, Baltimore MD 21208 (301) 484–0411.**

Board of Jewish Education. Baltimore com central servs agy for J edu, affiliated with Am Assn for J Edu. To advance & improve J edu in Orthodox, Conservative, Reform & communal schs in Baltimore City & Cty, & Howard, Ann Arundel & Carroll Ctys. Consultation & supervision; information & research; tests, measurements & edu pub; library of audio visual aids; Dept of Special Edu; Dept of Early Childhood; Dept of Co-Curricular Activities; Aaron H. Leibtag Resource Ctr; Dept of Professional Servs; Youth Ins & Academy for Reform J Studies; Dept of Parent & Family Edu; Newcomers Edu Prog; Master Teacher Prog; assistance to local public schs in Holocaust & social studies; aid to the Russian J stu in sch. Organized in 1921. Pres: Larry M. Wolf; 1st VP: Marcia Rothstein; 2nd VP: Dr Jerry M. Cohen; Sec: Richard G. Manekin; Treas: Dr Noah Lightman; Exec VP: Dr Hyman Chanover; Exec Dir: Rabbi Herbert Birnbaum; Assc Exec Dir: Dr Henry Tyrangiel; Dir of Resource Ctr, & Parent & Family Edu: Mira Fraenkel; Art Consultant: Elaine Gittlen; Supervisor One Day Classes: Beryl Gottesman; Adm, Youth Ins & Russian Schooling: Rita Kipper; Dir of Special Edu: Samuel S. Litov; Dir of Elementary Level Co-Curricular Activities: Leo Reich; Dir of Early Childhood Edu: Rena Rotenberg; Resource Asst: David Schapiro; Dir of Social Studies & Heb Edu: Sarah M. Siegman; Dir of Post Elementary Co-Curricular Activities: Sandy Vogel; Controller: Martin I. Yospa. **5800 Park Heights Ave, Baltimore MD 21215 (301) 367–8300.**

Chizuk Amuno Congregation. Conservative Syn affiliated with United Syn of Am. Rel Servs; Solomon Schechter Day Sch; Heb Sch; Early Childhood Edu Dept; Youth Dept; Brotherhood; Sisterhood; PTA; over 50 clubs; Young Couples Club; Adult Edu progs. Est in 1871; founding mems of the United Syn of Am. Rabbi Joel H. Zaiman; Hazzan: Abraham Salkov; Pres: Sigi R. Strauss; 1st VP: Irwin M. Sussman; VPs: Mende Lerner, Dr Irvin Pollack; Treas: Bernard B. Cohen; Asst Treas: Patsy Gilbert; Sec: Bette Miller; Exec Dir: Stanley I. Minch; Edu Dir: Louis I. Sternfield; Youth Dir: Cheryl Skolnick. **8100 Stevenson Rd, Baltimore MD 21208 (301) HU6–6400.**

Chizuk Amuno Congregation School. For information on the Cong, see – Chizuk Amuno Congregation, Baltimore, MD. **8100 Stevenson Rd, Baltimore MD 21208 (301) 486–6400.**

Chizuk Amuno Congregation School Library. 8100 Stevenson Rd, Baltimore MD 21208 (301) 486–6400.

Har Sinai Congregation. Affiliated with UAHC. 723 mems. Rabbis: Floyd L. Herman, A. Shusterman; Cantors: Barry Greenberg, Henry Cooper; Pres: Donald E. Milstein; Edu: Edwin Cohen; Sisterhood Pres: R.E. Segal; Brotherhood Pres: Stewart Sachs. **6300 Park Heights Ave, Baltimore MD 21215 (301) 764–2882.**

Hurwitz House. Comprehensive care facility; subsidiary of Levindale Hebrew Geriatric Ctr & Hosp. To provide personal care & nursing supervision to those elderly who do not require total institutional care. Residents participate in fulfilling their own personal needs for activities of daily living & prepare their own breakfasts; lunch & dinner are served daily with dietary laws observed. A van is available for transportation. Group living arrangement with 23 beds. Staff includes licensed practical nurse, aide on each shift, 2 utility men. In addition, adm & consultation are provided by the Levindale Hebrew Geriatric Ctr & Hosp. Hurwitz House began operating in Oct 1973 as a three-yr experimental proj. The facility consists of two bldgs located on one acre of land situated in a residential area near shops, theaters & servs. Adm: Louis Balk. **133 Slade Ave, Baltimore MD 21208.**

Jewish Historical Society of Maryland, Inc. To preserve papers & documents concerning the local J com. Speakers Bureau; two major meetings a yr; occasional seminars, special events; Oral Hist Library with interviews of distinguished people in the com. Est in 1960. Semi annual magazine; Newsletter. Restored the Lloyd St Syn, oldest existing syn in MD, & maintains it as a mus. Pres: Morton S. Oppenheimer; VPs: Col Philip Sherman, Helen Sollins, Joseph R. Hirschmann; Treas: Robert L. Weinberg; Sec: Mrs E. B. Hirsh; Fin Sec: Jerome Schloss; Exec Adm: Joan Lippman. **5800 Park Heights Ave, Baltimore MD 21215 (301) 466–4443.**

Levindale Hebrew Geriatric Center & Hospital. To provide modern facilities for intensive med care. Social servs; pharmacy; x-ray lab; sheltered workshop; chaplaincy prog; physical, med & occupational therapy provided by Sinai Hosp; dietary laws observed. 273 beds. Staff includes med dir, house physicians, psychiatric staff, over 150 on the nursing staff. Levindale had its beginnings in the Hebrew Friendly Inn est in 1890 to temporarily house the many new J immigrants to Baltimore. As some elderly J required com care, rms were set aside at the Inn to take care of them. A Home for Aged Incurables was organized in 1914. In the early 1920's the J Chil Soc which occupied the present Levindale site, reorganized its chil care prog, abandoning its orphanage. Levindale, named after the Exec Dir of the Assc J Charities Louis H. Levin, became a home for the aged with the merger of the Hebrew Friendly Inn & Aged Home, & the Home for the Aged Incurables. Additions increased the num of bldgs fr four to eight, & the bed capacity to 230. In 1962 the bed capacity was 267; an additional bldg was dedicated in 1975 bringing the total capacity to 273. In 1970 the Adult Day Treatment Ctr was opened as an alternate to nursing home inpatient placement. In 1973 the Shirley & Philip Hurwitz House, a 23 bed group home, was dedicated. This facility provides for those elderly who do not require the total & intensive care of the main bldgs. Pres: Gordon J. Salganik; 1st VP: Robert S. Ginsburg; VPs: Gilbert Sandler, Sander L. Wise; Treas: Jonas Brodie; Asst Treas: Dr Arthur Bushel; Sec: Dr William S. Parker; Exec Dir: Stanford A. Alliker. **Belvedere & Greenspring Ave, Baltimore MD 21215 (301) 466–8700.**

Maryland Council, Jewish National Fund. To further tree planting in Is, land reclamation, & edu with the Heb schs & Christian coms. Lectures; shows; dinners; cantors concerts; Women's Auxiliary; Young Leadership. 700 mems; 300 families; 10,000 individuals; 4 local groups; 3 state groups. 3 employees; 400 volunteers. 60 yrs in MD. Pub JMF Newsletter (bi-monthly). Pres: Sidney Kaplan; Exec VP: Bernhard Kiewe; Treas: Ben Schuster; VPs: Suzanne Mensh, Llen Quille. **14 Old Court Rd, Baltimore MD 21208 (301) 486–3317.**

Moses Montefiore Emunath Israel Woodmoor Hebrew Congregation. Modern Orthodox. To meet the needs of the suburban family by upholding a complete spiritual, edu & social prog mixed with the tradition of modern Orthodox J. Daily Rel Servs; Adult Edu; Talmud classes; annual Scholar-in-Residence Weekend; Intl Communication Seminars; individual, marital, family counseling; Brotherhood; Sisterhood. The Moses Montefiore Hebrew Cong was est in 1888 by Russian immigrants in S Baltimore City. The Cong merged with Cong Emunath Is & Woodmoor Hebrew Cong to become Moses Montefiore Emunath Is Woodmoor Hebrew Cong & moved to its present location in 1965. Bldg facilities include a library, sanctuary with permanent seats of 200, social hall, classrms, & chapel. Pub Bulletin (4 times a year). Rabbi Everett Ackerman; Cantor Israel Friedman; Pres: Samuel Stone; Chr: Max Scheinberg. **3605 Coronada Rd, Baltimore MD 21207 (301) 655–4484.**

National Conference of Synagogue Youth – Atlantic Seaboard Region. Central body for youth groups of Traditional congs. To articulate the timeless Torah message in an idiom, style, fervor & spirit that reaches the hearts of Am J youth. Library of youth pubs; Jr NCSY for pre-teens; Sr NCSY for pre-collegiates; regional conventions; Shabbatons; conclaves; leadership seminars; NCSY in Is – the Is Summer Seminar; Proj Yedid which reaches out to alienated J youth & provides positive informal J experiences; com outreach to HS, cols, young adults, & families; J Stu Assn for HS stu which devs & disseminates edu materials on issues relevant to J stu; campus sponsored progs; cult-activity monitoring of col campuses in conjunction with Hillel; com alert & edu serving the HS & col campuses, syns, J orgs, & the J com at large in response to missionary activities – providing counseling for missionary & cult group mems & families, Hotline, pamphlets for youth & parents, & library of anti-missionary materials. Over 900 mems. Over 150 volunteer youth leaders & advs. F in 1961, & since that time has provided more than 10,000 J youngsters with positive J experiences. Keeping Posted With NCSY; Advisors' Newsletter; Mitsvos Ma'asiyos; Holiday Series; Jewish Thought Series; Leadership Manual Series; Texts for Teen Study. Proj Yedid pubs a newsletter to keep all com leaders & J com orgs aware of the activity of missionary & cult groups. The Atlantic Seaboard Region of NCSY has been awarded 'Region of the Yr' four times in eight yrs. Dir NCSY & Consultant for Proj Yedid: Rabbi Yitzchok Lowenbraun; Assc Dir: Bonnie Sue Pollak; Asst Dir: Rabbi Jeff Mendell. **5713 Park Heights Ave, Baltimore MD 21215 (301) 542–8678.**

National Council of Jewish Women, Inc – Baltimore Section. Oldest J women's volunteer org in the US. The org is the largest affiliate mem of the Intl Council of J Women. Dedicated to com serv, edu, social action & the strengthening of the spirit of J. Aliza Brandwine Ctr for Parent-Infant Dev provides a prog for chil & their parents that enriches chil rearing skills & parenting strengths; Concord House Commissary enables residents to purchase non-perishable staple goods on a non-profit basis; Council Day Care Ctr offers a model training prog of quality day care located at Towson State Univ; First Step offers servs to youths & their families to prevent young people fr becoming involved in delinquent activities; Florence Crittenton Home benefits fr two agy projs: an edu & social prog for residents, & a research & interview survey of past recipients of the home's servs; House of Ruth offers a temporary crisis shelter for abused women & their chil; Meals-on-Wheels serves kosher meals to home-bound, aged & infirm; NW Sr Ctr provides progs, recreation, crafts, social activities & information & referral servs; Single Now provides an edu & social org for divorced & widowed men & women; WICS (Women In Com Servs) recruits & screens underprivileged women who are sch dropouts & enables them to acquire skills needed to obtain jobs; WISH (Women In Self Help) provides an anonymous telephone serv for adult women who need help; other servs include world-wide guided trips that incorporate points of special interest for mems & their families, Council Thrift Shop, Gift Fund Cards, public affairs com servs, legislation & social action, edu, discussions, ins, lecture groups & bk clubs. The org focuses on problems & issues confronting the local J com, & supports progs in Is. F in 1893 by Hannah Greenbaum Solomon. Future com servs include a Gan Yeladim (Garden of Chil) which will provide yr round day care servs, & NEED (Nutrition, Edu, Exercise & Discussion), a professionally run prog designed for women who have had mastectomies. Pres: Gladys Nathan; VP Public Affairs: Lucia Kerzner; VP PR: Margery Dellon; Public Affairs & Prog Cttee: Betty-Jean Bavar, Carol Bernstein, Ilene Brave, Lee Ehudin, Lois Greenebaum, Barbara Hettleman, Penne Klipper, Hannah Magram, Ann Ries, Wendy Rosen, Sharon Sagal, Carol Sandler, Sharon Schreter, Elyce Stern, Gail Sureff; Exec Adm: Florence Coplan. **7241 Park Heights Ave, Baltimore MD 21208 (301) 358–0707.**

Ner Israel Rabbinical College. 400 Mt Wilson Lane, Baltimore MD 21208 (301) 484–7200.

Pioneer Women – Na'amat. The training & edu of the Is woman & her family so that each can be best equipped to lead productive lives. For additional information, see – Pioneer Women Na'amat, New York City, NY. **6810 Park Heights, Baltimore MD 21215 (301) 358–3337.**

Seaboard America-Israel Chamber of Commerce – Baltimore – Washington. Offers assistance to mem US firms interested in economic activity in & with Is. Provides extensive trade assistance; pub market research reports; aids in dev trade & investment between US & Is. For additional information, see – American-Israel Chamber of Commerce & Industry, Inc, New York City, NY. **1000 Haverhill Rd, Baltimore MD 21229 (301) 525–2110.**

Sinai Hospital of Baltimore. Non-profit, acute care gen hosp. Affiliated for training & edu with: Johns Hopkins Univ Sch of Med, Univ of MD Sch of Med, Harford Com Col Sch of Nursing, Essex Com Col, Townson State Univ, Loyola Col. Approved for Training & Edu by: Am Med Assn for Interns & Residents Training, Council of Am Med Edu of the AMA, Midstates Assn of Cols & Secondary Schs. Mem: Am Hosp Assn, MD Hosp Assn, MD-DC-DE-VA Hosp Assn, Council of Teaching Hosps, Assn of Am Med Cols. To provide the com with the best health care in the spirit of the Heb word Tsadakah – generosity & social responsibility in the broadest sense – for all who need it, without regard to age, race, sex, rel, or natl origin. Anesthesiology, Cardiac Diagnostic Ctr, Cardio-Pulmonary Lab, Coronary Care Unit, Cystoscopy, Dentistry, Drug Dependency Prog, Electrocardiography, Electroencephalography, Emergency Servs, Home Care, Intensive Care Unit, Obstetrics & Gynecology, Orthopedics, Pathology, Pediatrics, Primary Care Ctr, Psychiatry, Radiology, Radiation Therapy, Respiratory Therapy, Neurology, Nuclear Med, Rehabilitation Med, Research, Respiratory Care, Social Work, Surgery, Urology; auxiliary; volunteers; official shock-trauma ctr for the NW section of the Baltimore met area; med assistance to com orgs; Sch of Radiologic Tech; Sch of Respiratory Care Tech; research. 516 beds & 53 bassinets. Over 600 physicians & dentists; 13 chiefs of servs; over 100 residents; 530 nurses; & about 1,300 technical & support personnel. The Hebrew Benevolent Soc laid the cornerstone for the Hebrew Hosp & Asylum in 1866, a ten-rm bldg at Monument St & Hopkins Ave (now Broadway). The Hosp grew over the yrs, & in 1926 the name was changed to Sinai Hosp. After WWII it was decided to build a new hosp in the NW section of the city. The present facility occupies a 50 acre campus. Chr: Eugene M. Feinblatt; 1st V Chr: Ellen L. Zamoiski; 2nd V Chr: Dr M. Gordon Wolman; Treas: Robert L. Weinberg; Asst Treas: David H. Bernstein; Asst Sec: Jo-Ann Orlinsky; Bd of Dirs: Hon Rosalie S. Abrams, Irving J. Applefeld, David H. Bernstein, Hon Clarence W. Blount, Jonas Brodie, Suzanne F. Cohen, Charles W. Cole Jr, Richard Davison, Manuel Dupkin II, Robert C. Embry Jr, Dr Spencer Foreman, Samuel L. Frank, Herbert D. Fried, Robert S. Ginsburg, Robert M. Goldman, Harold Goldsmith, David L. Greif II, Ellen Halle, Barbara L. Himmelrich, Janet L. Hoffman, Dr John B. Imboden, Joseph S. Kaufman, Herschel L. Langenthal, Carolyn Manuszak, Arthur S. Mehlman, Harvey M. Meyerhoff, Robert D. Myers, Irving Neuman, Dr William S. Parker, Arnold I. Plant, Malcolm D. Potter, T. Scott Pugatch, Ellen Rappaport, Henry A. Rosenberg Jr, Stanford Z. Rothschild Jr, Alan R. Sachs, Barbara Shapiro, Ronald M. Shapiro, Dr Leon G. Sheer, Shale D. Stiller, Alvin Wolpoff, Jack N. Zemil. **Belvedere Ave at Greenspring, Baltimore MD 21215 (301) 367–7800.**

Solomon Schechter Day School. Affiliated with Solomon Schechter Day Schs Assn. Prin: Louis

Sternfield; Chr: Henry Shor. **8100 Stevenson Rd, Baltimore MD 21208 (301) 486–6400.**

The Talmudical Academy of Baltimore. Accredited by the State of MD Dept of Edu. To prepare the stu for productive lives & careers as Am & as J. Rel edu prog; intensive secular prog leading to a diploma & entrance to col; field trips; Shabbat & holiday progs; sports activities. Nursery through twelfth grade. F in 1917 as the first Orthodox Heb day sch outside of NYC; relocated in 1967 to present campus in Pikesville, MD. Facilities include: ten acre suburban campus, dormitory for 100 stu with resident supervisor & counselor, sci lab, three libraries, gym, nursery & K playrooms, lecture halls, syn, auditorium & stage, athletic facilities, meat & dairy cafeterias, infirmary, & air conditioned classrooms. **4445 Old Ct Rd, Baltimore MD 21208 (301) 484–6600, 7410.**

Temple Emanuel. Affiliated with UAHC. 219 mems. Rabbi Gustav Buchdahl; Cantor Alvin Donald; Pres: Alan L. Katz; Edu: Sidney Bravmann; Sisterhood Pres: Eleanor Spunt; Brotherhood Pres: Ralph Jandorf. **3301 Milford Mill Rd, Baltimore MD 21207 (301) 922–3642.**

Temple Oheb Shalom. Reform Temple affiliated with UAHC, Central Conf of Am Rabbis, Natl Fed of Temple Sisterhoods, Natl Fed of Temple Brotherhoods, Natl Fed of Temple Youth. Rel Servs; edu progs; Sisterhood; Youth Group; Adult Edu; Afternoon Sch; Sun Sch; Sisterhood; Brotherhood; Sr Citizen Group; library containing 300 vols (Judaica). 1150 families; 550 stu. 50 employees; 200 volunteers. F 1853 led by Rabbis Benjamin Szold; Wm. Rosenaur; Abraham D. Shaw; Donald R. Berlin; Cantors A. Keyser, Schulman, Benjamin Grobani, Melvin Luterman. Pub Temple Topics Bulletin (monthly). Facilities include kitchen, auditorium seating 500, sanctuary seating 1,000. Exec Adm: Jesse Harris; Pres: Frank J. Bamberger, Leona Morris; VP: Stewart Greenebaum; Treas: Howard Rubenstein; Asst Treas: Norman Shapiro. **7310 Park Heights Ave, Baltimore MD 21208 (301) 358–0105.**

Yeshiva Institute of Baltimore. Chassidic style day sch with a ten grade intensive J study prog for boys 3½ to 14, & a standard secular studies prog. To provide an intensive high quality Torah edu with Yiddish instruction; to imbue the stu with the traits of warmth, understanding & tolerance which will enable them to guide & counsel their fellow young people. J & secular study prog, 11 mo a yr, six days a week; character bldg & com progs; Yiddish language curriculum & mastery of Aramaic; optional one mo summer prog which combines learning with physical edu, & arts & crafts; tutorial & reading specialist prog for slow learners; total & partial scholarships. 200 boys. F in 1952 as the Yeshiva Shearith Hapleita by a group of eight Holocaust survivors under the guidance of Rabbi Isaac Sternhell. Until five yrs ago, the sch shared its secular dept with another day sch but is now independent. The Yeshiva has occupied various quarters & now rents facilities fr Moses Montefiore Woodmoor Hebrew Cong. Five yr old boys at the sch can read Heb fluently & name every vol of the Talmud; second graders learn all 613 commandments by heart, & are taught what they mean. Prin: Rabbi Velvel Rosen; Prin Gen Studies: Rabbi David Meister; Exec Dir Dev: Rabbi Yisroel Reznitsky; Adm: Rabbi Gershom Flamm; Pres: Ernest Margareten; Chr of Exec Cttee: Lawrence Isbee; Exec Cttee: Zelic Ellenbogen, Rabbi Nosson Nussbaum, Rabbi Tzvi Willner; Sec: Mrs Boruch Zohn. **Edu Ctr, 3605 Coronado Rd, Baltimore MD 21207 (301) 922–0547; Exec Ctr: 6216 Baltimore Ave, Baltimore MD 21215 (301) 358–9330.**

Bethesda

Bethesda Jewish Congregation. Liberal non-affiliated Cong. High Holyday Servs open to the com; Fri Night Servs & discussion groups; Rel & Heb Sch – 2 days per week; Adult Edu – Heb, Talmud & Ethics; com holiday celebrations including a seder; library containing 700 vols (J encyclopedias, hist, philosophy, fiction, holidays). 118 families; 107 stu grades K–9. 18 employees. Pub BJC Newsletter (monthly). Facilities are shared (permanent off) in the Bradley Hills Presbyterian Church – sanctuary, kitchen, social hall, lounge classrms available to Cong. Rabbi Dr Roger E. Herst; Pres: Judith Gottlieb; Adm Sec: Maran Ostchega; Prin: Ruth Frenkel. **6601 Bradley Blvd, Bethesda MD 20817 (301) 469–8636.**

Congregation Beth El of Montgomery County. Affiliated with United Syn of Am. Rabbi Samuel Scolnic; Asst Rabbi: Aaron Pearlstein; Pres: Paula S. Eicher; Edu Dir: Noach Ravin. **8215 Old Georgetown Rd, Bethesda MD 20014 (301) 652–2606.**

Magen David Sephardic Congregation. To provide J of com with a rel, cultural & social ctr in the spirit of the unbroken Sephardic historic faith which has been sustained & preserved throughout the ages. Est in 1966 by 10 Sephardic J. Pres: Samy Yman; 1st VP: Sami Totah; 2nd VP: Ralph Colen; Treas: David Rebibo; Corsp Sec: Gwen Zuares; Rec

Sec: Luna Diamond; Mems at Large: Mercedes Bensimon, Suzanne Amsellem, Annie Totah; Trustees: Albert Emsellem, Elie Silvera. **PO Box 41019, Bethesda MD 20014 (301) 588–0446.**

United Jewish Appeal – Federation of Greater Washington, Inc. Mem of CJF. Organized 1935. Pres: Melvin S. Cohen; Exec VP: Elton J. Kerness. **6935 Arlington Rd, Bethesda MD 20014 (301) 652–6480.**

Bowie

Nevey Shalom. Affiliated with United Syn of Am. Cantor Dr Leonard Woolf; Pres: Allan Firestone; Edu Dir: Rabbi David Meister; Youth Dir: Paula Horowitz. **12218 Torah Lane, Bowie MD 20715 (301) 262–9020.**

Temple Solel. Affiliated with UAHC. 145 mems. Rabbis: Stuart G. Weinblatt, Louis J. Cashdan; Pres: Paul Rubin; Edu: Bernard Lebowitz; Sisterhood Pres: Susanne Lieberman. **PO Box 578, Bowie MD 20715 (301) 262–7878.**

Chevy Chase

Ohr Kodesh Congregation. Conservative Cong affiliated with United Syns of Am. Rel Servs; edu prog; Sisterhood; Chil Day Ctr; Adult Edu classes; HS classes; progs for all ages 2–17; col age prog; Mid Life Singles group; retired group; library containing 3500 vols(Judaica). 575 families; 2000 individuals. 16 employees. F 1948 as the Montgomery Cty J Com; changed name to Ohr Kodesh in 1959. Pub Ohr Kodesh Bulletin (biweekly). Facilities include kosher kitchen, sanctuary, chapel, auditorium, classrms, library, gym. First syn in Montgomery Cty MD. Rabbi Tzvi H. Porath; Exec Dir: Joseph Miller. **8402 Freyman Dr, Chevy Chase MD 20815 (301) 589–3880.**

Ohr Kodesh Congregation, Library. Library contains 3500 vols (Judaica). For information on the Cong, see – Ohr Kodesh Congregation, Chevy Chase, MD. **8402 Freyman Dr, Chevy Chase MD 20815 (301) 589–3880.**

Pioneer Women – Na'amat. The training & edu of the Is woman & her family so that each can be best equipped to lead productive lives. For additional information, see – Pioneer Women Na'amat, New York City, NY. **Ohr Kodesh Synagogue, 8402 Freyman Dr, Chevy Chase MD 20015 (301) 565–3130.**

Temple Shalom. Affiliated with UAHC. 400 mems. Rabbi Bruce E. Kahn; Cantor Saul Rogolsky; Pres: Alan Pressman; Edu: Ann Rubin; Sisterhood Pres: Jackie Hefter; Brotherhood Pres: Arthur Sturm. **8401 Grubb Rd, Chevy Chase MD 20015 (301) 587–2273.**

College Park

B'nai B'rith Hillel Federation Jewish Student Center. To meet the social, cultural & rel needs of the Univ of MD J com; to be a ctr of J concern & campus activity. Stu of all J persuasions & affiliations. The ctr facility has a kosher dining club. Dir: Rabbi Robert Saks; Assc Dirs: Jeremy Brochin, Rabbi Moishe Silverman; Pres Joint Com Bd: Edward Raskin; Pres Hillel Stu Org: Jared Yurow. **7612 Mowatt Lane, PO Box 187, College Park MD 20740 (301) 422–6200.**

Columbia

Temple Beth Shalom, The Meeting House. Affiliated with United Syn of Am. Rabbi Noah Golinkin; Pres: Madeline Snyder. **5885 Robert Oliver Pl, Columbia MD 21045.**

Temple Isaiah. Affiliated with UAHC. 240 mems. Rabbi Stephen Fuchs; Cantor Solomon; Pres: Saul Lubitz; Sisterhood Pres: Sara R. Sadowsky. **5885 Robert Oliver Pl, Columbia MD 21045 (301) 730–8277.**

Cumberland

Ber Chayim Congregation. Affiliated with UAHC. 55 mems. Rabbi Edwin Schoffmann; Pres: Benjamin Feldman; Edu: Edwin Schoffmann; Sisterhood Pres: Bernice Friedland. **107 Union St, Cumberland MD 21502 (301) 722–5688.**

Beth Jacob. Affiliated with United Syn of Am. Rabbi Edwin Schoffman; Pres: Dr Gerald Katz. **11 Columbia St, Cumberland MD 21502 (301) 722–6570.**

Elderburg

Beth Sholom. Affiliated with United Syn of Am. Pres: Allan Cohen. **925 Streaker Rd, Elderburg MD 21784.**

Gaithersburg

Gaithersburg Hebrew Congregation. Affiliated with United Syn of Am. Rabbi Dr I. David Oler; Cantor Saul Finn; Pres: Gerald R. Goldgraben; Edu Dir: Dr Shlomo Cohen; Youth Dir: Ahuva Abrams. **9915 Apple Ridge Rd, Galthersburg MD 20760 (301) 869–7699.**

Greenbelt

Mishkan Torah Congregation. Reconstructionist Cong affiliated with United Syn of Am, Bd of J Edu (Washington area), J Fed of Reconstructionist Congs & Havurot. Rel Servs; Rel Sch; Nursery Sch; Sisterhood; Men's Club; Chavurah; Adult Edu, youth progs, confirmation prog; library containing 2,500 vols (varied bks). 110 stu in grades K–10. 20 employees. F 1947 with the merger of the Greenbelt Hebrew Cong & the JCC of Prince George Cty. Name changed to Mishkan Torah, which means "Sanctuary of the Torah", in 1968. Pub Trumpet (monthly). Facilities include kosher kitchen, sanctuary, rel sch bldg, gift shop, teen lounge. Rabbi Steven Bayar; Cantor Phil Greenfield; Pres: Murray Shapiro; Exec VP: Diane Kritt; Prog VP: Micheal Bargteil; Fin Sec: Colin Alter; Prin Rel Sch: Evelyn Herschler; Exec Sec: Linda Bargteil. **Ridge & Westway Rds, Greenbelt MD 20770 (301) 474–4223.**

Mishkan Torah Congregation, Library. Library contains 2,500 vols (varied bks). For information on the Cong, see – Mishkan Torah Cong, Greenbelt, MD. **Ridge & Westway Rds, Greenbelt MD 20770 (301) 474–4223.**

National Congress of Jewish Deaf. 9102 Edmonston Ct #302, Greenbelt MD 20770.

Hagerstown

B'nai Abraham. Affiliated with UAHC. 131 mems. Rabbi Harvey Rosenfeld; Pres: Gerald I. Falke; Sisterhood Pres: Carolyn Boro; Brotherhood Pres: David Handler. **53 E Baltimore St, Hagerstown MD 21740 (301) 733–5039.**

Kensington

Temple Emanuel. Reform Temple affiliated with UAHC. Rel Servs; edu progs; Sisterhood; Brotherhood; youth groups; pastoral counseling; Family Concern Cttee; com outreach progs; library. 533 families; 319 stu. 26 employees; several volunteers. F 1952. Pub Kol Korei (monthly bulletin). Facilities include kitchen, sanctuary, social hall, library, sch, gift shop. Rabbi Leon M. Adler; Cantor Abrasha Robofsky; Edu Dir: Elayne Flax; Pres: Shirley Ifshin; 1st VP: Dorothy Mulitz; 2nd VP: Arthur Korotkin; 3rd VP: Lenore Cohen; 4th VP: Ruth Klein; Sec: Leah Valadez; Treas: Melvyn Cohen; Fin Sec: Lois Simpson. **10101 Connecticut Ave, Kensington MD 20895 (301) 942–2000.**

Temple Emanuel Library. For information on the Temple, see – Temple Emanuel, Kensington, MD. **10101 Connecticut Ave, Kensington MD 20895 (301) 942–2000.**

Lexington Park

Congregation Beth Israel. Affiliated with United Syn of Am. Pres: Jerry Diamond; Edu Dir: Dr Frank Gunzburg. **335 Midway Dr, Lexington Park MD 20653 (301) 863–8886.**

Olney

B'nai Shalom of Olney. Affiliated with United Syn of Am. Rabbi Philip Pohl; Pres: Gail Bloom. **3701 Olney-Laytonsville Rd, Olney MD 20832 (301) 774–0879.**

Potomac

Beth Sholom of Potomac. 11825 Seven Locks Rd, Potomac MD 20854 (301) 882–5666.

Beth Sholom of Potomac Library. 11825 Seven Locks Rd, Potomac MD 20854 (301) 882–5666.

Congregation Har Shalom. Affiliated with United Syn of Am. Rabbi Leonard Cahan; Cantor Cal Chizever; Rabbi Emeritus Morris Gordon; Pres: R. Barry Wertlieb; Exec Dir: Murray H. Knopf; Prin: Melanie Berman; Youth Dir: Dennis Kay. **11510 Falls Rd, Potomac MD 20854 (301) 299–7087.**

Congregation Har Shalom Library. For information on the Cong, see – Congregation Har Shalom, Potomac, MD. **11510 Falls Rd, Potomac MD 20854 (301) 299–7087.**

Randallstown

American Mizrachi Women – Sarah Ribakow Chapter. Women's rel zionist org. To est & provide vocational & academic edu in Is; to provide social servs to the coms serviced by the many progs in Is. Educates women to the needs of Is; provides threefold prog in Is for newcomers, chil, youth; provides other servs including chil restoration, youth aliyah, social servs, adult welfare, academic & vocational edu. Before 1926 the org was an arm of Mizrachi Men. In 1973 the org name was changed fr Mizrachi Women's Org of Am. The Am Mizrachi Women was the first to est a HS for girls in Palestine, a settlement house for immigrants in Jerusalem, a rel com ctr in Haifa, a Golden Age Prog, an accelerated Teachers Prog for rel teachers to work in border dev areas, & the first to use the Head Start Prog for underprivileged chil. There are three chapters in Baltimore. Exec Sec: Deborah Ansel.

8415 Allenswood Rd, Randallstown MD 21133 (301) 655–4141.

Beth Israel Congregation Hebrew School. 9411 Liberty Rd, Randallstown MD 21133 (301) 922–6571.

Beth Israel Congregation Hebrew School Library. 9411 Liberty Rd, Randallstown MD 21133 (301) 922–6571.

Beth Israel Mikro Kodesh Congregation. Affiliated with United Syn of Am. Rabbi Seymour L. Essrog; Cantor Elias Roochvarg; Pres: Searle E. Mitnick; Exec Dir: Kenneth A. Sodden; Edu Dir: Goldie Gorn; Nursery Sch Dir: Sharon K. Edlow. **9411 Liberty Rd, Randallstown MD 21133 (301) 922–6565.**

Reisterstown

The Reisterstown Jewish Center. Affiliated with United Syn of Am. Rabbi David Leiberman; Pres: Gladys Kaplan. **528 Gwynnwest Rd, Reisterstown MD 21136 (301) 833–5307.**

Rockville

B'nai Israel Congregation. Affiliated with United Syn of Am. Rabbi Matthew Simon; Cantor Robert Kieval; Pres: Dr Lawrence Thomas; Dir of Ritual Activities: Seymour M. Panitz. Exec Dir: Stuart Kleiner; Prog Dir: Diane L. Schilit; Edu Dir: Barry Krasner. **6301 Montrose Rd, Rockville MD 20852 (301) 649–3440.**

B'nai Israel Congregation Library. For information on the Cong, see – B'nai Israel Congregation, Rockville, MD. **6301 Montrose Rd, Rockville MD 20852 (301) 649–3440.**

Beth Tikvah. Affiliated with United Syn of Am. Rabbi Howard Gorin; Cantor Mark Levi; Pres: Gerald Kaiz; Exec Dir: Irving R. Mollen; Edu Dir: Mordecai Schreiber; Youth Dir: Elaine & Leroy Moses. **2200 Baltimore Rd, Rockville MD 20853 (301) 762–7338.**

Charles E. Smith Jewish Day School. Coeducational col prep sch with half day gen studies & half day J studies; affiliated with the Bd of J Edu of Greater Washington. To dev individual potential in all subjects, & to apply these concepts to daily living. Jr varsity & varsity sports; yearbook; Natl Hon Soc; literary magazine in English & Heb; Stu Govt; MD Math League; Volunteer Prog; Stu Choir; Special Prog for Academically Resourceful Kids; Learning Disabilities Ctr; special Heb & English classes for Russian, Israeli & Iranian stu. 800 stu grades K-12. Faculty of over 80. Est in 1965. Facilities include libraries in English & Heb; sci labs; computer ctr; gymnasium; theater; art studio. Prin: Dr Jay B. Stern; Asst Prin Gen Studies: Dr Shulamith Elster; Asst Prin Judaic Studies: Dr Richard Wagner; Col Counselor: Phylis Homes. **1901 E Jefferson St, Rockville MD 20852 (301) 881–1403.**

Jewish Community Center of Greater Washington. Multi function agy affiliated with the JWB. Two primary goals: to maintain the creative survival of the J people on the Am & world scene; to insure that each individual is give the opportunity, while taking part in an enjoyable experience, to grow & dev as a person, intellectually & physically. Health & physical edu; J studies; cultural arts; recreational & informal edu. 12,066 mems. The forerunners of the JCC of Greater Washington were the Young Men's Hebrew Assn & the Young Women's Hebrew Assn est in 1913. In 1917, when WWI broke out, the Y est a Servicemen's Ctr in downtown Washington. In 1922 the need for larger & permanent quarters was recognized. In 1925 the cornerstone was layed for the Ctr. In 1938 the original bldg was greatly enlarged. In 1959 the name of the Ctr was changed fr JCC of DC to the JCC of Greater Washington. In 1964 plans for the new bldg were suggested. Pres: Lesley Israel; VP for Adm: Philip N. Margolius; VPs: Edward Kaplan, Richard A. Schuman, Beth C. Sloan, Stefan F. Tucker; Sec: Leslie Kaplan; Asst Sec: Geraldine Polinger; Treas: Stephen R. Grayson; Asst Treas: Sidney Rothman; Exec Dir: Robert H. Weiner; Asst Dir: Eleanor B. Sirkis; Dir of Adm: Cyma R. Heffter. **6125 Montrose Rd, Rockville MD 20852 (301) 881–0100.**

Jewish Community Center of Greater Washington, Kass Judaic Library. For information on the Ins, see – Jewish Community Ctr of Greater Washington, Rockville, MD. **6125 Montrose Rd, Rockville MD 20852 (301) 881–0100.**

Jewish Day School of Greater Washington Library. For information on the Sch, see – Jewish Day School of Greater Washington, Rockville, MD. **1901 E Jefferson St, Rockville MD 20852 (301) 881–1403.**

Jewish Funeral Directors of America. 1170 Rockville Pike, Rockville MD 20852 (301) 340–1400.

Jewish Social Service Agency & Jewish Foster Home. Voluntary org affiliated with United Way. To provide social servs for the Washington area J population. Chil Guidance Clin: offers a full range of evaluation & treatment servs for chil up to age 15 & their families, with serv available to families of any race, rel or ethnic background. Adoption: unmarried parent serv which provides counseling to unmarried parents who want assistance in planning around adoption, or alternative plans for their unborn or young chil; provides servs to married couples, & non J parents who would like their chil placed in a J home. Foster Care for Emotionally Disturbed Chil: provides for placement of chil in specially selected & trained foster family homes; provides therapy, by a social worker under psychiatric supervision, for the chil & counseling for the foster parents & the chil own parents. Residential Treatment: provides for chil who are so emotionally disturbed that they must be removed fr their homes & the com. Family & Marriage Counseling: provides counseling for J families or families of mixed marriage. The Warm Line: offers servs so that parents of babies & pre schoolers can dial the J Social Serv Agy & talk with a professional social worker or psychologist about everyday problems associated with chil rearing. Outreach for Disabled Persons & Their Families: provides resource information & referral, assisted referrals & counseling for disabled persons & their families, support groups for parents. The Parent to Parent Prog: maintains a com wide support system to provide immediate help for new parents. Adolescent Mental Health Servs: provides evaluatio therapy for adolescents with emotional & behavioral problems who are referred to the prog. Friend to Friend: provides young people, as volunteer friends, to visit handicapped youngsters who are isolated fr their peer group, & provides young adult male volunteers for fatherless J chil. Financial Assistance: gives assistance to all J families who are in need & to whom there are no other resources available. J Family Life Edu: provides servs in the form of discussion groups & speakers to syns, orgs & individuals in the com. Servs to the Aging: helps the elderly maintain their independence & continue to function in the mainstream of life; provides help with problems caused by loss of loved ones, ill health, & changes due to retirement; provides for group or individual counseling. Homemaker Servs: helps elderly people who are temporarily ill or incapacitated & who cannot take care of their daily chores of living. Meals on Wheels: offers delivery to the home bound of two meals a day five days a week. Friendly Visitors: provides volunteers to visit people, either isolated at home or in an ins, who have withdrawn fr active participation in com life. Discussion Leaders: provides volunteers who serve as discussion group leaders in nursing homes, ins, sr citizens housing facilities, or who do a variety of other com servs such as provide transportation, plan recreation, plan parties & do off work. Widow to Widow Outreach: focuses on helping a newly widowed person, woman or man, to adjust to the trauma inherent in the loss of a spouse, the problem of bereavement, social & economic adjustments & other similar problems. Interfaith Couples Counseling: tries to help the couple explore & discuss concerns & issues for future decisions; provides for group workshops. Newcomer Resettlement: provides the immigrants with housing, furniture & clothing; gives access to the Agy's panel of med Drs & dentists; aids in applying for Social Security & Medicaid; helps newcomer to become enrolled in English language classes, find employment; provides financial assistance until they become self sufficient & independent. Loans: provides for scholarship loans, business loans, business advice. Jac J. Lehrman Home Health Serv: offers skilled nursing; med, social workers; home health aides; speech, physical & occupational therapists (there are 85 patients in the Lehman Home Health Serv). Professionally trained social workers, psychiatrists & psychologists. Pres: Irvin A. Lavine; VP for Prog: Irving P. Cohen; VP for Adm: Lawrence I. Kasdon; VP for Finance: Jerome Snider; Treas: Mrs Stuart B. Levi; Sec: Gilbert Lessenco; Exec Dir: George M. Pikser; Dir Professional Servs: Mervin Moss; Adm Off: Hannah I. Schweizer. **6123 Montrose Rd, Rockville MD 20852 (301) 881–3700.**

Temple Beth Ami. Reform Cong affiliated with UAHC. Dedicated to the dev of a vital & innovative style of J life. Rel Sch with grades K–10th; youth activities for chil ages 12–18; Brotherhood; Sisterhood; edu, social & cultural progs; library. 300 families; 520 stu in the rel sch. Full time Rabbi & Dir of Edu; part time Dir of Music; Rel Sch Teachers; two Secs; Bookkeeper; Youth Advs. Est in 1971 following the philosophy of liberal J. The Cong moved to their new bldg in 1980. Temple facilities include a sanctuary, social hall, kitchen, adm off. Rabbi Jack Luxemburg; Pres: Judith Graham; 1st VP: Ed Sondik; 2nd VP: Stuart Treby; 3rd VP: Kathy Dick; Rec Sec: Buzz Karpay; Fin Sec: Yvonne Oppenheimer; Treas: Paul Yentis; Dir of Edu: Phylis Green; Dir of Music: Sue Roemer; Sisterhood Pres: Madeline Weinstock; Brotherhood Pres: Elliot Allentuck. **800 Hurley Ave, Rockville MD 20850 (301) 340–6818.**

Temple Beth Ami Library. For information on the Temple, see – Temple Beth Ami, Rockville, MD. **800 Hurley Ave, Rockville MD 20850 (301) 340–6818.**

Salisburg

Beth Israel Congregation. Conservative Syn affiliated with United Syn of Am. Rel Servs; J Edu; Adult Edu; Sisterhood; USY group; social activities; Presch; Afternoon Sch; library containing 400 vols (Judaica). 130 mems; 130 families; 320 individuals; 42 stu in grades K–8. 4 employees. F 1921. Pub Beth Israel Bulletin (weekly). Facilities include sanctuary seating 140 with additional seating in social hall (seating 400), kosher kitchen, classrms, library, youth lounge, gift shop. Rabbi Maurice Schwartz; Pres: Harvey Needleman; Sisterhood Pres: Mrs Jack Wennerston. **Camden Ave & Wicomico St, Salisbury MD 21801 (301) 742–2564.**

Silver Spring

American Jewish Journal. Periodical pub. **1220 Blair Mill Rd, Silver Spring MD 20910 (301) 585–1756.**

College of Jewish Studies of Greater Washington. The only J communal ins of higher learning offering J & Hebraic studies in the Greater Washington area for col credit. Sponsored by the Bd of J Edu; beneficiary of the UJA Fed of Greater Washington; undergrad div offered in cooperation with Baltimore Hebrew Col. To train & prepare teachers of J & Hebraic studies for all types of schs; to prepare stu with the necessary undergrad requirements to enter rabbinical or other professional schs; to conduct col level courses for adults in order to dev a knowledgeable lay leadership in the com; to conduct courses to enrich the J background of J professionals in the J communal agy of Greater Washington. UnderGrad Div – depts in: Bible, Edu, Heb, Hist & Sociology, Philosophy & Rabbinics; Teacher Certification Prog (by special arrangement, stu fulfilling the necessary requirements are granted diplomas & degrees through the Baltimore Hebrew Col which confers: Academic Diploma, Teacher Diploma, Bachelor of Heb Literature, Bachelor of Arts, Teacher License). Ulpan Ins – prog in conversational Heb using the Habet Usham audio-visual method (confers Heb Language Certificate & Heb Language Diploma). J Enrichment for Professionals – courses for persons engaged in J com work. Academic Confs – biennial academic conf dealing with a topic pertinent to J scholarship in modern life. Kalat Seva – prog for retirees consisting of lectures & discussions on J topics. Faculty of 17. The Col is comprised of what was formerly known as the J Teachers Ins, & Washington Branch of Baltimore Hebrew Col. Chr: Dr Harvey Ammerman; Dean: Rabbi Jacob I. Halpern; Bd of Trustees: Mark Blumkin, Carl Freeman, Dr Isaac Franck, Dr Isaiah Frank, Judge Stanley Frosh, Dr Leon Gerber, Rabbi Joshua Haberman, Sylvia Hassan, Dr Howard Hausman, Dr Amihud Kramer, Leo Kramer, Rabbi I. David Oler, Esther Plotkin, Abe Pollin, Morris Rodman, Rebecca Safer, Bernard S. White. **9325 Brookville Rd, Silver Spring MD 20910 (301) 589–3180.**

Congregation Har Tzeon Agudath Achim. To further the rel, spiritual, cultural & social life of the Silver Spring J com. Sisterhood; Men's Club; USY; Kadima; Machar; Young Married; Singles Group; Rel Sch; Adult Edu; Couples Club. Over 500 families. Agudath Achim was organized on Sept 24, 1939 in the Brightwood area of Washington. It was granted a charter on Oct 9, 1939, & in Jan 1940 bought its first bldg. Har Tzeon was granted a charter on Oct 29, 1951. They moved into their present bldg in 1968. The two congs merged in 1977. Rabbi Reuben Landman; Rabbi Emeritus H. J. Waldman; Cantor Moshe Meirovich; Prin: Barry Krasner; Pres: Marvin Waldman; 1st VP: Robert Abrams; 2nd VP: Edwin Morgenstern; Treas: Paul D. Kagen; Asst Treas: Solomon Freishtat; Fin Sec: Stewart Sherman; Corsp Sec: June Morgenstern; Rec Sec: Ellie Green; Trustees: Mona Freishat, Ernest Green, Ernest Greenwald, Joyce Katz, Lillian Greenwald; Delegates at Large: Evelyn Block, Gerson Cohen, Jonathon Fine, Morton Katz, Natalie Cantor, Ruth Shapiro, Shirley Sindell, Fred Wolpert; Adm Servs: David Shudrich; Budget & Finance: Stanley Galef; Edu: Gerson Cohen; Memorialization & Dedication: Samuel Hyman; Rites & Rituals: Fred Wolpert; Ways & Means: Roncia Schwartz; Bldg & Grounds: Colman Fisher, Larry Abramson; Report Editor: Frieda Greenberg; Membership: Ruth Shapiro, Shirley Sindell; Pres of Sisterhood: Joyce Katz; Pres of Men's Club: Leon Scharff; Publicity: Irwin & Shirley Schumacher. **1840 University Blvd W, Silver Spring MD 20902 (301) 649–3800.**

Israel Aliyah Center. 8730 Georgia Ave, Suite 304, Silver Spring MD 20911 (301) 589–6136, 6007.

Jewish Week. Periodical pub. **8630 Fenton St, Suite 611, Silver Spring MD 20910 (301) 565–9336.**

Midrasha Community Hebrew High School of Greater Washington. Sponsored by the Bd of J Edu of Greater Washington; beneficiary of the UJA Fed of Greater Washington. To provide an intensive J edu experience for the J stu who attend public HS for their gen edu. Jr Midrasha prog for stu in grades 7–8 – curriculum with Bible, Hist, Heb & Talmudic Literature; Sr Midrasha prog for 9–12 grades – curriculum with courses in the following areas: Heb Studies – Heb Language, Classical & Modern Literature, Talmudic-Medieval Literature & Contemporary Heb Literature; J Social Studies – Hist, Is, Yiddish Language & Culture, Philosophy, Law & Archaeology; Rel Studies – courses on Observance & Ritual. Sch also provides preparation for stu who wish to participate in the Natl Bible Contest; prog for Day Sch grads; Hebrew Theatre – annually performs a Broadway musical in Heb; other activities including stu govt (K'nesset), extra curricular activities, study-ins, confs. Courses conducted in the Heb studies & the J social studies areas may be accepted by Montgomery Cty Public Schs for HS elective credit; stu who complete the course in Leadership Training through Dance may obtain Physical Edu credit. The Diploma, Certificate, or Letter of Certification is awarded depending on the num of credits earned. Pres: Dr Jules Cahan; Prin: Rabbi Jacob I. Halpern; Bd of Dirs: Stanley Abramowitz, Mark Blumkin, Jules Cahan, Sydney Davis, Phyllis Frank, Neil Garson, Harry Gelboin, Maxine Haberman, Sylvia & Zev Hendel, Alan Hirshfeld, Fradel Kramer, Marie & Sam Kramer, Aviva Kaufman-Penn, Jonathan Levin, Herbert Ozur, Jack Trombka, Ruth White. **9325 Brookville Rd, Silver Spring MD 20910 (301) 589–3180.**

Mikveh of Greater Washington. To provide facilities for immersion & information on taharat hamishpacha & J family life. Mikvah available by appointment for any J, male or female; tevilat kelim; tours of the facilities & disucussions of its use for women's groups, men's groups, mixed groups fr teenagers up; free Speakers' Bureau to discuss J family life, J survival & related topics at meetings of local J orgs; one-to-one discussions & learning sessions for brides or engaged couples. 400 families. 1 employee. Pub Newsletter (bi-monthly). Facilities include 2 mikvaot, 3 dressing rms, hairdryers, vanity table, attendant's residence. Pres: Jonathan Adler; House Chr: Linda Rishe; Treas: Annette Linzer; Edu Chr: Devorah Adler; Newsletter Editor: Pamela Pelcovitz. **8901 Georgia Ave, Silver Spring MD 20910 (301) 587–2014.**

Shaare Tefila Congregation. Affiliated with United Syn of Am. Rabbi Martin S. Halpern; Cantor Gershon E. Levin; Pres: Maurice Potosky; Exec Dir: Harold Fink; Edu Dir: Rabbi Albert M. Dimond. **11120 Lockwood Dr, Silver Spring MD 20901 (301) 593–3410.**

Temple Israel. Conservative Syn affiliated with United Syn of Am; United Syn, Seaboard Region; J Com Council of Greater Washington. To establish & maintain a syn & such rel, edu, social & recreational activities as will help further the cause & objectives of the Syn & Conservative Judaism. Rel Servs daily, Sabbath, Festival, Holy Days; edu prog; Consolidated Rel Sch; Presch; Sisterhood; Men's Club; PTA; USY; Adult Edu classes; speakers; Havurot; library containing 3,600 vols (gen, comprehensive J subjects). 650 mems; 600 families; 50 individuals; 68 afternoon stu in grades K–9. Approximately 15 employees; approximately 20 volunteers on a regula basis, plus many fr Sisterhood for special events. F 1951 as the Langley JCC & in March 1952 became Langley Hebrew Cong; in April 1957 changed name to Temple Israel. Pub The Light (monthly), Hineni (by Sisterhood, monthly). Facilities include kosher kitchen, sanctuary seating 425, chapel, gift shop, presch playground, ballrm, social hall. United Syn, Solomon Schechter Award for Social Action – Soviet J Prog; Is Bond & UJA Fed Awards. Rabbi Lewis A. Weintraub; Cantor Jerome Barry; Exec Dir: Blanche Abel; Prin: Barry Krasner; Youth Dir: Ellen Kagen; Mashgiach: Aharon Yakov; Pres: Jack Ventura; 1st VP: Norma Ozur; 2nd VP: Leon Altschuler; Treas: Harvey Rosenthal; Fin Sec: Walter Sacks; Recording Sec: Faye First. **420 Univ Blvd E, Silver Spring MD 20901 (301) 439–3600.**

Temple Israel Library. Library contains 3,600 vols (gen, comprehensive J subjects). For information on the Temple, see – Temple Israel, Silver Spring, MD. **420 Univ Blvd E, Silver Spring MD 20901 (301) 439–3600.**

Temple Hills

Congregation Shaare Tikvah. Affiliated with United Syn of Am. Rabbi Ralph Dalin; Pres: Bernard R. Shore; Edu Dir: Bernard Kaufman; Youth Dir: Hannah Kaufman. **5404 Old Temple Hills Rd, Temple Hills MD 20031 (301) 894–4303.**

MASSACHUSETTS

Accord

Congregation Shaaray Shalom. Affiliated with UAHC. 137 mems. Rabbi Stephen A. Karol; Pres: Harvey Kurr. **PO Box 15, Accord MA 02018 (617) 749–8103.**

Amherst

Chabad House. Lubavitch com servs ctr. Blends Chassidic fervor & warmth with tradition & learning, to show that every J, fr whatever background he or she comes fr, is an integral part of the body of Is. Anti-missionary work; adult edu; Sabbath seminars; holiday progs; day camp; youth groups; syns; kosher kitchen; counseling; chaplaincy; Mitzvah Campaigns; hosp & prison visitations; sr citizens encounters; speakers bureau. Rabbi Y. Deren. **30 N Hadley Rd, Amherst MA 01002 (413) 253–9040.**

National Yiddish Book Center. Library, bk distributor, Yiddish resource ctr. A non-profit agy for the preservation & promotion of Yiddish culture. The Ctr coords a world-wide campaign to collect unwanted & discarded Yiddish bks & return them to active use. It is the world's only comprehensive source of used & out-of-print Yiddish bks. A regular catalogue of available titles is distributed to stu, scholars & libraries in 20 countries on five continents. The Ctr sponsors a wide range of cultural & edu activities, including translation projs, the dev of curriculum materials, & the sponsorship of 'Elderhostel' progs in Yiddish Culture for older adults; maintains a library of 20,000 vols in Yiddish literature, gen Yiddish holdings. 1,500 mems; 40 local groups. 5 employees; 120 'Zamlers' (volunteer bk collectors). The Ctr was f in the spring of 1980 by a small group of graduate stu & scholars responding to the gen unavailability of essential Yiddish bks. The Ctr's original Bd was comprised of faculty mems & adms from Amherst, Hampshire, Mt Holyoke & Smith Cols & the Univ of MA. Pub Der Pakn-treger (The Book Peddler, quarterly), Catalogue of Used & Out-of-Print Yiddish Books (quarterly); Afn Veg/Zamler's Newsletter (bi-monthly). The Ctr is located in the former East St Sch in Amherst MA. Facilities include a library, exhibition space, the Aliza Greenblatt Reading Rm, which is open to the public. Collected more than 150,000 priceless Yiddish bks in first two yrs of operation. Emerged as the world's ctr for the physical recovery & preservation of Yiddish culture. Exec Dir: Aaron Lansky; Asst Dirs: Nansi Glick, Sharon Kleinbaum; Hon Chr: Isaac Bashevis Singer; Pres: Dean Joseph Marcus; VPs: Dean Richard Tice Alpert, Prof Haim Gunner; Hon Chr: Isaac Bashevis Singer. **Old East St School, PO Box 969, Amherst MA 01004 (413) 253–9201.**

Andover

Temple Emanuel. Reform Temple affiliated with UAHC. To further the faith of J through edu, social & rel programming. Rel Servs – Sabbath & all holidays, plus Sun morning minyan; edu progs sponsored by special cttees as well as Temple Sisterhood which supports Temple, natl & intl progs; Temple Brotherhood which supports local, natl & intl progs such as J Chataugua Soc; youth groups ranging in age fr 13 to 18 yrs; temple choirs for adults & chil; Presch; Afternoon Sch; library containing approx 2,000 vols (varied subjects). 475 mems (400 families, 75 individuals); 300 stu in grades K–10. 7 full-time employees, 20 part-time employees. F 1920 in Lawrence MA; in 1957 rebuilt in Lawrence; now in new bldg (1979) in Andover MA. Pub Temple Bulletin (bi-weekly). Facilities include sanctuary with permanent seating for 300; social hall which expands to seat additional 1,000 people, fully equipped kitchen available for kosher catering, Judaica shop to provide items of J interest. Rabbi Harry A. Roth; Cantor Norman Brody; Pres: Helen Wertheimer; 1st VP: Donald Sherman; 2nd VP: Dr Martin Hayman; 3rd VP: Jack Hayman; 4th VP: Lewis Gack; Treas: Arthur Heifetz; Asst Treas: Robert Goldstein; Rec Sec: Anne Goldstein; Fin Sec: Howard Ponty; Asst Fin Sec: Stuart Labell; Adm: Elaine Mandell. **7 Haggetts Pond Rd, Andover MA 01810 (617) 470–1356.**

Temple Emanuel Library. Library contains almost 2000 vols (varied). For information on the Temple, see – Temple Emanuel, Andover, MA. **7 Haggetts Pond Rd, Andover MA 01810 (617) 470–1356.**

Ayer

Congregation Anshe Sholom. To provide facilities for observance of holy days, festivals, memorial servs, social contacts; to serve as a campaigner for support to Is & other J causes; to be a liaison with the gen com. Rel Servs. Incorporated in MA in 1945 with a membership of over 30 families. Pres: Ida K. Naparstek; VP & Treas: Leon R. Slarskey; Sec: J. Maurice Naparstek; Trustees: Samuel Slarskey, Carl A. Black, Edwin B. Coltin, George C. Saul, Richard Slarskey, Gabis Max Schwartz, Leo Schwartz; Trustee & Dir: J. David Naparstek; Dirs: Louis Slarskey, Hyman Slarskey, Steven Slarskey, Dr Gerald B. Berenson, Murray Green, Ed Wheeler; House Cttee: Walter Naparstek, Joseph Schwartz. **Ayer MA 01432.**

Belmont

Beth El Temple Center. Reform Temple affiliated with UAHC. Rel Servs; adult & chil edu (Presch, Afternoon Sch); Brotherhood; Sisterhood. 400 families; 20 stu. 3 employees. F more than 40 yrs ago; new bldg in 1965. Pub Bulletin. Facilities include kosher kitchen, sanctuary seating 1200, gift shop, classrm. Rabbi Eail G. Grollman DD; Cantor Baruch Greisdorf; Pres: Norman Goldstein; Dir of Edu: Evelyn Bell. **2 Concord Ave, Belmont MA 02178 (617) 484–6668.**

Beverly

Temple B'nai Abraham. Conservative Syn affiliated with United Syn of Am. To provide a house of meeting, study & prayer to our com. Rel Servs; Rel Sch; Brotherhood; Sisterhood; youth groups; Adult Edu; library containing 1,000 vols (Judaica). 550 mems; 285 families; 135 stu. F 1900 as Cong Sons of Abraham & Isaac. Facilities include kosher kitchen, social halls, classrms, sanctuary, gift shop, library, chapel, youth lounge. Rabbi Louis Zivic; Prin: Marilyn Vener; Pres: Robert Landau; VPs: Esther Calish, Robert Gordon; Treas: Myron Glichouse; Sec: Naomi Kaplan. **200 E Lothrop St, Beverly MA 01915 (617) 927–3211.**

Boston

Anti-Defamation League of B'nai B'rith – New England Regional Office. Dedicated in purpose & prog to translating the Am heritage of democratic ideals into a way of life for all Am, & to countering assaults on the safety, status, rights & image of J. For additional information, see – Anti-Defamation League of B'nai B'rith, New York City, NY. **72 Franklin St, Suite 504, Boston MA 02110.**

B'nai B'rith Hillel Foundation, Boston University. To encourage an atmosphere in which one can find one's Jewishness; to help the J stu at the Univ take real responsibility for his or her J dev. Provides the J stu with opportunities to meet socially; maintains information ctr for the State of Is; provides astora & psychological counseling, rel servs, kosher meals; acts as a protectio agy with problems of anti-Semitism & anti-J missionary activity; helps organize the Univ UJA campaign; sponsors speakers, panels, films, dances, chorale, drama groups, series of inter-varsity athletics, wide variety of classes on various topics of J concern, social servs for the elderly, Holocaust Information Week. A variety of leaflets, posters, newsletters, & ads in Boston Univ Free Press throughout the academic yr. Hillel occupies a four floor bldg. The bldg houses lounges, an auditorium, dining rms, offs, & a caretakers residence. Dir: Rabbi Joseph Polak; Dir of Stu Activities: Vicki L. Ehrlichman; Sec: Ellen W. Horowitz. **233 Bay State Rd, Boston MA 02215 (617) 266–3880.**

B'nai B'rith Hillel Foundations of Greater Boston. Regional off est by Combined J Philanthropies of Great Boston to oversee the campus prog in met Boston. To est a strong prog which will involve a maximum num of J stu. Engages & supervises staff; sets policy; determines fiscal needs; maintains good PR with the local J com; promotes the interests of the Hillel Council of Met Boston, Natl Hillel, & the individual Hillel Founs (Hillel Council of Met Boston consists of 55–60 mems of the Greater Boston J com who are committed to encouraging effective & rewarding progs in the area); allocates funds appropriated for Hillel by Combined J Philanthropies; plans & est priorities for future progs. There are six Hillel Founs in met Boston: Boston Univ, Brandeis Univ, Harvard Univ, MA Ins of Tech, Northeastern Univ, & Tufts Univ. Three outreach workers serve J stu at twelve cols & five grad schs. Progs & servs include: edu, cultural, rel, & social activities; kosher meals; counseling; courses; lectures; Is programming; Soviet J action; Holocaust programming; movies; annual J Arts Festival; libraries; grad groups; Is dance groups; J arts & crafts; choral groups; leadership training; dances; parties; brunches; stu groups which visit nursing homes, work with J chil; Orthodox, Conservative & Reform Servs; Shabbat dinners;

Oneg Shabbats; holiday celebrations; Heb Table Talks. In the early 1940's when Univs would allow no rel activities on campus, space was rented in downtown Boston to serve as Hillel Ctrs for Boston Univ, Simmons Col, & Tufts Univ. In a few yrs there were three Hillel Rabbis in the area – one to serve Harvard & MA Ins of Tech, one for Boston Univ, & one for Simmons Col, Tufts Univ, & Wellesley Col. By 1947 funds had been raised to purchase a bldg for Harvard Univ & MIT J stu. By 1949 enough funds had been raised to construct a Hillel house on the Boston Univ campus. In the late 1940's & early 1950's, some of the area's ins provided space for campus clergymen. MIT Hillel separated fr Harvard. When Brandeis Univ opened in 1948, there was a Hillel off in the stu union. Until 1959 the local orgs were associated with Natl Hillel. Since the local Fed would only support local orgs, the Hillel Council of Met Boston was f. In 1971 Combined J Philanthropies of Greater Boston funded a regional off known as the B'nai B'rith Hillel Founs of Greater Boston. Through this off, the Hillel Council of Greater Boston was reorganized in 1972. Weekly calender pub in a Boston newspaper. Exec Dir: Rabbi Richard J. Israel; Exec Asst: Evelyn S. Karp; Pres: Clarence Jacobson; Treas: Prof Marshall Goldman; VPs: Prof Franklin Fisher, Harvey Freishtat, Michael Rukin; Sec: Marjorie Paley; Asst Treas: Harry Silverman; Exec Bd: Prof Alan Feld, Dr Doris Shay, Rabbi Richard J. Israel, Stephen Denker, Prof Suzanne Greenberg, Henry Morgenthau, Prof Naomi Banks. **233 Bay State Rd, Boston MA 02215 (617) 266–3882.**

Beth Israel Hospital. Non-profit ins providing care for patients of any race, creed, color, or nationality; conducts edu & research activities which promote patient care. Major teaching hosp of Harvard Med Sch. Surgery; Obstetrics/Gynecology; Orthopedics; Psychiatry; Neurosurgery; Neuromed, Med & Surgical Intensive Care Units; Home Care Prog; Special Care Nursery; Gen Med Ctr for ambulatory care & outpatient speciality clins; 24-hr Emergency Unit. Est 1916 by the Boston J com, & became affiliated with Harvard Med Sch in 1928. Since 1973, the oldest clin research facility in the US – Harvard's Thorndike Labs – have been located at Beth Is. A Clin Research Ctr maintains 10 beds for patients directly involved in sci study. Over 20,000 inpatients receive treatment each yr. There are 452 adult inpatient beds & 54 bassinets. As a teaching hosp, Beth Is provides training to over 1,200 stu each yr. Pres: Dr Mitchell T. Rabkin; Exec VP, Dir: David Dolins; Bd of Trustees–Chr of the Bd: Norman B. Leventhal; 1st V Chr: Eliot Snider; V Chrs: David Kosowsky, Phillip J. Nexon, Frank A. Morse, George J. Katz; Treas: Alan W. Rottenberg; Asst Treas: Henry T. Mann; Sec: Jay E. Orlin; Asst Sec: Steven J. Cohen, Allan S. Bufferd. **330 Brookline Ave, Boston MA 02215 (617) 735–4431.**

Charles River Park Synagogue. Traditional ("Conservadox") Syn. Only functioning J cong in Downtown Boston – the resurrection of an old shul which was torn down by urban renewal. To provide all urban J with a J cong. Rel Servs – Sabbath & weekdays; Fri evening communal Sabbath dinners for Bostonians & visiting tourists staying at nearby hotels (only such serv in Boston); Sun Brotherhood breakfasts; classes; com Passover Seder; regular series of courses & Shiurim; library containing 1,500 vols Judaica & Hebraica). 200 mems; 60 families; 80 individuals. 1 employee. F 1891 as Beth Hamedrash Hagadol – N Russell St Syn; destroyed in 1958; rebuilt as Charles River Park Syn in 1971. Pub Holiday Bulletin. Facilities include kosher kitchen for Sabbath meals. Rabbi Allan L. Nadler. **55 Martha Rd (Amy Ct), Boston MA 02114 (617) 523–0453.**

Charles River Park Synagogue Library. Library contains 1,500 vols (Judaica & Hebraica). For information on the Syn, see – Charles River Park Synagogue, Boston, MA. **55 Martha Rd (Amy Ct), Boston MA 02114 (617) 523–0453.**

Combined Jewish Philanthropies of Greater Boston, Inc. Mem of CJF. Organized 1895; reorganized 1961. Pres: Ruth B. Fein; Exec VP: David H. Rosen. **72 Franklin St, Boston MA 02110 (617) 542–8080.**

Government of Israel Trade Center. Dev of trade relations between US & Is. For additional information, see – Government of Israel Trade Center, New York City, NY. **Statler Off Bldg, 20 Providence St, Boston MA 02116 (617) 426–3636.**

Israel Aliyah Center. 31 St James Ave, Park Sq Blvd, Suite 450, Boston MA 02116 (617) 423–0868, 7491.

Jewish Advocate. Periodical pub. **251 Causeway St, Boston MA 02114 (617) 227–5130.**

Jewish Community Center of Greater Boston. Non-profit org with an open enrollment policy. To improve the quality of life in the J com; to strengthen J family life & identity. Edu, physical, social, cultural, recreational & civic activities; Dept for Is programming; summer activities consisting of two day camps & one camp for the elderly; nursery schs which are located throughout the Greater Boston area; servs for the elderly including a hot lunch prog, sheltered workshop, day care servs for fragile older adults, classes, interest groups, clubs & orgs; servs for chil, teens, families, handicapped, & new immigrants. 12,000 people of all ages; com wide serv progs reach an additional 10,000 annually; 600 chil in the nursery schs. F in 1963, & is in direct line of J agy est in Boston since the 1870's. Pres: Abbott N. Kahn; VPs: Joel D. Berkowitz, Dorothy G. Kagen, David M. Saltiel, Paula Sidman; Treas: Margery Katzenberg; Asst Treas: Alan R. Goldstein, Alan J. Maslow; Sec: Myrna Schultz; Asst Sec: Steven Grossman, Alberta Shapiro; Exec Dir: Sydney Gale; Asst Dirs: Alan Mann, Kayla Niles; Dirs: Helaine Allen, Edward Arnold, Sandra Berbeco, Robert Berish, George J. Bernstein, Richard K. Blankstein, Julian Cohen, Lloyd David, Neicei Degen, Madelyn Donoff, Dianne Epstein, Morton R. Godine, Harriet Gould, Bernard L. Green, Rose T. Greenberg, Jill Grossman, Henry Heller, Edward B. Jaye, Dr Hyman R. Kamens, Dr S. Charles Kasdon, Arthur Lang, Ruth J. Levin, Joseph B. Manello, Betty Marvin, Adele Newman, Jay E. Orlin, Dorothy Pearlstein, Ronald Pressman, Robert Romanow, Marvin P. Rumpler, Robert Sage, William R. Sapers, Lewis Sassoon, Donald L. Saunders, Lee Scheinbart, Alan M. Schwartz, Annette Schwartz, Steven Schwartz, Ronald Segal, Linda Sharkansky, Norton Sherman, Sidney Shneider, Edwin N. Sidman, Judith Slater, Rabbi Bernard Spielman, Merton Tarlow, Jay F. Theise, Dr Avraham Tuchman, Oscar Wasserman, Lawrence A. Weiner, Melvin Weinstein, Kennith Wexler; Hon Pres: Morton W. Goldberg, Leonard Kaplan, Howard Rubin, Sherman H. Starr, Isadore Z. Wasserman; Hon Bd Mems: David W. Bernstein, Arnold R. Cutler, Alvin M. Glazerman, John Grossman. **72 Franklin St, Boston MA 02110 (617) 542–1870.**

The Jewish Educational Ventures. 462 Boylston St, Boston MA 02116 (617) 536–6252.

Massachusetts Council of Rabbis. To unify J com activities. Rabbinical Ct divorce; conversions; seminars; kashruth; supervision. 50 mems. Pres: Rabbi Dr Samuel J. Fox; VP: Yehuda Kelemer; Sec: Meir Gross; Treas: Jacob Mann. **611 Washington St, Boston MA 02111 (617) 426–9586.**

Mizrachi – Hapoel Hamizrachi of New England. Rel Zionist org affiliated with branch of Rel Zionist of Am. To aid Is, especially rel ins; to give Passover relief. Edu progs; charity fund raising; counseling servs; banquet. 1,000 mems; 700 families; 10 local groups. 1 employee; 25 volunteers. Pres: Albert M. Stern; Co-Chr: Stanley Rabinowitz; Treas: Samuel Kurr; Sec: Hellen Morrison. **611 Washington St, Boston MA 02111 (617) 426–9148.**

New England Zionist Federation. 17 Commonwealth Ave, Boston MA 02116.

Pioneer Women – Na'amat. The training & edu of the Is woman & her family so that each can be best equipped to lead productive lives. For additional information, see – Pioneer Women Na'amat, New York City, NY. **294 Washington St, Boston MA 02108 (617) 426–1059.**

Rabbinical Council of Massachusetts (Vaad Harabonim). Orthodox supervision of kashruth, certification (kosher) of food products, Beth Din, rel information serv. Supervision of kashruth in catering establishments, bakeries, restaurants, meat markets, com & serv ctrs; kosher certification for many food & ind products on local & natl level; Rabbinical Ct on matters such as divorce, family disputes, arbitration cases, rel decisions & social issues; counseling; chaplaincy progs; edu progs on com-wide scale; resource for rel information to J & non-J, to the press, to media both locally & nationally; library containing 2,000 vols (Rabbinical Ct Library). Pres: Rabbi Saul Weiss; Adm: Rabbi Abraham Halbfinger. **177 Tremont St, Boston MA 02111.**

Rabbinical Council of Massachusetts (Vaad Harabonim), Library. Library contains 2000 vols (Rabbinical Ct Library). For information on the Ins,. see – Rabbinical Council of Massachusetts, Boston, MA. **177 Tremont St, Boston MA 02111.**

Temple Israel. Affiliated with UAHC. 1735 mems. Rabbis: Bernard H. Mehlman, Ronne Friedman, Roland B. Gittelsohn; Cantor Murray F. Simon; Pres: Justin L. Wyner; Edu: David A. Katz; Adm: Norman Fogel; Sisterhood Pres: Joy Rachlin; Brotherhood Pres: Arthur Schatz. **Longwood Ave at Plymouth St, Boston MA 02215 (617) 566–3960.**

Temple Israel Library. For information on the Temple, see – Temple Israel, Boston, MA. **Longwood Ave at Plymouth St, Boston MA 02115 (617) 566–3960.**

Zionist House. Non-profit facility that houses agy associated with furthering the interest of the State of Is. Much of the annual operating budget is provided by the Combined J Philanthropies. To edu Am about Is. Maintains a data bank about life in Is & world wide J conditions; holds exhibitions of Is art, photography, & films; provides loan kits explaining Is soc & culture to public sch systems; Scholar in Residence Proj coords the appearance of Is culture & academic figures; maintains 5,000 vol library; sponsors interfaith confs; reps the Is point of view in radio &

TV progs; sponsors Zionist Awareness Week; supports activities of Young Adult Zionists, MA & Is Cultural Soc, & the Aliyah Council; for Is stu in Boston, acts as an information ctr, & provides a free Is stu med prog. F in 1946. Zionist House is a five story bldg in which is located the regional offs of Am Zionist Fed, the Zionist Org of Am, New England Hadassah Youth Commis (Young Judaea), Mizrachi Women, Weizman Ins, & J Ctr for Arts. The auditorium is available to J groups & orgs for meetings, lectures, confs & symposia concerning Is. Pres: Bernard Garber; VPs: James Shulman, Benjamin Ulin, Rae Ginsburg; Sec: Judah Stone; Treas: Benjamin Nigrosh; Trustees: Sarah Ansell, Samuel Bahn, Susan Berk, Harvey Burg, Maurice Cohen, Sidney Govenar, Stanley Hatoff, Avis Jacobson, Morris Michelson, Helen Levin Michelson, Miriam Portman, Dorothy Rossyn, Rabbi Murray Rothman, Henry Silverman, Dorothy Spector, Lawrence Suttenberg, Alvin Tamkin, Peter Ulin. **17 Commonwealth Ave, Boston MA 02116 (617) 267-2235.**

Braintree

Temple B'nai Shalom. Affiliated with United Syn of Am. Rabbi Ephraim Greenberg; Pres: Bob Gorfinkle; Exec Dir: David Chafetz; Edu Dir: Marvin Ashes; Youth Dir: Maxine Spitzer. **41 Stores Ave, Braintree MA 02184 (617) 843-3687.**

Brighton

Daughters of Israel. To fulfil the halachaic requirements of mikveh & the edu of families & young people on the use of the mikveh. Edu progs for family life; mikveh. 500 mems. 3 employees; 5 volunteers. The mikveh was built in 1945 to fulfil the needs & requirements for the Greater Boston area. Facilities include two ritualariums & four baths with other health & beauty aids. Rabbi Mayer Horowitz. **101 Washington St, Brighton MA 02135 (617) 734-5100.**

Lubavitch Youth Organization. An outreach org that familiarizes J men & women & chil with J practices & philosophy. Affiliated with the Chabad Lubavitch Movement. To bring the Light of Torah & J tradition to all corners of the world; to battle against assimilation, apathy & indifference to J living. In gen this ins offers: Operation Helping Hand – gives aid to Russian immigrants; on campus progs – provides kosher foods, Fri night to Sun retreats, lectures, Shabbat servs & counseling; celebrations of holidays – sponsors seminars on Passover laws, holds Purim Party, sponsors Toys for Tots for chil in the hosp at Chanukah, helps with bldg of succas, distributes prayers bks for holidays; marriage & family counseling; Adult Edu Prog; helps est kosher kitchens in private homes; Mitzvah Mobile – introduces J men to the wearing of Tefillin, distributes rel articles, maintains traveling J library & audio visual ctr; Succamobile; & summer day camp. Rabbi Chaim Pruss. **42 Kirkwood Rd, Brighton MA 02135 (617) 787-2667.**

Brockton

Temple Beth Emunah. Affiliated with United Syn of Am. Rabbi H. David Werb; Cantor Gerhard Gluck; Pres: William Kracoff. **Torrey & Pearl Sts, Brockton MA 02401 (617) 583-5810.**

Temple Beth Emunah Library. For information on the Temple, see – Temple Beth Emunah, Brockton, MA. **Pearl & Torrey Sts, Brockton MA 02401 (617) 583-5810.**

Temple Israel. Affiliated with UAHC. 266 mems. Rabbi H. Bruce Ehrmann; Cantor Maurice Singer; Pres: Alvin Barber; Edu: Dr Lawrence J. Levine; Sisterhood Pres: Sharon Sohmer; Brotherhood Pres: Marvin Liberman. **184 W Elm St, Brockton MA 02401 (617) 587-4130.**

Brookline

American Jewish Historical Society. 21 Blake Rd, Brookline MA 02146.

American Jewish Historical Society Library. 21 Blake Rd, Brookline MA 02146.

American Physicians Fellowship, Inc. 2001 Beacon St, Brookline MA 02146 (617) 232-5382.

Congregation Beth Pinchas. Chassidic Cong affiliated with New England Chassidic Ctr. Worship according to the Orthodox J faith. Daily pryer;Sisterhood;counseling servs; library containing 1,000 vols (J sacred bks & commentaries). 200 families. 3 employees, 15 volunteers. F in 1914 by the 1st Bostoner Rebbe, Grand Rabbi Pinchos David Horowitz. The 1st location was in the W End; subsequently the Cong moved to Dorchester. In 1946, the present Bostoner Rebbe, Grand Rabbi Levi Horowitz, succeeded his father. In 1961 the Ctr's present location at Beacon St was acquired. Pub Sisterhood Bulliten (monthly). Rabbi Levi Y. Horowitz; Asst Rabbi R. Mayer Horowitz; Pres: Hershell Miller; Dayan: Rabbi Nephtali Horowitz. **1710 Beacon St, Brookline MA 02146.**

Congregation Kehillath Israel. Affiliated with United Syn of Am. Rabbi Manuel Saltzman; Cantor

Moshe Weiss; Pres: William Weiner; Edu Dir: Susan Rodenstein. **384 Harvard St, Brookline MA 02146 (617) 277–9155.**

Hebrew College. 43 Hawes St, Brookline MA 02146 (617) 252–8710.

Hebrew College, Jacob & Rose Grossman Library. 43 Hawes St, Brookline MA 02146 (617) 252–8710.

Jewish Times. Periodical pub. **118 Cypress St, Brookline MA 02146 (617) 566–7710.**

Kehillath Israel Congregation, Minnie W. Epstein Library. For information on the Cong, see – Kehillath Israel Cong, Brookline, MA. **384 Harvard St, Brookline MA 02146 (617) 277–9155.**

Lubavitch Yeshiva. 9 Prescot St, Brookline MA 02146 (617) 731–5330.

Machsikei Torah Institute. Ctr of learning for young adults primarily geared to beginners who are seeking to enhance their knowledge of J. Classes conducted daily; separate progs for men & women. F in 1969. **1710 Beacon St, Brookline MA 02146.**

Maimonides School. J & gen studies, K through 12th grade. To foster the dev of young people within whom rel & gen edu, commitment to J, & the desire to contribute to soc are organically linked. J studies include: Bible, Prophets, Talmud, Hist & Philosophy of the Siddur (prayer bk), & regular sessions devoted to a wide range of topics & issues in contemporary J thought; daily syn servs; gen studies include: English, French & Advanced Placement French, Latin, Social Studies (including J Hist), Mathematics, Algebra, Geometry, Trigonometry, Pre-Calculus, Advance Placement Calculus, Life Sci/Ecology, Introduction to Physical Sci, Biology, Chem, Physics, special sci progs for the stu who demonstrates an unusual talent & interest, Physical Edu; extra curricular activities include: varsity & jr basketball teams, intramural field hockey prog, math team, stu govt, Shabbatonim, speakers prog, sch outings, outreach & charitable fund raising progs; other progs include: scholarship prog & three day a week hot lunch prog; activities under the direction of the local JCCinclude: woodwork, ceramics, Is dancing, & dramatics. 400 boys & girls. 62 teachers; consultants in mental health, early childhood & special edu; librarian. F in 1937 by Rabbi Dr Joseph B. Soloveitchik. The campus covers four acres & includes 25 classrms, a sci lab, computer facilities, recreational areas, & a syn. Pub Kol Rambam (monthly). Pres: Samuel C. Feuerstein; Chr Bd of Dirs: Maurice H. Savel; V Chr Bd of Dirs: Stanley H. Sydney; VPs: Abraham Levovitz, Dr Bernard D. Kosowsky, Sidney Blechner; Treas: S. Joseph Solomont; Assc Treas: Samuel Kurr; Corporate Sec: Dr Benjamin E. Bahn; Dir of Gen Studies: Dr Kalman Stein; Exec Dir: Deanne Stone; Asst to the Exec Dir: Deanne Stone. **Philbrick Rd, Brookline MA 02146 (617) 232–4414.**

New England Chassidic Center. Social serv agency. To provide the Boston com with all the servs affiliated with gmilat chesed. Sabbaton Prog; visiting lecturers; kashruth information; counseling; edu progs. 2500 mems. 2 employees, 15 volunteers. Est in 1918. The org has gained fame for its Shabbaton prog – a unique method of involving col youth in experiencing a traditional Shabbat. Tens of thousands of young people have participated in this prog in the US & in the world. Spiritual leader: Bostoner Rebbe, Grand Rabbi Levi Y. Horowitz; Pres: Edward M. Sharzer. **1710 Beacon St, Brookline MA 02154 (617) 566–9182.**

ROFEH. Med referral serv & family housing for patients affiliated with New England Chassidic Ctr. To provide the best possible physicians & med care while simultaneously serving the mental & physical needs of the immediate family. Consultation & conseling regarding the choice of physicians; setting up appointments; providing translators for patients fr abroad; providing housing & direction for the families of the ill. F 1948 by Grand Rabbi Levy Y. Horowitz, the Bostoner Rebbe, as a proj of the New England Chassidic Ctr, & inc 1979 as an independent org to enable seriously ill patients fr all parts of the world to make contact with the proper med servs in Boston. Facilities include apts & bedrms, kitchenettes for families whose mems are undergoing med treatment in Boston. Pres: Rebetzin Rachel Horowitz; VP: Rabbi Mayer Horowitz; Dir: Rebetzin Sima Horowitz. **1710 Beacon St, Brookline MA 02146 (617) 566–9182.**

Temple Beth Zion. Affiliated with United Syn of Am. Rabbi Aivadia Rosenberg; Cantor Morris Michelson; Pres: Noah N. Sallop; Exec Dir: Harry Tarutz; Edu Dir: Abraham Woolf; Youth Dir: Israel Arnold. **1566 Beacon St, Brookline MA 02146 (617) 566–8171.**

Temple Ohabei Shalom. Affiliated with UAHC. 735 mems. Rabbis: Dov Taylor, Albert S. Goldstein; Cantor Alex Zimmer; Pres: Daniel Deykin; Edu: Serene Victor; Adm: Stanley Gaynor; Sisterhood Pres: Joan Wasserman; Brotherhood Pres: Stanley Goldberg, Jerry Weinberg. **1187 Beacon St, Brookline MA 02146 (617) 277–6610.**

Temple Sinai. Affiliated with UAHC. 283 mems. Rabbi Frank M. Waldorf; Cantor Mark Kagan; Pres: Jay P. Sage; Edu: Jane Taubenfeld; Adm: Joan M. Kunitz; Sisterhood Pres: Janet Pearlman, Mollie Sibley, Iris Wasserman; Brotherhood Pres: Abbe Cohen. **50 Sewall Ave, Brookline MA 02146 (617) 277–5888.**

Torah Institute of New England. Col level studies affiliated with the New England Chassidic Ctr. To educate col youth, both men & women, in J & to acquaint them with the traditional J faith. An entire series of classes fr beginning to intermediate level in Bible, Talmud, Halacha & Mussar; library contains 10,000 vols (J sacred bks & commentaries). 85 stu. 4 employees. F 1969. Facilities include lecture halls & library. Dean: Rabbi Mayer Horowitz; Registrar: Rabbi Abraham Hershoff. **1710 Beacon St, Brookline MA 02146 (617) 734–5100.**

Torah Institute of New England, Library. Library contains 10,000 vols (J sacred bks & commentaries). For information on the Ins, see – Torah Institute of New England, Brookline, MA. **1710 Beacon St, Brookline MA 02146 (617) 734–5100.**

UAHC Northeast Council. Rel & edu org serving J congs throughout the US & Canada. To encourage & aid the org & dev of J congs; to promote J edu, & enrich & intensify J life; to foster other activities for the perpetuation & advancement of J. For additional information, see – UAHC – Union of American Hebrew Congregations, New York City, NY. Pres: Robert Summit; Dir: Rabbi Paul J. Menitoff. **1330 Beacon St, Suite 355, Brookline MA 02146 (617) 277–1655.**

Yal-Day-New. Day Care Ctr; Orthodox prog licensed by the State of MA. Our goal is to provide loving child care & presch edu in an observant, J environment. Half-time & full-time care for chil between the ages of 3 mo & 4 yrs. 32 families; 32 chil between 3 mo & 4 yrs. 10 employees; 2 volunteers. F 1980 by a group of parents. Pres: Menachem Fishbein; Treas: Stephen Brenner, Nadine Brenner; Rec Sec: Deborah Kram; Enrollment Off: Gail Fishbein. **62 Green St, Brookline MA 02146 (617) 232–6019.**

Burlington

Temple Shalom Emeth. Affiliated with UAHC. 82 mems. Pres: Marvin Getman; Edu: Abby Brown; Brotherhood Pres: Richard Milesky. **PO Box 216, Burlington MA 01803 (617) 272–7454.**

Cambridge

Am Tikva. Com of gay & lesbian J in the Boston area; mem of the World Congress of Gay & Lesbian J Org. To provide a place for gay & lesbian J. To affirm important aspects of their identitiy, their gayness & their Jewishness. To serve the spiritual, cultural, edu & social needs of the mems. Sabbath evening servs; holiday celebrations; discussions; classes; social activities. 40 men & women. Est in 1977. Quarterly newsletter. **PO Box 11, Cambridge MA 02238 (617) 353–1821.**

Association for Jewish Studies. Widener Library, Harvard University, Cambridge MA 02138 (617) 495–2985.

Fellowship in Israel for Arab-Jewish Youth. 45 Francis Ave, Cambridge MA 02138 (617) 354–1198.

Canton

Temple Beth Abraham. Affiliated with United Syn of Am. Rabbi Joel Chernikoff; Pres: Joel Z. Kessel. **1301 Washington St, Canton MA 02021 (617) 566–8171.**

Chestnut Hill

Bureau of Jewish Education. Key edu resource for Greater Boston's diverse J com; Affiliated with the Am Assn for J Edu. To promote J edu. Frequent sch visits & classrm observations to monitor events & trends in Greater Boston's J schs; curriculum dev by BJE professional staff, & Boston's J Edu who work together to prepare materials in Heb language, J hist, Bible, ethics & prayer, & plan progs for J living experiences; teachers & prins orgs work to foster a sense of mutual support & common purpose among J edu & the BJE; In-Serv Professional Training Workshops give edu a chance to explore new methods & ideas with their colleagues; the Master Teacher Prog produces videotape cassettes of outstanding teachers to provide tangible role models for other instrs to observe; informal edu progs, through confs & com wide events, keeps provocative issues & trends in J edu before the eyes of the com; BJE sponsors progs including: karati, annual J Bk Read-a-thon, contests such as the Natl Bible Contest & the Soviet J Creative Arts Contest, Shabbatonim – weekend learning by living experiences sponsored by the BJE, Chevra Camp progs, drama, discussion, Israeli dancing & calligraphy (a few of the rich variety of J learning experiences available to youngsters during winter vacations); Para Professional Training Prog trains teens to serve as teacher aides & tutors in their rel schs using a yr long course & supervised apprenticeship to prepare youth for positions of responsibility; Proj Shalom gives stu the opportunity to work as volunteers in more than 20 different social servs orgs in Greater Boston; SWAP, Suburban W Area Progs, sponsors mini courses, workshops, trips, teen council meetings & special events which bring teenagers fr ten W area coms together for J edu; BJE's J Edu Resource & Adv Ctr maintains a continuously updated collection of bks, films, filmstrips, slides, records, audio & videotapes; BJE sponsors courses & workshops that range fr advanced training for working prins to holiday mini courses for one day a week teachers; BJE sponsors progs including edu conf, professional growth progs, in-serv courses & materials creating workshops offered on a yr round basis at the Ctr. 12,000 stu fr nursery sch through HS; 1,500 in the Prog of J Studies for HS stu; 1,000 J edu; 70 schs in 40 Greater Boston cities & towns – Conservative, Independent, Reform, & Orthodox day schs. Est in 1920 & sponsored by the Federated J Charities, precursor to today's Combined J Philanthropies of Greater Boston. The second central agy for J edu in the country, the Boston BJE, achieved recognition as a leader in Am J edu. BJE est the precedent of setting standards of achievement through uniform examinations for stu of Boston's J schs. BJE professionals consulted with edu to determine the direction of J edu. Together they est a Code of Practice, guaranteeing J edu professional status, benefits & standards, & developed an exemplary set of curricula for schs. The modern progs have been designed cooperatively by BJE professionals, teachers, rabbis, adms, sch cttees, & social workers – all people who believe that the strength of the J com is tied to the challenge of providing quality edu. Pres: N. Ronald Silberstein; VPs: Dr Phillip A. Lief, Sumner Milender; Treas: Hadassah Blocker; Sec: Norman B. Cohen; Exec Dir Emeritus: Dr Benjamin J. Shevach; Exec Dir: Louis Newman; Sr Consultant & JERAC Dir: Dr Daniel J. Margolis; Edu Consultants: Esther Karten, Hasia Kronberger; Dir HS Progs: Susan L. Shevitz; Com Edu & Media Specialist: Jeffrey Liberman. **824 Boylston St, Chestnut Hill MA 02167 (617) 277–3100.**

Congregation Mishkan Tefila. Conservative Cong affiliated with United Syn of Am. Sisterhood; Brotherhood; Couples Club; PTA; Heb HS; Rel Sch; Nursery Sch; Sr Citizens Org; Youth Prog. 2,500 people. Rabbi; Cantor; Exec Dir; Edu Dir; Youth Dir; Music Dir; teaching staff of 10. F in 1858. The third oldest cong in Greater Boston, Mishkan Tefila was the first Conservative cong in New England. The original Syn began in a tenement house on Oswego St in the S End. The Cong was located at various sites. In 1925 the Seaver St Temple in Roxbury was dedicated. The present bldg was dedicated in 1958. The Cong is the leading fundraiser of any syn in the Greater New England area for Is Bonds, JTS, & Combined J Philanthropies. Rabbi Richard M. Yellin; Cantor Gregor Shelkan; Pres: Leo Karas. **300 Hammond Pond Pkwy, Chestnut Hill MA 02167 (617) 332–7770.**

New England-Israel Chamber of Commerce and Industry, Inc – Boston. Offers assistance to mem US firms interested in economic activity in & with Is. Provides extensive trade assistance; pub market research reports; aids in dev trade & investment between US & Is. For additional information, see – American-Israel Chamber of Commerce & Industry, Inc, New York City, NY. **PO Box 40, Chestnut Hill MA 02167 (617) 738–5344.**

Temple Emeth. Affiliated with United Syn of Am. Rabbi Alan Turetz; Cantor Simon Kandler; Pres: Louis Epstein; Exec Dir: Alan M. Albert. **194 Grove St, Chestnut Hill MA 02167 (617) 469–9701.**

Concord

Concord Area Jewish Group. Rel, cultural, social, edu, interfaith & social action progs. 150 families; 60 stu in grades 1–7. 8 employees. Formerly Concord-Lincoln Study Group. Pub Newsletter (monthly). Meetings held at First Parish Unitarian in Concord MA. Rabbi Michael Jonathan Luckens; Pres: Susan Markson; VP: David Orlinoff. **PO Box 1339, Concord MA 01742.**

Fall River

Temple Beth El. Affiliated with United Syn of Am. Rabbi Jonathan A. Panitz; Cantor Richard A. Wolberg; Pres: Jason Sigal. **385 High St, Fall River MA 02720 (617) 674–3529.**

Temple Beth El, Ziskind Memorial Library. For information on the Temple, see – Temple Beth El, Fall River, MA. **385 High St, Fall River MA 02720 (617) 674–3529.**

Fitchburg

Jewish Federation of Fitchburg. 40 Boutelle St, Fitchburg MA 01420 (617) 342–2227.

Framingham

Congregation Bais Chabad. Orthodox Cong; mem of Lubavitch Youth Org; affiliated with Yeshiva Achei

Tmimim of Worcester MA. To spread Yiddishkeit. Rel Servs; Heb Sch; Sisterhood; Adult Edu; Presch; library containing 300 vols (Talmud, Shulchan Aruch, Halachic Responsa, Chassidic philosophy); counseling servs. 60 families; 55 stu in grades K–6. 6 employees. F 1916; previous name was Bais Chabad Ctr. Pub Annual Journal, Women of Chabad Newsletter (monthly). Facilities include kosher kitchen, sanctuary seating, rel articles shop. Rabbi Yakov Lazaros; Pres: Mike Seigel; VPs: Jeffrey Karsin, Leonard Auers; Chr: Mark Goldman; Asst Chr: Edward Weinberger; Treas: Sidney Katz; Gabbai: Joseph Seigenbaum. **74 Joseph Rd, Framingham MA 01761 (617) 877–8888.**

Greater Framingham Jewish Federation. Mem of CJF. Organized 1968; inc 1969. Pub Jewish Reporter. Pres: Dr Lawrence M. Stone. **76 Salem End Rd, Framingham MA 01701 (617) 879–3301.**

Lubavitch Youth Organization. An outreach org that familiarizes J men & women & chil with J practices & philosophy. Affiliated with the Chabad Lubavitch Movement. To bring the Light of Torah & J tradition to all corners of the world; to battle against assimilation, apathy & indifference to J living. In gen this ins offers: Operation Helping Hand – gives aid to Russian immigrants; on campus progs – provides kosher foods, Fri night to Sun retreats, lectures, Shabbat servs & counseling; celebrations of holidays – sponsors seminars on Passover laws, holds Purim Party, sponsors Toys for Tots for chil in the hosp at Chanukah, helps with bldg of succas, distributes prayers bks for holidays; marriage & family counseling; Adult Edu Prog; helps est kosher kitchens in private homes; Mitzvah Mobile – introduces J men to the wearing of Tefillin, distributes rel articles, maintains traveling J library & audio visual ctr; Succamobile; & summer day camp. Rabbi Z. Wilschanski. **74 Joseph Rd, Framingham MA 01701 (617) 877–5313.**

Temple Beth Am. Affiliated with UAHC. 585 mems. Rabbi Alfred L. Friedman; Pres: Barry Levitt; Edu: Ike Eisenstein; Sisterhood Pres: Barbara Schwartz; Brotherhood Pres: Richard Constant. **300 Pleasant St, Framingham MA 01701 (617) 872–8300.**

Temple Beth Sholom. Affiliated with United Syn of Am. Rabbi Dr Murray Levine; Cantor Jack Kessler; Pres: Joel Dubrow; Edu Dir: Dr Sarah Lieberman; Youth Dir: Nancy Bayer. **Pamela Rd, Framingham MA 01701 (617) 877–2540.**

Gloucester

Temple Ahavath Achim. Affiliated with United Syn of Am. Rabbi Myron S. Geller; Pres: Bernard Chapnick. **86 Middle St, Gloucester MA 01930 (617) 281–0739.**

Great Barrington

UAHC Eisner Camp Institute. Dir: Cantor Norman Swerling. **Brookside Rd, Great Barrington MA 01230 (413) 528–1652; 838 Fifth Ave, New York NY 10021 (212) 249–0100.**

Greenfield

Temple Israel of Greenfield, Inc. Affiliated with United Syn of Am. Rabbi Kalman Newfield; Pres: John Landes. **27 Pierce St, Greenfield MA 01301 (413) 773–5884.**

Haverhill

Haverhill United Jewish Appeal, Inc. Mem of CJF. Pres: Manuel M. Epstein; Exec Sec: Rabbi Abraham I. Jacobson. **514 Main St, Haverhill MA 01830 (617) 373–3861.**

Temple Emanu-El. Reform Temple affiliated with UAHC, JWB. To provide a center of J rel life as well as social & recreational progs. Rel Servs; Rel Edu Sch; Presch; confirmation; Afternoon Sch; Sun Sch; Adult Edu; Sisterhood; B'nai B'rith; Brotherhood; Young Couples; Sr Citizens Group; social action; support for Russian families relocating to Haverhill; library containing 1350 vols. 365 mems (240 families; 125 individuals); 18 presch stu; 27 stu in grades 1–4; 39 stu in grades 5–10. 8 employees. F 1937; added com ctr in 1950. Pub Temple Topics (bi-weekly). Facilities include sanctuary seating 423, chapel, library, gymnasium, games rm, locker rm, showers, 2 kitchens, assembly rm, 7 classrms. Rabbi Ira Korinow; Rabbi Emeritus Abraham Jacobson; Pres: Kenneth Salk; VPs: Robert Edelstein, Manuel Epstein, Adeline Watnick; Treas: Vinson Grad; Asst Treas: Marvin Brindis; Exec Dir: Mark W. Weisstuch; Sec: Judy Rutstein. **514 Main St, Haverhill MA 01830 (617) 373–3861.**

Temple Emanu-El Library. Contains 1350 vols (various). For information on the Temple, see – Temple Emanu-El, Haverhill, MA. **514 Main St, Haverhill MA 01830 (617) 373-3861.**

Holyoke

Combined Jewish Appeal of Holyoke. 378 Maple St, Holyoke MA 01040 (413) 534–3369.

Congregation Sons of Zion. Affiliated with United Syn of Am. Rabbi Mark D. Finkel; Cantor Dr David

Koffman; Pres: Sidney Paul. **378 Maple St, Holyoke MA 01040 (413) 534–3369.**

Hull

Temple Beth Sholom. Affiliated with United Syn of Am. Rabbi David H. Weisenberg; Cantor Judah Rinek; Pres: Lawrence Kellem; Exec Dir: Sidney Silbert; Edu Dir: Daniel Colman. **600 Nantasket Ave, Hull MA 02045 (617) 925–0091.**

Hyannis

Cape Cod Synagogue. Affiliated with UAHC. 290 mems. Rabbi Harold L. Robinson; Cantor Bruce Malin; Pres: David J. Silverman; Edu: Bruce Malin; Sisterhood Pres: W. Elkins. **145 Winter St, PO Box 61, Hyannis MA 02601 (617) 775–2988.**

Cape Cod Synagogue Library. For information on the Syn, see – Cape Cod Synagogue, Hyannis, MA. **145 Winter St, PO Box 61, Hyannis MA 02601 (617) 775–2988.**

Hyde Park

Temple Adas Hadrath Israel. Affiliated with United Syn of Am. Rabbi Myer Levetin; Pres: Norman Kristal Exec VP: Ivan Kirsch. **28 Arlington St, Hyde Park MA 02136 (617) 364–2661.**

Lawrence

Congregation Anshai Sfard & Sons of Israel. Affiliated with United Syn of Am. Rabbi Benjamin H. Tumin; Pres: Louis Spector. Sch Prin: Chaya Foxbruner. **492 Lowell St, Lawrence MA 01841.**

Jewish Community of Greater Lawrence. Mem of CJF. Organized 1906. Pres: Sidney Swartz; Exec Dir: Irving H. Linn. **580 Haverhill St, Lawrence MA 01841 (617) 686–4157.**

Leominster

Agudat Achim. Affiliated with United Syn of Am. Rabbi Loel M. Weiss; Pres: Matthew Faberman; Edu Cttee Chr: Gail Korn. **268 Washington St, Leominster MA 01453 (617) 534–6121.**

Leominster Jewish Community Council, Inc. Mem of CJF. Organized 1939. Pres: Martin J. Shaeval; Sec/Treas: Howard J. Rome. **268 Washington St, Leominster MA 01453 (617) 534–6121.**

Lexington

Temple Emunah. Affiliated with United Syn of Am. Rabbi Richard Meirowitz; Pres: Lloyd Gilson; Edu Dir: Carolyn Keller. **9 Piper Rd, Lexington MA 02139 (617) 861–0300.**

Temple Isaiah. Affiliated with UAHC. 425 mems. Rabbi Cary D. Yales; Pres: Marshall Derby; Edu: Lois Edelstein; Adm: Phyllis Silver; Sisterhood Pres: S. Pearlman; Brotherhood Pres: Roger Appell. **55 Lincoln St, Lexington MA 02173 (617) 862–7160.**

Temple Isaiah, Rabbi Haskell M. Bernat Library. For information on the Temple, see – Temple Isaiah, Lexington, MA. **55 Lincoln St, Lexington MA 02173 (617) 862–7160.**

Longmeadow

B'nai Jacob. Affiliated with United Syn of Am. Rabbi Gary Greene; Cantor Dr Theodore A. Perry; Pres: Archie Shapiro; Youth Dir: Judy Greene. **2 Eunice Dr, Longmeadow MA 01106 (413) 567–0058.**

Lowell

Temple Beth El. Affiliated with United Syn of Am. Rabbi James M. Lebeau; Cantor Stephen Thompson; Pres: Joel R. Shyavitz; Youth Dir: Harriet Shanzer. **105 Princeton Blvd, Lowell MA 01851 (617) 453–0073.**

Temple Emanuel. Affiliated with UAHC. 80 mems. Rabbi Everett Gendler; Pres: Alyn Rovin; Edu: Ruth Schwartz. **101 W Forest St, Lowell MA 01851 (617) 454–1372.**

Malden

Temple Ezrath Israel. Affiliated with United Syn of Am. Cantor Chaim Razin; Rabbi Emeritus Mayer S. Baer; Pres: Raymond Dreezer. **245 Bryant St, Malden MA 02148 (617) 322–7205.**

Temple Tefereth Israel. 430 mems. Rabbi Thomas P. Leibschutz; Cantor Sheldon H. Chandler; Edu: Jack L. Sparks; Adm: Sylvia Lyons; Sisterhood Pres: Cheryl Berman; Brotherhood Pres: Hyman Silverman. **3539 Salem St, Malden MA 02148 (617) 322–2794.**

Temple Tifereth Israel Religious School. Affiliated with UAHC. To produce rel sch grads who will feel comfortable being J; be committed to personal morality & social justice; be motivated to continue pursuit of J knowledge; want to join & contribute to the J com; identify with J of the past; feel pride in J accomplishments; recognize an obligation to J world wide; feel obligated to carry J traditions into the future; know enough Heb & ceremonies to feel comfortable participating in home & syn observances. Primary through grade nine; Bar/Bat Mitzvah; Confirmation; student paricipation: one stu fr each class in grades 4–9 sits on the Prin's Council, grades 3–7 conduct one Erev Shabbat or Shabbat Morning Serv for the Cong, reps fr each grade sit on the Justice Council & these stu maintain on-going communications fr the Prin to the stu on matters relating to Tzedakah & distribution of Keren Ami Funds. Progress reports of chil in grades 1–9 are sent to the parents twice during the year. Rabbi Thomas P. Leibschutz; Prin: Jack L. Sparks. Chr Edu Cttee: Donna Stone. **3539 Salem St, Malden MA 02148 (617) 322–2794.**

Marblehead

Jewish Federation of the North Shore, Inc. Mem of CJF. Organized 1938. Pres: Gerald Ogan; Exec Dir: Dr Gerald S. Ferman. **4 Community Rd, Marblehead MA 01945 (617) 598–1810.**

North Shore Jewish Community Center. Multi serv. For all the J in the area to engage in social, recreational, cultural & edu activities. Parenting & Chil Servs – Prepared Childbirth, Our Babies Ourselves for mothers & infants together, Mommy & Me for mothers & toddlers, Systematic Training for Effective Parenting; infant/toddler chil care: part time to full time chil care for chil ages one mo to two yrs nine mo; Presch: three & five mornings a week progs for chil two yrs nine mo to five yrs old; Presch Extended Day; K Enrichment: supplementary prog to complement the public sch K; aftersch & vacation progs for youngsters 5 to 12: classes in kite making, batik, painting, drawing, pottery, screenprinting, cooking, needlecrafts, carpentry & nature crafts. Youth Prog – clubs: Young Judea, 4–5–6, biking, jogging, & bowling; progs & activities for young people ages 12 through 17: youth lounge & snack bar, Sun night youth sports league, specialized courses for teens, dances, movies, trips & vacation progs. Sr Adults – social clubs, discussion groups, trips, exercise classes, recreation for the legally blind, fine arts classes, dance classes, choral group, health series & kaballah series. Single Adults – social group, Widowed to Widowed outreach self help prog & support groups for single parents. The Ctr sponsors – edu sessions: estate planning, seminar for adult chil of aging parents, & workshops; cultural events: concert series, J music festival, dramatic performances, exhibitions, mus & gallery trips, Artist in Residence Prog, Chanukah crafts fair, film series; trips to Is, visit Is prepared prog; & day & weekend travel; holiday celebrations; lecture series; adult classes: pottery, painting, drawing, sculpture, ulpan, wine tasting, yoga; health & physical edu: exercise classes, sports clubs, gymnastics, aquatics progs, competitive basketball & volleyball, paddleball, ski club, fitness progs, aerobic exercises, family roller skating, annual road race, swimming & health fair; Health Club; Tennis Club. Kings Plaza branch is an outgrowth of a com desire for a facility for all J to comfortably engage in social, recreational, cultural & edu activities. Activities include Presch & K Enrichment, toddler playgroups, parent-toddler progs, parenting progs, family days, racquetball & basketball, woodworking, cooking, drama, teen lounge & leadership dev, Couples Club, club groups for chil, & arts progs. F in 1911. The Ctr's facilities include indoor & outdoor swimming pools, tennis cts, basketball cts, locker rms, meeting rms, lounges, classrms, 14 acres in Marblehead, a 112 acre camping facility in Middleton. The health club facilities include a fully equipped gymnasium, steam rm, sauna, hydrocollator, private lockers, sun deck, infra red lamps, ultra violet sun lamps, private lounge, volleyball ct, paddleball & handball cts, & grooming & rest facilities. Pres: Ernest Weiss; VPs: Michael Eschelbacher, Michael Goshko, Gerald Posner, Barbara Schneider, Dr Howard Rosenkrantz; Treas: Irwin Cohen; Sec: Dr Charles Leidner; Hon Pres: Eli A. Cohen; Hon VP: Robert I. Lappin, John Rimer; Exec Dir: Dr S. Morton Altman; Prog Dir: Beverly P. Shapiro. **Community Rd, Marblehead MA 01945 (617) 631–8330.**

Temple Emanu-El. Reform Cong affiliated with UAHC. Rel Servs; Rel Sch K–12th grade, including Confirmation class & Post Confirmation; Adult Edu classes; Sisterhood; Men's Club; social events; library; youth groups for grades 7–12; Sr Adult Group; Adult Bat Mitzvah Class; Class with Confirmation Parents; Rel Sch workshops for holidays & festivals; family & Cong celebrations with suppers for Purim & Hanukkah; Shabbat worship servs created & conducted once a mo by a different grade of the Rel Sch; Israeli dancing taught. F in 1954. Bulletin (newsletter for the Cong). Rabbi Dr Robert W. Shapiro; Edu Dir: Gerald Orlen; Pres: Robert J. Smith; VPs: Jack Fischer, Marcia Michelson, Harris R. Tregor; Treas: Mitchell Comins; Fin Sec: Eugene Barden; Rec Sec: Barbara Cantor; Corsp Sec: Anita Barkan; Chr Sch Cttee: Burton M. Harris; Pres Sisterhood: Ruth Metz; Pres Brotherhood: Robert Lamkin; Bd of Trustees: Nancy Appeal, Lois Baker, Emily Cantor, David H. Cohen, Annette Feinstein, Marilyn Gerber, Lois Giller, Harris

Goldman, Martin C. Goldman, David Goldstein, Alfred Gross Jr, Buster Gross, Carla Herwitz, David Herwitz, Philip Kaminsky, Sandra Kanosky, Paul Levenson, Joan Livingston, Robert Livingston, Stanley Metz, Louis A. Patterson, Dr Alan Radack, Joel Saxe, Sandra Schauer, Lila Shapiro, Edward Snow, Jason Snyder, Harold Stavisky, Wendy Stavisky. **393 Atlantic Ave, Marblehead MA 01945 (617) 631–9300.**

Temple Sinai. Affiliated with United Syn of Am. Rabbi Meyer Strassfeld; Cantor Jack Chomsky; Pres: Jacob Saval. **1 Community Rd, Marblehead MA 01945 (617) 631–7539.**

Marlborough

Temple Emanuel. Affiliated with United Syn of Am. Cantor Rauol Shorr; Pres: Kenneth Honer; Edu Dir: Alan Swart. **150 Berlin Rd, PO Box 596, Marlborough MA 01752 (617) 485–7565.**

Medford

Temple Shalom Medford Jewish Community Center. Syn affiliated with United Syn of Am. To enrich J by working, praying & being together. Daily Rel Servs; Choir; Jr Cong; rel activities; Rel Sch; Adult Edu; Day Camp; Nursery Sch; library; social activities; Young Adults Group; youth groups, USY; Sisterhood. People of all ages. Est in Jun 1944. Weekly newsletter; bi-monthly bulletin. Temple facilities include a sanctuary, auditorium, kitchen, brides rm, chapel, classrooms, lounge. Rabbi Saul Leeman; Cantor Charles Lew; Pres: Benjamin Averbook; 1st VP: Mrs Melvin Aarons; 2nd VP: Dr Max Perlitsh; 3rd VP: Mrs Joel Saperstein. **475 Winthrop St, Medford MA 02155 (617) 396–3262.**

Medway

Congregation Agudath Achim. Est in 1921 & grew to membership of 45 families. At no time did the J com have a rabbi, except for a few yrs, for teaching the chil their rel background, reading & writing Heb, & preparing them for their Bar Mitzvahs. During the yrs, a learned man would tutor the chil privately. The residents thrived as a rel com through the yrs of 1930–1970 after which time it declined. Now there are only servs on the High Holidays. **13 Holliston St, Medway MA 02053.**

Melrose

Melrose Jewish Center. Affiliated with UAHC. 40 mems. Rabbi Michael Greenwald; Pres: Karl Geller. **21 E Foster St, Melrose MA 02176 (617) 665–4520.**

Milton

Shalom House. 68 Smith Rd, Milton MA 02186 (617) 333–0477.

Temple Shalom of Milton. Affiliated with United Syn of Am. Rabbi Jerome Weistrop; Cantor & Exec Dir: Irving Kischel; Pres: Selwyn W. Glincher; Dir: Irving Kischel; Youth Dir: Nancy Ginsberg. **180 Blue Hill Ave, Milton MA 02187 (617) 698–3394.**

Natick

Temple Israel Library. For information on the Temple, see – Temple Israel, Natick, MA. **145 Hartford St, Natick MA 01760 (617) 653–8591.**

Temple Israel of Natick. Affiliated with United Syn of Am. Rabbi Harold S. Kushner; Cantor Robert S. Scheer; Pres: Allan B. Strachman; Ritual Dir: Lester Schwartz; Edu Dir: Shimon Simons; Youth Dir: Barbara Rutberg. **145 Hartford St, Natick MA 01760 (617) 653–8591.**

Needham

Temple Aliyah. Affiliated with United Syn of Am. Rabbi Ira A. Korff; Cantor Henry Gelman; Pres: Andrew Newman. **1664 Central Ave, Needham MA 02192 (617) 444–8522.**

Temple Beth Shalom. Reform Syn affiliated with UAHC. Dedicated to spiritual, edu, & social enrichment for a full & meaningful J life. Rel Servs; Jr, Youth & Adult Choirs; Rel Sch grades K – Confirmation grade 10; Adult Edu prog, chavarut groups, study groups, & seminars; library; social activities; Nursery Sch; 7th grade Youth Group; Jr Youth Group for grades 8 & 9; Sr Youth Group for grades 10–12; progs include conclaves, retreats, study groups, socials; Brotherhood; Sisterhood; The Garden Club which maintains the Temple grounds & provides flower arrangements for the sanctuary & social hall, & offers courses to adults & youth; Parent Teacher Cttee; The Couples Club which provides an introduction to Temple life thru progs for couples; Col Group with the purpose of perpetuating the friendships made during the yrs at Temple Beth Shalom. The first permanent J settlement in Needham was est in 1897 by immigrants. In the beginning, the people attended nearby congs or hired tutors to provide rel training for their chil. In 1945 the Needham J Com Group was est, the foun of Temple Beth Shalom. In 1953 the first High Holiday Servs were held & a yr later, a Sun Sch with 14 chil was begun. In 1955 the Group was inc as the Needham JCC, & joined the UAHC. Servs were held at various churches. The Cong, consisting of sixty families, purchased a 2½ acre site where the Temple now stands. In 1957 the JCC was renamed Temple Beth Shalom. The first bldg was dedicated in 1960. In 1965 the Temple moved into its present sanctuary & sch bldg. Rabbi Rifat Sonsino; Prin: Roselyn Garber; Music Dir: Howard Worona; Pres: Marvin G. Rumpler; 1st VP: David Shapiro; 2nd VP: Edward Ginn; 3rd VP: Linda Lourie; 4th VP: Herbert Kahn; Treas: Edward Cherenson; Sec: Eleanor Shufro; Fin Sec: Murielle Gerard; Asst Fin Sec: Lucille Sands. **Highland Ave at Webster St, Needham MA 02194 (617) 444–0077.**

New Bedford

Tifereth Israel Congregation. Affiliated with United Syn of Am. Rabbi Dr Bernard Glassman; Cantor Jeffrey R. Shapiro; Pres: Arthur Mindlin; Edu Dir: Ethan Adler; Youth Dir: Wendy Garf-Lipp. **145 Brownell Ave, New Bedford MA 02740 (617) 997–3171.**

Newton

Solomon Schechter Day School. 60 Stein Circle, Newton MA 02159 (617) 891–8980.

Solomon Schechter Day School, Aaron Kushner Library. 60 Stein Circle, Newton MA 02159 (617) 891–8980.

Temple Emanuel. Affiliated with United Syn of Am. Pres: Alan M. Edelstein; Exec Dir: Sharon Sugarman; Edu Dir: Martin Federman. **385 Ward St, Newton MA 02159 (617) 332–5770.**

Temple Reyim. Affiliated with United Syn of Am. Rabbi Dr Philip Kieval; Cantor Martin Robbins; Pres: Kenneth E. Karger; Edu Dir: Esther Saltzman; Youth Dir: Jay Fridkis. **1860 Washington St, Newton MA 02166 (617) 527–2410.**

Temple Shalom. Affiliated with UAHC. 681 mems. Rabbis: Murray I. Rothman, David A. Whiman; Pres: Joel Baron; Edu: David A. Whiman; Adm: Sylvia J. Riese; Sisterhood Pres: Bernice Altshuler; Brotherhood Pres: Mandel Lofchie. **175 Temple St, Newton MA 02165 (617) 332–9550.**

Wasserman Library. 1860 Washington St, Newton MA 02166.

Newton Center

Temple Beth Avodah. Affiliated with UAHC. 395 mems. Rabbi Robert M. Miller; Pres: Bonnie Millender; Edu: Joan Azran; Sisterhood Pres: Marcia Clayman, Natalie Kurtz, Gail Satter; Brotherhood Pres: Jason Hochberg. **45 Pudding Stone LA, Newton Center MA 02159 (617) 527–0045.**

Newton Highlands

National Council of Jewish Women. Women's volunteer org. Dedicated in the spirit of J to advancing human welfare & the democratic way of life. Activities are organized around five prog priorities: women's issues, chil & youth, aging, J life, & Is. Women's Issues – major concerns are: ratification of the Equal Rights Amendment; protection of the right of every women to have access to safe & legal abortion; removal of gender related discrimination in all areas of life; provision of edu progs on the prevention of domestic violence & treatment for its victims, widow to widow counseling, & progs for single parents. Chil & Youth – primarily concerned with: the rights, needs & quality of life of the nation's chil & youth; juvenile justice, especially the treatment of adolescent girls; foster care; variety of projs that support servs to the young people in their coms; advocacy efforts needed to effectively change the way chil are treated under the law. Is – primarily concerned with: carrying out numerous edu & social welfare progs in Is; continuation of its long term strong advocacy for the State of Is; furtherance of current major proj in Is – the Research Ins for Innovation in Edu which is part of The Heb Univ Sch of Edu. J Life – places emphasis on: J edu & the problems of Soviet J; J edu progs for individuals of various ages & interests designed to assist people in exploring their understanding of & attitudes toward J & rekindling their interest in their rel; resettlement of Soviet J immigrants, & advocacy on behalf of those J who are refused permission to leave the USSR. Aging – primarily focussed on dev & support of: legislation on behalf of older adults, day ctrs, housing for the elderly, adult edu, enrichment progs, volunteer placement progs, sheltered employment projs, nutrition & transportation servs, multipurpose ctrs, nursing homes, ombudsman progs & self training for & by the elderly. **950 Boylston St, Newton Highlands MA 02161 (617) 244–8000.**

North Adams

Congregation Beth Israel. Affiliated with United Syn of Am. Rabbi Arthur Haselkorn; Pres: Burton D. Shapiro. **265 Church St, North Adams MA 01247 (413) 663–5830.**

North Chelmsford

Congregation Shalom. Affiliated with UAHC. 61 mems. Rabbi Terry R. Bard; Pres: Daniel Diamond;

Edu: Malcolm Roberts; Sisterhood Pres: Esther Wikander. **Richardson Rd, North Chelmsford MA 01863 (617) 251–8091.**

North Dartmouth

Jewish Federation of Greater New Bedford, Inc. Mem of CJF. Organized 1938; inc 1954. Pres: Joel Karten; Exec Dir: Steven J. Edelstein. **467 Hawthorn St, North Dartmouth MA 02747 (617) 997–7471.**

Northampton

Congregation B'nai Israel. Affiliated with United Syn of Am. Rabbi Allan Morse; Pres: Melvin Prouser; Youth Dir: Sherry Hyman. **253 Prospect St, Northampton MA 01060 (413) 584–3593.**

Norwood

Temple Shaare Tefilah. Affiliated with United Syn of Am. Rabbi Moshe Birnbaum; Pres: Harvey Mintzer; Youth Dir: Dr Harold Goldstein. **556 Nichols St, Norwood MA 02062 (617) 762–8670.**

Peabody

Temple Beth Shalom. Affiliated with UAHC. 320 mems. Rabbi Burton L. Padoll; Pres: Gerald Webber; Edu: Norman Wean; Sisterhood Pres: Marlene Koslow; Brotherhood Pres: Ronald Tanzer. **489 Lowell St, Peabody MA 01960 (617) 535–2100.**

Temple Ner Tamid. Affiliated with United Syn of Am. Rabbi Abraham Morhaim; Cantor Sam Pessaroff; Pres: David L. Goldberg; Edu Dir: Ury Rath; Youth Dir: Marc Titlebaum. **368 Lowell St, Peabody MA 01960 (617) 532–1293.**

Pittsfield

Congregation Knesset Israel. Affiliated with United Syn of Am. Rabbi Arthur Rulnick; Cantor David Weissman; Pres: C. Jeffrey Cook. **16 Colt Rd, Pittsfield MA 01201 (413) 445–4872.**

Jewish Community Council. Mem of CJF. Organized 1940. Pres: Alan Lipton; Acting Exec Dir: Rhoda Kaminstein. **235 E St, Pittsfield MA 01201 (413) 442–4360.**

Temple Anshe Amunim. Affiliated with UAHC. 175 mems. Rabbi Harold I. Salzmann; Cantor Julian Gabler; Pres: Gerald A. Denmark; Edu: Jacob Franklin; Sisterhood Pres: Barbara Kalib; Brotherhood Pres: David Kalib. **26 Broad St, PO Box 544, Pittsfield MA 01202 (413) 443–9400.**

Plymouth

Congregation Beth Jacob. Affiliated with UAHC. 99 mems. Rabbi Lawrence Silverman; Pres: Lawrence Winokur; Edu: Fred Sarke; Sisterhood Pres: Sheila Finer. **8 Pleasant St, PO Box 284, Plymouth MA 02361 (617) 746–1575.**

Quincy

Adas Shalom. Affiliated with United Syn of Am. Rabbi Samuel Kenner; Pres: Harry A. Hershenson. **435 Adams St, Quincy MA 02169 (617) 471–1818.**

Temple Beth El. Affiliated with United Syn of Am. Rabbi David J. Jacobs; Cantor Morris Semigran; Pres: Herbert Hodess; Youth Dir: Mrs Mitchell Rulnick. **1001 Hancock St, Quincy MA 02169 (617) 479–4309.**

Randolph

Temple Beth Am. Conservative Cong affiliated with United Syn of Am. Daily Morning & Evening Rel Servs; Jr Cong; Heb Sch; Nursery Sch; Sisterhood; Brotherhood; USY; Adult Edu; com functions; library. 700 families. Rabbi Bernard Spielman; Hazzan Thomas Berkson; Pres: Martin L. Horowitz; Edu Dir: Terri M. Swartz; Sexton: Herman Goldberg; Exec Sec: Claire Finstein. **871 N Main St, Randolph MA 02368 (617) 963–0440.**

Temple Beth Am Library. For information on the Temple, see – Temple Beth Am, Randolph, MA. **871 N Main St, Randolph MA 02368 (617) 963–0440.**

Temple Beth David of the South Shore. Affiliated with UAHC. 97 mems. Rabbi Marc E. Saperstein; Pres: Gerald Issokson; Edu: Lawrence J. Levine; Sisterhood Pres: P. Zalvan; Brotherhood Pres: Al Rothman. **PO Box 284, Randolph MA 02368 (617) 828–2275.**

Roslindale

The Recuperative Center. Skilled nursing facility, specializing in recuperation & rehabilitation; constituent agy Combined J Philanthropies, Am Health Care Assn, Am Hosp Assn, MA Fed of Nursing Homes, Assn of MA Homes for the Aged, MA Public Health Assn, Boston Soc for Gerontological Psychiatry, MA Assn of Older Am; accredited by the Joint Commis on Accreditation of Hosps. To prepare patients who are recovering fr acute illness to return to independent living, or to an appropriate long term setting. Physical therapy; occupational therapy; speech therapy; recreational therapy; full activities prog; skilled nursing (24 hrs); med dir; social serv dept (planning & counseling); holiday observances; Fri night Kiddush. 81 beds. 100 employees; volunteers (The Recuperative Ctr Assn (Women's & Men's Auxiliaries). F in 1955 by the J Women's Health Assn, now The Recuperative Ctr Assn; f originally in 1907 as the J Anti-Tuberculosis Assn. Pub Newsletters to membership twice a yr. Facilities include kosher kitchen, gift shop, cafeteria, dining rm on each patient unit, chapel, beauty parlor, recreation rm, TV lounges on each patient unit, air-conditioned throughout, terr & accessible spacious landscaped grounds, free parking. Pres: A. Raymond Tye; Exec Dir: Gregory C. Karr; Med Dir: Lester A. Steinberg MD; Treas: Benjamin Daniels. **1245 Centre St, Roslindale MA 02131 (617) 325–5400.**

Salem

The Journal. Newspaper serving the N Shore J Com. The newspaper covers features & varied subjects fr local working mothers to the subject of the J of Ethiopia. Mailed to 7,000 homes in 21 cities & towns N of Boston. F by the J Fed of the N Shore in 1975. The idea was born at a Young Leadership retreat, when it was decided that a newspaper is essential to an 'ideal' J com. The Journal, which is pub every two weeks, has fulfilled many prior expectations particularly in educating & bldg a sense of com. Though there is no direct charge for the 20 page newspaper, many readers pay for the newspaper indirectly through their pledges to the Fed. Editor in Chief: Alan J. Jacobs; Pres Bd of Overseers: Ernest Rosenthal; Chr Editorial Review: Barbara Wolf; Business Mgr: Janice Wyner. **140 Washington St, Salem MA 01970 (617) 744–5675.**

Temple Shalom. Affiliated with United Syn of Am. Rabbi Samuel S. Kenner; Cantor Irving Ackerman; Pres: Norman F. Cohen; Edu Dir: Sylvia Zippor. **287 Lafayette St, Salem MA 01970 (617) 744–9709.**

Sharon

Temple Adath Sharon. Affiliated with United Syn of Am. Rabbi Arnold Fine; Pres: Arthur Shulman; Edu Dir: Susan Feldman. **18 Harding St, Sharon MA 02067 (617) 784–2517.**

Temple Israel. Affiliated with United Syn of Am. Rabbi Barry Rosen; Cantor Harold Lew; Pres: Evelyne Wersted; Edu Dir: Irving Skupsky; Youth Dir: Manfred Sheff. **125 Pond St, Sharon MA 02067 (617) 784–3986.**

Temple Sinai. Affiliated with UAHC. 450 mems. Rabbi Daniel L. Kaplan; Cantor Robert E. Solomon; Pres: Laura Dickerman; Edu: Martha Aft; Sisterhood Pres: Margaret Davidi; Brothehood Pres: Fred Lezberg. **100 Ames St, PO Box 414, Sharon MA 02067 (617) 784–6081.**

Somerville

Havurat Shalom. J com house. A rel com committed to study, prayer & serious discussion of rel questions. Rel Servs, using Philip Birnbaum's Daily Prayer Bk, with a fair amount of free form davening in Heb, & singing. Servs are fully egalitarian. Activities include holiday & festival observances; weekly classes; periodic potluck suppers; first Sat of each mo – a vegetarian/dairy potluck lunch open to non-mems; social events; retreats; library. The House was est in 1968 as an experimental house of study & prayer aiming to provide an alternative both to large syns & to the rabbinical seminaries. The aim to supply rabbinical training was eventually dropped. While three or four tenants live at the Havurat House, Havurat Shalom is not a commune. Mems live in the neighborhood of the Havurat House & participate regularly in the group's activities. Membership involves the payment of dues, participation in the upkeep of the house, leading Servs, & other activities. Corsp Sec: Debra Cash. **113 College Ave, Somerville MA 02144.**

Springfield

Heritage Academy. Heb Day Sch. To offer J chil a superior bi-cultural edu & to instill in the chil a love for learning. To raise a new generation of J knowledgeable & proud of their Heb & Am heritage. The sch strives to integrate the best & newest in J & secular edu; speech therapist & psychologist servs are available. K–8th grade. Formerly known as the Springfield Hebrew Day Sch est in 1950 by a group of J parents & the local rabbinate. The sch was est as an alternative to the public sch system. In 1965 the Academy purchased Wesson residence which is the present site. **302 Maple St, Springfield MA 01105 (413) 737–5309.**

Jewish Weekly News. Periodical pub. **PO Box 1569, Springfield MA 01101 (413) 739–4771.**

Kesser Israel Synagogue. Orthodox Syn. Rel Servs; Sisterhood. 150 mems. 5 employees. F 1899. Pub The Kesser Crown (monthly). Facilities include kosher kitchen, sanctuary, gift shop. Pres: Harold

Chernock; VPs: Joseph Izenstein, Walter Heafitz; Treas: George Steinberg; Fin Sec: Daniel Friedson; Corsp Sec: Harry Aizenstat. **19 Oakland St, Springfield MA 01108 (413) 732–8492.**

Lubavitch Youth Organization. An outreach org that familiarizes J men & women & chil with J practices & philosophy. Affiliated with the Chabad Lubavitch Movement. To bring the Light of Torah & J tradition to all corners of the world; to battle against assimilation, apathy & indifference to J living. In gen this ins offers: Operation Helping Hand – gives aid to Russian immigrants; on campus progs – provides kosher foods, Fri night to Sun retreats, lectures, Shabbat servs & counseling; celebrations of holidays – sponsors seminars on Passover laws, holds Purim Party, sponsors Toys for Tots for chil in the hosp at Chanukah, helps with bldg of succas, distributes prayers bks for holidays; marriage & family counseling; Adult Edu Prog; helps est kosher kitchens in private homes; Mitzvah Mobile – introduces J men to the wearing of Tefillin, distributes rel articles, maintains traveling J library & audio visual ctr; Succamobile; & summer day camp. Rabbi D. Edelman. **15 Elwood Dr, Springfield MA 01108 (413) 737–7998.**

Sinai Temple. Affiliated with UAHC. 555 mems. Rabbis: Howard G. Kaplansky, Herman Snyder; Cantor Emily S. Mekler; Pres: Michael F. Bader; Edu: Judy Ehrenberg; Sisterhood Pres: Margot Roesberg; Brotherhood Pres: Seymour Weiner. **1100 Dickinson St, Springfield MA 01108 (413) 736–3619.**

Sinai Temple Library. For information on the Temple, see – Sinai Temple, Springfield, MA. **1100 Dickinson St, Springfield MA 01108 (413) 736–3619.**

Springfield Jewish Federation, Inc. Mem of CJF. Sponsors United Jewish Welfare Fund. Organized 1938. Pres: Alan Curtis; Exec Dir: Robert Kessler. **1160 Dickinson St, Springfield MA 01108 (413) 737–4313.**

Temple Beth El. Affiliated with United Syn of Am. Rabbi Barry Dov Lerner; Cantor Morton Shames; Pres: Sheldon S. Goldberg MD; Exec Dir: M. George Koplin; Youth Dir: Edward J. Finkel. **979 Dickinson St, Springfield MA 01108 (413) 733–4149.**

Temple Beth El Library. For information on the Temple, see – Temple Beth El, Springfield, MA. **979 Dickinson St, Springfield MA 01108 (413) 733–4149.**

Stoneham

Temple Judea. Affiliated with United Syn of Am. Rabbi Samuel Kenner; Pres: Arnold Goldstein; Edu Dir: Debbie Trachtenberg. **188 Franklin St, Stoneham MA 02180 (617) 665–5752.**

Stoughton

Ahavath Torah Congregation. Affiliated with United Syn of Am. Rabbi Harold Schechter; Cantor Stanley Sadinsky; Pres: Lewis Litwack; Edu Dir: Iris Katz; **1179 Central St, Stoughton MA 02072 (617) 344–8733.**

Sudbury

Congregation Beth El. Affiliated with UAHC. 170 mems. Rabbi Lawrence Kushner; Cantor Lester B. Bronstein; Pres: Neil G. Frieband; Edu: Lester B. Bronstein; Sisterhood Pres: Marilyn Novak. **Hudson Rd, Sudbury MA 01176 (617) 443–9622.**

Swampscott

Hillel Academy of the North Shore. Affiliated with Solomon Schechter Day Schs Assn. Prin: Dr Bennett Solomon; Chr: Dr Stephen Alpert. **837 Humphrey St, Swampscott MA 01907 (617) 599–3837.**

Jewish Rehabilitation Center for Aged of the North Shore, Inc. Non-sectarian geriatric ctr of the N Shore com of MA. To provide complete health, nursing & social care for the elderly residents of the N Shore com of MA. Med care; physical therapy prog utilizing the most advanced rehabilitative equipment; occupational therapy prog of knitting, painting, crafts projs & exercises; beauty & barber shop; bingo; card games; movies; sing-a-longs; workshops; poetry sessions; art & writing clubs; picnics; Bar-B-Q's; mazel tov parties; rel servs; day trips & shopping sprees via the Home's minibus. 167 residents. JRC engages the servs of a physical, occupational & a speech therapist; a beautician is available four days a week for both men & women; a volunteer manicurist comes to the Home weekly; staff includes Drs, nurses, social workers, rotating staff of dentists, podiatrist who visits the Home weekly, psychiatrists, activities consultant. The Home was conceived in the early 1940's by a group of men & women fr Lynn who foresaw the need for a facility to house & care for the growing num of the com sick & elderly. They selected, as a suitable home, a 14 rm three story structure. In 1945 they drew up the incorporation papers which stressed that the Home was non-sectarian. A few rms were set aside for returning wounded vets who wanted to live in a rel atmosphere where their dietary laws could be maintained. By 1951, however, the Home had changed its emphasis becoming less of a convalescent facility & more of a permanent residence for the elderly. The name was then changed to the J Home for the Aged. The name was again changed to the J Rehabilitation Ctr for Aged of the N Shore. After more than seven yrs of planning, fund raising & bldg, the new geriatric ctr opened its doors in 1972. An 87 bed second floor addition was dedicated in 1977. Facilities include med & podiatric equipment, dental offs, kosher kitchen, private & semi private rms, lounges, family sitting rms, chapel, solarium, landscaped grounds. The 1,200 mems of the Ladies Auxiliary have given both financial & personal assistance that has brought much to make life more meaningful & hopeful to the elderly residents. The JRC has an active & enthusiastic volunteer force whose efforts supplement those of the professional staff. Pres: Louis E. Stahl; 1st VP: Samuel Shapiro; 2nd VP: Louis Rudolph; 3rd VP: Howard Kaplan; 4th VP: Rita Reiser; Treas: Victor Cohen; Asst Treas: Melvin Pierce; Sec: Jeffrey Shub; Asst Sec: Miriam Lehman; Pres Ladies Auxiliary: Carole Weiner; Exec VP: Jack Chilnick; Adm: Julian Rich. **330 Paradise Rd, Swampscott MA 01907 (617) 598–5310.**

Temple Beth El. Conservative. Dedicated to the fellowship of God through the brotherhood of man. Rel Servs; Rel Sch offering pre-Heb Sun Sch & 3 day Heb Sch: Rabbi Israel Harburg Library; Adult & Chil Choir; cultural, rel & social activities. F in 1926, oldest Conservative Temple on the N Shore. Rabbi Ephraim I. Bennett; Cantor Robert H. Albert; Edu Dir: Mark S. Casso; Pres: Robert S. Soltz; VPs: Katharine Borten, Arthur Epstein, Morris Goldfield, Richard Hillman, Eric Kahn; Treas: Donald Fine; Asst Treas: Leonard Cohen; Rec Sec: Diana Caplan; Fin Sec: Saul Toby. **55 Atlantic Ave, Swampscott MA 01907 (617) 599–8005.**

Temple Beth El, Rabbi Israel Harburg Library. For information on the Temple, see – Temple Beth El, Swampscott, MA. **55 Atlantic Ave, Swampscott MA 01907 (617) 599–8005.**

Temple Israel of Sawmpscott & Marblehead. Conservative Syn affiliated with United Syn of Am. Daily, Sabbath, Holyday Rel Servs; Com Heb Sch of the N Shore; Brotherhood; Sisterhood; library (J non-fiction, fiction, encyclopedias). 700 families; 135 stu; 3 regional groups. 7 employees. F 1946. Pub Temple Israel Bulletin (fortnightly). Facitilies include main sanctuary seating 400 (expandable to 1400), chapel seating 100, main auditorium, smaller social hall, gift shop, 8 classrms, 3 off rms, youth group lounge, 2 full kosher kitchens. Rabbi Sanford D. Shanblatt; Cantor Harry Lubow; Pres: Dr S. Jerome Zackin; Prin: Dr Sarah Lieberman; Organist: Minna Smith. **837 Humphrey St, Swampscott MA 01907 (617) 595–6636.**

Taunton

Congregation Agudath Achim. Conservative Cong affiliated with United Syn of Am, Associated Syns of MA. To contribute to the perpetuation of J & the J people through worship, study, & communal solidarity. Rel Servs on Sabbaths, Festivals & High Holy Days; Rel Sch for ages 4–7 (1 day per week), 8–13 (3 days per week),ages 14–16 (1 evening per mo); Adult Edu progs; Brotherhood; Sisterhood; Hadassah; B'nai B'rith Women; B'nai B'rith Youth Org; UJA; Is Bonds; Social Action Cttee; choir; gift shop; cemetery; library containing 750 vols (reference, chil section, gen Judaica, fiction & non-fiction). 135 mems. F 1910; cornerstone for syn laid July 13, 1913; bldg occupied 1914; J Com House dedicated April 1957; syn underwent major renovation 1981–1982 with newly refurnished vestry & sanctuary & expanded pulpit. Pub News – Cong Agudath Achim (semi-monthly Sept–Jun); New Year Greeting Book (all High Holy Days). Facilities include syn bldg; sanctuary seating 400 (including balcony), vestry, meeting rm, kosher kitchen, J Com House, gym/social hall with 375 person capacity, library, rabbi's study, business off, classrms, meeting rms. Increase of 25% in membership since 1981; Rabbi Benjamin Lefkowitz; Chr of the Bd: Phyllis Rubin; Pres: Alfred Garshick; 1st VP: Lewis Boyar; 2nd VP: Benjamin Ashapa; Sec: Harvey Zides; Fin Sec: Herman Pine; Treas: Gordon Amgott; **36 Winthrop St, Taunton MA 02780 (617) 822–3230.**

Congregation Agudath Achim, Sisterhood of Congregation Agudath Achim Library. 36 Winthrop St, Taunton MA 02780 (617) 822–3230.

Vineyard Haven

Marthas Vineyard Hebrew Center. Affiliated with UAHC. 73 mems. Pres: Edward Zinaman. **Center St, Vineyard Haven MA 02568 (617) 693–0745.**

Wakefield

Temple Emanuel. Affiliated with United Syn of Am. Rabbi Reuven Kimelman; Cantor Dr Zev Raviv; Pres: Benjamin L. Weiner. **120 Chestnut St, Wakefield MA 01880 (617) 245–1886.**

Waltham

American Jewish Historical Society. Dedicated to the collection, preservation & dissemination of information on the hist, settlement, & life of J in N Am. Library housing more than 60,000 vols, 4 million pages of manuscripts, 250 paintings & artifacts, restored Am Yiddish films, thousands of newspapers & periodicals; edu activities; permanent exhibit: The Colonial Period in American Jewry; changing exhibits; confs; lectures; slide tape shows. Intl membership of 3,400. F in 1892. American Jewish History (quarterly scholarly journal); Colonial Jewry; series on early urban J hist; works on the J experience in Latin Am; 72 vol reprint series of bks describing the relationships between Am & the Holy Land fr Colonial times to the est of the State of Is. Located on the campus of Brandeis Univ. Facilities include: reading rm, 2 exhibition areas, conf rm/slide-tape show viewing gallery. Pres: Ruth B. Fein; Chr: Saul Viener; Sec: Rosemary Krensky; Assc Sec: Morton R. Godine; Treas: Hirsh Sharf; Dir: Bernard Wax. **2 Thornton Rd, Waltham MA 02154 (617) 891–8110.**

American Jewish Historical Society Library. Library contains 60,000 bks, reference, manuscripts, photos. For information on the Soc, see – American Jewish Historical Society, Waltham, MA. **2 Thornton Rd, Waltham MA 02154 (617) 891–8110.**

Brandeis University. Col of Arts & Sci – the only J sponsored, non-sectarian ins of higher learning in Am; accredited by the New England Assn of Schs & Cols. To be a place of learning where research is pursued, bks written, & the creative instinct is encouraged & developed in its stu & faculty. Grad Sch of Arts & Sci: offers courses of study leading to the master's & doctoral degrees; Rosentiel Basic Med Sci Research Ctr; The Florence Heller Grad Sch for Advanced Studies in Social Welfare: offers both a master's degree in Human Servs Mgmnt & a doctoral prog in Social Welfare; Sch of Creative Arts; Sch of Humanities: offers the undergrad a systematic introduction to the literary & philosophical heritage; Sch of Sci: provides the basic sci training to qualify stu for entry into grad sch or work at the intermediate level in their sci fields; Sch of Social Sci; Preprofessional Edu: provides progs in Architecture, Business & Mgmnt, Law, Med & Dentistry, Preparation for Teaching; The Jacob Hiatt Ins in Is: provides a prog emphasizing the social sci for stu who have completed at least four semesters of work in an accredited col or univ. Brandeis ASOR Archaeological Semester (located in Jerusalem); other progs include: physical edu, study abroad, summer sch, adult edu. Special progs, facilities, assns: mem of the Lowell Ins Cooperative Broadcasting Council; Patrons & Friends of the Rose Art Mus which helps the Univ exhibit each spring a major exhibition featuring an important contemporary artist; Gersh & Lemberg Chil Ctr; Ziskind Prog for Continuing Edu in J Studies; Am J Historical Soc (the Soc Hq & library are housed on the Brandeis campus). Trust Funds include: Edith Barbara Laurie Theater Arts Trust Fund, George & Charlotte Fine Endowment Fund. Endowed Schs & Ins: Crown Sch of Grad Studies in Am Civilization; Danielsen Sch of Philosophy, Ethics & Rel Thought; Fierman Sch of Chem; Fischer Sch of Physics; Kutz Sch of Biology; Lown Sch of Near Eastern & J Studies; Swig Sch of Pol Sci; The Tauber Ins. Fellowship & scholarship progs include: The Abr L. Sachar Intl Fellowship Prog which is a selective prog that supports Brandeis grad & undergrad stu abroad during a period of study or research complimentary to their edu in Brandeis; Saval-Sacher Summer Research Scholarship Prog which enables qualified Brandeis undergrads to conduct research for their sr hons theses, during the summer between jr & sr yrs, in any area of the world outside of the US; Wein Intl Scholarship Prog which is designed to further intl understanding, to provide foreign stu with opportunities to study in the US, & to enrich the intellectual & cultural life of the Brandeis campus. Special scholarships, fellowships, endowments & awards include: Brewer Cohen Undergrad Award, Joseph & Bessie Gerber Glass Prelaw Endowed Scholarships, Francis L. Hiatt Memorial Scholarship Endowment, Lemberg Scholarship Endowment, Joe & Emily Lowe Foun Scholarship in Fine Arts, Stephen P. Mugar Scholarship Endowment Fund, Harry & Mildred Remis Scholarship & Fellowship Endowment Fund in the Creative Arts, Rogoff Scholarship Endowment Fund, Maurice H. & Anna B. Salva Scholarship for Soviet Emigre Stu, Lew & Edie Wasserman Scholarship Fund, Jack I. & Lillian Poses Creative Arts Awards Lectureships & Lectureship Funds: Louis Dembitz Brandeis Memorial Lectures, Harry B. Helmsley Lecture Series, The Alexander L. & Fannie B. Shluger Memorial Lecture, The Nathan Straus Lectureship Fund, The Martin Weiner Distinguished Lectureship Fund, The Eleanor R. Roosevelt Memorial Lectureship. Visiting Professorships: Jacob Ziskind Professorship which brings to the campus distinguished academic figures fr sister univs both in the US & abroad, Fannie Hurst Fund for visiting professorship which supports visiting profs in the area of creative writing & theater arts, Shirley & Maurice Saltzman Artist in Residence Fund which supports prominent visiting artists who work with & guide stu majoring in the field of fine arts. Other programs, servs include: job placement, rel activities, stu orgs, stu activities, psychological counseling, athletic progs. F in 1948. The univ is named for the Supreme Ct Justice Louis Dembitz Brandeis. Brandeis received accreditation in the shortest time possible in 1953, & received Phi Beta Kappa recognition just 13 yrs after it was f. The Rosentiel Basic Med Sci Research Ctr was made possible in 1968 through the gift of the late Lewis S. Rosentiel. The Florence Heller Grad Sch for Advanced Studies in Social Welfare was est in 1959. The Jacob Hiatt Ins in Is was f in 1961 by Brandeis Trustee Jacob Hiatt of Worcester MA. The Abram L. Sachar Intl Fellowship Prog was instituted in 1969 by the Trustees of the Univ. The Wien Intl Scholarship prog was created in 1958. Stu pub: The Justice Campus Newspaper; Yearbook; Kether (the Brandeis literary journal); Artemis (a women's newspaper). The Brandeis Univ Press has pub: The Modernization of French Jewry; Consistory and Community in the Nineteenth Century; Images in American Culture, Essay in Memory of Philip Rahv; Kabbalah & Art; The Model Country; Jose Batlley Ordonez; Essays in Jewish Intellectual History. Campus facilities include: Abelson Physics Bldg; Adm Ctr; Bass Physics Bldg; Bassine Biology Ctr; Brown Bldg; Brown Social Sci Ctr; Brown Terrarium; Dreitzer Art Gallery; Edison Chem Bldg, Epstein Campus Servs Ctr; Faculty Ctr; Feldberg Computer Ctr; Fellows Garden; Ford Hall; Foster Biomedical Research Labs; Friedland Research Ctr; Gerstenzang Library of Sci which houses 100,000 vols; Goldfarb Library which houses humanities & social sci collections, & over 700,000 vols; Golding J Ctr; Golding Med Outpatient Servs Bldg; Goldman-Schwartz Art Studios; Goldsmith Mathematics Ctr; Hayden Sci Court; Heller Sch; Kalman Sci Ctr; Kosow Biochem Bldg; Kutz Hall; Lecks Chem Bldg; Lemberg Hall; Lown Sch of Near Eastern & J Studies; Mailman House; May Memorial Hall; Olin-Sang Am Civilization Ctr; Pearlman Hall; Pollack Fine Arts Teaching Ctr; Rabb Grad Ctr; Rapaporte Treas Hall; Rose Art Mus; Rosentiel Basic Med Sci Research Ctr; Sachar Intl Ctr; Shiffman Humanities Ctr; Schwartz Hall; Slosberg Music Ctr; Spingold Theater Arts Ctr; Stoneman Infirmary; Sydeman Annex; Ullman Amphitheatre; Wolfson-Rosensweig Biochem Bldg; Yalem Physics Bldg; Memphis Tract; Gordon Field; Linsey Sports Ctr; Marcus Playing Field; Shapiro Athletic Ctr; Rieger Tennis Cts; residence halls; dining facilities, separate kosher kitchen; bookstore; post off & stu mailrm; stu ctr; three chapels: Berlin (J) Bethlehem (Catholic) & Harlan (Protestant). Brandeis is regarded today as one of the finest small, private research univs in the US. Pres of the Univ: Marver H. Bernstein; Chancellor Emeritus of the Univ: Abram L. Sachar; Bd of Trustees–Chr: Henry L. Foster; V Chrs: Edwin E. Hokin, Irving Schneider; Sec: Stanley H. Feldberg. **Brandeis Univ, Waltham MA 02154 (617) 647–2177.**

Brandeis University – National Women's Committee. Non-profit volunteer org. To raise funds in support of the Univ Libraries. 65,000 women in 123 chapters. Est in 1948. The chapters hold fund raising activities which include auctions, bk sales, art exhibits, travel luncheons, & tours. They have contributed over 18 million dollars to Brandeis Univ Libraries. Pres: Elaine Lisberg; VPs: Maureen Durwood, Hannelies Guggenheim, Hermine Hoffman, Jeanne Nisenson, Adrienne Rosenblatt, Phyllis Shapiro, Lorraine Whitehill, Mollie Wilson; Treas: Janice Fineman; Asst Treas: Anne Falkof; Sec: Sara Jane Milder; Hon Dirs: Hannah Abrams, Ruth Rose, Romayne Goldberg, Ethel Rosenfeld, Rose Margolis, Beady Berler, Anne Margolis, Estelle Stern, Jen Kowal, Esther Schwartz; Exec Dir: Carol Rabinovitz. **Waltham MA 02254 (617) 647–2194.**

Brandeis University – University Libraries. Libraries contain more than 775,000 volumes including microtexts, microfilm holdings, periodicals, newspapers. Started with initial 2,000 volumes housed in a remodeled stone stable in 1948. Dir of Lib Servs: Bessie K. Hahn; Assc Univ Lib: Rupert F. Gilroy; On the Jacob & Bertha Goldfard Foun: Asst Univ Lib: Phyllis Cutler; Head Circulation Dept: Mark R. Alpert; Head Judaica Dept: Charles Cutter. **Brandeis Univ, 415 S St, Waltham MA 02254.**

Wayland

Temple Shir Tikva. Affiliated with UAHC. 120 mems. Rabbi Michael Mayersohn; Pres: Ed Safran. **PO Box 265, Wayland MA 01778 (617) 358–7719.**

Temple Shir Tikva Library. For information on the Temple, see – Temple Shir Tikva, Wayland, MA. **PO Box 265, Wayland MA 01778 (617) 358–7719.**

Wellesley Hills

Temple Beth Elohim. Affiliated with UAHC. 280 mems. Rabbi Ronald M. Weiss; Pres: Allan W. Drachman; Edu: Claire D. Robbins. **10 Bethel Rd, Wellesley Hills MA 02181 (617) 235–8419.**

Temple Beth Elohim Library. For information on the Temple, see – Temple Beth Elohim, Wellesley Hills, MA. **10 Bethel Rd, Wellesley Hills MA 02181 (617) 235–8419.**

West Newton

Temple Shalom of Newton. 175 Temple St, West Newton MA 02165.

Temple Shalom of Newton Library. 175 Temple St, West Newton MA 02165.

West Roxbury

Hillel B'nai Torah. Affiliated with United Syn of Am. Rabbi Oscar L. Bookspan; Pres: Max Goren; Youth Dir: Charlene Magier. **120 Corey St, West Roxbury MA 02132 (617) 323–0486.**

Westborough

Congregation B'nai Shalom. Affiliated with UAHC. 80 mems. Rabbi Debra R. Hachen; Pres: Ted Lemoff. **9 Charles St, Westborough MA 01581.**

Westwood

Temple Beth David of Dedham, East Westwood. Affiliated with UAHC. 161 mems. Rabbi Henry A. Zoob; Pres: Shirley Siroka; Edu: Roberta Gorden. **40 Pond St, PO Box 459, Westwood MA 02090 (617) 329–1938.**

Worcester

Congregation Beth Israel. Affiliated with United Syn of Am. Rabbi Baruch G. Goldstein; Pres: Joseph Cohen; Exec Dir: Abe Kravitz; Youth Dir: Dr Kenneth Farbman. **Jamesbury Dr & Kinnicutt Rd, Worcester MA 01609 (617) 756–6204.**

Jewish Civic Leader. Periodical pub. **11 Harvard St, Worcester MA 01609 (617) 791–0953.**

Lubavitch Youth Organization. An outreach org that familiarizes J men & women & chil with J practices & philosophy. Affiliated with the Chabad Lubavitch Movement. To bring the Light of Torah & J tradition to all corners of the world; to battle against assimilation, apathy & indifference to J living. In gen this ins offers: Operation Helping Hand – gives aid to Russian immigrants; on campus progs – provides kosher foods, Fri night to Sun retreats, lectures, Shabbat servs & counseling; celebrations of holidays – sponsors seminars on Passover laws, holds Purim Party, sponsors Toys for Tots for chil in the hosp at Chanukah, helps with bldg of succas, distributes prayers bks for holidays; marriage & family counseling; Adult Edu Prog; helps est kosher kitchens in private homes; Mitzvah Mobile – introduces J men to the wearing of Tefillin, distributes rel articles, maintains traveling J library & audio visual ctr; Succamobile; & summer day camp. Rabbi H. Fogelman. **24 Creswell, Worcester MA 01602 (617) 752–5791.**

Solomon Schechter Day School of Worcester. Affiliated with Solomon Schechter Day Schs Assn. Prin: Mark Silk; Chr: Alan Cooper. **633 Salisbury St, Worcester MA 01609 (617) 799–7888.**

Temple Emanuel. Affiliated with UAHC. 1065 mems. Rabbis: Stanley M. Davids, Steven A. Fox, Joseph Klein; Pres: Joseph Coff; Edu: Howard Adelman; Adm: Harold Press; Sisterhood Pres: Roberta Kunen; Brotherhood Pres: Kenneth Jacobson. **280 May St, Worcester MA 01602 (617) 755–1257.**

Temple Emanuel Library. For information on the Temple, see – Temple Emanuel, Worcester, MA. **280 May St. Worcester MA 01602 (617) 755–1257.**

Temple Sinai. Affiliated with UAHC. 172 mems. Rabbi Gary A. Glickstein; Cantor Harriet Katz; Pres: Arthur Wolpert; Edu: Selma Parker; Adm: Carolyn Solod; Sisterhood Pres: Audrey Shack. **661 Salisbury St, Worcester MA 01609 (617) 755–2519.**

Worchester Jewish Federation, Inc. Mem of CJF. Sponsors Jewish Welfare Fund (1939). Organized 1947; inc 1957. Pres: Harold N. Cotton; Acting Exec Dir: Steven Gelfand. **633 Salisbury St, Worcester MA 01609 (617) 756–1543.**

MICHIGAN

Alpena

Temple Beth El. Affiliated with UAHC. 8 mems. Pres: Morton Fivenson. **610 S 3rd St, Alpena MI 49707 (517) 354–5106.**

Ann Arbor

B'nai B'rith Hillel Foundation at the University of Michigan. To promote the welfare, cultural, rel, communal activities & interests of J stu at the Univ of MI. Shabbat, Holiday Servs; Beit Midrash offering 15 non credit courses each semester; annual concert series; weekly Shabbat dinners; speakers; films; social progs. Four full time professionals; Gov Bd composed of stu, com mems, faculty & staff. F 1931; moved to present bldg in 1951. Dir: Michael Brooks; Chr Gov Bd: Armand Lauffer. **1429 Hill St, Ann Arbor MI 48104 (313) 663–3336.**

Beth Israel Congregation. Conservative Syn affiliated with Unite Syn of Am. Rel, edu, cultural, social, & charitable activities; Sun Morning & Afternoon Sch; library. F 1916. Rabbi Allan David Kensky; Sch Dir: Harlene Adiv; Pres: Susan Coran; VPs: Howard Liss, Victor Gallatin, Eugene Stearns, Yetta Miller; Rec Sec: Henry Gershowitz; Corsp Sec: David Copi; Treas: Herbert S. Amster; Asst Treas: Selma Sussman; Bd of Dirs: Gerald Abrams, Carol Finerman, Melvyn Gluckman, Susie Guiora, Jeffrey A. Pike, Bertram Pitt, David E. Schteingart. **2000 Washtenaw, Ann Arbor MI 48104 (313) 663–5543, 665–9897.**

Beth Israel Congregation Library. For information on the Cong, see – Beth Israel Congregation, Ann Arbor, MI. **2000 Washtenaw, Ann Arbor MI 48104 (313) 663–5543, 665–9897.**

Chabad House. Lubavitch com servs ctr. Blends Chassidic fervor & warmth with tradition & learning, to show that every J, fr whatever background he or she comes fr, is an integral part of the body of Is. Anti-missionary work; adult edu; Sabbath seminars; holiday progs; day camp; youth groups; syns; kosher kitchen; counseling; chaplaincy; Mitzvah Campaigns; hosp & prison visitations; sr citizens encounters; speakers bureau. Rabbi A. Goldstein. **715 Hill, Ann Arbor MI 48103 (313) 995–3276.**

Hebrew Day School of Ann Arbor. Conservative day sch affiliated with Solomon Schechter Day Schs Assn. To provide a well balanced course of study, both J & secular, & dedicated to the philosophy of traditional J combined with a modern evolutionary outlook. Focuses on socialization, developmental & learning skills by means of J structures & concepts to instill in chil a deep sense of K'lal Yisrael, love of all J, & loyalty to Is. Classes for K–6; structure of public sch curriculum followed with more in-depth concentration on stu personal interest; dev of fluent knowledge of Heb. Heb. 45 stu in grades K–6. 10 employees; 3 volunteers. F 1975. Only day sch in MI outside of Detroit area. Dir: Marlene Gitelman; Pres: Barbara Bergman; VPs: Elana Sussman, Phil Bloch; Treas: Steve Gerber. **1920 Austin, Ann Arbor MI 48104 (313) 668–6770.**

Temple Beth Emeth. Affiliated with UAHC. 220 mems. Rabbi Ralph Mecklenburger; Presidents: Irving Fox, Marilyn K. Scott; Sisterhood Pres: Bobbi Heilveil, Marilynn Klein. **2309 Packard Rd, Ann Arbor MI 48104 (313) 665–4744.**

Temple Beth Emeth Library. For information on the Temple, see – Temple Beth Emeth, Ann Arbor, MI. **2309 Packard Rd, Ann Arbor MI 48104 (313) 665–4744.**

Battle Creek

Temple Beth El. Affiliated with UAHC. 39 mems. Rabbi Donald P. Cashman; Pres: Ken Shackman; Edu: Diane Fogel; Sisterhood Pres: Marlene

Aronoff. **306 Capital Ave NE, Battle Creek MI 49017 (616) 963–4921.**

Bay City

Temple Israel. Affiliated with United Syn of Am. Rabbi Dov Edelstein; Rabbi Emeritus Jossef Kratzenstein; Pres: Mark M. Jaffe. **2300 Center Ave, Bay City MI 48706 (517) 893–7811.**

Benton Harbor

Temple B'nai Shalom. Affiliated with United Syn of Am. Rabbi Robert Wolcoff; Pres: Michale Lieberman; Youth Dir: Michael Radorn. **2050 Bdwy, Benton Harbor MI 49022 (606) 925–8021.**

Birmingham

Sally Allan Alexander Beth Jacob School for Girls. Day sch. To offer full Heb prog based on Orthodox J belief. Complete col prep prog; full course of commercial subjects including Typing, Bookkeeping, Shorthand, Computer Prog. Enrollment of 217 stu grades 1–12. F in 1940 by Pearl Rothenberg. Started as two hour instruction after public sch; dev into day sch. In 1977 Mr & Mrs N. Allan bought the bldg & dedicated it to the memory of their deceased daughter Sally Allan Alexander. Presidium: Max Carmen, David Cohen, Joseph Nusbaum; Exec Dir: Rabbi Norman Kahn; Prin: Rabbi Sholom Goldstein; Asst Prin: Rabbi Samuel E. Cohen. **32605 Bellvine Trail, Birmingham MI 48010 (313) 644–3113.**

Temple Beth El. Reform Temple with Col of J Studies affiliated with UAHC, Central Conf of Am Rabbis, Natl Assn of Temple Adms, Natl Assn of Temple Edu, Natl Fed of Temple Youth, Natl Fed of Temple Sisterhoods. To perpetuate Reform Judaism & uphold the belief in & worship of The one God. Rel Servs; edu progs; Sisterhood; Brotherhood; singles, older adults, youth progs; weekend Rel Sch; library containing 32,000 vols (Leonard Simons Rare Bk Collection, Judaica). 5,500 mems; 1820 families; 6 regional groups; 910 stu presch through grade 12. 120 employees (many part-time); 550 volunteers. 1st J Cong f 1850 in MI. Pub Temple Bulletin (bi-weekly), Mirror (Brotherhood monthly). Facilities include sanctuary seating 1,900, chapel seating 250, auditorium seating 850, large kitchen, 35 sch classrms, large library, small auditorium seating 110, gift shop, archives, braille bindery, mus, youth lounge, nursery sch. One of the largest & most prominent Reform congs in the world. Sr Rabbi Dannel Schwartz; Assc Rabbi Norman T. Roman; Rabbi Emeritus Richard C. Hertz; Cantor John Redfield; Exec Dir: Marvin S. Walts; Edu Dir: Alan Waldman; Music Dir: Jason Tickton. **7400 Telegraph Rd, Birmingham MI 48010 (313) 851–1100.**

Temple Beth El, Prentis Memorial Library. Library contains approximately 32,000 vols (Leonard Simons Rare Bk Collection, bks on Judaica). For information on the Temple, see – Temple Beth El, Birmingham, MI. **7400 Telegraph Rd, Birmingham MI 48010 (313) 851–1100.**

Brighton

Congregation Solel. Affiliated with UAHC. 25 mems. Rabbi Joseph Gutmann; Pres: Arnie Rubin. **c/o Mr Arnie Rubin, 304 W Washington St, Howell MI 48843 (517) 546–2527.**

Detroit

Anti-Defamation League of B'nai B'rith – Michigan Regional Office. Dedicated in purpose & prog to translating the Am heritage of democratic ideals into a way of life for all Am, & to countering assaults on the safety, status, rights & image of J. For additional information, see – Anti-Defamation League of B'nai B'rith, New York City, NY. **163 Madison Ave, Suite 120, Detroit MI 48226.**

Jewish Home for Aged. 19100 W Seven Mile Rd, Detroit MI 48219 (313) 532–8112.

Jewish Home for Aged Library. 19100 W Seven Mile Rd, Detroit MI 48219 (313) 532–8112.

Jewish Welfare Federation of Detroit. Mem of CJF; sponsors Allied Jewish Campaign. Organized 1899. Pres: Judge Avern L. Cohn; Exec VP: Sol Drachler; Exec Dir: George M. Zeltzer. **Fred M. Butzel Memorial Bldg, 163 Madison, Detroit MI 48226 (313) 965–3939.**

Sinai Hospital of Detroit. Major health care facility. Mem agy of the J Welfare Fed of Detroit; mem of the Met NW Detroit Hosps Corp (Quadrangle); affiliated with the Wayne State Univ Sch of Med. Not only to care for the sick, but to enhance the health of the well through health edu & health promotion progs. Depts: Cardiovascular, Thoracic Surgery; Dental & Oral, Maxillofacial Surgery; Obstetrics & Gynecology; Ophthalmology; Psychiatry; Radiology; Med including subspecialties: Cardiology, Dermatology, Endocrinology, Gastroenterology, Hematology, Immunology, Internal Med, Med Oncology, Nephrology, Neurology, Pulmonary Med & Rheumatology; Rehabilitation Med. Facilites &

Progs: Schiffman Clin, an ambulatory care facility, provides med care for the com regardless of the patient's ability to pay; kosher kitchen; facilities for performing ritual circumcisions; research; health edu progs: arthritis edu classes, cardiac rehabilitation classes, cardiopulmonary resuscitation instruction, diabetes edu classes, health fairs, prenatal & prepared childbirth classes, speakers bureau, stroke edu classes, tay-sachs screening progs; Servs With Love, a volunteer serv, providing daily reassurance calls to the aged & homebound in the com; accredited med & dental residency progs: Anesthesiology, Diagnostic Radiology, Dentistry, Gen Surgery, Internal Med, Obstetrics & Gynecology, Ophthalmology, Oral Surgery, Orthopedic Surgery, Pathology, Physical Med & Rehabilitation, Plastic Surgery, Psychiatry, Therapeutic Radiology. Nursing stu fr Wayne State Univ Sch of Nursing, Mercy Col & Sinai's Shapiro Sch of Nursing train at the Hosp. Hosp also serves as clin training site for stu fr various cols & univs in allied health professions: dietetics, med tech, radiology tech, respiratory care, occupational therapy, physical therapy, med records adm, speech pathology, pharmacy, music therapy, recreation therapy, social work, psychology. 607 beds; 21,000 patients are admitted every yr; over 3,400 babies are born yearly; more than 14,500 in-patient & out-patient surgical procedures are performed every yr. The Shiffman Clin handles more than 30,000 visits a yr. Med & dental staff of over 850 physicians & dentists, 135 residents, 3,000 employees, 800 employees in the nursing div, resident chaplain, rabbi. The auxiliary, the Sinai Hosp Guild, has a membership of 5,000. The Guild operates the Gift Shop & Gift Cart. The Dept of Volunteer Servs places nearly 500 volunteers in 35 hosp areas. Opened in 1953. Sinai occupies a 36 acre site in NW Detroit. Exec VP: Irving A. Shapiro; VP of Adm: Arnold N. Kimmel; Public Affairs Coord: Marianne Z. Kestenbaum. **6767 W Outer Dr, Detroit MI 48235 (313) 493–5500.**

Temple Israel. 17400 Manderson Rd, Detroit MI 48235 (313) 863–7769.

Temple Israel Library. 17400 Manderson Rd, Detroit MI 48235 (313) 863–7769.

East Lansing

Congregation Shaarey Zedek. Affiliated with United Syn of Am. Com cong for Traditional & Liberal J. Serves as a rel ctr & house of worship for Lansing J of Traditional, Conservative & Reform backgrounds. Traditional Servs Fri evening & Sat morning; Liberal Servs Fri evening; Traditional Liberal High Holy Day Servs; Family Night Servs; Chil Prog in Edu: Sun Sch; 10th grade Confirmation class; four yr Enrichment Prog through grade 11; mid-week Heb Prog with training for Bar/Bat Mitzvah; Adult Edu. Over 300 families; 160 chil enrolled in edu progs. F over 50 yrs ago. Temple & facilities situated on 10 acres, includes a sanctuary seating 280, social hall, kitchen, library, gift shop, off, 10 classrooms. Rabbi Edward Chesman; Cantor Bruce Wetzler; Rabbi Emeritus Dr Philip Frankel; Pres: Dr Harold Shnider; Business VP: Arthur Kramer; Rel VP: Dr Martin Pearlman; Edu VP: Thea Glicksman; Fin Sec: Ira Ginsburg; Corsp Sec: Judy Frank; Treas: Sherwood Berman; Rec Sec: Gussie Shanker; Trustees: Dr Norman Abeles, Stuart Morrison, Norman Sernick, Dr Eric Goldstein, Gerald Simon, Dr Elaine Cherney, Burton Altman, Dan Gutter, Sid Rosenberg; Sisterhood Pres: Florence Rudman; Bd of Edu – Pres: Dr Bill Rosenthal; Corsp Sec: Dr Larry Schiamberg; Fin Sec: Harvey Goldstein; Harry Harris Prog Coord & Sisterhood Rep: Joan Mayor; Cong Bd Reps: Thea Glicksman, Ruth Polin, Janet Abramson. **1924 Coolidge Rd, East Lansing MI 48823 (517) 351–3570.**

Congregation Shaarey Zedek, Religious School Library. For information on the Cong, see – Congregation Shaarey Zedek, East Lansing, MI. **1924 Coolidge Rd, East Lansing MI 48823 (517) 351–3570.**

Greater Lansing Jewish Welfare Federation. Mem of CJF. Organized 1939. Pres: Anita Baron; Exec Dir: Louis T. Friedman. **PO Box 975, East Lansing MI 48823 (517) 351–3197.**

Kehillat Israel. Affiliated with United Syn of Am. Pres: Dr Allan B. Singer. **855 Grove St, East Lansing MI 48823 (517) 315–3221.**

Farmington

Hillel Day School. Affiliated with Solomon Schechter Day Schs Assn. Prin: Rabbi Robert Abramson; Chr: Ellen Glen. **32200 Middlebelt Rd, Farmington MI 48018 (313) 851–2394.**

Farmington Hills

Adat Shalom Synagogue Library. Library contains 10,000 vols (Judaica). For information on the Syn, see – Adat Shalom Synagogue, Farmington Hills, MI. **29901 Middlebelt Rd, Farmington Hills MI 48024 (313) 851–5100.**

Adat Shalom Synagogue. Conservative Syn affiliated with United Syn of Am, Syn Council of Greater Detroit. Rel Servs; edu progs; Nursery/summer camp; Men's Club; Sisterhood;

youth progs; kosher catering; library containing 10,000 vols (Judaica). 137 families; 130 stu in Nursery – Parent Toddler Progs. 14 employees. F 1943 as Adas Shalom. Pub Voice (monthly). Facilities including kosher kitchen, sanctuary seating 1,500, social hall, gift shop, multi-purpose rm, sch. Rabbi Efry Spectre; Cantor Larry Vieder; Pres: Dr Milton Shiffman; Exec Dir: Alan Yost; VP: Joel Gershenson. **29901 Middlebelt, Farmington Hills MI 48018 (313) 851–5100.**

The Birmingham Temple. J Humanist Cong. Affiliated with Soc For Humanistic J. Full servs with Cong celebrating all traditional holidays with exception of Simchat Torah; Bar/Bat Mitzva training, Confirmation training; life cycle celebrations; Adult Edu; social activities, social action prog, & com involvement. F in 1963. Rabbi Sherwin T. Wire. **28611 W Twelve Mile Rd, Farmington Hills MI 48018 (313) 417–1410.**

Society for Humanistic Judaism. 28611 W Twelve Mile Rd, Farmington Hills MI 48018.

Flint

Beth Israel Congregation Religious Library. For information on the Cong, see – Beth Israel Cong, Flint, MI. **5240 Calkins Rd, Flint MI 48504 (313) 732–6310.**

Congregation Beth Israel. Affiliated with United Syn of Am. Rabbi Hillel Rudavsky; Cantor Sholom Kalib; Pres: Edwin Schreiber; Edu Dir: F. Pinhas Fellus. **G–5240 Calkins Rd, Flint MI 48504 (313) 732–6310.**

Flint Jewish Federation. Mem of CJF. Organized 1936. Pres: Malcolm Isaacs; Exec Dir: Alan J. Hersh. **120 W Kearsley St, Flint MI 48502 (313) 767–5922.**

Temple Beth El. Affiliated with UAHC. 258 mems. Rabbi Gerald H. Schuster; Pres: Theodore Rosenberg; Edu: Golda Shapiro; Sisterhood Pres: Elaine Fishler. **501 S Ballenger Highway, Flint MI 48504 (313) 232–3138.**

Grand Rapids

Chabad House. Lubavitch com servs ctr. Blends Chassidic fervor & warmth with tradition & learning, to show that every J, fr whatever background he or she comes fr, is an integral part of the body of Is. Anti-missionary work; adult edu; Sabbath seminars; holiday progs; day camp; youth groups; syns; kosher kitchen; counseling; chaplaincy; Mitzvah Campaigns; hosp & prison visitations; sr citizens encounters; speakers bureau. Rabbi Y. Weingarten. **1549 Michigan NE, Grand Rapids MI 49503 (616) 458–6575.**

Congregation Ahavas Israel. Affiliated with United Syn of Am. Rabbi Philip Sigal; Cantor Stuart Rapaport; Pres: Morris Kleiman. **2727 Michigan Ave NE, Grand Rapids MI 49506 (616) 949–2840.**

Jewish Community Fund of Grand Rapids. Mem of CJF. Organized 1930. Pres: Joseph N. Schwartz; Exec Sec: Mrs William Deutsch. **1121 Keneberry Way SE, Grand Rapids MI 49506 (616) 949–5238.**

Temple Emanuel. Affiliated with UAHC. 275 mems. Rabbi Albert M. Lewis; Cantor Asher Moss; Pres: Roger Beutner; Sisterhood Pres: Lee Romer. **1715 E Fulton St, Grand Rapids MI 49503 (616) 459–5976.**

Huntington Woods

American Committee for Shaare Zedek in Jerusalem – Detroit Committee. To help future generations meet the health needs of Jerusalem and Israel. Continuing support of century old hospital which moved in 1979 fr old quarters to new $55 million ultra modern medical complex overlooking Jerusalem. Offers total patient & community care. University affiliated teaching hospital contains main hospital building planned for more than 500 beds, emergency shelter, outpatient clinics, school of nursing, clinical labs, research ins, central library, facilities. Ensures the full observance of J tradition. Open to all irrespective of their rel, race or natl origin. **13128 Wales, Huntington Woods MI 48070 (313) 544–8412.**

Ishpeming

Temple Beth Sholom. Affiliated with UAHC. 42 mems. Pres: Daniel J. Arnold; Edu: Retha Weiss. **c/o Dr Daniel Arnold, 80 Edgewood Dr, Marquette MI 49855 (906) 486–6246.**

Jackson

Temple Beth Israel. Reform Temple affiliated with UAHC. To promote & perpetuate the teachings of Reform Judaism as practiced by the Cong affiliated with the UAHC. Rel Servs; Rel Sch weekly; midweek Heb classes for Rel Sch stu; Sisterhood; B'nai B'rith; full range of edu activities for youth & adults; library containing 1500 vols (gen/scholarly collection for adults; young adult & juvenile titles &

sch texts). 85 families; 40 stu in K–10th grade. 1 full-time employee; 2 part-time employees. F October 17, 1861 as Hebrew Cong Beth Israel. At the time of the death of Pres Abraham Lincoln, resolution dated April 23, 1865 was issued under name of Cong Beth Israel; later & presently known as Temple Beth Israel. Pub Temple Voice (bi-monthly). Facilities include sanctuary seating 150, open back of sanctuary seating 300. Maintains prison syn for the MI Dept of Corrections. Pres: Robert LaZebnik; 1st VP: David Sher; 2nd VP: Louis Landman; Treas: Michael Marcellino; Rec Sec: Sharon Keys; Corsp Sec: Herbert Heuman. **801 W Michigan Ave, Jackson MI 49202 (517) 784–3862.**

Temple Beth Israel Library. Library contains 1,500 vols (scholarly collection for adults; juvenile titles, sch texts). For information on the Temple, see – Temple Beth Israel, Jackson, MI. **801 W Michigan Ave, Jackson MI 49202 (517) 784–3862.**

Kalamazoo

Congregation B'nai Israel. Affiliated with UAHC. 43 mems. Pres: Donald Goldsmith; Edu: Joyce Alpiner; Sisterhood Pres: Shirley Weiss. **2232 Crosswind Dr, Kalamazoo MI 49008 (616) 344–9762.**

Congregation of Moses. Affiliated with United Syn of Am. Rabbi Richard Spiegel; Pres: Dr Martin Gall; Edu Dir: Janet Skulnick. **2501 Stadium Dr, Kalamazoo MI 49008 (616) 312–5463.**

Congregation of Moses Library. For information on the Cong, see – Congregation of Moses, Kalamazoo, MI. **2501 Stadium Dr, Kalamazoo MI 49008 (616) 312–5463.**

Kalamazoo Jewish Federation. Mem of CJF. Organized 1949. Pres: Harvey Skulnick. **c/o Congregation of Moses. 2501 Stadium Dr, Kalamazoo MI 49008 (616) 375–5715.**

Livonia

Livonia Jewish Congregation. Affiliated with United Syn of Am. Pres: Helen Bayles. **31840 W Seven Mile Rd, Livonia MI 48152 (313) 477–8974.**

Midland

Temple Beth El. Affiliated with United Syn of Am. Rabbi Marc Rubenstein; Pres: Charles Jonas; Edu Dir: Carol Messing. **2505 Bay City Rd, Midland MI 48640 (517) 496–3720.**

Mount Pleasant

Temple Benjamin. Affiliated with United Syn of Am. Pres: Arthur Silverberg; Edu Dir: Gary Shapiro. **502 N Brown St, PO Box 246, Mount Pleasant MI 48858.**

Muskegon

Congregation B'nai Israel. Affiliated with UAHC. 102 mems. Rabbi Alan Alpert; Pres: Robert Scolnik. **391 W Webster, Muskegon MI 49441 (616) 722–2702.**

Oak Park

Congregation B'nai Moshe. Affiliated with United Syn of Am. Rabbi Stanley M. Rosenbaum; Cantor Louis Klein; Pres: Dr Leonard S. Demak; Exec Dir: Marvin Schader; Edu Dir: Rabbi Bernard Moskowitz; Youth Dir: Sharon Levine. **14390 W Ten Mile Rd, Oak Park MI 48237 (313) 548–9000.**

Congregation Beth Shalom. Affiliated with United Syn of Am. Rabbi David A. Nelson; Cantor Samuel L. Greenbaum; Pres: Dr Barbara Goodman; Edu Dir: Cyril Sevetter; Youth Dir: Karen Knoppow. **14601 W Lincoln Rd, Oak Park MI 48237 (313) 547–7970.**

Congregation Beth Shalom Library. For information on the Cong, see – Congregation Beth Shalom, Oak Park, MI. **14601 W Lincoln Rd, Oak Park MI 48237 (313) 547–7970.**

Jewish Federation Apartments, Inc. Mem agy of J Welfare Fed. To provide housing for sr citizens able to live independently. Provides residence for over 200 sr citizens & rent subsidy where required, five meals a week, assistance in emergencies. F in 1971 with 168 unit bldg. Additional 100 unit bldg opened in Dec 1979, & a new bldg with 103 apts planned for completion 1983. Facilities include library, store for residents. Residents plan own bingo games, movie nights, birthday & holiday progs. Pres: Sheldon P. Winkelman; VPs: Joseph Garson, Michael Perlman, Dr Hershel Sandberg; Sec: Rose L. Greenberg; Asst Sec: Emanuel Feinberg; Treas: Joel Gershenson; Asst Treas: Isadore Silverman; Bd Mems: Doris August, William Avrunin, Tillie Brandwine, Gerald Brody, Philip Handleman, Samuel Hechtman, Joseph H. Jackier, Dr Eva Kahana, Rose Kaplan, Bess Krolik, Jack Lefton, Janet B. Levine, Miriam Mondry, Lester Morris, Jack A. Robinson, Norman Rosenfeld, Harvey Sabbota, Barbara J. Safran, Neil Satovsky, Mark E. Schlussel, Freddy Shiffman, Gilbert B. Silverman, Leo P. Sklar, Leah

Snider, Jack I. Zwick; Rep Jr Div: Norman D. Ash, Lawrence Lax; Agy Rep: Ann Caplan, Sylvia Jaffe; J Welfare Fed: Samuel Cohen, Sol Drachler, Allen Juris; Exec Dir: Helen Naimark; Adm Asst: Connie Howard; Bldg Supt: Mike Cloonan; Adm Sec: Nancy Klein. **15100 W Ten Mile Rd, Oak Park MI 48237 (313) 967–4240.**

Jewish Historical Society of Michigan. Dedicated to the study, research, collection, preservation & commemoration of the hist of the J people in the state of MI. Prog of historical commemoration which includes erection of historical markers at sites of historic significance in the state; maintenance of The MI J Genealogical Index; collection & preservation of documents & papers of individual J & J orgs of MI; participation with local J schs in the teaching of local J hist; provision of speakers on local J hist. F in 1959. Michigan Jewish History (a semi–annua journal). Pres: Phillip Applebaum; VPs: Walter E. Klein, Leonore Miller; Treas: Ida Levine; Rec Sec: Esther Klein; Corsp Sec: Gertrude F. Edgar; Fin Sec: Mrs Abraham S. Rogoff; Dirs: Mrs Morris Adler, Leonard Antel, Laurence B. Deitch, Walter L. Field, Leon Fram, Miriam Hamburger, Mrs Louis LaMed, Reuben Levine, Richard Maddin, Harold Norris, Patricia Pilling, Bette Roth, Abraham Satovsky, Oscar D. Schwartz, Howard B. Sherizen, Leonard Simons, Adelle W. Staller, Devera Stocker, George M. Stutz, Saul Sugar; Editor: Phillip Applebaum; F: Allen A. Warsen. **24680 Rensselaer, Oak Park MI 48237 (313) 548–9176.**

Lubavitch Center. Rabbi B. Shemtov. **14000 W Nine Mile Rd, Oak Park MI 48237 (313) 548–2666.**

Pioneer Women – Na'amat. The training & edu of the Is woman & her family so that each can be best equipped to lead productive lives. For additional information, see – Pioneer Women Na'amat, New York City, NY. **25900 Greefield, Rm 205D, Oak Park MI 48237 (313) 967–4750.**

Temple Emanu-El. Reform Syn. Affiliated with UAHC.Rel Sch; Heb Sch; Adult Edu progs; social, youth auxiliaries. 594 mems. F in 1952. Rabbi Lane Steinger; Cantor/Edu Dir: Norman Rose; Rabbi Emeritus Milton Rosenbaum; Pres: Allan Tushman; Rel VP: Stanley Finkelstein; Fin VP: Terry F. Howard; Adm VP: Aaron Kahn; Rec Sec: Brand Marwil; Corsp Sec: Dr Eli M. Isaacs; Fin Sec: Elaine Grand Stulberg; Treas: Donald Cohen; Sisterhood Pres: Shonnette K. Weisman; Brotherhood Pres: Carl Scott; Couples Club Pres: Shelly & Don Friedman; Youth Group Pres: David Baum; Bd of Trustees: Lewis Barr, Richard Braun, Judge Jessica R. Cooper, Renee Eisenberg, Larry H. Ferstenfeld, Arthur H. Friedman, Sydney L. Harris, Jerry Hersh, Jason Horton, Samuel Leiter, Dr Ellsworth Levine, Phyllis Levy, Jeffrey Mossoff, Mark E. Reizen, Robert Rosen, Dr Ezra Shaya, Margaret Stark, Karyn B. Werner. **14450 W Ten Mile Rd, Oak Park MI 48237 (313) 967–4020.**

Young Israel of Greenfield. Part of Met Council of Young Is, Detroit. To organize Am J youth in model syns with social edu ctrs for the perpetuation of Traditional J. Adult Edu; Youth Prog. Began in the early 1920's; first minyan was in the basement of the Mogain Abraham Syn. The group relocated at various times in various locations following the movement of the J com. The Young Is of Oak-Woods was est in 1953, & Young Is of Southfield was est in 1977. Rabbi Emeritus Joshua Sperka; Sr Rabbi Samuel H. Prero. **15140 W Ten Mile Rd, Oak Park MI 48237 (313) 967–3655.**

Young Israel of Oak-Woods. Part of Met Council of Young Is, Detroit. To organize Am J youth in model syns with social edu ctrs for the perpetuation of Traditional J. Adult Edu; Youth Prog. Began in the early 1920's first minyan was in the basement of the Mogain Abraham Syn. The group relocated at various times in various locations following the movement of the J com. The Young Is of Oak-Woods was est in 1953, & Young Is of Southfield was est in 1977. Rabbi James I. Gordon. **24061 Coolidge, Oak Park MI 48237.**

Petoskey

B'nai Israel Congregation. Affiliated with UAHC. 25 mems. Pres: Melvin Holden; Sisterhood Pres: Irene Levine. **Corner Wavkazoo & Mich, Petoskey MI 49770.**

Pontiac

Temple Beth Jacob. Affiliated with UAHC. 158 mems. Rabbi Richard A. Weiss; Pres: David Schwartz; Edu: Susan Roth; Sisterhood Pres: Judy Schwartz. **79 Elizabeth Lake Rd, Pontiac MI 48053 (313) 332–3212.**

Saginaw

Saginaw Jewish Welfare Federation. Mem of CJF. Organized 1939. Pres: Norman Rotenberg; Fin Sec: Mrs Laney Spear. **1424 S Washington Ave, Saginaw MI 48601 (517) 753–5230.**

Temple B'nai Israel. Affiliated with United Syn of Am. Rabbi Marc Rubenstein; Cantor Martin Glancz;

Pres: Dr Malcolm Pike; Edu Dir: Dr Allen Solomon. **1424 S Washington Ave, Saginaw MI 48601 (517) 753–5230.**

Temple Beth El. Affiliated with UAHC. 8 mems. Pres: Leo A. Kahan. **c/o Mr Leo A. Kahan, 100 S Washington, Saginaw MI 48607 (517) 754–5171.**

Southfield

Congregation Beth Achim. Affiliated with United Syn of Am. Rabbi Milton Arm; Cantor Max Shimansky; Pres: George J. Rossman; Exec Dir: Louis Ellenson; **21100 W Twelve Mile Rd, Southfield MI 48076 (313) 352–8670.**

Congregation Beth Achim, Joseph Katkowsky Library. For information on the Cong, see – Congregation Beth Achim, Southfield, MI. **21100 W Twelve Mile Rd, Southfield MI 48076 (313) 352–8670.**

Congregation Shaarey Zedek. Affiliated with United Syn of Am. Rabbi Irwin Groner; Cantor Chaim Najman; Pres: Harvey L. Weisberg; Exec Dir: Thomas Jablonski; Edu Dir: Marvin Kasoff; Youth Dir: Teri Bornstein. **27375 Bell Rd, Southfield MI 48034 (313) 357–5544.**

Congregation Shaarey Zedek, Learning Resource Center. For information on the Cong, see – Congregation Shaarey Zedek, Southfield, MI. **27375 Bell Rd, Southfield MI 48076 (313) 357–5544.**

Detroit Jewish News. Periodical pub. **17515 W 9 Mile Rd, Suite 865, Southfield MI 48075 (313) 424–8833.**

The Midrasha College of Jewish Studies. Accredited by Iggud (The Natl Assn of Heb Col, & THe Natl Bd of License). Courses leading to the degrees: Bachelor of Heb Literature, Bachelor of J Studies with assc degrees in those areas, Heb Teaching Certificate. Four Depts: Language & Literature, Teacher Training, J & Rel Studies, Midrasha on Wheels offering non-credit courses for adults; cooperative prog with other ins of learning for transfer of credits; Bargman Memorial Lecture Series; Teacher's Ins providing a seminar for those teaching in Heb Schs; Mini-Mester; workshops; seminars; J studies library. Over 240 stu. F in 1948 by Albert Elazar as an outgrowth of the United Hebrew Sch System of Detroit. Initially located in Detroit, the Col moved to its present location in 1969. The Col houses a library of over 35,000 vols. Pres: Dr Gerald A. Teller; Dean: Dr Stanley Kupinsky; Chr: Rose Kaye; Bursar: Isadore J. Goldstein; Bd of Dirs: Rabbi Milton Arm, Mandell Berman, Barbara Berry, Leonard Demak, Stanley Frankel, Dr Barbara Goodman, Rabbi Irwin Groner, Hilda Hamburger, Dr Martin Hart, Marvin R. Hoffman, Norman D. Katz, Milton Lucow, Irving Panush, Abraham Pasternak, Matilda Rubin, Rose Schiller, Edwin Shifrin, David Tanzman, Julian S. Tobias, Barbara Wachler, Janice Waxenberg. **21550 W Twelve Mile Rd, Southfield MI 48076 (313) 352–7117.**

The Midrasha College of Jewish Studies Library. 35,000 vols in Heb, English & Yiddish with a large up-to-date collection on Heb language & literature, & pedagogic materials. For information on the Ins, see – Midrasha College of Jewish Studies, Southfield, MI. **21550 W Twelve Mile Rd, Southfield MI 48076 (313) 352–7117.**

National Association of Jewish Family, Children's & Health Professionals. 24123 Greenfield, Southfield MI 48075 (313) 559–1500.

United Hebrew Schools. Detroit's met area's communally sponsored & operated system of afternoon Heb schs affiliated with the Assn for J Edu. To prepare stu for a satisfying & creative J life, & to lay the basis for active participation in communal living. Included in the UHS structure are the Nursery Sch, four elementary schs, Central Hebrew HS, Midrasha Col of J Studies, Hebrew HS Dept with two divs – Hebraic & J (in the Hebraic div the emphasis is on Heb language, literature, study of the Bible & other original sources of the J tradition; in the J div the emphasis is on developing an understanding & an appreciation of the cultural heritage through the study of classical & modern J literature), part time study, independent study. Other progs include: Kfar Ivri – a Heb speaking camp offering a four week prog for boys & girls; Tour of Is – full time stu who maintain a grade average of 'B' or above are eligible to participate in a prog which combines a tour of Is with a prescribed prog of intensive Hebraic studies; Div of Advanced Heb Studies of the Midrasha – after successfully completing this course the stu is awarded a scholarship to attend an eight week collegiate summer prog at the Hebrew Univ in Jerusalem; The J Vocationsl Serv – offers the following to the HS stu: vocational & career counselin employment servs, identification of academic & personal problems, & initiation of referrals where indicated & approved by parents. Stu enrolled in a regular sch prog at the United Hebrew Schs HS or at the Cong Shaarey Zedek Rel Schs HS will be permitted to take courses at either sch provided that it meets the needs of the stu prog & the interest of the sch. Prin: Yosef Levanon; Librarian: Sarah Bell; Pres: Julius J. Harwood; VPs: Mrs Maxwell B. Bardenstein, Dr Paul C. Feinberg, Mel Seidman; Sec: Marvin R. Hoffman; Treas: Jerome Acker; Asst Treas: Albert L. Lieberman; Superintendent: Dr Gerald A. Teller; Exec Sec: Isadore J. Goldstein; Bd of Dirs: Jerome Acker, Mrs Irwin Alpern, Mrs Jules Altman, Dr Fred Averbuch, Mrs Maxwell B. Bardenstein, Mrs Henri Bernard, Dr Lawrence Berkove, Jeffrey Borin, Morris J. Brandwine, Perry Cohen, Mark Eichner, Harold Elson, Joseph Epel, Dr Paul C. Feinberg, Mitchell Felman, Donald Fox, Stanley D. Frankel, Morris Friedman, Mrs Max Garber, Gordon I. Ginsberg, Mrs Edward Gold, Dr Barbara Goodman, Dr Dan Guyer, Julius J. Harwood, Marvin R. Hoffman, Mrs Sidney Kaye, Jerry Konoppow, Frederick Kunick, G. Vernon Leopold, Albert L. Lieberman, Mrs Gerald Loomus, Milton Lucow, Stanley H. Marx, Dr Stephan Morse, Graham Orley, Abraham Pasternak, Mrs Saul Raimi, Michael Schwartz, Mel Seidman, I. William Sherr, Edwin Shifrin, Mrs Nathan Soberman, Mrs Zvi Steiger, David Tanzman, Julian S. Tobias, Marshall Wallace, Dr Alan Weiner, Benjamin Weiss; Adv Cttee: Rabbi Milton Arm, Mandell L. Berman, Rabbi Irwin Groner, Norman D. Katz, Norbert Reinstein, Rabbi Stanley Rosenbaum, Rabbi Efry Spectre, Rabbi Morton F. Yolkut. **21550 W 12 Mile Rd, Southfield MI 48076 (313) 354–1050.**

Young Israel of Southfield. Part of Met Council of Young Is, Detroit. To organize Am J youth in model syns with social edu ctrs for the perpetuation of Traditional J. Adult Edu; Youth Prog. Began in the early 1920's; first minyan was in the basement of the Mogain Abraham Syn. The group relocated at various times in various locations following the movement of the J com. The Young Is of Oak-Woods was est in 1953, & Young Is of Southfield was est in 1977. Rabbi Feivel Wagner. **27705 Lahser, Southfield MI 48076.**

Traverse City

Congregation Beth El. Affiliated with UAHC. 35 mems. Pres: Terry Tarnow. **c/o Mrs Terry Tarnow, 3545 Orchard View, Traverse City MI 49685 (616) 946–9586.**

Warren

The American Friends of Haifa University. 8701 E Eight Mile Rd, Warren MI 48089 (313) 758–1048.

West Bloomfield

B'nai Israel. Affiliated with United Syn of Am. Rabbi Philip Blachorsky; Pres: Dr Leonard Gaba; Edu Dir: Stanley Conn. **4200 Walnut Lake Rd, West Bloomfield MI 48033 (313) 681–5353.**

Congregation Beth Abraham-Hillel-Moses. 5075 W Maple Rd, West Bloomfield MI 48033 (313) 851–6880.

Congregation Beth Abraham-Hillel-Moses, Kaufman Library. 5075 W Maple Rd, West Bloomfield MI 48033 (313) 851–6880.

The Detroit Zionist Federation. Local branch of the AZF. Zionist renewal. Regularly sponsored events include Zionist Edu Shabbat, co-sponsorship of com Is Independence Day celebration, Jerusalem Day celebration; programming includes a Scholar-in-Residence fr Is. 13 affiliated orgs representing 12,000 mems. Est in the early 1970's. Pres: Dr Milton J. Steinhardt; VPs: Morris Lieberman, Rabbi E. Finkelman, Julian Cohen, Simon Cieck, Uriel Levi; Sec-Treas: Michael Poss; Chr Exec Cttee: Sol P. Lachman. **6600 W Maple Rd, West Bloomfield MI 48033 (313) 661–1000.**

Jewish Community Center. Serv org to provide for the leisure-time recreational, informal-recreational, & cultural needs of the J com. To help the J individual dev creatively, & committed to strengthening J identification & group survival, & promoting J cultural & rel values. The Ctr aims to enrich the life of the J group & of Am soc as a whole. Constructive progs using social group work, recreation, physical edu, informal & formal edu to meet the leisure-time need of its mems; library. F 1933. Main Branch in West Bloomfield; Jimmy Prentis Morris Branch in Oak Park. Pres: Thomas I. Klein; Exec Dir: Dr Morton Plotnick; Asst Exec Dir: Gary A. Leo; Dir Jimmy Prentis Morris Branch: Eugene Jaffe; Chr Exec Cttee: Joel D. Tauber; VPs: Lawrence Jackier, Robert Naftaly, Robert Slatkin, Charles G. Stone; Sec: Edie Mittenthal; Treas: Shirley Zirkin; Mems at Large: Peter M. Alter, Sidney Freedland, Richard J. Maddin; Bd of Dirs: Peter M. Alter, Jerome M. Ash, James August, Milton Barnett, Jeffrey Borin, Mrs Stanley Burkoff, Robert M. Citrin, Dr Mark Diem, Mark Eichner, Dolores Farber, Burton D. Farbman, Donald Fox, Judy Frankel, Baylee Franklin, Sidney Freedland, Harold Gales, Linda Gershenson, Fred L. Goldenberg, Barbara K. Goldman, Sheldon A. Goldman, Mrs Sidney Goldman, Stephen Grand, Judith Grant Granader, David M. Gubow, Dr Martin Hart, Samuel Hechtman, Austin Hirschhorn, Lawrence Jackier, Richard A. Kahn, Lee Kepes, Thomas I. Klein, Mrs Harold Kukes, Mrs Maurice Kurzman, Linda Lee, Alden M. Leib, Richard J. Maddin, Dr Harris Mainster, Philip S. Minkin, Edie Mittenthal, Denny

Munson, Robert H. Naftaly, Mrs Milton Nathanson, Lillian Jaffe Oaks, Mrs Leo Orecklin, Norman Pappas, Irving Pokempner, Mark Y. Segel, Herbert Shapiro, Robert Shapiro, Margie Shell, Hellen Singer, Robert G. Slatkin, Jerry Soble, Dr Louis Soverinsky, Bernard Stollman, Charles G. Stone, Marvin Talan, Joyce Weckstein, Melba Winer, Carol Sloman Wolfe, Shirley Zirkin; Life Hon Dirs: Mrs Aaron Deroy, Irwin Shaw; Hon Dirs: Rabbi Leon Fram, Rabbi Joshuas Sperka. **6600 W Maple Rd, West Bloomfield MI 48033 (313) 661–1000.**

Jewish Community Center, Meyers Memorial Library. For information on the Ins, see – Jewish Community Center, West Bloomfield, MI. **6600 W Maple Rd, West Bloomfield MI 48033 (313) 661–1000.**

Temple Israel. Affiliated with UAHC. 1743 mems. Rabbis: M. Robert Syme, Harold S. Loss, Leon Fram; Cantor Harold Orbach; Pres: Stanley Millman; Edu: Joel Wittstein; Adm: Frank L. Simons; Sisterhood Pres: Carol R. Cooper; Brotherhood Pres: Robert Gunsberg. **5725 Walnut Lake Rd, West Bloomfield MI 48033 (313) 661–5700.**

Temple Kol Ami. Affiliated with UAHC. 281 mems. Rabbi Ernst J. Conrad; Pres: Daniel Krause; Edu: Sol Dovitz; Sisterhood Pres: Gail Cohen. **5085 Walnut Lake Rd, West Bloomfield MI 48033 (313) 661–0040.**

MINNESOTA

Aitkin

Camp Tikvah of the Minneapolis Jewish Community Center. Resident camp which offers three sessions dedicated to creating a total J environment where chil between the ages of 9–15 can learn various skills about themselves & the environment through diverse camping progs. Dir: Joel Miller. **Camp add: Aitkin MN; City add: 4330 Cedar Lake Rd, Minneapolis MN 55416 (612) 377–8330.**

Duluth

Jewish Federation & Community Council. Mem of CJF. Organized 1937. Pres: James Glazman; Sec Adm: Oriana Borup. **1602 E 2nd St, Duluth MN 55812 (218) 724–8857.**

Temple Israel. Syn & Rel Sch affiliated with UAHC & with United Syn of Am. One day a week prog on Sun mornings during the sch yr. Curriculum stresses holidays, hist, Is & values; Heb language & Bar/Bat Mitzvah training is taught weekday afternoons following public sch. 308 mems; 75 stu ranging in age fr 4–15. Staff of 8. Temple Is is a merged cong of a Reform syn & a Conservative syn. The merger took place in 1974. Rabbi Jon Konheim; Prin: Kitty Altman; Rel Sch Bd Chr: James Glazman; Pres: Dr Richard Eisenberg. **1602 E 2nd St, Duluth MN 55812 (218) 724–2956.**

Edina

Women's American ORT – Minneapolis Region. Org for Rehabilitation through Training. Supports vocational schs in twenty two countries including Is. Pres: Cheri Rolnick; Exec Cttee Chr: Bonnie Litton. **7317 Cahill Rd, Edina MN 55435 (612) 941–7158.**

Hibbing

Agudath Achim Synagogue. Affiliated with United Syn of Am. Pres: Dr Bernard Halper. **2320 Second Ave W, Hibbing MN 55746 (218) 263–9237.**

Minneapolis

Adath Jeshurun Congregation. Affiliated with United Syn of Am. Rabbi Arnold M. Goodman; Asst Rabbi: Moshe Silberschein; Cantor Morton Kula; Pres: Norman Pink; Exec Dir: Alex Meirovitz; Youth Dir: Sheila Radman. **3400 Dupont Ave, Minneapolis MN 55408 (612) 824–2685.**

Adath Jeshurun Congregation Library. For information on the Cong, see – Adath Jeshurun Congregation, Minneapolis, MN. **3400 Dupont Ave, Minneapolis MN 55408 (612) 824–2685.**

American Jewish World. Weekly Am-J newspaper. Editor: Norman Gold. **4820 Minnetonka Blvd, Minneapolis MN 55416 (612) 920–7000.**

American-Israel Chamber of Commerce & Industry of Minnesota, Inc. Offers assistance to mem US firms interested in economic activity in & with Is. Provides extensive trade assistance; pub market research reports; aids in dev of trade & investment between US & Is. For additional information, see – American-Israel Chamber of Commerce & Industry, Inc, New York City, NY. **130 S 10th St, Minneapolis MN 55403 (612) 332–1284.**

Anti-Defamation League of B'nai B'rith – Minnesota & Dakotas. Jewish Community Relations Council. Dedicated in purpose & prog to translating the Am heritage of democratic ideals into a way of life for all Am, & to countering assaults on the safety, status, rights & image of J. For additional information, see – Anti-Defamation League of B'nai B'rith, New York City, NY. **15 S 9th St Bldg, Minneapolis MN 55402.**

Beth El Synagogue. Conservative Syn affiliated with United Syn of Am. To serve rel & J needs of mems & com. Rel Servs; edu progs; Women's League; Men's Club; Couples Club; youth groups; Presch; K; Rel Sch; USY youth group; Syn Day Care; Syn Skills Prog; library containing 5,000 vols. 1300 mems. 12 employees. F 1924. Pub Shofar (weekly). Facilities include kosher kitchens, sanctuary seating 638, classrms, gyms. Rabbi Kassel Abelson; Rabbi Marc Sack; Cantor Neil Newman; Exec Dir: Harold Bernstein. **5224 W 26th St, Minneapolis MN 55416 (612) 920–3512.**

Beth El Synagogue Library. Library contains 5000 vols. For information on the Syn, see – Beth El Synagogue, Minneapolis, MN. **5224 W 26th St, Minneapolis MN 55416 (612) 920–3512.**

Congregation Bet Shalom. Affiliated with UAHC. 65 mems. Rabbi Norman M. Cohen; Pres: John Lonstein. **c/o John Lonstein, 1559 Pennsylvania Ave N, Minneapolis MN 55427 (612) 336–4391.**

Hillel Foundation, University of Minnesota. Sponsored locally by the United J Fund of St Paul, & the Minneapolis Fed for J Servs, & internationally by B'nai B'rith Hillel Founs. Provides J stu & faculty mems with a prog of edu, rel, cultural, & social activities; provides opportunities for personal growth, counseling; maintains referral servs. Exec Dir: Rabbi Moshe Adler; Dir of Stu Activities: Vicki Goldish. **1521 University Ave SE, Minneapolis MN 55414 (612) 336–4691.**

Histadrut Israel Labor Campaign. Regional Dir: Alen Herman. **4517 Minnetonka Blvd, Minneapolis MN 55416 (612) 927–4927.**

Israel Aliyah Center. 4330 Cedar Lake Rd S, Minneapolis MN 55416 (612) 377–8330.

Jewish Community Relations Council, ADL of Minnesota & the Dakotas. Speakers Bureau & Resource Ctr. To preserve & translate into greater effectiveness the ideals of Am democracy; to combat anti-Semitism & all forms of racial & rel bigotry; to dev understanding of the modern & ancient nation of Is; to publicize the plight of Soviet J. Audio visual materials, pubs, & speakers on the subjects of prejudice, intergroup understanding, Is the land & its people, Soviet J; support for edu prog in Is. Est in 1975. Pres: Robert Latz; VP: Bonnie Heller; Sec: Morley Friedman; Treas: Howard Kahn; Exec Dir: Morton W. Ryweck; Asst Dirs: Samuel I. Horowitz, Marcia Yugend; Bd of Dirs: Arnold Aberman, Robert Ansel, Fred Baron, Rabbi Stephan Barack, Dr Harold Barrie, Hyman Berman, Michele Bix, Stanely Breen, David Cooperman, Lois Devitt, Jean Druker, Walter Eldot, Manley Feinstein, Dr Stephen Feinstein, Harold Field Jr, Marvin Fineberg, Eileen Freidson, Morley Friedman, Martin Garden, Burton Genis, Larry Gibson, James Glazman, Bonnie Heller, Howard Kahn, Merril Kuller, Robert Latz, John Levine, Annette Newman, Marvin Pertzik, Sol Pogoriler, Gary Porter, Dorothy Rose, Clare Savitt, Byron Schneider, Idell Silberman, Jackie Sinykin, James Stein, Gary Tankenoff, Michael Weinberg, Alan Weinblatt, Carol Wirtschafter, Helen Ziff. **15 S 9th St Bldg, Suite 400, Minneapolis MN 55402 (612) 338–7816.**

Jewish National Fund. Land reclamation & afforestation in Is. Raises funds through the sale of tree certificates, bond transfers, bequests & life insurance assignments; supports special projs including recreation areas, watch towers, roads & devs in frontier areas. Regional Dir: Zev Vinitsky. **425 Hennepin Ave, Suite 1100D, Lumber Exchange Bldg, Minneapolis MN 55401 (612) 339–0862.**

Kenesseth Israel Congregation. Orthodox Syn. To conduct Orthodox servs in accordance with & through its progs further the ideals of Halachic J. Daily Rel Servs; Adult Edu, weekly classes & lectures; youth activities for pre K–HS; special progs for collegiates & post grads; Sisterhood; social activities. Est in 1888, it is known as the Mother of Synagogues, one of the oldest syns in Minneapolis. Monthly bulletin. Communal mikvah is housed in the bldg. Rabbi Jerome M. Herzog; Pres: Edmund A. Gottlieb; 1st VP: Victor Mintz; 2nd VP: Dr Max Donath; Sec: Max Gutman; Treas: Jack Baumgarten. **4330 W 28th St, Minneapolis MN 55416 (612) 920–2183.**

Minneapolis Federation for Jewish Services. Mem of CJF. Organized 1929; inc 1930. Pres: Morris Sherman; Exec Dir: Herman Markowitz. **811 LaSalle Ave, Minneapolis MN 55402 (612) 339–7491.**

Mount Sinai Hospital of Minneapolis. Teaching affiliate of the Univ of MN & an internal med teaching affiliation with Hennepin Cty Med Ctr. To serve the patient's total needs with deep concern for the quality of care. Acupuncture Clin; Adult Med Surgical Unit; Ambulatory Care Ctr; Surgery Unit; Anesthesiology; Blood Bank; Cardiac Rehabilitation Unit; Cardiopulmonary Lab; Clin Labs; Clin Psychology; Coronary Care Unit; CT Scanner; Dental Clin; Diabetic Unit; Electrocardiography; Electroencephelograph; Emergency Servs; Endoscopy Suite; Gastroenterology Lab; Health Servs; Intensive Care Unit; Kidney Dialysis; Neurology Clin; Nuclear Med/ultrasound; Occupational Therapy; Open Heart Surgery Facility;

Pediatric Unit; operating rms; physical therapy; radiology; recovery rm; respiratory therapy; special procedures rm; social servs; med library. Med Stu & Residency Training Progs: Clin Pathology, Gastroenterology, Gen Surgery, Internal Med & Neurology. Health Care Professional Residency Progs: Hosp Adm; Lab, Med Record Adm, Nursing, Occupational Therapy, Physical & Respiratory Therapy. F in 1951. In 1978 a comprehensive Diabetic Metabolic Disease Care Ctr was opened. The Hosp has a 273 bed capacity. Guest housing is available at reasonable prices for patients & family in a Hosp owned house adjacent to the Hosp. **2215 Park Ave, Minneapolis MN 55404 (612) 339–1692.**

Philip & Florence Dworsky Center for Jewish Studies, University of Minnesota. To foster scholarship in the field of J studies. The Ctr sponsors three progs: Harold Goldberg Memorial Prize for Excellence in J Studies awarded to the stu who writes the best paper in an annual competition; David & Kalman Goldenberg Scholar in Residence Prog which brings in a prof in a field of J studies for one week; The Florence G. Dworsky Grant-in-Aid in J Studies which supports faculty scholarship & pubs in the field. Dir: Tzvee Zahavy. **178 Klaeber Ct, 320 16th Ave SE, Minneapolis MN 55455.**

Programs in Israel Committee. Under auspices of J Com Relations Council, ADLof MN & the Dakotas. Works with Twin Cities' Shaliach whose major concern is interviewing, recruiting & placing MN youth in a prog in Is. **MN JCC, 4330 S Cedar Lake Rd, Minneapolis MN 55416 (612) 377–8330.**

State of Israel Bonds. 1488 Northwestern Bank Bldg, Minneapolis MN 55402 (612) 338–8475.

The Talmud Torah of Minneapolis. Supplementary Heb sch affiliated with the Am Assn for J Edu, supported by Minneapolis Fed for J Servs. To provide a strong background in Heb, J thought & values as well as giving stu a strong J identity. Mekhina Prog for 1st & 2nd grades; Elementary Prog for 3rd–7th grades; HS for 8–10th grades; Bet Midrash for 11th & 12th graders including advanced studies in Heb literature, Bible, Rabbinics, J thought, & elective prog; Maba 3 wk camping prog; Learn & Play summer prog; J is Alive & Well in Minnesota – a prog in which J chil fr small towns are given an opportunity to experience a larger J com; English as a Second Language prog for newcomers; library; J teachers ctr. 450 stu 1st–12th grade. Est in 1894 as a one rm cheder. The Sch was officially named in 1913. Pres: Herbert A Kohn; 1st VP: Evelyn Flom; 2nd VP: Morton Silverman; Sec: Donna Leviton; Treas: Dr Nathan Freidson; Exec Dir: Rabbi Avraham Ettedgui; Assc Dir: Rabbi David Younger; Business Mgr: Nancy Peilite. **8200 W 33rd St, Minneapolis MN 55426 (612) 935–0316.**

The Talmud Torah of Minneapolis Library. For information on the Ins, see – Talmud Torah of Minneapolis, Minneapolis, MN. **8200 W 33rd St, Minneapolis MN 55426 (612) 935–0316.**

Temple Israel. Affiliated with UAHC. Rel Servs; edu progs; Sisterhood; Men's Club; couples club; Camp Teko (summer camp); Rel Sch; Heb Sch; library containing 5,000 vols (Judaica). 1850 mems. F 1878. Pub The Temple Call (bulletin). Facilities include kitchen; sanctuary; chapel; several social hall; Rel Sch. Rabbis: Max A. Shapiro, Stephen H. Pinsky, Daniel G. Zemel; Cantor Arnold Katz; Pres: Edwin Sherman; Edu: Frances P. Finstad; Sisterhood Pres: Myrna Abrams; Brotherhood Pres: David Abramson. **2324 Emerson Ave S, Minneapolis MN 55405 (612) 377–8680.**

Torah Academy. Day sch affiliated with Torah Umesorah. To challenge & dev the stu minds & reinforce their positive J identity; to provide J chil with preparation to meet the moral ethical challenges of life through the learning of Torah. Gen & J Studies. 210 stu fr K-Jr HS. Est in 1945 by a group of people concerned about the future of J in Minneapolis. Prin Dir: Rabbi Heshy Dachs; Pres: Rabbi Jay Roberts. **8200 W 33rd St, Minneapolis MN 55426 (612) 933–6630.**

Northfield

Jewish Students of Carleton. Rel, social & cultural ctr for J stu on the Carleton campus, & Northfield residents. Housing in the J Stu Ctr; Holiday Servs; Shabbat dinners; weekend retreats; informal J study groups; library resource ctr. Faculty Adv: Janet Garfinkel. **Carleton Col, Northfield MN 55057 (507) 645–4431.**

Rochester

B'nai Israel Synagogue. Reform Cong affiliated with UAHC. To edify & enrich the worshippers' spiritual, personal & communal lives as J. Rel Servs; edu progs; Rel Sch; Heb Sch; youth group; gift shop; B'nai B'rith Men's Lodge; Adult Discussion Group; library containing 500 vols (variety of subjects). 80 mems; 25 stu aged 5–14 yrs old. 3 employees. F 1910 as Hebrew Cong of Rochester; 1919 became B'nai Israel Syn. Pub Bulletin (monthly). Facilities include sanctuary (can accomodate 250 for High Holidays), kitchen, library, rabbi's study, four classrms, recreation rm, gift shop, off. A young, active cong. We see J fr all over the world who come for the med servs of the Mayo Clinic staff. Rabbi Sol Goodman; Pres: David Fellman; VP: Marilyn Handwerger; Sec: Brian Fishman; Treas: Ed Stollof. **621 2nd St SW, Rochester MN 55901 (507) 288–5825.**

St. Louis Park

B'nai B'rith International District Six. 1433 Utica Ave S, Suite 57, St Louis Park MN 55416 (612) 546–1616.

B'nai B'rith Minnesota-Wisconsin Council. J serv org. To unite world J for the advancement of the J people, & to help create a better world for all people. Coordinating body for the 17 men's lodges in the Twin Cities & throughout MN & western WI. Pres: Monroe Schlactus; Adm Sec: Ruth Hollischer. **1433 Utica Ave S, Suite 57, St Louis Park MN 55416 (612) 546–1616.**

B'nai B'rith Youth Organization. Chr Bd of Dir: Steve Cohen. **3546 Dakota Ave S, St Louis Park MN 55416 (612) 929–3334.**

B'nai Emet Synagogue. Affiliated with United Syn of Am. Rabbi Sylvan D. Kamens; Cantor Shalom Markovits; Pres: Alice Flom; Chr of the Bd: Lorraine Astren; Adm: Sybil Korengold; Edu Dir: Steve Toberman. **3115 Ottawa Ave S, St Louis Park MN 55416 (612) 927–7309.**

Chaplaincy Service to State Institutions. Provides chaplaincy servs to residents of state mental & penal ins, out-of-town & syn unaffiliated patients at the Univ of MN Hosp, local hosps & nursing homes; provides chemical dependency counseling; maintains volunteer cttee. Dir: Rabbi Barry I. Woolf. **2640 Quentin Ave S, St Louis Park MN 55416 (612) 922–0322.**

Shaare Shalom Congregation. Affiliated with United Syn of Am. Pres: Dr Stanley Finkelstein. **2524 Aquila Ave S, St Louis Park MN 55426 (612) 546–4022.**

St. Paul

Adath Israel Orthodox Synagogue. Sisterhood; Youth Group. Rabbi Asher Zeilingold; Pres: Irving Rosenblum; Sisterhood Pres: Evelyn Zylberberg. **2337 Edgcumbe Rd, St Paul MN 55116 (612) 698–8300.**

Bais Chana Women's Ins. 11 wk summer live & learn prog & 5 wk winter prog to give women, who do not have a yeshiva background, an opportunity to experience total J living & learning. Est 1976. Prin: Rabbi Manis Friedman. **15 Montcalm Ct, St Paul MN 55116 (612) 698–3858.**

Gan Israel Day Camp. Camp of Merkos-Lubvitch House. Half-day for chil 3-5; full day for chil 5-11 during the mo of July & Aug. Dir: Rabbi Gershon Grossbaum. **15 Montcalm Ct, St Paul MN 55116 (612) 698–3858.**

Hebrew House of Macalester College, Chavurat Or Hadash. Live-in Hebrew house. Edu, social & rel programming for the J com at Macalester Col. Houses 8 stu a semester. Facilities include a J library & kosher kitchen. Coord: Cindy Lazebnik. **37 Macalester St, St Paul MN 55105 (612) 647–6464.**

Jewish Community Center Day Camps. Camp Centerland – half-day camp for ages 3,4, & 5 with choice of three or five day prog; Camp Butwin – located on country day camp site for chil 5-7, K through grade 2; Camp Adventure – advanced prog located on a country day camp site including overnights for grades 3-6. Dir Camp Centerland: Sue Muenzer; Dir Camp Butwin: Ken Weintraub. **1375 St Paul Ave, St Paul MN 55116 (612) 698–0751.**

Jewish Community Center of St. Paul. Social group work agy. To serve the pre-sch chil, youth, young adults, adults, & sr citizens of the com. Cultural, recreational & edu activities; Health Club; three summer camping progs; three & five day nursery sch; extended day activity prog for pre-sch chil; special chil group involving recreational & social experience for brain damaged, retarded or autistic chil including activities in physical edu, swimming, drama, music & celebration of J holidays. A three mo complimentary membership is offered to all new residents of St Paul. Membership scholarships are available. Exec Dir: Burton Garr; Pres: Gary Bloom. **1375 St Paul Ave, St Paul MN 55116 (612) 698–0751.**

Jewish Family Service. To provide professional counseling & social servs to individuals & families for improvement of personal adjustment & family relationships, & for sustaining life adjustment in the face of disabling conditions. Individual counseling; married couple & family therapy; assistance in planning options; home care servs; resettlement of emigrees; group therapy for young adult singles; edu group seminars on life adjustment problems; consultation on prog planning; edu workshops on mental health & J family life themes for com orgs. Fees are based on ability to pay. Exec Dir: Sidney

N. Hurwitz; Pres: Les Novak. **1546 St Clair Ave, St Paul MN 55105 (612) 698–0767.**

Jewish Vocational Service. The only approved vocational counseling agy in St Paul certified by the Intl Assn of Counseling Servs, Inc; mem agy of the Natl Assn of J Vocational Servs. Edu & vocational counseling; scholarship selection; job placement; sheltered workshops for the aged at Sholom, Inc, & Leisure League; aptitude & psychological test batteries; group guidance progs. Professionally trained counselors & psychologists with masters degrees. As a serv to the gen com, JVS has contracts with the City of St Paul to provide counseling & job placement servs at the Career Guidance & Training Ctr, to provide edu & vocational guidance for vets, & to conduct the Career Opportunities Preparation for Employment Prog for the United Way. Exec Dir: Benjamin Lasoff; Pres: Bernard Grodin. **1821 University Ave, St Paul MN 55104 (612) 645–9377.**

Lubavitch Cheder Day Sch. St Paul's only Heb day sch. Est in 1977. Prin: Rabbi Shlomo Benet. **15 Montcalm Ct, St Paul MN 55116 (612) 698–3858.**

Lubavitch House. Houses the Hq of Upper Midwest Regional Off; maintains weekly Shabbatons & various J edu classes. Dir: Rabbi Gershon Grossbaum. **15 Montcalm Ct, St Paul MN 55116 (612) 698–3858.**

Merkos L'inyonei Chinuch Lubavitch. Hq of Upper Midwest Regional Off. Ongoing outreach progs. Maintains various ins – Lubavitch House, Bais Chana Women's Ins, Lubavitch Cheder Day Sch, Gan Israel Day Camp, Drake Univ J Stu Ctr at Des Moines IA. Regional off est in 1962 by the Lubavitcher Rebbe. The Lubavitch Digest. Dir: Rabbi Moshe Feller. **15 Montcalm Ct, St Paul MN 55116 (612) 698–3858.**

Mikvah Association of St. Paul. Ritual immersion pool (a completely modern facility). Pres: Reuven Hoch. **1516 Randolph Ave, St Paul MN 55105 (612) 698–6163.**

Minnesota Rabbinical Association. Statewide assn of rabbis. Discussion of important issues pertinent to J & to the local J coms; interest in all areas of J life; responsive to those situations which may arise in Is, Russia, the US & other J coms; participation with other J agy to help bring about the true sense of K'lal Yisrael. Pres: Rabbi Mordecai Miller. **Temple of Aaron Cong, 616 S Mississippi River Blvd, St Paul MN 55116 (612) 698–8874.**

Mount Zion Hebrew Congregation. Reform Temple. Affiliated with UAHC. Sisterhood; Youth Group; Rel Sch; Heb Sch. 658 mems. Rabbi Leigh Lerner; Cantor Holly Callen; Adm: David Savage; Edu Dir: Susan Gordon; Pres: Joseph C. Harris; Sisterhood Pres: Judy Kane. **1300 Summit Ave, St Paul MN 55105 (612) 698–3881.**

Mount Zion Temple, Bloom Memorial Library. For information on the Temple, see – Mt. Zion Temple, St Paul, MN. **1300 Summit Ave, St Paul MN 55105 (612) 698–3881.**

Shaare Shalom Congregation. Conservative Syn. Rel Sch. Pres: David Itzkowitz. **1922 Sargent, St Paul MN 55105 (612) 699–1014.**

Sholom Home, Inc. Long-term care agy; licensed for both skilled nursing care & intermediate care. Physical & occupational therapy; recreational servs; Northstar Workshop in conjunction with the J Vocational Servs; staff med servs; day commuter & home delivery meals prog; prime food contractor of the JCCCongregate Dining Prog. 302 residents. The Home is a merger of the J Home for the Aged of the NW & the George Kaplan Sholom Residence. Exec Dir: Harold Sobel; Pres: Sig Harris. **1554 Midway Pkwy, St Paul MN 55108 (612) 646–6311.**

Sons of Jacob Congregation. Conservative Syn. Men's Club; Sisterhood; Youth Prog; Rel Sch. Pres: Nate Neren; Sisterhood Pres: Francis Sains; Men's Club Pres: Moe Katz. **1466 Portland Ave, St Paul MN 55104 (612) 646–0498.**

St. Paul United Jewish Fund & Council. Central planning, coordinating, & financing org for most of the health, welfare, cultural, & recreational servs in the com. Anything that concerns J people & the com of St Paul is the concern of the UJFC. United J Fund Campaign – annual drive proceeds used to help finance local, state & natl J com servs as well as welfare progs overseas & in Is; Young Leadership Prog – dev & trains young people in com leadership. F in 1935. Directory of Jewish Agencies, Organizations & Institutions in St Paul. Activities are implemented through active yr-round cttee such as social planning-budgeting, leadership dev, endowments. Exec Dir: Kimball Marsh; Pres: Donald Mains. **790 S Cleveland Ave, Suite 201, St Paul MN 55116 (612) 690–1707.**

The Talmud Torah of St. Paul. Independent, communal supplementary J sch. To teach positive attitudes toward all J movements. The sch stresses Heb language, J practices, classical J texts, Is & Zionism. Heb & J Studies; Adult Edu. 400 stu presch-

HS. Est 50 yrs ago as a product of a merger of smaller J communal ins. The Talmud Torah houses the Jesse B. Calmenson Library, Moadon Hebrew Activity Ctr, Capp Hebrew Curriculum Dev Prog, a natl prog to create & implement an elementary level Heb curriculum in the Heb language. In Sept 1982 the Talmud Torah opened a J communal day sch. Prin: Ruth Gavish; Exec Dir: Rabbi Joel Gordon; Pres: Barry Glaser; VPs: Sandra Aaron, Dr Neil Arnold, R. David Unowsky; Treas: Dr James C. Smith; Sec: Linda Schloff; Life Mems: David B. Bishoff, Irwin E. Gordon, Ethel Levey, Harry Rosenthal, Harold Smith; Bd of Dirs: Harvey Berwin, Rabbi Ely Braun, Sheila Brod, Jane Broude, Ida Raye Chernin, Ardyce Ehrlich, Richard Fisch, Eunice Gelb, Jules Goldstein, Max Goodman, Steven S. Goodman, Bernard Grodin, Jean Kanter, Stanley Kaplan, Elliott Karasov, Phylis Karsov, Bernard Karon, Miriam Kieffer, Lawrence Kuller, Elizabeth Latts, William Leder, Rabbi Leigh Lerner, Joyce Levitan, Lee Litman, Suzanne Malmon, Stuart Marofsky, Rabbi Joel Newman, Dr Norman Newman, Arnold Orloff, Rabbi Bernard Raskas, Nancy Reich, Dr Paul Rosenblatt, Barbara Rutzick, Sandra Rutzick, David Sanders, Dr Laurence Savett, Larry Steinberg, Lloyd Stern, Rolla Unowsky, Nancy Waldman, Edward Zamansky, Rabbi Asher Zeilingold. **636 S Mississippi River Blvd, St Paul MN 55116 (612) 698–8807.**

The Talmud Torah of St. Paul, Jesse B. Calmenson Memorial Library. For information on the Ins, see – The Talmud Torah of St Paul, St Paul, MN. **636 S Mississippi River Blvd, St Paul MN 55116 (612) 698–8807.**

Temple of Aaron. Conservative Syn affiliated with United Syn of Am. Sisterhood; Youth Prog; Rel Sch. Rabbi Bernard S. Raskas; Assc Rabbi Mordecai Miller; Pres: Sanford Brody; Sisterhood Pres: Fran Rosen. **616 S Mississippi River Blvd, St Paul MN 55116 (612) 698–8874.**

United Jewish Fund & Council. Mem of CJF. Organized 1935. Pres: Donald Mains; Exec Dir: Kimball Marsh. **790 S Cleveland, St Paul MN 55116 (612) 690–1707.**

Workmen's Circle. Workers-oriented fraternal org. Maintains credit unions; supports ORT, City of Hope, & Sholom Home. Pres: Irving Waldman. **790 S Cleveland Ave, Suite 225, St Paul MN 55116 (612) 699–5146.**

Zionist Organization of America. To promote the philosophy of Zionism on local, natl & intl levels. To solidify world J coms with the Is com through cultural, edu, & historical doctrines. Natl Exec Cttee: Adeline Fremland; Treas: Joseph Fremland. **1595 Highland Pkwy, St Paul MN 55116 (612) 698–3234.**

Webster

Herzl Camp. Three sessions each for different age range: 9-11, 12-13, 14-16. MaBa session (intensive Heb prog) incorporated in first session; Kadimah session during second & third session; Ozo prog (counselor in training) during entire period for those entering 12th grade. Dir: Andrew Halper. **Camp add: Webster WI (715) 866–1795; City add: 1698 Grand Ave, St Paul MN 55101 (612) 698–3895.**

MISSISSIPPI

Biloxi

Congregation Beth Israel. Conservative Syn. Rel Servs; Sun Sch; Heb Sch. 48 families. Est in 1958. Cong Beth Is, one of the few Conservative syns in MS, is located in a met area close to one of the largest Air Force Bases & also close to the tourist business on the Gulf of Mexico. Officiating Rabbi – Pres: Abraham H. Silver; Chazzan, Treas: Martin Goldin; Sec: Rose Datlof. **Camellia & Southern Ave, PO Box 851, Biloxi MS 39533 (601) 388–5574.**

Clarksdale

Congregation Beth Israel. Affiliated with UAHC. 68 mems. Rabbi Max Selinger; Pres: Harry Lipson Jr; Sisterhood Pres: Leah Ehrich. **PO Box 165, 401 Catalpa St, Clarksdale MS 38614 (601) 624–5862.**

Cleveland

Temple Adath Israel. Affiliated with UAHC. 56 mems. Rabbi Moses M. Landau; Pres: Eva Kamien; Sisterhood Pres: K.P. Levingston. **201 S Bolivar Ave, Cleveland MS 38732 (601) 843–2005.**

Columbus

B'nai Israel. Affiliated with UAHC. 25 mems. Pres: Julie Brookhadt; Sisterhood Pres: Ellen Sonkin. **717 Second Ave N, Columbus MS 39701 (601) 328–8355.**

Greenville

Hebrew Union Congregation. Affiliated with UAHC. 154 mems. Pres: Dave Davidow; Edu: Jeanne Mayer; Adm: B.C. Goldstein; Sisterhood Pres: Leslie Mosow. **PO Box 212, 504 Main St, Greenville MS 38701 (601) 332–4153.**

Greenwood

Congregation Beth Israel. Affiliated with UAHC. 15 mems. Pres: David Pachter. **c/o David Pachter, 506 E Harding St, Greenwood MS 38930 (601) 453–5749.**

Hattiesburg

Congregation B'nai Israel. Affiliated with UAHC. 59 mems. Rabbi Samuel A. Rothberg; Pres: Richard Feinberg; Sisterhood Pres: Linda Shemper. **PO Box 1753, Hattiesburg MS 39401 (601) 583–0375.**

Jackson

Beth Israel Congregation. Affiliated with UAHC. 224 mems. Rabbis: Richard J. Birnholz, Perry E. Nussbaum; Pres: William B. Howell; Edu: Richard J. Birnholz; Sisterhood Pres: Gilda Hesdorffer. **PO Box 12329, Jackson MS 39211 (601) 956–6215.**

Jackson Jewish Welfare Fund, Inc. Mem of CJF. Organized 1945. Pres: Louis H. Shornick. **PO Box 12329, Jackson MS 39211 (601) 956–6215.**

Lexington

Temple Beth El. Affiliated with UAHC. 15 mems. Pres: Edward Schur; Sisterhood Pres: J. Stern. **224 Ct St S, Lexington MS 39095.**

Meridian

Congregation Beth Israel. Affiliated with UAHC. 67 mems. Rabbis: Joseph Levenson, Leo Turitz; Pres: Sam Feltenstein; Sisterhood Pres: A. Herzog. **PO Box 3456, Meridian MS 39301 (601) 483–3193.**

Natchez

Congregation B'nai Israel. Affiliated with UAHC. 29 mems. Pres: Gerald Krouse; Sisterhood Pres:

Sarah Pasternack. **PO Box 1003, Natchez MS 39120 (601) 445–5407.**

Port Gibon

Congregation Gemiluth Chasadim. Affiliated with UAHC. 4 mems. Pres: Karl Weil. **Port Gibson MS 39150.**

Utica

UAHC Jacobs Camp Institute. Dir: Macy B. Hart. **Box C, Utica MS 39175 (601) 885–6042.**

Vicksburg

Jewish Welfare Federation. 1210 Washington St, Vicksburg MS 39180 (601) 636–7531.

Temple Anshe Chesed. Affiliated with UAHC. 85 mems. Rabbi Allan H. Schwartzman; Pres: Benjamin R. Wendrow; Sisterhood Pres: Judy Rankin. **2414 Grove St, Vicksburg MS 39180 (601) 636–1126.**

MISSOURI

Chesterfield

Tpheris Israel Chevra Kadisha Congregation. Orthodox Cong; founding mem of Union of Orthodox Cong, founding mem of Vaad Hoeir of St Louis. Pioneering for Torah J in W St Louis Cty. Rel Servs – daily morning, Fri & Sat evenings, Sat & Sun mornings; Youth Group; Sisterhood; Men's Club; library containing 1,000 vols (Talmud & Rabbinic works). 125 families. 3 employees. F 1883, merger of several syns. Pub Newsletter (quarterly). Facilities include kosher kitchen, sanctuary seating 450 (High Holidays), 150 (Shabbath) . Special Awards from Union of Orthodox Cong of Am as pioneering cong. Rabbi David S. Zlatin; Pres: Charles Neuman; VPs: Merle Hartstein, Sam Turken, John Krombach, Roberta Fine; Treas: Irv Schulman; Sec: Robert Tregman; Shammash: I. Altman; Gabbaim: Morris Galler, Harry Neuman; High Holiday Gabbai: Henry Grossberg; Sisterhood Pres: Sylvia Rosen; Youth Group Adv: Elaine Sandler. **14550 Ladue Rd, Chesterfield MO 63017 (314) 469–7060**

Clayton

Anti-Defamation League of B'nai B'rith – Missouri-S Illinois Regional Office. Dedicated in purpose & prog to translating the Am heritage of democratic ideals into a way of life for all Am, & to countering assaults on the safety, status, rights & image of J. For additional information, see – Anti-Defamation League of B'nai B'rith, New York City, NY. **225 S Meramec, Clayton MO 63105.**

Jefferson City

Temple Beth El. Affiliated with UAHC. 8 mems. Pres: Robert S. Herman; Edu: Barbara Herman. **c/o Mr Robert S. Herman, 1005 Adams St, Jefferson City MO 65101 (314) 636–3821.**

Joplin

United Hebrew Congregation. Affiliated with UAHC. 58 mems. Pres: Jay Rosenberg; Sisterhood Pres: Shirley Baum. **702 Sergeant St, Joplin MO 64801 (417) 624–1181.**

Kansas City

Beth Shalom Congregation. Conservative Syn affiliated with United Syn of Am. Daily, Fri Evening, Sat Morning & Holiday Servs; Choir; Beth Shalom Sch including Nursery, Bar/Bat Mitzvah, HS; Adult Edu including Ins of J Studies; Sisterhood Bat Torah; Havurot; Parent Edu Prog; Kabbalat Shabbat & Family Dinners; Stuart J. Hersh Memorial Lecture; Heb Literacy Classes; Conversion & Gen Information Class; Sisterhood; Men's Club; youth groups: United Syn Intermediates for 7th & 8th graders; USY, Leaders Training Fellowship – an elite group of 9–12th graders who wish to study more; Mishpacha Sr Group; New Group for Young Singles; Young Marrieds; Young Parents. F in 1878 as a burial soc which grew into both Cong Ohav Sholom & Beth Shalom. Originally known as Cong Keneseth Is, the first syn was built in 1902. A split in the Cong led to the formation of Beth Shalom which later remerged with Keneseth Is & built a new syn dedicated in 1927. Population shifts signaled a necessity to move; 46 acres were purchased SW of Kansas City in 1955. Sch facilities were completed in 1962; in 1968 the ground breaking ceremony for the sanctuary, assembly hall, chapel, & off took place. In 1971 the bldg was dedicated. The Scroll (bi-weekly newspaper). JTS maintains an off in the syn. Facilities include the Main Sanctuary seating 1,280, Katz Memorial Chapel seating 250, Cumonow Social Hall seating 1,000, Commons Rm seating 270, gift shop, library. Two tapestrie decorate the sanctuary – Genesis designed by Tel Aviv artist Kopel Gurwin & created by 70 women of the Sisterhood, & The Revelation at Sinai by artist Janet Kuemmerlein dedicated in honor of Mr & Mrs Lewis Goldberg. Rabbi Dr Morris B. Margolies; Assc Rabbi Henry B. Balser; Cantor Dr Hyman I. Sky; Exec Dir: Lawrence H. Trope; Edu Dir: Sarah Small; Prog & Youth Dir: Patsy Dunn; Librarian: Fran Wolf; Pres

Neil Miller; VPs: Sylvan Siegler, Neil Sosland, Dr Larry Jacobson; Treas: Michael Azorsky; Sec: Saul Ellis; Parliamentarian: Dr Herbert Winer; Historian: Elaine Polsky; Hon Treas: Hymie Sosland. **9400 Wornall Rd, Kansas City MO 64114 (816) 361–2990.**

Beth Shalom Congregation, Blance & Ira Rosenblum Library. For information on the Cong, see – Beth Shalom Congregation, Kansas City, MO. **9400 Wornall, Kansas City MO 64114 (816) 361–2990.**

Chabad House, Jewish Education Center. Orthodox Ins affiliated with Chabad Lubavitch HQ, Bklyn NY. To advance J knowlege & identity. Weekly & Holiday Servs; Sun Sch; Presch; Camp Gan Is; campus outreach; Russian immigrant progs; Adult Edu classes; hosp chaplaincy; library containing 300 vols (Judaica – adult & chil) 300 mems; 150 families; 5 regional groups, 2 state groups: 30 presch stu; 25 Sun sch stu; 50 adult edu. 6 employees; volunteers (Neshei Chabad). F in Kansas City in 1970. Pub Torah Times (weekly); Chabad Happening (bi-monthly). Facilities include stu housing, kosher kitchen, gift shop, library, sanctuary, chil game rm, classrms. Rabbi Shalom Winesberg; Rabbi Ben Zion Friedman; Chr: Neil Sosland. **8901 Holmes Rd, Kansas City MO 64131 (816) 333–7117.**

Jewish Community Relations Bureau. Involved in the areas of anti-Semitism, church-state relations, Is, Soviet J, civil rights, civil liberties, urban affairs, & other social action issues. Offers assistance to individuals who may be experiencing problems in these areas; maintains speakers bureau; distributes literature to interpret Judaism & J issues to the gen com. Chr: William G. Levi; V Chr: Sheila Greenbaum, Harvey Kaplan; Sec: Richard P. Atlas; Exec Dir: David H. Goldstein; Asst Dir: Judy Hellman; Mems: Alice Jacks Achtenberg, Frank J. Adler, Janet Davis Baker, Rabbi Herbert I. Berger, Rabbi Edward Paul Cohn, Dr Steven G. Cohn, Deborah R. Engelhardt, Paul Flam, Mark H. Gilgus, Barry A. Glasberg, Meyer L. Goldman, Susan L. Goldsmith, Loeb H. Granoff, Sharon Greenwood, Sharon Hellman, Harlene J. Hipsh, Sanford P. Krigel, Peter S. Levi, Hilary M. Lewis, Dr Harris Mirkin, Lynnly B. Picow, Elaine Polsky, Scott A. Raisher, Milton Rydell, Mark R. Singer, Phyllis Stevens, Lorraine Stiffelman, R. Hugh Uhlmann, Walter M. Ulin, Rabbi Michael Zedek; Adv Bd: Irving Achtenberg, Bert Berkley, Irwin E. Blond, Morris Cohen, Harvey Fried, Nathan S. Goldberg, Herbert Horowitz, Ann R. Jacobson, Abe J. Kaplan, Chester B. Kaplan, Ward A. Katz, Joseph Koralchik, Sevi Krigel, Kurt Levi, Rabbi Morris B. Margolies, Rodney T. Minkin, Stanley A. Morantz, James D. H. Reefer, Ruth G. Shechter, Harry Sheskin, Mendel Small, Beth K. Smith, Joseph Solsky, Donald H. Tranin, Evelyn Wasserstrom; Ext-Officio: Albert Goller, Sol Koenigsberg. **25 E 12th St, Kansas City MO 64106 (816) 421–5808.**

Jewish Federation of Greater Kansas City. Mem of CJF. Organized 1933. Pres: Albert Goller; Exec Dir: Sol Koenigsberg. **25 E 12th St, Kansas City MO 64106 (816) 421–5808.**

Kansas City Jewish Chronicle. Periodical pub. **PO Box 8709, Kansas City MO 64114 (913) 648–4620.**

Menorah Medical Center. Non-profit, gen acute care hosp with a 430 licensed bed capacity. To deliver quality health care to all persons without regard to race, creed, color or ability to pay. Three med ctrs in Neurology, Oncology, & Cardiopulmonary; Special Procedures Lab; Intensive Care Unit; Psychiatric Care; Outpatient Clins. 400 physicians. On Sept 7, 1931 Menorah Hosp opened its doors to the public. By 1932 the Hosp had a total of 167 active & courtesy staff physicians on the med staff. In Mar 1952 the name of the Hosp was changed to Menorah Med Ctr. In 1962 the Menorah N addition to the hosp was officially opened. In 1975 the Menorah Tower addition to the hosp was constructed. Menorah has an active Women's Auxiliary which provides numerous servs to both the Hosp & the com. Pres: Norman C. Schultz; Exec Dir: Robert Tell. **4949 Rockhill Rd, Kansas City MO 64110 (816) 276–8000.**

The New Reform Temple. Affiliated with UAHC. 250 mems. Rabbi Edward P. Cohn; Pres: Richard M. Levin. **7100 Main St at Gregory, Kansas City MO 64114 (816) 523–7809.**

The New Reform Temple Library. For information on the Temple, see – The New Reform Temple, Kansas City, MO. **7100 Main St at Gregory, Kansas City MO 64114 (816) 523–7809.**

The Temple Congregation B'nai Jehudah, Library. For information on the Cong, see – The Temple Congregation B'nai Jehuda, Kansas City, MO. **712 E 69th St, Kansas City MO 64131 (816) 363–1050.**

The Temple, Congregation B'nai Jehudah. Affiliated with UAHC. 1487 mems. Rabbis: Michael R. Zedek, Mark H. Levin, William B. Silverman; Cantor Paul C. Silbersher; Pres: Jerome Cohen; Edu: Robert E. Tornberg; Adm: Frank J. Adler; Sisterhood

Pres: Nancy Ruben; Brotherhood Pres: Lawrence R. Gelb. **712 E 69th St, Kansas City MO 64131 (816) 363–1050.**

Olivette

Genesis of St. Louis. Affiliated with UAHC. 47 mems. Rabbi Robert Blinder; Pres: Charlotte Cohen; Edu: Jean Chase. **c/o Mrs Charlotte Cohen, 14 High Acres, Olivette MO 63132 (314) 994–0787.**

Sedalia

Temple Beth El. Affiliated with UAHC. 14 mems. Rabbi Abe Rosenthal; Pres: Phil Scissors. **232 S Dundee St, Sedalia MO 65301 (816) 826–3392.**

Shawnee Mission

Kansas City Jewish Chronicle. Weekly J newspaper for the benefit & readership of J in Western MO & Eastern KS. To inform, educate, amuse & inspire the J readership. F in 1920. The newspaper is privately owned although it works closely with the J Fed of Greater KS City, Is Bonds, & the Rabbinical Assn of Greater KS City. Editor & Pres: Milton Firestone; Pub & VP: Stanley J. Rose. **7375 W 107 St, Shawnee Mission KS 66212 (913) 648–4620; mailing add: PO Box 8709, Kansas City MO 64114.**

Springfield

United Hebrew Congregation. Affiliated with UAHC. 57 mems. Rabbi Solomon K. Kaplan; Cantor Ernest Tarrasch; Pres: Harry Federow; Edu: Sandra Asher; Adm: Steve Broidy; Sisterhood Pres: Gloria Martin. **931 S Kickapoo, Springfield MO 65804 (417) 866–4760.**

St. Joseph

B'nai Sholom. Pres: Sol Stein. **615 N 10th St, St Joseph MO 64501.**

Temple Adath Joseph. Affiliated with UAHC. 117 mems. Rabbi Wolfgang Hamburger; Pres: Gary Rosenthal; Sisterhood Pres: Louise Leibowitz. **17th & Felix Sts, St Joseph MO 64501 (816) 279–3179.**

United Jewish Fund of St. Joseph. Mem of CJF. Organized 1915. Pres: Simon Polsky; Exec Sec: Ann Saferstein. **2903 Sherman Ave, St Joseph MO 64506 (816) 279–3436.**

St. Louis

B'nai B'rith Hillel Foundation. 6300 Forsyth Blvd, St Louis MO 63105 (314) 726–6177.

B'nai B'rith Hillel Foundation Library. 6300 Forsyth Blvd, St Louis MO 63105 (314) 726–6177.

B'nai El Temple. Affiliated with UAHC. 465 mems. Rabbis: Jerrold M. Levy, Bertram Klausner; Pres: Boris Tureen; Edu: Janet Newman; Sisterhood Pres: Trudy Levy; Brotherhood Pres: Lewis Levey. **11411 Highway 40, St Louis MO 63131 (314) 432–6393.**

B'nai El Temple Library. For information on the Temple, see – B'nai El Temple, St Louis, MO. **11411 Highway 40, St Louis MO 63131 (314) 432–6393.**

Brith Sholom Kneseth Israel Congregation. Affiliated with United Syn of Am. Rabbi Benson Skoff; Cantor Paul Stone; Pres: Yusef Hakimian; Exec Dir: Milton Rossner. **1107 Linden Ave, St Louis MO 63117 (314) 725–6230.**

Central Agency for Jewish Education. 225 S Meramec, Suite 400, St Louis MO 63105 (314) 862–0606.

Central Agency for Jewish Education, Klausner Library. 225 S Meramec, Suite 400, St Louis MO 63105 (314) 862–0606.

Congregation B'nai Amoona. Conservative Syn affiliated with United Syn of Am. Rel Servs; Rel Sch; Presch. 1,000 families. F in 1882 as an Orthodox Syn & fr 1916 has identified itself with the Conservative movement. The Cong maintains two bldgs – the edu complex houses the Rel Sch & the Solomon Schechter Day Sch of St Louis, adm offs of the Syn, the rabbi's & hazzan's studies; the sanctuary is located at 524 Trinity in Univ City. Erected in 1950, it is one of the earliest examples of modern syn architecture to be found in the US with extensive use of concrete & glass. Rabbi Bernard Lipnick; Assc Rabbi Jeffrey Cohen; Cantor Leon S. Lissek; Pres: Maurice Gordon; Exec Dir: Phillip Polsky; Edu Supervisor: Rabbi Jeffrey Cohen; Prin Lower Grades Prog: Sherry Hecht; Prin Upper Grades, Prog & Youth Dir: Dana Scott. **324 S Mason Rd, St Louis MO 63141 (314) 576–9990.**

Congregation Kol Am. Affiliated with UAHC. 130 mems. Rabbi Bruce Diamond; Pres: Carl Smith. **11155 Clayton Rd, St Louis MO 63131 (314) 569–0797.**

Jewish Community Relations Council. Social servs agy. Constituent agy of Natl J Com Relations Adv Council funded by J Fed. To promote understanding & support for Is; to assist Russian J; to secure equal opportunity; to improve inter-group relations; to combat anti-Semitism. Intl com relations concerns: progs to support Is & efforts on behalf of Soviet J; church-state & interreligious relationships: concern for protection of rel liberty for all Am especially the rel rights of J, cooperation with other rel groups & individuals on projs of mutual concern including provision of information material & speakers to the Christian com, provision of material on the Holocaust to cols & HS, distribution of sch calendar indicating J Holy Days to schs; equal opportunity: activities to gain civil rights & housing & employment for all Am, com efforts to eliminate hunger; J security & anti-Semitism: monitoring of various hate groups, investigation of instances of alleged discrimination & counseling of victims of discrimination. The Council consists of 13 constituent orgs & six reps-at-large. The J Com Relations Council began with coordination within the St Louis com against pro-Nazi, anti-Semitic groups during the 1930's. Following WWII, the agy broadened its outlook & attempted to secure equal rights for all citizens. With creation of the State of Is, the Council embarked on edu progs relating to the importance, needs & views of the State. Recently, the Council conducted campaigns to aid Soviet J. Exec Dir: Norman A. Stack. **722 Chestnut St, Suite 1019, St Louis MO 63101 (314) 241–2584**

Jewish Federation of St. Louis. Mem of CJF. Includes St Louis County. Organized 1901. St Louis Light. Pres: Harris J. Frank; Exec VP: Martin S. Kraar. **411 N Seventh St, Suite 1700, St Louis MO 63101 (314) 621–8120.**

Missouri Jewish Post & Opinion. Periodical pub. **8235 Olive St, St Louis MO 63132 (314) 993–2842.**

Pioneer Women – Na'amat. The training & edu of the Is woman & her family so that each can be best equipped to lead productive lives. For additional information, see – Pioneer Women Na'amat, New York City, NY. **8123 Delmar Blvd, St Louis MO 63130 (314) 721–5856.**

Solomon Schechter Day School of St. Louis. Affiliated with Solomon Schechter Day Schs Assn. Prin: Rabbi Howard Siegel; Chr: Harold Guller. **324 S Mason Rd, St Louis MO 63141.**

St. Louis Center for Holocaust Studies. Edu resource ctr affiliated with St Louis J Fed. To intelligently communicate to all peoples the hist & lessons of this human tragedy. Focuses attention on: coordinating Holocaust related progs & projects in St Louis area; developing Holocaust curriculum material for use in J, Catholic & public schs; assisting teachers, academics, clergymen, youth group leaders, stu, artists & lay people in the org of Holocaust related events; maintaining a library & multi-media resource ctr; coordinating an Oral Hist Proj; bringing in films, lecturers & exhibitions to the St Louis area & programming the annual Yom Hashoa Commemoration. Library contains 5,000 vols (Holocaust, 2nd World War, fascism & anti-Semitism). 3 employees. Est by the St Louis J Fed in 1977. Facilities include audio-visual resource ctr, teachers' learning rm, library, exhibition hall & meeting rms. Major Holocaust audio-visual resource ctr in the US; published an interfaith, interdiscipline curriculum on St Maximillian Kolbe. Dir: Warren Green; Chr: Bernard Levin. **10957 Schuetz Rd, St Louis MO 63141 (314) 432–0020.**

St. Louis Center for Holocaust Studies, Library. Library contains 5,000 vols (holocaust, WWII, fascism & anti-Semitism). For information on the Ctr, see – St Louis Center for Holocaust Studies, St Louis, MO. **10957 Schuetz Rd, St Louis MO 63141 (314) 432–0020.**

Temple Emanuel. Reform Temple affiliated with UAHC. Rel worship servs, child & adult edu & gen life enhancement. Worship Servs; edu; counseling by rabbi; occasional social events; Sun Sch; library containing 3,000 vols (gen J). 350 families; 180 stu in grades K–10. 5 employees; 15 volunteers. F 1956. Pub Emanuscript (monthly). Facilities include kitchen, sanctuary seating 1000, 20 classrms. Rabbi J.R. Rosenbloom; Pres: Richard Marx; VPs: William Nussbaum, David Levy; Treas: Robert Scharff; Sec: Zena Hellman. **12166 Conway Rd, St Louis MO 63141 (314) 432–5877.**

Temple Emanuel Library. Library contains 3,000 vols (gen J). For information on the Temple see– Temple Emanuel, St Louis MO. **12166 Conway Rd, St Louis MO 63141 (314) 432–5877.**

Temple Israel. Reform J Cong affiliated with UAHC. Dedicated to the serv of God & to the enhancement of J faith by its mems. Sisterhood; Brotherhood; Youth Group; Singles Group; Young Married Group; Retirees Group. 1553 mems. F 1886. Owns 111 acre camp ground near Troy MO; summer camp also maintained. Rabbi Alvan D. Rubin, Rabbi Gary A. Huber, Rabbi Martin W. Levy; Pres: Paul P. Weil; 1st VP: Merle L. Silverstein; 2nd VP: Arthur A. Silverman; 3rd VP: Irwin B. Hoffman; Treas: Louis

B. Loebner; Asst Treas: Warner Isaacs; Sec: Mrs Harold W. Dubinsky; Asst Sec: Sanford A. Silvertein. **10675 Ladue Rd, St Louis MO 63141 (314) 432–8050.**

Temple Shaare Emeth. Reform J Cong affilited with UAHC. Complete prog of worship & edu activities including a Rel Sch of 825 stu, mid-week Heb Sch of 225 stu, & Nursery Sch of 125 stu. 1,500 families. F in 1867. Sr Rabbi Dr Jeffrey Stiffman; Asst Rabbis: Rabbi James Stone Goodman, Rabbi Susan Talve; Cantor Edward R. Fogel; Dir of Edu: Marsha Grazman; Exec Dir: Jeanette Bleiweiss; Pres: Bernard Pasternak. **11645 Ladue Rd, St Louis MO 63141 (314) 569–0010.**

UAHC Midwest Council. Rel & edu org serving J congs throughout the US & Canada. To encourage & aid the org & dev of J congs; to promote J edu, & enrich & intensify J life; to foster other activities for the perpetuation & advancement of J. For additional information, see – UAHC – Union of American Hebrew Congregations, New York City, NY. Pres: Ted Pallet; Dir: Rabbi Eric Yoffie; Asst Dir: Rabbi Ronald Klotz. **8420 Delmar Blvd, Suite 304, St Louis MO 63124 (314) 997–7566.**

United Hebrew Congregation. Affiliated with UAHC. 1626 mems. Rabbis: Jerome W. Grollman, Kenneth E. Ehrlich; Cantor Murray Hochberg; Pres: Stanley Laiderman; Edu: Lois Winthrop; Adm: Richard J. Weinstein; Sisterhood Pres: Eleanor Kean; Brotherhood Pres: Gene Pattiz. **225 S Skinner Blvd, St Louis MO 63105 (314) 726–4666.**

University City

Nusach Hari – B'nai Zion Congregation. Orthodox Cong affiliated with Union of Orthodox J Cong of Am. Sun Torah Sch; Adult Edu Prog including Bible class, Talmud & Shulchan Aruch classes; Sisterhood; Men's Club; PTA; NCSY Youth Group. Nusach Hari was f as a minyan of men fr Russia & davened in accordance with the liturgy of the ARI in 1901; the syn was chartered as a cong in 1905; Bnai Zion Cong was organized as a minyan in 1908 & chartered in 1918; merger took place in 1961. Rabbi Aaron Borow; Pres: Adolph Gelb; Hon Pres: Hyman Spritz; Hon VP: Sol Klarfeld; Hon Gabbai: Aaron Fishman; VPs: Sam Bluestein, Alan Zarkowsky, Dr Craig Berkin, Lenny Alper; Sec: Myron Yolkut; Treas: Joel Schraier; Sgt-at-Arms: Byron Cohen; Gabbaim: Walter Richtman, Howard Belsky; Trustees: Irving Abitz, Irvin Alper, Maurice Apple, Louis I. Cohen, Hyman Feder, Marvin Goldstein, Sol Klarfeld, Joseph Novack, Sidney Silverman, Hyman Spritz; Bd of Dirs: Margaret Adelstein, Ben Adelstein, Lenny Alper, Morris Belsky, Sol Benjamin, Julius Berg, Dr Craig Berkin, Mildred Drifon, Mike Frederick, Morris Fredlich, Esther Gelb, Betty Goldstein, Victor Grossman, Paul Lelchook, Leon Lumerman, Ronald Makovsky, Ruth Mendelson, Emanuel Millman, Morris Mitchell, Joseph Needle, Ruth Novack, Ted Pevnick, Joe Radman, Walter Richtman, George Rosenberg, Dina Rothman, Dr Robert Rubin, Jack Rubin, Frank Schneider, Ann Schneider, Dan Schultz, David Sherp, Phyllis Silverman, Bess Spritz, Paul Spritz, Dr Herbert Sunshine, Dr Mark Tversky, Charles Waxman, Scott Waxman, Jack Yakovitz; Hon Bd mem: Sophie Osheroff. **8630 Olive Blvd, University City MO 63132 (314) 991–2100.**

Shaare Zedek. Affiliated with United Syn of Am. Rabbi Zalman M. Stein; Pres: H. David Hartstein; Adm Dir: Mollie Frohlichstein; Edu Dir: Doris Zinn. **829 N Hanley Rd, University City MO 63130 (314) 727–1747.**

MONTANA

Billings

Beth Aaron. Affiliated with UAHC. 45 mems. Rabbi Samuel Horowitz; Pres: Martha Robinson. **1148 N Bdwy, Billings MT 59101 (406) 248–6412.**

Butte

B'nai Israel Congregation. 327 W Galena St, Butte MT 59701 (406) 792–9330.

NEBRASKA

Lincoln

Congregation B'nai Jeshurun. Reform Temple affiliated with UAHC. Rel Servs; Sisterhood; edu progs; Rel Sch; com involvement; library containing 400 vols. 105 mems. F 1884. Pub Bulletin (monthly). Facilities include sanctuary, rabbi's study, library, classrms, kitchen, gift shop. Rabbi Kenneth White. **20th & South Sts, Lincoln NE 68502 (402) 435–8004.**

Congregation Tifereth Israel. Affiliated with United Syn of Am. Rabbi Mark J. Bisman; Pres: Harry Allen. **3219 Sheridan Blvd, Lincoln NE 68502 (402) 423–8569.**

The Lincoln Jewish Welfare Federation, Inc. Mem of CJF. Organized 1931; Inc 1961. Pres: Gerald Grant; Exec Dir: Herbert F. Gaba. **PO Box 80014, Lincoln NE 68501 (402) 435–0230.**

Omaha

Anti-Defamation League of B'nai B'rith – Plains State Regional Office. Dedicated in purpose & prog to translating the Am heritage of democratic ideals into a way of life for all Am, & to countering assaults on the safety, status, rights & image of J. For additional information, see – Anti-Defamation League of B'nai B'rith, New York City, NY. **333 S 132nd St, Omaha NE 68154.**

Beth El Synagogue. Affiliated with United Syn of Am. Rabbi Kenneth Bromberg; Cantor Emil Berkovits; Pres: Kenneth Sacks; Exec Dir: Merle Potash; Edu Dir: Stanley Mitchell; Youth Dir: Dr Raymond Goldstein. **210 S 49th St, Omaha NE 68132 (402) 553–3221.**

Jewish Community Center. 333 S 132 St, Omaha NE 68154 (402) 334–8200.

Jewish Federation of Omaha. The central fundraising, planning, & budgeting agy for the Omaha J Com. Bureau for the Aging; Com Relations Cttee; Dept of J Edu; JCC; J Family Servs; J Fed Library; J Press. Conducts an annual Fed Campaign which raises funds to meet J obligations in Omaha, across the nation & overseas. Est in 1903. Pres: Paul G. Cohen; 1st VP: Don W. Greenberg; VPs: Sanford Friedman, Howard Kaslow; Sec: Marvin Polikov; Treas: Paul Epstein; Exec Dir: Louis B. Solomon. **333 S 132nd St, Omaha NE 68154 (402) 334–8200.**

Jewish Federation of Omaha Library. 16,000 bks, 1,100 bound periodical vols, 2,500 records, 600 films, 1,000 filmstrips, 1,000 pamphlets; Subjects: J rel & philosophy, Biblical commentary & research, J literature, fiction, J art, hist & Is; subscribes to 70 journals & five newspapers; interlibrary loan; copying servs; collections on Comparative Rel, Marc Chagall, Holocaust. Staff has compiled a detailed expansion of Weine classification for Holocaust collection. Open to public. Index to Jewish Press (Omaha). For information on the Ins, see – Jewish Federation of Omaha, Omaha, NE. Library Dir: Edythe Wolf. **333 S 132nd St, Omaha NE 68154 (402) 334–8200.**

Temple Israel. Affiliated with UAHC. 674 mems. Rabbis: Sidney H. Brooks, Barry L. Weinstein; Cantor Harold I. Firestone; Pres: Michael M. Erman; Sisterhood Pres: Joie Simon; Brotherhood Pres: William Wasserkrug. **7023 Cass St, Omaha NE 68132 (402) 556–6536.**

NEVADA

Las Vegas

Congregation Ner Tamid. Affiliated with UAHC. 215 mems. Rabbi Melvin Hecht; Pres: David Wasserman; Sisterhood Pres: Phyllis H. Mark. **4412 S Maryland Pkwy, Las Vegas NV 89109 (702) 733–6292.**

Jewish Family Service Agency. Non-sectarian counseling agy affiliated with the Assn of J Family & Chil Agy, & Combined J Appeal. To strengthen the individual, the family & the com. Individual & group counseling on a variety of family problems: parent chil problems, single parent-chil relationships, individual, widow, marital & pre-marital problems, divorce, parenting & needs, & problems of the older population; homemaker mgmnt servs; information & referral servs, pipeline to Drs, lawyers, psychiatrists, public health, welfare, housing authorities, & other social servs & com orgs; volunteer prog; case advocacy; family life edu; Russian resettlement. The agy is in the process of setting up a home health care prog for the sr & disabled in the com. Est in 1977 by leaders of the J com who felt there was a need for an agy to provide counseling & concrete supportive servs to the com. Exec Dir: Alan L. Morger; Bd of Dirs: Marti Ashcraft, Dr Alvin Blumberg, Naomi Cherry, Jerry Countess, Fay Cramer, Blanche H. Feinberg, Dr Marv Glovinsky, Ruth Goldfarb, Ruth Hanusa, Bea Levinson, Arthur Liebert, Marc H. Ratner, Harvey Riceberg, Alan Roselinsky, Gertrude Rudiak, Linda Silvestri, Mary Stivers, Les Sully, Dr John Van Vactor, Eli Welt, Flora Mason, Herb Pastor, Ruth Pearson, Myrna Williams. **1555 E Flamingo Rd, Suite 125, Las Vegas NV 89109 (702) 732–0304.**

Jewish Federation of Las Vegas. Mem of CJF. Organized 1973. Pub Jewish Reporter. Pres: Hon Bill Hernstadt; Exec Dir: Jerome D. Countess. **1030 E Twain Ave, Las Vegas NV 89109 (702) 732–0556.**

Las Vegas Israelite. Periodical pub. **PO Box 14096, Las Vegas NV 89114 (702) 876–1255.**

Temple Beth Sholom. Conservative Temple affiliated with United Syn of Am. Rel Servs; Presch Nursery; Pre-K; Heb Sch, Primary–HS; Bar/Bat Mitzvah training; Sun Sch, K–Pre Confirmation & Confirmation; USY, Jr USY, AZA, BBG youth groups; summer prog for chil in Camp Sholom, Kinder Kamp & Camp Masada; Adult Edu classes; Sisterhood; Men's Club; Sr Group; Adult & Youth Choirs. Bulletin. The Temple's faclities include a recreation ctr, social hall, library & reading rm; Memorial Park Cemetery Grounds. Rabbi Kalman Appel; Cantor Simon Bergman; Pres: Herb Kaufman; Exec Dir: Leo A. Wilner. **1600 E Oakey Blvd, Las Vegas NV 89104 (702) 384–5070.**

Reno

Temple Emanu-El. Affiliated with United Syn of Am. Rabbi Irnie A. Nadler; Cantor Sam Silverberg; Pres: Dr Leonard Schapiro; Edu Dir: Marty Gutride; Youth Dirs: David & Beverly Brondz. **1031 Manzanita Lane, at the corner of Lakeside Dr, Reno NV 89509 (702) 825–5600.**

Temple Sinai. Reform Temple affiliated with UHAC, Natl Fed of Temple Sisterhoods. To offer a full range of servs to Reform J; to represent Reform J in northern NV. Shabbat & Festival Servs; life-cycle ceremonies; Rel Sch grades K–10; Adult Edu; Sisterhood; library containing 300 vols (Judaica). 90 mems; 40 stu in grades K–10. 2 employees. F 1962; bldg dedicated 1970. Pub Sentinel (monthly). Facilities include sanctuary seating 150; Judaica shop; kitchen. Rabbi Paul Tuchman; Rel Sch Dir: Eric Hobson; Pres: Ruth Dickens; Sisterhood Pres: Maggi Kennedy. **PO Box 3114, Reno NV 89505 (702) 747–9927.**

NEW HAMPSHIRE

Claremont

Temple Meyer David. High St, Claremont NH 03743 (603) 542–6773.

Concord

Temple Beth Jacob. Affiliated with UAHC. 129 mems. Rabbi Arnold M. Fertig; Cantor Donna Goldfarb; Pres: Joann Myers; Edu: Gayle Crane; Sisterhood Pres: Marlene Larsen. **67 Bdwy, Concord NH 03301 (603) 228–8581.**

Dover

Temple Israel. 4 & Grove Sts, Dover NH 03820 (603) 742–3976.

Laconia

Temple B'nai Israel. Affiliated with UAHC. 56 mems. Pres: Manuel F. Gordon. **PO Box 160, Laconia NH 03246 (603) 524–1276.**

Manchester

Jewish Federation of Greater Manchester. Mem of CJF. Organized 1974. Pres: Arnold Cohen; Exec Dir: Robert D. Jolton. **698 Beech St, Manchester NH 03104 (603) 627–7679.**

Temple Adath Yeshurun. Affiliated with UAHC. 354 mems. Rabbi Arthur Starr; Cantor Gerald Weinberg; Pres: Bernard Rakoff; Edu: Beth Ann Salzman; Sisterhood Pres: Millie Rosenberg; Brotherhood Pres: Lee Dorson. **152 Prospect St, Manchester NH 03104 (603) 669–5650.**

Temple Israel. Affiliated with United Syn of Am. Rabbi Richard Polirer; Pres: Charlotte Gross; Exec Dir: Rabbi Richard Polirer. **678 Pine St, Manchester NH 03104 (603) 622–6171.**

Nashua

Temple Beth Abraham. Affiliated with United Syn of Am. Rabbi Gerald Weiss; Pres: Arthur Krulik; Exec VP: Ronald Weiss; Edu Dir: Marlene Shaw; Youth Dir: George Kessler. **4 Raymond St, Nashua NH 03060 (603) 883–8184.**

Portsmouth

Temple Israel. Affiliated with United Syn of Am. Rabbi Arnold Bienstock; Pres: Louis Schwartz. **200 State St, Portsmouth NH 03801.**

NEW JERSEY

Aberdeen

Temple Beth Ahm. Affiliated with United Syn of Am. Rabbi Gary L. Atkins; Cantor Jeffrey Shiovitz; Pres: Stuart A. Abraham; Prin Rel Sch: Helayne Sotnikoff. **550 Lloyd Rd, Aberdeen NJ 07747 (201) 583–1700.**

Temple Beth Ahm Library. For information on the Temple, see – Temple Beth Ahm, Aberdeen, NJ. **550 Lloyd Rd, Aberdeen NJ 07747 (201) 583–1700.**

Temple Shalom. Affiliated with UAHC. 570 mems. Rabbi Henry M. Weiner; Pres: Norman Katz; Edu: Ruth Birnbaum; Sisterhood Pres: Rynda Klein; Brotherhood Pres: Elliott Rosenthal. **5 Ayrmont Lane, Aberdeen NJ 07747 (201) 566–2621.**

Atlantic City

Community Synagogue. Affiliated with United Syn of Am. Rabbi Aaron N.H. Krauss. Pres: Saul H. Cohen. **901–903 Pacific Ave, Atlantic City NJ 08401 (609) 345–3282,3.**

Jewish Record. Periodical pub. **1537 Atlantic Ave, Atlantic City NJ 08401 (609) 344–5119.**

Bayonne

Bayonne Jewish Community Council. Mem of CJF. Pres: Dr Raphael Levine; Exec Dir: Alan J. Coren. **1050 Kennedy Blvd, Bayonne NJ 07002 (201) 436–6900.**

Jewish Family & Counseling Service of Jersey City-Bayonne. Mem of Assn of J Family & Chil Agy. To strengthen J families & individuals in Jersey City & Bayonne. Individual & family counseling; information & referral servs; J family life edu servs; consultant to J com agy. Est 1976. Exec Dir: Leah Meir; Caseworker: Aryeh Meir; Pres: Claire Frank; VPs: Abe Nutkis, Sarah Eisenberg; Rec Sec: Ruth Seftel; Corsp Sec: Shirley Porte; Treas: Edward Walker; Hon Pres: Mrs Ellis Taube, Mrs Joseph Preminger; Bd of Dirs: Pearl Abramson, Rev Meyer Auerbach, Charles Berkowitz, Mr & Mrs Mel Blum, Joel Chasis, Mrs Edward Chester, Alan J. Coren, Lothar Daniel, Nina Dobkin, Mr & Mrs Isaiah Eisenberg, Mrs Janice Epstein, Mr & Mrs Buddy Frank, Claire Frank, Hon David Friedland, Louis Heyman, Hyman Lebowitz, Max Lourie, Mrs Solomon Mangel, Mr & Mrs Joseph Novick, Alan Paul, Morris Pesin, Arnold A. Piskin, Mrs Elliot Porte, Lewis S. Ripps, Mary Sager, Dr Harry Schneider, Mrs Nathan Susskind, George Tilton, Mrs Anita Tosk, Mrs Herman Wapnowitz. **1050 Kennedy Blvd, Bayonne NJ 07002 (201) 436–1299.**

Temple Beth Am. Affiliated with UAHC. 152 mems. Rabbi Harold F. Caminker; Cantor Lee Fowler; Pres: David Levinson; Sisterhood Pres: Gloria Glanzer; Brotherhood Pres: Herman Zablotsky. **111 Ave B, Bayonne, NJ 07002 (201) 858–2020.**

Temple Emanu-El of Bayonne. Affiliated with United Syn of Am. Rabbi Zachary I. Heller; Cantor Marshall Wise; Pres: Phyllis Levine. **735 Kennedy Blvd, Bayonne NJ 07002 (201) 436–4499.**

Yeshiva of Hudson County. 5 Bergen Ct, Bayonne NJ 07002.

Yeshiva of Hudson County Library. 5 Bergen Ct, Bayonne NJ 07002.

Belleville

Ahavath Achim. Affiliated with United Syn of Am. Rabbi Noah M. Burstein; Pres: Joseph Berkowitz. **125 Academy St, Belleville NJ 07109 (201) 759–9731.**

Bergenfield

Bergenfield-Dumont Jewish Center. Affiliated with United Syn of Am. Rabbi Dr Jerome H. Blass;

Cantor David Barbalatt; Pres: Wallace D. Ross; Edu Dir: Sara Soltes. **169 N Washington Ave, Bergenfield NJ 07621 (201) 384–3911.**

Bloomfield

Temple Ner Tamid. Affiliated with United Syn of Am & UAHC. Rabbis Nathan H. Fish, Steve C. Kushner; Cantor Kevin D. Wartell; Pres: Gerald M. Stein; Edu Dir: Susan L. Nanus; Youth Dir: Ronald Sheps. **936 Broad St, Bloomfield NJ 07003 (201) 338–6482.**

Boonton

Temple Beth Sholom. Affiliated with United Syn of Am. Rabbi Gerald Chirnomas; Pres: Steve Weitzman; Edu Dir: Bruce Degan. **Harrison St, Boonton NJ 07005 (201) 334–2714.**

Bound Brook

Congregation Knesseth Israel. Affiliated with United Syn of Am. Rabbi Aaron Decter; Cantor Bernard Knee; Pres: Nachum Bar–Din; Edu Dir: Rabbi Shmuel Shimoni. **229 Mountain Ave, Bound Brook NJ 08805 (201) 356–1634.**

Bricktown

Temple Beth Or. Affiliated with United Syn of Am. Rabbi Robert E. Fierstien; Pres: Alan Taubenkimel. **200 Van Zile Rd, Bricktown NJ 08723 (201) 458–4700.**

Bridgeton

Congregation Beth Abraham. Affiliated with United Syn of Am. Rabbi Samuel M. Burstein DD; Pres: Ed Fisher; Edu Dir: Irving Silverman; Exec Sec: Diane Randolph. **Fayette St & Belmont Ave, Bridgeton NJ 08302 (609) 451–7652.**

Bridgewater

Solomon Schechter Day School of Central New Jersey. Affiliated with Solomon Schechter Day Schs Assn. Prin: Lauren Siwoff; Chr: Dr Daniel Frimmer. **North Bridge St, PO Box 6007, Bridgewater NJ 08807 (201) 722–2089.**

Temple Sholom. Affiliated with United Syn of Am. Rabbi Ronald H. Isaacs PhD; Cantor Natan Fetman; Pres: Arthur A. Gertzman; Edu Dir: Tina Zegas; Youth Dir: Allan Halperin. **PO Box 6007, North Bridge St, Bridgewater NJ 08807.**

Caldwell

Congregation Agudath Israel of West Essex. Affiliated with United Syn of Am. Rabbi Alan Silverstein; Rabbi Emeritus Morris Werb; Cantor Bruce Ruben; Pres: Mayer Kass; Exec Sec: Deena Hollander. **20 Academy Rd, Caldwell NJ 07006 (201) 226–3600.**

Carteret

Carteret Jewish Community Center. Affiliated with United Syn of Am. Rabbi Hyman Weissman; Pres: Sam Breslow. **Leick & Noe Sts, Carteret NJ 07008 (201) 541–5500.**

Cedar Grove

Temple Shalom of West Essex. Reform Temple affiliated with UAHC. Rel Servs Fri evening, Sat, holidays; Thanksgiving Interfaith Servs; Holocaust Memorial Day Yom Ha'Shoa Servs; Rel Sch K-9th grade; Nursery Sch; Bar/Bat Mitzvah; Confirmation prog; summer progs; col servs; library; Adult Edu; youth groups; Brotherhood; Sisterhood; holiday gatherings; Shabbatons; parties; dances; Purim Carnival; picnics; assistance in times of need. Approximately 375 families with 290 chil attending classes. 35 J families formed a social group in 1953, & in 1954 the J com of Cedar Grove held their first rel servs at a local church. In 1956 the original bldg was erected. The Cong chose the name Temple Shalom of Cedar Grove. In 1968 the name of the Cong was changed to Temple Shalom of W Essex. In Jun of 1972 the sanctuary, Oneg Shabbat area, social hall, library & offs were dedicated. The Nursery Sch was initiated in 1973. In 1978 ground was broken for a new wing to provide an all-purpose rm, youth lounge, storage space & expanded classrm space. The Ad Book; Membership Brochure; memorial bk 'These We Remember' pub for the Yizkor Memorial Serv on Yom Kippur; Shabbat Shalom flyer; The Shofar (monthly bulletin); Treasures/Acquisitions bk in the library containing photographs & descriptions of the Cong's major ritual & art objects including name of donor, historical details, & information on the artist/craftsman. Syn facilities include: large sanctuary, memorial alcove, mus, judaica shop, Benefactor's Wall, bride's rm. Rabbi Norman Patz; Pres: Dr Arthur Fost; VPs: Carol Beyer, Henry Brott, Howard Unker; Sec: Paula Cummis; Treas: Bruce Pritikin; Comtroller: Jerry Abrams; Trustees Chr: Robert Podvey; Trustees: Harold Adler, Jacob Balk, Alan Greene, Ronald Kaplan, Bernard Koslowsky, Philip Kupchik, Edward Maged, Samuel Oolie; Edu Dir: Norman Greenberg; Adm Sec: Dorothey Schept. **760 Pompton Ave, Cedar Grove NJ 07009 (201) 239–1321.**

Cherry Hill

Bureau of Jewish Education. A dept of J Fed of S NJ. The central agy of the J com in the area of J edu. To promote & improve the delivery of J edu heritage so that fellow J strike deep roots into J past, identify Jewishly at present, & convey this knowledge & experience to the next generation. Funds for specialists provided to schs; maintains library, media ctr; pedagogic conf; Edu Council; Teacher Creativity Ctr; Ins of J Studies; related servs including teacher licensure, edu consultation, communications, teacher recruitment, special edu, family edu, J edu for Russian immigrants, J edu for HS stu, cooperation with other agy in planning: Yom Ha'Shoah, Walkathon, Yom Ha'atzmaoot, J Bk Month. Affiliated schs: Beit Ya'akov; Beth El; Beth Jacob; Beth Is; Beth Tikvah; Beth Torah; Har Zion; JCC Nursery; Kellman Academy; Midrashah; M'Kor Shalom; Sons of Is; Temple Beth Shalom; Temple Emanuel, C.H.; Temple Emanu-El, Will; Temple Sinai. Pres: Dr Bertram Greenspun; VPs: Dr Harris Colton, Leonard Feldman, Morton Mann; Exec Dir: Reuven Yalon; Midrashah Prin: Steven Wenick; Edu Consultant: Beverly Rose; Special Edu Head Teacher: Deborah Shrier; Teacher Creativity Ctr Dir: Dalia Eichhorn; Librarian: Rene Batterman; Sec: Arlene Cooper. **2393 W Marlton Pike, Cherry Hill NJ 08002 (609) 662–6300.**

Congregation Beth El. Affiliated with United Syn of Am. Rabbi Howard Kahn; Cantor Louis Herman; Pres: Herbert V. Kolosky; Exec Dir: Sidney Someth; Edu Dir: Rabbi Isaac Furman. **PO Box 481, 2901 W Chapel Ave, Cherry Hill NJ 08003.**

Harry B. Kellman Academy. Affiliated with Solomon Schechter Day Schs Assn. Prin: Rabbi Isaac Furman; Chr: David Roitman. **2901 W Chapel Ave, Cherry Hill NJ 08002 (609) 667–1300.**

Jewish Community Center. Social, cultural & recreational progs; summer day camp prog; pre-sch nursery; clubs; hobby classes; specialized courses; lectures; sr citizen orgs. Ctr servs as a meeting place for orgs. A 90 day complimentary membership & free brochure are available to new residents of the J com. Facilities include: swimming pool, gymnasium & health club. Pres: Bertram Berman; Exec Dir: Argje Shaw. **2395 W Marlton Pike, Cherry Hill NJ 08002 (609) 662–8800.**

Jewish Community Relations Council, Jewish Federation of Southern New Jersey. A beneficiary of Allied J Appeal of Southern NJ. Serves as the instrument through which the J com maintains relations with the gen com; attempts to be rep of all shades of opinion within the J com by seeking representation fr every J org; gives public expression on views & issues of concern such as Soviet J, Middle E, church state relations, civil liberties & anti-Semitism; seeks to build support on these critical issues; welcomes & encourages comment & inquiries. Exec Dir: Alan Respler; Pres: Dr Jacob Farber; VPs: Miriam Davis, Mark Jacobs, Evelyn Levit. **2393 W Marlton Pike, Cherry Hill NJ 08002 (609) 665–6100.**

Jewish Family Service. Counseling & guidance to individuals, couples & families; servs to the elderly & ill; emergency fin assistance; assistance to new Am requiring help with their resettlement; J Family Life Edu Prog. **2393 W Marlton Pike, Cherry Hill NJ 08002 (609) 662–8611; Burlington Cty Ext 2 E River Dr, Willingboro NJ 08046 (609) 871–1450.**

Jewish Federation of Southern New Jersey. Central org of the J com. To enrich the quality of J life. Planning, budgeting, est & maintenance of all communal & social welfare servs on behalf of the entire J com; sponsors yearly campaign of Allied J Appeal which supports local, natl & overseas agy & servs. Pres: Leonard Wolf; Exec VP: Stuart Alperin. **2393 W Marlton Pike, Cherry Hill NJ 08002 (609) 665–6100.**

Jewish Geriatric Home. To provide for the happiness & care of individuals no longer able to live in their own home & who require the specialized care that only a quality nursing home can provide. Med & social servs; rel & cultural progs. **3025 W Chapel Ave, Cherry Hill NJ 08002 (609) 667–3100.**

Temple Emanuel. Affiliated with UAHC, & with PA Council of Reform Syns, & the Fed of Reform Syn of Greater Phila. To provide an inspiration & a rel focus in the tradition of the Reform J Movement. Sabbath & Holiday Rel Servs; Rel Sch – primary grades K–2, intermediate grades 3–5, Shabbat Studies for grades 6–7, Confirmation Academy for grades 8–10, Confirmation Class, Jr & Sr Study Series for grades 11 & 12; Heb Dept for grades 3–12; Jr & Sr HS Dinners with the Rabbi; Happy Days which provides Shabbat celebrations for chil K–5 & their families; Teen Canteen for 6th–8th graders to get together on Shabbat evening for dinner, Havdalah & social activity; Pre-Sch for 3 & 4 yr olds; Adult Edu; Sisterhood; Sisterhood Study Group; Brotherhood; Temple Youth Group; Young Couples Club; Havurah; Singles Again Group; Human Resources Cttee; library; panels & speakers. 700 families. F in 1950 in Camden NJ. After seven yrs in temporary quarters, ground breaking ceremonies for the construction of the present bldg took place on Nov

10, 1957. The bldg was completed in the fall of 1959. Since then, two additional wings have been added. Temple facilities include two large auditoriums with stage & a kitchen for social functions. For the High Holidays, the auditorium & sanctuary becomes one large place of worship seating 1,000 people. The bldg also contains the rabbis' studies, a small chapel, an adm off, classrooms, & a youth lounge. New stained glass windows in the sanctuary symbolize the Six Days of Creation. Rabbi Edwin N. Soslow; Assc Rabbi & Edu Dir: Jerome P. David; Rabbi Emeritus Dr Herbert M. Yarrish; Prin Rel Sch: Helene Cohen; Cantor Robert Gerber; Pres: Shirley Chess; VPs: Ruth Bogutz, David Fendrick, Florence Greenberg; Treas: Brian Baratz; Rec Sec: Rhoda Abrams; Corsp Sec: Yvonne Cooper; Trustees: Arthur Abramowitz, Barry Bannett, Elaine Bobrove, Pearl Braunstein, Martin Brody, Dr Stanton Dietch, Judy Gerson, Arlene Greenwood, Franklin Hess, Lee Hymerling, Donald Kapel, Dr Gary Kaplan, Robert Karpf, Irving Koffler, Robert Paul, Arthur Pierce, Herbert Ray, Lucille Ray, Dr Henry Raich, Gerald Rosenfield, Edward Sattin, Dr Matthew Shechtman, Howard Simonoff, Bonnie Weiner; Sisterhood Pres: Lucille Ray; Brotherhood Pres: Dr Matthew Shechtman. **Cooper River Pkwy & Donahue, Cherry Hill NJ 08002 (609) 665–0888.**

Temple Emanuel Library. For information on the Temple, see – Temple Emanuel, Cherry Hill, NJ. **Cooper River Pkwy & Donahue, Cherry Hill NJ 08002 (609) 665–0888.**

The Voice. To dev an enlightened & informed J com on vital issues. Pub every two weeks. Reaches every known J family in Camden & Burlington Ctys. **2393 W Marlton Pike, Cherry Hill NJ 08002 (609) 665–6100.**

Cinnaminson

Temple Sinai. Affiliated with United Syn of Am. Heb sch; Nursery Sch; accredited library of over 1,000 bks. 10 teachers; 2 specialists in music, & arts & crafts. Est 1962. The new Jack Balaban Library dedicated by Faith & Ray Silverstein Mar 22, 1974. Rabbi Lewis Bornstein; Prin: Fred Reiss; Nursery Teachers: Nancy Davis, Lynn Grobman; Nursery Aides: Sunny Johnson, Bobbi Herman; Librarian: Elaine Cohen. **New Albany Rd & Rt 130, Cinnaminson NJ 08077 (609) 829–0658, 0310.**

Temple Sinai Library. For information on the Temple, see – Temple Sinai, Cinnaminson, NJ. **New Albany Rd & Rt 130, Cinnaminson NJ 08077 (609) 829–0658.**

Clark

Temple Beth Or. Affiliated with United Syn of Am. Rabbi Jonathan D. Porath; Cantor Herbert Zaiman; Pres: Bernard Burkhoff; Adm: Lorraine Loshin; Edu Dir: Deborah Miller; Youth Dirs: Sandy & Greta Pollack. **111 Valley Rd, Clark NJ 07066 (201) 381–8403.**

Cliffside Park

Temple Israel Community Center. Affiliated with United Syn of Am. Rabbi Samuel Fraint; Pres: Jeffrey Schwartz; Edu Dir: Ora Kiel. **207 Edgewater Rd, Cliffside Park NJ 07010 (201) 945–7310.**

Clifton

Beth Sholom Reform Temple. Affiliated with UAHC. 150 mems. Rabbi Stanley Skolnik; Cantor Donn Rosensweig; Pres: Alfred L. Berman; Edu: Emanuel Frankel; Brotherhood Pres: Steven Zeisel. **733 Passaic Ave, Clifton NJ 07012 (201) 773–0355.**

Clifton Jewish Center. Conservative Syn affiliated with United Syn of Am, Natl Women's League. Rel Servs; edu progs; Sisterhood; Men's Club; adult activities; Kadima Youth Group; USY group; Women's & Men's Org; Sr Citizen Group; library containing 3,000 vols in all areas of J life & academic disciplines. 400 mems; 85 stu. 15 employees. Pub Bulletin (bi-monthly). Facilities include kosher kitchens, sanctuary, chapel, gym, meeting rms, ball rm. Pres: David Curland; VPs: Murray Bedrin, Herbert Gochman, Murray Goteiner, Dr Robert Ramer, Sally Thor; Exec Dir: Doris Jaffe. **18 Delaware St, Clifton NJ 07011 (201) 772–3131.**

Clifton Jewish Center, Library. Library contains 3,000 vols in all areas of J life & academic disciplines. For information on the Ctr, see – Clifton Jewish Center, Clifton, NJ. **18 Delaware St, Clifton NJ 07011 (201) 772–3131.**

Daughters of Miriam Center for the Aged. Orthodox ins accredited by the Commis on Accreditation of Hosps; Rehabilitation Facilities; Joint Commis on Accreditation of Hosps; approved by the Am Dental Assn. To provide domiciliary, hosp & skilled nursing care for aged & chronically ill men & women on an inpatient & outpatient basis; to maintain & operate all facilities devoted to the foregoing purposes in accordance with the J faith & in faithful adherence to & observance of the precepts, traditions, customs & dietary laws thereof.

Geriatric Ctr that includes a long term care facility, day care prog, Sheltered Workshop, sr citizen apts, Outpatient Dept; Daily Rel Servs (full time rabbi); Sabbath Servs, Oneg Shabbat, Holiday Servs; Torah Study Group; Bible Study Group; Seders with family; arts & crafts; exercise classes; dramatics, choral groups; movies; discussion groups, parties & socials; outings; holiday celebrations; cultural events; horticulture; work activities; Sheltered Workshop; psychiatry; dentistry; podiatry; physiatry; occupational therapy; physical therapy; audiologist; dietician; inhalation therapy; speech therapy; social casework; family counseling; x–ray, EKG: library containing 2000 vols (Heb reference, fiction, large print, AV material). 3000 mems; 680 families; 3 regional groups; 15 col level – affiliation progs; 318 hosp beds; 55 med day care clients; 300 apt tenants 420 employees; 150 volunteers (full-time med dir; dietician). F as Daughters of Miriam Home for the Aged, Paterson NJ 1921; merged with B'nai Israel Home for the Aged, Passaic NJ in 1957. Pub annual Report & Ad Journal; Chronicle (quarterly). Facilities include kosher kitchen, sanctuary, gift shop, coffee shop, 13 acres, 8 bldgs, skilled nursing facility, sr citizen housing. Pres: Arthur Bodner; Exec VP: Harvey Adelsberg; Sr VP: Joel J. Steiger; VPs: Melvin Opper, Stanley Berenzweig, Milton Kleinman; Treas: Jack Birnberg. **155 Hazel St, Clifton NJ 07015 (201) 772–3700.**

Daughters of Miriam Center for the Aged, Library. Library contains 2,000 vols (Heb, reference, fiction, large print, AV materials). For information on the Ctr, see – Daughters of Miriam Ctr for the Aged, Clifton, NJ. **155 Hazel St, Clifton NJ 07015 (201) 772–3700.**

Jewish Family Service. Non-profit org serving the J coms of Passaic, Clifton, Garfield, Lodi, Rutherford, Little Falls, Wallington, & W Paterson NJ. Constituent agy of J Fed of Greater Clifton-Passaic. Individual, family & marital counseling; referrals & counseling for elderly & their chil; Passover assistance to needy; re-settlement of Russian immigrants; homemaker prog; liaison with local Fed & YMHA; referral to & cooperation with local agy & ins; J Family Life Edu Progs. One full time & one part time worker. F in 1947. Originally, the JFS was comprised of volunteers who provided servs to the com & assistance to newly arrived immigrants. In later yrs, the agy formally incorporated an exec dir/social worker plus a part time social worker. Pres: Bernice Moskowitz; VPs: Ivan Nelson, Sidney Rudolph; Sec: Pamela Sendowski; Exec Dir: Benita M. Burstein; Treas: Bobbi Hack. **199 Scoles Ave, Clifton NJ 07012 (201) 777–7638, 7961.**

Jewish Federation of Greater Clifton-Passaic. Mem of CJF. Sponsors United Jewish Campaign. Organized 1933. Pres: Morris Macy; Exec Dir: Marden Paru. **199 Scoles Ave, Clifton NJ 07012 (201) 777–7031.**

Passaic-Clifton YM-YWHA. Social serv com ctr affiliated with J Welfare Bd, NYC; J Fed of Greater Passaic-Clifton. To meet the needs of our membership in social, recreational & cultural areas. Prog servs through various depts: Nursery Sch; Chil Dept; Teen-Tween; Adult; Cultural Arts – concerts, plays, etc; Older Adults – nutrition prog; Physical Edu – gym, pool, exercise rm; Health Club; Day Camp; Nursery Camp; Teen Travel Camp; library containing 700 vols (Judaica). 3000 mems; 700 Families, 1000 individuals. 15 full-time, 80 part-time employees; 150–200 volunteers serv on approximately 25 cttees. Pub News N Notes (monthly). Facilities include kosher kitchen, auditorium, gym, pool, exercise rm, massage rm, meeting rms, ceramics rm. Pres Marvin Book; VPs: Herbert Cohen, Marc Rinzler, Cecily Cohn, Morris Yamner; Treas: Jacqueline Klein; Record Sec: Nina Adamoff. **199 Scoles Ave, Clifton NJ 07012 (201) 779–2980.**

Closter

Temple Beth El. Affiliated with UAHC. 420 mems. Rabbi Fredric Pomerantz; Cantor Shlomo Bar-Nissim; Pres: Marlys Lehmann; Edu: Evelyn L. Rotstein; Sisterhood Pres: Sandy Schneider; Brotherhood Pres: Burt Bruman. **221 Schraalenburgh Rd, Closter NJ 07624 (201) 768–5112.**

Colonia

Temple Ohev Shalom. Affiliated with United Syn of Am. Rabbi Philip Brand; Pres: Robert Zimmerman. **220 Temple Way, Colonia NJ 07067 (201) 388–7222.**

Temple Ohev Shalom, Hofmann-Dezube Memorial Library. For information on the Temple, see – Temple Ohev Shalom, Colonia, NJ. **220 Temple Way, Colonia NJ 07067 (201) 388–7222.**

Cranford

Solomon Schechter Day School of Essex & Union. Affiliated with Solomon Schechter Day Schs Assn. Prin: S. Hirsch Jacobson; Chr: Dr Judith Lax. **721 Orange Ave, Cranford NJ 07016 (201) 272–3400.**

Temple Beth El. Conservative Syn affiliated with United Syn of Am. Rel Servs; edu progs; Rel Sch; Nursery Sch; Sisterhood; Men's Club; Youth Group; Presch; library containing 2,500 vols (J subjects). 1400 mems; 400 families. 12 employees. F 65 yrs ago. Pub Bulletin (weekly). Facilities include sanctuary, social hall, gift shop, basketball ct, kosher kitchen, library, chapel, youth lounge, classrms, off. Rabbi Ronald Hoffberg; Cantor Ralph Nussbaum; Pres: Stan Eigenberg; VP: Marty Scher; Prin: Darlene Margolis. **338 Walnut Ave, Cranford NJ 07016 (201) 276–9231.**

Temple Beth El Library. Library contains 2,500 vols (J subjects). For information on the Temple, see – Temple Beth El, Cranford, NJ. **338 Walnut Ave, Cranford NJ 07016 (201) 276–9231.**

Deal Park

Jewish Federation of Greater Monmouth County. Mem of CJF. Organized 1971. Pres: Ruth Rosenfeld; Exec Dir: Marvin Relkin. **100 Grant Ave, Deal Park NJ 07723 (201) 531–6200,1.**

Dover

Adath Israel – Dover Jewish Center. Affiliated with United Syn of Am. Pres: Alan R. Beckerman. **18 Thompson Ave, Dover NJ 07801 (201) 366–0179.**

East Brunswick

East Brunswick Jewish Center. Affiliated with United Syn of Am. Rabbi Chaim A. Rogoff; Cantor Marvin Richardson; Pres: Harvey M. Flug; Edu Dir: Steven A. Solomon; Youth Dir: Ginny Kamis. **511 Ryders Lane, East Brunswick NJ 08816 (201) 257–7070.**

East Brunswick Reform Temple. Affiliated with UAHC. 370 mems. Rabbi Eric M. Milgrim; Cantor Roger J. Weisberg; Pres: Arnold P. Brown; Edu: Pauline Tannenbaum; Sisterhood Pres: Sheryll Levine. **PO Box 337, East Brunswick NJ 08816 (201) 251–4300.**

East Brunswick Reform Temple Library. For information on the Temple, see – East Brunswick Reform Temple, East Brunswick, NJ. **PO Box 337, East Brunswick NJ 08816 (201) 251–4300.**

Solomon Schechter Day School of East Brunswick. Affiliated with Solomon Schechter Day Schs Assn. Prin: Barbara Summers; Chr: Eileen Seaman. **511 Ryders Lane, East Brunswick NJ 08816 (201) 238–7971.**

East Orange

Jewish Community Federation of Metropolitan New Jersey Library. For information on the Ins, see – Jewish Community Federation of Metropolitan New Jersey, East Orange, NJ. **60 Glenwood Ave, East Orange NJ 07017 (201) 673–6800.**

Jewish Community Federation of Metropolitan New Jersey. Mem of CJF. Sponsors United Jewish Appeal. Organized 1923. Pub Morris-Sussex Jewish News. Pres: Clarence Reisen; Exec VP: Dr Donald Feldstein. **60 Glenwood Ave, East Orange NJ 07017 (201) 673–6800.**

Temple Sharey Tefilo. Affiliated with UAHC. 506 mems. Rabbi Charles A. Annes; Cantor Theodore L. Aronson; Pres: Annette S. Littman; Edu: Theodore L. Aronson; Adm: Florence Seglin; Brotherhood Pres: Joel Scharf. **57 Prospect St, East Orange NJ 07017 (201) 678–0005.**

Temple Sharey Tefilo, Edward Ehrenkrantz Memorial Library. For information on the Temple, see – Temple Sharey Tefilo, East Orange, NJ. **57 Prospect St, East Orange NJ 07017 (201) 678–0005.**

East Windsor

Beth El Synagogue. Conservative Cong affiliated with United Syn of Am. To encourage social serv & rel observance; to maintain a syn for divine worship, a sch for instruction in rel doctrine, & dev of J culture; to dev the moral, mental & physical welfare of its mems. Daily & Shabbat Servs; Afternoon & Sun Sch for chil up to HS age; youth groups; Couples Club; Adult Edu; Sisterhood. Est in 1915 as First United Hebrew Assn, Hightstown NJ. Pub Shalom (monthly). Rabbi Ronald Roth; Sch Adm: Myra Epstein; Sec: Jessie Ingber. **50 Maple Stream Rd, East Windsor NJ 08520 (609) 443–4454.**

Edison

Edison Jewish Community Center – Congregation Beth El. Affiliated with United Syn of Am. Rabbi Jerry Lauterbach; Pres: Joseph Cohen; Edu Dir: Joel Klausner; Youth Dir: Myra D'Agostino. **91 Jefferson Blvd, Edison NJ 08817 (201) 985–7272.**

Jewish Federation of Northern Middlesex County. Mem of CJF. Sponsors United Jewish Appeal. Organized 1975. Pub Jewish Voice Pres: Gerald Grossman; Exec Dir: Arthur Eisenstein. **100**

Menlo Park, Suite 101-102, Edison NJ 08837 (201) 494–3920.

Temple Emanu-El. Affiliated with UAHC. 450 mems. Rabbi Alfred B. Landsberg; Cantor Martha Novick; Pres: Bernice Slater; Edu: Michael Farhi; Sisterhood Pres: Sherrill Bressman, Frumet Sachs; Brotherhood Pres: Jerome Levitt. **100 James St, Edison NJ 08817 (201) 549–4442.**

Elberon

Temple Beth Miriam. Affiliated with UAHC. 375 mems. Rabbi Joseph Goldman; Cantor Walter Blazer; Pres: Joseph Bergman; Edu: Andrew Edison; Adm: Hannah Buckman; Sisterhood Pres: Carol Krupnick. **PO Box 2097, Elberon NJ 07740 (201) 222–3754.**

Elizabeth

Temple Beth El. Affiliated with UAHC. 121 mems. Pres: Ide Vogelstein, Beulah L. Passman, Leatrice Lieberman; Sisterhood Pres: Ide Vogelstein. **1374 North Ave, Elizabeth NJ 07208 (201) 354–3021.**

Elmwood Park

Elmwood Park Jewish Center. Affiliated with United Syn of Am. Rabbi Stephen A. Leon; Pres: Samuel Lubliner; Exec Sec: Edith Feinberg; Youth Dir: Sandra Gilbert. **100 Gilbert Ave, Elmwood Park NJ 07407 (201) 797–7320.**

Englewood

Congregation Ahavath Torah of Englewood, NJ. Orthodox Cong. Rel Servs; cultural progs; Sisterhood activities; Afternoon Sch. 350 families. 6 employees. F 1887. Pub Bulletin (quarterly). Facilities include sanctuary, kosher kitchen, gift shop. Rabbi Isaac L. Swift; Cantor V. Konikov. **240 Broad Ave, Englewood NJ 07631 (201) 569–1315.**

Moriah School of Englewood. 53 S Woodland St, Englewood NJ 07631 (201) 567–0208.

Moriah School of Englewood Library. 53 S Woodland St, Englewood NJ 07631 (201) 567–0208.

The Solomon Schechter Day School of Bergen County. Conservative day sch. Wide range of edu progs with full curriculum in gen & J studies. 120 chil K through grade 7. Est in 1974. Originally located in Teaneck NJ; relocated in 1982 to larger facilities in Englewood NJ. Pres: Jerome Kantor; Prin: Howard Goldberg; Gen Studies Dir: Jane Abraham. **147 Tenafly Rd, Englewood NJ 07631 (201) 871–1152.**

Temple Emanu-El. Affiliated with United Syn of Am. Rabbi Arthur Hertzberg; Cantor Kurt Silbermann; Pres: Mort Krell; Edu Dir: Rabbi Aryeh Meir. **147 Tenafly Rd, Englewood NJ 07631 (201) 567–1300.**

United Jewish Fund of Englewood & Surrounding Communities. Mem of CJF. Organized 1952. Pres: Norman Gurman; Exec Dir: Seymour J. Colen. **411 E Clinton Ave, Englewood NJ 07670 (201) 569–1070.**

Englishtown

Temple Shaari Emeth. Affiliated with UAHC. 550 mems. Rabbi Philip Schechter; Cantor Wayne S. Siet; Pres: Harvey Price; Edu: Gail Teicher; Adm: Ruth Blotsky; Sisterhood Pres: Toby Hanover; Brotherhood Pres: Ron Kerstein. **PO Box 393, Englishtown NJ 07726 (201) 462–7744.**

Temple Shaari Emeth Library. For information on the Temple, see – Temple Shaari Emeth, Englishtown, NJ. **Craig Rd, PO Box 393, Englishtown NJ 07726 (201) 462–7744.**

Fair Lawn

Congregation B'nai Israel. Affiliated with United Syn of Am. Rabbi Stanley Bramnick; Cantor Irving Weisberger; Pres: Edward Rosenblatt; Edu Dir: Marlene Klein. **Pine Ave & 30th St, Fair Lawn NJ 07410 (201) 797–9735.**

Fair Lawn Jewish Center. Affiliated with United Syn of Am. Rabbi Simon Glustrom; Cantor Max Rubin; Pres: Norman Krameisen; Exec Dir: Henry Ascher. **10–10 Norma Ave, Fair Lawn NJ 07410 (201) 796–5040.**

Temple Avoda. Affiliated with UAHC. 250 mems. Rabbi Selig Salkowitz; Pres: Gunter Hecht; Edu: Arlene Rifkin; Brotherhood Pres: Harvey Miller. **10–10 Plaza Rd, Fair Lawn NJ 07410 (201) 797–9716.**

Temple Beth Sholom. Affiliated with United Syn of Am. Rabbi Robert Aronowitz; Cantor Harold Brown; Pres: Jacques Marlowe. **40–25 Fair Lawn Ave, Fair Lawn NJ 07410 (201) 797–9321.**

Fairfield

The New Jersey YMHA-YWHA Camps. 21 Plymouth St, Fairfield NJ 07006.

The New Jersey YMHA-YWHA Camps, Library. 21 Plymouth St, Fairfield NJ 07006.

Flanders

Mount Olive Jewish Center. Affiliated with United Syn of Am. Rabbi Sidney D. Shanken; Pres: Michael H. Snyderman; 1st VP: Mark Roffman; Edu Dir: Linda Snyderman, Judy Greenberg; Youth Dir: Lee Mund. **PO Box 152, Pleasant Hill Rd, Flanders NJ 07836 (201) 584–0212.**

Flemington

Flemington Jewish Community Center. Affiliated with United Syn of Am. Rabbi Gershon Baron; Pres: Steve Rubin. **PO Box 567, Flemington NJ 08822 (201) 782–6410.**

Fort Lee

Jewish Community Center of Fort Lee. Affiliated with United Syn of Am. Rabbi Irving Spielman; Cantor Meir Berger; Pres: Herbert Feuerstein; Exec Dir: Carl Hess; Edu Dir: Dov Nahari. **1449 Anderson Ave, Fort Lee NJ 07024 (201) 947–1735.**

Jewish Community Center of Fort Lee Library. For information on the Ins, see – Jewish Community Center, Fort Lee, NJ. **1449 Anderson Ave, Fort Lee NJ 07024 (201) 947–1735.**

Franklin Lakes

Temple Beth Rishon. 225 Forest St, Franklin Lakes NJ 07417.

Temple Beth Rishon Library. 225 Forest St, Franklin Lakes NJ 07417.

Glen Rock

Glen Rock Jewish Center. Affiliated with United Syn of Am. Rabbi Hyman J. Krantz; Pres: Stephen Haber; Edu Dir: Sarah Helpern; Youth Dir: Stanley Hittman. **682 Harristown Rd, Glen Rock NJ 07452 (201) 652–6624.**

Haddon Heights

Temple Beth Sholom. Affiliated with United Syn of Am. Rabbi Albert L. Lewis; Asst Rabbi Nathan Rose; Cantor Samuel Lavitsky; Pres: Rochelle Tobolsky. **White Horse Pike & Green St, Haddon Heights NJ 08035 (609) 593–6113.**

Temple Beth Sholom, Goldberg Memorial Library. For information on the Temple, see – Temple Beth Sholom, Haddon Heights, NJ. **White Horse Pike & Green St, Haddon Heights NJ 08035 (609) 547–6113.**

Highland Park

Highland Park Conservative Temple & Center. Affiliated with United Syn of Am. Rabbi Yakov R. Hilsenrath; Cantor Morris Rosenblatt; Pres: Karl Ringel; Exec Dir: Reuben S. Silver; Youth Dir: Howard Buechler. **201 S 3rd Ave, Highland Park NJ 08904 (201) 545–6482.**

Jewish Federation of Raritan Valley. Mem of CJF. Organized 1948. Pub Jewish Journal. Pres: Irvin Baker; Exec Dir: Dr Jonathan Spinner. **2 S Adelaide Ave, Highland Park NJ 08904 (201) 246–1905.**

Hightstown

Congregation Beth Chaim. Affiliated with UAHC. 360 mems. Rabbi Eric B. Wisnia; Pres: Richard Stoller; Edu: Arthur Finkle; Sisterhood Pres: Cindy Gordon. **PO Box 128, Hightstown NJ 08520 (609) 799–9401.**

Hillside

Hillside Jewish Center. Orthodox Syn. Daily minyan each morning; teachings & gatherings; adopted twin city in Is (Alonshvuth located near Gush–Etzyon) in cooperation with Sinai Cong & Shomrei Torah; Syn houses Kollel Zecher Naftali, an ins for writing the first encyclopedia of J phil & ethics. Rabbi Eli Carlebach; VPs: Moishe Furer, David H. Kahanne. Pres Twin–city Proj: Dr Joseph Payser. **1550 Summit Ave, Hillside NJ 07205.**

The Kollel Zecher Naftali. Cttee for preparation & pub of the first Encyclopedia of J Phil, Homiletics, Chassidus, & Ethicals Writing. To perpetuate all stories & episodes of our ancestors concerning J life, life in the shtetl, the Chassidic rabbis, & the thoughts & feelings of our martyrs who died in WWII (that which has been gathered fr survivors). 30 scholars working full–time in Jerusalem, Haifa & Bklyn. 300 mems; 30 sponsors. Seven bks completed. F Rabbi Eli Carlebach; Dean of the Kollel: Rabbi Eli Fisher. **1550 Summit Ave, Hillside NJ 07205.**

Temple Shomrei Torah. Affiliated with United Syn of Am. Rabbi Dr H. Beryl Lasker; Cantor Ralph Schlossberg; Pres: Stanley Blechman. **910 Salem Ave, Hillside NJ 07205 (201) 351–1945.**

Howell

Solomon Schechter Academy of Ocean & Monmouth Counties. Affiliated with Solomon Schechter Day Schs Assn. Prin: Dr Constance Skor; Chr: Marilyn Sosis. **101 Kent Rd, Howell NJ 07731 (201) 370–1767.**

Irvington

Congregation Agudath Israel. Orthodox Syn. To est & maintain an Orthodox cong & syn for worshipping according to traditional Orthodox manner. Provides edu for youngsters in Torah, culture, Heb language, J law, hist; assists mems in times of distress; provides burial places for mems & families; provides com ctr for advancement of J social interests. Est in Newark in 1924; relocated in 1969 to Irvington due to changes in J population. Pres: William Bilow; VP: Joseph Spinard; Treas: Benjamin Meyerson; Fin Sec: Harry Dobbrin; Rabbi Yaakov I. Zakheim. **1125 Stuyvesant Ave, Irvington NJ 07111.**

Temple B'nai Israel. Affiliated with United Syn of Am. Cantor Moshe Weinberg; Pres: Sidney Prestup; Exec Dir: Jerome W. Holzman. **706 Nye Ave, Irvington NJ 07111 (201) 327–9656.**

Iselin

Beth Sholom. Affiliated with United Syn of Am. Rabbi David M. Steinhardt; Pres: Phil Schreiber. **90 Cooper Ave, Iselin NJ 08830 (201) 283–0239.**

Jersey City

B'nai Jacob. Affiliated with United Syn of Am. Rabbi Dr Solomon Herbst; Cantor Isaac Steinberg; Pres: Arthur Smith. **176 West Side Ave, Jersey City NJ 07305 (201) 435–5725.**

Jewish Hospital & Rehabilitation Center of New Jersey. A voluntary, non-sectarian, non-profit ins. The Ctr is dedicated to: serv to the com, perception of & response to its need; the best possible med, nursing & rehabilitative servs by keeping up with the latest sci dev & med advances; the tradition of high quality care & treatment assured by the continuing presence of a dedicated & highly skilled staff across the entire spectrum of med, nursing, rehabilitative, & social work disciplines; the willingness to listen, to learn, to educate all concerned – the offs & dirs, the staff, the patients, their families, the com; the pride of achievement. Med & nursing; radiology; lab; nuclear med; respiratory & inhalation therapy; cystoscopy; dentistry; podiatry; pharmaceutical; cardiac stress tests & rehabilitation; intensive care; Total Eye Care Clin; Nutrition Prog; Day Care Ctr for Handicapped & Aged; occupational therapy; physical therapy; diversional therapy; speech pathology; audiology & audiometrics; social servs; ambulatory care servs; ancillary servs: lab, pharmacy, radiology, med library, & Drs offs; Recreational Prog; Volunteer Prog; Outreach Progs: Total Eye Care Clin, med evaluation servs, Cardiac Stress Testing Prog, Nutrition Prog, Day Care Prog, Social Servs Dept; Chil Ctr for Special Servs which serves handicapped chil through 21 yrs of age. Bergen Cty Unit, located in River Vale, provides an extended care facility of 50 beds. 150 bed special hosp; five bed intensive care unit; 250 bed facility for skilled nursing care, including 75 set aside in a fully equipped ctr for rehabilitation. Drs, registered nurses, practical nurses, nurses aides, therapists in rehabilitation specialties, technicians, & social workers. F in 1915 as the Hebrew Orphan's home of Hudson Cty. The original bldg was used by orphans until 1949. The first group of aged people was moved fr an inadequate bldg to a bldg on Summit Ave. When this bldg was outgrown, the Lerner Bldg was erected in 1932. In 1941 the Kahn Infirmary was built for the sick aged. In 1949 the Yager Bldg was constructed to provide custodial, med & nursing servs. In 1961 the 150 bed Gross Hosp Pavilion was added in order to meet the increasing com need for additional health servs. Within a few yrs of this time, the name of the Hebrew Home & Hosp was changed to its present name. In Aug of 1970 the Rehabilitation & Skilled Nursing Facility was completed & ambulatory care servs for the com were initiated. The opening of this wing added 152 beds to the med complex. In Jun of the same yr, a 50 bed nursing home was opened in River Vale. A kashruth policy is strictly adhered to in the dietary dept of all units. J holidays are observed & prayer servs are conducted in the Hosp syn daily, on Sabbath & the holidays. Pres: Jack Siegel; Exec VP: Charlotte B. Simon; Assc Adm: Charles P. Berkowitz; Treas: Sydney A. Rose; Med Dir: Dr Michael L. Wagner; Pres of the Med Staff: Dr Eli A. Wallack; Sr VP: Louis Adler; Fin Sec: Mrs Murray Gillette. **Hudson Cty Complex, 198 Stevens Ave, Jersey City NJ 07305 (201) 451–9000.**

Jewish Standard. Periodical pub. **40 Journal Sq, Jersey City NJ 07306 (201) 653–6330.**

Rogosin Yeshiva High School. 25 Cottage St, Jersey City NJ 07306 (201) 798–0055.

Rogosin Yeshiva High School Library. 25 Cottage St, Jersey City NJ 07306 (201) 798–0055.

Temple Beth El. Affiliated with UAHC. 391 mems. Rabbi Samuel A. Berman; Cantor Abraham Berman; Pres: Louis Silverman; Sisterhood Pres: Madeline Mazer; Brotherhood Pres: Harold Mandel. **2419 Kennedy Blvd, Jersey City NJ 07304 (201) 333–4229.**

United Jewish Appeal. Mem of CJF. Organized 1939. Chr: Mel Blum; Exec Sec: Madeline Mazer. **71 Bentley Ave, Jersey City NJ 07304 (201) 332–6644.**

Kearny

B'nai Israel of Kearny & N Arlington. Affiliated with United Syn of Am. Presidium: Dr Milton Lerner, Max Yurman, M. Sumner. **780 Kearny Ave, Kearny NJ 07032 (201) 998–3813.**

Lake Hiawatha

Lake Hiawatha Jewish Center. Affiliated with United Syn of Am. Rabbi Herman Savitz; Cantor Samuel A. Grossman; Pres: Dr Jospeh Weisberg; Edu Dir: Roberta Schudrich; Youth Dir: Bernard Ulrich. **Lincoln Ave, Lake Hiawatha NJ 07034 (201) 334–0959.**

Lake Hopatcong

Lake Hopatcong Jewish Community Center. Affiliated with United Syn of Am. Rabbi Nathan Zolondek; Pres: Leonard Frankel; Youth Dir: Sandy Leon. **PO Box 333, Lake Hopatcong NJ 07843 (201) 398–8700.**

Lakewood

Beth Medrash Govoha of America. Post-secondary yeshiva accredited by Assn of Advanced Rabbinical & Talmudic Sch (AARTS); licensed by Dept of Higher Edu, State of NJ. To furnish an environment conducive to the intensive study of Torah at an advanced level & to encourage the study of Torah & its observance worldwide. Sponsors adult edu classes in addition to its regular edu progs in rabbinical & Talmudic studies; library contains 14,000 vols (Judaica). 904 stu. F 1943 by Rabbi Aaon Kotler, who served as Rosh Yeshiva until Nov 1962. Upon his passing, his son, Rabbi Shneur, assumed leadership. Each served exactly 19 yrs, 7 months, 1 day until his death. Rabbi Malkiel Kotler became Rosh Yeshiva in June 1982. Pub Alumni Newsletter (bi-monthly), Torah Journal (semi-annually). Facilities include Beth Medrash bldg, dining hall-auditorium, dormitory, residence halls for marrieds. World's largerst advanced Talmudic yeshiva; world's largest kollel for married stu (over 440); many branches across the USA, in Canada & abroad. Rosh Yeshiva: Rabbi Malkiel Kotler; Dean of Stu: Rabbi Nathan Wachtfogel; Exec Bd Chr: Dr Ernst L. Bodenheimer; VP: Elias Klein; Sec: Naftaly Baruch; Treas: Nochim Zeldes; Registrar: Jacob Bursztyn. **617 6th St, Lakewood NJ 08701 (201) 367–1060.**

Beth Medrash Govoha of America, Library. Library contains approx 14,000 vols (Judaica). For information on the Ins, see – Beth Medrash Govoha of Am, Lakewood, NJ. **617 6th St, Lakewood NJ 08701 (201) 367–1060.**

Congregation Ahavat Shalom. Affiliated with United Syn of Am. Rabbi Raphael Miller; Pres: Michael Nussbaum; Edu Dir: Mrs M. Snider; Youth Dir: C. Gruber. **Forest Ave & 11th St, Lakewood NJ 08701 (201) 363–5190.**

Congregation Sons of Israel. Orthodox Cong affiliated with Union of Orthodox J Congs of Am. To be a vehicle for the continuity of Torah study & commitment to Mitzvot, & a Beacon of Light for all who seek to be guided in the aforementioned paths. Rel Servs; youth activities; sr nutrition lunch daily; edu progs; Adult Edu; sr citizen residence; women's org; library containing 400 vols. 300 families; 200 stu in grades K–8; approx 150 sr citizen residents. 8 employees. F 1905. Pub Synagogue News (monthly). Facilities include sanctuary, kitchen, auditorium, chapel, gift shop, Chevra Kadisha, funeral sanctuary, Tahara rm automated with mikvah. Rabbi Pesach Z. Levovitz; Cantor Aaron Lieber; Pres: Ira Wolfson. **Madison Ave & 6th St, Lakewood NJ 08701 (201) 364–2230.**

Ocean County Jewish Federation. Mem of CJF. Pres: Michael Levin; Exec Dir: Michael Ruvel. **301 Madison Ave, Lakewood NJ 08701 (201) 363–0530.**

Temple Beth Am. Reform Cong affiliated with UAHC. To further the dev of Reform J in Lakewood NJ area, & to inculcate into its mems knowledge of J & a love for the J people. Sabbath Servs; Bar/Bat Mitzvah; Confirmation; Sisterhood; Men's Club; Adult Edu; youth groups; Rel Sch; other progs of prayer & edu. 328 mems. Est in 1949 & moved to different locations until permanent temple was built in 1952. Rabbi Stanley Yedwab; Hon Pres, OCJF Rep: Joseph Kohn; Pres: Barry Rosenzweig; VPs: Everett Rogove, Stuart Ozegowsky, Toby Olin; Treas: Roberta Krantz; Fin Sec: Harriet Glassman; Rec Sec: Jacqueline Elbaum; Corsp Sec: Jerome Price. **Madison at Carey, Lakewood NJ 08701 (201) 363–2800.**

Ledgewood

United Jewish Federation of Morris-Sussex. Mem of CJF. Pres: Dr Irwin Roseman; Exec Dir: Michael P. Shapiro. **500 Route 10, Ledgewood NJ 07852 (201) 584–1850.**

Leonia

Congregation Adas Emuno. Affiliated with UAHC. 66 mems. Rabbi Fredric S. Dworkin; Cantor Ian Cosman; Pres: Philip G. Elkins. **254 Broad Ave, Leonia NJ 07605 (201) 461–4045.**

Congregation Sons of Israel. Affiliated with United Syn of Am. Rabbi Zelick L. Block; Pres: Henry Postrong. **150 Grand Ave, Leonia NJ 07605 (201) 592–9700.**

Linden

Suburban Jewish Center – Temple Mekor Chayim. Affiliated with United Syn of Am. Rabbi Judah Kogen; Cantor Irving S. Rothman; Pres: Franklin Felder. **Deerfield Academy Terr, Linden NJ 07036 (201) 925–2283.**

Livingston

Anti-Defamation League of B'nai B'rith – New Jersey Regional Office. Dedicated in purpose & prog to translating the Am heritage of democratic ideals into a way of life for all Am, & to countering assaults on the safety, status, rights & image of J. For additional information, see – Anti-Defamation League of B'nai B'rith, New York City, NY. **513 W Mt Pleasant Ave, Livingston NJ 07039.**

Temple Beth Shalom. Affiliated with United Syn of Am. Rabbi Samuel L. Cohen; Cantor Henry Butensky; Pres: Martin Barber; Exec Dir: Donald I. Lowy; Edu Dir: Isaac Friedman; Youth Dir: Allan & Patti Lowy. **193 Mt Pleasant Ave, Livingston NJ 07039 (201) 992–3600.**

Temple Emanu-El. Affiliated with UAHC. 515 mems. Rabbi Peter Kasdan; Cantor Louis E. Davidson; Pres: Robert Neuville; Edu: Aimee Neibart; Adm: Lillian Scheffer; Sisterhood Pres: Sheila Kasdan. **264 W Northfield Rd, Livingston NJ 07039 (201) 992–5560.**

Temple Emanu-El Library. For information on the Temple, see – Temple Emanu-El, Livingston, NJ. **264 W Northfield Rd, Livingston NJ 07039 (201) 992–5560.**

Lyndhurst

Lyndhurst Hebrew Center. Affiliated with United Syn of Am. Rabbi David Brown; Pres: Dr Bernard Glick. **333 Valley Brook Ave, Lyndhurst NJ 07071 (201) 438–9582.**

Mahwah

Beth Haverim. Affiliated with UAHC. 65 mems. Rabbi Milton Weinberg; Pres: Larry Heppen; Edu: Steven Issman; Sisterhood Pres: Jane Simon. **PO Box 332, 59 Masonicus Rd, Mahwah NJ 07430 (201) 327–4333.**

Margate

Congregation Beth Israel. Affiliated with UAHC. 350 mems. Rabbi Mark L. Shook; Pres: Robert Mayer; Edu: Amy J. Schlecker; Adm: Edna Deutsch; Sisterhood Pres: Eleanor Thierman; Brotherhood Pres: Charles Thierman. **8401 Ventnor Ave, PO Box 1, Margate NJ 08402 (609) 823–4116.**

Temple Beth El. Affiliated with United Syn of Am. Rabbi Mark H. Kunis; Pres: Daniel Roseman; Edu Dir: Charles Danenberg. **500 N Jerome Ave, Margate NJ 08402 (609) 823–2725.**

Temple Emeth Shalom. Affiliated with UAHC. 249 mems. Rabbi Seymour M. Rosen; Pres: Irving H. Newborn; Edu: Ina Rosen; Sisterhood Pres: L. Tahasnik; Brotherhood Pres: Myer Feldman. **8501 Ventnor Ave, Margate NJ 08402 (609) 822–4343.**

Marlboro

Ohav Shalom. Affiliated with United Syn of Am. Cantor Neil Ben Isvy; Pres: Martin Wallack; Edu Dir: Gabriella Kaldor; Youth Dir: Dov Furer. **PO Box 98, Marlboro NJ 07746 (201) 536–2300.**

Marlton

Beth Tikvah – Mt Laurel. Affiliated with United Syn of Am. Rabbi Gary Gans; Pres: Norman Levithan; Edu Dir: Gail Kernish. **Evesboro–Medford Rd, Marlton NJ 08053 (609) 983–8090.**

Maywood

Temple Beth Israel. Affiliated with United Syn of Am. Rabbi Len Rosenthal; Pres: Seigfried Kling. **34 W Magnolia Ave, Maywood NJ 07607 (201) 845–7550.**

McAfee

Temple Shalom. Affiliated with UAHC. 40 mems. Pres: Harvey Wasserman. **PO Box 93, McAfee NJ 07428 (201) 827–5655.**

Merchantville

Congregation Beth Jacob. Affiliated with United Syn of Am. Rabbi Lester Hering; Cantor Seymour Schwartzman; Pres: Bernard Platt. **109 E Maple Ave, Merchantville NJ 08109 (609) 662–4509.**

Metuchen

Temple Neve Shalom – JCC. Affiliated with United Syn of Am. Rabbi Gerald L. Zelizer; Cantor Mordecai Goldstein; Pres: Mildred Holtzman; Exec Dir: Roy Kern; Edu Dir: David Schwartzmer; Youth Dir: Dr Edgar Alster. **250 Grove Ave, Metuchen NJ 08840 (201) 548–2238.**

Millburn

Congregation B'nai Israel. Affiliated with United Syn of Am. Rabbi Victor A. Mirelman; Cantor Joshua Steele; Rabbi Emeritus Dr Max Gruenwald; Pres: Dr Gilbert Sugarman; Adm: Natalie Tambor. **160 Millburn Ave, Millburn NJ 07041 (201) 379–3811.**

Congregation B'nai Israel, Gruenewald Library. For information on the Cong, see – Congregation B'nai Israel, Milburn, NJ. **160 Milburn Ave, Milburn NJ 07041 (201) 379–3811.**

Montclair

The Charles Bierman Home for Aged People. Intermediate care facility (boarding home) licensed by State of NJ for retired persons. To provide a family atmosphere in a comfortable setting specifying continuance of independence of residents with the focus on dignity & respect of retired residents. Daily socialization progs: discussion groups, exercise groups, choral groups, arts & crafts, birthday parties, J holiday progs, Fri night servs, trips to syns, theater trips, concert & mus trips; personal care servs: medication distribution, bathing, dressing, making beds, awake coverage. F 1936 by Milton Bierman, son of philanthropist Charles Bierman. Home began in compliance with his wishes & concern for frail J elderly. Med facilities not available. Pub Ner Tamid (6 times a year). Pres: Edward Blau; Exec Dir: Seymour Krieger; Prog Dir: Sandra Orgle **10 Madison Ave, Montclair NJ 07042 (201) 744–6333.**

Congregation Shomrei Emunah. Conservative Syn affiliated with United Syn of Am. Seeks to est & perpetuate on the Am scene a contemporary form of J faithful to the spirit of tradition, & responsive to the needs of the modern age. Rel servs; pre-sch prog; Sisterhood; library with 1000 vols. 150 families. F in 1905 by Abraham Kurnish, a J resident of Montclair who lost a mem of his family, & was in need of a minyan. Ten men formed &, after servs, talked about forming a corporate body for worship, study, edu, & mutual support. In 1905 the Cong incorporated under the name of Cong Shomar Ammuna of Bloomfield & Montclair. First Shabbat servs held in quarters behind shop of com's 1st pres. In 1906 Heb Sch f with 13 pupils. In 1907 land was purchased, & in 1910 the first Servs were held in new syn. In 1914 syn was remodeled to add needed facilities for communal functions. In 1949 the cornerstone of a new bldg was laid; the official dedication was held in Feb of 1953. Pub Kol Emunah (monthly). Rabbi Perry R. Rank; Rabbi Emeritus Dr Jeshaia Schnitzer; Pres: Dr Michael S. Kogan. **67 Park St, Montclair NJ 07042 (201) 746–5031, 7862.**

Morganville

Solomon Schechter Day School of Marlboro. Affiliated with Solomon Schechter Day Schs Assn. Prin: Alan Kurland; Chr: Joseph Eisenstein. **PO Box 94, Morganville NJ 07751.**

Temple Rodeph Torah. Affiliated with UAHC. 70 mems. Pres: Richard M. Herzog. **PO Box 23, Morganville NJ 07751 (201) 536–2417.**

Morristown

Lubavitch Students Organization. 226 Sussex Ave, Morristown NJ 07960 (201) 540–0877.

Morristown Jewish Community Center. Affiliated with United Syn of Am. Rabbi Sheldon Weltman; Cantor Maimon Attias; Pres: Dr Lawrence D. Kornreich; Exec Dir: Erma Krief; Edu Dir: Marjorie Elkind; Youth Dir: Dave & Doris Cooper. **177 Speedwell Ave, Morristown NJ 07960 (201) 538–9292.**

Morristown Jewish Community Center Library. For information on the Ctr, see – Morristown Jewish Community Center, Morristown, NJ. **177 Speedwell Ave, Morristown NJ 07960 (201) 358–9292.**

Rabbinical College of America. Rabbi M. Herson. **226 Sussex Ave, Morristown NJ 07960.**

Temple B'nai Or. Affiliated with UAHC. 425 mems. Rabbis: Z.D. Levy, Melanie W. Aron; Pres: Ronald Levy; Edu: Melanie W. Aron; Adm: Shirley E. Bloom; Sisterhood Pres: Davida Ginsburg; Brotherhood Pres: Seymour Rosenthal. **Overlook Rd, Morristown NJ 07960 (201) 539–4539.**

Mt. Holly

Temple Har-Zion. Affiliated with United Syn of Am. Rabbi Herschel J. Matt; Cantor Dr Paul Bender; Pres: Sam Podietz. **High & Ridgeway Sts, Mt Holly NJ 08060 (609) 267–0660.**

Mt. Laurel

Congregation M'kor Shalom. Affiliated with UAHC. 387 mems. Rabbi Fred J. Neulander; Cantor Anita Hochman; Pres: David Garfield; Edu: Beverly A. Solomon. **Church & Fellowship Rds, Mt Laurel NJ 08054 (609) 235–0590.**

Congregation M'kor Shalom Library. For information on the Cong, see – Congregation M'kor Shalom, Mt Laurel, NJ. **Church & Fellowship Rds, Mt Laurel NJ 08054 (609) 235–0590.**

New Brunswick

Anshe Emeth Memorial Temple. Affiliated with UAHC. 500 mems. Rabbi Bennett F. Miller; Cantor Joel Gordon; Pres: Louis Goldstein; Edu: Sandra Schlanger; Adm: Marilyn Asofsky. **222 Livingston Ave, New Brunswick NJ 08901 (201) 545–6484.**

Association for the Sociological Study of Jewry. Dept of Sociology, University College, Rutgers University, New Brunswick NJ 08903.

Community Jewish School. Non-profit, cooperative sch & com affiliated with the Conf of Secular J Orgs. To help the chil dev positive attitudes & emotions toward J through an understanding & appreciation of & through an identification with their J heritage. Classes for chil, & adult discussion sessions on Sun mornings; curriculum dev by parents & teaching staff including J hist, customs, holidays & beliefs, current J thinking & events, music, singing, dancing, creative writing, acting, & cooking. Emphasis is placed upon J secularism & humanitarianism, celebration of holidays together as a sch & com. All mems are encouraged to participate in at least one of the standing or ad hoc cttees. All families are scheduled during the yr for Sun morning duties involving clean-up & hospitality. F in 1970. Bd of Dirs – Pres:Steve Lefelt; VP: Harry Herz; Curriculum: Ruth Edenbaum; Personnel: Marty Edenbaum; Treas: David Harris; Membership: Ellen Kaplan; Secs: Ruth Miller, Carol Lefelt; Adult Edu: Bernie Miller; Mems at Large: Steve Rosenthal, Sandra French. **PO Box 961, New Brunswick NJ 08903.**

Jewish Historical Society of Raritan Valley. To dev an interest in preserving the hist of the central NJ area. Annual spring meetings with guest lecturers; oral hist proj with 36 tapes; hist exhibits set up upon request; maintenance of Central Jersey J Archives. Est 1977. Central J Archives opened to public in 1981; stored in Central NJ J Home for the Aged. The Jewish Scene in NJ's Raritan Valley: 1698–1948; The Rural Jewish Community in the Raritan Valley. Pres: Ruth Marcus Patt; VP: Dr Lawrence Zimmer; Sec: Dr Doris Kahn; Treas: Herman Harris. **1050 George St, New Brunswick NJ 08901 (201) 247–0288.**

New Milford

Beth Tikva – New Milford Jewish Center. Affiliated with United Syn of Am. Daily Shabbat & Festival Rel Servs; Rel Sch fr age 6; youth groups fr 5th grade through HS; Sisterhood; Men's Club; Golden Age Club for sr citizens; Adult Edu; host activities for B'nai B'rith & Hadassah. Est 1952; met in homes of mems & in public bldgs. 1st bldg completed in 1955, & larger bldg in 1965. Rabbi Harold D. Halpern; Cantor Leonard Reiter; Pres: Larry Pick. **435 River Rd, New Milford NJ 07646 (201) 261–4847.**

Newark

Beth David Jewish Center. Affiliated with United Syn of Am. Rabbi Julius Eidenbaum; Cantor Mordecai Finerman; Pres: Rita Siegel. **828 Sanford Ave, Newark NJ 07106 (201) 372–9360.**

Newark Beth Israel Medical Center. 545 bed tertiary care facility. Major teaching affiliate of Col of Med & Dentistry of NJ. Mem of J Com Fed of Met NJ & beneficiary of its annual UJA campaign. Recognized referral ctr for cardiovascular disease; large Artificial Kidney Ctr for adults & chil; regional Transplant Ctr with full-time organ procurement prog; 5-cty recognized Perinatal Ctr with 22-bed Neonatal Intensive Care Nursery; maternal/fetal obstetrical floor; 5 bed Pediatric Intensive Care Unit; Oncology Ctr (with linear accelerator) specializing in med, surgical & radiation therapies; complete inpatient & outpatient Com Mental Health Ctr; 33 outpatient specialty clins; Dental Clin; Women's Health Ctr. Bd of Trustees of 45 men & women in all professions. 1,000 mem Auxiliary contributing hours & funds for special projs. Staff of 2,000; med staff of over 400 attending Drs & dentists; 600 mem nursing staff. F in 1901 as teaching hosp for J interns. 2 yrs later Sch of Nursing f; discontinued 1970. Responsible for major contributions in areas of Rh factor & hemophilia. Pioneered prototype of 1st Am-made nuclear powered pacemaker with US Atomic Energy Commis. First 15 units implanted Apr, 1973. Med Ctr now takes up entire 2 block area; has multi-level modern parking garage. Pres Bd of Trustees: Robert Marks; Exec Dir: Lester Bornstein; Pres of Med Staff: Dr Thomas C. Rommer; Pres of Auxiliary: Mrs Donald Brief. **201 Lyons Ave, Newark NJ 07112 (201) 926–7175.**

Newton

Jewish Center of Sussex County. Affiliated with United Syn of Am. Rabbi Philip Samuel-Siegel; Pres: Arthur Heyderman. **13 Washington St, PO Box 334, Newton NJ 07860.**

North Bergen

Temple Beth Abraham. To foster a Traditional & Orthodox J among mems, & encourage ideals of J among the young. Incorporated Feb 5, 1931 as the Talmud Torah of N Bergen; remained in a small converted house until 1943. In Jun 1947 ground was broken for the new syn; thereafter re-named Temple Beth Abraham in memory of Abraham Srulowitz, father of Harry Srulowitz who made the first donation toward the new bldg. In 1951 Rabbi Zigelman was named spiritual leader; through his direction the Cong grew & prospered. In 1967 further expansion was called for. Through efforts of mems, dedication for a new addition was held in 1970. Pres: Sidney Schlanger; 1st VP: Sidney Kliegler; 2nd VP: Henry Klein; 3rd VP: Adolph Glattstein; Rec Sec: Norman Soffen; Fin Sec: William Horowitz; Treas: Joseph Schonberger; Rabbi Abraham I. Zigelman. **8410 Fourth Ave, North Bergen NJ 07047 (201) 869–2425.**

North Brunswick

Congregation B'nai Tikvah. JCC of N & S Brunswick; Conservative Syn affiliated with United Syn of Am. Rel Servs; Ins for Adult Studies; Sisterhood; Men's Club; several youth groups. Est 1980 as a merger between 3 previous J orgs in com: Cong Shaari Shalom, Temple Beth Shalom, JCC of N Brunswick. Pres: Marvin Stark; VPs: David Offenberg, Nancy Kivor, Stanley Sorkin, Barbara Bergman; Rabbi Andrew Warmflash; Hazan David Tucker; Rel Sch Adm: Sara Feigenbaum; Trustees: Howard Kalish, Harold Kizner, Steven Mendelow, David Offenberg, Samson Rosenzweig, Stephen Sobel, Stanley Sorkin. **Box 3028, North Brunswick NJ 08902 (201) 297–0696.**

Oakhurst

Temple Beth El. Affiliated with United Syn of Am. Rabbi Murray Ezring; Cantor Sidney Schulman; Pres: Lois Barrett; Edu Dir: Ann Lieberman; Youth Dir: Dorothy Secol. **301 Monmouth Rd, Oakhurst NJ 07755 (201) 531–0300.**

Ocean

Temple Beth Torah. Conservative Syn affiliated with United Syn of Am. J living, J edu. Rel Servs; Rel Sch (afternoon sch); Sisterhood; Men's Club; Sr Club; youth groups. 529 families; 267 stu in grades K–8. 8 employees plus 12 teachers. F 1982. Pub The Bulletin (weekly). Facilities include kosher kitchens, sanctuary, social hall, library, classrms. Rabbi Jacob Friedman; Cantor Arnold Schraeter; Pres: Rabbi Shapiro; Adm: Florence Morrows; Prin: Philip Dickstein. **1200 Rodeld Ave, Ocean NJ 07712 (201) 531–4410.**

Temple Beth Torah Library. For information on the Temple, see – Temple Beth Torah, Ocean, NJ. **1200 Roseld Ave, Ocean NJ 07712 (201) 531–4410.**

Old Bridge

Beth Ohr. Affiliated with United Syn of Am. Rabbi Herman Cohen; Cantor Marvin Brogin; Pres: Ira Marshal. **300 Route 516, Old Bridge NJ 08857 (201) 257–9867.**

Paramus

Congregation Beth Tefillah. Orthodox Syn. Rel Servs; adult classes: Bible, Philosophy, Talmud; once a mo Coffee & Culture Group; Shabbat morning courses; folk dancing; Nursery for ages 2–4; Sisterhood. 40 families. Organized in 1969 with 10 families seeking more traditional Orthodox observance. Rabbinical stu were sent fr Yeshiva Univ each weekend to lead rel servs held in homes of mems. In Dec 1969 the Cong purchased house on Midland Ave. In 1973 the syn was enlarged. Rabbi Benjamin Yasgur; Torah Reader: Morton Kolber; Pres: Alan Bloomberg; VP: Dr Jonathan Cohen; Treas: Harold Unger; Sec: Paul Herman; Sisterhood Pres: Gaby Strauss. **241 Midland Ave, Paramus NJ 07652 (201) 265–4100.**

Frisch School. Yeshiva. To promote awareness of human affairs & concern for problems of humanity; to promote respect & understanding of democratic ideals, ins, & traditions of the US; to promote understanding & appreciation of the creativity of mankind; to provide atmosphere & experience through which stu can dev self-awareness & ability to relate to others; to promote commitment to & appreciation for the Torah; to communicate the unity of J people throughout the world; to communicate centrality of Is as the J homeland, & to dev responsibility for the country. Offers both Torah & col prep edu on secondary sch level, grades 9–12. F 1971. Opened with 9th & 10th grades Sept 1972. Prin: Dr Rabbi Menahem Meier; Pres: Joseph Nelson. **Frisch Ct, Paramus NJ 07652 (201) 845–0555.**

Frisch School, Library. Library contains 6,000 vols. For information on the Sch, see – The Frisch School, Paramus, NJ. **Frisch Ct, Paramus NJ 07652 (201) 845–0555.**

Jewish Community Center of Paramus. Affiliated with United Syn of Am. Rabbi Aryeh Gotlieb; Cantor Nathan Gottlieb; Pres: Adalph Berman; Exec Dir: Marvin Todd; Edu Dir: Helen Josephs; Youth Dir: Laurence Grossman. **E 304 Midland Ave, Paramus NJ 07652 (201) 262–7691.**

Parlin

Temple Ohav Shalom, Sayreville Jewish Center. Affiliated with United Syn of Am. Rabbi Robert S. Port; Pres: Maxine A. Persons; **PO Box 34, Parlin NJ 08859 (201) 727–4334.**

Parsippany

Temple Beth Am. Affiliated with UAHC. 209 mems. Rabbi Daniel Franzel; Pres: Fred Garodnick; Edu: Irving Barocas; Sisterhood Pres: Bonnie Morris. **PO Box 50, 879 S Beverwyck Rd, Parsippany NJ 07054 (201) 887–0046.**

Passaic

Congregation Ahavas Israel, Passaic Park Jewish Community Center. Traditional Syn. Daily Rel Servs – morning, evening, Shabbat, Rosh Chodesh; Men's Club; Sisterhood. 250 mems (200 families, 50 individuals). F 1926. Facilities include sanctuary seating 650, daily chapel, ballroom, gift shop, kosher kitchen. Rabbi Kenneth D. Poplace; Rabbi Emeritus Israel Gerstein; Pres: Louis Goodman; Men's Club Pres: William Darman; Sisterhood Pres: Arlene Bitterman. **181 Van Houten Ave, Passaic NJ 07055 (201) 777–5929.**

Paterson

Congregation B'nai Jeshurun. Affiliated with UAHC. 233 mems. Rabbi Martin Freedman; Cantor Mimi Frishman; Pres: Edward Wexler; Edu: Sheldon Shuck; Adm: Dorothy Levy; Sisterhood Pres: Janet Bauer; Brotherhood Pres: Barry Kessler. **152 Derrom Ave, Paterson NJ 07504 (201) 279–2111.**

Temple Emanuel of North Jersey. Affiliated with United Syn of Am. Rabbi Dr David H. Panitz; Cantor Abraham Weisman; Pres: Cecil A. Gordon; Exec Dir: Kalman Black. **151 E 33rd St, Paterson NJ 07514 (201) 684–5564.**

Perth Amboy

Congregation Beth Mordecai. Affiliated with United Syn of Am. Cantor Edward W. Berman; Pres: Jerome Gumpel. **224 High St, Perth Amboy NJ 08862 (201) 442–2431.**

Pine Brook

Pine Brook Jewish Center. Affiliated with United Syn of Am. Pres: Donald Lebowitz; Edu Dir: Gloria Bernstein. **Changebridge Rd, Pine Brook NJ 07058 (201) 227–3520.**

Plainfield

Temple Beth El. Affiliated with United Syn of Am. Rabbi Moshe Sambar; Pres: James Shrager. **225 E Seventh St, Plainfield NJ 07060 (201) 756–2333.**

Temple Sholom. Affiliated with UAHC. 380 mems. Rabbi Gerald A. Goldman; Cantor Emilie Coopersmith; Pres: Luna Kaufman; Edu: Norman Pianko. **815 W 7th St, Plainfield NJ 07063 (201) 756–6447.**

Pompton Lakes

Congregation Beth Shalom. Affiliated with United Syn of Am. Rabbi Bernard Schecter; Pres: Louis M. Lees; Youth Dir: Michael Fisch. **21 Passaic Ave, Pompton Lakes NJ 07442 (201) 835–9785.**

Congregation Beth Shalom Library. For information on the Cong, see – Congregation Beth Shalom, Pompton Lakes, NJ. **21 Passaic Ave, Pompton Lakes NJ 07405 (201) 835–9785.**

Princeton

The Jewish Center. Conservative Syn & com ctr; non-affiliated cong. To promote J life through full range of rel, cultural, edu & social activities. Rel Servs; Adult Edu progs; Sr Citizen Drop-In Lounge; Mercer Cty Col extension site; Women's Div; Men's Club; counseling servs; nursery class; Youth Group (grades 4–12); physical edu activities; Is affairs; social concerns; publications; film series; Heb language training; adult Bar/Bat Mitzvah; library containing several hundred vols (Judaica). 460 families; 225 stu. 8 part-time employees. F about 25 yrs ago; original name B'nai Zion, changed to The J Ctr. Pub 3–4 bulletins (annually); Newsletters, flyers (bi-weekly); Adult Education brochure (annual). Facilities include gift shop, lounge, nursery, library, adult library, central off, classrms, adm offs, display case for Judaica, social hall, kosher kitchen, nursery play yard, large parking lot, rabbi's & cantor's studies (expansion underway of present facilities). Widely recognized for extensive J Adult Edu Prog. Rabbi Melvin Jay Glatt; Cantor Robert Freedman; Pres: Arthur Meisel; VP: Marc Citron; Prin: Judith B. Rin; Adm: Paula Wachtel; Sec: Elaine Lesnever; Treas: David Lieberman. **457 Nassau St, Princeton NJ 08540 (609) 921–0100.**

Yavneh House. Servs for rel stu body of Princeton Univ. To unite rel J stu in fellowship & common purpose; to facilitate the observance of Torah J; to aid in the solution of problems common to these stu; to promote a deeper understanding of the intellectual & spiritual bases of traditional J; to engender a sense of com responsibility, & to encourage participation in activities of Am, Is, & worldwide J com; to promote fellowship with rel J stu on other campuses. 3 Daily Minyans, Shabbat Servs, Holiday observance; kosher dining facilities offering 14 meals per week; classes in J subjects; J library. Kosher dining has over 100 mems. Organized in 1961 by stu to serve the needs of rel J stu of Princeton. Rabbi & mems of com aided stu by renting a house off-campus. In 1971 facilities moved on campus; kosher kitchen opened that year. Pres: Steven M. Weiss; Treas: Burton Rubin; VP: Sharon Lubadh; Shabbat Gabbai: Charles Walter; Stu Kashrut Supervisors: Raphael Wenger, Jeffrey Gluck; Press Sec: Matt Saal; Corsp Sec: Michael Bayme; Minister of Edu: David Landes. **83 Prospect Ave, Princeton NJ 08540 (609) 452–3610.**

Rahway

Temple Beth Torah – Rahway Hebrew Congregation. Affiliated with United Syn of Am. Rabbi Jacob Rubenstein; Cantor Solomon Sternberg; Pres: Sy Vogel. **1365 Bryant St, Rahway NJ 07065 (201) 574–8432.**

Ramsey

Beth Sholom. Affiliated with United Syn of Am. Rabbi Martin Merin; Pres: Jack Berger; Edu Dir: Esther Taragin. **Maple St & Plaza Lane, Ramsey NJ 07446 (201) 327–7759.**

Randolph

Hebrew Academy of Morris County. Affiliated with Solomon Schechter Day Schs Assn. Prin: Moshe Schreiber; Chr: Dr Elliot Milgram. **146 Dover–Chester Rd, Randolph NJ 07869 (201) 584–5530.**

Red Bank

Congregation B'nai Israel.PO Box 252, Red Bank NJ 07701.

Congregation B'nai Israel, Dorothy L. Spiwak Memorial Library. PO Box 252, Red Bank NJ 07701.

Ridgefield Park

Temple Emanuel. Affiliated with United Syn of Am. Rabbi Mark Kiel; Pres: Amy Lederhendler. **120 Park St, Ridgefield Park NJ 07660 (201) 440–9464.**

Ridgewood

Temple Israel of Ridgewood. Affiliated with United Syn of Am. Rabbi Allan Schranz; Cantor Elihu Flax; Pres: Marvin Amsterdam. **475 Grove St, Ridgewood NJ 07450 (201) 444–9320.**

Ringwood

Lakeland Hills Jewish Center. Affiliated with United Syn of Am. Rabbi Nathaniel Sprinzen; Pres: Kenneth Kurzweil. **PO Box 115, Ringwood NJ 07456 (201) 835–4786.**

River Edge

Temple Sholom. Affiliated with UAHC. 353 mems. Rabbi Joseph Rudavsky; Pres: Martin Besen; Edu: Helga Newmark; Brotherhood Pres: Mel Solomon. **385 Howland Ave, River Edge NJ 07661 (201) 489–2463.**

United Jewish Community of Bergen County. Mem of CJF. Inc 1978. Pres: Arthur Joseph; Exec VP: Dr James Young. **111 Kinderkamack Rd, PO Box 176, N Hackensack Station, River Edge NJ 07661 (201) 488–6800.**

River Vale

Jewish Historical Society of Raritan Valley. To dev an interest in preserving the hist of the central NJ area. For additional information, see – Jewish Historical Society of Raritan Valley – Jersey City, NJ. **Bergen Cty Unit, 185 Westwood Ave, River Vale NJ 07675 (201) 666–2370.**

Rockaway

White Meadow Temple. Affiliated with United Syn of Am. Rabbi Jacob Weitman; Cantor Lyle Rockelr; Pres: Hyman Zelnick; Edu Dir: Rabbi Harvey Horn; Youth Dir: Errol Schnurman. **153 White Meadow Rd, Rockaway NJ 07866 (201) 627–4500.**

Rumson

Congregation B'nai Israel. Affiliated with United Syn of Am. Rabbi Jack M. Rosoff; Cantor Michael Chernofsky; Pres: Joel Engel; Exec Adm: Miriam Friedman. **Hance & Ridge Rds. Rumson NJ 07760 (201) 842–1800.**

Dorothy L. Spiwak Memorial Library of Sisterhood, Congregation B'nai Israel. To support & enrich adult & juvenile edu progs of the Syn; to contribute to the dev of J social, intellectual, & spiritual values; to contribute to the knowledge of J Am heritage; to stimulate appreciation of J in Heb & English. Facilities for over 4,500 bks, periodicals & pamphlets; circulation, reading, display & work areas. Part-time librarian to assist K through adults. Est 1961 with its collection in a case in the lobby of the syn, staffed by volunteers. In 1971 library cttee organized for preparation for a move into new wing of the syn. Chr: Isolina Karpel; Librarian: Mildred Howitt. **Hance & Ridge Rds, Rumson NJ 07760 (201) 842–1800.**

Rutherford

Temple Beth El. Affiliated with United Syn of Am. Rabbi Steven J. Shaw. **185 Montross Ave, Rutherford NJ 07070 (201) 438–4931.**

Scotch Plains

Temple Israel of Scotch Plains & Fanwood. Affiliated with United Syn of Am. Rabbi Clifford B. Miller; Cantor Milton Kurz; Pres: Lewis M. Markowitz; Edu Dir: Benjamin Margolis; Youth Dir: David Tannenbaum. **1920 Cliffwood St, Scotch Plains NJ 07076 (201) 889–1830.**

Short Hills

Congregation B'nai Jeshurun. Affiliated with UAHC. 1232 mems. Rabbis: Barry H. Greene, Stephen W. Goodman, Ely E. Pilchick; Cantor Norman Summers; Pres: Jerry Harwood; Edu: Elaine Kadison; Adm: Martin Halpern; Sisterhood Pres: Sharon Kleinberg; Brotherhood Pres: F. Rick Brous. **1025 S Orange Ave, Short Hills NJ 07078 (201) 379–1555.**

Congregation B'nai Jeshurun Library. For information on the Cong, see – Congregation B'nai Jeshurun, Short Hills, NJ. **1025 S Orange Ave, Short Hills NJ 07078 (201) 379–1555.**

Somerset

Central New Jersey Jewish Home for the Aged. Nursing Home affiliated with J Fed of Central NJ, N Middlesex, Raritan Valley & Somerset Counties; Am Assn of Home for the Aging; NJ Assn of Non-Profit Homes for the Aged; J Homes & Housing for the Aging. To provide the finest care that can be provided for the J elderly in the central NJ area both socially & physically in a J environment. Med servs provided with in-house Drs; social work; counseling; Rel Servs held 3 times a day as well as on all Holidays; glot kosher meals provided 3 times a day; edu progs: Bat Mitzvah lessons for those residents interested; HS graduation for those residents interested; library containing 750 vols, (gen subjects); daily activities designed according to residents individual interests. 125 Beds. 150 full-time & part-time employees; over 200 volunteers. The Central NJ J Home for the Aged opened in March 1975. Pub Cnai Lites (monthly resident newsletter). Facilities include kosher kitchen, daily sanctuary seating 50, holiday sanctuary seating 250, gift shop, physical therapy rm; recreation rm with kitchen. Exec Dir: Eliott V. Solomon; Asst Adm: Judith Tucker; Pres: Sol Kramer; 1st VP: David Koplowitz; VPs: Doris Arshan, Margit Feldman, Emanuel Germinsky. **380 DeMott Lane, Somerset NJ 08873 (201) 873–2000.**

Temple Beth El. Affiliated with United Syn of Am. Rabbi Martin Schlussel; Pres: Irwin Cohen; Edu Dir: Dr Edgar Alster. **1495 Amwell Rd, Somerset NJ 08873 (201) 873–2225.**

Somerville

Jewish Federation of Somerset County. Mem of CJF. Organized 1960. Pres: Gilbert Pelovitz; Exec Dir: Moshe M. Ziv. **2 Division St, PO Box 874, Somerville NJ 08876 (201) 725–2231.**

Temple Beth El. Affiliated with UAHC. 225 mems. Rabbi Michael L. Abraham; Pres: Michael Feldman; Edu: Janet Halpern, Edward Malberg; Sisterhood Pres: Jolane Bernheimer. **67 Rte 206 S, Somerville NJ 08876 (201) 722–0674.**

South Orange

Beth El of the Oranges & Maplewood. Affiliated with United Syn of Am. Rabbi Jehiel Orenstein; Cantor Morris Levinson; Pres: Herman Lebersfeld; Edu Dir: Saul Troen. **222 Irvington Ave, South Orange NJ 07079 (201) 763–0111.**

Congregation Beth El Library. For information on the Cong, see – Congregation Beth El, South Orange, NJ. **222 Irvington Ave, South Orange NJ 07079 (201) 763–0111.**

Congregation Oheb Shalom. Affiliated with United Syn of Am. Rabbi Dr Alexander M. Shapiro; Cantor Henry R. Rosenblum; Pres: Richard Weitzman; Exec Dir: Naomi Reisberg; Edu Dir: Saul B. Troen. **170 Scotland Rd, South Orange NJ 07079 (201) 762–7067.**

Congregation Oheb Shalom Library. For information on the Cong, see – Congregation Ohev Shalom, South Orange, NJ. **170 Scotland Rd, South Orange NJ 07079 (201) 762–7067.**

Temple Israel of the Oranges & Maplewood. Affiliated with UAHC. 400 mems. Rabbi Herbert Weiner; Cantor Abraham Levitt; Pres: David Greenstone; Edu: Arie Ben-Shalom; Sisterhood Pres: Natalie Grapek; Brotherhood Pres: Theodore H. Rose. **432 Scotland Rd, South Orange NJ 07079 (201) 763–4116.**

Spotswood

Monroe Township Jewish Center. Affiliated with UAHC. 70 mems. Pres: Len Ziven. **PO Box 71, Spotswood NJ 08884 (201) 251–0594.**

Springfield

Temple Sha-arey Shalom. Affiliated with UAHC. 291 mems. Rabbi Howard Shapiro; Cantor Irving Kramerman; Pres: Lawrence Malin; Edu: Elaine Snepar; Sisterhood Pres: Lois Schneider; Brotherhood Pres: David Belasco. **78 S Springfield Ave, Springfield NJ 07081 (201) 379–5387.**

Succasunna

Temple Shalom. Reform Syn affiliated with UAHC. To provide a spiritual ctr that seeks to bring relevance to the beliefs & practices of J rel traditions; to provide through its many cttee, progs, activities, & edu facilities, opportunities for experiencing, studying & appreciating J heritage. Fri Evening & Sat Rel Servs, Oneg Shabbat; Family Servs; High Holy Day Servs; Rel Sch: Pre-K; K; 1st – 7th grades; HS prog for 8th – 10th grades; Bar/Bat Mitzvah; Confirmation; library; Story Hour for pre-schoolers; Sisterhood; Brotherhood; youth groups; Choir; L'Chaim Sr Citizen Club; Col Outreach Prog; cemetery property available. F in 1960 by 10 J families Roxbury Reform Temple – Temple Shalom in order to fulfill spiritual needs & provide for chil J edu. Within 3 yrs, the Sisterhood, Brotherhood, & Youth Group formed while holding servs at various rel & com facilities. In 1965 construction began on S Hillside Ave, & original structure was expanded in 1976. The Menorah (monthly information bulletin). Bldg facilities include: sanctuary with seating capacity of over 300, large social hall, kitchen, adm offs, library, 13 classrooms, all-purpose rm. Rabbi Joel E. Soffin; Pres: Eugene Friedman; 1st VP: Ronald Bronstein; Cttee & Chr – Bldg & Grounds: Steve Redan; Ritual: Howard Rauchberg; Ways & Means: Robert Doniger; 2nd VP: Susan Zuckerman; Cttee & Chr – Adult Edu: Randy Brooks; Publicity & Historian: Stuart Bauer; Social Action: Honey Devins; 3rd VP: Robert Gold; Cttee & Chr – Rel Sch: Joel Zamlong; Youth: Allan Monack; Membership: Irene Bolton; Sec: Sandi Monack; Treas: Marcia Saltz; Asst Treas: Judi Shinberg; Trustees: Phyllis Vogel, Edward Gates, Dick Satz; Sisterhood Pres: Barbara Gold; Brotherhood Pres: Steve Tabakin. **215 S Hillside Ave, Succasunna NJ 07876 (201) 584–5666.**

Temple Shalom, Edna Goldblatt Salzman Memorial Library. For information on the Temple, see – Temple Shalom, Succasunna, NJ. **215 S Hillside Ave, Succasunna NJ 07876 (201) 584–5666.**

Summit

Summit Jewish Community Center. Affiliated with United Syn of Am. Rabbi William B. Horn; Cantor Albert Mulgay; Pres: Murray Mohl; Edu Dir: Victor Cohen. **67 Kent Pl Blvd, Summit NJ 07901 (201) CR3–8130.**

Temple Sinai. Affiliated with UAHC. 285 mems. Rabbi Morrison D. Bial; Cantor Glenn A. Groper; Pres: Robin Green; Edu: Constance R. Reiter; Sisterhood Pres: Marilyn Svach; Brotherhood Pres: Harvey Feuer. **208 Summit Ave, Summit NJ 07901 (201) 273–4921.**

Teaneck

Congregation Beth Am. Affiliated with UAHC. 143 mems. Rabbi Deborah R. Prinz; Cantor Kenneth Butensky; Pres: Carlene Fleishman; Edu: Barbara Bar-Nissin. **510 Claremont Ave, Teaneck NJ 07666 (201) 836–5752.**

Congregation Beth Sholom. Affiliated with United Syn of Am. Rabbi Kenneth E. Berger; Pres: Stuart Weiner. **Rugby Rd & Rutland Ave, Teaneck NJ 07666 (201) 833–2620.**

Congregation Beth Sholom Library. For information on the Cong, see – Congregation Beth Sholom, Teaneck, NJ. **Rugby Rd & Rutland Ave, Teaneck NJ 07666 (201) 833–2620.**

Jewish Center of Teaneck. Syn & JCC affiliated with United Syn of Am. To become a true 'Syn Ctr' stimulating the J com to full participation in all aspects of J life, & providing servs & functions to make such participation possible. Daily Shabbat & Holiday Servs; two Jr Congs for 7–12 yrs of age & 12 yrs & older; Shabbat lunches; Shabbatons which include sleep–ins over Fri night & weekends at nearby campgrounds; Chil Edu: nursery for ages 3–5, Pre Heb for ages 5–7, Elementary Heb Sch for ages 8–12, Heb HS for ages 12–15; Adult Forum Progs: four or five progs yearly of special interest including speakers, musical progs & films; Adult Ins For J Studies: mini courses which include J Hist, Talmud, J Ethics, Conversational Heb & Modern Heb Literature; youth activities: club prog for boys & girls grades 3–7 which includes gym activities, lounge games, holiday celebrations, & arts & crafts; Kadima: youth prog for boys & girls in 7th & 8th grades which includes social, edu & athletic progs; USY: youth prog for 9–12 graders which includes social, edu, cultural & athletic progs, col trip, Purim Carnival, hosting of an area dance, edu workshops; Jr Sisterhood: a serv org for girls in HS; After Sch Prog: gym, ceramics, arts & crafts; Athletic Dept: gym hrs for mens basketball & paddle ball, open gym time, open & organized swimming, athletics for youth groups & competitive meets, sponsorship of a basketball league; Men's Club; Sisterhood; Couples Club; Horeynu (Our Parents) Group; Kosher Nutrition Prog; Seder for Russian Emigres; Post Mastectomy Prog; library; annual Shabbat Dinner & Dinner Dance. F in 1933. In 1949, due to an increase in membership, a larger facility was built. In a short time, even that proved insufficient & the bldg that now houses the sanctuary was started in 1955. Facilities include an auditorium with stage, pool, sauna, gift shop, & gym. Local J orgs make use of the large auditorium in the ctr for their functions. Rabbi Dr Judah Washer; Pres: Milton Polevoy; VPs: Herbert Stern, Kurt Heilbronner, Martin Kornheiser; Treas: Martin L. Cohen; Fin Sec: Hyman Sobel; Rec Sec: Adele Golbey; Corsp Sec: Dr Alan Bloom; Auditor: Milton Bornstein. **70 Sterling Pl, Teaneck NJ 07666 (201) 833–0515.**

Temple Emeth. Affiliated with UAHC. 433 mems. Rabbi Louis J. Sigel; Cantor Donald M. Slonim; Pres: Eileen Nahm; Edu: Gail S. Kahn; Brotherhood Pres: Lawrence Lipsitz. **1666 Windsor Rd, Teaneck NJ 07666 (201) 833–1322.**

Tenafly

Congregation Beth Chavairuth. Affiliated with UAHC. 53 mems. Rabbi Avraham Soltes; Pres: Henry Lehmann. **c/o Mr Henry Lehmann, 49 Leonard Ave, Tenafly NJ 07670 (201) 569–8323.**

Jewish Community Center on the Palisades. Non-profit J social servs agy. Dedicated to enriching J life, perpetuating J by instilling pride in & understanding of the J heritage. Adult Edu; Nursey Sch; physical edu; sports: game rms; swimming; tennis; softball; baseball; select classes & activities; teen socials; holiday celebrations. The JCC serves as a training ground for grad & undergrad stu in the fields of early childhood edu, health & recreation, & social work. Facilities include a weight & exercise rm, game rms, an indoor & outdoor swimming pool, tennis cts, baseball field, teen lounge, stereo rm, par course, racquetball cts, picnic area, nature trails, gymnasium, sauna rms, gym, squash ct, indoor jogging track, health clins, & basketball cts. Pres: Herny Taub; VPs: Dr Sandra Gold, Charles Klatskin, Ilene Fish, Dr Martin Levitt, Myron Rosner; Treas: Dr Louis Greenwald; Sec: Paula Braverman; Bd of Trustees: Norman Seiden, Benjamin Casser, Jules Casser, Helen Eisenberg, Eleanor Epstein, Ira Fish, Charles Klatskin, Philip Rothman, Leonard Rubin, John Saril, Herbert Schwartz, Joseph Skaller, Henry Taub, Fred Thomases; Bd of Advs: Renato Cohen, Nathan Baker, Hyman Goodman, Wilson Kaplen, Harold Meltzer, Dr Carl Rothschild, C. Conrad Schneider, Inge Trachtenberg; Bd of Dirs: Naomi Bartnoff, Fran Bash, Murray Beer, Frances Bernstein, Martin Bernstein, Dr Al Bodenstein, Alan Cohen, Jerry Cohen, Sanford Dorf, Marvin Eisman, Mark Epstein, Rusti Fand, Eliot Frankel, Harold Gabe, Linda Gabriel, Mel Gerstein, Seymour Graye, Sylvia Heidenberg, Erich Holzer, Esther Kaplan, Dr Edward Kaplow, Ruth Kurtzman, Leonard Marcus, Reuven Merker, Ralph Miller, Dianne Nashel, Robert Oliff, Stephen Ollendorf, Carole Owens, David Ralby, Praticia Rosen, Dr Seligman Rosenberg, Daniel Rubin, Adele Salitan, Dr Burton Scherl, Sid Schonfeld, Leonard Schwartz, Stanley Shirvan, Stephen Silver, Leslie Simon, Laurence Skaller, Norbert Steinberger, Henry Voremberg, Ruth Warshauer, Norton Waltuch, Bernard Weinflash, Robert Zuckerman; Exec Dir: David Dubin; Asst Exec Dirs: Michael Witkes, Gil Landau; Dir of Adm: Walter Krug. **411 E Clinton Ave, Tenafly NJ 07670 (201) 569–7900.**

Temple Sinai of Bergen County. Affiliated with UAHC. 600 mems. Cantor Nathaniel Benjamin; Pres: Sandra Barsky; Edu: David K. Ressler; Adm: Janet Koplik; Sisterhood Pres: Ellen Marcus; Brotherhood Pres: Joseph Josefsberg. **1 Engle St, Tenafly NJ 07670 (201) 568–3035.**

United Jewish Fund of Englewood & Surrounding Communities. Fund raising & creative programming: Proj Renewal (Neve Yosef in Haifa); Russian absorption; Scholar-in-Residence; Young Leadership Dev Prog; Missions to Is; Walkathon for Is; other activities of a pol & social action nature. Inc in 1953 although hist began much earlier since the local com of Englewood organized fund raising campaign for Palestine & local J needs in 1938. Exec Dir for JCC & UJA, George Hantgan, was employed in 1950. Since then, the Fund enlarged its scope of activities & has been consistently among the top leadership in per-capita fund raising. Runs yearly fund raising campaign through separate men's, women's & youth divs. Fund's allocations reflect broad range of interests with emphasis towards Is. Exec Dir: Sy Colen; Exec Consultant: George Hantgan; Pres: Norman Gurman; VPs: Helen Kaplan, Adele Salitan, Judith Vogel, William Weiss; Treas: Dr Richard Rosenbluth; Sec: Dr Burton Scherl; Hon Pres: Sam Lieben; Natl Cabinet: Raymond Kaplan, Norman Seiden; Women's Div Pres: Adele Salitan; General Chr: Norman Waltuch; Women's Div Chr: Yaffa Reisfield; Bd of Trustees – Exec Cttee: Helen Eisenberg, Valerie Hyman, Rita Merendino, Dr A. Harry Passow, Leonard Rubin, Leona Schiller, Henry Taub, Florence Thomases, Rudolph Treitel, Norton Waltuch; Bd of Advs: Naomi Bartnoff, Daniel Blackstone, Paula Braverman, Benjamin Casser, Deborah Forman, Nellie Greenberg Gellerman, Abe Ginsburg, Dr Jules Hirsch, Dr Edward Kaplow, Dr Gerlad M. Litzky, Dr Elias Reiner, Philip Rothman, John Saril, Sidney Slauson, Betty Steinberg Tell, Norbert Steinberger, Inge Trachtenberg, Michael Trachtenberg. **411 E Clinton Ave, Tenafly NJ 07670 (201) 569–1070.**

Tinton Falls

Monmouth Reform Temple. Affiliated with UAHC. 205 mems. Rabbi Sally J. Priesand; Pres: Stuart Tuchband; Edu: Terry Layman, Sally J. Priesand; Sisterhood Pres: Sheila Fink; Brotherhood Pres: Bernard Brandwene, Barry Kahn. **332 Hance Ave, Tinton Falls NJ 07724 (201) 747–9365.**

Monmouth Reform Temple Library. For information on the Temple, see – Monmouth Reform Temple, Tinton Falls, NJ. **332 Hance Ave, Tinton Falls NJ 07724 (201) 747–9365.**

Toms River

Congregation B'nai Israel. Conservative Syn affiliated with United Syn of Am, & World Council of Syns. Dedicated to the edu & spiritual life of its mems, & the J rel com. Cong works with gen com to help perpetuate ideals of J throughout the world. Daily, Shabbat, Festival Rel Servs; Nursery Sch; Talmud Torah; Heb HS; Ins of Adult J Studies; USY & Kadima youth clubs; Sisterhood affiliated with Women's League for Conservative J. F in 1949 as outgrowth of the com of J Farmers. Facilities include sanctuary, social hall, library, classrooms, youth lounge. Rabbi Richard Hammerman; Cantor Daniel Green; Prin: Hannah Felder; Syn Sec: Alice Tulecki; Pres: Robert Foxman; 1st VP: Henry Goldfarb; 2nd VP: Ruth Guenzburger; Treas: Harold Isaacson; Rec Sec: Robert Ullman; Fin Sec: Esther Federovitch; Corsp Sec: Carla Friedman; Gabbai Rishon: Aron Weiss; Gabbai Shani: Solomon Guttman. **1488 Old Freehold Rd, Toms River NJ 08753 (201) 349–1244.**

Trenton

Adath Israel Congregation. Affiliated with United Syn of Am. Rabbi Donald D. Crain; Cantor Irving Feller; Pres: Albert Z. Segal. **715 Bellevue Ave, Trenton NJ 08618 (609) 599–2591.**

Adath Israel Congregation, Hyman & Jennie Green Library. For information on the Cong, see – Adath Israel Congregation, Trenton, NJ. **715 Bellevue Ave, Trenton NJ 08618 (609) 599–2591.**

Congregation Brothers of Israel. Affiliated with United Syn of Am. Rabbi Howard Hersch; Cantor Mark Spindler; Asst Rabbi & Edu Dir: Rabbi Jeffrey Kravitz; Pres: Sylvia Geser; Youth Dir: Alan Isaacs. **499 Greenwood Ave, Trenton NJ 08609 (609) 695–3479.**

Congregation Brothers of Israel Library. For information on the Cong, see – Congregation Brothers of Israel, Trenton, NJ. **499 Greenwood Ave, Trenton NJ 09609 (609) 695–3479.**

Har Sinai Hebrew Congregation. Affiliated with UAHC. 551 mems. Rabbi Bernard Perelmuter; Cantor Marshall M. Glatzer; Pres: Harold G. Orland; Adm: Bea Littman; Sisterhood Pres: Eva Adelberg, Rita Getty, Marion Wilner. **491 Bellevue Ave, Trenton NJ 08618 (609) 392–7143.**

Har Sinai Hebrew Congregation Library. For information on the Cong, see – Har Sinai Hebrew Congregation, Trenton, NJ. **491 Bellevue Ave, Trenton NJ 08618 (609) 392–7143.**

Jewish Federation of the Delaware Valley. Mem of CJF. Organized 1929. Pres: Martin Okean; Exec Dir: Charles P. Epstein. **999 Lower Ferry Rd, PO Box 7365, Trenton NJ 08628 (609) 883–9110.**

Union

Congregation Beth Shalom. Affiliated with United Syn of Am. Rabbi Dr Elvin I. Kose; Cantor Richard Dondes; Pres: Lewis Schwarz; Edu & Youth Dir: Rabbi Lawrence Weiss. **Vauxhall Rd & Plane St, Union NJ 07083 (201) 686–6773.**

Jewish Federation of Central New Jersey. Affiliated with Council of J Feds. Dedicated to strengthening the spirit of human helpfulness among the J people. The purposes are: to engage all the major J groups within the J com in a cooperative process to fulfill the goals & aspirations of the J com; to review the operations, principles & standards of the Fed local beneficiary agy & other such orgs & agy as function within the Fed com, so as to assist & strengthen them in serving the interests of the com as a whole; to raise funds for the support of overseas, natl & local J philanthropic agy & progs. Fundraising; planning; com relations; com dev. 22 towns. 14 employees; hundreds of volunteers. F in 1945 as the Elizabeth Jewish Council; changed name to Eastern Union Cty J Council in 1956, to Union Cty J Council in 1972, & to J Fed of Central NJ in 1973. Pres: Emanuel C. Pachman; VPs: Marilyn Flanzbaum, Richard Goldberger, Murray Pantirer, Richard Samuel; Campaign Chr: Larry Goldberger; Assc Camp Chr: Dr George Pogosky; Women's Div Pres: Gladys Moore; Treas: Marvin Share; Asst Treas: David Tannenbaum; Sec: Alfred Gelfoun; Asst Sec: Jerry Tarlowe; Staff includes Exec VP: Burton Lazarow; Assc Dir: Diana Cohen. **Green Lane, Union NJ 07083 (201) 351–5060.**

Temple Israel of Union. Conservative Syn. Heb Sch; Sisterhood; Men's Club; Teen Age Club; AZA, BBG youth groups; Leisure Timers (sr citizens). Est 1960. Rabbi Meyer H. Korbman; Cantor Hillel J. Sadowitz; Pres: William Feldman; VP: Michael Zuckerman. **2372 Morris Ave, Union NJ 07083 (201) 687–2120.**

Ventnor

Congregation Beth Judah. Affiliated with United Syn of Am. Rabbi Alan B. Lucas; Cantor Edmond A. Kulp; Pres: Jack Fleishman; Exec Dir: Bernice F. Salins; Edu Dir: Carole Letzter; Youth Dir: Linda S. Kulp. **6725 Ventnor Ave, Ventnor NJ 08406 (609) 822–7116.**

Ventnor City

Federation of Jewish Agencies of Atlantic County. Mem of CJF. Organized 1924. Pres: Judge Gerald Weinstein; Exec Dir: Murray Schneier. **5321 Atlantic Ave, Ventnor City NJ 08406 (609) 822–7122.**

Verona

Jewish Community Center of Verona. Affiliated with United Syn of Am. Rabbi Michael Laxmeter; Pres: Herman Sebiri; Youth Chr: Bonnie Yorke. **56 Grove Ave, Verona NJ 07044 (201) 239–0754.**

Vineland

Beth Israel Congregation. Affiliated with United Syn of Am. Rabbi Dr Murray J. Kohn; Pres: Irving Zislin; Edu Dir: Allan Cohen; Youth Dir: David Kotok. **1015 Park Ave, PO Box 465, Vineland NJ 08360 (609) 691–0852.**

Beth Israel Congregation Library. For information on the Cong, see – Beth Israel Congregation, Vineland, NJ. **1015 E Park Ave, PO Box 465, Vineland NJ 08360 (609) 691–0852.**

The Jewish Federation of Cumberland County. Mem of CJF. Incorporating the Jewish Community Council & Allied Jewish Appeal. Inc 1971. Pres: Dr David Rosenberg; Exec Dir: Melvyn May. **629 Wood St, Suite 204, Vineland NJ 08360 (609) 696–4445.**

Warren

Mountain Jewish Center. To fulfill the need for J identity; to provide servs in a meaningful, traditional, yet contemporary, atmosphere. Rel Edu prog: Sun Sch, Heb Sch, Bar/Bat Mitzvah, Sun Simcha for presch chil; Fri Night Sabbath Servs are held twice each mo with women taking an active part in the ritual; Men & Women's Div provide cultural, social & fundraising events. Est in 1970 by families fr Watchung Hills area. In 1975 a small house situated on a 7 acre fruit orchard was purchased. In 1981 a new bldg was erected comprising one large rm to accommodate the need for a larger sanctuary & all-purpose rm. All the rms in the house are used as classrooms. Rabbi Dr Bruce Charnov; Pres: Barbara Cohen; VP: Dr Martin Harris; Corsp Sec: Jean Horowitz; Rec Sec: Jana Fromm; Treas: Dr Abe Morganoff; Adm Dir: Celia Menasha; Adult Activities: Louise Small; Bldg Dir: Norman Wechsler; Edu Dir: Charlee Harris; Rel Dir: Joel Werbel; Ways & Means

Dir: Philip Seagull; Women's Div Pres: Pat Reeves; Men's Div Pres: Marvin Schaab. **104 Mt Horeb Rd, Warren NJ 07060 (201) 356–8777.**

Washington Township

Temple Beth Or. Affiliated with UAHC. 385 mems. Rabbi H.P. Berkowitz; Cantor Donn Rosenzweig; Pres: John Lee; Edu: Barbara Schweber; Sisterhood Pres: Phyllis Simmons, Sharon Schwart; Brotherhood Pres: Robert Berkowitz. **56 Ridgewood Rd, Washington Township NJ 07675 (201) 664–7422.**

Temple Beth Or, Arthur E. Merke Memorial Library. For information on the Temple, see – Temple Beth Or, Washington Township, NJ. **56 Ridgewood Rd, Washington Township NJ 07675 (201) 664–7422.**

Wayne

Jewish Federation of North Jersey. Mem of CJF. Formerly Jewish Community Council. Sponsors United Jewish Appeal Drive. Organized 1933. Pres: Marge Bornstein; Exec Dir: Leon Zimmerman. **One Pike Dr, Wayne NJ 07470 (201) 595–0555.**

Options Publishing. Options, The Jewish Resource Newsletter (monthly pub) offers all Am J a chance to learn about the opportunities for & the benefits of being J today; reports the who, what & where available for a J lifestyle. Bks: Friends of the Jews; Conversations with My Soul. Publisher: Betty J. Singer. **Box 311, Wayne NJ 07470 (201) 694–2327.**

Temple Beth Tikvah. Reform Temple affiliated with UAHC. 462 mems. Rabbi Israel Dresner; Cantor Charles D. Romalis; Pres: Alvin Edelstein; Edu: Phillip Schimmel; Sisterhood Pres: Barbara Goldstein, Roslyn Gorovitz; Brotherhood Pres: William Rothenberg. **PO Box 3182, 950 Preakness Ave, Wayne NJ 07470 (201) 595–6565.**

Wayne Conservative Congregation. Affiliated with United Syn of Am. Rabbi Carl Astor; Pres: Barry Mersky. **8 Mayfair Dr, Wayne NJ 07470 (201) 696–2500.**

West Caldwell

Hebrew Youth Academy. 1 Henderson Dr, West Caldwell NJ 07006.

Hebrew Youth Academy Library. 1 Henderson Dr, West Caldwell NJ 07006.

West End

Congregation B'nai Sholom. Affiliated with United Syn of Am. Rabbi Jonathan Waxman; Pres: Linda J. Maltzman; Edu Dir: M. Eichel. **213 Lenox Ave, West End NJ 07740 (201) 229–2700.**

West Orange

Daughters of Israel – Pleasant Valley Geriatric Center. Multi-purpose geriatric care facility – beneficiary agy of the UJA of Met NJ, & United Way of Essex & W Hudson. To provide total geriatric care, & to make the lives of the residents as pleasant & meaningful as possible. Daughters of Is Pleasant Valley Home: 24-hour nursing & personal care, 24-hour med coverage, psychiatry, dentistry, podiatry, ophthalmology, physical therapy, pharmacy, x-ray, social servs, work activity ctr, syn servs, rel progs, holiday observance, arts & crafts, recreational & cultural progs, beauty & barber shops, housekeeping servs, kosher meals, special & therapeutic diets, special care for mentally impaired, convenience shop, banking servs, volunteer servs, Women's League. Herr Congregate Living Prog: assisted residential living prog for those elderly people who do not need the servs of a nursing home, but who are unable to live completely on their own. Geriatric Assessment Ctr: full range of diagnostic servs for the elderly of the com. Daughters of Is Sr Day Ctr: provides transportation to & fr the Geriatric Ctr, kosher lunch, med & nursing servs, social servs & referrals, recreational progs. Franzblau Ctr for Continuing Edu in conjunction with Montclair State Col offers seminars for professionals in the field of long-term care, granting continuing edu credit in the States of NY & NJ. Daughters of Is Pleasant Valley Home has a bed capacity of 283. Herr Adult Day Ctr serves up to 100 elderly people per day. Home f in 1906, & in 1982 the name was changed fr Daughters of Is Pleasant Valley Home to Daughters of Is Pleasant Valley Geriatric Ctr. The Geriatric Assessment Ctr opened in the Spring of 1982. Pres: Lester H. Lieberman; VPs: Sanford Grossman, Harold L. Hoffman, Benedict M. Kohl, Daniel M. Peyton; Treas: Donald Cohen; Sec: Edward Blake, Daniel Kram. **1155 Pleasant Valley Way, West Orange NJ 07052 (201) 731–5100.**

Jewish Academy of Arts & Sciences, Inc. 123 Gregory Ave, West Orange NJ 07052 (201) 731–1137.

Jewish Center of West Orange. Affiliated with United Syn of Am. Rabbi Stanley L. Asekoff; Cantor Elihu Feldman; Pres: Murray Gottlieb; Edu Dir: Pearl Witkin. **300 Pleasant Valley Way, West Orange NJ 07052 (201) 731–0160.**

YM-YWHA of Metropolitan New Jersey. Mem & beneficiary of J Com Fed of Met NJ & UJA, United Way of Essex & W Hudson, mem of JWB. To provide an environment for the enrichment of the J family & its individual mems; to respond to the needs of these families to strengthen the Am J com. Nursery Sch; chil care; arts; dance; music; comprehensive physical edu prog; discussion groups; clubs; sci; J family programming. Approximately 2,500 J families; mems of all ages. Est in Newark NJ in 1877 to provide social, recreational, & cultural servs to the J com. Exec Dir: Jack Boeko; Asst Exec Dirs: Rhoda Goodman, Sandy Silverstein; Pres: Harriet Rosenthal; VPs: Mrs Frank Lautenberg, Judith Lieberman, Jerry Schultz, Philip Talkow; Sec: Howard Menaker; Asst Sec: Paul Rosenberg; Treas: Mrs George Newman; Asst Treas: Joel Leibowitz; Bd of Dirs: Vicki Abrams, Jan Ball, Jerry Ben-Asher, Benjamin Bendit, Robert Berkowitz, Horace Bier, Philip Brous, Leon Cooperman, David Dondershine, Barbara Friedman, Steven Gering, Mrs Burton Gillete, Arnold Golber, Stephen Greenberg, Murray Hecht, Kenneth Heyman, Enid Denholtz Horne, Gerald Jaffe, Sima Jelin, Mrs Samuel Larner, Audrey Leiwant, William Lester, Lionel Levey, Vivian Levin, Leon Mendelbaum, Albert Millman, Walter Nachtigall, Lorraine Netko, Harriet Perlmutter Pilchik, Stephen Ploscowe, Genie Reichman, Elizabeth Reisen, Mitzi Reisen, Davie Rocker, Barbara Rothfeld, Frank Schlesinger, Sanford Schoenback, Samuel Schultz, Elinor Seevak, Stephen Seiden, Ruth Snyder, Ethel Somberg, Irving Stein, Stanley Strauss, Muriel Walter, Alan Weill, Leah Weiss, Leonard Wilf, Jeffrey Zissu, Rhea Karlin Zukerman. **760 Northfield Ave, West Orange NJ 07052 (201) 736–3200.**

Westfield

Temple Emanu-El of Westfield. Reform Cong affiliated with UAHC. Rel Servs; Sisterhood; youth groups; Men's Club; Rel Sch; library; 14 chavurot groups; Nursery Sch; Friendship Club; Bar/Bat Mitzvah; Confirmation. 800 families. The first meeting for discussing the est of the Temple was held on Feb 16, 1950 with 31 families represented at the meeting. Money was the major problem. The women thought that a women's group was the likely choice to organize social activities for the essential fund raising purposes. The Sisterhood was organized in 1951. When the J com applied for a bldg permit, a cttee of neighbors objected to the creation of a place of worship, & prepared to circulate a petition to be presented to the town council. In the beginning, servs were held in private homes. Later, they were offered the use of a church. When an elder fr the church was presented with the petition, he was opposed to it saying the J are good friendly people. The petition was never presented to the council. In 1953 the temple was formally dedicated. In 1954 the Sisterhood joined the Natl Fed of Temple Sisterhoods. The Men's Club was est in 1953. Adult Edu consisted of an arts & crafts workshop, & an extra curricular activity for chil was a social dance class for 6th graders. In 1955 the first youth group was organized & a cradle group was also organized to see that pre-schoolers enjoyed holidays through party celebrations. In 1955 there were 267 stu in the Rel Sch. In the mid 1950's an Adult Edu Cttee was formed. Home discussion groups were formed. A com forum was est by the Temple to bridge the gap between the J com & the non J world. In 1956 ground was broken for the new sch bldg. In 1957 a Nursery Sch was opened under the sponsorship of the Temple. In 1958 the Golden Age Club was est & in 1959 renamed the Friendship Group. Temple activities were growing & a temple bulletin was distributed to the mems of the Temple. The Rel Sch bldg was dedicated on May 3, 1959. In the early 1960's the Rel Sch innovated a prog for 9th graders with mems of the Cong lecturing on J subjects of interest. A class for retarded chil was started on Sat mornings, open to any chil in the Union Cty area. A new temple was dedicated on Oct 7, 1966. During the mid 1960's the Rel Sch became more structured. Report cards were standardized, a formal curriculum was est, & Heb was mandatory. Confirmation was extended to tenth grade thereby increasing the total num of yrs of rel edu. The sch received accreditation fr the UAHC. A craft show was initiated as a fund raising proj. The Temple joined the J Com Council of Westfield-Mountainside. On the High Holy Days or at a Sisterhood Sabbath, the pres of the Sisterhood would sit on the binah. In 1970 women started to receive aliyaot. Women started wearing a tallit on the bimah. In 1974 the Chavurah movement was started. In 1976 a Sat morning minyan began in the Lehr Library. On Sept 10, 1978 the Temple library was named in memory of Fritz Lehr. Sisterhood cook bks: Look Who's Cooking & Not By Bread Alone. Rabbi Charles Kroloff; Cantor Don Decker; Pres: Eileen Nathanson; Exec Dir: Robert F. Cohen. **756 E Broad St, Westfield NJ 07090 (201) 232–6770.**

Temple Emanu-El of Westfield, Fritz Lehr Library. For information on the Temple, see – Temple Emanu-El of Westfield, Westfield, NJ. **756 E Broad St, Westfield NJ 07090 (201) 232–6770.**

Westwood

Temple Emanuel. 111 Washington Ave, Westwood NJ 07675 (201) 664–2880.

Temple Emanuel, Ada L. Goldberg Library. 111 Washington Ave, Westwood NJ 07675 (201) 664–2880.

Willingboro

Congregation Beth Torah. Affiliated with United Syn of Am. Rabbi Avraham Kapnek; Pres: Dr Mitchell Litt. **Beverly-Rancocas Rd, Willingboro NJ 08046 (609) 877–4214.**

Temple Emanu-El. Reform Cong affiliated with UAHC. Dedicated to the continued survival of the J people, & to the progressive principles of Reform J. Rel Sch; Nursery Sch; Men's Club; Adult Edu classes; Sisterhood; Couples Club; Youth Prog. 290 mems. In 1959 a group of 5 families broke off fr a larger group in Willingboro (then called Levittown) to form a Reform cong. They met in homes & public bldgs. Rel servs were held at the Municipal Bldg with High Holy Days servs held at St Paul's Methodist Church. The Cong received its charter in 1959 fr UAHC, with a membership of 40 families. The first rabbi was sent by UAHC to conduct Shabbat servs, followed by stu rabbis who spent weekends in Willingboro. Rabbi Richard Levine came in 1964 to become the permanent rabbi. Pres: Sam Silverstein; 1st VP: Arnold Kimmel; 2nd VP: Lenard Israel; 3rd VP: Michael Negin; Treas: Joseph Rothenberg; Fin Sec: Florence Klein; Rec Sec: Janet Maslow; Corsp Sec: Bernice Olinsky; Business Mgr: Arlene Circus; Rabbi Richard Levine. **John F. Kennedy Way, Willingboro NJ 08046 (609) 871–1736.**

Woodbridge

Congregation Adath Israel. Affiliated with United Syn of Am. Rabbi Milton Kula; Pres: Mrs Joseph Goldberg; Coord: Jack Turner. **424 Amboy Ave & S Park Dr, Woodbridge NJ 07095 (201) 634–9601, 3893.**

Woodbury

Beth Israel. Affiliated with United Syn of Am. Rabbi Mitchell Smith; Cantor Kenneth Eckstein; Pres: Robert Snyder. **PO Box 143, High & Warner Sts, Woodbury NJ 08096 (609) 848–7272.**

Woodcliff Lake

Temple Emanuel – Pasack Valley. Affiliated with United Syn of Am. Rabbi Dr Andre Unger; Cantor Mark Biddleman; Pres: Naomi Antonoff; Edu Dir: Mathew Kanig. **87 Overlook Dr, Woodcliff Lake NJ 07675 (201) 664–2880.**

NEW MEXICO

Albuquerque

Congregation Albert. Affiliated with UAHC. 438 mems. Rabbis: Paul Citrin, David Shor; Pres: Steven K. Moise; Sisterhood Pres: Kathy Goldenberg; Brotherhood Pres: Louis Druxman. **1006 Lead Ave SE, Albuquerque NM 87106 (505) 243–3533.**

Congregation B'nai Israel. Affiliated with United Syn of Am. Rabbi Isaac H. Celnik; Cantor Sam Ross; Pres: Charles N. Glass; Youth Dir: Harold Baskin. **4401 Indian Sch Rd NE, Albuquerque NM 87110 (505) 266–0155.**

Jewish Community Council of Albuquerque. Mem of CJF. Organized 1938. Pres: Elvin Kanter; Exec Dir: Elisa M. Simon. **600 Louisiana Blvd SE, Albuquerque NM 87108 (505) 266–5641.**

Las Cruces

Temple Beth El. PO Box 1029, Las Cruces NM 88003 (505) 524–3380.

Los Alamos

Los Alamos Jewish Center. 2400 Canyon Rd, Los Alamos NM 87544 (505) 662–2140, 6434.

NEW YORK

Albany

Albany Jewish Community Center. To be a common meeting ground for all segments of the J com; to enhance the quality of J life; to dev progs which contribute to personal growth & individual dignity on the part of all those who participate; to take responsibility for the dev of future leadership for the J & gen com. Over 300 activities for all age groups: Nursery Sch for ages 3–5; Pre-Sch for 18 mo–3 yrs; sponsors BBYO; Jr HS prog; adult programming: culture progs, Yiddish; Sr Adult Dept; summer day camp; music; dance; progs for widows; J single parent progs; J Singles; health, physical edu; aquatics. Pres: Kenneth Altman; VPs: Marvin Patack, Herman Ungerman, Dr Irving Ratchick; Sec: Eugene Karp; Treas: Sanford Bookstein, David Lobel; Bd Mems: Al Abrams, Dr Mort Arenstein, Norm Brickman, Jules Feinstein, Arnold Ferrer, Elaine Freedman, Marvin Freedman, Dr Warren Geisler, Herbert Goldstein, Alvin Goodman, Arnold Grushky, Hon Joseph Harris, George Kasselman, Al Kaufman, William Kogen, Dr Lawrence Kotlow, Joseph Mandelbaum, Dr Lawrence Marwill, Miriam Mebel, Bonnie Ostroff, Sol Rosenfeld, William Rosenblum, Ann Silk, Sidney Stein III, Michael Urbach, Bayla Wilcove. **340 Whitehall Rd, Albany NY 12208 (518) 438–6651.**

Albany Jewish World. Periodical pub. **1104 Central Ave, Albany NY 12205 (518) 459–8455.**

B'nai Sholom, The New Reform Congregation. Affiliated with UAHC. 106 mems. Rabbi Harry D. Rothstein; Cantor Martin Somerdin; Pres: Franklin Steinhardt. **420 Whitehall Rd, Albany NY 12208 (518) 482–5283.**

Chabad Lubavitch. Lubavitch com servs ctr. Blends Chassidic fervor & warmth with tradition & learning, to show that every J, fr whatever background he or she comes fr, is an integral part of the body of Is. Anti-missionary work; adult edu; Sabbath seminars; holiday progs; day camp; youth groups; syns; kosher kitchen; counseling; chaplaincy; Mitzvah Campaigns; hosp & prison visitations; sr citizens encounters; speakers bureau. Rabbi Y. Rubin. **122 S Main St, Albany NY 12208 (518) 482–5781.**

Congregation Ohev Sholom. Affiliated with United Syn of Am. Rabbi Baruch Frydman; Cantor Daniel Chick; Pres: David L. Diamond. **New Krumkill Rd, Albany NY 12208 (518) 489–4706.**

Greater Albany Jewish Federation. Mem of CJF. Sponsors Jewish Welfare Fund. Organized 1938. Pres: Joan Rosenstein; Exec Dir: Dr Steven R. Windmueller. **19 Colvin Ave, Albany NY 12206 (518) 459–8000.**

Temple Beth Emeth. Affiliated with UAHC. 1094 mems. Rabbis: Martin I. Silverman, Bernard H. Bloom; Cantor Howard M. Stahl; Pres: Audrey P. Kaufman; Edu: Norma Ball, Bernard H. Bloom; Adm: Norman M. Paul; Sisterhood Pres: Dorry Kotzin; Brotherhood Pres: Mordecai Bressler. **100 Academy Rd, Albany NY 12208 (518) 436–9761.**

Temple Beth Emeth Library. For information on the Temple, see – Temple Beth Emeth, Albany, NY. **100 Academy Rd, Albany NY 12208 (518) 436–9761.**

Temple Israel. Affiliated with United Syn of Am. Rabbi Hayyim Kieval; Pres: Eugene Z. Grens; Edu Dir: Rabbi Paul Silton. **600 New Scotland Ave, Albany NY 12208 (518) 438–7858.**

Amenia

Beth David Congregation. Affiliated with UAHC. 33 mems. Cantor Jerome Steiner; Pres: Irving Saperstein . **PO Box 76, Amenia NY 12501 (914) 373–8264.**

Amherst

Temple Sinai. Affiliated with UAHC. 244 mems. Rabbi Joseph Herzog; Pres: Betty Goodman. **50 Alberta Dr, Amherst NY 14226 (716) 834–0708.**

Amityville

Beth Sholom Center of Amityville & the Massapequas. Affiliated with United Syn of Am. Rabbi Leon Spielman; Pres: Bernard Barash. **79 Cty Line Rd, Amityville NY 11701 (506) AM4–2891.**

Amsterdam

Sons of Israel. Rabbi Samuel A. Bloom; Pres: Morris B. Olender. **355 Guy Park Ave, Amsterdam NY 12010 (518) 842–8691.**

Temple of Israel. Affiliated with UAHC. 22 mems. Pres: Carl Salmon. c/o **Mrs Carl Salmon, 166 Locust Ave, Amsterdam NY 12010.**

Armonk

Congregation B'nai Yisrael. Affiliated with UAHC. 115 mems. Rabbi Douglas E. Krantz; Cantor Kerry Mc Divitt; Pres: Michael J. Gross; Edu: Reese Berman, Marianne Rich. **485 Bedford Rd, Box 7, Armonk NY 10504 (914) 273–2220.**

Astoria

Congregation Beth El of Astoria. To disseminate J values & ideology as well as democratic principles in the com. Golden Age Club; Sisterhood; Men's Club; fund raising, annual Bazaar; luncheons; card parties; bus trips; annual Journal Dinner. Est in 1917. Pres: Ludwig Katz; 1st VP: Fred Halberstadt; 2nd VP: Morris Schnabel; Treas: Herman Samet; Rec Sec: Julius Fischer; Hon Trustees: Jacob Eisner, Edward A. Marks, Stanley Stitzer; Bd of Trustees: Charles Rosner, Julius Fischer, William Aron, Harold Garson, Abraham Goodman, Irving Hecht, Norbert Karten, Sam Leitner, William Mandel, Sam Milden, Jonas Podhorzer, Nathan Reder, Sam Roth, Kaufman Rothberger, Irving Siegel, Martin Sorgen, Leo Sternberg, Joseph Teitelbaum, Julian Wager, Zoltan Wieder, Louis Ziegler; Rabbi Harold J. Furst; Gabbais: Fred Halberstadt, Jacob Safier. **30–85 35th St, Astoria NY 11103 (212) 278–8930.**

Atlantic Beach

Jewish Center of Atlantic Beach. Orthodox Cong affiliated with Union of Orthodox J Congs. Rel Servs; Sisterhood; Adult Edu progs; Afternoon Sch; library (variety of rel subjects in Heb & Eng). 215 mems (185 families; 30 individuals); 35 stu. 8 employees. Cong 34 yrs old. Pub Bulletin (monthly with weekly supplement). Facilities include kosher kitchen, sanctuary seating 500, gift shop. Rabbi Sol Roth; Cantor Pinchus Cohen; Pres: Samuel Borenstein; Bd Chr: Hermann Merkin; Ritual Dir: Murray Voroba. **Park St & Nassau Ave, Atlantic Beach NY 11509 (516) FRI–0972.**

Auburn

Congregation B'nai Israel. Affiliated with United Syn of Am. Pres: Edward Knecht; Edu Dir: Ernest J. Lowenstein; Chr Ritual Cttee: A. Leon Goldman. **PO Box 101, 8 John Smith Ave, Auburn NY 13021 (315) 253–6675.**

Babylon

Congregation Beth Sholom. Affiliated with United Syn of Am. Rabbi Richard Smith; Pres: Jack Diamond; Edu Dir: Gerri Stief; Youth Dir: Jack Siegal. **441 Deer Park Ave, Babylon NY 11702 (516) 587–5650.**

Baldwin

Baldwin Jewish Center. Affiliated with United Syn of Am. Rabbi J. Leonard Romm; Cantor Robert Brown; Pres: Owen Diringer; Edu Dir: Stanley Chazan. **885 E Seaman Ave, Baldwin NY 11510 (516) 223–5599.**

Central Synagogue of Nassau County. Reform Syn & Academy of Adult J Studies affiliated with UAHC, LI Fed Temple Youth, Chautauqua Society, Nat1 Fed of Temple Brotherhoods, Natl Fed of Temple Sisterhoods. To perpetuate the heritage of J as interpreted progressively, & to avail the mems of opportunities to live a J way of life in a contemporary Am setting. Sabbath Eve & Morning Servs; Festival Eve & Morning Servs; Sisterhood; Men's Club; Singles Group; Youth Group; Rel Sch grades K–10; Adult Edu; Couples Club; Social Action Group; Blood-Bank prog; library containing 10,000 vols (Judaica plus). 310 families; 290 individuals; 250 stu in grades K–10. 11 employees. F 1936 as Central Syn of Nassau Cty; present facility built in 1952. Pub The Bulletin (bi-weekly). Facilities include sanctuary, chapel, auditorium, lounge, gift shop, sch wing. Pres: Walter Levy; 1st VP: Elliott Winograd; 2nd VP: Eugene P. Friedman; Treas: Richard A. Oppenheimer; Sec: Evelyn Bishop; Off Mgr: Fredda Wolk; Rel Sch Prin: Leonard Berkman. **430 DeMott Ave, Baldwin NY 11510 (516) 766–4300.**

Central Synagogue of Nassau County, Library. Library contains 10,000 vols (Judaica). For information on the Syn, see – Central Synagogue of Nassau County, Baldwin, NY. **430 DeMott Ave, Baldwin NY 11510 (516) 766–4300.**

South Baldwin Jewish Center – Congregation Shaarei Shalom. Affiliated with United Syn of Am. Rabbi A. David Arzt; Cantor Mordechai Edry; Pres: Jerome Warshawsky; Edu Dir: David Fischberger; Youth Dir: Dona Schwab. **2959 Grand Ave, Baldwin NY 11510 (516) 223–8688.**

Batavia

Temple Emanu-El. Affiliated with United Syn of Am. Pres: Jeffrey D. Oshlag. **124 Bank St, Batavia NY 14020 (715) 343–7027.**

Bay Shore

Jewish Centre of Bay Shore. A Conservative Cong affiliated with the United Syn of Am. To perpetuate J faith & traditions, provide facilities for J com dev, & aid for the J people in need here & abroad. Rel Servs & instruction; rel edu of chil; fund raising functions; Choir; Sisterhood; Men's Club; Grandmother's Club; Morning Minyon; Youth Group for teenagers. Est in 1919 as United Hebrew Cong of Bay Shore, NY; changed to J Ctr of Bay Shore in Aug 1933. Servs were held in various locations in the area before being held in a large house on the property on which the syn now stands. The present syn was built in 1951, & the present Heb Sch bldg, The Mary Seley Memorial Hebrew Sch, in 1959. Rabbi & Prin of Heb Sch: Rabbi Israel Jacobs; Cantor Uri Lemberger; Pres & Adm of Exec Bd: Albert Beja; 1st VP: Aaron Siben; 2nd VP: Richard Foster; 3rd VP: Nancy Rabin; 4th VP: Philip Fleishman; Treas: Murray Kramer; Fin Sec: Adolph Schuster; Sec: Jack Zadeck; Off Mgr: Patricia Makowski. **34 N Clinton Ave, Bay Shore NY 11706 (516) 665–1140.**

Sinai Reform Temple. Affiliated with UAHC. 207 mems. Rabbi Benjamin A. Kamin; Cantor Sharon Ruth Kohn; Pres: Gerald F. Hoffer; Edu: Paul Shapiro; Sisterhood Pres: Shelley Katz; Brotherhood Pres: Don Kent. **39 Brentwood Rd, Bay Shore NY 11706 (516) 665–5755.**

Sinai Reform Temple Library. For information on the Temple, see – Sinai Reform Temple, Bay Shore, NY. **39 Brentwood Rd, Bay Shore NY 11706 (516) 665–5755.**

Bayside

Bayside Jewish Center. Traditional–Orthodox Cong affiliated with Yeshiva Univ; Schs accredited by J Bd of Edu of NY. To advance Traditional Judaism, Zionism, State of Is, yeshivos & J edu. Rel edu for adults & chil; Sisterhood; Men's Club; Young Couples Group; Singles Group; Married Couples Group; Col-age Cong; Presch; HS; Afternoon Sch: Hadassah; B'nai B'rith, Knights of Pythias; Sr Citizens; discussion groups, Bible & Talmud classes; Adults Ins; J War Vets; single & youth progs; library of 10,000 vols (Judaica). 350 mem families; 1400 individuals; 75 stu grades 1 to 8; 20 stu HS; 125 col age. 18 employees. F in 1938. Pub The Voice (weekly). Facilities include 3 kosher kitchens, sanctuary seating 1200, chapel seating 125, jr sanctuary seating 200, gift shop, 2 ballrooms, 11 classrms, library, offs. Rabbi Dr William A. Orentlicher; Pres: Robert Stock; VP: Sidney Ahelsan. **204th St & 32nd Ave, Bayside NY 11361 (212) FL2–7900.**

Bayside Jewish Center, Library. Library contains 10,000 vols (Jewish). For information on the Ctr, see – Bayside Jewish Center, Bayside, NY. **204th St & 32nd Ave, Bayside NY 11361 (212) FL2–7900.**

Jewish Center of Bayside Hills. Affiliated with United Syn of Am. Rabbi Samuel Smerling; Cantor Maimon Attias; Pres: Anna Simon; Edu Dir: Jacqueline Mailman. **48th Ave & 212th St, Bayside NY 11364 (212) 225–5301.**

Oakland Jewish Center. Affiliated with United Syn of Am. Rabbi Irwin Isaacson; Cantor Alfred Burger; Pres: Murray Winderman; Exec Dir: Hans Weinberg; Edu Dir: Frieda Berkman; Youth Dir: Bruch Schneider. **61–35 220th St, Bayside NY 11364 (212) 225–7800.**

Bedford

Temple Shaaray Tefila. Affiliated with UAHC. 125 mems. Rabbi David E. Greenberg; Pres: Frank Neubauer; Edu: David E. Greenberg. **PO Box 416, Bedford NY 10506 (914) 666–3133.**

Bellmore

Bellmore Jewish Center. Affiliated with United Syn of Am. Rabbi Bernhard Presler; Cantor Mordechai Fuchs; Pres: Irving Schneider; Exec VP: Elaine Kaye; Edu Dir: Richard Skolnik; Youth Dir: Harold Margulies. **2550 Centre Ave, Bellmore NY 11710 (516) 781–3072.**

Shaarei Shalom, the East Bay Reform Temple. Affiliated with UAHC. 160 mems. Rabbi Paul Kushner; Cantor Lynn Karpo; Pres: Harriet Shangold; Edu: Joan L. Davidson. **2569 Merrick Rd, Bellmore NY 11710 (516) 781–5599.**

Bethpage

Bethpage Jewish Community Center. Affiliated with United Syn of Am. Rabbi Bruce Ginsburg; Cantor Boris Fisch; Pres: Julius Farber; Youth Dir: Ron Grotsky. **600 Bdwy, Bethpage NY 11714 (516) WE8–7909.**

Binghamton

The Jewish Federation of Broome County. Mem of CJF. Organized 1937; inc 1958. Pres: Dr Donald A. Bronsky; Exec Dir: Stanley H. Bard. **500 Clubhouse Rd, Binghamton NY 13903 (607) 724–2332.**

Temple Concord. Affiliated with UAHC. 250 mems. Rabbi Elihu Schagrin; Pres: Edward R. Levene; Sisterhood Pres: Jean Hecht; Brotherhood Pres: Lewis C. Hecht. **9 Riverside Dr, Binghamton NY 13905 (607) 723–7355.**

Temple Israel. Affiliated with United Syn of Am. Rabbi Jacob Hurwitz; Pres: Leonard Feld; Edu Dir: Jacob Spitz. **Deerfield Pl, Binghamton NY 13903 (607) 723–7461.**

Brewster

Chavurah Beth Chai (Mahopac). Affiliated with UAHC. 37 mems. Rabbi Avram Arian; Pres: Charles Sandmel. **c/o Mr Charles Sandmel, RFD 6 Brewster Hill Rd, Brewster NY 10509 (914) 279–8307.**

Putnam County Temple, Jewish Center. Affiliated with UAHC. 75 mems. Rabbi Solomon B. Acrish; Pres: Harold Kapp; Edu: Sylvia Welsher. **Route 22, Brewster NY 10509 (914) 279–4585.**

Briarcliff Manor

Congregation Sons of Israel. Conservative Cong affiliated with United Syn of Am. To establish & maintain a traditional syn & provide for the edu, rel, social & recreational activities of its mems. Rel Servs Sabbath-Fri evenings, Sat mornings; Holiday Servs; weekday minyan Mon & Thurs; edu progs; Nursery Sch; Sunday Sch for K–2nd grade; Afternoon Rel Sch for 3–7 grades; HS for grades 8–10; Adult Edu progs; social functions; library containing 2,000 vols. 340 mems; 320 families; 20 individuals; 50 stu in grades K–2; 133 stu in grades 3–7; 30 stu in grades 8–10. F 1891 in Ossining; first location – Hunter St, second location – Waller St fr 1922, third location – present address fr 1960. Pub The Bulletin (monthly). Facilities include sanctuary seating 100 (opens to 750), chapel, social hall, milk & meat kosher kichens; 7 classrms. Rabbi Daniel Issac; Cantor Nancy Abramson; Pres: Alan Duke; VPs: Paul Rosen, David Lubell, Michael Kirsch; Treas: David Eisendrath; Sec: Marilyn Grossman. **1666 Pleasantville Rd, Briarcliff Manor NY 10510 (914) 762–2700.**

Congregation Sons of Israel, Library. Library contains 2,000 vols. For information on the Cong, see – Congregation Sons of Israel, Briarcliff Manor NY. **1666 Pleasantville Rd, Briarcliff Manor NY 10501 (914) 762–2700.**

Briarwood

Brit Trumpeldor Betar of America, Inc. 85–40 149th St, Briarwood NY 11435.

Bronx

Ahav Tsedek of Kinsbridge. 3425 Kingsbridge Ave, Bronx NY 10463 (212) 543–6969.

Albert Einstein College of Medicine – Yeshiva University. Prepares physicians, conducts research in health sci, provides patient care, awards MD. Clinical facilities & affiliates encompass Bronx Municipal Hosp Ctr (Abraham Jacobi Hosp, Nathan B. van Etten Hosp), Montefiore Hosp & Med Ctr (adm Hosp of Albert Einstein Col of Med), Bronx-Lebanon Hosp Ctr, Bronx Psychiatric Ctr, Bronx Chil Psychiatric Ctr. Ins within the Col include: Belfer Ins for Advanced Biomed Studies (1978) which integrates & coordinates the Med Col post-doctoral research & training prog in the biomed sci; Camp David Ind for Intl Health (1980) which trains sci & physicians fr Egypt, Is & US as grad fellows in clinical & biomed research at Med Col, emphasizing improvement of med serv throughout ME. Med Col also maintains agy & ins serving the com including: Irwin S. & Sylvia Chanin Ins for Cancer Research which is one of the largest med sch-affiliated cancer research ctrs in E; the Rose F. Kennedy Ctr for Research in Mental Retardation & Human Dev which brings together under one roof sci & clinicians concerned with genetic, prenatal, biochem, neurological, psych, & environmental aspects of mental retardation & other forms of aberrant dev; Florence & Theodore Baumritter Kidney Dialysis Research Ctr; Ctr for Social Research in Rehabilitation Med; Chil's Evaluation &

Rehabilitation Clin; Einstein-Montefiore Diabetes Research & Training Ctr; Genetic Counseling Prog; Ins of Neurotoxicology; Liver Research Ctr. Med Col f in 1958. For information on the Univ, see – Yeshiva University, New York City, NY. **Bronx Ctr, Eastchester Rd & Morris Park Ave, Bronx NY 10461.**

Beth El, The House of Yah. 1231 Franklin Ave, Bronx NY 10456 (212) 681–4912.

Bronx Park E Chotiner Jewish Center. 2256 Bronx Park E, Bronx NY 10451 (212) 655–9934.

Castle Hill Jewish Community Center. 486 Howe Ave, Bronx NY 10473 (212) 892–2372.

Co-op City Jewish Center. Affiliated with United Syn of Am. Rabbi Fred Ackerman; Pres: Sidney Rogofsky. **900 Co-op City Blvd, Bronx NY 10475 (212) 671–4579.**

Community Center of Israel. 2440 Esplanade, Bronx NY 10469 (212) 882–2400.

Congregation B'nai Israel of Bronx. 1570 Walton Ave, Bronx NY 10452 (212) 583–8993.

Congregation B'nai Israel of Edenwald. 1014 E 227th St, Bronx NY 10466 (212) 881–4921.

Congregation Sons of Israel. 2521 Cruger Ave, Bronx NY 10467 (212) 231–6213.

Congregation Toras Chaim of Co-op City. 620 Baychester Ave, Bronx NY 10475 (212) 671–0310.

Conservative Synagogue Adath Israel of Riverdale. Affiliated with United Syn of Am. Rabbi Dr Shlomo Balter; Cantor Gordon D. Piltch; Pres: Martin S. Wolpoff; Exec Dir: Mildred Barowsky; Edu Dir: Joan Freeman Cohen; Youth Dir: Perry Netter. **250th St & Henry Hudson Pkwy, Bronx NY 10471 (212) K13–8400.**

Daughters of Jacob. A voluntary non-profit & non-sectarian geriatric ctr. Affiliations: Fed of J Philanthropies of NY, NY Assn of Homes for the Aging, Am Assn of Homes for the Aged, Central Bureau for the J Aged, Beth Is Med Ctr, Natl Assn of J Homes for the Aged. Teaching affiliations: Bronx-Lebanon Hosp Ctr Dept of Psychiatry, City Col of NY Sociological Lab, Cornell Univ-NY Hosp Sch of Nursing, Hunter Col Sch of Health Sci Physical Therapy Sch, Fordham Sch of Social Work, J Theological Seminary, State Univ of NY at Stony Brook Health Sci Ctr Sch of Nursing, St John's Univ Col of Pharmacy & Allied Health Professions, Yeshiva Sch of Social Work. To help each person achieve the best possible quality of life – physically, mentally & spiritually. Skilled nursing care; Intensive Care Unit; Audiology; Dentistry; Dietary; Electrocardiography; Occupational Therapy; Physical Therapy; Optometry; Pharmacy; Podiatry; Social Work Servs; Speech Therapy; X–ray; health related facility for ambulatory residents who require supportive servs; rel servs on Sabbath & all holidays; dietary laws of Kashruth; leisure time & recreation activities; volunteer servs. Guild & the Mother's Day Group raise funds to provide gifts to the elderly patients & residents. Findlay House: 214 one-rm efficiencies & 13 one-bedrm apts with lunch & dinner served daily, housekeeping servs (sheets, pillowcases & towels provided weekly), nurse on duty daily, cultural & edu & recreational activities, library, lounge, auditorium, beauty & barber shop. Findlay Plaza: 131 one-rm efficiencies & 32 one-bedrm apts with dining rm, canteen, library, lounge, auditorium, cultural, edu & recreational activities. 305 skilled nursing beds; 210 health related beds. Staff of 546; 260 volunteers. The Home of the Daughters of Jacob was f in 1896. The present nursing home bldg was constructed in 1973. Findlay House was built in 1971. In 1979 the original bldg of the Daughters of Jacob Geriatric Ctr was completely renovated & reopened as Findlay Plaza. All bldgs are linked together by overhead pedestrian bridges. Current – newsletter pub quarterly. Facilities of the 13 story skilled nursing & health related facility include: adm suite, nursing offs, classrm, gift shop, med library, snack bar, multipurpose auditorium, personnel off, diagnostic & treatment facilities, day suite, dining & recreation rm, barber & beauty shop, clin rms. Exec Dir: Gerald Gottlieb; Chr: Jules Raynes; Pres: Miriam Halberstadt; 1st VP: Martin Chelnick; 2nd VP: Alice Dworsky; 3rd VP: Sylvia Fein; Treas: Matthew B. Rosenhaus; Assc Treas: Mrs Philip Vogelman; Sec: Irving Kessler; Asst Sec: Howard Modlin; Hon 1st VP: Walter H. Weinstein. **1160 Teller Ave, Bronx NY 10456 (212) 293–1500.**

Gun Hill Jewish Center. Orthodox Syn. F in 1931 by Miriam & the late Samuel Feldman. Rabbi Moisha Fuchs; Sisterhood Pres: Miriam Feldman; Syn Cttee: Abraham Gruber, Sol Feigenbaum, Murray Bleiberg, Neil Harrow, Harry Falek, Joseph Feuerstein, Max Telmar, Julius Weiner. **3380 Reservoir Oval E, Bronx NY 10467.**

Hebrew Hospital for Chronic Sick, Inc. Accredited by The Joint Commis on Accreditation of Hosps. To provide long term health care for those afflicted with chronic disease; to create a home-like atmosphere, & to care for the physical, emotional, spiritual & social needs of each person. 24 hour med coverage; Dental Servs; Social Servs Dept; Pharmacy; Clin Lab; Radiology; Ophthalmology; Optometry; Podiatry; Special Med Consultations; Electrocardiogram; Nursing Care; Physical Therapy; Occupational Therapy; Speech & Hearing Servs; Recreational Progs which include arts & crafts, discussion periods, sing-a-longs, entertainment & movies; Special monthly activities which include parties, field trips, resident council activities & coalition meetings; rel servs; full range of health related care servs for residents who do not require skilled nursing care. Full time med dir; physicians fr all major fields of med specialization; nurses; pharmacists; therapists; speech pathologist; audiologist. F in 1928. Facilities include an activity rm, dining rm, patio, patient day rms, beauty & barber shop, private & semi-private rms. Trained volunteers often assist in activities & provide special servs. Chr: Leo Schneider; V Chr: David A. Spector; Pres: Yetta Littman; Sec: Harry Goldsmith; Treas: Sydney Drazen; Gen Counsel: Frederick Katz; Bd of Dirs: David Blasband, Philip Brass, Sydney Drazen, Herbert Drexler, Thomas Elmezzi, Harry Goldsmith, Arnold Goldstein, Samuel Goldstein, Seymour D. Gort, Jerome Jakubovitz, Frederick Katz, Yetta Littman, Joseph A. Perlman, Jack E. Rosenfeld, Peter L. Schaffer, Leo Schneider, David A. Spector, Hon Morris E. Spector, George J. Strauch, Milton H. Wohl; Hon Dirs: Bernard E. Alpern, Hon Alfred M. Ascione; Exec Dir: Richard Shedlovsky; Asst Exec Dir: Martin F. David; Controller: Steven H. Bloom; Med Dir: Dr Paul Hurwitz. **2200 Givan Ave, Bronx NY 10475 (212) 379–5020.**

Intervale Jewish Center of Bronx. To provide a place for the remaining J of the neighborhood. Rel Servs; Social Ctr; fin assistance to the needy. Incorporated as the Minsker Cong of the Bronx in 1916. The name of the Syn was changed in 1948. The sole remaining syn in the S Bronx. Pres: Moishe Sacks; VP: Melachi Parkus; Sec-Treas: Mrs Ray Darginsky; Trustees: Sidney Flisser, Hanich Horowitz, Moishe Sacks. **1024 Intervale Ave, Bronx NY 10459.**

Jack & Pearl Resnich Gerontology Center. Albert Einstein College of Med. Yeshiva University. Coordinates Albert Einstein Col of Med activities relating to aging, including the dev of a serv network for the chronically impaired elderly. For information on the Med Col, see – Albert Einstein College of Medicine, Bronx, NY. **Bronx Ctr, Eastchester Rd & Morris Park Ave, Bronx NY 10461.**

Jacob H Schiff Center. 2510 Valentine Ave, Bronx NY 10457 (212) 295–2510.

Mikvah-Ritualarium. 708 Mace Ave, Bronx NY 10467 (212) 798–6173.

Ohel Torah Synagogue. To teach Torah J. Daily Rel Servs; Adult Edu; Youth Group; Sisterhood; Chevrah Mishnays; Talmud class; cultural events; rel instruction for chil. F in 1937. Rabbi Isaac Gottlieb; Pres: Nathan Shain; Servs Chr: Adolf Haller; Gabboim: Sam Sopher, Louis Moskowitz. **629 W 239th St, Bronx NY 10463.**

Sephardic Shaare Rahamim Congregation, Inc. Morning & Evening Daily Rel Servs; Bar Mitzvah preparation; Heb Ulpan; Sisterhood; dancing; discussions; vocational workshops for the aged; week-end & day trips; movies; social activities; adult edu: gemarah, J law; youth groups. 400 mems. Est in the Bronx in the 1930's. In 1971 the Cong relocated in Co-op City. Among the mems of the Cong are Askenazim who prefer the Sepharadic style. Mems of the Cong come fr Turkey, Rhodes & Greece. Rabbi Abraham Ben Haim; Pres: Victor Alhadeff; Fin Sec: Isaac Benbasset. **100 Co-op City Blvd, Bronx NY 10475 (212) 671–8882.**

Sholem Aleichem Folk Institute, Inc. 3301 Bainbridge Ave, Bronx NY 10467.

Sue Golding Graduate Division of Medical Sciences – Yeshiva University. Offers advanced study in biological sci; awards PhD; Six-yr Med Sci Training Prog prepares stu for research & teaching career & offers combined MD fr Einstein-PhD fr Sue Golding. F 1957. For information on the Med Col, see – Albert Einstein College of Medicine, Bronx, NY. **Bronx Ctr, Eastchester Rd & Morris Park Ave, Bronx NY 10461.**

Temple Beth El of Co-op City. Affiliated with UAHC. 65 mems. Rabbi David L. Dunn; Cantor Dennis Tobin; Pres: Beulah Friedman; Edu: Harold Leids; Sisterhood Pres: Edith E. Kace. **920–1 Baychester Ave, Bronx NY 10475 (212) 671–9719.**

Temple Emanuel at Parkchester. Affiliated with United Syn of Am. Rabbi Joseph P. Schonberger; Cantor Joseph A. Green; Pres: Leon Kaye. **2000 Benedict Ave, Bronx NY 10462 (212) 828–3400.**

Temple Judea. Modern Liberal Syn affiliated with the UAHC. Rel Servs; Choir; Adult Edu, offers courses in Bible, Heb, J Philosophy, Hist & Significant Movements in J Life; Rel Sch for chil ages

5 to 13; Sisterhood; Men's Club; Temple Youth Group. 99 mems. Rabbi Dr Israel Renov; Pres: Muriel Billig; Sisterhood Pres: Doris Solomon; Brotherhood Pres: Leo Bochner. **615 Reiss Pl, Bronx NY 10467 (212) 881–5118.**

Traditional Synagogue of Co-op City. 115 Einstein Loop, Bronx NY 10475 (212) 379–6920.

Young Israel of Parkchester. A constituent of the Natl Council of Young Is. To further J on the Am scene. Full schedule of servs, morning & evening; day & evening classes, lectures; Men's Club; Women's League; sr citizens progs. Young Is is the largest adult J ins in Bronx. F in 1940; The first syn to adopt a syn in Is – Young Is of Rishon L'Zion. Rabbi Maurice L. Schwartz; Pres: Fred Kutner; VPs: Max Spielberger, Sidney Klugman; Treas: Albert Hein; Corsp Sec: Frank Nussbaum; Sec: Abraham Gewertz; Fin Sec: Samuel Pausack. **1375 Virginia Ave, Bronx NY 10462 (212) 822–9576.**

Young Israel of Riverdale. 4502 Henry Hudson Pkwy E, Bronx NY 10471 (212) 548–4765.

Young Israel of the Concourse. Grand Concourse at 165th St, Bronx NY 10451 (212) 293–9700.

Yugntruf. A world-wide org of Yiddish-speaking youth. To ensure the survival of Yiddish as a living language & culture. Literature clubs; Yiddish songfests, picnics, dances & social gatherings, lectures, video-tape progs, full-time field-worker available for programming. F in 1964 to give young people an opportunity to come together & speak Yiddish, read & study Yiddish works, & write, sing, dance, act, & create in Yiddish. Yugntruf (quarterly journal in Yiddish). Editor: Itzek Gottesman; NY Chr: Hershel Glasser; Natl Chr: Dr J.V. Mallow; Sec: Rukhl Schaechter. **3328 Bainbridge Ave, Bronx NY 10467 (212) 654–8540.**

Brooklyn

Adelantre – The Judezmo Society. To stimulate interest in all aspects of Sephardic linguistics, literature, hist, music & folkways. Pubs material on Sephardic J. Est in 1975 by David Bunis & Stephen Levy. A Guide to Reading & Writing Judezmo; Ke xaber (a newsletter); Working Papers in Sephardic & Oriental Jewish Studies; Words of the Sephardim, A Series of Annotated Selections. **4594 Bedford Ave, Bklyn NY 11235.**

Agudas Nshei Ub'nos Chabad770 Eastern Pkwy, Bklyn NY 11213 (212) 493–9250.

Ahavath Sholom. Affiliated with UAHC. 176 mems. Rabbi Eric H. Hoffman; Pres: Gerald Prezioso, Charlotte Russell, Grace Schneider; Sisterhood Pres: Mary Margolis. **1609 Ave R, Bklyn NY 11229 (212) 375–4500.**

Akiva Jewish Culture Clubs of the New York City Public High Schools. Sponsored by the Assn of Orthodox J Teachers. To promote J identity & pride among teenagers in NYC public HS; to expose young people with little or no J knowledge to a prog of various J content. Weekly, bi-weekly or monthly clubs meet after sch: speakers on J identity; films; plays; music; exhibits; J mus; Is dancing; Shabbatons. 20 clubs throughout the city with an average membership of 25–30 teenagers. J faculty mems in HS serve as volunteer club advs. Chr: Zev Schlifstein; Co-Chr: Morton Horowitz; Dir: Max Lew; Dir, Speakers Bureau: Moishe Greenwald; Coord, Scholarships: Dr Fred Bohensky; AOJT Consultant: Jerry Mann. **1577 Coney Island Ave, Bklyn NY 11230 (212) 258–3585.**

American Friends of Yeshivat Zvi Hatzadik. 3100 Brighton 3rd St, Bklyn NY 11235.

American Friends of Yeshivat Zvi Hatzadik, Library. 3100 Brighton 3rd St, Bklyn NY 11235.

Ari Ezer Congregation. 1885 Ocean Pkwy, Bklyn NY 11223 (212) 376–4088.

Association of Orthodox Jewish Teachers. 1577 Coney Island Ave, Bklyn NY 11230 (212) 258–3585.

Ave N Jewish Community Center. 321 Ave N, Bklyn NY 11230 (212) 339–7747.

B'nai Israel Jewish Center. 3192 Bedford Ave, Bklyn NY 11210 (212) 258–2748.

B'nai Israel Jewish Center of East Flatbush, Inc. 357 Remsen Ave, Bklyn NY 11201 (212) 342–4554.

Bais Rochel School for Girls. 225 Patchen Ave, Bklyn NY 11233 (212) 453–0250.

Bais Yaakov Khal Adas Yereim. 563 Bedford Ave, Bklyn NY 11211 (212) 782–2486.

Bais Yaakov Khal Adas Yereim Kindergarten. 570 Bedford Ave, Bklyn NY 11211 (212) 384–7187.

Bais Yaakov of Brooklyn. 1362 49th St, Bklyn NY 11219 (212) 435–7776.

Bais Yaakov of Brooklyn Annex. 4910 14th Ave, Bklyn NY 11219 (212) 854–1219.

Bais Yaakov of Ferndale. 1676 52th St, Bklyn NY 11234 (212) 851–5180.

Baith Israel Anshei Emes. Affiliated with United Syn of Am. Rabbi Howard Gorin; Pres: Nancy Fink. **236 Kane St, Bklyn NY 11231 (212) TR5–1550.**

Bay Ridge Jewish Center – Sheiris Israel. Affiliated with United Syn of Am. Rabbi Dr David M. Feldman; Cantor Leon Gottesman; Pres: Samuel A. Diamond; Edu & Youth Dir: Gregg Flom. **405 81st St, Bklyn NY 11209 (212) 836–3103.**

Beach Haven Jewish Center. 723 Ave Z, Bklyn NY 11223 (212) 375–5200.

The Ben Yehuda School. Solomon Schechter Day Sch for gifted & talented J chil. To create an atmosphere which will encourage the growth of an integrated J personality on Am soil. Bicultural edu for gifted chil grades K–8 – curriculum strives to improve quality of thinking, feeling & living; provides pupil participation; classes consist of Health, Art, Music, Language, Arts, Social Studies, Sci, Math, Heb Studies, Bible, Heb Literature, J Hist, J subjects, trips. F by a group of J men & women brought together by a common interest in a fuller & more satisfactory bicultural edu for gifted & talented J chil. Housed in the spacious, well-equipped, fireproof structure of Bay Ridge J Ctr. Pres: Dr Amnon Abramowitz; Treas: H. Russell Cammer; Sec: Saul Bodner; Prin: Dr Hayim Abramowitz. **405 81st St, Bklyn NY 11209 (212) 238–1504.**

Beth Am – Labor Zionist Center. 1182 Brighton Beach Ave, Bklyn NY 11235 (212) 646–9409.

Beth Am – Labor Zionist Center & Day School. 1182 Brighton Beach Ave, Bklyn NY 11235 (212) 743–4442.

Beth Chana. A girls sch affiliated & sponsored by the Klausenberger Chasidim; registered by the NY State Dept of Edu. Gen Studies Dept for secular subjects; Limudei Kodesh Dept with classes conducted in Yiddish; Heb & English classes; all day K; hot lunches – dining rm & kitchen; buses; playground; summer camp in Catskills. Prin: Rabbi M. Scheiner; Hon Pres: Gherson Weiss, Rabbi Benjamin Wulliger; Pres: Hersh Knopfler; VPs: Erno Nussenzweig, Wolf Mayer; Sec: Jacob Steinmetz; Treas: Leibel Lederman; Comptroller: Mordechai Taub; Chr of the Bd: Chaim Silberman; Exec Dir: Benjamin Paskesz; Bd of Dirs: Juda Brisk, Israel Grossman, Jacob Hollender, Z. Mutzen, Jacob Levy, Tovia Moskovitz, Benjamin Paskesz, Joseph Perlmutter, Chaim Silberman, Hershel Spitzer, Mordchai Tessler, Jacob E. Unsdorfer, S.M. Lovi, Chaim Deutsch. **620 Bedford Ave, Bklyn NY 11211 (212) 522–7422.**

Beth El Elementary School. 457 Grand Ave, Bklyn NY 11238 (212) 789–1259.

Beth El Jewish Center of Flatbush. Affiliated with United Syn of Am. Rabbi Phillip Listokin; Cantor Etan Yungerman; Asst Rabbi Moskowitz; Pres: Ben Yuter. **1981 Homecrest Ave, Bklyn NY 11229 (212) ES5–0120.**

Beth El Talmudic Institute. 1981 Homecrest Ave, Bklyn NY 11224 (212) 339–9117.

Beth Hatalmud. 2127 82nd St, Bklyn NY 11227 (212) 259–2525.

Beth Jacob Academy High School of Brooklyn. 4419 18th Ave, Bklyn NY 11204 (212) 435–8478.

Beth Jacob Day School. 550 Ocean Pkwy, Bklyn NY 11224 (212) 633–6555.

Beth Jacob of Boro Park. 1413 45th St, Bklyn NY 11219 (212) 853–7197.

Beth Jacob of Flatbush. 1823 Ocean Pkwy, Bklyn NY 11224 (212) 645–2009.

Beth Jacob School. 616 Bedford Ave, Bklyn NY 11211 (212) 625–8390.

Beth Jacob Teachers Seminary of America. 132 S 8th St, Bklyn NY 11211 (212) 388–2701.

Beth Kirsch Pre-School & Day Camp. 1014 E 15th St, Bklyn NY 11230 (212) 377–8426.

Beth Rachel School for Girls. 165 Clymer St, Bklyn NY 11211 (212) 782–8811.

Beth Rachel School of Boro Park. 5301 14th Ave, Bklyn NY 11219 (212) 438–7822.

Beth Rivkah Elementary School. 2270 Church Ave, Bklyn NY 11026 (212) 856–4451.

Beth Rivkah Schools. 310 Crown St, Bklyn NY 11225 (212) 771–9000.

Beth Sarah School. 5801 16th Ave, Bklyn NY 11204 (212) 851–5198.

Beth Sholom Peoples Temple. Affiliated with UAHC. 220 mems. Rabbis: Albert J. Lowenberg, Emanuel Schenk; Pres: Rhea Cohen; Sisterhood Pres: S. Chase; Brotherhood Pres: Sigfried Katz. **Bay Pkwy & Benson Ave, Bklyn NY 11214 (212) 372–7164.**

Bialik School. Affiliated with Solomon Schechter Day Schools Assn. Prin: Miriam Vatkin; Chr: Irving Listman. **500 Church Ave, Bklyn NY 11218 (212) 853–7100.**

Bobower Yeshiva. 1533 48th St, Bklyn NY 11219 (212) 438–8411.

Boro Park Progressive Synagogue Congregation B'nai Sholom. Affiliated with UAHC. 62 mems. Rabbi Charles J. Shoulson; Cantor Bernard Tannenbaum; Pres: Max Loeb; Sisterhood Pres: Sara Goldman. **1515 46th St, Bklyn NY 11219 (212) 436–5082.**

Brooklyn Heights Synagogue. Affiliated with UAHC. 241 mems. Rabbi David Glazer; Pres: Herbert Glantz; Edu: David Glazer, Reuven Firestone; Adm: Stanley Levenson; Sisterhood Pres: Therese Meyer. **117 Remsen St, Bklyn NY 11201 (212) 522–2070.**

The Brooklyn Jewish Center. Affiliated with United Syn of Am. Rabbi Israel H. Levinthal; Pres: Benjamin Markowe; Exec Sec: Stanley C. Bresnick. **667 Eastern Pkwy, Bklyn NY 11213 (212) 493–8800.**

Brotherhood Research Institute, Inc. Collects copies of sermons fr clergymen of all faiths. At present, the Ins has 10,000 sermons, & 5 million clippings on the J rel. Material is stored in 3 separate bldgs. Pres: Gerald Kaplan; VP: Roslyn Lubrano; Sec/Treas: Joann Lubrano. **2879 W 12th St, Bklyn NY 11224 (212) 372–5280.**

Canarsie Jewish Center. 965 E 107th St, Bklyn NY 11236 (212) 272–2848.

Center for Holocaust Studies, Inc. 1605 Ave J, Bklyn NY 11230 (212) 338–6494.

Central Yeshiva Beth Joseph Rabbinical Seminary. 1427 49th St, Bklyn NY 11219.

Chabad Lubavitch World Headquarters, Merkos L'Inyanei Chinuch Machne Israel. An outreach org that familiarizes J men & women & chil with J practices & philosophy. To bring the light of Torah & J tradition to all corners of the world; to battle against assimilation, apathy & indifference to J living. In gen this ins offers: Operation Helping Hand – gives aid to Russian immigrants; on campus progs – provides kosher foods, Fri night to Sun retreats, lectures, Shabbat servs & counseling; celebrations of holidays – sponsors seminars on Passover laws, holds Purim Party, sponsors Toys for Tots for chil in the hosp at Chanukah, helps with bldg of succas, distributes prayer bks for holidays; gives marriage & family counseling; Adult Edu Prog; helps est kosher kitchens in private homes; Mitzvah Mobile – introduces J men to the wearing of Tefillin, distributes rel articles, maintains a traveling J library & audio visual ctr; Succamobile; summer day camp. **770 Eastern Pkwy, Bklyn NY 11213 (212) 493–9250,1, 772–5995,6.**

Chevra Shomrei Emunei Anshe Lomza. 474 E 96th St, Bklyn NY 11212 (212) 343–8401.

Chevra Torah Anshe Chesed V'anshei Radishkow. 731 Montauk St, Bklyn NY 11235 (212) 934–8116.

Committee for the Furtherance of Torah Observance. 1430 57th St, Bklyn NY 11219 (212) 851–6428.

Community Temple Beth Ohr. Affiliated with UAHC. 80 mems. Rabbi Herbert H. Rose; Cantor Paula Stark; Pres: Jerome T. Levy; Sisterhood Pres: Hermine Ginsberg; Brotherhood Pres: Mal Cohen. **1010 Ocean Ave, Bklyn NY 11226 (212) 284–5760.**

Congregation & Talmud Torah Ahavath Achim. Orthodox Syn. To serve the com in its rel, edu & communal needs. Provides Daily Rel Servs, central meeting place for the J people; offers classes & lectures on varied J subjects. Est in 1920 & moved to its permanent bldg in 1928. Rabbi Israel Poleyeff; Rabbi Emeritus Dr Meyer Karlin; Cantor Oscar Trainer; Sexton: Rev Meyer Kabinowitz; Pres: Milton Aidlen; VPs: Reuben Hecht, Barnett Schneider, Irving Teller; Treas: Lloyd Somer; Fin Sec: Hyman Evinsky; Rec Sec: Ben Somer; Chief Gabbai: Ira Brand; Assc Gabbai: Meyer Levine. **1750 E 4th St, Bklyn NY 11223 (212) 375–3895.**

Congregation & Yeshiva Lev Someach, Inc. 674 E 2nd St, Bklyn NY 11218 (212) 438–4800.

Congregation & Yeshiva Yeshurin of Flatbush. To strengthen Torah, edu & chasidut in the Flatbush area. Torah edu for boys & girls; education of youth & public in Torah permeating way; daily & weekly classes; outstanding record for charity & Gemilas Chasudim; mikva free of charge. Est in 1949. All syn functions are free. Pres: Mordchai Friedman; VP: Smuel Kizelnik; Gabaim: Eli Abramzyk, Hirsh Wuliger; Treas: C. Steuer; Hon Pres: Alter Liberman. **1454 Ocean Pkwy, Bklyn NY 11230 (212) 375–9292.**

Congregation Adath Yeshurun of Flatbush. 3418 Ave N, Bklyn NY 11234.

Congregation Agudath Achim Talmud Torah. 865 50th St, Bklyn NY 11219 (212) 438–8718.

Congregation Agudath Sholom of Flatbush. 3714 18th Ave, Bklyn NY 11218 (212) 854–2226.

Congregation Ahavas Achim Anshei Sfard. Daily Rel Servs; Study Groups; Outreach Prog for Young People; participation in com & edu endeavors. F in 1925; serves the Canarsie J com. Rabbi Yaacov Chanes; Hon Pres: Abe Schwartz; Pres: Boris Stain; VP: K. Wechadtowsky; Gabbai: H. Kupfer, N. Glasser; Fin Sec: M. Elefant; Rec Sec: S. Guttenberg; Trustees: A. Schwartz, K. Wechadtowsky, S. Guttenberg. **1385 E 94th St, Near Ave L, Bklyn NY 11236 (212) 272–6933.**

Congregation Ahavas Moische. 612 Maple St, Bklyn NY 11203 (212) 771–7365.

Congregation Ahavath Achim. Orthodox Cong affiliated with Union of Orthodox J Congs of Am. To promote Orthodox J practice in all its aspects. Rel Servs daily; periodic edu progs; Sisterhood progs & activities; Talmud & Mishnayos classes daily; library containing 250 vols (Talmud, Halacha, Tanach, gen J subjects). 150 mems. F 1928 in same location it is presently located; additional edu facility built in 1948. Pub Newsletter (monthly). Rabbi Israel Poleyeff; Pres: Milton Aidlen; VPs: Barnett Schneider, Ira Friedman, Jack Silvera; Treas: Villiam Bratin; Fin Sec: Abe Strassfeld; Rec Sec: Ben Somer. **1750 E 4th St, Bklyn NY 11223 (212) 375–3895.**

Congregation Ahavath Achim Anshei Canarsie. 9420 Glenwood Rd, Bklyn NY 11236 (212) 257–9586.

Congregation Ahavath Israel. 2818 Ave K, Bklyn NY 11210 (212) 258–6666.

Congregation Ahavath Israel of Greenpoint Synagogue. 108 Noble St, Bklyn NY 11222 (212) 383–8475.

Congregation Atzei Chaim Siget. 4915 15th Ave, Bklyn NY 11219 (212) 438–9126.

Congregation B'nai Abraham. 409 E 53rd St, Bklyn NY 11203 (212) 495–2660.

Congregation B'nai Isaac. 54 Ave O, Bklyn NY 11204 (212) 232–3466.

Congregation B'nai Israel. 859 Hendrix St, Bklyn NY 11207 (212) 649–1144.

Congregation B'nai Israel. 1455 Geneva Loop, Bklyn NY 11239 (212) 642–8804.

Congregation B'nai Jacob of Flatbush. 3017 Glenwood Rd, Bklyn NY 11210 (212) 434–8855.

Congregation B'nai Josef. 1616 Ocean Pkwy, Bklyn NY 11223 (212) 627–9861.

Congregation Bais Yisroel of Rugby. 1821 Ocean Pkwy, Bklyn NY 11223 (212) 376–9689.

Congregation Baith Israel Anshei Emes. 236 Kane St, Bklyn NY 11231 (212) 875–1550.

Congregation Belz. 186 Ross St, Bklyn NY 11211 (212) 384–8193.

Congregation Beth David, Inc. 802 44th St, Bklyn NY 11220 (212) 851–8829.

Congregation Beth El of Borough Park. 4802 15th Ave, Bklyn NY 11219 (212) 435–9020.

Congregation Beth El of Flatbush. 2181 E 3rd St, Bklyn NY 11223 (212) 336–1926.

Congregation Beth Eliyoho. 111 Rutledge St, Bklyn NY 11211 (212) 855–0091.

Congregation Beth Elohim. Affiliated with UAHC. 523 mems. Rabbis: Gerald I. Weider, Eugene J. Sack; Cantor Norma Hirsh; Pres: George Harris; Edu: Donna Kleiner; Sisterhood Pres: Dorothy Feller, Helen Finkelman. **8th Ave & Garfield Pl, Bklyn NY 11215 (212) 768–3814.**

Congregation Beth Israel. 1424 51st St, Bklyn NY 11219 (212) 438–9087.

Congregation Beth Israel of Boro Park. 5602 11th Ave, Bklyn NY 11219 (212) 853–1720.

Congregation Beth Jacob Ohev Sholom. 284 Rodney St, Bklyn NY 11211 (212) 384–8715.

Congregation Beth Judah. 1960 Schenectady Ave, Bklyn NY 11234 (212) 338–3968.

Congregation Beth Medrash Chemed of Nitra. 2 Lee Ave, Bklyn NY 11211 (212) 384–9546.

Congregation Beth Medrash Gohova, Inc. 5113 16th Ave, Bklyn NY 11204 (212) 438–9619.

Congregation Beth Medrash Hagadol of Boro Park – The Mishkon Children's Home. Orthodox Cong. Rel Servs daily, Sabbaths, & Holidays; Oneg Shabbat progs, Achos – sisterhood to finance & sponser the rel needs of the Mishkon Chil Home of the JBFCS – Fed of J Philanthropists of NY. F in 1919 as a Bais Yesomim, & subsequently The Infants Home of Bklyn; as of Jan 83 it bacame Mishkon – JBFSC–Fed. Facilities include main sanctuary seating 275 (expandable to 700). Rabbi Nachum Zvi Josephy; Assc Rabbi Avrohom Katz; Pres: Hon Samuel Hirsch; VPs: Mayer Bock, Yehuda J . Fischbein, Meir Y. Gruenwald; Chr of Bd: Shlomo Markowitz. **1358 56th St, Bklyn NY 11219 (212) 438–9384, 851–6570.**

Congregation Beth Moses. 124 West End Ave, Bklyn NY 11235 (212) 769–9794.

Congregation Beth Shalom of Kings Bay. 2710 Ave X, Bklyn NY 11235 (212) 891–4500.

Congregation Beth Tikvah, Inc. 8800 Sea View Ave, Bklyn NY 11236 (212) 763–5577.

Congregation Beth Torah. Orthodox Cong affiliated with Union of Orthodox J Congs. To serve the Sephardic com. Rel Servs; youth progs; Torah classes; lectures; library with 150 vols (rel, hist). 250 families. 8 employees, 50 volunteers. F 1954. Pub Beth Torah Bulletin (5 times a yr). Facilities include kosher kitchen, sanctuary. Pres: Ike Antesy; VPs: Marcel Braha, Elliot Hanan; Treas: Isaac Kassin; Sec: Sheldon Goldman. **1061 Ocean Pkwy, Bklyn NY 11230 (212) 252–9840.**

Congregation Beth Yehuda, Inc. 62 Keap St, Bklyn NY 11211 (212) 625–8732.

Congregation Chasidei Belz. 662 Eastern Pkwy, Bklyn NY 11213 (212) 773–8561.

Congregation Chasidei Belz of Borough Park. 4814 16th Ave, Bklyn NY 11204 (212) 851–5345.

Congregation Chasidei Goor. 1317 49th St, Bklyn NY 11234 (212) 438–8199.

Congregation Chasidei Goor. 5104 18th Ave, Bklyn NY 11204 (212) 438–8818.

Congregation Etz Chaim of Flatbush. 1649 E 13th St, Bklyn NY 11229 (212) 339–4886.

Congregation Israel of Kings Bay. 3903 Nostrand Ave, Bklyn NY 11235 (212) 934–5176.

Congregation Kahal Adath Krasa. 1654 43rd St, Bklyn NY 11204 (212) 438–8880.

Congregation Kahal Yeraim of Borough Park. 1184 53rd St, Bklyn NY 11219 (212) 438–9499.

Congregation Kahal Yesode Hatorah. 4914 16th Ave, Bklyn NY 11204 (212) 851–9858.

Congregation Kehal Raatzfert. Orthodox Cong. Rel Servs; Yeshiva; Kolel – where young men receive a stipend for the complete daily study of the Torah; guest house. Est in 1962 & moved to its present location in 1978. The Torah World (an Orthodox monthly newspaper to strengthen rel). Rabbi A. Krausz; Pres: Martin Cohn; Sec: Joel Franzos. **182 Division Ave, Bklyn NY 11211 (212) 387–2217.**

Congregation Kesser Torah. 2310 Cortelyou Rd, Bklyn NY 11226 (212) 282–3958.

Congregation Khal Adas Yisroel. 4712 14th Ave, Bklyn NY 11219 (212) 633–2305.

Congregation Khal Chasidim of Brooklyn. 4820 15th Ave, Bklyn NY 11219 (212) 871–0110.

Congregation Kneses Israel of Seagate. 3803 Nautilus Ave, Bklyn NY 11224 (212) 372–1668.

Congregation Minyan Mir. 5401 16th Ave, Bklyn NY 11204 (212) 438–9173.

Congregation of Ohel Shalom. 4419 12th Ave, Bklyn NY 11219 (212) 854–7240.

Congregation Ohr Torah. 1520 48th St, Bklyn NY 11219 (212) 253–7176.

Congregation Petach Tikvah. 971 E 10th St, Bklyn NY 11230 (212) 253–7176.

Congregation Rozenoyer Adas Kodeishim. **1510 Ocean Pkwy, Bklyn NY 11230 (212) 336–1195.**

Congregation Sanz Klauzenburg. **1420 50th St, Bklyn NY 11219 (212) 438–9611.**

Congregation Shaari Israel. Conservative Syn affiliated with United Syn of Am. Est in 1929 & moved to its present bldg in 1931. Fr 1957 Rel Sch enrollment declined & was discontinued in 1976. The Syn has been honored by J Natl Fund as the largest fund raising syn for J Natl Fund in Bklyn. Rabbi Dr Abraham I. Feldbin; Pres: David Sakolsky; VP: Sol Laurentz; Chief Gabbai: George Rabinowitz; Treas: Mal Schoenberg; Fin Sec: George Rabinowitz; Rec Sec: Sidney Nadel; Bd of Trustees: Lewis Lamhut, Alexander Berkowitz, Abraham Cohen, Elias Goldberg, George Rabinowitz, Mal Schoenberg, David Sakolsky, Russell Teller, Nathan Weiner, Sidney Weiss, M. K. S. Altman, Louis Bernstein, Nat Boshak, Martin Ehrlichman, Marvin Fishman, Henry E. Klachkin, Abraham Kugal, Lewis Lamhut, Sidney Nadel, Alexander Altman, George Cohen, Morris Ellowitz, Sam Hersh, Sidney Lann, Israel Lanoil, Sol Laurentz, Sidney Nissen, Solomon C. Schoenberg. **810 E 49th St, Bklyn NY 11203 (212) NA9–0476.**

Congregation Talmud Torah Ohev Shalom. **1387 E 96th St, Bklyn NY 11236 (212) 251–1430.**

Congregation Tifereth Israel of Williamsburgh. **491 Bedford Ave, Bklyn NY 11211 (212) 384–8145.**

Congregation Yereim of Sea Gate, Inc. **3868 Poplar Ave, Bklyn NY 11201 (212) 372–9385.**

Congregation Yetev Lev. **4507 10th Ave, Bklyn NY 11211 (212) 438–8144.**

Congregation Yetev Lev Bikur Cholim. **152 Rodney St, Bklyn NY 11211 (212) 387–0546.**

Congregation Yetev Lev D'Satmar, Inc. **152 Rodney St, Bklyn NY 11211 (212) 384–9652.**

Congregation Ziv Yisroel. **4904 16th Ave, Bklyn NY 11204 (212) 438–9428.**

Crown Heights of Israel. **310 Crown St, Bklyn NY 11225 (212) 773–6520.**

East Midwood Jewish Center. Affiliated with United Syn of Am. Rabbi Dr Alvin Kass; Cantor Joseph Eidelson; Pres: Milton Krasne; Exec Dir: Bernard Panzer; Edu Dir: Dr Aryeh Rohn; Youth Dir: Tamara Feit. **1625 Ocean Ave, Bklyn NY 11230 (212) 338–3800.**

Eighteenth Ave Jewish Center. **3714 18th Ave, Bklyn NY 11218 (212) 438–9131.**

First Congregation Anshe Sfard of Borough Park. Traditional Orthodox Syn. To conduct traditional Orthodox servs according to the nusach Safarad; to lead classes; & to contribute charity around the world. Chevra Mishnayot; Daily Servs. First Cong Anshe Sfard supports UJA, Bonds for Is, J Natl Fund, yeshivot, hosps & ins for the sick, disabled, orphans, & the elderly both in Is & the US. Inc Jun 7, 1915. Rabbi David Singer; Cantor Mendel Klein; Assc Cantor Abraham A. Weinberger; Pres: Isidor Greenberger; 1st VP: Abraham Halpern; 2nd VP: Martin Weiner; Treas: Herman Weiss; Fin Sec: Jack Sternklar; Rec Sec: Rev Joseph Fischman; Exec Dir: Rev Joseph Fischman; Hon Pres: Morris Chasen, Samuel Klaus, Abraham Michaelson, Abraham Roth, Morris Schertz, David Silverman; Bd of Dirs: Siegfried Ausubel, Joseph Beer, Leonard Berger, Adolph Bernstein, Hugo Brecher, Jeno Briger, Ignatz Einhorn, Dr Jack Deutsch, Simon Friedman, Moses Frisch, Saul Fruchter, Frank Fuchs, Jack Gerstner, Yehuda Giladi, Joel Gold, Philip Gottesman, Murray Greenberger, George Guttman, Samuel Halpern, Joseph Klein, Sandor Klein, Maurice Laufer, Martin Lebowitz, Max Lewko, Chaim Lipman, Gershon Leobenberg, Andrew Lowinger, Nandor Mandell, Nathan Nachimson, Tzvi Perlstein, David Pfeifer, Aaron Prager, Jacob F. Rappoport, Morris Resnick, Mordchai Rosenberg, Jacob Rottenberg, Sol Rybak, Arnold Salamon, David Scharf, William Schleider, Max Segal, David Sherman, David Silverman, Sidney Smithline, Joseph Stern, Kalman Stern, Nathan Stern, Moshe Strassburger, Irving Tempelman, Jack Verschleisser, Milton Wagh, Leon Weinstock, Emanuel Wieder, Lewis Wolf. **4502 14th Ave Corner 45th St, Bklyn NY 11219 (212) GE6–2691, GE8–9033.**

Flatbush & Shaare Torah Jewish Center. Affiliated with United Syn of Am. Rabbi Irwin Feldman; Cantor Moshe Berger; Pres: Daniel Michaels; Exec Dir: Louis Sanders. **500 Church Ave, Bklyn NY 11218 (212) 871–5200.**

Hadar Hatorah Rabbinical Seminary. **824 Eastern Pkwy, Bklyn NY 11213.**

Harma Institute Sephardic Community High School. Girls HS. To present the vibrant value of J in everyday life; to provide each stu with the right amount of learning to form a well rounded citizen. Gen & Heb studies; Enrichment Prog; music; art; drama;

dancing; sports; special progs for immigrants. Est in 1967. Dean Adm: Rabbi Dr Hanania Elbaz; Hon Dean: Rabbi Dr Abraham Hecht; Co Prin: Dr Ernest A. Sharo; Pres: Elie Rofe; 1st VP: Elie Elbaz; 2nd VP: Abe Kassin; Chr of Finance: Mira Tawil; Treas: Hezkia Arochas; Trustees: S. Tawil, Rabbi Joseph Protowicz, Jesse Salem, Elie Esses, Rabbi Chaim Portowicz, Rabbi David Sebag, Sarah Elbaz. **2600 Ocean Ave, Bklyn NY 11229 (212) 743–3141,2.**

Hebrew Academy for Special Children. Umbrella org for four facilities. To provide edu, training & clin servs to mentally retarded chil & adults fr ages 10 mo & up. Summer Camp, Parksville NY (residential camp for retarded chil & adults) – prog includes sports, nature walks, pioneer camping, dramatics, picnics, night activities, trips, bowling, academic learning prog (staff includes psychologists, speech therapists, occupational therapists, physical therapist, physical edu instr, direct care counselor, & rehabilitation counselor). Workshops in Bklyn & Parksville NY (for mentally retarded adults who need a sheltered employment setup; certified & approved by the NY State Off of Vocational Rehabilitation, & the US Dept of Labor) – breakfast & hot lunches served daily; teaching of assembly skills, packaging skills with the use of simple & more complex machines; Personal Adjustment Training Prog which designs & implements a prog for each client; Transitional Workshop Prog developed with the hope that the clients will be able to get a job in a competitive work situation (staff includes certified personal adjustment training counselors, psychologist, special edu teachers & additional training personnel). Residential Sch, Parksville NY (for the adult mentally retarded; accredited by NY State Off of Mental Retardation & Developmental Disabilities) – provides personal care, med & dental care; nursing servs; psychological & psychiatric servs; provides training in attaining skills of independent living; Adult Edu; Pre-Vocational & Vocational Training; industrial therapy in on-site work activity ctr; Com Awareness Training which includes shopping prog, travel prog, public library, participation in NY State Special Olympics; Transitional Workshops; Recreation Prog (evenings, on the weekends & holidays) which includes training for skills of leisure time activities & field trips to places of social & cultivated interest; annual med, dental, eye & hearing checkups (staff includes houseparents, staff nurses, dentists, physicians, ophthalmologists, hearing specialists, other med specialists, psychiatrists & psychologists). Hebrew Academy for Special Chil, Bklyn NY – infant intervention group; early childhood classes; elementary & upper sch classes & pre vocational classes; speech & occupational therapy; physical therapy; adaptive physical edu; rehabilitation & vocational counseling; psychological servs; music therapy; nurse care; daily breakfasts & lunches (faculty includes special edu teachers, psychologists, physiatrist, speech therapists, rehabilitation counselor, physical therapists, occupational therapists, adaptive physical edu instrs, music therapists & a nurse). To provide the ancillary servs needed to complement effectively the special edu progs, there are four depts: Speech & Language, Occupational Therapy Prog, Physical Therapy Prog, Music Therapy Prog. Est in 1964. Psychologist Adm: Bernard M. Kahn. **1311 55th St, Bklyn NY 11219 (212) 851–6100.**

Hebrew Educational Society. To foster & strengthen J heritage; to help the J individual to dev creatively as a person, as a J, & as an Am citizen. Committed to the enhancement of J identification & group survival, & the intensification of J cultural, ethical & rel values. Friendship Club activities for boys & girls of all ages; hobby groups; special interest classes; adult activities: exercise classes, sports, conversational Heb, kosher gourmet cooking, oil painting; Sr Friendship Club for retired persons: trips, get-togethers, holiday celebrations; library contains 6000 vols (Judaica). 7000 mems; 1100 families; 2200 individuals. Pub HES Bulletin. Est in 1899 to integrate European J into the Am-J soc of Brownsville. Pres: Irving Tabb; VPs: Irving Schwartz, Martin Stone; Treas: Terry J. Wallin; Sec: Edwin H. Baumann; Exec Dir: Dr Murray H. Kiok. **9502 Seaview Ave, Bklyn NY 11236 (212) 241–3000.**

Israel Aliyah Center. 1416 Ave M, Bklyn NY 11230 (212) 336–1215.

Jewish American Record. Periodical pub. **PO Box 1100, 271 Camden Plaza E, Bklyn NY 11202 (212) 646–5184.**

Jewish Center of Mapleton Park, Congregation Beth Hamedrash Hagodol. 1477 W 8th St, Bklyn NY 11204 (212) 837–8875.

Jewish Communal Center. 1302 Ave I, Bklyn NY 11230 (212) 377–9429.

Jewish Community House of Bensonhurst. JCC affiliated with Fed of J Philantropies, JWB. To serve leisure time needs of the J com & membership. Rel Servs; nursery sch; day camp; chil progs; Council of J Orgs; traditional & holiday progs; sr citizen activities; cultural progs; library containing 2600 vols (Judaica). 5500 mems (650 families). 60 employees; 70 volunteers. Present bldg f & est in 1927. Facilities include nursery sch, library, exercise rms, steamrm, sauna, kosher kitchen, two gyms, meeting rms, auditorium, syn, 35 basketball teams in extensive sports & athletic prog; substantial Russian resettlement prog. Pres: Bernard Blumenthal; Chr Exec Cttee: Arthur J. Press; Acting Exec Dir: Philip J. Cohen; Exec Dir: Milton Gold; Health & Physical Edu Dir: Bill Balter; Sr Citizen Supervisor: Helen Harris; Presch Dir: Shirley Wolin; Day Camp & Chil Dir: Sylvia Langer; Is Culture Specialist: Haim Ayalon; Russian Resettlement Coord: Mira Volf; Rabbi Abraham Avrech. **7802 Bay Pkwy, Bklyn NY 11214 (212) 331–6800.**

Jewish Community House of Bensonhurst Library. Library with 2600 vols (Judaica subjects only). For information on the Ins, see – Jewish Community House of Bensonhurst, Bklyn NY. **7802 Bay Pkwy, Bklyn NY 11214 (212) 331–6800.**

Jewish Education Program. Orthodox serv org affiliated with Agudath Israel of Am. To foster J pride through J edu. Release hour classes for public sch chil on Weds; visitations & 'Ruach' seminars at numerous day schs & Talmud Torahs in the Tri-State area; Shabbatones for several hundred chil throughout the yr; placement & referral serv to help place chil in yeshivas & day schs; scholarship assistance; publications & records. 3,000 stu reached per yr. 5 employees; approx 500 volunteers. F Sept 1972. Pub JEP-Rothman Foundation Series (Lilmod Ul'lamade, Lishmor V'Laasos, Menucha V'Simcha), JEP's Mitzvah Manuals (monthly), Alef-Bet Workbook, Holiday Fun Book, 4 JEP records; 2 Uncle Moishy & The Mitzvah Men; Prof Green & the Simcha Machine (in records & cassettes). JEP is instrumental in placing over 100 chil annually into Heb day schs & J summer camps. Dir: Rabbi Mordechai Katz; Exec Dir: Rabbi Yosef C. Golding; Rabbinical Adv: Rabbi Yisroel Belsky; Exec Sec: Mrs C. Aranoff. **425 E 9th St, Bklyn NY 11218 (212) 941–2600.**

Jewish Journal. Periodical pub. **16 Court St, Bklyn NY 11241 (212) 624–7991.**

Jewish Pharmaceutical Society of America. 525 Ocean Pkwy, Bklyn NY 11218 (212) 436–8320.

Jewish Press. Periodical pub. **338 3rd Ave, Bklyn NY 11215 (212) 858–3300.**

Kingsbrook Jewish Medical Center. Major med complex serving both acute & long term patients fr all age groups. Rehabilitation Med; Recreational Therapy; Med, Surgical, Radiological Servs; Dentistry; Ophthalmology & Neuro-Ophthalmology; Oncology; Orthopedic Surgery; Pediatric Metabolic Unit for victims of Tay-Sachs Disease; Genetic Counseling. Acute Div contains 351 beds; the skilled nursing facility, the David Minkin Rehabilitation Ins, contains 538 beds. F in 1926 as the J Sanitarium for Incurables. F to give Orthodox J patients an environment in which they could observe J dietary laws & other rel traditions, the 250 bed ins accepted patients without regard to race, creed or color. An Orthodox J Syn was opened on the premises in 1928. The Ins has undergone several name changes over the yrs, fr J Sanitarium for Incurables, to J Sanitarium & Hosp for Chronic Diseases, to J Chronic Disease Hosp, to Kingsbrook J Med Ctr. In the planning, is the erection of a 200-bed comprehensive geriatric diagnostic & treatment facility. The Ctr's research div, the Isaac Albert Research Ins, has received intl recognition for its work in disorders such as Tay-Sachs. In 1981 the NY State Dept of Health designated the Med Ctr a "unique specialty teaching hosp," one of only four in NY State & two in NYC. Pres: David Minkin; VPs: Irving Evall, Joseph E. Forman, Philip D. Held, Jack J. Holland, Louis Silver; Treas: Henry Kronhaus; Assc Treas: Abraham B. Kerne; Sec: Henrietta Klein; Chr Exec Cttee: Philip D. Held; Chr Bd of Trustees: Hon Jeremiah B. Bloom; Exec Dir: Harold A. Schneider; Dir of PR: Edward N. Mintz. **Rutland Rd & E 49th St, Bklyn NY 11203 (212) 756–9700.**

Kingsway Jewish Center. Orthodox Cong affiliated with Union of Orthodox J Congs of Am. Daily Rel Servs & classes; Adult Edu; youth activities; Sisterhood; Young Families Group; gym & pool athletic prog; summer day camp; catering hall. Approx 250 mems. F 1928; bldgs built between 1936–70. Pub Kingsway Light (monthly). Facilities include syn, sch, catering halls, gymnasium, swimming pool, outdoor playground & pool, auditorium, library, offs. Rabbi Milton H. Polin; Cantor Moshe Hecht; Pres: Melvin Ness; Bd Chr: Jonas Steigman; Sisterhood Pres: Minnie Ezer. **2810 Nostrand Ave, Bklyn NY 11229 (212) 258–3344.**

Long Island Jewish World. Periodical pub. **1029 Brighton Beach Ave, Bklyn NY 11235 (212) 769–6000.**

Machne Israel, Inc. 770 Eastern Pkwy, Bklyn NY 11213 (212) 493–9250.

Maimonides Medical Center. Voluntary non-profit hosp; primary teaching affiliate of the State Univ of NY, Downstate Med Ctr, Col of Med; a major ins of the Fed of J Philanthropies. Anesthesiology; Com Med & Com Health Servs; Preventive Med; Obstetrics & Gynecology; Pediatrics,

Hematology/Oncology, Neonatology; Psychiatry; Rehabilitation Med; Med Servs: Cardiology, Dermatology, Gastroenterology, Hematology/ Oncology, Infectious Diseases, Metabolism & Endocrinology, Neurology, Neuromuscular Disease, Pulmonary Disease, Renal Disease, Rheumatology & Immunology, Radiology, Neuroradiology, Nuclear Med; Surgical Servs: Breast Surgery, Dentistry, Head & Neck Surgery, Neurosurgery, Ophthalmology, Orthopedic Surgery, Otolaryngology, Pediatric Surgery, Plastic Surgery, Podiatry, Proctology, Thoracic & Cardiovascular Surgery, Urology; Kidney Dialysis; Developmental Ctr which is designed for families of chil & adults with signs of faulty mental dev; Emergency Care Ctr; Outpatient Servs; Com Mental Health Ctr; Nursing Edu which servs as an in servs edu prog to maintain & improve nursing skills (clin training provided for nursing stu fr several affiliated cols); Paramed Training; research prog; com involvment; social servs; home care; outreach prog. Staff include 595 med staff, 221 house staff, 677 nurses, 74 LPN nurses. F in 1947 as a result of a merger between Beth Moses & Is Zion Hosp of Bklyn using the facilities of the former Is Zion Hosp. The 670 bed Med Ctr is comprised of the Goldberg Bldg, the Kronish & Aron Pavilions, the Dr Abraham Gellman Pavilion, the Emergency Care Ctr, the Neimeth Research Ins, the Neinken Outpatient Ctr, & two bldgs for stu & staff housing. The Med Ctr complex also includes its renowned Com Mental Health Ctr. Adjacent to the Med Ctr campus is the 500 bed Brenner Pavilion of the Met J Geriatric Ctr which has a close relationship with the Hosp. A close relationship is also maintained with the nearby Coney Island Hosp. Pres: David Wassner; Hon Chr of the Bd: Jack R. Aron, Hilda M.F. Bell, Fred J. Isaacson, Mortimer L. Neinken; Hon VPs: Hyman Meskin, Morris Furman; Chr Exec Cttee: Clarence D. Bell; VPs: David Kosh, David Lubart, James A. Stein; Treas: Richard L. Hirsch; Assc Treas: Irving Kanarek; Sec: Benjamin Eisenstadt; Asst Sec: Alan J. Seelenfreund; Trustees: Jack R. Aron, Clarence D. Bell, Hilda M. F. Bell, William Blanksteen, Gail Chasin, Marius Decker, Benjamin Eisenstadt, Nathan Escava, Eugene Fixler, Jeannette Frank, Morris Furman, Richard L. Hirsch, Fred J. Isaacson, Irving Kanarek, Mortimer N. Klaus, Bernard Klebanow, David Kosh, Israel Lefkowitz, David Lubart, John T. Magliocco, Charles Mathalon, Hyman Meskin, Paul Mishkin, Mortimer L. Neinken, Daniel Z. Nelson, David J. Platzer, Walter D. Richards, Al Schreiber, Alan J. Seelenfreund, James A. Stein, Ronald J. Stein, Ronald S. Tauber, David Wassner; Exec VP: Lee W. Schwenn; 1st VP: Frank W. Hays; VP Dev: James L. Neiman. **4802 Tenth Ave, Bklyn NY 11219 (212) 270–7679.**

Mesifta Heichal Hakodesh. 851 47th St, Bklyn NY 11220 (212) 438–9097.

Mesivta Teshiva Rabbi Chaim Berlin Rabbinical Academy. 1593 Coney Island Ave, Bklyn NY 11230.

Mikvah Israel of Boro Park. 1351 46th St, Bklyn NY 11219 (212) 871–6866.

Mikvah Israel of Brighton Beach. 245 Neptune Ave, Bklyn NY 11235 (212) 769–8599.

Mikvah Mayon of Papa. 115 Rutledge St, Bklyn NY 11211 (212) 624–9262.

Mirrer Yeshiva Central Institute. 1791–5 Ocean Pkwy, Bklyn NY 11223 (212) 645–0536.

National Committee for the Furtherance of Jewish Education. To re-establish & strengthen J faith, principles, identity, commitment & pride. Released Time – a prog to reach out to lost J youngsters; Hadar Hatorah – rabbinical ins for advanced Torah studies; Machon Chana – women's ins for the study of J; Vocational Div; camps; Colony of Hope – ins in Kfar Chabad Is for orphaned girls & girls fr troubled & disturbed backgrounds; Boys Village – ins in Kfar Chabad Is for gifted & troubled youngsters; Anti Ahmad – anti conversion; Poor & Sick Fund; Free Loan Fund; Brides Fund; Toys for Hospitalized Chil; Orphans & Chil Fund; Keren Torah Fund – provides scholarships; counseling; family servs & aids; immigrant serv; Mercy Corps – provides assistance for the aged & needy that is unobtainable fr other sources. Est in 1940 by the Lubavitcher Rebbe. Edu & prayer booklets; the column Focus in the J Press NY, & B'nai B'rith Messenger, Los Angeles; special radio prog twice a week. Presidium: Gil Aronowitz, Herman H. Cohen, Hon Julius Hellenbrand, J. James Plesser, Samuel C. Rubin; VPs: Solomon Z. Ferziger, Shelly S. Goren, Mel Hoffman, Joseph Kivel, George Silberberg, Herbert Weiss; Sec: Morris Drucker; Treas: Ben Dubovsky, Martin Rieber; Exec VP: Rabbi Jacob J. Hecht; Exec Sec: Chaya S. Popack; Chr of the Bd: Morris Hoberman; Bd of Dirs: Paul Bernstein, Sanford C. Bernstein, Hon Bernard M. Bloom, Hon Jeremiah B. Bloom, Samuel Eisenstat, Godfrey Dallek, Hon Harold Fischer, Eugene Goldenberg, Fred Goldschmidt, Stanley Goldstein, Harold E. Hirsch, Abe Lager, Anne Lager, Sol Palitz, Warren Palitz, Jack Peerless, Fred Pilevsky, Theodore Present, Joseph Pruzansky, Ira Rennert, Arthur Rogers, Michel S. Schwartz, Saul P. Steinberg, Herbert B. Weiss, Paul Wildstein, Hirsch Wolf, Jacob Wolk; Legal Counsel: Leon Brickman, Samuel Eisenstat,

Solomon Z. Ferziger, Arnold J. Goldstein, Fred Queller; Budget & Finance: Jeffrey Glick, Herbert Hauser, Joseph Hirsch, Morris Hoberman, Phillip Hoenig, Marvin Leiberman, J. James Plesser, George Rennert; Auditors: Marvin Leiberman; Membership: Hon Julius Hellenbrand, Milton Kramer; Prog Consultant: Mordechai Fogel; Dir of Dev: Rabbi Faivel Rimier; PR: David A. Weiss. **824 Eastern Pkwy, Bklyn NY 11213 (212) 735–0200.**

National Council of Beth Jacob Schools, Inc. 1415 E 7th St, Bklyn NY 11230 (212) 979–7400.

Ocean Avenue Jewish Center – Congregation Pri Eitz Chaim. Orthodox Syn. Heb Sch; HS; Sr Ctr; Sisterhood; Men's Club; Mr & Mrs Club; Chevra Mishnayot; Daily Servs three times a day. 180 mems. The Cong has been in existence for 59 yrs. The bldg facilities include a sanctuary, Beth Hamedrash, ballroom, off, classrms. Rabbi Melvin I. Burg; Cantor Joel Kaplan; Pres: Karl Forseter; Exec VP: Harry Osofsky; Hon Pres: Murray Singer, Isidore Klomberg; Hon VPs: Dr Sol E. Feldman, Phil Kaplan; VPs: Joseph Hecht, Norton Goodman, Michael Levine, Jerome Poch; Sec: Oswalt Heymann; Treas: Cy Fisher; Gabbai: Jacob Pock; Sergeant At Arms: Harold Bialstock; Chr Bd of Dirs: Jerome Frier; Chr Ritual Cttee: Ludwig Friedman. **2600 Ocean Ave, Bklyn NY 11229 (212) 743–5533.**

Ocean Parkway Jewish Center. Affiliated with United Syn of Am. Cantor Benjamin Berger; Pres: Tobias Herstik. **550 Ocean Pkwy, Bklyn NY 11218 (212) 436–4900.**

Oceanview Jewish Center. 3100 Brighton St, Bklyn NY 11235 (212) 646–9639.

Oholey Shem Yeshiva Congregation. 5206 12th Ave, Bklyn NY 11219 (212) 435–1639.

The Organization for Torah Ethics. To promote knowledge & undestanding of Mitzvot between man & his friend; to contribute towards uniting the Torah com. Supplies material to yeshivot & syns all over the world; organizes gatherings. Est in 1971. Literature & posters in Heb, English & Yiddish. Chr: Rabbi Yuda Dick; Treas: Romi A. Kohn; Exec Sec: Rabbi Jacob Kalisch; Rabbinical Adv Cttee: Rabbi Moshe Bick, Rabbi Yitzchok Naftali Knopfler, Rabbi Elchanan Herzman. **928 46th St, Bklyn NY 11219 (212) 438–1574.**

Orthodox Torah Services & Advocacy for the Retarded. Orthodox parent advocate group affiliated with Bd of J Edu, Aguadath Israel, Torah Umsorah, Fed of J Phil Ohel, Women's League, Miskon, YMHA Central Queens, Bais Issac Zvi. To make the public aware of the needs of the Orthodox mentally retarded & their families; to be a liaison to any org that deals with the J retarded; to be a political activist to get progs for the J retarded; to help organize J edu progs for the retarded. Maintains two progs for chil from 3 to 12, one in Bais Issac Zvi in Boro Park (Sun 10am–2pm for special edu) & one in YMHA Central Queens (Sun & two afternoons for special edu); runs parent workshops & seminars; holds conf in conjunction with Fed, Agudath & AOJS. 150 families. F 1980. Pub OSTARNewsletter (quarterly). Pres: Betty Pollack; VP Public Affairs: Gaffney Pnina; VP Fund Raising: Gaffney Aaron; VP: Tasya Stone; Treas: Leona Stern; Fin Sec: Carla Schipper; Bd Chr: Dr Arthur Feinerman. **1717 15th St, Bklyn NY 11229 (212) 376–0557, 434–0570.**

Pioneer Women – Na'amat. The training & edu of the Is woman & her family so that each can be best equipped to lead productive lives. For additional information, see – Pioneer Women Na'amat, New York City, NY. **3858 Nostrand Ave, Bklyn NY 11229 (212) 769–9604.**

Progressive Shaari Zedek Synagogue. Reform Temple. To study & practice the principles of liberal J. Rel Servs; Rel Sch; Sisterhood; Men's Club; Social Club; Adult Edu. Rabbi Ferenc Raj. **1395 Ocean Ave, Bklyn NY 11230 (212) 377–1818.**

Prospect Park Temple Issac. 1419 Dorchester Rd, Bklyn NY 11226 (212) 284–8032.

Rabbi Harry Halpern Day School. Affiliated with Solomon Schechter Day Schools Assn. Prin: Dr Aryeh Rohn; Chr: Milton Krasne. **1625 Ocean Ave, Bklyn NY 11230.**

Rabbi Nachman of Braslav Library. 5019 10th Ave, Bklyn NY 11219.

Remsen Heights Jewish Center. 1115 E 87th St, Bklyn NY 11236 (212) 763–2244.

School of Biblical Instruction. 157 Leonard St, Bklyn NY 11206 (212) 782–5663.

Sea Breeze Jewish Center. 311 Sea Breeze Ave, Bklyn NY 11224 (212) 372–9749.

The Sephardic Home. Home for the aged. Arts & crafts; cooking & baking progs; gardening; weaving; sewing; cookouts; picnics; trips to temples, theatres, mus; lectures; birthday & anniversary parties; personal servs; physical therapy; kosher food; special diets; Orthodox Servs. Social workers;

physicians; skilled nurses; Ladies Auxiliary volunteers. In 1948, the Sephardic people began a campaign to build a home for the Sephardic aged. They were inspired by the knowledge that their aged were unhappy in various old age homes due to differences in culture, language & food. The 1st bldg was opened on Aug 16, 1951 with 58 beds. On Mar 29, 1960 a new 173 bed facility opened. On Sept 8, 1969 the Lasha Pavilion was opened giving residents a spacious lounge, & added recreational space. In 1974, due to lack of space, the Jacob A. & Jeanne E. Barkey Wing was opened adding 99 additional beds. Facilities include: beauty parlor & barber shop; spacious lounge; garden; terr; auditorium; dining rm; syn; clin; kosher kitchen. Pres: Abe Cassuth; Chr of the Bd: Irving Russo; Exec Dir: Herbert Freeman. **2266 Cropsey Ave, Bklyn NY 11214 (212) 266–6100.**

Sephardic Institute. Syn, HS. HS: To provide not only stu who can read, write & compute but also to make them human beings with refined characters & deep loyalty to their families & com. Beth Medrash for col age youth; ctr for adult edu; youth progs. Sephardic HS: Rel Studies; English; Social Studies; Math; Business courses; elective & advanced placement courses; Art; Health Edu; Physical Edu; Oceanography; library; Guidance Dept; voluntary Mishmar Prog, evening Torah study group, early morning group, & girls evening group; extra curricular prog; basketball team; trips; Shabbat Servs; Parents Assn. 275 stu in the HS. Faculty of 22. F in 1969 as a com ctr. The HS was f in 1973. The girls div was est in 1977. In 1979 the Parents Assn was formed. The NY State Dept of Edu granted full accreditation in 1980. Sephardic Scoop – sch newspaper issued four times a yr. Facilities include Beth Medrash, cafeteria, auditorium, specialty rms, labs, offs & a computer rm. The Sephardic HS is a div of the Sephardic Ins. The main focus of the Ins has become the HS. Prin: Rabbi Moshe Shamah; Asst Prin J Studies: Rabbi Norman Amsel; Asst Prin Gen Studies: Dr Daniel J. Vitow; Exec Dir: Rabbi Ronald Barry; Pres: David Hidary; Chr: Joseph Beyda; Adm Asst: Sally Ashkenazi; Exec Cttee: Mickey Abraham, Harry Ashkenazie, Jack Marc Benun, Jack Morris Benun, Joseph Benun, Ronnie Benun, Ralph Betesh, Joseph Bijou, Morris Cabasso, Murray Dweck, Leo Esses, Manny Hamowy, Abe S. Kassin, Morris Matalon, Dr Robert Matalon, Marc Mishaan, Jack C. Mizrachi, Joseph Shemueli, Mayer I. Sutton, Sam A. Sutton. **511 Ave R, Bklyn NY 11223 (212) 998–8171.**

Shaare Zion Congregation. 2030 Ocean Pkwy, Bklyn NY 11223 (212) 376–0009.

Shellbank Jewish Center. 2121 Bragg St, Bklyn NY 11235 (212) 891–8666.

Shevet Y'hudah Resnick Institute of Technology. Sch of Tech. To train stu in modern tech in a Torah environment. Counseling; stu loan; library; computer prog; electronic tech. F by Rabbi Schneerson in 1963. Facilities include lecture rms, computer rms, electronic lab. Dir: Rabbi Elliot Amsel; Registrar: Esther Gewirtzman; Fiscal Off: Miriam Perlow; Guidance Counselor: Rabbi Paul Gruber; Job Dev: Rabbi Arnold Gewirtzman; Bd of Dirs – Pres: Rabbi Philip Harris Singer; VP: Rabbi Sholom B. Schneerson; Sec: Herman Weisner; Treas: Rabbi A.M. Greenhut; Rabbi Eli Carlebach, Sonia Schneerson, David Yarmush; Bd of Govs: Rabbi Joseph Levinson, Dr Adolf Razdow, Rabbi Sholom Rottenberg, Rabbi Meir Rottenstreich, Martin P. Schanbach, Michael H. Steinhardt; Edu Adv Bd: Ari Cohen, Prof S. Engelson, Dr E. Feldman, Charles G. Marrara, Alvan Segal. **670 Rockaway Pkwy, Bklyn NY 11236 (212) 342–6878.**

Shore Park Jewish Center. 2959 Ave Y, Bklyn NY 11235 (212) 648–2900.

Shulamith School for Girls. The oldest Heb girls elementary yeshiva in the US. To indoctrinate J daughters with a Torah true Orthodox edu, a love of Is & a love of its people. Enrollment of nearly 600 stu. Est in 1928; in 1979 a HS was est. Hon Pres: Ber Mandel, Rabbi Arthur Schick; Pres: Richard Jacobs; Chr of the Bd: Leo Schachter; VPs: Chaim Fortgang, Sy Knapel, Joseph Piontnica, Nathan B. Silberman; Hon Chr of the Bd: Max Hershdorfer, Herbert Knobel; Hon VPs: Julius Bienenfeld, Mortimer Chrein, George Hershkowitz, Moses Polansky, Israel Schmell, Moshe Semel, Myron Weiss; Co-Treas: Sheldon Fliegelman, Arnold Kalish; Fin Sec: Joshua Danziger; Rec Sec: Naomi Gurin; Exec Dir: Rabbi Moshe Zwick; Elementary Prin: Rabbi David Rogoff; HS Prin: Dr Susan R. Katz; Chr, Bd of Edu: Rabbi Gedalia D. Schwartz; Asst Elementary Prin: Batya Nekritz; Asst Adm: Hannah Kalish; Bd of Govs: Daniel Eckhaus, Simon Geldwerth, George Gottlieb, Bernard Leibman, Herman Lerner, Sidney Lieberman, William Michaelson, Bernard Resnick, Irving Saidlower, Dr Irving Schmierer, Bertha Schraeter, Morris Surick, Sylvia Weinreb, Alexander Weinreb, Sam Weinstock, Gerald Weisberg; Bd of Dirs: Nathan Bienenfeld, David Braun, Robert Danzger, Robert David, Noach Dear, Martin Elefant, Solomon Feder, Kalman Finkel, Emerick Goldstein, Libby Green, Sandor Hirth, Jacob Kaminetsky, Kenneth Kaplan, Stanley Kaplan, Henry Katz, Harry Klein, Henry Kwitel, Eugene Lerman, Edward Lieberman, George Mayer, Rubin Margules, Egon

Pfeifer, Al Reingold, Dr Arthur Rosenbaum, David Rosenberg, Renate Ross, Shirley Schachter, Avram Schreiber, Dr Robert Schulman, Hillel Schwartz, Arthur Shinensky, David Silverman, Nechama Steinhardt, Helen Tepler, Michael Tepler, Abraham Weiss, Margie Yaari; Bd of Edu: Dr Pincas Doron, Solomon Feder, Esther Fessel, Stanley Fogel, Rabbi E. Gottlieb, Richard Jacobs, Dr Sholem Kaminetzky, Ber Mandel, Harvey Morgenstern, Dr Monty Penkower, Rabbi Shimon Rabin, Naomi Rabin, Aaron Rosenfeld, Rabbi Jacob Rabinowitz, Dr Reuben Rudman, Sarah Saperstein, Malkie Silberman, Dr Richard Staum, Melvin Steinhardt, Miriam Sunshine, Margie Yaari, Rabbi Stuart Zweiter. **1350–1353 50th St, Bklyn NY 11219 (212) 853–7070, 7071, 1130, 7156.**

Solomon Schechter High School. Affiliated with Solomon Schechter Day Schools Assn. Prin: Rabbi Ari Korenblit, Dr Sandra Keller; Chr: Dr Stephen Weinstock. **500 Church Ave, Bklyn NY 11218 (212) 854–3500.**

Tabernacle Beth El. 85 Fountain Ave, Bklyn NY 11208 (212) 277–8035.

Talmud Torah Sons of Israel. 2115 Benson Ave, Bklyn NY 11214 (212) 372–4830.

Talmud Torah Tifereth Israel of West Flatbush. 1915 W 7th St, Bklyn NY 11223 (212) 339–1927.

Talmud Torah Toldois Yaakov Yosef. 105 Heyward, Bklyn NY 11206 (212) 852–0502.

Telshe Alumni Bais Hamedrash, Inc. 5218 16th Ave, Bklyn NY 11204 (212) 438–8937.

Temple Ahavath Sholom. Reform Temple affiliated with UAHC. To promote the spiritual, edu, ethical & social aims of Reform Judaism. Friday Evening & Sat Morning Servs every Sabbath, & Evening & Morning Servs on the Holy Days; Rel Sch on Sun mornings & weekday afternoons, K through Confirmation (tenth grade); Bar/Bat Mitzvah; Adult Edu classes; Distinguished Speakers Series in Fall & Spring; Sisterhood; Brotherhood; Jr & Sr Youth Groups; Parent-Teachers Assn; Social Action Cttee; outreach to the unaffiliated; library containing 1,000 vols (gen Judaica). 200 mems (150 families, 50 individuals); 50 stu in K–grade 10. 16 employees; 50 volunteers. F 1912. Pub Messenger (monthly), Religious School Bulletin (quarterly). Facilities include sanctuary seating 1000, chapel seating 100, vestries, offs, library, 10 classrms, gymnasium, kosher kitchen. Rabbi Eric H. Hoffman; Pres: Gerald Prezioso; Pres: Grace Schneider; VPs: Charlotte Russell, Alan Kaye, Abraham Levitt; Sec: Sandra Platt; Treas: Lucille Schreibman. **1609 Ave R, Bklyn NY 11229 (212) 375–4500.**

Temple Beth Abraham. Affiliated with United Syn of Am. Rabbi Samuel Berger; Cantor Efrim Berkovitch; Pres: Louis Smith. **301 Sea Breeze Ave, Bklyn NY 11224 (212) 266–6544.**

Temple Beth El of Bensonhurst. 1656 W 10th St, Bklyn NY 11223 (212) 232–0019.

Temple Beth El of Manhattan Beach. Affiliated with United Syn of Am. Rabbi Leonard Goldstein; Pres: Henry Hyman; Edu Dir: Gerald Sutofsky. **111 West End Ave, Bklyn NY 11235 (212) TW1–3500.**

Temple Beth Emeth. Affiliated with UAHC. 234 mems. Rabbi William Kloner; Cantors: Ira S. Bigeleisen, Walter A. Davidson; Pres: Clifford Greenspan; Sisterhood Pres: June E. Greenspan; Brotherhood Pres: Leonard Drucker. **83 Marlborough Rd, Bklyn NY 11226 (212) 282–1596.**

Temple Emanu-El of Canarsie. 1880 Rockway Pkwy, Bklyn NY 11236 (212) 251–0450.

Temple Hillel of Flatlands. 2164 Ralph Ave, Bklyn NY 11221 (212) 768–2400.

Temple Shaare Emeth Annex. 6012 Farragut Rd, Bklyn NY 11226 (212) 444–9519.

Temple Sholom of Flatbush. Affiliated with United Syn of Am. Rabbi Alan F. Lavin; Cantor Berel Bokow; Pres: Carl Schechter. **2075 E 68th St, Bklyn NY 11234 (212) 251–0370.**

Toldos Yakov Yosef. 5323 12th Ave, Bklyn NY 11219 (212) 438–8312.

Tomer Devora High School. A tri-lingual rel HS for girls; affiliate of Skwere Mosdos. To make the stu cognizant of her responsibility to herself, her family, her sch, her com, her country & the J nation; Torah commitment is the essential goal of the sch. Academic & vocational courses are offered including Algebra, Geometry, Social Studies, English, Typing, Sewing, Wig Styling, Consumer Law, Business English; Methods of Teaching; J Studies; extra curricular & co-curricular activities, stu govt, social action & com involvement, Visits to the Sick Cttee, various volunteer progs for families & area ins. Independent research is encouraged in accordance with the personal interest of the stu. F initially as an extension of Tomer Devora Elementary Sch with the elementary sch to be its feeding sch. The ins now draws some of its stu fr other US cities & fr Europe. Stu newspaper in both English & Yiddish appears monthly. **1462 50th St, Bklyn NY 11219 (212) 538–4600.**

Union Temple. Affiliated with UAHC. 525 mems. Rabbis: Jay J. Sangerman, A.S. Dreyfus; Cantor Avery Tracht; Pres: Irving Gerstman; Edu: Jay J. Sangerman; Sisterhood Pres: A. Forman; Brotherhood Pres: Harold Silvey. **17 Eastern Parkway, Bklyn NY 11238 (212) 638–7600.**

Yad L'Achim – Boro Park-Flatbush. Orthodox charity org for Is. "A hand to aid my brothers in Israel". Fund-raising for ctrs in Is main offs. 12 Ctrs in Is perform the following activities: edu – guarding & registering chil in rel ins, following up with progress of stu, organizing Ohalei Torah for thousands of yeshiva stu during their vacation; spreading Torah – dev 'Yeshivot L'am', organizing lectures for women, organizing meetings to discuss Yiddishkeit, holding assemblies on rel topics, sponsoring Shabbatons in the settlements; anti-missionary action – maintaining div for preventive care, div for caring for families & chil, div for gathering information; absorption – conducting discussions for Russian, Gruzians, Iranians & Western immigrants, making home visits & presentations at immigration ctrs, maintaining libraries with Russian & English bks; Torah publications – publishing. 3 employees; 5 volunteers. F in Is 1950; in NY 1960; initially known as Peilei Machne Hatorati; later changed to Peyilim of Yad L'achim. Pub newsletters of activities in Is; wall calendars. Exec Dir: Rabbi Aaron M. Krausz; Other offs: W. Tessler, L. Markovits. **4702 16th Ave, Bklyn NY 11204 (212) 633–0776,7.**

Yavne Hebrew Theological Seminary. A sch for higher J learning, training of rabbis & teachers as J leaders for the Am com. Est 1923 in NY. Otzar Ha-She'Eloth-U-Teshuvot (Compedium Responsarum). Branch: Machon Maharshal in Jerusalem. Pres: Rabbi Nathan Shapiro; Exec Dir: Rabbi Solomon Shapiro; Dirs: Ray Dorn, Joseph Friedland, Max Friedman, Rabbi Joseph Grossman, Rabbi Jacob Holzman, Joseph Kurzon, Rabbi Samuel Meyer, Rabbi Irwin Pechman, Rabbi Morris Reinitz, Rabbi Abraham Schoen, Abraham Schwebel, Philip Schwebel, Rabbi David Shapiro, Rabbi Max Stauber, Rabbi Sol Steinmetz, Judith Suson-Rabiner, Nathan Tuchinsky; Is Cttee – Chr: Rabbi Joshua F. Sachs, Rabbi S.Y. Zevin, Prof A.S. Hartum, Prof J.J. Rivlin, Dr Y. Berman, Dr H. Gevaryahu, Dr Ch. Lipshitz, S.Z. Shragai, Walter Williams, J.L. Levy, Moshe Lieber, Joshua Levy, Y.D. Mann, Reuven Mass, Joseph Rivlin, Rabbi Nathan Shapiro. **510 Pahill Rd, Bklyn NY 11218 (212) GE6–5610.**

Yeshiva of Bensonhurst, Inc. 2025 79th St, Bklyn NY 11214 (212) 232–7400.

Yeshiva of Eastern Pkwy. 3121 Kings Highway, Bklyn NY 11235 (212) 377–9151.

Yeshiva of Flatbush Joel Braverman High School & Elementary School. A private rel day sch. To dev in its stu a positive attitude to J values & an identification with the Torah way of life; to imbue its stu with a love for the Torah, the J people & the land of Is; to train stu in the highest standards of secular studies in order for the stu to function successfully in the Am soc. Secular & J studies with all Judaic content taught in Heb; Mishmar prog; advance placement course seminars; stu govt org; sports; art; sewing; music; dance; eurythmics; choir; marching band. Over 2,200 stu fr nursery through 12th grade; over 800 stu in the HS div & 1,400 stu in the elementary div. 120 faculty mems in the elementary sch. The elementary sch was est in 1927. The sch's F conceived & executed a new concept of total edu: a mixture of J heritage, modern Heb language & culture, & the gen culture of Western civilization to produce a modern Torah true J. In 1950 the HS was est. Pub Kol Hatalmid – a literary journal in Heb; Pegasus – a literary journal in English; Phoenix – the sch newspaper. HS facilities in the Joel Braverman Bldg, a fully air-conditioned four story structure above ground & three levels underground, include a swimming pool, gymnasium, auditorium with seating for 700, Beth Hamedrash, four sci labs, two demonstration rms, library with over 21,000 vols. Pres Bd of Trustees: Allen Bodner; Adm: G. Eisenberg; Prin Gen Studies: Dr Abraham Zamichow; HS Prin: Rabbi David Eliach; Head Elementary Sch: Yeshayahu Ephraim Greenfeld. **1609 Ave J, Bklyn NY 11230 (212) 377–4466.**

Yeshivah of Crown Heights. Dedicated to the highest ideals of Torah learning, J traditional observance & character bldg; aims towards a blending of rel J heritage together with the finest of Am democratic traditions; aims to foster a love for knowledge & study & a rounded approach to Torah. Nursery; K; complete 8 yr curriculum of J & secular subjects; field trips; audio/visual aids. Experienced & licensed teachers. Sch facilities include: spacious air-conditioned & modern classrooms; gymnasium; library; dining hall; early childhood facilities; playground. Pres: Alexander Schlesinger; Chr, Bd of Trustees: Irving Horowitz; VPs: Sidney Friedlander, Hyman Golombeck, Rabbi Israel

Grossman, Gerald Hersher, Matthew Kleinman; Treas: Milton Linder; Sec: Meyer Benezra; Bd of Edu: Hon Herbert Berman, Israel Cohen, Lionel Cohen, Martin Feldman, Nathan Grossbard, Mike Kaplan, Michael Keltz, Charles Liss, Harvey Lubin, George Meissner, Kurt Penner, Bernard Rappaport, Borah Rothberg, Morris Simnowitz, William Stulbach, Sam Wolf; Dean: Rabbi Myron Rakowitz; Exec Dir: Naomi Benezra. **6363 Ave U, Bklyn NY 11234 (212) 444–5800, 5802, 5813.**

Yeshivath Torah Vodaath & Mesivta Rabbinical Seminary. 425 E 9th St, Bklyn NY 11218 (212) 941–8000.

Young Israel of Avenue J. 1721 Ave J, Bklyn NY 11230 (212) 338–2056.

Young Israel of Coney Island. Orthodox Cong affiliated with Natl Council of Young Is. To make all Jews Jewish. Rel Servs; com progs; library containing 150 vols (Judaism). 60 mems; 100 families; 8 individuals. 2 employees; 3 volunteers. F 1945; now the only Orthodox syn in Coney Island; all others have closed due to change in neighborhood. Facilities include kitchen & meeting rm. Pres & Natl Liason VP: Stanley I. Schumsky; 1st VP: Herbert Rock; 2nd VP: Hyman Pisark; Treas: Benjamin Gilman; Sec: Michael Feinstein. **2801 Surf Ave, Bklyn NY 11224 (212) HI9–1949.**

Young Israel Synagogue. 66 E 89th St, Bklyn NY 11236 (212) 496–4287.

Buffalo

Beth Am Temple. Affiliated with UAHC. 335 mems. Rabbi Daniel E. Kerman; Pres: Hubert Gerstman; Edu: Rosalyn Levy; Sisterhood Pres: Diana L. Young. **4660 Sheridan Dr, Buffalo NY 14221 (716) 633–8877.**

Beth Zion Temple. Affiliated with UAHC. 1592 mems. Rabbis: Martin L. Goldberg, Jeffrey Bennett; Pres: Ralph Halpern; Edu: Daniel G. Kantor, Joseph A. Poisson; Adm: Gertrude Schultz; Sisterhood Pres: Ruth Rachman; Brotherhood Pres: Jack Goldstein. **805 Delaware Ave, Buffalo NY 14209 (716) 886–7150.**

Beth Zion Temple Library. For information on the Temple, see – Beth Zion Temple, Buffalo, NY. **805 Delaware Ave, Buffalo NY 14209 (716) 886–7150.**

Buffalo Jewish Review. Weekly newspaper. F in 1919. Editor: Steve Lipman. **15 E Mohawk St, Buffalo NY 14203.**

Chabad House. Lubavitch com servs ctr. Blends Chassidic fervor & warmth with tradition & learning, to show that every J, fr whatever background he or she comes fr, is an integral part of the body of Is. Anti-missionary work; adult edu; Sabbath seminars; holiday progs; day camp; youth groups; syns; kosher kitchen; counseling; chaplaincy; Mitzvah Campaigns; hosp & prison visitations; sr citizens encounters; speakers bureau. Rabbi N. Gurary. **3292 Main St, Buffalo NY 14214 (716) 833–8334.**

Jewish Federation of Greater Buffalo, Inc. Affiliated with CJF, United Way of Buffalo & Erie Cty, Buffalo Chamber of Commerce. To edu & set policy for local J com; to raise funds for maintaining local & overseas social serv agy. Com relations – educates com, both J & non-J, regarding J issues of Is, oppressed J, Church/State & intergroup relationships, J security; fund-raising – conducts annual United J Fund Campaign as local branch of the United J Appeal; planning & budgeting – allocates funds to local, natl & intl J concerns through planned approach; leadership dev – finds new leadership participants in the local com, trains them for posts in local J orgs & educates regarding current J issues; Women's Activity Cttee – prepares local J com calendar, conducts annual visit of disabled Is vets. 21 employees; 500 volunteers. F 1903. Pub The Federation News (bi-monthly). Pres: Gordon Gross; VPs: Harold Axlerod, Leonard Kaminker, Ann Holland Cohn, Martin Trossman; Sec: David Brown; Fin Sec: Irving Fudeman; Treas: Robert Fine; Planning & Budgeting Dir: Jonathan Biatch; Asst Treas: Neil Rudin; Asst Fin Sec: Morris Rombro. **787 Delaware Ave, Buffalo NY 14209 (716) 886–7750.**

Temple Beth El of Greater Buffalo. Affiliated with United Syn of Am. Rabbi Samuel I. Porath; Cantor Gerald DeBruin; Pres: Howard I. Levine; Exec Dir: Ruth Fridman; Edu Dir: Janet Adler; Youth Dir: Lisa Rodwin. **2368 Eggert Rd, Buffalo NY 14150 (716) 836–3762.**

Temple Beth Zion Religious School. To give each stu an intensive J edu. Formal & informal edu progs; special edu prog; club progs; folk dancing; sports; J music; J cooking; grades 11 & 12 have a special dept which is divided into three tracks: Teacher Aides Training Prog, HS Seminar Prog, club leaders & specialists; library contains 800 vols. 700 stu fr presch–12th grade. F 1850. Dir of Edu: Joseph A. Poillon.**700 Sweet Home Rd, Buffalo NY 14226 (716) 836–6565.**

Temple Shaarey Zedek. Affiliated with United Syn of Am. Rabbi Sholom Stern; Cantor Aryeh Grayewsky; Pres: J. Herbert Scheer; Exec Dir: Jerome

Frank; Edu Dir: Shay Mintz; Youth Dir: Karla Wiseman. **621 Getzville Rd, Buffalo NY 14226 (716) 838–3232.**

Temple Sinai. Reconstructionist Syn affiliated with the Reconstructionist Fed of Congs & Fellowships, & UAHC. Fri Evening, Sat Morning Servs. Est in 1952. Rabbi Joseph D. Herzog; Pres: Betty Goodman; 1st VP: Julius Falk; 2nd VP: Norman Ablove; 3rd VP: Arthur Wasserman; Sec: Alva Finkelstein; Treas: Donald Kertman. **50 Alberta Dr, Buffalo NY 14226 (716) 834–0708.**

Catskill

Temple Israel. Affiliated with UAHC. 58 mems. Rabbi Philip Schlenker; Pres: Isidor N. Oren. **Spring St, Catskill NY 12414 (518) 943–5758.**

Cedarhurst

Israel Music Foundation. 109 Cedarhurst Ave, Cedarhurst NY 11516 (516) 569–1541.

National Tay-Sachs & Allied Diseases Association. Non-profit health org. To conduct progs of public & professional edu into the genetic disease Tay-Sachs & medically allied diseases. Provide edu on Tay-Sachs disease; acts as a referral agy for lay & professionals; promotes genetic screening; supports International Quality Control & Reference Sample Ctr for laboratories conducting Tay-Sachs testing; supports parent outreach & on-going parent support groups; provides referrals for med & genetic supports to families of affected chil. 2 employees. Pub What Every Family Should Know; Prevent a Tragedy; Test Center Guide; Breakthrough. Natl Pres: Steven Laver; Exec VP: Michael Sheff; Fin VP: Harvey Greenstein; Fund VP: Rose Weisfeld; Edu VP: Frances Berkwits; Chapter Dev VP: Jayne Mackta; Rec Sec: Joan Citrenbaum. **92 Washington Ave, Cedarhurst NY 11516 (516) 569–4300.**

Temple Beth El. Affiliated with United Syn of Am. Rabbi Gilbert S. Rosenthal; Cantor Tibor Kelen; Pres: Allan Rodolitz; Exec Dir: Morton Engle; Edu Dir: Mira Rosenfeld; Youth Dir: Edward Edelstein. **Bdwy & Locust Ave, Cedarhurst NY 11516 (516) 569–2700.**

Chappaqua

Temple Beth El. Affiliated with UAHC. 453 mems. Rabbis: Dennis Ross, Chaim Stern; Cantor Kenneth Cohen; Pres: Stanley Amberg; Sisterhood Pres: Elisabeth R. Weseley; Brotherhood Pres: Herbert Green. **220 Bedford Rd, Chappaqua NY 10514 (914) 238–3928.**

Clifton Park

Congregation Beth Shalom. Affiliated with United Syn of Am. Rabbi Robert Bronstein; Pres: Barry Forman; Edu Dir: Deborah Epstein; Treas: Richard Marshall. **PO Box 82, Clifton Park Ctr, Clifton Park NY 12065 (518) 371–0608.**

Commack

Commack Jewish Center. Affiliated with United Syn of Am. Rabbi William Berman; Cantor Leon Wolk; Pres: Burton Young; Edu Dir: Rabbi Murray Apelbaum. **83 Shirley Ct, Commack NY 11725 (516) 543–3311.**

Temple Beth David. Affiliated with UAHC. 700 mems. Rabbis: Mark Winer, Donald A. Weber; Cantor Peter Taormina; Pres: Hyman Needleman; Edu: Jacob Eckstein; Sisterhood Pres: Sue Weiner; Brotherhood Pres: Harold Guberman. **100 Hauppauge Rd, Commack NY 11725 (516) 499–0915.**

Cronton-on-Hudson

Temple Israel of Northern Westchester. Liberal Reform Syn. Dedicated to all aspects of contemporary J life, study & action. Rel Servs; study. F in 1947 as Temple Is of the Town of Cortlandt. Rabbi Dr Michael A. Robinson; Cantor Michael Schiff; Edu Dir: Sheila Phillips; Adm Sec: Sally Schechter; Pres: Dr Jacob Judd; VP: John Gochman; Sec: Oscar Scherzer. **Glengary Rd, Cronton-on-Hudson NY 10520 (914) 271–4705.**

DeWitt

Congregation Beth Sholom. Affiliated with United Syn of Am. Pres: Dr Edward Mofson; Edu Dir: Dr Ronald Ramer. **5205 Jamesville Rd, PO Box 271, DeWitt NY 13214 (315) 446–9570.**

Congregation Beth Sholom – Chevra Shas Library. For information on the Cong, see – Congregation Beth Sholom, DeWitt, NY. **5205 Jamesville Rd, PO Box 271, DeWitt NY 13214 (315) 446–9570.**

Deer Park

Suffolk Jewish Center. Conservative syn ctr; unaffiliated. Rel Sch – K-Bar/Bat Mitzvah age; Sisterhood; Youth Group; Daily Servs; Adult Edu. Est in 1956. Rabbi Gabriel Maza; Cantor Stuart M. Kanas; Sexton: Lou Hahn; Pres: Theodore Newman; 1st VP: Seymour Schnee; 2nd VP: Irwin Natter; Sisterhood Pres: Marsha Milstein; Chr Bd of Edu: Seymour Schnee. **330 Central Ave, Deer Park NY 11729 (516) 667–7695.**

Dix Hills

Dix Hills Jewish Center. Affiliated with United Syn of Am. Rabbi Nathaniel Steinberg; Pres: Serge Kreisberger; Edu Dir: Rachel Segal; Youth Dir: Stuart Zucker. **Vanderbilt Pkwy & De Forest Rd, Dix Hills NY 11746 (516) 499–6644.**

Temple Beth Torah. Affiliated with UAHC. 422 mems. Rabbi Marc A. Gellman; Cantor Dana Troupe; Pres: Harold Kopman; Edu: Doris Dornfeld; Sisterhood Pres: Joanne Levant; Brotherhood Pres: Jack Meisner. **35 Bagatelle Rd, Dix Hills NY 11746 (516) 643–1200.**

Dobbs Ferry

Greenburgh Hebrew Center. Affiliated with United Syn of Am. Rabbi Lyle Fishman; Cantor Sidney Rosenfeld; Pres: Fran Singer; Edu Dir: Lilyan Brower; Youth Dir: Eleanor Heller. **515 Bdwy, Dobbs Ferry NY 10522 (914) 693–4260.**

Douglaston

Marathon Jewish Community Center. Conservative ins affiliated with United Syn of Am. Rel Servs; edu prog; Sisterhood.550 mems. F 1953. Rabbi Hillel A. Cohen; Cantor Avshalom Zfira; Pres: Murray I. Ostrin. **245–37 60th Ave, Douglaston NY 11362 (212) 428–1580.**

Dunkirk

Temple Beth El. Affiliated with United Syn of Am. To provide rel servs & rel instruction; to foment a sense of com among the mems; to foment bonds of brotherhood with the State of Is & with coreligionists everywhere; to promote social interaction & intellectual activities among mems; to foster, in as much as possible for the small J com, good relations with non-J rel & cultural ins. Rel Servs; Rel Sch; Heb Sch; Post Bar Mitzvah classes; Study Group – a small group of mems meet monthly to discuss a bk of J interest that has been read by all; Talmud – on Sat afternoons a small group studies & discusses under the leadership of the rabbi; social & fundraising activities; Fri Night Servs held approximately once a mo fr Sept to May, sometimes to hear lectures, participate in discussions, & sometimes specifically aimed at chil participation. 40 families. The Dunkirk Hebrew Com Org was formed in 1918. In 1919 a bldg was bought by the Org for the purpose of rel servs. The Dunkirk Hebrew Com moved to its present site in 1932. In 1955 the sanctuary was dedicated & the name Temple Beth El was officially adopted. Rabbi Samuel Levenberg; Pres: Clark M. Zlotchew; VP: William Chazanoff; Treas: Yvonne Wilensky; Sec: Leonard Light; Fin Sec: Martha Light; Bd of Trustees: Warren Beyer; Esther Kozlowski, Irving Jacobs, Lillian Zeman.**507 Wahshington Ave, Dunkirk NY 14048 (716) 366–6646.**

East Hampton

Jewish Center of the Hamptons. Affiliated with UAHC. 135 mems. Pres: Evan Frankel. **44 Woods Lane, PO Box 871, East Hampton NY 11937 (516) 324–9858.**

East Meadow

Anti-Defamation League of B'nai B'rith – Long Island Regional Office. Dedicated in purpose & prog to translating the Am heritage of democratic ideals into a way of life for all Am, & to countering assaults on the safety, status, rights & image of J. For additional information, see – Anti-Defamation League of B'nai B'rith, New York City, NY. **2310 Hempstead Turnpike, East Meadow NY 11554.**

East Meadow Jewish Center. Conservative Syn affiliated with United Syn of Am, accredited Heb sch & nursery sch by Bd of J Edu, LI Principals Assn. To perpetuate J. Rel Servs; edu progs; Sisterhood; Men's Club; Youth Group; Sr Citizens Group; Young Couples Group; Presch; HS; Afternoon Sch; library containing 3,300 vols (Judaica). 625 families; 189 stu in grades K–10. 30 employees. F July 9, 1953. Pub Observer (monthly), Inner Circle (monthly Sisterhood paper). Facilities include kosher kitchen, sanctuary, gift shop, nursery sch bldg. Awards fr United Syn for Youth. Awards fr Yeshiva Univ, Is Bonds, JTS, Hadassah, Town of Hampstead for com serv. Rabbi Dr Israel Nobel; Cantor Paul Carus; Pres: Henry Frankenberg; Nursery Sch Dir: Enid Offenbach; Edu Dir: Rabbi Irvin S. Beigel. **1400 Prospect Ave, East Meadow NY 11554 (516) 483–4205.**

East Meadow Jewish Center, Library. Library contains 3300 vols (Judaica, Is, hist of the J people, J literature, chil literature, Bible & Bible stories, biographies, J fiction, etc.) For information on the Ctr, see – East Meadow Jewish Center, East Meadow, NY. **1400 Prospect Ave, East Meadow NY 11554 (516) 483–4205.**

Suburban Park Jewish Center. Conservative Syn. Rel Servs; edu progs; Sisterhood; Afternoon Sch. 135 families; 50 stu. 9 employees. F 1958. Pub Shema (monthly). Facilities include kosher kitchen, sanctuary. Rabbi David Rosen; Pres: Manny Effron. **400 Old Westbury Rd, East Meadow NY 11554 (516) 796–2626.**

Temple Emanu-El of East Meadow. Reform Cong affiliated with UAHC. Rel Servs; edu progs; Sisterhood; counseling servs; HS; Afternoon Sch. 650 families; 500 stu. Pub Voice (monthly). Facilities include kosher kitchen; sanctuary; auditorium, gift shop, sch. Pres: Norman Konsker; VPs: Gerald Hayden, Jacqueline Lakretz, Stanford Schwartz. **123 Merrick Ave, East Meadow NY 11554 (516) 794–8911.**

East Northport

East Northport Jewish Center. Affiliated with United Syn of Am. Rabbi Stanley Wernick; Cantor Philip Friedman; Pres: Stanley Goldick. **328 Elwood Rd, East Northport NY 11731 (516) 368–6474.**

East Rockaway

Hewlett-East Rockaway Jewish Center Library. For information on the Ctr, see – Hewlett-East Rockaway Jewish Center, East Rockaway, NY. **295 Main St, East Rockaway NY 11518 (516) 599–2634.**

Hewlett-East Rockaway Jewish Center, Congregation Etz Chaim. Affiliated with United Syn of Am. Rabbi Dr Stanley Plater; Cantor Emanuel Perlman; Pres: Stanley L. Cohen; Exec Dir: Robert Fox; Edu Dir: Mordecai Mahfouda; Youth Dir: Stanley Blumenstein. **295 Main St, East Rockaway NY 11518 (516) 599–2634.**

Ellenville

Congregation Ezrath Israel. Orthodox Syn affiliated with the Union of Orthodox J Congs of Am. Rel Servs; edu & social progs for youth & elderly; Men's Club; Sisterhood; library; mikveh; meeting place for J orgs; Heb Sch. 300 families. Est in 1907 under the name Ellenville Hebrew Aid Soc. The name was changed after the est of the State of Is. The Syn is active in raising funds for Is. In 1979 the Cong adopted Netivot, a com in the Negev. Rabbi Herman Eisner; Asst Rabbi Kenneth Stein; Hon Pres: Julius Slutsky; Hon VP: Manuel Rosenstock; Pres: Stanley C. Rosenstock. **31 Center St, Ellenville NY 12428 (914) 647–4450.**

Elmhurst

Emanu-El of Queens. Affiliated with UAHC. 60 mems. Rabbi Leah Kroll; Pres: Edwin Devorin; Edu: Allan Fisk. **91–15 Corona Ave, Elmhurst NY 11373 (212) 592–4343.**

Elmira

Congregation Shomray Hadath. Conservative Cong affiliated with United Syn of Am. To serve as a House of Prayer, Study & Fellowship for the Elmira J com within the standards of Conservative Judaism. Rel Servs – daily, Sabbath & Holidays; Talmud Torah – K thru HS; Sisterhood; Adult Edu; social activities; library with 750 vols (Judaica). 235 families. 10 employees. F 1883. Pub Double Triangle (monthly). Facilities include sanctuary, 2 social halls, daily chapel, 5 classrms, youth house, 2 kosher kitchens, off. Rabbi Ronald Androphy; Pres: David Schofield; Chr Bd: Ruth Golos; Rabbi Emeritus Mordecai Simckes. **Cobbles Park, Elmira NY 14905 (607) 732–7410.**

Elmira Jewish Welfare Fund, Inc. Mem of CJF. Organized 1942. Pres: Dr Edward J. Grandt; Exec Dir: Ernest G. Budwig. **PO Box 3087, Grandview Rd Ext, Elmira NY 14905 (607) 734–8122.**

Temple B'nai Israel. Affiliated with UAHC. 155 mems. Rabbi Philip Aronson; Pres: Marilyn Rabinowitz; Edu: Janice Weisenfeld; Sisterhood Pres: Susan King. **900 W Water St, Elmira NY 14905 (607) 734–7735.**

Elmont

Jewish Current Events. Periodical pub. **430 Keller Ave, Elmont NY 11003.**

Temple B'nai Israel. Affiliated with UAHC. 235 mems. Rabbi Samuel Kehati; Cantor Morris Gesell; Pres: Florence Gould; Edu: Gary Chattman; Sisterhood Pres: Carolyn S. Brenner; Brotherhood Pres: I. Leonard Messer. **Elmont Rd, Baylis Ave, Elmont NY 11003 (516) 354–1156.**

Far Rockaway

Bayswater Jewish Center – Congregation Darchay Noam. Affiliated with United Syn of Am. Cantor Reuven Caspi; Pres: Arthur Sudran; Edu Dir: Melvin Hyman. **2355 Healy Ave, Far Rockaway NY 11691 (212) GR1–7771.**

Jewish Community Council of the Rockaway Peninsula, Inc. A non-partisan, non-pol body for communication & action for the 34 J fraternal & social servs agy & orgs on the Rockaway Peninsula. Provides direct servs on a non-sectarian basis to those in need, & advocates on issues of importance to the com; information & referral advocacy for the poor; shopping & escort servs for the frail & elderly; street fair; energy assistance prog; cooperation with other orgs for the betterment of the com; housing resettlement for Russian immigrants; housing referral; participation in neighborhood housing proj. 34 J orgs & social serv agy located on Rockaway Peninsula. Inc in 1973. Com newsletter. Exec Dir: Alan Grossman; Pres: Irving Baron; 1st VP: Irving Kitzner; VPs: Norman Solomon, Yitchak Klein, Norman Blaustein, Marilyn Stadtmauer, Bernard Hoenig; Rec & Fin Sec: Muriel Shube; Treas: Bernard Klein. **257 Beach 17th St, Far Rockaway NY 11691 (212) 327–7876.**

Jewish Community Services of Long Island. A counseling agy devoted to helping families with personal & emotional problems. For additional information, see – Jewish Community Services of Long Island – Rego Park NY. **1600 Central Ave, Far Rockaway NY 11691 (212) 327–1600.**

Pioneer Women – Na'amat. The training & edu of the Is woman & her family so that each can be best equipped to lead productive lives. For additional information, see – Pioneer Women Na'amat, New York City, NY. **1931 Mott Ave, Far Rockaway NY 11691 (212) 471–8453.**

Young Israel of Far Rockaway. Orthodox Syn affiliated with Natl Council of Young Is. Daily Servs (twice a day, 365 days a yr); youth activities; Sisterhood; Daf Yomi; lectures & classes in Torah/Talmud throughout the week; library containing approx 2,500 vols (Judaica). 175 families. 4 full-time employees, 8 part-time employees. F 1964 in temporary housing; syn built 1970. Pub Ha-Or (bi-monthly). Facilities include kitchen, full gyms, sanctuary seating 400, Beth Midrash seating 100, 3 classrms, coffee house in basement. Consistent winners in YI Basketball League; on-going clothing drive for Is. Rabbi Dr Yitzchak M. Goodman; Pres: Norman Solomon; 1st VP: Akiva Salomon; 2nd VP: Shelley Kreinberg. **716 9th St, Far Rockaway NY 11691 (212) 471–6724.**

Young Israel of Far Rockaway, Library. Library contains 2,500 vols (Judaica). For information on the Ins, see – Young Is of Far Rockaway, NY. **716 9th St, Far Rockaway NY 11691 (212) 471–6724.**

Farmingdale

Farmingdale Jewish Center. Affiliated with United Syn of Am. Rabbi Paul Teicher; Cantor Herbert Harris; Pres: Howard Linett; Edu Dir: Henry Hamlin; Youth Dir: Joel Sehreck. **425 Fulton St, Farmingdale NY 11735 (516) 694–2343.**

Pioneer Women – Na'amat. The training & edu of the Is woman & her family so that each can be best equipped to lead productive lives. For additional information, see – Pioneer Women Na'amat, New York City, NY. **45 Conklin St, Farmingdale NY 11735 (516) 735–2675.**

Floral Park

Bellerose Jewish Center. Affiliated with United Syn of Am. Rabbi Alvin M. Poplack; Cantor Abraham Ranani; Pres: David Bogart. **254–04 Union Turnpike, Floral Park NY 11004 (212) 343–9001.**

Temple Sholom. Affiliated with UAHC. 140 mems. Rabbi Michael L. Kramer; Cantor Rinaldo Tazzini; Pres: Mel Gerard; Edu: Jack Goldstein; Adm: Richard Frankel; Sisterhood Pres: Mollie Rogers; Brotherhood Pres: Alvin Dunaisky. **263–10 Union Turnpike, Floral Park NY 11004 (212) 343–8660.**

Florida

Temple Beth Shalom, Hebrew Community Center. Affiliated with UAHC. 100 mems. Rabbi Ronald Gerson; Pres: Paul Klein; Sisterhood Pres: Miriam Munzer. **Roosevelet Ave, Florida NY 10921 (914) 651–7817.**

Flushing

American Association of Professors of Yiddish. A 1309 Queens Col, Flushing NY 11367 (212) 520–7067.

Congregation Shaarai Tefila – Temple Gates of Prayer. Affiliated with United Syn of Am. Rabbi Albert Thaler; Cantor Jacob Ven Zion Mendelson; Pres: Dr Saul Futterman; Exec Dir: Ann Burns. **38–20 Parsons Blvd, Flushing NY 11354 (212) 359–1160.**

Electchester Jewish Center, Inc. Affiliated with United Syn of Am. Rabbi Joseph J. Spevack; Cantor Kurt Flaschner; Pres: Philip Lefkowitz; Exec Dir: Joseph Weber; Edu Dir: Barbara Eulau. **65–15 164th St, Flushing NY 11365 (212) TU6–4454.**

Free Synagogue of Flushing. Affiliated with UAHC. 270 mems. Rabbis: Charles Agin, Max Meyer; Pres: Martin Silverman; Edu: Charles Agin; Adm: Ruth Wunder; Sisterhood Pres: Joyce

Schenkman; Brotherhood Pres: Bertram Goldblatt. **41–60 Kissena Blvd, Flushing NY 11355 (212) 961–0030.**

The Hillcrest Jewish Center. Affiliated with United Syn of Am. Rabbi Israel Mowshowitz; Asst Rabbi Mordecai Efron; Cantor Alan Mayersdorf; Pres: Judge Leon A. Berman; Edu Dir: Elliot Prager; Youth Dir: Bert Rosenberg. **183–02 Union Turnpike, Flushing NY 11366 (212) 380–4145.**

Hollis Hills Jewish Center. Affiliated with United Syn of Am. Rabbi Dr H. Joseph Simckes; Cantor Sol Zim; Pres: Stanley B. Hendler; Sexton: Frank Strassfeld; Youth Dir: Steve Wohl. **210–10 Union Turnpike, Flushing NY 11364 (212) 776–3500.**

Hollis Hills Jewish Center Library. For information on the Ctr, see – Hollis Hills Jewish Center, Flushing, NY. **210–10 Union Turnpike, Flushing NY 11364 (212) 776–3500.**

Israel Center of Hillcrest Manor. Affiliated with United Syn of Am. Rabbi Michael P. Strasberg; Cantor Ira Greenberg; Pres: Rudolph A. Kovacs; Edu Dir: Rabbi Michael Strasberg; Spiritual Dir: Rev. M. Scheinkopf. **167–11 73rd Ave, Flushing NY 11366 (212) 969–8085.**

The Jewish Center of Kew Gardens Hills. Affiliated with United Syn of Am. Rabbi I. Usher Kirshblum; Cantor Akiva Lefkowitz; Pres: Theodore Roslyn; Chr Bd of Ed: Bernard Newman; Youth Dir: Yaakov Thompson. **71–25 Main St, Flushing NY 11367 (212) 263–6500.**

Queensboro Hill Jewish Center. Affiliated with United Syn of Am. Rabbi Aharon Shapiro; Cantor Joseph Kahan; Pres: Samuel Cohen. **156–03 Horace Harding Blvd, Flushing NY 11367 (212) H15–4141.**

Rabbi Simon Hevesi Jewish Heritage Library. 5,000 monographs in English, Heb & Yiddish; subscriptions to 25 periodicals; subjects encompass archaeology, rel, philosophy, J & Is Hist, Middle E relations, Holocaust, Heb language, Yiddish literature, Talmudic commentaries & seforim; 25 films; 80 filmstrips; 6 slide sets; over 50 phonograph records; com lectures. Serves over 300 each mo. Est in 1977 when Assemblyman Hevesi received the 1st yearly appropriation for creating this resource. The official opening was on Dec 2, 1979. In the summer of the same yr, Queens Col became the adm agy & moved the collection to its 1st branch at the J Ctr of Kew Gardens Hills. Steering Cttee: Alan Hevesi, Saul Cohen, Ernest Schwarcz, Rabbi Usher Kirschblum, Rabbi Fabian Schonfeld, Ellen Moskowitz, Nehemiah Ben-Zev, Rabbi Simon Hevesi, Shoshana Kaufman, Paul Klapper, Harold Baron. **71–25 Main St, Flushing NY 11367 (212) 793–4752.**

The Solomon Schechter School of Queens. Affiliated with Solomon Schechter Day Schs Assn. To provide the kind of edu which will encourage its stu to contribute to & participate in Am soc & at the same time understand, cherish & live by J tradition. High level gen studies: Math, Social Studies, Foreign Languages, Sci, Music & Art; Intensive J Studies Prog: Heb Language, Prophets & Torah, Heb Literature, J Traditions & Observances; library – English & Heb; fully-equipped sci lab; holiday observance; prayers. Enrollment of 545 chil fr 20 coms. Staff of 55. F in 1955 by leaders of the Conservative J cong in Central Queens. A small group of dedicated teachers, parents & stu began to dev a vibrant edu ins. Pres: Solomon Heiferman; VPs: Elliott Goldstein, Fred Katzner, Abe Malamut, Sol Turetsky; Sec: Ann Low; Treas: Norman Gursen; Prin of English Dept: Frieda Lieberman; Prin of J Dept: Rabbi Abraham Sofer. **76–16 Parsons Blvd, Flushing NY 11366 (212) 591–9800.**

Temple Beth Or of the Deaf. Affiliated with UAHC. 175 mems. Pres: Charles Grant; Adm: Alfred A. Weinrib; Sisterhood Pres: Wendy Bachman. **c/o Temple Beth Sholom, 171–39 Northern Blvd, Flushing NY 11358 (212) 776–4400.**

Temple Beth Sholom. Affiliated with UAHC. 337 mems. Rabbi Bruce Goldwasser; Cantor Hilda Abrevaya; Pres: Victor Lowenstein; Edu: Irwin Maiman; Sisterhood Pres: Francis Harris, Francine Schwartz; Brotherhood Pres: Sol Solarsh. **171–39 Northern Blvd, Flushing NY 11358 (212) 463–4143.**

Utopia Jewish Center. Affiliated with United Syn of Am. Rabbi Solomon Goldman; Cantor Israel Flusberg; Pres: Irving Heller; Edu Dir: Dr Elly Schischa; Youth Dir: William Goldstein. **64–41 Utopia Pkwy, Flushing NY 11365 (212) 461–8347.**

Young Israel of Kew Gardens Hills. Syn. Adult Edu; Primary Sch; youth activities; Free Loan Fund; Young Is Ltd Med Insurance; Young Is Blood Prog; Benevolent Assn. Rabbi Fabian Schonfeld; Exec Sec: Pearl Hametz; Pres: Jerry Sklar; 1st VP: Jacob Weinstein; Assc VPs: Sol Englander, Norman Gittler; Treas: Morris Lopata; Fin Sec: Naftali Flaumenhaft; Rec Sec: Ephraim Love; Corsp Sec: Larry Sheldon; Hon Pres: Leon Blatt, Herbert L. Cohen, Nathaniel Geller, Dr Murray Grossman, Issac Hametz, Irving

Kahan, Joseph M. Reiner, Nathan Saperstein, Harry Spett, Alex Steinberg, Dr Hyman Zahtz, Leo Ziegel, Joseph Zimilover; Gabbyim: David Englander, Stuart Friedman, Jack Rapp; Bd of Dirs: Seymour Fried, Eugen Gluck, Norman Gross, Rabbi Emanuel Holzer, David Kallus, William Kantrowitz, Eugene Leitman, Gerald Moskowitz, Jack Polinsky, Alex Schechter, Al Scheinfeld, Sol Spierer. **150th St & 70th Rd, Flushing NY 11367 (212) BO1–9723, 9761.**

Forest Hills

Congregation Machane Chodosh. Orthodox Syn. Rel Servs; edu progs; Sisterhood; youth groups; library containing 1,000 vols (Judaica). F 1939. Pub Kehillah News (monthly, Sept–June); Annual Journal. Facilities include sanctuary, auditorium, kosher kitchen, library & classrms. Spiritiual Leader: Rabbi Manfred Gans; Pres: Sol Wachenheimer; VPs: Arthur F. Pagelson, Otto Israel, Erick Liebenstein; Editor: Susan Moses; Corsp Sec: Sali Rothschild; Rec Sec: Leo Zentman; Treas: William Leib. **67–29 108th St, Forest Hills NY 11375 (212) 793–5656.**

The Forest Hills Jewish Center. Affiliated with United Syn of Am. Rabbi Dr Ben Zion Bokser; Asst Rabbi Gerald Skolnik; Cantor Erno Grosz; Pres: Roy Clements; Edu Dir: Hyman J. Campeas; Youth Dir: Arthur Lederer. **106–06 Queens Blvd, Forest Hills NY 11375 (212) 263–7000.**

Temple Isaiah. Affiliated with UAHC. 390 mems. Rabbi Mayer Perelmuter; Cantors: Judith K. Rowland, Boris Voronorsky; Pres: Irving Miller; Edu: Lee Korobkin; Adm: Marcia Weinroth; Sisterhood Pres: Joan Murray; Brotherhood Pres: Robert Newman. **75–24 Grand Central Pkwy, Forest Hills NY 11375 (212) 544–2800.**

Franklin Square

Franklin Square Jewish Center. Affiliated with United Syn of Am. Rabbi Abraham B. Shoulson; Cantor Larry Adler; Pres: David Lagnado. **Pacific & Lloyd Sts, Franklin Square NY 11010 (516) FL4–2322.**

Freeport

Congregation B'nai Israel of Freeport. Conservative Cong affiliated with United Syn of Am. To serve the rel, cultural & social needs of the Freeport J com. Shabbat Servs, festivals, daily minyan; Sisterhood; Men's Club; Mr & Mrs Club; Golden Circle; USY, Kadima youth groups; boy scout troop; cub scout pack; Rel Sch ages 5–13; confirmation for post Bar/Bat Mitzvah; Heb HS, adult edu progs through a Women's Ins & Akiba Sch. Organized in 1915, the Cong originally was located at Bdwy fr 1920–1956. Thereafter, the Cong moved to its present location. Rabbi Reuven M. Katz; Cantor Harry Altman; Pres: Marvin H. Cohen; VPs: Eileen Ardbaum, Henrietta Goldstein, Allen Goldstein, Neal Goodman, Seymour D. Siskind; Treas: Vivian Garf; Fin Sec: David B. Freeman; Rec Sec: Phyllis Mond; Chr Bd of Trustees: Stanley Ardbaum. **91 N Bayview Ave, Freeport NY 11520 (516) MA3–4200.**

Union Reform Temple. Affiliated with UAHC. 280 mems. Rabbi Lawrence Colton; Cantor Sheri Blum; Pres: Barbara Levine; Edu: Donald S. Milrod; Sisterhood Pres: Marcia Levenberg; Brotherhood Pres: Douglas Sherman. **475 N Brookside Ave, Freeport NY 11520 (516) 623–1810.**

Fresh Meadows

Fresh Meadows Jewish Center. Affiliated with United Syn of Am. Rabbi Robert E. Fine; Cantor Morris Romalis; Pres: Albert Esterow; Edu Dir: Solomon Lasky; Youth Dir: Hal Malis. **193–10 Peck Ave, Fresh Meadows NY 11365 (212) 357–5100.**

Garden City

Garden City Jewish Center. Affiliated with UAHC. 67 mems. Rabbis: David W. Nelson, Meyer Miller; Pres: Morgan Y. Himelstein; Edu: David W. Nelson; Sisterhood Pres: Ann Markon, Rose Zelenetz. **168 Nassau Blvd, Garden City NY 11530 (516) 248–9180.**

Geneva

Temple Beth El. Reform Temple affiliated with UAHC; mem of the Geneva Council of Churches & Syns. Rel Servs; edu progs; Rel Sch; Sisterhood. library (Judaica – literature, reference bks). 71 families; approx 250 individuals; 35 stu in Rel Sch. 2 full-time employees; 7 part-time employees). F 1947. Pub Temple Topics (11 issues a yr). Facilities include sanctuary, 4 classrms, rabbi's study, library, social hall, kitchen, caretaker's apt. Rabbi Garson Herzfeld; Bd Chr: Ira Mitchell; Pres: Perry Myers; VP: Barry Budgar; Bd of Edu Chr: Genevieve Russo. **755 S Main St, Geneva NY 14456 (315) 789–9710.**

Glen Cove

Congregation Tifereth Israel. Affiliated with United Syn of Am. Rabbi Maurice Weisenberg; Cantor Maurice Casuto; Pres: Phillip Windler; Edu

Dir: Robert O. Brooks; Youth Dir: Dr Myron Polkes. **Hill St & Landing Rd, Glen Cove NY 11542 (516) 676–5080.**

North Country Reform Temple. Affiliated with UAHC. 197 mems. Rabbi Laurence Kotok; Cantor Jan Mahler; Pres: Harold Berkowitz; Edu: Jack Sotsky; Sisterhood Pres: Michele Siskind; Brotherhood Pres: David Medina. **Crescent Beach Rd, Glen Cove NY 11542 (516) 671–4760.**

Glendale

Forest Park Jewish Center. Orthodox Syn. To provide for the rel needs of the young & old as well as to try to bring back into fold those who may have strayed away. Daily Minyan, morning & evening; Afternoon Heb Sch; Adult Edu Prog; youth activities; Sisterhood. Est in 1956. The Voice (monthly newsletter). Rabbi Y.A. Sladowsky; Editor: Bettina Schwarzachild; Pres: Irving Pernick; VP: Jack Pallay. **90–45 Myrtle Ave, Glendale NY 11227 (212) VI7–6273.**

Glens Falls

Greater Glens Falls Jewish Welfare Fund. Mem of CJF. Organized 1939. Chr: Sunny Buchman. **PO Box 525, Glens Falls NY 12801 (518) 792–4624.**

Shaarey Tefila. Affiliated with United Syn of Am. Rabbi Gerald Solomon; Pres: Dr. Allan Korot. **68 Bay St, Glens Falls NY 12801 (518) 792–4945.**

Temple Beth El. Affiliated with UAHC. 121 mems. Rabbi Richard J. Sobel; Pres: Linda Agranov; Edu: Sheldon Binns; Sisterhood Pres: Leslie Munzer. **3 Marion Ave, Glens Falls NY 12801 (518) 792–4364.**

Gloversville

Knesseth Israel Synagogue. Affiliated with United Syn of Am. Rabbi Milton Feierstein; Pres: Marian Finkle. **34 E Fulton St, Gloversville NY 12078 (518) 725–0649.**

Knesseth Israel Synagogue Library. For information on the Syn, see – Knesseth Israel, Gloversville, NY. **34 E Fulton St, Gloversville NY 12078 (518) 725–0649.**

Great Neck

Temple Beth El. Affiliated with UAHC. 1350 mems. Rabbis: Jerome K. Davidson, David J. Gelfand; Cantor B. Ostfeld–Horowitz; Pres: Myron Pomerantz; Edu: Irene S. Dicker, Eric Feldheim; Adm: Ann Finkelstein; Sisterhood Pres: Joan Hessekiel; Brotherhood Pres: Stewart M. Chodosch. **5 Old Mill Rd, Great Neck NY 11023 (516) 487–0900.**

Temple Beth El, Arnold & Marie Swartz Library. For information on the Temple, see – Temple Beth El, Great Neck, NY. **5 Old Mill Rd, Great Neck NY 11023 (516) 487–0900.**

Temple Emanuel. Affiliated with UAHC. 690 mems. Rabbis: Robert S. Widom, Robert A. Jacobs; Cantor Henry Weintraub; Pres: Herbert W. Riemer; Edu: Charles G. Sussman; Adm: Robert A. Jacobs; Sisterhood Pres: Stephanie Reyer; Brotherhood Pres: Warren Werner. **150 Hicks Lane, Great Neck NY 11024 (516) 482–5701.**

Temple Isaiah of Great Neck. Affiliated with UAHC. 155 mems. Rabbi Harold Spivack; Cantor Milton M. Friedman; Pres: Irma L. Wolfe; Edu: Esther Raviv; Adm: Florence R. Levy. **PO Box 229, Great Neck NY 11022 (516) 487–8709.**

Temple Israel Library. 108 Old Mill Rd, Great Neck NY 11023 (516) 582–7800.

Temple Israel of Great Neck. For information on the Temple, see – Temple Israel of Great Neck, Great Neck, NY. Affiliated with United Syn of Am. Rabbi Mordecai Waxman; Cantor Benjamin Siegel; Asst Rabbi: Robert Summer; Pres: Murray Damast; Exec Dir: Vivian Krasnow; Edu Dir: Rabbi Miriam Charry; Youth Dir: Rabbi Lavey Derby. **108 Old Mill Rd, Great Neck NY 11023 (516) 582–7800.**

Guilderland

Hebrew Academy of the Capital District. Affiliated with Solomon Schechter Day Schools Assn. Prin: Dvorah Heckelman, Dr Jeanne Jacobson; Chr: Linda Hershberg. **2211A Western Ave, Guilderland NY 12084 (518) 456–6816.**

Harrison

Jewish Community Center of Harrison. Affiliated with United Syn of Am. Rabbi Norton D. Shargel; Cantor Bernard Dienstag; Pres: Leo Gilberg. **Union Ave, Harrison NY 10528 (914) 835–2850.**

Hastings-on-Hudson

Temple Beth Shalom. Affiliated with UAHC. 167 mems. Rabbi Edward Schechter; Cantor Abraham Blumenfeld; Pres: Allan Janger; Adm: Dorothy

Ettlinger. **740 N Bdwy, Hastings-on-Hudson NY 10706 (914) 478–3833.**

Hauppauge

Temple Beth Chai. Affiliated with United Syn of Am. Rabbi Jacob Goldstein; Pres: Barry Musher. **870 Townline Rd, Hauppauge NY 11787.**

Hempstead

Jewish Community Services of Long Island. A counseling agy devoted to helping families with personal & emotional problems. For additional information, see – Jewish Community Services of Long Island – Rego Park, NY. **50 Clinton St, Hempstead NY 11550 (516) 485–5710.**

Henrietta

Temple Beth Am. Affiliated with United Syn of Am. Rabbi Dr Meyer Minkowich; Pres: Bruce D. Nelson; Sch Chr: Judy Greenspan; Treas: Dennis Kovel. **3249 E Henrietta Rd, PO Box 177, Henrietta NY 14467 (716) 334–4855.**

Herklmer

Temple Beth Joseph. Affiliated with United Syn of Am. Rabbi L. Dimpson; Pres: Sam Heller. **327 N Prospect St, Herklmer NY 13350 (315) 866–4270.**

Hewlett

Congregation Beth Emeth. Affiliated with United Syn of Am. Rabbi Morris Pickholz; Cantor Andrew Beck; Pres: Gloria Feinsmith. **36 Franklin Ave, Hewlett NY 11557 (516) 374–9220.**

Hicksville

Hicksville Jewish Center. Affiliated with United Syn of Am. Rabbi Joseph Grossman; Pres: Clifford Luban. **6 Maglie Dr, Hicksville NY 11801 (516) WE1–9323.**

Holliswood

Society for the History of Czechoslovak Jews, Inc. To capture the modern hist of J of Czechoslovakia. Studies the hist of the Czechoslovak J in its economic, rel, pol, social & cultural aspects; collects material for such study; disseminates all types of information by way of pub of bks & pamphlets; advances the knowledge of Czechoslovak J hist. J historical research in Czechoslovakia came to an abrupt end with the Nazi occupation of 1939, when the Soc for the Hist of the J in the Czechoslovak Republic, est in Prague by the Historian Prof Samuel Steinherz, was dissolved. The successor of that org is the Soc for the Hist of Czechoslovak J which was f in 1961. Pub The Jews of Czechoslovakia, I & II. Hon Pres: Prof Guido Kisch; Pres: Lewis Weiner; VPs: Hugh Colman, Walter Kauders, George Miller, Joseph C. Pick, William W. Reiner; Sec & Treas: Joseph Abeles; Bd of Dirs: Rose Abeles, Stephen S. Barber, Albert Bergman, Kurt Bock, Prof John H. Buchsbaum, Robert Eisner, Frances Epstein, Emil Glauber, Prof Fred Hahn, Paul Hartmann, Bertha Jellinek, Rabbi Dr Leo Jung, Ilka Kubicek, Irma Miller, Hanna Moller, Dr Alexander Muller, Zdenka Munzer, Rabbi Norman Patz, Fred Popper, Lisa Popper, Dora Spitzer, Joseph Stein, Dr Karel Steinbach, Rabbi Dr Hugo Stransky, Grete Sturc, Jiri Traub, Bruno Wolfe. **c/o Lewis Weiner, 87–08 Santiago St, Holliswood NY 11423 (212) 468–6844.**

Temple Israel of Jamaica. Affiliated with UAHC. 416 mems. Rabbi Ronald Millstein; Cantor Leo Postrel; Pres: Donald Kahaner; Edu: Albert Loew; Adm: Sam Feldman; Sisterhood Pres: Gloria Lempke; Brotherhood Pres: Edward Alexander. **188–15 McLaughlin Ave, Holliswood NY 11423 (212) 776–4400.**

Honeoye Falls

Jewish Community Center of Greater Rochester. Markus Park, Honeoye Falls NY 14472 (716) 624–3668.

Hornell

Beth El Temple. Affiliated with United Syn of Am. Pres: Robert E. Hammond. **12 Church St, Hornell NY 14843 (607) 324–2236.**

Howard Beach

Howard Beach Jewish Center. Affiliated with United Syn of Am. Rabbi Maurice D. Simckes; Pres: Dr David Lehon; Exec Dir: Dave Alexander. **162–05 90th St, Howard Beach NY 11414 (212) 845–9443.**

Hudson

Jewish Welfare Fund of Hudson, N.Y. Joslen Blvd, Hudson NY 12534 (518) 828–6848.

Huntington

Huntington Hebrew Congregation. Affiliated with United Syn of Am. Rabbi Tobias Rothenberg;

Cantor Stephen Stein; Pres: Howard A. Baker; Edu Dir: Roslyn Grossman; Youth Dir: Lee Paseltiner. **510 Park Ave, Huntington NY 11743 (516) HA7–1089.**

Temple Beth El of Huntington. Affiliated with UAHC. 504 mems. Rabbi Barton Shallat; Cantor Leon M. Perlman; Pres: Jacqueline Brandman; Edu: Helene Shein; Sisterhood Pres: Naomi Specht; Brotherhood Pres: Robert Perlmutter. **660 Park Ave, Huntington NY 11743 (516) 421–5835.**

Temple Beth El of Huntington, Rabbi Schatz Memorial Library. For information on the Temple, see – Temple Beth El, Huntington, NY. **660 Park Ave, Huntington NY 11743 (516) 421–5835.**

Ithaca

B'nai B'rith Hillel at Ithaca College. Affiliated with B'nai B'rith Hillel Founs. To foster J com & activity on campus. Rel Servs; edu progs; counseling; social, cultural, Zionist activities; activities on issues relating to oppresed J; library containing 800 vols (plus subscriptions to 8 periodicals). 200 affiliates; 1300 J stu out a population of 4700. 1 employee (Dir/Adv); faculty & stu volunteers. Pub Jewish Connection (bi-weekly). Facilities include chapel seating 200; help with kosher meals. Pres Faculty Adv Bd: David Berman; Treas: John Rosenberg; Fund Raising: Harvey Fireside. **Muller Chapel, Ithaca NY 14850 (607) 273–3190.**

B'nai B'rith Hillel Foundation at Cornell University. Hillel Foundation – Univ J Chaplaincy; affiliated with B'nai B'rith Hillel. To foster J awareness at Cornell Univ; to be a focal point of J life on campus; to involve & edu J stu & faculty in matters of J concern; to represent Jews & Judaism to the larger com. Rel Servs; cultural & edu progs; counseling; social progs; library containing 1,500 vols (gen Judaica). 3200 J stu at Cornell. 3 employees. F 1929. Pub occasional calendars & listings of upcoming events. Facilities include library & off space in Anabel Taylor Hall, a bldg used cooperatively by a num of rel groups. Dir: Rabbi Laurence Edwards; **Anabel Taylor Hall, Ithaca NY 14853 (607) 256–4227.**

Temple Beth El. Unaffiliated . Rel Servs; edu progs; Sisterhood; social activities; 2-days-a-week Rel Sch. 190 families; 101 stu in grades K–10. 1 full-time employee; several part-time employees. F 1924; merged group; bldg completed in 1929; only cong in Tompkins Cty. Pub Temple Beth El Bulletin (monthly). Facilities include kosher kitchen, sanctuary, classrm space, library, gift shop. Rabbi Scott L. Glass; Pres: David B. Gersh. **Court & Tioga Sts, Ithaca NY 14850 (607) 273–5775.**

Jackson Heights

Beth Hillel Congregation. Affiliated with UAHC. 39 mems. Pres: Edwin Wolff; Sisterhood Pres: Belle Glasser. **23–38 81st St, Jackson Heights NY 11370 (212) 899–6666.**

Jewish Center of Jackson Heights. Affiliated with United Syn of Am. Cantor Gary Zener; Pres: Yale Marienhoff; Youth Dir: Bruce Sklover. **34–25 82nd St, Jackson Heights NY 11372 (212) 429–1150.**

Jamaica

Conservative Synagogue of Jamaica. Affiliated with United Syn of Am. Rel sch; youth activities; Men's Club; Sisterhood; Young Couples Group; USY Youth Group; Adult J Edu. F in 1974 as a result of a merger of 2 previously long-est cong in the area: the Jamaica J Ctr f in 1922, & the Jamaica Estates Hebrew Ctr f in 1926. The Jamaica J Ctr was the 2nd of its kind in the country, housing in its complex a syn, sch, & an outstanding complex of social & sports facilities. The present syn operates in the bldg originally built by the Jamaica Estates Hebrew Ctr & underwent an expansion in 1981–82. Chr of the Bd: Sylvan Bloom; Pres: Arthur Flug; VPs: Derle Siegelbaum, Steven Kasavana, Arnold Lazar; Comptroller: Kenneth Kopelson; Treas: Samuel Verter; Asst Treas: Jack Niedelman; Sec: Florence Lazar; Asst Sec: Hannah Trachtenberg; Rabbi Isidoro Aizenberg; Cantor Louis Teichman; Exec Dir: Morris Hoppenfeld. **182–69 Wexford Terr, Jamaica NY 11432 (212) 739–7500.**

The International Synagogue at John F. Kennedy Airport. To serve as a house of prayer & meditation for the millions of travelers fr all parts of the world who arrive at Kennedy Airport. Serves as a house of prayer for those arriving & departing; represents J to visitors fr far flung coms throughout the world; house of study; meeting house for J groups & orgs; ctr for J orgs; place where J Am com can welcome Is & European J leaders; Airport Cong sponsors servs & social/cultural activities. Dedicated in 1967. The NY Bd of Rabbis, with mems fr the three branches of J, agreed to sponsor syn. Rabbi Israel Mowshowitz, Spiritual Leader of Hillcrest J Ctr & then Pres of the NY Bd of Rabbis, headed a fund-raising drive; the J com responded generously. Is selected the Syn for inauguration of its 25th & 30th anniversary celebrations in the US. Interesting architecture reflecting both old & new styles; Ferkauf Mus houses: gifts fr J coms throughout the world, Ferkauf Library, Judaica collection, J periodicals, & gifts fr ambassadors to the United Nations; hung over the ark are 10 bronze plagues portraying the Ten Commandments sculptured by Chaim Gross; stained glass windows by Is artist Ami Shamir; artistic doors designed by Ludwig Wolpert. Hon Pres: Rabbi Israel Goldstein, Rabbi Israel Mowshowitz; Pres: Hon Charles H. Silver; VPs: Abraham L. Malamut, William S. Miller, Max Stern, Mortimer Marcus; Chr of the Bd: Rabbi Harold I. Saperstein; Sec: Rabbi Harold H. Gordon; Chaplain: Rabbi Eugene J. Cohen. **JFK Airport, Jamaica NY 11430 (212) 656–5044, 879–8415.**

Rochdale Village Jewish Center. Affiliated with United Syn of Am. Pres: Jerry Zisner. **167–10 137th Ave, Jamaica NY 11434 (212) 528–0200.**

Jamestown

Temple Hesed Abraham. Affiliated with UAHC. 69 mems. Rabbi Donald Heskins; Pres: Neil R. Power. **215 Hall Ave, Jamestown NY 14701 (716) 484–1800.**

Jericho

Jericho Jewish Center. Affiliated with United Syn of Am. Rabbi Stanley Steinhardt; Cantor Israel Goldstein; Pres: Herbert Nussbaum; Edu Dir: Samuel Goldberg; Youth Dir: Ellen Siber. **N Bdwy, Jericho NY 11753 (516) WE3–2540.**

Solomon Schechter Day School of Nassau County. Affiliated with Solomon Schechter Day Schools Assn. Prin: Rabbi Albert Berliner; Chr: Allan Bernstein. **Barbara Lane, Jericho NY 11753 (516) 935–1441.**

Temple Or Elokim. Reform Cong affiliated with UAHC. Rel Sch; Adult Edu; youth groups; special edu progs; Sisterhood; Men's Club; Choirs; cultural progs; social action progs. 300 families. Est in Jericho NY by a group of 50 people who had moved fr the city. Rabbi Philip J. Bentley; Cantor Marvin Antosofsky. **18 Tobie Lane, Jericho NY 11753 (516) 433–9888, 9587.**

Kiamesha Lake

Hebrew Day School of Sullivan & Ulster Counties. To prepare the youths of Sullivan & Ulster ctys to be proud, educated Am J. Classes nursery–8th grade. Est in 1955. Prin & Dir: Rabbi Irving H. Goodman; English Prin: Rose Gibber; Pres: Joseph Heller; Chr of the Bd: Melvin Bien; VPs: Theodore Katz, Sigurd Koesterich, Nat Lebowitz; Sec: Paul Garfinkel, Irving Podhurst. **Kiamesha Lake NY 12751 (914) 794–7890.**

Kings Park

Congregation Etz Chaim of Kings Park. Orthodox Cong. Rel Servs; Youth Groups; Heb Sch; Sun Sch; Nursery Sch; Adult Edu. Est in 1974. Rabbi Raphael Wizman; Pres: Abraham Gruber; VP: Robert Miller. **44 Meadow Rd, Kings Park NY 11754 (516) 269–9666.**

Kings Park Jewish Center, Inc. Affiliated with United Syn of Am. Rabbi Gordon Papert; Pres: Marvin Shapiro; Exec Dir: Zenia Roth; Edu Dir: Marsha Grill; Youth Dir: Art Segal. **Route 25A, PO Box 301, Kings Park NY 11754 (516) 269–1133.**

Kingston

Congregation Ahavath Israel. Affiliated with United Syn of Am. Rabbi Joel Weintraub; Cantor L. Larry Jacobs; Pres: Carl Lipton. **100 Lucas Ave, Kingston NY 12401 (914) 338–4409.**

Jewish Federation of Greater Kingston, Inc. Mem of CJF. Inc 1951. Pres: Dr Joseph Cohen; Exec Dir: Jane Myerson. **159 Green St, Kingston NY 12401 (914) 338–8131.**

Temple Emanuel. Affiliated with UAHC. 300 mems. Rabbi Jonathan Eichhorn; Cantor John F. Park; Pres: Conrad I. Heisman; Edu: Leonard Zimet; Adm: Jaqueline Olsen; Sisterhood Pres: Joan Plotsky. **243 Albany Ave, PO Box 1421, Kingston NY 12401 (914) 338–4271.**

Lake Placid

Lake Placid Synagogue. Traditional Syn. Rel Sch; Sisterhood. 45 Families; 5 Stu. The only organized & fully active cong in Essex & Franklin Ctys. Rabbi Dr Selig S. Auerbach; Pres: Ronald M. Urfiner; Pres of Sisterhood: Renee Ring. **30 Saranac Ave, Lake Placid NY 12946 (518) 523–3876.**

Lake Success

Lake Success Jewish Center. Affiliated with United Syn of Am. Rabbi Seymour Baumrind; Pres: Seymour Arenstein; Edu Dir: Michael Kluger; Youth Dir: Alan Gish. **354 Lakeville Rd, Lake Success NY 11020 (516) 466–0569.**

Larchmont

Beth Emeth Synagogue. Affiliated with United Syn of Am. Rabbi Hershel E. Portnoy; Pres: Theodor Brown. **2111 Boston Post Rd, Larchmont NY 10538 (914) 834–1093, 834–2543.**

Larchmont Temple. Affiliated with UAHC. 490 mems. Rabbis: H. Leonard Poller, Vicki Hollander; Cantor Edward Graham; Pres: Samuel Stein; Edu: Vicki Hollander; Adm: Ellen Gardner; Sisterhood Pres: N. Abraham; Brotherhood Pres: Lawrence Turk. **75 Larchmont Ave, Larchmont NY 10538 (914) 834–6120.**

Laurelton

Laurelton Jewish Center. Affiliated with United Syn of Am. Rabbi Geoffrey Goldberg; Cantor Henry Belasco; Pres: Seymour Ponemon. **134–49 228th St, Laurelton NY 11413 (212) 527–0400.**

Lawrence

The Brandeis School. Conservative J day sch affiliated with Solomon Schechter Day Schs Assn. Gen studies; J studies. 400 stu nursery–12th grade. Est in 1936 by Rabbi Miller. Headmaster: Frederick S. Nathan; Pres Bd of Trustees: Arthur Riegel; Chr Bd of Edu: Edmund Wolf; Exec Dir: Raphael Ellenbogen. **25 Frost Lane, Lawrence NY 11559 (516) 371–4747.**

Congregation Beth Sholom, Inc. Orthodox Cong affiliated with Union of Orthodox J Cong of Am. To promote Orthodox ideals & to serve the Orthodox com. Rel Servs; Heb Sch; Sisterhood; youth groups; edu progs; library of 700 vols (mostly Judaica). 300 families. F 1928 as Cong Derech Yosher; name changed to Cong Beth Absolom. Cong Beth Absolom Bulletin. Facilities include kosher kitchen, sanctuary, chapel, ballrms, lounge, library. Rabbi Dr Gilbert Klaperman; Cantor Marcus Ehrlich; Sexton: Rev Joseph Glazer; Pres: Harry Epstein; Exec VP: Herbert Linn; Sr VP: Frank Herman; VPs: Hon Herbert Warshavsky, Hon Howard Legum; Treas: Hyman G. Weiner; Sec: William Weinberger; Chr of Bd: Eli Gurian; Sisterhood Presidium: Caroline Geltman, Mrs Ray Kotel, Tema Wolfson. **390 Bdwy, Lawrence NY 11559 (516) 569–3600.**

Congregation Shaaray Tefila. Orthodox Syn. Organized in 1910. After utilizing temporary facilities for servs & classes, the syn was constructed in 1915 at Central Ave, Far Rockaway NY. The Ctr Bldg was completed in 1925. It housed the Heb Sch & various youth & social activities. The original syn was destroyed by fire in 1969, & the Cong relocated at Central & Lord Ave, Lawrence NY. The new edifice was completed in 1980. Rabbi Dr Walter S. Wurzburger; Pres: Dr Jacob Becker; Chr of the Bd: Leo Goldschmidt; V Chr of the Bd: Ray Ehrlich; VPs: Irving Ross, Raymond Woloch, Bernard Klein; Treas: Milton Kramer; Asst Treas: Arthur Jacobs; Chr Finance Cttee: Irwin Selevan; Sec: David Wohlner. **Central & Lord Ave, Lawrence NY 11559 (516) 239–2444.**

Temple Israel. Affiliated with UAHC. 900 mems. Rabbi Joel Zion; Cantor David Benedict; Pres: Alvin J. Baron; Sisterhood Pres: Flora Bender, Rose Mack; Brotherhood Pres: John Malino. **140 Central Ave, Lawrence NY 11559 (516) 239–1140.**

Temple Israel Library. For information on the Temple, see – Temple Israel, Lawrence, NY. **140 Central Ave, Lawrence NY 11559 (516) 239–1140.**

Temple Sinai of Long Island. Affiliated with UAHC. 417 mems. Rabbis: Mark N. Goldman, Abram V. Goodman; Cantor Michael F. Trachtenberg; Pres: Stanley Singer; Edu: Audrey B. Bernstein; Sisterhood Pres: Barbara L. Steiker. **131 Washington Ave, Lawrence NY 11559 (516) 569–0267.**

Levittown

Israel Community Center of Levittown. Affiliated with United Syn of Am. Rabbi Eugene S. Katz; Cantor Emery Gelbman; Pres; Mona F. Bloom; Youth Dir: Karl Weinstein. **3235 Hempstead Turnpike, Levittown NY 11756 (516) 731–2580.**

Little Neck

Little Neck Jewish Center. Affiliated with United Syn of Am. Rabbi Abraham B. Eckstein; Cantor Julian Raber; Pres: Dr Donald Forman; Edu Dir: Bernice Witten. **49–10 Little Neck Pkwy, Little Neck NY 11362 (212) BA4–0404.**

Long Beach

American Veterans of Israel. 548 E Walnut St, Long Beach NY 11561 (516) 431–8316.

Congregation Beth Sholom of Long Beach & Lido. Affiliated with United Syn of Am. Rabbi Dr Amos Miller; Pres: Hubert J. Brandt. **700 E Park Ave, Long Beach NY 11561 (516) 432–7464.**

Temple Beth El of Long Beach. Orthodox Syn affiliated with Union of Orthodox J Cong, NCSY Youth Group, B'nai Akivah. To provide good fellowship between young & old, single & married, poor or rich. Daily minyan morning & evening; Sr Citizen Prog including 5-days-a-week lunch, Meals-on-Wheels, counseling; women's folk dancing; library containing 600 vols (assorted). 150 mems (110 families, 40 individuals). 5 employees; 20 volunteers (Bingo). F 1927. Pub Beth El Bulletin (10 times a yr). Facilities include kosher kitchen (Parkside Caterers), sanctuary seating 300 (expandable to 700 for High Holiday); separate bingo. Rabbi Abraham Kulchick; Cantor: Abraham Brun; Pres: David Fisch; Chr of Bd: William Brainin; Off Chr of Bd: Stanley Schwartz; Sisterhood Pres: Lucy Kaplow; Chr Bd: Merle Fisch. **570 W Walnut St, Long Beach NY 11561 (516) 432–2191, 1678.**

Temple Emanu-El. Affiliated with UAHC. 312 mems. Rabbi Bernard Kligfeld; Cantor Mikhail Manevich; Pres: Irwin Klenosky; Edu: Bernard Kligfeld; Sisterhood Pres: Racille Mason; Brotherhood Pres: William Ross. **455 Neptune Blvd, Long Beach NY 11561 (516) 431–4060.**

Temple Zion. Orthodox Syn. To promote Torah & love for fellow man. Est in 1948. Dr Rabbi Samuel Horowitz; Pres: Leon Jasper. **62 Maryland Ave, PO Box 389, Long Beach NY 11561.**

Long Island City

American Jewish Public Relations Society. PO Box 6117, Long Island City NY 11106 (212) 728–2863.

Astoria Center of Israel. Affiliated with United Syn of Am. Rabbi Jacob Polish; Cantor George Lidenblatt; Pres: Morris Kemp; Exec Dir: Richard Cohen. **27–35 Crescent St, Long Island City NY 11102 (212) AS8–2680, 278–2261.**

Lynbrook

Congregation Beth David. Affiliated with United Syn of Am. Rabbi Louis D. Diament; Cantor Abraham B. Shapiro; Pres: Joseph Schneider; Youth Dir: Joan Sidney. **188 Vincent Ave, Lynbrook NY 11563 (516) 599–9464.**

Temple Emanu-El. Affiliated with UAHC. 762 mems. Rabbis: Stuart M. Geller, Harold I. Saperstein; Pres: Allen Hochberg; Edu: Stuart M. Geller, Elaine B. Mandel; Sisterhood Pres: Linda Bandler; Brotherhood Pres: Robert Stone. **Saperstein Plaza, Lynbrook NY 11563 (516) 593–4004.**

Mahopac

Jewish Center of the Mahopacs – Temple Beth Shalom. Affiliated with United Syn of Am. Rabbi Philip Fleisher; Pres: Ralph C. Horowitz; Edu Dir: Irwin Wander. **Rd 10, PO Box 245, Mahopac NY 10541 (914) 628–6133.**

Malverne

Malverne Jewish Center. Affiliated with United Syn of Am. Rabbi Theodore Steinberg; Cantor & Youth Dir: Martin Cooper; Pres: Norman Liben. **1 Norwood Ave, Melverne NY 11564 (516) 593–6364.**

Mamaroneck

Westchester Jewish Center. Affiliated with United Syn of Am. Rabbi Irving Koslowe; Pres: Saul Schargel. **Rockland & Palmer Ave, Mamaroneck NY 10543 (914) 698–2960.**

Manhasset

Temple Judea. Affiliated with UAHC. 524 mems. Rabbi Eugene Lipsey; Cantor Richard H. Berman; Pres: Stanley Sibell; Edu: Raphael Cohen; Sisterhood Pres: Honey Rabinowitz; Brotherhood Pres: Dave Beegel. **333 Searingtown Rd, Manhasset NY 11030 (516) 621–8049.**

Massapequa

Congregation Beth El. Affiliated with United Syn of Am. Rabbi Gary Creditor; Cantor Arthur Fogel; Pres: Abraham Bloomstone; Edu Dir: Max Klein; Youth Dir: Barbara Gerstel. **99 Jerusalem Ave, Massapeque NY 11758 (516) 541–0740.**

Temple Judea. Affiliated with UAHC. 410 mems. Rabbi Sanford H. Jarashow; Cantor Robert Applestone; Pres: Fred Zivitofsky; Edu: Victor Ravens; Sisterhood Pres: Ellen Jackson; Brotherhood Pres: Howard Miller. **Jerusalem & Central Ave, Massapequa NY 11758 (516) 798–5444.**

Temple Sinai. Affiliated with UAHC. 113 mems. Rabbi Leonard Stern; Pres: Ivan Hametz; Sisterhood Pres: Irma Kulakoff. **270 Clock Blvd, Massapequa NY 11758 (516) 795–5015.**

Melville

South Huntington Jewish Center. Affiliated with United Syn of Am. Rabbi Morris Shapiro; Cantor Saul Rubenstein; Pres: Celia K. Scher; Edu Dir:

Howard Teplitz; Youth Dir: Dr Arnold Suchow. **2600 New York Ave, Melville NY 11747 (516) HA1–3224.**

Merrick

Temple Beth Am, Patricia Morris Memorial Library. For information on the Temple, see – Temple Beth Am, Merrick, NY. **Nerrick & Kirkwood Ave, Merrick NY 11566 (516) 378–3477.**

Merrick Jewish Center – Congregation Ohr Torah. Affiliated with United Syn of Am. Rabbi Charles A. Klein; Cantor Jacob Tessler; Pres: Helen B. Drogin; Edu & Youth Dir: Robert I. Spitz. **225 Fox Blvd, Merrick NY 11566 (516) 379–8650.**

Temple Beth Am. Affiliated with UAHC. 530 mems. Rabbi Sanford E. Saperstein; Cantor Irving Spenadel; Pres: Barbara Bashe; Edu: Barbara Greene, Ruth Silverberg; Sisterhood Pres: Gloria Datlow; Brotherhood Pres: Fredric S. Knauer. **Merrick & Kirkwood Ave, Merrick NY 11566 (516) 378–3477.**

Temple Israel of South Merrick. Affiliated with United Syn of Am. Rabbi Sheldon Thall; Cantor Tyrone Bauer; Pres: Leslie I. Kessler; Edu Dir: Rabbi David Barbalet; Youth Dir: Jerry Kaye. **2655 Clubhouse Rd, Merrick NY 11566 (516) 378–1963.**

Middle Village

Jewish Center of Forest Hills West. Affiliated with United Syn of Am. Rabbi Samuel Geffen; Pres: George Mattaway. **63–45 Dry Harbor Rd, Middle Village NY 11379 (212) NE9–2110.**

Middletown

Temple Sinai (Middletown Hebrew Association). Conservative Syn affiliated with United Syn of Am. A house of God, Study & Brotherhood providing for a continuing quest for spiritual peace & enlightenment. Rel Servs; Sisterhood; Men's Club; Presch; Afternoon Sch; home of local chapters of Hadassah, B'nai B'rith Men & Women; Boy Scouts; B'nai B'rith Youth, ORT; secular & rel groups for all age groups; a variety of social edu, cultural activities offered in cooperation with the J Fed of Greater Orange Cty; facilities rented to responsible com groups for meetings; catering facilities; library containing 3000 vols (bks of J interest). 350 families; 220 stu in Afternoon Sch, 75 stu in Nursery Sch. 30 full & part time employees; up to 75 volunteers. F 1917 as the Middletown Hebrew Assn; moved to new bldg in 1969 with new name, Temple Sinai. Pub Temple Sinai Newsletter (monthly), plus house organs fr each constituent org. Facilities include gym, chapel, library, nursery, social hall, 8 classrms, various lounges, offs. Largest & oldest Conservative syn in the area. Rabbi Joel M. Schwab; Cantor Harold Stein; Exec Dir: Roy Fromer; Sisterhood Pres: Sue Matoren; Men's Club Pres: Joel Lovitch; Pres: Rubin Shafran; 1st VP: Irving Fox; 2nd VP: Dr Robert Kulak; Treas: Hon Elaine Slobod; Rec Sec: Linda Dlugatz; Fin Sec: Charles Judelson; Corsp Sec: Stuart Lederman. **75 Highland Ave, Middletown NY 10940 (914) 343–1861.**

Temple Sinai, Library. Library contains 3,000 bks of J interest. For information on the Temple, see – Temple Sinai, Middletown, NY. **75 Highland Ave, Middletown NY 10940 (914) 343–1861.**

Monroe

Beth Ropshitz & Congregation Kahal Kdushas Yom Tov, Library. Library contains over 7000 vols on Talmudical, Halacha & interpretation. For information on the Cong, see – Beth Ropshitz Congregation Kahal Kdushas Yom Tov, Monroe, NY. **4 Raywood Dr, Monroe NY 10950 (914) 782–5494.**

Beth Ropshitz & Congregation Kahal Kdushas Yom Tov. Orthodox Cong. To provide the immediate com with a proper Orthodox place of worship. Daily minyan, morning & evening; nightly & weekly lectures; Jr Get-together every Shabbos for Oneg Shabbos & lectures; yearly Sisterhood fundraising party for the upkeep of mikvah; daily morning use of mikvah; library containing over 7,000 vols (Tamudical, Halacha & interpretation). 70 families. Facilities include Beth Hamedrash & mikvah. Rabbi Chaim Rubin; Adm: M. Friedman; Chr of Bd: A. Meisels. **4 Raywood Dr, Monroe NY 10950 (914) 782–5494.**

Congregation Eitz Chaim. Affiliated with United Syn of Am. Rabbi Gerald Lerer; Pres: Daniel S. Gershkowitz; Edu Dir: Cary Falber. **251 Spring St, Monroe NY 10950 (914) 783–7424.**

Temple Beth El – Monroe Temple of Liberal Judaism. Reform Temple affiliated with UAHC. Rel Servs; youth & adult edu; Sisterhood; Men's Club; Youth Group; Pre-Bar/Bat Mitzvah through Confirmation; library containing 1,000 vols. 200 families; 70 individuals; 265 stu in grades K–10. 3 employees; 270 volunteers. F 1944; formerly known as Monroe J Com Council. Pub Bulletin (bi-monthly), Newsletter (bi-weekly). Facilities include sanctuary, kitchen, social hall, rel sch classes, library, gift shop. Rabbi Dr Kurt Metzger; Pres: David L. Levinson; 1st VP: Jack Nizewitz; 2nd VP: Herbert Weissman; Fin

Sec: Joan Birnbaum; Rec Sec: Jane Itzka; Corsp Sec: Maryellen Lucks. **314 N Main St, Monroe NY 10950 (914) 783–2626.**

Monsey

Adolph H. Schreiber Hebrew Academy of Rockland. An Orthodox day sch, known in Heb as Yeshivat Hadar Avraham Tzvi. The sch is strongly committed to the cultivation of an Orthodox J life-style, to the furtherance of the Heb Language, & to the est of strong & positive ties to modern Is. Edu for boys & girls nursery age – grade 8; rel studies; intensive secular prog in accordance with the laws of NY State. Over 400 stu. F in 1953. Dean: Rabbi Nachum Muschel; Pres: Dr David L. Koplon; Chr of the Bd: Rabbi Hyman Fein; VPs: Dr Jack Prince, Max Thurm, Dr Mandell I. Ganchrow; Fin Sec: William Roth; Treas: Steven Rothschild; Rec Sec: Leon Schwartz; Corsp Sec: Dr Laurence Gordon; Exec Dir: Rabbi Howard Gershon; Bd of Dirs: Alvin Blumenfeld, Dr Oscar Hausdorf, Jerry Jacobs, Dr Murray Kuhr, Dr Nathan I. Meiselman, Dr Stephen Novick, Wallace Pruzansky, Ralph Rothschild, Dr Herbert Schlussel, Elliot N. Schreiber, Dr William Schwartz, Dr Joseph Tuchman; Bd of Govs: Irving Eisenman, Arthur Fein, Joseph Goldstein, Jakob Landa, Rabbi Irving Levy, Sylvia Schreiber, Henry Zeisel. **70 Highview Rd, Monsey NY 10952 (914) 357–1515.**

American Biblical Encyclopedia Society. 24 W Maple Ave, Monsey NY 10952 (914) 425–8079.

American Torah Shelemah Committee. 24 W Maple Ave, Monsey NY 10952 (914) 352–4609.

B'nai Jeshurun Synagogue of Monsey NY. To encourage strict practice of the Torah following Ashkanaz tradition. Rel, charitable & social activities in the com & to J throughout the world. Servs conducted daily. Est in 1957. Pres: David Paikin; VP: Emanuel Frankel; Sec: Jay Levy; Treas: Fred Golin; 1st Gabbai: Emanuel Polack; 2nd Gabbai: Philip Soskin. **Park Lane, PO Box 423, Monsey NY 10952.**

Beth Medrosh Elyon (Academy of Higher Learning & Research). 73 Main St, Monsey NY 10952.

Community Synagogue of Monsey. 15 Cloverdale Lane, Monsey NY 10952.

Shaarei Torah of Rockland. 1 School Terr, Monsey NY 10952 (914) 356–9773.

Shaarei Torah of Rockland Library. 1 School Terr, Monsey NY 10952 (914) 356–9773.

Monticello

Jewish Community Center of Monticello. Edu, cultural & physical improvement for all age groups. Serves as clearing house for com servs & activities; promotes J identity & awareness. Nursery sch; day care; swimming pool; classes; sports; lectures; concerts; exhibitions; lending library; fund raising; Chanukah dinner; Purim Seudah; youth groups; singles clubs. Est in 1934. The present bldg was built in 1962. Monthly newsletter. Pres: Jane Gorden; VP: Howard Garchik; Sec: Enid Hersh; Treas: Jeffrey Kaplow; Exec Coord: Sylvia Chayat. **Park Ave, Box 208, Monticello NY 12701 (914) 794–4560.**

Temple Sholom. Affiliated with UAHC. 190 mems. Rabbi Robert Schenkerman; Pres: Monis Brafman. **Port Jervis & E Dillon Rds, PO Box 664, Monticello NY 12701 (914) 794–8731.**

Mount Kisco

Temple Shaaray Tefila. Reform Syn. Rel Sch. 150 families. Est in 1975 & has recently acquired an estate which will serve as its permanent home. Rabbi David E. Greenberg; Pres: Frank Neubauer; VPs: Nina Trimer, Diane Berkowitz, Alan Siskinz; Treas: Jerry Gros; Sec: Paul Keppler; Rel Sch Prin: Marilyn Shebshaievitz. **Route 172, Mount Kisco NY 10549 (914) 666–3133.**

Mount Vernon

Congregation Brothers of Israel. Orthodox Syn. Daily Rel Servs; Sisterhood; lectures. Mems fr Mt Vernon, Bronx, Yonkers, Eastchester, New Rochelle, Scarsdale. Est in 1892; the oldest syn in Westchester Cty. Rabbi Dr Solomon Freilich; Pres: Harvey Bayer. **116 Crary Ave, Mount Vernon NY 10550 (914) 667–1302, 664–8945.**

Emanu-El Jewish Center. Affiliated with United Syn of Am. Rabbi David Haymovitz; Cantor David Schwarzmer; Pres: Murray Mintz. **261 E Lincoln Ave, Mount Vernon NY 10552 (914) 667–0161.**

Free Synagogue of Westchester. Affiliated with UAHC. 340 mems. Rabbi James Perman; Cantor Lee Schwartz; Pres: Phyllis S. Heller; Edu: Sidney Starr; Adm: Jeanne Sambor; Sisterhood Pres: Judith Steinman; Brotherhood Pres: Bernard Schwartz. **500 N Columbus Ave, Mount Vernon NY 10552 (914) 664–1727.**

Sinai Temple. Affiliated with UAHC. 294 mems. Rabbi Cyrus Arfa; Cantor Metika Freeman; Pres: Ellen L. Heffan; Sisterhood Pres: Ronna R. Dienstfrey; Brotherhood Pres: Norman Krasne. **132 Crary Ave, Mount Vernon NY 10550 (914) 668–9471.**

Nanuet

Nanuet Hebrew Center. Affiliated with United Syn of Am. Rabbi Simon Potok; Cantor Mark E. Levine; Pres: Chuck Drachman. **34 S Middletown Rd, Nanuet NY 10954 (914) 623–3735.**

Neponsit

The West End Temple. Affiliated with UAHC. 311 mems. Rabbi Joseph Weiss; Cantor Stuart Rauch; Pres: Mildred Jaffe; Edu: Sheldon Friedberg; Sisterhood Pres: Rhoda Hammer; Brotherhood Pres: Jesse Plutzer. **147–02 Newport Ave, Neponsit NY 11694 (212) 634–0301.**

New City

New City Jewish Center. Conservative Syn in existence for 24 yrs. Afternoon Heb Sch; Heb HS; Youth Group for 6th grade & up; Nursery Sch; Adult Edu Series; Sisterhood; Men's Club; Sr Citizens group; library. 677 families. Rabbi Henry A. Sosland; Cantor Hal Rifkin; Edu Dir: Leslie Goldress; Pres: Eugene Zinbarg; Exec VP: Stanley Scheff; Fin VP: Harvey Nuland; Treas: Byron Zabusky; Fin Sec: Murray Cohen; Pres Men's Club: Mel Katz; Pres Sisterhood: Elaine Binder; Mem VP: Donald Mondschein. **Old Schoolhouse Rd, New City NY 10956 (914) 634–6140, 3619.**

New City Jewish Center Library. For information on the Ctr, see – New City Jewish Center, New City, NY. **Old Schoolhouse Rd, New City NY 10956. (914) 634–6140, 634–3619.**

Solomon Schechter Day School of Rockland County. Affiliated with Solomon Schechter Day Schs Assn. Prin: Meir Efrati; Chr: Denny Herzberg. **Route 45, New City NY 10956 (914) 353–5500.**

Temple Beth Sholom. Reform Temple affiliated with UAHC. Fri Evening & Sat Morning Servs; Sisterhood; Brotherhood; Rel Sch, nursery – 10th grade; Jr & Sr youth groups. 470 mems. Est in 1959. Rabbi David E. Fass; Cantor Jerry Heller; Edu Dir: Edward Feldstein; Pres: Arthur Dresner; VPs: David Scheichet, Isabell Freireich, Carol Bell; Treas: Mel Komitor; Fin Sec: Michael Newman; Rec Sec: Joan Kossoff; Corsp Sec: Helen Harris. **228 New Hempstead Rd, New City NY 10956 (914) 638–0770.**

New Hyde Park

Jewish Institute for Geriatric Care. Non-profit facility for the ill & elderly affiliated with Home and Hosp Daughters of Is. To serve older people. Med, rehabilitation, nursing, therapy, social, & daily health servs for outpatients. Est in 1972. Maintains 527 beds. Exec VP: David Glaser. **271–11 76th Ave, New Hyde Park NY 11042; Queens (212) 343–2100, Nassau (516) 437–0090.**

Long Island Jewish Hillside Medical Center. Teaching hosp. Committed to the highest standards of med & to the humanity of med. Emergency servs, med & psychiatric observation areas, a cardiac care rm & a trauma rm; cancer prog; diagnosis & treatment of heart disease; Neonatal Unit; Pediatric Dept; adolescent servs; dentistry for handicapped chil; research projs; provision of med servs & professional edu at Queens Hosp; drug treatment; kidney dialysis. Hillside Div of LIJ – a 203 bed psychiatric facility; outpatient depts: psychiatric emergency rm; after hospitalization prog; day hosps, one for adults, one for adolescents & another for the chronically ill in Queens; clins that treat every psychiatric problem, & com outreach facilities in Queens & Nassau Ctys which deal with the stress of troubled personalities, family relationships, chil-rearing, drug & alcohol abuse. Est in 1954. In 1959 LIJ became a mem of a country-wide network of leading med ctrs organized to exchange information on the effectiveness of various treatment progs for leukemia. In 1975 the Natl Cancer Ins awarded funds to LIJ to study the feasibility of creating a Regional Cancer Prog. In 1974 LIJ & Blue Cross Blue Shield est a prepaid full coverage health plan. This became the first Health Maintenance Org to qualify under NY State Law. An emergency & cardiac care ctr were completed in 1979. The Hillside Div is known throughout the country for pioneering work in the dev of drugs for mental illness. Bd of Trustees – Chr: Irving L. Wharton; Pres: Dr Robert K. Match; V Chr: Martin C. Barell, Arthur G. Cohen, Eli B. Cohen, Arthur Garson, Irving Schneider, Michael Stein, Joseph S. Wohl; Treas: Stanley B. Gary; Assc Treas: Stephen Shalom; Sec: Elihu H. Moldin; Asst Sec: Oscar Katz; Chr Emeriti: Gustave M. Berne, Jack Liebowitz, Aaron L. Solomon; Trustees: Saul J. Beldock, John M. Bendheim, Leo V. Berger, Selig S. Burrows, Sol C. Chaikin, Alexander Cohen, Benjamin Duhl, Arthur Fatt, Robert Frankel, Rosalie Greenberg, Aaron Gural, Joseph Gurwin, Hon Bertram Harnett, Leo Hausman, Gilbert Helman, Milton M. Herman, Kaufman Ray Katz, Arnold

Kramer, Arthur Levien, H. Bert Mack, William Mack, Hon Charles Margett, Leonard Nedal, Hon Samuel Rabin, Andrew Saul, Irwin Schnurmacher, Anne Sonfield, Saul P. Steinberg, Martin B. Swarzman, Gilbert Tilles, Hon Sol Wachtler, Alfred Wohl, Leonard Zahn. **270–05 76th Ave, New Hyde Park NY 11040 (212) 343–6700.**

New Hyde Park Jewish Community Center. Conservative ins affiliated with United Syn of Am. Rel Servs; Adult Edu progs; Sisterhood. 155 mems. 5 employees. F 1929. Pub Bulletin of the New Hyde Park Jewish Community Center (monthly). Facilities include sanctuary; classrms; ballroom; kosher kitchen; gift shop. Rabbi Dr. Leonard J. Aronson; Cantor Herbert Weiser; Pres: Hyman Portnoy; Off Mgr: Shirley Powell. **100 Lakeville Rd, New Hyde Park NY 11040 (516) 354–7583.**

Temple Emanuel. Affiliated with UAHC. 282 mems. Rabbi David E. Powers; Cantor Ephraim Steinhauer; Pres: Jack Helitzer; Brotherhood Pres: Louis Handelsman. **3315 Hillside Ave, New Hyde Park NY 11040 (516) 746–1120.**

New Paltz

Ahavath Achim. Affiliated with United Syn of Am. Pres: Larry Meltzer. **Church St, New Paltz NY 12561 (914) 883–6437.**

New Rochelle

Beth El Synagogue of New Rochelle, Inc. Affiliated with United Syn of Am. Rabbi Emeritus Dr David I. Golovensky; Cantor Lawrence Avery; Pres: Harry Gingold; Exec Dir: Harvey D. Silton; Edu Dir: Jack Gruenberg. **Northfield Rd at N Ave, New Rochelle NY 10804 (914) BE5–2700.**

Temple Israel. Affiliated with UAHC. 1350 mems. Rabbis: Amiel Wohl, William L. Rothschild, Jacob K. Shankman; Cantors: Sumner A. Crockett, Helene Reps; Pres: Walter A. Bobrow; Edu: Dorothy Axelroth; Adm: Rhoda Royal; Sisterhood Pres: Carol Kurzman; Brotherhood Pres: Kenneth Keenan. **1000 Pinebrook Blvd, New Rochelle NY 10804 (914) 235–1800.**

Temple Israel Library. For information on the Temple, see – Temple Israel, New Rochelle, NY. **1000 Pinebrook Blvd, New Rochelle NY 10804 (914) 235–1800.**

United Home for Aged Hebrews. Geriatric ins. Med, rehabilitation & social servs prog; recreational & therapeutic progs. Est in 1919 by a group of Austrian J. Facilities include: 134 bed skilled nursing facility; 138 bed health related facility; 135 unit low income housing apt for Sr citizens. Pres: Herbert B. Platzner; Exec Dir: Saunders T. Preiss; Chr Bd of Dirs: Robert S. Savin; Co-Chr Bd of Dirs: George M. Friedland; Hon Chr Bd of Dirs: Arnold L. Ginsburg, Alfred J. Green, Saul Kramer, Max M. Low; VPs: Jerome S. Koch, Leroy Kramer, Joel Langer; Sec: Peter A. Tomback; Treas: Donald Duberstein; Bd of Dirs: Richard Albert, Sanford Batkin, Frederic S. Bogart, Richard Bross, Marcy Chanin, Leroy Fadem, Solomon J. Freedman, Marvin S. Glickman, Erwin L. Klineman, Mrs Joseph Levy, Morris S. Latzen, Robert K. Low, Jack Manne, Elton Meltzer, Arnold Miller, Henry H. Minskoff, Samuel R. Patent, Roy R. Raizen, J. George Spitzer, Joseph Wasley, Mitchell Wollman; Med Staff Pres: Dr Pellegrino Tozzo; Dir of Surgery: Dr Alan B. Levitt; Dir of Med: Dr Daniel Sherber; Sec: Dr Charles Forman; Med Dir: Dr Frank A. Napolitano; Asst Dir: Neil Dworkin. **60 Willow Dr, New Rochelle NY 10805 (914) 632–2804.**

Westchester Jewish Community Services, Inc. A state licensed, non-sectarian chil guidance & family mental health clin which is available to all Westchester residents of all ages. For additional information, see Westchester Jewish Community Services, Inc. – White Plains, NY. **271 North Ave, New Rochelle NY 10802 (914) 632–6433.**

New York City

Academic Committee on Soviet Jewry. 345 E 46th St, NYC NY 10017 (212) 557–9013.

Academy for Jewish Religion. 112 E 88th St, NYC NY 10028 (212) 722–5811.

The Academy for Jewish Studies Without Walls. Independent J studies through correspondence; sponsored by the Am J Cttee. To provide both J & non-J with a flexible edu framework for the serious study of J hist & J thought, through independent study & correspondence. Courses offered: Biblical Thought, Talmudic Thought, Modern J Thought, J Christian Encounter, Hasidism, Bioethical Issues in the Rabbinic Tradition, Hist of Am J, Zionism, Hist & Ideology, Am J Experience in Literature; Summer Seminar Prog on Am col campuses. F in 1974 in assn with the Univ of Haifa. In 1978 the sch severed its relationship with Haifa Univ. The Academy submitted its courses to the Prog on Non Collegiate Sponsored Instruction of the Univ of the State of NY for review & accreditation. Since then, the sch offerings have been recommended for credit by the Prog on Non Collegiate Sponsored Ins, & listed & described in the special guide which is distributed to 3,000 cols in all 50 states. In 1981 the Academy sponsored seminars in Aspen, CO & Williams Col in MA, & three courses at Skidmore Col. Stu who wish to apply credits earned at the Academy toward a col degree need to check with the appropriate official at their univ. Future plans include study seminars at Israeli univs. Adm Dir: Yehuda Rosenman; Asst Dir: Dr Gladys Rosen; Chr: Dr Edward Bloustein. **165 E 56th St, NYC NY 10022 (212) 751–4000.**

Agudas Israel World Organization. 471 West End Ave, NYC NY 10024 (212) 874–7979.

Agudath Israel of America. Affiliated with the World Agudath Is Movement. To perpetuate authentic J & to come to grips with all current issues in accordance with Torah tradition; to solve all problems facing J as individuals & as a people in the spirit of the Torah; to be the prime advocate for the rel rights of J. Commis on J Legislation & Civic Action maintains a constant vigil to protect the rights of Orthodox J, protects shichita, kosher slaughtering of meat, works for consumerism guarantees that what is sold as kosher is not misrepresented, protects the rights of Sabbath observers in the public & private employ, obtains the proper recognition for J higher edu & makes certain that hosps respect the rel needs of the J; Rel Welfare Aid to Is, through its sister org in Is, maintains a wide range of servs including Torah edu for chil & adults, trade schs, chil ins & aid for the needy & immigrants; The Agudath Natl Youth Commis trains J youth for leadership roles in their coms &, led by 1,700 volunteers, sponsors Pirchei Agudath Is for boys, Bnos Agudath Is for girls, & Zeirei Agudath Is for adolescent boys, summer overnight camps Agudah for boys & Bnos for girls; the J Edu Prog provides an outreach proj aimed at J unaffiliated youth; Torah edu network enables men & women to study Torah in their home com through telephone hook ups, tapes & correspondence with the aid of volunteers who teach every level of J knowledge fr begining to intensive advanced Talmud study; Commis on Sr Citizens offers kosher lunch prog, informative & referral progs, Meals-on-Wheels prog, visitation serv, household chores, cultural progs, legal advice, med progs & special events for J & civic holidays; Cope, a career opportunities & preparation for employment prog, offers on-the-job training, vocational edu, classroom training, placement, career guidance, counseling, aid for immigrants, job club; Cope Vocational Ins, licensed by the NY State Edu Dept, operates two divs which offer training in many areas including sec servs, computer programming, & kosher catering; Fresh Start Training prog helps women who are widowed or divorced to cope with their new responsibilities; Proj Rise, a Russian immigrant prog, provides rel articles, circumcisions, summer camps, edu experiences, personal counseling, & an Adopt-a-Family Prog; Prog Yad sends parcels to J in E Europe for Passover & yr round; Russian Immigrant Rescue Fund supports projs & facilities for the rel absorption of Soviet J in Is; Torah Action Prog involves youngsters in helping Russian J in need; Orthodox J Archives documents material about the world's Orthodox J & the rescue of J during the Holocaust; audio visual library. 25,000 young people in the youth groups; 200 chapters nation wide. Exec staff of 200. F in 1912 in Poland; est on the lower E Side of Manhattan in 1922. The Daf Yomi prog, the world's largest united adult Torah study prog, was f in 1924. Das Yiddishe Vort which features articles of comment & biographical & historical essays; The Jewish Observer (pub monthly); pocket sized vols of the Talmud; monthly Russian language bulletin; Agudah News Reporter; news letter on activities issued by Social Servs Proj; bulletins (issued by the Public Information Dept on the Torah position on contemporary issues); Judaiscope which, when completed, will be a library dealing with the Torah approach to a broad range of current social & ethical concerns – the first two vols, The Torah Personality, & Seasons of the Soul, have already been pub. Presidium: Rabbi Moshe Feinstein, Rabbi Moshe Horowitz, Rabbi Shneur Kotler, Rabbi Chaskel Besser, Rabbi Yaakov Perlow; Pres: Rabbi Moshe Sherer; Chr of Vaad Hanhala: Rabbi Shlomo Oppenheimer; Co-Chr of Vaad Hanhala: Rabbi Josef Frankel; Hon VPs: Rabbi Judah Altusky, Rabbi Yeruchem Gorelick, Rabbi Pinchos Hirschprung, Rabbi Yaakov Kamenetzky, Rabbi Mordechai Lubart, Rabbi Chaim Lubinsky, Rabbi Benjamin Paler, Rabbi Yaakov Ruderman, Rabbi Israel Spira, Rabbi Elya Svel, Rabbi Peretz Yogel; VPs: Mendel Berg, Dr Ernst L. Bodenheimer, Rabbi Leib Cywiak, Benjamin Fishoff, Louis Glueck, Rabbi Yaakov Goldstein, Chaim Hertz, David Klein, Julius Klugmann, Shmuel Roth, Menachem Shayovich; Treas: Eugene Fixler, William K. Friedman, Aaron Seif, David Singer; Sec: Eli Basch, Avrohom Halpern; Offs at Large: Avrohom Fruchthandler, Dr Bernard Fryshman, Rabbi Edwin Katzenstein, Joseph Neumann, Al Reider, Alan J. Rosenberg, Leon Scharf, Nochum Stein, David H. Turkel, Dr Aaron Twerski, Willy Wiesner; Gen Sec: Joseph Friedenson; Exec Dir & Sec: Rabbi Boruch B. Borchardt; Adm Dir: Rabbi Shmuel Bloom; Dir of Govt & Public Affairs: Rabbi Menachem Lubinsky; Editor, The Jewish Observer: Rabbi Nisson Wolpin. **5 Beekman St, NYC NY 10038 (212) 964–1620.**

Algemeiner Journal. Periodical pub. **404 Park Ave S, NYC NY 10016 (212) 689–3390.**

Altro Health & Rehabilitation Services, Inc. Affiliated with many private & governmental ins. Beneficiary of the Soc of the Fed/UJA Joint Campaign & the Greater NY Fund/United Way. To help the needy person achieve the ability of self-support while obviating a dependence on charity. Provides treatment progs to persons suffering relapsing, exacerbating chronic illness. Rehabilitation Workshops – Machine Shop: provides vocational training for individuals with particular mechanical dexterity; Mechanical Assembly & Packaging; trains psychologically handicapped, emotionally disturbed, educationally disadvantaged & mildly retarded individuals to learn & perform a useful range of jobs that are viable in the industrial com; Print Shop: clients are trained in all facets of quality reproduction; Data Processing: client trainees begin with keypunching, verification & data entry, & then proceed to tabulating operations & console operation; Garment Shop: clients in training are guided, monitored & progressed through the prog by rehabilitation & technical support staff; Com Support System: a residence based Care Mgmnt & Day Treatment Prog which provides the regressed, discharged psychiatric patients with a full range of progs; Continuing/Day Treatment: a socialization/cognitive skill dev prog; Work Activities Ctr: patients with limited rehabilitation potential are able to constructively engage their time in ergotherapeutic tasks. F in 1913, Altro's primary servs were to those suffering fr tuberculosis. In the 1940's & 1950's, when tuberculosis was diminishing, Altro adjusted its primary servs to persons suffering cardiac disability. For nearly a quarter century since then, the Agy's major servs are for the mentally ill & disabled. The garment prog began in 1915 & is the pioneer vocational training prog among Altro's five current work shops. The data processing prog began as an independent section in Altro's Work Shops in 1967. Bd of Dirs – Pres: George S. Greenberg; VPs: Ann Eliasoph, J. Harold Garfunkel, Alan S. Jaffe, Robert Saltzman; Asst Treas: Alan R. Kahn; Asst Sec: Peter S. Kolevzon; Dirs: Mrs Alexander Bing III, Alex Burger, Peter Claman, Jacques Coleman, Mrs James C. Hirsch, Walter Hirshon, Erwin Kaufman, Lewis Levene, Madeleine M. Low, William J. Oppenheim, Mrs Martin Paskus, Allan Retzky, Martin Sachs, Robert Saltzman, Mrs Michael Schultz, Ann F. Thomas, Mrs David W. Unterberg, John Wasserman, Judy Temel; Altro Work Shops Offs – Chr of the Bd: George S. Greenberg; Pres: Dr Jeffrey R. Solomon; VPs: Alan S. Jaffe, William H. Oppenheim, Ray M. Rahman, Robert Saltzman; Treas: J. Harold Garfunkel; Asst Sec: Peter S. Kolevzon; Dir of Vocational Servs: Jay Sloma; Adm Asst: Raymond Falk; Altro Health & Rehabilitaton Servs Adm – Exec VP: Dr Jeffrey R. Solomon; Asst Dirs: Shirley Abel, Ray M. Rahman, Dr Barry Roff; Asst Dir of Clin Servs: Nellie Matus; Manhattan Borough Dir: Estelle Reingold; CSS Proj Dir: Arthur Gabler; Com Servs Coord: Richard Africk; Quality Assurance Coord: Diane Carn; Exec Asst: Dorine Bennett. **345 Madison Ave, NYC NY 10017 (212) MU4–0600.**

American Academy for Jewish Research. 3080 Bdwy, NYC NY 10027 (212) 749–8000.

American Associates Ben Gurion University of the Negev. A non-profit org. To promote & support the Univ's comprehensive dev & research goals throughout the US. 2,500 mems. Est in 1973. Reporter (pub three times a yr). Pres: Aron Chilewich; Chr Exec Cttee: Bobbie Abrams; VPs: Lane Kirkland, Richard B. Stone; Treas: Michael Jaffe; Sec & Counsel: Frederick Siegmund. **Natl Off – 342 Madison Ave, Suite 1923, NYC NY 10173 (212) 687–7721.**

American Association for Jewish Education. 114 Fifth Ave, NYC NY 10011 (212) 675–5656.

American Association of Rabbis. A non-profit professional & fraternal org of rabbis in the US & Canada. The advancement & preservation of J in its highest ideals & traditions through Torah; encouragement & fostering of observance of J in the home & com; support of Is as the spiritual home of the J people & as a haven of refugee for those J seeking spiritual & physical redemption fr tyranny; perpetuation of Heb as the primary language of prayer & study; encouragement of fraternal relations among rabbis. Provides a placement serv for mem rabbis; maintains Halachic Beth Din for rel & domestic needs; encourages participation with other rabbinical orgs. Pres: Rabbi David Schectman; VP Canadian Region: Rabbi Dr Harold Lerner; VP Eastern Region: Rabbi David Dunn; VP Southern Region: Rabbi Dr Maxwell Berger; VP Midwestern Region: Rabbi Gideon M. Goldenholz; Sec: Rabbi Robert Chernoff; Treas: Rabbi Joseph Spector.**350 Fifth Ave, Suite 3308, NYC NY 10001 (212) 244–3350.**

American Committee of OSE, Inc. 8 W 40th St, Suite 1107, NYC NY 10018 (212) 565–3904.

American Committee for Rescue & Resettlement of Iraqi Jews . 1200 Fifth Ave, NYC NY 10029 (212) 427–1246.

American Committee for Shaare Zedek in Jerusalem. To help future generations meet the health needs of Jerusalem and Israel. Continuing support of century old hospital which moved in 1979 fr old quarters to new $55 million ultra modern medical complex overlooking Jerusalem. Offers total patient & community care. University affiliated teaching hospital contains main hospital building planned for more than 500 beds, emergency shelter, outpatient clinics, school of nursing, clinical labs, research ins, central library, facilities. Ensures the full observance of J tradition. Open to all, irrespective of their rel, race or natl origin. Natl Pres: Charles H. Bendheim; Chr Natl Bd of Dir: Ludwig Jesselson; Pres: Rabbi Dr Leo Jung; Chr: Bernard W. Leymore; Co-Chr: Michael S. Strauss; Hon Co–Chr: Joshua J. Shapiro; Sec: Isaac Strahl; VPs: Sidney Adler, Marc Breuer, Moshe Krausz, Henry Wimptheimer; Treas: Norbert Strauss; Asst Treasurer: Steven B. Rothschild. **49 W 45th St, NYC NY 10036 (212) 354–8801.**

American Committee for the National Sick Fund of Israel . 60 E 42nd St, Suite 1144, NYC NY 10165 (212) 599–3670.

American Committee for the Weizmann Institute of Science, Inc. 515 Park Ave, NYC NY 10022 (212) 752–1300.

The American Conference of Cantors. Affiliate of the UAHC. Through Joint Placement Commis, serves congs seeking cantors & music dirs; sponsors associate membership & Guild of Temple Musicians consisting of music dirs & organists serving Reform congs. **838 Fifth Ave, NYC NY 10021 (212) 249–0100.**

American Congregation of Jews From Austria. 188 W 95th St, NYC NY 10025 (212) 663–1920.

American Council for Judaism. Research & edu org. To advance the universal principle of a Judaism free of nationalism, & the civic, cultural & social integration into Am ins of Am of J faith. Research progs; pub progs; adv progs; library containing 1,000 vols on J in Am & other countries; media files on same subject. Pub Issues (quarterly); Special Interest Report (monthly). Pres & Chr of Bd: Clarence L. Coleman, Jr; VPs: Jeannette D. Naman, Bert E. Reuler, August B. Rothschild, Stanley R. Sundheim, Max E. Tonkon; Treas: Eliot D. Bernat; Sec: Alan V. Stone. **307 Fifth Ave, NYC NY 10016 (212) 889–1313.**

American Far Eastern Society. 259 W 30th St, NYC NY 10001 (212) 244–6225.

American Federation of Jewish Fighters, Camp Inmates, & Nazi Victims, Inc. To heighten awareness of the Holocaust & Resistance among J & non-J youth & among the gen public by teaching & stimulating more extensive studies on the subject. Disseminates materials & information on the subject; conducts lecture tours on campuses & other edu settings (in cooperation with AZYF); promotes & implements the concept that 27 Nissan be permanently affixed as Yom HaShoa; provides information, posters, booklets & prog packets on how to organize & observe Yom HaShoa; collects pages of testimony which records names of martyrs, coms, orgs & ins destroyed during the Holocaust; sponsors Eli & Diana Zborowski Professional Chair in Interdisciplinary Holocaust studies at Yeshiva Univ – more than a dozen courses & annual summer ins; formulates Holocaust curriculum for NYC HSs; provides progs in schs & univs including kits; provides witnesses for US Dept of Justice to help in the prosecution of former Nazis living in Am; participates in intl events such as the Gathering of J Holocaust survivors in Jerusalem, & Liberators of Auschwitz; active in furthering Remembrance through membership in such bodies as the US Holocaust Memorial Council; helps to meet the need of making the record of the Holocaust as clear, exact, authentic & complete as possible. Est in 1971 by survivors of the Holocaust determined that the tragedy that befell the J people should never be a forgotten lesson for all humanity. To accomplish their goal, in 1972 the F asked Yad Vashem to prepare a mobile exhibition on the Holocaust & Resistance to be shown in Canada & the US. The Holocaust & Resistance; An Outline of Jewish History in Nazi Occupied Europe; Pedagogic Bulletin on Holocaust Instruction; Martyrdom & Resistance (bi-monthly newspaper). Hon Pres: Eli Zborowski; Pres: Solomon Zynstein; Chr: Joseph Tekulsky; VPs: Abe Foxman, Benjamin Meed, Sam Skura; Treas: Isaac Pulvermacher; Sec: Ernist Honig; PR: Ben Geizhals; Bd of Dirs: Simon Baker, Frank Blaichman, Roman Blum, Robert Born, Anshel Borzykowski, Irving Broner, Henry Burstyn, Henry Cook, Max Dachinger, Charles Feder, Mark Feigen, Alex Friedman, Harry Gluck, David Handelsman, Max Hilfstein, Joe Holm, Mischa Jaffe, David Josefowicz, David Klein, Al Kooper, Felix Laski, Isaac Mendelson, Dr Coleman Orchier, Blanche Rantz, Mark Reiman, Max Rosenbaum, Alex Schlessinger, Dr Hillel Seidman, Julius Stohl, Mark Winchester, Hirsch Wolf. **823 United Nations Plaza, NYC NY 10017 (212) 490–2525.**

American Federation of Jews from Centra Europe, Inc. Acts as a liaison & coordinating agy for all social, cultural & welfare orgs f by J immigrants fr Central Europe in the US. Affiliated with Research Foun for J Immigration Convention. Seeks to protect the rights & represent the interest of its mems. Aid in the fields of restitution & indemnification; support of liberalized immigration prog; analysis & interpretation of laws, govt decrees, legal decisions which affect constituents; cultural activities; public conf; migration hist research; presentation of awards. Staff of two. F in 1941. Bks & booklets. Pres: Curt C. Silberman; Hon Pres: Max Gruenewald; VPs: Walter Strauss, Albert U. Tietz, Franz Winkler, Henry J. Zacharias; Exec VP: Herbert A. Strauss; Treas: Stephen S. Wertheimer; Asst Treas: Albert O. Philipp; Sec: Alfred Prager; Chr Finance Cttee: Howard John Fields; Exec Cttee: Hansi Baruch, Fred S. Bodenheimer, Jerry Brunell, Bernard N. Cohn, Rudolph David, Erna F. Einstein, Lotte Elsas, Helmut Erlanger, Hans J. Frank, Fred Grubel, Kurt H. Grunebaum, Hans Hammelbacher, Gustav Jacoby, Edith Kosterlitz, Robert L. Lehman, K. Peter Lekisch, Fred W. Lessing, Joseph Maier, Gertrud Mainzer, Sig Mayer, Albert Meinhardt, Eugene E. Noymer, Joachim Prinz, Stephen Rosskamn, Ismar Schorsch, Henry Siegman, Hermann E. Simon, Eric S. Sondheimer, Rudolph F. Stahl, Werner Stein, Hans Steinitz, Frederick C. Tuchmann, Fritz Weinschenk, Norbert Wollheim. **570 Seventh Ave, NYC NY 10018 (212) 921–3871.**

American Federation of Polish Jews. c/o United Jewish Appeal of NY, 220 W 58th St, NYC NY 10019 (212) 265–2200.

American Friends of Boy's Town Jerusalem. 475 Fifth Ave, NYC NY 10017.

The American Friends of Haifa University. Pres: Sigmund Strachlitz. **206 Fifth Ave, NYC NY 10010 (212) 696–4022.**

American Friends of Israel. 850 Third Ave, NYC NY 10022 (212) 752–7430.

American Friends of the Alliance Israelite Universelle. 61 Bdwy, Rm 811, NYC NY 10006 (212) 425–5171.

American Friends of the Haifa Maritime Museum, Inc. Tax exempt org. To foster & disseminate information in the US about the cultural activities of the Natl Maritime Mus in Haifa, Is; to provide support for the Mus progs such as exchange of scholars, acquisition of new exhibits & promulgation of sci pubs. Lectures, films, exhibitions; raising of funds. F in 1977. Pres: Prof Edward Neufeld; VP: Franklin Feldman; Treas: Sol Cooper; Sec: Dr A. Joseph Berlau; Bd of Dirs: Kenneth Abrahami, Stanley Beck, Jane W. Boris, Dr Gerald M. Branower, Dr Michael Ben-Eli, Dr Avram M. Cooperman, Earle Field, Justin Goldman, Isidore Greenberg, Ernest Herzfeld, Kenneth Janowitz, Dr Peter Laderman, David S.J. Neufeld, Dr Michael Papo, Devorah Sherman, Jeffrey Small, Leonid Tarassuk; Bd of Hon Govs: Saul Bellow, Leonard Bernstein, R. Buckminster Fuller, Hon Arthur J. Goldberg, Rev Theodore M. Hesburgh, Robert B. Inverarity, Hon Philip M. Klutznick, Edwin A. Link, Senator Daniel Patrick Moynihan, Roberta Peters, Hon Simon H. Rifkind, Jonas Salk, Hon William E. Simon, Edward Teller, John Updike, Adm Elmo R. Zumwalt; Editor of the Bulletin: Paul Sherman. **18 E 74th St, PO Box 616, NYC NY 10021 (212) 776–4509.**

American Friends of the Hebrew University. 11 E 69th St, NYC NY 10021 (212) 472–9800.

American Friends of the Israel Museum. 10 E 40th St, Suite 1208, NYC NY 10016 (212) 683–5190.

American Friends of the Jerusalem Mental Health Center – Ezrath Nashim, Inc. 10 E 40th St, NYC NY 10016 (212) 725–8175.

American Friends of Yad Benjamin – Educational Center of Poale Agudath Israel. 147 W 42nd St, NYC NY 10036 (212) 279–0816,7.

American Friends of Yeshivat Sha'alvim. 156 Fifth Ave, Suite 811, NYC NY 10010 (212) 924–9475.

American Histadrut Cultural Exchange Institute. 33 E 67th St, NYC NY 10021 (212) 628–1000.

The American Israel Friendship League. An independent non-sectarian org initiated by Bnai Zion. To promote people to people progs between the US & Is; to create friendship & understanding between their citizens. Distributes bks & periodicals to over 2,000 Am univ libraries, funds seminars & discussion groups that will bring Am into closer communications with Is, presents an annual award to an individual who has made an outstanding contribution to Am-Is friendship. **136 E 39th St, NYC NY 10016 (212) 725–1211.**

American Israeli Lighthouse. 30 E 60th St, NYC NY 10022 (212) 838–5322.

American Jewish Alternatives to Zionism. 133 E 73rd St, Suite 404, NYC NY 10021 (212) 628–2727.

The American Jewish Committee. A human relations agy. To ensure the security & dignity of J in all parts of the world & advance democratic principles & ins in the US. Fights anti-Semitism & all forms of prejudice; works overseas in Europe, Is, Latin Am & within the UN, to protect the rights of J & advance human rights; strives to prevent catastrophes affecting J the world over; mobilizes nationwide support for Is; seeks to further understanding among Israelis & J in the US & elsewhere; seeks to help J maintain & enrich their J identity &, at the same time, achieve full integration into Am life; encourages progs to help the underprivileged while resisting the imposition of racial or rel quotas in employment, edu & other areas of Am life; develops progs to help stem the decline of Am cities & coalitions for energy conservation; monitors the influence of Arab petro-dollars on Am economic, political & edu life. Ins on Pluralism & Group Identity works closely with leaders of the ethnic minorities on progs designed to maintain their ethnic heritage & improve the quality of their lives; Natl J Family Ctr encourages research & exchange of information on the Am family, promotes US policies in support of family life; Academy for J Studies Without Walls offers summer seminars & correspondence courses in J hist & related subjects; Jacob & Hilda Blaustein Ctr for Human Relations Research monitors threats to freedom the world over & encourages basic research & action progs to enhance freedom for people everywhere; William E. Wiener Oral Hist Library has more than 1,000 memoirs documenting the J experience in the 20th century. 50,000 mems fr more than 600 coms, organized in 80 chapters & units. Staff of 400 worldwide. F in 1906 by 50 prominent Am J leaders who were concerned about the pogroms in Russia & global anti-Semitism. American Jewish Year Book; Commentary; Present Tense. Pres: Maynard I. Wishner; Chr Bd of Govs: Howard I. Friedman; Chr Natl Exec Council: Theodore Ellenoff; Chr Bd of Trustees: Gerard Weinstock; Treas: Robert L. Pelz; Sec: Mervin H. Riseman; Assc Treas: Elaine Petschek; Exec VP: Bertram H. Gold; VPs: Stanford M. Adelstein, Morton K. Blaustein, Robert D. Gries, David Hirschhorn, Miles Jaffe, Harris L. Kempner Jr, Hamilton M. Loeb Jr, John H. Steinhart, Emily W. Sunstein, George M. Szabad, Elise D. Waterman; Hon Pres: Morris B. Abram, Arthur J. Goldberg, Philip E. Hoffman, Richard Maass, Elmer L. Winter; Hon VPs: Nathan Appleman, Ruth R. Goddard, Andrew Goodman, James Marshall, William Rosenwald; Hon Chr Natl Exec Council: Max M. Fisher; Hon Treas: Maurice Glinert; Exec VP Emeritus: John Slawson. **165 E 56th St, NYC NY 10022 (212) 751–4000.**

The American Jewish Committee, Blaustein Library. For information on the Ins, see – The American Jewish Committee, New York City, NY **165 E 56th St, NYC NY 10022 (212) 751–4000**

American Jewish Congress. A J com relations agy; a democratic & rep instrument of the Am J com. To help build a J homeland, fight anti-Semitism & all forms of racism, foster a postive sense of J identity & work toward full equality in a free soc for all Am. Defends the rights of the J poor & provides them with free legal counsel; supports the Equal Rights Amendment & the Women's Agenda; promotes adult J edu: exhibits, Heb & Yiddish language records, J bk fairs & study guides for chapter discussions on great J bks; encourages greater funding for J edu; helped f the Natl Conf on Soviet J; works to secure free emigration, rel & cultural rights for Soviet J; sponsors Overseas Travel Prog which offers 250 departures on person-to-person group tours to J coms in 40 countries; concentrates its efforts on bldg public understanding of Is needs for security, dignity & peace; fights the Arab boycott; played an important roll in drafting an effective federal anti-boycott bill; f the Commis on Com Interrelations; est the Louis Waterman Wise Youth Hostel in Jerusalem which draws thousands of young people fr all over the world; holds citizenship prog for immigrant chil; sponsors pilot projs which bring Moslem, Christian & Druze youth in Is into contact with young J & sponsors a special prog for the widows & chil of fallen Is soldiers. Recent additions to the hostel include a garden pavilion & Steinberg Cultural Bldg; Martin Steinberg Cultural Ctr in NY provides a meeting place for young J people engaged in J music & dance, painting & sculpture, poetry, fiction & film making; houses the Charles & Bertie Schwartz J Reading Rm & the Bernard L. Madoff J Music Library. F in 1918 by Rabbi Stephen Wise, Justice Louis Brandeis & other distinguished Am J. The Palestinians: What is Real and What is Politics; Boycott Report – periodic review of current dev affecting the boycott; Congress Monthly – a journal free to mems; Judaism (a quarterly); pubs directories, in NY & major cities throughout the country, of servs & facilities available to the J aged. Pres: Howard M. Squadron; Chr Governing Council: Jacqueline K. Levine; Co Chr Governing Council: Paul S. Berger, Jack M. Elkin, Alvin Gray; Treas: Clarence Goldberg; Co-Treas: Bernard Madoff; Sec: Joseph Gerofsky; Corsp Sec: Harold Becker; Exec Dir: Henry Siegman; Assc Exec Dir: Phil Baum; Gen Counsel: Will Maslow; Sr VPs: Theodore Bikel, Leona F. Chanin, Abraham Goldstein, Stanley H. Lowell, Theodore R. Mann, Henry Rosovsky, Howard Samuels; VPs: Jo Amer, David Barlas, Martin Begun, Barbara Cullen, Edith Frank, Joel Garver, Mollie Gersh, Murray A. Gordon, Chiae Herzig, Frank Horny, Lila Horwitz, David Kahn, Sylvia Kaplan,

Ralph Kingsley, Joel H. Levy, Amram Nowak, Walter Roth, Alan Shecter, Arthur Susswein, Marion Wilen, Frank Winston, Judith L. Wolfe, Louis E. Yavner; Hon Pres: Israel Goldstein, Arthur Hertzberg, Arthur J. Lelyveld, Irving Miller, Joachim Prinz; Hov VPs: Paul G. Annes, Benjamin S. Kalnick, Max A. Kopstein, Leon Kronish, Esther Polen, Harry Schacter, Virginia Snitow, Lillian Steinberg; Hon Co-Chr Governing Council: Morris Michelson; Hon Treas: Benjamin M. Halpern; Dir of Communications: Israel E. Levine. **Stephen Wise Congress House, 15 E 84th St, NYC NY 10028 (212) 879–4500.**

American Jewish Correctional Chaplains Association. 10 E 73rd St, NYC NY 10021 (212) 879–8415.

American Jewish History Center of the Jewish Theological Seminary. c/o Special Projects, Jewish Theological Seminary, **3080 Bdwy, NYC NY 10027 (212) 749–8000.**

The American Jewish Joint Distribution Committee, Inc. The major philanthropic arm of the Am J com for overseas J needs. To serve the world J com. JDC conducts & sponsors progs of relief, rescue, rehabilitation & J edu to the J com world wide. Afghanistan: Passover supplies; Algeria: sr care, welfare; Argentina: Golden Age Clubs, com ctrs, schs & seminaries, professional manpower dev; Austria: Soviet emigrant care & maintenance; Belgium: stu aid; Brazil: schs; Burma: relief & welfare; Cambodia: seed rice; Chile: schs, sr care, chil residence, rabbinical servs; China: WWII survivor relief; Denmark: refugee integration; Egypt: Passover supplies, welfare; Ethiopia: health & welfare, J edu; Finland: rabbinical servs; France: J edu, health & welfare, sr care, youth progs, chil welfare, WWII refugee relief, manpower dev; Great Britain: representation; Greece: Passover supplies; Hong Kong: liaison; Hungary: kosher kitchen, health & welfare, WWII survivor relief, rel supplies; Italy: Soviet emigrants – health & maintenance, Yiddishkeit, Passover Supplies, Italian J – young adult servs, WWII refugee relief, resource ctrs; India: schs, hot lunch prog, sr care; Is: com ctrs, edu, geriatrics, mental health, manpower dev, yeshivot, youth servs; Morocco: J edu, sr care, summer camps, pre-sch classes, health & welfare; Norway: transmigrant relief; Portugal: WWII survivor relief, health care, com ctrs; Rumania: servs to aged, health & welfare, kosher kitchens; Spain: WWII survivor relief, health care; Sweden: transmigrant relief; Switzerland: liaison intl agy; Thailand: Cambodian refugee relief; Tunisia: sr care, J edu, health & welfare, Passover supplies; Uruguay: schs, com ctrs, sr care; Yugoslavia: servs to aged, Passover supplies, com ctr. JDCsupports: ORT – Org for Rehabilitation through Training; The Alliance Israelite Universelle – a French J secular edu org; Ozar Hatorah – a religiously oriented J edu org; Lubavitcher schs. F in 1914 in response to the needs of the J coms in Palestine & Eastern European which were suffering fr persecution & hunger. The JDC receives funds fr Am J through the UJA. The JDC also receives funds fr the World J Relief, J Trust Corp for Germany Ltd of England, United J Relief Agy of the Canadian J Congress, & coms in Latin Am. Pres: Henry Taub; Exec VP: Ralph I. Goldman; Chr of the Bd: Donald M. Robinson; Hon Pres: Edward Ginsburg, Edward M. Warburg, Jack D. Weiler; VPs: Heinz Eppler, Pauline B. Falk, Harold Friedman, Patricia A. Gantz, Herbert H. Schiff, Stephen Shalom, Marshall M. Weinberg; Hon VPs: Irving Kane, William Rosenwald, Judge Nochem S. Winnet; Hon Exec VP: Samuel L. Haber; Co-Treas: Herbert M. Singer, Elaine K. Winik, Henry L. Zucker; Hon Treas: Joseph I. Lubin, Irving H. Sherman; Sec: Emanuel Goldberg; Asst Sec: Herbert Katzki; Exec Cttee: Dr Abram J. Abeloff, Joseph Ain, Herschel W. Blumberg, Arthur Brody, Marilyn Brown, Edgar L. Cadden, Dr Martin Cherkasky, Martin E. Citrin, Maurice M. Cohen, Amos Comay, Irwin S. Field, Max M. Fisher, Sylvia Hassenfeld, Jerold C. Hoffberger, Max W. Jacobs, Saul Kagen, Carl Leff, Sidney E. Leiwant, Harry R. Mancher, Morton L. Mandel, Joseph Meyerhoff, Raquel H. Newman-Naymark, Bert Rabinowitz, Howard Rubin, Edward Sanders, Laurence A. Tisch, Elizabeth R. Varet, Barbi Weinberg, Hon Milton A. Wolf, Louis I. Zorensky. **60 E 42th St, NYC NY 10017 (212) 687–6200.**

The American Jewish Joint Distribution Committee, Library. For information on the Ins, see – The American Joint Distribution Committee, New York City, NY. **60 E 42nd St, NYC NY 10017.**

American Jewish League Against Communism. 39 E 68th St, NYC NY 10021 (212) 472–1400.

American Jewish League for Israel. To unite all those who, notwithstanding differing philosophies of J life, are committed to the historical ideals of Zionism. Works for the welfare of Is as a whole & is not identified with any pol party. Hon Pres: Seymour R. Levine; Chr Exec Cttee: Eleazar Lipsky; Chr of Bd: Samuel Rothberg. **595 Madison Ave, NYC NY 10022.**

American Jewish Public Relations Society. Dedicated to the advancement of professional standards for public information & interpretation of J affairs in the United States & abroad. F in 1957.

Pres: Avi Feinglass; VPs: Barbara Rogoff, Martin Warmbrand; Treas: Hyman Brickman; Sec: Toby Willig; Exec Cttee: David Bicofsky, George Friedman, Norma Harrop, Lionel Koppman, Paul Kresh, Hy Kuperstein, Irving Leos, Martha Loewenstein, Evelyn Musher, Robert Smith, Dorothy Steinberg, Arthur Weyne, Mary Wisotsky, Frank Wundohl. **234 Fifth Ave, NYC NY 10001 (212) 697–5895.**

American Jewish Society for Service. An independent natl social servs org. To give young people a way to practice charity & an opportunity to perform the J tradition of humanitarian servs to the deprived & calamity stricken regardless of their color or creed. Conducts three or four voluntary summer work camps which include rel, edu & recreational progs. Camp sessions last seven weeks with 16 to 18 boys & girls in each camp; projs undertaken usually include construction or repair of bldgs. Camp Dir, two counselors & a cook in each camp. F in 1950. Projs in the past have included bldg a sch, a gymnasium, single family homes, barns, recreational facilities, a com ctr, & installation of water systems, construction of additional facilities for an inter-racial camp for underprivileged chil, repairing flood & tornado damage. Campers have worked in 30 states & 14 Indian reservations. Some scholarships are available. Chr of the Bd: Henry Kohn; Pres: E. Kenneth Marks; VP: Frederic S. Nathan; Treas: Sidney H. Shloss Jr; Sec: Leveritt A. Wallace; Exec Dir: Harry Elly Saltzman; Dirs: Amanda Jane Berger, Robert W. Bloch, Rabbi Herman J. Blumberg, Audrey Brenner, Carl Brenner, Michael Clarke, Dr Edward G. Cohen, Carole Convissor, Scott Elias, Edward Fogel, Edward R. Freedman, Irma Gertz, Lawrence G. Green, Irving Greenblatt, Stanley S. Herr, Dr Harold L. Hirsh, Steven Klein, Max Kleinbaum, Henry Kohn, Rabbi Arthur J. Lelyveld, E. Kenneth Marks, Michael F. Mayer, Frederic S. Nathan, Ralph Pessach, Jane Plitt, David Z. Rosensweig, Erica Rosenthal, David Schulson, Sidney H. Shloss Jr, Sanford Solender, D. Hays Solis Cohen Jr, David Tafler, Leveritt A. Wallace, Richard Weinert. **15 E 26th St, NYC NY 10010 (212) 683–6178.**

American Mizrachi Women. 817 Bdwy, NYC NY 10003 (212) 477–4720.

American Organization of Tour Operators to Israel. 18 E 48th St, NYC NY 10017 (212) 758–6464.

American ORT Federation. Committed to the task of ORT – bldg & operating a global network of schs & training progs to provide quality vocational & technical edu to J in need throughout the world. Provides vocational & technical edu to more than 100,000 J men, women & chil in 26 countries on 5 continents. Stu at ORT schs learn skills ranging fr mechanics & welding to communications & computer tech. Largest ORT operation is in Is where more than 75,000 stu attend over 100 ORT schs & training ctrs &, in addition, there is the ORT Sch of Engineering in Jerusalem; in France, ORT maintains vocational & technical training progs serving thousands of French J, many originally fr economically deprived J coms in N Africa; in Latin Am, ORT maintains progs ranging fr creative edu to carpentry to advanced courses in med electronics, & data processing; in the US, Bramson ORT Technical Ins in NYC, a two-yr tech col accredited by the NY State Bd of Regents, trains J stu in tech-intensive fields such as biomed electronics, computer operations & advanced optics. Combined tuition & maintenance scholarships are available. F in Tsarist Russia in 1880 to train the poverty-stricken J of Eastern Europe in ind & agriculture. ORT Bulletin; ORT Yearbook. Pres: Alvin L. Gray; VPs: Shelley Appleton, Stanley Black; Sec: Rudy Reis; Dir of PR: Avi Feinglass. **817 Bdwy, NYC NY 10003 (212) 677–4400.**

American Red Magen David for Israel 888 Seventh Ave, NYC NY 10019 (212) 757–1627.

American Sephardi Federation. 521 Fifth Ave, NYCNY 10017 (212) 697–1845.

American Society for Jewish Music. 155 Fifth Ave, NYC NY 10010 (212) 533–2601.

American Society for Technion – Israel Institute of Technology. 271 Madison Ave, NYC NY 10016 (212) 889–2050.

American Society of Sephardic Studies. 500 W 185th St, NYC NY 10033 (212) 960–5236.

American Trade Union Council for Histadrut. 33 E 67th St, NYC NY 10021 (212) 628–1000.

American Veterans of Israel. To keep the mems of the group together. Reunions in US & Canada; meetings on Yom Haatzmaoot, Chanukah & other occasions; memorial servs at grave of Colonel David Marcus; memorial plaque in forest in Harel; close ties with Israeli govt; reception for Is vets coming to the US for treatment; major proj – Agudah Lmaan Hachayal; connections with mems who returned to Is on aliyah. 500 mems; est category of hon mem. Started in 1949 by mems of Machal who returned to the US & Canada. Immediately after, non-Israelis who served in the Aliyah-Bet were included in group. Newsletter. Pres: Louis Brettler; VP: Maximilian

Tocker; Treas: Stanley Cohen; Sec: Samuel Alexander; Special Events: Harry Eisner. **15 E 26th St, NYC NY 10010 (212) 532–4949.**

American Veterans of the Jewish Legion – Hagdud Haivri League, Inc. c/o Dr Judah Lapson, 1776 Bdwy, NYC NY 10019.

American Zionist Federation. Coordinating agy of the Am Zionist Movement encompassing 16 natl mem orgs. Constituent orgs: Am J League for Is, Am Mizrachi Women, Am for Progressive Is-Hashomer Hatzair, Am Sephardi Fed, Assn of Parents of Am Israelis, Assn of Reform Zionists of Am – ARZA, B'nai Zion, Emunah, Hadassah, Labor Zionists Alliance, N Am Aliyah Movement, Pioneer Women, Rel Zionists of Am, Telem – Movement for Zionist Fulfillment, United Zionists-Revisionists of Am, Zionist Org of Am. To motivate Am J to accept the Zionist principles that all the J in the world are one people with Is as the ctr of J life. Provides a Speakers Bureau which keeps the com at large informed with up-to-date information on the Middle E & Is; supports agy assisting J who need or want to settle in Is; encourages the est of ins & data for edu in J, Heb & culture of the J people; furthers the efforts of fund raising orgs supporting J edu, youth progs & advancing J welfare; supports progs encouraging Am J youth to participate in Zionist work & activities nationally & locally; promotes research, study & discussion of Zionist ideals & aims. Close to one million Am J. F in 1939. **515 Park Ave, NYC NY 10022 (212) 371–7750.**

American Zionist Youth Council. 515 Park Ave, NYC NY 10022 (212) 751–6070.

American Zionist Youth Foundation Resource Center. 515 Park Ave, NYC NY 10022 (212) 751–6070.

American Zionist Youth Foundation, Inc. The AZYF strives to instill in young J a strong sense of J identity & a deep devotion to the land of Is. Individual departments within the Foun reach out to Am J youth in a variety of ways. Sponsors edu progs & servs for Am J youth including tours to Is, progs of volunteer serv or study in leading ins of sci, scholarship, & arts; sponsors field workers who promote J & Zionist programming on campus; prepares & provides specialists who present & interpret the Israeli experience for com ctrs & feds throughout the country; provides supportive servs for the Zionist Youth groups in Am. F 1963. Pub Activist Newsletter; Guide to Educational & Programming Material; Programs in Israel. Chr: Bernard S. White; V Chr: Henry Everett, Raymond Patt, Bess G. Rothbaum, Rabbi Israel Miller; Treas: Arthur Levine; Sec: Eli Zborowski. **515 Park Ave, NYC NY 10022 (212) 751–6070.**

American-Israel Chamber of Commerce & Industry, Inc. Offers assistance to mem US firms interested in economic activity in & with Is. Provides extensive trade assistance; pub market research reports; aids in dev of trade & investment between US & Is; gives annual natl convention/dinner at which firms contributing to the growth of exports fr Is to US are honored by Govt of Is Trade Ctr. In cooperation with the Govt of Is Trade Ctr, pub Israel Quality (a quarterly economic newsletter). **500 Fifth Ave, NYC NY 10110 (212) 354–6510.**

American-Israel Cultural Foundation. 485 Madison Ave, NYC NY 10022 (212) 751–2700.

Americans for Progressive Israel. 150 Fifth Ave, NYC NY 10011 (212) 255–8760.

Ampal – American Israel Corp. 10 Rockefeller Plaza, NYC NY 10020.

Anti-Defamation League of B'nai B'rith. Dedicated in purpose & prog to translating the Am heritage of democratic ideals into a way of life for all Am, & to countering assaults on the safety, status, rights & image of J. Is: maintains comprehensive prog to keep the Am public informed about Is & the Middle E conflict; conducts natl advertising, direct mail campaigns; distributes specially prepared analyses, surveys, reviews & digests to public opinion molders in communications, govt, human relations, edu, rel, ind & labor; distributes Op-Ed page & letters to the editor commentaries; initiates direct meetings with editors, church reps & govt officials; maintains library of audio-visual materials on Is, radio & TV progs. Interrel understanding: participates in the Intl J Cttee on Interrel Consultations which meets regularly with Vatican officials; dev prog to eliminate anti-Semitic references & nuances fr sermons, texts & other church literature; provides for incorporation of accurate information on J & Judaism in col & seminary curricula through textbks, audio-visual aids & other edu material; conducts seminars & workshops on J & the contemporary J com; supports Catholic-J & Protestant-J relations cttee in cities throughout the country; conducts study tours of Is for Christian clergy & rel writers; promotes interrel memorial servs in churches & coms around the country to observe the Holocaust. Discrimination: works to implement anti-discrimination laws; monitors & seeks to dev affirmative action progs to provide access to edu & employment for minorities & women without resorting to quotas & artificial means; acts as a consultant &

provides audio-visual & printed materials on intergroup relations & human relations training techniques to business & industrial mgmnt; monitors, & makes public, violations of local, state & federal laws by social clubs which discriminate on racial & rel grounds; trys to ensure fair employment practices on behalf of those who observe the Sabbath & other rel holidays. Sch curriculum: integrates study about the Holocaust into the curriculum of secondary schs; sponsors Ctr for Studies on the Holocaust; sends edu package of multimedia materials on J & other minorities for teachers & stu; monitors the treatment of minorities in curricula & textbks; makes printed & audio-visual materials on racial & ethnic groups available for gen sch use; develops simulation games; uses filmed situations & specially dev manuals to assist sch systems in recognizing & resolving classrm conflicts based on interracial, ethnic & socio-economic tensions; devs methods & materials for helping teachers discover & correct their own negative attitudes as well as those of their stu; counsels edu & adms at all sch levels. Extremism: performs annual audits of assaults against J ins & private property; works to expose anti-democratic as well as anti-J groups; research & counteraction efforts directed at extremist groups. Soviet & Latin Am J: prepares reviews & analyses of USSR policy & trends, & helps mobilize public support in behalf of Soviet J through ADL contacts with the media & other opinion molders. Latin Am Affairs Dept: works to keep human rights violations in the public eye. Civil rights: serves as a bridge between racial & ethnic groups; pubs manuals for mayors; holds confs & seminars; sets up human relations progs for police officials; acts frequently as witness at governmental hearings on equal opportunity, legislation & enforcement. 27 regional offices in the US, a European off in Paris, an Is off in Jerusalem, affiliated offs in Latin Am, & a consultant in Rome. Professionals in the fields of civil rights, communications, edu, intl affairs, law, rel, research & investigation, urban affairs & social sci; volunteers consisting of leaders of the Am J com, including reps of B'nai B'rith. F in 1913. ADL Bulletin; Facts – in-depth reports on the activities of anti-Semitic orgs & individuals; Rights – reports on cases of anti-J discrimination & remedial action taken; Law – surveys nationwide legislative & judicial devs in areas of ADL concern; Face to Face – an interrel bulletin; International Reports; Nuestro Encuentro – a Spanish-language pub to build a bridge of understanding between the J com & Hispanic-Am; scholarly bks; pamphlets; reports; research studies; sch aids. Catalogues listing available printed & audio-visual materials may be obtained fr any League off. Natl Chr: Maxwell E. Greenberg; Hon Chr: Seymour Graubard, Burton M. Joseph; Natl Dir: Nathan Perlmutter; Assc Natl Dir: Abraham H. Foxman; Chr Natl Exec Cttee: Kenneth J. Bialkin; Hon V Chr: Leonard L. Abess, Rudy Boschwitz, Edgar M. Bronfman, Maxwell Dane, Lawrence A. Harvey, Bruce I. Hochman, Jacob K. Javits, Philip M. Klutznick, Carl Levin, Howard M. Metzenbaum, Samuel H. Miller, Bernard Nath, Robert R. Nathan, Abraham A. Ribicoff, Benjamin S. Rosenthal, William Sachs, Melvin H. Schlesinger, S.O. Shapiro, Theodore H. Silbert, Sidney R. Yates; V Chr: Jerry Dubrof, Nat Kameny, Max M. Kampelman, Kaygey Kash, Philip Krupp, Larry M. Lavinsky; V Chr, Natl Exec Cttee: Donald R. Mintz; Hon Treas: Benjamin Greenberg, Richard M. Lederer Jr; Treas: Charles Goldring; Asst Treas: Norman J. Gray; Sec: Martin L.C. Feldman; Asst Sec: Alvin J. Steinberg. **823 United Nations Plaza, NYC NY 10017 (212) 490–2525.**

Associated YM-YWHAs of Greater New York. For the aged, provides 18 sr citizen ctrs, meals prog, preventive & rehabilitative physical & mental health care servs, edu progs, involvement of the physically handicapped in the sr ctr progs, transportation servs, help to prevent crime against the elderly, assistance to the victims of crime, & integration of the visually handicapped aged in normal activites; provides servs for Russian immigrants; provides information, referral & counseling for poor, aged & one parent families; provides servs to Orthodox residents; maintains servs to youth & chil which include Kadima Prog, handicapped progs, Russian chil counseling, mental health, extra-curricular activities; maintains volunteer progs; sponsors seven camps which serve chil, youth & the elderly; sponsors older adult vacati progs. Servs reach 65,000. Com Ctrs: E Flatbush-Rugby YM-YWHA; Emanu-El Midtown YM-YWHA; Gustave Hartman YM-YWHA, May Hartman Sr Ctr; Henrietta & Stuart Hirschman YM-YWHA of Coney Island; Kings Bay YM-YWHA, A. David Benjamin Sr Ctr; Mosholu-Montefiore Com Ctr; Samuel Field YM-YWHA; Shorefront YM-YWHA of Brighton-Manhattan Beach; YM-YWHA of Greater Flushing; Bay Terrace Extension Ctr; YM-YWHA Of Mid-Westchester; Yonkers JCC. Affiliate: YM-YWHA Of Lower-Westchester. Assc Camps: Tillie & Alexander Block Vacation Ctr, Marguerite & Maurice B. Hexter Vacation Ctr, Coeur D'alene Camp, Camp Poyntelle-Ray Hill, Lewis Village, Hattie & Max Lewis Campgrounds, Ella Fohs Camps, Henry I. Moses Camp for the Aged. Sr Citizens Ctrs: Rockaway Pk Sr Ctr, Roy Reuther Houses Y Prog, Queens; Marble Hill Sr Ctr, Bronx; Brighton-Manhattan Beach Sr Ctr; Midwood Sr Ctr; Storefront Servs Ctr, Bklyn. F in 1957. The 1st Pres dream was to create 11 new JCC in Greater NY – this took 21 yrs. Pres: Lester Pollack; Chr of the Bd: Mrs Leonard H. Bernheim,

Milton B. Eulau, Sidney J. Silberman, Robert F. Weinberg; V Chr of the Bd: Irving Brodsky; Assc Chr of the Bd: Nathan S. Ancell, Calmon J. Ginsberg, Alfred R. Goldstein, Harold Korzenik, Michael A. Loeb, John H. Slade, Mrs Robert D. Steefel, Peter V. Tishman, Dr Ruth Weintraub; Chr of Exec Cttee: Stephen M. Peck; VPs: Mrs Stanley J. Behrman, Thoma R. Block, Richard Eisner, Susan Halpern, Larry Silverstein, Michael J. Weinberger; Sec: Richard H. Alexander; Asst Secs: Joseph Gluckman, I. Stanley Krieger, Alfred L. Plant, Leslie Steinau; Treas: Eli Weinberg; Asst Treas: Peter Feldman, Herbert M. Paul, Stephen R. Reiner, Alfred A. Rosenberg, Raymond Sagov, Stephen L. Wald; Hon Pres: James A. Block; Hon Chr of the Bd: Lawrence B. Buttenwieser, Irving M. Felt, Saul Horowitz; Assc Hon Chr of the Bd: John H. Gutfreund, Frederick A. Klingenstein; Hon VPs: Leo R. Fink, Benjamin S. Hornstein, Joseph L. Mailman, Mrs A. Louis Oresman, Mrs Milton Weill; Hon Treas: Jerome Gevirman; Hon Trustees: Edwin M. Appel, Mrs Edwin M. Appel, Mrs Nathan Appleman, Alfred R. Bachrach, Sidney B. Becker, William L. Bernhard, Ernest Blum, Samuel Field, Eugene Grant, Mrs Gustave Hartman, Sol R. Kaplan, Lee Paul Klingenstein, Samuel Lemberg, Mrs Alvord N. Luria, Peter L. Malkin, Jack Mintz, V. Henry Rothschild, Eugene Tuck, Mrs Thomas Wall, Kenneth Weiser, George Weissman. **130 E 59th St, NYC NY 10022 (212) 751–8880.**

Association of Advanced Rabbinical & Talmudic Schools. 175 Fifth Ave, NYC NY 10010 (212) 477–0950.

Association of Jewish Anti-Poverty Workers. 18 E 41st St, Rm 806, NYC NY 10017 (212) 686–2777.

Association of Jewish Book Publishers. 1646 First Ave, NYC NY 10028 (212) 799–6517.

Association of Jewish Center Workers. Affiliated with Conf of J Communal Servs. Pres: David Eskenazi; Exec: Herman Zimmerman. **15 E 26th St, NYC NY 10010 (212) 532–4949.**

Association of Jewish Chaplains of the Armed Forces. 15 E 26th St, Rm 1423, NYC NY 10010 (212) 532–4949.

Association of Jewish Community Relations Workers. 55 W 42nd St, Suite 1530, NYC NY 10036 (212) 490–2525.

Association of Jewish Family & Children's Agencies. 200 Park Ave S, NYC NY 10003 (212) 674–6659.

Association of Jewish Libraries. To promote librarianship & improve library servs & professional standards in the field of J; to serve as a ctr for the dissemination of J library information & guidance; to promote pub of literature which will aid the J library; to keep mems abreast of the latest dev in J librarianship. There are two divs, the Research & Special Library Div representing J Univ & Research Libraries & J collections in larger libraries, & the Syn Sch & Ctr Library Div representing the bulk of membership & serving the smaller, more popular libraries. Offers a variety of comprehensive resources to help the J Librarian in the form of an annual convention, a semi annual pub, & a list of professional manuals, systems & booklist sources; presents annual award to the author of an outstanding juvenile bk in J, annual scholarship grant to a qualified library sch stu planning to enter the field of J. Over 500 mems in the two divs. F in 1965. AJL Bulletin (pub twice yearly); AJL Newsletter (pub 4 times yearly); Convention Proceedings; Literature of the Holocaust for Juvenile & Young Adult Collections. The AJL is interested in Heb language search capabilities, & a resolution was adopted at their convention requesting that search titles in the Heb language be made possible. Pres: Barbara Y. Leff; VP/Pres Elect: Philip E. Miller; Treas: Mary Guilbert Brand; Corsp Sec: Edith Lubetski; Rec Sec: Linda P. Lerman; Membership: Carole G. Ozeroff; Publicity & PR: Rose Sobol; Research & Special Library Div – Pres: Edith Degani; VP: Charles Cutter; Sec: Richard W. Marcus; Syn, Sch & Ctr Div – Hon Pres: Miriam Leikind; Pres: Rita C. Frischer; VP Pres-Elect: Hazel B. Karp; Sec: Anita Wenner. **c/o Natl Foun for J Culture, 122 E 42nd St, Rm 1512, NYC NY 10168 (212) 490–2280.**

Association of Jewish Sponsored Camps, Inc. To provide camping servs to the people of the Greater NY Met Area. Camps for chil, teenagers & sr citizens. There are also camps for retarded chil & adults, for the physically disabled & emotionally disturbed. The camps offer J cultural progs, daily study & Heb instruction. The Assn disseminates information to the public & promotes the dev of the edu, spiritual, social welfare, & recreational aspects of camping. The Assn is comprised of 38 mem camps: AZYF, Block & Hexter Vacation Ctr, Bronx House-Emanuel Camps, Cejwin Camps, Camp Chavatzeleth, Cummings Campgrounds, Camp Dora Golding, Camp Edward Isaacs, Eisner Camp Ins, Camp Ella Fohs, Camp HASC, Camp Hatikvah, Camp HES, Camp Isabella Freedman, Camp Kinder Ring, Camp Kinderland, Camp Leah, Camp Louemma, Massad Camps, Camp Mikan Recro, Camp Mogen Avraham, Camp Morasha, Camp Moshava, Camp Naaleh, Camp Oakhurst, Camp Poyntelle-Ray Hill

Lewis, Camp Rainbow, Camp Ramah, Ramapo Anchorage Camp, Camp Shomria, Camp Sternberg-Spatt, Suprise Lake Camp, Camp Sussex, Tarbuth Foun, Camp Tel Yehudah, Camp Young Judea-Sprout Lake. The camps range fr Orthodox to the Reform. Seminars for camp professionals are conducted on a regular basis. The Exec Dir acts as a consultant to the mem camps. Pres: Arnold M. Heller; 1st VP: Abbott L. Lampert; 2nd VP: Miriam Sehecter; Sec: Joy Helman; Treas: Joy Henshel; Exec Dir: Asher O. Melzer. **130 E 59th St, NYC NY 10022 (212) 751–0477.**

Association of Orthodox Jewish Scientists. 116 E 27th St, NYC NY 10016 (212) 889–1364.

Association of Reform Zionists of America. A constituent of the World Zionist Org & its territorial union, the Am Zionist Fed; an affiliate of UAHC. To work in cooperation with other orgs in a com-wide effort to insure Is security & economic well-being; to work to build a strong Reform J in Is, & to eradicate the official discrimination against non-Orthodox rel J imposed under Is law by an entrenched Orthodox est; to work to est creative links between Am & Is Jews. 65,000 mems in cong chapters throughout the US. Est in 1977 to be the primary link between Am's 1 million Reform J & Is, & to be the Reform J voice in the World Zionist Org. ARZA's delegation to the 29th World Zionist Congress in Feb 1978 introduced a successful resolution which for the 1st time put WZO on record as favoring equal treatment for all branches of rel J. Newsletter; Leadership Update. Pres: Rabbi Roland B. Gittelsohn; VPs: Donald S. Day, Tracy H. Ferguson, Ruth Nussbaum, Rabbi David Polish; Treas: Norma U. Levitt; Assc Treas: L. Kenneth Rosett; Sec: Theodore K. Broido; Exec Dir: Rabbi Ira S. Youdovin. **838 Fifth Ave, NYC NY 10021 (212) 249–0100.**

Association of Yugoslav Jews in the U.S.A. 247 W 99th St, NYCNY 10025 (212) 865–2211.

B'nai B'rith Career & Counseling Services. Philanthropically supported, non-profit edu & vocational counseling serv. Provides counseling assistance to youngsters & adults fr age 12 through the retirement yrs. The prog consists of individual, confidential interviews, & a battery of aptitude, interest & personality tests/ inventories with an evaluation session at the conclusion. All professionals on staff are required to have a minimum of a Masters Degree in counseling, guidance, psychology or a related field with previous experience. Est in 1938. Dist Exec Dir: Peter Mandelbaum; Asst Dir: Margot Gellman; Chr of the Natl Commis: Milton W. Kadish; Adv Bd Chr: Shirley Diamond; V Chr: Sanford Siegal, Dorothy Weinstein; Treas: Phyllis M. Siegal; Sec: Shirley Wanetik; Exec Cttee: Ralph DeNat, Bernard Goldstein, Lillian Jay Greene, Seymour Lesser, Arthur A. Nerson, Anne Rubinstein, Irving Rubinstein Sr, Rita Salberg, Rae Saltzman, Harriette Simon, Howard Thomashauer; Adv Bd: Gusti Ackermann, Jerry Beatus, Michael Bershad, Carrie Bock, Arthur Bookman, Marvin Braunstein, Jocelyn Chait, Morton Cohen, Daniel Fine, Evelyn Finkelstein, Anne S. Gold, Herman Gold, Morris Goldberg, Gloria Goldwater, George Gordon, Trudy Gordon, Yvette Halperin, Florence Halpern, Rita Jorrisch, Lee Kahn, Irving Krakoff, David Lack, Irene Levy, Bernard Lickver, Mathilda Luboff, Toni Mann, Malvina Mark, Leonore Mazer, Charles Merinoff II, Herman M. Metz, Sydell Miller, Cliff Muller, Ruth Perel, Seymour Reich, Debbie Rice, Ann Scher, Shirley Schnee, Milton Siegel, Thelma Siegel, Victor Silibovsky, Esther Sitzer, Harold Stangler, Sally Sterman, Harold Storch, Anne Swerdlove, Elmer Tannenbaum, Rabbi Malcolm Thomson, Stanley Vogel, David Wanetik, James Weinberg, Anita Weisbord, Harry Weisbord, Edith Wilner, Louis M. Zwiebach. **823 United Nations Plaza, NYC NY 10017 (212) 490–0677.**

B'nai Jeshurun Day School. Affiliated with Solomon Schechter Day Schs Assn. Prin: Rabbi William Berkowitz; Chr: Dr Jules Hirsch. **270 W 89th St, NYC NY 10024.**

B'nai Yiddish Society. 41 Union Sq, NYC NY 10003 (212) 989–3162.

B'nai Zion. Am Zionist fraternal org; Assn: Brith Abraham; mem of the World Zionist Congress. Associated with Hadassah & the Am J League for Is. Americanism, Fraternalism & Zionism; committed to supporting & continuing the democratic way of life in Am, the strengthening of the State of Is, & the preservation of the identity of the J people. provides med & life insurance progs; supports the study of Heb; promotes tours & study trips to Is; conducts in-depth seminars on issues of concern to the J com; supports UJA, Is Bonds & the J Natl Fund; gives medals & awards to Am pursuing advanced studies in Heb; raises money for projs in the US & Is. The Bnai Zion Foun est & helps maintain the Bnai Zion Home for Retarded Chil in Rosh Ha'ayin, Is; supports the Bet Halochem Rehabilitation Ctr for Disabled Veterans near Tel Aviv; est the Cardiac Rehabilitation Ctr of the Haifa Med Clin; has been instrumental in founding a chain of Maccabi sports ctrs in Is; has built a series of Kupat Cholim Health Clins; est Kfar Bnai Zion, a highly successful agricultural settlement in Is; aided in the est of the artists' colony at Ein Hod, as well as its Sch of

Applied Arts & its new stu hostel; maintains the beautiful Am-Is Friendship House as a ctr for Zionist meetings, edu functions, festivals & cultural gatherings. Available for mems only: tax sheltered retirement accounts, travel dept, blood bank, med servs, welfare fund, cemetery lots, singles div, social progs & seminars. 40,000 mems. F in 1908 at a convention chaired by Judah Magnus who became the first pres of the Hebrew Univ in Jerusalem, & Rabbi Stephen S. Wise. The group is the oldest Zionist fraternal org in the US. Bnai Zion organized the first J insurance co in Palestine, & in 1921 helped launch the first major Am fund raising effort for the J com in Palestine. That effort was the direct forerunner of the UJA. Bnai Zion Voice; The Bnai Zion Traveler – a periodic up-date on travel tips, information & review of org highlights. The Annual Award Dinner presents an award to someone who has achieved greatly in promoting the ideals of Americanism & Zionism. Pres: Sidney Weiner; Exec VP: Herman Z. Quittman; VPs: George O. Arkin, Fred Kahan, Dorothy S. Levine, Hon Herbert Tenzer, Jack Wilcox; VP Fin: Mike Funk; Natl Sec: Mel Parness; Treas: Ernest Zelig; Assc Treas: Werner Buckold, Bertram Ordan; Counsel: Raymond M. Patt; Trustees: Rabbi Willian Berkowitz, Harold Bernstein, Louis K. Bleecker, Hon Abraham J. Multer, Paul Safro, Sumner Zabriskie. **136 E 39th St, NYC NY 10016 (212) 725–1211.**

Bar/Bat Mitzvah Pilgrimage World Zionist Organization. 515 Park Ave, NYC NY 10022 (212) 752–0600.

Bar-Ilan University in Israel. 527 Madison Ave, NYC NY 10022 (212) 751–6366.

Baron De Hirsch Fund. 386 Park Ave S, NYC NY 10016 (212) 532–7088.

Beit Midrash L'Torah, Jerusalem Torah College for Men. Located in Jerusalem. Affiliated with & sponsored by the Torah Edu Dept of the World Zionist Org. To provide each stu with a warm understanding environment in which he may achieve his individual goals in learning. Beginners classes available to univ stu. Offers Gemara, Halacha & a broad spectrum of J studies; provides monthly tours & two major trips sponsored by the J Agy, with selected visits to settlements, kibbutzim families & yeshivot. F in 1969. Classes are generally given in Heb with provisions made for those who are weak in the language. Special emphasis is on stu involvement with the youth & families of the poorest sections of Jerusalem. Dean: Rabbi Moshe Horowitz. **Torah Dept, World Zionist Org, 515 Park Ave, NYC NY 10022 (212) 752–0600.**

Benjamin N. Cordozo School of Law – Yeshiva University. Prepares stu for progessional practice of law or other activities in which legal training is useful; grants JD. F 1976. For information on the Univ, see – Yeshiva University, New York City, NY. **Brookdale Ctr, 55 Fifth Ave, NYCNY 10003.**

Bernard Revel Graduate School – Yeshiva University. Offers grad work in Judiac studies, J edu, Semitic languages, literatures, cultures; confers MS, MA, PhD, EdD. Units within the sch include: Block Edu Prog (1980) which under a grant fr LA Pincus Fund for the Diaspora, J Agy, trains J edu adm for serv throughout US; Harry Fischel Sch for Higher J Studies (1945) which offers summer grad work in Judaic studies, J edu, Semitic languages, literatures, & cultures. F in 1937. For information on the Univ, see – Yeshiva University, New York City, NY. **500 W 185th St, NYCNY 10033 (212) 960–5285.**

Beth Am, The Peoples Temple. Affiliated with UAHC. 90 mems. Rabbis: Burt A. Siegel, Israel R. Margolies; Pres: Hans H. Joseph; Edu: Burt A. Siegel; Sisterhood Pres: Dora Stokes. **178 Bennett Ave, NYC NY 10040 (212) 927–2230.**

Beth Din of America. 1250 Bdwy, NYC NY 10001 (212) 594–3780.

Beth Israel Medical Center. Facility affiliated with Mount Sinai Sch of Med & Fed of J Philanthropies. Gen & specialized med servs; three abuse progs; chaplaincy servs. Est in 1890 by a group of J civic leaders for the needs of the large J immigration fr E Europe. In 1929 Beth Is moved to its present location. Beth Is maintains 966 beds, kosher kitchen, & nursing sch. Pres: Charles H. Silver; VPs: Samuel Hausman, Howard N. Blitman, Max J. Etra, Mitchell Flaum, Morton P. Hyman, David B. Kriser, Robert A. Krissel, Richard Netter, Seymour J. Phillips, Michael E. Schultz, Herbert M. Singer; Sec: Jack A. Rothenstein; Asst Sec: Robert L. Ginsberg; Treas: Abaraham L. Malamut; Asst Treas: Sidney Kraines. **10 Nathan D. Perlman Pl, NYC NY 10003 (212) 420–2000.**

Bialystoker Center, Home & Infirmary for the Aged. Sr citizen residence & infirmary (nursing home) affiliated with AAHA, NAJHA, NYAHA. To provide a pleasant, well-equipped residence & infirmary for the elderly. Med servs; physical therapy; recreational facilities; rel servs; in-house rabbi; edu lectures; entertainment prog; ladies auxiliary; library containing approx 200 vols (mostly Yiddish literature). 1500 mems. 110 employees; 10 volunteers. In 1928 the Bialystoker Relief Soc became the Bialystoker Ctr, which merged with Bialystoker Bikur Cholim. Pub The Bialystoker Stimme (semi-annual). Facilities include kosher kitchen, syn, physical therapy rm, main dining hall & smaller dining halls, auditorium. Gen Sec: Izaak Pybal; Adm: Yehoshua Schachter; Chaplain: Rabbi Charles Shoulson. **228 E Bdwy, NYC NY 10002 (212) 475–7755.**

The Bialystoker Synagogue. 7 Wilet St, NYC NY 10002 (212) 475–0165.

Black-Jewish Information Center. 16 E 85th St, NYC NY 10028 (212) 879–4577.

Bnei Akiva of North America. A youth movement of the Rel Zionists of Am – Mizrachi – Hapoel Hamizrachi, composed of thousands of rel J youth. Believes that through rel commitment & work on the land of Is, J youth can achieve fulfillment & self-realization. Through extensive edu programming, Bnei Akiva instills in its mems the idea of chalutzic aliya, & endeavors to bring to Is an immigration of Am youth who are rel, pioneering, idealistic, & committed to J; continues to bring J identity & pride to J young people. Sends garinim; forms garinim; shlichim, emissaries fr the world movement in Is, acts as advs & organizers. Prog includes: edu minyanim; outings; Shabbatons; weekends; special events; social activities; activities & experiences about J & Is; natl convention; kumsitzes; seminars; Purim carnival; holiday celebrations; visiting hosp & old-age homes; Yom HaShoa, Yom Yerushalayim, Yom Ha'atzmaoot activities; Walk for Is participation; participation in local rallies for Is & Soviet J; special interest groups in drama, music, choir, arts & crafts, scouting; 5 summer camps; natl seminar; sponsorship of a yearly work-study prog on a rel kibbutz; tours in Is; participation in other Is progs – sch & yeshivas, ulpans & volunteer progs; summer prog; leadership training prog. 50 branches in 15 cities in N Am. F in Feb of 1950 & originally called Hashomer Hadati. The movement's origins began in Poland in 1928. Pub Zraim; Akivon; Hamivasher; Meohalai Torah. Natl Dir: Danny Mayerfeld; Edu Dir: Alan Silverman; Edu Shaliach: Kadish Goldberg. **25 W 26th St, NYC NY 10010 (212) 889–5260.**

Bnos Agudath Israel. Div for girls within Natl Commis on Youth – Agudath Is of Am. To serve as a training ground for responsible leadership roles in the com. More than 25,000 youths led by 1,700 volunteer leaders benefit from activities. Sponsors weekly progs which prepare youth for a life dedicated to loyal J serv & responsible voluntarism. Summer camp – Camp Agudah in New York's Catskill Mountains accomodates large number of youngsters from poor homes – the materially impoverished as well as the spiritually deprived. For additional information, see – Agudath Israel of America, New York City, NY. **5 Beekman St, NYC NY 10038 (212) 964–1620.**

Brith Abraham. 136 E 39th St, NYC NY 10016 (212) 725–1211.

The Brotherhood Synagogue. Affiliated with United Syn of Am. To meet the needs of Am J. Rel edu; edu for the mentally retarded; com servs helping Black J, Russian immigrants, & Falasha J of Ethiopia. Over 800 mems. Est in 1954 by Rabbi Block & 23 mems. The Syn has pioneered in the field of rel edu for the mentally retarded. The Syn is located in a landmark bldg, the former Friends Meeting House, which has been renovated & restored. Rabbi Irving J. Block; Pres: Dr Gerald J. Friedman; Chr of Bd of Trustees: Prof Julius J. Marke. **28 Gramercy Park S, NYC NY 10003 674–5750.**

Bund Archives of the Jewish Labor Movement. Atran Ctr for J Culture. An ins of documentation & research. The bk & manuscript collection of the Archives is one of unique significance for the study of J pol & labor activities beginning in the late 19th century. The heart of the collection, comprising hundreds of linear feet of manuscript material & periodicals, was twice saved fr the Nazis during the 1930's – 1940's & brought to the US after WWII. The Bund Archives has continuously existed for over 80 yrs. Pub Bulletin of the Bund; Archives of the J Labor Movement. Dir: Dr Benjamin Nadel. **25 E 78th St, Rm 502, NYC NY 10021 (212) 535–0850.**

Business & Professional ORT. 817 Bdwy, NYC NY 10003 (212) 677–4400.

Camp Morasha. Chil summer camp at Lake Como PA sponsored by Met NY Commis on Torah Edu & the Rabbinic Alumni of RIETS. Runs summer camps; also runs Gesher Morasha at Kfar Batya, Is in cooperation with Torah Edu Dept of World Zionist Org. **2540 Amsterdam Ave, NYC NY 10033.**

Camp Moshava of Bnai Akiva of North America. Orthodox camp affiliated with Am Camping Assn, & Assn of J Sponsored Camps. To provide a full prog of recreational & cultural activities in a rel chalutzic atmosphere that emphasizes the importance of close & meaningful friendships. Full sports progs including baseball, basketball, tennis, soccer, volleyball, swimming, boating, canoeing, archery, riflery; camping; music; drama; nature; agriculture; scouting; arts & crafts; dancing; radio;

woodworking; hiking; nature study; chunuch; Rel Servs; roller skating; library. 350 mems grades 3–10. 80 employees. F 45 yrs ago. Facilities include glatt kosher kitchen, gym, basketball & tennis cts, baseball field, archery & riflery ranges, lake, radio station, indoor & outdoor syns, lounges, large dining hall, canteen, library, infirmary. Training of leaders of various youth movements. Dir: Sid Weg. **25 W 26th St, NYC NY 10010 (212) 683–4484.**

Camp Sussex, Inc. A free overnight summer camp. To insure a healthy & rewarding summer for the campers, embodying ideals of leadership, responsibility, & true friendship. The summer is divided into two three week sessions for chil 7–12 yrs of age, & one two week session for teenagers 13–15 yrs of age; prog includes swimming; boating, handball, volleyball, softball, tennis, basketball, arts & crafts, ceramics, dramatics, hiking, photography, cookouts, camping, olympics, hockey, gymnastics, Sabbath Servs, med servs, nutritious meals adhering to dietary laws, laundry servs. Over 800 chil a summer. The staff is made up of qualified individuals fr cols & univs across the country. F in 1923. Facilities include over 250 acres of greenery, a natural spring fed lake, a fully equipped infirmary with qualified med personnel, athletic fields & equipment, swimming pool, cabins accommodating up to nine campers & three staff mems. Many of the counselors are former campers who receive fin aid through its unique col scholarship prog. An alumni org consisting of former campers & staff mems has been formed. This group meets monthly & has been instrumental in fundraising as well as maintaining friendships & providing leadership. Pres: Elliot Lippin; Life Pres: Hon Benjamin Shalleck, Leonard Amsterdam; Exec VP Chr of the Bd: Howard Lippin; VP & Exec Sec: Cecile Patterson; VPs: Nat Fuchs, Jack Geizler, Helen Ludmerer, Daniel Cohen, Sharon Izzo, Jerry Patterson, Judy Saphir, Selma Gold, Murray Lederman, Mickey Brande, Evelyn Bernstein, Ruby Bernstein, Marion Grill, Leonard Jacoby, Edna Mayers, Candy Shalleck, Bob Silver; Hon Treas: Max Grill; Treas: Joseph Pollack; Social Sec: Yetta Fuchs; Sec: Roz Lederman; Chief Med Dir: Dr Richard Saphir; Hon Med Dir: Dr Harold Ratner; Exec Camp Dir: Dr Stuart Lisbe.**Exec off – 1140 Bdwy, NYC NY 10001 (212) 683–8528.**

Cantors Assembly – Jewish Theological Seminary of Am. An org of professional cantors affiliated with United Syn of Am. To be concerned with the traditions of J worship; to maintain the highest standard for Hazzanim; to promote the welfare of its mems; to enhance & enlarge J liturgical music. Has pub over 50 vols of liturgical music to serve the Hazzanim, chorus, cong & rel schs; provides musical texts, tapes & Hazzanim for rel servs in Ramah camps; maintains Placement Bureau for Hazzanim; gives scholarship aid; musical library in preparation. Organized in 1947. The Journal of Synagogue Music. Pres: Abraham Shapiro; VP: Ivan Perlman; Sec: Harry Weinberg; Treas: Saul Z. Hammerman; Exec VP: Samuel Rosenbaum. **150 Fifth Ave, NYC NY 10011 (212) 691–8020, 749–8000.**

The Center for Russian Jewry – Student Struggle for Soviet Jewry. Stages rallies & demonstrations to bring the plight of Soviet J to the public; conducts edu progs, Adopt a Russian Family Prog; sends Right to Identity J materials packets into the USSR; documents the Kremlin's mail & phone blockades; briefs tourists going to the USSR; creates specialty groups for particular refuseniks or prisoners in great need or in specialized professions; serves as Russian J experts to US Congress; also works for Rumanian J emigration; encourages progs for Russian J absorbtion in Is & Am. Est in 1964 by a group of young people who learned fr the Holocaust never to be silent again in the face of a threat to J survival. Prog Material; Handbook; Lists & Photo Bks of Refuseniks & Prisoners. Chr: Rabbi Shlomo Riskin; V Chr: Paul W. Freedman, Morey Schapira, Rabbi Charles Sheer, Rabbi Avraham Weiss; Treas: Paul W. Freedman; Sec: Martin Koenig, David Nussbaum; Natl Dir: Jacob Birnbaum; Natl Coord: Glenn Richter; Coords: Alan Alter, Stuart Apfel, Sheldon Benjamin, Zev Brenner, Larry Domnitch, Rachel Eisenberg, Israel Fridman, Akiva Garber, Phyllis Hymoff, Andy Kane, Steven Karp, Mark Levitt, David Makofsky, Jon Michaeli, Joel Michaels, Allan Miller, Warren Moskowitz, Ellen Pincus, Michael Sabin, Randy Schaal, Rose Segal, David Stahl, Ruth Wang, Sanford Zwickler. **210 W 91st St, NYC NY 10024 (212) 799–8900.**

Central Conference of American Rabbis. Professional rabbinic assn of Reform rabbis throughout the US, Canada & abroad. The Conf is one of three natl orgs within Reform J working closely with the Congregational Union, UAHC & the seminary HUC-JIR. To preserve & promote J; to encourage all efforts for the dissemination of its teachings in a liberal spirit; to advance the cause of J learning; to foster cooperation among rabbis; to serve the welfare of its mems. Maintains Rabbinical Pension Plan; relates the views & positions of its mems to the J & gen coms throughout the country; provides placement servs as a co-partner with UAHC & the Col Ins in the Joint Commis on Placement; pubs liturgical, homiletic & scholarly bks; maintains funds for the emergency or ongoing needs of its mems; acts as liaison between its mems & other natl J orgs;

sponsors annual convention. 1,200 rabbis serving about 700 congs. In addition to its org on a natl level, the Conf is divided into 11 regional assns of Reform rabbis. F in 1889 by Rabbi Isaac Mayer Wise. A uniform prayer bk for Reform congs was created in 1892. A second vol for the High Holidays was pub in 1894. Gates of Prayer; Gates of Repentance; Passover Haggadah; Shaarei Ha-Bayit; Shaarei Bina; Anim Zemirot: Songs & Hymns for Gates of Prayer; Tadrich Le-Kiddush Ha-Chayim; Shabbat Manual; Rabbi's Manual; Reform Judaism: A Historic Perspective; Contemporary Reform Jewish Thought; CCAR Yearbook; CCARJournal (pub quarterly). The Conf makes available to its mems the following documents: Suggestions for Procedure in Rabbinical-Congregational Relationships, Placement Guidelines, Negotiating a New Contract, Guidelines for Rabbinic Interviews, Code of Ethics for Rabbis, Guide to Synagogue Decorum, CCAR Constitution, Reform Judaism: A Centenary Perspective, Publications of the Central Conference. CCAR has held special progs on Family Life, Aging & Planning for Retirement, a four day seminar on Preserving Life & the Right to Die, & a two day seminar on Between Universalism & Particularism: Towards a Language of Survival. Pres: Herman E. Schaalman; VP: W. Gunther Plaut; Rec Sec: Jack Stern Jr; Fin Sec: Sylvan D. Schwartzman; Treas: Meyer Heller; Exec VP: Joseph B. Glaser; Adm Sec: Elliot L. Stevens; Exec VP Emeritus: Sidney L. Regner. **21 E 40th St, NYC NY 10016 (212) 684–4990.**

Central Sephardic Jewish Community of America. 8 W 70th St, NYC NY 10023 (212) 787–2850.

Central Synagogue. Affiliated with UAHC. 1200 mems. Rabbis: Sheldon Zimmerman, Lynne Landsberg, David J. Seligson; Cantor Richard Botton; Pres: John H. Ball; Edu: Arnold Bergman; Adm: Barry E. Kugel; Brotherhood Pres: Robert Gordon. **123 E 55th St, NYC NY 10022 (212) 838–5122.**

Central Synagogue, Friedman Library. For information on the Syn, see – Central Synagogue, New York City, NY. **123 E 55th St, NYC NY 10022 (212) 838–5122.**

Central Synagogue, Religious School. For information on the Syn, see – Central Synagogue, New York City, NY. **123 E 55th St, NYC NY 10022 (212) 838–5122.**

Central Yiddish Culture Organization. 25 E 78th St, NYC NY 10021 (212) 535–4320.

Chatham Jewish Center – Congregation Beth Sholom. Affiliated with United Syn of Am. Rabbi Irvin Brandwein: Pres: Min Fishman; Sec: Gail Burbaum. **217 Park Row, NYC NY 10038 (212) 233–0428.**

Chevra Bechurim B'nai Menashe Ahauas Achim. 225 E Bdwy, NYC NY 10007 (212) 349–0089.

Civic Center Synagogue. 49 White St, NYC NY 10013 (212) 966–7141.

Commission on Social Action of Reform Judaism. Affiliate of parent body of Reform Judaism. To translate principles of Judaism into action in our coms, the nation & the world. Servs include edu progs, research progs, preparation of literature. Approx 80 mems; 13 regional groups; approx 500 local groups. 4 employees; several volunteers. F 1953. Pub Briefings (irregular). Dir: Albert Vorspan; Assoc Dir: Rabbi David Saperstein; Chr: Alexander Ross; V Chrs: Constance Kreshtool, Rabbi Charles Kroloff. **838 Fifth Ave, NYC NY 10021 (212) 249–0100.**

Commission on Status of Jewish War Orphans in Europe – American Section. 47 Beekman St, NYC NY 10038 (212) BA7–7800.

Committee for the Implementation of the Standardized Yiddish Orthography. Implementation of standardized Yiddish orthography in all writing & in all printed bks, periodicals & other publications. F 1951. Chr: Dr Mordkhe Schaechter; Sec: Leybl Kahn. **Philosophy hall, Columbia Univ, Rm 406, NYC NY 10027.**

Community Synagogue Center. 325 E 6th St, NYC NY 10003 (212) 473–3665.

The Conference of Jewish Communal Service. Serves as the umbrella org for eight major professional groups. To improve the quality & raise the level of professional servs to the Am J com as their contribution to enriching & perpetuating J life. Serves as the broadly based professional forum for all philosophies which have significance & relevance to the field of J communal servs; provides for natl & local exchange of information, experience & interpretation through natl pub of a journal, special reports & studies, annual confs & through local J communal professional forums & local professional enrichment study courses; involves its mems in a continuing collective effort to identify & anticipate needs for J communal servs, & stimulates the creation of progs to meet those needs; provides opportunities for increased knowledge of J hist, tradition & values, & encourages deeper personal, as well as professional, involvement in J life;

influences the nature & content of edu & training for J communal servs; helps give clearer definition to careers in the field through contact with schs, seminars & other ins; creates opportunities for mems to enjoy health & welfare benefits. 3,100 individual professionals; 320 local & natl J communal servs agy & orgs. F in 1899 as the Natl Conf of J Charities. The Conf is the only center for all who have a new professional experience to test, a new idea to propose, or wish to question or reaffirm an old concept. Journal of Jewish Communal Service. For information on the Intl Org, see – International Conference of Jewish Communal Service, New York City, NY. Pres: Daniel Mann; VPs: Saul Hofstein, Ferne Katheman, Belle Likover, Ethel Taft; Sec & Asst Sec: Sid L. Brail, Joseph L. Weinberg; Treas & Asst Treas: Herbert Shore, Alan D. Bennett; Exec Dir: Joel Ollander. **15 E 26th St, NYC NY 10010 (212) 683–8056.**

Conference of Presidents of Major American Jewish Organizations. 515 Park Ave, NYC NY 10022 (212) 752–1616.

Conference on Jewish Material Claims Against Germany, Inc. 15 E 26th St, NYC NY 10010 (212) 679–4074.

Conference on Jewish Social Studies. 250 W 57th St, Rm 904, NYC NY 10019 (212) 247–4718.

Congregation Ansche Chesed. 251 W 100th St, NYC NY 10025 (212) 864–6637.

Congregation B'nai Israel. 335 E 77th St, NYC NY 10021 (212) 570–6650.

Congregation B'nai Israel Chaim. 353 W 84th St, NYC NY 10024 (212) 874–0644.

Congregation B'nai Jeshurun. 270 W 89th St, NYC NY 10024 (212) 787–7600.

Congregation Beth Hamedrash of Inwood. 1781 Riverside Dr, NYC NY 10035 (212) 567–9776.

Congregation Beth Hamedrosh Hagodol. 60 Norfolk St, NYC NY 10002 (212) 647–3330.

Congregation Beth Hamedrosh Hagodol of Washington Heights, Inc. 610 W 175th St, NYC NY 10033 (212) 927–6000.

Congregation Beth Hillel & Beth Israel, Inc. To promote J among its mems, to maintain a prog of ongoing edu in J. Rel Servs; adult & youth edu; chevra kadisha; Sisterhood; cultural prog. 600 mems. The origins of Cong Beth Hillel began in 1939 when Samson Schmidt, a former resident of Munich, & a friend of the Chief-Rabbi of the liberal J com of Munich, initiated discussions with other former Munich J in NYC on organizing a new cong. The new cong started with the High Holy Day Servs of 1940, which were held in a rented hall. The hall was filled close to the seating capacity of 800, & three Torah scrolls fr Germany were dedicated. Rel orientation, syn servs, melodies & rituals were those of S German, conservative J. Sermons were given in German. Social progs were offered to mems; a Heb sch was started with 20 chil; a Sisterhood was organized & a bulletin was pub. In the early 1940's a youth group & Chevra Kadisha were started. The first burial plots were purchased in Cedar Park Cemetery. Over the yrs, the Cong membership grew. Membership increased fr about 200 families in 1940 to 750 in 1948. In 1943, the bulletin was enlarged & English appeared in its pages. A two story bldg was purchased in 1946. In 1947 the upper floor became available for the Heb Sch & weekday servs. During 1948 the sanctuary was constructed. The syn was dedicated on Sept 26, 1948. A Shabbat Youth Serv was initiated in 1949. In 1950 a Class Lernen was begun. A Young People's League was started in 1950 & the first com Seder took place in 1951. Concerts, bazaars, holiday festivities, dinner dances, youth group & Heb Sch presentations & progs were sponsored annually. Guest sermons & lectures were given by visiting rabbis & scholars. The Heb Sch consisted of six grades, post grad courses & a yearly enrollment of 80 to 130 stu. The Parent Assn gave strong support to the sch. The bulletin increased in size & English became the predominant language. German alternated with English sermons. In 1957 the first annual Kristallnacht Memorial Serv was held. In 1961 the Family Club was started. Membership started declining fr 730 families in 1962 to 450 in 1979. Enrollment in the Heb Sch in 1960 was about 120; by 1970 the Sch, Youth Servs & Parent Assn ceased to exist. The Cong adapted to the changing conditions by intensifying older progs & moving into new areas. The Cong also increased their role in com activities. In 1969 major reconstruction of access to the lower social hall was carried out. Cong Beth Is of Washington Heights was started by Cantor Jack Schartenberg when he arranged for & led High Holidays Servs in Oct of 1948. Heartened by the popularity of the Holiday Servs, many of the worshipers expressed the desire to est a permanent cong. On Nov 30th, with an initial membership of 66 people, the Cong was f. A place to hold servs was rented. On Jan 29, 1949 the dedication took place & by that time membership had already doubled.

Membership rose to 600 mems. Beth Is gave its mems the opportunity to practice in a Kehillah life such as experienced & practiced in the European congs of old. A Heb Sch was f which grew fr 7 stu to an enrollment of 150. Cemetery grounds were purchased. A Chevra Kadisha, Sisterhood & Parents Assn were est. To strengthen the Cong, regular shiurim & study groups were maintained, sermons & lectures were delivered, a library of J literature & of film-strips was est, a newsletter was pub, & for youth, a Sun Morning Breakfast Club, recreation evenings, Oneg Shabbos, youth groups & an annual Youth Shabbos were organized. In Jan 1955 the Syn on 181st St was dedicated. A nation wide trend of city decline & moving to the suburbs affected the membership of the Cong. Membership started to decline & in Jan of 1979 Cong Beth Hillel & Beth Is joined together for weekday servs. Subsequently, the congs merged. Pub Habayit (4 times a year); Rabbi News Letter. Rabbi Shlomo Kahn; Pres: Oscar Wortsman. **571 W 182nd St, NYC NY 10033 (212) 568–3933.**

Congregation Beth Israel. 347 W 34th St, NYC NY 10001 (212) 297–0016.

Congregation Beth Simchat Torah. GPO Box 127O, NYC NY 10001 (212) 929–9488.

Congregation Beth Simchat Torah, Eugene Berman Memorial Library. GPO Box 127O, NYC NY 10001 (212) 929–9488.

Congregation Darech Amuno. 53 Chase Manhatten Plaza, NYC NY 10005 (212) 242–6425.

Congregation Emanu-El of the City of New York. Reform Cong affiliated with the UAHC. Daily Rel Servs (special Chil Servs are held on the High Holidays); Family Worship Servs (each Fri evening the Sabbath Servs are broadcast on the radio); Rel Sch for stu fr the ages 5 to 15; prog of lectures, classes & discussions; guest speakers; Nursery Sch; Parents Org; The Stettenheim Library; The Lehman Mus; Women's Auxiliary; Men's Club; Temple Soc (a group for single adults in their middle yrs); Jr Soc; Collegiate Soc; Emanu-El League (social, intellectual & rel progs for young single adult mems of the Cong); Choir; 2 cemeteries maintained. 3,158 families. F in 1845. Consolidated with Temple Beth El in 1927. The present structure was dedicated in 1930. A six story Rel Sch bldg was completed in 1964. Temple Bulletin; The Ark – the stu yearbook. Facilities include an auditorium seating 2,500 people, a chapel seating 350 people, a memorial hall seating 1,500 people, a kitchen, banquet facilities; an eight story Com House containing an assembly hall seating 450, Temple offs, rabbis study, gen library, 10 classrooms, minor assembly halls & a meeting rm; the Rel Sch Bldg containing 33 classrooms, auditorium seating 1,000, mus, & a recreation rm accommodating 630 persons. Rabbi Dr Ronald B. Sobel; Assc Rabbi David M. Posner; Asst Rabbi Richard S. Chapin; Rabbi Emeritus Dr Nathan A. Perilman; Cantor Howard Nevison; Pres: Edwin A. Malloy; Hon Pres: Alfred R. Bachrach, Alvin E. Coleman, Maxwell M. Rabb; VPs: John B. Oakes, Milton Pollack, Mervin H. Riseman, Mrs Frederick H. Theodore; Hon VPs: A. Alan Lane, Benjamin Lazrus, Ira A. Schur; Treas: Walter S. Mack; Sec: Herbert C. Bernard; Trustees: Robert A. Bernhard, Alfred Eisenpreis, Daisy J. Elkan, Leonard H. Goldenson, Mortimor S. Gordon, John L. Loeb, David E. Marrus, Robert B. Menschel, Hon Robert M. Morgenthau, Mrs Donald E. Newhouse, Morton Pepper, Robert Rubinger, Oscar S. Straus II; Adm VP: Henry Fruhauf; Asst Adm: Hilary M. Kohen; Funeral Dir: Charles S. Salomon. **1 E 65th St, NYC NY 10021 (212) 744–1400.**

Congregation Emes Wozedek Inc. 560 W 166th St, NYC NY 10032 (212) 928–9785.

Congregation Emunath Israel. 236 W 23rd St, NYC NY 10111 (212) 292–9882.

Congregation Erste Lutowiska Machzika Hadas. 262 Delancey St, NYC NY 10002 (212) 982–0007.

Congregation Habonim. Affiliated with UAHC. 680 mems. Rabbi Bernard N. Cohn; Cantor Erwin Hirsch; Pres: Ralph Stein; Adm: Lotte Marshall; Sisterhood Pres: Marion Lust; Brotherhood Pres: Rudolph Mariam. **44 W 66th St, NYC NY 10023 (212) 787–5347.**

Congregation K'hal Adath Jeshurun. 90 Benett Ave, NYC NY 10033 (212) 923–8984.

Congregation Kehilath Jeshurun. Orthodox Cong. Rel; cultural; edu. 625 families. Est in 1881 & moved to its present location in 1901. The Cong f the Ramaz Sch, a yeshiva for boys & girls. Rabbi Haskel Lookstein; Cantor Avrum Davis; Ritual Dir: Israel D. Rosenberg; Exec Dir: Robert J. Leifert; Hon Pres: Harry W. Baumgarten, Max J. Etra, Nathan Saltzman; Pres: Samuel M. Eisenstat; VP: Joseph Lorch; Treas: Irwin B. Robins; Sec: Benjamin Brown; Bd of Trustees: Harry W. Baumgarten, Milton Berkowitz, Max J. Etra, A. Phillip Goldsmith, Nathan Goldsmith, Steven R. Gross, Harry Green, Dr William F. Herzig, Norman Jaspan, William G. Lebowitz,

Edward Low, Benjamin Mandelker, Joseph H. Moss, Myron Poloner, Hon George Postel, Henry M. Rem, E. David Rosen, Joseph Roth, Nathan Salzman, Frederick Schwartzberg, Irwin Shapiro, Romie Shapiro, Elgin Shulsky, Leon Sigall, Arthur C. Silverman, Samuel Silverstien, Samuel Singer, Dr Meyer Texon, Mrs Jess Ward; Assc Trustees: Frederic H. Baumgarten, Mrs A. Milton Brown, Norman Bulow, Tova Bulow, Charles Censor, Joshua S. Deutsch, Stanley Gurewitsch, Dr Norman Javitt, Dr Bernard Kabakow, Alfred N. Kahn, Stephen J. Kule, David H. Levy, Mrs Meyer Texon, Raymond Ward; Hon Trustees: Hyman I. Bucher, Mrs Joseph H. Lookstein, Samuel A. Marcus. **125 E 85th St, NYC NY 10028 (212) HA7–1000.**

Congregation Machzikei Torah. 851 W 181th St, NYC NY 10033 (212) 927–6740.

Congregation Morya. 2228 Bdwy, NYCNY 10024 (212) 729–6909.

Congregation Nodah Bi Yehuda, Inc. Orthodox Cong. Daily Rel Servs; Mishna class; Gemarra class. F in 1939 by refugees fr Nazi Germany. The Cong owns a cemetery. Rabbi Simon Romm; Pres: Isadore Gettinger; VPs: Zoltan Lieberman, Sol Frommer, Phillip Feldheim; Gaboim: Benjamin Gatterer, Yakob Feingold; Treas: David Shedlo; Sec: J. Suss; Chr of the Bd: Moritz Weissman. **392 Ft Washington Ave, NYC NY 10033.**

Congregation Ohab Zedek. Orthodox Cong. To make the stand of uncompromising Orthodoxy more popular & more palatable to modern soc. Daily Rel Servs; Shiurim; lectures; breakfasts; Adult Edu; charity org; social welfare group; voluntary Chevra Kadisha; Beginners Minyan; Beginners Shiurim; hosp visitors group. F in 1874 on the lower E Side. The Syn was originally composed of J of Hungarian origin but eventually came to include J fr all parts of Europe. In 1912 the Cong moved to Harlem, & in 1926 to its present site after merging with Cong Pinchas Eliyahu. An additional sch bldg was constructed in 1939. A full hist & archives of the Cong is maintained as part of the Natl Orthodox Archives. Rabbi Avrohom Marmorstein. **118 W 95th St, NYC NY 10024.**

Congregation Ohav Shalom. 270 W 84th St, NYC NY 10024 (212) 877–5850.

Congregation Ohave Sholaum. 4624 Bdwy, NYC NY 10040 (212) 567–0900.

Congregation Orach Chaim. 1459 Lexington Ave, NYC NY 10028 (212) 722–6566.

Congregation Ramath Orah. 550 W 110th St, NYC NY 10025 (212) 222–2470.

Congregation Rodeph Sholom. 7 W 83rd St, NYC NY 10024 (212) 362–8800.

Congregation Shaare Hatikvah Ahavath Torah v'Tikvoh Chadoshoh, Inc. 711 W 179th St, NYC NY 10033 (212) 927–2720.

Congregation Shaare Zedek. Affiliated with United Syn of Am. Rabbi Edward M. Gershfield; Cantor David Levine; Pres: Fred L. Botterman; Exec Dir: Alexander C. Elishewitz. **212 W 93rd St, NYC NY 10025 (212) 874–7005.**

Congregation Shearith Israel. 8 W 70th St, NYC NY 10023 (212) 873–0300.

Congregation Shearith Israel Library. 8 W 70th St, NYC NY 10023 (212) 873–0300.

Congregation Smuel Josef Vchayah. 587–B Fort Washington Ave, NYC NY 10033 (212) 927–9012.

Congregation Talmud Torah Adereth El. 135 E 29th St, NYC NY 10016 (212) 685–0241.

Congregation Zichron Ephraim. 163 E 67th St, NYC NY 10021 (212) 737–6900.

Congregation Zichron Moshe. 342 E 20th St, NYC NY 10003 (212) 475–9330.

Congress for Jewish Culture. 25 E 78th St, NYC NY 10021 (212) 879–2232.

Conservative Synagogue of Fifth Avenue. Affiliated with United Syn of Am. Rabbi Richard Margolis; Cantor Robert L. Cohen; Pres: I. E. Edelstein. **11 E 11th St, NYC NY 10003 (212) 929–6954.**

Consulate General of Israel. 800 Second Ave, NYC NY 10017 (212) 697–5500, 5169.

Consultative Council of Jewish Organizations. 61 Bdwy, NYC NY 10006 (212) 425–5170.

Council for Jewish Education. J council affiliated with Am Assc for J Edu, & The Conf of Communal Servs. To improve & strengthen the quality of J life in Am by advancing J edu. Arranges natl & regional confs; participates in communal activities for the cause of J edu; conducts edu projs;

represents the J edu profession in natl & intl bodies. Est in 1926. Pub Jewish Education; Sheviley Hahinuch. Pres: Rabbi Matthew Clark; VPs: Fradle Freidenreich, Dr Leon Spotts, Elliot S. Schwartz, Rabbi Irwin E. Witty; Sec: Bernard Ducoff; Treas: Dr Solomon Goldman; Exec Sec: Dr Philip Jaffe; Comptroller: Jack M. Horden. **114 Fifth Ave, NYC NY 10011 (212) 675–5656.**

Council of Jewish Federations, Inc. Assn of 200 Feds, Welfare Funds & Com Councils which serve nearly 800 coms & embrace over 95% of the J population of the US & Canada. To strengthen the work & the impact of J Feds through leadership in developing progs to meet the changing needs in the J com; through the exchange of successful experiences to assure the most effective com servs; through est guidelines for fundraising & operation; through joint natl planning & action on common purposes dealing with local, regional, natl, & intl needs. Direct consultation in the area of finance & adm; staff visits, consultation, & natl study reports aimed at identifying & meeting communal servs needs for chil, youth, families, & aged; assistance to Feds in establishing & strengthening Endowment Funds; recruitment, in-serv training & placement of qualified personnel for positions in Fed; adm of the Federal matching grant prog for Soviet immigrants; joint day-long CJF-UJA PR Ins which bring new ideas & techniques to coms; development of reports on innovative approac toward leadership dev; leadership seminars aimed at strengthening the women's role in all aspects of the com; staff, budget research & reporting servs to the Large City Budgeting Conf which includes 29 of the largest Feds working together to analyze the progs & finances of 32 natl & overseas agy, & dev recommendations on funding them; objective analyses of the prog, cost & income of the 60 major natl & overseas beneficiary agy to which coms allocate funds; an interchange with J coms abroad in planning, financing & com org; orientation to Fed leadership on the structure of CJF & the servs available to coms; consultation servs in specific functional areas of Fed concern; data & information compilation & analysis; natl guidelines dev by using local experiences as a primary resource; information exchange & edu through workshops, Bd retreats & inter-Fed consultation; assistance to lay & professional leadership in identifying & creating new resources; in intl affairs relative to Is & the Middle E, coordination of central planning strategy & progs of the natl com relations, & local com relations agy; help to the J Agy in strengthening its fiscal planning & budget procedures, initiate new & coordinating arrangements in the activities of the Agy, & undertake changes in administrative procedures, especially regarding immigration & absorption; maintenance of interchanges with J coms abroad to bring to them Am experience in com org, planning, financing & servs. In 1932 a small group of leaders of 29 local J Feds met to form a natl instrument called the Council of J Feds. A basic task of the Council was to help unorganized coms which wanted Feds to est them. Within a few yrs, that mission was accomplished. The Council's membership rose to 200. In 1936 the Fed leaders committed themselves to help the German J to leave Germany. Whem WWII ended, the Fed immediately started to rebuild the shattered coms for those who wanted to remain in Europe, & to resettle the others. In order to help do this as effectively as possible, CJF set up an Ins on Overseas Studies. It brought in experts fr govt & univs to make independent appraisals of needs, current policies & servs, especially in Is, & to advise on how Am J aid could be used for greatest results. In 1944 the CJF organized the Natl J Com Relations Adv Council. CJF leaders took part in the economic conf in Jerusalem in 1950 which set the future framework of financial aid to Is. It included the est of Is Bonds. Around 1960 CJF est the Natl Foun for J Culture & the Natl Council of Cultural Agy. In 1966 CJF helped to merge the J Agy in the US with the United Is Appeal. CJF set up a special cttee & staff in 1967 to help Feds of every size to est endowment funds. In 1969 CJF had a main role in proposing designing & staffing the Conf on Human Needs. In 1970 CJF est a fund to finance innovative campus based projs. In 1971 CJF joined with others to help reorganize the Natl Conf on Soviet J. In 1973, after the flood in Wilkes-Barre & the surrounding areas, CJF sent in leaders & staff to assess the needs, to help the J com obtain govt & gen aid, to coord the assistance of other natl J bodies. After the Yom Kippur War, CJF mobilized a special fund to make possible public information progs. The CJF est the Washington Action Off in 1976. Around 1980 CJF embarked on a prog to assist Feds in developing com support systems to strengthen the J family. CJF has given natl leadership in planning, providing guidelines & aiding in developing specific servs such as apts for the elderly. The major link between CJF & its mem Feds is a yr round delegate system comprised of about 700 local leaders, elected annually by their Feds, who determine the Council's policies, progs & finances, & help to implement them. Pres: Martin E. Citrin; VPs: Joe Ain, Madlyn Barnett, Irwin H. Goldenberg, Harry A. Levy, Harry R. Mancher, Albert B. Ratner, Esther Leah Ritz, Fred Sichel, I. Jerome Stern, Peggy Tishman; Sec: Perry Sloane; Treas: Charles H. Goodman; Exec VP: Carmi Schwartz; Assc Exec VPs: Darrell D. Friedman, Charles Zibbell. **575 Lexington Ave, NYC NY 10022 (212) 751–1311.**

Council of Jewish Organizations in Civil Service, Inc. 45 E 33rd St, NYC NY 10016 (212) 689–2015.

Council of Young Israel Rabbis. 3 W 16th St, NYC NY 10011 (212) 929–1525.

Dor Hemshech, United States. 515 Park Ave, NYC NY 10022 (212) 752–0600.

Dror Young Zionist Organization. 215 Park Ave S, NYC NY 10003 (212) 777–9388.

East 55th Street Conservative Synagogue. Affiliated with United Syn of Am. Rabbi Reuven Siegel; Cantor Stephen Merkel; Pres: Cecil B. Porcelain. **308 E 55th St, NYC NY 10022 (212) 752–1200.**

East End Temple. Affiliated with UAHC. 165 mems. Rabbi Bruce K. Cole; Cantor Robert Spiro; Edu: Bruce K. Cole; Sisterhood Pres: Elizabeth Gross; Brotherhood Pres: Murray Bittman. **398 Second Ave, NYC NY 10010 (212) 254–8518.**

East Side Torah Center. Center of Slutzker Shul, Yeshivah Konvit Yehuda Wolf Institute, Jacob David School. Orthodox Syn & com ctr affiliated with Union of Orthodox J Cong, Bd of Jewish Ed, Fed of J Torah Umesorah. Rel, edu, recreational, communal & fraternal servs (fr 2 to 10 yrs old); the Hilda Weinberg Sisterhood; Men's Club; the Rabbanit Miriam Nulman Adult Ins of J Studies; the Chevra Shaas – Talmud Society; the Chevra Mishnayos; the Chevra Tehillim/Psalms of David; the J Code Law Society; the Slutzker Men & Women's Societies; Presch; Day Sch; HS; Afternoon Sch; library containing 5,000 vols (Heb, Judaica). 2500 mems; 600 families; 100 individuals; 240 stu. 20 employees; 36 volunteers. F 1890. Pub Monthly Letter, Yearbook. Facilities include syn, chapel, classrms, social halls, study halls, libraries, kitchen, dining hall, gift shop. Rabbi Dr Shlomo Nulman; Pres: Saul Mark; VPs: Sam Eis, Jack Lebewohl, Joseph Mittman, Eugene Singer; Sec: Melvin Schurberg; Corsp Sec: George Axelrod; Treas: Herbert Zolty; Bd of Dirs Chr: Joel J. Silver. **313 Henry St, NYC NY 10002 (212) 473–1000.**

East Side Torah Center Library. Library contains 5,000 vols (Heb, Judaica). For information on the Ctr, see – East Side Torah Center, NYC, NY. **313 Henry St, NYC NY 10002 (212) 473–1000.**

Economic Minister, Government of Israel. 350 Fifth Ave, NYC NY 10118 (212) 560–0630.

The Educational Alliance, Inc. Provider of social servs. Affiliated with Fed of J Philanthropies. Social & edu activities; welfare servs; youth servs; physical edu; rel sch; servs for pre-delinquent youth, drug & alcoholic abusing youth & young adults, mentally retarded & disabled youth & young adults; art sch; photography ins; craft workshops; lectures & discussion series. 10,000 mems of all ages. Est in 1889 by German J philanthropists to aid E European J immigrants. It provided them with many social servs including summer camp facilities. The Edu Alliance, financed by a federal govt loan, built The David Podell House, a ten story apt house for the elderly. This proj provides social servs, edu, & recreational facilities for the elderly. The Edu Alliance has set up special progs for the Orthodox J com & for the Israelis living in NYC. Pres: James J. Ross; VPs: Martha V. Bartos, Arnold Chase, Mrs J. Harold Garfunkel, Lawrence Greenfield, Benjamin Grund, Leonard J. Hankin, Stanley Herzman, Ralph Lippman, Ernest Rubenstein, Henry N. Sachs, Wilbert Tatum; Treas: Jerome E. Kranz; Asst Treas: Eugene Schorr; Sec: Linda Lynn; Asst Sec: Mrs Gerald Walpin; Trustees: Dr Katherine Behrens, Charles Benenson, Miriam Birnbaum, Walter J. Brownstone, Mrs Israel Cummings, Elliot H. Fixler, George Freedman, Martin J. Freund, Howard Ganek, Randolph Guggenheimer Jr, Dr Jerry Hochbaum, Murray L. Jacobs, Richard Karp, Charles Kleiman, Amos Landman, Stanley H. Levy, Maurice Magid, Deborah W. Meier, Joseph S. Oettinger, Samuel S. Perelson, Robert Pilpel, Mrs Norman Pleshette, Jonathan Rose, Charles I. Rostov, Howard Schneider, Michael Sher, Sheldon Silver, Bruce Slovin, Carl M. Spero, William Stern, Marcia Warner, Benjamin Weiss; Hon Trustees: Mrs Randolph Guggenheimer, Stanley R. Jacobs, Donald B. Strauss, Frank A. Weil, Robert Wolf; Exec Dir: Robert Meltzer; Asst Exec Dir: Daniel Morris. **197 E Bdwy, NYC NY 10002 (212) 475–6200.**

Emet – Rabbi Herzog World Academy. Publishing Talmudic Encyclopedia & other bks of J interest. **122 W 76th St, NYCNY 10023 (212) 435–0115.**

Emunah Women of America. 370 Seventh Ave, NYC NY 10001 (212) 564–9045.

Federated Council of Beth Jacob Schools. 142 Broome St, NYC NY 10002 (212) 473–4500.

Federated Council of Israel Institutions, Inc. Central fundraising org. Handles & executes estates, wills & bequests for traditional ins in Is; acts as clearing house for information on budget, size, functions, traditional edu, welfare & philanthropic ins in Is; works closely with the Is Govt & overseas dept of the Council of J Fed & Welfare Funds, NY. Est in 1940. Pres: David L. Meckler; VPs: Rabbi Dr J. B. Soloveitchik, Rabbi Dr Solomon Reichman, Rabbi Dr Manuel Laderman; Treas: Rabbi Z. Shapiro; Dev Consultant: Rabbi Julius Novack. **15 Beekman St, NYC NY 10038 (212) 227–3152.**

Federation Employment & Guidance Service. Vocational serv agy. Guidance; psychological testing; job placement; day developmental & day training; residences; vocational rehabilitation; skills training & supportive servs; library. Employment is found for the handicapped, retarded, disadvantaged, new immigrant & drug abuser. Staff of 600. Est in 1934. Pres: Judge Caroline K. Simon; VPs: Martin I. Bresler, Dr Irving M. Clyne, William S. Friedman, Mrs Milton N. Scofield, James S. Tisch; Chr of the Bd: Richard M. Bleier; Sec: Sarah Sussman; Asst Sec: Robert M. Warner; Treas: Mrs Frederick Wm. Greenfield; Asst Treas: Burton M. Strauss; Bd of Dirs: William L. Bernhard, Michael I. Bernstein, Helen J.R. Clyman, Fenimore Fisher, Bernie Hutner, Fred Landau, Mrs Arthur Levitt, Alice Rush Levy, Howard M. Leibman, Walter A. Miller, Joseph Oettinger, Stuart Oltchick, Michael Saphier, Anthony M. Schulte, Mrs Bernard Spitzer, Joseph Stein Jr, Philip Wagner; Hon Dir: Robert Rau; Exec Dir: Alfred P. Miller; Deputy Assc Exec Dirs: Gail Magaliff, Bernice Sherman; Asst Exec Dirs: Benjamin Greenblatt, Rae Linefsky, Gladys Siff. **114 Fifth Ave, NYC NY 10011 (212) 741–7110.**

Federation of Jewish Philanthropies of New York. Mem of CJF. Includes Greater NY, Westchester, Nassau & Suffolk Counties. Organized 1917. Pres: Mrs Laurence A. Tisch; Exec VP: William Kahn. **130 E 59th St, NYC NY 10022 (212) 980–1000.**

Federation of Jewish Women's Organizations. 55 W 42nd St, NYC NY 10036 (212) 736–0240.

Ferkauf Graduate School – Yeshiva University. Sch of professional psych which offers MA in gen psych, Doctor of Psych progs in clin & sch psych, PhD progs in clinical, dev-experimental, sch, social, health & bilingual edu-dev psych. Includes: Chil Ctr which helps chil with learning & sch-related problems; Yeshiva Univ Ctr for Psych & Psychoedu Servs offering psychological counseling, diagnostic evaluation, & psychotherapy. F in 1957. For information on the Univ, see – Yeshiva University, New York City, NY. **Brookdale Ctr, 55 Fifth Ave, NYC NY 10003.**

Fifth Avenue Synagogue. Orthodox Cong. To adhere to all the requirements of J law & tradition; to present J through its worship & classes with beauty, dignity & meaning. Rel Servs; Mishnah & Halacha classes; Rel Sch; youth activities; Young People's Group for singles & couples; Adult Edu Prog with classes in Torah, Talmud & various discussion groups; Men's Club; Women's Club; social events such as breakfasts, luncheons & lectures. 300 families. Est in 1958, its bldg was built before 1960. The Syn is one of the leading Orthodox congs in the US. Rabbi Dr Nisson E. Shulman; Cantor Joseph Malovany; Ritual Dir: David Finkelstein; Chr: Henry Hirsch; Pres: Ira Leon Rennert; Hon Pres: Hermann Merkin, Victor Barnett, Adolph A. Krejtman; VPs: S. Daniel Abraham, Leon Jolson, Rabbi Solomon Trau; Asst to the Pres: Harry Boren; Treas: David Hirsch; Sec: Josef B. Cohen; Pres Women's Club: Mrs Jerry S. Needleman; Pres Men's Club: Hyman Bravin. **5 E 62nd St, NYC NY 10021 (212) TE8–2122, 3113.**

First Roumanian American Congregation. 89 Rivington St, NYC NY 10002 (212) 673–2835.

Fort Tryon Jewish Centre. 524 Fort Washington Ave, NYC NY 10013 (212) 795–1391.

The Foundation for the Advancement of Sephardic Studies & Culture, Inc. To encourage the academic study of the hist & culture of the Sephardim, & to strengthen the identity of youth of Spanish-J origin; the Foun supports acknowledgements of the Sephardic contribution to Western hist & culture, in order that the experience of the Sephardim be more well known & better understood, so its traditions & rel will thrive. F in 1962 as an Ad Hoc Cttee for the Advancement of Sephardic Studies & Culture; f by Louis Levy & David Barocus with the inspiration & suggestions of Prof Mair Benardette. Several bks & pubs on the hist, culture & rel of the Sephardim. Pres: Louis Levy; Sec: Rev Dr Marc Angel; Assc Dir: Dr J. de H. Halio y Torres. **599–601 Bdwy, NYC NY 10012.**

Foundation for the Jewish National Fund. 42 E 69th St, NYC NY 10021.

The Free Sons of Israel. J natl fraternal order in the US. To assist its mems in translating into practice the J spiritual heritage & freedom; to help J to freedom both in the US & abroad; to advance the principles of human equality on a world wide basis; to join experience in human understanding with the advances in social sci & communications, & the influence of laws to achieve these ends; to protect

J fr oppression. Hosp, med & surgical benefits; scholarships for mems & their wives & chil; blood bank for the use of all mems & their families; low cost life insurance for mems, their wives & their chil; money saving med & dental specialist plans; aid in placing sr citizen mems in homes; aid in placing ailing mems of their families in convalescent homes; Chanukah & Purim festivals; teenage sports & dances for chil; projs & progs for the betterment of youth; various athletic activities; participation in lodge & inter lodge athletic tournaments; use of gymnasium facilities; active participation in charities through the Foun Fund of the Free Sons of Is; social action in the pursuit of freedom for the individual; burial benefits for mems & their families; cultural activities; ladies auxiliaries; Free Sons Hebrew Awards; Foun Fund; distribution of toys to handicapped chil; active participation with charitable orgs & affiliation with homes for sr citizens, convalescent homes, summer camps for sr citizens, & summer camps for needy chil; travel servs. The Free Sons of Is is divided into two separately functioning divs, the Fraternal Div & the Insurance Fund. It is comprised of some 46 subordinate lodges with a membership of about 10,000 men & women. F in 1849 by a small group of J who felt the need of a friendly home in Am. The Free Sons of Is is the oldest natl J fraternal order in the US. Free Sons Reporter which disseminates information on the latest happenings in the lodges. **150 Fifth Ave, NYC NY 10011 (212) 260–4222.**

Free Synagogue. 30 W 68th St, NYC NY 10023 (212) 877–4050.

Friends of Bellevue Hospital Synagogue. First Ave & 27th St, NYC NY 10016 (212) 685–1376.

Fund for Higher Education. 1500 Bdwy, Suite 1900, NYC NY 10036 (212) 354–4660.

Fur Center Synagogue. 228 W 29th St, NYC NY 10001 (212) 560–9236.

Garin Yardin – Young Kibbutz Movement. 215 Park Ave S #1806, NYC NY 10003 (212) 777–9388.

Garment Center Congregation. 205 W 40th St, NYC NY 10018 (212) 391–6966.

Government of Israel Investment Authority. Dev of trade relations between US & Is. For additional information, see – Government of Israel Trade Center, New York City, NY. **350 Fifth Ave, NYC NY 10118 (212) 560–0610.**

Government of Israel Trade Center. Dev of trade relations between US & Is. In cooperation with American-Israel Chamber of Commerce & Industry, pub Israel Quality – a quarterly economic newsletter giving information on trade dev, new products, results of product research, announcements concerning awards in science & industry, information on new patents granted, gen news of the industry, business opportunities with Is (imports, exports, investments, joint ventures, know-how). **350 Fifth Ave, NYC NY 10118 (212) 560–0660.**

The Greater New York Conference on Soviet Jewry. Coordinating body of Soviet J activities for J org & com groups throughout the NY met area. The work of the org is made possible through the financial support of the UJA of Greater NY & the Fed of J Philanthropies. The repatriation to Is of those Soviet J who wish to leave the Soviet Union, & the devotion to one cause – the rights & well being of nearly 3 million Soviet J men & women. Cttee of Conscience: in the forefront of the org's efforts to free Soviet prisoners of conscience; NY Legislators Coalition for Soviet J: lends essential support to publicizing the plight of the refuseniks & obtaining their rights to emigrate; Adopt-a-Prisoner: sends petitions, letters & telegrams to US & Soviet officials, & to mems of Congress: Action Hotline: a taped message, gives the latest news fr the Soviet Union, & describes the met area's upcoming events & recommended programming. Freedom Vigils: syns, orgs & stu groups conduct the Rosh Chodesh prayer servs in front of the off of the Soviet airline; Soviet Press Vigil: information gathering serv monitors the Soviet media for remarks on J, Judaism & Is; Commis on Soviet J Life: formed to attain for the J com in the Soviet Union its right to teach, practice, worship & observe, & to provide teachers, J texts & ritual articles; Freedom Parcels: provides kosher food, bks & holiday materials necessary for preserving J life; Youth Prog: mobilizes young people to do volunteer work, organizes activities in support of Soviet J on col campuses; Proj Yachad: encourages personal links with Soviet J; Soviet Olim Tour: brings former prisoners of conscience to NY to generate support for Soviet J; Bar/Bat Mitzvah Prog: symbolically allows Soviet J youth to participate in local Bar/Bat Mitzvah ceremonies, & Holiday Commemorative materials, designed to remind chil & adults of the plight of Soviet J, are distributed to local ins & orgs; com & professional outreach groups: provide com groups with staff assistance, prog ideas, resources, pub & media contacts; NY Legal Coalition for Soviet J: gives legal assistance to J refuseniks; NY Med & Mental Health Cttee: assists Soviet J med & mental health professionals to leave the USSR. Other progs & facilities include annual solidarity Sun rally for Soviet J; research library containing an extensive collection of material concerning J life & Soviet J;

speakers bureau; briefing serv. Parcels & preprinted postcards are sent to Soviet J prisoners of conscience by affiliated agy, syns, schs & youth groups; thousands of telegrams which are stored in telegram banks & are sent to Soviet officials whenever the rights of Soviet J are violated. 85 constituent orgs in the NY area. F in 1971 by leaders of the NY UJA & Fed of J Philanthropies. ActionPack (monthly newsletter); Currents (monthly bulletin); Synagogue Bulletin – provides monthly columns on Soviet J movement for use in temple & syn newsletters; Conscience of Congress – documents the efforts of NY area mems of Congress on behalf of J prisoners of conscience; Policy Reports – disseminates special reports & devs in the movement; Jewish Survey – Russian language magazine. Soviet Jewry Update is broadcast three times a week on a NY radio station. Chr: Dr Seymour P. Lachman; Rec Sec: Naomi Cohen; Corsp Sec: Nechi Shudofsky; Fin Sec: David Weil; Treas: Irwin Robins; Exec Bd: Irving Adelsberg, David Bar-Illan, Martin S. Begun, Shirley Billet, Dr Judith Bleich, Louis Ehrenkrantz, Barry Farber, Cecile Feder, Hon Stanley Fink, Amy Goldberg, Barbara Goldstein, Nahum Gordon, Hon Kennith Gribetz, Rabbi Reuven Grodner, Alvin Hellerstein, Rabbi David Hill, Dr Albert Hornblass, Bernard Kabak, Nat Kameny, George Klein, Jay Kriegel, Larry Lavinsky, Naomi Levine, Irwin Loitz, Matthew Maryles, Hon Milton Mollen, Nat Nagler, Larry Newman, Toby Newman, Hon Steven Orlow, Joel Plavin, Rabbi Alvin M. Poplack, Dr Harold Proshansky, Rabbi Sol Roth, Axel Schupf, Hon Sheldon Silver, Rabbi Ronald Sobel, Dorothea Steindl, Stanley Stone, Joshua Vogel, Lou Weiser, Rabbi Avi Weiss, Samuel Wigder; Exec Dir: Zeesy Schnur; Asst Dir: Bina Presser. **8 W 40th St, NYC NY 10018 (212) 354–1316.**

The Greater NY Conference on Soviet Jewry – Research Library. Maintains extensive files on individual refusenik cases, prisoners of conscience & human rights violations of Soviet J. Library contains extensive collection of bks, pamphlets & periodicals in Russian, English & Heb concerning J life & Soviet J. Material available to schs, univs, journalists, others; consulting servs to private individuals & govt agys. For information on the Ins, see – The Greater NY Conference on Soviet Jewry, New York City, NY. **8 W 40th St, NYC NY 10018 (212) 354–1316.**

Hadassah. The Women's Zionist Org of Am affiliated with: Am Assn for J Edu, Am Council for Voluntary Agy for Foreign Serv, Am Zionist Fed, Conf of Pres of Major Am J Orgs, Gen Fed of Women's Clubs, Natl Council of Women in the US, Natl J Com Relations Adv Council, United Nations Assn of the USA, World Zionist Org, World Confederation of United Zionists. Conducts edu progs in US; provides health, edu & com servs in Is; provides basic J edu as a background for intelligent & creative J living in Am; built & maintains, in Jerusalem, the Hadassah – Hebrew Univ Med Ctr with campuses at Kiryat Hadassah for healing, teaching & research including Med Sch, Henrietta Szold Sch of Nursing, Sch of Dentistry, & facilities on Mt Scopus which include an occupational therapy ctr, rehabilitation ctr & gen hosp; maintains a network of clins & com health ctrs; operates the Hadassah Com Col, Seligsberg / Brandeis comprehensive co-edu HS & Vocational Guidance Ins in Jerusalem; acts as principal agy in US for support of youth aliyah villages & day-care ctrs for immigrants & deprived youth; participates in J Natl Fund land purchase & reclamation progs; sponsors Hashachar – Zionist movement for Am youth fr ages 9–25; provides a residence for Am youth who come to Is for work & study. Over 370,000 mems with 1,600 local groups. Staff of 150. F in 1912. Hadassah Magazine; Hadassah Headlines; study guides. Pres: Frieda S. Lewis; Treas: Beatrice I. Feldman; Sec: Rosalie Schechter; Rec Sec: Evelyn W. Sondheim; VPs: Sylvia Doppelt, Florence S. Goodman, Mrs Franklin B. Moosnick, Ruth Popkin, Emma K. Retchin, Mrs Benjamin Zamost; Hov VPs: Mrs Moses P. Epstein, Charlotte Jacobson, Mrs Siegfried Kramarsky, Mrs Max N. Matzkin, Dr Miriam Freund Rosenthal, Mrs Herman Shulman, Bernice S. Tannenbaum; Washington Rep: Mrs Joseph Rose; Exec Dir: Aline Kaplan; PR Dir: Lenore Kahn. **50 W 58th St, NYC NY 10019 (212) 355–7900.**

Hadassah House Library. For information on the Ins, see – Hadassah, New York City, NY. **50 W 58th St, NYC NY 10019 (212) 355–7900.**

Hadassah Zionist Youth Commission. 50 W 58th St, NYC NY 10019 (212) 355–7900.

Hashachar. Zionist movement for Am youth. Sponsored by Hadassah. For additional information on the Ins, see – Hadassah, New York City, NY. **50 W 58th St, NYC NY 10019 (212) 355–7900.**

Hashomer Hatzair Socialist Zionist Youth Movement. 150 Fifth Ave, #710, NYC NY 10011 (212) 929–4955.

Hebrew Actors Union. 31 E Seventh St, NYC NY 10003 (212) 674–1923.

The Hebrew Arts School. To preserve & cultivate J art & culture. Group & individual instruction in piano, orchestral instruments, classical & folk guitar & recorder; classes in music fundamentals, creativity & composition, choral & instrumental ensemble groups; dance; art & theatre. Chil, adults, lay people & professionals fr all races, rel & cultures. Part time faculty of over 90 professionals. F in 1952. The Sch's initial focus on chil was so successful that its prog has been expanded over the yrs to reach a broader cross section of New Yorkers. Facilities include classrms, piano & instrumental studios, dance & art studios, a recital hall & a concert hall. Through its teacher training & pub divs, its distinguished concert series & innovative outreach progs, the Sch contributes to the growth & enjoyment of the J arts everywhere. Several schs in the US & in Is have modeled themselves after The Hebrew Arts Sch. Dir: Dr Tzipora H. Jochsberger; Hon Chr of the Adv Bd: Leonard Bernstein; Adv Bd: Tzvi Avni, David Bar-Illan, Paul Bne-Haim, Jacob Druckman, Prof Emma D. Sheehy, Anna Sokolow, Robert Starer, Isaac Stern, Hugo Weisgall, Dr Eric Werner; Bd of Trustees – Chr: Dr Abraham Goodman; Hon Pres: Marcus Rottenberg; Pres: Philip Esterman; VPs: Norman P. Friedman, Fred J. Issacson, Romie Shapiro; Treas: Louis B. Resnick; Sec: Hon Benjamin Wm. Mehlman; Bd of Trustees: Gerald Bregman, Dr Victor Goodhill, Connie Goodman, Leonard Goodman, Ruth Goodman, Dr Tzipora H. Jochsberger, Jean Claude Landau, Solange Landau, Charles D. Lieber, Ulla Merkin, Reba I. Rottenberg, Martha K. Selig, Leonard P. Shaykin, Elie Wiesel, Stephen J. Ziff; Friends Exec Bd – Hon Pres: Lily Mars, Reba I. Rottenberg; Co-Pres: Lea Cohen, Helen Esterman, Blanche Shapiro; VPs: Bertha Daniels, Helen Juran, Evelyn R. Mehlman, Sue M. Shapiro; Corsp Sec: Naomi Weber; Exec Bd: Fran P. Bell, Sallie Blumenthal, Ruth Camche, Miriam Colman, Esther B. Cory, Dorothy Delbaum, Sylvia Dissick, Vivian Fink, Connie Goodman, Ruth Goodman, Susan Radvany Greer, Alva Hirschberg, Rudy Lowenstein, Sarah G. Lowenthal, Mary Marcus, Leona Nager, Aviva Sella, Beatrice Vare. **129 W 67th St, NYC NY 10023 (212) 362–8060.**

Hebrew Culture Foundation. 515 Park Ave, NYC NY 10022 (212) 752–0600.

Hebrew Free Burial Association. c/o Harry Moskowitz, 1170 Bdwy, NYC NY 10001 (212) 686–2433.

Hebrew Tabernacle Congregation. Affiliated with UAHC. 250 mems. Rabbi Robert L. Lehman; Cantors: Henry Ehrenberg, Fred Herman; Pres: Ernest Hartog; Edu: Fred Herman; Sisterhood Pres: Elsa F. Katz; Brotherhood Pres: Ernest Marso. **551 Fort Washington Ave, NYC NY 10033 (212) 568–8304.**

Hebrew Union College – Jewish Institute of Religion. Ins of higher learning in Am Reform J. Accredited by the Middle States Assn of Cols & Secondary Schs, the N Central Assn of Cols & Secondary Schs, the Western Assn of Schs & Cols; affiliated with the Univ of Cincinnati, the Greater Cincinnati Consortium of Cols & Univs, the Univ of Southern CA, Washington Univ, NY Univ, & the Hebrew Univ. Dedicated to the study of J in the spirit of free inquiry. Rabbinic Sch: five yr prog leading to the Master of Arts degree & Ordination. The stu are required to spend their first academic yr at the HUC-JIR campus in Jerusalem Is. Facilities & progs include library containing 110,000 vols; Hebrew Union Col Press, Sacred Music Press; lectures; concerts; films & other public events which enrich the cultural & intellectual life of the com. The J Ins of Rel was f in 1922 by Rabbi Stephen S. Wise; the sch merged with the HUC in 1950. A new ctr in Washington Square was completed in 1979. The Hebrew Union College Annual; scholarly bks by mems of the faculty & alumni pub by Hebrew Union Col Press; Chronicle – periodical reporting col activities. Facilities include classrms & seminar rms, auditorium-chapel, conf ctr, adm & faculty offs, stu-faculty lounge, rehearsal halls. Dean: Rabbi Paul M. Steinberg; Pres: Rabbi Alfred Guttschalk PhD; Asst to the Pres: Harold Epstein; Bd of Gov – Chr: Richard J. Scheuer; Exec Dean: Dr Eugene Mihaly. **One W 4th St, NYC NY 10023 (212) 873–0388.**

Hebrew Union College – Jewish Institute of Religion, Klau Library. Contains approximately 110,000 vols; holds large Judaica collection rich in modern Heb literature. Annual journal of HUC-JIR Libraries – Studies in Bibliography & Booklore, appearing since 1953, is the only learned journal devoted to J bibliography pub in US. For information on the Col, see – Hebrew Union College – Jewish Institute of Religion, New York City, NY. **One W 4th St, NYC NY 10012 (212) 873–0388.**

The Hebrew Union College Press. Pub scholarly bks by mems of faculty & alumni. **One W 4th St, NYC NY 10012 (212) 873–0388.**

Hebrew University – Technion Joint Maintenance Appeal. 11 E 69th St, NYC NY 10021 (212) 988–8418.

Herut – USA. 41 E 42nd St, NYC NY 10017 (212) 687–4502.

Herzliah – Jewish Teachers Seminary. 69 Bank St, NYC NY 10014.

HIAS, Inc. The worldwide J migration agy operating through a global network of offs, cooperating cttee, & affiliated orgs in 47 countries on six continents. To rescue, reunite & resettle J. Serves as the overseas arm of settlement agy such as the J Immigrant Aid Servs of Canada, Fed of Australian J Welfare Soc, & J Refugee Cttee in Europe & Latin Am; helps thousands of J to migrate fr Eastern Europe, the Middle E, N Africa, & elsewhere; at request of US Govt, assists non J refugees; helps many Iranian J gain admission to the US & other countries for family reunions, & aids those already in the US to comply with the immigration laws; offers pre-migration servs including: processing letters of invitation, visa documentation, consular representation, intervention with govt agy, transportation, reception, family reunion & settlement; offers post migration servs including: adjustment of status, naturalization & protection fr deportation. HIAS helps locate missing relatives & friends worldwide & is on the alert with rescue plans should trouble erupt for J coms in areas of potential strife around the world. Formerly known as United HIAS Servs or Hebrew Sheltering & Immigrant Aid Soc. HIAS has resettled an estimated 4,000,000 J. In recent yrs, most HIAS assisted migrants have been fr the Soviet Union. Pres: Edwin Shapiro; Exec VP: Leonard Seidenman; VP Finance: Irving Haber. **200 Park Ave S, NYC NY 10003 (212) 674–6800.**

Hineni. To foster J identity & strengthen ties between the J of the Diaspora & J of Is. Pubs, recordings, tapes, video-tapes & films to educate & inspire; classes for family & youth in Bible & J related subjects; Singles Prog; weekly TV show reaching 62 Am coms; annual tour to Is; progs on col campuses for youth. Progs fr coast to coast in the US; chapters in NY, Los Angeles, Miami, Johannesburg S Africa, Sydney Australia, & Jerusalem. F in 1973 by Rebbetzin Esther Jungreis. Pres: Rebbetzin Esther Jungreis; Exec Dir: Barbara Janov. **155 E 38th St, NYC NY 10016 (212) 557–1190, 275–6464.**

Histadruth Ivrith of America. 1841 Bdwy, NYC NY 10023 (212) 581–5151.

Horace M. Kallen Center for Jewish Studies. Ctr of Hebrew Teachers Ins & J Teachers Seminary & People's Univ. **69 Bank St, NYC NY 10014.**

Ichud Habonim Labor Zionist Youth. 575 Sixth Ave, NYC NY 10011 (212) 255–1796.

International Conference of Jewish Communal Service. Branches in Is, N Am, Australia, Europe, Latin Am & S Africa. The ICJCS came into being in 1965–66 in response to a felt need of J communal workers in the world for better understanding of each other's problems, progs & servs, & for more effective communication with professional colleagues. With the support of the Conf of J Communal Servs, concrete steps were taken to est this intl body; a rep cttee was formed of leaders of J agy throughout the world. The 1st worldwide conf was held in Aug 1967. Other confs have taken place in 1971, 1975, 1978, & 1981. Pres: Ralph Goldman; Assc Pres: Yehuda Dominitz; VPs: Ferne Katleman, Zev Hymowitz, Melvin Carlowe, Irving Kessler, Florence Mittwock, Alberto Senderey, Adam Loss; Secs: Gerald Bubis, Shmuel Friedman; Treas: Zvi Feine, Arthur Rotman. **15 E 26th St, NYC NY 10010 (212) 683–8056.**

International Council on Jewish Social & Welfare Services. 200 Park Ave S, NYC NY 10003 (212) 674–6800.

International League for the Repatriation of Russian Jews. 315 Church, NYC NY 10013 (212) 431–6866.

Inwood Hebrew Congregation. Affiliated with United Syn of Am. Rabbi: Ascher M. Yager; Presidium: Abraham Shafran, Emanuel Rizick, Joseph Rosenkranz. **111 Vermilyea Ave, NYC NY 10034 (212) 569–4010.**

Israel Folk Dance Institute. 515 Park Ave, NYC NY 10022 (212) 371–5650.

Israel Foundation Fund (Keren Hayesod), Inc. 515 Park Ave, NYC NY 10022 (212) 688–0800.

Israel Government Tourist Office. 350 Fifth Ave, NYC NY 10118 (212) 560–0650.

Israel Program Center. 515 Park Ave, NYC NY 10022 (212) 751–6070.

Israeli Community of Mizrachi – Hapoel Hamizrachi. 25 W 26th St, NYC NY 10010 (212) 679–2050.

Israeli Students Organization in the U.S.A. & Canada. 515 Park Ave, NYC NY 10022 (212) 688–6796.

Jerusalem Institutions for the Blind (Keren-Or, Inc). 1133 Bdwy, Suite 1227/1228, NYC NY 10010 (212) AL5–1180.

The Jerusalem Post. 110 E 59th St, NYC NY 10022 (212) 355–4440.

Jewish Association for Services for the Aged. To help older adults to remain in the com. Operates

21 social serv offs which provide counseling, information & referral on such matters as health servs, personal & fin problems & housing; other servs include 21 ctrs offering daily kosher hot lunch, & edu, social, recreational & cultural activities; Meals-on-Wheels; home chore serv; home attendants; mgmnt of three apt complexes: Scheuer House & Friendset House in Coney Island, & Brookdale Village in Far Rockaway; Public Information Dept which provides information to public on issues affecting the aged, publicizes JASA activities with goal of improving the image of the elderly, legal advice & representation to indigent elderly; Assn of Older J Immigrants fr the Soviet Union; Coalition of Social Action Cttee in 80 sr ctrs; information & social action on legislative issues of concern to older adults. Serves more than 50,000 elderly & their families per yr. F in 1968 by Fed of J Philanthropies to fill the unmet needs of the J elderly. The three apt complexes total 1,512 subsidized units for the well elderly. Two more bldgs are under construction. **40 W 68th St, NYC NY 10023 (212) 724–3200.**

Jewish Book Council. Bk ctr affiliated with JWB. To meet the needs of readers, authors & publishers of J bks. Acts as clearinghouse for librarians, professionals, & lay readers; J Bk Mo celebrates the bks of the J people through exhibits, bk fairs & special progs; presents Natl J Bk Awards for bks of outstanding scholarship & literary merit. 2 employees. Est in 1943. Jewish Book Annual; Jewish Books In Review which is featured bi-monthly in JWB Circle. Pres: Blu Greenberg; Dir: Ruth Frank. **15 E 26th St, NYC NY 10010 (212) 532–4949.**

Jewish Braille Institute of America. Library & social welfare agy. Endorsed by Natl Fed of Temple Sisterhoods, Women's League for Conservative Judaism, Women's Branch of the Union of Orthodox J Cong of Am; mem of Am Assn of Workers for the Blind, Assn for the Edu of the Visually Handicapped, Natl Fed of the Blind. Seeks to serve the rel & cultural needs of the J blind by pub bks & other material in braille, large print & sound cassettes in English & Heb. Youth Edu Prog including Bar & Bat Mitzvah preparation in braille & large print; counseling on col & grad sch admission as well as specialized materials prepared for J studies stu, rabbinical stu, & cantorial stu; assistance to elderly blind & visually impaired & to agy serving them; production of rel pub including prayerbks & haggadahs in braille & large type; maintenance of lending libraries in English & Heb braille, sound cassettes in English, Heb, Yiddish & other languages, large print in English & Heb; assistance in dev of libraries for blind & partially sighted in Is; direct aid to scholars & stu in Is; edu materials provided to meet specific needs of blind Is vets; assistance to Is agy in acquiring specialized materials for the blind produced in US & other countries; advisory servs to J communal agy; resource for non–J seminarians studying Heb language & J traditions; accredited as non–governmental observer at UN; sponsors intl literature competitions for blind writers to encourage their creative expression; maintains library of 90,000+ braille vols, 65,000+ sound cassettes, Judaica. 20 employees; volunteer braillists, recorders & large print specialists org through local Sisterhoods of 3 branches of Judaism. F in 1931 by Leopold Dubov. Pub Jewish Braille Review (monthly); JBI Voice (monthly sound recording); Or Chadash (irregular issue sound cassette in Heb for distribution in Is. Facilities include Waxman Fragrance Garden; Lamport Sound Studio. Pres: Dr Jane Evans; Exec VP: Gerald M. Kass; Lib Dir: Richard Borgersen. **110 E 30th St, NYC NY 10016 (212) 889–2525.**

Jewish Braille Institute of America, Library. Lending library contains 90,000+ braille vols in English & Heb; 65,000+ sound cassettes in Heb, English, Yiddish & other languages; large print vols in English & Heb; special brailling & recording of materials requested but not available fr other agy or libraries. For information on the Ins, see – Jewish Braille Institute of America, New York City, NY. Library Dir: Richard Borgessen. **110 E 30th St, NYC NY 10016 (212) 889–2525.**

The Jewish Center. Orthodox Cong affiliated with Union of Orthodox J Congs of Am. To provide rel, social & intellectual resources for mems & friends interested in Orthodox Judaism. Daily Servs (morning & evening); classes on all levels; lecture series on topics of contemporary interest; Sisterhood; very active Singles Prog; youth groups for 3 ages (chil, pre-teen, teen); library containing 1,500 vols (Judaica). 250 mems (200 families, 50 individuals). F 1917 by Mordecai Kaplan. Pub The Jewish Center Bulletin (bi-monthly). Facilities include 2 sanctuaries, offs, 2 kitchens. Rabbi Jacob J. Schacter; Rabbi Emeritus Leo Jung; Exec Dir: Rabbi Irving Wietschner; Sexton: Rabbi Joseph Wermuth; Chr of Bd: Morris L. Green; Pres: Martin Schwarzschild; VPs: Abe Tennenbaum, Dr Irwin Gribetz; Sec: Arthur Degen; Acting Treas: J. Peter Lunzer; Bulletin Editor: Hadassah Gold. **131 W 86th St, NYC NY 10024 (212) 724–2700.**

Jewish Chautauqua Society. 838 Fifth Ave, NYC NY 10021 (212) 249–0100.

Jewish Child Care Association of New York. J sectarian outreach agy offering a comprehensive range of chil care servs to the met J com. Affiliated with the Fed of J Philanthropies, beneficiary of the UJA-Fed, & certified by Council on Accreditation of Servs for Families & Chil. Support is also received fr private & public funding sources. Central Intake & Referral Servs: responds to families seeking placement without the assistance of a com or a professional; provides information on servs of agy; provides staff of social workers, psychiatrists & psychologists who determine & place chil in appropriate facilities. Edu & Scholarship Prog: provides financial grants to young people who have left JCCA facilities; provides consultation & guidance on special edu needs for col & vocational prog stu, & offers support for grad stu on a selective basis. Family Day Care Serv: provides day care servs for presch chil, & after sch supervision of sch age chil in licensed day care homes; gives parents case work servs on chil dev, parent-chil relationships, & personal problems. Preventive Servs Prog: offers servs to rehabilitate, strengthen & support families; provides case work treatment & counseling; makes referrals & works with hosps, camps & com ctrs as needed; provides fin assistance, transportation help, housing relocation, day care, recreational aid, edu remediation & homemaker servs. Psychiatric Clin: licensed mental health clin offers diagnostic treatment for chil & families; offers consultations & training prog for the professional staff; supports research & dev progs of the agy; provides edu, tutorial & vocational counseling servs through progs attached to the psychiatric clin. Two Together: provides one to one reading tutoring for disabled chil. Adoption Servs: recruits suitable adoptive homes; consults with undercare divs & is a liaison with the com on adoption matters. Health Care Servs, & Psychiatric & Psychological Serv: assigns staff to all divs of the agy who assume responsibility for diagnosis & treatment of chil & families under care; performs other servs including remedial edu, speech therapy & vocational & edu counseling. Nannahagen Sch & Day Treatment Prog: offers day prog consisting of individual, family & group therapy, & special edu & recreational servs for Westchester chil fr K to 14 yrs of age with severe emotional & learning handicaps. Group Homes: provides home for adolescents who leave ins & live in com, attend regular or special schs, or work in open or sheltered jobs in the com, or are provided training to dev work skills; gives med & dental care, psychiatric & psychological servs, rel edu & col or technical scholarships to group home residents. Foster Home Serv: offers screened & trained foster parents; & also provides casework counseling, remedial edu, med, psychiatric & psychological servs & rel training. Developmentally Disabled Prog: provides group homes which offer professionally supervised care, habilitation, rehabilitation, & a full range of clin servs for the retarded, autistic & disabled young people (dietary laws are observed & other J cultural & rel practices are maintained). Youth Residence Ctr: provides com based residential & treatment facility for young men & women aged 16 to 21 with servs including individual casework, vocational counseling, psychotherapy, pharmacotherapy, med & dental care, vocational guidance & col or technical sch scholarships. Pleasantville Cottage Sch: serves emotionally disturbed chil age 8 to 15 with a prog which includes on-ground sch, recreation such as sports, summer day camp, arts & crafts, supervised social activities & outings, rel edu & special events. Pleasantville Diagnostic Ctr: admits boys 7 to 14 yrs of age for 60 day diagnostic & assessment prog. Edenwald Ctr: provides residential treatment ctr for mildly & moderately retarded, emotionally disturbed chil age 8 to 16. Childville Residential Treatment Ctr: offers intensive treatment for severely emotionally disturbed boys & girls ages 6 to 10 (public sch & special edu teachers on premises). Childville Progress Houses: provides group homes for chil age 10 to 14 who are ready to leave the residential treatment ctr. 2,551 chil & families served. Today's agy was formed through a series of mergers of nineteenth & early twentieth century ins & agy. Pres: Daniel A. Pollack; Chr of Bd: Noel Rubinton; Exec VP: David Roth; VPs: Sanford B. Ehrenkranz, Mrs David Sher, Alan V. Tishman; Treas: Stephen Sokoloff; Asst Treas: Robert Maslow; Sec: Michael Saphier; Asst Sec: Mrs Norman D. Broder; Trustees: Richard L. Berman, Mrs Edward B. Bermas, Howard N. Blitman, Henry B. Bobrow, Elmer Coley, Leonard S. Elman, Mrs David L. Finkelman, John L. Freeman, Mrs Nathan Gordon, George J. Greenberg, Walter E. Harris Jr, Thomas S. Karger, Frederick Katz, David Kosh, Mrs Martin Kraus, Phillip A. Laskawy, Robert H. Lehman, Hope W. Levene, Robert A. Lewis, Mrs Milton Miller, Henry Necarsulmer, Donald L. Newborg, Judge Louis Otten, Walter D. Richards, Mrs Alfred A. Rosenberg, Norman Rosow, Richard L. Scherzer, Adolph Schimel, Benjamin P. Schoenfein, Herman D. Schultz, Howard L. Schwartz, Isaac Sherman, Dorothy Silverman, Phillip Silverman, Melvin H. Small, Mrs Carl M. Spero, Paul B. Zeisler Jr; Asst Exec Dirs: Eileen Nagel, Harvey Steinberg. **345 Madison Ave, NYC NY 10017 (212) 490–9160.**

Jewish Community Relations Council of New York. Central coord body for 33 NY J orgs. Central coord & resource body for the J com in the met NY area. Commis on Govt Relations; Commis on Intergroup Relations; Commis on Intl J Concerns; Speakers Bureau; Commis on Equal Opportunity; Commi on J Security; Task Force on Missionaries &

Cults; J Com Cable Corp; Universal Torah Registry; J Coalition on Higher Edu; Ombudsman; Media Relations; Commis on Legal & Legislative Issues. 33 regional groups. 10 employees. F 1976. Pub regular bulletins, alerts & backgrounders; Newsletter on Cults & Missionaries (quarterly). Schroder Award 1982; Citation NYC Police Dept 1981; Tribute – FEGS 1980. Exec Dir: Malcolm Hoenlein; Pres: Laurence A. Fisch. **111 W 40th St, Suite 2600, NYC NY 10018 (212) 221–1535.**

Jewish Conciliation Board of America. 120 W 57th St, NYC NY 10019 (212) 582–3577.

Jewish Currents. Periodical pub. **22 E 17th St, Suite 601, NYC NY 10003 (212) 924–5740.**

Jewish Defense League. 76 Madison Ave, NYC NY 10016 (212) 686–3041.

Jewish Education Service of North America. The central natl serv agy for coordination, promotion & research in Am J edu. The promotion of higher standards of J edu. Natl Curriculum Research Ins evaluates projs; devs staff & curriculum progs; conducts teacher training progs; sponsors confs on supplementary HS edu; co-sponsors the Natl Conf on J Day & Resident Camping; has contracted with the US Govt to dev a new J curriculum for US military personnel & their dependents; provides consultive servs to local J coms through the central agy for J edu or directly to Fed cttees for J edu. Shteinshleifer Testing Bureau assesses the progs & achievements of stu in Heb schs & Heb day schs. Natl Edu Resource Ctr makes materials available in the curricular & methodological areas, & distributes edu packets (the ctr is open to visitors by reservation); disseminates worthwhile projs developed by local J edu agy. Dept of Com Servs, Information & Studies provides staff mems who visit coms for consultation, in-depth studies & reviews of edu systems; originates task forces; maintains research projs. Dept of Personnel Servs administers the placement of edu personnel in central agy & communal schs; administers the Natl Bureau of License & the Fellowships in J Edu Leadership Prog; issues statistics on salaries. F in 1939 as the Am Assn for J Edu. It consisted of 18 natl orgs, 51 central communal agy, & an at-large membership. In 1978 a study cttee was appointed to consider the future of the org. The cttee recommended a reorganization. On Jul 1, 1981 a new Bd of Dirs held an organizational meeting. Nine units of a curriculum on the Holocaust for HS classes: The Nazi Totalitarian State, The Destruction of European Jewry 1933–1945, Civil Self-Defense, Armed Resistance, The Response of the Free World, What It Means To Be A Jew After Auschwitz, The Righteous Among the Nations, The Uniqueness of the Holocaust, The Antecedents of Nazi Anti-Semitism; Zionism & Israel – A Series of Mini-Courses on Three Themes; The Pedagogic Reporter (issued four times a yr); Curriculum Newsletter; SAFRA – A Review of Jewish School Materials; the Masada Learning Materials Kit; Home Start – subscription series mailed before each of the three major holidays includes stories & storybks (or recorded narration), handicraft projs, recipes & cooking ideas, games, recorded music & historical information. Natl Curriculum Research Ins – Dir: Dr Shimon Frost; Methods & Materials: Fradle Freidenreich; Pedagogic Reporter: Dr Mordecai Lewittes; Dir Personnel Servs: Dr Hyman Pomerantz; Com Servs, Information & Studies – Dir: Dr George Pollak; Press & Publicity & J Edu News: Gary Gobetz; Mgmnt & Adm – Dir: Milton Weinstein; Coord of Dev & Planning: Robert L. Kern. **114 Fifth Ave, NYC NY 10011.**

Jewish Educators Assembly of America. 155 Fifth Ave, NYC NY 10010 (212) 533–7800.

Jewish Foundation for Education of Women. 120 W 57th St, NYC NY 10019 (212) 265–2565.

Jewish Frontier. Monthly Am Labor Zionist Journal. F in 1934. The journal has played, over the last century, a leading role in Am J & Zionist pub as the voice of progressive Zionist ideas in N Am. Editor: Mitchell Cohen; Literary Editor: Lilian Elkin; Mgr: Mark Seal. **114 Fifth Ave, NYC NY 10011 (212) 243–2741,2, 989–0300.**

Jewish Guild for the Blind. 15 W 65th St, NYC NY 10023 (212) 595–2000.

Jewish Information Bureau, Inc. Independent (non-profit) clearinghouse on all subjects relating to Judaism & J communal affairs. To render free serv to the public on all matters pertaining to Jews & Judaism; to foster a wider knowledge of J things by collecting & disseminating authentic facts relating to J life & hist, laws, customs, literature, etc. 350 mems. The Bureau was f in 1932 by Bernard G. Richards, noted author, prolific journalist, pioneer Zionist & an original organizer of the Am J Congress. Pub Index (quarterly). Since its founding, the Bureau has answered (as of Nov 1982) approx 650,000 questions from all over United States & overseas. Asst Dir: Steven Wise; Sec: Ruth Eisenstein; Treas: Myron Eisenstein. **250 W 57th St, NYC NY 10019 (212) 582–5318.**

Jewish Labor Bund. 25 E 78th St, Suite 501, NYC NY 10021 (212) 535–0850.

Jewish Labor Committee. **25 E 78th St, NYC NY 10021 (212) 535–3700.**

Jewish Media Service. National Jewish Welfare Broad, **15 E 26th St, NYC NY 10010 (212) 532–4949.**

Jewish Ministers Cantors Association of America, Inc. To perpetuate the Cantorial profession in its traditional form. Assistance to needy cantors; library of cantorial & Heb music. First cantorial org in the US; est in 1896. Kol Lakol (bulletin). Pres: Rev David Rosenzweig; Exec Dir: Rev Irving Obstbaum; Legal Consultant: Rev Abraham Gartenhaus; Musical Dir: Seymour Silbermintz; 1st VP: Rev Henry Butensky; 2nd VP: Rev Isidor Schneidor; Treas: Rev Sholom Gruen; Fin Sec: Rev Lawrence Spern; Rec Sec: Rev Samuel Gomberg; Parliamentarian: Rev Ephraim Yavneh; Bd of Dirs: Rev Chaskele Ritter, Rev Charles Block, Rev Kenneth Butensky, Rev Paul Carus, Rev Abraham Friedman, Rev Joseph Kahan, Rev Barry Kallenberg, Rev Samuel Morginstin, Rev Matus Radzivilover, Rev Eleazar Schulman, Rev Binyamin Siller, Rev Abraham Veroba, Rev Samuel Vigoda, Rev Sol Wechsler; Bd of Advs: Rev Zvee Aroni, Rev Michael Alexandrovich, Rev Abraham Brun, Rev Maurice Ganchoff, Rev Kalman Kalich, Rev David Kusevitsky, Rev Noah Schall; Auditing & Budget: Rev Samuel Gomberg, Rev Lawrence Spern; Concerts: Rev Irving Rogoff, Rev Moshe Stamm; Cultural & Edu: Rev Sholom Gruen; Ensemble: Rev Lawrence Spern; Ethics: Rev Charles Bloch; Legislative: Rev Benjamin Alpert, Rev Eleazer Schulman; Membership: Rev Murray Bazian, Rev Binyamin Siller; Memorial: Rev Samuel Morginstin; Placement & Pub Rev Irving Obstbaum. **3 W 16th St, NYC NY 10011 (212) 675–6601.**

The Jewish Museum. Dedicated to collecting, preserving, interpreting & presenting art & artifacts which represent the richness & diversity of J life throughout the ages. Permanent collection includes ceremonial objects, antiquities, paintings, prints, drawings, sculpture, photographs, textiles, decorative arts & coins & medals fr around the world. The Natl J Archive of Broadcasting collects & displays significant TV & radio progs of J content & interest of the past 35 yrs. The Mus provides sch progs for specific grade levels & curriculum needs, interpretive materials & guided tours; special family workshops which enable parents & chil to learn together about J holidays, traditions & crafts; adult progs, created in conjunction with exhibitions, which feature lectures by curators & other prominent guest speakers, films & concerts; The Tobe Pascher Workshop in which resident artists create original ceremonial objects & conduct classes for amateur & professional craftsmen; Volunteer Prog in which a group of people assist in many phases of the Mus operation, hold positions in the Mus Shop, at the Information Desk, as guides in the Edu Prog, & as curatorial & adm assts. Mus Shop contains graphics by artists, a wide range of bks on J art, hist & culture, contemporary ceremonial objects, posters, toys, jewelry, Is crafts, & J Mus exhibition catalogues. Mus est in 1904 in the Library of The J Theological Seminary of Am. A family residence was donated in 1944 for use as The J Mus &, under the auspices of the J Theological Seminary of Am, the Mus opened its doors to the public in 1947. A sculpture court outside the mansion was installed in 1959, & the Vera & Albert A. List Bldg was added four yrs later to provide additional space for exhibitions & progs. Newsletter (bimonthly). Dir of Edu: Andrew Ackerman; Coord of Adult Progs: Margo Bloom.**1109 Fifth Ave, NYC NY 10028 (212) 860–1888.**

Jewish Music Council. Council affiliated with JWB. To enrich Am J Culture by highlighting its musical heritage. Plans progs for musical activities; annually sponsors & promotes the J Music Festival encourages composition of new musical works & academic research in J music; promotes fine performances of J music of high quality in concerts, radio, TV, & recordings; offers information on J music to individuals & groups in the US & abroad. Est in 1944. Highlighting Jerusalem With Music; Israeli Music – A Program Aid; Ernest Bolch Creative Spirit – A Program Source Book; Music Program Aids – A Bicentennial Arts Resource; Jewish Music Movement in America; The Yiddish Folksong – An Illustrated Lecture; Jewish Music Programs; Music Program Aids; Resource Cultural Arts Agencies & Funding Data; Resource Materials on Music of the Sephardic & Oriental Jews; Jewish Music Programs; Quarter Century of Synagogue Music in America; Bibliography of Instrumental Music of Jewish Interest; Bibliography of Publications & Other Resources on Jewish Music; Bibliography of Jewish Vocal Music; The Historic Contribution of Russian Jewry to Jewish Music; Supplement – The Historical Contribution of Russian Jewry to Jewish Music; The Cantorial Art; A. W. Binder – His Life & Work; The Music of Abraham Ellstein & Max Helfman; Jewish Music Concert Programs; Four American Jewish Composers – Their Life & Work; A Jewish Composer by Choice; Jewish Folk Song Resources; Jewish Music Concert Programs; Musical Gems of the Sabbath; Oneg Shabbat; The Scope of Jewish Music; Music of the Synagogue. Chr: Leonard Kaplan; Dir: Irene Weiner; Hon V Chr: Judith K. Eisenstein, Julius Schatz, Lazar Weiner, Max Wohlberg; V Chr: Norman Belnik, Theodore Bikel, Irving H. Cohen, Tzipora

Jochsberger, Hadassah B. Markson, Joseph Mlotek, Richard Neuman, Albert Weisser; Pres: Robert L. Adler; Exec VP: Arthur Rothman. **15 E 26th St, NYC NY 10010 (212) 532–4949.**

Jewish National Fund. Land reclamation & afforestation in Is. Raises funds through the sale of tree certificates, bond transfers, bequests & life insurance assignments; supports special projs including recreation areas, watch towers, rds & dev in frontier areas. **42 E 69th St, NYC NY 10021 (212) 879–9300.**

Jewish Philanthropic Fund of 1933. To raise money, primarily through testamentary dispositions; to support progs previously financed by J Restitution Successor Org & J Trust Corp. Provides a natl com fund to finance preservation & extension of social servs to immigrant J. F by J immigrants fr Central Europe who fled Nazi oppression. Fr 1955 to 1962, more than two million dollars was received fr J Restitution Successor Org & J Trust Corp to build homes for the aged, build group residences, est sheltered workshops & recreation facilities, provide med & hosp care; render related servs. Exec Off: Herbert A. Strauss. **570 Seventh Ave, NYCNY 10018.**

Jewish Post of New York. Periodical pub. **101 Fifth Ave, NYC NY 10003 (212) 989–6262.**

The Jewish Publication Society of America. Non–profit edu ins devoted to J culture. To provide significant, worthwile & informative bks of J content in the English language so that the J rel, hist, literature & culture will be understood & read & known. For further information, see – The Jewish Publication Society of America, Philadelphia, PA. **60 E 42nd St, Rm 707, NYC NY 10165 (212) 687–0809.**

Jewish Reconstructionist Foundation. 432 Park Ave S, NYC NY 10016 (212) 889–9080.

Jewish Restitution Successor Organization. 15 E 26th St, NYC NY 10010 (212) 679–4074.

Jewish Socialist Verband of America. 45 E 33rd St, NYC NY 10016 (212) 686–1536.

Jewish Student Press Service. 15 E 26th St, Suite 1350, NYC NY 10010 (212) 679–1411.

Jewish Teachers Association. Profesional org of teachers fr all levels of edu; mem of Council of J Orgs in Civil Serv. To defend teachers against anti-Semitism; to further Holocaust edu & foster J issues in edu. To protect teachers fr abuse of the seniority rights; to provide legal counsel to protect teachers fr discrimination; to fight the encroachment of anti-Semitism in the field of edu; to promote the extension & encouragement of courses in J studies in the public schs throughout the US; to provide scholarships to stu for study in Israel; to provide bks on J studies to public schs throughout the country; to provide cultural & instructional materials; to encourage the growth of J studies progs; to encourage teachers to assume an active role in J communal & rel efforts. 28,000 mems. 4 employees; 27 volunteers. F 52 yrs ago. Pub Morim (3 times a yr). Pres: Dr Beverly Lipschitz; VP: Mrs Ronnie Simmons; Treas: William Leinwand, **45 E 33rd St, NYC NY 10016 (212) 684–0556.**

Jewish Telegraphic Agency, Inc. J news agy intl wire serv. To provide information about the lives, fate & well being of J in all countries; to serve as a bridge linking J coms together in order to assure cohesion & solidarity; to provide an avenue, through its press, to world public opinion; to dispel the prejudice, malice & misinformation that has accumulated against the J people. Provides on the spot coverage, analysis & special interviews on J happenings; presents day to day activities of J serv orgs in their effort to aid communal needs; reports news fr all sources, & presents all views. JTA has correspondents in N Am, S Am, Western Europe, S Africa, Australia, Is & several E European countries; JTA prepares material which is sent to Is where it is used by the Heb language press, radio & TV; JTA produces a weekly series of features & commentaries by experts in fields dealing with the US, Europe, Is, & with sports, cooking, movies, rel, humor, & the arts; provides in depth analysis on topics of gen interest to the J com. Est in 1917 in Holland & was the first news agy to gather & distribute news to J throughout the world. The JTA in NY produces the Daily News Bulletin 5 times a week; Weekly News Digest; Community News Reporter. JTA uses Rueters facilities to transmit fr its intl hq in NY to its bureaus throughout the world. In addition, it has wire facilities within the US. JTA reports are read by more than 1,000,000 people daily, & may be characterized as the 'eyes & ears' of the J people. It is said that, by its influence on the J & non J press, the JTA makes it impossible for J rights to be attacked anywhere without the outside world learning about it. Pres: Martin S. Fox; Exec VP: John Kayston; Chr of the Bd: William M. Landau; Chr Exec Cttee: Robert H. Arnow; VPs: Raymond Epstein, Philip Slomovitz, Melvin M. Swig, Marshall Weinberg; Sec: Julius Berman; Treas: Abraham

Goodman; Editor: Murray Zuckoff; Editor in Chief Emeritus: Boris Smolar. **165 W 46th St, NYC NY 10036.**

The Jewish Theological Seminary of America. Conservative rabbinical seminary accredited by Middle States Assn of Cols & Secondary Schs; chartered Bd of Regents NY State. Establishing & maintaining a theological seminary for the prepetuation of the tenets of the J religion; the cultivation of Hebrew literature; the pursuit of biblical, rabbinic, theological & archaeological research; the intergation of J & gen philosophy & learning; the advancement of J scholarship; the est of a library; the fostering of the study of J sacred music; the edu & training of J rabbis & teachers; the ordination of rabbis; the promotion of better understanding among people of different rel & ethnic backgrounds & the fostering of deeper insights into the philosophy & thought of rel; the est & maintenance of a col of liberal arts. Rel Servs; Rabbinical Sch; Graduate Sch; Cantors Ins & Seminary; Col of J Music; Seminary Col of J Studies; Prozdor (HS). Maintains the J Mus; Melton Research Ctr in J Edu; Bernstein Ctr & Brand Foun Ins of Dept of Pastoral Psychiatry; library containing 250,000 vols, 10,000 manuscripts, 10,000 incunabula in fields of Hebraica & Judaica. 600 stu. 300 employees. F in 1886 to insure the preservation in Am of the knowledge & practice of historical J. The Seminary was planned as a native ctr for the training & edu of J leaders responsible to the com of Am J. As the com grew & its needs increased, the Seminary's concerns were reflected in its revised charter of 1902, which included among its new responsibilities the perpetuation of the tenets of the J rel, the cultivation of Heb literature, the pursuit of biblical & archaeological research, the advancement of J scholarship, the est of a library for the edu & training of J rabbis & teachers. Pub Conservative Judaism, Seminary Progress (monthly); Seminary Bulletin (6 per yr). Chancellor & Pres of the Faculties: Dr Gerson D. Cohen; Chancellor Emeritus: Dr Louis Finkelstein; V Chancellor & VP of the Faculties: Dr Simon Greenberg; V Chancellor: Dr David C. Kogen; V Chancellor & Pres of the Univ of Judaism: Dr David Lieber; V Chancellors: Rabbi Stanley J. Schachter, Rabbi Yaakov G. Rosenberg; Provost: Dr Ismar Schorsch VPs: David Gordis, Morton Leifman. **3080 Bdwy, NYC NY 10027 (212) 678–8000.**

The Jewish Theological Seminary, Library. For information on the Seminary, see – Jewish Theological Seminary, New York City, NY. **3080 Bdwy, NYC NY 10027 (212) 678–8000.**

Jewish Welfare Board. 15 E 26th St, NYC NY 10010 (212) 532–4949.

The Joint Passover Association of the City of New York. Gives aid for the Passover holiday to the J needy; serves as a link between the needy & social servs agy. Est over 50 yrs ago to meet the needs of the J com; replaced the inadequate servs of many independent J groups. **33 W 60th St, NYC NY 10023 (212) 586–2900.**

Keren Or, Inc. 1133 Bdwy, NYC NY 10010 (212) 255–1180.

Labor Zionist Alliance. Seeks to enhance J life, culture, & edu in the US & Canada; to aid in bldg the State of Is as a cooperative commonwealth, & to aid its labor movement organized in the Histadrut; to support efforts toward a more democratic soc throughout the world; to further the democratization of the J com in Am & the welfare of J everywhere; to work with labor & liberal forces in Am. Youth: Habonim & Dror – summer camps; edu & culture – schs & seminaries; Zionist activites; com servs; alliance awards; Is scholarships; pubs; stu assistance; fraternal servs; aliyah assistance. Beneficiaries include: Habonim, Dror, Chai Commis, J Frontier, Yiddisher Kempher, N Am Stu Union, Network, J Stu Press Serv, J Teacher's Seminary, Folk Sch of NY, Kinneret, Yiddish Dictionary Cttee, Congress for J Culture, Edu Material & Bks, Heb Prog, Yivo Ins, Natl Cttee of J Folk Sch, Yugentruf, Zukunft, Hadoar, Louis Segal Edu Cttee, Is Scholarships, Farband Awards, Am Zionist Fed, Conf of Pres of Major J Orgs, Natl Conf on Soviet J, Am Section-World J Congress, Farband Med Ctr, Assn of Am & Canadians in Is, Ghetto Fighters, Ihud Olami, Am Academic Assn for Peace in the Middle E, Fed of J Philanthropies, Am ORT. Pub The Jewish Frontier; the Yiddisher Kemfer. Pres: Dr Ezra Spicehandler; Exec Sec: Frieda Karp. **114 Fifth Ave, NYC NY 10011 (212) 989–0300.**

League for Safeguarding the Fixity of the Sabbath. 122 W 76th St, NYC NY 10023.

League for Yiddish, Inc. Cultural ins. To encourage the use of Yiddish as a living language. Conducts classes in Yiddish; sells Yiddish bks; provides resource ctr. Est in 1935 as the Freeland League for J Territorial Colonization to rescue J escaping Nazi onslaught. In time, the org became a cultural movement. The name was changed in 1979. Afn Shvel (quarterly). Exec Dir: Dr Mordkhe Schaechter; Pres: Nathan Turak; Deputy Exec Dir: Leybl Kahn. **200 W 72nd St, Suite 40, NYC NY 10023 (212) 787–6675.**

League of Labor Israel. 575 Sixth Ave, NYC NY 10011 (212) 989–0300.

Leo Baeck Institute, Inc. 129 E 73rd St, NYC NY 10021 (212) 744–6400.

Lilith – The Jewish Women's Magazine. Periodical pub. **250 W 57th St, NYC NY 10019 (212) 757–0818.**

Lincoln Square Synagogue. 200 Amsterdam Ave, NYC NY 10023 (212) 874–6100.

Machon Gold College for Women. Located in Jerusalem. Affiliated with & sponsored by the Torah Edu Dept of the World Zionist Org. To train stu to learn on their own. Basic prog offers courses in Tanach, Mishna, Halacha, Hist, Zionism, Yediat Haaretz, Women in J Law, & Heb Literature; the Pedagogic Prog offers similar courses with greater emphasis on Heb language & teaching skills, observing classes & stu teaching; conducts bi-monthly tours & two major trips, one to the Gallil & one to the S; sponsors visits to kibbutzim, moshavim, new settlements & dev towns; sponsors volunteer prog at hosps, schs & absorption ctrs. Grads of the Prog receive a Heb Teacher's Diploma fr the Ministry of Edu. Over 100 women stu. One bldg houses the classrms, dormitory, library, dining rm, syn & lounge. Dean: Dr Gavriel Cohen. **Torah Dept, World Zionist Org, 515 Park Ave, NYC NY 10022 (212) 752–0600.**

Manhattan Day School. Full J & secular studies curriculum with J studies courses conducted in Heb; 3 pre- ꞏn levels including half day nursery for 3 yr olds, full day nursery for 4 yr olds & K for 5 yr olds; regular prog for grades 1–8. F in 1943 to serve the needs of the Manhattan J com. Most sch grads go on to Yeshiva HS. Pres: Charles Bendheim; Dean: Rabbi Shlomo Riskin; Prin: Rabbi David Kaminetsky; Chr, Bd of Dirs: Max Stern; VPs: Barry Eisenberg, Aaron Green, Myron Smith. **310 W 75th St, NYC NY 10023 (212) 595–6800.**

The Marsha Stern Talmudical Academy – Yeshiva University High School for Boys. Offers four-yr col preparatory curriculum with a complete J studies prog leading to an academic HS Diploma with NY State Regents endorsement. Also incorporates special P'TACH Prog enabling boys with mild learning disabilities to receive full benefit of regular J all-day HS edu. F 1916. **2540 Amsterdam Ave, NYC NY 10033.**

The Martin Steinberg Center of the American Jewish Congress. Ctr for J artists. To create a warm & supportive com for artists; to study & experience J culture & tradition; to dev new artists & help bring out their work. Workshops; films; art festivals; study groups; coffee house; library; music archives. Est in 1976. Jewish Arts Newsletter. The Ctr has produced a series of radio progs & three films. Chr Adv Bd: Bernard Madoff; Co-Chr: Rabbi Balfour Brickner; Prog Chr: Amram Nowak; Dir: Jeff Oboler; Adm Assc: Chava Miller. **15 E 84th St, NYC NY 10028 (212) 879–4500.**

Max Weinreich Center for Advanced Studies. 1048 Fifth Ave, NYC NY 10028.

Medem Jewish Socialists Group. Democratic socialist org affiliated with J Labor Bund. To further dev of secular J culture & the language Yiddish. lectures; forums. It is named after Vladimir Medem, a leader of the Bund. Co-pub of the journal Jewish Socialist Critique. Sec: Daniel Soyer. **25 E 78th St, NYC NY 10021 (212) 535–0850.**

Memorial Foundation for Jewish Culture. Serv org affiliated with J orgs. To assure a creative J future by promoting J scholarship & edu research. Institutional grants for research, pub, edu; univ J studies to help univs est & expand depts of J studies; documentation & commemoration of the Holocaust to encourage research on the Holocaust; com servs scholarships; doctorial scholarships; post rabbinical scholarships; fellowships in J culture. Est in 1964 by the Conf on J Material Claims Against Germany as a living memorial to the six million J who died in the Holocaust. Pres: Dr Nahum Goldman; VPs: Leon Dulzin, Dr Solomon Gaon, Philip M. Klitznick; Treas: Jack J. Spitzer; Sec: Rabbi Israel Miller; Exec Dir: Dr Norman E. Frimer. **15 E 26th St, NYC NY 10010 (212) 679–4074.**

Mendel Gottesman Library. For information on the Univ, see – Yeshiva University, New York City, NY. **Yeshiva Univesity, 500 W 185th St, NYC NY 10033.**

Mesorah. Natl collegiate youth org of the Union of Orthodox Jewish Cong of Am. Fights intermarriage, & missionary influences on & off the campus. **45 W 36th St, NYC NY 10018 (212) 563–4000.**

Metropolitan Synagogue. Affiliated with UAHC. 235 mems. Rabbis: Judah Cahn, Charles J. Davidson; Cantor Norman J. Atkins; Pres: Barnie Brody. **10 Park Ave, NYC NY 10016 (212) 679–8580.**

Mikvah of Mid Manhattan. 234 W 78th St, NYC NY 10024 (212) 799–1520.

Mikveh of Washington Heights. 536 W 187th St, NYC NY 10033 (212) 568–1780.

Millinery Center Synagogue. 1025 Sixth Ave, NYC NY 10025 (212) 921–1580.

Mizrachi Palestine Fund. 200 Park Ave S, NYC NY 10003 (212) OR3–8100.

The Mount Sinai Medical Center. Affiliated with Beth Is Med Ctr, Vets Adm Med Ctr Bronx NY, City Hosp Ctr at Elmhurst, The J Home & Hosp for Aged, Joint Diseases N Gen Hosp, Hosp for Joint Diseases Orthopaedic Ins. Depts: Anatomy, Anesthesiology, Biophysics, Biomathematical Sci, Com Med, Dentistry, Dermatology, Health Care Mgmnt, Microbiology, Med Edu, Med, Neoplastic Diseases, Neurology, Neurosurgery, Obstetrics & Gynecology, Ophthalmology, Orthopaedics, Otolaryngology, Pathology, Pediatrics, Pharmacology, Physiology & Biophysics, Psychiatry, Radiology, Radiotherapy, Rehabilitation Med, Surgery, Urology. 1,200 beds; 36,000 inpatients annually; 100,000 outpatients annually; 475 med stu; 22 MD & PhD stu; 61 PhD stu. 1,400 physicians; 2,400 faculty at the Sch of Med. In 1852 a group of nine J New Yorkers secured a charter for the charitable & sci soc known as The J Hosp in NY, later to be known as the Mount Sinai Hosp. Mount Sinai opened on May 17, 1855 in its first home at 138 W 28th St. The Hosp treated more patients at no charge than any other private ins in NY in the 1880's. The recognition Mount Sinai was achieving as a leading ins of patient care, research & edu was built yr by yr on a tradition of philanthropy. In 1962 it was decided to open the Sch of Med. In its early yrs, the Hosp est a reputation as a leading med research ctr. Mount Sinai was the first hosp to have full time chiefs of servs, & among the first to offer residency progs. Its social work dept was the first in NY. The Hosp's Sch of Nursing, now closed, was one of the first to be chartered in NY State. In the 1970's, the new med sch & the hosp were combined to form an integrated med ctr. Chr: Alfred R. Stern; Chr Emeritus: Alfred L. Rose; V Chr: Mrs Jack R. Aron, William T. Golden, Fredrick A. Klingenstein, Henry A. Loeb, Stephen M. Peck; Sec: M. Ronald Brukenfeld; Treas: Edgar M. Cullman; Assc Treas: William Wishnick. **Fifth Ave & 100 St, One Gustave L. Levy Place, NYC NY 10029 (212) 650–6500.**

National Academy for Adult Jewish Studies. 155 Fifth Ave, NYC NY 10010 (212) 260–8450.

National Association of Hebrew Day School Adms. 22 E 28th St, NYC NY 10016 (212) 673–1405.

National Association of Hebrew Day School PTA'S. 229 Park Ave S, NYC NY 10003.

National Association of Jewish Vocational Services. 225 Park Ave S, 16th Fl, NYC NY 10003 (212) 475–2400.

National Association of Temple Adms . Org of professional exec of Reform congs; affiliated with the UAHC. Undertakes research progs on syn mgmnt; Research Studies Cttee pubs periodic surveys on finance, publicity & PR practices, Bd & cttee structure, use of facilities; Congregational Survey Serv offers an evaluation serv to UAHC congs; othe servs include workshops for the training of lay leaders, placements. Journal pub quarterly. **838 Fifth Ave, NYC NY 10021 (212) 249–0100.**

National Association of Temple Educators. Affiliate of the UAHC. Collates & evaluates the latest devs in curricula, administration, teaching methods, audio–visual techniques, & the use of art forms in rel edu; gives placement servs, consultations. NATE News (a quarterly magazine). Mems: Dirs of edu, principals, & rabbis involved in rel edu fr mem congs of the UAHC. **838 Fifth Ave, NYC NY 10021 (212) 249–0100.**

National Bureau of Federated Jewish Women's Organizations. 55 W 42nd St, NYC NY 10036 (212) 736–0240.

National Commission on Torah Education. Rabbi Isaac Elchanan Theological Seminary. Under RIETS, serves as a lay group concerned with Torah edu in all of its ramifications; advocates Torah educator's interests with local & natl umbrella agys; cooperates with Torah educators; serves as a resource for J curriculums & materials dev. **2540 Amsterdam Ave, NYC NY 10033.**

National Committee for Labor Israel. 33 E 67th St, NYC NY 10021 (212) 628–1000.

National Conference of Synagogue Youth. Youth movement of the Union of Orthodox J Congs of Am. Inspiring J youth to be proud, practicing J & responsible citizens. An effective instrument for J revival & return. Over 300 annual conclaves, Shabbatons & seminars; unique progs such as camp seminars, regional & natl conventions, NY Torah Experience, NCSY Goes to Yeshiva, leadership training seminars, Torah fund projs, bks, records & pubs; special programs including: The Our Way Prog for the J Deaf, Russian Outreach Progs, Collegiate Commis. 365 Chapters & 16 regions throughout US & Canada. **45 W 36th St, NYC NY 10018 (212) 563–4000.**

National Conference of Yeshiva Principals. 229 Park Ave S, NYC NY 10003 (212) 674–6700.

National Conference on Soviet Jewry. Coordinating agy for major natl J orgs & local com groups in the US acting on behalf of Soviet J through public edu & social action. Seeks to aid Soviet J who seek their right to leave for Is & elsewhere; to combat rising anti-Semitism in the USSR; to help J live in the Soviet Union with their rights, privileges & freedoms accorded other rel & natl minority groups; to help protect the civil & personal rights of J within the USSR. Sponsors special progs & projs; organizes public meetings & forums; monitors trends in emigration as well as accumulates, evaluates & processes information concerning Soviet J. Est in 1964 as the Am J Conf on Soviet J & reorganized as NCSJ in 1971. The NCSJ has rallied support for the Jackson-Vanik amendment which has given tens of thousands of Soviet J a new life; sponsors the Washington based Congressional Wives for Soviet J; maintains a Washington off in close communication with the current Adm, Congress & Washington based experts; conducts private briefings, implemented the Adopt-A-Prisoner of Conscience Proj & administers the Soviet J Research Bureau. Chr: Theodore R. Mann; V Chrs: Osias G. Goren, Rabbi David Hill, Donald Lefton, Thelma C. Wolf, Nan Wood; Treas: Bobbie Abrams; Fin Sec: Margery Kohrman; Sec: Robert B. Goldmann; Exec Dir: Jerry Goodman; Assc Dirs: Myrna Shinbaum, Mark Heutlinger; PR Dir: Robin S. Wilansky; Exec Cttee: Lucille Brotman, Rabbi David Goldstein, Neil Greenbaum, Lawrence Jackier, Nicholas Lane, Jules Lippert, Richard Neiter, Stuart Raskas, Mervin Riseman, Herbert Rosenthal, Rita Salberg, Herbert Setlow, Joseph Smukler, Nancy Steiner, Will Stern. **10 E 40th St, Suite 907, NYC NY 10016 (212) 679–6122.**

National Council for Jewish Education. 114 Fifth Ave, NYC NY 10011 (212) 675–5656.

National Council for Torah Education. c/o Religious Zionists of America, 25 W 26th St, NYC NY 10010 (212) 289–1414.

National Council of Jewish Women. Women's volunteer org. Dedicated in the spirit of J to advancing human welfare & the democratic way of life. Activities are organized around five prog priorities: women's issues, chil & youth, aging, J life & Is. Women's Issues – major concerns are: ratification of the Equal Rights Amendment, protection of the right of every women to have access to safe & legal abortion, removal of gender related discrimination in all areas of life, provision of edu progs on the prevention of domestic violence & treatment for its victims, widow to widow counseling & progs for single parents. Chil & Youth – primarily concerned with: the rights, needs & quality of life of the nation's chil & youth;, juvenile justice, especially the treatment of adolescent girls; foster care; variety of projs that support servs to the young people in their coms; deeply committed to advocacy efforts needed to effectively change the way chil are treated under the law. Is – carries out numerous edu & social welfare progs in Is; has long been a strong advocate for the State of Is; furthers major proj in Is – The Research Ins for Innovation in Edu which is part of The Hebrew Univ Sch of Edu. J Life – places emphasis on: J edu & the problems of Soviet J; J edu progs for individuals of various ages & interests designed to assist people in exploring their understanding of & attitudes toward J & rekindling their interest in their rel; involvement in the resettlement of Soviet J immigrants & in advocacy on behalf of those J who are refused permission to leave the USSR. Aging – primary focus is on dev of servs f & supports: legislation on behalf of older adults, day ctrs, housing for the elderly, adult edu, enrichment progs, volunteer placement progs, sheltered employment projs, nutrition & transportation servs, multipurpose ctrs, nursing homes, ombudsman progs & self training for & by the elderly. 100,000 mems in 200 cities. F by Hannah Solomon in 1893. NCJW Milestones: In 1894 NCJW was the first J women's group to est Sabbath schs. In 1903 formed Port & Dock Dept to help women arriving alone in US. In 1904 est permanent Immigrant Aid Station on Ellis Island; made the first organized effort for the J blind; & pioneered penny lunch stations in schs. In 1906 NCJW probation off for delinquent chil accepted in municipal courts. In 1920 developed first voluntary Farm & Ritual Work Prog to assist J farmers. In 1923 convened first European Conf of Natl Orgs for J Women. In 1938 helped form German J Chil Aid. In 1945 organized Ship-A-Box Prog to provide edu toys & materials for J K in many countries. In 1946 est Fellowship Prog to train social workers & edu fr eight countries; opened homes in Paris & Athens for girls victimized by Nazis; & launched first network of Golden Age Clubs. In 1947 provided funds to help est Sch of Edu at the Hebrew Univ. In 1952 launched Freedom Campaign to combat threats to civil liberties. In 1957 became the first natl J women's org to sponsor Meals-On-Wheels. In 1960 conducted a nationwide survey of the needs of out-of-sch, unemployed youth, resulting in action prog A Start for Youth. In 1961 helped plan the first White House Conf on the Aging. In 1963 built Hebrew Univ HS in Jerusalem; launched Sr Servs Corps Pilot Prog, later to become Retired Sr Volunteer Prog. In 1964 participated in the est of Women in Com Servs interagy effort to recruit & screen applicants for Fed Job Corps. In 1968 est NCJW Research Ins for Innovation in Edu at the

Hebrew Univ. In 1976 sponsored the Natl Symposium on Status Offenders in Washington DC& NCJW Colloquium on Educating the Disadvantaged bringing together for the first time the Israeli Minister of Edu & the US Commissioner of Edu. In 1977 initiated J Women's Caucus at Intl Women's Yr Conf in Houston. In 1978 present at signing of US – Is Memorandum of Understanding of Edu. In 1979 received grants to dev training models for volunteers in Soviet Resettlement & Foster Care Advocacy projs. In 1980 received grants to study adolescent girls in juvenile justice system; & NCJW played the leading role in the first Natl White House Conf on Families. In 1981 renewed ten yr contract with The Hebrew Univ of Jerusalem for support of the NCJW Research Ins for Innovation in Edu, & est two Chairs at NCJW Research Ins for Innovation in Edu. Windows On Day Care; Children Without Justice; Innocent Victims; Women Helping Women; Monitoring the Juvenile Court; Domestic Violence – An NCJW Response; Community Partners – The Staff/Volunteer Team in Soviet Jewish Resettlement; Options in Living Arrangements: Housing Alternatives for the Elderly. Pres: Shirley I. Leviton; VPs: Shirley Joseph, Barbara Mandel, Florence Schornstein, Elaine Sterling, Claire Wolf; Rec Sec: Bette Miller; Asst Rec Sec: Diane Marowitz; Treas: Lenore Feldman; Asst Treas: Nan Wood; Exec Dir: Dadie Perlov. **15 E 26th St, NYC NY 10010 (212) 532–1740.**

National Council of Young Israel. 3 W 16th St, NYC NY 10011 (212) 929–1525.

National Council on Art in Jewish Life. Artists Assn. To sustain & expand the exploding interest & utilization of the J visual arts. Servs as the umbrella org for J Visual Artists Assn, Pomegranate Guild of Judaic Needlework. Assists syn, com ctrs, artists, mus, galleries, publishers & collectors with problems & questions concerning Judaic art; conducts art shows, seminars; supplies speakers & disseminates information & dates on all aspects of art as it pertains to J culture; serves as a reference for J ins regarding resources & creative artisans, craftpersons & artists; maintains library (articles on J art, bks, pamphlets). 1000 mems. 10–12 volunteers. Celebrates 18th anniversary in 1983. Chr: Harry C. Waterston; Exec VP Julius Schatz; V Chrs: Dr Moshe Davidowitz, Dr Mark Podwal. **15 E 84th St, NYC NY 10028 (212) 879–4500.**

National Federation of Jewish Mens Clubs, Inc. Affiliated in the Conservative movement with United Syn of Am, the J Theological Seminary of Am, & the World Council of Syns. To weld existing separate men's clubs into a strong well-knit body & to guide them toward their highest social, cultural & rel objectives. Sponsors the Home Library of Conservative J, Leaders Training Fellowship, J Youth Resource Ctr, Academy of Leadership – a traveling learning experience which visits all areas of N Am, speakers bureau, the Heb Literacy Campaign – a prog for J adults which enables them to learn & read Heb & participate in Fri Night Servs. Supports USY, Boy Scouts, Atid & Ramah. 30,000 mems in approximately 350 clubs in 14 regions throughout the US, Canada & Mexico. Est in May of 1929 in NYC. The Torchlight (a quarterly magazine); Innovations & Spiritual Readings for Opening Prayers at Meetings; Men's Club Manual & Hand Book for Organized Synagogue Men; Sabbath in Jewish Life; When Religion Becomes Vital; Jewish Ethical Living; How to Be a Good Jewish Father; The Jewish Dietary Laws; Roads to Jewish Survival; Implementation Guide for Hebrew Literacy Campaign; Shalom Aleichem, the Textbook for Hebrew Literacy Campaign; Guides to Men's Club Sabbath; Programming with a Purpose; A Guide to Men's Club Programming; 'How To' Manuals; Digest of Materials for Effective Administration of Clubs & Regions; Installation Service; Model Constitution; Academy of Leadership pamphlets; Responsibility of Jewish Laity. **475 Riverside Dr, Suite 244, NYC NY 10115 (212) 749–8100.**

National Federation of Temple Brotherhoods. Affiliate of the UAHC. To strengthen the progs of its 500 congregational men's clubs & intensify the interest of J laymen in their temple & their faith. Leadership training; leader's workshops; retreats; biennial convention; Lecture Bureau; Temple Attendance Kit to help increase attendance at workship servs; J Chautaugua Soc (JCS) – five–phase prog to create better understanding & appreciation of J & Judaism among people of all faiths. JCS assigns rabbis to lecture on J at more than 2,000 cols; sponsors 110 resident lectureship courses on J for col credit; donates J reference bks to col libraries; fills request to send rabbis to serve as counselor-teachers & chaplains at 450 Christian church summer youth & Boy Scout camps; produces motion pictures on J ethical themes for local public serv TV & group showings. 500 congregational clubs; 70,000 members; Natl Bd of Dirs & professional staff; 16 regional councils, Brotherhood (a quarterly magazine). JCS has produced 33 films (7 have been adapted to radio). The films & tapes are distributed through 106 volunteer local distributors in the mayor cities. Pres: David N. Krem. **838 Fifth Ave, NYC NY 10021 (212) 249–0100.**

National Federation of Temple Sisterhoods. Women's agency of Reform Judaism; affiliate of the

UAHC. Serves J & humanitarian causes. Provides rel edu aids, advice on Sisterhood problems, leadership training, speakers bureau, family edu, prog materials, study guides; F & patron of J Braille Ins of Am Inc, which operates progs on behalf of the J & non–J blind; works on behalf of the HUC–JIR; Youth, Edu & Sisterhood Fund (YES). Fund beneficiaries include: Natl Fed of Temple Youth; rabbinic stu at the HUC–JIR, overseas rabbinic stu of the World Union, & NFTS prog dev. Rep organization of 630 Reform Temple Sisterhoods with more than 110,000 members throughout the US & in cities of Canada, Panama, Netherlands, Antilles, Guatemala, Argentina, the United Kingdom, Belgium, Holland, Israel, Republic of S Africa, Rhodesia, India, Australia & New Zealand. Oldest affiliate of the UAHC. Pres: Constance Kreshtool. **838 Fifth Ave, NYC NY 10021 (212) 249–0100.**

National Foundation for Jewish Culture. 122 E 42nd St, NYC NY 10017 (212) 490–2280.

National Foundation for Jewish Culture, Library. Chanin Building, Rm 1512, 122 E 42nd St, NYC NY 10017.

National Hebrew Culture Council. 1776 Bdwy, NYC NY 10019 (212) 247–0741.

National Jewish Commission on Law & Public Affairs. 71 Bdwy, NYC NY 10006 (212) 269–0810.

National Jewish Community Relations Advisory Council. 443 Park Ave S, NYC NY 10016 (212) 684–6950.

National Jewish Resource Center. To strengthen the internal life of the Am J com; to serve & enrich J leadership through its two main ctrs: Shamor & Zachor. For additional information on Shamor & Zachor, se Shamor, The Center for Jewish Enrichment, NYC, NY; Zachor: Holocaust Study & Commemoration, New York City, NY. Consultant to the J com in helping J communal bodies & groups to enrich their J content progs & work more closely together; lobbyist for the J com by proposing new progs & strategies for adoption by existing groups; initiator of its own progs where a vacuum of leadership or of organizational capacity has existed; edu of com leaders by inspiring & broadening the ranks of leadership through deepening their J identity, & by increasing their experience & their knowledge; sponsor of Shamor J Leadership Enrichment which includes Chevra (soc for the advancement of J thought), leadership study groups, ins, retreats, confs, resource materials; sponsor of Zachor Holocaust Study & Commemoration which includes liturgy & ritual, faculty seminars, consultations, resource materials. Mems include Natl orgs such as the UJA, the Council of J Fed, local feds & programming alliances, cong, & rabbinical bodies, & ins such as the YM-YWHA. F in 1973 by Irving Greenberg, Elie Wiesel & Steven Shaw. Tri-annual Shoa magazine. Chr: Irvin Frank; Pres: Edwin Ellman; V Chr: Jeffrey Boyko; Dir: Dr Irving Greenberg; Hon Chr: Elie Wiesel; Asst Dir: Rabbi Anson Laytner; Staff Assc for Zachor: Susan Grossman. **Suite 216, 250 W 57th St, NYC NY 10107.**

New Jewish Agenda. Political & edu org. To be a progressive voice in the J com & a J voice among progressives. Edu progs on a wide range of issues including ME peace, nuclear disarmament, anti–Semitism, J feminism. 2500 mems. 3 employees. Started at a f conference in Dec 1980; merged with Shalom Network in July 1982. Pub Agenda Newsletter (quarterly); Shalom Network Newsletter (6 times a yr) provides information on the peace movement in Is. **1123 Bdwy, Rm 1217, NYC NY 10010 (212) 620–0828.**

New World Club. 2121 Bdwy, NYC NY 10023 (212) 873–7400.

New York Association for New Americans. 225 Park Ave S, NYC NY 10003 (212) 674–7400.

The New York School of Education – HUC-JIR. Created to meet the edu needs of Reform congs for dirs of rel educ, principals & teachers. Offers certification prog & prog leading to degree of MA in Rel Edu. For information on the Col, see – Hebrew Union College – Jewish Institute of Religion, New York City, NY. Dean: Rabbi Paul M. Steinberg. **One W 4th St, NYC NY 10012 (212) 873–0388.**

New York Society for the Deaf. A voluntary non-profit org; receives fin support fr the Fed of J Philanthropies of NY. To provide generic servs on a non-sectarian basis to the deaf com in the Met NY area. Servs include: information & referral, for both deaf & hearing people, on all facilities & available servs; sign language interpreters serv which provides certified & other sign language interpreters for all purposes including legal & med specialities on a 24 hour, seven day a week basis; Am sign language instruction; personal & family counseling under the direction of a certified social worker who can communicate with the deaf; job placement & vocational counseling; Tanya Towers, a housing prog for elderly deaf & other elderly & disabled; Berger Deaf Scholars Prog which provides scholarships for deaf persons seeking grad degrees through NY Univ Deafness Research & Training Ctr; group work with deaf of all ages by qualified workers at facilities for social, edu & athletic progs; psychological testing which determines intelligence, aptitude & emotional quotients of the deaf; advocacy on behalf of the deaf; meeting accommodations for Hebrew Assn of the Deaf & its Sisterhood; rel worship in sign language for deaf of J com; summer camping prog for deaf chil & adults; Substance Abuse Proj; Elderly Deaf & Deaf Blind progs. Est in 1911 & inc by a special act of the NY State Legislature in 1913. The org operates under a total communications policy which encourages deaf persons to communicate by any means comfortable to them including sign language, finger spelling, lip reading, speech, writing, mime, gesture, & body language. Exec Dir: Joel D. Ziev; Pres: Dr Jerome D. Schein; Chr of the Bd: Joseph G. Blum; VPs: Robert S. Caress, Julian Lynton, Col Joseph I. Sonnenreich; Sec: Bella Nusbaum; Treas: Nathan C. Belth. **344 E 14th St, NYC NY 10003, Teletypewriter Phone for the Deaf (212) 673–6974, Phone for the Hearing (212) 673–6500.**

Noar Mizrachi. 25 W 26th St, NYC NY 10010 (212) 689–1914.

North American Aliyah Movement. 515 Park Ave, NYC NY 10022 (212) 752–0600.

North American Federation of Temple Youth. 838 Fifth Ave, NYC NY 10021 (212) 249–0100.

North American Jewish Council. 515 Park Ave, NYC NY 10022 (212) 751–6070.

North American Jewish Students Appeal. Central fund raising mechanism for natl, independent, J stu orgs which insures accountability of public J communal funds used by these agy; assists stu undertaking projs of concern to the J com; advises & assists J orgs in determining stu proj feasibility & impact; fosters dev of J stu leadership in the J com. Beneficiaries include local & regional J stu projs on campuses throughout N Am: J Stu Press Serv; N Am J Stu Network; Stu Struggle for Soviet J; Response; Yugntruf; Stu Coalition for Soviet J; Genesis 2; Focus; Tampa J Stu Union. Chr: Suzanne Parelman; V Chr: Alan Molod, Jacqueline Levine, Gordon Zacks; Sec: Nat Kameny; Pres: Steven M. Cohen; Exec Dir: Roberta Shiffman; Trustees: Donald Benjamin, Jerry Benjamin, Robyn Berenstein, Theodore Bikel, Harvey Blitz, Margo Bloom, Emma Burstyn, Susan Dessel, Julius Eisen, Daniel Elazar, Edith Everett, David Factor, Leonard Fein, Moses Feuerstein, Irwin Field, Carl Glick, Mark Gold, Paul Goldberg, William Goldenberg, Robert Goldman, Jonathan Groner, Rabbi Oscar Groner, Susan Grossman, Rabbi Arthur Hertzberg, Malcolm Hoenlein, Sanford Hollander, Albie Hornblass, Richard Horowitz, S. Hal Horowitz, Anne Jacobs, Bobie Klotz, Jeffrey Lautman, Helaine Lender, Bud Levin, Robert Levy, Deborah Lipstadt, Avi Lyon, David Makovsky, Richard Manekin, Andi Minkoff, Sam Norich, Nell Norry, Harvey Paretzky, Michael Pelavin, Natalle Pelavin, Allen Pollack, Mitchell Rasansky, Glenn Richter, Gary Rubin, Janice Rudy, Stuart Schear, Lois Schlar, Leslie Schnur, Robert Schrayer, David Shapiro, Arden Shenker, Joel Sherman, Reena Wein, Sinkah Weintraub, Barbara Wiener, Elaine Winik. **15 E 26th St, Suite 1350, NYC NY 10010 (212) 679–2293.**

North American Jewish Students' Network. 15 E 26th St, Suite 1350, NYC NY 10010 (212) 869–8610.

Orthodox Jewish Archives – Agudath Israel of America. Documents hist of the world movement; includes material about Orthodox J nationally & internationally; maintains major section on the rescue of J during the Holocaust yrs. Has received important collections of papers on the rescue work of Orthodox J & agys. Est early 1978. For information on the Ins, see – Agudath Israel of America, NYC NY. **5 Beekman St, NYC NY 10038 (212) 964–1620.**

Ozar Hatorah, Inc. 411 Fifth Ave, NYC NY 10016 (212) 684–4733.

P'eylim-American Yeshiva Student Union. 3 W 16th St, NYC NY 10011 (212) 989–2500.

P'TACH Program, Marsha Stern Talmudical Academy Yeshiva University HS. Special edu prog for boys in a Yeshiva setting. To integrate boys with mild learning disabilities into the regular classes & activities of the sch by offering each stu an individual edu prog. Resource Ctr facilities: stu receive tutorial assistance including supplementary lessons, assignments & special adm of tests & alternative classes; individualized instruction; J & gen studies; pre-vocational training; industrial arts; vocational training, sports prog; stu council; guidance & counseling servs; dormitory & food facilities. F in 1979 by a parents group, Parents for Torah for All Chil, in cooperation with Yeshiva Univ HS for Boys, Manhattan & its parent body Yeshiva Univ. A NY State HS diploma is awarded to those who pass the Regents Competency Test in English & Mathematics. A certificate of attendance is awarded to those not fulfilling NY State HS diploma requirements but indicating those courses that the stu has completed. Those stu who receive passing grades on the HS Equivalency Examinations are eligible for NY State HS Equivalency Diplomas. There is also a P'TACH Prog for girls with learning disabilities. Prin: Rabbi David L. Weinbach; Asst Prin: Rabbi George B. Finkelstein; P'TACH Prog Dir: Joel Dickstein; Pres: Cynthia Zalisky; Chr Professional Adv Cttee: Dr Joel Rosenshein; Chr Bd:

Dr Melvin Hyman; Chr Prog Steering Cttee: Rabbi Burton Jaffa. **Amsterdam Ave & 186th St, NYC NY 10033 (212) 960–5337.**

Park Avenue Synagogue. Affiliated with United Syn of Am. Rabbi Judah Nadich; Cantor David Lefkowitz; Pres: Martin Milston; Exec Dir: Barrie Modlin. **50 E 87th St, NYC NY 10028 (212) 369–2600.**

PEC Israel Economic Corporation. 511 Fifth Ave, NYC NY 10017 (212) 687–2400.

P.E.F. Israel Endowment Funds, Inc. A tax exempt non-profit public charity. Secondary sch scholarships for chil of Oriental extraction; grants for applied sci, ins of learning including univ & yeshivoth, hosps & health care facilities, ins for the blind & disabled & aged & needy, innovative teaching, archaeological exploration, cultural ins, welfare of soldiers, & women's orgs. The beneficiaries range fr such major ones as the Hebrew Univ, various HS scholarship funds coordinated by the Edu & Culture Ministry to the Soldiers Welfare Assn. They have also included medium sized orgs such as the Yad Sarah Org for Free Loan Med Equipment, ILAN, & the Intl Culture Ctr for Youth in Jerusalem. F in 1922. P.E.F. assets are about $10,000,000. Contributions, both small & large, may be sent to P.E.F. with a recommendation by the donor for use in Is. Chr: Julius Weiss; Pres: Sidney Musher; VPs: Sidney B. Becker, Sydney A. Luria, Joshua Morrison; Treas: Howard L. Perlmutter; Asst Treas: William Gold, Sheldon S. Gordon; Sec: Burt Allen Solomon; Asst Sec: Isabelle Clarke; Trustees: Aaron Baroway, Sidney B. Becker, Mrs Abner Brenner, Benjamin V. Cohen, Moses P. Epstein, William Lee Frost, Mrs Eli Ginzberg, Simon Glick, Ezra Goodman, Philip Goodman, Sheldon S. Gordon, Milton M. Gottesman, Marc L. Hurwitz, Irving H. Isaac, Abraham J. Kremer, Ralphe E. Loewenberg, Sydney A. Luria, Boris Margolin, Marcus D. Mason, Joshua Morrison, Sidney Musher, Irving S. Norry, Stella Rabinowitz, William Rosensohn, Dr Abram L. Sachar, Stephen Shalom, Burt Allen Solomon, Dr Henry Sonneborn III, Mary Ann Stein, Richard B. Stone, Stephen Stulman, Julius Weiss, Herbert L. Werner, Robert L. Zinn.**342 Madison Ave, Suite 1010, NYC NY 10173 (212) 599–1260.**

Pioneer Women – Na'amat. The sister org of Na'amat in Is. A mem of the Conf of Pres of Major Am J Orgs, the Am Zionist Fed, the Natl Conf on Soviet J; a participant in all natl Is fundraising campaigns. The training & edu of the Is woman & her family so that each can be best equipped to lead productive lives. Day care ctrs for chil fr three mo to five yrs of age; chil care ctrs; day-night homes to provide the parentless child, during his earliest yrs, with the warm & loving care which will allow him to dev into a healthy & happy adult; group work with adolescent girls aged 14–18 through a club prog which provides a structured environment for the teenager who is having problems coping with her emerging adulthood & has nowhere to turn for guidance; after sch clubs which provide the sch age chil with a place to study in a comfortable, quiet, supervised atmosphere; three agricultural schs, all operated as regular four yr coeducational boarding schs where all stu follow a course of study which is divided into half day sessions – one half devoted to academic studies & one half day to courses in agriculture, gardening, botany; Vocational Sch Network which provides various types of edu & training; vocational training for women which is provided through a great variety of courses in fields where jobs are readily available; club work among the Arab & Druze women in Is; special prog for teenage Arab girls which combines academic courses with practical vocation training; com ctrs which provide social servs & bring together the different immigrant groups; The Mother Chil Summer Camp which provides mothers of large deprived families a short vacation, accompanied by her two youngest chil; Advancement of the Woman & Family In Soc Prog which works mostly with semi-literate woman faced with the care of large families in small apts, limited funds, & husbands reared in Eastern values of male supremacy, through weekly group sessions in which the women are acquainted with contemporary methods of family care, as well as provided a forum for discussion of their mutual family problems. 800,000 active mems world wide; 20,000 youngsters in 500 day nurseries. Moetzet Hapoalot was first est in Is in 1921. Four yrs later, Pioneer Women was f in the US as its overseas arm. In 1976 Moetzet Hapoalot changed its name to Na'amat. In 1976 Friends of Pioneer Women, the men's affiliate, was organized. Natl Pres: Phyllis Sutker; Natl VP Membership: Gloria Elbling; Natl VP Prog: Phyllis Frank; Natl VP Org: Edythe Rosenfield; Natl VP Allied Funds: Judith Telman; Natl VP Na'amat: Harriet Green; Natl Treas: Annette Navis; Natl Fin Sec: Zelda Lemberger; Natl Sec: Dorothy Margolis; Natl Exec Dir: Shoshonna Ebstein. **200 Madison Ave, NYC NY 10016 (212) 725–8010.**

Pirchei Agudath Israel. Div for boys within Natl Commis on Youth – Agudath Is of Am. To serve as a training ground for responsible leadership roles in the com. More than 25,000 youths led by 1,700 volunteer leaders benefit from activities including weekly progs which prepare youth for a life dedicated to loyal J serv & responsible voluntarism; summer camp – Camp Agudah in New York's Catskill Mountains accomodates a large num of youngsters from poor homes – the materially improvished as well as the spiritually deprived. For information on the Ins, see – Agudath Israel of America, New York City, NY. **5 Beekman St, NYC NY 10038 (212) 964–1620.**

Poale Agudath Israel of America. 156 Fifth Ave, NYC NY 10010 (212) 924–9475.

Project Ezra. Independent, non-profit org serving the J elderly on the Lower E Side. To relieve the elders of poverty & social & emotional isolation. Volunteer Prog: approximately 50 volunteers are involved on a weekly basis with Ezra clients; stu groups help before major J holidays delivering food packages, cleaning up syns & participating in holiday preparations. Case Work: assigns a case supervisor to clients who are especially needy. Nursing Prog: participates in the City Col nursing prog for registered nurses who are receiving BA degrees – nurses visit clients on a weekly basis during the sch semester. Special projs: works with syns & schs hosting progs for Ezra clients which provides an opportunity for the homebound elderly to leave their neighborhoods; buses & special vans for the disabled are provided. Small groups: provides for Craft Group, Peer Volunteer Group, Writing Workshop, J Studies Group, Oneg Shabbat. Serves approximately 200 elders. Paid staff & volunteers. Est in 1976. Bd of Dirs: Alison Alpert, Misha Avramoff, Susie Kessler, Lois Lowenstein, Zev Mindlin, Kay Newman, Rina Pianko, Terrie Raphael, Sheila Rubin, Jayne Skoff. **197 E Bdwy, NYC NY 10002 (212) 982–4124.**

Project RISE – Russian Immigrant Services & Education. Prog of Agudath Is of Am. To restore the J roots of refugees fr Communist Russia. Helps in gaining employment, provides monthly bulletin in Russian language, sponsors after–sch prog through JEP for Russian immigrant chil in Brighton Beach Coney Island area, provides all rel articles, circumcisions, summer camps, edu experiences, personal counseling, 'adopt-a-family' prog; sends parcels to J in Eastern Europe through Proj YAD, and packages with special kosher Passover food to Soviet Russia; supports proj & facilities for rel absorption of Soviet J in Is through Russian Immigrant Rescue Fund. For information on the Ins, see – Agudath Israel of America, New York City, NY. **5 Beekman St, NYC NY 10038 (212) 964–1620.**

Rabbi Isaac Elchanan Theological Seminary. Affiliate of Yeshiva University. Leading sch in nation for preparaion of Orthodox rabbis to minister to the needs of J com in US & other countries. Ctr for intensive Torah study in classic spirit of J; trains scholars, teachers, & researchers with a rich grounding in original sources, who will perpetuate & enhance J scholarship; serves com needs with a network of auxiliary prog & special projs; grants Semikhah (ordination). Includes: Semikhah Prog which is a three yr intensive study of Talmud & Codes; Brookdale Chaplaincy Internship Prog designed for prospective Rabbis who wish to develop skills necessary for working effectively with aged (sponsored by Brookdale Foun); Caroline & Joseph S Gruss Ins in Jerusalem for advanced Talmudic Studies; Marcos & Adina Katz Kollel (Ins for Advanced Research in Rabbinics) which provides intensive training in Talmudic research for stu planning to become teacher-scholars (roshei yeshiva), or enables young men with other career interests to engage in advanced Talmudic scholarship. Special academic progs include: Kollel l'Horaah (Yadin Yadin) – an intensive two-yr prog which trains selected, especially gifted young Talmud scholars to prepare for the roles of posekim, decisors of J law; Chaver Prog which develops edu J laity through a post-col yr of concentrated J learning in areas related to stu chosen profession; Maybaum Sephardic Fellowship Prog which trains rabbis for serv in Sephardic com – courses in Sephardic Halakhah, Spanish or Arabic, & other pertinent areas; Cantorial Training Ins which provides professional training of cantors & other music personnel for the J com, & awards Assoc Cantor's Certificate & Cantorial Diploma. A major prog is the Sephardic Community Activites Prog which dev congs in US & Canada & Latin Am; conducts an Annual Sephardic Cultural Festival; offers adult edu courses & youth activities; provides lecturers, rabbis, cantors, & teachers to Sephardic com; sponsors conf of syn leaders & Sephardic scholars; promotes Sephardic culture & language through Spanish-language materials, home study groups, & other outreach progs. F 1896. For information on Div of Communal Servs, see – Rabbi Isaac Elchanan Theological Seminary, Div of Communal Services, New York City, NY. **2540 Amsterdam Ave, NYC NY 10033.**

Rabbi Isaac Elchanan Theological Seminary – Div of Communal Services. Serves J com in US, Canada, Is, S & Central Am, Australia & S Africa with special attention to outreach to the young, serv to the elderly, & other edu, communal, rel & soc progs. Depts include: Dept of Rabbinic Servs which provides progs for the personal & professional dev of men in the rabbinate & related fields, including counseling for students considering careers in J com serv, & a Rabbinic placement serv for pulpit positions, Hillel, mil & civilian chaplaincy, & J com agys; Dept of Syn Servs which offers guidance & assistance to syns through field visitiation, contact with lay leaders, dev of programming material for com leaders, assists in establishment of new com, provides for special needs of the Sephardic com; Dept of Youth Servs which assists syn & coms in establishing & strengthening youth activities & provides direct outreach progs to countries mentioned above; Dept of Edu Servs which provides for J edu needs by recruiting, advising, & placing adm & teachers in sch & agy settings, servs professional edu bodies, advances J edu through dev of resource materials & programming servs for educators, offers counseling servs to young men & women considering a career in J edu; Dept of Cantorial Servs which places cantors, baalei tefilah, & multifunctional staff in full-time, part-time, & seasonal positions; serves as liason to Cantorial Council of Am. For information on Seminary, see – Rabbi Isaac Elchanan Theological Seminary, New York City, NY. **2540 Amsterdam Ave, NYC NY 10033.**

Rabbinical Alliance of America – Igud Harabonim. Ortrhodox rabbinical org. To provide support servs to mems of the rabbinate; to take stand on issues of importance to the J com; to further the cause of Orthodox J Torah observance without compromise. The Rabbinical Alliance maintains a Beit Din (Rabbinical Ct) for serv to the J com by providing for Gittin (J Divorces), a court of arbitration for disputes; Din Torahs provides family & marriage counseling; publishes Torah articles & journals; performs activities in support of the rabbis in their positions; engages in public relations activities on behalf of J causes. 504 mems. F 1942. Pres: Rabbi Abraham B. Hecht; Exec VP: Rabbi Saul Eisner. **156 Fifth Ave, NYC NY 10010 (212) 242–6420, 255–8313.**

Rabbinical Assembly. 3080 Bdwy, NYC NY 10027 (212) 749–8000.

Rabbinical Council of America. 1250 Bdwy, NYC NY 10001 (212) 594–3780.

Ramaz. Day sch. To provide a high quality J & gen edu. 865 stu nursery–12th grade. Est in 1937 by Cong Kehilath Jeshurun. F & first Dir was Rabbi Joseph H. Lookstein. Prin: Rabbi Haskel Lookstein; Adm: Dr Noam Shudofsky; Bd of Trustees – Hon Chr: A. Phillip Goldsmith, Joseph Lorch; Chr: Lawrence A. Kobrin; V Chr: Melvin D. Newman; Treas: Arthur C. Silverman; Fin Sec: Ira Rennert; Sec: Steven Gross; Mems of Bd: Estanne Abraham, George A. Baumgarten, Hal Beretz, Albert H. Bernstein, Benjamin Brown, Dr Perry Davis, Joshua Deutsch, Nancy N. Dubler, Samuel Eisenstat, Alfred M. Frankel, Rae Gurewitsch, Alvin K. Hellerstein, Prof Louis Henkin, George Jacobs, Lillian Jacobs, Morton Kassover, Dr Samuel Klagsbrun, Walter Koppel, Morris L. Kramet, Dr Terry Ann Krulwich, Ezra G. Levin, Bleda Lindenbaum, Edith Lipiner, Myron B. Poloner, Robert Riederman, Marcella Rosen, Howard Rubenstein, Nathan Salzman, Frances Schub, Fred Schwartzberg, Irwin Shapiro, Judy Tanz, Herschel Waldman, Dr Frederick Zuckerman; Life Trustees: Harry W. Baumgarten, Max J. Etra, Irving Kobrin, Max Sadinoff, Elgin Shulsky, Samuel Singer; Hon Trustees: Hon Robert Abrams, Hon Harrison J. Goldin, Nathan Goldsmith, Mrs Joseph H. Lookstein, Raphael Recanati; Parents Council Pres: Rochelle Fang. **125 E 85th St, NYC NY 10028 (212) 427–1000; The Rabbi Joseph H. Lookstein Upper Sch: 60 E 78th St, NYC NY 10021.**

Ramaz School Library. For information on the Sch, see – Ramaz, New York City, NY. **60 E 78th St, NYC NY 10021.**

Reconstructionist Federation of Congregations & Fellowships. 432 Park Ave S, NYC NY 10016 (212) 889–9080.

Reconstructionist Rabbinical Association. (In Heb: Hevrat Ha Rabbinim L'shikum Ha Yehadut). To advance J as a rel civilization in consonance with the values of tradition & the spirit & requirements of the times; to work in co-operation with the J Reconstructionist Foun, the Fed of Reconstructionist Congs & Havurot, & the Reconstructionist Rabbinical Col in the furthering of the above goal; to promote & encourage the interchange of ideas & J learning among its mems; to foster fellowship & co-operation among rabbis, J scholars & others who serve the J com; to serve the welfare of its mems. Annual convention; mid-yr meetings; local RRA meetings; Bet-Din for resolution of problems. 80 & increasing; comprised of alumni of the RRC, rabbis serving congs or havurot affiliated with the Fed of Reconstructionist Cong & Havurot, faculty of the RRC, rabbis graduated fr recognized rabbinical ins who wish to identify with & work towards the goals of the Assn. Est in 1975 by grads of the Reconstructionist Rabbinical Col in Phila, & other interested rabbis. Membership then was 22. Quarterly journal: Ra'ayonot. Pres: Rabbi Elliot Skiddell; VP: Rabbi Kenneth Berger; Rec Sec: Rabbi Linda Holzman; Corsp Sec: Rabbi Michael Swartz; Treas: Rabbi Gary Gerson. **423 Park Ave S, Suite 1206–08, NYC NY 10016 (212) 889–9080.**

Reform Jewish Appeal. 838 Fifth Ave, NYC NY 10021 (212) 249–0100.

Religious Zionists of America. 25 W 26th St, NYC NY 10010.

Research Foundation for Jewish Immigration, Inc. Edu foun. Holds jointly with the Ins Fur Zeitgeschichte in Munich, archives of 25,000 biographies of outstanding emigres of the Nazi period; maintains oral hist collection on J immigration since 1933; trains research asscs; maintains master file. F in 1971 for the preparation, research, writing & editing of the hist of German-J immigrants of the Nazi period, & their resettlement & acculturation. Jewish Immigrants of the Nazi Period in the U.S.A.; International Biographical Dictionary of Central European Emigres 1933–1945. Sec & Coord of Research: Herbert A. Strauss; Bd of Dirs: Hans J. Frank, Max Gruenewald, Fred W. Lessing, Joseph Maier, Gerald Mayer, Curt C. Silberman, Hermann E. Simon, Herbert A. Strauss, Albert U. Tietz, Franz Winkler. **570 Seventh Ave, NYC NY 10018 (212) 921–3871.**

Research Institute of Religious Jewry, Inc. 471 West End Ave, NYC NY 10024 (212) 874–7979.

Rika Breuer Teachers Seminary. Advanced J edu & teacher training for women. Provides the opportunity for young women to pursue advanced J studies in the true Torah spirit, & to acquire the solid grounding in Torah they vitally need for J living in the modern world; seeks to dev its stu as personalities with the knowledge of & firm loyalty to Torah values, & the enthusiastic desire to serve Klall Yisrael in their spirit. Traditional disciplines: Chumash, Nach, Dinim, Heb, Hist, Post-Biblical Literature & Thought; contemporary problems & issues courses; music; arts & crafts; home-study & assignments; study groups; guest lectures; seminary weekends; vocational training progs; specialized training in edu; social activities. 109 evening div stu; 66 day div stu. Opened in Sept of 1963 as an evening ins, with an enrollment of 33 stu. A day div was added in Sept 1964 with an enrollment of 10 fulltime stu. Since then, the ins has grown rapidly by drawing stu fr the area as well as out of town. Facilities: auditorium, library, dormitory. Prin: Rabbi Joseph Elias; Faculty: Rabbi Solomon Carlebach, Rabbi Chaim Elbaum, Rabbi Eliyahu Glucksman, Rabbi Joseph Leiser, Rabbi Yaakov Posen, Rabbi Eliezer Perr, Leah Halberg, Rivka Samson, Nechama Salomon, Esther Sorscher. **95–103 Bennett Ave, NYC NY 10033.**

Rodeph Sholom Congregation. Affiliated with UAHC. 900 mems. Rabbis: Gunter Hirschberg, Seth L. Bernstein; Cantor Ephraim Biran; Pres: Norman I. Schafler; Edu: Irwin Shlachter; Adms: David N. Fischer, Jack Eisenberg; Sisterhood Pres: Barbara Lustig; Brotherhood Pres: Herbert Levy. **7 W 83rd St, NYC NY 10024 (212) 362–8800.**

Roumanian Jewish Federation of America, Inc. 210 W 101th St, NYC NY 10025 (212) 866–2214.

The Sacred Music Press, Hebrew Union College – Jewish Institute of Religion. Pub arm of Sch of Sacred Music. **One W 4th St, NYC NY 10012 (212) 873–0388.**

The School of Sacred Music – HUC-JIR. Trains cantors & syn music dir; awards the degrees of Bachelor of Sacred Music & Master of Arts (with specialization in Sacred Music); offers 'Life Experience' Prog designed to enable cantors of long experience & training to earn the Bachelor of Sacred Music degree in less than usual period. Cantor Certification Program est to set standards among cantors. The Prog in Sacred Music in Los Angeles offers special courses for syn professionals, organists & choir directors. For information on the Col, see – Hebrew Union College – Jewish Institute of Religion, New York City, NY. Dean: Rabbi Paul M. Steinberg. **One W 4th St, NYC NY 10012 (212) 873–0388.**

Selfhelp Community Services. Multipurpose, not-for-profit agy serving aged persons. Social servs; homemaking & housekeeping servs; housing. F in 1936 by refugees, Nazi victims fr Germany & Austria, with the assistance of prominent persons of other rel affiliations. Pres: K. Peter Lekisch; VP: Eric S. Sondheimer; VP & Consultant to the Bd: Kurt G. Herz; VP & Treas: K. Fred Netter; Co-Treas: Edward G. Newman; Asst Treas: Frederick Baum, Ernest M. Grunebaum; Sec: Olga Warmbrunn; Exec Dir: Lawrence Matloff; Assc Dir: Richard S. Aronson; Deputy Dir: Gabriele D. Schiff; Bd of Dirs: Erich J. Aschkenasy, Ella Auerbach, Rudolph Baer, H. Fred Baerwald, Fritz Bamberger, Ursula Bamberger, Dennis A. Baum, Frederick Baum, Matha Bergmann, Ernest Bial, Ellen Blum, Arthur Bondi, Hilda Bondi, Herman Cahn, Robert Dallos, Herman Z. Elbin, Fred S. Fallek, Howard John Fields, Lotte Fields, Ernest Frank, Hans J. Frank, Evelyn Wolf Frankel, Alfred D. Furth, Marie Galpern, Ernest M. Grunebaum, Kurt H. Grunebaum, Frank F. Guthery, Kurt Gutmann, Frank Harris, Max Heine, Frederick Herman, Kurt G. Herz, Hannah Hirschfield, Max H. Hull, Eva Jacoby, Manfred Joel, Stephan Jacoby, Frida Kahn, Anne Kamberg, George Klein, Paul A. Kohlmann, Walter Leipzig, K. Peter Lekisch, Lotte Lekisch, Fred W. Lessing, Joan Lessing, Lee Levi, Heinz Levy, Adolph Lowe, Erwin Lowe, Lizzie Lowenstein, Annemarie Maass, Gertrud Mainzer, Alfred F. Mayer, Irma

Mayer, Reggie Mayer, Mark J. Millard, K. Fred Netter, Edward G. Newman, Arnold Ostwald, Ernest P. Poll, Kurt Preuss, Paul Roche, Ernest Rosenberg, Stephanie Rosenblatt, Samuel Sadin, Gustave Schindler, Hans Schindler, Martha K. Selig, Karen Shewer, Rita Shewer, Dennis Smetana, Eric S. Sondheimer, Werner A. Stein, John Steiner, Hans Steinitz, Henry J. Stern, Ernest C. Stiefel, Toni Stolper, Herbert Strauss, Albert U. Tietz, Frederick Tuchmann, Alice Ullmann, Helen Vogel, Olga Warmbrunn, Erwin Weil, Gisela Weil, Bernard F. Weissman, Marguerite Wyler, Henry Zacharias, John H. Zorek. **44 E 23rd St, NYC NY 10010 (212) 533–7100.**

Sephardic House at the Congregation Shearith Israel in the City of New York. A natl org dedicated to fostering Sephardic hist & culture. To present Sephardic culture in an authentic, creative & meaningful fashion. Maintains pub prog; encourages progs of Sephardic interest & provides resource people to other orgs; sponsors classes & public progs including: Judeo-Spanish literature, Judeo-Arabic folklore, the hist & culture of the Moroccan J, Sephardic Torah commentary, Sephardic mysticism, the J of Syria, Greek J, the songs & traditions of Yemenite J, progs of contemporary J concern. F in the fall of 1978. Sephardic House is based at Cong Shearith Is – the Spanish & Portuguese Syn f in 1654. Sephardic House Newsletter. Dir: Rabbi Dr Marc D. Angel. **8 W 70th St, NYC NY 10023 (212) 873–0300.**

Seven Arts Feature Syndicate & World Wide News Service. Periodical pub. **165 W 46th St, Rm 511, NYC NY 10036 (212) 247–3595.**

Shaaray Tefila Temple. Affiliated with UAHC. 708 mems. Rabbi Harvey M. Tattelbaum; Cantor Steven Puzarne; Pres: Michael Jaffe, Edu: Janie H. Trencher; Adm: Shirley Chernela; Sisterhood Pres: Ruth Bradfield; Brotherhood Pres: David B. Pinter. **250 E 79th St, NYC NY 10021 (212) 535–8008.**

Shamor, The Center for Jewish Enrichment – Natl J Resources Ctr. To deepen the self-awareness & knowledge of Am J. Creates programs for decision makers in J com to stimulate personal J growth through learning & rel experience which cross existing lines of affiliation, & to identify & train emerging leaders through the following progs: Chevra – Society for the Advancement of J Thought, Dialogue, & Community brings together Orthodox, Conservative, & Reform rabbis, academics, & other secular leaders to discuss critical issues facing J com (consists of regular study circles, annual conference, series of adult edu outreach progs); Leadership Study Groups; offers top lay & professional leadership of UJA/Fed progs extended study groups; institutes & retreats; conferences; resource materials which includes an eight-part video series on J leaders throughout hist. Monthly series of Holiday & Personal Growth Guides; Policy Studies. For information on the Ins, see – National Jewish Resources Center, New York City, NY. **250 W 57th St, Suite 216, NYC NY 10107 (212) 582–6116.**

Sherut La'am College Graduate Programme. American Zionist Youth Foundation, 515 Park Ave, NYCNY 10022 (212) 751–6070.

The Society for the Advancement of Judaism. Mother Syn of the Reconstructionist movement in J; affiliated with the Fed of Reconstructionist Congs & Fellowships, & the United Syn. To promote J as the evolving rel civilization of the J people. Rel Sch; library; Adult Edu prog, celebrations of all holidays. 400 families. Formed in 1922. Reconstructionist J blends J tradition with a rel humanistic perspective. It stresses the importance of J peoplehood, Is, the Heb language, J ritual, & J custom. Rabbi Dr Alan W. Miller; Cantor Eliezer Kornreich; Chr of the Bd: Norman A. Schoor; Co-Chr: Noel Berman, Linda Rosenfeld Shulsky; Sec: Sheila Bassman; Treas: Aaron Ziegelman; Comptroller: Joel G. Shapiro; Adm: Jane Canter. **15 W 86th St, NYC NY 10024 (212) SC4–7000.**

The Society for the Advancement of Judaism, Library. For information on the Ins, see – The Society for the Advancement of Judaism, New York City, NY. **15 W 86th St, NYC NY 10024 (212) SC4–7000.**

Southern Brooklyn Community Organization – Agudath Israel of America. To preserve ethnic neighborhoods through effective local org & dev. Works toward est housing, block assns, crime prevention. Particularly successful in Boro Park com, & has gained national reputation as model prog for saving neighborhoods fr erosion through interethnic cooperation. For additional information on the Ins, see – Agudath Israel of Am, New York City, NY. **c/o Agudath Israel of Am, 5 Beekman St, NYC NY 10038 (212) 964–1620.**

Soviet Jewry Research Bureau – National Conference on Soviet Jewry. Monitors trends in emigration; accumulates, evaluates & processes information concerning Soviet J. For additional information on the Ins, see – National Conference on Soviet Jewry, New York City, NY. Chr: Charlotte Jacobson. **10 E 40th St, Suite 907, NYC NY 10016 (212) 679–6122.**

State of Israel Bonds. Sold to individuals, institutions & orgs for purpose of maintaining & developing the State of Israel. To provide a central source of investment capital for Is historic progs of econ dev & immigrant absorption. Sells stock of govt owned Is corporations through its affiliate, Capital for Israel, Inc. **215 Park Avenue S, NYC NY 10003 (212) 677–9650.**

Stephen Wise Free Synagogue. Affiliated with UAHC. 648 mems. Rabbis: Balfour Brickner, Helene Ferris, Edward E. Klein; Cantor Ellen L. Stettner; Pres: Stanley H. Slom; Edu: Myra Carp; Adm: Henry E. Ziegler; Sisterhood Pres: Leah Zayde; Brotherhood Pres: George Pretzfelder. **30 W 68th St, NYC NY 10023 (212) 877–4050.**

Stern College for Women. 245 Lexington Ave, NYC NY 10016 (212) 481–0514.

Stern College for Women, Hedi Steinberg Library. 245 Lexington Ave, NYC NY 10016 (212) 481–0514.

Stone-Sapirstein Center for Jewish Education – Yeshiva University. With the Stone-Sapirstein Chair in J Edu, sponsors innovative courses & coordinates a range of educational, internship, guidance, serv, & outreach progs in J edu at Yeshiva Univ. For additional information on the Univ, see – Yeshiva University, New York City, NY. **500 W 185th St, NYC NY 10033.**

Sutton Place Synagogue. Affiliated with United Syn of Am. Rabbi David B. Kahane; Cantor Kenneth L. Kuransky; Pres: Warren Alpert; Exec Dir: Harriet Janover. **225 E 51st St, NYC NY 10022 (212) 593–3300.**

Synagogue Council of America. 432 Park Ave S, NYC NY 10016 (212) 686–8670.

Synagogue of the Jewish Theological Seminary. Affiliated with United Syn of Am. Rabbi Stanley J. Schachter; Pres: Alan Strook. **3080 Bdwy, NYC NY 10027 (212) RI9–8000.**

Tel-Hai Fund, Inc. 47 W 34th St, NYC NY 10001 (212) 594–2879.

Temple Ansche Chesed. Affiliated with United Syn of Am. Cantor Charles B. Bloch; Pres: Dr Emil Lehman. **West End Ave & 100th St, NYC NY 10025 (212) 865–0600.**

Temple Israel of the City of New York. 112 E 75th St, NYC NY 10021 (212) 249–5000.

Temple of Universal Judaism. 15 Rutherford Pl, NYC NY 10003 (212) 673–1810.

Temple Shaaray Tefila. Reform Cong. To strengthen one's J identity by transmitting a deep sense of purpose & warmth. Rel Servs; Oneg Shabbat; monthly Family Worship Servs; Choir; Rel Sch for grades K–7; stu in grades 7, 8 & 9 participate annually in a weekend study retreat with the rabbi, edu dir & mems of the Rel Sch faculty; Bar Mitzvah/Birkat Habat ceremony; Youth Group for grades 9–12 includes social, edu, cultural & rel activities; Adult Edu; Lecture Series; Adult Bar & Bat Mitzvah classes; library; Social Action Commis – to aid the victims of the com & the world at large who need support; Sisterhood – participates in the Neighborhood Interfaith Prog, provides servs to the blind, provides scholarships for young people for attendance on camping trips planned by the Rel Sch as well as trips planned on a natl level, provides flowers for the altar, decorates the Sukkah; Men's Club – sponsors servs for the residents of the DeWitt Nursing Home, & sponsors Meals-on-Wheels prog, participates in the philanthropic & humanitarian concerns of the NY J com, world J, as well as areas of social concern in the neighborhood; Singles Group; Sr Group; brunch; Shabbat dinner; theater party; Purim dance; dinner dance. F in 1845 as a result of the continued growth & diversity of the J com of NYC at that time. The Temple began as an Orthodox cong & in 1921 joined the Reform movement. Originally located on Wooster St, the Temple was forced to relocate due to the northward movement of the J com. The Cong first moved to W 82nd St & in 1958 to the E Side. In 1963 its com house & sch house were formally dedicated. The first organized J women's group in NYC was f in the 1840's by Shaaray Tefila women. Rabbi Harvey M. Tattelbaum; Stu Rabbi: Eric H. Gurvis; Stu Cantor: Steven Puzarne; Pres: Michael Jaffe; VPs: Morton Asch, Paula Levitt; Treas: Martin Galett; Asst Treas: Alfred Plant; Sec: Edward Bradfield; Asst Sec: Reuben Samuel; Chr of the Bd: Carl A. Morse; V Chr of the Bd: Hyman Gamso; Trustees: Joel Bickel, Howard Brownstein, Ronda Fox, Hyman W. Gamso, Dr Michael Gershon, Simone Hartman, Melville I. Haupt, Mrs Hortense Hochstein, Michael Katzman, Theodore Kaufman, Mollie Levinson, Carl A. Morse, Dr Charles Nechemias, Leo Panzirer, Ernest Pinter, Helen Radin, John Samuelson, Harriette Schecter, Simone Shalita, H. Roger Spiegal, Diana Stein, Jay H. Tanenbaum, Allen Vogel, Dr Louis Weiss; Hon Pres: Robert K. Raisler; Hon Trustees: George Bragman, Aaron W. Davis, David W. Fisherman, Mrs Alvin Freirich, Jules L. Gerson, Carl Grossberg, Leon Juster, Gerard Oestreicher, Robert K. Raisler, I. Arnold Ross; Temple Adm: Shirley Chernela; Edu

Dir: Laura M. Kizner; Sisterhood Pres: Ruth Bradfield. **250 E 79th St, NYC NY 10021 (212) LE5–8008.**

Theodor Herzl Institute. 515 Park Ave, NYC NY 10022 (212) 752–0600.

Tonya Soloveitchik, Yeshiva University. High School for Girls. Located at the Olga Gruss Lewin Educational Center. To offer an academic HS diploma while providing a unique col prep prog of J & gen studies. The essential goal of the sch is Torah commitment. Prep & hons level progs in J studies; general prog includes hons level in several areas & Chumash, Navi/J Hist, Mishna/Dinim, Heb Language & Literature, J Philosophy, & J Ethics, & Contemporary J Hist; English, Social Studies, Mathematics, Biology, Chem, Physics, Advanced Biology, French, Spanish, Pre-Law, Talmud, Typing, Home Economics, Driver Edu, Art Appreciation courses & Physical & Health Edu prog; Twelfth Yr Prog, a reduced early admissions prog which lets qualified stu take all gen studies at Stern Col but continue J prog at YUHS; Individual Course Plan allows stu to take one course each semester at Stern Col or qualified stu may take full prog at Stern Col; Guidance Prog; clubs; sch trips· assembly progs; Hannukah & Purim to the People Prog for sr citizen homes; prog by guest edu on J interest topics; library; scholarship prog. Est in 1959. The Courier-Hamevaser – stu newspaper; the G.O. (Gen Org) Newsletter; The Elchanet – sr yrbk; Hamagid – an explication of the weekly Sidra; literary magazine. Facilities in the air conditioned bldg include two sci labs, audio-visual rm, infirmary, conf & stu activity rms, stu lounge, large multi-purpose area housing auditorium with fully equipped stage, gymnasium & lunchrm. Rabbi David L. Weinbach, Rivkah Blau. **425 Fifth Ave, NYC NY 10016 (212) 481–3746,9.**

Torah Umesorah – National Society for Hebrew Day Schools. 229 Park Ave S, NYC NY 10003 (212) 674–6700.

Torah Va'Avodah Institute. Orthodox Ins sponsored by Bnei Akiva of North America. To train HS srs in the skills of youth leadership, Zionism & rel. Rel Servs; edu progs in rel, Zionism & youth leadership; full sports prog; swimming; arts & crafts; camping; music; drama; dancing; choir; scouting & nature; library. 125 stu grade 12; 3 families. 20 employees. Facilities include glott kosher kitchen, indoor & outdoor syns, lounge, large dining hall, tennis, volleyball, handball & baseball, basketball & soccer cts, new large swimming pool, lake, canteen, teaching facilities, library, infirmary. Dir: Sid Weg. **25 West 26th St, NYC NY 10010 (212) 683–4484.**

Touro College. 30 W 44th St, NYC NY 10036 (212) 575–0190.

Town & Country Synagogue – Tifereth Israel. Affiliated with United Syn of Am. Rabbi Henry Glazer; Cantor Louis Moss; Pres: Justin Colten. **334 E 14th St, NYC NY 10003 (212) 677–8090.**

UAHC – Union of American Hebrew Congregations. Rel & edu org serving J congs throughout the US & Canada. Patron body of the HUC – JIR. Affiliates: Natl Fed of Temple Sisterhoods, Natl Fed of Temple Brotherhoods, J Chautauqua Soc, Natl Fed of Temple Youth, Natl Assn of Temple Adms, Natl Assn of Temple Edu, Am Conf of Cantors, World Union for Progressive J, ARZA Assn of Reform Zionists of Am. To encourage & aid the org & dev of J congs; to promote J edu, & enrich & intensify J life; to foster other activities for the perpetuation & advancement of J. Provides needed progs for syns & on-going consultation to individual mem congs. Edu: pubs a suggested curriculum for the congregational edu prog K to adult; provides summer teacher training ins, speakers for teacher edu prog, edu clearing house for ideas & progs, curricular assistance & consultation servs to Reform day schs. Natl Teacher & Prin Certification Prog: provides study materials, discussion guides & other J learning materials for adult edu. Worship (5 point prog to serve the liturgical needs of the mem congs): conducts research on the content & form of servs, explores & analyses the theological problems implicit in prayer & rel belief, assists congs in making the most effective use of the Union Prayer Bks, serves as a clearing house for the creative ideas of individual congs, conducts workshops & seminars. Youth activities: sponsors N Am Fed of Temple Youth for teenagers between the ages of 15½–18 with more than 500 temple youth groups, each of which is affiliated with one of the 21 NFTY regional feds in the US & Canada; sponsors nine UAHC Camps for Living J. UAHC provides several summer, six & one-yr progs abroad: the NFTY Is Academy; NFTY Intl Ins including Is & Europe, Mitzvah Corps in Is, Archaeological Seminar, NFTY Ulpan, Confirmation Class Study Tour in Is, NFTY Eisendrath-Intl-Exchange prog offering HS stu the opportunity to study & live in Is with stu fr Is spending an equal period of time living with NFTY mems & attending sch in N Am, The Academy Yr in Is on a Kibbutz for stu who have completed one yr of col. Col progs: maintains communal residences & chavurot on campuses; conducts weekend seminars, summer progs, mid-winter leadership trip to Is. Rel action: assists congs in establishing social action cttee; directs the work of the Commis on Social Action of

Reform J; provides bks, pamphlets, filmstrips & other prog materials relevant to contemporary social problems. Rel Action Ctr in Washington DC: maintains close liaison with govt agy & personnel. Interrel Affairs: works with the natl agy of Protestantism & Roman Catholicism on matters of J & interrel concern; stimulates interrel endeavors regionally & in Reform J congs in the areas of rel thought & action; produces filmstrips of J for Christian groups; pubs articles on matters of Christian-J interest, produces Adventures in J on a weekly half-hour radio prog. Syn adm: aids congs in the adm & financing of syns; provides information & literature on such areas as dues structures, fund raising, constitutions, membership campaigns, Bd & cttee structure, insurance, cemetery operation, maintenance & operation of bldgs; pubs Syn Research Surveys; maintains Architects Adv Panel, Accredited List of Syn Artists & Craftsmen, Syn Art & Architectural Library, traveling art exhibits & films about J art. Aging Progs: aids congs in programming for their older mems. Prog of Outreach: aids in the dev of new congs; maintains Syn Resources Loan Fund to assist small congs in obtaining the full time servs of an ordained rabbi. Task Force On Outreach: welcomes converts to J, seeks out mixed married couples, plans special progs to bring the message of J to any who wish to examine or embrace it. 750 congs; 13 regional councils & four feds. F in Cincinnati in 1873 by Rabbi Isaac Mayer Wise with an initial membership of 34 congs located in 28 cities. In 1950 the Org moved its hq to NYC where it occupies its own bldg known as the House of Living Judaism. Reform Judaism – newspaper sent to every mem-family of a Reform syn; What's Happening? – update information on current creative progs in J edu, sent to UAHC congs four times a yr; Compass – journal of edu approaches & teaching suggestions pub three times a yr; Experimental Education Editions – creative curricular units sent ten times a yr to subscribing congs; Keeping Posted – monthly periodical of J edu; largest pub of J textbks in N Am; trade bks of special interest for adults & young people; audio-visual edu materials & teaching aids. Transcontinental Music, a div of the UAHC, is the largest publisher of syn & other J music in the world. Pres: Rabbi Alexander M. Schindler; Chr: Donald S. Day; V Chrs: Robert L. Adler, Alan V. Iselin, Joseph Kleiman, Norma Levitt, Alfred N. Miller, E.M. Rosenthal, Charles J. Rothschild Jr, Jocelyn Rudner, Melvin S. Strassner, Howard M. Wilkoff; V Pres: Albert Vorspan; Adm Sec: Theodore K. Broido; Treas: Gilbert Tilles; Assc Treas: L. Kenneth Rosett; Hon Chrs: Judge Emil N. Baar, Irvin Fane, Dr S.S. Hollender, Earl Morse; Hon V Chrs: Hyman J. Bylan, Max L. Koeppel, Richard M. Stern; Hon Mems: J.S. Ackerman, Dr Harold Faigenbaum, Arthur J. Goldberg, Myron S. Goldman, Dr Maurice Jacobs, Maurice J. Klein, Sol Levites, Howard M. Metzenbaum, Philip M. Meyers, A.B. Polinsky, Sydney W. Roos, Bernard G. Sang, Dr Hiram B. Weiss; Adm: Donald S. Day. **838 Fifth Ave, NYC NY 10021 (212) 249–0100.**

UAHC New Jersey-West Hudson Valley Council. Area council of natl org – a rel & edu org serving J congs throughout the US & Canada. To encourage & aid the org & dev of J congs; to promote J edu, & enrich & intensify J life; to foster other activities for the perpetuation & advancement of J. For additional information, see – UAHC (Union of American Hebrew Congregations), New York City, NY. Pres: Martin Strelzer; Dir: Rabbi Karen L. Fox. **838 Fifth Ave, NYC NY 10021 (212) 249–0100.**

UAHC New York Federation of Reform Synagogues. NY fed of natl org – a rel & edu org serving J congs throughout the US & Canada. To encourage & aid the org & dev of J congs; to promote J edu, & enrich & intensify J life; to foster other activities for the perpetuation & advancement of J. For additional information, see – UAHC (Union of American Hebrew Congregations), New York City, NY. Pres: Leonard Spring; Dir: Rabbi Bernard Zlotowitz; Assc Dir: Rabbi Allen S. Kaplan. **838 Fifth Ave, NYC NY 10021 (212) 249–0100.**

Union of Orthodox Jewish Congregations of America. The central spokesman & serv org of the Orthodox syn in N Am. To defend the rights & interests of Orthodox J on the local, regional, natl & intl levels. Sixteen separate regional offs serviced by local dirs implement the Union's progs throughout N Am. Syn servs: provides adult & youth progs, supplies information & experience on syn & com problems, provides field visits & consultations which furnish guidance for construction of new bldgs & est of new congs, provides consultations on adult edu progs & retreats; Natl Conf of Syn Youth prog: 300 annual conclaves, Shabbatons, seminars, Return To Rel J Movement; Our Way Prog for the J Deaf; Russian Outreach Prog; Col Commis; Kashrut Certification Prog: supervises & certifies over 3,000 food products with the cooperation of the Rabbinical Council of Am; Is Prog: Is ctr, located in the Bernard & Sarah Falk Ctr in Jerusalem, provides meeting place, youth ctr, seminar ctr, coffeehouse, movement hq, learning ctr, central Am syn, aliyah & guidance ctr, recreation, reading & information library; Is Commis: educates the public on behalf of Is through press releases, pubs & seminars; NCSY Is Summer Seminar; Aliyah Dept: promotes aliyah to Is, furnishes films, lectures & consultations; Torah Study Commis: promotes & devs new concepts & progs of adult edu & daily Torah study for the syn & individual; Funeral Standards Commis: protects the rights of each J to a proper J funeral with est natl standards, pub grievance procedures & edu pubs; Mitzvah Prog Cttee: distributes mitzvah aids at no charge. F in 1898. Jewish Action (a quarterly newspaper); News Reporter – gives lists & details of the newest kosher foods & servs available; Passover Products Directory & Consumer Products Directory – bring the latest kashruth information to the public; Keeping Posted with NCSY – a monthly youth movement bulletin; NCSY Youth pubs; Jewish Life (quarterly magazine); Luach & Limud Torah Diary – a monthly pub offering a prog of daily Torah study; manuels & pubs on syn adm, constitutions, budgeting, fund raising, prog dev, adult edu & planning for syn progs. The trademark of the Union is the most widely accepted, not for profit, kashruth symbol in the world. Pres: Julius Berman; Chr Bd of Dirs: Nathan K. Gross; Chr Bd of Govs: Marcos Katz; Hon Pres: Harold M. Jacobs, Joseph Karasick, Moses I. Feuerstein, Max J. Etra, Dr Samuel Nirenstein; Hon Chr of the Bd: Samuel C. Feuerstein, Samuel L. Brennglass; Hon VPs: Dr Bernard Lander, Irving Stone, David Politi, Emanuel Reich; Sr VPs: Bernard W. Levmore, Marvin Herskowitz, Sheldon Rudoff, Fred Ehrman, George B. Falk, David Fund; VPs: Solomon T. Scharf, Michael C. Wimpfheimer, Max Richler, Dr David Luchins, Ronald Greenwald, Marcel Weber, Sanford Deutsch, Sidney Kwestel, Mayer Sutton, Larry Brown; Treas: Dr Jacob B. Ukeles; Sec: Harvey Blitz; Fin Sec: Joseph Miller; Exec VP: Rabbi Pinchas Stolper; Natl Assc VPs: Herman Herskovic, Al H. Thomas, Earl Korchak, Joel M. Schreiber, Jack M. Nagel, Marcus Rosenberg. **45 W 36th St, NYC NY 10018 (212) 563–4000.**

Union of Orthodox Rabbis of the U.S. & Canada. 235 E Bdwy, NYC NY 10002 (212) 964–6337.

Union of Sephardic Congregations. 8 W 70th St, NYC NY 10023 (212) 873–0300.

United Charity Institutions of Jerusalem. 1141 Bdwy, NYC NY 10001 (212) 683–3221.

United Hebrew Trades of the State of New York. 853 Bdwy, NYC NY 10003 (212) 674–2753.

United Israel Appeal, Inc. Steward for Am J support for immigrants to Is & Israel's disadvantaged. Disbursement of funds collected on its behalf for the resettlement of refugees in Is through its operating agy, the J Agy; est of over 700 K, nurseries, com ctrs & schs to serve Is chil through the Is Edu Fund; allocation of funds to Proj Renewal for forging closer ties between specific distressed neighborhoods & their twinned Am coms; resettlement of refugees fr the Soviet Union & other E European countries in Is; participation in various other agys, such as Am Council of Voluntary Agy for Foreign Serv, Excess Property Prog of the US Govt, the Consortium for Com Self-Help. Since 1925; one of f & principal beneficiary of United J Appeal. Chr: Jerold C. Hoffberger; V Chrs: Charlotte Jacobson, Frank R. Lautenberg; Hon Chrs: Melvin Dubisky, Max M. Fisher; Treas: Jack D. Weiler, Paul Zuckerman; Sec: Morris L. Levinson; Exec V Chr: Irving Kessler; Assc Exec V Chr: Harold Goldberg. **515 Park Ave, NYC NY 10022 (212) 688–0800.**

United Israel World Union. 507 Fifth Ave, Rm 903, NYCNY 10017 (212) 688–7557.

United Jewish Appeal. To serve as the Am J com principal fund raising agent in the United States for support of humanitarian progs & servs in Is, through the work of the J Agy for Is, & in J coms in 26 nations around the globe, through the Am J Joint Distribution Cttee. Provides prominent Is & Am personalities as campaign speakers through the Speakers Bureau; provides printed communications, audio-visual productions, broadcast materials, graphic design, award incentives, & background materials, through the Public Relations Dept; provides planning, programming & producing climate-setting special events through the Creative & Edu Progs Dept; maintains an archives & records ctr; provides fin information & demographic data on current & potential donors for major gift progs & major missions to Is through the Research Dept. 43 yrs of serv. Natl Chr: Robert E. Loup; Pres: Herschel Blumberg; Exec V Chr: Irving Bernstein. **1290 Ave of the Americas, NYC NY 10104 (212) 757–1500.**

United Jewish Appeal – Federation of Jewish Philanthropies Campaign, Inc. Mem of CJF. Organized 1974. Pres: Lawrence B. Buttenweiser; Chr of Bd: James L. Weinberg; Chr of Exec Cttee: Harry R. Mancher; Exec VP & Camp Dir: Ernest W. Michel; Exec VP: William Kahn. **130 E 59th St, NYC NY 10022 (212) 980–1000.**

United Jewish Appeal of Greater New York, Inc. Mem of CJF. Includes Greater NY, Westchester, Nassau & Suffolk Cts. Organized 1939. Pres: Elaine Winik; Exec VP: Ernest W. Michel. **130 E 59th St, NYC NY 10022 (212) 980–1000.**

United Order True Sisters, Inc. Cancer serv. A fraternal, fund raising & philanthropic serv org. To assist in arresting cancer, & to serve cancer patients regardless of race, color or creed. About $300,000 a yr is contributed to hosps & research ctrs for equipment, treatment, care & rehabilitation of cancer patients; sponsors two post doctoral fellowships in cancer immunology; provides outpatient cancer clin to administer chemotherapy to indigent cancer patients & any True Sister mem or mems of her family who may require aid; conducts cultural, edu & social progs on both local & natl level; sponsors teas, fashion shows, bowling parties, leadership workshops, seminars, concerts, art & antique shows, discussion groups & theatre parties. Workshops have been set up throughout the US for the making of dressings & various handiwork items needed by cancer patients. 45 lodges & 3 groups fr coast to coast. No paid workers. F in 1846 by a group of women of German birth or descent who were mems of Cong Emmanual in NY. Est as a secret soc because the giving or receiving of charity is traditionally a secret matter. Originally named Immanual, the org was guided by men until 1851 when the Grand Lodge was formed. A second Lodge was est in Phila in 1851. In 1874 the first lodge in the Middle W was f. The official language of the Lodges was German until 1892 when the first English speaking group was organized. In 1918 the use of German was discontinued. A natl clubhouse was dedicated in 1927. The Cancer Serv was est in 1947. In 1966 the first cancer outpatient clin was est. The group is the oldest women's org in the US. The Echo has been issued since 1881. Hosps serviced by the org include: Research Foun of Chil Hosp, Washington DC; Tel Hashomer, Is; Detroit Memorial Hosp; Sinai Hosp & William Beaumont Hosp, MI; the J Hosp of St Louis. Pres: Dorothy Giuriceo; 1st VP: Anita Sporn; 2nd VP: Sylvia Fishgall; Sec: Anita Baar; Treas: Hazel Saville; Fin Sec: Paula Robinson; Monitress: Nana Klein. **150 W 85th St, NYC NY 10024 (212) 362–2520.**

United Parent-Teachers Association of Jewish Schools. 426 W 58th St, NYC NY 10019 (212) 245–8200.

United Sons of Israel. 41 Union Sq, NYC NY 10003 (212) 255–6648.

United States Committee Sports for Israel, Inc. 823 United Nations Plaza, NYC NY 10017 (212) 687–9625.

United Synagogue Commission on Jewish Education. 155 Fifth Ave, NYC NY 10010 (212) 260–8450.

United Synagogue of America. 155 Fifth Ave, NYC NY 10010 (212) 533–7800.

United Synagogue Youth. c/o United Synagogue of America, Dept of Youth Activities. **155 Fifth Ave, NYC NY 10010 (212) 533–7800.**

United Tiberias Institutions Relief Society. 195 Henry St, NYC NY 10002 (212) 349–8755.

Village Temple. Affiliated with UAHC. 298 mems. Rabbi Dennis N. Math; Cantor Elliot D. Levine; Pres: Robert Pesner; **33 E 12th St, NYC NY 10003 (212) 674–2340.**

Vocational Institute & Project COPE. Prog of Agudath Is of Am. To train the unemployed & underemployed for meaningful livelihoods. Fed funded proj has helped thousands of applicants through: on-the-job-training, vocational edu, classrm training, placement, career guidance, counseling, testing, immigrants' desk, job club, pubs. Ins maintains COPE Vocational Institute, licensed by NY State Edu Dept, which operates two divs offering training in areas such as sec servs, computer programming, kosher catering; The Fresh Start Training Prog for displaced homemakers which has helped many women who have suddenly lost their husbands through death or divorce. **5 Beekman St, NYC NY 10038 (212) 964–1620.**

Washington Heights Congregation. 815 W 179th St, NYC NY 10033 (212) 923–4407.

Washington Market Synagogue. 410 W 14th St, NYC NY 10014 (212) 243–2507.

West Side Institutional Synagogue. Est in 1937; originally est in Harlem in 1917. Rabbi Dr O. Asher Reichel. **120–138 W 76th St, NYCNY 10023 (212) 877–7652,3.**

Women's American ORT. The largest of voluntary groups in 40 nations supporting the global ORT prog. Autonomous membership affiliate of the Am ORT Fed composed primarily of Am J men. The Fed is linked with the World ORT Union Hq in Geneva, Switzerland. To build the ORT prog overseas, promote quality edu in the US, & to rejuvenate vocational edu in the US. Supports 800 ORT vocational & technical schs in 24 countries on five continents, including technical assistance progs in developing nations; mobilizes natl campaigns promoting public edu with emphasis on freedom of choice & quality options; provides testimony at Congressional hearings to insure public funding; utilizes the mass media to advocate public support for edu; participates in US Off of Career Edu Conf; recognizes outstanding ins & individuals in vocational & career edu; developed the new & innovative

Bramson ORT Technical Ins in NYC; distributes natl pubs highlighting current issues in edu; produced L'Chaim to Life, a documentary tracing ORT's concern for sustaining J coms through vocational edu; holds Career Fairs at schs & shopping malls; sponsors orientation seminars for parents, stu & coms; maintains speakers bureau; produces materials for the media; provides direct servs to schs & stu. Over 140,000 mems in over 1,200 chapters in the US. Est in Bklyn NY in 1927 with three women whose husbands were active in ORT. Facts & Findings; Highlights; Insights; The Merchandiser; Women's American ORT Reporter. Natl Pres: Beverly Minkoff; Hon Pres: Florence Dolowitz; Chr Natl Exec Cttee: Gertrude White; Exec VP, Exec Dir: Nathan Gould; VPs: Claire Baumel, Jane Birnbaum, Reese Feldman, Naomi Finger, Jojo Fruchtman, Sandy Isenstein, Elinor Katz, Marilyn Lawit, Anita Levine, Marla Levine, Edith Liberman, Beverly Pechenik, Gerri Prince, Claire Pyser, Ann Shenfeld, Leona Shomer, Ruth Taffel; Treas: Miriam Pressman; Fin Sec: Barbara Silver; Rec Sec: Bea Forrest; Corsp Sec: Margery Kohrman; Parliamentarian: Ferne Kron; Offs-at-Large: Eileen Brown, Rhoda Rappaport Louise Stein. **1250 Bdwy, NYC NY 10001 (212) 594–8500.**

Women's League for Conservative Judaism. Parent body of 800 Sisterhoods of Conservative Syns; associated with the J Theological Seminary, United Syn of Am, World Council of Syns. Dedicated to perpetuation of traditional J & translation of its high ideals into practice. Leadership, & speaker training courses to dev & maintain a high level of leadership & strengthen activities in Sisterhoods; guidance & consultation servs to Sisterhoods; adult edu guidance & materials for the est of women's classes & progs; guidance & materials for setting up & operation of bookshops, libraries & discussion groups; guidance in organizing & operating gift shops; dev & circulation of patterns & directions for handicrafts with Judaic motifs; guidance & materials to encourage practice of the ethics & ceremonies of J in the home; support for Is through edu & economic aid; dev of an informed, activated body of women through guidance & direction in applying J ethical teachings to local, natl & intl issues affecting the J & gen coms; non govt observer at the United Nations; guidance to Canadian affiliates; guidance for youth edu & activities; servs to the visually handicapped; support to com servs. 200,000 worldwide. F in 1918 as J Women's League of the United Syn of Am. Pres: Mrs Murray Kweller; VPs: Mrs Rubin Auerbach, Mrs Harry Bloom, Mrs Irving Chaiken, Mrs Burton Citak, Mrs Stanley Karesh, Mrs Norman Levine, Mrs Bernard Liedman, Mrs Paul Perman, Mrs Alan Shulman, Mrs Robert Turker, Mrs Morris Weintraub, Mrs Jack Wolfstein; Rec Sec: Mrs William Rosenberg; Fin Sec: Mrs Irving Fine; Treas: Mrs Burton Seelig; Hon Pres: Mrs Barnett E. Kopelman. **48 E 74th St, NYC NY 10021 (212) 628–1600.**

Women's League for Conservative Judaism, Library. For information on the Ins, see – Women's League for Conservative Judaism, New York City, NY. **48 E 74th St, NYC NY 10021 (212) 628–1600.**

Women's League for Israel, Inc. Projs for the social, economic & edu welfare of Is youth. Homes in Jerusalem, Tel Aviv, Haifa & Nathanya where young people find a place to live & receive vocational training, guidance & placement, & instruction in Heb; Com ctr in Haifa: prog includes clubs, ceramics, dramatics & various other hobbies; Com ctr in Hatzor: culture & recreational ctr for 7,000 chil & adults; Natl Rehabilitation & Vocational Training Ctr at Nathanya: includes a dormitory, evaluation ctr, classrms & workshops, progs for physically & emotionally handicapped & normal girls to dev their aptitudes, nonresident use of the ctr's evaluation & vocational training facilities; Weaving Workshop for the Blind: enables sightless men & women to gain economic & social independence; Ins for Edu & Social Workers: provides col level courses for men & women who will work with alienated youth, retarded chil & the parents of these chil; Hebrew Univ Bldgs: at Hebrew Univ the building of a cafeteria accommodating 600 stu at each of at least three lunch sessions per day providing subsidized nutritious meals, stu ctr comprised of a gymnasium bldg & activities bldg & a hq bldg for the stu org; three women's dormitory wings. Hebrew Univ Progs: Rose Isaacs Chair in Sociology at Hebrew Univ which provides for teaching, & research; Scholarship Endowment Fund which gives priority to disabled vets; Bk Endowment Fund which provides text bks & reference materials in the library of the Sch of Social Work; pilot prog for minimally brain damaged teenagers in the Jerusalem Home. 5,000 Am women mems. F in 1928 for girls coming to build a J State. The first Home, in Haifa, was completed in 1932. Pres: Mrs Herman Schwartzman; Exec Bd Chr: Mrs Richard E. Miner; Assc Bd Chr: Mrs Harold Smith; VPs: Mrs Martin Anopolsky, Mrs Stanley Berg, Mrs Mark Fischer, Fay Inkeles, Mrs Bernard Majteles, Mrs Murray Mandelbaum, Mrs Benjamin Payson, Mrs Daniel Rednor, Mrs Arthur Schumer, Mrs Melvin Starr; Fin Sec: Mrs Eugene Cohen; Treas: Mrs Irving Berg; Assc Treas: Mrs Sidney Landes, Mrs Jesse Schwartz; Sec Exec Bd: Helen B. Harris; Bd of Govs: Bea Alexander, Mrs Isidore Arons, Mrs David Berlin, Mrs Harry Blum, Mrs Myron Bruck, Mrs Shim Engelmeyer, Mrs Melvin Epstein, Mrs Chaim Gross, Elinor Guggenheimer, Mrs Charles J. Hallen, Mrs

Bernard R. Jankoff, Mrs Irving Kaplan, Mrs Irving Kaufman, Mrs Sheldon Kay, Mrs Lawrence Klosk, Mrs Joseph Liskin, Mrs Milton Lunden, Mrs Hyman Mindich, Mrs David Pinsky, Mrs Solomon Rabinowitz, Mrs Meyer I. Resnick, Mrs Irving Rosenstein, Mrs Max Shulman, Mrs Della Slater, Mrs Irving Sofer, Mrs Henry Sonneborn III, Lita Starr, Mrs Harry A. Straus, Mrs Charles Strier, Theresa Waldfinger; Exec Dir: Bernice Backon; FL Rep: Ruth Sperber; Is Rep: Dita Natzor. **1860 Bdwy, NYC NY 10023 (212) 245–8742.**

Women's Social Service for Israel. 240 W 98th St, NYC NY 10025 (212) 666–7880.

World Confederation of Jewish Community Centers. 15 E 26th St, NYC NY 10010 (212) 532–4949.

World Confederation of United Zionists. 595 Madison Ave, NYC NY 10022 (212) 371–1452.

World Council of Synagogues. 155 Fifth Ave, NYC NY 10010 (212) 533–7800.

World Federation of Bergen-Belsen Associations. PO Box 333, NYC NY 10021 (212) 752–0600.

World Federation of Hungarian Jews. 136 E 39th St, NYC NY 10016 (212) 683–5377.

World Jewish Congress. Intl org. Branches in 66 countries. To foster the unity of the J people, to strive for the fulfillment of its aspirations, & to ensure the continuity & dev of its rel, spiritual, cultural & social heritage, & to that end it seeks to: intensify the bonds of world J with Is as the central creative force in J life; to strengthen the ties of solidarity among J coms everywhere; to secure the rights, status, & interests of Jews & J coms & to defend them wherever they are denied, violated, or imperiled; to encourage & assist the creative dev of J social, rel & cultural life throughout the world; to coordinate the efforts of J coms & orgs with respect to the pol, economic, social, rel & cultural problems of the J people; to represent & act on behalf of its participating coms & orgs before governmental, intergovernmental & other intl authorities with respect to matters which concern the J people as a whole. The World J Congress strives to cooperate with all peoples on the basis of the universal ideals of peace, freedom & justice. Intl org f 1936; Am section f 1939. **One Park Ave, NYC NY 10016 (212) 679–0600.**

World Organization for Jews From Arab Countries, Inc. To bring information before world forums concerning the problems & the rights of the J fr Arab countries; to press demands for compensating J fr Arab countries in any negotiations. Est in 1975 to represent J fr Arab countries. US Pres: Dr Heskel M. Haddad. **Off of the Pres – 1200 Fifth Ave, NYC NY 10022 (212) 427–1246; Exec Off – 165 E 56th St, NYCNY 10022 (212) PL1–4000.**

World Union for Progressive Judaism. Intl counterpart of the UAHC. Serves Liberal & Progressive J outside N Am; affiliates in 25 countries. Est in 1926. Pres: Gerard Daniel. **838 Fifth Ave, NYC NY 10021 (212) 249–0100.**

World Union of General Zionists. ZOA House, 4 E 34th St, NYC NY 10016.

World Zionist Organization. Exec Dir: Karen Rubinstein. **515 Park Ave, NYC NY 10022 (212) 752–0600.**

Wurzweiler School of Social Work – Yeshiva University. Offers grad progs in social group work, social casework, & com social work; grants MSW, DSW. Programming includes: Block Edu Prog providing field instruction in J com in US, Canada, Is & offering MSW; Master of Social Work for Clergy (1979) which provides training in counseling for clergymen; Yeshiva Univ Gerontological Ins (1976) which offers an interdisciplinary prog for professionals, fosters & coordinates univ-wide research, study, & activities related to process & problems of aging (grants Post-MS certificate in Gerontolgy). F in 1957. For information on the Univ, see – Yeshiva Univ, New York City, NY. **Brookdale Ctr, 55 Fifth Ave, NYC NY 10003.**

Yavneh – National Religious Jewish Students Association. 25 W 26th St, NYC NY 10010 (212) 679–4574.

Yeshiva University. An independent non-sectarian ins under J auspicies chartered by the State of NY. To maintain the quality & character of a small ins & yet have the facilities of a large univ. Yeshiva Col: liberal arts & sci curricula for men, joint BA-MA progs; grants Bachelor of Arts & Bachelor of Sci degrees. Erna Michael Col of Hebraic Studies: offers progs of Hebraic studies for men who wish to train for edu leadership; awards Heb Teachers Diploma & Assc in Arts, Bachelor of Arts & Bachelor of Sci degrees. James Striar Sch of Gen J Studies: offers a special prog of J studies for men with limited Hebraic background (stu may apply credits toward their bachelor's degrees); grants Assc in Arts degree. Yeshiva Prog/Mazer Sch of Talmudic Studies: offers a four yr course of study for men with an advanced background in J studies emphasizing intensive analysis of Talmudic texts & commentaries in the original Heb & Aramaic (stu may apply credits toward their bachelor's degrees). Stern Col for Women: liberal arts & sci curricula including courses in J studies, joint BA-MA progs; awards Bachelor of Arts & Bachelor of Sci degrees; also awards Assc in Arts degree & Heb Teachers Diploma. Teachers Ins for Women: trains professional personnel for positions of leadership in edu & com agy work; awards Heb Teacher's Diploma & Bachelor of Sci in Edu degree. Bernard Revel Grad Sch: offers grad work in Judaic studies, J edu, Semitic languages, literatures, cultures; confers Master of Sci, Master of Arts, Dr of Edu & Dr of Philosophy degrees. Block Edu Prog: trains J edu adms for serv throughout the US; grants Dr of Edu degree. Harry Fischel Sch for Higher J Studies: summer grad work in Judaic studies, J edu, literatures, cultures; confers Master of Sci, Master of Arts, Dr of Edu & Dr of Philosophy degree. Albert Einstein Col of Med: prepares physicians, conducts research in the health sci, provides patient care; awards Dr of Med degree; offers stu exchange progs with three Is ins – Sch of Med Ben Gurion Univ of the Negev, Hadassah Med Sch Hebrew Univ, & Shaare Zedek Med Ctr. Belfer Ins for Advanced Biomedical Studies: integrates & coords the Med Col's postdoctoral research & training progs in the biomedical sci, seeks to dev new & innovative postgraduate edu projs & open new areas of sci inquiry; awards certificate at terms completion. Camp David Ins for Intl Health: trains scientists & physicians fr Egypt, Is & the US as grad fellows in clin & biomed research at Einstein Col & emphasizes the improvement of med servs throughout the Middle E. Sue Golding Grad Div of Med Sci: advanced study in the biological sci, awards Dr of Philosophy degree, provides six yr Med Sci Training Prog which prepares stu for a research or teaching career; offers combined Dr of Med degree fr Einstein & Dr of Philosophy degree fr Sue Golding. Wurzweiler Sch of Social Work: grad progs in social group work, social casework, com social work; grants Master of Social Work & Dr of Social Welfare degrees. Block Edu Prog: provides field instruction in J coms within the US, Canada, Europe & Is; grants Master of Social Work degree. Master of Social Work for Clergy: provides training in counseling for clergymen of all denominations holding full time positions, offers courses during two summers & fieldwork over three academic yrs. Yeshiva Univ Gerontological Ins: offers an interdisciplinary prog for professionals holding master's degrees in such fields as social work, psychology, counseling, nursing or holding ordination; grants Post Master's Certificate in Gerontology. Ferkauf Grad Sch: sch of professional psychology offering Master of Arts prog in gen psychology, Dr of Psychology progs in clin & sch psychology, & Dr of Philosophy progs in clin, developmental-experimental, sch, social, health & bilingual edu-developmental psychology. Benjamin N. Cardozo Sch of Law: prepares stu for the professional practice of law or other activities in which legal training is useful; grants Dr of Law Degree. Rabbi Isaac Elchanan Theological Seminary (affiliated): ministers to the needs of J com in the US & other countries & provides a ctr for intensive Torah study in the classic spirit of J – grants Semikhah (Ordination); Kollel l'Horaah: an intensive two yr prog which trains selected, especially gifted young Talmud scholars to prepare for the roles of decisors of J law. Chaver Prog: devs educated J laity through a post col yr of concentrated J learning in areas related to the stu chosen profession, Maybaum Sephardic Fellowship Prog: trains rabbis for servs in Sephardic coms here & abroad. Cantorial Training Ins: provides professional training of cantors & other music personnel for the J com; awards Assc Cantors Certificate & Cantorial Diploma. Div of Communal Servs: serves J coms in the US, Canada, Is, So & Central Am, Australia & S Africa with special attention to outreach to the young, servs to the elderly & other edu, communal, rel & social progs. Yeshiva Univ HS (affiliate): a separate HS for boys & girls offers a four yr col prep curriculum with a complete J studies prog leading to an academic HS Diploma with NY State Regents Endorsement; P'TACH Prog enables boys & girls with mild learning disabilities to receive the full benefit of a regular J all day HS edu. Yeshiva Univ of Los Angeles: Menachem Begin Sch of J Studies, Yeshiva Prog, Beit Midrash Prog, Kollel, with stu pursuing Bachelor of Arts degree at col of their choice. Simon Wiesenthal Ctr for Holocaust Studies at YULA: offers progs of lectures, discussions & films bringing to stu & com the hist & lessons of the Holocaust; a major resource, it includes a reference library, documentation & exhibit area, lecture hall & multimedia facility. YULA HS with boys & girls divs. Libraries: seven libraries housing 850,000 vols, periodicals & other materials in all branches of the arts & sci & J; interlibrary exchanges & loans. Mus: a permanent display of 10 scale-model Syns Through the Centuries, spanning the 3rd to 19th centuries; ceremonial objects & rare bks; wall size cybernetic map; audio visual presentations & film theater; Torah Scroll of the Baal Shem Tov; & changing exhibits on various themes. 7,000 stu in all the schs. 1,200 faculty mems. Est in 1886 as Yeshiva Eitz Chaim, an elementary day sch offering J & gen studies. Ten yrs later, the Rabbi Isaac Elchanan Theological Seminary was f & in 1915 the two schs merged under the name of the latter. The elementary sch prog was eliminated. Liberal arts studies were initiated in 1928

& univ status was achieved in 1945. In 1954 a col of liberal arts & sci for women was f. **500 W 185th St, NYC NY 10033 (212) 960–5285.**

Yeshiva University Libraries. Seven libraries house some 850,000 vols, periodicals, other materials in all branches of art, sci, Judaica. Part of the OH Col Library Ctr, a computerized bibliographic network of catalog data of libraries throughout US; also part of the Met Reference & Research Library Agy. Named as a Govt Selective Depository Library by US Govt Printing Off. For information on the Univ, see – Yeshiva Univ, New York City, NY. **500 W 185th St, NYC NY 10033.**

Yeshiva University Museum. Teaching mus. To preserve, & interpret to contemporary audiences, J life, hist & culture as it is reflected in fine art, folk art, ceremonial objects, textiles, manuscripts, bks & photographs. Permanent collection contains ceremonial silver, paintings, 10 scale models of historic syns, textiles & costumes, archives, slide library, bks & manuscripts. Each yr the Mus has a major special exhibition with an edu component; smaller exhibits are held in the Mus galleries throughout the yr fr Sept to Jun; edu activities include tours, workshops, teachers kits & an outreach prog. On permanent display: Models of ten syns dating fr third century Syria to 19th century Florence, the first display ever assembled; electronic map that traces the migration of the J during 3,500 yrs of dispersion; rare ceremonial objects including the Torah Scroll of the Baal Shem Tov. Changing exhibits have included: J Ceremonies & Celebrations, J Life Through Hist, The Holy Place. F in 1973. Exhibition catalogue: The Jewish Wedding; Purim: The Face & the Mask (winner of the 1981 Natl J Bk Award); Families & Feasts; Paintings by Oppenheim & Kaufman; See & Sanctify; Exploring Jewish Symbols; Daily Life in Ancient Israel. Curatorial Asst: Leah Monderer. For information on the Univ, see – Yeshiva Univ, New York City, NY. **2520 Amsterdam Ave, NYC NY 10033 (212) 960–5390, 5429.**

Yeshiva University Research Institute. A developing ins in the applied sci. For information on the Univ, see – Yeshiva University, New York City, NY. **500 W 185th St, NYC NY 10033.**

Yiddishe Shprakh. Journal devoted to problems of standard Yiddish (in Yiddish) pub by Yivo Ins for J Research. Editor: Mordkhe Schaechter. **1048 Fifth Ave, NYC NY 10028 (212) 535–6700.**

Yiddisher Kultur Farband. 853 Bdwy , NYC NY 10003 (212) 228–1955.

Yivo Institute for Jewish Research. To expand to meet the needs of a growing public. Max Weinreich Ctr for Advanced Studies; research ins; multilingual library of 300,000 vols (rare vols dating back to 16th century, Yiddish language, E European studies); archive which includes numerous items rescued from Nazi destruction – 22,000,000 itmes; public progs (lectures, confs, etc); exhibitions; information servs. 5,000 mems; 3 regional groups; 3 state groups; 40 stu. F 1925. Pub Yivo Annual; Yedeas (irregular). Exec Dir: Samuel Norich; Asst Dir: Hannah Fryshdorf; Chr of Bd: Joseph Greenberger. **1048 Fifth Ave, NYC NY 10028 (212) 535–6700.**

Yivo Institute for Jewish Research Library. Library contains 300,000 vols (rare vols dating back to 16th century, Yiddish language, E European studies). For information on Ins, see – Yivo Institute for Jewish Research, New York City, NY. **1048 Fifth Ave, NYC NY 10028 (212) 535–6700.**

Yorkville Synagogue B'nai Jehuda. 352 E 78th St, NYC NY 10021 (212) 249–0760.

Young Israel of Fifth Ave. 3 W 16th St, NYC NY 10011 (212) 929–1525.

Young Israel of Manhattan. 225 E Bdwy, NYC NY 10002 (212) 732–0960.

Young Israel of the West Side. 210 W 91th St, NYC NY 10024 (212) 787–7513.

Young Men's & Young Women's Hebrew Association. 1395 Lexington Ave, NYC NY 10028 (212) 427–6000.

Young Men's & Young Women's Hebrew Association, Library. 1395 Lexington Ave, NYC NY 10028 (212) 427–6000.

Zachor, Holocaust Study & Commemoration – Natl J Resources Ctr. To serve a growing network of Holocaust ctrs & progs; to incorporate the consciousness of the Holocaust into contemporary J culture. Current progs include: liturgy & ritual to commemorate the Holocaust; faculty seminar series on the Holocaust to commemorate the Holocaust; faculty seminar series on the Holocaust which meets monthly at CUNY's Graduate Ctr as a forum for leading scholars; consultations on Holocaust memorials & ctrs. Shoah, a journal of Holocaust studies pub tri-annually; American Youth & the Holocaust – a new study assessing Holocaust curricula; series of six trigger films for teaching the Holocaust produced in conjunction with Holocaust

Edu Proj of Louisville KY. For information on the Univ, see – Yeshiva University, New York City, NY. **250 W 57th St, Suite 216, NYC NY 10107 (212) 582–6116.**

Zebulun Israel Seafaring Society, Inc. 485 Fifth Ave, Suite 522–530, NYC NY 10017.

Zeirei Agudath Israel. Div for adolescent boys within Natl Commis on Youth – Agudath Is of Am. To serve as a training ground for responsible leadership roles in the com. More than 25,000 youths led by 1,700 volunteer leaders benefit from activities; weekly programs which prepare youth for a life dedicated to loyal J serv & responsible voluntarism; summer camp – Camp Agudah in New York's Catskill Mountains accomodates large number of youngsters from poor homes – the materially improvished as well as the spiritually deprived. For information on the Ins, see – Agudath Israel of America, New York City, NY. **5 Beekman St, NYC NY 10038 (212) 964–1620.**

Zionist Archives & Library of World Zionist Organization – American Section. 515 Park Ave, NYC NY 10022 (212) 753–2167.

Zionist Organization of America. 4 E 34th St, NYC NY 10016 (212) 481–1500.

Newburgh

Congregation Agudas Israel. Orthodox Cong affiliated with Union of Orthodox J Congs of Am, J Fed of Orange Cty NY. To create a wholesome rel com. Daily Morning & Evening Rel Servs; afternoon Talmud Torah; day sch affiliate; Daughters (sisterhood); Men's Club; NCSY Youth Group; ongoing Adult Edu prog; com serv support; Is Commis; social activities; library with 1000 vols (Judaica). 350 mems; 120 stu – elementary & secondary ages. Original cong founded at the beginning of the century; eventually Sons of Israel & Agudas Achim merged in 1964 to form Agudas Israel. Pub Bulletin (monthly). Facilities include main sanctuary, small sanctuary, furnished auditorium, meat & dairy kosher kitchens, 3 classrms, rabbi's study, Chevra Kadisha; elementary edu awards. Rabbi Daniel Kramer; Cantor Endre Stamler; Prin: Zalman Zager; Daughters Pres: Shelley Sosnick; Pres: Hyman Slavin; Chr of Bd: Michael Dubroff; Men's Club Pres: Joel Carmen. **290 North St, Newburgh NY 12550 (914) 562–5604.**

The Jewish Federation of Newburgh & Middletown, Inc. Mem of CJF. Organized 1925. Pres: Gerald Kreisberg. **360 Powell Ave, Newburgh NY 12550 (914) 562–7860.**

Newburgh Hebrew Day School. Orthodox day sch affiliated with Torah Umesorah, Cong Agudas Israel. To foster quality J edu & practice. Pre-nursery; Nursery; Pre-k; K; first grade; library of 200 vols (gen & Judaica). 40 stu. 4 employees; volunteers. Begun in 1980 by mems of Cong Agudas Israel as successor to local prog run by Hebrew Day Sch of Orange Cty. Newsletter (monthly). Facilities include 3 classrms (rented). Dean: Rabbi Daniel Kramer; Pres: Michael Dubroff; VPs: Sally Mayer, Mona Rieger. **290 North St, Newburgh NY 12550 (914) 562–5515.**

Temple Beth Jacob. Affiliated with UAHC. 347 mems. Rabbi Hirshel L. Jaffe; Cantor William Satzman; Pres: Gerald S. Hecht; Edu: Sidney I. Cardoza; Sisterhood Pres: Ellen Bernstein, Jane Spevak. **344 Gidney Ave, Newburgh NY 12550 (914) 562–5516.**

Niagara Falls

Jewish Federation of Niagara Falls, New York, Inc. Mem of CJF. Organized 1935. Pres: Robert D. Wisbaum; Exec Dir: Miriam Schaffer. **Temple Beth Israel, Rm 5, College & Madison Ave, Niagara Falls NY 14305 (716) 284–4575.**

Temple Beth El. Affiliated with UAHC. 64 mems. Pres: William A. Rosenthal; Edu: Eva Posener; Sisterhood Pres: Helen Zeplowitz. **720 Ashland Ave, PO Box 1062, Niagara Falls NY 14302 (716) 282–2717.**

Temple Beth Israel. Affiliated with United Syn of Am. Rabbi Jerome Kestenbaum; Pres: Samuel Wineburgh; Exec Dir: Michael Kranitz; Edu & Youth Dir: Hadria Lunken. **College & Madison Ave, Niagara Falls NY 14305 (716) 285–9894.**

North Bellmore

Temple Beth El of Bellmore. Affiliated with United Syn of Am. Rabbi Harvey Goldscheider; Cantor David Hiesiger; Pres: Lawrence M. Greebel; Edu Dir: Rabbi Albert Block; Youth Dir: Barbara Gerstel. **1373 Bellmore Rd, North Bellmore NY 11710 (516) 781–2650.**

North Syracuse

Congregation Ner Tamid of the Suburban Jewish Center. Conservative rel prog includes High Holy Day, Holiday, Fri Evening Servs; Sabbath & Holiday Morning Servs are also scheduled on occasion – Servs conducted by mems; Bar/Bat Mitzvah; chil parties for Chanukah & Purim; family seder on 2nd evening of Passover; cultural & social progs including installation dinner & mid-yr dinner; youth social progs; Sisterhood; Sun breakfasts; Rel Sch, K-HS. 50 families. F in 1955 by a small group of N Suburban J families who recognized the need to educate their chil in the traditions of J & to participate in social, cultural & rel activities. The Cong acquired a site at W Taft Rd in 1963, & completed the present 2-story bldg in 1968. Pres: Stuart Krupkin; 1st VP: Jonathan Carmen; 2nd VP: Dianne Stolusky; Treas: Larry Suffness; Sec: Elaine Russell; Rel Sch Adm: Larry Leviton, Joan Leviton; Rel Dir & Pubs: Elihu Cohen. **5061 W Taft Rd, North Syracuse NY 13212 (315) 458–2022.**

Nyack

Jewish Peace Fellowship. PO Box 271, Nyack NY 10960 (914) 358–4601.

Oakdale

B'nai Israel Reform Temple. Affiliated with UAHC. 185 mems. Rabbi Steven Moss; Pres: Donald Meyers; Edu: Alice Lambert; Sisterhood Pres: Nancy Meyers, Carol Reiss; Brotherhood Pres: Martin Hochheiser. **96 Biltmore Ave, PC Box 158, Oakdale NY 11769 (516) 589–8948.**

Oceanside

Congregation Shaar Hashamayim. Orthodox Syn. To teach mems & youth Orthodox ritual, prayers & love of J. Heb Sch; ladies org; youth groups. Est in 1964. Rabbi Dr Elihu Kasten; Assc Rabbi Avi J. Kasten. **3309 Skillman Ave, Oceanside NY 11572 (516) RO4–6888.**

Oceanside Jewish Center, Inc. Affiliated with United Syn of Am. Rabbi Azriel C. Fellner; Cantor Yitzhak Lefkowitz; Pres: Donald L. Rubin; Exec Dir: Rosalind Keyes. **2860 Brower Ave, Oceanside NY 11572 (516) 764–4213.**

Oceanside Jewish Center, Library. For information on the Ctr, see – Oceanside Jewish Center, Oceanside, NY. **2860 Brower Ave, Oceanside NY 11572 (516) 764–4213.**

Temple Avodah. Affiliated with UAHC. 460 mems. Rabbi Philmore Berger; Cantor Joseph Sopher; Pres: Edmund Fried; Edu: Howard Dornfeld; Adm: Charlotte Tischler; Sisterhood Pres: Sari Golos, Barbara Kaplan; Brotherhood Pres: Mervin Knecht. **3050 Oceanside Rd, Oceanside NY 11572 (516) 766–6809.**

Old Bethpage

Society of Jewish Science. A Cong that represents a scholarly but humble approach to learning; a deep but calm approach to emotional life, & a thorough but non-labored approach to health. To promote the mental, physical & emotional well being of individuals through enlightment, hope & faith; to apply the teachings of J to everyday life. Discussion groups; lectures; counseling & healing; social gatherings; servs. F in 1922 by Rabbi Morris Lichtenstien. After his death in 1938, his wife Tehilla became the spiritual leader. Distinct fr other branches of J, this Cong permits among its followers a wide latitude of beliefs with respect to traditional J teachings. Its adherents come fr & continue to practice Orthodox, Conservative, Reform & Reconstructionist tenets. J Sci provides a unique opportunity for people to practice their faith; it also is consistent with major historical, philosophical, & sci themes of man's cultural heritage. Leader: Abraham Goldstein; Exec Dir: Dr Ethan Gologor. **Box 114, 825 Round Swamp Rd, Old Bethpage NY 11804 (516) 249–6262.**

Temple Beth Elohim. Affiliated with UAHC. 403 mems. Rabbi Louis Stein; Pres: Barbara Hershman; Sisterhood Pres: Lydia Struhl. **926 Round Swamp Rd, Old Bethpage NY 11804 (516) 694–4544.**

Old Westbury

Old Westbury Hebrew Congregation. Affiliated with United Syn of Am. Rabbi Melvin Kieffer; Cantor Marvin Savitt; Pres: Howard Futterman; Edu Dir: Isadore Popack. **21 Old Westbury Rd, Old Westbury NY 11590 (516) 333–7977.**

Olean

B'nai Israel Congregation. Affiliated with UAHC. 48 mems. Rabbi Allen H. Podet; Pres: Glen Miller; Edu: Sydell Miller; Sisterhood Pres: Roberta Blumenthal. **127 S Barry St, Olean NY 14760 (716) 372–3431.**

Oneonta

Beth El. Affiliated with United Syn of Am. Rabbi Dr Max Rothschild; Pres: Shaledon Edison; Edu Dir: Mrs. Deborah Kornfeld. **83 Chestnut St, Oneonta NY 13820 (607) 432–5522.**

Orangeburg

Orangetown Jewish Center. Affiliated with United Syn of Am. Rabbi Pesach Krauss; Cantor

Jeffrey Zucker; Pres: Murray Ginsberg; Exec Dir: Murray Ginsberg; Edu Dir: Murray Atik; Youth Dir: Ed Kaplan. **Independence Ave, Orangeburg NY 10962 (914) 359–5920.**

Ossining

Congregation Anshe Dorshe Emes. Mem of the Reconstructionist Foun. To foster the basic tenets of J Reconstructionism: belief in One impersonalized God who is not a human being nor has human attributes; belief in Torah as continuous learning; belief in Ethics & ethical behavior regardless of rewards or punishments; belief in Charity in the broadest sense of doing for one's family, com, nation, Is & the world; belief in Patriotism to one's country & com. Fri Evening, Sat Morning, High Holy Days & Festival Servs; Rel Sch for ages 6–15; Bar/Bat Mitzvah; Sisterhood; adult classes; Winter Nursery; Summer Camp & Nursery; Quakerbridge Players drama group. The Cong was chartered in 1965 as an out-growth of an adult edu group which predates the Cong by 20 yrs. Cong has female Rabbi who is the first female chaplain candidate in the US Army Reserves. Rabbi Bonnie Koppell; Pres: Harry Leibowitz; Exec VP: Elliot S. Grossman; VPs: Ruth Leibowitz, Karen Kahn; Sec: Robert Garber; Treas: Lewis Hilton; Asst Treas: Erwin Damsky; Exec Sec: Gerald Klein; Chr, Membership Cttee: Dr Elliot S. Grossman. **100 S Highland Ave, Ossining NY 10562.**

Oswego

Congregation Adath Israel. Affiliated with United Syn of Am. Pres: S. Shapiro. **E Third & Oneida, Oswego NY 13126 (315) 342–0371.**

Oyster Bay

Oyster Bay Jewish Center. Conservative Syn affiliated with United Syn of Am. Rel servs; edu prog for chil & adults including Afternoon Sch; youth activities; J cultural & social activities; com & ecumenical events. 140 mems (120 families, 20 individuals), 80 stu. 9 employees. F 1964. Pub Bulletin (monthly), Calendar (bi-weekly). Facilities include sanctuary, kosher kitchen, classrms, social rms, off. Rabbi Harold M. Kamsler DD; Cantor Sidney Kamil; Pres: Robert I. Mandel; Exec VP: Dr Ronald Feldman; Edu VPs: Dr Michael Falcove, Dianne Fleck; Fin Sec: Alfred Kuhn; Treas: Walter Belous; Sisterhood Pres: Sandra Mandel. **Berry Hill Rd, Oyster Bay NY 11771 (516) 922–6650.**

Ozone Park

Temple Sons of Jacob. Affiliated with United Syn of Am. Rabbi Morris Reinitz; Pres: Stanley A. Gertz. **97–44 75th St, Ozone Park NY 11416 (212) AX6–8334.**

Patchogue

Temple Beth El of Patchogue. Affiliated with United Syn of Am. Rabbi Bernard Stefansky; Pres: Dr Robert M. Starr; Edu Dir: Barry Chernoff; Youth Dir: Steve Rosenberg. **45 Oak St, Patchogue NY 11772 (516) 475–1882.**

Young Israel of Patchogue. Orthodox Cong affiliated with Natl Council of Young Is. To provide traditional Judaism – rel, edu, social & cultural. Rel Servs – daily, Sabbath & Holidays; Adult Edu; Sisterhood; youth groups (elementary & HS); library containing 100 vols (Judaica). 50 mems (40 families, 10 individuals). F 1974. Facilities include sanctuary, study hall, kitchen. Rabbi Howard Wolk. **28 Mowbray St, Patchogue NY 11772 (516) 654–0882.**

Pearl River

Beth Am Temple. Affiliated with UAHC. 185 mems. Rabbi Alan J. Katz; Pres: Joel L. Weinstein; Edu: Jack Perel; Adm: Joel L. Weinstein; Sisterhood Pres: Barbara List; Brotherhood Pres: Stanley Popeil. **60 E Madison Ave, PO Box 236, Pearl River NY 10965 (914) 735–5858.**

Pelham

American Association for Ethiopian Jews. To aid Ethiopian J & to preserve their culture; to inform world J about their plight so that action may be taken. Conducts charitable progs to support absorption of Ethiopian J in Is; maintains speakers bureau & files of articles, correspondence, records, & photographs of Ethiopian J. About 12 chapters throughout the US; affiliates in Canada, Australia, France & Is; 50 bd mems. F in 1975. The org is a merger of Am Pro-Falasha Cttee & the Friends of Beta-Is (Falasha) Com in Ethiopia. Annual information paper – The Falasha Update; selected literature & reprints. **340 Corlies Ave, Pelham NY 10803 (914) 738–0956.**

Pelham Jewish Center. Affiliated with United Syn of Am. Rabbi Mark Diamond; Pres: Michael C. Sloane; Edu Dir: Dr Ron Becker. **451 Esplanade, Pelham NY 10803 (914) PE8–0870.**

Penn Yan

Jewish Community Center of Greater Rochester. Camp Seneca Lake, Penn Yan NY 14527 (315) 536–9981.

Plainview

Manetto Hill Jewish Center. Affiliated with United Syn of Am. Rabbi Eli Libenson; Pres: Paul Gaynes. **244 Manetto Hill Rd, Plainview NY 11803 (516) 935–5454.**

Plainview Jewish Center. Conservative Cong affiliated with United Syn of Am. To teach the principles of J; to provide a gathering place; to support Is through edu, Is Bonds & UJA. Social, cultural & rel activities; Sisterhood; Men's Club; Rel Servs; Sr Citizen Prog; Rel Sch; youth activities. Est in 1953. Rabbi Julius Golberg; Cantor Morris Wolk; Edu Dir: Joseph S. Schapiro; Pres: Dorothy Turker; 1st VP: Jerold Kaniuk; 2nd VP: Gerald Rosenberg; 3rd VP: Jerome Ginsberg. **95 Floral Dr, Plainview NY 11803 (516) 938–9610.**

Plattsburgh

Temple Beth Israel. Affiliated with UAHC. 78 mems. Rabbi Yossi J. Liebowitz; Pres: Laura T. Schiff; Edu: Michael White; Adm: Pearlie Rabin; Sisterhood Pres: Phyllis Freedman, Zahava Harrison. **Bowman & Marcy Lane, Plattsburgh NY 12901 (518) 563–3343.**

Pomona

Pomona Jewish Center. Affiliated with United Syn of Am. Rabbi Mordecai Kieffer; Pres: Richard Weinberger; Youth Dir: Jerry Marcus. **106 Pomona Rd, Pomona NY 10970 (914) 354–2226.**

Port Chester

Congregation Knesset Tifereth Israel. Affiliated with United Syn of Am. Rabbi Alfredo S. Winter; Pres: David B. Rosen; Edu Dir: Avi Nahumi. **575 King St, Port Chester NY 10573 (914) 939–1004.**

Port Jefferson

North Shore Jewish Center. Affiliated with United Syn of Am. Rabbi Martin Edelman; Cantor Martin Ehrlich; Pres: Leonard Lustig; Exec Dir: Harry Hauser; Edu Dir: Harvey Goldstein. **385 Old Town Rd, Port Jefferson NY 11776 (516) 928–3737.**

Port Jervis

Beth El. Affiliated with United Syn of Am. Rabbi Murray Lieberman; Pres: Murray Luger. **88 E Main St, Port Jervis NY 12771 (914) 856–1722.**

Port Washington

Community Synagogue. Affiliated with UAHC. 520 mems. Rabbis: Martin S. Rozenberg, David E. Lipman; Cantor Jacob Yaron; Pres: Allan Stone; Edu: David E. Lipman; Adm: Alice Alpert; Sisterhood Pres: Cynthia Magazine; Brotherhood Pres: Gerald Adelberg. **150 Middle Neck Rd, Port Washington NY 11050 (516) 883–3144.**

Community Synagogue Library. For Information on the Ins, see – Community Synagogue, Port Washington, NY. **150 Middle Neck Rd, Port Washington NY 11050 (516) 883–3144.**

Port Jewish Center. Affiliated with UAHC. To strengthen & encourage the observance of the principles of J in personal conduct, in family life, & in relations with soc. Rel Servs every other Fri night; Rel Sch twice a week. 50 mems. Est in 1969. Pres: Mildred Kupperberg; VP: Jonathan Helfat; Treas: Marvin Becker; Sec: Janet Effman. **PO Box 852, Port Washington NY 11050 (516) 883–5117.**

Sh'ma. Periodical pub. **PO Box 567, Port Washington NY 11050 (516) 944–9791.**

Temple Beth Israel. Affiliated with United Syn of Am. Rabbi Neil Kurshan; Cantor Baruch Blum; Pres: Gilbert Hammer. **Temple Dr, Port Washington NY 11050 (516) 767–1708.**

Potsdam

Congregation Beth El. Conservative Syn unaffiliated. Rel Servs; Rel Sch; Sisterhood; Speakers Prog. 40 families; 29 rel sch stu. F 1955. Pres: Donald Rosenthal; VP: Ronald Ein; Sec: Jack Kolplowitz; Treas: Morris Pinto; Pres of Sisterhood: Judith Glasser. **81 Market St, Potsdam NY 13676.**

Poughkeepsie

Jewish Community Center. Ctr for the J com affiliated with JWB. To foster & dev J living within the highest ideals of Am democracy; to improve spiritual, moral & social welfare for its mems. Meeting place for the com. 700 mems. Est in 1923; moved to present bldg in 1964. The ctr's facilities include a gym, pool, health club, nursery sch, classrooms, meeting rms, kitchen, auditorium, banquet rm, exercise rm, gameroom. The JCC houses the Poughkeepsie Com Hebrew Sch, Mid Hudson Hebrew Day Sch, J Welfare Fund, Is Bonds. Pres: Eugene Fleishman; Exec Dir: Richard L. Rubin; Prog Supervisor Cultural & Social Activities: Deborah Kehr; Prog Supervisor Health & Physical Edu

Activities: Douglas Domiani; Camp Dir: Robert Finkelstien; Bd of Dirs – Pres: Dr Martin Zweifler; VPs: Phyllis Arnoff, Marilyn Hankin, Herbert Stoller; Sec: Emaline Grecco; Treas: Samuel Silver. **110 S Grand Ave, Poughkeepsie NY 12603 (914) 471–0430.**

Jewish Welfare Fund of Dutchess County. Organized 1941. Pres: Mrs Terry Fleisher. **110 Grand Ave, Poughkeepsie NY 12603 (914) 471–9811.**

Mid-Hudson Hebrew Day School. Affiliated with Solomon Schechter Day Schools Assn. Prin: Susan Helman; Chr: Marilyn Schwartz. **110 Grand Ave, Poughkeepsie NY 12603 (914) 454–0474.**

Temple Beth El. Affiliated with United Syn of Am. Rabbi Erwin Zimet; Cantor Joseph Wieselman; Pres: Iby Heller; Edu Dir: Rabbi Richard Spiegel. **118 Grand Ave, Poughkeepsie NY 12603 (914) 454–0570.**

Vassar Temple. Affiliated with UAHC. 300 mems. Rabbi Stephen A. Arnold; Pres: Elaine Lipschutz; Edu: Mary Solomon; Sisterhood Pres: Adrianne Bourstein. **140 Hooker Ave, Poughkeepsie NY 12601 (914) 454–2570.**

Putnam Valley

Reform Temple of Putnam Valley. Affiliated with UAHC. 26 mems. Rabbi Abraham Krantz; Cantor Norma Scheingold; Pres: Donald Solomon. **PO Box 232, Church Rd, Putnam Valley NY 10579 (914) 528–9721.**

Rego Park

Jewish Community Services of Long Island. A counseling agy devoted to helping families with personal & emotional problems. Deals with: couples in troubled marriages, chil with behavior problems, widows coping with loneliness, single parents struggling to keep their families together, families in fin crisis, couples in second marriages, working mothers adjusting to responsibilities, chil reacting to divorce, confused young adults. Special servs: home economist to assist with budgeting; homemakers for times of med emergency; progs for drug abusers; assistance to Russian & Iranian J with resettlement problems; financial help to the needy at Passover; prog for chronically ill & homebound men & women; respite servs for families with retarded relative living at home. Served in 1981 more than 10,000 families. Staff of over 125 – professional social workers, psychologists & psychiatrists. Organized in 1942 with a staff of 5. JCSLI is the 2nd largest J family agy in the US. Exec Dir: George Rothman; Asst Exec Dir: Melvin Frankel; Com Relations Dir: Marion Cohn; Pres: Saul Beldock; VPs: Howard Fleischman, Benjamin Gertz, Morton Moskin, Mrs Henry Pearce; Treas: Victor Levin; Sec: Diane Ringler; Dirs: Charles Altman, Martin Barell, Herbert Bienstock, Ruth Coller, Francis Ehrenberg, Stanley Gertz, Arthur Gilmore, Morris Ginsberg, Charles Greenbaum, Lawrence Gross, Rosalind Gurwin, John Kase, Hon Emil Levin, Milton Levin, Victor Levin, Harold Litwin, Ben Marcus, Hon Charles Margett, Rabbi Israel Mowshowitz, Hon Samuel Rabin, Joseph Rogers, Ina Ross, Emanuel Seideman, Aaron Solomon, Morton Weissman, Irving Wharton. **97–45 Queens Blvd, Rego Park NY 11374 (212) 896–9090.**

Long Island Jewish Press. Periodical pub. **95–20 63rd Rd, Rego Park NY 11374.**

Sephardic Jewish Brotherhood of America, Inc. 97–29 64th Rd, Rego Park NY 11374 (212) 459–1600.

Westchester Jewish Tribune. Periodical pub. **95–20 63rd Rd, Rego Park NY 11374.**

Richmond Hill

Congregation Beth Israel. Affiliated with United Syn of Am. Rabbi Joseph M. Reich; Cantor Chaim Schnek; Pres: Irving Mendelson. **88–01 102nd St, Richmond Hill NY 11418 (212) 847–9688.**

Riverdale

Kinneret Day School. Co-edu prog for ages 3–13. Pre-sch for ages 3–5; regular prog for grades 1–8: J subjects; Heb; Yiddish; music; language; reading; math; sci; social studies; edu trips; holiday projs; sci fairs; participation in after-sch YM-YWHA progs; transportation. Fully licensed staff including librarian, gym & music teachers. F in 1947 by the Labor Zionist Movement. First pres was Chaim Greenberg. Prin: Asher Abramowitz; Chr of the Bd: Morris Zeigel. **2600 Netherland Ave, Riverdale NY 10463 (212) 584–0900,1.**

Riverdale Temple. Liberal Syn affiliated with the Reform wing of J. To retain the best of the traditions of the J experience. Singles Group; Sisterhood; Men's Club; Youth Group; Adult Edu; Nursery Sch; Rel Sch; Heb Sch; Summer Prog; Parents Assn; Temple Jr; Jr Cong; Young Married Group; library. Est in 1947 by a group of J families devoted to the ideals of their heritage. The Cong moved to its present site in 1954. Monthly bulletin. Temple facilities include a sanctuary, auditorium, social hall, lounge. Rabbi Stephen D. Franklin; Hon & F Pres: Hon Francis J. Bloustein; Pres: Marvin Goodman; VPs: Charles S. Baron, Michael S. Mishkin, Dennis S. Neier; Treas: J. William Jaffe; Fin Sec: Mrs Charles Mandel; Assc Fin Sec: Mrs Benjamin Silverman; Rec Sec: Mrs Charles Baron. **246th St & Independence Ave, Riverdale NY 10471 (212) 548–3800.**

SAR Academy. A rel day sch. Teaching the tenets of Torah J; inspiring the stu to love & revere God; inspiring the stu to study the Torah & to fulfill their rel obligations as J as set forth in the written & Oral Torah; inspiring the stu to be committed & concerned J & to be sensitive to the needs not only of the Am-J com, but also of J throughout the world; instilling in the stu a special love & concern for the State of Is; providing stu with the broadest & most effective gen edu & imbuing them with a respect for democratic ins & the fundamental concepts of a free soc, using the most progressive & appropriate edu methods available. J & gen studies; mini-courses; workshops; opportunities for independent study. Est in Sept of 1969 when 3 yeshivot merged. Prin: Rabbi Sheldon Chwat; Assc Prin: Rabbi Yonah Fuld; Asst Prin: Audrey Schurgin; ELC Coord: Gloria Kestenbaum; Exec Dir: Michael Schreck; Chr, Bd of Trustees: Ludwig Jesselson; V Chr Bd of Trustees: A. Stanley Gluck; Pres: Jack Bendheim; Chr Exec Cttee: Dr Norman Kahan; V Chr Exec Cttee: David Goldsmith; VPs: George Berman, David Gordon, Edmond Lang, Sidney Newman; Treas: Dr Bernard Weiner; Fin Sec: Marvin Hochberg; Sec: Theodore Mirvis; Bd of Trustees: Joshua Aber, Abraham Atik, Dr Harvey Benovitz, Nathan Berger, Joseph Bezborodko, Max Boritzer, Ludwig Bravmann, Sydell Brooks, Dr Isaac Chavel, Esther Farber, Harry Feder, Harry First, Irving Fishman, Dr Stephen Glasser, Dr Edwin Goldstein, Rabbi Irving Greenberg, Herbert Hirsh, Eveline Hochstein, Helene Isaacs, David Kahan, Stanley Langer, Eva Lefkowitz, Harriet Mandel, Samuel Mandel, Rubin Marcus, Michael Marton, Rabbi Henry Michaelman, Marc Moller, Robert Newton, Ronald Nussbaum, Martin Packer, Tobias Shapiro, Alfred Schoen, Manfred Schuster, Elizabeth Shapiro, Rabbi Charles Sheer, Marilyn Sopher, William Spier, Avrum Stein, Milton Steinberg, Kurt Stern, Ina Tropper, Jack Ukeless, Rabbi Abner Weiss, Harry Wild, Martin Wolpoff, Abraham Zion. **655 W 254th St, Riverdale NY 10471 (212) 549–5160, 548–0894.**

Riverhead

Temple Israel of Riverhead. Affiliated with United Syn of Am. Rabbi Harry Lazaros; Pres: Irwin B. Abrams. **490 Northville Turnpike, Riverhead NY 11901 (516) 727–3191.**

Rochester

Beth Hakneses Hachodosh. Orthodox Cong. To provide a cong setting in which the congregants can lead a J life; to help foster & strengthen the belief in G-d. Rel Servs (daily, Sabbath, Holidays); Adult Edu; public lectures; youth progs; Sisterhood; 3 libraries (totalling 650 vols). 200+ mems; 80 families; 10 individuals. 1 employee. F 1885. Pub Bulletin (5 times a yr). Facilities include sanctuary seating 280, kosher kitchen, youth library. Has been the standard bearer of Torah observance in Rochester NY; influential in est Yeshiva HS. Rabbi Mark Jablon; 1st Gabbai: Rabbi Nathan Meltzer; 2nd Gabbai: Moshe Japha; Pres: Gerald Bodzin; 1st VP: Dr Richard Mandelbaum; 2nd VP: Dr Richard Mosak; Treas: Beryl Vilinsky; Fin Sec: Gerhard Victor; Sec: Barbara Hollander. **19 St Regis Dr N, Rochester NY 14618 (716) 271–5390.**

Beth Hamedresh Beth Israel. Affiliated with United Syn of Am. Rabbi A. Solomon; Pres: Harry Aronow; Edu Dir: Myer Asper. **1369 E Ave, Rochester NY 14610 (716) 244–2060.**

Congregation Beth Shalom. Orthodox Syn. Shabbat Servs, Kiddush; Jr Cong; Adult Edu; Nursery Sch for ages 2½–5; Bar/Bat Mitzvah; Heb Sch; Sun Sch; Sisterhood; Men's Club; PTO Group; Couples Club; Young Adult Club; youth activities; NCSY Youth Group. The Cong was f on July 11, 1929 in order to fulfill the needs of a growing com. Property was purchased fr St John's Episcopal Church. At this time the Cong numbered 65 mems. A new syn bldg was completed in 1954. In 1963 the rel sch bldg was formally dedicated. In 1970 Beth Shalom was bombed causing heavy damage; the mems helped to re-build. 1971 brought the ground-breaking ceremony of the Agudas Achim Sanctuary, & on Oct 12, 1975 it was dedicated. In 1978 the Cong merged with Cong Tiphereth Is. Facilities include: Goldstein Gardens; Golberg Memorial Library; banquet & wedding facilities; Garden Rm; Bride's Rm. Rabbi Shaya Kilimnick; Cantor Chaim Gartenhaus; Pres: Dr Jack Azar; Fin Adm: Irving Goldstein. **1161 Monroe Ave, Rochester NY 14620 (716) 473–1625.**

Hillel School. 191 Fairfield Dr, Rochester NY 14620 (716) 271–6877.

Hillel School Library. 191 Fairfield Dr, Rochester NY 14620 (716) 271–6877.

JCC of Greater Rochester, Israel Emiot Memorial Yiddish Library. houses 1,500 bks in Yiddish. Dir of Library Servs: Alice Palokoff. **1200 Edgewood Ave, PO Box 18026, Rochester NY 14618 (716) 461–2000.**

Jewish Community Center of Greater Rochester, Feinbloom Library. Judaica in English & Heb contains: 2,500 vols gen interest bks (large print bks, & Russian & Heb language bks are borrowed fr the Rochester Public Library System); current periodicals; bks to support JCCprogs dealing with divorce, death, parenting & personal growth; special progs include chil storytimes, adult discussion groups, Chil J Bk Mo Read-a-thon; library reference servs; acts as consultant to teachers & professionals within the J & gen com. Staff consists of one part-time library dir; eight volunteers who provide a variety of servs & receive in-serv training fr the library dir. F in 1936 as the Horace Wolf Library. When the JCC moved to its present location in the early 1970's, the library received its current name. The Yiddish collection was housed in the Feinbloom Library until 1981 when a special rm was dedicated to Israel Emiot who had been the JCC Scholar-in-Residence for many yrs. The Library has recently received a certificate of merit fr the Natl J Bk Council. Dir of Library Servs: Alice Palokoff. **1200 Edgewood Ave, PO Box 18026, Rochester NY 14618 (716) 461–2000.**

Jewish Community Center of Greater Rochester, New York. Facilities include kosher kitchen, sports facility, art gallery, auditorium, Nursery Sch (day care for all housed in JCC), Feinbloom Library with 3,000 bks (J & gen interest). Dir: Leonard Freedman; Pres Bd of Dir: Linda Cornell Weinstein; Chr Library Cttee: Anne Berger; Library Dir: Alice Palokoff. **1200 Edgewood Ave, Rochester NY 14618 (716) 461–2000.**

Jewish Community Federation of Rochester New York, Inc. Central servs agy for the J com. The J Com Fed supports Rochester Area Hillel Foun, J Family Servs, Bureau of J Edu, JCC of Greater Rochester, J Home & Infirmary. The Fed operates through six depts: Dept of Com Relations, Dept of Internal Affairs, Dept of Planning & Budgeting, United J Welfare Fund, Women's Assn, Endowment Prog. Pres: Neil J. Norry; VPs: Dr Seth Borg, Ethel Kowal, Elliott Landsman, Nathan Robfogel; Sec: Etta Atkin; Asst Sec: Dr Jack Azar; Treas: Michael Futerman; Asst Treas: Alvin Kaufman; Exec Dir: Henry M. Rosenbaum; Bd of Dirs: Dr Peter Z. Adelstein, Hanon Berger, Rabbi Philip S. Bernstein, Frances Blanchard, Dr Murray I. Blanchard, Roberta Borg, Priscilla A. Brown, Judy Columbus, Harold S. Feinbloom, Leon M. Germanow, Rita Glazer, Carol Goldberg, Emanuel Goldberg, Nathalie Goldberg, Hon Harry D. Goldman, John L. Goldman, Joseph Goldstein, Robert Gordon, Frank S. Hagelberg, Harold M. Hecker, Helen Hecker, Warren H. Heilbronner, Dr Joshua Hollander, Rabbi Henry Hyman, M. Orry Jacobs, Elliott Landsman, Morris Levinson, Philip M. Liebschutz, Sanford J. Liebschutz, Arthur M. Lowenthal, Donald Margolis, Dr Lawrence F. Markus, Rabbi Judea B. Miller, Irving S. Norry, Neil J. Norry, Beryl Nusbaum, Ella Oken, Bertram A. Rapowitz, Ruth B. Rosenberg, Linda Rubens, Irving Ruderman, Elizabeth M. Schwartz, Dr Morris J. Shapiro, Harriet J. Sherman, Myron S. Silver, Joseph E. Silverstein, Florence Sturman, Leon H. Sturman, Justin L. Vigdor, Seymour Weinstein, Carolyn R. Zaroff. **50 Chestnut St, 1200 Chestnut Plaza, Rochester NY 14604 (716) 325–3393.**

Jewish Ledger. Periodical pub. **1427 Monroe Ave, Rochester NY 14618 (716) 275–9090.**

Temple B'rith Kodesh. Reform Temple affiliated with UAHC. To serve as a house of worship, house of study, house of assembly. Rel Sch Sun morning & Heb Sch 3 days a wk, after sch; Adult Edu; Sisterhood; Morning Adult Edu; Bat Mitvah prog; Braille group; Brotherhood; Havura; Married Couples Club; youth groups; sr adult groups; Nursery Sch; Presch; HS; Afternoon Sch; mus; library containing approx 8,000 vols (Judaica & rel). 1,000 families; 262 individuals; 395 stu in grades K–10; 34 nursery; 20 stu midrasha. 78 employees. F 1848 as Jews Syn; first changed its name to Greentree Schule, then to Cong B'rith Kodesh & now Temple B'rith Kodesh. Pub Bulletin (semi-monthly). Facilities include kitchen, sanctuary, gift shop, mus, classrms, adult lounge, multi-purpose rms, library, auditorium, chapel. Rabbi Judea B. Miller; Rabbi Robert J. Eisen; Rabbi Emeritus Philip S. Bernstein; Exec Sec: Jerome B. Gordon; Prin: Aaron D. Braveman; Pres: Lawrence S. Scott; VPs: Thomas Fink, Mrs Donald Rubens, Mrs Peter Schwartz; Treas: Burton Gordon; Sec: Mrs Mark Lewin; Staff Assc: Harold G. Movsky. **2131 Elmwood Ave, Rochester NY 14618 (716) 244–7060.**

Temple B'rith Kodesh Library. Library contains approx 8,000 vols (Judaica & rel). For information on the Temple, see – Temple B'rith Kodesh, Rochester, NY. **2131 Elmwood Ave, Rochester NY 14618 (716) 244–7060.**

Temple Beth David. Affiliated with United Syn of Am. Rabbi Laurence M.Skopitz; Pres: Calvin Rosenbaum; Edu Dir: Sandra Levy. **3200 St Paul Blvd, Rochester NY 14617 (716) 266–3223.**

Temple Beth El. Conservative Syn affiliated with United Syn of Am. To harmonize J life & modern thought in the spirit of rel. Daily Servs; library; Rel Sch – Nursery-HS; Adult Edu Prog; Sisterhood; Men's Club; USY; Havurah – small fellowship groups that meet monthly for purposes of discussion, socializing & mutual support; Mishpachah – a group in which the entire family joins for a light meal & family fun, discussion or other projs; Haverim – a group that offers an opportunity for men & women who have leisure day time to meet together. 750 stu in the Rel Sch. The Cong was inc in Mar of 1916 & purchased a bldg in Nov of 1916. Destroyed by fire in 1960, the syn was rebuilt & dedicated in 1963. Syn facilities include two meeting rms, dining rm, lobby, gift shop, auditorium, chapel, mus, class rms, audio-visual rm, off rms, 700 permanent seats, & rm for an additional 2,000 seats. Rabbi Shamai Kanter; Hazzan: Neil Norry; Pres: Norman M. Spindelman; Exec Dir: Joseph H. Bronstein; VP: Julian Gordon. **139 Winton Rd S, Rochester NY 14610 (716) 473–1770.**

Temple Beth El Library. For information on the Temple, see – Temple Beth El, Rochester, NY. **139 Winton Rd S, Rochester NY 14610 (716) 473–1770.**

Temple Emanu-El of Irondequoit. Affiliated with UAHC. 124 mems. Rabbi William E. Blank; Pres: Renate Livingston; Edu: Wilfred Newman; Brotherhood Pres: Lawrence Slotnick. **2956 St Paul Blvd, Rochester NY 14617 (716) 266–1978.**

Temple Sinai. Affiliated with UAHC. 275 mems. Rabbi Ned J. Soltz; Cantor Martha R. Birnbaum; Pres: Ann Braverman; Edu: Jane Schuster. **363 Penfield Rd, Rochester NY 14625 (716) 381–6890.**

Temple Sinai Library. For information on the Temple, see – Temple Sinai, Rochester, NY. **363 Penfield Rd, Rochester NY 14625 (716) 381–6890.**

Rockaway Park

Robert Gordis Day School. Affiliated with Solomon Schechter Day Schs Assn. Prin: Rabbi Allan Blaine; Chr: Dr Irwin Wiener. **445 Beach 135th St, Rockaway Park NY 11694 (212) 634–7711.**

Temple Beth El of Rockaway Park. Affiliated with United Syn of Am. Rabbi Allan Blaine; Cantor Jacob Singer; Pres: Dr Leonard M. Levin–Epstein; Exec Dir: Oscar Wexman. **445 Beach 135th St, Rockaway Park NY 11694 (212) 634–8100.**

Rockville Centre

Central Synagogue. Affiliated with UAHC. 650 mems. Rabbis: Lewis C. Littman, George B. Lieberman; Cantor Joy H. Parks; Pres: Arthur E. Kahn; Edu: Leonard C. Berkman; Adm: Fredda Wolk; Sisterhood Pres: Nina Roll; Brotherhood Pres: Herbert Kahn. **430 DeMott Ave, Rockville Centre NY 11570 (516) 766–4300.**

The Helen Blau Memorial Library of Central Synagogue of Nassau County. Ctr for Judaica on LI. 4,000 bks; filmstrips; records; maps; annual progs for J Bk Mo; Bk Fair. Est in 1947, & is in its present location since 1960. Librarian: Barbara Gresack; Co-Chr Library Cttee: Lauretta Sack, Rose Werne. **430 DeMott Ave, Rockville Centre NY 11570 (516) R06–4300.**

Temple B'nai Sholom. Affiliated with United Syn of Am. Pres: Howard Ratner; Exec Sec: Diane Tropper. **100 Hempstead Ave, Rockville Centre NY 11570 (516) 764–4100.**

Temple B'nai Sholom Library. For information on the Temple, see – Temple B'nai Sholom, Rockville Centre, NY. **100 Hempstead Ave, Rockville Centre NY 11570 (516) 764–4100.**

Rome

Adas Israel. Affiliated with United Syn of Am. Rabbi Manfred Wimer; Pres: Irving Eitches. **705 Hickory St, Rome NY 13440 (315) 337–3170.**

Rosedale

Rosedale Jewish Center. Affiliated with United Syn of Am. Rabbi Samuel Smerling; Pres: Donald Weinzimer. **247–11 Francis Lewis Blvd, Rosedale NY 11422 (212) 528–3983.**

Roslyn

Shelter Rock Jewish Center. Affiliated with United Syn of Am. Rabbi Myron M. Fenster; Cantor David Weg; Pres: Irving M. Solomon; Edu Dir: Hy Krebs; Youth Dir: Harvey Goodman. **Shelter Rock & Searingtown Rds, Roslyn NY 11576 (516) 741–4305.**

Roslyn Heights

Temple Beth Sholom. Conservative Temple. Rel Servs; edu progs (including Afternoon Sch); Sisterhood; Men's Club. Over 800 families. Pub Beth Sholom News (bi-monthly). Facilities include kosher kitchen for catering, gift shop. Rabbi Dr Joseph P. Sternstein; Pres: Stephen Seltzer; Exec VP: Arthur Goldberg. **Roslyn Rd, & N State Pkwy, Roslyn Heights NY 11577 (516) 621–2288.**

Temple Sinai of Roslyn. Affiliated with UAHC. 1025 mems. Rabbis: Norman Kahan, Judith S. Lewis; Cantor Mark Ostfeld-Horowitz; Pres: Martin Marlowe; Edu: Helene Tarasow; Adm: Edwin A. Kohen; Sisterhood Pres: Rhoda Braverman; Brotherhood Pres: Leonard Gordon. **425 Roslyn Rd, Roslyn Heights NY 11577 (516) 621–6800.**

Rye

Community Synagogue. Reform Syn affiliated with UAHC. Rel Servs; edu progs; Sisterhood; Afternoon Day Sch. 500 families; approximately 350 stu. 56 employees. Pub Community News (monthly). Facilities include sanctuary, auditorium, kitchen, gift shop. Rabbi Robert A. Rothman DD, DHL; Cantor Bruce Halev; Prin: Marilyn Scheffler; Adm: Arlena Leiter; Pres Exec Bd: Francis Fraenkel; Exec VP: Jay Schwab; VPs: William Lurie, Ronald Cohen; Treas: Walter Loeb; Fin Sec: Sel Hubert; Rec Sec: Bonnie Marcus; Corsp Sec: Irene Weiss. **200 Forest Ave, Rye NY 10550 (914) 967–6262.**

Emanu-El of Westchester. Affiliated with UAHC. 316 mems. Rabbi Daniel S. Wolk; Cantor Earl Rogers; Pres: Morton A. Kornreich; Edu: Lawrence Davis; Adm: Elizabeth S. Talbot. **Westchester Ave, Rye NY 10580 (914) 967–4382.**

Sag Harbor

Temple Adas Israel. Affiliated with UAHC. 15 mems. Rabbi Joseph Ginsberg; Pres: Donald Katz; Edu: Amy R. Perlin. **Elizabeth St & Atlantic Ave, Sag Harbor NY 11963 (516) 725–0054.**

Saratoga Springs

Temple Sinai. Affiliated with UAHC. 41 mems. Pres: Carol L. Pinsley; Edu: Kathy Doyle. **509 Bdwy, PO Box 224, Saratoga Springs NY 12866 (518) 584–8730.**

Sayville

Temple Shalom. Conservative Temple affiliated with United Syn of Am. Commitment to J values, & search for a more meaningful existence. Rel Servs; Sisterhood; com servs; Rel Sch; Heb HS; youth activities. 145 families. Est in 1960. Kol Shalom – a magazine sent monthly to mems. Rabbi Jeffrey Wartenberg; Pres: Manny Balfour; VPs: Edward Raskin, Murray Cohen; Treas: Eugene Weiss; Sec: Harriet Kessler; Co-Pres Sisterhood: Toby Klausner, Tina Steiner. **225 Greeley Ave, Sayville NY 11782 (516) 567–3207.**

Scarsdale

Scarsdale Synagogue – Tremont Temple. Affiliated with UAHC. 160 mems. Rabbi Stephen A. Klein; Pres: William V. Lewit. **2 Ogden Rd, Scarsdale NY 10583 (914) 725–5175.**

The Sephardic Community of New Rochelle-Scarsdale. Syn. To maintain the Sephardic heritage for future generations. Rel Servs. 15 families. F in 1977; the first Sephardic minyan est in Westchester Cty. The backgrounds of the families consist of Syrians fr Aleppo, Iraqis, Moroccans, & Egyptians. The Syn possesses a Sefer Torah fr Iraq over 106 yrs old, which has been restored. Pres: Albert Shammah; VP: Albert Asher; Treas: Debrah Dweck. **c/o Young Israel of Scarsdale, 1313 Daisy Farms Rd, Scarsdale NY 10583 (914) 723–6273.**

Westchester Reform Temple. Affiliated with UAHC. 780 mems. Rabbis: Jack Stern Jr, Peter G. Weintraub; Cantor Joseph Boardman; Pres: Joseph Bernstein; Adm: Claire Franzman; Sisterhood Pres: Merle Brenner; Brotherhood Pres: Louis I. Rubins. **255 Mamaroneck Rd, Scarsdale NY 10583 (914) 723–7727.**

Westchester Reform Temple Library. For information on the Temple, see – Westchester Reform Temple, Scarsdale, NY. **255 Mamaroneck Rd, Scarsdale NY 10583 (914) 723–7727.**

Young Israel of Scarsdale. 1313 Daisy Farms Rd, Scarsdale NY 10583 (914) 723–6273.

Schenectady

Congregation Agudat Achim. Affiliated with United Syn of Am. Rabbi Samuel Kieffer; Pres: William I. Rowen. **2117 Union St, Schenectady NY 12309.**

Congregation Gates of Heaven. Oldest J cong in Schenectady; affiliated with UAHC. Rel Sch now enrolls about 300 stu, taught in 19 classes with 9 extra classes for Heb instruction; Sisterhood; Brotherhood; Mr & Mrs Club; Youth Group; com affairs; meeting space available for various J orgs. The first J families of Schenectady worshipped in private homes for several yrs until they est a cong in 1854; two yrs later it was inc as Cong Shaarai Shamayim. Immediately after, a burial plot was purchased. The constitution of the Cong was recorded in 1862. The first syn bldg on E Ferry St was purchased in 1865; a new syn was erected on N Col St in 1892 due to more J families in the area. Originally Orthodox, the syn gradually turned more liberal. In 1907 the syn became affiliated with UAHC. In 1920 the former Christian Sci Temple of Parkwood Blvd was purchased; an addition was built 15 yrs later doubling the seating capacity. The Cong moved to Eastern Pkwy & Ashmore Ave in 1956. The original inc name of Shaarai Shamayim was dropped in 1920, & changed to Cong Gates of Heaven. The Sisterhood was organized in 1897 as the Ladies Auxiliary; the Brotherhood in 1924 (originally the Men's Club); & the Mr & Mrs Club in 1952. Rabbi Dr Michael M. Szenes; Edu Dir: Judith Morag; Pres: Julius Jermanok; 1st VP: Sanford Fialkoff; 2nd VP: Paul Swartz; 3rd VP: Ann Cramer; Fin Sec: Stanley Strauss; Treas: Gordon Zuckerman; Fin Sec: Ernest Kahn. **Eastern Pkwy & Ashmore Ave, Schenectady NY 12309 (518) 374–8173.**

Jewish Federation of Greater Schenectady. Mem of CJF. Sponsors UJA & Federated Welfare Fund. Organized 1938. Pres: Neil M. Golub; Exec Dir: Haim Morag. **2565 Balltown Rd, Schenectady NY 12309 (518) 393–1136.**

Shenorock

Hebrew Congregation of Somers, Inc. Affiliated with United Syn of Am. Rabbi Geoffrey Goldberg; Pres: Dr Leonard Sonnenberg; Edu Dir: Roberta Roberts. **Mervyn Dr & Cypress Lane, Shenorock NY 10587 (914) 248–5166.**

Smithtown

Jewish Community Services of Long Island. A counseling agy devoted to helping families with personal & emotional problems. For additional information, see – Jewish Community Services of Long Island – Rego Park NY. **22 Lawrence Ave, Smithtown NY 11787 (516) 724–6300.**

Temple Beth Sholom of Smithtown. Conservative Syn affiliated with United Syn of Am; a Syn which expresses itself in a liberal, progressive way. Rel Sch; USY youth groups; Chai Club; Nursery Sch; Adult Edu; PTA. 600 families fr the Greater Smithtown area. Rabbi Elliot T. Spar; Rabbi Kenneth A. Emert; Cantor Israel Rosen; Exec Dir: Bernard Gutmaker; Pres: Donald Berman; VP: Ben Wieder; Fin Sec: Dr Sanford Scheman; Rec Sec: Stephen Abramson; Corsp Sec: Sheila Eckstein; Trustees: Barry Berger, Charles Falk, Eve Fischthal, Dena Goldberg, Marsha Klass, Judith Lazar, Gerald Rosenberg, Ira Sloane, Martin Teitelbaum, Arthur Williams, Barbara Winawer; Hon Pres: Dr Jack M. Hanover; Sisterhood Pres: June Goldman; Men's Club Pres: Richard Pomeranz. **PO Box 764, Edgewood Ave & River Rd, Smithtown NY 11787 (516) 724–0424.**

South Fallsburg

Yeshiva Gedolah Zichron. To instill Torah values, providing secular edu & developing each stu individual potential. Four-yr HS Prog; Elementary Sch; Rabbinical Seminary; Kolel Post Grad Sch; Post Fellowship Prog. 300 stu. 14 Heb teachers; 10 gen studies teachers. Est in 1969. Yeshiva facilities include a study hall, J library, lecture rms, classrooms, sci lab, kosher kitchen & dining hall, dormitories, gymnasium. Chr of the Bd: Simon Kaplan; Dean: Rabbi Jeruchim Gorelick; Rosh Yeshiva: Rabbi Abba Gorelick; Bais Medrash Col – Rosh Yeshiva: Rabbi Eli Wachtfogel; Dean of Men: Rabbi Elya Goldschmidt; Dir of Research: Rabbi Ben Tzion Kokis; Instr: Rabbi Gershon Neuman; Mesivta HS Dept – Menahel: Rabbi Asher Bornstein; HS Gen Studies Dept – Prin: James F. Brennan; Cheder Elementary Sch Div – Menahel: Rabbi Tzvi M. Kirsch; Prin Gen Studies: Chanie Trieger; Adm – Exec Dir: Robert D. Gibber; Adm: Rabbi Elisha Dorfman; Comptroller: Rosalind Bley. **Laurel Park Rd, South Fallsburg NY 12779 (914) 434–5240.**

Spring Valley

Jewish Community Center of Spring valley. Affiliated with United Syn of Am. Rabbi Hillel Friedman; Cantor David Rosenzweig; Pres: Sam Warsoff; Exec Dir: Dr Irving Kriesberg; Edu Dir: Ira Blassberg; Youth Dir: Mitchel Schwartz. **250 N Main St, Spring Valley NY 10977 (914) 356–3710.**

Jewish Community Center of Spring Valley Library. For information on the Ctr, see – Jewish Community Center of Spring Valley, Spring Valley , NY. **250 N Main St, Spring Valley NY 10977 (914) 356–3710.**

Shaarey Tfiloh Congregation. Conservative Cong. Rel Servs; edu progs; Men's Club; Sisterhood; youth progs; Adult Edu & public forums; Afternoon Sch; library containing 1,800 vols (primarily Judaica). 250 families; 160 stu in grades 1–6. F 1962; facilities enlarged 3 times. Pub Kol Shaarey Tfiloh (monthly). Facilities include main chapel seating 760, lower sanctuary seating 96, 8 rm sch suite & principal's off; Judaica library (professionally organized); kitchen facilities for 300 – meat &/or dairy, gift shop, youth lounge. Learning disabled chil taught as separte prog. Rabbi Solomon Zeides; Cantor Edward Kaplan; Prin: Zelda Perel. **972 S Main St, Spring Valley NY 10977 (914) 356–2225.**

Shaarey Tfiloh Congregation, Library. Library contains 1,800 vols (primarily Judaica). For information on the Cong, see – Shaarey Tfiloh Congregation, Spring Valley, NY. **972 S Main St, Spring Valley NY 10977 (914) 356–2225.**

Temple Beth El. Affiliated with UAHC. 891 mems. Rabbis: Louis Frishman, Sara R. Perman; Cantor George Weinflash; Pres: William Weltman; Edu: David Iskovitz; Sisterhood Pres: Sheila Kleinman; Brotherhood Pres: Barry Miller. **415 Viola Rd, Spring Valley NY 10977 (914) 356–2000.**

Staten Island

B'nai Jeshurun Congregation. Affiliated with United Syn of Am. Rabbi Wayne Allen; Cantor Harvey Waldman; Pres: Arthur Klapper. **275 Martling Ave, Staten Island NY 10314 (212) YU1–5550.**

Bais Yaakov School of Staten Island. 1111 Capodanno Blvd, Staten Island NY 10314.

Bais Yaakov School of Staten Island Library. 1111 Capodanno Blvd, Staten Island NY 10314.

Congregation B'nai Israel. Conservative – Traditional Syn; affiliated with United Syn of Am. To foster & interpret historical, traditional J with a modern approach; to serve the needs of young & old through rel, cultural, & social activities; to be dedicated to serv, God & man. Daily Minyan; Nursery Sch; 6 hour Talmud Torah; Heb HS; Jr HS Youth Group; HS Youth Group; ORT; Hadassah; Sisterhood; Men's Club; Couples Club; Adult Edu Ins; Ba'al Koreh Ins; Chevrah Kadisha. F in Feb of 1935 as the S Shore Hebrew Alliance. Incorporated as Cong B'nai Is in 1943, & was affiliated with United Syn of Am. Bis Hunnert un Zwanzing-A Ritual Guide to Funerals and Mourning; Shabbat Shalom-Friday Night Home Service; Chag Kasher V'Sameach – A packet of Halachot & Dinim/Minhagim for Passover. Rabbi Jeffrey Rappoport; Pres: Marvin Shindelman; Sisterhood Pres: Rita Eisenberg; Men's Club Pres: Stuart Maitin; Prin: Rabbi Tzvi Berkowitz; Ritual Dir: Sheldon Weinstein. **45 Twombly Ave, Staten Island NY 10306 (212) 987–8188,9.**

Jewish Community Center of Staten Island. Nursery Sch; Music Ins; Learning Ins for Disabled Chil; summer camps; family park complex; physical edu; sr adult progs; cultural arts; recreational progs for various age groups. Over 6,000. Est in 1928 as an edu, cultural & recreational agy for the J com of Staten Island. Physical facilities: main bldg in original location with nursery sch next door. A S Shore extension is being opened about 10 miles fr main location; the family park camp-complex is 5 miles away. Pres: Dr Ronald Leventhal; Chr of the Bd: Allan Weinglass; Treas: Alan Bernikow; Sec: Diane Teitelbaum; VPs: Nancy Avis, Dr Dennis Blommfield, R. Randy Lee, Herbert Schiff; Exec Dir: Lewis Stolzenberg; Adm Dir: Harold Garber; Dir of Edu: Susan Bender. **475 Victory Blvd, Staten Island NY 10301 (212) 981–1500.**

Temple Emanu-El of Staten Island. Conservative Temple affiliated with United Syn of Am, Council of J Org of Staten Island. To enhance the J consciousness, committment & practice of its mems. Rel Servs; Jr Cong; Heb Sch; Men's Club; Sisterhood, Adult Edu; cemetery, com serv projects; B'nai B'rith Youth Group. 300 families; 7 employees. F 1907. Pub Temple Mail (monthly). Facilities include kosher kitchen sanctuary seating 400, chapel seating 40, 4 classrms, ballrm, 2 lane bowling alley. Rabbi Gerald Sassman; Cantor Jack Schwartz; Pres: Hyman Doctor. **984 Post Ave, Staten Island NY 10302 (212) 942–5966.**

Temple Israel. Affiliated with UAHC. 318 mems. Cantor Jan Meyel; Pres: Leonard Leef; Rabbis: Milton Rosenfeld, Marcus Kramer; Edu: Daniel Drobner; Sisterhood Pres: Margaret Eichler, Vivian Gaines; Brotherhood Pres: Leslie Meyerberg. **315 Forest Ave, Staten Island NY 10301 (212) 727–2231.**

Stony Brook

B'nai B'rith Hillel Foundation at the State University of New York. Org & chaplaincy for J col stu; mem of the B'nai B'rith Hillel Founs. To provide social, rel, cultural & edu progs & counseling to J stu & faculty at SUNY – Stony Brook. Shabbat & Holiday Servs; kosher dining hall; J social events; lectures & discussions; J Free Univ courses; Is progs; seminars & institutes; counseling; referral; J stu newspaper; library containing 800 vols (varied Judaica). 4,000 individuals; 1 local group. 3 employees. Formerly a B'nai B'rith Hillel Counselorship est in 1968; upgraded to B'nai B'rith Hillel Foun in 1975. Pub The Shining Star (quarterly), Hillel Calendar (monthly). Facilities include suite of offs & lounge, kosher dining rm, other univ facilities. Hillel Dir: Joseph Topek; Outreach: Marcia Prager; Adm: Barbara Szostek. **Interfaith Center, Humanities 165, SUNY – Stony Brook, Stony Brook NY 11794 (516) 246–6842,3.**

Temple Isaiah. Reform Temple affiliated with UAHC, BJE of Greater NY, Suffolk Cty J Assn. To promote Judaism in all relations of life by means of public & private worship, by rel edu, & through social welfare activities & such other means as shall serve to convey the teachings of Judaism. Afternoon Sch – grades K–12 with curriculum covering: J people, hist, holiday orientation, study of Torah. 492 families, 430 stu grades K–7, 70 stu grades 8–12. 24 employees. F 1965 by 38 families; constructed first bldg & acquired Holocaust Torah in 1967; completed current facility, a work of architecture contemporary with its time, in 1976. Pub Bulletin (monthly Sept–June). Facilities include sanctuary seating 250, gift shop, catering kitchen, social hall for receptions, stage, cemetery. Pres: Mal Taylor; VPs: Bruce Howard, Hal Ziegler, Barbara Yarmus, Bob Klomp; Treas: Martin Lieberman; Fin Sec: Lori Rosenthal; Corsp Sec: Renee Plevin; Rec Sec: Marilyn Rosenzweig. **1404 Stony Brook Rd, Stony Brook NY 11790 (516) 751–8518.**

Suffern

Congregation Sons of Israel. Affiliated with United Syn of Am. Rabbi Paul E. Schuchalter; Pres: Martin Weiss; Youth Dir: Martin Boltax. **Suffern Place, Suffern NY 10901 (914) 357–9827.**

Reform Temple of Suffern. Affiliated with UAHC. 67 mems. Rabbi Elyse Frishman; Pres: Jay Meyers; Edu: Elyse Frishman. **70 Haverstraw Rd, PO Box 472, Suffern NY 10901 (914) 357–5872.**

Syosset

Jewish Community Services of Long Island. A counseling agy devoted to helping families with personal & emotional problems. For additional information, see – Jewish Community Services of Long Island – Rego Park NY. **175 Jericho Turnpike, Syosset NY 11791 (516) 364–8040.**

Midway Jewish Center. Affiliated with United Syn of Am. Rabbi Ezra Finkelstein; Cantor Morris Dubinsky; Pres: Milton Ackerman; Edu Dir: Rabbi Abraham Soffer; Youth Dir: Jeff Schwartz. **330 S Oyster Bay Rd, Syosset NY 11791 (516) 938–8390.**

North Shore Congregation. Affiliated with UAHC. 515 mems. Rabbi Daniel Fogel; Cantor Phyllis P. Cole; Pres: Howard Jacoby; Edu: Irene Blanco; Sisterhood Pres: Fran Costigan; Brotherhood Pres: Howard Kane. **83 Muttontown Rd, Syosset NY 11791 (516) 921–2282.**

North Shore Congregation, Charles Cohn Memorial Library. For information on the Cong, see – North Shore Congregation, Soysset, NY. **83 Muttontown Rd, Syosset NY 11791 (516) 921–2282.**

Syracuse

The Rabbi Jacob H. Epstein School of Jewish Studies. To dev a sense of loyalty to the J people & to the values that bind the J people together; to learn what J values are, & to adapt these values to everyday living in a pluralistic soc; to broaden & deepen the teenagers knowledge of source material in the J tradition: Hist, Torah & Talmud; to build a sense of responsibility toward social agy & J rel ins; to strengthen the teenagers identification with the local J com; to build a continuing commitment to the State of Is within the framework of Am soc; to enable stu to use Heb language more effectively; to build a sensitivity to, & understanding of, the points of view of other groups within & outside of J; to teach stu to examine & question their own beliefs in keeping with our tradition; to motivate stu to accept study as a life long pursuit. Comprehensive prog of J edu for teenagers ages 13–18; non-matriculated prog; matriculation prog. Pres: Dr Myron Lichtblau; VP: Ted Zucker; Treas: Harvey Delson; Sec: Richard Serlin; Edu Dir: Ronald Remer. **PO Box 161, Syracuse NY 13214.**

Sephardic Group of Syracuse. Orthodox Cong affiliated with Young Is of Syracuse. To promote Sephardic customs; to attract more Sephardim to become more actively involved in rel practices & J matters; to give love & support for Is & J unity. Rel Servs on High Holy Days & special occasions. About 20 families; origins of mems include: Libya, Egypt, Greece, Morocco, Syria, Turkey, some Ashkenazim. Est in Feb 1968 by Moshe Habib upon his arrival in NY fr Libya. Hazan Moshe Habib; Pres: David Peppi; Treas: Victor Azria. **c/o Mr Habib, 119 Doll Pkwy, Syracuse NY 13214 (315) 446–0760.**

Syracuse Jewish Federation, Inc. Mem of CJF. Organized 1918. Pres: Alan S. Burstein; Exec Dir: Barry Silverberg. **2223 E Genesee St, PO Box 5004, Syracuse NY 13250 (315) 422–4104.**

Temple Adath Yeshurun. Conservative Syn affiliated with United Syn of Am. To make a rel, cultural, social & edu home for the com. Daily minyan; Shabbat & Holiday Serv; Bar/Bat Mitzvah class; Men's Club; Sisterhood; Shoresh Youth (grades 4&5); Kadima Youth (grades 6–8); USY (grades 9–12); Temple Srs; Temple Adath New Group (young families); a J Alternative (J singles

18–35); Rabbi's Commission on Human Needs; Pre-sch; HS; Afternoon Sch. 900 mems; 175 stu in grades K–7. 15 employees. In 1870 began as Cong of Kadisha, & in 1872 chartered under name of Cong Adath Yeshurun. The first Rabbi was Rabbi Joseph Herman Hertz, first graduate of the JTS, & later Chief Rabbi of the British Empire. Pub Temple Adath Bulletin (monthly), Temple Adath & You (weekly). Facilities include sanctuary seating 750 (seats 2800 in ballrm & sanctuary for High Holidays); ballroom seating 2100 auditorium style, 1800 dinner style; kosher kitchen; 7 approved kosher caterers. Rabbi Chalres Sherman; Cantor Harold Lerner; Pres: Arnold Goldberg; Exec Dir: Steven S. Greene; Edu Dir: Chana Elefant. **450 Kimber Rd, Syracuse NY 13224 (315) 445–0002.**

Temple Society of Concord. Reform Temple. Affiliated with UAHC. The oldest J cong in Syracuse. Fri Evening, Sat, Holiday Servs, Oneg Shabbat; monthly Sabbath Servs & Dinner; Rel Sch; Confirmation; Bar/Bat Mitzvah; youth groups; Sisterhood; Brotherhood; Chaverim group; Adult Edu & J classes; support group for single parents; cemetery; memorials. 756 mems. Est in 1839 when Syracuse had an approximate population of 11,000 people. The 1st rel servs were held in a small store. By 1951 the Cong had built & dedicated their 1st temple on the corner of Harrison & S State Sts. Facilities include: modern meeting rm & social hall with seating capacity for 300, equipped kitchen, lounge, library, rel sch bldg. Rabbi Thecdore S. Levy; Asst Rabbi, Edu: Laurence A. Schlesinger. **910 Madison St, Syracuse NY 13210 (315) 475–9952.**

Temple Society of Concord, Lois Arnold Gale Memorial Library. For information on the Temple, see – Temple Society of Concord, Syracuse, NY. **910 Madison St, Syracuse NY 13210 (315) 475–9952.**

Tarrytown

Temple Beth Abraham. Affiliated with UAHC. 358 mems. Rabbi Paul R. Siegel; Cantor Jerome Holland; Pres: Burton Litwin; Edu: Roberta Rods; Adm: Iris Gerissman; Sisterhood Pres: Donna Ferris. **25 Leroy Ave, Tarrytown NY 10591 (914) 631–1770.**

Temple Beth Abraham, Joseph Dean Wolar Library. For information on the Temple, see – Temple Beth Abraham, Tarrytown, NY. **25 LeRoy Ave, Tarrytown NY 10591 (914) 631–1770.**

Troy

Congregation Berith Sholom. Reform Cong affiliated with UAHC. Rel Servs; Sisterhood; Brotherhood; Sun Sch; Heb Sch. The Rel Soc & Cong of Baris Sholem in the City of Troy was inc in 1866. The Cong was the successor of Anshe Chesed, the first J org in Troy. In 1870 a lot was purchased & the present structure was erected there. The corner stone laying ceremony took place on Jun 12, 1870. The dedication of the bldg took place on Sept 22, 1870. The Cong took on the Reform character, which had the effect of isolating them fr the later new-comers in Troy, who were for the most part very Orthodox J fr Eastern Europe. A Sun Sch was started. In 18S3 the women of Berith Sholom organized a sisterhood. In 1920 the Temple joined the UAHC. In 1921 a brotherhood was formed. As a result of an increase in membership there was a need to expand & improve facilities. In 1953 an addition was made in the form of a sch annex; in 1963 the entire interior of the temple was renovated & modernized; in 1965 stained glass windows were installed. Rabbi Jonathan H. Gerard; Pres: Charles S. Ehrlich; VPs: Dorothy Jacobson, Dr Robert Loewy; Treas: Arthur Danzig; Fin Sec: Ruth Marinsky; Rec Sec: Marcia Ehrlich; Corsp Sec: Barbara Marshall; Ritual Cttee: Joseph Rosner. **167 Third St, Troy NY 12180 (518) 272–8872.**

Temple Beth El. Affiliated with United Syn of Am. Cantor Leo Spangelet; Pres: Dr Abraham Singer; Edu Dir: Rina Pridor. **409 Hoosick St, Troy NY 12180 (518) 272–6113.**

Troy Jewish Community Council, Inc. Mem of CJF. Organized 1936. Pres: Dr Louis Cohen. **2430 21st St, Troy NY 12180 (518) 274–0700.**

Tuckahoe

Genesis – Agudas Achim. Affiliated with United Syn of Am. Rabbi Dr Edward Neufeld; Pres: Arthur Scholder; Ritual Dir: Samuel Kamchi; Edu Dir: Yehuda Arnon; Sec: Marjorie Ronin. **25 Oakland Ave, Tuckahoe NY 10707 (914) WO1–3766.**

Upper Nyack

Congregation Sons of Israel. Conservative Cong affiliated with United Syn of Am. A Conservative syn serving Nyack – Valley Cottage, NY area. Rel Servs; edu progs for chil, teens & adults; Sisterhood; social & cultural progs; cemetery. 200 individuals; 120 chil in Rel Sch. 3 full-time employees, 8 part-time employees. F 1891. Pub Bulletin (monthly). Facilities include kosher kitchen, sanctuary, social hall, sch bldg. Rabbi Michael Gold; Cantor Jay Goldstein; Edu Dir: Bernie Rapp. **300 N Bdwy, Upper Nyack NY 10960 (914) 358–3767.**

Temple Beth Torah. Reform Temple affiliated with the UAHC, Assn of J Libraries. To promote the practice of Judaism. Sabbath & Holiday Servs; youth groups; Sisterhood; Men's Club; Pre-sch; Afternoon Sch; Evening Sch for high schoolers; library with 750 vols (general). 300 families; 400 stu. 25 employees. F 1965. Pub Alenu (monthly bulletin), Newsletter (weekly). Facilities include sanctuary seating 600, social area accomodating 250 at tables, Judaica shop, kitchen. Rabbi George M. Stern; Cantor Don A. Croll; Pres: David Firstenberg; Edu: Molly Karp; VPs: Stern Silverberg, Gerald Tenser, Lee Ostroff; Youth Group Adv: Ira Oustatcher; Men's Club Pres: Ernie Blitzer, Stu Korn; Editor: Dan Mufson; Sisterhood Pres: Susan Korn. **Route 9W, Upper Nyack NY 10960 (914) 358–2248.**

Temple Beth Torah Library. For information on the Temple, see – Temple Beth Torah, Upper Nyack, NY. **Route 9W, Upper Nyack NY 10960 (914) 358–2248.**

Utica

Jewish Community Council of Utica, New York, Inc. Mem of CJF. Sponsors United Jewish Appeal of Utica. Organized 1933; inc 1950. Pres: Cecily Eidelhoch. **2310 Oneida St, Utica NY 13501 (315) 733–2343.**

Temple Beth El. A Conservative Syn est for the worship of God, the study of Torah & the practice of righteous deeds. Affiliated with United Syn of Am. Morning & Evening Minyans; Family Rel Servs; Bar/Bat Mitzvah; minyan breakfast seminars; Is Independence Day celebrations; guest speakers & groups; Rel Sch grades 2–8; Jr Cong; Tutorial Prog; Heb HS; scholarships to Is; Sisterhood; Men's Club; USY Youth Group; Young Couples progs; Adult Edu. 100 stu enrolled in Rel Sch & at neighboring com HS which Temple co-sponsers. In 1902 a cong calling itself Beth El met at the Foster Bldg. In 1912 Fri Evening Servs & a Heb sch were est. In 1919 the founding group organized a rel soc to reconcile J tradition with the demands of modern life. The Temple joined the United Syn in 1921. In 1923 they purchased a cemetery. In 1927 the present temple site was purchased. In Aug of 1930 the 1st Servs were held in the new bldg; 2 yrs later the 1st Heb sch & the 1st chil study group were held.Pres: Victor H. Flax; 1st VP: Nettie Schwartz; 2nd VP: Michael Silverman; Treas: William Trapanick; Sec: Ellen Samuels; Rabbi Dr Edgar J. Weinsberg; Hazzan David Katchen. **1607 Genesee St, Utica NY 13501 (315) 724–4751, 6883.**

Temple Emanu-El. Reform Temple affiliated with UAHC. Rel Servs; edu progs for chil & adults; Sisterhood; Brotherhood; Youth Group; rabbinic counseling; cemetery; library containing 500 vols (Judaica). 220 families; 75 stu grades K–10. F 1950 as a Reform Syn. Pub Bulletin (monthly). Facilities include sanctuary seating 225 (expandable to 650), social hall, gift shop, 8 classrms. Rabbi Henry Bamberger; Pres: Gloria Schaeffer; 1st VP: Julius Reiner; 2nd VP: Dr Scott Silver. **2710 Genesee St, Utica NY 13502 (315) 724–4177.**

Valley Stream

Temple Gates of Zion. Affiliated with United Syn of Am. Rabbi Simon Resikoff; Cantor David J. Mann; Pres: Samuel Benowitz; Exec Dir: Evelyn Epstein; Edu Dir: Stuart L. Margolies; Youth Dir: Jim Stember. **322 N Corona Ave, Valley Stream NY 11580 (516) 561–2308.**

Temple Hillel. Affiliated with United Syn of Am. Rabbi Morris S. Friedman; Cantor Rudolph Dresdner: Asst Rabbi & Edu Dir: Rabbi Solomon Aidleson; Pres: Benjamin Tarlow; Exec Dir: Cecil Walkenfeld; Youth Dir: Evan Shore. **1000 Rosedale Rd, Valley Stream NY 11581 (516) 791–6344.**

Temple Hillel Library. For information on the Temple, see – Temple Hillel, Valley Stream, NY. **1000 Rosedale Rd, Valley Stream NY 11581 (516) 791–6344.**

Temple Hillel Southside Jewish Center. Affiliate cong of the United Syn of Am. Servs to the com, to the people of Is & to the State of Is. Daily, Shabbat & Holiday Servs; daily morning minyan breakfasts; library; J mus; bk & discussion group; Sisterhood & Evening Circle; Men's Club; USY; Rel Sch; Sun Sch; PTA; Adult Edu; basketball team; Teen Lounge; Jr Cong Servs. 1,000 families. F in 1955 in a converted garage. In 1956 a permanent bldg was erected housing the Syn & the Heb Sch. In Oct of 1956 the Syn received a charter of affiliation fr the United Syn of Am. In 1957 the first issue of the Temple bulletin was published. In 1959 the name of the Syn was changed to Temple Hillel S Side Ctr. Due to an increase in membership, a larger facility was needed. In Sept of 1960 the new Temple Hillel was dedicated. In 1972 the new Minyan Chapel was consecrated. The Holocaust Wall in the Main Sanctuary was dedicated on Holocaust Day in Apr of 1979. Southside Jewish Center Bulletin; The Temple Herald (pub monthly). Facilities in the temple include a ballroom & an all purpose rm. The Men's Club has donated six ambulances to Is. Rabbi Morris S. Friedman; Asst Rabbi & Edu Dir: Solomon Aidelson; Cantor Rudolph Dresdner; Exec Dir: Cecil Walkenfeld; Pres: Benjamin Tarlow; Exec VP:

Emanuel Scherman; VPs: Irving Schlussel, Paul Burton, Martin Popofsky, David Atlas; Treas: Arnold Miller; Fin Sec: Abraham Goldberg; Sec: Sol Deutsch; Trustees Chr: Cyrus Wolf; Co-Chr: Joseph Berman; Trustees: William Barnett, Leonard Bergman, Sy Bochner, Beth Cohen, Steve Cohen, Susie Feibusch, Rhoda Fleischer, Leo Girshek, Henry Goldberg, Egon Henner, Melvin Hoffman, Stanley Ifcher, Jerry Kaller, Mac Klar, Jack Klein, Jerome Koffler, Al Land, Lenore Malamud, Meyer Marks, Myron Oshinsky, Joan Perlmutter, Elaine Popofsky, Julius Rossberg, Gloria Schlussel, Helen Schlussel, Dorothy Schwartz, Arlene Schweitzer, Sol Shmulewitz, Ted Shuster, Arthur Singer, Sid Stein, Leonard Tannenbaum, Muriel Tannenbaum, Eugene Zweig. **1000 Rosedale Rd, Valley Stream NY 11581 (516) 791–6344.**

Vernon

Westchester Jewish Community Services, Inc. A state licensed, non-sectarian chil guidance & family mental health clin which is available to all Westchester residents of all ages. For additional information, see Westchester Jewish Community Services, Inc. – White Plains, NY. **9 W Prospect Ave, Mt Vernon NY 10550 (914) 668–8938.**

Wantagh

The Suburban Temple. Affiliated with UAHC. 670 mems. Rabbi Robert A. Raab; Cantor Bernard Barr; Pres: Stanley S. Fox; Edu: Susanne Heiman; Sisterhood Pres: Lillian Rattner; Brotherhood Pres: Victor Breitburg. **2900 Jerusalem Ave, Wantagh NY 11793 (516) 221–2370.**

Wantagh Jewish Center. Affiliated with United Syn of Am. Rabbi Mordecai Rubin; Cantor Henry Wahrman; Pres: Jerry Tack; Edu Dir: Solomon Feld; Youth Dir: Debbie Friedman. **3710 Woodbine Ave, Wantagh NY 11793 (516) SU5–2445.**

Warwick

UAHC Kutz Camp Institute. Dir: Rabbi Allan L. Smith; Co-Dir: Paul Reichenbach. **Bowen Rd, Warwick NY 10990 (914) 986–1174; 838 Fifth Ave, NYC NY 10021 (212) 299–0100.**

Watertown

Congregation Degel Israel. Affiliated with United Syn of Am. Rabbi Morris C. Katz; Pres: Simon Finkelman. **557 Thompson Blvd, Watertown NY 13601 (315) 782–2860.**

West Amherst

Bureau of Jewish Education of Greater Buffalo. 2600 N Forest Rd, West Amherst NY 14228 (716) 689–8844.

Bureau of Jewish Education of Greater Buffalo, Library. 2600 N Forest Rd, West Amherst NY 14228 (716) 689–8844.

West Hempstead

Jewish Community Center of West Hempstead. Affiliated with United Syn of Am. Rabbi Stephen C. Lerner; Cantor Haskell Rosenbloom; Pres: Jack Abramson; Edu Dir: Solomon Silverman. **711 Dogwood Ave, West Hempstead NY 11552 (516) 481–7448.**

Nassau Community Temple. Affiliated with UAHC. 200 mems. Rabbi Leonard Troupp; Cantor Mindy J. Fliegelman; Pres: Bert Taras; Edu: Ellen Tutsch; Sisterhood Pres: Sue Taras; Brotherhood Pres: Max Hirsch. **240 Hempstead Ave, West Hempstead NY 11552 (516) 485–1811.**

Westbury

Community Reform Temple. Affiliated with UAHC. 238 mems. Rabbi Michael L. Klein-Katz; Pres: Alan Gurvis; Edu: Daphna Schneider; Sisterhood Pres: Karen Davis; Brotherhood Pres: Ira Warshawsky. **712 Plain Rd, Westbury NY 11590 (516) 333–1839.**

Temple Beth Torah. Affiliated with United Syn of Am. Rabbi Michael Katz; Cantor Kalman Fliebelman; Pres: David Norflus. **243 Cantiague Rd, Westbury NY 11590 (516) ED4–7979.**

Temple Sholom. Affiliated with United Syn of Am. Rabbi Dr M. Aranov; Cantor Ivor Lichtman; Pres: Dr Alfred A. Magaliff; Exec Dir: Michael Scheeler. **675 Brookside Ct, Westbury NY 11590 (516) ED4–2800.**

White Plains

Jewish Community Center of White Plains. Affiliated with UAHC. mems. Rabbis: Maurice Davis, Lawrence W. Schwartz; Cantor Raymond Smolover; Pres: Bernice Brussel; Edu: Karen Rossel; Adm: Mathew Gruber; Sisterhood Pres: Marilyn Ptak; Brotherhood Pres: Leonard Kratz. **252 Soundview Ave, White Plains NY 10606 (914) 949–4717.**

Solomon Schechter Day School of Westchester. Affiliated with Solomon Schechter Day

Schools Assn. Prin: Dr Elliot Spiegel; Chr: Leo Salon. **30 Dellwood Rd, White Plains NY 10605 (914) 948–3111.**

Solomon Schechter School of Westchester. 20 Soundview Ave, White Plains NY 10606 (914) 948–2846.

Solomon Schechter School of Westchester, Library. 20 Soundview Ave, White Plains NY 10606 (914) 948–2846.

Temple Israel Center Library. 280 Old Mamaroneck Rd, White Plains NY 10605 (914) 948–2800.

Temple Israel Center of White Plains. Affiliated with United Syn of Am. Rabbi Arnold S. Turetsky; Cantor Abraham Mizrahi; Pres: Dr Saul Shapiro; Exec Dir: Lionel Semiatin; Edu Dir: Gabriel Schonfeld; Youth Dir: Helise Lieberman. **280 Old Mamaroneck Rd, White Plains NY 10605 (914) 948–2800.**

Westchester Jewish Community Services, Inc. A state licensed, non-sectarian chil guidance & family mental health clin which is available to all Westchester residents of all ages. It is the 9th largest family counseling agy under J auspices in the US. Individual, group, couple, chil & family therapy; marital & premarital counseling; sex therapy; chemotherapy; crisis intervention; information & referral; edu career counseling; workshops for women; psychoeducational evaluation & assistance to chil with learning problems; pre-nursery sch; outreach prog in the home to prevent chil abuse & neglect; geriatric servs: counseling for the aged & their families, guidance on specialized placement needs, provision of homemaker-home health aid servs to help the elderly & the chronically mentally ill; family life edu progs: works toward the prevention of marital difficulties & aids in adjustment to: changing mores & lifestyles, job change or loss, broken or reblended families, bereavement, single family stresses, divorce, confusion around family & social roles, problems of aging parents; com consultation servs to nursery schs, rel schs, Y's, temples, syns, public schs on chil & family problems; Passover assistance & other special assistance to J in need; self-help progs offering mutual support for: families of Alzheimer Disease victims, & the widowed & their chil through counseling servs & interesting cultural & social progs, families of chil in cults who receive counseling (no de-programming or legal assistance offered); com residences for: the frail elderly who receive support servs & homemaker aid daily, moderately to severely retarded adults who receive training according to their ability. Professional staff of 100 including psychiatric social workers, psychologists, psychiatrists, edu therapists, chil dev specialists, & an edu-vocational counselor. Est in 1946 to meet the needs of the J com in Westchester. Pres: Judy Tenney; VPs: Herbert Werner, Myron Blum, Lynn Kroll; Treas: Charles W. Pachner; Sec: Donald M. Landis; Exec Dir: Oscar Rabinowitz; Asst Exec Dir: Ronald Gaudia; Med Dir: Dr Harry A. Mendelsohn; Coord Chil Psychiatry: Dr Nina Evans; Com Relations: Marjorie Gilbert; Dir of Geriatric Servs & Dir of Com Servs: Renee Pollack. **172 S Bdwy, White Plains NY 10605 (914) 949–6761.**

Woodlands Community Temple. Affiliated with UAHC. 315 mems. Rabbi Peter J. Rubinstein; Cantor Burton A. Borovetz; Pres: Bob Rosen; Edu: Dina Katz; Adm: Joan Mann. **50 Worthington Rd, White Plains NY 10607 (914) 592–7070.**

Whitestone

Whitestone Hebrew Center. Affiliated with United Syn of Am. Rabbi James R. Michaels; Cantor Dov Propis; Pres: Lewis Charney. **12–45 Clintonville St, Whitestone NY 11357 (212) 767–1500.**

Williamsville

Congregation Havurah. Affiliated with UAHC. 62 mems. Pres: Barry Muskat. **6320 Main St, Williamsville NY 14221 (716) 634–3010.**

Woodbury

Kibbutz Library. PO Box 64, Woodbury NY 11797.

Woodhaven

Hebrew Veterans of the War with Spain. 87/71 94th St, Woodhaven NY 11421 (212) VI7–6692.

Yonkers

Congregation Oheb Zedek of Yonkers NY. To maintain an Orthodox syn with the servs of a rabbi. Adult Edu; youth activities. Est in 1887. Pres: Dr Joakim Issacs; 1st: VP Daniel Klein; 2nd VP: Joel Resenwasser; 3rd VP: David Baumzer; Treas: Steven Lesh; Sec: Samuel Frank; Gabboim: Sidney B. Klein, David Klein; Rabbi Ephraim Kanarfogel. **63 Hamilton Ave, Yonkers NY 10705 (914) YO3–1951.**

Lincoln Park Jewish Center. Affiliated with United Syn of Am. Rabbi Solomon Sternstein; Cantor Max Pincus; Pres: Harvey Fuchs. **311 Central Park Ave, Yonkers NY 10704 (914) 965–7119.**

Midchester Jewish Center. Affiliated with United Syn of Am. Rabbi Harry Bolensky; Pres: Saul Kahn. **236 Grandview Blvd, Yonkers NY 10710 (914) SP9–3660.**

Northeast Jewish Center of Yonkers, Inc. Affiliated with United Syn of Am. Rabbi Dr Joseph Wise; Pres: Leonard Gelles; Exec Dir: Si Sternbush; Edu Dir: Dr Joseph Wise. **11 Salisbury Rd, Yonkers NY 10710 (914) DE7–0268.**

Temple Emanu-El. Reform Cong affiliated with UAHC. Rel Servs; Rel Sch, Bar/Bat Mitzvah, Confirmation; Choir; UJA & Is Bond progs; sculpture garden. Rabbi, exec dir, edu dir, music dir, cantor, bkkeeper, secs & custodians. At the end of the 19th century & the beginning of the 20th century, J of Germanic coms came to Yonkers. They found the existing Hungarian Syn unresponsive to their desires & needs. In 1901, under the guidance of Rabbi Ignatz & citizen Leon Block, they formed a new cong called The Staff of Aaron. A fire destroyed the bldg in 1939. The name was changed to Emanu-El of Yonkers. After WWII Emanu-El constructed the third of its sanctuaries, & artists & craftsmen were commissioned to fashion works that would effectively & dramatically express the hist & purpose of J. Today, Yonkers is a city witnessing the movement of the upper & middle class to more secure & satisfying areas. Many of the 'elders' of the City who est & maintained the Temple have also moved to retirement areas, cities in the southern & western states. Rabbi Klausner est the Emanuel Press seeking to combine art, story & music with the spirit & intent of traditional prayers in a series of pubs, including: A Holyday Prayer Book for Children, An American Haggadah, A Sabbath Bar Mitzvah Prayer Book, The New Marriage Ketubah; video-tape curriculum for syn edu progs. Rabbi Abraham J. Klausner. **306 Rumsey Rd on the Pkwy, Yonkers NY 10705 (914) 963–0575.**

Westchester Jewish Community Services, Inc. A state licensed, non-sectarian chil guidance & family mental health clin which is available to all Westchester residents of all ages. For additional information, see Westchester Jewish Community Services, Inc. – White Plains, NY. **20 S Bdwy, Yonkers NY 10701 (914) 423–4433; 475 Tuckahoe Rd, Yonkers NY 10710 (914) 793–3565.**

Yorktown Heights

Temple Beth Am. Mem of UAHC. 124 mems. Rabbi Leonard Schofer; Cantor Naomi Gross; Pres: Saul Gussak; Edu: Alvin Marcus; Adm: Marilyn Campbell; Brotherhood Pres: Lou Karmazin. **Church St, PO Box 433, Yorktown Heights NY 10598 (914) 962–7500.**

Westchester Jewish Community Services, Inc. A state licensed, non-sectarian chil guidance & family mental health clin which is available to all Westchester residents of all ages. For additional information, see Westchester Jewish Community Services, Inc. – White Plains, NY. **2000 Maple Hill St, Yorktown Heights NY 10598 (914) 632–6433.**

Yorktown Jewish Center. Affiliated with United Syn of Am. Rabbi Stanley Urbas; Pres: Leonard Douglas; Edu Dir: I. Pomper; Youth Dir: R. Rose. **2966 Crompond Rd, Yorktown Heights NY 10598 (914) 245–2324.**

NORTH CAROLINA

Asheville

Asheville Jewish Community Center. Com ctr affiliated with JWB. To strengthen J identity. Edu activities providing neutral forum so that all in com can meet & discuss issues that effect com; summer camp; youth activities; sr club; library containing 250 vols (Judaica & Is). 85 families; 15 stu in grades 3–7; 15 HS stu. 2 full-time employees; 2 part-time employees. F 1940. Pub Center of Things (monthly); Centerpeace (annual); Feyers (bi-weekly). Exec Dir: Francine Sherwood; Pres: Joe Knight; Adm Asst: Bonnee Oveibeck; Progs Asst: Pat Samuels; Audio-Visual: Paul Samuels; Prog VP: Jan Schochet; Sec: Elissa Brown. **236 Charlotte St, Asheville NC 28801 (704) 253–0701.**

Beth Israel Synagogue. Affiliated with United Syn of Am. Rabbi Paul Grob; Pres: Jack Feingold. **229 Murdock Ave, Asheville NC 28804 (704) 252–8431.**

Congregation Beth Ha-Tephila. Affiliated with UAHC. 126 mems. Rabbi Paul M. Kaplan; Pres: Hyman Dave; Brotherhood Pres: Sidney Schochet. **43 N Liberty St, Asheville NC 28801 (704) 253–4911.**

Federated Jewish Charities of Asheville, Inc. Mem of CJF. Pres: Ronald Goldstein. **236 Charlotte St, Asheville NC 28801 (704) 253–0701.**

Chapel Hill

Durham-Chapel Hill Jewish Federation & Community Council. Mem of CJF. Pres: Symoine K. Laufe. **1721 Allard Rd, Chapel Hill NC 27514 (919) 929–4774.**

Charlotte

American Jewish Times – Outlook. Periodical pub. **PO Box 33218, Charlotte NC 28233 (704) 372–3296.**

Charlotte Jewish Federation. Mem of CJF. Organized 1940. Pres: Richard Klein; Exec Dir: Marvin Bienstock. **PO Box 220188, Charlotte NC 28222 (704) 366–0358,7.**

North Carolina Hebrew Day Academy. Affiliated with Solomon Schechter Day Schs Assn. Prin: Eleanor Weinglass; Chr: Robert Bernhardt. **PO Box 220176, Charlotte NC 28222 (704) 366–6390.**

Temple Beth El. Affiliated with UAHC. 290 mems. Rabbi Harold I. Krantzler; Pres: Mark Perlin; Edu: Fairlyn Levine; Adm: Judy C. Honeycutt; Sisterhood Pres: Iris Friedlander; Brotherhood Pres: Alan Shuart. **1727 Providence Rd, Charlotte NC 28207 (704) 366–1948.**

Temple Beth Shalom. Affiliated with UAHC. 38 mems. Rabbi Robert A. Seigel; Pres: Irwin Pepper; Edu: Albert Behar; Adm: Sidney Abramsky. **3600 Fairview Rd, Charlotte NC 28211 (704) 366–5560.**

Temple Israel. Affiliated with United Syn of Am. Rabbi Richard K. Rocklin; Cantor Frank Birnbaum; Pres: Marvin Barman; Edu Dir: Arthur Tirsun; Youth Dirs: Sherman Levine, Arlene Karp. **1014 Dilworth Rd, Charlotte NC 28203 (704) 376–2796.**

Clemmons

Blumenthal Jewish Home for the Aged, Inc. Skilled & intermediate care; physical therapy; respiratory therapy; social servs; recreation; podiatry; dentistry; Respite Prog where temporary care is provided. 132 Residents. The Home was conceived by the NC Assn of J Women, & the NC Assn of J Men in 1957, & opened its doors in 1965. The Home is situated on an 118 acre country estate. The Home is non-sectarian though preference is given to J fr NC or their relatives. **7870 Fair Oaks Dr, PO Box 38, Clemmons NC 27012 (919) 766–6401.**

Durham

Beth El Congregation. Affiliated with United Syn of Am. Rabbi Steven Sager; Cantor Paul Grob; Pres: Dr Joel Schwartz. **PO Box 1762, Watts & Markham Ave, Durham NC 27702 (919) 682–1238.**

Judea Reform Congregation. Liberal Cong affiliated with UAHC, the Durham Congs in Action, & the Chapel Hill Interfaith Council. Rel Servs; Couples Group; Singles Group; Women's Group; Men's Club; Anshe Mitzvah Study Group; Youth Group; Syn Sch; yearly retreat called Shabbaton in the mountains of western NC; Academy offering a bi-annual six week series of mini-courses (three courses are offered in each session). 300 families; 150 stu in the sch. F in 1961 as the second syn in the Durham Chapel Hill area. The Cong began with a few dozen families. The syn was built in 1968. In 1980 the Cong erected a new sanctuary addition. Pub Journal (monthly). Rabbi John S. Friedman; Rabbi Emeritus Efraim Rosenzweig; Pres: Jim Davis; VPs: Judith Ruderman, Ron Chandross; Treas: Jack Schuman. **2115 Cornwallis Rd, Durham NC 27705 (919) 489–7062.**

Gastonia

Temple Emanuel. Affiliated with UAHC. 71 mems. Rabbi Israel J. Gerber; Pres: Charles Katzenstein; Sisterhood Pres: Bernice Zeitlin. **320 South St, Gastonia NC 28052 (704) 865–1541.**

Goldsboro

Temple Oheb Sholom. Affiliated with UAHC. 27 mems. Rabbi M. Reuben Kesner; Pres: Sam Samelson; Sisterhood Pres: R.S. Kadis. **PO Box 2063, Goldsboro NC 27530 (919) 867–9975.**

Greensboro

B'nai Shalom Synagogue Day School. Affiliated with Solomon Schechter Day Sch Assn, & Southern Assn of Cols & Schs. To ensure that the grads will be learned, sensitive, secure, understanding, & proud Am & J. Gen & J Studies; Physical Edu; Music Prog; Arts & Crafts Prog; field trips to local points of interest; guest speakers. 51 stu K–6th grade. The Day Sch was conceived in 1969 by nine families. It was to be a regional ins to serve the J families of the area. The sch, first called NC Hebrew Academy, opened in 1970 at Beth David Syn with two small classes. The name was changed a few yrs later to Bnai Is Syn Day Sch, & finally to its present name. The Sch has been housed at Beth David Syn, the Presbyterian Church of the Covenent, & Temple Emanuel. Today they have a permanent location – the Beth David Syn's Kagan Bldg. The sch has been approved by the NC Dept of Public Instruction. Pres: David Kaplan; VP Fund Raising: Merryl Shaffir; VP Adm: Kenneth Miller; VP Edu: Ann Kabat; Fin Sec: Alan Bardy; Rec Sec: Polly Strasser; Treas: Ronald Green; Bd of Dirs: Frank Nelson, James Rosenberger, Harmon Feig, Jerry Baggish, Lee Kabat, Steven Mackler, Nat Shaffir, Sharon Kaiser, Stuart Cook; Dir: Susan Cook. **804 Winview Dr, Greensboro NC 27410 (919) 855–5091.**

B'nai Sholom Synagogue, Inc. Affiliated with United Syn of Am. Pres: David M. Kaplan; Chr Bd of Edu: Susan Green. **PO Box 10214, Greensboro NC 27408 (919) 855–5091.**

Beth David Synagogue. Affiliated with United Syn of Am. Rabbi Edward H. Feldheim; Pres: Michael A. Berkelhammer. **804 Winview Dr, Greensboro NC 27410 (919) 297–0007.**

Greensboro Jewish Federation. Mem of CJF. Organized 1940. Pres: Joanne K. Bluethenthal; Exec Dir: Sherman Harris. **713–A N Greene St, Greensboro NC 27401 (919) 272–3189.**

Temple Emanuel. Affiliated with UAHC. 320 mems. Rabbi Arnold Task; Pres: Leonard Guyes; Edu: Victor B. Cohen; Sisterhood Pres: Linda Silverstein; Brotherhood Pres: Michael T. Marshall. **713 N Greene St, Greensboro NC 27401 (919) 275–6316.**

Hendersonville

Congregation Agudas Israel. Affiliated with United Syn of Am. Pres: Morris Kaplan. **PO Box 668, 328 N King St, Hendersonville NC 28793 (704) 693–9838.**

High Point

High Point B'nai Israel Synagogue. Conservative Syn. Pres: Fred Schwartzberg; Rabbi Robert Sandman; Edu Dir: Rabbi Robert Sandman. **1207 Kensington Dr, High Point NC 27260 (919) 883–1966.**

High Point Jewish Federation. Camp Chr: Harry Samet. **PO Box 2063, High Point NC27261 (919) 431–7101.**

Kinston

Temple Israel. Affiliated with UAHC. 41 mems. Rabbi Robert D. Shafran; Pres: Joseph Goldwasser. **PO Box 903, Kinston NC 28501 (919) 523–2057.**

New Bern

B'nai Sholem Congregation. Affiliated with UAHC. 16 mems. **505 Middle St, New Bern NC 28560 (919) 637–5663.**

Raleigh

The American Friends of Haifa University. PO Box 18137, Raleigh NC 27619 (919) 876–7270.

Beth Meyer Synagogue. Affiliated with United Syn of Am. Rabbi Abe W. Schoen; Pres: David Zendels. **PO Box 2045, 806 W Johnson St, Raleigh NC 27602 (919) 832–6498.**

Temple Beth Or. Affiliated with UAHC. 200 mems. Rabbi Martin P. Beifield Jr; Pres: Norman S. Pliner; Edu: Gizella Abramson; Sisterhood Pres: Harriet Lasher. **5315 Creedmoor Rd, Raleigh NC 27612 (919) 781–4895.**

Rocky Mount

Temple Beth El. Affiliated with UAHC. 36 mems. Rabbi David Kraus; Pres: J. Hertzberg; Sisterhood Pres: Betti K. Hertzberg. **Sunset Ave at Pine, PO Box 291, Rocky Mount NC 27801 (919) 446–7675.**

Salisbury

Temple Israel. Affiliated with United Syn of Am. Rabbi Avery Waldman; Pres: Lee Goldman; Edu Dir: Lea Silverburg. **PO Box 815, 1600 Brenner Ave, Salisbury NC 28144 (704) 633–1152.**

Statesville

Congregation Emanuel. Affiliated with United Syn of Am. Rabbi Israel Gerber; Pres: Dr Cecil Ram. **PO Box 5171, Kelly St & West End Ave, Statesville NC 28677 (704) 873–7611.**

Weldon

Temple Emanu-El. Affiliated with UAHC. 21 mems. Rabbi David Kraus; Pres: Ellis Farber. **Eighth & Sycamore Sts, Weldon NC27890.**

Wilmington

Temple of Israel. Affiliated with UAHC. 78 mems. Rabbi Mordecai M. Thurman; Pres: Max Kahn; Edu: Mordecai M. Thurman; Sisterhood Pres: Regina Harris. **1 S 4th St, Wilmington NC 28401 (919) 762–0000.**

Winston-Salem

Beth Jacob Congregation. Affiliated with United Syn of Am. Pres: Dr Bernard Agress. **1833 Academy St, Winston-Salem NC 27103 (919) 725–3880.**

Temple Emanuel. Reform Cong affiliated with UAHC. Rel Servs: Rel Sch. 141 mems. A group of people recognizing the need for a liberal serv, planned & convened the first Reform serv. Regular meeting quarters were secured at the First Natl Bank Bldg, & in 1934 the Reform Cong welcomed its first permanent Rabbi. Plans & funds for a temple were started. During the yrs, the Cong outgrew the quarters in the First Natl Bldg & used larger halls for the High Holidays. By 1947 Cong Emanuel had grown into an org of almost 100 families with a Sun Sch enrollment of 52 chil. Bldg plans, which were shelved during WWII, were later revived & Temple Emanuel was dedicated on May 9, 1952. In 1971 the Cong erected the annex to provide improved facilities for the Rel Sch, & the bldg was completed in 1972. Pub Bulletin (monthly). Rabbi Stephen F. Moch; Pres: Ira Citron; Treas: Milton Goldberg; Sec: Marcia Epstein. **201 Oakwood Dr, Winston-Salem NC 27103 (919) 722–6640.**

Winston-Salem Jewish Community Council. Pres: Barry Eisenberg. **620 Lankashire Rd, Winston-Salem NC 27106 (919) 765–6685.**

NORTH DAKOTA

Bismarck

Bismarck Hebrew Congregation Religious School. N 5th St, Bismarck ND 58501 (701) 223–1768.

Fargo

Temple Beth El. Affiliated with UAHC. 100 mems. Pres: Michael B. Herbst. **809 S 11 Ave, Fargo ND 58103 (701) 232–0441.**

Grand Forks

B'nai Israel Synagogue. 601 Cottonwood Ave, Grand Forks ND 58201 (701) 775–5124.

Minot

Minot Hebrew Congregation. Affiliated with United Syn of Am. Pres: Harold Porter. **205 8th St SE, Minot ND 58701.**

Temple Beth Israel. 6th St & First Ave SE, Minot ND 58701 (701) 838–8798.

OHIO

Akron

Akron Jewish Community Federation. Mem of CJF. Organized 1935. Pres: Herman Rogovy; Exec Dir: Steven Drysdale. **750 White Pond Dr, Akron OH 44320 (216) 867–7850.**

Beth El Congregation. Affiliated with United Syn of Am. Rabbi Abraham D. Feffer; Cantor Stephen J. Stein; Pres: Richard V. Levin; Edu Dir: Libby Portnoy; Youth Dirs: Eric & Myrna Scheinbart. **464 S Hawkins Ave, Akron OH 44320 (216) 864–2105.**

Beth El Congregation Library. For information on the Cong, see – Congregation Beth El , Akron, OH. **464 S Hawkins Ave, Akron OH 44320 (216) 864–2105.**

Temple Israel. Affiliated with UAHC. 730 mems. Rabbis: Mark A. Golub, Morton M. Applebaum; Cantor Gedaliah Gertz; Pres: David Meckler; Edu: Arlene Corsover; Sisterhood Pres: Doris L. Dannis; Brotherhood Pres: Terry Zimmerman. **133 Merriman Rd, Akron OH 44303 (216) 762–8617.**

Ashtabula

Tifereth Israel Congregation. Affiliated with UAHC. 20 mems. Pres: Irving A. Goodman. **713 Prospect Ave, PO Box 739, Ashtabula OH 44004.**

Beachwood

The Agnon School. Com J day sch. To strengthen the J identity of its pupils through the experience of the J people as an historical, sociological, rel & cultural entity; to encourage each chil to make the most of his inner resources allowing him to explore & dev his potential, both creative & intellectual. The ultimate goal of the sch is the dev of responsible young J adults who have a deep & abiding commitment to their J & to their Am heritage, who are knowledgeable Judaically, identifying with J culture, rel & nationhood including the State of Is. Presch through 8th grade; offers full prog of J & gen studies. Approximately 200 stu. Est in 1969 with 19 stu. The sch accepts chil fr all J families. The teacher pupil ratio never exceeds 17 to 1. The sch is an edu & not a theological ins. There is no attempt to indoctrinate stu, but rather to teach, inform & provide them with the basis for intelligent choices. Dir: Illana Sebo; Pres: Dr Arthur Rosner; VPs: Ian Abrams, Marc Freimuth, Lawrence Lake; Sec: Sheldon Hartman. **26500 Shaker Blvd, Beachwood OH 44122 (216) 464–4055.**

Cleveland College of Jewish Studies. Ins of higher J studies & J teacher edu affiliated with the Bureau of J Edu. To educate teachers for the com schs; to offer a prog of adult edu in the entire com; to provide a cadre of scholars who serve as a resource for the com. Beth Midrash Le-Morim, The Heb Teacher Training Dept, conducts lectures in Heb & areas of study including Bible, Edu, Heb Literature & Language, J Hist, J TQHOUGHT, & Rabbinics; Dept of J Studies gives courses in English in the areas of Bible, Edu, Heb Literature, J Hist, J Thought, & Rabbinics; Heb Ulpan Dept offers beginning, intermediate & advanced levels of Heb language study; library. Est in 1952 as an independent agy for J teacher edu & higher J study. The Heb Teacher Training Sch was f in 1925. In 1947 the Heb Teacher Training Sch, & the J Teachers Ins were merged into the Cleveland Ins of J Studies. In 1952 the Ins moved into its new home. In 1964 the name of the Ins was officially changed to Cleveland Col of J Studies. The Col was granted accreditation by the Am Assn of Hebrew Training Col, & its Heb teachers certificate was recognized by the Natl Bd of License. In 1971 the Col was granted authorization by the Bd of Regents of the State of OH to confer three Baccalaureate degrees & two Masters degrees. In 1975 the Col moved into its own bldg with Akiva HS & Agnon Day Sch. Chr Bd of Govs: Dr Eli Reshotko; V Chr of the Bd: Alice Fredman, Ray Leventhal; Sec:

Phyllis Berlas; Treas: Dan A. Polster; Bd Mems: Philip J. Arnoff, Mrs Nathan J. Arnold, Alan D. Bennett, Mrs Harlan Bradley, Stanley Busch, Mrs Eli Cohen, Rabbi Frederick Eisenberg, Barnett Garson, Samuel H. Givelber, Allan J. Goldberg, Mrs Gilbert Green, Mrs Sheldon Hartman, Dr Richard Katzman, Dr Aaron Leash, Dr Daniel Litt, Fred Livingstone, Theodore Luntz, Robert Madow, Milton Maltz, Dr Herbert Mayers, Conrad Morgenstern, Nathan Oscar, Dr Leatrice B. Rabinsky, Dr Howard Schwartz, Nathan Shafran, Prof Morris G. Shanker, Paul L. Shapiro, Mrs Neal Stonehill, Harry L. Terkel, Harold Ticktin, Mrs Leonard W. Yarus, Stanley Wertheim, Milton Wish; Hon Bd Mems: Mrs Sigmund Braverman, Mrs Barnett R. Brickner, Nathan Brilliant, Joseph Horwitz, Bennet Kleinman, Joseph H. Persky, Leighton A. Rosenthal, Dr Irving B. Tapper, Maurice W. Terkel. **26500 Shaker Blvd, Beachwood OH 44122 (216) 464–4050.**

Cleveland College of Jewish Studies Library. Library contains 22,000 vols (Hebrew, Yiddish, Judaica) For information on the Col, see – Cleveland College of Jewish Studies, Beachwood, OH. **26500 Shaker Blvd, Beachwood OH 44122 (216) 464–4050.**

Congregation Beth Aynu. Affiliated with United Syn of Am. Rabbi Milton Rube; Cantors (laymen): Albert Bender, Don Gurney; Pres: Robert C. Weiss; Exec Dir & Sch Prin: Leonard Steiger. **25400 Fairmount Blvd, Beachwood OH 44122.**

Jewish Library Association of Greater Cleveland. 24735 Twickenham Dr, Beachwood OH 44122.

The Suburban Temple. Reform Cong. Devoted to the concept that it be large enough to offer a full spectrum of spiritual & edu opportunities yet be small enough to provide total responsiveness to its mems need, plus a continuing personal relationship between its mems & the Rabbi. Rel Sch, K–9th grade; Ben or Bat Torah; Rel Servs; family activities, Sukkah Decorating & Dinner, family Shabbat dinners, Chanukah Family Dinner & Decorating Party, Purim Carnival, Presch afternoons, family picnic, Sun family lunches, Chil Party With the Rabbi series, family worship Servs, sports speakers; Womens Cttee activities: luncheons & bk review, sewing group, rug hooking, study groups with Rabbi Oppenheimer, Torah Convocation, Taping for the Blind, special prog meetings, & Mother Daughter Luncheon & Fashion Show; youth activities: retreats, study sessions, socials, cultural events; Jr Temple Youth Group; library. Over 500 families. In 1945, a small study group, mems of Cleveland's largest Reform cong met to form a new cong whose size would be rigidly limited. The reasons for its size limitations were: to provide every mem full opportunity for participation in the workings & activities of the Cong, to make it possible for every mem to have a personal relationship with the Rabbi & to present the Cong the opportunity for continuing participation in the affairs of the Rel Sch. The Temple became an entity in 1948 & became a functioning enterprise the following Fall. In 1955 the present bldg was dedicated. Because of its unique construction, the sanctuary can seat up to 1,000. Rabbi Michael A. Oppenheimer; Rabbi Emeritus Myron Silverman; Adm: Loree B. Resnik; Pres: Mina S. Segal; VPs: Alan R. Daus, David L. Margolius, Robert D. Markus; Treas: Lawrence G. Kirshbaum; Sec: James L. Grunzweig; Bd of Trustees: Laura Berick, Jack Bialosky, Louis J. Bloomfield, Barrett Brown, Dr Stanley L. Brown, Zolman Cavitch, Dr Richard L. Cohen, Martin J. Cohn, Philip C. Cristal, David H. Dietz, Alice Effron, Jerome C. Frankel, Thomas E. Galvin, James H. Glueck, Irene Goldhamer, Lynn Heiman, Gilbert Kaplan, Leslie Karmel, Pamela Katz, Judith G. Kossoff, Doris Lieber, Sue Manheim, Rachel Oppenheimer, Stanley M. Proctor, Gerald Rosenwater, Robert M. Rubin, Barbara Schreibman, Richard A. Skall, Bernard A. Weingart, Ira J. Wieder, John T. Wise. **22401 Chagrin Blvd, Beachwood OH 44122 (216) 991–0700.**

The Suburban Temple, Gries Library. For information on the Temple, see – The Suburban Temple, Beachwood, OH. **22401 Chagrin Blvd, Beachwood OH 44122 (216) 991–0700.**

UAHC Northeast Lakes Council – Detroit Federation. Rel & edu org serving J congs throughout the US & Canada. To encourage & aid the org & dev of J congs; to promote J edu, & enrich & intensify J life; to foster other activities for the perpetuation & advancement of J. For additional information, see – UAHC – Union of American Hebrew Congregations, New York City, NY. Pres: Marshall Madison, Dr Stuart Falk; Dir: Rabbi David S. Hachen. **25550 Chagrin Blvd, Suite 108, Beachwood OH 44122 (216) 831–6722.**

Canton

Jewish Community Federation of Canton. Mem of CJF. Organized 1935; reorganized 1955. Pres: Harriet B. Narens; Exec Dir: Revella R. Kopstein. **2631 Harvard Ave NW, Canton OH 44709 (216) 453–0133.**

The Shaaray Torah Synagogue. Conservative Cong, mem of United Syn of Am. To enrich the lives of the mems & help them grow spiritually; to edu in Torah & to make worship a meaningful experience. Rel Servs; Men's Club; Sisterhood; Couples Club; USY Youth Group; Sun Sch; library. 370 families. F in 1894 as Anshe Shalom, an Orthodox cong. In 1904 the name of the Syn was changed to Shara Torah & after 1940 to its current spelling. In 1923 a fire destroyed the syn. Larger accommodations were acquired in 1924. In 1934 the Cong was forced to leave its premises because it could not meet its mortgage payments. For three yrs, Servs were held in temporary quarters. In 1937 a new bldg was erected. In 1940 the first Sun sch classes were held, & in 1946 the Syn joined the Conservative movement. The present syn was built in 1960. The clubs affiliated with the Syn each have their own set of offs & calender of events including rel, edu, social & fund raising events. Pub The Scribe (bi-monthly). Facilities include kosher kitchen, sanctuary seating 400, chapel seating 70, social hall with raised stage, gift shop, Sisterhood rm, Sun Sch classrms. Rabbi Mordecai Miller; Rabbi Emeritus Nathan Jacobson; Baal Tefillah: Bruce Braun; Chr of the Bd: Arnold R. Shifman; Pres: William S. Rudner; Sr VPs: Mrs Rena Stein, Allan Rudner, Raymond G. Wilkof; VP Finance: Ron Fi Rec Sec: Carole Sheidlower; Sec's: Mary Jane Morgan, Rosemary Vandegrift **432 30th St NW, Canton OH 44709 (216) 492–0310.**

The Shaarey Torah Synagogue Library. Library contains 5,000 vols (Heb, Yiddish & Judaic reference & literature). For information on the Syn, see – The Shaarey Torah Synagogue, Canton, OH. **432 30th St NW, Canton OH 44709 (216) 492–0310.**

Stark Jewish News. Periodical pub. **PO Box 9112, Canton OH 44711 (216) 494–7792.**

Temple Israel. Affiliated with UAHC. 420 mems. Rabbis: John H. Spitzer, Paul Gorin; Cantor Eugene Sirak; Pres: Robert I. Friedman; Edu: Bilha Ron; Adm: Chloe Shapiro; Sisterhood Pres: Hannah Jolly; Brotherhood Pres: Neal Libster. **333 25th St NW, Canton OH 44709 (216) 455–5197.**

Temple Israel Library. For information on the Temple, see – Temple Israel, Canton, OH. **333 25th St NW, Canton OH 44709 (216) 455–5197.**

Cincinnati

Adath Israel Congregation. Affiliated with United Syn of Am. Daily Rel Servs; Rel Edu; library. F in 1847. Facilities include a lobby, sanctuary, three halls, chapel which seats 125 people, Bd rm, youth lounge, dairy kitchen, meat kitchen, rel sch bldg & gift shop. Rabbi Sindey Zimelman; Edu Dir: Rabbi Pesach Sobel; Ritual Dir: Rabbi Joel Epstein; Pres: David Spitzberg; VPs: Jerry Bogdan, Bernard Gessiness, David Jacobson, Gerald M. Lerer, Donald N. Miller, Dr Sidney Peerless, William Schneiderman; Fin Sec: Edwin L. Drill; Treas: Narvin I. Emden; Rec Sec: Mrs Alvin Meisel; Corsp Sec: Mrs Abrom Dombar. **3201 E Galbraith Rd, Cincinnati OH 45236 (513) 793–1800, Rel Sch Off: (513) 793–1805.**

Adath Israel Congregation, Leshner Library. 3201 E Galbraith Rd, Cincinnati OH 45236 (513) 793–1800.

The American Israelite. Newspaper. Local, natl & intl J news & features. Est in 1854; the oldest English J weekly in Am. 98% of all homes of the J faith in Greater Cincinnati are paid subscribers of the Am Israelite. Editor: Henry C. Segal; News Dir: Phyllis Singer; Advertising Mgr: Mary Bradley. **906 Main St, Rm 505, Cincinnati OH 45202 (513) 621–3145.**

American Jewish Archives. To est the facts as they actually are & to promote the study of these materials which will further a knowledge of the Am J, not only for the purpose of understanding the present period in the long hist of the J people, but also so that we may grasp the ethos of Americanism & so make another contribution to the hist of humanity. Reading rm for 10 readers; microfilm readers & reader printer; Xerox & microfilm copies; seven million pages of documentation, supplemented by a special collection of approximately 200 microfilm reels fr other sources; 10,000 photographs; 1,300 sound recordings; select list of records & papers of special importance & interest: Jacob Schiff papers 1914–1920, Felix Warburg papers 1895–1937, Louis Marshall papers 1891–1930, Annie Nathan Meyer papers 1858–1950, Horace Kallen papers 1902–1975, Kivie Kaplan papers 1948–1975, Julian Morgenstern papers 1900–1974, Adolph S. Ochs papers 1893–1939, UAHC records 1873–1952, World Union for Progressive Judaism 1925–1965, & Heb Union Col records 1875–1947. F in 1947 in the aftermath of WWII at a time when the J of Am faced the responsibility of preserving the continuity of J life & learning in the western hemisphere. Guide to the Holdings of the American Jewish Archives; Manuscript Catalogue of the American Jewish Archives; Guide to the Picture Collections of the American Jewish Archives; Guide to the Sound Recordings of the American Jewish Archives. The period of the Am J Archives in the Western Hemispheric J experience, 15th century to the present. 75% of the holdings are fully & 10% partially processed & accessible through card catalogues & inventories. Use of some of the collections is restricted, according to the wishes of either the donors or the dir of the Archives. Dir: Dr Jacob R. Marcus; Assc Dir: Abraham J. Peck. **3101 Clifton Ave, Cincinnati OH 45220.**

The American Jewish Committee. US human relations org. To combat bigotry; to protect the civil & rel rights of J & all people at home & abroad. Studies on energy, Arab influence, interpretation of Is, & threat of the moral majority continue the work of the Cttee in making the world safe for J by supporting the foun of strong, stable democracies. Natl agy, 50,000 mems in 100 coms; Cincinnati Chapter 1,100 mems. F in 1906 when the oppression of J in the Kishinev pogrom spurred a group of prominent Am J to undertake a unique act of rescue. Some of the Cttee's achievements include the f of the Joint Distribution Cttee after WWI, the minority rights provisions in the Paris Peace Treaties, the admission of 100,000 Holocaust survivors to Palestine, the first documented exposure of Soviet anti-Semitism, the participation in Vatican II which changed forever the image of the J in Catholic teaching. Chr: Eleanor S. Lazarus; V Chrs: Dabby Blatt, Ronald F. Graceman, Dr Kenneth J. Newmark, Melvin L. Schulman; Hon V Chr: Norma B. Moss; Treas: Robert D. Stern; Sec: Peggy F. Selonick; Southern OH-KY Area Dir: Nancy C. Hahn. **105 W Fourth St, Suite 1008, Cincinnati OH 45202 (513) 621–4020.**

American Jewish Periodical Center. Depository of film on which are preserved J newspapers, periodicals pub in US since first such periodical issued in 1823. Outstanding Spinoza collection & other specialized collections of J music & J Americana. **3101 Clifton Ave, Cincinnati OH 45220 (513) 221–1875.**

Bureau of Jewish Education. 1580 Summit Rd, Cincinnati OH 45237 (513) 761–0203.

Bureau of Jewish Education, Dr Moses Zalesky Memorial Library. 1580 Summit Rd, Cincinnati OH 45237 (513) 761–0203.

Chabad House. Lubavitch com servs ctr. Blends Chassidic fervor & warmth with tradition & learning, to show that every J, fr whatever background he or she comes fr, is an integral part of the body of Is. Anti-missionary work; adult edu; sabbath seminars; holiday progs; day camp; youth groups; syns; kosher kitchen; counseling; chaplaincy; Mitzvah Campaigns; hosp & prison visitations; sr citizens encounters; speakers bureau. Rabbi Sholom B. Kalmanson. **1666 Summit, Cincinnati OH 45237 (513) 821–5100.**

Congregation B'nai Tzedek. Affiliated with United Syn of Am. Rabbi Kurt Stone; Pres: Louis Nidich. **1580 Summit Rd, Cincinnati OH 45237 (513) 821–0941.**

Congregation Ohav Shalom. Daily Rel Servs; activities for every age; classes in J instruction; participant in many natl & local ins that serve the com. Est in 1881 in rented quarters. After several moves, the Cong purchased a structure. At the beginning of the 20th Century, the Cong moved into a new J area & around the 1950's, the Cong est itself in the Roselawn section of the city after completing a million & a half dollar structure. Rabbi Bernard Greenfield; Pres: Martin Ruben; 1st VP: Melvin Shapiro; 2nd VP: Benjamin Krauss; Treas: Louis Franklin; Fin Sec: Sam Nedelman; Rec Sec: Harold Kirzner; Gabbaim: Gordon J. Schilmeister, Irwin E. Harris; Bd of Dirs: Robert Barnett, Mrs Phil Bayliss, Sidney Binik, Sol J. Blatt, Leonard Borden, Aaron Brown, Alfred Carl, Louis Carl, Philip Cohen, Dr William Cohen, Jules Conison, Louis Feldman, Aaron Fingerman, H. Irving Fox, Isadore Fox, Leslie Fox, Louis Franklin, Dr Alan Freid, Arthur Friedman, Stanley T. Funk, William Gallop, Dr Joseph Ginsberg, Dr Alvin Goldey, Albert Goldfarb, Fred Goldfarb, Irwin E. Harris, Jack Hoffman, Maurice Hoffman, Jacob Hoodin, Gene Kichler, Harold Kirzner, Hyman Kirzner, Sam Klayman, Sidney Kohn, Ben Krauss, Mrs Ben Krauss, Jack Kuresman, Jack Levine, Ralph Lipsky, Ted Lipsky, Edward Malkis, Kenneth Mitman, Max Mitman, Ben Nedelman, Sam Nedelman, Irvin Neuerman, Max C. Nogen, William Okrent, Mrs Morris Plotnick, Elliott Polaniecki, Irvin Rauchman, Jack B. Robinson, Hank Rolnick, Abe Rosen, Frank Ruben, Martin Ruben, Steve Ruben, Howard Rubin, Ben Schilmeister, Gordon J. Schilmeister, Melvin Shapiro, Dr Lee Shonfield, Nathan Shostack, Max Siegel, Louis Sigman, Irvin Singer, Jack Skolnick, Abe Skurow, Louis Skurow, Sam T. Sloan, Max Slovin, David Tessel, Ben Torf, Robert Tulch, Coleman Ullner, Bernie Weller, Harold Winkler, Edwin Winterfeldt, David C. Young, Stanley Zeidman. **1834 Section Rd, Cincinnati OH 45237 (513) 531–4676.**

Hebrew Union College – Jewish Institute of Religion. Ins of higher learning in Am Reform J. Accredited by the Middle States Assn of Cols &

Secondary Schs, the N Central Assn of Cols & Secondary Schs, the Western Assn of Schs & Cols; affiliated with the Univ of Cincinnati, the Greater Cincinnati Consortium of Cols & Univs, the Univ of Southern CA, Washington Univ, NY Univ & the Hebrew Univ. Dedicated to the study of J in the spirit of free inquiry. Rabbinic Sch: five yr prog leading to the Master of Arts degree & Ordination, with the stu required to spend their first academic yr at the HUC–JIR campus in Jerusalem Is. The Grad Sch: awards Dr of Philosophy, Dr of Heb Letters & Master of Arts degrees; Leading institution of Judaic scholarship; important ctr for interfaith dialogue. Prominent for scholarship on J origins of early Christianity. Stu body of around 92 with equal number of J & Christians most of whom are preparing for careers in univ & seminary teaching & research. Klau Library: contains 300,000 vols; Am J Periodical Ctr: preserves Am J periodicals & newspapers on microfilm, houses the Spinoza collection & other collections of J music & J Americana; Am J Archives: houses 4,000,000 pages of documents. Other serves & facilities include: guidance & counseling; stu activities; stu orgs; social & cultural ctivities: lectures, concerts, films, & other public events which enrich the cultural & intellectual life of the com. HUC-JIR maintains two schs in Jerusalem, Is – the Sch of J Studies: serves rabbinic & other stu of the Am campuses of the Col; & servs as the ctr of the Col Academic Yr, a prog for Am col undergrads, & also offers a prog leading to the degree of Master of Arts in J Studies for Israeli grad stu. The Nelson Glueck Sch of Biblical Archaeology: serves as an Am ctr for postgrad study in the fields of Bible, archaeology & the hist of ancient Is. F in 1875 by Rabbi Isaac Mayer Wise. His original idea was to est a J univ with various faculties & with secular & rel depts. However, his plans had to be abandoned & Rabbi Wise confined himself to bldg the first rabbinic sch in Am. In 1881 the sch moved into its first permanent home. In 1913 new bldgs were dedicated: the Adm Bldg & the Bernheim Library (now the Am J Archives). In 1924 the Freiberg Gymnasium was added. After 1933 the Col embarked on a prog of rescuing as many J scholars as possible & bringing them to Am. In 1950 the JIR & HUC merged. The Am J Archives was est on the Cincinnati campus in 1948. The Jerusalem Sch of HUC was est in 1963. The Hebrew Union College Annual; Studies in Bibliography & Booklore; American Jewish Archives; Hebrew Union College Press which pubs scholarly bks by mems of the faculty & alumni; Chronicle (periodical reporting Col activities). Facilities include the Classrm Bldg which also houses the S.H. & Helen R. Scheuer Chapel, Sisterhood Dormitory, New Dormitory, Dalsheimer Rare Bk Bldg, Adm Bldg, & Freiberg Gymnasium. Pres: Alfred Gottschalk PhD; Exec VP: Rabbi Uri D. Herscher DHL; Exec Dean for Academic Affairs: Rabbi Dr Eugene Mihaly PhD; Natl Dir Dev & Information: Harold Epstein; Exec Sec: Rissa Alex; Acting Dean Rabbinic Sch: Rabbi Kenneth E. Ehrlich; Dean Grad Sch: Rabbi Herbert H. Paper PhD; Chr Bd of Overseers: Abraham S. Braude; Chr Bd of Govs: Jules Backman. **3101 Clifton Ave, Cincinnati OH 45220 (513) 221–1875.**

Hebrew Union College – Jewish Institute of Religion, Klau Library. One of most extensive J libraries in world. Contains approximately 300,000 vols, among them 160 incunabula, & almost 6,000 manuscripts. Outstanding Spinoza collection & other specialized collections of J music & J Americana. Annual journal of HUC-JIR Libraries – Studies in Bibliography & Booklore, appearing since 1953, is the only learned journal devoted to J bibliography pub in US. **3101 Clifton Ave, Cincinnati OH 45220 (513) 221–1875.**

Hebrew Union College Student Association. 3101 Clifton Ave, Cincinnati OH 45220 (513) 221–1875.

Isaac M. Wise Temple. Affiliated with UAHC. 1299 mems. Rabbis: Alan D. Fuchs, Ronald W. Kaplan, Albert A. Goldman; Pres: David J. Schiebel; Edu: M.M. Singer; Sisterhood Pres: Winifred Barrows; Brotherhood Pres: Tom Carsch. **8329 Ridge Rd, Cincinnati OH 45236 (513) 793–2556.**

Isaac M. Wise Temple, The Ralph M. Cohen Memorial Library. For information on the Temple, see – Isaac M. Wise Temple, Cincinnati, OH. **8329 Ridge Rd, Cincinnati OH 45236 (513) 793–2556.**

Jewish Federation of Cincinnati & Vicinity. Mem of CJF. A merger of Assc J Agy & J Welfare Fund. Organized 1896; reorganized 1967. Pres: Melvin Schulman; Exec VP: Harold Goldberg. **200 W 4th St, Cincinnati OH 45202 (513) 381–5800.**

The Jewish Hospital of Cincinnati. A non-sectarian 619 bed acute care com teaching hosp. Sch of Nursing offering a two yr diploma prog; Chil Psychiatric Ctr; various com edu progs on a wide array of health care topics; kosher Meals-on-Wheels prog providing meals to bedridden & elderly persons confined to their homes; May Ins Med Research; Urodynamic Testing Lab; Div of Peripheral Vascular Surgery; Peripheral Vascular Lab; Cardiac Rehabilitation Unit providing a complete three phase comprehensive Cardiac Rehabilitation Prog; CT Scanner; 12 bed Adolescent Psychiatric Treatment

Unit; Cancer Ctr; Tel-Hosp consisting of a telephone edu prog exclusively provided by the Hosp for the greater Cincinnati area describing in excess of 100 med procedures; Laser Ctr; Neuro-Physiology & Audiology Ctr with principle emphasis in the multi-disciplinary areas of Otolaryngology & Neurology, & providing a hosp based audiometric serv. Est in 1850 as the first J sponsored hosp in the US. Initially, the motivating force behind the org of the Hosp was a deep concern within the J com about the health & welfare of the indigent J of Cincinnati. Today, patients treated at the Hosp Ctr represent a broad cross section of the Greater Cincinnati com. In its early yrs, the Hosp relocated several times, & in 1890 it moved to its present site. In 1891 the Sch of Nursing was est as the first nursing sch in the country associated with a private hosp. In 1917 the Hosp installed the first electrocardiograph in a Cincinnati hosp. In 1920 the Psychopathic Ins, presently known as the Chil Psychiatric Ctr, was f as the first inpatient home within a med setting in the US. The first Drinker Respirator to be used in Cincinnati was installed in 1931, marking a major advance in the treatment of respiratory problems. In 1928 the Hosp est a Heart Clin. In 1939 the May Ins for Med Research was f & was the first research ins est on the campus of a private hosp. In 1970 the Burnet Ave Pavillion & the new wing of the Chil Psychiatric Ctr were dedicated. In 1977 the first Urodynamics Testing Lab in Cincinnati was est. In 1978 a new Div of Peripheral Vascular Surgery & a Peripheral Vascular Lab were est to better serve an increasing vol of patients requiring this area of med expertise. In 1980 the Cardiac Rehabilitation Unit was opened, the Hosp aquired a CT Scanner, the Adolescent Psychiatric Treatment Unit was opened, the Cancer Ctr was approved by the Am Col of Surgeons, & the Tel-Hosp was implemented. In 1981 the Laser Ctr was est & the Neuro-Physiology & the Audiology Ctr were opened. Chr: Robert Kanter; Pres: Warren C. Falberg; V Chr: Robert Senior, Bernard L. Dave; Treas: Robert W. Heldman; Bd of Trustees: Benjamin Gettler, Leonard S. Meranus, Lee Schimberg, Gretchen Dinerman, David W. Ellis Jr, Roslyn Harkavy, Paul Heiman, Thomas S. Heldman, Dr Asher O. Hoodin, Miriam Katz, Robert Leshner, Robert E. Levinson, Dr Samuel J. Mantel Jr, Joe Mendelsohn III, Dr Sidney A. Peerless, Dr Harold Pescovitz, Dr Edward H. Saeks, Paul G. Sittenfeld, Jacob K. Stein, Charles H. Stix, S. Charles Straus, Alan Wolf, Nancy Youkilis; Hon: David J. Joseph Jr, Edward Kuhn, Philip M. Meyers. **The Jewish Hosp, 3212 Burnet Ave, Cincinnati OH 45229 (513) 872–3220.**

New Hope Congregation. Orthodox Syn affiliated with Union of Orthodox Congs of Am. To preserve the tradition of former German Orthodoxy. Daily Servs; Sisterhood; Youth Group affiliated with NCSY. 110 mems (57 families, 53 individuals). F 1939. Pub semi-annual bulletin. Facilities include kosher kitchen, sanctuary. The only Chevra Kadisha in town. Rabbi Rev Manfred Rabenstein; Pres: Jerry Schottenfels; Bd Chr: Ernst Kahn; Sisterhood Co-Pres: Flora Rabenstein, Ruth Kropveld, Ruth Teitz. **1625 Crest Hill Ave, Cincinnati OH 45237 (513) 821–6274.**

Northern Hills Synagogue – Congregation B'nai Avraham. Conservative Cong affiliated with United Syn of Am. Rel Servs; edu, social & youth activities. 175 families. F in 1960 as Northern Hills Syn – Cong Beth El. In 1967 the Syn merged with the Norwood Syn Cong B'nai Avraham. Pub Shavua Tov (weekly). Rabbi Gershom Barnard; Rabbi Emeritus Henry E. Barnies; Pres: Harvey Singer; VPs: Ira Grann, Edith Neusner, Larry Knapp. **715 Fleming Rd, Cincinnati OH 45231 (513) 931–6038.**

Rockdale Temple, K K Bene Israel. Affiliated with UAHC. 975 mems. Rabbis: Howard A. Simon, Norman M. Cohn, Victor E. Reichert; Pres: James Rosenthal; Edu: Estelle Levine; Adm: Bess Greene; Sisterhood Pres: Harriet F. Miller; Brotherhood Pres: Herman Kleinfeld. **8501 Ridge Rd, Cincinnati OH 45236 (513) 891–9900.**

Rockdale Temple, Sidney G. Rose Library. For information on the Temple, see – Rockdale Temple, Cincinnati, OH. **8501 Ridge Rd, Cincinnati OH 45236 (513) 891–9900.**

Sephardic Beth Shalom Congregation. Traditional Sephardic Cong. To conduct Sephardic Servs during Yamim Noraim & major festivals; to maintain the Sephardic cemetery of Cincinnati. Rel Servs. 104 mems; 48 families; 8 individuals. F 1906; sanctuary built in 1933. Facilities include sanctuary seating 150. Pres: Lena Azouz; VP: Albert Ouziel; Treas: Yetta Holo; Fin Sec: Neama Yerushalmi; Sec: Sylvia Ouziel. **PO Box 37431, Cincinnati OH 45222 (513) 793–6936.**

Temple Sholom. Affiliated with UAHC. 385 mems. Rabbis: Donald Splanksy, Stanley Brav; Pres: Harold E. Sterne; Edu: Edna Ora; Sisterhood Pres: Gladys Warshauer; Brotherhood Pres: Sal Wertheim. **3100 Longmeadow Lane, Cincinnati OH 45236 (513) 791–1330.**

Temple Sholom Library. For information on the Temple, see – Temple Sholom, Cincinnati, OH. **3100 Longmeadow Lane, Cincinatti OH 45236 (513) 791–1330.**

The Valley Temple. Affiliated with UAHC. 205 mems. Rabbi Solomon T. Greenberg; Pres: Robert Gugenheim Jr; Edu: Robert Ratner. **145 Springfield Pike, Cincinnati OH 45220 (513) 761–3555.**

The Valley Temple, Library. For information on the Temple, see – The Valley Temple, Cincinnati, OH. **145 Springfield Pike, Cincinnati OH 45220 (513) 761–3555.**

Cleveland

American Committee for Shaare Zedek in Jerusalem – Mid-Central Region. To help future generations meet the health needs of Jerusalem and Israel. Continuing support of century old hospital which moved in 1979 fr old quarters to new $55 million ultra modern medical complex overlooking Jerusalem. Offers total patient & community care. University affiliated teaching hospital contains main hospital building planned for more than 500 beds, emergency shelter, outpatient clinics, school of nursing, clinical labs, research ins, central library, facilities. Ensures the full observance of J tradition. Open to all, irrespective of rel, race or natl origin. **Euclid Ave, Cleveland OH 44115 (216) 566–9357.**

American-Israel Chamber of Commerce & Industry, Inc. Offers assistance to mem US firms interested in economic activity in & with Is. Provides extensive trade assistance; pub market research reports; aids in dev of trade & investment between US & Is. For additional information, see – American-Israel Chamber of Commerce & Industry, Inc, New York City, NY. **10800 Brookpark Rd, Cleveland OH 44130 (216) 267–1200.**

B'nai B'rith Cleveland Hillel Foundation. 11291 Euclid Ave, Cleveland OH 44106 (216) 231–0040.

B'nai B'rith Cleveland Hillel Foundation Library. 11291 Euclid Ave, Cleveland OH 44106 (216) 231–0040.

Bellefaire. Residential treatment & chil care ctr. To discharge the chil with the emotional maturity & cognitive skills necessary to function responsibly & productively in the adult world. Operates treatment, intervention & edu serv for chil & adolescents ages 8–18: Bellefaire Residential Treatment Ctr for Emotionally Disturbed Chil – 90 chil; The Bellefaire Sch: an ungraded special edu ctr – 105 chil; Day Treatment Ctr & Family Therapy Prog – 20 families; Individual Foster Care Prog – 10 chil; five Group Foster Homes – 30 chil; Group Residence – 10 chil; Adoption Servs; Outpatient Diagnostic & Therapy Serv – 150 clients; Presch & K Day Care Prog – 70 chil; Emergency Shelter Prog; Wilderness Camp; outreach servs – 60 chil. Est in 1868 as a home for chil orphaned by the Civil War, it changed its mission to a chil treatment ctr during WWII. Chil living with their parents in nearby coms commute to the Bellefaire Sch & attend day treatment activities after the sch day. Most of the chil admitted to the Bellefaire system are classified as emotionally or behaviorally handicapped, & all have histories of failures in home settings, sch & social adjustment. The Agy is admitting an increasing num of chil with chronic physical problems in combination with their emotional ones including juvenile diabetes, spina bifida, hemophelia & anorexia nervosa. Chr: Frank E. Joseph; V Chr: I. S. Anoff; Pres: David I. Warren; VPs: David Friedman, Mrs Harlan Sherman; Sec: David Nachman; Treas: Gerald B. Chattman; Exec Dir: Dr Samuel M. Kelman; Asst Dir: Raymond S. Fant; Dir of Treatment Servs: Dr Lawrence J. Schreiber; Dir of Residential Treatment: Edward J. Kubicka; Dir of Com Servs: Robert J. Cohen; Prin: Vincent Julian; Dir of Adm & Mgmnt: William Shlensky; Dir of Dev: Martin B. Omansky; Dir of Natl & Adm Projs: Ellen K. Markus. **22001 Fairmount Blvd, Cleveland OH 44118 (216) 932–2800.**

Beth Israel – The West Temple. Reform Cong affiliated with UAHC. To discover & introduce rel & cultural values of J. Rel Servs; special Family Servs on Sukkot, Chanukah & Purim; com Seder; Choir; Rel Sch fr K through HS; Shabbatons; Confirmation & Consecration Servs; BITSY, Sr Youth Group; Adult Edu classes, providing Elementary Heb, Basic J, Torah, Sabbath & holiday workshops; library; Sisterhood; gift shop; Com Edu Prog; Social Action Cttee; J Information Ctr which provides information about & exposure to J communal life for the gentile com, & has held ins for public sch teachers & provided source materials on the Holocaust to schs & public libraries; social activities. 140 families; 100 stu in the Rel Sch; 100 women in the Sisterhood. F in 1954. The Rel Sch was est in 1955. In 1957 the Conservative Cong Bnai Is merged with Beth Is. The combined congs f a home in the present temple which was dedicated in May of 1958. In Oct of 1965 an addition providing eight more classrooms was dedicated. Since 1956 the Temple has presented over 1,000 Com Edu Progs to acquaint its neighbors with the tenets of J. A monthly bulletin informs the Cong of J thinking on important issues & notifies the mems of Cong news & activities. Rabbi David Rose; Pres: Sol Gorland; Sisterhood Pres:Charlotte Feldman; Sec Bd of Trustees: Paul Buchsbaum. **14308 Triskett Rd, Cleveland OH 44111 (216) 941–8882.**

Beth Israel – The West Temple Library. For information on the Temple, see – Beth Israel – The West Temple, Cleveland, OH. **14308 Triskett Rd, Cleveland OH 44111 (216) 941–8882.**

Bureau of Jewish Education. Central agy responsible for the com planning & servs for J edu. Advocates J edu through publicity, PR & by the personal participation of lay leaders & staff in Fed & other communal bodies; provides PR to promote scholarship & prog activities; provides for staff supervision, leadership dev & Bd-staff interaction; engages in a continuing assessment of its own priorities; engages in long range planning for J edu; coords edu servs to syn schs; assesses syn edu goals & needs; serves the J & gen coms; provides speakers on edu matters & J content areas, assigns its staff as guest teachers in syn schs & the Col of J Studies; sponsors & arranges sch participation in local & natl contests; supervises & coords the Welfare Fund Campaign in schs & pupil participation in the Walkathon; pubs & distributes edu materials; helps public schs with curriculum materials; prepares & reproduces materials for schs & other J orgs; provides staff for leadership roles in local & natl professional bodies; presents com-wide progs; administers & awards over $35,000 annually for scholarships & loans for Is study progs, & scholarships for J camping; publicizes, administers & enrolls schs & families in the com Is Incentive Savings Plan to help stu in Cleveland J schs finance a combination study/travel visit to Is; sponsors summer Heb language & Is study experience (the Is Study Prog); provides consultation to teachers with techniques & methods to enhance quality of instruction, & makes classrm visits to evaluate achievement & methods; conducts teacher workshops; locates teaching resources & coords their use; helps sch dirs evaluate curriculum & improve sch org; evaluates credentials to determine the salaries of individual teachers; issues licenses to Heb teachers; evaluates the abilities of teachers for referral to sch dirs; devs & carries out teacher recognition progs to enhance the stature of the J teacher; awards outstanding teacher projs; carries out research activities; maintains bus system providing transportation for congregational schs, communal schs, camps & other summer progs. Instructional Material Ctr: shows teachers how to create teaching aids, & creates, mass produces & distributes to schs material for stu learning projs, charts & edu displays; Media Ctr: maintains collection of films, film strips, slides, video tapes & print items. 22 affiliated schs. Staff of 12, support staff of 10. Organized in 1924. Hamoreh, monthly pub, informs teachers of new edu dev & presents new ideas for teaching & for improving effectiveness in the classrm. Pres: N. Herschel Koblenz; VPs: Norman E. Gutfeld, Dr Jack W. Jaffe, Stanley E. Wertheim; Treas: Hal H. Myers; Assc Treas: Irvin A. Leonard; Sec: Dr Dale Cowan; Bd of Trustees: Sue Arnold, Elliot Azoff, Judy Becker, Linda Bensoussan, Sharlet Berman, Jean Bloomfield, Kenneth Bravo, Armond Budish, Dr Dale Cowan, Paul Dennis, Michael Diamant, Rabbi Frederick Eisenberg, Monroe Elbrand, Hilda Faigin, Dr Walter Forman, Rita Frankel, Rabbi Sherman Frankel, Marc Freimuth, Myron Friedman, Michael Fromm, Norma Geller, Fred Gevelber, Samuel Givelber, David Goldish, Linda Goldman, Evy Gordon, Harley Gross, Norman E. Gutfeld, William Haas, Marvin Hertz, Lois Jacobson, Dr Jack W. Jaffe, Rabbi Paul Joseph, Simon Kadis, Ziona Kadis, Amy Kaplan, Marvin Karp, Keeva Kekst, N. Herschel Koblenz, Judy Kossoff, Murray Koval, Lawrence Lake, Jordan Lefko, Irvin A. Leonard, Harriet Leventhal, Dr Howard Levin, Gail Levine, Lawrence Lichtig, Michael J. Linden, Melville Moses, Dr Dieter Myers, Hal H. Myers, Edmund C. Paller, Zachary Paris, Martin Pincus, Harold Polster, Charles A. Ratner, Neil Rembrandt, Lawrence Rich, Dr Tena Rosner, Rabbi Daniel Schur, Rabbi Herbert Schwartz, Paul L. Shapiro, Adrienne Sharp, Martin Silverman, Edward Simon, Dr Abba Spero, Frank Stern, Dr Chaim Sukenik, Lawrence Turbow, Ieda Warshay, Edmund Weisler, Avi Weiss, Steven Werber, Dr Sally Wertheim, Stanley Wertheim, Michael Wieder, Florence Wish, Dr Jerry Wolkoff. **2030 S Taylor Rd, Cleveland OH 44118 (216) 371–0446.**

Chabad House. Lubavitch com servs ctr. Blends Chassidic fervor & warmth with tradition & learning, to show that every J, fr whatever background he or she comes fr, is an integral part of the body of Is. Anti-missionary work; campus ctr; adult edu; stu dormitory; sabbath seminars; holiday progs; day camp; nursery for ages 2 to 4; youth groups; J library; syns; kosher kitchen; Russian Immigrant Aid Soc; counseling; chaplaincy; Mitzvah Campaigns; hosp & prison visitations; sr citizens encounters; speakers bureau. Est in Cleveland in 1972 by the Lubavitch movement. They purchased their own facility in 1973. The Chabad Women's Div was est in 1973. In 1974 Camp Chabad was f. The Chabad Russian Div was created in 1974. In 1977 the Chabad on Case Western Reserve Campus was purchased. The Kosher Kitchen opened in 1978. In 1980 the Chabad Nursery opened. Chabad is an acronym of the Heb words meaning Wisdom, Understanding & Knowledge. Exec Dir: Rabbi Leib Alevsky; Spiritual Leader: Rabbi Sholom B. Chaiken; Adm Dir: Rabbi Lipa Brennan; Dir Col Dept: Rabbi Mordechai Mendelson; Russian Immigrant Aid Soc: Mrs Z. Kazen; Women's Div: Devorah Alevsky; Torah

Nursery: Shoshana Estreicher; Dir Chabad House of Akron: Rabbi Dan Rotenberg. **2057 Cornell Rd, Cleveland OH 44106 (216) 721–5050.**

The Cleveland Hebrew Schools. Affiliated with the Bureau of J Edu & the J Com Fed. Three day week prog; classes fr K through sixth grade to prepare stu to read, write & converse in Heb, to study the Bible in Heb, to participate in prayers, & to become familiar with J holidays & traditions, to teach the hist & meaning of modern day Is, & to prepare the stu for their Bar or Bat Mitzvah; Outreach Prog to serve the edu needs of J chil in outlying areas; prog for the edu of handicapped chil & for those with learning disabilities. For over 90 yrs, The Cleveland Hebrew Schs, a communal sch serving chil of all ideological backgrounds, has been dedicated to the concept of intensive afternoon Heb edu. Pres: Mrs Milton Wish; Exec VP: Mrs Samuel M. Frankel; VPs: Dr Herbert Mayers, Edmund C. Paller, Manuel Rock, Mrs Harry Wiederhorn, Milton Wish; Treas: Harley Gross; Sec: Marvin Hertz; Pres Beth Aynu: Robert C. Weiss; Superintendent: Judith Shamir; Bd of Trustees: Mrs Albert Assayag, Elliot Azoff, Mrs Sam M. Baron, Mrs Frank Buchwald, Samuel M. Frankel, Rina Frankel, Dr Judith Gerblich, Mrs Steven Goldstine, Mrs Larry Goodman, Sanford Gordon, Harley Gross, Morton J. Gross, Mrs Donald Harris, Marvin M. Hertz, Keeva Kekst, Mrs Hyman Lupeson, Dr Herbert Mayers, Stan Meirson, Tamar Meirson, Samuel H. Miller, Conrad Morgenstern, Edmund C. Paller, Sheldon Pierson, Mrs David Resnik, Manuel Rock, Marshall Rosenberg, Mrs Philip Rosenberg, Leighton A. Rosenthal, Mrs Marvin Schinagle, Mrs Barry Siegel, Leonard Skolnik, Mrs Eric Smith, Morton J. Weisberg, Robert C. Weiss, Mrs Harry Wiederhorn, Dr David Willen, Mrs Raymond Willen, Milton Wish; Hon Mems: Joseph Barrat, Howard I. Chesler, Ben M. Coben, Suggs I. Garber, Max I. Goldfarb, Esther Haber, Helen Levine, Jerome Silberman, Florence Wish. **25400 Fairmount Blvd, Cleveland OH 44122 (216) 464–8050.**

The Cleveland Jewish Archives. The Archives is a prog of The Western Reserve Historical Soc. To collect the papers of J & the records of J ins & orgs in the Greater Cleveland area. Collections available for scholarly research; major manuscript accessions include: Autobiographical Narratives & Am Letters, Business & Professional Men & Women, Business, Clubs & Assns, Early Cleveland Family Papers 1850–1900, Family & Miscellaneous Personal Papers 1900 to the present, Genealogy, Schs, Social Servs Orgs, Syns, Zionism. Est in 1976. Fr 1976 through 1980 this proj was funded by special grants made fr local founs. In 1981 the J Com Fed of Cleveland est a permanent fund to finance the Archives. History of the Jews in Cleveland; Merging Traditions – Jewish Life in Cleveland; A Contemporary Narrative, 1945–1975 & Pictorial Record, 1939–1975. Dir Hist Library: Kermit J. Pike. **10825 E Blvd, Cleveland OH 44106 (216) 721–5722.**

Cleveland Jewish Community Center. 3503 Mayfield Rd, Cleveland OH 44118.

Cleveland Jewish News. Periodical pub. **13910 Cedar Rd, Cleveland OH 44118 (216) 371–0800.**

Fairmount Temple. Affiliated with UAHC. 2125 mems. Rabbis: Arthur J. Lelyveld, Frederick A. Eisenberg, Stuart A. Gertman; Cantor Sarah J. Sager; Pres: Stanley E. Wertheim; Edu: Judith G. Lichtig; Adm: Si Wachsberger; Sisterhood Pres: Ileen Kelner; Brotherhood Pres: Harvey Relman. **23737 Fairmount Blvd, Cleveland OH 44122 (216) 464–1330.**

Fairmount Temple Library. For information on the Temple, see – Fairmount Temple, Cleveland, OH. **23737 Fairmount Blvd, Cleveland OH 44122 (216) 464–1330.**

The Jewish Community Federation of Cleveland. J Information Servs: a prog offering accurate & up-to-date information & referral servs about resources available in the J & gen com; Cleveland Shalom: a proj that extends hospitality & provides information to new J residents in the Cleveland area. The Information Servs was est in 1975, & continues to be sponsored by The J Com Fed of Cleveland. Cleveland Shalom was est in 1972, & is currently sponsored by the Cleveland Section, Natl Council of J Women, & the J Information Servs of the J Com Fed. J Information Servs Assc: Arlene Jaffe; Pres: Lawrence H. Williams; VPs: Max M. Axelrod, Victor Gelb, Henry J. Goodman; Treas: Marilyn Bedol; Assc Treas: Aileen M. Kassen; Exec Dir: Stanley B. Horowitz. **2030 S Taylor Rd, Cleveland OH 44118 (216) 371–3999.**

Jewish Community Federation, Library. 1750 Euclid Ave, Cleveland OH 44115 (216) 566–9200.

The Mount Sinai Medical Center. Affiliated with Case Western Reserve Univ Sch of Med & The J Com Fed. Dedicated to broad progs of patient care, teaching & research. A wide range of special diagnostic & therapeutic facilities; teaching ins – the Med Ctr offers first yr post grad & residency progs in mostmed-surgical specialties as well as training of other health care specialists. More than 16,000 patients are admitted annually to the Med Ctr & 45,000 patient visits are made to its outpatient clin. Staff of 400 physicians; 2,000 employees. F in 1903 by mems of the J Women's Hosp Soc, Mt Sinai began as a 29 bed health unit. Fr its very beginning, Mt Sinai's growth & dev as a major med ins has been supported primarily by philanthropic contributions fr the J com. In 1916 a new 160 bed hosp was opened in Cleveland's med, edu & cultural area, Univ Circle, & through the yrs it has expanded steadily in response to advances & innovations in med & to growing com needs. The Med Ctr now maintains 500 beds. Mt Sinai is in the midst of a renovation & modernization prog which will permit the physical complex to continue to keep pace with new demands on space created by modern tech & more specialized staff. Chr of the Bd of Trustees: Edwin M. Roth; Pres: Barry M. Spero. **Univ Circle, Cleveland OH 44106 (216) 795–6000.**

Pioneer Women – Na'amat. The training & edu of the Is woman & her family so that each can be best equipped to lead productive lives. For additional information, see – Pioneer Women Na'amat, New York City, NY. **13969 Cedar Rd, Rm 208, Cleveland OH 44118 (216) 321–2002.**

The Suburban Temple. Affiliated with UAHC. 502 mems. Rabbi Michael Oppenheimer; Pres: Mina Siegel; Edu: Holly Friedlander; Rabbis: Randall M. Falk, Kenneth A. Kanter; Adm: Loree B. Resnik; Sisterhood Pres: Sue Manheim. **22401 Chagrin Blvd, Cleveland OH 44122 (216) 991–0700.**

Temple Emanu-El. Affiliated with UAHC. 647 mems. Rabbis: Daniel A. Roberts, Alan S. Green; Cantor Irving Bushman; Pres: Lawrence Berman; Edu: Sylvia F. Abrams; Adm: William S. Gibberman; Sisterhood Pres: Marjorie Rosenbaum; Brotherhood Pres: Richard Brastoff. **2200 S Green Rd, Cleveland OH 44121 (216) 381–6600.**

Temple Emanu-El, Sindell Library. For information on the Temple, see – Temple Emanu-El, Cleveland, OH. **2200 S Green Rd, Cleveland OH 44121 (216) 381–6600.**

The Temple Library. For information on the Temple, see – The Temple, Tifereth Israel, Cleveland, OH. **University Circle, at Silver Park, Cleveland OH 44106 (216) 791–7755.**

The Temple, Tifereth Israel. Affiliated with UAHC. 1635 mems. Pres: Charles Evans; Rabbis: Daniel J. Silver, Jonathan S. Woll, Paul Joseph; Edu: Mona Senkfor, Paul Joseph; Adm: Marvin Linder; Sisterhood Pres: Connie Friedman; Brotherhood Pres: Lewis S. Sternberg. **University Circle, at Silver Park, Cleveland OH 44106 (216) 791–7755.**

Women's American ORT – Cleveland Region. Vocational training prog of the J people affiliated with Women's Am ORT, Inc. To be concerned with the ideals of the ORT prog & its edu purposes & provide substantive efforts in support of the global ORT network. Conducts fund raising activities; fosters & reinforces quality edu, career orientation & technical training as vehicles to improve the quality of life; combats the rise of anti-Semitism; works to help alleviate the plight of Soviet J. 4,000 mems in 30 chapters in the Cleveland area. Est in 1957 as a Region. Ort's technical & vocational schs serve over 100,000 stu in Is, US, France, India, Morocco & Latin Am. Pres: Patricia Kaplan; Exec Cttee Chr: Charlene Press. **23715 Mercantile Rd, Cleveland OH 44122 (216) 464–7360.**

Workmen's Circle. A fraternal org affiliated with the Bureau of J Edu & J Com Fed. To emphasize the idealism & intellectuality of secular J life. & work actively for social justice & human dignity for all. The org is committed to the enrichment of J life in every form of secularist expression through J edu, Yiddish language & culture. Actively involved in the issues facing Is, J in the Soviet Union & everywhere the J com exists; provides Excess Major Med Plan, Hosp Indemnity Plans, Life & Hosp Insurance Plans, Ltd Med Expense Policy, Disability Income & Retirement Annuity Plans, Legal Servs Benefits, Credit Union, Cemetery Coverage, Optical Plan. Supports I.L. Peretz Yiddish Schs with a curriculum which includes J Social Studies, Yiddish Language, Heb Language, celebration of J Holidays, J Music, Dramatics & Literature; renders brotherly & fraternal aid. 850 mems in 6 branches in the Cleveland/Akron area. F in 1900 in NY, & in about 1905 in Cleveland. Pub The Call (semi-annual), Calendar Newsletter (monthly), The Jewish Daily Forward. Regional Dir: Marilyn Baruch; S Dir: Esther Schachner; Chr: Dominic Gianasi; V Chr: Elaine Weiss; Dist Sec: Max Wohl; Rec Sec: Ben Parker. **1980 S Green Rd, Cleveland OH 44121 (216) 381–4515.**

Young Israel. 14141 Cedar Rd, Cleveland OH 44121 (216) 382–5740.

Young Israel, Esther Kohn Estricher Memorial Library. 14141 Cedar Rd, Cleveland OH 44121 (216) 382–5740.

Cleveland Heights

Congregation Beth Am. Conservative Syn affiliated with United Syn of Am. Rel Servs; Rel Sch;

library. 525 families. Est in 1933. Pub Kol (monthly). Rabbi Michael Hecht; Cantor Martin Leubitz; Pres: A. Bernard Peters; Exec VP: Margaret Bohnen; VPs: Ronald Newman, Estelle Leutenberg, Jack Weingold; Treas: Seymour Birnbaum; Gen Sec: William Friedson; Rec Sec: Garth Ireland; Fin Sec: Robert Solomon; Exec Dir: Larry Leibowitz; Edu Dir: Mervyn Berger. **3557 Washington Blvd, Cleveland Heights OH 44118 (216) 321–1000.**

Congregation Beth Am Library. Library contains 4,000 vols. For information on the Cong, see – Congregation Beth Am, Cleveland Heights, OH. **3557 Washington Blvd, Cleveland Heights OH 44118 (216) 321–1000.**

Council Gardens. Non-profit, non-sectarian 130 bed suite apt complex for persons 62 yrs of age & over. Independent living with dignity for older persons. 24 hour coverage by staff, including exec dir, a resident nurse & a resident superintendent; podiatrist servs; beauty salon; barber shop; check cashing servs; weekly satellite bank; postage sales; transportation provided for grocery shopping three days a week with staff assistance for carrying parcels to tenants doors; meals served three nights a week; bingo; lectures; entertainment; Ship A Box Sewing Group; movies; music; monthly Fri Evening Servs; Oneg Shabbat; annual picnic; bus trips; holiday progs; continuing edu provided by col level lecture courses. Council Gardens Tenants Assn provides a link to the Bd of Trustees & helps plan progs, special events & various activities. Est in 1963. Council Gardens is housed in eight one story garden apts & one four story mid rise bldg. The Adm Bldg contains a dining rm, lounge, kitchen, activities rm, library, beauty-barber salon, offs & the resident nurses quarters. There are 56 efficiency apts, 62 one bedroom apts & 12 two bedroom apts. Four apts are available for disabled persons of any age. All apts are equipped with smoke detectors. Natl Council of J Women – Cleveland Section volunteers have been active since Council Gardens began. **2501 N Taylor Rd, Cleveland Heights OH 44118 (216) 382–8625.**

Hadassah – Greater Cleveland Chapter. The women's Zionist org of Am. Progs & projs coordinated with natl Hadassah. Conducts edu progs in US, health edu & com servs in Is; provides basic J edu as a background for intelligent & creative J living in Am; built & maintains in Jerusalem the Hadassah-Hebrew Univ Med Ctr; supports clins & com health ctrs; operates the Hadassah Com Col, Seligsberg/Brandeis Comprehensive Co-edu HS, & Vocational Guidance Ins in Jerusalem; acts as principal agy in US for support of youth aliyah villages & day-care ctrs for immigrants & deprived youth; participates in J Natl Fund land purchase & reclamation progs; sponsors Hashachar, a Zionist youth movement. Pres: Sandra L. White. **1855 S Taylor Rd, Cleveland Heights OH 44118 (216) 321–9000.**

The Oheb Zedek Taylor Road Synagogue. Modern Orthodox Syn. To bring the message of Orthodoxy to the mems. Daily Rel Servs; Torah Edu for all ages; Mens Club; Sisterhood; Mr & Mrs Club; Young Married couples groups; youth groups; NCSY youth group; guest speakers. 700 families. F in 1904. Congs Knesset Is, Shaarey Torah, Agudas B'nai Is, Chibas Jerusalem, Agudas Achim subsequently joined the Oheb Zedek Cong to form The Taylor Rd Syn. Facilities include an auditorium & kosher catering facilities for the entire J com. Rabbi Dr Louis Engelberg; Pres: Sidney Silverstein; VPs: William Haas, Jerome Wolf, Henry Polster; Fin Sec: Leland Freedman; Treas: Bernard Potash; Rec Sec: Louis Wolinsky; Cantor: Rev Stuart Friedman; Edu Dir: Rabbi Gerald Porath. **1970 S Taylor Rd, Cleveland Heights OH 44118 (216) 321–4875.**

The Park Synagogue. Conservative Syn affiliated with JTS. To further the belief & understanding of Traditional J. Rel Servs; edu progs; Couples Club; Men's Club; Sisterhood; Parents League; Nursery Sch; Lillian Ratner Montessori Presch; Park-Ratner Day Sch; Park Day Camp; youth activities; HS; Afternoon Sch; Summer Day Camp; library containing 15,000 vols (reference, Judaica, biography, hist, fiction, Is, chil section). 1,800 families; 7,000 individuals; 600 stu in grades K–12. 240 employees. F 1869; originally known as Anshe Emeth Beth Tefilo Cong; later as The Cleveland J Ctr. Pub Park Bulletin (semi-monthly). Facilities include 3 kosher kitchens, 2 auxiliary kitchens, gift shop, sanctuary seating 985, chapel seating 150, theatre seating 600, ballroom seating 800, 2nd ballroom seating 350, gym. Sr Rabbi Armond E. Cohen; Asst Rabbi Kenneth A. Stern; Cantor Elliot Joel Portner; Pres: Bernard M. Loewenthal; Exec Dir: Jacob Berger; Ritual Supervisor: Eli Z. Levy. **3300 Mayfield Rd, Cleveland Heights OH 44118 (216) 371–2244.**

Park Synagogue, Rachel & Charles Kravitz Memorial Library. Library contains 15,000 vols (reference, Judaica, biography, hist, fiction, Is, chil section). For information on the Syn, see – The Park Synagogue, Cleveland Heights, OH. **3300 Mayfield Rd, Cleveland Heights OH 44118 (216) 371–2244.**

Solomon Schechter Day School of Cleveland. Affiliated with Solomon Schechter Day Schs Assn.

Prin: Murray Kudroff; Chr: Dr Coleman Brosilow. **3557 Washington Blvd, Cleveland Heights OH 44118 (216) 371–1364.**

Yavne Teachers' College for Women. To train the mind & mold the character of young J women through a thorough & multifaceted exposure to their rich heritage; to imbue its stu with a sense of mission & dedication to the perpetuation of knowledge & ideals so that these young women may set standards of excellence as they enter into the edu coms of the world. Counseling & guidance; health servs; Stu Placement Off: assistance to qualified stu in securing part time work to help defray sch expenses, assistance to graduating srs & alumnae in securing career positions; special lecture series; stu orgs & activities; weekly Ongei Shabbat, Shabbatonim & com progs; Depts: Bible, Edu – Elementary & Secondary, English, Heb, Hist, Philosophy, Physical & Health Edu, Rel, Speech. Yavne Teachers Seminary, under the auspices of the Rabbinical Col of Telshe, came into being in Lithuania following WWI. It was fully licensed by the govt & drew stu fr all over Europe. With the Nazi invasion of Lithuania, the sch was closed. In Sept of 1958 Yavne Teachers' Seminary was reopened in Cleveland OH. In Apr of 1969 the name of the ins was changed to the Yavne Teachers Col for Women. There is a stu residence hall located in suburban Cleveland. The sch also arranges for accommodations in private homes. Full & partial Yavne scholarships & loans are available, & are awarded on the basis of academic & personal promise & fin need. Stu of Yavne present an annual play which is written, produced & directed by the stu themselves under the guidance of a faculty adv. Proceeds fr the play go to the Stu Scholarship Fund. Pres: Rabbi Mordecai Gifter; VP: Rabbi Seymour Gewirtz; Dean: Rabbi Moshe Einstadter; Dean of Stu: Cheya Ausband; Dir of Health & Med Servs: Dr Henry C. Romberg; Dir of Admissions & Registrar: Rabbi Shlomo Davis. **1970 S Taylor Rd, Cleveland Heights OH 44118 (216) 943–5300.**

Columbus

Anti-Defamation League of B'nai B'rith – OH-KY-IN Regional Office. Dedicated in purpose & prog to translating the Am heritage of democratic ideals into a way of life for all Am, & to countering assaults on the safety, status, rights & image of J. For additional information, see – Anti-Defamation League of B'nai B'rith, New York City, NY. **1175 College Ave, Columbus OH 43209.**

B'nai B'rith Hillel Foundation. J Stu Ctr. To promote & provide a source of J identity & identification for the OH State Univ stu. J studies; J social & cultural progs; Israeli dancing; intl dancing; Rel Servs; Is & Social Action Prog; Grad Stu Group; Chabbad; Hakesher Com of Reform Stu; Heb Club; Betar Zionist; Dinner Club; Is Club; Stu Chai Campaign; rel, social & cultural activities. F in 1925, & is the third oldest Hillel in the US. J stu newspaper – Oasis, J stu newspaper. Dir: Rabbi Howard Alpert; Dir of Stu Activities: Sally Chasman; Adm Asst: Gilda Abramson; Pres: Joseph Paul; VPs: Nelson Genshaft, Dan Nemzer, Richard Fishman; Sec: Geraldine Keller; Treas: Barry Goldin; Bldg Cttee: Eydie Garlikov; Faculty Adv: Reuben Ahroni. **46 E 16th Ave, Columbus OH 43201 (614) 294–4797.**

Columbus Hebrew School. Non-denominational & non-ideological com sch. To transmit J literacy & Hebraic culture, & to instill a sense of belonging to the J com & to the J people. Five-yr curriculum including Heb language skills, Biblical narratives & concepts, understanding & familiarity with the prayer bk; J holidays & events; J arts; Bar/Bat Mitzvah instruction, Special Edu Prog. Classes are conducted at 3 branches geographically located to serve the J com: Agudas Achim in Bexley, Beth Tikvah in Worthington, & Temple Is on the Eastside. **1125 College Ave, Columbus OH 43209 (614) 231–7764.**

Columbus Jewish Federation. Mem of CJF. To maintain, provide & strengthen the servs that assure the continuity & vitality of local & world wide J. Annual campaign; Young Men's Div; Women's Div; Aging Servs; New Am Resettlement; Com Relations Cttee which deals with inter-group relations, inter-racial, & inter-rel activities, & also deals with anti-Semitism, edu, civil rights & the multitudinous activities whereby the J com relates to the non J com of Columbus; the Is Dept Cttee which concentrates on edu work enriching J activities with an Israeli flavor & an Israeli component, as well as reaching out to the non J com & youth who live & study in Central OH edu ins; the Com Scholarship Cttee which functions to help subvent tuition costs for com & communal servs applicants; Council of Orgs which plans & coords organizational concerns & issues which affect the orgs & the com; Young Leadership Dev Prog which provides knowledge & information on current issues through various sessions led by local & natl leaders; field placement for grad work; Young Leadership Award. Pres: Bernard K. Yenkin; VPs: Millard Cummins, Judith Swedlow, Jack L. Wallick, Benjamin L. Zox; Treas: N. Victor Goodman; Asst Treas: Irving Barkan; Sec: Lawrence D. Schaffer; Asst Sec: Stanley Schwartz Jr; Bd of Trustees: Merom Brachman, Dr Robert Friedman, Robert Glick, Ben Goodman, Dennis B. Mellman, Karen Moss, Rabbi Samuel W. Rubenstein, Gary

Robins, Judith Swedlow, Marilyn Skilken, Dr Jeffrey Tilson, Norman Traeger, Dr Albert Tyroler, Alan Weiler, Benjamin L. Zox; Term Ending 1983: Irving Barkan, Diane Cummins, Ira O. Kane, Victor Krupman, Richard Kohn, Arthur Loeb, Julius Margulies, Cynthia Paine, Goerge Rosenberger, Ellen Siegal, Irving Schottenstein, Jack L. Wallick, Alan Wasserstrom, Joyce L. Zacks, Sol D. Zell. **1175 College Ave, Columbus OH 43209 (614) 237–7686.**

Columbus Torah Academy. To produce a generation of chil well grounded in the learning & culture of both their J & their Am heritage. Intensive J edu & gen elementary & jr high courses; Conversational Heb, Bible, Prophets, Hist, Customs, Prayers; gen subjects include all those taught in OH schs. F in 1958. **181 Noe-Bixby Rd, Columbus OH 43213 (614) 864–0299.**

Congregation Ahavas Sholom. Daily Rel Servs; guest lecture series; discussion groups on issues in contemporary J; adult classes in classical J texts; pre holiday workshops; all night Shavuous Torah study; Purim & Hanukkah parties; weekly teenage Torah study; Sun morning youth groups; Sisterhood study groups & activities; holiday programming for new Am families; Family Shabbatons; S.E.E.D. – three week summer Torah study prog: full day study & recreation prog for chil, evening classes for adults; gift shop; Chevra Kadisha. F in 1914. Rabbi Marvin I. Possick; Rabbi Emeritus Julius Baker; Pres: Pearson Press; VP: Michael Berenstein; Treas: Aaron Yablok; Fin Sec: Morton Rising; Rec Sec: Claire Bain. **2568 E Broad St, Columbus OH 43209 (614) 258–4815.**

Congregation Tifereth Israel. Affiliated with United Syn of Am. To teach & promote J patterns of life that are based on the laws & traditions of the J people as expressed & interpreted throughout hist. Daily Rel Servs; babysitting servs during all Shabbat & Holiday Morning Servs; Rel Sch for grades K through 7; Bar or Bat Mitzvah Servs; HS for grades 8 through 12; Adult Edu classes: Heb, Yiddish, Bible, Prayer Bk, J Hist, & J Law. Special class also offers Bar & Bat Mitzvah opportunities to adults. Special progs include guest lectures, Scholar-In-Residence, & weekends of study & discussion; Men's Club; Sisterhood; Young Mems for those under 40; USY Youth Group; Kadima, Pre-USY prog for stu in 7th & 8th grade; library; Choir; Jr Cong for grades 1, 2 & 3; Young Peoples Syn for grades 4, 5 & 6; Chevra Kaddisha; catering servs; library. 200 stu in the edu prog; 200 mems in the Men's Club. Est in the early 1900's. The Cong occupies the oldest syn bldg in Columbus. The edu prog is a pilot sch of the Melton Research Ctr for J Edu of the J Theological Seminary. In 1981 the Cong completed major renovation & redecorating of the social hall. Facilities include sanctuary seating 1800. Pub Tifereth Israel Forum (monthly), Rabbi's Newsletter (monthly). Rabbi Harold J. Berman; Rabbi Emeritus Nathan Zelizer; cantor Jack Chomsky; Edu Dir: Merrill Shapiro; Exec Dir: Arthur W. Flicker; Adm: Anne Covel; Hon Pres for Life: Samuel M. Melton; Pres: Harold Mindlin; 1st VP: Paul G. Rehmar; 2nd VP: Dr L. Robert Polster; Treas: Michael S. Marlin; Sec: Alan T. Radnor; Bd of Trustees: I. C. Benis, Judy Blair, Ralph Cobey, Marilyn Fishman, Arthur Flicker, Ben Goodman, Leslie Gutter, Heinz Hoffman, B. Marvin Horkin, Dr Arthur Kamlet, Herman Katz, Marvin A. Katz, Renee Levine, Richard Lieberman, Charles Margulis, Mark Masser, Neil Moss, Samuel Oppenheimer, Sondra Osipow, Lawrence W. Polster, Martin J. Polster, Dr Martin Derrow, Harriet Felsenthal, Edward Fishman, Dr Norman Hosansky, Marvin Resnik, Paula Weinstein, Carol Radnor, Ralph J. E. Rothschild, Edward F. Schlezinger, Harold M. Schneider, Joan Shell, Joseph Sniderman, Alvin Solove, Larry Solove, Diane Tyroler, Jack L. Wallick, William Wasserstorm, Mark Weinstein, Arthur B. Westerman, Dr Gerald Winer, Sidney Wolpert, Gordon G. Zeidman; Coord Adult Edu: Evelyn Nateman; USY Kadima Adv: Lynn Isenberg. **1354 E Broad St, Columbus OH 43205 (614) 253–8523.**

Congregation Tifereth Israel, Minnie Cobey Memorial Library. Library contains 6,000 vols. For information on the Cong, see – Congregation Tifereth Israel, Columbus, OH. **1354 E Broad St, Columbus OH 43205 (614) 253–8523.**

Heritage House. J home for the aged – retirement ctr, nursing home & skilled nursing care facility. To provide life with dignity; to meet the needs of the growing num of elderly mems of the J com who require its prog of quality care. Servs include med, psychiatry, podiatry, dentistry, nursing, social work, occupational therapy prog. Facilities include therapeutic landscaped gardens including barrier free pathways leading to gazebos, fountains, a grandchil playground, wheelchair planters for gardening. The home sponsors Outreach Progs, Short Stay Progs of Post Hosp Recuperation, Vacation Stay, J Holiday Stay, the Geriatric Servs Org, Retired Sr Volunteer Prog, & Meals on Wheels. 146 residents. The home was selected by the OH Dept of Health to be the area training ctr for the training of nursing home staff in a nine-cty area. **1151 College Ave, Columbus OH 43209 (614) 237–7417.**

Heritage Tower. Sr citizen housing adm by the The J Com Sr Citizens Housing Corp. Rae & Jerome

Health Assessment Clin; volunteer prog. 118 residents. Opened on Oct 25, 1978. The ground floor of the eight-story bldg is devoted to com areas including the living rm mall, coffee-convenience food shops, beauty/barber shop, craft areas, game rm & com dining rm. **1145 College Ave, Columbus OH 43209.**

The Jewish Center. To provide an identification with J life for people of all ages through a wide variety of social, cultural, edu & recreational activities. Pre-sch; all-day chil care facility; summer day camp; sch vacation progs; BBYO; Singles Club; Single Parents & Kids (SPAK) group; Golden Age Club; Nutrition Involving Columbus Elderly (NICE) prog, provides kosher lunches daily to 100 sr adults; classes in Art, Music & Dance; Gallery Players; J Ctr Com Orchestra; Intl Film Series; guest speakers; art exhibits; bkstore; servs to Russian J immigrant com including holiday workshops, discussions, English classes & sports progs. 600 mems; over 624,000 per year visits (average of 2,080 visits per day). More than 30 highly-trained, experienced professionals, cttee mems, volunteers. F in 1913. Monthly newsletter in Russian. Facilities include gymnasium, health club, handball & racquetball cts, indoor & outdoor swimming pools, bowling alleys, tennis cts & athletic fields. **1125 College Ave, Columbus OH 43209 (614) 231–2731.**

Jewish Family Service. Confidential agy to solve problems of the J family. Operates through two major depts: Clin Servs & Vocational Servs – Clin Servs Dept: helps in personal adjustment problems, family counseling, J family life edu; Vocational Servs Dept: provides career & edu planning, employment counseling & career change counseling. Sponsors VITAL prog (Volunteers In Training, Absorption & Living). **1175 College Ave, Columbus OH 43209 (614) 237–7686.**

Ohio Jewish Chronicle. Periodical pub. **2831 E Main St, Columbus OH 43209 (614) 237–4296.**

Temple Beth Shalom. Affiliated with UAHC. 59 mems. Rabbi Howard L. Apothaker; Pres: James Dowell; Edu: Howard L. Apothaker; Adm: Constance Freundlich. **3100 E Broad St, Columbus OH 43209 (614) 231–4598.**

Temple Israel. Reform Cong affiliated with UAHC. Rel Servs; Rel Sch; Heb Sch; Adult Edu, lectures & seminars; Sisterhood; Brotherhood; Young Folks Temple League; Youth for Temple Leadership; Potpourri Sr Group; library. 1000 mems. Est in 1846 by a small group of immigrant J who came largely fr Germany. The Cong took the name of Bnai Yeshurun, which later in its hist was changed to Bnai Is. The Cong remained intact until 1868, during which it worshipped in various rms. In 1868, due to disagreement, the Cong split. Nineteen of the mems withdrew & organized the Cong of Bnai Is in 1870. For the purpose of erecting a place of worship, a lot was purchased. The mems of the original Cong who had formed the separatist group, now rejoined, making a total membership of 33 people. The cornerstone was laid in 1870. The Temple accommodated 300 persons. For 30 yrs this temple satisfied the needs of the Cong. During this time the membership grew until it almost reached the 100 mark. It then became evident that a larger syn was necessary. The bldg was sold in 1901 & a lot was purchased. While the new structure was being built, Servs were held at a church. The cornerstone was laid in 1903. In 1904 the temple was dedicated. The new bldg accommodated 750 people. The temple is the oldest in the city of Columbus. The Temple Bulletin (pub bi-weekly). Rabbi Harvey S. Goldman; Rabbi Robert D. Levy; Cantor Alane S. Katzew; Rabbi Emeritus Dr Jerome D. Folkman; Temple Adm: Barbara Soloway; Pres: Seyman L. Stern; 1st VP: Raymond Wells; VPs: Robert S. Aronson, James Brenner; Sec: Beverly Shafran; Asst Sec: Rita Cohen; Treas: George Rosenberger; Asst Treas: Marvin Pliskin; Rel Sch Prin: Joan Folpe; Presch Dir: Linda Hayon; Foun Pres: Robert A. Glick; Sisterhood Pres: Hope Ellen Kaplan; Brotherhood Pres: Fred Summer; Bulletin Editor & Temple Is Historian: Mildred W. Tarshish. **5419 E Broad St, Columbus OH 43213 (614) 866–0010.**

Temple Israel, Meta Marx Lazarus Library. For information on the Temple, see – Temple Israel, Columbus, OH. **5419 E Broad St, Columbus OH 43213 (614) 866–0010.**

Dayton

Beth Abraham Synagogue. Conservative Syn affiliated with United Syn of Am. Daily Rel Servs; Rel Sch; cemetery privileges; Men's Club; USY Youth Group for 9th–12th graders; Kadima Youth Group for 7th & 8th graders; Sisterhood; social, rel & cultural activities; Adult Edu Prog; weekly Bible Classes; Youth Chorale. Est in 1897 when a few men formed a new cong. After yrs of wandering fr one hall to another, the Cong secured a small frame structure in 1913, the yr Dayton had its great flood. With the old bldg ruined, a new bldg campaign was organized which culminated in the Wayne Ave Syn. Following the flood, the J population shifted to Dayton View. In 1924 Dayton View Ctr was organized. The House of Abraham, Cong Beth Jacob, & the Dayton View Ctr formed an assn in 1941. The Mearick Mansion was acquired to serve as the temporary home for this rel org which now consisted of the Dayton View Ctr & the House of Abraham, to be known as the Beth Abraham Syn Ctr. The Mearick Mansion was temporarily remodeled to function as a Syn & Sun Sch & home for other related activities, & a bldg prog & campaign was est. Recently, the Syn purchased the old Rel Sch & the land it stood upon behind the syn. Facilities include the Burick-Zusman Chapel, housing for sch facilities of the Hillel Academy, Kravitz Library, & kosher facilities for syn & com functions. Rabbi Samuel B. Press; Cantor Jerome B. Kopmar; Ritual Dir: Rev Ernest A. Adler; Exec Dir: Shirley F. Gotlieb; Prin Rel Sch: Rochelle Wynne; Pres: Gerald H. Wilks; 1st VP & Treas: Dr Michael Jaffe; 2nd VP: Sherman Vangrov; Sec: Norman Feuer; Sisterhood Pres: Joan Marcus; Men's Club Pres: Jack Rubin; Chevra Kadisha Pres: Harold I. Jacobson; Chorale Stu Dir: Randy Goodman. **1306 Salem Ave, Dayton OH 45406 (513) 275–7403.**

Beth Abraham Synagogue, Kravitz Library. For information on the Syn, see – Beth Abraham Synagogue, Dayton, OH. **1306 Salem Ave, Dayton OH 45406 (513) 275–7403.**

Beth Jacob Synagogue. Traditional Syn. Rel Sch; Sisterhood; Men's Club; Tallis & Tefillin Club; library; gift shop. **7020 N Main St, Dayton OH 45415 (513) 274–2149.**

Bureau of Jewish Education. A div of the J Fed of Greater Dayton. Edu Progs; teacher's training; Adult Edu Ins; Com Heb Sch; coord of progs with day schs & Sun schs; Resource Ctr; library containing 35,060 vols. 11 employees. Exec Dir: Dr Yosef Batzir; Chr: Richard Flagel; Heb Sch Chr: Barbara Miller; Adult Edu Ins Chr: Dr Jack Goldfrank; Budget Cttee Chr: Howard Sanderow. **4501 Denlinger Rd, Dayton OH 45426 (513) 854–2021.**

Bureau of Jewish Education Library. Library contains 35,060 vols. For inforamtion on the Bureau, see – Bureau of Jewish Education, Dayton OH. **4501 Denlinger Rd, Dayton OH 45426 (513) 854–2021.**

Community Hebrew School. Afternoon Sch; library containing 470 vols (Heb texts & Hebraic studies). 163 stu grades 1–8. 9 employees; volunteer Bd of Edu, Va'ad Ha–Horim. Dir: Dr Yosef Batzir; Chr: Barbara Miller. **4501 Denlinger Rd, Dayton OH 45426 (513) 854–2021.**

Community Relations Council. J com spokesman with the com-at-large. Serves J interests in public life; expresses J opinion on matters of communal concern. **Jesse Philips Bldg, 4501 Denlinger Rd, Dayton OH 45426 (513) 854–4150.**

Convenant House. J home for the aged. 24-hr med care; sections for the well-aged, those needing nursing care, & for the acutely ill; kosher kitchen. **Jesse Philips Bldg, 4501 Denlinger Rd, Dayton OH 45426 (513) 854–4150.**

Dayton Jewish Center. Nursery Sch; Day Camp; Day Care; chil & youth progs; single adult & adult edu progs; sr adult prog; health & physical edu prog for all ages. **Jesse Philips Bldg, 4501 Denlinger Rd, Dayton OH 45426 (513) 854–4150.**

Dayton Jewish Chronicle. Periodical pub. **118 Salem Ave, Dayton OH 45406 (513) 222–0783.**

Hillel Academy. 100 E Woodbury Dr, Dayton OH 45414.

Hillel Academy Library. 100 E Woodbury Dr, Dayton OH 45414.

Jewish Family Service Division of the Jewish Federation of Greater Dayton. Social serv agy affiliated with Assn of J Family & Chil Agy & mem United Way. To help families & individuals cope with & effect change necessitated by the stresses of contemporary life, so that they may be enabled to live personally satisfying & socially useful lives. Counseling: individual adjustment, marital, parent/child, fin, vocational, resettlement, adoption &/or home studies, problems of the aged, divorce & group; admissions to Covenant House (J home for the aged); Sr Lunch Prog; Havurah; Family Life Edu progs; scholarship loans (for Dayton only); Brandeis Univ loans (for Dayton only); financial aid (minimal, for Dayton only); help to the needy; Assc Membership Drive; appropriate referrals; resettlement of J Soviet refugees. 3 employees. J Fed of Greater Dayton, Inc, formerly known as the J Com Council of Dayton, is the umbrella agy for all of the divs located on an 85 acre campus. Dir: Sheldon W. Switkin; Counselor: Michael Novak; Sec: Vanessa Rosensweet; Chr: Dr Melvin Lipton; V Chr: Ruth Rosenfeld; Treas: Gerald Jacobson; Sec of Bd: Blanche Shear. **4501 Denlinger Rd, Dayton OH 45426 (513) 854–2944.**

Jewish Federation of Greater Dayton Inc. Mem of CJF, central org of the J com. To further the welfare of the J com; to coord social, welfare & cultural progs; to foster cooperation among J orgs; to coord fund raising activities on the local & natl level; to stimulate participation & interest in all com wide activities. Conducts the annual United J Campaign; implements progs in leadership dev; sponsers J edu & com relations; supervises com planning & budgeting; maintains a J Com Calendar; divs include: Com Relations Council, J Com Complex, United J Campaign & Women's Cttee, J Family Serv, Bureau of J Edu; administers an endowment prog; maintains library. Est in 1910 with health & welfare agy as beneficiaries. Facilities include J Ctr (which includes Health Club, Pre-sch, youth adult progs & physical activities), Covenant House (J home for the aged), future site of Covenant Manor (apts for sr citizens); kosher kitchens located in Covenant House & in the Jesse Philips Bldg which also houses library, Health Club, gym, classrms for Bureau of J Edu & Pre-sch, youth & adult lounge, game rm, racquet ball cts, meeting & prog rms, playground, lodge, outdoor pool & snack area, baseball diamond & soccer area, running track, offs. Pres: Bernard Goldman; VPs: Charles Abramovitz, Bernard Rabinowitz, Larry Zusman; Treas: Milton Isaacson; Asst Treas: Ronnie Harlan; Sec: Lawrence Burick; Asst Sec: Richard Potasky; Exec Dir: Peter H. Wells; Asst Exec Dir: Bruce J. Yudewitz; Staff Assc: Carol Pavlofsky; Dir of Operations: Harris S. Abrahams. **Jesse Philips Bldg, 4501 Denlinger Rd, Dayton OH 45426 (513) 854–4150.**

Jewish Federation of Greater Dayton, Arthur Beerman Memorial Library. For information on the Ins, see – Jewish Federation of Greater Dayton, Dayton, OH. **Jesse Philips Bldg, 4501 Denlinger Rd, Dayton OH 45426 (513) 854–4150.**

Shomrei Emunah Young Israel. Orthodox Cong. **1706 Salem Ave, Dayton OH 45406 (513) 274–6941.**

Temple Israel. Affiliated with UAHC. Rel Sch; Sisterhood; Men's Club; gift shop; library. 1028 mems. Rabbis: P.I. Bloom, Lawrence P. Karol; Cantor Jay Weiss; Pres: Alan Klein; Edu: Shirley Schatz; Sisterhood Pres: Stephanie Meiselman; Brotherhood Pres: Howard Faust. **1821 Emerson Ave, Dayton OH 45406 (513) 278–9621.**

Temple Israel South Branch. Reform Temple. **1136 W Centerville Rd, Dayton OH 45959 (513) 434–9067.**

Temple Israel, Rabbi Louis Witt Memorial Library. For information on the Temple, see – Temple Israel, Dayton, OH. **1821 Emerson Ave, Dayton OH 45406 (513) 278–9621.**

United Jewish Campaign. Fundraising arm of the J Fed. Annual Campaign secures funds to meet the financial needs of its local, natl & overseas beneficiary agy; Women's Cttee organizes & conducts women's participation in the Campaign, plans yr-round edu progs, & devs responsible leadership for all orgs. **Jesse Philips Bldg, 4501 Denlinger Rd, Dayton OH 45426 (513) 854–4150.**

East Liverpool

Congregation Beth Shalom. Affiliated with UAHC. 43 mems. Pres: Richard Feldman; Sisterhood Pres: Harriette Feldman. **PO Box 309, East Liverpool OH 43920 (216) 386–6820.**

Elyria

Temple B'nai Abraham. Affiliated with United Syn of Am. Rabbi Sidney Rackoff; Cantor Martin Cohen; Pres: Kenneth Frankel; Edu Dir: Regina Rackoff. **PO Box 5, 530 Gulf Rd, Elyria OH 44036 (216) 366–1177.**

Euclid

Temple Ner Tamid. Affiliated with UAHC. 160 mems. Rabbi Stephen S. Goldrich; Cantor Samuel Levine; Pres: Lloyd Cooper; Brotherhood Pres: Irwin Gale. **24950 Lake Shore Dr, Euclid OH 44132 (216) 261–2280.**

Fremont

Temple Beth Israel. Affiliated with United Syn of Am. Pres: Robert Gilberg. **514 Birchard Ave, Fremont OH 43420 (419) 332–6302.**

Granville

Ohev Israel Temple. Affiliated with UAHC. 32 mems. Pres: Elliot Davidoff; Adms: Joy Binkovitz, Caryn Bloomberg; Sisterhood Pres: Caryn Bloomberg. **c/o Elliot Davidoff, 324 Mt Parnassus, Granville OH 43023 (614) 326–4501.**

Kent

Hillel Foundation, Kent State University Jewish Student Center. To interest J in Judaism. Rel Servs; Sun Brunch; Women's Coffee House; Brew Blasts; Intl J Cooking Class; Jazzerdance; Computer Dating Servs; Self Defense Class; movies; alternate Tues nights free supper & speaker. Dir: Rabbi Gerald Turk. **202 N Lincoln, Kent OH 44240 (216) 678–0397.**

Kenwood Station

Congregation Etz Chayim. PO Box 2882, Kenwood Station OH 43606.

Congregation Etz Chayim Library. PO Box 2882, Kenwood Station OH 43606.

Lima

Federated Jewish Charities of Lima District. Organized 1935. Pres: Morris Goldberg. **2417 W Market St, Lima OH 45805 (419) 224–8941.**

Temple Beth Israel. Affiliated with UAHC. 94 mems. Rabbi Sol H. Oster; Pres: Marvin A. Lotzoff; Edu: Beverly Hersh; Sisterhood Pres: Nancy Mayerson; Brotherhood Pres: David H. Goldberg. **Lakewood Ave at Glenwood, Lima OH 45805 (419) 223–9616.**

Lorain

Agudath B'nai Israel. Affiliated with United Syn of Am. Rabbi Robert Bronstein; Pres: Samuel Rosen; Admin Sec: Ruth M. Sepsenwol. **1715 Meister Rd at Pole Ave, Lorain OH 44053 (216) 282–3307.**

Agudath B'nai Israel Congregation, Lewis P. Jacoby Memorial Library. For information on the Cong see – Agudath B'nai Israel Congregation, Lorain, OH. **1715 Meister Rd, Lorain OH 44052 (216) 282–3307.**

Mansfield

B'nai Jacob Congregation. Affiliated with UAHC. 92 mems. Rabbi Gary Loeb; Pres: Louis Stephan; Edu: Ann Schwartz. **973 Larchwood Rd, Mansfield OH 44907 (419) 756–7355.**

Temple Emanuel. Affiliated with UAHC. 16 mems. Pres: J.B. Morris; Sisterhood Pres: Esther Garber. **Cook Rd at Larchwood, PO Box 1665, Mansfield OH 44901 (419) 756–7266.**

Marion

Temple Israel. Affiliated with UAHC. 40 mems. Pres: Robert Kirshen; Sisterhood Pres: Diane Smith. **c/o Mr Art Radwin, 730 Harding Rd, Marion OH 43302 (614) 382–3629.**

Mayfield Heights

B'nai Jeshurun Congregation. Affiliated with United Syn of Am. Rabbi Jacob Shtull; Cantor Gary Paller; Pres: Henry Gruen; Edu Dir: Esther Schachner; Youth Dir: Warren Sklar. **1732 Lander Rd, Mayfield Heights OH 44124 (216) 449–6200.**

Mayfield Hillcrest Synagogue. Affiliated with United Syn of Am. **1732 Lander Rd, Mayfield Heights OH 44124 (216) 449–6200.**

Mayfield Hillcrest Synagogue, Rabbi Enoch H. Kronheim Memorial Library. Affiliated with AJL. To serve the mems of the Cong; to provide fiction & non-fiction bks & materials. Library contains 3,000 vols (Judaica – adult & juvenile). 1 employee; 3 volunteers. F 1961. Librarian: Polly Wilkenfeld; Library Chr: Erna Einstein. **1732 Lander Rd, Mayfield Heights OH 44124 (216) 449–6200.**

Mentor

Am Shalom. Affiliated with UAHC. 63 mems. Cantor Walter Boninger; Pres: Marvin Plasco; Edu: Terry Pollack. **PO Box 454, Mentor OH 44060 (216) 255–4129.**

Middletown

Temple Beth Sholom. Affiliated with UAHC. 60 mems. Rabbi Gordon L. Gladstone; Pres: Kenneth Cohen. **610 Gladys Dr, Middletown OH 45042 (513) 422–8313.**

Pepper Pike

B'nai Jeshurun Congregation – The Temple on the Heights. Conservative Cong affiliated with United Syn of Am. Rel Servs daily; Sisterhood; Afternon Rel Sch; Weekend Rel Sch; USY; Kadima; library (Judaica). 1200 families; 400 stu in grades K–12. 19 employees plus 30 teachers. F 1866. Pub The Tidings (monthly). Facilities include kosher kitchens, 2 sanctuaries, social hall, gift shop. Rabbi Herbert N. Schwartz; Cantor Yehuda Shifman; Pres: Earl M. Linden; Exec Dir: Bruce M. Hennes; Edu Dir: Judith Holzer. **27501 Fairmount Blvd, Pepper Pike OH 44124 (216) 831–6555.**

Brith Emeth Temple. 17575 Shaker Blvd, Pepper Pike OH 44124.

Brith Emeth Temple, Goldy & Max Smith Library. 17575 Shaker Blvd, Pepper Pike OH 44124.

Piqua

Anshe Emeth Congregation. Affiliated with UAHC. 24 mems. Pres: Herman Barr. **c/o Mr**

Herman Barr, 1409 Nicklin, Piqua OH 45356 (513) 773–4253.

Portsmouth

Congregation B'nai Abraham. Affiliated with UAHC. 40 mems. Pres: Louis Orloff; Sisterhood Pres: Sherry Orloff. **c/o Mr Michael Mearan, 325 Masonic Bldg, Portsmouth OH 45662 (614) 354–1671.**

Sandusky

Oheb Shalom Congregation. Affiliated with UAHC. 56 mems. Cantor Andrew Krause; Pres: Richard Pohl; Edu: Effie Shiff; Sisterhood Pres: Golda Stein. **1521 E Perkins Ave, Sandusky OH 44870 (419) 433–6051.**

Springfield

Beth El Synagogue. Affiliated with United Syn of Am. Pres: Max Beloff. **2424 N Limestone St, Springfield OH 45505 (513) 399–7512.**

Temple Sholom. Affiliated with UAHC. 111 mems. Rabbi Paul D. Caplan; Pres: Irene Klaben; Edu: Edward Leventhal; Sisterhood Pres: Sharon L. Broock. **2424 N Limestone St, Springfield OH 45503 (513) 399–1231.**

Steubenville

Jewish Community Council. Mem of CJF. Organized 1938. Pres: Morris Denmark; Exec Sec: Mrs Joseph Freedman. **PO Box 472, Steubenville OH 43952 (614) 282–9031.**

Temple Beth Israel. Affiliated with UAHC. 90 mems. Rabbis: David B. Kaplan, Rieven Slavkin; Pres: Morris Denmark; Sisterhood Pres: Alan Silberman; Brotherhood Pres: Raymound Reich. **300 Lovers Lane, Steubenville OH 43952 (614) 264–5514.**

Sylvania

Jewish Welfare Federation of Greater Toledo. Mem of CJF. To solicit, collect, receive & hold money & property, & to allot & disburse same to local, regional, natl & overseas agy for the maintenance of J rel, charitable, literary & edu purposes; to foster cooperation among J orgs; to engage in com planning & to take such steps as are necessary to implement such planning. Financing, budgeting, coordination, & leadership dev for the JCC, J Family Servs, Toledo Bd of J Edu, & Darlington House; annual campaign through the United J Fund on behalf of over 40 natl & overseas beneficiaries as well as various local servs; Endowment Prog. Est in 1907; reorganized in 1960. Pres: John M. Bloomfield; VPs: Robert D. Gersten, Charles Kaminsky; Sec: Marla Levine; Treas: Barry Z. Liber; Exec Dir: Alvin S. Levinson; Assc for Budgeting & Planning: Sydney Mostov; Bd of Trustees: Bill Osterman, Mike Berebitsky, Phyllis Horwitz, Nora Romanoff, Marcia Liber. **6505 Sylvania Ave, PO Box 587, Sylvania OH 43560 (419) 885–4461.**

The Temple, Congregation Shomer Emunim. Reform Temple affiliated with UAHC. Temple for prayer, study, edu to evoke a bond of love for our rel & its traditions. Rel Servs; edu progs; Rel Sch; Sisterhood; Brotherhood; Chavurah Group; Youth Group; Braille Group; library with 6,000 vols (Judaica). 709 families; 280 stu grades K – 12. 11 employees plus 29 on Rel Sch staff. F 1875 by 60 families; first sanctuary built 1884; after a move to larger quarters, temple built & dedicated in 1917; moved to present temple occurred in 1973. Pub The Temple Bulletin (weekly). Facilities include sanctuary, chapel, social hall, lounge, 2 kitchens, resource ctr, classrms, JCC Presch, JCC Day Care. Rabbi Alan M. Sokobin, Rabbi Thomas J. Friedman, Rabbi Emeritus Leon I. Feuer; Pres: Arthur P. Solomon; VPs: Rosemary Bramson, Gordon I Levine; Hon VP: Lawrence Raskin; Sec: Marvin Cohen; Treas: Jack Treuhaft. **6453 Sylvania Ave, Sylvania OH 43560 (419) 885–3341.**

The Temple, Temple Resource Center. Library contains 6,000 vols of Judaica. For information on the Temple, see – The Temple, Congregation Shomer Emunim, Sylvania, OH. **6453 Sylvania Ave, Sylvania OH 43560 (419) 885–3341.**

Toledo

Darlington House – The Toledo Jewish Home for the Aged. To provide care for the infirmed J aged in NW OH, regardless of financial ability, with warmth & dignity. Provides skilled care for the infirmed J aged who need institutionalized care & for the well aged who reside at Pelham Manor, & day care supervision for the aged who live independently. The House has a Day Care Prog, Physical Therapy Dept, Occupational Therapy Dept & Social Servs Prog. F in 1936, & is licensed for 116 beds. The Home views itself as more than just a facility that cares for the infirmed aged but also as a social servs provider for the J com. The Home has a holistic concept of med emphasizing the social components of care. The House also has 100 apt units at Pelham Manor. The Manor is connected to the House by an underground tunnel. Pres: Sam Webne; 1st VP: Roy Treuhaft; 2nd VP: Stephen H. Wiener; Sec: Mrs Samuel Ganden; Treas: Richard I. Green; Fin Sec: Mrs Bernard Treuhaft; Exec Dir: Meyer E. Pollack; Med Dir: Dr Eli C. Abramson; Dental Consultant: Harmon J. Rusgo; Podiatrist: Samuel F. Korman; Consulting Pharmacist: Max J. Hersh; Bd of Trustees: Allen M. Adler, Mrs Louis Axonovitz, Robert A. Billstein, Dr Lawrence Birndorf; Mrs Joe Bloom, Morton Bobowick, Guy Michael B. Davis, Dr Francis W. Epstein, Yale Feniger, Marcus L. Friedman, Rabbi Edward H. Garsek, Mrs Theodore Gersz, Judge George M. Glasser, Rabbi Dr Morton Goldberg, Mort Goldman, Leo Goldner, Arnold Gottlieb, Mrs Harold A. Gross, Marvin Jacobs, Rabbi Nehemiah Katz, Dr Joel Kestenbaum, Sidney Kezur, Ben Magdovitz, Allan Miller, Jay Miller, Dr Richard E. Myers, Stanford H. Odesky, Rabbi Dr Fishel Pearlmutter, Norman Perlmutter, Lester M. Radovsky, Mrs Zale Reinstein, Janet C. Rogolsky, Theodore M. Rowen, Mrs Simon Sack, Myer Shiff, Rabbi Alan M. Sokobin, Arthur P. Solomon, Joseph Tochtermann, Roy Treuhaft, Larry Weinberg, Richard L. Wittenberg; Hon Pres: Dr A.H. Steinberg; Hon VP: Mrs Alfred H. Billstein; Hon Sec: Mrs Herman Ernstein; Hon Trustees: Mrs Jerome M. Kobacker, Mrs Goodman Liber, Norman R. Thal Sr. **2735 Darlington Rd, Toledo OH 43606 (419) 531–4465.**

Temple B'nai Israel. Affiliated with United Syn of Am. Rabbi Dr Fishel A. Pearlmutter; Cantor Israel J. Barzak; Pres: Richard F. Bernstein; Exec Dir: Howard J. Moskowitz PhD. **2727 Kenwood Blvd, Toledo OH 43606 (419) 531–1677.**

Temple B'nai Israel, Michael Lichtenstein Memorial Library. For information on the Temple see – Temple B'nai Israel, Toledo, OH. **2727 Kenwood Blvd, Toledo OH 43606 (419) 531–1677.**

Toledo Jewish News. Periodical pub. F 1951. Monthly. Pub under the Jewish Welfare Federation. **2506 Evergreen St, Toledo OH 43606.**

Twinsburg

Temple Beth Shalom. Affiliated with UAHC. 46 mems. Pres: Charles Newman. **PO Box 315, Twinsburg OH 44087.**

University Heights

Jewish Vocational Service. Helps people prepare resumes; coaches people on how to be effective during an interview; suggests methods for making a positive search; advises people of employment opportunities; works closely with those in the process of career changes; works closely with stu to provide financial aid information & resources, as well as helping them to obtain paid employment; works with the stu to help choose appropriate cols or guide them to alternative non-traditional schs or progs; deals with people who are coming into the job market, but are unclear what their goals are or even how to go about searching for employment; helps immigrants assess their skills & teaches them how to market these skills in the economy. F in 1939 & has served as the focal point in working with J & non-J to help them in all facets of improving themselves in the job market. Pres: David Goldberg; VPs: Nina Gibans, Alan S. Sims; Sec: Dr Carol Kleiner Willen; Treas: Richard Rivitz; Asst Treas: Vivian Solganik; Bd of Trustees: Howard Abrams, Marshall Bedol, Dr Art Blum, Robert Bogolmony, Dr Dan Butler, Bruce B. Felder, Lawrence Friedman, Jean Heflick, Lawrence Katz, Sheldon S. Mann, Arthur Mayers, Michael Peterman, Richard Phillips, Dr Jeffrey Ponsky, Charles Rosenberg, Bernard Rutman, Rhoda Shapiro, Robert Silverman, William Stern, Morry Weiss, June Weiner, Dr Ralph Wolpaw, Kenneth Zeisler; Hon Life Trustee: Miriam S. Klein; Hon Bd Mem: Meyer Sarkin; Exec Dir: Allan Bellin. **13878 Cedar Rd, University Heights OH 44118 (216) 321–1381.**

Warren

Beth Israel Temple Center. Affiliated with United Syn of Am. Rabbi Michael Stevens; Pres: Dr Bernard Schultz. **2138 E Market St, Warren OH 44483 (216) 395–3877.**

Jewish Federation. 3893 E Market St, Warren OH 44483.

Wickliffe

Rabbinical College of Telshe, Inc. 28400 Euclid Ave, Wickliffe OH 44092 (216) 943–5300.

Worthington

Congregation Beth Tikva. Affiliated with UAHC. 165 mems. Rabbi Anthony D. Holz; Pres: Gilbert Nestel. **6121 Olentangy River Rd, Worthington OH 43085 (614) 885–6286.**

Youngstown

Congregation Rodef Sholom. Affiliated with UAHC. 760 mems. Rabbi Sidney M. Berkowitz; Cantor Lawrence Ehrlich; Pres: Nathan Monus; Sisterhood Pres: Gay S. Birnbaum; Brotherhood Pres: Sanford Schwaber. **Elm & Woodbine Sts, Youngstown OH 44505 (216) 744–5001.**

Jewish Community Center. 505 Gypsy Lane, Youngstown OH 44505 (216) 746–2351.

Jewish Community Center, Schwartz Judaic Library. 505 Gypsy Lane, Youngstown OH 44505 (216) 746–2351.

Ohev Tzedek – Shaarei Torah. Affiliated with United Syn of Am. Rabbi Mitchell H. Kornspan; Pres: Morton H. Sands. **5245 Glenwood Ave, Youngstown OH 44512 (216) 758–2321.**

Temple El Emeth. Affiliated with United Syn of Am. Rabbi Samuel Meyer; Cantor David Axelrad; Pres: Sam D. Roth. **Fifth & Fairgreen, Youngstown OH 44515 (216) 744–5055.**

Youngstown Area Jewish Federation. Mem of CJF. Organized 1935. Pres: Bertram Tamarkin; Exec Dir: Stanley Engel. **PO Box 449, Youngstown OH 44501 (216) 746–3251.**

Youngstown Jewish Times. Periodical pub. **PO Box 777, Youngstown OH 44501 (216) 746–6192.**

Zanesville

Congregation Beth Abraham. Affiliated with United Syn of Am. Rabbi Avrim Hartstein; Pres: Arthur Rogovin. **1740 Blue Ave, Zanesville OH 43701 (614) 453–5391.**

OKLAHOMA

Ardmore

Jewish Federation. 23 B St SW, Ardmore OK 73401.

Temple Emeth. Affiliated with UAHC. 23 mems. Pres: Walter Neustadt Jr; Sisterhood Pres: L. Isenberg. **421 Stanley, Ardmore OK 73401 (405) 223–3064.**

Muskogee

Temple Beth Ahaba. Affiliated with UAHC. 15 mems. Pres: Fanny Lu Yaffe. **c/o Mrs Fanny Lu Yaffe, 4131 S Robb, Muskogee OK 74401 (918) 682–1432.**

Oklahoma City

Emanuel Synagogue. Affiliated with United Syn of Am. Rabbi David Maharam; Pres: Robert Wasserman; Edu & Youth Dir: Mark Goodfriend. **900 NW 47th St, Oklahoma City OK 73118 (405) 528–2113.**

The Oklahoma City Jewish Community Council. A planning & coordinating agy serving Greater OK city residents of the J faith for philanthropic, social, cultural & edu advancement of the J com, & to foster cooperation with civic, social serv, governmental & rel groups in the com. To strengthen relations with all groups to benefit the entire com. Maintains a calendar of J com activities; maintains a reference library of bks, periodicals, magazines on various aspects of J life in Am; assists in relocations of persons of J faith in cooperation with non-sectarian local agy; acts as referral agy for chil placement & of aged in Oklahoma City & surrounding coms; provides social & cultural activities for single adults, adults & sr citizens. Area served: primarily Greater Oklahoma City with casework extended to surrounding small coms. Servs also rendered to J persons in ins outside OK City. Eligibility is primarily for J, but servs often rendered to other mems of the com in referrals to natl J hosps for treatment. Organized in Apr of 1943. Pres: Maynard Greenberg; 1st VP: Dr Joel W. Corn; 2nd VP: Robert Greenberg; 3rd VP: Dr Carl Rubenstein; Sec: Mrs Richard Shifrin; Treas: Mrs Milton Schonwald; Exec Dir: Earnest Siegel; Bd of Dirs: Mrs Donald Bloustine, Mrs Robert Bravo, Albert Cohen, Charles Fagin, Mrs Steve Fineberg, Richard Fleischaker, Mrs Alan Gold, Dr Richard Goldstein, Mrs Irwin Green, Robert Heiman, Alfred Karchmer, Rabbi David Maharam, Mrs E. L. Merlin, Dr Allan Metz, Royal Miller, Don Nevard, Dr Sam Oleinick, Rabbi David Packman, Mrs Carl Rubenstein, David Schneider, Mrs Ben Shanker, Marcel Silberman, Joseph B. Singer, Mrs Joseph L. Singer, Mrs Robert Wasserman, Blake Yaffe. **11032 Quail Creek Rd 201, Oklahoma City OK 73120 (405) 755–6030.**

Southwest Jewish Chronicle. Periodical pub. **324 N Robinson St, Suite 313, Oklahoma City OK 73102 (405) 236–4226.**

Temple B'nai Israel. Affiliated with UAHC. 405 mems. Rabbis: A.D. Packman, Joseph Levenson; Pres: Morris Blumenthal; Edu: Yona Z. Lahav; Sisterhood Pres: Barbara Wernick; Brotherhood Pres: David Schneider. **4901 N Pennsylvania Ave, Oklahoma City OK 73112 (405) 848–0965.**

Ponca City

Temple Emanuel. Affiliated with UAHC. 21 mems. Pres: Sophye Locke; Edu: Martin Felsenthal. **PO Box 1081, Ponca City OK 74601 (405) 765–5898.**

Tulsa

Congregation B'nai Emunah. Affiliated with United Syn of Am. Rabbi Arthur D Kahn; Pres: Dr Marcel Binstock; Edu & Youth Dir: Yehuda Biran. **1719 S Owasso Ave, PO Box 52430, Tulsa OK 74152 (918) 583–7121.**

Jewish Federation of Tulsa. Mem of CJF. Sponsors United Jewish Campaign. Organized 1938. Pres: Howard Raskin; Exec Dir: Nathan Loshak. **2021 E 71st St, Tulsa OK 74136 (918) 495–1100.**

Temple Israel. Affiliated with UAHC. 526 mems. Rabbis: Charles P. Sherman, Norbert L. Rosenthal; Cantor Harry Se Pres: Herbert Miller; Edu: Nachama S. Moskowitz; Sisterhood Pres: Darlene Rudner; Brotherhoo Pres: Al Tilkin. **2004 E 22nd Pl, Tulsa OK 74114 (918) 747–1309.**

Temple Israel, Jay Allan Myers Memorial Libra For information on the Temple, see – Temple Israel, Tulsa, OK. **2004 E 22nd Pl, Tulsa OK 74114 (918) 747–1309.**

OREGON

Eugene

Hillel Campus Interfaith Ministry at the University of Oregon. To foster a deeper & wider identity & identification of its constituency to Judaism & J causes. Weekly Outreach – information table at the Stu Union; celebrations of all holidays; Kiddushim & dinners; Heb & J courses; interfaith activities with campus interfaith minorities; Rosh Hodesh monthly gathering for women; counseling. Est Sept 1, 1980. Dir: Alice Haya Kinberg; Pres J Stu Union: Bob Gittelson; AZYF Rep: Paul Barish; Programming: Terry Steinberg; Hillel Rep Fundraiser: Joeann Furie. **Koinonia Ctr, 1414 Kincaid St, Eugene OR 97401 (503) 484–1707.**

Temple Beth Israel. Affiliated with United Syn of Am. Rabbi Myron Kinberg; Cantor Yitzhak Hankin; Pres: Thomas G. Barkin; Exec Dir: Nancy Higgins. **2550 Portland St, Eugene OR 97401 (503) 485–7218.**

Medford

Rogue Valley Jewish Community Congregation. Affiliated with UAHC. 60 mems. Pres: Charlotte Osborne. **PO Box 1094, Medford OR 97501 (503) 779–7648.**

Portland

Congregation Neveh Shalom. Conservative Syn affiliated with United Syn of Am. To provide an environment for J observance & learning within the framework of the Conservative movement. Rel Servs; edu & social progs; Pre-sch; Rel Sch; Adult Edu; youth activities; Lecture & Bk Review Series; young mems progs; library. In 1869 Cong Ahavai Shalom was f as the first Conservative cong in the Pacific NW. Cong Neveh Zadek was f in 1895. The two merged to become Neveh Shalom in 1961. Rabbi Joshua Stamfer; Cantor Marc Dinkin; Mems Dir: Sylvia Pearlman; Presch Dir: Leah Rubin; Prog Dir: Sandy Fields; Pres: Richard Brownstein. **2900 SW Peaceful Lane, Portland OR 97201 (503) 246–8831.**

Congregation Neveh Shalom, Feldstein Library. For information on the Cong, see – Congregation Neveh Shalom, Portland, OR. **2900 SW Peaceful Lane, Portland OR 97201 (503) 246–8831.**

Havurah Shalom. Affiliated with UAHC. 56 mems. Rabbi Roy Furman; Pres: Joan Rosenbaum. **8085 SW Ridgeway Dr, Portland OR 97225.**

Jewish Education Association. Constituent agy of the J Welfare Fed of Portland; affiliated with the Am Assn for J Edu. To provide a Heb edu for J boys & girls in Portland. Pres: Naomi Samuels; VP: Ivan B. Inger; Sec: Sandra Bennet; Treas: Rodney T. Cox; Dir: Ceal Ettinger. **6651 SW Capitol Highway, Portland OR 97219 (503) 244–0126.**

Jewish Federation of Portland. Mem of CJF. Includes State of OR & adjacent WA coms. Organized 1920; reorganized 1956. Pres: Jonathan Newman; Exec Dir: David Roberts. **4850 SW Scholls Ferry Rd, Suite 304, Portland OR 97225 (503) 297–8104.**

Temple Beth Israel. Affiliated with UAHC. 914 mems. Rabbis: Emanuel Rose, Alan L. Berg; Cantor Judith B. Schiff; Pres: Bernardine Brenner; Edu: Rachel Tal; Adm: Joy Alkalay; Sisterhood Pres: Sally Vidgoff; Brotherhood Pres: Richard L. Garfinkle. **1931 NW Flanders St, Portland OR 97209 (503) 222–1069.**

Salem

Salem Jewish Congregation – Temple Beth Sholom. Rel Servs; Sun Heb Sch. 75 families. The Salem Aid Soc was formed in 1930. In 1934 it was reorganized as the Salem J Cong, with the principle purpose of 'Jewish aid of this city'. A hall was rented for the Cong's activities. A Sun Sch was begun in 1935 & in the following yr the Cong began holding weekly Servs. In 1940, the Cong formally inc & acquired the land on which its syn now stands. Several J orgs are affiliated with the Cong & use its facilities. Servs follow a Conservative format. Pres: Ronald G. Rubel; VP: Gilbert B. Feibleman; Sec: Raymond L. Robert; Treas: Dr Martin J. Mehr; B'nai B'rith Women Rep: Alice Gruber; Trustees: Tedd Linn, Sid Schain, Esther Baruch, Martin Rosenberg, Millie Estrin. **1795 Broadway NE, Salem OR; mailing add: PO Box 102, Salem OR 97308.**

PENNSYLVANIA

Abington

Old York Road Temple Beth Am. Reform Cong affiliated with the UAHC. Rel Servs; Rel Sch; Adult Edu; library; rel, edu & social activities; Sisterhood; Brotherhood. 675 families; 650 chil in the Rel Sch. The Temple was started as the Old York Rd JCC in 1946 by a small group of people in Willow Grove. In 1950 the present bldg was purchased & the name was changed to Old York Rd Temple. In 1951 the first full time rabbi joined the Cong. Soon after, the chapel, ark & pulpit were dedicated. Rabbi Harold B. Waintrup; Cantor Jodi Sufrin; Exec Dir: Marcia Goldman; Sch Prin: Arthur Beyer; Music Dir: Ronald Nelson; Pres: Michael Krassenstein; Exec VP: Joseph G. Rosenfeld; VP Ways & Means: Michael Slobodien; VP Rel: Elaine Fox; VP Edu: Mark Elfont; VP Mems: Jan Black; VP Com Affairs: Sandra Gold; Treas: Marvin Levin; Fin Sec: Stanley Schneiderman; Sec House & Grounds: Donald Dafilou; Legal Counselor: Eugene M. Schloss Jr; Sisterhood Pres: Dena Richman; Brotherhood Pres: Gerald Sapers; Parents Assn Pres: Libby Pearlman; Chavarim Pres: Sheila Honer. **971 Old York Rd, Abington PA 19001 (215) 886–8000.**

Old York Road Temple Beth Am Library. For information on the Temple, see – Old York Road Temple, Abington, PA. **971 Old York Rd, Abington PA 19001 (215) 886–8000.**

Solomon Schechter Day School of Philadelphia. Affiliated with Solomon Schechter Day Schs Assn. Prin: Dr Steven Brown; Chr: Betsy Cohen. **971 Old York Rd, Abington PA 19001 (215) 886–2355.**

Allentown

Congregation Keneseth Israel. Affiliated with UAHC. 442 mems. Rabbi Herbert Brockman; Cantor Geroge A. Mason; Pres: Alan H. Schragger; Edu: Jeanette Eichenwald; Adm: Judith A. Murman; Sisterhood Pres: Sheila Saunders; Brotherhood Pres: Jeffrey Bindell. **2227 Chew St, Allentown PA 18104 (215) 435–9074.**

Congregation Keneseth Israel Library. For information on the Cong, see – Congregation Keneseth Israel, Allentown, PA. **2227 Chew St, Allentown PA 18104 (215) 435–9074.**

Jewish Federation of Allentown, Inc. Mem of CJF. Organized & inc 1948. Pres: Fred Sussman; Exec Dir: Ivan C. Schonfeld. **702 N 22nd St, Allentown PA 18104 (215) 435–3571.**

Temple Beth El. Affiliated with United Syn of Am. Rabbi P. Michael Meyerstein; Cantor Joseph Bach; Pres: Michael Prokup; Exec Dir: Ben Tanback. **17th & Hamilton Sts, Allentown PA 18104 (215) 435–3521.**

Altoona

Agudath Achim Synagogue. Affiliated with United Syn of Am. Rabbi M. Herbert Berger; Pres: Yale Schulman. **1306 17th St, Altoona PA 16601 (814) 944–5317.**

Federation of Jewish Philanthropies. Mem of CJF. Organized 1920; reorganized 1940. Pres: Donald Devorris. **1308 17th St, Altoona PA 16601 (814) 944–4072.**

Temple Beth Israel. Reform Cong affiliated with UAHC. Weekly Sabbath Worship Servs; holiday observances; chil edu progs; adult edu progs. 125 families. F in 1874. Rabbi Gary M. Klein; Rabbi Emeritus Dr Nathan Kaber; Pres: Michael Kranich; 1st VP: Alan Krier; 2nd VP: Jules Patt; Sec: Charlotte Morris; Treas: Louis Miller; Sisterhood Pres: Pam Patt; Cemetery Chr: Harold Rosend. **3004 Union Ave, Altoona PA 16602 (814) 942–0057.**

Ambridge

Beth Samuel Jewish Center. Affiliated with United Syn of Am. Rabbi Martin Sofer; Pres: David L. Chamovitz; Edu Dir: Marcia Chamovitz. **PO Box 219, 810 Kennedy Dr, Ambridge PA 15003 (412) 266–9871.**

Beaver Falls

Agudath Achim Congregation. Affiliated with United Syn of Am. Rabbi David G. Shapiro; Pres: Isador Soodek. **PO Box 293, Beaver Falls PA 15010 (412) 846–5696.**

Beth Sholom Congregation. Affiliated with UAHC. 18 mems. Pres: Max Trobe; Sisterhood Pres: Brenda Siegel. **c/o Mrs L. Goldstein, 1409 8th Ave, Beaver Falls PA 15010 (412) 846–0068.**

Bensalem

Congregation Tifereth Israel of Lower Bucks County. Affiliated with United Syn of Am. Rabbi Gerson Schwartz; Pres: Arline Ravitch. **2909 Bristol Rd, Bensalem PA 19020 (215) 752–3468.**

Bethlehem

Brith Sholom Community Center. Affiliated with United Syn of Am. Rabbi Alan Juda; Cantor & Exec Dir: David Green; Pres: Dr Joseph Goldstein. **PO Box 5323, Brodhead & Packer Ave, Bethlehem PA 18015 (215) 866–8000,9.**

Bloomsburg

Beth Israel Congregation. To get the J population involved in preserving the J heritage. Talmud Torah which meets Sun mornings & evenings for chil ages six through twelve; Fri Evening Servs on the first Fri of each mo. The Syn has a relationship with Ohev Shalom Cong in Berwick, whereby the Syn hosts Rosh Hashanhah & Yom Kippur Servs on alternating yrs. 20 families. Est in the mid 1930's. Pres: Martin Satz; Treas: Louis Doublestein; Sec: Leonard I. Comerchero. **144 E 4th St, Bloomsburg PA 17815 (717) 784–5778.**

Bradford

Temple Beth El. Affiliated with UAHC. 76 mems. Rabbi Joshua Marenof; Pres: Joseph Brauser; Edu: Dan Lohr. **PO Box 538, 111 Jackson Ave, Bradford PA 16701 (814) 368–8204.**

Broomall

Congregation Beth El Suburban. Affiliated with United Syn of Am. Rabbi Samuel K. Wohlgelernter; Cantor Morris Diamond; Pres: Harold C. Sampson; Edu Dir: Michael A. Shore. **715 Paxon Hollow Rd, Broomall PA 19008 (215) 246–8700.**

Temple Sholom. Affiliated with UAHC. 300 mems. Rabbi Mayer Selekman; Cantor Sandy Gold; Pres: Stan Shapiro; Edu: Neal Kahn; Adm: Norman Sassler; Sisterhood Pres: Saralee Braun; Brotherhood Pres: Ed Kresch. **55 N Church Rd, Broomall PA 19008 (215) 356–5165.**

Butler

B'nai Abraham. Affiliated with United Syn of Am. Rabbi Eliezer Ben-Yehuda; Pres: Bernard Levin. **519 N Main St, Butler PA 16001 (412) 287–5806.**

Butler Jewish Welfare Fund. 148 Haverford Dr, Butler PA 16001 (412) 287–3814.

Carnegie

Ahavath Achim. Affiliated with United Syn of Am. Pres: Harris Tisherman. **Lydia & Chestnut Sts, Carnegie PA 15106 (412) 276–9777.**

Chambersburg

Congregation Sons of Israel. Conservative Syn affiliated with the United Syn of Am. To foster, teach & perpetuate the J rel. Rel Servs; Rel Sch; Sisterhood; ctr for rel & J activities. Chartered in 1919 as the first & only syn in Franklin Cty. On May 30, 1919, the Cong purchased its first facility. The present site was acquired in 1939. The first full time rabbi was engaged in 1940. In the same yr, a Mennonite resident of Chambersburg made & installed the present Ark which is hand-made without the benefit of a single machine tool. Until 1946 there was no formal rel sch; rel instruction was given by the rabbi. A formal full time Heb & Sun sch was organized in 1946 by Rev Cantor Samuel Tobey. Rabbi Robert Chernoff; Pres: Barret Silver; VPs:Jeffery Brener, Stephen Andrews; Sec: Robert Radbill; Treas: Alex Dessel; Sisterhood Pres: Mrs Ronnie Bornstein. **King & Second Sts, Chambersburg PA 17201 (717) 264–2915.**

Cheltenham

Congregation Melrose B'nai Israel. Conservative Cong affiliated with United Syn of Am. Rel Servs (adult & youth); edu progs (Sun Sch, Heb

Sch, Adult Edu); Sisterhood; Men's Club; Adult Bat Mitzvah classes; Rosh Chodesh class for women; library (hist, fiction, J & Heb content). 300 mems; 45 stu – primary to 5th grades. 10 employees. F 1967; formerly B'nai Israel of Olney. Pub The Shofar (monthly). Facilities include kosher kitchen, sanctuary, gift shop, smaller chapel, classrms, 2 offs (sch & syn). Rabbi Isaac Moseson (Prin); Cantor Joshua Gordon; Pres: J. Robert Klein; VPs: Joseph Pressman, Seymour Kasinetz, Edythe Kaplan; Treas: Harry Cylinder; Fin Sec: Len Cohen. **2nd St at Cheltenham Ave, Cheltenham PA 19012.**

Coatesville

Beth Israel Congregation. Conservative Syn affiliated with United Syn of Am. Rel Servs; Women's League; USY & Kadima youth groups; Sun Sch; Heb Sch; Confirmation Class; Adult Studies. 125 families. Est in 1916; the current bldg was opened in 1924. The Syn is the only cong in Coatesville & serves the entire Coatesville J com. The syn houses Hadassah & B'nai B'rith chapters. Rabbi Linda Holtzman; Pres: Melvyn Goldstein; VP: David Cohen; Treas: Richard Kramer; Sec: Florence Goldfine; Fin Sec: Elizabeth Endy. **Fifth Ave & Harmony Sts, Coatesville PA 19320 (215) 384–1978.**

Coraopolis

Ahavath Sholom Temple. Affiliated with UAHC. 38 mems. Pres: M/M Mack Yogman. **Fleming St & Vance Ave, Coraopolis PA 15108 (412) 264–4100.**

Doylestown

Temple Judea of Bucks County. Affiliated with UAHC. 107 mems. Rabbi Morton M. Rosenthal; Pres: George Lowenstein; Edu: Keith Kessler. **Swamp Rd, PO Box 215, Doylestown PA 18901 (215) 348–5022.**

Dresher

Temple Sinai. Affiliated with United Syn of Am. Rabbi Sidney Greenberg; Cantor Nathan Chaitousky; Pres: Seymour Saslow; Exec Dir: Harvey L Brown; Edu & Youth Dir: Faith Rubin. **Limekiln Pike & Dillon Rd, Dresher PA 19025 (215) 643–6510.**

Eagleville

Eagleville Hospital & Rehabilitation Center. Main on-campus prog is a 126 bed hosp offering a short term drug free prog for men & women; Off-campus progs include: Outpatient Serv which provides comprehensive clin servs & individualized treatment progs for individuals & families with drug or alcohol problems; Family & Youth Progs including Lincoln Sch which is an alternative edu prog administered in cooperation with the Norristown Area Sch Dist, Family Resource Ctr which strengthens family relationships through parenting edu & through individual & family therapy, Com Edu & Prevention Servs which provide prevention & intervention (with parents, teachers, stu & com groups in Montgomery Cty), & Vocational Edu & Rehabilitation Servs providing adult basic edu & preparation for employment, Family House which provides a home for recovering alcohol & drug dependent women & their chil, Post Residential Treatment Facilities which provide facilities for Eagleville clients completing the Candidate Prog who need traditional living as they return to look for work, & resume their normal course of life. Eagleville as a health servs ins was f in 1909 when a few families fr the J com in Phila raised funds to create a tuberculosis sanatorium. The need for Eagleville's tuberculosis beds diminshed in the mid 1960's when the natl epidemic of tuberculosis was coming under control. The idea of alcoholism as a field of work was introduced. Eagleville opened in its new mission in Jul 1966. Within a couple of yrs, the agenda of the Hosp was broadened to include drug addiction & drug abuse. Over the course of several yrs, out patient facilities, halfway houses, transitional progs, & a variety of special progs & com based servs were created. Many of its progs were honored by being used as models throughout the country. One of Eagleville's unique contributions was to take a generic approach to the problems of substance abuse by finding the common elements in alcoholism, heroin addiction & other substance abuse problems. Eagleville has also gained respect as a training ctr. Pres Bd of Dirs: Jonathan A. Kane; Exec Dir: Dr Donald J. Ottenberg; Med Dir: Dr William S. Allerton; Dir Adm Servs: Albert P. Black; Dir Fiscal Affairs & Dev: J. Kevin Fee. **100 Eagleville Rd, PO Box 45, Eagleville PA 19408 (215) 539–6000.**

East Stroudsburg

Temple Israel. Affiliated with United Syn of Am. Rabbi Steven Westman; Pres: Arthur Jolley. **PO Box 368, 660 Wallace St, East Stroudburg PA 18360 (717) 421–8781.**

Easton

Bnai Abraham Synagogue. Conservative Syn affiliated with United Syn of Am. To serve the J edu, rel, cultural & social needs of membership. Rel Servs; rel edu for all age levels (presch – adult); Sr Citizens Group; Sisterhood; USY youth prog; nursery prog; library containing 2500 vols (gen Judaica). 260 mem; 60 stu in grades K–5. F 1888; large new facility completed in 1965. Pub B'nai Abraham Bulletin (monthly). Facilities include sanctuary seating 210 (expandable to 550). auditorium, nursery sch, kosher kitchen, library, gift shop, chapel, class rms, offs. Rabbi Jonathan A. Schnitzer; Cantor Morris Siegel; Pres: Seymour Jacowitz. **16th & Bushkill Sts, Easton PA 18042 (215) 258–5343.**

Bnai Abraham Synagogue, Library. Library contains 2500+ vols (gen Judaica). For information on the Syn, see – Bnai Abraham Synagogue, Easton, PA. **16th & Bushkill Sts, Easton PA 18042 (215) 258–5343.**

Jewish Community Council of Easton, Pennsylvania and Vicinity. 16th & Bushkill Sts, Easton PA 18042 (215) 253–4235.

Temple Covenant of Peace. Reform Temple affiliated with UAHC. Sisterhood; Temple Youth Group. 195 mems (125 families, 70 individuals); 50 stu; hosp with 389 beds; 22 bassinets; annual outpatient visits 100,000; 12 sr citizen residents. 3 employees. F 1839. Pub Temple Bulletin (monthly). Facilities include sanctuary seating 150 (expandable to 600 seats), social hall, gift shop. Rabbi Jerald Bobrow; Pres: Dr David H. Feinberg; VP: Dr Robert Stein. **1451 Northampton St, Easton PA 18042 (215) 253–2031.**

Elkins Park

Beth Jacob Schools of Philadelphia. Accredited by Torah Umesorah Natl Soc for Hebrew Day Schs, PA Dept of Private Edu; mem of the Col Bd. To provide a thorough & meaningful elementary edu to J girls & boys, & an academic, religiously inspiring secondary edu. Early childhood edu – using a multi sensory language experience approach; elementary schs – full Judaic & gen studies, highly individualized classes, extra curricular activities, Sun progs & sports, remedial prog; Girls HS Div – full academic col prep prog, stu govt, com serv progs, dramatic productions & other com oriented activities; Boys Hs Div – full academic col prep prog, sports prog, mishmor & beth hamidrash prog; summer camping – many outdoor sports prog, indoor gym prog, arcade video games, pool; library containing 4000 vols (gen, ref & Judaica). 170 families; 90 stu in Presch; 200 stu grades 1–8; 70 in girls' HS; 45 in boys' HS. 75 employees. F 1945; accredited 1950; moved to present 10 acre campus in 1975. Pub curriculum guides (bi-annually); Hamitzpeh Bulletins (bi-monthly); Parentogram Bulletins (bi-weekly). Facilities include early childhood ctr; 4 classrms; offs; gym; dining rm; elementary sch – 26 classrms, 900 seat auditorium, 2 gymnasia, library; HS – 10 classrms, computer ctr, offs, Beth Midrash Sanctuary seating 200, lab; main gym – full basketball ct, locker & shower rms, wrestling rms, 600 seat bleechers. Pres: Rabbi Abraham Shemtoy; Dean: Rabbi Nochem Kaplan; V Prin: Dr Gladys Morse; Exec Dir: Lawrence Caroline. **Montgomery Ave at High Sch Rd, Elkins Park PA 19117 (215) ME5–6805.**

Beth Jacob Schools of Philadelphia – Learning Resource Center. Full time co-ed Heb day sch setting for mildly learning disabled chil ages 7–12. Easy flexibility or mainstreaming into regular classes. All bicultural edu needs met in one location; full time licensed counselor. Dir: Rabbi Jacob Schwab. **High Sch Rd & Montgomery Ave, Elkins Park PA 19117 (215) 635–6805.**

Beth Jacob Schools of Philadelphia, Library. Library contains 4000 vols (gen, reference & Judaica). For information on the Schs, see – Beth Jacob Schools of Philadelphia, Elkins Park, PA. **Montgomery Ave at High Sch Rd, Elkins Park PA 19117 (215) ME5–6805.**

Beth Sholom Congregation. Affiliated with United Syn of Am. Rabbi Aaron Landes; Cantor David F. Tilman; Pres: Samuel Spielman; Exec Dir: Stanley Cluck; Edu & Youth Dir: Saundra Sterling Epstein. **Old York & Foxcroft Rds, Elkins Park PA 19117 (215) 887–3625.**

Beth Sholom Congregation, Joseph & Elizabeth Schwartz Library. For information on the Cong, see – Beth Sholom Congregation, Elkins Park, PA. **Foxcroft & Old York Rds, Elkins Park PA 19117 (215) 887–3625.**

Congregation Adath Jeshurun. Affiliated with United Syn of Am. Rabbi Seymour Rosenbloom; Cantor Charles Davidson; Pres: William Karsif; Exec Dir: Lewis Coren; Edu Dir: Rabbi Arthur Ruberg; Youth Dir: Robert Russock. **York & Ashbourne Rds, Elkins Park PA 19117 (215) 635–6611.**

Congregation Adath Jeshurun, Gottlieb Memorial Library. For information on the Cong, see – Congregation Adath Jeshurun, Elkins Park, PA. **York & Ashbourne Rds, Elkins Park PA 19117 (215) 635–6611.**

Congregation Keneseth Israel. Reform Cong affiliated with UAHC. All usual syn servs & activities; Rel Sch for retarded; Cong of the Deaf; weekly FM radio Sabbath Serv; Temple Judea Mus; library containing 15,000 vols. 1600 mems; 620 chil in grades K–12. 50 employees. F 1847. Pub Bulletin (tri-weekly). Facilities include sanctuary seating 900 (expandable to 2,400); chapel seating 200; basketball, gift shop, Sr Rabbi Simeon J. Maslin; Assc Rabbi Steven M. Fink; Cantor & Music Dir: Richard Allen; Pres: Michael M. Goldberg; VPs: Jan E. DuBois, Miriam Finkel, Dr I. Ezra Staples; Sec: Connie Kay; Assc Sec: Steven J. Serling; Treas: Norman J. Brody; Assc Treas: Howard Sichel; Dir of Rel Edu: Rabbi Ruth N. Sandberg; Exec Adm: William Ferstenfeld. **York Rd & Township Line, Elkins Park PA 19117 (215) 887–8700.**

Congregation Keneseth Israel Library. Library contains 1,500 vols. For information on the Cong, see – Congregation Keneseth Israel, Elkins Park, PA. **York Rd & Township Line, Elkins Park PA 19117 (215) 887–8700.**

Forman Hebrew Day School. Affiliated with Solomon Schechter Day Schs Assn. Prin: Sora Landes; Chr: William Forman. **Old York & Foxcroft Rds, Elkins Park PA 19117 (215) 887–6981.**

Rodelph Shalom. To provide J identification, opportunities for worship experience, holiday observances. Classes for hearing impaired chil who are of pre–Bat/Bar Mitzvah age on Sun. Reform cong sch open to any chil in J com. Prog leads to Bar or Bat Mitzvah ceremonies for those families who desire them. Edu Dir: Rabbi Patrice E. Heller. **8201 High Sch Rd, Elkins Park PA 19117 (215) CA4–1010, 627–6747.**

Ellwood City

Tree of Life Congregation. Affiliated with United Syn of Am. Pres: Herman Feldman; Exec Dir: Dr Peter Roff. **Beatty St, Ellwood City PA 16617 (412) 758–7329.**

Erdenheim

Beth Tikvah – B'nai Jeshurun. Conservative Syn affiliated with United Syn of Am. To dev in ourselves responsibility for the righteous use of the blessings with which God has endowed us; to be ethical & moral people of our world; to live up to traditional J standards of virtue & piety both in our home & in our dealings with others; to encourage our chil to further their moral & spiritual growth & to accept with joy their heritage as J; to worship God in sincerity & truth; to support J as a potent influence for truth, justice, freedom & tranquility among nations; to be able to express our rel traditions in terms of understandable experience relevant to our present day needs. Nursery prog for ages 2 through 4; Heb Sch; Adult Edu prog; USY Youth Group; Sisterhood; Men's Club; Young Adults group; dances; art shows; fashion shows; Shabbat retreats; Sun brunches; Sat lunches; Daily, Shabbat, & Holiday Servs; Oneg Shabbat refreshments following Servs. 300 families. Beth Tikvah-B'nai Jeshurun has been serving the J com in Phila NW suburbs since 1956. The merged cong was formed in 1974 by the union of Beth Tikvah in Erdenheim & B'nai Jeshurun of Mount Airy, the successor to B'nai Jeshurun of Strawberry Mansion. Syn library contains over 5,000 vols of J interest. There is a yearly production of a Broadway show put on by Syn mems. Rabbi Robert Layman; Cantor Bernard Walters; Edu Dir: David Kaye; Pres: Aron Hoffman Exec VP: Fred Donaldson; VPs: Gerald Bleiman, Shirley Cohn; Fin Sec: Miriam Hirsch; Corsp Sec: Sandra Dresser; Rec Sec: Lee Waters; Treas: Milton Stander. **1001 Paper Mill Rd, Erdenheim PA 19118 (215) 836–5677; 242–0512.**

Erie

Congregation Brith Sholom. Affiliated with United Syn of Am. Rabbi Leo Heim; Cantor Morris Markowitz; Pres: I. Michael Brown. **3207 State St, Erie PA 16508 (814) 454–2431.**

Jewish Community Council of Erie. Mem of CJF. Organized 1946. Pres: Bobbi Pollock. **701 G Daniel Baldwin Bldg, 1001 State St, Erie PA 16501 (814) 455–4474.**

Temple Anshe Hesed. Reform Cong affiliated with the UAHC. To further the ideals of J through liberal interpretation. A full gamut of congregational activities; library. 252 mems. In 1855 there were enough J settlers residing in Erie to form the first rel org. This org was called The Anshe Hesed Soc. The Soc was inc in 1862. The Soc had no rabbi until 1861. The Cong held servs in rented halls until a syn was purchased, but it was soon resold. The Cong had the dilemma in common with most J congs – the conservative element opposed the Reform movement & the progressive element was attracted by it. The Cong aligned itself with the Reform movement with the org of the Anshe Hesed Reform Cong in 1875. In 1882 the cornerstone for a new temple was laid. In 1884 the temple was completed & dedicated. Due to its need for space, the temple had many remodelings & in 1924 a plan was adopted to form a cttee to report on a site for a new temple. A lot was chosen. Several adjustments were made in this temple to conform to the needs of a growing cong. The Curruck Memorial was added in 1958 & the beautification of the sanctuary took place in 1970. After careful consideration, it was decided to completely renovate the sanctuary & add a passageway. Rabbi Bradley N. Bleefeld; Pres: Dr James L. Schuster; VPs: Walter Harf, Herbert Rubinfield, Barbara Pollock; Treas: John Pless; Sec: Bonnie Lechtner; Edu Dir: Janice Mandel. **10th & Liberty Sts, Erie PA 16502 (814) 454–2426.**

Temple Anshe Hesed Library. For information on the Temple, see – Temple Anshe Hesed, Erie, PA. **10th & Liberty Sts, Erie PA 16502 (814) 454–2426.**

Feasterville

Congregation Beth Chaim. Jewish Cong affiliated with Yeshiva Univ Syn Council, J Fed of Lower Bucks Cty. To foster the practice of Judaism by the individual, in the home & as a com. Family Servs; Rel Sch; Sisterhood; Men's Club; counseling servs; boy scouts; kosher catering facilities; adult classes; library containing 1,000 vols (Judaica). 375 families; 250 stu in grades Aleph through Confirmation. 25 employees; 550 volunteers. F 1956. Facilities include kosher kitchen, sanctuary seating 800, hall for rent, gift shop, meeting rm & banquet facilities for rent. Rabbi Maurice E. Novoseller; Cantor Marving L. Verbit; Prin: David Dion; Pres: Michael M. Berue; Sisterhood Pres: Marilyn Levin; Men's Club Pres: Edward Gertz. **350 E St, Feasterville PA 19047 (215) 355–3626.**

Greensburg

Congregation Emanu-El Israel. Affiliated with UAHC. 140 mems. Rabbi Barry R. Friedman; Pres: Charlotte Fiedler; Edu: Janet Engelhart; Sisterhood Pres: Virginia Lieberman. **222 N Main St, Greensburg PA 15601 (412) 834–0560.**

Hanover

Hanover Hebrew Congregation. Affiliated with United Syn of Am. Pres: Moris Quint. **179 Second Ave, Hanover PA 17331.**

Harrisburg

Beth El. Affiliated with United Syn of Am. Rabbi Jeffrey A. Wohlberg; Cantor Asher Balalban; Pres: Morton D. Rosen; Edu Dir: Nachum Chasan; Exec Dir: Rhea Gross; Youth Dir: Joel Burcat. **2637 N Front St, Harrisburg PA 17110 (717) 232–0556.**

Chisuk Emuna Congregation. Conservative Cong affiliated with United Syn of Am. The Syn is committed to fostering the furtherance of J tradition & teachings within the J com. Rel Servs 3 times every day of the yr; Youth Group; Brotherhood; Sisterhood; Adult Edu prog. F 1883. Rabbi Asher Ostrin; Cantor Philip Wittlin; Pres: Ormond N. Urie; VPs: Edward Dunietz, J. Yale Gordon; Rec Sec: George Rosen; Fin Sec: Paul Singer; Treas: Harvey Danowitz. **Fifth & Division Sts, Harrisburg, PA 17110. Mailing Add: PO Box 1807, Harrisburg PA 17105 (717) 232–4851.**

Jewish Family Service of Harrisburg. Non-profit multi function private social servs agy affiliated with the Assn of J Family & Chil Agy. To meet the needs of mems of the J com of all ages. Offers counseling servs to help individuals, families & groups cope with crisis & stress. Administers the following progs – Refugee Resettlement Prog: performs tasks such as finding an apt, food, clothing, furniture, language dev, sch for chil, rel exposure, & job dev; kosher Meals-on-Wheels: provides hot kosher meals to the convalescent, elderly & handicapped who are unable to prepare adequate meals for themselves; J Family Life Edu presents the com with a wide range of subjects aimed at enriching family life, expanding personal awareness & averting family problems. Est in 1965 when the Hebrew Ladies Aid Soc of Harrisburg recognized a need for professional servs in the com. In 1973 the United J Com purchased the J Family Servs bldg & servs were expanded. Progs are implemented through coordination between professional staff, the use of psychiatric & psychological & social work consultants, & the dedicated energies of hundreds of com volunteers. Pres: Neil Weber; VP: Burton Morris; Treas: Norman Scher; Sec: Pearl Lehrman; Bd Mems: Etta Abrams, Stephanie Bryan, Ed Dunietz, Frances Goldberg, Florence Melitzer, Barry Nussbaum, Martin Rosenschien, Elliott Singer, Steven Wassner, Charles Wilson; Ex Officio: Rabbi Charles Mintz, Rabbi Asher Ostrin, Rabbi David Silver, Rabbi Jeffrey Wohlberg, Margaret Sherman; Exec Dir: Shirley D. LeBlanc; Staff Workers: Marsha Shapiro, Eva Siegel; Off Mgr: Deanne M. Ifshin. **3332 N 2nd St, Harrisburg PA 17110 (717) 233–1681.**

Reform Temple Ohev Sholom. Affiliated with UAHC. 285 mems. Rabbi Charles D. Mintz; Pres: William L. Kanenson; Edu: Pearl Lehrman; Sisterhood Pres: Phyllis Berman, Pearl Lehrman, Diana Sauertieg; Brotherhood Pres: Martin Binder. **2345 N Front St, Harrisburg PA 17110 (717) 233–6459.**

United Jewish Community of Greater Harrisburg. Mem of CJF. Organized 1933. Pres: S. Robert Grass; Exec Dir: Avrom B. Fox. **100 Vaughn St, Harrisburg PA 17110 (717) 236–9555.**

Havertown

Suburban Jewish Community Center, B'nai Aaron. Affiliated with United Syn of Am. Rabbi Morris V. Dembowitz; Cantor Jacob Goldstein; Pres: Martin Feldman; Exec & Edu Dir: Marvin Zukerman. **560 Mill Rd, Havertown PA 19083 (215) 528–5011.**

Hazelton

Agudas Israel Congregation. Affiliated with United Syn of Am. Pres: Bernard Cury. **Pine & Oak Sts, Hazelton PA 18201 (717) 454–9294.**

Hazleton

Beth Israel Congregation. Affiliated with UAHC. 108 mems. Rabbi Richard L. Klein; Pres: Ernest Scheller Jr; Sisterhood Pres: Janice Bowman; Brotherhood Pres: Herman Stone. **98 N Church St, Hazleton PA 18201 (717) 455–3971.**

Jewish Community Council. Mem of CJF. Organized 1960. Pres: Anthony Coffina. **Laurel & Hemlock Sts, Hazleton PA 18201 (717) 454–3528.**

Honesdale

Congregation Beth Israel. Affiliated with UAHC. 44 mems. Pres: Leonard Weiss; Sisterhood Pres: Paula Roos. **PO Box 311, Honesdale PA 18431 (717) 253–2222.**

Jenkintown

Beth Sholom Congregation. 1300 families; 3000 individuals; 500 stu. Congregational facilities including library & conf rm. **Foxcroft & Old York Rds, Jenkintown PA 19117 (215) WA4–2223.**

Beth Sholom Congregation, Joseph & Elizabeth Schwartz Library. Mem of J Library Assn of Greater DE Valley, Assn of Libraries, Natl Assn of Church & Syn Libraries. To provide bks, records (music) & art to the Cong & its many edu progs. Supplements all progs of major 1300 family cong. Special prog this yr is to exhibit J art on specially built art walls (exhibitions change every 3 weeks). Contains 6000 vols (bks & records of J interest only). 2 employees; 1 volunteer. Facilities include library rm with conf rm attached. Recipient of 1982 award by Natl Assn of Church & Syn Libraries as Outstanding Congregational Library in US. **Foxcroft & Old York Rds, Jenkintown PA 19117 (215) WA4–2223.**

Johnstown

Beth Sholom Congregation. Affiliated with UAHC. 100 mems. Rabbi Rav A. Soloff; Cantor Solomon C. Epstein; Pres: Isadore Glosser; Sisterhood Pres: Ethel Schwartz; Brotherhood Pres: Isadore Glosser, Milton Heyman. **700 Indiana Ave, Johnstown PA 15905 (814) 536–0647.**

Beth Sholom Congregation Library. For information on the Cong, see – Beth Sholom Congregation, Johnstown, PA. **700 Indiana St, Johnstown PA 15905 (814) 536–0647.**

The United Jewish Federation of Johnstown. Cultural progs; UJA & State of Is Bonds campaigns; Endowment Fund; pol activities; financial assistance; progs for local or transient people; stu scholarship awards in PA & in Is; adult edu progs. In 1938 the Johnstown J Com Council was organized for the purpose of conducting various activities, other than rel progs, as a united J com. The Council sponsored such events as lectures, charity drives, & was involved in social activities. In the early 1970's the Council legally changed its form & became known as The United J Fed of Johnstown. Pres: Isadore Glosser; 1st VP: I. Samuel Kaminsky; 2nd VP: Cynthia Friedman; Sec: Linda Engel; Treas: Harvey Supowitz; Fin Sec: Nathan Edelstein; UJA Treas: Lester Goldstein. **1334 Luzerne St Ext, Johnstown PA 15905 (814) 255–1447.**

King of Prussia

Temple Brith Achim. Reform Syn affiliated with UAHC. To est a visible J presence in the King of Prussia area; to offer an excellent J edu to chil & adults; to create a comfortable spiritual atmosphere where Reform J can worship in their own way & can share in the J experience. Rel Servs; Sun Sch; Bar/Bat Mitzvah training; Adult Edu prog. Est as Brotherhood Temple Brith Achim in 1971 when several families got together seeking a unique approach to experiencing their J. The mems of the Cong met in borrowed quarters with a part time rabbi. As more families joined the Cong the facilities became less adequate. A full time rabbi was employed. A syn bldg was completed in 1982. Newsletter. Rabbi Hava L. Pell; Pres: Gail Moyer; 1st VP: Howard Rosenblum; 2nd VP: Evan Komito;

Treas: Ron Drucker; Rec Sec: Judy Salzer. **481 S Gulph Rd, PO Box 268, King of Prussia PA 19406 (215) 337–2222.**

Kingston

Temple B'nai B'rith of Wilkes Barre. Affiliated with UAHC. 225 mems. Rabbi Arnold Shevlin; Pres: Marshall S. Jacobson; Adm: Elizabeth Patton; Sisterhood Pres: Ilene Cheokes. **408 Wyoming Ave, Kingston PA 18704 (717) 287–9606.**

Kunkeltown

UAHC – Harlam Camp Institute. Dir: Arie Gluck. **1, Kunkeltown PA 18058 (717) 629–1390; 117 S 17th St, Phila PA 19103 (215) 563–8726, 8183.**

Lafayette Hill

Congregation Or Ami. Affiliated with UAHC. 322 mems. Rabbi Seymour Prystowsky; Cantor Nathaniel A. Entin; Pres: Maxine Petersohn; Edu: Julian Swiren; Brotherhood Pres: Matthew Bennett. **PO Box 156, 708 Ridge Pike, Lafayette Hill PA 19444 (215) 828–9066.**

Congregation Or Ami Library. For information on the Cong, see – Congregation Or Ami, Lafayette Hill, PA. **PO Box 156, 708 Ridge Pike, Lafayette Hill PA 19444 (215) 828–9066.**

Lancaster

The Lancaster Jewish Community Center. To help every human being fulfill his or her potential; to involve the entire com in the Ctr prog. Nursery Sch; Day Camp; Sr Citizens Org; Physical Edu Progs fr pre-sch through adult; Crafts; Cooking; Dramatics; Conversational Heb; J Hist; Money Investment. Formed on Jan 2, 1944 & located at 219 E King St, Lancaster PA. In Apr 1974 moved to present location; expansion of 2nd floor completed in 1979. Pub Federation Newspaper (monthly). Pres: Dr Jack Fischel; 1st VP: Stanley Berk; 2nd VP: Dr Jules Yavil; Sec: Barry Leibowitz; Treas: Scott Dichter; Exec Dir: Paul L. Speigal. **The Mary Sachs Bldg, 2120 Oregon Pike, Lancaster PA 17601 (717) 569–7352.**

Lancaster Jewish Federation. Mem of CJF. Organized 1928. Pres: David Halperin; Exec Dir: Paul L. Spiegal. **2120 Oregon Pike, Lancaster PA 17601 (717) 569–7352.**

Temple Beth El. Affiliated with United Syn of Am. Rabbi Paul Rosenfeld; Pres: Dr Berel Arrow; Edu Dir: Judith White. **25 N Line St, Lancaster PA 17602 (717) 392–1379.**

Temple Shaarai Shomayim. Affiliated with UAHC. 211 mems. Rabbi David Sofian; Pres: Max Migdon; Edu: David Sofian; Sisterhood Pres: Ellen Steinman. **508 N Duke St, Lancaster PA 17602 (717) 397–5575.**

Langhorne

Jewish Federation of Lower Bucks County. Mem of CJF. Organized 1956; inc 1957. Pres: Dr David Rothstein; Exec Dir: Elliot Gershenson. **One Oxford Valley, Suite 212, Langhorne PA 19047 (215) 757–0250.**

The Woods Schools. Schs for mentally & physically handicapped chil & adults. Ins provides teachers for rel instruction on Sun. Residents attend servs at the Temple once a mo. **Route 213, Langhome PA 19047 (215) 757–3731.**

Lansdale

Congregation Beth Israel. Affiliated with United Syn of Am. Rabbi Jacob Rosner; Pres: Betty London. **1080 Sumneytown Pike, Lansdale PA 19446 (215) 855–8328.**

Latrobe

Beth Israel. Affiliated with United Syn of Am. Pres: Robert R. Mendler. **414 Weldon St, Latrobe PA 15650 (412) 539–1450.**

Lebanon

Congregation Beth Israel. Affiliated with United Syn of Am. Rabbi Nason Goldstein; Pres: Dr Murray Grosky; Edu Dir: Dr Joseph Clark; Youth Dir: Sarah Schneider; Off Mgr: Thelma Marks. **411 S 8th St, Lebanon PA 17042 (717) 273–6669.**

Levittown

Congregation Beth El. Affiliated with United Syn of Am. Rabbi William Fierverker; Pres: Seymour S. Kaplan; Edu & Youth Dir: Rabbi Howard Rosenbaum. **21 Penn Valley Rd, Levittown PA 19055 (215) 945–1172.**

Temple Shalom. Affiliated with UAHC. 255 mems. Rabbi Gordon L. Geller; Cantor David Wisnia; Pres: Lois Ginsburg; Edu: Warren Politz; Adm: Gordon L.

Geller; Sisterhood Pres: Lois Frank; Brotherhood Pres: Stan Margulies. **Edgely Rd off Mill Creek Pkwy, Levittown PA 19507 (215) 945–4154.**

Lock Haven

Beth Yehuda Synagogue. Affiliated with UAHC. 43 mems. Rabbi Steven D. Abrams; Pres: Joseph Klevansky. **320 W Church St, Lock Haven PA 17745 (717) 748–3908.**

McKeesport

Temple B'nai Israel. Reform Temple affiliated with UAHC, CCAR, NATA. Rel, edu, social. Rel Servs; Adult Edu; Sisterhood; chil Heb sch; conversion classes; visiting the sick; cemetery; Sun Rel Sch at Heb Ins Pittsburgh; library containing 1,000 vols (non-fiction Judaica). 250 families; 35 students grades K–10. 7 employees. F 1912 as Temple B'nai Israel. Pub Temple Talk (monthly). Facilities include kitchen not serving treyfot – but uses one set of dishes, 400 permanent sanctuary seats, social hall, sch bldg, 10 classrms, off, additional classrms at rabitat for weekday Heb. Rabbi Leonard Winograd; Hazzanit Cathy Bomstein; Pres: Dr Daniel Spiegel; Exec Sec: Judy Selkowitz; VP: Richard Rubinstein. **536 Shaw Ave, McKeesport PA 15132 (412) 678–6181.**

Media

Congregation Beth Israel. Reconstructionist Syn affiliated with Fed of Reconstructionist Congs & Fellowships, & Reconstructionist Rabbinical Col of Phila. To strive for creative servs; to advance a humanistic approach to J; to maintain a consistency between J values & beliefs, & the way in which daily life is conducted both in & out of the syn. Rel Servs; Heb Sch for chil eight through 13; Presch; teenagers meeting with the rabbi for a Shabbat dinner & discussion once a mo; Adult Edu; Chil Seder; lecture series; music evenings; tennis parties; picnics, & a retreat in Jun. F in 1929. Women & men are equally encouraged to participate in the responsibilities & voluntary activities of the Syn. This principle extends to such events as Bar/Bat Mitzvah ceremonies, marriage & divorce proceedings, calling to the Torah, & counting of the minyan. The Cong maintains a unique relationship with the Reconstructionist Rabbinical Col. Rabbinic interns fr the Col are provided with the opportunity to share their varied & often fresh ideas with the Cong. Rabbi Dr Sidney Schwarz; Pres: Burton Cohen. **Gayley Terr, Media PA 19063 (215) L06–4645.**

Merion Station

Akiba Hebrew Academy. Independent com day sch. To prepare stu to take their places in their coms as leaders & active citizens who have knowledge & skill as well as sensitivity & commitment to J culture, to Am culture & to the human needs of the world around us. Gen & J studies; in the sr yr advanced placement courses are offered in European Hist, Biology & Calculus; col courses are offered in Psychology & in Rel; Work Prog: srs are placed as volunteer interns in social servs or edu agy throughout the city for six weeks; physical & health edu; assemblies; progs; Shabbatonim; sports; intramural athletics; stu assn; interest groups including Jr & Adult Great Bks, World J Cttee, Computer Club, stu pub, sch chorus, drama groups, Sci Club & others. 309 stu grades 6–12. 42 teachers. Est in 1946 by mems of the J com of the Greater Phila area to provide an intensive prog of J studies integrated with a comprehensive prog of col prep studies. Pub Akiva Update (semi-annual). Pres: Adena Potok; Prin: Dr Steven C. Lorch; Asst Prin: Robert A. Gordon; Col Counselor-Certified Sch Psychologist: Helen Tigay. **223 N Highland Ave, Merion Station PA 19066 (215) 839–3540.**

Akiba Hebrew Academy, Library. For information on the Ins, see – Akiba Hebrew Academy, Merion Station, PA. **223 N Highland Ave, Merion Station PA 19066 (215) 839–3540.**

Monongahela

Temple Beth Am. Affiliated with UAHC. 75 mems. Pres: Sidney Ackerman. **c/o Mr Sidney Ackerman, Rd 1 Box 615, Monongahela PA 15063 (412) 379–5312.**

Monroeville

Temple David. Reform Temple affiliated with UAHC, Natl Fed of Temple Sisterhoods, Natl Fed of Temple Youth. To perpetuate Judaism by providing opportunities for worship, study, com concerns & social interaction. Rel Servs; adult & chil rel edu progs; Sisterhood; Men's Club; Youth Group; Young Couples Club; Singles; Sr Citizens Club; Mitzvah Cttee; Havurah; counseling servs (rabbi); library with 1675 vols (gen & Judaica); Presch; Afternoon Sch. 290 families; 177 stu in grades k–10. 6 employees. F 1957 as a "conservatively" Reform Temple to serve the J families in the E suburbs. Original bldg was constructed in 1959 with two expansions in 1970 & 1981 to add additional classrms, off space, separate sanctuary & new library. Pub Temple David Bulletin (fortnightly). Facilities include kitchen, social hall, gift shop, 8 classrms, library, Rel Sch off, Temple off, rabbi's study, sanctuary seating 200, larger sanctuary area seating 800. Rabbi Jason Z. Edelstein; Pres: Linda Jacobs; Exec VP: Barbara Shuman; Fin VP: Eric Udren; Rel Sch VP: Grace Moritz; Worship & Ritual Practice VP: Bruce Antonoff; Fin Sec: Margery Swetlitz; Rec Sec: Elizabeth Murray; Treas: Jan K. Hurwitz; Sisterhood Pres: Barbara Berkowitz; Men's Club Pres: Joseph Cohen. **4415 Northern Pike, Monroeville PA 15146 (412) 372–1200.**

Temple David, Library. Contains 1675 vols (fiction, non-fiction, youth & adult; additionally there are reference bks, 143 vols of J encyclopedias, the Babylonian Talmud, Am encyclopedias, Hist of the J, The World of the Bible). For information on the Temple, see – Temple David, Monroeville, PA **4415 Northern Pike, Monroeville PA 15146 (412) 372–1200.**

Narberth

Beth Am Israel. Affiliated with United Syn of Am. Rabbi Andrew M. Sacks; Cantor Sheldon M. Levin; Pres: Michael B. Albert. **1301 Hagys Fork Rd, Narberth PA 19072 (215) 667–1651.**

New Castle

Temple Israel. Affiliated with UAHC. 61 mems. Pres: Robert Ziman. **908 Highland Ave, New Castle PA 16101 (412) 652–7551.**

United Jewish Appeal of New Castle, PA. Mem of CJF. Organized 1967. Chr: Ruth-Ann Fisher. **PO Box 5050, New Castle PA 16105 (412) 658–8389.**

New Kensington

Beth Jacob Congregation. Affiliated with United Syn of Am. Rabbi Irving Dick; Pres: Dr Jon Schwartz; Edu Dir: Mrs Melvin Goldberg. **1040 Kenneth Ave, New Kensington PA 15068 (412) 335–8525.**

Newtown

Shir Ami, Bucks County Jewish Congregation. Affiliated with UAHC 300 mems. Rabbi Elliot M. Strom; Pres: Ruth Fives; Edu: Steven Weintraub; Sisterhood Pres: Lenora Schwartz; Brotherhood Pres: Arthur Pollack. **101 Richboro Rd, Newtown PA 18940 (215) 968–3400.**

Norristown

Jewish Community Center. Family oriented syn ctr. Affiliated with United Syn of Am. Daily Rel Servs; High Holiday Servs at four age levels; scouting; Kadimah for 11 & 12 yr olds; USY camp & summer activity scholarships; contact with collegians; playgroups for ages 18 mo to 2½ yrs; daily nursery sch; Heb classes; Sun classes; arts & crafts; trips; adult classes, J studies & Heb; classes in cooking, bridge, aerobic dancing; Couples Club; Womens League; Men's Club; com serv projs. Pres: Rabbi Dr Irving Archinow; Rabbi Emeritus Harold M. Kamsler; Cantor Uri Naor; Edu Dir: Shoshana Silberman; 1st VP: Alvin Schwartz; 2nd VP: Jerome Kerner; Treas: Ralph Petersohn; Rec Sec: Stanley Ershler; Corsp Sec: Albert Markowitz; Solicitor: Raymond Pearlstine; Bd of Dirs: Israel Abramovitz, Lillian Abramovitz, Bernard Allmayer, Sandy Archinow, Robert Bamford, Silas Bolef, David Cardis, Morton Check, Robert Cohen, Sam Danzig, Robert Davis, Nathan Dubner, Reba Dubner, Julian Ehrenberg, Robert Elfenbein, Charles Elgart, Richard Fine, Irving Fliegelman, Leonard Friedman, Alan Gelman, Annalee Ginsberg, Morris Gerber, Jerome Gluckman, Jerome Heitner, Dr Mark Hite, Leonard Huber, Emanuel Katz, Jack Kronick, Ethel Ladov, Dr Morris Ladov, Dr Irwin Peikes, Thelma Peikes, Benjamin Petersohn, Harry Pure, Paul H. Rudberg, David Sandler, Martin Schaffer, Faith Schreiber, Harold Schreiber, M. Eugene Seltzer, George Stickeler, Bernard Tepper, Carole Tepper, Leonard Tose, Jay I. Weiss, Philip D. Weiss, Sylvan P. Weiss, William Wolfe; Gabbaim: Israel Abramovitz, Nathan Dubner, Robert Goldblatt, Paul Rudberg, Jack Korn. **Brown & Powell Sts, Norristown PA 19401 (215) 275–8797.**

Penn Valley

Beth Am Israel. Conservative Syn affiliated with United Syns of Am. Rel Servs; Sisterhood; Men's Club; Youth Group; Afternoon Sch; library containing 2,000 vols (Judaica). 150 families; 400 individuals; 120 stu. 10 employees. F 1925. Facilites include kosher kitchen, sanctuary, gift shop. Rabbi Andrew M. Sacks; Cantor Sheldon Levin; Pres: Michael Albert. **1301 Hagysfosd Rd, Penn Valley PA 19072 (215) 667–1651.**

Beth Am Israel, Library. For information on the Syn, see – Beth Am Israel, Penn Valley, PA 19072 (215) 667–1651.

Har Zion Religious School. Har Zion for chil with learning disabilities meets twice a week (Tues, Sun). Conservative cong sch open to chil whose families are affiliated with any syn. 3–day–a–week prog available leading to Bar/Bat Mitzvah; individual instruction in phonetics; class prog for holidays, Shabbat Servs, music & art. Edu Dir: Sara H. Cohen.

Hagys Ford at Hollow Rd, Penn Valley PA 19072 (215) 667–5002, 839–1340.

Har Zion Temple. Affiliated with United Syn of Am. Rabbi Gerald I. Wolpe; Asst Rabbi Elliot Skiddell; Cantor Isaac I. Wall; Pres: Ralph S. Snyder; Exec Dir: Phillip Redelheim; Edu Dir: Sara H. Cohen. **Hagys Fork Rd at Hollow Rd, Penn Valley PA 19072 (215) MO7–1651.**

Philadelphia

Adath Shalom. Affiliated with United Syn of Am. Cantor Mendel Litman; Pres: Samuel Cader. **Marshall & Ritner Sts, Phila PA 19148 (215) 463–2224.**

Adath Tikvah Montefiore Congregation. Affiliated with United Syn of Am. Rabbi Bruce Harbater; Pres: Samuel Perlman. **Hoffnagle St & Summerdale Ave, Phila PA 19152 (215) PL2–9191.**

Adath Tikvah Montefiore Congregation, Richard Jonathan Cohen Memorial Library. For information on the Cong, see – Adath Tikvah Montefiore Congregation, Philadelphia, PA. **1742 Bergen St, Phila PA 19152.**

Adath Zion Branch of the United Hebrew Schools. Class for chil with learning disabilities on Sun. Com sch available to any chil in J com. Prin: Marilyn Grobman. **Pennway & Friendship Sts, Phila PA 19111 (215) 742–8500.**

Ahavath Israel of Oak Lane. Affiliated with United Syn of Am. Pres: Jacob H. Beratan. **6735 N 16th St, Phila PA 19126 (215) WA4–7675.**

American Committee for Shaare Zedek in Jerusalem – Mid-Atlantic Region. To help future generations meet the health needs of Jerusalem and Israel. Continuing support of century old hospital which moved in 1979 fr old quarters to new $55 million ultra modern medical complex overlooking Jerusalem. Offers total patient & community care. University affiliated teaching hospital contains main hospital building planned for more than 500 beds, emergency shelter, outpatient clinics, school of nursing, clinical labs, research ins, central library, facilities. Ensures the full observance of J tradition. Open to all irrespective of rel, race or natl origin. **1518 Walnut St, Suite 900, Phila PA 19102 (215) 735–3306.**

The American Friends of Haifa University. 226 W Rittenhouse Square, Suite 2301, Phila PA 19103 (215) 735–8074.

American Jewish Press Association. 226 S 16th St, Phila PA 19102 (215) 893–5700.

American-Israel Chamber of Commerce & Industry, Inc – Philadelphia Chapter. Offers assistance to mem US firms interested in economic activity in & with Is. Provides extensive trade assistance; pub market research reports; aids in dev of trade & investment between US & Is. For additional information, see – American-Israel Chamber of Commerce & Industry, Inc, New York City, NY. **1845 Walnut St, Phila PA 19103 (215) 299–1700.**

Anti-Defamation League of B'nai B'rith – PA-WV-DE Regional Office. Dedicated in purpose & prog to translating the Am heritage of democratic ideals into a way of life for all Am, & to countering assaults on the safety, status, rights & image of J. For additional information, see – Anti-Defamation League of B'nai B'rith, New York City, NY. **225 S 15th St, Phila PA 19102.**

Associated Camping Services. 401 S Broad St, Phila PA 19147 (215) 546–6600.

B'nai B'rith Career & Counseling Services. Provides testing & counseling of the individual; extensive in-depth tests are given in order to formulate edu & career plans for the individual. Est in 1938 to provide edu & career counseling to J youth. The agy has provided an internship experience for over 25 doctoral stu in Temple Univ Sch of Psychology, Counseling Psychology, & Univ of PA Psychological Servs Prog. Pres: Stephen D. Rudman; VPs: Harry Hirsch, Alan Lessack, Rosalie Michaelson; Sec: Rose G. Weinstein; Treas: Bayle H. Weiner; Exec Dir: Dr Julius Romanoff. **1405 Locust Rd, Suite 1507, Phila PA 19102 (215) 545–1455.**

Beth David Reform Congregation. Affiliated with UAHC. 310 mems. Rabbi Henry Cohen; Cantor Henry Pordes; Pres: Lionel Prince; Edu: Milt Gerwertz; Sisterhood Pres: Sylvia Helfand; Brotherhood Pres: Robert Benowitz, Murry Saltzman. **5220 Wynnefield Ave, Phila PA 19131 (215) 473–8438.**

Beth David Reform Congregation, Jewel K. Markowitz Library. For information on the Cong, see – Beth David Reform Congregation, Philadelphia, PA. **5220 Wynnefield Ave, Phila PA 19131 (215) 473–8438.**

Beth Emeth Congregation. Affiliated with United Syn of Am. Rabbi Herman L. Horowitz; Cantor

Hershel A. Weitz; Pres: Stanley Koltoff; Edu Dir: Raphael Becker; Youth Dir: Ira Pogachefski. **Bustleton & Unruh Ave, Phila PA 19149 (215) 338–1533.**

Beth Judah of Logan. Affiliated with United Syn of Am. Rabbi Samuel P. Cohen; Cantor Yehuda L. Mandel; Pres: Philip D. Katz. **4820–30 N 11th St, Phila PA 19141 (215) DA9–4545.**

Beth T'fillah Branch of the United Hebrew Schools. Class for chil with learning disabilities on Sun. Com sch available to any child in the J com. Prin: Harvey Litcofsky. **7630 Woodbine Ave, Phila PA 19151 (215) 477–9146.**

Beth Torah Temple. Affiliated with UAHC. 495 mems. Rabbi Bernard Solis Frank; Cantor Faith Steinsnyder; Pres: Michael Aaronson; Edu: Jerry Segal; Sisterhood Pres: Bea Evantash; Brotherhood Pres: Irv Chasen. **608 Welsh Rd, Phila PA 19115 (215) 677–1555.**

Brith Sholom. J fraternal soc for men & women 16 yrs of age & over. Sponsors a sr citizens home in Phila & med rehabilitation ctr for Israeli vets in Haifa; com relations; organized sports prog; social activities; fraternal benefits; civic & communal activities; Is & J affairs; humanitarian causes; public speaking; leadership training progs; vacation outings; tours; dinners; dances; art exhibits; provocative speakers; bk reviews; films; musical concerts; pop music; comedy; dramatics; volunteer servs for thousands of serv men & vets on post, off post, & in hosps. 3 state groups, 98 local groups. Staff of three. F in 1905 & formerly known as the Independent Order of British Sholom. Outstanding accomplishments include: contributed a 65 acre tract of land for the est of Eagleville Sanatorium; rescued 50 chil, aged five to 14, fr the Nazi crematoriums; est a lab for cancer research at the Albert Einstein Col of Med, Yeshiva Univ, NY; purchased land in pre-Is for the est of farm coms which still flourish in modern Is; built & maintained the multi million dollar Brith Sholom House for sr citizens in Phila; sponsored the construction of the Brith Sholom Beit Halochem in Haifa to rebuild the bodies & spirit of Is permanently wounded paraplegics, amputees & the unsighted. Brith Sholom News (weekly); Community Relations Digest. Natl Pres: David Saner; Exec Dir: Joshua Eilberg. **3939 Conshohocken Ave, Phila PA 19131 (215) 878–5696.**

Bustleton Somerton Synagogue. Affiliated with United Syn of Am. Rabbi Howard Lifshitz; Cantor Dr Samuel Romirowsky; Pres: Dr Martin M. Roffman; Edu Dir: Norma Tabakin. **Tomlinson Rd & Ferndale St, Phila PA 19116 (215) 677–6886.**

Center City YM & YWHA Branch. 401 S Broad St, Phila PA 19147 (215) 545–4400.

Congregation Beth Ahavah. Serves the rel & social needs of gay & lesbian J in Phila; mems of the World Congress of Gay & Lesbian J Orgs. Rel Servs; Communal Seder at Passover; ritual observances of the festivals; social activities; edu prog; First Fri of each mo is designated Women's Night; women gather for their own separate celebration of Rosh Chodesh. 50 mems. Est in 1975. An elected bd of five offs is responsible for all syn activities including the conducting of Servs. Beth Ahavah participates with other gay & lesbian orgs in the work of advancing the civil & human rights of sexual minorities. Through continuing dialogue with all elements of the J com, it hopes to contribute to a more enlightened understanding of sexual preference, & to a reintegration of all gay & lesbian J into K'lal Yisrael. **PO Box 7566, Phila PA 19101 (215) 922–3872.**

Congregation Beth T'fillah of Overbrook Park. Affiliated with United Syn of Am. Rabbi Arthur J. S. Rosenbaum; Cantor & Exec Dir: Harry Weinberg; Pres: Irvin Tessler. **7630 Woodbine Ave, Phila PA 19151 (215) 477–2415.**

Congregation Brith Israel. Affiliated with United Syn of Am. Rabbi William Greenburg; Cantor Shimon Berris; Pres: Samuel J. Strak. **Roosevelt Blvd & D Sts, Phila PA 19120 (215) 329–2230.**

Congregation Emanu-El. Affiliated with United Syn of Am. Rabbi Fredric Kazan; Pres: George Horowitz. **Old York Rd & Stenton Ave, Phila PA 19141 (215) LI8–1658.**

Congregation Ramat El. Affiliated with United Syn of Am. Rabbi Dr Louis L. Sacks; Pres: Maurice Simon; Exec Dir: Julius Schecter. **Johnson & Ardleigh Sts, Phila PA 19119 (215) LI9–8800.**

Congregation Rodeph Shalom. Affiliated with UAHC. 1753 mems. Rabbis: Richard F. Steinbrink, Patrice E. Heller, Brooks R. Susman, David H. Wice; Pres: Ivan H. Gabel; Adm: Stanley Brenner; Sisterhood Pres: Anne Zaslow; Brotherhood Pres: Morton Collier. **615 N Broad St, Phila PA 19123 (215) 627–6747.**

Congregation Rodeph Shalom Library. 1338 Mt Vernon St, Phila PA 19123.

Congregation Shaare Shamayim. 9768 Verree Rd, Phila PA 19115.

Congregation Shaare Shamayim, Library. **9768 Verree Rd, Phila PA 19115.**

David G. Neuman Senior Center. **6600 Bustleton Ave, Phila PA 19149 (215) 338–9800.**

Downtown Children's Center. Administered by the Fed Day Care Serv. Group day care for presch chil in the ctr bldg; summer day care for sch-age chil; family day care for 3 yr olds; group homes for sch-agers, chil attending a local public sch are housed in group homes in the neighborhood for after sch & vacation care; counseling & referral servs; Parents Assn activities. Day care to 56 chil three to eight yrs old. F in 1911 as a completely volunteer prog. In 1916 the facility's present home was purchased. In 1924 it became a mem of the Fed of J Charities & J Family Servs & became responsible for intake. In 1953 the name was changed fr Downtown Hebrew Day Nursery to its present name. In 1973 the Bd merged with the Samuel Paley Day Care Ctr & became part of Fed Day Care Serv. **366 Snyder Ave, Phila PA 19148 (215) 389–1018.**

The Dropsie University. The only independent grad ins in Am – non-sectarian & nontheological, & completely dedicated to Heb, Biblical, J, & Ancient & Contemporary Near Eastern Studies. Approved by the Dept of Public Instruction of the Commonwealth of PA, & accredited by the Middle States Assn of Col & Secondary Schs. The promotion of & instruction in the Heb & cognate languages & their respective literatures. Offers the following advanced degrees: Master of Arts, Master of Arts in J Studies, Dr of Philosophy; Depts: Biblical Studies, Hellenistic Studies, Rabbinic Studies, Medieval J Studies, Arabic & Islamic Studies, Heb Language & Literature, Modern J Hist & Middle Eastern Studies, Ancient Near Eastern Studies, Rel Thought; Ctrs: The Joseph & Sally Handleman Communications Ctr for the Study of Man's Humanity, The Abraham I. Katsh Ctr for Manuscript Research; Lib: The Fannie & Victor Tomshinsky Library contains more than 150,000 vols of bks & periodicals; Progs: Col Work-Study Prog; Scholarship & Fellowship Progs. Faculty of 16; visiting scholars fr univs in the US & abroad participate in the Univ academic prog through public lectures, formal classes & scholarly colloquia. F in 1907 under the terms of the will of Moses Aaron Dropsie which directed the est of a col in Phila for the promotion of & instruction in the Heb & cognate languages & their respective literature, with admission of stu without discrimination on account of creed, color or sex. Originally called The Dropsie Col for Hebrew & Cognate Learning, the ins was officially renamed in 1969. The main bldg was erected in 1911. An annex was acquired in 1961, & in 1977 the former Mikveh Is Syn bldg, which shared a common campus with the univ, was acquired. The campus is included in the official Natl Register of Historic Places. The Jewish Quarterly Review pub articles & reviews of J literature, hist & rel, Heb philology & related subjects; Jewish Apocryphal Literature consists of a series of vols each containing text, translations & commentaries: The First Book of Maccabees, Aristeas to Philocrates, The Third & Fourth Books of Maccabees, The Second Book of Maccabees, The Book of Tobit, The Book of Judith. The main bldg houses classrms, offs, an auditorium, & a rare bk rm. The annex houses classrms, library, faculty & stu lounges, & offs. Pres of Univ: Dr David M. Goldenberg; Exec VP: Nobel Smith; VPs: Jules Broundy, Zvi Levavy; Treas: Morris J. Root; Sec: Joseph B. Saltz; Chr of Exec Cttee: Albert J. Wood; Chr of Bd: Isadore L. Kirschner; Pres Phila Friends of The Dropsie Univ: Mildred Stenson; Bd of Trustees: Isaac Auerbach, Herman Badillo, Veachey R. Bloom, Fred Blume, Burton Caine, Stuart Caine, Walter D. Cherry, Aaron N. Cohen, Betsy Z. Cohen, Irving Cohen, Mary Cohen, Phillip Forman, S. Harry Galfand, David A. Goldstein, Elinor C. Guggenheimer, Joseph Handleman, Paul L. Jaffe, Robert Y. Kamin, Seymour Kaplan, Raymond Klein, Phillip M. Klutznick, Leon Korngold, Phyllis Kosloff, Marvin Lundy, Lawrence Marwick, Robert N.C. Nix Jr, Theodore Norman, Ruth Rabb, Samuel Rosenblum, Moe Septee, Murray H. Shusterman, Beryl Simonson, Philip Slomovitz, Philip S. Snyder, Harry Stern, William B. Thomas, Saul Volchok, Emanuel Weinstein, Marvin Weitz. **Broad & York Sts, Phila PA 19132 (215) 299–0110.**

Federation of Jewish Agencies. To preserve the J heritage & to assure the well being of J everywhere. Allocation of funds to agy concerned with health care, servs to the aged including housing, help for homeless & neglected chil, day care for chil, immigrant absorption, aid to the handicapped, family counseling, mental health, vocational training & leisure time activities for youths & adults; allocation of fin support to the Rabbinate & the Chaplaincy Serv, & the Hillel Prog on local col campuses; allocation of funds for local & natl agy which fight for human rights & combat anti-Semitism & bigotry; support for natl cultural, edu & com relations agy. Overseas agy supported by the Fed carry on the tasks of immigrant resettlement & rescue & relief. The FJA Leadership Dev Cttee, composed of men & women between the ages of 21 & 40, conducts edu courses & progs designed to dev effective leadership training. The FJA Women's Council, a leadership group charged with interpreting the Fed to the gen com, & the Business & Professional Woman's Coalition for J career women who want to be active within the organized J com, conduct FAJA fundraising activities. FAJA provides centralized local servs for its local constituent agy & neighboring coms through its Electronic Data Processing Ctr, printing facilities of its Production Dept, & the communications resources of its Dept of PR. F in 1901 as the Fed of J Charities uniting nine agy into one com effort to help the Phila J com, & to aid immigrants fleeing the pogroms of Eastern Europe. In 1957 the FJC & the Allied J Appeal, which had been organized in 1938 to aid refugees fr Nazi oppression, were merged into a single entity which became the present Fed of J Agy. Two Am J newspapaers: Jewish Exponent & The Jewish Times of the Greater Northeast; Inside (a quarterly magazine). The Fed maintains a thrift shop. Pres: Edward H. Rosen; VPs: Bernard Borine, Marvin N. Demchick, Joel Gershman, Teddy M. Kaiserman, Robert J. Reichlin, Shirley Shils; Exec VP: Robert P. Forman; Treas: Mitchell E. Panzer; Assc Treas: Bennett L. Aaron; Sec: Alan H. Molod; Assc Sec: Miriam A. Schneirov; Gen Chr: Jerome P. Epstein, Mark I. Solomon; Campaign Dir: Alvin H. Gilens; Dir of PR: Phyllis B. Menduke. **226 S 16th St, Phila PA 19102 (215) 893–5600.**

Federation Day Care Services. Administers four day care progs: Samuel Paley Day Care Ctr, Northern Hebrew Day Nursery, Downtown Chil Ctr, & NE Family Day Care. Constituent of the Fed of J Agy, & a mem of the Chil Welfare League of Am. To strengthen family life through daytime care provided for chil & through its relationship to parents; to incorporate J values & traditions in its progs. Supplements the care, & the edu & recreational experiences which parents provide for chil; administers progs for presch & sch age chil which give the chil opportunities to participate in experiences which help them fulfill their capacity to learn & to grow intellectually, socially, emotionally & physically. Caring (quarterly periodical). Exec Dir: Norman S. Finkel. **Jamison Ave & Garth Rd, Phila PA 19116 (215) 676–7550.**

Germantown Jewish Center. Affiliated with United Syn of Am. Rabbi Sanford H. Hahn; Pres: Judge Abraham J. Gafni; Edu Dir: Louise Goldman. **Lincoln Dr & Ellet St, Phila PA 19119 (215) 814–1507.**

Germantown Jewish Center, Quitman Library. For information on the Ins, see – Germantown Jewish Center, Philadelphia, PA. **Lincoln Dr & Ellet St, Phila PA 19119 (215) 814–1507.**

Government of Israel Trade Center. Dev of trade relations between US & Is. For additional information, see – Government of Israel Trade Center, New York City, NY. **225 S 15th St, Phila PA 19102 (215) 546–4300.**

Gratz College. 10 St & Tabor Rd, Phila PA 19141.

The Hebrew Sunday School Society of Greater Philadelphia. Edu ins. To help chil participate happily, intelligently & creatively as J in modern life; to encourage the spiritual growth of every J chil; to teach the basic tenets of the J rel, & their application & practice in our daily life; to instill an abiding love for & lasting loyalties to J traditions; to encourage a deep sense of identificaiton with the J people, leading to continuity & survival. Sun morning prog: Hist, Heb Reading, Customs-Ceremonies, Current Events, Bar/Bat Mitzvah preparation; rel instruction provided for J clients with special needs (emotionally disturbed, handicapped, mentally retarded, learning disabled) at the Elwyn Sch, Ken-Crest Sch, Overbrook Sch for the Blind, Pathway Sch, PA Sch for the Deaf, Devereux Sch & Woodhaven State Sch. F by Rebecca Gratz in 1838. The Hebrew Sun Sch Soc is the oldest edu ins of its kind in the US. Provides rel edu in the greater Phila area for elementary & HS pupils, K–12, of unaffiliated families not receiving any other type of J edu. Pres: Dr Daniel Isaacman; Chr: Daniel C. Cohen. VPs: Mrs Gilbert Grossman, Mrs Robert Mosenkis; Treas: Mrs Carl S. Dash; Asst Treas: Mrs Bernard L. Babbit; Corsp Sec: Mrs Fredric Krupnich; Rec Sec: Mrs Allen D. Kohn, Mrs Harold J. Spangenberg; Social Sec: Mrs Jerome Miller; Exec Dir: Dr Jerome I. Leventhal. **1729 Pine St, Phila PA 19103 (215) 735–7972.**

Israel Aliyah Center. 225 S 15th St, Suite 2528, Phila PA 19102 (215) 546–2088.

Jewish Community Relations Council. Com relations arm of the organized J com; a constituent of the Fed of J Agy. To safeguard the rights of J, & to work in the broader com on behalf of the common good. Coords the activities of 35 major J orgs & interprets public policy positions on a wide range of issues of concern to the J com; devs the broadest possible backing for continuing economic, military & diplomatic support of Is; provides the Phila com with opportunities to learn about the democratic nature of Israeli soc, & heightens the com awareness of the centrality of Is to the well being & security of the world J com; provides a central resource in the Greater Phila area for information & edu to aid J in the Soviet Union; works for equal opportunity & urban affairs; supports quality integrated edu in the Phila public schs; concerned with the issues of anti-

Semitism, job & sch discrimination, Am Nazis & Nazi war criminals, freedom of speech, rights of coms to protect themselves, crime & justice, & abuses of civil rights & civil liberties; maintains channels of communication with other rel groups & works cooperatively with them on shared concerns; works to preserve the historical separation of church & state guaranteed by the US Constitution; Memorial Cttee & Holocaust Programming administers: activities of the Memorial Cttee for the Six Million J Martyrs, annual Yitzkor Ceremony, Teaching Conf on the Holocaust, Mordechai Anielewicz Creative Arts Competition, PA Commemoration of The Holocaust, Youth Symposium on the Holocaust; provides com servs, holiday calenders; maintains Speakers Bureau, JCRC Youth Council. F in 1939. JCRC has neighborhood divs in Eastern Montgomery Cty, NE & NW, & Main Line Delaware Ctys. Pres: Marion A. Wilen; VPs: Dr Norma Furst, Bennett G. Picker, James A. Rosenstein, Arnold J. Silvers, Horace A. Stern, Barry E. Ungar; Treas: Janet H. Zolot; Sec: Dr Bernard P. Dishler. **1520 Locust St, Phila PA 19102 (215) 545–8430.**

The Jewish Employment & Vocational Service. To provide facilities for scientific & practical adjustments of people to jobs; to provide facilities for a better understanding of the job seekers abilities & personal characteristics; to learn of employment opportunities in Phila; to find all the com resources where suitable training can be secured; to provide & seek opportunities for the placement of job seekers. Ctr for Career Servs: offers counseling, vocational testing & career planning help to stu, women re-entering the work force, people who need or want to change careers, & recent col grads. Sch of Home Care Mgmnt: trains people to care for the sick & elderly. Work Adjustment Ctr: provides a vocational habilitation prog for mentally retarded persons who receive training in activities of daily living & learning to become responsible for themselves, with those who can function at a higher level enrolled in a food servs training prog (the Ctr offers Phila's only vocational habilitation prog for the blind retarded). Achievement Through Counseling & Treatment prog for drug & alcohol abusers: offers individual, group & family therapy, psychiatric & med treatment, outpatient detoxification, & vocational exploration & counseling; administers a prog for out-of-sch, out-of-work youth, aiming to place them in competitive employment. The Vocational Research Ins: devs & distributes, nationally & internationally, several systems which evaluate vocational potential. AP Orleans Vocational Ctr: servs the handicapped, unskilled & unemployed. JEVS Schs of Business & Trades located at the Ctr: provide training in clerical skills, data processing, word processing, air conditioning & refrigeration, electronics, food preparation & servs, machining, bldg maintenance, heating & maintenance plumbing, & residential & commercial electricity. Russian & Indochinese immigrants receive English language instruction. The Orleans Ctr has two special cooperative arrangements: a Physical Therapy Prog administered at the Ctr by Moss Rehabilitation Hosp, & a production workshop administered by the Orleans Ctr staff at the Phila Geriatric Ctr. Several thousand clients each yr. In 1941 25 people signed Articles of Incorporation for the Employment & Vocational Bureau. Although refugees were the first priority, it soon became apparent that many Am also needed the servs of the Bureau. With the end of WWII came returning GIs who also required vocational servs. In 1951 the Bureau changed its name to the J Employment & Vocational Serv. During the 1950's the Serv provided vocational guidance for youth, waged campaigns & highlighted job placement for the elderly. In 1956 the Serv est a workshop where vocationally handicapped men & women could learn about work in an industrial environment. In the late 1950's & early 1960's the State Bureau of Vocational Rehabilitation began referring clients to the JEVS Work Adjustment Ctr, & the US Dept of Labor funded a JEVS prog for out-of-work & out-of-sch youth. In the 1960's the Exec Adv Cttee was formed to eliminate discrimination in hiring & promotion at the exec level. The 1970's were a time of tremendous growth & dev for the Serv. A clin for drug abusers became a comprehensive out-patient treatment ctr. Skill training & English language instruction were introduced in the 1970's. In 1979 the AP Orleans Vocational Ctr opened. Chr of the Bd: Warren L. Eisenberg; Pres: Robert M. Segal; VPs: Dr Walter Gershenfeld, Richard B. Laden, Mrs D. Gerald Scott; Treas: Morton J. Simon Jr; Asst Treas: Peter Rothberg; Sec: Lewis J. Gordon; Dirs: Steven J. Batzer, Martin Bayersdorfer Jr, Michael M. Baylson, Alan H. Bernstein, Julian S. Bers, Howard Bregman, Howard B. Brownstein, Dr Sarle H. Cohen, Charles Conston, Mrs Robert P. Frankel, Diane S. Freedman, Ronald S. Gross, Mrs Alvin P. Gutman, M. Gilbert Herbach, Alexander Herskovitz, William Kaplan, Dr Benjamin J. Katz, Lewis J. Laventhol, Herman Lazarus, Dr Roy T. Lefkoe, Dorie Lenz, Daniel Lepow, Benjamin S. Loewenstein, Karlyn W. Messinger, Lester Pomerantz, Benjamin Prager Jr, Stephen H. Saks, Howard D. Scher, Dr Rosalind Schulman, Ben Stahl, Alan A. Steinberg, Leon C. Sunstein Jr, Carolyn E. Temin, Isadore Wiener, Alvin E. Wolf Jr; Hon Dirs: Donald S. Cohan, Alfred J. Goldsmith, Dr Saul S. Leshner, Leon J. Perelman, Mrs Edwin H. Weil, Dr Seymour L. Wolfbein; Exec Dir: Ephrain H. Royfe. **1624 Locust St, Phila PA 19103 (215) 893–5900.**

Jewish Exponent. Weekly newspaper owned by the Fed of J Agy. To bring the J population closer together. Brings news of J throughout the world, & news of local activities to readers; covers current events, rel events, holidays, J bks & authors. Printed in Phila since 1887. Editor: Marc S. Klein; Managing Editor: Albert H. Erlick; Sr Editor: Sandra Sherman; News Editor: David Gross; Graphics Editor: Maralin Krowll; Entertainment Editor: Michael Elkin; Rel Editor: Ian Blynn; Fri Editor: Jane Biberman; Business Dir: Richard Waloff; Advertising Mgr: Byron Fink; Controller: Paul Frimark; Sales Mgr: Rita Breskman; Creative Dir: Lenore Chorney; Production Mgr: Julie A. Gismondi; Pres: Irvin J. Borowsky; Chr of the Bd: David H. Solms; VPs: Milton B. Creamer, Ann Eisman, Charles Conston, Dr Edward B. Shils; Treas: Stanley D. Ferst; Sec: Ramon R. Obod; V Chr: Teddy Kaiserman. Asst Treas: Bennett L. Aaron; Asst Sec: Lucille Berger; **226 S 16th St, Phila PA 19102 (215) 893–5700.**

Jewish Family Service of Philadelphia. To help preserve & strengthen J family life. Marital counseling: guidance & counseling for marriages in trouble & counseling to identify the problems, determine their causes, & institute methods of resolving them; parent-chil counseling: counseling for chil who exhibit aberrant behavior, fight, sulk, are withdrawn or react in puzzling ways (there are reasons which J Family Serv professionals are ready to determine); family group counseling: individual & joint sessions of family mems with a skilled JFS counselor; group counseling: group sessions available for discouraged & lonely elderly persons, couples with marital problems, maladjusted chil, wayward youngsters, single parents, & for sch chil slow in developing learning skills; personal counseling; servs for older persons: housekeeper & homemaker assistance, friendly visitors, protective servs, transportation, handyman help, podiatry care, temporary financial assistance, & emergency med & emotional care; business counseling & loans: business advice, direction & loans to individuals & families; homemaker servs: a professionally trained homemaker to help a family during a crisis; resettlement of new Am: economic assistance & counseling for newly arrived J refugees & immigrants; Adopt-A-Family: responsibility for helping newcomers assumed by a local family; servs for offenders & their families: counseling, representation in juvenile ct, parole sponsorship, job placement & temporary fin assistance; J family life edu: J Family Serv tries to anticipate family problems before they emerge, & gain voluntary acceptance of appropriate preventive measures. Skilled JFS discussion leaders give talks to organized groups, & information & refferral servs are maintained. F in 1869. Pres: Arnold M. Kessler; VPs: Joan P. Wohl, Carl Schneider, Ivan Gabel; Sec: Charlotte V. Bernstein; Treas: Daniel B. Behrend; Solicitor: Robert Wachter; Exec Dir: Benjamin R. Sprafkin; Assc Exec Dir: Judith Kasser. **1610 Spruce St, Phila PA 19103 (215) KI5–3290.**

The Jewish Publication Society of America. Non-profit edu ins devoted to J culture. To provide significant, worthwhile & informative bks of J content in the English language so that the J rel, hist, literature & culture will be understood & read & known. As the prime pub of J bks of quality in the English speaking world, JPS has issued a body of works for all tastes & requirements. Its many titles include biographies, histories, novels, art bks, holiday anthologies, bks for young readers, rel & philosophical studies, translations of scholarly & popular classics, JPS Bible. Est in 1888. Nearly eight million vols divided among some 800 titles have been pub & distributed around the world. Editor: Maier Deshell; Special Projs Editor: Chaim Potok; Pres: Muriel M. Berman; VPs: Stuart E. Eizenstat, Norma F. Furst, Norman Oler, Charles R. Weiner, Robert S. Rifkind; Treas: Robert P. Frankel; Sec: Marlene F. Lachman; Chr Exec Cttee: Robert P. Abrams; Hon Pres: Edwin Wolf 2nd, Joseph M. First, William S. Fishman, Jerome J. Shestack, A. Leo Levin, Edward B. Shils; Exec VP: Bernard I. Levinson; Exec Dir Emeritus: Lesser Zussman; Bd of Trustees: Robert P. Abrams, Arlin M. Adams, Muriel M. Berman, Edward J. Bloustein, Burton Gaine, Harold Crammer, Jack L. Cummings, Stuart Eizenstat, Edward E. Elson, Joseph M. First, Libby G. Fishman, William S. Fishman, Max Frankel, James O. Freedman, Norma F. Furst, J. E. Goldman, Louis Henkin, Irwin T. Holtzman, Lawrence E. Irell, Max M. Kampelman, Jay I. Kislak, Marlene F. Lachman, Jack Lapin, A. Leo Levin, Roberta Levy, Richard Maass, Theodore R. Mann, Joseph L. Mendelson, Martin Meyerson, Alan H. Molod, Rela G. Monson, Norman Oler, Mitchell E. Panzer, David Reichert, Robert S. Rifkind, Julius Rosenwald 2nd, Jonas Salk, Bernard G. Segal, Daniel Segal, Ruth Septee, Irving S. Shapiro, Stanley I. Sheerr, Jerome J. Shestack, Edward B. Shils, Harry Starr, Marvin Wachman, Jerry Wagner, Charles R. Weiner, Edwin Wolf 2nd, Gerald I. Wolpe. **117 S 17th St, Phila PA 19103 (215) 564–5925.**

Jewish Ys & Centers of Greater Philadelphia, Adult Services & Research Dept. Joseph A. Daroff Campus of Adult Studies: among the nation's largest schs for sr adults with over 1,000 sr adults registered as stu, & over 70 courses offered on four campuses. Retired Sr Volunteer Prog: places 600 sr adults as volunteers in over 50 public & non-profit private agy where they serve as teacher aides, reading aides or friendly visitors, provide telephone reassurance to shut ins, make gifts for institutionalized individuals, provide off help. Orgs & Clubs: 33 orgs ranging in size fr 40 to 300 mems usually meeting on a weekly basis with the primary objectives of socialization, com servs & pol action. Sr Adult Council: represents the united voice of the retired J population of Phila & gives it a source of power through which it can question the order priority of social servs in the J com & hold J social serv agy accountable to the consumers. JYC Sr Adult Pol Action Cttee: arm of the Sr Adult Council which plans & carries out pol action progs for the Council. Multi Servs Ctrs: concentrates on a variety of servs for the aged such as health, casework, transportation, nutrition, servs for the homebound, recreation, socialization, edu, medicaid & foodstamps, with information & referral in one bldg so that they are available, accessible & delivered in a friendly neighborhood setting. Outreach: with the help of volunteers & staff, tries to locate isolated older adults, visit them, help them to overcome the barriers which prevent them fr using available servs, provides tele-care progs for the homebound whereby they are telephoned on a daily or weekly basis by one of the sr adult mems. Research is conducted to determine the impact of a volunteer role upon the health, morale, & social contacts of retired people. One & two day ins are held in the following areas: physical edu, sexuality & aging, communication, assertiveness training. Chr Gilbert Goldstein; Dir: Dr Seymour Kornblum; Pres: Mrs Charles Conston; Exec VP: Samuel I. Sorin. **401 S Broad St, Phila PA 19147 (215) 545–4400.**

JWB Armed Services Committee. 401 S Broad St, Phila PA 19147 (215) 545–4400.

KO Kosher Service. Kosher supervising org. A non-profit org to facilitate the availability of kosher food & servs. Supervise kosher facilities at various firms & edu the com about the laws of kashruth, & about available foods & servs. 150 mems. 6 employees. F 1945. Pres: Rabbi Maurice E. Novoseller; VP: Rabbi Amiel Novoseller; F: Rabbi David S. Novoseller, Rabbi Sholom Novoseller, Rabbi Moshe Schnall; 1st Exec Dir: Rabbi Norman J. Novoseller. **5871 Drexel Rd, Phila PA 19131.**

Lubavitch Center. Rabbi A. Shemtov. **7622 Castor Ave, Phila PA 19152 (215) 725–2030.**

Multi-Service Center. Marshall & Porter Sts, Phila PA 19148 (215) 468–6285.

Museum of American Jewish History. The only ins in the US whose sole purpose is public edu on Am J hist. To collect, preserve, exhibit, & interpret the hist of the J people in the US. Permanent exhibit: The American Jewish Experience fr 1654 to The Present; changing exhibits; confs; musical performances; workshops; films; lectures. Located on Phila Independence Mall, the Mus attracts a natl & intl audience. There have been over 60,000 visitors since the Mus opening. Chartered in 1973, the Mus opened its doors to the public on Jul 4, 1976. The Mus receives support fr memberships & gifts as well as grants fr govt agy & private founs. Pres Bd of Trustees: Hillard Madway; Pres Emeritus: Ruth B. Sarner; VPs: Phyllis Yusem, Lyn Ross, Robert Zimmerman; Sec: Daniel Cohen; Treas: Neal Cupersmith. **Independence Mall E 55 N 5th St, Phila PA 19106 (215) 923–3811.**

Ner Zedek – Ezrath Israel. Affiliated with United Syn of Am. Rabbi David Wachtfogel; Cantor Sidney Karpo; Pres: Martin Titman; Edu Dir: Ray Levin. **Bustleton & Oakmont Sts, Phila PA 19152 (215) RA8–1155.**

Northeast Family Day Care. An independent branch of the Fed Day Care Servs. Dedicated to the welfare of the chil & his family. Family day care prog; counseling servs to parents. 38 chil. Although it provided day care servs prior to 1978, the facility expanded its prog in that yr when it became a separate branch of the Family Day Care Servs. **Jamison Ave & Garth Rd, Phila PA 19116.**

Northern Hebrew Day Nursery. Administered by the Fed Day Care Servs. Group day care ctr for presch chil; counseling & referral servs; Parents Assn activities. 60 chil aged three to five. On Nov 3, 1921, 14 women met to est a day care ctr that would be conducted in the traditional J manner. After two yrs of solicitation & fund raising, the membership was enlarged & a house was bought. On Mar 16, 1923 the Northern Hebrew Day Nursery opened. Care was given to needy chil aged 3–13. Servs were voluntary. At first there was no fee, but eventually parents began to make contributions. The Nursery was inc Dec 24, 1923. In 1936 the original bldg was expanded & two adjacent properties were purchased, providing space for 50 chil. Due to a population shift, a new site was purchased in Jun of 1954, & in Sept of 1955 the new facility opened. After another 23 yrs there was another population shift. In 1977 the nursery merged with Fed Day Care Servs. Ground was broken in Jun 1978 for a new bldg, & on Oct 31, 1978 a uniquely designed modern facility was opened in the NE area. Outdoor facilities include a playground & a picnic area. Future plans include day care for sch age chil. **10800 Jamison Ave, Phila PA 19116.**

Oxford Circle Jewish Community Center. Affiliated with United Syn of Am. Rabbi J. Harold Romirowsky; Cantor Irving Grossman; Pres: Joseph Sternberg; Exec Dir: Sylvia Reibstein; Edu Dir: Sheldon Senoff. **1009 Unruh Ave, Phila PA 19111 (215) FL2–2400.**

Pennsylvania Federation of Temple Youth. A Fed of youth groups fr Reform congs in the PA Council of the UAHC. It is one of 21 youth regions of NFTY (N Am Fed of Temple Youth), the youth affiliate of the UAHC. To provide Reform youth with an organizational tie to the Am J com, an opportunity to learn & experience J traditions, a forum in which to discuss J issues, & a social environment in which to meet other Reform J. Retreat Weekends; week-long Summer Encampment; Study Weekends; Leadership Weekends. 26 active youth groups with a total membership of 558 HS people. The offs are HS stu who are elected by their peers annually. The Fed was originally part of MAFTY (Mid-Atlantic Fed of Temple Youth), but separated in 1964 to form its own region. Dir of Youth & Camp: Arie Gluck. **PA Council UAHC, 2111 Architects Bldg, 117 S 17th St, Phila PA 19103 (215) LO3–8183.**

Pinemere Camp of the Middle Atlantic Region of J.W.B. The regional sleep away camp for the J Y's & Ctrs of the area for chil aged seven to 14. To provide a J living experience in a majority setting for chil fr non-met & rural coms who otherwise live their entire childhood in a minority setting. Eight week session or two four week sessions; rel servs; group work oriented prog; photography workshop; sports; outdoor living & nature prog; day & overnight canoeing trips; arts & crafts. Est in 1943. Facilities include 159 acres of woodland, 8¾ acre lake, swimming pool, three all weather tennis cts, all weather basketball ct, athletic fields for all land sports, three camper dev overnight camp site areas, arts & crafts ctr, ceramics workshop, nature bldg for exhibits & lectures, recreation hall with an indoor & outdoor stage, outdoor chapel, kosher kitchen, health ctr, adm bldg & a conf ctr. The health & conf ctrs are dual purpose bldgs used for yr round camping progs which are open to the constituent agy of Pinemere Camp. Together these bldgs house 88 people, dormitory style. Pres: Martin Sonnenfeld; 1st VP: Donald V. Selkow; VPs: John Benowitz, Stephanie Cohen, Alfred J. Green, Dr Stephen M. Holden, Frank H. Menaker Jr, Irving Refowich; Sec: Robert Rockmaker; Treas: Joel H. Tapper; Hon Pres: Fabian I. Fraenkel, Ian Lipton, Dick M. Richards, Louis Rubin; Exec Dir: Robert H. Miner. **R.D. #3, Stroudsburg PA; winter add: 438 W Tabor Rd, Phila PA 19120 (215) 924–0402.**

Pioneer Women – Na'amat. The training & edu of the Is woman & her family so that each can be best equipped to lead productive lives. For additional information, see – Pioneer Women Na'amat, New York City, NY. **1405 Locust St, Rm 1117, Phila PA 19102 (215) 545–1328.**

Raymond & Miriam Klein Branch, Myer & Rosaline Feinstein Center. Jamison St & Red Lion Rd, Phila PA 19116 (215) 698–7300.

Reconstructionist Rabbinical College. Grad sch for the edu & training of rabbis & J com leaders. To train & ordain rabbis for servs in every aspect of the J com & at the same time to equip them with the necessary academic training which qualifies them to teach J studies at a col or univ; to make J studies relevant to the demands of contemporary J & gen life. Curriculum leading to ordination or Dr of Hebrew Letters degree which is based on a dual prog of studies combining course work in rabbinic subjects at the Col with a prog of grad studies at a major univ in the Phila area (stu are encouraged to spend a yr in Is prior to graduation); Prog of study which includes: Biblical Period, Rabbinic Period, Medieval Period, Modern Period, Contemporary Period; Seminars in Reconstructionism; Dept of Practical Rabbinics; Guest Lecturer Prog; Mordecai M. Kaplan Library which includes collections in biblical studies, rabbinics, J hist, theology & philosophy, & maintains over 200 gen & specialized periodicals; communal serv, congregational, & edu internships; Col Council which considers all matters relating to the prog of studies & makes recommendations, & serves as a clearing house for faculty stu relations; Stu Assn; Placement Cttee. Est by Charter in 1968 by the J Reconstructionist Foun. The Women's Org of the J Reconstructionist Foun provides fin aid to the Col & sponsors the Reconstructionist Univ Fellowship. The Phila Friends of the Col support the Col & sponsor the Ins of J Studies. F J Reconstructionist Movement: Rabbi Mordecai M. Kaplan; Pres Emeritus: Rabbi Ira Eisenstein; Pres: Ira Silverman; Dean: Ronald Brauner; Co-Chr Bd of Govs: Lavy M. Becker, Peter A. Kessner; Sec: Joseph Singer; Treas: William Seltzer; Registrar, Librarian: Jennifer Gabriel; Dir of Stu Affairs: Rabbi Rebecca Trachtenberg Alpert; Dir, Dept of Biblical Civilization: Rabbi Ivan Caine; Dept of Rabbinic Civilization: Dr Sol Cohen; Acting Dir, Dept of Medieval Civilization: Dr Howard Kreisel; Dir, Dept of Modern Civilization: Dr Stephen Murray Poppel; Dir, Dept of Contemporary Civilization: Dr Robert I. Weiner. **2308 N Board St, Phila PA 19132 (215) 223–8121.**

Reconstructionist Rabbinical College, Mordecai M. Kaplan Library. For information on the Ins, see – Reconstructionist Rabbinical College, Phila, PA. **2308 N Broad St, Phila PA 19132 (215) 223–8121.**

Samuel Paley Day Care Center. Administered by the Fed Day Care Serv. Not only to educate the young chil but also to show a concern for his social & psychological dev, & support for his family. Group day care for the presch & the younger sch age chil; Early Intervention Dept for group day care for presch chil who need both treatment & daytime care; extension day care for sch age chil at a Mini Branch; summer day care for yr round sch age chil & the brothers & sisters of presch chil; Parent Assn activities; Weekend Family Swim Club. 230 chil in yr round prog, & 240 during the summer; enrolls chil ages 3 through 11. F in Nov 1923 in a two story row house. The facility was then called the Strawberry Mansion Hebrew Day Nursery. It became a constituent of the Fed of J Charities in 1927. 10 yrs later, the nursery moved to a larger bldg. At the same time, the need for a more professional staff was recognized & implemented. The nursery was one of the first to use case work for intake & follow up, & provide servs to the entire family. Admissions were based on med & psychological factors as well as economic needs. Because of a shift in the J population, a pilot prog was instituted in the new J area in 1959. In 1961 the Strawberry Mansion Day Care House closed its doors. The pilot prog begun in 1959 conclusively proved the need in the NE com for a day care ctr. In 1966 the Samuel Paley Day Care Ctr was opened. The bldg, including an addition constructed in 1974, is on a seven acre plot that includes presch & sch age playgrounds, a wading pool, & a regulation swimming pool. **Strahle & Horrocks Sts, Phila PA 19152 (215) RA5–8930.**

School of Observation & Practice. Jointly managed by Gratz College & the United Hebrew Schs. Class for chil with learning disabilities on Sun. Com sch available to any chil in J com. Prin: Sylvia Silovitz. **701 Byberry Rd, Phila PA 19116 (215) 677–7261.**

The Society for the Sociological Study of Jewry. Scholarly org of social researchers. Mems are sociologists, but other social scientists participate as well. Journal specializing in empirical studies of J soc & culture – Contemporary Jewry. Dir: Samuel Z. Klausner. **3718 Locust Walk, Phila PA 19104.**

Society Hill Synagogue – Agudath Ahim/Ohr Hadash. Reconstructionist Conservative Syn, unaffiliated. To provide rel, edu, cultural & social nourishment for modern J who respect tradition but not conventional forms. Sabbath Worship Servs; Fri night & Sat morning (Sat only, July/Aug); Servs on Holidays following Is calendar; cultural prog with various courses; Rel Sch twice-weekly plus cantor's training to become Bar/Bat Mitzvah; Presch; cultural & social celebrations for Holidays (worship servs use Conservative Siddur with English liturgical supplement (Sermon dialogue Lail Shabbat, Torah/Haftara dialogue Yom Shabbat); library containing 1,000 vols (almost exclusively Judaica & J fiction). 310 families; 120 individuals; 90 stu through Bar Mitsvah; 10 HS stu. 7 employees. Changed fr church to Agudas Ahim/Oir Hudos in 1911 (Roumanian Orthodox). In 1967 added name Society Hill Synagogue (pronounced Heb name as in Israeli Heb), unaffiliated Conservative; since then, growing identification as Reconstructionist. Pub SHS Newsletter (monthly). Facilities include sanctuary seating 750. Rabbi Ivan Caine; Adm: Keith Rand; Pres: Jay Baer; VPs: Marilyn Steiner, Irving Shapiro; Treas: Peter Piven. **418 Spruce St, Phila PA 19106 (215) 922–6590.**

Talmudical Yeshiva of Philadelphia. Gen & J studies. 180 stu. F in 1953 as a Beth Medrash only. In 1955 a HS was added. Enrollment is limited intentionally to be able to maintain personalized contact between Rabbeim, Roshei Yeshiva & stu. Virtually all stu attend full time 7:30–23:00, residing in dormitories. Roshei Yeshiva: Rabbi Elya Svei, Rabbi Shmuel Kamenetsky; Prin: Rabbi Uri Mandelbaum; Exec Dir: Rabbi Shmuel Lieberman; Pres: Erwin Weinberg; Exec VP: Dr Albert Schild; VPs: Dr S. I. Askovitz, Julius Idstein, Rev Louis Joseph, Samuel J. Korman, Rabbi Joseph Rothstein, Dr Nathan Steinberg; Treas: George Gornish; Fin Sec: Isaac Friedman; Rec Sec: H. Jay Wenick; Corsp Sec: Dr Eli M. Mandelbaum; Bd of Trustees: Leonard Goldfine, Marvin I. Levinthal, Rev Harry Mauskopf, Morris J. Root, Harry Solomon, Sol Swerlick; Bd of Dirs: Samuel Back, Dr Joseph Brown, Bernard B. Brownstein, Dalk Feith, Jack Goldstein, Gerald Cornish, Harry J. Greenstein, Joseph Grossman, Harry A. Kalish, Alvan Kamis, Lawrence Katz, Dr Abba Krieger, Dr Joseph Mandelbaum, Manfred Mauskopf, Norman T. Meketon, Rabbi Bernard Meth, Mitchell E. Panzer, Julius L. Popowich, Max J. Reiser, Rabbi Chaim Tzvi Rosenberg, Abner Schreiber, Aaron Shapiro, Rabbi Abraham Slivko, Sam Sokoloff, Jack Steinbreg, Rev Naftali Ungar, Aaron Vegh, David Weinberg, A. Joseph Weinberger, Gilbert I. Yaros, William Zuckerman, Jack H. Zweig. **6063 Drexel Rd, Phila PA 19131 (215) GR7–1000.**

Temple Beth Torah. Class for chil with learning disabilities on Sun. Reform cong sch open to families affiliated with a cong & to J com–at–large pending available space. Prin: Jerome Segal. **608 Welsh Rd, Phila PA 19115 (215) 677–1555.**

Temple Beth Zion Beth Israel. Affiliated with United Syn of Am. Rabbi Herbert Rosenblum; Cantor Mark Kushner; Pres: Leo Lorona; Exec Dir: Mrs Daniel P. Parker; Edu & Youth Dir: Mark H. Levene. **SW Corner 18th & Spruce Sts, Phila PA 19103 (215) PE5–5148,9.**

Temple Beth Zion Beth Israel Library. For information on the Temple, see – Temple Beth Zion Beth Israel, Philadelphia, PA. **18th & Spruce Sts, Phila PA 19103 (215) 735–5148.**

Temple Israel – Wynnefield. Affiliated with United Syn of Am. Rabbi Samuel H. Berkowitz; Cantor Joseph Abramson; Pres: Albert Pearson. **901 Woodbine Ave, Phila PA 19131 (215) 877–3200.**

Temple Judea. Affiliated with UAHC. 400 mems. Rabbi Edward M. Maline; Pres: Alvin Waxman; Edu: Joel Alpert; Sisterhood Pres: R. Sobelman; Brotherhood Pres: Robert Sobelman. **6928 Old York Rd, Phila PA 19126 (215) 224–3040.**

Temple Menorah. Affiliated with United Syn of Am. Rabbi Abraham H. Isrealitan; Cantors: Julius Wahlberg, Josef Trasken; Pres: Stanley Kamens; Exec Dir: Betty Barnett. **4301 Tyson Ave, Phila PA 19149 (215) MA4–9600.**

Temple Sholom. Affiliated with United Syn of Am. Rabbi Pinchos J. Chazin; Cantor David Lebovic; Pres: Dr Stanley I. Goodhart; Edu Dir: Esther Weintraub; Youth Dir: Joseph Saffren. **Large St & Roosevelt Blvd, Phila PA 19149 (215) 288–7600.**

Tikvoh Chadoshoh. Affiliated with United Syn of Am. Rabbi Dr Willim Eisenberg; Cantor Gustav Florsheim; Pres: Herbert H. Oser. **5364 W Checo Ave, Phila PA 19138 (215) GE8–1508.**

UAHC Pennsylvania Council – Philadelphia Federation. Rel & edu org serving J congs throughout the US & Canada. To encourage & aid the org & dev of J congs; to promote J edu, & enrich & intensify J life; to foster other activities for the perpetuation & advancement of J. For additional information, see – UAHC – Union of American Hebrew Congregations, New York City, NY. Pres: David Cohen, Dr I. Ezra Staples; Dir: Rabbi Richard Address. **2111 Architects Bldg, 117 S 17th St, Phila PA 19103 (215) 563–8183.**

United Hebrew Schools & Yeshivos of Philadelphia. Dedicated to the principle that an authentic J identity can best be acquired by studying the classics of J Thought with an emphasis on Heb language. To help a stu feel competent to interact with all aspects of the J com, having developed an appreciation for & dedication to Am J communal life, & the State of Is & World J. The United Heb Schs & the Sch of Observation & Practice offer a three day per week prog of study that extends over the course of five yrs. The curriculum features a prep primary class & also provides stu with an enrichment prog of indivualized tutorial assistance. The curriculum of the schs includes the study of Heb Language, Bible, Rabbinic & Contemporary Literature, Hist, Liturgy, Ethics, Customs & Ceremonies, & Current Events, workshops in the arts. Gratz Col was f in 1895 & is the oldest Heb teachers col in the western hemisphere. While primarily a teachers col for all types of J schs, it also provides a prog of studies for young men & women who will take their places as informed, knowledgeable J & lay leaders of the J com. The United Hebrew Schs was est in 1919 when the Associated Talmud Torahs were est. The Sch of Observation & Practice was est in 1909. It serves as a demonstration sch for both curricular experimentation, innovative methods & media. The Sch is designed to serve as a model for those schs serviced by the Div of Com Servs of Gratz Col, & provides Gratz Col stu of J edu with a unique opportunity for classroom observation & practice teaching. Exec Dir United Hebrew Schs: Morton Schulman; Pres: Natalie L. Hodes; VP: Philip Resnikov; Treas: Marc A. Krefetz; Coordinating Consultant Gratz Col: Dr William B. Lakritz. **701 Byberry Rd, Phila PA 19116 (215) OR7–7261.**

United States Committee, Sports for Israel. 341 S 18th St, Phila PA 19103 (215) 546–4700, 4739, 4771.

Young Israel of Wynnefield. Orthodox Syn affiliated with Natl Council of Young Is. Rel Servs; edu progs; Sisterhood. 60 families. F 1961. Facilities include sanctuary seating for 90 men & 75 women. Pres: Alter Diament; VP: Arnold Miller; Treas: Stewart Schoenbrun; Sec: Helmut Bodenheim. **5300 Wynnefield Ave, Phila PA 19131 (215) 473–3511.**

Phoenixville

B'nai Jacob Library. For information on the Cong, see – Congregation B'nai Jacob, Phoenixville, PA. **Starr & Manavon Sts, Phoenixville PA 19460 (215) 933–5550.**

Congregation B'nai Jacob. Affiliated with United Syn of Am. Rabbi Mitchell Rominowsky; Pres: Dr

Joel W. Eisner. **Starr & Manavon Sts, Phoenixville PA 19460 (215) 933–5550.**

Pittsburgh

Associated American Jewish Museums, Inc. Maintains regional collections of J art, historical & ritual objects; maintains a central catalogue of such objects in the collections of J mus throughout the US; helps J mus acquire, identify & classify objects; arranges exchanges of collections, exhibits, & individual objects among J mus; encourages the creation of J art, ceremonial & ritual objects. Pres: Walter Jacob; VP: William Rosenthall; Sec: Robert H. Lehman; Treas: Jason Z. Edelstein. **303 LeRoi Rd, Pittsburgh PA 15208.**

B'nai B'rith Hillel Foundation. 315 S Bellefield Ave, Pittsburgh PA 15213 (412) 621–8875.

B'nai B'rith Hillel Foundation Library. 315 S Bellefield Ave, Pittsburgh PA 15213 (412) 621–8875.

Beth El Congregation. Affiliated with United Syn of Am. Rabbi Stephen Steindel; Cantor Herman Weissberg; Pres: Alexander Silverman: Edu Dir: Moshe Bettan. **1900 Cochran Rd, Pittsburgh PA 15220 (412) 561–1168.**

Congregation Adath Jeshurun & Congregation Cnesseth Israel. Orthodox Syn affiliated with Union of Orthodox Congs. To disseminate Judaism. Rel Servs; 3 daily & all Sabbaths & Holidays; Adult Edu; daily classes in Mishna; weekly classes in Talmud; weekly class in current events; pre-holiday workshops; classes in J Law; Sisterhood; Men's Club; Chevra Mishna; Chevra Thillim; Chevra Kadisha; Minyanaires; Adath Jeshurun Cemetery; Cnesseth Israel Cemetery; Sr Citizen Club; library containing over 1,000 vols (Judaica). 300 mems (250 families; 50 individuals). 5 employees. F 1916. Pub Adath Jeshhurun News (5 times a yr). Facilities include main sanctuary seating 1,000, small sanctuary seating 300, kosher kitchen, social hall seating 300, 5 classrms, Bd rm, off, rabbi's study, Sisterhood gift shop. Rabbi Dr Morris A. Landes; Cantor Joseph Fish; Pres: Ben Karik; 1st VP: Leonard Lipsky; 2nd VP: Ruben Simon; Treas: Edwin Finer; Fin Sec: Arnold Kansebaum; Rec Sec: Henry Melnick. **5643 E Liberty Blvd, Pittsburgh PA 15206 (412) 361–0173.**

Congregation B'nai Israel. Affiliated with United Syn of Am. Rabbi Richard M. E. Marcovitz; Cantor Mordecai G. Heiser; Pres: Arnold N. Wagner; Edu Coord: Maxima Ofer; Youth Dir: Claryne Karsh. **327 N Negley Ave, Pittsburgh PA 15206 (412) 661–0252.**

Congregation Beth Shalom. Conservative Syn affiliated with United Syn of Am. Committed to the enhancement of the quality of J life. Rel Servs; spiritual guidance; communal & family oriented programming; J elementary edu & adult edu. 850 families. Rabbi Moshe V. Goldblum; Cantor Moshe Taube; Bar Mitzvah Teacher: Rabbi Morris Sklar; Edu Dir: Dr Justin H. Lewis; Exec Dir: Mark Stern; Pres: Harriet N. Kruman; Exec VP: Alan Greenwald; 1st VP: Marrianne Silberman; 2nd VP: Milton Eisner; 3rd VP: Yale Rosenstein; Sec: Samuel Nathenson; Treas: David Graff; Asst Treas: Judity Palkovitz. **5915 Beacon St at Shady Ave, Pittsburgh PA 15217 (412) 421–2288.**

Dor Hadash. Reconstructionist Cong belonging to the Reconstructionist Fed. Rel Servs; study groups. Servs are led by volunteers fr the Cong. All activities are voluntary. A stu rabbi fr the Reconstructionist Rabbinical Col in Phila visits the Cong three times a yr. F in 1963 as an independent cong leaning toward Reconstructionism. Monthly bulletin. Pres: Avis Kotovsky; VP: Larry Saroff; Sec: Regina Belle; Treas: Leonard Belov. **PO Box 8223, Pittsburgh PA 15217.**

Holocaust Center of Greater Pittsburg. 234 McKee Pl, Pittsburgh PA 15213 (412) 681–8000.

Jewish Family & Children's Service of Pittsburgh. Counseling; outreach to youth; psychiatric out-patient serv; adoption servs; casework servs; kosher Meals-on-Wheels; referral to com resources; immigration serv. Est 1937. Fees are on a sliding scale. Dir of Professional Servs: Shirley R. Imber; Supervisor of Aged Servs: Nancy Frank. **234 McKee Pl, Pittsburgh PA 15213 (412) 683–4900.**

Lubavitch Youth Organization. An outreach org that familiarizes J men & women & chil with J practices & philosophy. Affiliated with the Chabad Lubavitch Movement. To bring the Light of Torah & J tradition to all corners of the world; to battle against assimilation, apathy & indifference to J living. In gen this ins offers: Operation Helping Hand – gives aid to Russian immigrants; on campus progs – provides kosher foods, Fri night to Sun retreats, lectures, Shabbat servs & counseling; celebrations of holidays – holds seminars on Passover laws, gives Purim Party, sponsors toys for tots for chil in the hosp at Chanukah, helps with bldg of succas, distributes prayers bks for holidays; marriage & family counseling – sponsors adult edu prog; helps est kosher kitchens in private homes; Mitzvah Mobile – introduces J men to the wearing of Tefillin, distributes rel articles, maintains travelling J library & audio visual ctr; Succamobile; summer day camp. Rabbi I. Altein. **5819 Douglas St, Pittsburgh PA 15213 (412) 521–5252.**

Parkway Jewish Center. Affiliated with United Syn of Am. Rabbi Moshe Weingarten; Pres: Mitchell Hoffman. **300 Princeton Dr, Pittsburgh PA 15235 (412) 823–4338, 9709.**

Pioneer Women – Na'amat. The training & edu of the Is woman & her family so that each can be best equipped to lead productive lives. For additional information, see – Pioneer Women Na'amat, New York City, NY. **6328 Forbes Ave, Pittsburgh PA 15217 (412) 521–5253.**

Pittsburgh Jewish Publication & Education Foundation. 315 S Bellefield Ave, Pittsburgh PA 15213 (412) 687–1000.

Rodef Shalom Congregation. Reform Cong affiliated with UAHC. Rel Servs; Rel Sch for chil in grades 1–10; HS for grades 11 & 12; special mid week Heb prog for boys & girls who will be Bar or Bat Mitzvah; Adult Edu Prog which consists of lectures, symposia, forums, classes, breakfasts & films; special progs for teenagers, col age singles, singles & retired people; Sisterhood which provides floral decorations for the pulpit, does braille work, typing for the partially sighted, accomplishes bookbinding, & maintains a sewing group & other activities; Brotherhood which supports a boy scout troop, provides ushers for servs, guides visiting groups through the Temple, maintains a Blood Assurance Prog & other activities; Jr Cong which conducts its own additional prog of edu, social & rel activities including a nursery for young chil during servs, sponsors a scholar in residence, conducts servs in nursing homes & special rel demonstrations. The Cong sponsors Mothers Day Out Prog which is open to the com, & an annual dinner on behalf of Is bonds. 1650 mems. Chartered in 1856, it is the oldest J cong in Western PA. It occupied several downtown sites before moving to its present site in 1907. The sanctuary, which was completed in that yr, has been designated as a Pittsburgh landmark & is the only structure designed for J purposes so designated in Pittsburgh. In 1938 a sch bldg was added, & an activities bldg, a library, a social hall & additional classooms were added in 1956. Bulletin. Facilities include a sanctuary that seats approximately 1,500 persons, a chapel that seats 100, an assembly hall which seats approximately 550 persons & has small stained glass windows which are replicas of windows in German syns destroyed by the Nazis, a large assembly hall which can accommodate 700 for dinner, three libraries with combined holdings exceeding 10,000 vols, a small mus, & a bk & gift corner. Rabbi Walter Jacob; Assc Rabbi Mark N. Staitman; Rabbi Emeritus Solomon B. Freehof; Rel Sch Prin: Saul Simon; Exec Sec: Vigdor Kavaler; Pres: Allen H. Berkman; VPs: Lester Herrup, Gerald Ostrow; Treas: Stanley R. Gumberg; Sec: Robert M. Frankel; Asst Sec-Treas: Mrs Edward L. Waisbrot; Bd of Trustees: M. L. Aaron, Richard N. Adelsheim, Stuart A. Arnheim, Mark B. Aronson, Norman L. Berger, Allen H. Berkman, Harold S. Bigler, A. A. Bluestone, Louis B. Brody, Dr Sidney N. Busis, Charles L. Deaktor, Robert M. Frankel, Dr Solomon B. Freehof, Stanley R. Gumberg, Lester Herrup, Dr Walter Jacob, Norman T. Kanel, Irving M. J. Kaplan, Joel W. Katz, Alan Z. Lefkowitz, Mrs Alex D. Lowy Jr, Alan Marcus, Mark E. Mason, Edgar W. Michaels, Gerald Ostrow, Albert I. Raizman, Mrs Jack S. Rashba, Mrs S. Jay Rogal, Mrs Lawrence J. Rosen, Stanley W. Rosenbuam, Samuel B. Roth, Leonard H. Rudolph, Bonnie Schwartz, Mrs Edward L. Waisbrot, Mrs Robert H. Wolf. **Fifth & Morewood Ave, Pittsburgh PA 15213 (412) 621–6566.**

Rodef Shalom Congregation, Glick Memorial Library. For Information on the Cong, see – Rodef Shalom Congregation, Pittsburgh, PA. **4905 Fifth Ave, Pittsburgh PA 15213 (412) 621–6566.**

Solomon Schechter Day School of Pittsburgh. Affiliated with Solomon Schechter Day Schs Assn. Edu Dir: Ruth Gumerman; Chr: Al Smolover. **Beacon at Shady St, Pittsburgh PA 15217.**

Temple Emanuel. Affiliated with UAHC. 600 mems. Rabbis: William Sajowitz, Mark Mahler; Pres: Shirley Bleiberg; Adm: Louise A. Sperling; Sisterhood Pres: Ferne Friedman; Brotherhood Pres: Ruben Abramovitz. **1250 Bower Hill Rd, Pittsburgh PA 15243 (412) 279–7600.**

Temple Emanuel Library. 1250 Bower Hill Rd, Pittsburgh PA 15243 (412) 279–7600.

Temple Sinai. Affiliated with UAHC. 491 mems. Rabbis: Stephan F. Barack, Aaron B. Ilson; Pres: Herman Greenberg; Edu: Fran Borovetz; Sisterhood Pres: Delores R. Smooke; Brotherhood Pres: Gilbert Dansker. **5505 Forbes Ave, Pittsburgh PA 15217 (412) 421–9715.**

Tree of Life. Affiliated with United Syn of Am. Rabbi Solomon M. Kaplan; Cantor Harry P.

Silversmith: Pres: Harvey A. Wolsh; Exec & Edu Dir: David Dinkin; Youth Dir: Dr Iris Nahemow. **Wilkins & Shady Ave, Pittsburgh PA 15217 (412) 521–6788.**

The United Jewish Federation of Greater Pittsburgh. The central fund raising, budgeting, planning & coordinating agy for the J com of Pittsburgh. Est in 1955 as a result of a consolidation of the United J Fund previously est in 1936, & the Fed of J Philanthropies previously est in 1912. Pres: Leonard H. Rudolph; VPs: Gerald S. Ostrow, Sylvia M. Robinson, Howard T. Shapiro; Treas: Sylvia Busis; Asst Treas: Marilyn S. Latterman; Sec: Stanley C. Ruskin; Asst Sec: Ruth Schacter; Bd of Dirs: Michael J. Aranson, Meyer Berger, Marshall L. Berkman, Edward Berman, Harold S. Bigler, Harold Y. Black, Joseph E. Berman, Dr Sidney N. Busis, Donald Butler, Gertrude F. Caplan, Dr David L. Chamovitz, David I. Cohen, Jesse J. Cohen, Amos Comay, R. Joel Coslov, Saul Elinoff, Marcella L. Finegold, Dr Ellen Frank, Frederick N. Frank, Dr Michael A. Friedberg, Gilbert Gerber, Edwin I. Grinberg, Bernard M. Halpern, Ethel A. Halpern, Irving J. Halpern, David G. Hast, Dr Stanley A. Hirsch, Dean J. Hirschfield, Dr Larry E. Hurwitz, Harry Kamin, Richard E. Kann, Robert Kaplan, Marshall P. Katz, Dr Laibe A. Kessler, Albert S. Klein, Ronald Kottler, Elliott B. Kramer, Nicholas Lane, Bernard B. Latterman, Earl M. Latterman, Aaron P. Levinson, Harriet D. Levinson, Edward J. Lewis, Jerome B. Lieber, Harry Markovitz, Bernard S. Mars, Jack A. Meyers, Dr Bernard I. Michaels, Dr Charles J. Miller, David J. Millstein, Donald I. Moritz, Leon L. Netzer, Ivan J. Novick, Natalie E. Novick, Dr Richard S. Pataki, Edward A. Perlow, James C. Polacheck, Irwin W. Porter, Donald Pripstein, Raymond Rackoff, Fred M. Rock, Sally S. Rock, Alvin Rogal, Samuel B. Roth, Joseph Rubenstein, Julian H. Ruslander, David S. Shapira, Robert D. Shapiro, Joel Smalley, Albert Smolover, Arthur Sonnenklar, Rabbi Stephen E. Steindel, Harriett H. Wedner, Arlene P. Weisman, Flossie C. Wolf, John M. Wolf, Louis Zeiden; Exec VP: Howard M. Rieger; Assc Dir: Saul Weisberg. **234 McKee Pl, Pittsburgh PA 15213 (412) 681–8000.**

Yeshivah Achai Tmimim. 2410 Fifth Ave, Pittsburgh PA 15213 (412) 681–2446.

Young Peoples Synagogue of Pittsburgh. Orthodox Cong. To promote traditional J in all facets of life; to encourage young men & women to participate actively in all phases of the syn Servs; to stimulate participation in other forms of J communal life; to strengthen the bonds with our brethren in Is & with the J people everywhere; to exemplify J by emphasizing the principles of righteousness & brotherhood in soc at large. 375 mems. F in 1946 by the Young Men's Club of the Hapoel Hamizrachi of Pittsburgh. The Syn is a participatory syn with the mems organizing & running the Servs. Pres: David Milch; VP: Jordan Dern; Treas: Sidney Deutsch; Sec: Leonard Feldman; Gabbai: Walter Vogal. **6401 Forbes Ave, Pittsburgh PA 15217.**

Pottstown

Congregation Mercy & Truth. Affiliated with United Syn of Am. Rabbi Max W. Wasser; Pres: David S. Kaplan. **575 N Keim St, Pottstown PA 19464 (215) 326–1717.**

Pottsville

Oheb Zedek Synagogue Center. Pres: Gerald Ravitz MD; Edu Dir: Mrs Bruce Edelson. **2300 Mahantongo St, Pottsville PA 17901 (717) 622–4320.**

United Jewish Charities. 2300 Mahantongo St, Pottsville PA 17901 (717) 622–5890.

Reading

Congregation Oheb Sholom. Affiliated with UAHC. 295 mems. Rabbi Alan G. Weitzman; Pres: Ellis Friedman; Edu: Steven Gaynes; Sisterhood Pres: Annalee Aarons; Brotherhood Pres: Ted Sherman. **13th St & Perkiomen Ave, Reading PA 19602 (215) 373–4623.**

Jewish Federation of Reading PA, Inc. Mem of CJF. Sponsors United Jewish Campaign. Pres: Dr David N. Farber; Exec Dir: Roy Stuppler. **1700 City Line St, Reading PA 19604 (215) 921–2766.**

Kesher Zion Synagogue. Conservative Syn. To advance the teachings & philosophy of Conservative J. Rel Servs; Rel Sch; Presch for chil between the ages 3 & 5; Sisterhood, meetings, progs & projs; library; Adult J Studies, divided into two semesters in each of which courses dealing with Heb Language, Prayerbook, Bible, J Hist, Literature & Music are given; guest speakers; class on the Ethics of the Fathers every Sabbath during summer & spring; post Bar & Bat Mitzvah classes; chil drama & choir groups; Bk Review Club; concerts; cultural progs; Oneg Shabbats; USY Youth Group. 500 families. Formed in 1930 through a merger of the Kesher Is & B'nai Zion Congs. The Syn is the largest J cong in Reading. Monthly Bulletin. Facilities include a sanctuary, chapel, sch wing, social hall, reading rm, auditorium, kitchen, Is art & gift shop, & bk shop. Rabbi Dr Joseph Renov; Cantor Ben Klonsky; Pres:

Jack Schnee; VPs: Moses Rabinovitch, Dr Gary Lattin; Sec: Alan Strauss; Asst Sec: Janet Kaplan; Treas: William Lidman; Asst Treas: Dr Gordon Perlmutter. **1245 Eckert & Perkiomen Ave, Reading PA 19602 (215) 372–3818.**

Richboro

Ohev Shalom of Bucks County. Affiliated with United Syn of Am. Rabbi Elliott Perlstein; Cantor Eric Snyder; Pres: Mitchell Ziegler; Edu Dir: Cheryl Levine; Youth Dir: Sara Steiner. **944 2nd St Pike, Richboro PA 18954 (215) 322–9595.**

Ohev Shalom of Bucks County Library. For information on the Cong, see – Ohev Shalom of Bucks County, Richboro, PA. **944 2nd St Pike, Richboro PA 18966.**

Scranton

Hillel Academy. Day sch. To provide J edu for chil ages 5 through 17 regardless of rel affiliation. Curriculum includes: Heb Language, Liturgy, Bible, J Observances, Holocaust, Is Today, Talmud, & J Ethics; auxiliary activities: Choir, Natl Bible Contest, holiday gatherings, & Is edu trips. F in 1978 as a com afternoon Heb sch, an outgrowth of the local Reform, Conservative & Orthodox Heb schs. Hon Chr: M.L. Hodin; Chr: Edward Novick; V Chr: Aaron Glassman; Sec: Judith Seitchik; Treas: Joseph Dubin; Exec Dir: Rabbi Melvin Sachs. **900 Gibson St, Scranton PA 18510 (717) 343–7837.**

Jewish Community Center. To dev & conduct a comprehensive prog of activities utilizing the skills & methods of social group work, edu, & recreation aimed at assisting individuals to achieve an affirmative identification with J life & a deep appreciation of their responsibilities as citizens of the com, the state & the nation. Grade Sch Dept with youth activities for jr high & HS youngsters; special progs for adults; physical edu for all ages; recreational progs; social progs; cultural events; concerts & art exhibits; com events, Health Fair, Mayorality Debate, Heart Clin & Cancer Detection Series; Gus & Lena Weinberger Scholarship Fund for stu requiring additional aid for supplemental col activities such as bks & registration fees rather than full support for a yrs tution. 2,400 mems ranging in age fr birth to late 90's. The agy was est as the YMHA in 1909. It was incorporated in 1914 & the name was changed to the JCC in 1949. The JCC moved to the present location in 1957. The JCC participates with the Heart Assn, Cancer Soc, Retarded Chil & numerous other communal groups in Scranton offering progs of interest to the com of a health, edu & cultural nature. Chr of the Bd: Joseph Dubin; 1st Vice Chr: Sam Harris; 2nd Vice Chr: Bernard Hochman; Treas: Louis Dinner; Asst Treas: Edward Novick; Asst Sec: Mrs Harold Sprung; Sec: Seymour Brotman; Exec Dir: Seymour Brotman. **601 Jefferson Ave, Scranton PA 18510 (717) 346–6595.**

The Jewish Home of Eastern Pennsylvania. A skilled nursing facility licensed by the Commonwealth of PA, Medicare & Medicaid. To provide skilled nursing care to mems of the J faith residing in E PA. Occupational therapy; some physical therapy; syn on the premises with Daily, Shabbat & Holiday Servs; strict dietary servs; kosher Meals-On-Wheels for citizens of Scranton & Wilkes-Barre. In 1916 an org of J women f an ins to be called, at that time, the J Home for the Friendless, for the purpose of giving assistance to & providing a home for the orphans & aged of both sexes. In 1944 the Home ceased to house chil, & devoted its attention to the aged. The total num of chil cared for in 23 years was 124. In 1961 the name of the org was changed to the J Home of E PA. Between 1964 & 1981 a new facility & additions were constructed & added. Exec Dir: Herman C. Margulies; Assc Exec Dir: Samuel K. Sandhaus; Pres: J. Milton Swartz; VPs: Sanford Cohen, Nathan I. Kuss, Ernest Weisberger, Max Fisher, Dr David S. Wagner, Julius Simon; Treas: Irwin Alperin; Asst Treas: Jerry Weinberger; Sec: Harold Sprung; Asst Sec: Mrs Benno C. Levy; Hon Chr: Dr Bernard Shair, Seymour Hollenberg. **1101 Vine St, Scranton PA 18510 (717) 344–6177.**

Scranton-Lackawanna Jewish Council. Mem of CJF. Includes Lackwanna County. Organized 1945. Pres: Jack Plotkin; Exec Dir: Seymour Brotman. **601 Jefferson Ave, Scranton PA 18510 (717) 961–2300.**

Temple Hesed. Affiliated with UAHC. 295 mems. Rabbi Milton Richman; Pres: John Appleton; Sisterhood Pres: S. Kaplan; Brotherhood Pres: Dov Giloni. **Lake Scranton Rd & Knox St, Scranton PA 18505 (717) 344–7201.**

Temple Israel. Affiliated with United Syn of Am. Rabbi Dr Simon H. Shoop; Asst Rabbi Dan Grossman; Cantor Mark Keller; Pres: Leonard Krieger; Edu Dir: Rabbi Melvin Sachs; Youth Dir: Rabbi Dan Grossman. **Gibbon St & Monroe Ave, Scranton PA 18510 (717) 342–0350.**

Sharon

Shenango Valley Jewish Federation. 840 Highland Rd, Sharon PA 16146 (412) 346–4754.

Temple Beth Israel. Affiliated with UAHC. 207 mems. Rabbi Samuel I. Weingart; Pres: Dorothy Bolotin; Sisterhood Pres: Darlene Rabinowitz. **840 Highland Rd, Sharon PA 16146 (412) 346–4754.**

Spring House

Beth Or. Affiliated with UAHC. 384 mems. Rabbi Robert A. Alper; Pres: Dolores P. Solomon; Edu: William Dodies; Sisterhood Pres: Carole Chasen; Brotherhood Pres: David Magen. **Penllyn Pike & Dager Rd, Spring House PA 19477 (215) 646–5806.**

Springfield

Delaware County JCC – Cong Ner Tamid. Affiliated with United Syn of Am. Rabbi Joseph Teichman; Cantor Emanuel Menkes; Pres: Bea Ernest. **300 W Woodland Ave, PO Box 266, Springfield PA 19064 (215) 543–4241.**

Starlight

B'nai B'rith Perlman Camp. To make the camping experience stimulating, rewarding & fun; to foster pride in heritage, learn more about Judaism, & meaningfully practice the rituals of religious heritage; to learn how to participate in group living. Sports; variety of BBYO & B'nai B'rith activities including leadership training conferences, the AZA & BBG Intl Conventions, adult ins of Judaism. Located on 15 acre spring-fed lake. **Camp add: Starlight PA; Natl Off: 1640 Rhode Island NW, Washington DC 20036 (202) 857–6600.**

Trevose

Bikur Holim. Social serv. To visit the institutionalized, physically, mentally or emotionally ill; to help make arrangements for Israelis who need special med attention in Am. 15 mems. 15 volunteers. F 1958. Pres: David S Novoseller; VP: Joseph Novoseller; Sec: Rachel Kaim. **David & Jerome Rds, Trevose PA 19047 (215) 357–7131.**

Chevra Kadisha Holy Society of Bucks County. Social serv. To care for & bring the deceased to J burial; to aid the family through their onan period & shiva period. Provides minyan at home of mourner; provides for Tahara; adv on burial in Is; edu on the above matters; maintains library containing 100 vols (death, mourning & Yiskor). 8 mems. 8 volunteers. F 1977. Pres: Zena Reba Miryam Novoseller; VP: David S. Novoseller; Treas: Joshua M. Novoseller; Sec: Rachel Royce Novoseller. **400 David Dr, Trevose PA 19047 (215) 357–7130.**

Congregation B'nai Yoshia. Orthodox Cong. To help transplant & maintain an E European oriented Orthodox shul in the Bucks Cty & Phila PA area. Rel Servs; Daf Yomi; library containing 2,000 vols (Sifre Kodesh). 50 families. 6 volunteers. F 1930. Facilities include seating capacity of 50, Bais Medrash study hall facilities. Rabbi Maurice E. Novoseller; Sisterhood Pres: Shirley Novoseller; Men's Club Pres: Joseph Novoseller; Sec: Zachary Novoseller; Treas: Joshua Novoseller. **David Dr & Jerome Rd, Trevose PA 19047 (215) 357–7131.**

Congregation B'nai Yoshia, Library. Library contains 2,000 vols (Sifre Kodesh). For information on the Cong, see – Congregation B'nai Yoshia, Trevose, PA. **David Dr & Jerome Rd, Trevose PA 19047 (215) 357–7131.**

Jewish Chaplaincy of Bucks Cty. Social serv. To visit & counsel the institutionalized. 15 mems. F 1963. Chief Chaplain: Maurice E. Novoseller; Chaplains: Zachary Novoseller, Joseph Novoseller, David Novoseller, Joshua Novoseller, Shirley Novoseller, Rachel Novoseller. **800 David Dr, Trevose PA 19047 (215) 357–7131.**

Jewish Library & Laboratory of Judaism. Library – mus. To house & collect bks on J topics; to gather J incunabla & semi-incunabla; to gather & store for research rare & old bks of biblical commentary. Provides, for study, research, understanding, appreciation & emulation, a laboratory of Judaism (full size displays of living Judaism) including: a kitchen obviously designed & set up to facilitate kosher cooking; a display of a Shabbos table, including all the ritual items that distinguish it fr a week-day dining setting; a bedrm that is identifiable as a J bedrm & a posting of the laws pertaining to it; seasonal displays including Hanuka in the home, Sukkot settings, Rosh Hashona preparations, Purim for the family. Maintains a library containing 12,000 vols (every possible & remote relevancy to Judaism). 20 mems. 8 volunteers. F 1965. Facilities include reading desks & reading rms for research. Pres: Rabbi Maurice E. Novoseller; VP: Zachary Novoseller; Sec: Haya M. Novoseller; Treas: Shirley Novoseller. **800 David Dr, Trevose PA 19047 (215) 357–7130.**

Mikvah Association of Lower Bucks Cty. Mikvah. To maintain a mikvah for com use; to disseminate edu concerning the sanctity of the family & its inception in concept & practice. 14 mems. 10 volunteers. F 1960. Facilities include mikvah & relevant facilities. Pres: Shirley Novoseller; VP: Haya M. Novoseller; Sec: Rachel Novoseller; Halacha Adv: Rebettzin Pesia Novoseller. **400 Jerome Rd, Trevose PA 19047 (215) 357–7130.**

Vaad Hakashrus of Delaware Valley. Rel Servs. To supervise the kosher facilities of local firms. 25 mems. F 1975. Rav Hamachshir: Maurice E. Novoseller; Pres: Haya Novoseller; VP: Rachel Novoseller; Mashgichim: Zachary Novoseller, Joseph Novoseller, David Novoseller. **400 David Dr, Trevose PA 19047 (215) 357–7130.**

Uniontown

Temple Israel. Affiliated with UAHC. 54 mems. Rabbi Sion A. David; Pres: Lucille Cooper; Sisterhood Pres: Eunis Freeman; Brotherhood Pres: Norman Belfer. **119 E Fayete St, Uniontown PA 15401 (412) 437–6431.**

United Jewish Federation. c/o Jewish Community Center, 406 W. Main St, Uniontown PA 15401 (412) 438–4681.

Upper Darby

Temple Israel of Upper Darby. Affiliated with United Syn of Am. Rabbi Martin Rubenstein; Cantor William Lieberman; Pres: Shirley Kleinman. **Bywood Ave & Walnut St, Upper Darby PA 19082 (215) FL2–2125.**

Wallingford

Congregation Ohev Shalom. Affiliated with United Syn of Am. Rabbi Louis A. Kaplan PhD; Cantor Jonas Garfinkle; Pres: Melvin Rudman. **2 Chester Rd, PO Box 157, Wallingford PA 19086 (215) 874–1465.**

Washington

Beth Israel Congregation. Affiliated with United Syn of Am. Rabbi Alberta A. Goldman; Pres: Sherman H. Siegel. **265 North Ave, Washington PA 15301 (412) 225–7080.**

Wayne

Or Shalom, The Conservative Synagogue of the Main Line. Affiliated with United Syn of Am. Rabbi David Goldstein; Cantor Barry Krieger; Pres: George Sall; Edu Dir: Cecile Dalton; Youth Dir: Benson Goldberg. **PO Box 476, Wayne PA 19087 (215) 296–3041.**

White Oak

Tree of Life Sfard Congregation. Affiliated with United Syn of Am. Rabbi Chaim Burstein; Pres: Jerome Simon; Exec Dir: Mona Naimark. **2025 Cypress Dr, White Oak PA 15131 (412) 673–0938.**

Wilkes-Barre

Jewish Federation of Greater Wilkes-Barre. Mem of CJF. Sponsors United Jewish Appeal. Organized 1935. Pres: Eugene Roth; Exec Dir: Monty Pomm. **60 S River St, Wilkes-Barre PA 18701 (717) 824–4646.**

Ohav Zedek Synagogue. Orthodox Syn affiliated with Union of Orthodox J Cong of Am. Daily Rel Servs; edu progs; active Sisterhood; active youth progs; library containing 500 vols (mostly rel). 235 families; 105 individuals; 12 stu in Rel Sch. 9 employees. Over 100 yrs old. Pub Ohav Zedek News (7 times a yr). Facilities include kosher kitchen, sanctuary seating 900. Rabbi Israel Kestenbaum; Cantor Shimon Vogel; Pres: Sidney Kirshner; 1st VP: Murray Ufberg; 2nd VP: Howard Greenberg; Treas: Edward Felder; Fin Sec: Nathan Schiowitz; Rec Sec: Sydall Minkoff. **242 S Franklin St, Wilkes-Barre PA 18702 (717) 825–6619.**

Temple Israel. Affiliated with United Syn of Am. Rabbi Dr Abraham D. Barras; Cantor Aaron Griver; Pres: Dr Burton S. Benovitz; Adm: Sally Connor. **239 S River St, Wilkes-Barre PA 18702 (717) 824–8927.**

Williamsport

Beth Ha-Sholom. Affiliated with UAHC. 80 mems. Rabbi David L. Schwartz; Pres: Morton Rauff; Sisterhood Pres: Sarah Eiseman. **425 Center St, Williamsport PA 17701 (717) 323–7751.**

Ohev Shalom Congregation. Affiliated with United Syn of Am. Rabbi Norman E. Singer; Co–Pres: David Brumberg, William Pickelner. **Cherry & Belmont, Williamsport PA 17701 (717) 322–4209.**

Wynnewood

Main Line Reform Temple Library. For information on Temple Beth Elohim, see – Main Line Reform Temple, Wynnewood, PA. **410 Montgomery Ave, Wynnewood PA 19096 (215) 649–7800.**

Main Line Reform Temple, Beth Elohim. A liberal Reform Cong affiliated with UAHC. Committed to J edu & the deepening of commitments to God & our people. Rel Sch of over 900 chil; 2 youth groups & a col youth group; Young Singles Group; Older Singles Group; Sr Citizens Group; library. Cong has a large Sisterhood & Brotherhood, & is affiliated with ARZA. Over 1,100 families. F 1951. Sr Rabbi Max Hausen; Asst Rabbi Susan Abramson; Rabbi Emeritus Theodore Gordon; Cantor Merril Fisher; Cantor Emeritus Samuel Kligfeld; Adm: Shirley Haas; Pres: Arthur J. Berlin; 1st VP: Lawrence S. Simon; 2nd VP: Robert J. Pludo; 3rd VP: Jules R. Lippert; Treas: Martin M. Thorner; Fin Sec: Mrs Jerome A. Gold; Rec Sec: Ruth B. Seidelman. **410 Montgomery Ave, Wynnewood PA 19096 (215) 649–7800.**

Temple Beth Hillel – Beth El. Affiliated with United Syn of Am. Rabbi Marshall J. Maltzman; Cantor Alan Edwards; Pres: Saul N. Clair; Edu Dirs: Louis & Marjorie Surden; Youth Dirs: Richard & Beth Rizisboard; Off Mgr: Jacqueline Student. **Remington Rd & Lancaster Ave, Wynnewood PA 19096 (215) MI9–5300.**

York

Ohev Sholom Synagogue. Affiliated with United Syn of Am. Rabbi Thomas Werthman; Pres: Stuart M. Segal; Youth Dir: Marlene Denenberg. **2251 Eastern Blvd, York PA 17402 (717) 755–2714.**

Temple Beth Israel. Affiliated with UAHC. 205 mems. Rabbis: Irwin N. Goldenberg, Eli L. Cooper; Pres: Max Einhorn; Sisterhood Pres: Lynne Shapiro; Brotherhood Pres: Mark D. Frankel. **2090 Hollywood Dr, York PA 17403 (717) 843–2676.**

York Council of Jewish Charities, Inc. Pres: Tim Grumbacher; Exec Dir: Allen Dameshek. **120 E Market St, York PA 17401 (717) 843–0918.**

Zieglerville

JYC Camps Arthur & Reeta. Zieglerville PA 19492 (215) 545–4400.

RHODE ISLAND

Barrington

Temple Habonim. Affiliated with UAHC. 95 mems. Rabbi James Rosenberg; Pres: Richard Carr; Adm: James Rosenberg; Sisterhood Pres: Alexis Hafken. **165 Meadow Rd, Barrington RI 02806 (401) 245–6536.**

Cranston

Temple Sinai. Affiliated with UAHC. 315 mems. Rabbi George J. Astrachan; Cantor Remmie Brown; Pres: Irving J. Waldman; Edu: Marilyn Moskol; Sisterhood Pres: Gloria Staub; Brotherhood Pres: Phillip Geller. **30 Hagen St, Cranston RI 02920 (401) 942–8350.**

Temple Sinai Library. For information on the Temple, see – Temple Sinai, Cranston, RI. **30 Hagen St, Cranston RI 02920 (401) 942–8350.**

Temple Torat Yisrael. Conservative Syn affiliated with United Syn of Am. To serve as the rel, edu, cultural ctr for our 772 households & be the dynamic focus of their inner spiritual needs. Daily minyan; Rel Servs; edu progs; Sisterhood; Men's Club; library containing 5,000 vols (Judaica). 772 mems (600 families, 100 individuals). 25 employees. F 1952 as Cranston J Ctr; in 1966 name changed to Temple Beth Torah; in 1981, after merger, became Temple Torat Yisrael. Pub Bulletin (15 issues a yr). Facilities include kosher kitchen, sanctuary seating 258 (expanded to 1,500 on High Holydays), gift shop. Rabbi Gerald B. Zelermyer; Cantor Stephen Freedman; Pres: Dorothy Bookbinder; VP Mem: James Galkin; VP Fin: Stephen Yarlas; VP Ways & Means: Frank Prosnitz; Prin: Lonna S. Picker. **330 Park Ave, Cranston RI 02905.**

Temple Torat Yisrael, Library. Library contains 5,000 vols (Judaica). For information on the Temple, see – Temple Torat Yisrael, Cranston, RI. **330 Park Ave, Cranston RI 02905.**

Kingston

B'nai B'rith Hillel Foundation at the University of Rhode Island. To provide a complete rel, social, cultural & edu prog for the 1,000 J stu & 200 J faculty mems & their families. Rel Servs; kosher meals; socials; classes; lectures; concerts; counseling; Is prog; UJA-Fed fund raising prog; lobby for campus J needs; library containing 1,000 vols (Judaica). 200 families; 1,000 stu (900 undergrad, 100 grad). 2 full-time employees; 3 part-time employees. URI Hillel was f in 1949 in an attempt to serve the J needs on campus; in 1968, the prog became a full-time prog. Pub A Nickel Stogie (monthly), total circulation 8,000. Facilities include kosher kitchen (under the supervision of the RI Bd of Kashruth), chapel, off, coffee house. URI Hillel & J Chaplain Dir: Rabbi Chaim Casper; URI Hillel Adv Bd Pres: Bertram M. Brown; URI Hillel Stu Bd Pres: Kevin Leff. **34 Lower Col Rd, Kingston RI 02881 (401) 792–2740.**

Middletown

Temple Shalom. Affiliated with United Syn of Am. Rabbi Marc S. Jagolinzer; Pres: Stephen Schneller. **221 Valley Rd, PO Box 372, Middletown RI 02840 (401) 846–9002.**

Newport

Society of Friends of Touro Synagogue. To maintain the oldest syn in N Am & promote awareness of its preeminent role in Am rel liberty. Maintenance & upkeep of bldgs, grounds, personnel in keeping with the Touro Syn, & to maintain the premises in their character as a Natl Historic Site in accordance with the designation of the US Dept of the Interior, March 5, 1946; provides for raising & allocating funds for the printing of articles, booklets & material on Touro Syn; commemorates each yr, on or about August 19th, the pronouncement by George Washington on rel liberty in his letter to the Hebrew Cong in Newport August 19, 1790; receives manuscripts, relics, pictures & other articles of interest to further the objectives of the corp for preservation, information & use of the public. The Sephardic J Cong of Newport was f in 1658. Rel Servs were held in homes or rented bldgs. In 1677 the Newport J bought a cemetery plot. In 1763 the syn was dedicated. The Cong chose the name Yeshuat Is. After the Revolutionary War, the city of Newport declined. Many of the inhabitants left including the J com. At the end of the 18th century the syn was closed. In 1822 Abraham, the son of Reverend Isaac Touro who had officiated at the syn dedication, died & left a $10,000 fund for the care & preservation of the syn. His brother Judah, who died in 1854, left another $10,000 for the salary of a minister & for care of the cemetery. In 1883 the syn was permanently reopened. New immigration fr Central & Eastern Europe had again brought J to Newport. The com took the name Cong Jeshuat Is & maintained continuity with its predecessor. This Cong also follows the Sephardic tradition. The syn is open to visitors. Guides provided by the Soc of Friends of Touro Syn are available to lead tours. Pres Emeritus: Judge Samuel Barnet; Pres: Aaron J. Slom; VP: Herbert Epstein; Exec Dir for Natl Affairs: Dr Martin Greenfield; Treas: Saul Schweber; Asst Treas: Mrs Samuel Gillson; Sec: Rabbi Theodore Lewis; Co-Counsel: Judge Alexander G. Teitz, Owen B. Landman; Exec Cttee: Dr Martin Greenfield, Edgar J. Nathan 3rd, Saul Fine, Samuel Friedman, Joseph Galkin, Ben Helfner, Michael Josephson, Howard N. Kay, Bernard Kusinitz, Mrs Jack Werner. **85 Touro St, Newport RI 02840 (401) 847–4794.**

Providence

Bureau of Jewish Education of Rhode Island. 130 Sessions St, Providence RI 02906 (401) 331–0956.

Bureau of Jewish Education of Rhode Island, Library. 130 Sessions St, Providence RI 02906 (401) 331–0956.

International Association of Hillel Directors. c/o B'nai B'rith Hillel Foundation, 80 Brown St, Providence RI 02906 (401) 863–2344.

The Jewish Community Center of Rhode Island. Agy which provides for the leisure time, recreational, informal edu & cultural needs of the J com. Affiliated with United Way, Natl JWB, RI Council of Com Servs, J Fed of RI. To help the J individual dev creatively as a person, as a J & as a citizen. Sports & Fitness Prog; social group work; Nursery Sch; informal edu; creative & graphic arts; volunteer servs; J experiences. Skilled professional staff. F in 1925. Exec Dir: Ramon F. Berger; Pres: Mark S. Mandell; VPs: Joel Roseman, Mathew Shuster; Treas: Aaron Weintraub; Sec: Michael Nulman. **401 Elmgrove Ave, Providence RI 02906 (401) 861–8800.**

Jewish Federation of Rhode Island. Mem of CJF. Organized 1945. Pres: Melvin Alperin; Exec Dir: Elliot Cohan. **130 Sessions St, Providence RI 02906 (401) 421–4111.**

Rhode Island Jewish Historical Association. J historical resource ctr. To collect & preserve bks, records, pamphlets, letters, manuscripts, prints, photographs, paintings & any other historical material relating to the hist of J of RI; to encourage & promote the study of such hist by lectures & otherwise; to pub & diffuse information as to such hist. Provides a repository for its collection; lectures before Heb schs, temple Sun schs, men's clubs & orgs; provides tour of hq for stu; aids stu in local cols in doing research work involving RI J hist; cooperates with JCC, Fed of RI, Bureau of J Edu in supplying needed information; sets up exhibits with photographs & memorabilia fr archives. Chartered in 1951 & was the first local J historical soc in the US. Remember When? (a monthly column); Rhode Island Jewish Historical Notes; Newsletter. The Assn holds an annual meeting which features a noted speaker, usually on a subject of RI J hist. The Assn furnishes a research scholarship each yr to a stu in the social sci, usually fr a local univ. Pres: Dr Marvin Pitterman; VP: Geraldine Foster; Rec Sec: Florence Zachs; Corsp Sec: Stella Glassman; Treas: Bertha Kasper; Librarian & Archivist: Eleanor F. Horvitz. **130 Sessions St, Providence RI 02906.**

Solomon Schechter Day School of Rhode Island. Affiliated with Solomon Schechter Day Schs Assn. Prin: Rabbi Alban Kaunfer, Ada Cutler; Chr: Daniel Kaplan. **99 Taft Ave, Providence RI 02906 (401) 751–2470.**

Temple Beth El. Affiliated with UAHC. 944 mems. Rabbi Leslie Y. Gutterman; Pres: Edward S. Goldin; Edu: Seymour Krieger; Adm: Samuel J. Stepak; Sisterhood Pres: Melba Meister; Brotherhood Pres: Stanley Bleeker. **70 Orchard Ave, Providence RI 02906 (401) 331–6070.**

Temple Beth El, William G. Braude Library. For information on the Temple, see – Temple Beth El, Providence, RI. **70 Orchard Ave, Providence RI 02906 (401) 331–6070.**

Temple Emanu-El. Affiliated with United Syn of Am. Rabbi Wayne M. Franklin; Asst Rabbi Alvan H. Kaunfer; Cantor Ivan E. Perlman; Pres: Donald M. Robbins; Exec Dir: Irwin B. Giffen; Youth Dirs: Gail & Richard Perlman. **99 Taft Ave, Providence RI 02906 (401) 331–1616.**

Warwick

Temple Beth Am Beth David. Affiliated with United Syn of Am. To provide a place of worship, edu & social activities for J families in the area; to provide guidance in the understanding & practice of J. Rel Servs; Men's Club; Sisterhood; USY Youth Group; Warwick Social Sr; Rel Sch; Pre Rel Sch for ages four to seven. F in the 1950's as the Warwick J Com Assn. After its first few yrs of utilizing rented temporary quarters, a permanent Temple was constructed on the current site. In 1980 the Temple merged with a cong in nearby Providence RI & the name was officially changed to Temple Beth Am Beth David. Currently under construction is an addition to the existing bldg which will house a permanent sanctuary for more than 300 congregants. It will open onto the area currently occupied by the combination sanctuary & social hall so that during the High Holy Days it will be able to accommodate more than 1,100 persons. Rabbi Milton L. Kroopnick; Cantor Jack S. Smith; Pres: Arthur Poulten; 1st VP: Fred Kamin; 2nd VP: Alan Horowitz; 3rd VP: Mrs Robert Sock; 4th VP: William Scheraga; Fin Sec: Morris Zenofsky; Treas: Robert Silverman; Rec Sec: Mrs Robert Greenstein; Corsp Sec: Mrs Joseph Cohen; Men's Club Pres: Jerry Aron; Sisterhood Pres: Suzanne Glucksman; Warwick Social Sr Pres: Lester Aptel. **40 Gardiner St, Warwick RI 02888 (401) 463–7944.**

Woonsocket

Congregation B'nai Israel. Affiliated with United Syn of Am. Cantor Philip Macktaz; Pres: Richard R. Ackerman; Edu Dir: Deborah Rubenstein; Youth Dir: Mrs Roy Schoenfeld. **224 Prospect St, Woonsocket RI 02895 (401) 762–3651.**

SOUTH CAROLINA

Anderson

Temple B'nai Israel. Affiliated with UAHC. 40 mems. Pres: David Friedman. **Oakland Ave, PO Box 491, Anderson SC 29622 (803) 226–0310.**

Beaufort

Beth Israel. Affiliated with United Syn of Am. Rabbi Dr Henry Guttman; Pres: Dr H. D. Lipsitz. **PO Box 387, Beaufort SC 29003.**

Charleston

Charleston Jewish Federation. Mem of CJF. Organized 1949. Pres: David Cohen; Exec Dir: Steven Wendell. **1645 Millbrook Dr, PO Box 31298, Charleston SC 29407 (803) 571–6565.**

Kahal Kadosh Beth Elohim. Reform Cong affiliated with UAHC. Rel Servs; Archives Mus: contains historic documents, minute bks & memorabilia, ceremonial objects & paintings; Raisin Memorial Library; Youth Lounge; Rel Sch. F in 1749 in private quarters. In 1775 the Cong used an improvised syn adjacent to the modern temple grounds. In 1792 construction of the permanent temple was started & two yrs later it was dedicated. The bldg was destroyed in the Charleston fire of 1838 but was replaced in 1840 by the present bldg. Mems of the Cong f Charleston's Hebrew Benevolent Soc in 1784, & in 1801 est the Hebrew Orphan Soc both of which are still in existence. A Heb sch where secular & rel subjects were taught functioned fr the middle of the 18th century. In 1838 the second oldest J Sun Sch in the US was organized. The syn became, in 1841, the first Reform cong in the US & was one of the founding congs of the UAHC. The temple was the first in Am to include a musical instrument in worship. The syn is the second oldest in the US & the oldest one in continuous use. In 1980 it was designated a Natl Historic Landmark. Rabbi William A. Rosenthall. **86 Hasell St, Charleston SC 29401 (803) 723–1090.**

Synagogue Emanu-El. Affiliated with United Syn of Am. Rabbi Alan L. Cohen; Cantor & Youth Dir: Edward Berkovits; Pres: Burnet Mendelsohn, Exec Sec: Constance C. Thompson; Edu Dir: Marcia Miller. **5 Windsor Dr, Charleston SC 29407 (803) 571–3264.**

Columbia

Beth Sholom Synagogue. Affiliated with United Syn of Am. Rabbi Dr Edward R. Kandel; Pres: Sherwood Stark. **5827 Trenhom Rd, Columbia SC 29206 (803) 782–2500,1.**

Columbia United Jewish Welfare Federation. Mem of CJF. Organized 1960. Pres: Frederick R. Blank; Exec Dir: Alexander Grossberg. **4540 Trenholm Rd, Columbia SC 29206 (803) 787–2023.**

Tree of Life Congregation. Reform Cong affiliated with UAHC. Rel Servs; edu progs; Sisterhood; Brotherhood; Temple Youth Group; library (only J content or authors). 250 families; 109 stu in grades K–Confirmation. 3 employees. F 1896. Pub Tree of Life Bulletin (monthly). Facilities include sanctuary seating 154, gift shop, offs, kitchen, social hall, library, Rel Sch, classrms, choir rm. Rabbi Howard A. Kosovske; Pres: Howard Weiss; VPs: Richard Helman, Edward Hertz; Treas: Joseph Sharnoff; Sec: Stephen Savitz; Adm: Ricka W. Robinson; Editor: Barbara Bleeck. **2701 Heyward St, Columbia SC 29205 (803) 799–2485.**

Florence

Temple Beth Israel. Affiliated with UAHC. 74 mems. Rabbi Sidney Strome; Pres: Leslie W. Levy; Edu: Sandra S. Levy; Sisterhood Pres: Sandra S. Levy; Brotherhood Pres: Bruce Siegal. **316 Park Ave, PO Box 3008, Florence SC 29502 (803) 669–9724.**

Georgetown

Temple Beth Elohim. Affiliated with UAHC. 24 mems. **c/o Sylvan Rosen, Atty at Law, Screven St, Georgetown SC 29440 (803) 546–7925.**

Greenville

Congregation Beth Israel. Affiliated with United Syn of Am. Rabbi Hyman Fishman; Pres: Hyman J. Brand; Edu Dir: Barry Nock. **425 Summit Dr, PO Box 83, Greenville SC 29602 (803) 232–9031.**

Temple Israel. Affiliated with UAHC. 90 mems. Rabbi James D. Cohn; Pres: Neil I. Steinberg; Sisterhood Pres: Susan Hellman. **115 Buist Ave, Greenville SC 29609 (803) 233–2421.**

Kingstree

Beth Or. Affiliated with United Syn of Am. Rabbi Alan Cohen; Cantor Edward Berkwotz; Pres: David S. Grossman. **107 Hirsch St, Kingstree SC 29556 (803) 354–6425.**

Spartanburg

Congregation B'nai Israel. Affiliated with United Syn of Am. Rabbi Max S. Stauber; Pres: Jack Tobin; Edu Dir: Helen Price. **145 Heywood Ave, Spartanburg SC 29302 (803) 582–7087.**

Congregation B'nai Israel Library. For information on the Cong see – Cong B'nai Israel, Spartanburg, SC. **145 Heywood Ave, Spartanburg SC 29302 (803) 582–7087.**

Sumter

Temple Sinai. Affiliated with UAHC. 73 mems. Rabbi Milton Schlager; Pres: Virginia M. Rosefield; Sisterhood Pres: Rae N. Denemark; Brotherhood Pres: Irwin Praeger. **11 Church St, PO Box 1673, Sumter SC 29150 (803) 773–2122.**

SOUTH DAKOTA

Aberdeen

Congregation B'nai Isaac. Affiliated with United Syn of Am. Pres: Herschel Premack. **PO Box 91, 202 N Kline, Aberdeen SD 57401 (605) 225–3404.**

Rapid City

Synagogue of the Hills. Affiliated with UAHC. 19 mems. Pres: Stanford Adelstein. **PO Box 1392, Rapid City SD 57709 (605) 342–3875.**

Sioux Falls

Jewish Welfare Fund. Mem of CJF. Organized 1938. Pres: Laurence Bierman; Exec Sec: Louis R. Hurwitz. **National Reserve Bldg, Sioux Falls SD 57102 (605) 336–2880.**

Mountain Zion Congregation. Affiliated with UAHC. 60 mems. Rabbi Stephen I. Forstein; Pres: Richard Hosen; Sisterhood Pres: Lya Rosenstein. **523 W 14th St, Sioux Falls SD 57104 (605) 338–5454.**

TENNESSEE

Blountville

B'nai Sholom Congregation. Affiliated with UAHC. 67 mems. Pres: Leo G. Shankman; Sisterhood Pres: Polly Horning. **Mt Tucker Addition, Rt 6 Box 563, Blountville TN 37617 (615) 323–7596.**

Brownsville

Adas Israel Congregation. Affiliated with UAHC. 7 mems. Pres: Robert Felsenthal; Sisterhood Pres: Dorothy Silverstein. **N Washington St, Brownsville TN 38012.**

Chattanooga

B'nai Zion Synagogue. Traditional Syn within the Conservative movement, affiliated with United Syn of Am. Rel Servs. F in 1888. The syn is the largest of the three Chattanooga congs. Rabbi Richard Sherwin; Cantor Louis M. Rothman; Pres: Robert H. Siskin; Adm: Dorothy Rice. **114 McBrien Rd, Chattanooga TN 37411 (615) 894–8900.**

Beth Shalom Congregation. Orthodox Syn affiliated with Union of Orthodox J Cong of Am. Rel Servs; social servs; edu servs; NCSY Chapter; cemetery; Chevra Kadisha; mikvah. 70 mems. F 1959. Pub Beth Sholom Congregation Bulletin (bi-monthly). Facilities include kosher kitchen, sanctuary, social hall, classrms, gift shop, mikvah. Rabbi Yitzchak Adler; Pres: Max Yagoda; VP: Phil Lutin; Sec: Harold Shapiro; Treas: Morris Ellman. **20 Pisgah Ave, Chattanooga TN 37411 (615) 894–0801.**

Chattanooga Jewish Day School. Com day sch serving grades K–6. To emphasize those beliefs & practices which unite J & to dev the joy & understanding which come fr such shared convictions. Gen & J studies provided so that each child receives a superior edu, learns self-discipline, personal acceptance & respect for tradition. The accent is on individual instruction in small classes in order to dev full learning potential & a positive attitude toward edu. F in 1974. A group of J parents & com leaders concerned for the secular & rel edu of their chil est a sch whose atmosphere would provide a quality edu in which each child's intellectual, spiritual, moral, physical & social dev would be promoted to its fullest. Prin: Beverly W. Milner; Teachers: Brenda Wilkes, Judith Gribben, Barbara Pettigrew, Heb: Chaim Charyn, Zehava Mirkin. **5326 Lynnland Terr, Chattanooga TN 37411 (615) 892–2337.**

Chattanooga Jewish Federation. Mem of CJF. Organized 1931. Pres: Tom Trivers. **5326 Lynnland Terr, Chattanooga TN 37411 (615) 894–1317.**

Mizpah Congregation. Affiliated with UAHC. 219 mems. Rabbis: Lloyd R. Goldman, Abraham Feinstein; Pres: Max Brener; Sisterhood Pres: H. Geismar. **923 McCallie Ave, Chattanooga TN 37403 (615) 267–9771.**

Jackson

Congregation B'nai Israel. Affiliated with UAHC. 51 mems. Pres: Gertrude Kisber. **PO Box 278, 401 W Grand St, Jackson TN 38301 (901) 427–6141.**

Knoxville

Heska Amuna Synagogue. Affiliated with United Syn of Am. Rabbi Mark Greenspan; Pres: Jerrold L. Becker; Edu Dir: Nancy Cohen. **3811 Kingston Pike, Knoxville TN 37919 (615) 522–0701.**

Jewish Welfare Fund, Inc. Mem of CJF. Organized 1939. Chr: Michael Feinman. **6800 Deane Hill Dr, PO Box 10882, Knoxville TN 37919 (615) 690–6343.**

Temple Beth El. Affiliated with UAHC. 194 mems. Pres: Clare G. Maisel; Sisterhood Pres: Elaine

Freeman. **PO Box 10325, 3037 Kingston Pike, Knoxville TN 37919 (615) 524–3521.**

Memphis

Anshei Sphard Beth El Emeth Congregation. Orthodox Syn. Daily Morning, Afternoon & Evening Servs; Shabbat Servs Fri evening, Sat morning & afternoon; Sisterhood; Men's Club; NCSY Youth Group; Sun Rel Sch, & 3 day a week Cheder. The syn is a merger of two of the oldest Orthodox congs in Memphis: the Beth El Emeth Cong which was f in 1860 & the Anshei Sphard Syn which was chartered in 1904. The congs merged in 1966; ground-breaking for the present site took place in 1969. The Cong maintains two cemeteries & a mikva. **120 E Yates Rd N, Memphis TN 38117 (901) 682–1611.**

B'nai B'rith Home & Hospital for the Aged. To assure the welfare & comfort of its elderly residents through a design for living which considers the essential dignity of the human being. Med servs; rel, social & recreational activities. The Home serves J aged fr AL, MS, TN, AR, LA, OK & TX. One must be at least 60 yrs of age & have lived in the serv area for one yr prior to application. Professional nurses & nursing assistants on a 24-hour a day basis; med dir; staff of med specialists. F in 1927. **131 N Tucker St, Memphis TN 38104 (901) 726–5600.**

Baron Hirsch Congregation. Orthodox Syn, modern but Traditional Cong. Daily Servs held morning & evening, Sabbath Servs Fri evenings & Sat mornings; Sabbath Servs also held at rel sch facility at 5631 Shady Grove Rd in E Memphis; Ladies Auxiliary; Men's Club; Rel Sch for K–10th grade; youth groups; Summer Camp; study progs; retreats; cultural progs; library; kosher facilities. F in 1890. Baron Hirsch Cong is the largest Orthodox syn in the US. The Cong maintains a cemetery & mikvah. **1740 Vollintine Ave, Memphis TN 38107 (901) 274–3525; Facility: 5631 Shady Grove Rd, Memphis TN 38117 (901) 683–4767.**

Beth Sholom Synagogue. Conservative Syn affiliated with United Syn of Am. Daily Evening Servs, Shabbat Servs Fri evenings & Sat mornings; Sun Morning Servs, Siddur & Tallis Club; Sisterhood; Youth Group; Sun Sch for Nursery Sch through Confirmation; Heb classes; special instruction for Bar/Bat Mitzvah. F in 1955 in order to est Conservative J in Memphis. It was the first new syn in the com since 1905. Rabbi Edmund Winter; Cantor Elliot Finkelstein; Pres: Charles O. Friedman; Exec Dir: Mayer Becker. **482 S Mendenhall Rd, Memphis TN 38117 (901) 683–3591.**

Hebrew Watchman. Periodical pub. **277 Jefferson Ave, Memphis TN 38103 (901) 526–2215.**

Jewish Community Relations Council. The voice of the Memphis J com in public & pol situations. To promote better understanding between the local J com & the com-at-large. Responsible for bettering relations between the J com & the gen public; works with such natl agy as the Am J Cttee, Anti-Defamation League, Natl J Com Relations Adv Council, & the Am Is Public Affairs Cttee; provides help & advice in handling anti-Semitic situations. **6560 Poplar Ave, Memphis TN 38138 (901) 767–5161.**

Jewish Service Agency. To provide social serv skills; to serve chil, the aged, new Am & whoever is touched by the pressures & tensions of an insecure world. Confidential servs for counseling people with marital problems, chil-rearing difficulties, adjustments to old age, problems of one parent families; career & vocational counseling; immigrant resettlement; Russian Resettlement Prog; homemaker servs; adoption planning; foster home placement; fin assistance. Fees are based on income. For those who are unable to pay, servs are free. **6560 Poplar Ave, Memphis TN 38138 (901) 767–5161.**

Jewish Student Union. Housed on the campus of Memphis State Univ; provides progs which reach out to col aged youth, stu, & faculty at all of Memphis' campuses including Memphis State Univ, Southwestern Univ, Univ of TN Ctr for Health Sci, & the Southern Col of Optometry. Servicemen at the Millington Naval Base are also served. Full-time professionally trained dir who provides leadership & guidance. **3606 Mynders, Memphis TN 38111 (901) 452–2453.**

Memphis Hebrew Academy. Day Sch for pre-K thru the eighth grade. J edu curriculum & gen studies; classes are also provided for Special Edu along with a Resource Prog for stu with varying learning disabilities. F in 1949. Close cooperation is maintained with the Memphis Bd of Edu & the Memphis State Univ Sch of Edu. **390 White Station, Memphis TN 38117 (901) 682–2409.**

Memphis Jewish Community Center. Beneficiary of the Memphis J Fed & the United Way. To provide leisure time recreational, cultural & edu progs for the entire J com. Summer day camp prog with specialty camps in sports, the fine & creative arts & a cross-country tween travel camp; pre-sch & K prog; sr citizen progs; adult edu classes; cultural & fine arts classes; medically supervised post-cardiac rehabilitation & preventive exercise classes;

individual & team sport activities. Located on over 20 acres of land. The Ctr facilities include: indoor & outdoor swimming pools, gymnasium, racquetball-handball cts, tennis cts, several multi-purpose athletic fields; modern health ctr facility; theatre; photography studio, fine & cultural arts wing. **6560 Poplar Ave, Memphis TN 38138 (901) 761–0810.**

Memphis Jewish Federation. Central coordinating, fundraising, social planning, & budgeting agy for the entire Memphis J com. To provide support & a linkage with the State of Is; to practice Tzedakah so that collectively the J com can meet today's needs; & to build a strong & viable united J com. Annual campaign benefitting over 60 social welfare, com relations & cultural agy in Memphis, the US, Is & around the world. The largest recipient of Fed Campaign funds is the UJA. Local beneficiaries include the JCC, B'nai B'rith Home & Hosp, Russian Resettlement Prog & J Vocational Servs, J Elderly Transportation System, Memphis J Housing Dev Corp, J Stu Union, Is Shaliach Prog, USO Prog at the Millington Naval Base, BBYO, J Com Relations Council, & all Memphis J edu ins. The Fed also sponsors J edu progs, leadership dev, com relations & maintains an ongoing census of the J com. The Memphis J Fed began as the J Welfare Fund, a communal fundraising body in 1935. The J Welfare Fund dates back to the Hebrew Benevolent Soc f in 1850. In 1977 the role & servs of the J Welfare Fund were broadened & the name changed to the J Fed. Handbook of the hist, structure, servs & facilities of the Memphis J Com & its orgs. Exec Dir: Howard M. Weisband; Pres: Dr George Matz; VPs: Martin Lichterman, Edward R. Young, Lewis Kramer; Treas: Robert Solmson; Sec: Sam Chafetz. **6560 Poplar Ave, Memphis TN 38138. Mailing add: PO Box 38268, Memphis TN 38138 (901) 767–5161.**

Memphis Jewish Housing Development Corp. Helping to meet the needs of a rising proportion of aged in population. Eleven story high-rise bldg with 150 units includes modern facilities & social servs in conjunction with other communal agy. Individuals will reside in own homes conforted by fact that they are in a happy & secure atmosphere. Facility started in May 1979. Funded by HUD. **6560 Poplar Ave, Memphis TN 38138 (901) 767–5161.**

State of Israel Bonds. Sold to individuals, institutions & orgs for purpose of maintaining & developing the State of Israel. To provide a central source of investment capital for Is historic progs of econ dev & immigrant absorption. Sells stock of govt owned Is corporations through its affiliate, Capital for Israel Inc. **5118 Park Ave, Box 17008, Memphis TN 38117 (901) 682–7841.**

Temple Israel. Reform Cong affiliated with UAHC. Rel Servs Fri night & Sat morning; Rel Sch on Sun morning fr nursery classes through grade 8; Pre-Confirmation & Confirmation classes; HS prog for grades 11 & 12; youth groups; adult edu classes; Sisterhood; Brotherhood; Jr Cong; Boy Scout Troop; library. 1434 mems. F in 1853, the Cong was first named B'nai Is. The Temple has occupied three bldgs since its founding. In 1976 the Cong moved to its present site. Rabbis: Harry K. Danziger, Harry A. Rosenfeld, James A. Wax; Cantor John M. Kaplan; Pres: Leo Bearman Jr; Edu: Barbara W. Mansberg; Adm: Joseph W. Boston; Sisterhood Pres: Leona Rosen; Brotherhood Pres: Sanford V. Lichterman. **1376 E Massey Rd, Memphis TN 38138 (901) 761–3130.**

Temple Israel Library. For information on the Temple, see – Temple Israel, Memphis, TN. **1376 E Massey Rd, Memphis TN 38138 (901) 761–3130.**

Yeshiva of the South. Col prep sch for HS level stu for the entire S; certified by the State of TN. Separate campuses for boys & girls (girls div is called Goldie Margolin Sch); five period prog plus three or four additional hours for J studies; boys housed in dorms, & girls housed in private homes; cultural bond with Is maintained through class work & correspondence with Is ins. F in 1964. **5255 Meadowcrest Cove, Memphis TN 38117 (901) 767–4140.**

Nashville

Jewish Federation of Nashville & Middle Tennessee. The central J voluntary org which provides fund raising, budgeting, planning & prog servs for Nashville & Middle TN. It is the rep body of individuals & orgs which works cooperatively in the interests of J survival. Affiliated with the Council of J Feds, Natl J Com Relations Adv Council, & Natl JWB. The enhancement of the quality of J life for the mems of the com; the advancement of social justice & maintenance of links with the J of Is & throughout the world. conducts annual fundraising campaign; allocates funds for J edu; sponsors com relations & planning, leadership dev, progs for the elderly; maintains Endowment Fund, J Stu Union, J Welfare Fund. Administrative staff. F in 1934 as the J Com Council & later changed its name to the present one. Pres: Morris Werthan II; 1st VP: Peter Weiss; 2nd VP: Sandy Averbuch; Treas: Carl Goldstein; Sec: Howard Safer; Bd of Dirs: Larry F. Alexander, Felicia Anchor, Gerald Averbuch, Sandy Averbuch, James Blumstein, Marilyn Dicker, Daniel Eisenstein, Robert D. Eisenstein, Stacey Evans, Gerald Fleischer, Lauren Fox, Lois K. Fox, Marvin Friedman, Rabbi

Melvin Glazer, Carl Goldstein, Joel C. Gordon, Barbara Grossman, Irma Kaplan, Dr Herman J. Kaplan, Louise Katzman, Jack W. Kuhn, Carolyn Levine, Sally Levine, Alex Limor, Eugene Pargh, David Perrine, Nedda Pollack, Howard Safer, Nan Speller, David Steine Jr, Harry Stern, Alvin Stillman, Ann Stillman, Peter Weiss, Bernard Werthan Sr, Bernard Werthan Jr, Libby Werthan, Morris Werthan II, Shirley Zeitlin; Exec Dir: Dr Jay M. Pilzer; Staff Assc: Joyce Fox, Susan Limor; Dir Endowment Fund: Benjamin Zucker. **3500 W End Ave, Nashville TN 37205 (615) 269–0729, 0901.**

Nashville Jewish Community Center. J com ctr with JWB, J Fed of Nashville, United Way of Nashville. To strengthen the moral, physical & cultural well-being of the mems; to emphasize & promote rel loyalties; to foster & develop the ideals of Am citizenship. Presch; child care; day camping; classes for all age groups; activities for all age groups fr infants through sr adults; cultural events for the com; health, physical edu & recreational activities; library containing 5,000 vols (Judaica). 1144 mems (783 families, 361 individuals). Employed staff varies seasonally; approx 90 volunteers. F 1902 as the Young Men's Hebrew Assn; in current facilities since 1951; will be moving to new facilities in the spring of 1984. Pub Center Brochures (3 times a yr), Center Scene (approx every 6 weeks). Facilities include kosher kitchen, auditorium, gymnasium, library, presch & child care, exercise rm, health club, day camp site, indoor & outdoor swimming pools, tennis cts, racquetball cts, athletic fields, meeting rms. Pres: Irma Kaplan; 1st VP: Mark Doyne; 2nd VP: Ruth Kornman; Sec: Diane Trachtman; Treas: Stewart Kresge; Dir: Robert Litvak. **3500 West End Ave, Nashville TN 37205 (615) 297–3588.**

Nashville Jewish Community Center, Library. Library Contains 5,000 vols (Judaica). For information on the Ctr, see – Nashville Jewish Community Center, Nashville, TN. **3500 West End Ave, Nashville TN 37205 (615) 297–3588.**

Observer. Periodical pub. **PO Box 15431, Nashville TN 37215 (615) 292–9861.**

The Temple, Congregation Ohabai Sholom. Affiliated with UAHC. A House of Prayer, a House of Study, & a House of Fellowship. To meet the J needs of our congregants at every stage of life; to enrich family life. Worship Servs; Rel Sch; Brotherhood; Sisterhood; Youth Group; Couples Club; Singles Group; Adult Edu; library containing 5,500 vols (Judaica). 800 mems. F in 1854. Pub The Temple Bulletin (weekly). Pres: Harris Gilbert; 1st VP: Bernard Werthan Jr; 2nd VP: Ernest Freudenthal; Sec: Elise Steiner; Treas: Dr Irwin Eskind; Rabbis: Dr Randall Falk, Kenneth Kanter; Cantor Peter Halpern; Edu & Adm: Richard M. Morin. **5015 Harding Rd, Nashville TN 37205 (615) 352–7620.**

West End Synagogue, Khal Kodesh Adath Israel. Affiliated with United Syn of Am. Rabbi Edward Ruttenberg; Cantor Stanley Weinberger; Pres: Alvin Fox; Exec Dir: Frances Burke; Edu Dir: Miriam Halachmi. **3810–12–14 West End Ave, Nashville TN 37205 (615) 269–4592.**

Oak Ridge

Congregation Beth El. Affiliated with United Syn of Am. Rabbi Daniel Zucker; Pres: Frances Silver; Edu Dir: Herbert Hoffman; Youth Dir: Roberta Steiner. **W Madison Lane, Oak Ridge TN 37830 (615) 483–4284.**

TEXAS

Abilene

Temple Mizpah. Affiliated with UAHC. 20 mems. Pres: Howard Tobin; Edu: Gail Tobin. **849 Chestnut, PO Box 1283, Abilene TX 79604 (915) 672–8225.**

Amarillo

Temple B'nai Israel. Affiliated with UAHC. 140 mems. Rabbis: Martin Scharf, Maurice Feuer; Cantor Norton Bicoll; Pres: Erwin Kohn; Edu: Roberta Scharf; Sisterhood Pres: Sheila Bicoll. **4316 Albert, Amarillo TX 79106 (806) 352–7191.**

Austin

Chabad House. Lubavitch com servs ctr. Blends Chassidic fervor & warmth with tradition & learning, to show that every, J fr whatever background he or she comes fr, is an integral part of the body of Is. Anti-missionary work; adult edu; sabbath seminars; holiday progs; day camp; youth groups; syns; kosher kitchen; counseling; chaplaincy; Mitzvah Campaigns; hosp & prison visitations; sr citizens encounters; speakers bureau. **2101 Nueces Ave, Austin TX 78705.**

Congregation Agudas Achim. Affiliated with United Syn of Am. Rabbi Joseph Caron–Wolre; Pres: Dan Fleschman; Youth Dir: Marilyn Stahl. **4300 Bull Creek Rd, Austin TX 78758 (512) 459–3287.**

Congregation Agudas Achim Library. For information on the Cong see – Congregation Agudas Achim, Austin, TX. **4300 Bull Creek Rd, Austin TX 78731 (512) 459–3287.**

Jewish Community Council of Austin. Mem of CJF. Organized 1939; reorganized 1956. Pres: Paul Gardner; Exec Dir: Sheldon Sklar. **5758 Balcones Dr, Suite 104, Austin TX 78731 (512) 451–6435.**

Temple Beth Israel. Affiliated with UAHC. 340 mems. Rabbi Louis Firestein; Pres: Leon Lebowitz; Sisterhood Pres: Joan Newburger; Brotherhood Pres: Benjamin Steinfeld. **3901 Shoal Creek Blvd, Austin TX 78756 (512) 454–6806.**

Temple Beth Israel, Simon Memorial Library. For information on the Temple, see – Temple Beth Israel, Austin, TX. **3901 Shoal Creek Blvd, Austin TX 78756 (512) 454–6806.**

Beaumont

Beaumont Jewish Federation. Central serv agy serving the Beaumont TX area which consists of about 225 J families. Raising & dispersing of funds for worthy J causes. Most funds generated go to the UJA with lesser amounts to various causes both in the US & in Is. Chartered in 1966. Preceded by United Palestine Appeal drives in the middle 1930's & an annual United J Appeal following WWII. Pres: Edwin M. Gale; Exec Dir: I. G. Harris. **PO Box 1981, Beaumont TX 77704 (713) 833–5427.**

Temple Emanuel. Affiliated with UAHC. 149 mems. Rabbi Herbert S. Rutman; Pres: Nelson Alter; Sisterhood Pres: Marsha Hoffer; Brotherhood Pres: Dennis Alter. **PO Box 423, Beaumont TX 77704 (713) 832–6131.**

Bellaire

Congregation Brith Shalom. Affiliated with United Syn of Am. Rabbi Herbert A. Yoskowitz; Cantor & Youth Dir: Erwin Halpern; Pres: Lorraine Josem Brown; Exec Dir: Karen Glina. **4610 Bellaire Blvd, Bellaire TX 77401 (713) 667–9201.**

Congregation Brith Shalom Library. For information on the Cong see – Congregation Brith Shalom, Bellaire, TX. **4610 Bellaire Blvd, Bellaire TX 77401 (713) 667–9201.**

I. Weiner Secondary School. Affiliated with Solomon Schechter Day Schs Assn. Prin: Marilyn Hassid; Chr: Michael Bloome. **4610 Bellaire Blvd, Bellaire TX 77401 (713) 668–0393.**

Brownsville

Temple Beth El. Affiliated with UAHC. 100 mems. Pres: Isaac Rabinovich; Sisterhood Pres: Marsha Alvarez. **PO Box 3851, Brownsville TX 78520 (512) 542–5263.**

Bruceville

UAHC Greene Family Camp. Dir: Loui Dobin. **Bruceville TX 76630 (817) 859–5411.**

Bryan

Congregation Beth Shalom. Affiliated with UAHC. 37 mems. Pres: William Bassichis. **PO Box 3523, Bryan TX 77801 (713) 846–7313.**

Corpus Christi

B'nai Israel Synagogue. Affiliated with United Syn of Am. Rabbi Stuart Keith Lipson; Cantor Bernard Kane; Pres: Leon Newman; Edu & Youth Dir: Rabbi Stuart Keith Lipson. **3434 Ft Worth St, Corpus Christi TX 78411 (512) 855–7308.**

B'nai Israel Synagogue, Kovner Library. For information on the Syn see – B'nai Israel Synagogue, Corpus Christi, TX. **3434 Ft Worth St, Corpus Christi TX 78411 (512) 855–7308.**

Combined Jewish Appeal of Corpus Christi. Mem of CJF. Organized 1962. Pres: Jesse Lieberman; Exec Dir: Andrew Lipman. **750 Everhart Rd, Corpus Christi TX 78411 (512) 855–6239.**

Corpus Christi Jewish Community Council. To support charitable & edu undertakings; to foster & dev J com life; to provide edu & recreational facilities for the youth of the com; to provide financial assistance for indigent, transient & needy local citizens; to aid the integration of new Am into the com; to raise & distribute money to J hosps, orphan homes, edu ins, & charitable & philanthropic orgs throughout the US & the world. Presch for ages 2½ – 5; summer day camp for ages 2½ – 12; summer operated swimming pool; Sick Loan Closet – hosp equipment is loaned out to the needy; Com Calender; activity bldg. Exec Dir: Andrew J. Lipman; Pres: Jack Solka. **750 Everhart Rd, Corpus Christi TX 78411 (512) 855–6239.**

Temple Beth El. Affiliated with the UAHC. Support, encouragement & promotion of public worship of the J rel. Rel Servs; Sisterhood; edu for all ages; social activities; com Seder on the second day of Passover. In the Spring of 1930, construction was started on the first J house of worship in Corpus Christi. The J house of worship was named Temple Beth El & Com Ctr. Rabbi Stephen E. Fisch; Rabbi Emeritus Sidney A. Wolf; Pres: Davie Lou Solka; 1st VP: Edward R. Birnberg; 2nd VP: Dr Lawrence F. Buxton; Sec-Treas: Henry Heffler; Trustees: Dr Myron H. Appel, Donald M. Feferman, Irving Fenster, Edmund H. Hecht, Sherlie Hurwitz, Joe B. Jessel, Elaine Kline, Kirk Kroloff, Carl Kuehn, Marvin Nebrat, Jeanne Nisenson, Ronald B. Sanders, Steven M. Solka, Rona Train, Helen Wilk. **1315 Craig St, Box 3214, Corpus Christi TX 78404 (512) 883–0831.**

Dallas

Akiba Academy of Dallas. Day sch. To ensure the survival, flourishing & identity of Am J in a changing world. Pre-sch with an optional afternoon prog; dual prog for K–8th grade with half the day devoted to J studies & half to academic subjects: Language Arts, Math, Sci & Social Studies with the addition of French for 7th & 8th grade stu. Music, Art, & Physical Edu are also part of the prog. In addition to the regular curriculum there is a prog for the academically gifted, a Sun Ins for learning disabled chil, field trips, stu assemblies, stu council, brownie & girl scout troops organized at the sch. 275 stu. 10–1 pupil-teacher ratio. The Academy began with 30 stu. The bldg was constructed in 1967 & has been continually expanding. It now consists of 19 classrms, library, sci lab, chapel & gymnasium/auditorium/lunch rm. Pres: Ronald S. Blumenthal; Exec VP: Raymond Lambert; VPs: Mike Goldfarb, Carole Ann Hoppenstein, Dr Jay M. Hoppenstein, Harry Kabler, Sol Schwartz, Bud Silverberg, Julius Tills; Sec: Leslie Schultz; Treas: Tony Abroms; Asst Treas: Jaime Hazan-Cohen; Prin: Rabbi Joshua Mosak; Dir of Guidance & Counseling: Rabbi David Leibtag; Presch Dir: Hanna Lambert; Bd of Dirs: Dr Donald Bernstein, Barbara Blumenthal, Ted Bogart, Eddie Fox, Harry Goldman, Jerald Goldman, Joe Goldman, Angel Kosfiszer, Leo Laufer, David Lenovitz, Paul Lewis, Barry Mellman, Sol Prengler, Dr Lionel Reiman, Philip Reinstein, Manuel Rohan, Shirley Rovinsky, Gary Schepps. **6210 Churchill Way, Dallas TX 75230 (214) 239–7248.**

Anti-Defamation League of B'nai B'rith – NW Texas-Oklahoma Regional Office. Dedicated in purpose & prog to translating the Am heritage of democratic ideals into a way of life for all Am, & to countering assaults on the safety, status, rights & image of J. For additional information, see – Anti-Defamation League of B'nai B'rith, New York City, NY. **Royal Central Tower, 11300 N Central Expressway, Dallas TX 75243.**

Congregation Shearith Israel. Affiliated with United Syn of Am. Rabbi Jordan S. Ofseyer; Asst Rabbi Edward Friedman; Cantor Sol Sanders; Pres: Bernard Levy; Exec Dir: Philip E. Shier; Edu Dir: Jack Molad; Youth Dir: Roy Hirschberg. **9401 Douglas Ave, Dallas TX 75225 (214) 361–6606.**

Congregation Shearith Israel, Dave Rubin Library. For information on the Cong see – Congregation Shearith Israel, Dallas, TX. **9401 Douglas, Dallas TX 75225 (214) 361–6606.**

Jewish Federation of Greater Dallas. Mem of CJF. Organized 1911. Pres: Ann Sikora; Exec Dir: Morris A. Stein. **7800 Northhaven Rd, Suite A, Dallas TX 75230 (214) 369–3313.**

National Association of Jewish Homes for the Aged. 2525 Centerville Rd, Dallas TX 75228 (214) 327–4503.

National Council of Jewish Women. Women's volunteer org. Dedicated in the spirit of J to advancing human welfare & the democratic way of life. Activities are organized around five prog priorities: women's issues, chil & youth, aging, J life, & Is. Women's Issues – major concerns are: ratification of the Equal Rights Amendment, protection of the right of every women to have access to safe & legal abortion, removal of gender related discrimination in all areas of life, edu progs on the prevention of domestic violence & treatment for its victims, widow to widow counseling, & progs for single parents. Chil & Youth – concerned with: the rights, needs & quality of life of the nation's chil & youth; juvenile justice, especially the treatment of adolescent girls; & foster care; variety of projs that support servs to the young people in their coms; advocacy efforts needed to effectively change the way chil are treated under the law. Is – carries out numerous edu & social welfare progs in Is; continues its strong advocacy for the State of Is; furthers current major proj in Is – the Research Ins for Innovation in Edu which is part of The Hebrew Univ Sch of Edu. J Life – places emphasis on: J edu & the problems of Soviet J; J edu progs for individuals of various ages & interests which have been designed to assist people in exploring their understanding of & attitudes toward J & to rekindle their interest in their rel; resettlement of Soviet J immigrants, & advocacy on behalf of those J who are refused permission to leave the USSR. Aging – primary focus is on dev servs for & supporting: legislation on behalf of older adults, day ctrs, housing for the elderly, adult edu, enrichment progs, volunteer placement progs, sheltered employment projs, nutrition & transportation servs, multipurpose ctrs, nursing homes, ombudsman progs & self training for & by the elderly. **7147 Brookshire Circle, Dallas TX 75230 (214) 369–8370.**

National Jewish Committee on Scouting. PO Box 61030, Dallas – Ft Worth Airport TX 75261 (214) 659–2000.

Solomon Schechter Academy of Dallas. Affiliated with Solomon Schechter Day Schs Assn. Prin: Lois Davidson; Chr: Ervin Donsky. **9401 Douglas Ave, Dallas TX 75225 (214) 369–8237.**

Temple Emanu-El. Affiliated with UAHC. 2100 mems. Rabbis: Gerald J. Klein, Jack Bemporad, Ellen Lewis, Levi Olan; Pres: Herbert S. Rosenthal; Adm: Joe Abrams; Sisterhood Pres: Ruth Pines; Brotherhood Pres: David Alkek. **8500 Hillcrest Rd, Dallas TX 75225 (214) 368–3613.**

Temple Emanu-El, Alex Weisberg Library. For information on the Temple, see – Temple Emanu-El, Dallas, TX. **8500 Hillcrest, Dallas TX 75225 (214) 368–3613.**

Temple Shalom. Affiliated with UAHC. 605 mems. Rabbis: Saul P. Besser, Mark S. Goodman; Pres: Phillip R. Warren; Adm: Margaret K. Spieth; Sisterhood Pres: Mara Levi; Brotherhood Pres: Harvey Flick. **6930 Alpha Rd, Dallas TX 75240 (214) 661–1810.**

Tiferet Israel Congregation. Traditional Syn. To utilize our heritage & to instill in the chil the standards necessary to make them better J. Daily Rel Servs; Oneg Shabbat (following the Fri evening servs a social hour is held to renew old friendships & to make new ones. A babysitting serv is available during the Oneg Shabbat Serv; Teenage Club; Pre-Teenage Club; Teenage & Pre-Teen Tephillin Serv & Breakfast; youth groups: Jr NCSY, Sr NCSY; library; Brotherhood; Sisterhood; Couples Club; Talmud Torah; Rel Sch: Sun Div beginning with 4 yr olds, Mid Week Div for chil fr second grade through B'nai Mitzvah, & a HS Div leading to Confirmation; Adult & Jr Choir; Adult J Edu; classes offered by the Rabbi to all those interested in furthering their knowledge in the J rel; In-Depth Adult Edu Prog for all citizens of Dallas; Cemetery Assn & Chevra Kadisha. Chartered in 1890; the oldest & largest Traditional syn in Dallas. Servs were first conducted in a private home on Sat only for three yrs. Property in N Dallas was bought in 1893. A 1½ story house on the lot was used for Servs until 1902. The house was torn down & rebuilt in 1902. The Cong remained there until 1937. Fr 1937 until 1956 the Cong was located in a masonry bldg in S Dallas. Since 1956 the Cong has been located at its present site. The Cong offers the most modern facilities in Dallas for all its mems & activities. Facilities for Bar & Bat Mitzvahs, weddings, confirmations, graduations, private parties. Rabbi Max Zucker; Cantor Ben Zion Lanxner. **10909 Hillcrest Rd, Dallas TX 75230 (214) 691–3611.**

UAHC Southwest Council. Rel & edu org serving J congs throughout the US & Canada. To encourage & aid the org & dev of J congs; to promote J edu, & enrich & intensify J life; to foster other activities for the perpetuation & advancement of J. For additional information, see – UAHC – Union of American Hebrew Congregations, New York City, NY. Pres: B.J. Tanenbaum Jr; Dir: Rabbi Lawrence I. Jackofsky. **13773 N Central Expressway, Dallas TX 75243 (214) 699–0656.**

El Paso

Congregation B'nai Zion. Conservative Syn affiliated with United Syn of Am. To provide rel & edu opportunities that are guided by the principles of Conservative J. Rel Servs (daily, Shabbat & Yom Tov); edu progs for youth & adults; Sisterhood; Men's Clubs; library (gen & Judaica). 440 mems; 90 stu in grades K–9. F 1900. Pub The Messenger (monthly). Facilities include sanctuary & chapel, ballrm, offs, classrms, kosher kitchen, mikveh, gift shop, library, youth rm. Rabbi Martin J. Berman; Cantor Edwin Gerber; Pres: Gary Weiser; VP: Jerry Rubin; Edu Dir: Elie Amar. **210–220 E Cliff Dr, El Paso TX 79902 (915) 532–3137.**

El Paso Texas Jewish Federation. Central com agy. The Fed is the parent body of the El Paso JCC, & the J Family & Chil Serv. Annual campaign to raise funds for J causes locally, nationally & in Is. Approximately 50% of funds raised are distributed to UJA. The J population is about 5,500 of a total population of about 400,000. Pres: Marvin Zinet; Pres Elect: Bernard Schoichet; VPs: Samuel Ellowitz, William Rosen; Sec: Beth Lipson; Treas: Charles Freithandler; Exec Dir: Howard Burnheim. **405 Mardi Gras Dr, El Paso TX 79920 (915) 584–4437.**

Temple Mount Sinai. Affiliated with UAHC. 450 mems. Rabbis: Kenneth J. Weiss, Floyd S. Fierman; Pres: William Rosen; Edu: Eileen Licht; Adm: Myrna Rasmussen; Sisterhood Pres: B.J. Cohen; Brotherhood Pres: Isadore Drayer. **4408 N Stanton, El Paso TX 79902 (915) 532–5959.**

Fort Worth

Ahavath Sholom. Affiliated with United Syn of Am. Rabbi Isadore Garsek; Pres: Bob kragen. **1600 W Myrtle, Fort Worth TX 76401.**

Beth El Congregation. Reform Cong affiliated with UAHC. To edu mems & the com about Judaism & specifically the practice of Reform Judaism. Shabbat Servs on Fri evenings; Rel Sch on Sun mornings; after sch Heb prog for Bar/Bat Mitzvah preparation; Adult Edu classes; inquirers & conversion classes; special edu, social & cultural events; Sisterhood; Brotherhood; Temple Youth. 400 families; 900 individuals; 67 stu in grades K–3; 48 stu in grades 4–6; 52 stu in grades 7–9; 6 Confirmation. 7 regular staff, 25 Rel Sch teachers. F 1902 as Reform J Syn. Pub Bulletin (monthly). Facilities include kitchen, 2 sanctuaries, social hall, numerous classrms. Rabbi Robert J. Schur; Pres: Sheldon Anisman; VPs: Edouard M. Propper, Irwin Krauss; Sec: Andrew Resnick; Treas: Edwin Wittenberg; Sisterhood Pres: Deidra Bihari; Brotherhood Pres: Gerald Zodin; Edu Dir: Ellen Mack. **207 W Bdwy, Fort Worth TX 76104 (817) 332–7141; Mailing Add: PO Box 2232, Fort Worth TX 76113.**

Jewish Federation of Fort Worth. Mem of CJF. Organized 1936. Pres: I.L. Freed; Exec Dir: Norman A. Mogul. **6801 Granbury Rd, Fort Worth TX 76133 (817) 292–3081.**

Texas Jewish Post. Weekly Newspaper. Serves all segments of the Dallas – Fort Worth met J coms. Pub Jimmy Wisch; Editorial Mgr: Rene Wisch. **PO Box 742, Fort Worth TX 76101.**

Galveston

Congregation B'nai Israel. Affiliated with UAHC. 178 mems. Rabbi Alan H. Greenbaum; Pres: E.R. Thompson Jr; Sisterhood Pres: R.M. Rose. **3008 Ave O, Galveston TX 77550 (713) 765–5796.**

Congregation B'nai Israel, Lakser Memorial Library. For information on the Cong, see – Congregation B'nai Israel, Galveston, TX. **3008 Ave O, Galveston TX 77550 (713) 765–5796.**

Congregation Beth Jacob. Affiliated with United Syn of Am. Rabbi Daniel Horwitz; Pres: Joe Ginsberg. **2401 Avenue K, Galveston TX 77550 (713) 762–7267, 4545.**

Galveston County Jewish Welfare Association. Mem of CJF. Organized 1936. Pres: Mrs E.I. Klein; Treas: Harry Pransky. **PO Box 146, Galveston TX 77553 (713) 744–8295.**

Halletsville

Temple Israel of Schulenburg. Affiliated with UAHC. 17 mems. Pres: Armond G. Schwartz. **c/o Mr Armand G. Schwartz, PO Box 385, Halletsville TX 77964 (713) 743–3864.**

Houston

Anti-Defamation League of B'nai B'rith – SW Regional Office. Dedicated in purpose & prog to translating the Am heritage of democratic ideals into a way of life for all Am, & to countering assaults on the safety, status, rights & image of J. For additional information, see – Anti-Defamation League of B'nai B'rith, New York City, NY. **4211 SW Freeway, Suite 209, Houston TX 77027.**

Congregation Shaar Hashalom. Affiliated with United Syn of Am. Pres: Joel M. Farber; Edu Dir: Howard Fireman; Youth Dir: Dave Rosenfeld. **16020 El Camino Real, Houston TX 77062 (713) 488–5861.**

Congregation Beth Am. Conservative Cong affiliated with the United Syn of Am. To provide a unique rel, edu & social environment for young & old. As a unique cong, provides an approach to Judaism that combines the beauty of Traditionalism in worshipping God with a liberal understanding, & a commitment to serve our fellowman. The syn provides a meaningful J experience for all ages in a manner that maintains our J heritage, while being responsive to the changing times & the changing needs of the Cong. Goal of sch: To provide the chil of mems with excellence in J edu & to help stu develop skills & knowledge to function as participating mems of the Am J com. Seeks to foster love of J & J learning, & desire to live an active & fulfilling J life. High Holy Day & Festival Servs, Shabbat Servs; Sun & Afternoon Rel Heb Sch – Sun Sch encompasses grades K–10 & the weekday After Sch Prog offers five yrs of study with chil usually entering the After Sch Prog when in the third grade; Adult Edu; Sisterhood; Men's Club; Kadima; USY; conversion classes; inter-religious affiliation with local churches. monthly Sun Breakfasts with noted guest speakers; monthly BK Circle, courses in Heb, Haftorah Trope, Life Cycle, Pirke Avot, Is & Arabs, Bible, Is Dance; weekly Oneg Shabbat following Servs: social functions held regularly – bowling, Chanukah Party, Las Vegas Night, special social events planned for new mems. 215 mems. Rabbi, Sec, Edu Dir, 16 teachers, 6 aides, 2 household. F in 1972 by a small group of J who had recently moved to Houston. Beth Am Midabare (monthly bulletin), Newsletter (bi-weekly). Facilities include a sanctuary seating 200, kosher kitchen, library with 1000 vols (Judaica); gift shop. Rabbi Edward S. Treister; Pres: Joel Katz: VPs: Ben Ostrofsky, Gay Braman; Edu Dir: Nomi Bulter; Sec: Lesley Winaker; Treas: Dan Kornhauser; Adm: Emily Lam. **1431 Brittmoore Rd, Houston TX 77043 (713) 461–7725.**

Congregation Beth Israel. Affiliated with UAHC. 1650 mems. Rabbis: Samuel E. Karff, Arthur P. Nemitoff; Hyman J. Schachtel; Cantor: Arthur Sergi; Pres: Alan M. Rauch; Edu: Kenneth A. Midlo, Shirley Barish; Adm: Doris P. Markoff; Sisterhood Pres: Suzanne Rockoff; Brotherhood Pres: Jacob Leon. **5600 N Braeswood Blvd, Houston TX 77096 (713) 771–6221.**

Congregation Beth Israel, Hyman Judah Schachtel Library. For information on the Cong, see – Congregation Beth Israel, Houston, TX. **5600 N Braeswood Blvd, Houston TX 77096 (713) 771–6221.**

Congregation Beth Yeshurun. Affiliated with United Syn of Am. Rabbi Jack Segal; Asst Rabbi Stephen Grundfast; Cantor George Wagner; Pres: Irving J. Weiner; Exec Dir: Ben Katz; Edu Dir: Michael Korman; Youth Dir: Boaz Hodes. **4525 Beechnut, Houston TX 77096 (713) 666–1881.**

Congregation Beth Yeshurun, Rubin Kaplan Memorial Library. For information on the Cong see – Congregation Beth Yeshurun, Houston, TX. **4525 Beechnut Blvd, Houston TX 77096 (713) 666–1881.**

Congregation Emanu-El. Reform Temple affiliated with UAHC. To promote interfaith relations; to educate & enlighten the non-J com. Besides regular congregational activities Cong Emanu-El has been involved in special projs: Festival of the Bible in the Arts in 1961, 1964 & 1971 where Biblically inspired art was displayed; Is Expo 73 honoring Is 25th anniversary with over 30,000 people of all races & rels attending this one week-long celebration; Am J Festival in 1976 telling the story of J contribution to Am life. A show 200 Yrs With Love was produced for the festival & presented as part of the official bicentennial celebration of the City of Houston. For this festival the Cong was awarded the Valley Forge Hon Certificate in Com Progs fr the Freedoms Foun. 1,800 families. F in 1944 with 190 families as charter mems. Land was purchased in 1945, & in 1949 the bldg was dedicated. The bldg then contained 20 classrms. In 1955 10 more were added & another 4 in 1970. In 1976 the Jackie & Freda Proler Chapel & the Robert I. Kahn Gallery were dedicated. In 1977 two TV specials dealing with rel dimensions of J life were produced. The Cong produces a weekly radio prog, The Voices of Temple Emanu-El, on station KTRH, presenting different facets of J. Pres: David L. May; Sr VP: Dolores Wilkenfeld; VPs: Mildred L. Cowen, Jay D. Hirsch, Dr Richard L. Plumb, Larry Sachnowitz; Treas: Dr Larry J. Greenfield; Sec: Michael Wilk; Hon Pres: Sanford I. Lack; Rabbi Roy A. Walter; Rabbi Emeritus Robert I Kahn. **1500 Sunset Blvd, Houston TX 77005 (713) 529–5771.**

Government of Israel Trade Center. Dev of trade relations between US & Is. For additional information, see – Government of Israel Trade Center, New York City, NY. **1 Greenway Plaza E, Houston TX 77046 (713) 840–0510.**

Houston Congregation for Reform Judaism. Affiliated with UAHC. 100 mems. Rabbi Lewis E. Bogage; Pres: Joseph Eichberg. **PO Box 27151, Houston TX 77027 (713) 782–4162.**

Israel Government Tourist Office. 4151 Southwest Freeway, Houston TX 77027 (713) 850–9341.

Jewish Civic Press. Periodical pub. **PO Box 35656, Houston TX 77035.**

Jewish Community Center of Houston. Presch; K; day care; parent edu; cultural classes & sport activities including art, music, dance, drama, tennis, soccer, basketball & other sports classes for all ages (leagues & tournaments for all sports); family recreation; scouting; cultural activities for chil & youth; cultural activities including concerts, theatre productions, films, etc of J content; J Book Fair; library containing 1200 vols of Judaica. 11,000 mems; 3000 families; 1400 individuals. 80 permanent & 300 seasonal employees; 100 volunteers. F 1936 as YM & YWHA. Pub Center News (bi-monthly). Facilities include 110,000 sq ft on 13 acres, 2 pools, 2 gyms, 350 seat theatre, kosher kitchens, snack bar, gift shop, tennis & racquetball cts, 2 health clubs, sch wing. Exec Dir: Jerry Wische; Assc Dir: Neil Perlman; Asst Dir: Stanley Rosenblatt; Pres: J. Lawrence Folloder; VPs: Linda Walter, Ann Kaufman. **5601 S Braeswood Blvd, Houston TX 77096 (713) 729–3200.**

Jewish Community Center of Houston, Rich Memorial Library. Library contains 1,200 vols of Judaica. For information on the Ctr, see – Jewish Community Center of Houston, Houston, TX. **5601 S Braeswood, Houston TX 77096 (713) 729–3200.**

Jewish Community North. Affiliated with UAHC. 120 mems. Rabbi Robert S. Sharff; Pres: Joel S. Henenberg. **PO Box 90448, Houston TX 77090 (713) 376–0016.**

Jewish Federation of Greater Houston. Mem of CJF. Sponsors United Jewish Campaign. Organized 1937. Pres: Stephen Kaufman; Exec Dir: Hans Mayer. **5601 S Braeswood Blvd, Houston TX 77096 (713) 729–7000.**

Jewish Hearld-Voice. Periodical pub. **PO Box 153, Houston TX 77001 (713) 661–3116.**

Lubavitch Center. Lubavitch com serv ctr. Blends Chassidic fervor & warmth with tradition & learning, to show that every J, fr whatever background he or she comes fr, is an integral part of the body of Is. Anti-missionary work; adult edu; sabbath seminars; holiday progs; day camp; youth groups; syns; kosher kitchen; counseling; chaplaincy; Mitzvah Campaigns; hosp & prison visitations; sr citizens encounters; speakers bureau. Rabbi S. Lazaroff. **109–50 Fondern, Houston TX 77071 (713) 981–1000.**

Noah's Ark. A magazine for J chil in K-6th grade. To present quality J oriented material, actively involving young people in J themes & topics. Each issue features a different theme of J content & includes original stories, simple recipes, bk reviews, mazes, puzzles, dot to dots, jokes, riddles, advice column, do it yourself crafts, contributions fr chil, Heb words of the mo, & a pen pal prog. Circulation of about 170,000. Subscribers include rel schs & young people all over the world. First issue pub in Sept 1977. Noah's Ark is included as a monthly supplement to about 15 English language J newspapers. Pub-Business Mgr: Linda Freedman Block; Publisher-Managing Editor: Debbie Israel Dubin. **Linda Block, 5514 Rutherglen, Houston TX 77096 (713) 729–6221; Debbie Dubin, 6330 Gulfton, Houston TX 77081 (713) 771–7143.**

Temple Sinai. Affiliated with UAHC. 41 mems. Rabbi Abraham Shaw; Pres: G.S. Cyprus; Edu: Howard Schwartzberg; Brotherhood Pres: John Biro. **PO Box 42888, Suite 111, Houston TX 77042 (713) 496–5950.**

United Orthodox Synagogues of Houston. Orthodox Cong affiliated with Union of Orthodox J Congs of Am. Combination of three syns: Adath Emeth, Adath Is & Beth Jacob. To further Orthodox

J in Houston. Over 550 families. Adath Emeth the oldest of the three syns was f in 1908 to conduct the needed Servs for the J com. The present bldg was completed in 1960. Pub UOS Bulletin (monthly). Rabbi Joseph Radinsky; Cantor Irving Dean; Pres: Michael Abramowitz; Sec: Mary Sacks, Parn Laibson; Treas: Sidney Reichenthal. **9001 Greenwillow, Houston TX 77096 (713) 723–3850.**

United Orthodox Synagogues of Houston, Library. Library contains 5,000 vols (Judaica). For information on the Syn, see – United Orthodox Synagogues of Houston, Houston, TX. **9001 Greenwillow, Houston TX 77096 (713) 723–3850.**

William S. Malev School of Religious Studies. Affiliated with Solomon Schechter Day Schs Assn. Edu Dir: Michael Korman; Prin: Cecile Jordan; Chr: Irving J. Weiner. **4525 Beechnut Blvd, Houston TX 77096 (713) 666–1884.**

Laredo

Agudas Achim. Affiliated with United Syn of Am. Rabbi Akiva N. Gerstein; Pres: Ralph Norton; Edu Dir: Rabbi Akiva N. Gerstein. **Laredo & Malinche Sts, Laredo TX 78040 (512) 723–4435, 2512.**

Temple B'nai Israel. Affiliated with UAHC. 8 mems. Pres: Patricia Sanditen. **c/o Mrs Dean Sanditen, 2120 Musser St, Laredo TX 78040.**

Longview

Temple Emanu-El. Reform Temple affiliated with UAHC. The maintenance & continuance of J tradition, beliefs & values. Rel Servs; Adult Edu; Sun Sch; Sisterhood; personal counseling by the Rabbi; library containing 1,000 vols (Judaica). 45 families; 25 stu. 1 employee. F 1957. Pub Temple Newsletter (monthly bulletin). Facilities include sanctuary seating 250, gift shop. Rabbi Kalman Dubov; Pres: Joost Gosschalk; VP: Mike Finfer; Sisterhood Pres: Joy Wolf; Sisterhood VP: Elaine Retting. **1205 Eden Dr, PO Box 423, Longview TX 75601 (214) 753–6512.**

Lubbock

Congregation Shaareth Israel. Affiliated with UAHC. 96 mems. Rabbis: Stephen E. Weisberg, Alexander Kline; Pres: Larry Solomon; Sisterhood Pres: Judy Weinstein. **PO Box 6192, 1706 23rd St, Lubbock TX 79413 (806) 744–6084.**

McAllen

Temple Emanuel. Affiliated with UAHC. 112 mems. Rabbi Jeffrey Elson; Pres: Alex Sidelnik; Edu: Karen R. Elson; Sisterhood Pres: Audrey Goldman. **1410 Redwood, PO Box 896, McAllen TX 78501 (512) 686–9432.**

Port Arthur

Congregation Rodef Shalom. Affiliated with UAHC. 60 mems. Rabbi Lothar Goldstein; Pres: John K. Levy; Sisterhood Pres: Dolores Wyde. **3984 Procter St, Port Arthur TX 77640 (713) 985–7616.**

Richardson

Congregation Beth Torah. Affiliated with United Syn of Am. Rabbi Gabriel Ben–Or; Pres: Norman Kramer; Edu Dir: Lee Rosenthal. **810 Lookout Dr, Richardson TX 75080 (214) 234–1541.**

San Antonio

Congregation Agudas Achim. Affiliated with United Syn of Am. Rabbi William E. Kaufman; Cantor Louis D. Goldhirsh; Pres: Wolford Sadovsky; Edu Dir: David Segal. **1201 Donaldson Ave, San Antonio TX 78228 (512) 736–4216.**

Golden Manor Jewish Home for the Aged. Skilled nursing home, licensed by the State Dept of Health; non-profit, non-sectarian facility. To meet the needs of the older population who require health & protective servs beyond that which is available to them in their own home, but not requiring hospitalization. To rehabilitate the aged to maximum self-care & to provide a stimulating, enriching environment. Laundry, beauty parlor, library, dining rms, Sabbath Servs & Holiday Servs; Ladies Auxiliary; 16 apt units with facilities for those who can manage independently but need the protection & security available fr being adjacent to the nursing home, & for those requiring maximum care & treatment; Meals-on-Wheels serv. Men & women 65 yrs of age or older may apply. A younger person may apply where special conditions warrant. The Home opened in the Spring of 1968. The bldg offers facilities specifically designed for the comfort of the older person fully ambulatory or in a wheel chair or with limited vision. Facilities include kosher & diet kitchens; lounges, game rms & dining rms. Exec Dir: Sue Bornstein; Pres: Robert Rosow; Pres Ladies Auxiliary: Lenore Rodis. **130 Spencer Lane, San Antonio TX 78201 (512) 736–4544.**

Jewish Community Center. To serve the leisure time, recreational, & informal edu needs in the J com beginning with the infant & continuing through to the older adult. Nursery Sch Prog; special interest groups for pre-sch age chil; classes for youth & adults; ongoing activities for sr citizens; summer camps: Kinder Camp (a half-day camp) for chil 2½ yrs thru 3 yrs 8 mo, Camp Chai I for chil 3 yrs 9 mo thru grade 2, Camp Chai II for chil in grades 3 & 4, Camp of the Arts for grades 5 thru 8, Tennis/Swim Camp for grades 4 thru 8; Sports Camp for grades 6 thru 8, & Tween Trips & Tours for grades 7 thru 9; scouting for boys & girls; special groups & servs for single adults & single parent families; Chil Care Prog for after sch care; servs for the J personnel in the Armed Forces. Membership is open to all interested individuals & families. Facilities are available to all J orgs. Housed on 5½ acres, the facilities include: meeting rms; nursery sch wing with kitchen; multi-purpose auditorium adjoining a kosher kitchen; arts & crafts rm; adult lounge; exercise/dance studio; gymnasium; 4 tennis cts lighted for night play; outdoor swimming facilities; picnic grounds & playground. Exec Dir: Irving Ginsberg; Asst Dir: Peter M. Merles; Pres: Aaron Charles. **103 W Rampart, San Antonio TX 78216 (512) 344–3454.**

The Jewish Day School of San Antonio. Com sch having an open enrollment policy; chartered by the State of TX as an independent edu ins. To offer chil in the San Antonio area the opportunity to integrate both gen & J studies during regular sch hours. Excellent & progressive curriculum to enable the chil to feel interaction & harmony between J & gen studies, & to appreciate the J contribution to the world. The curriculum is implemented in a modified open class setting. Prin: Dr Nissim Elbaz; Pres: David Kboudi. **703 Trafalgar Rd, San Antonio TX 78216 (512) 341–0735.**

The Jewish Family Service. To strengthen the quality of J family life. Counseling; information & referral servs; volunteer servs; family & emergency fin assistance; J Family Life Edu; resettlement of Soviet J & the Indochinese Boat People. Fees are based on a sliding scale. Exec Dir: Claire Frontman; Pres: Bennett Weissman. **8438 Ahern, San Antonio TX 78216 (512) 349–5481.**

The Jewish Federation of San Antonio. Mem of CJF. To coord & meet local, natl & overseas J philanthropic needs. Conducts an annual campaign on behalf of natl & overseas agy as well as local agy: Golden Manor Home for the Aged, JCC, J Day Sch of San Antonio, & the J Family Serv; com planning; edu; Women's Coordinating Cttee; Leadership Dev Group; Com Relations Council; Men's & Women's Div. Est in 1927. Jewish Journal. A large percentage of every dollar raised is allocated to the UJA which in turn supports four major overseas Am philanthropies: The J Agy, The Joint Distribution Cttee, HIAS & the NY Assn for New Am. Exec Dir: Hilda S. Heritch; Pres: Allen Bassuk; Gen Campaign Chr: Richard E. Goldsmith; Women's Div Chr: Irene Heintz; VPs: Paula Kaufman, Fred Kline, Mike Levy; Sec: Maxine Cohen; Treas: Phyllis Siegal; Dirs: Elsa Barshop, Stanley Blend, Maxine Carr, Stanley Cohen, Russel Davis, Alan Dreeben, Seymour Dreyfus, Candy Gardner, Arthur Gurwirtz, Philip Heintz, Bruce Hendlin, Judy Hoberman, Ruth Hoine, Helen Jacobson, Dr Norman Jacobson, Estelle Kaufman, Rabbi William E. Kaufman, William Kaufman, Dr Herbert Keyser, Martha Landsman, Leonard Leighton, Calvin Michelson, Marge Miller, Dr Paul Mohl, Sterling Neuman, Beth Novick, Dr Victor Ostrower, Judy Palans, Sandra Riordan, Bernard Rosenman, Raymond Schneider, Rabbi Arnold Scheinberg, Joan Schwartz, Lynn Stahl, Rabbi Samuel Stahl, Malcolm Steinberg, Rachel Weiner, Dr Martin Weinstein, Bennet Weissman. **8434 Ahern Dr, San Antonio TX 78216 (512) 341–8234.**

Temple Beth El. Affiliated with UAHC. 954 mems. Rabbis: Samuel M. Stahl, Morley T. Feinstein, David Jacobson; Pres: Janet Lieberman; Edu: Roberta L. Louis; Sisterhood Pres: Doris Toubin; Brotherhood Pres: Richard I. Miller. **211 Belknap Pl, San Antonio TX 78212 (512) 733–9135.**

Temple Beth El Library. 211 Belknap Pl, San Antonio TX 78212 (512) 733–9135.

Sherman

Temple Beth Emeth. Affiliated with UAHC. 26 mems. **304 N Rusk St, Sherman TX 75090 (214) 892–9326.**

Texarkana

Mount Sinai Congregation. Affiliated with UAHC. 41 mems. Pres: Harry Friedman; Adm: Ralph Brody; Sisterhood Pres: Evelyn Kennedy. **1310 Walnut St, Texarkana TX 75501 (214) 792–2394.**

Tyler

Ahavath Achim. Affiliated with United Syn of Am. Rabbi Kalman Taxon; Pres: Meyer Mellinger. **1014 W Houston St, Tyler TX 75702 (214) 597–4284.**

Federation of Jewish Welfare Fund. Organized 1938. Pres: Dr Barry Green. **PO Box 8601, Tyler TX 75711.**

Temple Beth El. Affiliated with UAHC. 90 mems. Rabbi Eugene H. Levy; Pres: Ron Serber; Sisterhood Pres: Sue Zimmerman. **1102 S Augusta, Tyler TX 75701 (214) 597–2917.**

Victoria

Temple B'nai Israel. Affiliated with UAHC. 38 mems. Pres: Robert H. Loeb Jr. **PO Box 2088, Victoria TX 77901 (512) 578–5140.**

Waco

Agudath Jacob. Affiliated with United Syn of Am. Rabbi Abraham Pollack; Cantor & Pres: Elliot Wolpo. **4925 Hillcrest Dr, Waco TX 76710 (817) 772–1451.**

Jewish Welfare Council of Waco. Mem of CJF. Organized 1949. Pres: Mrs Sam Chernoff; Exec Sec: Mrs Maurice Labens. **PO Box 8031, Waco TX 76710 (817) 776–3740.**

Temple Rodef Sholom. Liberal Cong affiliated with UAHC. To maintain a syn for worship, learning & fellowship in accordance with the practices of J. To stimulate love, understanding & loyalty to the principles of J as well as a sense of historical identity with our co-religionists everywhere. To be a symbol, rep & advocate of the lofty idealism that is our J ethical heritage & thereby to bring nearer the perfection of humanity in ourselves, in the wider com & in all mankind. Rel Servs; Rel Sch, the Sun Sch off a ten yr prog leading to Confirmation, Heb classes meet weekly; Bar & Bat Mitzvah instruction; social, cultural & servs activity for temple youth aged 14–17; Sisterhood sponsors monthly meetings, cultural & social progs, study group; library; Oneg Shabbat; Adult Edu including lectures, presentations by visiting scholars, study group series, bk review series, monthly Scripture Circle. In 1879 mems of a J lodge organized a cong to be named Rodef Sholom. The first syn was completed in 1881. By 1908 the structure was felt to be inadequate & a second temple was completed in 1910. In 1961 the present temple was dedicated. The temple receives streams of visitors of all denominations, church & col classes, sightseers & others who come to view & learn about the temple edifice, its symbols & the faith for which it stands. Newsletter. Facilities include a gift shop, social hall & a kitchen. Rabbi Mordecai Podet; Pres: Frank Levy; VPs: Arnold Miller, Maurice Labens; Sec-Treas: Harold Ginsburg; Bd of Trustees: Ruth Beasley, Mrs Nathan Brickman, Louis Englander, Abbye Freed, Charles Hart, Ira Levy, Bert Scheinbrum, Arthur Schwartz, Mrs Milton Spark; Sisterhood Pres: Mrs Maurice Labens; Cemetery Chr: James Fetter; Rel Sch Prin: Mrs Robert Rosen. **1717 N 41st St, Waco TX 76707 (817) 754–3703.**

UTAH

Salt Lake City

Congregation Kol Ami. Affiliated with UAHC & United Syn of Am. 370 mems. Rabbi Eric A. Silver; Cantor Maynard Gerber; Pres: Robert Fineman; Edu: Nomi Loeb. **2425 E Heritage Way, Salt Lake City UT 84109 (801) 484–1501.**

National Conference of Christians & Jews. 4326 Zarahemia Dr, Salt Lake City UT 84117 (801) 278–6165.

Salt Lake City Jewish Community Center. 2416 E 1700 S, Salt Lake City UT 84108 (801) 581–0098.

United Jewish Council & Salt Lake Jewish Welfare Fund. Mem of CJF. Organized 1936. Pres: Bruce Cohne; Exec Dir: Bernard Solomon. **2416 E 1700 S, Salt Lake City UT 84108 (801) 581–0098.**

VERMONT

Burlington

Ohavi Zedek Synagogue. Affiliated with United Syn of Am. Rel Servs; social servs; counseling; guidance; cemetery; welfare functions. F in 1885 for rel, edu & communal purposes. Rabbi Max B. Wall; Cantor Rodney J. Margolis; Pres: Stephen Halley; VP: Shallom Lewin; Treas: Bernard Cohen; Fin Sec: David Pearl; Rec Sec: Lenore Broughton; 1st Trustee: Myron Samuelson; 2nd Trustee: Samuel Epstein; Activities Dir: Barry Krikstone. **188 N Prospect St, Burlington VT 05401 (802) 864–0218.**

Rutland

Rutland Jewish Center. Affiliated with United Syn of Am. Rabbi Solomon Goldberg; Pres: James Chase. **96 Grove St, Rutland VT 05701 (802) 773–3455.**

South Burlington

Temple Sinai. Affiliated with UAHC. 75 mems. Rabbi James S. Glazier; Cantor Mark Leopold; Pres: Jules Broder; Adm: Eleanor Perl; Sisterhood Pres: Naomi E. Berman. **899 Dorset St, South Burlington VT 05401 (802) 862–5125.**

VIRGINIA

Alexandria

Agudas Achim Congregation. Conservative Cong affiliated with United Syn of Am. Daily Rel Servs; Men's Club; VIP Club for young adults; USY Groups; library; Rel Sch; Post Bar Mitzvah instruction leading to Confirmation & graduation fr Heb HS; Adult Edu including seminars, instruction in Heb, biblical & J oriented subjects in weekday classes & home study groups; Sisterhood which underwrites the Rel Sch, supplies furnishings for the kitchen & library, & acts as hostess for Syn functions; edu, rel & social activities. 300 families; 200 women in the Sisterhood; 100 mems in the Men's Club; 64 stu in the HS. Organized in 1914 by prominent J residents. The Cong is the oldest Conservative cong in N VA. After using several temporary facilities, a permanent bldg was built & dedicated in 1958. The Temple was one of the examples of outstanding Alexandria architecture pictured in "Virginia's Buildings". The Temple has been cited for its unique architectural design. Temple facilities include a social hall, kitchen & sanctuary. Rabbi Sheldon E. Elster; Pres: Gerson Serody; Fin VP: David Yaffe; Adm VP: Joseph Loeb; Edu VP: Estelle Rosoff; Ritual VP: Frank Walter; Treas: Neale Ainsfield; Parliamentarian: Ira Polon; Gabbaim: Joseph Loeb, Jerome Salkin, Jerome Chapman; Sisterhood Pres: Marcia Lazrus; CEAC VP: Rhoda Berson; Mems VP: Marilyn Steinthal; Ways & Means VPs: Paula Walter, Deborah Yaffe; Catering VP: Andrea Bregstone; Treas: Irene Janow; Rec Sec: Marilyn Feldman-Krug; Corsp Sec: Roxy Chitlik; Fin Sec: Nancy Landson; Parliamentarian: Ellen Wayne; Trustees: Gloria Sitrin, Elaine Stokols; Edu Dir: Solomon Rabinowitz. **2908 Valley Dr, Alexandria VA 22302 (703) 548–4122.**

Agudas Achim Congregation, Schoenberger Library. 2908 Valley Dr, Alexandria VA 22302 (703) 548–4122.

Beth El Hebrew Congregation. Affiliated with UAHC. 650 mems. Rabbi Arnold G. Fink; Cantor Michael Peerless; Pres: Ellen Feldstein; Edu: Gloria Eiseman; Adm: Marshall Levin; Sisterhood Pres: Joyce N. Gordon; Brotherhood Pres: Jerome Liess. **3830 Seminary Rd, Alexandria VA 22304 (703) 370–9400.**

Arlington

Arlington-Fairfax Jewish Congregation. Conservative Syn affiliated with United Syn of Am. the only cong in the Cty of Arlington. Adult Edu; Rel Sch; Sisterhood, Men's Club; youth groups. F in 1940; originally known as Oheb Shalom. Pub Chronicle (bi-monthly). Rabbi Dr Marvin I. Bash; Cantor Moshe Shore. **2920 Arlington Blvd, Arlington VA 22204 (703) 979–4466,7.**

Charlottesville

B'nai B'rith Hillel Foundation at the University of Virginia. J ins on campus. To enhance J life in its edu, cultural, rel & social dimensions. Rel, edu & cultural activities; rel servs; holiday observances; speakers; brunches; dinners; classes; coffee houses. Est in 1940. Dir: Rabbi Daniel Alexander; Chr Com Adv Bd: P. Thorner. **1824 University Circle, Charlottesville VA 22903 (804) 295–4963.**

Congregation Beth Israel. Reform Cong affiliated with UAHC. To provide a worship experience that is meaningful & pleasant for people of all branches of J. Rel Servs, the Fri Evening Servs is that of a Reform cong & Sat morning is a Conservative-Traditional Serv; Oneg Shabbat following the Fri Night Servs; Kiddush following the Sat Morning Servs; Heb Sch; Sun Sch; Adult Edu progs; rel, social, edu, social action, charitable, youth progs; library; Advanced Studies Class; Bar & Bat Mitzvah preparation. 165 families. Est in 1864. The present temple bldg was constructed in 1881. When the federal govt bought the land, the temple was moved 'brick by brick' to its present location. The annex bldg was purchased in 1976. With a relatively small J population to draw upon, Beth Is has always had a small membership, numbering under 60 until the 1970's. Servs have been led by mems, Hillel rabbis & by stu rabbis. The recent increase in mems & growing desire by the Cong for a full prog of J activities & J com life led to the hiring of the first full time rabbi since the 1880's. The Temple Bulletin. Facilities include a seating capacity of 180 in the sanctuary, social hall, gift shop, six classrms, kitchen, rabbi's study. Rabbi Sheldon Ezring; Pres: Robert Dwoskin; VP: Nancy Berry; Sec: Mimi Hirsch; Treas: Lou Simons; Trustees: Jack Hirsch, Harry O'Mansky, Leonard Milgraum; Dirs: Sheila Elkon, Mark Kruger, Judy Jacobson, Jon Whitman, Judy Schlussel, Bert Litman, Harriet Noble. **Third & Jefferson Sts, Charlottesville VA 22902 (804) 295–6382.**

Danville

Temple Beth Sholom. Affiliated with UAHC. 45 mems. Rabbi Larry Kaplan; Pres: Peter K. Howard; Sisterhood Pres: Harriette Kingoff. **127 Sutherlin Ave, Danville VA 24541 (804) 792–3489.**

Fairfax

Congregation Olam Tikvah Library. For information on the Cong see – Congregation Olam Tikvah, Fairfax, VA. **3800 Glenbrook Rd, Fairfax VA 22030 (703) 978–3333.**

Northern Virginia Jewish Community Center. Non-profit social servs agy. To serve the J com recreational, cultural, edu, social & physical needs under the supervision of a professionally trained & experienced staff. The JCC is dedicated to activities with J content that will enrich & further an appreciation of the spitirual, cultural, & ethical heritage & values of J as they apply to the J Am way of life. Early childhood classes for preschoolers & parents; J holiday workshops; special progs on Sun for chil ages 4–grade 6; activities for teens; summer camps; seminars; conversational Heb & Yiddish classes; J Single Adults Group; Young Couples Club; Choral Club; Hiking Club; servs for sr citizens. The first com wide event of the Ctr was the now annual Hanukah Happening in 1977. Until 1981, when a bldg was acquired, activities were held in schs & syns. Pres: Dr Chet Kessler; VP Adm: Bunni Latkin; VP Prog: Sharon Alperstein; VP Membership: Michael Hausfeld; VP Fund Raising: Paul Frommer; Sec: Herman Hohauser; Treas: Dr Ron Apter; Exec Bd Mems: Paul Arnstein, Dr David Zohn; Bd Mems: Arthur Altman, Dorothy Bennett, Judith Bernanke, Stephen Bodzin, David Brewer, Bernard Cohen, Eugene Davidson, Alvin Fuchsman, Manfred Gale, Dene Garbow, Donna Gary, Daniel Goldberg, Samuel Kastner, Jonathan Levine, Jon Luria, Harold November, Douglas Poretz, Estelle Rosoff, Irwin Samet, Dr Lawrence Shuman, Pearl Shuman, Douglas Samuelson, Mayer Smith; Dir: Adele M. Greenspon. **8822 Little River Turnpike, Fairfax VA 22031 (703) 323–0880.**

Falls Church

Temple Rodef Shalom. Affiliated with UAHC. 408 mems. Rabbi Laszlo Berkowits; Pres: Samuel A. Simon; Edu: Sylvia Rosenthal; Sisterhood Pres: Karen Hecker, Renee Perlstein; Brotherhood Pres: Sidney Lovick. **2100 Westmoreland St, Falls Church VA 22043 (703) 532–2217.**

Fredericksburg

Beth Sholom Temple. Affiliated with UAHC. 74 mems. Pres: William L. Stein; Edu: Gloria Schor; Sisterhood Pres: Elaine Klauber. **PO Box 481, Fredericksburg VA 22404 (703) 373–4834.**

Hampton

Rodef Sholom Congregation. Affiliated with United Syn of Am. Rabbi Steven C. Lindemann; Pres: M. David Levy. **318 Whealton Rd, Hampton VA 23666 (804) 826–5894.**

Harrisonburg

Beth El Congregation. Affiliated with UAHC. 57 mems. Pres: J. Gerald Minskoff; Edu: Janet Kohen; Sisterhood Pres: Janet Kohen; Brotherhood Pres: Robert Levine. **PO Box 845, Harrisonburg VA 22801 (703) 434–2744.**

Lynchburg

Agudath Sholom Congregation. Affiliated with UAHC. 109 mems. Rabbi Morris Shapiro; Pres: Rosel Schewel; Edu: David Rubinberg; Sisterhood Pres: Sonja Ornan. **PO Box 2262, Lynchburg VA 24501 (804) 846–0739.**

Martinsville

Ohev Zion Congregation. Reform Syn serving the J com within a radius of about 40 miles. Sabbath Servs; Rel Sch which meets twice a week; study groups; B'nai B'rith Lodge; Sisterhood; Youth Group. 50 families; 32 stu in the Rel Sch. The Rabbi also serves as Heb teacher & adm of the Cong. F in 1927 by the late Abe Globman. Rabbi Harold A. Friedman; Pres: Al Groden. **801 Parkview Ave, Martinsville VA 24112 (703) 632–2828.**

Newport News

Adath Jeshurun Synagogue. Orthodox Syn. To perpetuate Orthodox J. Daily Minyan Servs; Sun Sch; participates in com Heb Sch; NCSY Youth Group; Adult Edu classes; Men's Club; Ladies Auxiliary; Va'ad Hakashruth; mikvah. F in 1893; the first J Syn in Newport News. The Cong has been located at several locations: 1893–1926 – 2310–12 Lafayette Ave, 1926–1961 – 656 28th St, 1961–1982 – 1815 Chestnut Ave, & fr May 1982 – Nettles Rd. Rabbi Aryeh Weil; Chr: Barney Siegel; Men's Club Pres: Harvey Anker; Ladies Auxiliary Pres: Frances Rice; First Gabbai, Chevra Kadisha: Benjamin Brenner. **1815 Chestnut Ave, Newport News VA 23607 (804) 245–7485.**

Jewish Community Center of the Virginia Peninsula. Affiliate of JWB. To provide a place where fellow J can meet with pride. Singles Prog; summer camp: pre-K camp, Camp Kadima, Travel Camp; fun & games rm; social progs; pre-sch classes for ages two, three & four; youth after school classes: arts & crafts, ballet, cooking & sewing; Winterama providing winter vacation activities for K through 5th grade; Tweens Prog for 6th, 7th & 8th grades; BBYO; Adult Prog: CPR Prog, film festival, bridge classes, trips, health fair, Family Life Edu series; Sr Adult Dept; Athletic Prog including tennis, fitness class, volleyball league, ping pong tournament, youth soccer, bowling league, softball & swimming. Centerpiece. Pres: Jane Susan Frank; 1st VP: Kenneth Murov; VPs: Marty Damsky, Lois Ullman, Howard Waters, Sherry Sternberg, Jeff Deyong; Sec & Parliamentarian: Joanne Gordon; Bd Mems: Dr Arnold Abrams, Frona Adelson, Bunny Altman, Ginny Becker, Sidney Becker, Myrt Braslow, Dr Steve Dannenberg, Joel Divack, Jay Epstein, Richard Feldman, Leslie Frank, Betsi Garfinkel, Myra Kramer, Dorothy Lazzaro, Rabbi Charles Levi, Rhoda Mazur, Enid Milner, Karen Minkoff, Gary Nachman, Aaron Ostroff, Tzina Richman, Dale Satran, Steve Seltzer, Rossi Schlosser, Nathan Sharf, Rabbi Aryeh Weil; Exec Dir: Meyer L. Bodoff; Prog Coord: Bubba Guilford; Ctr Sec: Kathie Pipkin; Bookkeeper: Shirley Johnson; Presch Dir & Teacher: Carolyn Vassos; Presch Teachers: Margaret Lang, Debbie Parker; Housekeeper: Elizabeth Smith; Maintenance: Kenneth Wright. **2700 Spring Rd, PO Box 6680, Newport News VA 23606 (804) 595–5544.**

Jewish Federation of the Virginia Pensinsula. Mem of CJF. Organized 1942. Pres: Betty Levin; Exec Dir: James Wellen. **2700 Spring Rd, PO Box 6680, Newport News VA 23606 (804) 595–5544.**

Temple Sinai. Affiliated with UAHC. Rel Servs; Rel Sch; Sisterhood; Brotherhood; Youth Group; quarterly Family Shabbat Dinners; annual Family Chanukah Dinner; annual Boy & Girl Scout Sabbath; annual Candlelight Ball Fund Raiser; Passover Family Seder; annual Sisterhood Donor Banquet; annual Brotherhood Game Night; participant in Fed Forum Series; Rel Sch Purim Carnival; monthly Brotherhood Breakfasts; annual Temple Picnic; Brotherhood sponsors Temple Man of the Yr Award; Youth Group sponsors TYG Conclaves; annual Confirmation Servs; sponsors J Ins for non J; annual Col Sabbath; annual US Armed Forces Sabbath. Est in 1955. Monthly Bulletin. The Syn maintains a Biblical Garden & Gift Shop. The Cong is a mem of the Interfaith Com Rel Group. Temple Sinai sponsored a Vietnamese family. Rabbi Charles S. Levi; Pres: Abraham Leiss; VP: Joanne Ross; Sec: Lydia Shipman; Treas: Dianne Haley; Sisterhood Pres: Marilyn Cooper; Brotherhood Pres: Michael Haley. **11620 Warwick Blvd, Newport News VA 23601 (804) 596–8352.**

Norfolk

Beth El. Affiliated with United Syn of Am. Cantor Joseph Reich; Pres: Stanley Samuels; Edu Dir: Blanche Glickman. **422 Shirley Ave, PO Box 11206, Norfolk VA 23517 (804) 625–7821.**

Hebrew Ladies Charity Society. To dispense worthy charities; to help the poor & needy, financially & otherwise; to lend money upon surrender of collateral, without interest or charges through the Free Loan Fund, to worthy people in destitute circumstances; to supply milk to needy families; to contribute toward burial expenses & to erect tombstones in needy cases. Est in 1902. The work of the Soc is limited to the geographic area of Norfolk VA & neighboring suburbs. Pres: Carol A. Levitin; 1st VP: Mrs Donald Levy; 2nd VP: Mrs Jerome Isrow. **1321 Noble St, Norfolk VA 23518.**

Jewish Family Service of Tidewater, Inc. Social serv agy; accredited by Council of Accreditation. Affiliated with United J Fed of Tidewater Inc; United J Fed of Hampton/Newport News, Inc; Four Cities United Way, Norfolk VA; Portsmouth Area United Way, Portsmouth VA. To strengthen the J family. Counseling servs; J Family Life Edu progs; a variety of progs for the elderly. 500 families visits per yr. 100 volunteers. F 1916 by Hebrew Ladies Aid & Natl Council of J Women. Pres: Stanley Samuels; 1st VP: Martin Mendelsohn; 2nd VP: Joan London; Sec: Barbara Albinder; Treas: Gary Rubin; Exec Dir: Neil P. Newstein; Social Work Supervisor: Gail S. Cervarich; Sr Servs Coord: Diana Ruchelman; Volunteer Coord: Clare Krell. **7300 Newport Ave, Norfolk VA 23505 (804) 489–3111.**

Temple Israel. Affiliated with United Syn of Am. Rabbi Joseph Goldman; Cantor Isaac Danker; Pres: Leon I. Salzberg. **7255 Granby St, Norfolk VA 23505 (804) 489–4550.**

Temple Ohev Sholom. Affiliated with UAHC. 625 mems. Rabbi Lawrence A. Forman; Pres: Henry M. Schwan; Adm: Rita Cogan; Sisterhood Pres: R.L. Stein; Brotherhood Pres: Robert Brotman. **530 Raleigh Ave, Stockley Gardens, Norfolk VA 23507 (804) 625–4295.**

Temple Ohev Sholom Library. For information on the Temple, see – Temple Ohev Sholom, Norfolk, VA. **530 Raleigh Ave, Norfolk VA 23507 (804) 625–4295.**

United Jewish Federation, Inc of Norfolk & Virginia Beach. 7300 Newport Ave, PO Box 9776, Norfolk VA 23505 (804) 489–8040.

Petersburg

Congregation Brith Achim. Conservative Syn affiliated with United Syn of Am. Rel Servs; Rel Edu. 130 families. F in 1915. Rabbi Dr Oscar Fleishake **314 S Blvd, Petersburg VA 23805 (804) 732–3968.**

Congregation Brith Achim Library. For information on the Cong, see – Congregation Brith Achim, Petersburg, VA. **314 S Blvd, Petersburg VA 23805 (804) 732–3968.**

Portsmouth

Gomley Chesed Congregation. Affiliated with United Syn of Am. Rabbi Judah L. Fish; Pres: Harry R. Kocen; Exec Sec: Ronda J. Lacher. **3110 Sterling Point Dr, Portsmouth VA 23703 (804) 484–1019.**

Portsmouth Jewish Community Council. Rm 430, Dominion Natl Bank Bldg, Portsmouth VA 23704 (804) 393–2557.

Temple Sinai. Affiliated with UAHC. 71 mems. Rabbi Arthur Z. Steinberg; Pres: Edward B. Ostroff. **4401 Hatton Point Rd, Portsmouth VA 23703 (804) 484–1730.**

Reston

North Virginia Hebrew Congregation. Affiliated with UAHC. 175 mems. Rabbi Rosalind A. Gold; Pres: Stuart M. Patz; Edu: Ruth Hershkowitz; Sisterhood Pres: Ann Grossman. **1441 Wiehle Ave, PO Box 2758, Reston VA 22090 (703) 437–7733.**

Richmond

Anti-Defamation League of B'nai B'rith – N Carolina-Virginia Regional Office. Dedicated in purpose & prog to translating the Am heritage of democratic ideals into a way of life for all Am, & to countering assaults on the safety, status, rights & image of J. For additional information, see – Anti-Defamation League of B'nai B'rith, New York City, NY. **3311 W Broad St, Richmond VA 23230.**

Chabad Lubavitch. Lubavitch com servs ctr. Blends Chassidic fervor & warmth with tradition & learning, to show that every J, fr whatever background he or she comes fr, is an integral part of the body of Is. Anti-missionary work; adult edu; sabbath seminars; holiday progs; day camp; youth groups; syns; kosher kitchen; counseling; chaplaincy; Mitzvah Campaigns; hosp & prison visitations; sr citizens encounters; speakers bureau. Rabbi Jacob Kranz. **5311 W Franklin St, Richmond VA 23226 (804) 288–0588.**

Congregation Beth Ahabah. Affiliated with UAHC. 630 mems. Rabbi Jack D. Spiro; Pres: Harold P. Straus; Edu & adm: Harry A. Glasser; Sisterhood Pres: Nancy G. Levine; Brotherhood Pres: Daniel W. Dabansky. **1111 W Franklin St, Richmond VA 23220 (804) 358–6757.**

Congregation Kol Emes. Orthodox Syn. Daily Rel Servs. F in 1964 for the purpose of re-establishing J observance according to Halacha in this southern city. In the sanctuary there is a mechitzah (divider between men & women). The Cong maintains a mikvah in the bl-g. All J are welcome & hospitality is available for visitors fr out of town. Pub Guardian (monthly). Pres: Abraham J. Dere; Treas: Harold M. Marks; Sec: Harold Winer; Gabbai: Leonard Polevoy. **4811 Patterson Ave, Richmond VA 23226 (804) 353–5831.**

Congregation Or Ami. Affiliated with UAHC. 95 mems. Rabbi Beverly J. Lerner; Pres: Arthur J. Seidenberg. **3406 N Huguenot Rd, Richmond VA 23235 (804) 272–0017.**

Jewish Community Center. 5403 Monument Ave, Richmond VA 23226 (804) 288–6091.

Jewish Community Center Library. 5403 Monument Ave, Richmond VA 23226 (804) 288–6091.

Jewish Community Federation of Richmond. Mem of CJF. Organized 1935. Pres: Irwin Schapiro; Exec Dir: Roy Rosenbaum. **PO Box 8237, 5403**

Monument Ave, Richmond VA 23226 (804) 288–0045.

Masada Hillel. B'nai B'rith Hillel Foun at VA Commonwealth Univ which also serves the Univ of Richmond, J. Sargeant Reynolds Com Col, & Randolph-Macon Col. Shabbat & Holiday Servs; Is progs; lecture series; weekend retreats; coffeehouses; social progs; com servs; Richmond J Stu Appeal Campaign; Hillel Stu Council; J library; Drop-In Ctr; J Stu Residence Ctr; personal counseling; J Univ. **1103 W Franklin St, Richmond VA 23220 (804) 353–6477.**

Temple Beth El. Affiliated with United Syn of Am. Rabbi: Dr Myron Berman; Cantor Morris Okun; Pres: Dr Albert J. Wasserman; Exec Dir: Milton J. Lewis. **3330 Grove Ave, Richmond VA 23221 (804) 355–3564, 359–2119.**

Temple Beth El Religious School. 3330 Grove Ave, Richmond VA 23221 (804) 355–3564.

Roanoke

Beth Israel Synagogue. Affiliated with United Syn of Am. Rabbi Cary D. Kozberg; Pres: Dr Joseph H. Penn. **920 Franklin Rd SW, Roanoke VA 24016 (703) 343–0289.**

Jewish Community Council. Mem of CJF. Chr: Albert Lippmann. **PO Box 1074, Roanoke VA 24005.**

Temple Emanuel. Affiliated with the UAHC. Rel Servs Fri evenings & all holy days; joint Sun Sch K–9th grade (with Beth Is Syn, a Conservative syn in Roanoke); Heb Sch – 5th grade–Bar/ Bat Mitzvah; adult classes; Confirmation Class; Joint Youth Group; adult activities: Basic J Class, Bk Group; Sisterhood: monthly meetings, special fund raisers, dinners. The Reform J Cong of Roanoke had its beginning in 1890. 2 years later, Theodore Joseph, a sr rabbinical stu at the HUC officiated at Servs which were held in an upstairs hall at Jefferson & Campbell St. In the same year, a Ladies Guild was formed. In 1905 the new temple bldg at Franklin Rd was dedicated. In 1937 a new temple was dedicated at McClanahan Pl. In 1959 the present Temple Emanuel bldg was dedicated. On November 6, 1981 the Temple observed its 90th anniversary. Pres: Albert K. Lippmann; VP: H. Lawrence Davidson; Sec: Esther Natt; Treas: Dr Herbert Sudranski; Asst Treas: Susan Bulbin; Membership: Dr Bernard Goffen; Cemetery: Burton Albert; Rel Sch: Jane Bender; Finance: Jerome Barr; House: Robert Herskovitz; Intra-Com Relations: Gordon Shapiro; Pulpit: Fred Bulbin; Sisterhood Pres: Elaine Platt; Sisterhood Rep: Dixie Wolf; Social Action: Alan Gore; Com Council Rep: Dr Raphael Greenstein; Rabbi Gerry H. Walter; Cantor Allen Levin. **1163 Persinger Rd SW, Roanoke VA 24015 (703) 342–3378.**

Staunton

Temple House of Israel. Affiliated with UAHC. 28 mems. Pres: Alan D. Goldenberg; Sisterhood Pres: Rûth Sacks. **c/o Mr Alan D. Goldenberg, Mountainside Farm, Rt 1 Box 1896, Staunton VA 24401 (703) 885–6878.**

Tidewater

United Jewish Federation of Tidewater. Mem of CJF. Includes Norfolk, Portsmith & Virginia Beach. Organized 1937. Pres: Robert O. Copeland; Exec Dir: A. Robert Gast; Asst Exec Dir: Rachel Lindenthal. **7300 Newport Ave, PO Box 9776, Tidewater VA 23505 (804) 489–8040.**

Virginia Beach

Hebrew Academy of Tidewater. Com day sch accredited by State Bd of Edu – Commonwealth of VA. To inspire its students with a love of learning & to create within them an awarness of Judaism's rich & meaningful heritage. Edu prog in secular, Judaic & Heb studies for preschoolers through 7th graders; library containing 4,000 vols (Judaica; chil). 135 stu; 6 Pre-Nursery stu. 35 employees. F 1955; moved into its current facility in 1965. Pub Newsletter (monthly). Facilities include 4 classrms for early chil, 10 classrms, multi-purpose rm (servs as auditorium, gym), kosher kitchen & cafeteria, gift shop, art rm, computer ctr, library, learning ctrs, outdoors playground. Pres: Ed Stein; Adm VP: Dr Jay Laizer; Edu VP: Dr David Kruger; Prin: Rabbi Sackett; Asst Prin: Ada Michaels; Fin VPs: Joann & Bob Stein; Sec: Dr David Maizel; Treas: Jeffery Littman. **1244 Thompkins Lane, Virginia Beach VA 23464 (804) 424–4327.**

Hebrew Academy of Tidewater Library. Library contains 4,000 vols (Judaica, chil). For information on the Ins, see – Hebrew Academy of Tidewater, Virginia Beach, VA. **1244 Thompkins Lane, Virginia Beach VA 23462 (804) 424–4327.**

Kehillat Bet Hamidrash. Affiliated with United Syn of Am. Pres: Stephen A. Schechner MD; Edu Dir: Stephanie Tomasulo; Youth Dir: Ed Ornoff. **740 Arthur Ave, Virginia Beach VA 23452 (804) 424–9715.**

Temple Emanuel. Affiliated with United Syn of Am. Rabbi Arnold M. Turchick; Press: Charles J. Sidman; Youth Dir: Max Meyer. **25th St & Baltic Ave, Virginia Beach VA 23451 (804) 428–2591.**

Temple Emanuel, Leon Fine Memorial Library. For information on the Temple see – Temple Emanuel, Virginia Beach, VA. **25th St & Baltic Ave, Virginia Beach VA 23451 (804) 428–2591.**

Winchester

Beth El Congregation. Affiliated with UAHC. 39 mems. Pres: Irving Weiss. **528 Fairmont Ave, PO Box 1041, Winchester VA 22601 (703) 667–1043.**

Woodbridge

Congregation Ner Tamid. Affiliated with UAHC. 34 mems. Rabbi Samuel Volkman; Pres: Ira Schwab. **PO Box 54, Woodbridge VA 22194 (703) 494–3251.**

WASHINGTON

Aberdeen

Temple Beth Israel. Affiliated with UAHC. 10 mems. Pres: Jay Goldberg. **c/o Jay Goldberg, 1801 Sherwood Lane, Aberdeen WA 98520 (206) 532–7485.**

Mercer Island

Herzl – Ner Tamid Conservative Congregation. Affiliated with United Syn of Am. Rabbi Moshe Pomerantz; Cantor Errol Helfman; Pres: Irving A. Hirsch; Exec Dir: Walter Bernstein; Edu Dir: Richard Miller; Youth Dir: Sylvia & Robert Epstein. **PO Box 574, 3700 E Mercer Way, Mercer Island WA 98040 (206) 232–8555.**

Temple B'nai Torah. Affiliated with UAHC. 110 mems. Rabbi Jacob Singer; Cantor David M. Serkin; Pres: Doris Haykin. **6195 92nd Ave SE, Mercer Island WA 98040 (206) 232–7243.**

Seattle

Anti-Defamation League of B'nai B'rith – Pacific NW Regional Office. Dedicated in purpose & prog to translating the Am heritage of democratic ideals into a way of life for all Am, & to countering assaults on the safety, status, rights & image of J. For additional information, see – Anti-Defamation League of B'nai B'rith, New York City, NY. **918 Securities Bldg. Seattle WA 98101.**

ASUW Experimental College. Edu forum where people share ideas & skills. To provide a unique learning experience outside of the structured ins. Wide variety of classes such as: Auto Mechanics, Cooking, Investments, Dancing, Exercises, Photography, Self-Discovery, Yoga. Classes are open to stu & com mems of all ages. Experimental Col began as an off-campus edu alternative in the 1960's. In 1968 the Col became a part of Associated Stu Univ of WA (ASUW). Today it is the largest of its kind in the US. Each quarter over 500 non-credit courses are offered. Forum (quarterly catalog of classes). Dir: Julie Miller; Asst Dir: Jeff Slater. **103 HUB, Univ of WA, Seattle WA 98195 (206) 543–4375.**

B'nai B'rith Hillel Foundation. 4745 17th Ave NE, Seattle WA 98105 (206) 522–1060.

B'nai B'rith Hillel Foundation Library. 4745 17th Ave NE, Seattle WA 98105 (206) 522–1060.

Bikur Cholim Machzikay Hadath Congregation. 5145 S Morgan St, Seattle WA 98118 (206) 723–0970.

The Caroline Kline Galland Home. Skilled nursing facility serving the J Aged of the Pacific NW. Nursing care; restorative & social servs; weekly rel servs; The Seattle-King Cty Nutrition Proj for the Elderly: about 75 persons, for whom bus transportation is provided, attend kosher lunch; The Polack Adult Day Ctr. 145 J elderly. 125 full & part-time staff; over 50 volunteers are involved in the Kline Galland Home progs. F in 1915 on the site of the present Home with 7 residents. After a num of expansions, the num of residents accomodated rose to 25 in 1930, 40 in 1940 & 45 in 1956. In 1967 a new bldg with a bed capacity of 75 replaced the old structure. In 1976 a 70 bed addition was completed. Until 1956 the Home was managed by a live-in matron with restrictive rules & regulations. In 1956 a professional social worker was hired & the philosophy of care was changed. Social work serv, group programming, 24 hr nursing serv, psychiatric consultation & a panel of Drs were initiated. Originally the Home was funded by a bequest of one million dollars. The Home functioned under a trusteeship of Seattle Trust & Savings Bank & an Adv

Bd of four. In 1967 the Bd was enlarged to 15 representing all local syns & temples. In 1976 the Home was incorporated as a non-profit charitable org with an independent governing Bd of 27 elected by the J com. The original fund is used to supplement the operating budget of the Home. The Home has the largest budget of any J org in Seattle. The Home is used by the Univ of WA to provide clin experience for nurses, social work & med stu. There is also a work study prog with Yeshiva Univ of NY. Bd of Dirs – Pres: Barry Schneiderman; VP: Arva Gray; Treas: Harold Seligmann; Sec: Michael Cohen; Asst Sec: Kenneth Kahn; Mems: Deborah Arron, Becky Benaroya, Robert Block, Olga Butler, Carolyn Danz, Adelyne Freiberg, William Hardman, Edith Heinemann, Howard Keller, Richard Quint, Barry Schneiderman, Henry Wolf, Michael Cohen, Lilly De Jean, Arva Gray, Dr Kenneth Kahn, Morris Polack, Bernice Stern, Arthur Siegal, Meyer Twersky, Ira Alexander, Eleanor Cohon, Sol Esfeld, Sol Halfon, Paul Jassny, Harold Seligmann, Dr Doris Stiefel. **7500 Seward Park Ave S, Seattle WA 98118 (206) 725–8800.**

Central Organization for Jewish Education Chabad-Lubavitch Pacific Northwest. Activities span the states of WA, OR, MT, AK, & the provinces of British Columbia & Alberta in Canada. To be an anchor, a pillar of light & hope with which J of all classes & ages can identify. In Seattle, WA: Chabad House, fully staffed (open 7 days a week, 24 hours a day), provides rel servs, kosher meals, lectures, study sessions, counseling & 24 hour Hot Line for the stu of the Univ of WA & the com at large; Yeshiva Gedola provides the first post-HS full day J Studies Prog on the W Coast; Russian Refugee Prog provides Russian families with rel material, comfort & advice, weekly visitations, study sessions, weddings, Bar-Mitzvoth, circumcisions, pidyon haben; kosher deli in downtown Seattle; radio prog serves the NW with the first regularly scheduled broadcasts addressed to the J population of the Pacific NW; Nursery Sch. In Vancouver, British Columbia, the Org makes provisions for youth groups, campus activities, adult edu classes, nursery progs, daycamps; summer camps; hosp & prison visitations, est of kosher kitchens in some of the facilities; Mitzvah Campaign emphasizing the following ten precepts: J Edu, Torah Study, Tefillin, Mezuzah, Tzedokoh-Charity, Rel Edu Material, Lighting of Shabbot Candles, Kashrut, Observance of the Laws Pertaining to Family Purity, Ahavas Yisorel – the love & devotion to one's fellow J; Mitzvah Mobiles: to remind J about the observance of a particular holiday, to give them an opportunity to observe a mitzvah & to prompt them to acquaint themselves with their J heritage. Staff of 5 rabbis in Seattle & four in British Columbia. Chabbad was f in the 18th century by Rabbi Schneur Zalman of Laiadi. Rabbi Schneerson became the new leader of the Lubavitcher Movement after the passing away of his father-in-law in 1950. In 1953 the Rebbe f the Lubavitch Women's Org, & in 1955, the Lubavitich Youth Org. Challenge – two vols which describe Lubavitcher ins & activities in various parts of the world; 15 vols of selections fr the Rebbe's public addresses; bks & pubs of J interest, printed in many languages. The word Chabad is made up of three Heb Words – Chochmoh, Binoh, Dass (Wisdom, Understanding & Knowledge). Regional Dir: Rabbi Sholom B. Levitin; Adm: Rabbi Abe Kawka; Chabad House Rabbi: Rabbi Yechezkel Kornfeld; Dean Yeshiva Gedola: Rabbi Lieb Kaplan. **4541 19th Ave NE, Seattle WA 98105 (206) 527–1411.**

Chabad House. Lubavitch com servs ctr. Blends Chassidic fervor & warmth with tradition & learning, to show that every J, fr whatever background he or she comes fr, is an integral part of the body of Is. Anti-missionary work; adult edu; sabbath seminars; holiday progs; day camp; youth groups; syns; kosher kitchen; counseling; chaplaincy; Mitzvah Campaigns; hosp & prison visitations; sr citizens encounters; speakers bureau. Rabbi S.B. Levitin. **4541 19th Ave NE, Seattle WA 98105 (206) 527–1411.**

Congregation Beth Shalom. Affiliated with United Syn of Am. Rabbi Ira F. Stone; Pres: Murray Finkelstein; Edu Dir: Ethel Suhar. **6800 35th Ave NE, Seattle WA 98115 (206) 524–0075.**

Congregation Beth Shalom Library. For information on the Cong see – Congregation Beth Shalom, Seattle, WA. **6800 35th Ave NE, Seattle WA 98115 (206) 524–0075.**

Congregation Ezra Bessaroth. 5217 S Brandon St, Seattle WA 98118 (206) 725–3770.

Emanuel Congregation. 3412 NE 65 St, Seattle WA 98115 (206) 525–1055.

Jewish Education Council. Central bureau for J edu mem of J Edu Serv of N Am, Council of J Edu. To enhance & foster the highest ideals of J edu, & in particular, as it relates to J culture in the Greater Seattle met area. All-city com HS of J Studies; Teachers Ins of J Studies; Media Library & Resource Ctr; teachers seminars; scholarship progs; classes; Principals Assn; Seatle Cantors in Concert; Rabbinic Torah Night; coords Greater Seattle B'nai B'rith Scholar-In-Residence Prog; Com Rel Sch Enrollment Campaign; Soviet J Edu progs; J civics & identity progs; edu consulting servs; liaison with secular schs; outreach progs; adult edu classes & seminars; library containing approx 1,000 vols (Judaica & Hebraica). 300 mems; 75 HS stu. 2 full-time employees, 3 part-time employees plus sch faculty of 5. F 1970 as Cttee of J Fed of Greater Seattle; became independent agy in 1980. Pub Jewish Education Catalogue (annual); JECNewsletter (monthly). Exec Dir: Kay Pomerantz; Adm Asst: Ruth Bovarnick; Pres: Herbert Rosen; Treas: Miriam Roth; VPs: Joel Starin, Sharon Finegold, Alvin Katsman; Sec: Tina Kahn. **516 Securities Bldg, Seattle WA 98040 (206) 625–0665.**

Jewish Federation of Greater Seattle. Mem of CJF. Includes King County, Everett & Bremerton. Organized 1926. Pres: Francine Loeb; Exec Dir: Murray Shiff. **Securities Bldg, Suite 525, Seattle WA 98101 (206) 622–8211.**

Seattle Hebrew Academy. 1617 E Interlaken Dr, Seattle WA 98112.

Seattle Hebrew Academy Library. 1617 E Interlaken Dr, Seattle WA 98112.

Sephardic Bikur Holim Congregation. 6500 52nd St S, Seattle WA 98118 (206) 723–9661.

Temple B'nai Torah. 6195 92nd SE Mercer Island, Seattle WA 98112 (206) 232–7243.

Temple Beth Am. Affiliated with UAHC. 314 mems. Rabbi Norman D. Hirsh; Pres: Philip Dale; Edu: Gloria Aronson; Adm: Norma Dahl. **8015 27th Ave NE, Seattle WA 98115 (206) 525–0915.**

Temple De Hirsch Sinai. Affiliated with UAHC. 1441 mems. Rabbis: Earl S. Starr, James L. Mirel, Stephen Wylen, Raphael H. Levine; Cantor Melvyn Poll; Pres: Herbert L. Pruzan; Edu: Alisse Seelig; Adm: Bernard Feinberg; Sisterhood Pres: Cheri Mermelstein, Lee Weinstein; Brotherhood Pres: Steven Pruzan. **1511 E Pike St, Seattle WA 98122 (206) 323–8486.**

Spokane

Jewish Community Council of Spokane. Includes Spokane City. Sponsors United Jewish Fund. Organized 1927. Pres: C. Eugene Huppin. **521 Parkade Plaza, Spokane WA 99201 (509) 838–4261.**

Temple Beth Shalom. Affiliated with United Syn of Am. Rabbi Eugene Gottesman; Cantor Emeritus Leo Matzner; Pres: Jeff A. Morris; Edu & Youth Dir: Jay Weiner. **PO Box 8013, E 1322 30th Ave, Spokane WA 99203 (509) 747–3304.**

Tacoma

Temple Beth El. Affiliated with UAHC. 254 mems. Rabbi Richard Rosenthal; Pres: Lucille Hurst; Edu: Joan Garden; Sisterhood Pres: Snookey Simon. **5975 S 12th St, Tacoma WA 98465 (206) 564–7101.**

WEST VIRGINIA

Beckley

Temple Beth El. Affiliated with UAHC. 18 mems. Rabbi Isadore R. Wein; Pres: Sidney Fink. **Bellview Lane, PO Box 1363, Beckley WV 25801 (304) 253–9421.**

Bluefield

Congregation Ahavath Sholom. Affiliated with UAHC. 75 mems. Rabbi Elbert Sapinsley; Pres: Fred Gilbert; Sisterhood Pres: Deborah R. Jackson. **632 Albemarle St, Bluefield WV 24701 (304) 325–9372.**

Charleston

Congregation B'nai Jacob. Rel Servs; Men's Club; Ladies Auxiliary; Chevra Kaddisha. The origins of Cong B'nai Jacob date back to 1890 when a minyan was held at the home of Julius Nearman. Num increased & Servs for the High Holidays were held in a rented hall. In 1894 the frame temple on State St, built by the Hebrew Edu Soc, was vacated, & the Orthodox Cong rented it. A cong was organized with 17 charter mems. The following yr, the Temple was purchased & moved around the corner to Court St. By 1908 the Cong had grown to 60 mems. The Cong purchased the State St Methodist Church & the Syn functioned as an Orthodox Syn. There was a steady increase in membership. In 1934–36 the downstairs of the shul was remodeled to provide a social hall. A new brick addition was built on the Court St side for the whole length of the bldg which provided three classrms, off, library & a Beth Hamidrash. The membership grew fr 225 in 1931 to 408 at the close of Sept 1949. At the end of the 1940's the Cong erected a new syn. Pres: Morton Victorson; 1st VP: Gordon Sherman; 2nd VP: Stephen Max; Rec Sec: Jonathan Kurland; Fin Sec: Harry Kanner; Treas: Edwin Masinter; Bd of Trustees: Paul Aaron, Bruce Goffin, I.B. Gorsetman, Jacob Isacoff, Ted Kanner, Harry Lazaroff, Sanders Levine, Sanford Lewis, Ben Lieberman, Alvin Preiser, Harvey Siler, Morris Steiger, Sherwin Steiger; Pres Ladies Auxiliary: Mrs Morton Victorson; Pres Men's Club: Dr Kenneth Manges; Pres Chevra Kaddisha: Alex Diznoff. **Virginia & Elizabeth Sts, Charleston WV 25311.**

Federated Jewish Charities of Charleston, Inc. Mem of CJF. Organized 1937. Pres: Jerome Goldberg; Exec Sec: William H. Thalheimer. **PO Box 1613, Charleston WV 25326 (304) 346–7500.**

Clarksburg

Tree of Life Synagogue. Affiliated with United Syn of Am. Rabbi Jerome S. Fox; Pres: Hyman Rosen. **5th & W Pike Sts, Clarksburg WV 26301 (304) 622–3453.**

Fairmont

Fairmont Jewish Community Center. Affiliated with UAHC. 18 mems. Rabbi Jerome S. Fox; Pres: Henry Stern. **c/o Maxfields, 216 Broadview Ave, Fairmont WV 26554 (304) 363–5630.**

Huntington

B'nai Sholom Congregation. Conservative-Reform Temple affiliated with UAHC, United Syn of Am. Rel Servs; chil & adult edu; Sisterhood; B'nai B'rith & Hadassah orgs; NFTY youth group; col stu (J Stu Assn); library containing 1,000 vols (modern J literature, gen Judaica). 120 families; 50 individuals; 70 stu; 10 pre-sch stu. 1 employee; volunteer Rel Sch teachers. Ohev Sholom (Reform) F 1887; B'nai Israel (Conservative) F 1910; merger 1972. B'nai Sholom serves the entire J com of Huntington as its syn & meeting hall. Pub B'nai Sholom Newsletter (monthly). Facilities include sanctuary, chapel, social hall, classrms, Judaica shop, kosher kitchen. Rabbi Stephen Wylen; Pres: Paul Mayer; VP: Ike Lerner; Sec: Joyce Levy; Treas:

Morris Kuntz. **PO Box 2004, 10th Ave & 10th St, Huntington WV 25720 (304) 522–2980.**

Federated Jewish Charities. Organized 1939. Pres: William H. Glick; Sec: Andrew Katz. **PO Box 947, Huntington WV 25713 (304) 523–9326.**

Logan

Congregation B'nai El. Affiliated with UAHC. 11 mems. Pres: Edward I. Eiland; Sisterhood Pres: J.T. Fish. **PO Box 899, Logan WV 25601 (304) 752–2275.**

Martinsburg

Congregation Beth Jacob. Affiliated with UAHC. 15 mems. Pres: Max Apfeldorf. **126 W Martin St, PO Box 1147, Martinsburg WV 25401 (304) 267–4347.**

Parkersburg

Congregation B'nai Israel. Affiliated with UAHC. 49 mems. Pres: Richard C. Heller; Edu: Stevie Frank; Sisterhood Pres: Joanne Heller. **1703 20th St, Parkersburg WV 26101 (304) 428–1192.**

Congregation B'nai Israel Library. 1703 20th St, Parkersburg WV 26101 (304) 428–1192.

Welch

Emanuel Congregation. Affiliated with UAHC. 8 mems. Pres: M.D. Herzbrun. **Welch WV 24801 (304) 436–4768.**

Wheeling

Temple Shalom, Congregation Leshem Shomayim. Reform Cong affiliated with UAHC. Rel Servs; Rel Sch; Heb Sch; Sisterhood; Brotherhood; BBYO. 229 mems, 145 families. Temple Shalom is a merger between the former Reform Woodsdale Temple & the Conservative Syn of Is. The merger took effect in 1974. The Woodsdale Temple Cong L'shem Shomayim was originally the Eoff St Temple, Cong L'shem Shomayim which was f in 1849. The Syn of Is was originally Orthodox & was f in 1924. Pub Ha-Kol (monthly). facilities include kosher kitchen, J gift shop, sanctuary seating 134. Rabbi Daniel M. Lowy; Pres: Stanley G. Burech; VP: Edward Cohen; Treas: Seena Lewine; Sec: Arthur Beckerman. **23 Bethany Pike, Wheeling WV 26003 (304) 233–4870.**

United Jewish Federation of Ohio Valley. 20 Hawthorne Court, Wheeling WV 26003.

Williamson

B'nai Israel. Affiliated with UAHC. 39 mems. Pres: Saul Brown; Sisterhood Pres: Betty Rosen. **PO Box 21, Williamson WV 25661 (304) 235–2947.**

WISCONSIN

Appleton

Moses Montefiore Synagogue. Affiliated with United Syn of Am. Rabbi Melvin Eskovitz; Chr Bd of Trustees: Harlan K. Balkansky; Edu Dir: Lisa Weiner; Youth Dir: David Balkansky. **3131 N Meade St, Appleton WI 54911 (414) 733–1848.**

United Jewish Charities of Appleton. 3131 N Meade St, Appleton WI 54911 (414) 733–1848.

Beloit

B'nai Abraham. Affiliated with UAHC. 30 mems. Pres: David Cohen; Edu: Mollie Putterman. **Box 964, Beloit WI 53511 (608) 364–4916.**

Eau Claire

Temple Sholom. Affiliated with United Syn of Am. Rel Servs; Rel Sch. 40 families. For many yrs the Cong of Temple Sholom operated with no central location. In 1960, the Cong purchased a bldg to be used as a syn. Most Servs & progs are lay run. The cong has never had a rabbi. The syn houses a B'nai B'rith unit. Pres: Morton Sipress; Treas: Joseph Berney; Sec: Verna Merrin. **1223 Emery St, Eau Claire WI 54701 (715) 834–4667.**

Fond Du Lac

Temple Beth Israel. Rel Servs; Sisterhood; Rel Sch. 48 mems; 24 families. The Syn dates back to 1914 with the formation of the rel soc Kehilath Jacob. In 1922 the Soc decided to organize for the purpose of purchasing a place for com worship. The Kehiloth Jacob Syn, a one story frame house of two rms on the corner of Ruggles & Military Ave, was ready for the High Holydays of 1922. The house was torn down & a syn was built in 1925. In 1954 a home at 149 E Division St was purchased & used as a J ctr downstairs, & a home for the rabbi. In 1959 the home was torn down & work began on a new bldg. It was decided to change the name of the Temple fr Kehiloth Jacob Syn to Temple Beth Is. On Aug 7, 1960 the dedication of the cornerstone was held. Pres: Ben Sadoff; Exec VP: Peter Stone; Sec: Meyer Green; Treas: Jacob Hammes; Rabbi Morton Shalowitz. **Fond Du Lac, WI 54935.**

Green Bay

Congregation Cnesses Israel. Affiliated with United Syn of Am. Rabbi Barukh Schectman; Pres: Joann Glickman. **PO Box 1252, 222 S Baird St, Green Bay WI 54301 (414) 437–4841.**

Green Bay Jewish Welfare Fund. Treas: Betty Frankenthal. **PO Box 335, Green Bay WI 54305 (414) 432–9347.**

Kenosha

Beth Hillel Temple. Reform Syn affiliated with UAHC. Sabbath & Holiday Servs, monthly Family Worship Servs; Sisterhood; Chemerow Cultural Series, which presents a speaker or prog on a Sun evening; Rel Sch named Bet Shalom with stu fr Beth Hillel Temple of Kenosha & Beth Is-Sinai Cong of Racine (the sch meets half the yr in Racine & the other half in Kenosha on Sun mornings); weekday Heb classes held in Kenosha. 115 families. F in 1922. Temple facilities include a sanctuary, garb lounge, Founders Hall, classrms, library, Bd rm, rabbi's study. Rabbi Michael M. Remson; Pres: Michael Fisher; VP: Marvin Letven; Treas: Harold Nelson; Sec: Susan Shepanek; Fin Sec: Harriet Smoler; Trustees: Elynor Chemerow, Lenore Chulew, Irmgard Daniels, Dr Leslie Fai, Peter Friend, Florence Kassel, Adrienne Klafter, Peter Phillips, Robert Sullivan, Phillip Wilk; Hon Trustees: Harold Brosk, Harry Chemerow, Charles Lepp; Sisterhood Pres: Naomi Fisher. **Library Square, Kenosha WI 53140 (414) 654–2716.**

Kenosha Jewish Welfare Fund. Mem of CJF. Organized 1938. Pres: S. Michael Wilk; Sec Treas:

Mrs S.M. Lapp. **6537 7th Ave, Kenosha WI 53140 (414) 658–8635.**

La Crosse

Congregation Sons of Abraham. Rel Servs; Heb Sch; Sun Sch; Sch; adult classes; Women's League; serves as a ctr of J life & activities not only for J of La Crosse but also for the surrounding areas. Est in the beginning of the century with the arrival of Orthodox J fr Eastern Europe. Servs were first held in a private home. A syn bldg was procured in 1905 where Orthodox Servs were held until 1948. The Syn moved into its present location in 1948. Facilities include a social hall, classrooms, kitchen & boardroom. The Syn offers facilities to B'nai B'rith & UJA. Pres: Ed Neuman; VP: Mike Levenstein; Sec: Corine Neuman; Treas: Roger Ziff; Fin Cttee Chr: Bill Locketz; Maintenance: Hy Kaplan; Rabbinical Cttee Chr: Mike Levenstein; Bd of Trustees: Irving Balto, Dr Rudolph Keimovitz, Jordan Levin, Dee Peacock. **1820 Main St, La Crosse WI 54601.**

Madison

Beth Israel Center. Affiliated with United Syn of Am. Rabbi Charles Feinberg; Cantor Simcha Prombaum; Pres: Judith Kaufman; Youth Dir: Helene Moss. **1406 Mound St, Madison WI 53711 (608) 256–7763.**

Beth Israel Center, Library. For information on the Ins, see – Beth Israel Center, Madison, WI. **1406 Mound St, Madison WI 53711 (608) 256–7763.**

Chabad House. Lubavitch com servs ctr. Blends Chassidic fervor & warmth with tradition & learning, to show that every J, fr whatever background he or she comes fr, is an integral part of the body of Is. Anti-missionary work; adult edu; sabbath seminars; holiday progs; day camp; youth groups; syns; kosher kitchen; counseling; chaplaincy; Mitzvah Campaigns; hosp & prison visitations; sr citizens encounters; speakers bureau. Rabbi Y. Hecht. **613 Howard Pl, Madison WI 53703 (608) 251–6022.**

International Association of Hillel Directors. 611 Langdon St, Madison WI 53703 (608) 256–8361.

Madison Jewish Community Council, Inc. Mem of CJF. Organized 1940. Pres: Stanley Mintz; Exec Dir: Avrum Weiss. **310 N Midvale Blvd, Suite 325, Madison WI 53705 (608) 231–3426.**

National Association of Professors of Hebrew. 1346 VanHise Hall, Wisconsin-Madison, Madison WI 53706 (608) 262–3204.

Temple Beth El. Affiliated with UAHC. 444 mems. Rabbis: Kenneth D. Roseman, Manfred Swarsensky; Pres: Suzanne Blotner; Edu: Lawrence Kohn; Sisterhood Pres: Ina Smolker. **2702 Arbor Dr, Madison WI 53711 (608) 238–3123.**

Milwaukee

Anti-Defamation League of B'nai B'rith – WI-Upper-Midwest Regional Office. Dedicated in purpose & prog to translating the Am heritage of democratic ideals into a way of life for all Am, & to countering assaults on the safety, status, rights & image of J. For additional information, see – Anti-Defamation League of B'nai B'rith, New York City, NY. **1360 N Prospect Ave, Milwaukee WI 53202.**

Beth El Ner Tamid Library. For information on the Cong see – Beth El Ner Tamid Synagogue, Milwaukee, WI. **3725 N Sherman Blvd, Milwaukee WI 53216 (414) 442–4520.**

Beth El Ner Tamid Synagogue. Affiliated with United Syn of Am. Rabbi Louis J. Swichkow; Cantor Norton H. Siegel; Asst Rabbi & Youth Dir: Joel Schwab; Pres: Harold I. Rozansky. **3725 N Sherman Blvd, Milwaukee WI 53216 (414) 442–4520.**

Committee for the Economic Growth of Israel. PO Box 2053, 5301 N Ironwood Rd, Milwaukee WI 53201 (414) 961–1000.

Congregation Anshe Sfard. Orthodox Cong. Rel Classes; Sisterhood; Culture & Co (social group); Chavurah Group; Mr & Mrs Club. 280 mems, 100 families, 80 individuals. 3 employees. Bulletin (fortnightly). Facilities include kosher kithchen, gift shop, social hall. Rabbi David S. Shapiro; Asst Rabbi Gershon Segal; Cantor Moses Lichtman; Pres: Dr Bruce Fetter; Rel Dir: Kopel Weinstein. **3447 N 51st Blvd, Milwaukee WI 53216 (414) 444–9640.**

Congregation Beth Israel. Conservative Syn affiliated with United Syn of Am. To bring the traditional heritage into harmony with modern thought; to fulfill the conception of the syn as a House of Worship, a House of Learning, & a House of

Assembly. Daily Servs; Sch of J Studies for chil ages 5–16; Nursery Prog; Camp K'Ton Ton for chil 2½–5; Adult Edu; Havurah Prog; Sabbath Seders – families join together to experience the traditional Sabbath meal & its ritual; Scholar in Residence Prog; library; youth groups: Pre-USY for 7th & 8th graders, USY for 9th–12th graders; Men's Club; Sisterhood; Couples Club; Sr Group; Adult & Youth Choirs. 650 families. Monthly Bulletin; Annual Calendar. The Cong owns & maintains the Second Home Cemetery for use by the entire J com. Bldg facilities include the main sanctuary which can accommodate 1,900, Jacobson Chapel for daily servs, gift shop, multi purpose rm accommodating 1,400 for lecture & up to 600 for luncheons & dinners. The Cong maintains the Three Doors Caterers offering kosher cuisine. Rabbi Herbert G. Panitch; Cantor Carey Cohen; Edu Dir: Jeremy Alk; Pres: Fredrick J. Safer; VPs: Sidney Lawrence, Melvin Pomerantz, Milton Sattell, Burt Zuckerman; Treas: Sheldon Schnoll; Sec: Jay I. Miller; Trustees: Alfred Altman, Gerald Bass, Sidney Kohlenberg, Jack L. Marcus, Edward Pickett, Lynne Willens, Aaron Bodner, Al Hearst, Harry Lensky, Jack Spector, Louise Stein, Patti Weigler, Arthur Cohen, Sam Friedman, Sally Schnoll, Martin R. Stein, Judy Wolkenstein; Sisterhood Pres: Beverly Blankstein; Men's Club Pres: Ronald Durchslag. **6880 N Green Bay Ave, Milwaukee WI 53209 (414) 352–7310.**

Congregation Beth Israel, Isadore Blankstein Library. For information on the Cong, see – Congregation Beth Israel, Milwaukee, WI. **6880 N Green Bay Ave, Milwaukee WI 53209 (414) 352–7310.**

Congregation Emanu-El B'ne Jeshurun. Reform Cong. To function as a catalyst for spiritual growth through servs & progs that encourage the widest possible pursuit of truth. Rel Servs; Rel Sch; Sisterhood; Brotherhood; Adult Confirmation Prog; Adult J Studies; spiritual, edu, cultural & social progs. Cong Imanu-Al, f in 1850, & Ahabath-Emuno, f in 1854, joined together on Oct 5, 1856 to become Cong B'ne Jeshurun. Its liturgical ritual was the same as that used by Rabbi Isaac Mayer Wise's Cong in Cincinnati. Membership totalled 70 families. The Cong soon settled into its first syn bldg. In 1859 the Cong built a new syn & B'ne Jeshurun & Anshe Emeth, f in 1855, merged. The first Confirmation Serv was introduced in 1859 & mixed seating began. Almost all sermons & business meetings were conducted in German. In the late 1860's B'ne Jeshurun was the only cong in Milwaukee. This caused many struggles between the proponents of Reform J & the traditionalists in the Cong. This led to the breakaway of 35 mems who est Cong Emanu-El in 1869. B'ne Jeshurun built a larger syn in 1869 which was rebuilt in 1872. By the mid 1920's B'ne Jeshurun membership stood at 350 families. Cong Emanu-El, which stood for Reform J ritual & practice, held Servs in Field's Hall until the Cong erected its first bldg in 1872. The Cong added to the syn, central heating in 1881, electric lights in 1896, & a new com house & complete remodeling in 1892. Emanu-El remained at its E side site for 50 yrs. In the early 1920's membership stood at 250 mems. On Mar 30, 1923 the Cong held its first Servs in its new temple. In the 1920's B'ne Jeshurun began to liberalize its customs & practices. By the mid 1920's many of its mems were leaving the W side location for Emanu-El's more convenient site. When B'ne Jeshurun land was earmarked for the bldg of a courthouse, plans were made for the merger of the two congs. The merger was completed in 1927 & Cong Emanu-El B'ne Jeshurun became the official name of the combined syns. The membership now stood at 600 families. The memorial windows of the temple were installed in 1931. In 1948 a full time cantor joined the staff. Fr 1947 to 1970 membership grew to 1,300 families. In 1972 the Cong sold land that it had purchased about 20 yrs earlier as a possible site for a new bldg. The proceeds of the sale were set aside for a Prog Servs Dev Trust. In 1974 the Cong broke ground for an edu bldg addition & a remodeling of the syn. Between 1970 & 1980 the membership grew to 1,550 families. In 1981 the Cong held its 125th anniversary celebration. Life – a hist of the Cong. Facilities include: adm & rabbinical offs, modern classrms, arts & crafts ctr, music rm, youth lounge, library, kitchen, chapel, foyer & com hall. Rabbi Francis Barry Silberg; Rabbi Ronald C. Bluming; Cantor Nancy S. Hausman; Dir of Edu: Michael K. Fefferman; Adm: S. Bernard Lieberman; Archivist: Lillian Friedman; Group Servs Coord: Laurie Kestelman; Distinguished Servs Fellow: Dr Herman Weil; Librarian: Shirley Rumack; Organist: John Sheaffer; Sexton: Buzz Cody; Off Mgr: Anne Meyer; Bookkeeper: Gladys Beerman; Rabbi Silberg's Sec: Kathy Butt; Sch Sec: Cookie Cohen; Secs: Eileen Smitka, Beverly Ugent; Pres: Robert W. Kohn; VPs: Robert L. Hersh, Cese Holland, Florence Kesselman; Sec: Robert J. Lerner; Treas: William B. Braun; Sisterhood Pres: Jean Yagobian; Brotherhood Pres: Jeffrey S. Schuster; Trustees: Mimi Chernov, Doris H. Chortek, Donald V. Cohen, Renee Dygola, Marshall L. Gratz, Dr Louis Kagen, Edward S. Kapper, Helga Levings, Alan M. Levy, Ned Nashban, Jerold I. Perlstein, Irving H. Raffe, Robert Rellin, Lou Rosenblum, Sharon Sanderson, James F. Stern, Howard B. Tolkan, James H. Zucker; Hon Pres: Frankie Adashek, Ben L. Chernov, Lawrence S. Katz, Edward R. Prince. **2419 E Kenwood Blvd, PO Box 11698, Milwaukee WI 53211 (414) 964–4100.**

Congregation Emanu-El B'ne Jeshurun, Rabbi Dudley Weinberg Library. 2419 E Kenwood Blvd, PO Box 11698, Milwaukee WI 53211 (414) 964–4100.

Congregation Shalom. Affiliated with UAHC. 589 mems. Rabbis: Ronald M. Shapiro, Harry B. Pastor; Pres: Jacquelyn R. Gilbert; Edu: Jack Padek; Sisterhood Pres: Gail Spitzer; Brotherhood Pres: Albert Padek. **7630 N Santa Monica Blvd, Milwaukee WI 53217 (414) 352–9288.**

Congregation Sinai. Affiliated with UAHC. 291 mems. Rabbi Jay R. Brickman; Pres: Alfred Meyers; Edu: Max Gelles; Sisterhood Pres: Shari Cayle; Brotherhood Pres: Ted Bradbury. **8223 N Port Washington Rd, Milwaukee WI 53217 (414) 352–2970.**

Congregation Sinai Library. For information on the Cong, see – Congregation Sinai, Milwaukee, WI. **8223 N Port Washington Rd, Milwaukee WI 53217 (414) 352–2970.**

Jewish Community Center of Milwaukee. Com ctr with memberships in Adult Edu Assn, Am Assn of Health, Physical Edu & Recreation, Am Camjping Assn, Natl Assn of J Ctr Workers, Natl Assn of Social Work, Sr Action Coalition. To enhance & perpetuate J values, & cultural & edu self–fulfillment. Servs open to all Milwaukee area residents, resources & facilities permitting, although Ctr's prog directed to J goals. Various servs to com including sponsoring of chil & family resident & day camping; supervision Beth-Am Ctr on W side of Milwaukee; conducting many extension progs & activities in N suburban syns & schs; resettlement & acculturation of Soviet newcomers; involvement in J Vocational Serv–JCC Prog, & intensive servs to elderly. 2100 families; 6,500 individuals. 100 full & part–time employees; 200 volunteers F around 1894; originally f to administer to adjustment problems of immigrants. After several moves over the yrs & an increase in servs, moved to new Ctr bldg in 1955. Facilities include kosher dining rm, gymnasium, swimming pool, gift shop, auditoriums, club rms, nursery sch, men's & women's health ctrs, kosher restaurant. Pres: Marsha Sehler; Exec Dir: Morton S. Levin; VPs Bd of Dirs: William B. Braun, Sheri Levin; Sec Bd of Dir: Howard B. Tolkan; Treas: William H. Orenstein; PR Dir: Anne C. Schwartz. **1400 N Prospect Ave, Milwaukee WI 53202 (414) 276–0716.**

Jewish Family & Children's Service, Milwaukee WI. Social serv agy with membership in Family Serv Assn of Am, Child Welfare League of Am, Milwaukee J Fed, United Way of Greater Milwaukee Inc, Assn of J Family & Chil Agy. To enhance J family life & enable individuals & families to reach their "psycho-social" optimum functioning. Counseling servs – individual, family & marital counseling; aged servs – screening, counseling, home visits; Chil Dev Ctr – day care servs for chil aged 2 yrs 3 months to 5 yrs; resettlement – refuge & migration assistance; consultative servs to com agy, sch & professionals; Family Life Edu; stu training; library containing approx 300 vols (social welfare, mental health, Judaica). 35 employees; 350 volunteers. F 1867 as the Hebrew Relief Soc & was inc in 1889. The agy changed its name to the J Social Serv Assn in 1923 & to J Family & Chil Serv in 1948 when it was merged with the J Chil Home. Pub All In The Family (semi-annual newsletter). Pres: Joseph Bernstein; VPs: Marsha Sehler, Steven Appel; Treas: Stephen Chernof; Sec: Judy Guten; Exec Dir: Ralph Sherman; Asst Exec Dir: Elliot Lubar. **1360 N Prospect Ave, Milwaukee WI 53202 (414) 273–6515.**

Milwaukee Board of Jewish Education. 4650 N Port Washington Rd, Milwaukee WI 53212 (414) 962–8860.

Milwaukee Board of Jewish Education Library. 4650 N Port Washington Rd, Milwaukee WI 53212 (414) 962–8860.

Milwaukee Jewish Federation, Inc. Mem of CJF. Organized 1902. Pres: Mark E. Brickman; Exec VP: Melvin S. Zaret. **1360 N Prospect Ave, Milwaukee WI 53202 (414) 271–8338.**

The Milwaukee Jewish Home. Orthodox ins which serves the J aged in WI & is an affiliated agy of the Milwaukee J Fed. 24 hour skilled care; social servs; rel servs; physical therapy; occupational therapy; recreation activities; music; art; podiatry; sheltered workshop; dental servs. F in 1906. Pres: Sheldon L. Cohen; Exec VP: Nita L. Corre; 1st VP: Lawrence Appel; 2nd VP: Martin Stein; 3rd VP: Philip Rubenstein; Treas: Morris Silverman; Sec: Marshall Rotter. **1414 N Prospect Ave, Milwaukee WI 53202 (414) 276–2627.**

Temple Menorah. Traditional Temple. To create family worship – inspiring young & old to adhere to our heritage. Rel Servs (daily); Sisterhood; Men's Club; Adult Edu; Afternoon Sch; Sun Sch; pre-K; K; post Bar/Bat Mitzvah prog; youth progs; library containing 7000 vols (Heb, Yiddish, English, references, encyclopedias, film strips, tapes, records). 400 families; 157 stu. 12 teachers. F 1919; formerly Beth Hamedrash Hagadol B'nai Shalom –

Anshei Sfard – Degal Ephraim; changed to Temple Menorah in 1964. Facilities include sanctuary seating 421, social hall (combined with sanctuary 1100 seats on High Holy Days), kosher kitchen, gift shop, library. First J org to sponsor housing for sr citizens (150 units) Rabbi Dr Isaac N. Lerer; Asst Rabbi Gil–Ezer Lerer; Pres: William K. Appel; Adm: June German. **9363 N 76th St, Milwaukee WI 53223 (414) 355–1120.**

Temple Menorah, Library. Library contains 7,000 vols (Heb, Yiddish, English, references, encyclopedias, film strips, tapes, records). For information on the Temple, see – Temple Memorah, Milwaukee, WI. **9363 N 76th St, Milwaukee WI 53223 (414) 355–1120.**

Mukwonago

B'nai B'rith Beber Camp. To make the camping experience stimulating, rewarding & fun; to foster pride in heritage, learn more about Judaism, & meaningfully practice the rituals of religious heritage; to learn how to participate in group living as chil mature socially & physically. Sports; variety of BBYO & B'nai B'rith activities including leadership training conferences, the AZA & BBG intl conventions, adult institutes of Judaism. Located on 8 mile-long lake. **Camp add: Mukwonago WI; Natl Off: 1640 Rhode Island Ave NW, Washington DC 20036 (202) 857–6600.**

Oconomowoc

UAHC Olin-Sang-Ruby Camp Institute. Dir: Gerard Kaye. **600 Lac La Belle Dr, Oconomowoc WI 53066 (414) 567–6277; 100 W Monroe St, Chicago IL60603 (312) 782–1477.**

Oshkosh

Temple B'nai Israel. Affiliated with UAHC. 45 mems. Rabbi Steven J. Mason; Pres: Laurence Kates; Sisterhood Pres: Debbie Havins. **1121 Algoma Blvd, Oshkosh WI 54901 (414) 235–4270.**

Racine

Beth Israel Sinai Congregation. Affiliated with United Syn of Am. Rabbi Harold Markman; Pres: Jerome H. Brown. **944 S Main St, Racine WI 53403 (414) 633–7093.**

Racine Jewish Welfare Council. Mem of CJF. Organized 1946. Pres: Philip Cohen; Exec Sec: Betty Goldberg. **944 S Main St, Racine WI 53403 (414) 633–7093.**

Sheboygan

Congregation Beth El. Conservative Syn affiliated with United Syn of Am. Daily Rel Servs; adult classes; Heb Sch; Sisterhood; Chevra Kadisha. F in 1944. The Cong raises funds for UJA & Is Bonds. Gentile groups come for information on Judaism, Is & the J people. Rabbi Nathan A. Barack; Pres: Harold Hoffman; Sec: Ruth Benson. **1007 North Ave, Sheboygan WI 53081 (414) 452–5828.**

Jewish Welfare Council of Sheboygan. 1404 North Ave, Sheboygan WI 53081.

Superior

Temple Beth El of Superior Hebrew Congregation. Affiliated with United Syn of Am. Pres: Harry Bear. **603 Faxon Ave, Superior WI 54880 (715) 392–4279.**

Waukesha

Congregation Emanuel. Affiliated with UAHC. 60 mems. Rabbi Manfred Swarsensky; Pres: Peter Shelley; Edu: Arlene Shelley. **830 W Moreland Blvd, Waukesha WI 53186.**

Wausau

Mount Sinai Congregation. Affiliated with UAHC. 75 mems. Rabbi Lawrence N. Mahrer; Pres: David Fromstein. **622 4th St, Wausau WI 54401 (715) 845–7461.**

INSTITUTIONS IN CANADA

ALBERTA

Calgary

Beth Israel Congregation. Affiliated with United Syn of Am. Rabbi Louis I. Schechter; Pres: Dr Leonard Smith. **1325 Glenmore Terr SW, Calgary Alberta Canada T2V 4Y8 (403) 255–8688.**

Calgary Hebrew School. 1415 Glenmore Trail SW, Calgary Alberta Canada T2V 4Y8 (403) 252–3235.

Calgary Hebrew School Library. 1415 Glenmore Trail SW, Calgary Alberta Canada T2V 4Y8 (403) 252–3235.

Calgary Jewish Community Council. The official rep of J coms in Canada. Affiliated with the World J Congress. To dev the highest degree of peoplehood in the J of Canada by encouraging, carrying on & participating in activities of a natl, cultural & humanitarian nature. For additional information, see – Canadian Jewish Congress, Montreal Quebec Canada. Pres: Joe A. Spier; Exec Dir: Harry S. Shatz. **1607 90th Ave SW, Calgary Alberta Canada T2V 4V7.**

Pioneer Women – Na'amat. The training & edu of the Is woman & her family so that each can be best equipped to lead productive lives. For additional information, see – Pioneer Women Na'amat, New York City, NY. **1–703 56th Ave SW, Calgary Alberta Canada T2V 0G9 (403) 253–9060.**

Temple B'nai Tikvah. Affiliated with UAHC. 42 mems. Pres: Norm Yanofsky; Edu: Alvin Lander; Adm: Judy Bing. **7211 11th St SW, Calgary Alberta Canada T2V 1N2 (403) 252–1654.**

Edmonton

Beth Israel Synagogue. Orthodox Cong. Rel Servs held twice daily; NCSY youth progs; Sisterhood; Adult Edu classes; com Seders. The oldest syn in Edmonton, Cong Beth Is was organized in Aug of 1909. The cornerstone was laid for the syn, com mikvah & classrms in 1911. Semi-monthly bulletin. Bldg facilities include a kosher kitchen, social halls, auditorium & mikvah. **10219 119th St, Edmonton Alberta Canada T5K 1Z3 (403) 482–2470, 488–2840.**

Beth Shalom Synagogue. Conservative Cong. Rel Servs: Shabbat, holidays & Mon & Thurs mornings; Sun Sch; Sisterhood; gift shop; USY & Kadima youth groups. F in 1932. Beth Shalom used the facilities of the Talmud Torah bldg fr 1932 until 1950 where its own structure on 119th St & Jasper Ave is now located. In Feb of 1980 the bldg was damaged by fire &, fr then until reconstruction was completed in Apr 1981, servs were held at the JCC. Bi-weekly bulletin; special bulletin for Holy Days. **10219 119th St, Edmonton Alberta Canada T5K 1Z3 (403) 482–2470, 488–2840.**

Camp B'nai B'rith Pine Lake, Alberta. Summer camp run in two sessions, three weeks each. A camper may attend one or both sessions. Arts & crafts, athletics, canoeing & boating, drama & music, evening progs, Is programming, Shabbat Servs, Heb classes, holiday observance, kosher foods, med care, photography, horseback riding, swimming, tennis, watersking. The camp is located on the shores of Pine Lake surrounded by 132 acres of woodland. Camp mems are 8 yrs through 14 yrs. **Camp B'nai B'rith Off: 7200–156th St, Edmonton Alberta Canada T5R 1X3 (403) 487–0899.**

The Canadian Zionist Federation – Western. To promote the Zionist ideal among the J population in Canada; assist in strengthening the J State & the enrichment of Canadian J life through J edu, Is & Zionist information, promotion of aliyah & activities among J youth in Canada. Aliyah, Edu, Culture, Information, Tourism, Youth & Hechalutz & Pub & Is Trade Depts – progs of major activities throughout

Canada in these areas. Est in 1967. Chr: Dr Eli Adler. **7200 156th St, Edmonton Alberta Canada T5N 3R4 (403) 487–0901.**

Chevra Kadisha Chapel. Funeral & Burial Society for J Com of Edmonton. **12313 105th Ave, Edmonton Alberta Canada (403) 482–3065.**

Edmonton Beth Shalom Congregation. Affiliated with United Syn of Am. Rabbi Saul Hyman; Cantor Paul Graner; Pres: Larry Rollingher; Exec Dir: Harry Bloomfield; Youth Dir: Barry Vogel. **11916 Jasper Ave, Edmonton Alberta Canada T5K 0M9 (403) 488–6333.**

Edmonton Jewish Community Council. Com relations; com servs; com programming; J edu; J public library; univ chair in J studies; demographic survey; Heb language HS option; Holocaust Remembrance Cttee; Soviet J; J radio prog; J video prog; provision for distribution of kosher meat delivered fr Winnipeg. J population of approximately 5,800. The Com Council was est in 1953 in recognition of the need that planning together for human needs was more important & more significant than planning separately. Com Council co-produced 7 prog series 'On Being Jewish' shown on Edmonton's cable TV com channel Pres: David Grossman; Exec Dir: Hillel Boroditsky; Asst Exec Dir: Marc Silverberg. **7200 156th St, Edmonton Alberta Canada T5R 1X3 (403) 487–5120.**

Edmonton Talmud Torah. To foster in each stu a strong & positive sense regarding his or her identity. Pre-Sch Dept; Day Sch grades 1 to 6; Jr HS grades 7 to 9; gen & J studies. 250 stu. In 1912 the Edmonton Talmud Torah was est. For 13 yrs the Talmud Torah met in the basement of Beth Is Syn. In Sept of 1925 the cornerstone of the Talmud Torah bldg was laid. At that time there were only 135 J families in the com. In 1927 the Mothers Auxiliary was organized. The first graduation took place in 1928. Once again the growth of the com brought about the problem of expansion of sch facilities. On Apr 12, 1953 construction began on a new Talmud Torah bldg. The bldg was completed Sept 1, 1953. The Edmonton Talmud Torah est the first Heb Day Sch in Canada. The Sch has been with the Edmonton Public Sch Bd system since 1974. Facilities include classrooms, K-rm, an auditorium equipped with a stage, library, audio visual equipment & a kitchen. Prin: E. Mickelson; Heb Curriculum Coord: Yudith Sela; Pres: Stan Miller; VP Adm: Ron Ritch; VP Academic: Jack Goldberg; VP Fin: David Friedman; VP PR: David Seaberg; Treas: Jerry Cooper; Sec: Joan Goldstein. **1312 106th Ave, Edmonton Alberta Canada T5N 1A3 (403) 455–9114.**

Jewish Community Centre of Edmonton. Recreational, cultural & physical edu progs; day-care facilities, baby-sitting servs; pre-sch prog; holiday celebrations; birthday party servs; Summer Day-Camp Tikvah; Edmonton Chaverim – a group for J single adults ages 22 to 35; mini-seminars on contemporary matters affecting J com life; workshops on various topics including parent-teen dialogues, conversational Heb & J handicrafts. The bldg hosts the meetings of many of the J orgs in Edmonton. Located at the Ctr are the offs of the J Com Council, Canadian J Congress, UJA, Camp B'nai B'rith, Temple Beth Ora, Canadian Zionist Org, & State of Is Bonds. Facilities include a gymnasium, meeting rms, health club, tennis cts, lounges, racquet & squash ball cts, pool, kosher kitchen facilities & kosher snack bar. **7200 156th St, Edmonton Alberta Canada T5R 1X3 (403) 487–0585.**

Jewish Family Services. To solve problems of daily living. Counseling in the areas of marital conflicts, family relationships, teenage concerns, single parent problems, coping with divorce, coping with illness or death, sch adjustment problems; servs for the elderly, relocation of newcomers; settlement of new immigrants; provision of B'nai B'rith Camp scholarships, kosher Meals-on-Wheels, foster & adoptive homes for J chil, emergency fin assistance, legal aid information & referral. On Jan 4, 1955 a meeting was held at which a group of J citizens, concerned with helping people, agreed to the incorporation of the Edmonton J Welfare Soc as the organized social agy in Edmonton to help people in personal as well as financial difficulty. On Jan 17, 1955 the Edmonton J Welfare Soc was registered under the Alberta Socs Act. In Sept 1956 the J Com Council agreed to a partnership with the J Welfare Soc in establishing an off staffed by a qualified social worker. On Jan 28, 1961 the Welfare Soc went out of existence & the Agy was inc under the name J Family Serv. Exec Dir: Florence Shaffer; Pres: Judith Goldsand; VP: Shelby Smordin; Treas: Harry Nolan; Hon Sec: Daniel C. Abbott; Hon Bd Mems: Mrs S. Cooperman, Dr Max Dolgoy, Herbert Leon, Irving C. Lyons, Eugene Pechet, J.H. Shoctor, Mrs H. Singer; Bd Mems: Gloria Aaron, Sandy Bornstein, Max Dolinko, Fani Estrin, Cheryl Friedenthal, Alvin Fialkow, Susan Halpert, Joyce MacDonald, Dr Jack Miller, Patti Morgenstern, Laurie Mozeson, Norma Nozick, Robert Nozick, Vladimir Pokotinsky, Selwyn Romanovsky, Miriam Sheckter, Florence Singer, Barry Slawsky, Esther Starkman, Dorothy Tapper, Mal Wasserman. **606 McLeod Bldg, 10136 100th St, Edmonton Alberta Canada T5J OP1 (403) 424–6346, 9554.**

Jewish Senior Citizens Drop-In-Centre. To meet the primary needs & social programming wishes of the elderly of the Edmonton J Com. **10052 117th St, Edmonton Alberta Canada (403) 488–4241.**

Temple Beth Ora Congregation. Affiliated with the Canadian Council of Liberal Congs. Rel Servs conducted by lay leaders, with a stu rabbi conducting the High Holy Day Servs; Sun Sch. The Cong began in 1979 under the title of the Edmonton Fellowship for Reform J. The new name was adopted in Sept 1980. Regular Servs are held at the Edmonton JCC on alternate Fri. **7200 156th St, Edmonton Alberta Canada TSR 1X3 (403) 456–6916.**

BRITISH COLUMBIA

Richmond

Beth Tikvah Congregation & Centre Association. Affiliated with United Syn of Am. Pres: Stu Levitt; Edu Dir: Judy Majewski. **PO Box 94374, Richmond British Columbia Canada V6Y 2A8 (604) 271–6262.**

Beth Tikvah Synagogue of Richmond. Conservative Syn affiliated with the United Syn of Am. Rel Servs; Heb Sch; Nursey Sch Prog; USY Youth Group; Adult Edu Prog; social & cultural J activities. Rabbi Harvey Markowitz; Pres: Morlev Cofman. **9711 Geal Rd, Richmond British Columbia Canada V6Y 2A8 (604) 271–6262.**

Vancouver

Canadian Jewish Congress – Pacific Region. Regional off covering the Province of British Columbia; official rep of J com. Through Joint Com Relations, acts on anti-Semitism, provides interfaith edu & dialogue, sponsors media & inter-ethnic communication; coords J edu in the area; maintains Ethiopian J materials & slide show; through J Historical Soc, maintains pub & tape bank on early pioneers in British Columbia; through the Holocaust & Warsaw Ghetto Memorial, provides teaching aids on Holocaust, yearly Holocaust Symposium, memorial Servs for Holocaust victims; through the Soviet J Action Cttee, acts on behalf of J in USSR; the Congress also works with youth in the city on & off campus; sponsors Yiddish events; provides outreach to suburban coms; supervises kosher establishments & provides booklet on local servs & products; provides audio visual aids, library, Canadian J Life; maintains files on such issues as Nazi war criminals, Soviet J, J in Ethiopia & Argentina, Islam in N Am; helps people find speakers & progs for their org. Regional Chr: Irvine E. Epstein; V Chr: Dr Robert Krell, Prof Jon Wisenthal; Treas: Leon Kahn; Sec: Gwen Yacht; Exec Offs: Leon Getz, Sophie Waldman, Anita Waterman; Natl VP: Dr M.W. Steinberg; Hon Sec: Esmond Lando; Hon Bd: H. Altman, J. Balshine, M. Belkin, S. Belzberg, Dr A. Bogoch, J.H. Cohen, T. Cohen, H. Davis, J. Diamond, Mayor M. Evers, A. Fouks, Dr M. Fox, D.A. Freeman, Dr A. Hayes, P. Heller, S. Heller, A. Jackson, Dr J. Katz, M. Koffman, Prof S. Lipson, Justice A.A. Mackoff, Judge N.L. Oreck, Dr J.H. Quastel, D. Radler, L. Raphael, N. Rothstein, A. Sacks, J. Segal, Rabbi W. Solomon, Dr R. Waldman, I.M. Wolfe, M.J. Wosk, S. Zack; Exec Dir: Morris Saltzman; Asst Dir: Gwen Yacht. **950 W 41st St, Vancouver British Columbia Canada V5Z 2N7 (604) 261–8101.**

The Canadian Zionist Federation – Pacific. To promote the Zionist ideal among the J population in Canada; assist in strengthening the J State & the enrichment of Canadian J life through J edu, Is & Zionist information, promotion of aliyah & activities among J youth in Canada. Aliyah, Edu, Culture, Information, Tourism, Youth & Hechalutz & Pub & Is Trade Depts – progs of major activities throughout Canada in these areas. Est in 1967. Chr: Stan Korsch. **950 W 41st Ave, Vancouver British Columbia Canada V5Z 2N7 (604) 266–5366.**

Canadian Jewish Outlook. Periodical pub. **2414 Main St #4, Vancouver British Columbia Canada V5T 3E3 (604) 874–1323.**

Chabad House. Lubavitch com servs ctr. Blends Chassidic fervor & warmth with tradition & learning, to show that every J, fr whatever background he or she comes fr, is an integral part of the body of Is. Anti-missionary work; adult edu; Sabbath seminars; holiday progs; day camp; youth groups; syns; kosher kitchen; counseling; chaplaincy; Mitzvah Campaign; hosp & prison visitations; sr citizens encounters; speakers bureau. Rabbi I. Wineberg. **497 W 39th St, Vancouver British Columbia Canada (604) 324–2406.**

Congregation Beth Hamidrash. Sephardic Orthodox Syn. To bring together J of Sephardic origin living in Western Canada; to promote Sephardic culture & tradition. Rel Servs. Est in 1972 under the title of Sephardic Cong. The name was changed in 1976. Rabbi Avraham Tauby; Chief Hazzan: Gamliel Aharon; Pres: Moses Jacob; VP: Dr Avraham Benjamin; Sec: David Aboody; Treas: Marcel Acrech; Dirs: Victor Setton, Chaskel Kaufman, Dr David Haskell. **3231 Heather St, Vancouver British Columbia Canada V5Z 3K4 (604) 872–4222.**

Congregation Beth Israel. Conservative Cong affiliated with the United Syn of Am. The advancement of the cause of J in Am & the maintenance of J tradition in its historic continuity. Daily Rel Servs; Shabbat dinners; free baby sitting servs during Shabbat Morning Servs; lecture series; Rel Sch; Adult Edu; Talmud Study; Choir; Sisterhood; week-end retreats; Tallit & Tefillin; Men's Club; USY & Kadima youth groups; Havurah – a young couples & singles group that meets once a mo for informal learning. In Sept 1925 a group organized a new cong. Servs were held at the Com Ctr in Fairview & this led to the incorporation on Nov 30, 1932 of Cong Beth Is. In 1948 Beth Is erected its own bldg. Bulletin Congregation Beth Israel. The Syn maintains a mus. Rabbi Wilfred Solomon, Rabbi Jeffrey Hoffman; Hazzan Murray Nixon; Sch Adms: Dr Herbert Dank, Dr Marion Dank; Syn Adm: Helene Rosen. **4350 Oak St, Vancouver British Columbia Canada V6H 2N4 (604) 731–4161.**

Israel Aliyah Center. 950 W 41st Ave, Vancouver British Columbia Canada V5Z 2N7 (604) 266–5366.

Jewish Community Fund & Council of Vancouver. Mem of CJF. Organized 1932. Pres: Arnold Barkoff; Exec Dir: Morris Saltzman. **950 W 41st Ave, Vancouver British Columbia Canada V5Z 2N7 (604) 261–8101.**

Jewish Western Bulletin. Periodical pub. **3268 Heather St, Vancouver British Columbia Canada V5Z 3K5 (604) 879–6575.**

Pioneer Women – Na'amat. The training & edu of the Is woman & her family so that each can be best equipped to lead productive lives. For additional information, see – Pioneer Women Na'amat, New York City, NY. **950 W 41st St, Rm G, Vancouver British Columbia Canada V5Z 2N7 (604) 266–8308.**

Temple Sholom. Reform Cong. Affiliated with UAHC. To observe the traditions of J worship in ways which are relevant to modern men & women; to further the rel, cultural & historical bonds with the J people & the State of Is; to enrich our lives as individuals & as families through a sense of com, a sense of belonging & a commitment to J values. Rel Servs; Oneg Shabbat – a social period during which the spirit of Sabbath fellowship can be enjoyed by all who attend; Passover Seder; celebration of festivals with a potluck dinner; Rel Sch for chil in grades K–10; Bar/Bat Mitzvah Servs; Confirmation Servs; Youth Group for grades 9–12; Sisterhood; Brotherhood; Adult Edu; social action; J library; resource ctr. 180 mems. F in 1964. The Shofar (monthly bulletin). Rabbi Philip L. Bregman; Pres: Dr Sidney Kirson; Adm: Mrs Lee Harrison. **4426 W Tenth Ave, Vancouver British Columbia Canada V6R 2H9 (604) 224–1381.**

The Vancouver B'nai B'rith Hillel Foundation. J stu ctr. Affiliated with B'nai B'rith, N Am J Stu Network, Canandian Bureau. Rel, cultural, counseling & social activities among J stu, univ staff & faculty, & unaffiliated people in the Vancouver area. Monthly Oneg Shabbat; Shabbat Morning Servs every other week; Holiday Servs & celebrations; lunches & lunch hr progs; the Network Seminar; Is Week; classes in J subjects & Heb; counseling; weekly dinners & progs; inter-faith discussion; ping-pong; bd games; TV & stereo; weekend parties; place to study; place to meet people; stu retreats; counseling; progs for social action & com involvement. library containing approx 300 vols (J hist, rel, Zionism). 450 mems; 25 families; 400 individuals. 2 employees; 30 volunteers (Hillel Adv Bd). On Nov 10, 1946 Vancouver B'nai B'rith Lodge 668 & Vancouver Chapter 77 endorsed the Hillel prog & petitioned for counselorship at Univ of British Columbia. On Dec 10, 1946 the petition was granted by the Natl Hillel Commis & on Jul 14, 1947 the Vancouver B'nai B'rith Hillel Foun was registered as a soc. In Nov 1947 the first bldg to be constructed by the B'nai B'rith Hillel Foun was dedicated on the campus of the Univ of British Columbia in Vancouver. The Univ donated the land & the Univ architect planned the bldg. The funds for the construction of the bldg were raised by B'nai B'rith. Chr: Phyllis Sapers; Treas: Tillie Kositsky; Dir: Rabbi Daniel Siegel. **Box 43, Student Union Bldg, Univ of British Columbia, Vancouver British Columbia Canada V6T 1W5 (604) 224–4748.**

MANITOBA

Winnipeg

B'nai B'rith Youth Organization – Red River Region. To help its mems feel at home in the J com, identify themselves with the common aspirations of the J people & make contributions of distinctive J values to the mosaic of their country's culture; to help its mems enhance their knowledge & appreciation of J rel & culture; to afford its mems group life experiences which give them an understanding of & loyalty to the democratic heritage; to offer supervised leisure-time activities in which youth make happy adjustments to real life situations by making friends, exploring & expressing individual interest & developing skills; to provide learning experiences whereby youth become ethical & altruistic in human relationships, devoted & competent in the fulfillment of family & com responsibilities. Leisure time activities; edu classes & activities. BBG N'siah: Mia Elfenbaum; BBG S'ganit: Laurie Chess; BBG Katvanit & Gzbarit: Lisa Guttman; BBG Aim Chavairot: Carolyn Berkowitz; BBG Madricha: Nonnie Keynes; AZA Godol: Fraser Aronovitch; AZA S'gan: Mike Weidman; AZA Mazkir & Gizbor: Randall Swa4tz; AZA Moreh: Richard Buchwald; AZA Me'amen: Bryan Hershfield; AZA Kohane Godol: Murray Elfenbaum; Regional Dir: Arona F.B. Olfman. **207–235 Garry St, Winnipeg Manitoba Canada R3C 1H2 (204) 943–4066.**

Beth Israel Congregation. Affiliated with United Syn of Am. Rabbi Neal Rose; Pres: Jack Litvack; Edu Dir: Sandy Shuster. **1007 Sinclair St, Winnipeg Manitoba Canada R2V 3J5 (204) 582–2353.**

Canadian Jewish Congress – Manitoba Region. The official rep of J coms in Canada. Affiliated with the World J Congress. To dev the highest degree of peoplehood in the J of Canada by encouraging, carrying on & participating in activities of a natl, cultural & humanitarian nature. For additional information, see – Canadian Jewish Congress, Montreal Quebec Canada. **370 Hargrave St, Winnipeg Manitoba Canada R3B2K1.**

The Canadian Zionist Federation – Midwest. To promote the Zionist ideal among the J population in Canada; assist in strengthening the J State & the enrichment of Canadian J life through J edu, Is & Zionist information, promotion of aliyah & activities among J youth in Canada. Aliyah, Edu, Culture, Information, Tourism, Youth & Hechalutz & Pub & Is Trade Depts – progs of major activities throughout Canada in these areas. Est in 1967. Chr: Sid Ritter. **365 Hargrave St, Winnipeg Manitoba Canada R3B 2K3 (204) 943–6494.**

Chabad House. Lubavitch com servs ctr. Blends Chassidic fervor & warmth with tradition & learning, to show that every J, fr whatever background he or she comes fr, is an integral part of the body of Is. Anti-missionary work; adult edu; Sabbath seminars; holiday progs; day camp; youth groups; syns; kosher kitchen; counseling; chaplaincy; Mitzvah Campaigns; hosp & prison visitations; sr citizens encounters; speakers bureau. Rabbi A. Altein. **532 Inkster Blvd, Winnipeg Manitoba Canada (204) 586–1867.**

Congregation Shaarey Zedek. Syn affiliated with the United Syn of Am & JTS. Rel Servs; Sisterhood; USY & Kadima youth groups; Choir; Adult Edu; adult leisure progs; Confirmation Class; Shaarey Zedek Cemetery. Over 1,000 families. Staff of 16. F in 1889, the Cong is the oldest in Western Canada. The syn was formally dedicated in 1890. In 1913 the Cong amalgamated with Shaarey Shomayim & moved to the larger bldg at Dagmar & Henry which was enlarged to seat 700. The Sisterhood was est in 1920. Membership in the Syn continued to grow & in 1949 the Cong moved to its present site. In 1956 the Ramah Sch was opened; Monthly bulletin. Rabbi Eugene A. Wernick; Rabbi Louis Berkal; Exec Dir: Lona Shafer; Ritual Dir: Ephraim Tatelbaum; Bulletin Editor: Judy Wernick; Choir Dir: Sheila Roitenberg; Youth Dir: Philip Guberman; Pres: Paul Silver; VP: Greg Brodsky; Exec Cttee: Alan Bronstone, Mildred Devins, Easton Lexier, Donald Weidman, Marshall L. Wilder;

Sisterhood Pres: Miriam Segal. **561 Wellington Crescent, Winnipeg Manitoba Canada R3M 0A6 (204) 452–3711.**

Congregation Shaarey Zedek Library. For information on the Cong, see – Congregation Shaarey Zedek, Winnipeg Manitoba Canada. **561 Wellington Crescent, Winnipeg Manitoba Canada R3M OA6 (204) 452–3711.**

Herzlia-Adas Yeshurun Congregation. Orthodox Syn. Dedicated to furthering Winnipeg's J population with a J identity as well as J edu. Daily Rel Servs; Sisterhood; Men's Club; Choir; com progs; Adult Edu progs; NCSY youth group for ages 5–18; Torah Academy providing Heb Day Sch fr pre nursery, gen & J studies, swimming, Yamaha Music Sch, & french; Herzlia Academy Night Sch for J chil attending elementary public sch; Herzlia Academy Night Sch Extended Prog for stu in secondary & HS classes, univ progs; The Torah Ins of Winnipeg; Manitoba Ins of Torah with Kollel Prog; Adult Edu progs; library containing 2000 vols. 300 mem families. The cornerstone laying & official dedication ceremony for the Herzlia Academy took place on Dec 11, 1955. The Cong is the only Orthodox syn in the S end of Winnipeg. Rabbi & Prin: Ephraim Bryks; Pres: Sherman Greenberg; Sec: Tom Gillman; Bldg: Abe Silverman; Finance: Harry Tregobov. **620 Brock St, Winnipeg Manitoba Canada R3N 0Z4 (204) 489–6262, 6668.**

Jewish Child & Family Services. A resource for families & chil. Clin servs – helps in parent chil issues, separation & divorce, & problems of behavioral adjustment; marriage & pre-marriage counseling; servs for the elderly – provides counseling, daily phone check, friendly visits by volunteers, help with transportation, information & referral, & outreach progs; homemaker servs; Newcomer Prog – helps with initial housing, furnishings, edu, English language instruction, & integration into the larger J com; adoption; foster parents; residential treatment – provides residential care & treatment for chil with special needs; chil protecting servs – provide serv when parents have trouble in the care of their chil (JCFS can work with the entire family in the home situation), provides field training for stu fr the Sch of Social Work, Univ of Manitoba; social servs provided to the J day schs on a regular basis; volunteer prog – volunteers are involved in all Agy activities; information & referral – provides gen information regarding social servs & refers enquiries to the proper channel in cases where the JCFS is not directly involved; group work servs – brings together people in common circumstances; lobbying – works toward the provision of needed servs. Est in 1952. Funded by the United Way of Winnipeg, the Winnipeg J Com Council, the Province of Manitoba & the J Immigrant Aid Soc. **228 Notre Dame Ave, Suite 1001, Winnipeg Manitoba Canada (204) 943–6425.**

Jewish Post. Periodical pub. **PO Box 3777, Winnipeg Manitoba Canada R2W 3R6 (204) 633–5575.**

Jewish Public Library. 1725 Main St, Winnipeg Manitoba Canada R2V 1Z4.

Jewish Students Association, University of Manitoba & University of Winnipeg. To co-ordinate activities with J interests in mind. Involvement in com projs in a wide variety of areas; sponsorship of edu progs on issues of J concern. Campus Supervisor: Marsha Dozar; Campus Worker: Joan Sheps. **Rm 149 Univ Ctr, Univ of Manitoba, Winnipeg Manitoba Canada R3T 2N2 (204) 474–9325; Univ of Winnipeg, Winnipeg Manitoba Canada R3B 2E9 (204) 786–7811 Ext 428.**

Pioneer Women – Na'amat. The training & edu of the Is woman & her family so that each can be best equipped to lead productive lives. For additional information, see – Pioneer Women Na'amat, New York City, NY. **1727 Main St, Winnipeg Manitoba Canada R2V 1Z4 (204) 334–3637.**

Ramah Hebrew School. Com parochial sch serving S Winnipeg for grades K through six. To assist in the dev of each chil, both academically & socially, to their maximum potential; committed to the concept that every J chil must know his roots. Gen & J studies; visual aids; field trips; guest speakers; assemblies; songs; plays; weekly Fri progs which emphasize the Shabbat observance; observance of Pesach, Purim, Chanukah, Yom Haatzmaut, Yom Hazikaron & Holocaust; curriculum includes physical edu, music, french prog. 350 stu. Est in 1957. Prin: Rachel Fink; Chr: Morris Henoch; V Chr: Brian Fleishman; Fin Chr: William Silverberg; Sec: Anita Bakal, Sharon Shinewald. **705 Lankark St, Winnipeg Manitoba Canada R3N 1M4 (204) 453–4136.**

Rosh Pina Congregation. Affiliated with United Syn of Am. Rabbi Shalom Rappaport; Cantor Judah Smolack; Pres: Judge Marvin Garfinkel; Exec Dir: Mendel Rosenfeld; Edu Dir: Chaim Shiel; Prog Dir: Phyllis Spigelman; Youth Dir: Robyn Spigelman. **PO Box 3586, Station B, 123 Matheson Ave, Winnipeg Manitoba Canada R2W 3R4 (204) 589–6306.**

Temple Shalom. Affiliated with UAHC. 55 mems. Pres: Scotty Barlin. **921 Ash St, Winnipeg Manitoba Canada R3N 0S1 (204) 453–8260.**

Western Jewish News. Periodical pub. **PO Box 87, 400–259 Portage Ave, Winnipeg Manitoba Canada R3C 2G6 (204) 942–6361.**

Winnipeg Hebrew Schools. An elementary & collegiate day sch system for grades 7–12. Edu first & foremost. Gen & J studies; Shabbatons; Tzdakah Progs; J Awareness Seminars; sports; music; drama. 213 stu. Joseph Wolinsky Collegiate was est in 1957 as a continuation of the Talmud Torah elementary sch which has been in existence since 1907. The Sch operates in accordance with Orthodox J law while at the same time serving the entire spectrum of Winnipeg J youth. Prin: Jerry Cohen; V Prin: Rabbi Charles Grysman; Pres: Sid Halpern; VPs: Max Reich, Frank Steele; Chr Bd of Edu: I.S. Kleiman; Chr Scholarship Fund: Marilyn Cass; Pres PTA: Peggy Diamond; Co-Chr Collegiate Adv Bd: Oscar Grubert, Syd L. Morantz; Bd of Dirs: Yoram Barr, Arky Berkal, Jack Boroditsky, Marilyn Cass, Dr Louis Cogan, Peggy Diamond, Dr Charles Faiman, Phil Finkle, Sid Halpern, Sid Flackman, Irv Greenberg, Larry Hurtig, Harry Kaplan, Harold Kives, I.S. Kleiman, Dr Marvin Kohn, William Kowall, Judy Linhart, Rae Margolis, Rabbi Sholom Rappaport, Maz Reich, Norman Satran, Alan Schacter, David Segelbaum, Larry Shlafman, Lyle Smordin, Frank Steele, Dr Milton Tenenbein, David Waldman, Lewis Wasel; Exec Sec: Sue Weiss; Bd of Govs: Aaron Boroditsky, Marcus Bressler, Dr Morris Erenberg, Melvin Fenson, Irwin Green, Oscar Grubert, Phil Kravetsky, Joseph Margulius, Syd L. Morantz, Israel Pinczowski, Jack Silverberg, Abe Simkin, George Skulsky, Harry Stuart, Joseph Wiesenthal, Tamara Wiseman, Hymie Wolinsky, Saul B. Zitzerman. **427–437 Matheson Ave, Winnipeg Manitoba Canada R2W 0E1 (204) 586–5822, 582–2346, 589–4311.**

Winnipeg Jewish Community Council. Mem of CJF. Includes Combined Jewish Appeal of Winnipeg. Organized 1938; reorganized 1973. Pres: Marjorie Blankstein; Exec VP: Izzy Peltz. **370 Hargrave St, Winnipeg Manitoba Canada R3B 2K1 (204) 943–0406.**

NEW BRUNSWICK

Fredericton

Sgoolai Israel Synagogue. 213 Lynhaven Ct, Fredericton New Brunswick Canada E3B 2V5.

Sgoolai Israel Synagogue Library. 213 Lynhaven Ct, Fredericton New Brunswick Canada E3B 2V5.

Moncton

Tiferes Israel Synagogue. 50 Steadman St, Moncton New Brunswick Canada (506) 382–8324.

St. John

Congregation Shaarei Zedek. Affiliated with United Syn of Am. Rabbi Roger V. Pavey; Pres: L.I. Michelson. **PO Box 2041, 76 Carleton St, St John New Brunswick Canada E2L 3T5 (506) 657–4790.**

NOVA SCOTIA

Glace Bay

Congregation Sons of Israel. Rel Servs; Talmud Torah; Sun Sch activities; celebration of Is Independence Day; Commemoration of the Warsaw Ghetto. Nine stu in the Talmud Torah. In 1900 several J residents decided to build a syn & formed the org Sons of Is Soc of Glace Bay which was registered in 1901. The ground was broken in 1901 for the syn & in 1902 it was completed. It was the first syn for J residents in Cape Breton. After the erection of the syn, the num of J residents increased. Heb sch classes were held in the basement of the shul & as time progressed, it was necessary to have the servs of a rabbi, a teacher & sometimes a shames. In 1928 the present Talmud Torah bldg was erected. The Ladies Aid Soc played an important part in organizing socials & other projs to pay off the bldg debt. Pres & Chr of Exec: Dr Philip Simon; VP: Elliot Marshall; Rec Sec: Daniel Mendelson; Treas: Len Schelew; Fin Sec: Sandor Zilbert. **Prince St, Glace Bay Nova Scotia Canada B1A 2J6.**

Halifax

Atlantic Jewish Council. 5675 Spring Garden Rd, Halifax Nova Scotia Canada B3J 1H1 (902) 422–7491.

Beth Israel Religious School. 1480 Oxford St, Halifax Nova Scotia Canada (902) 422–1301.

Canadian Jewish Congress – Atlantic Region. The official rep of J coms in Canada. Affiliated with the World J Congress. To dev the highest degree of peoplehood in the J of Canada by encouraging, carrying on & participating in activities of a natl, cultural & humanitarian nature. For additional information, see – Canadian Jewish Congress, Montreal Quebec Canada. **5675 Spring Garden Rd, Halifax Nova Scotia Canada B3J 1H1.**

The Canadian Zionist Federation – Atlantic. To promote the Zionist ideal among the J population in Canada; assist in strengthening the J State & the enrichment of Canadian J life through J edu, Is & Zionist information, promotion of aliyah & activities among J youth in Canada. Aliyah, Edu, Culture, Information, Tourism, Youth & Hechalutz & Pub & Is Trade Depts – progs of major activities throughout Canada in these areas. Est in 1967. Chr: Ben Prossin. **Lord Nelson Arcade, 5675 Spring Garden Rd, Halifax Nova Scotia Canada B3J 1H1 (902) 422–7491.**

Shaar Shalom Congregation. Affiliated with United Syn of Am. Pres: E.M. Rosenberg MD. **1981 Oxford St, Halifax Nova Scotia Canada B3H 4A4 (902) 422–2580, 423–5848.**

Shaar Shalom Synagogue Library. 1981 Oxford St, Halifax Nova Scotia Canada B3H 4A4 (902) 423–5848.

ONTARIO

Downsview

Achdut HaAvoda – Poale Zion of Canada. 272 Codsell Ave, Downsview Ontario Canada M3H 3X2 (416) 636–4021.

Adath Israel Congregation. Affiliated with United Syn of Am. Rabbi Erwin Schild; Cantor & Edu Dir: A. Eliezer Kirshblum; Assc Rabbi & Youth Dir: Rabbi Harvey W. Meirovich; Pres: Ed Morrison; Exec Dir: Beatrice Solomon. **37 Southbourne Ave, Downsview Ontario Canada M3H 1A4 (416) 635–5340.**

The Bernard Betel Centre for Creative Living. Multi purpose ctr for the sr adult. Affiliate of the Toronto J Congress. To improve the quality of life of the sr mems of the com. Men's Club; weaving; Heb; pottery; woodwork; macrame; knitting & crochet; bowling; effective leadership; folk dancing; bridge; rug hooking; social afternoon; needlepoint; exercise class; ballroom dancing; quilting; mosaic tiles; painting; drawing; discussion group; musical variety show; fitness; yoga; Yiddish reading; choral group; human relations courses; counseling servs; referral servs; two kosher meals a day; outreach progs which aim to reach the isolated & lonely through a monthly bulletin, Dial-a-Friend, Dial-a-Craft, servs & home visiting cttee; volunteerism which places mems in vital jobs within both the ctr & com; Com Volunteers (men & women fr the com who devote many hours to the Ctr as advs & teachers). Information is available concerning housing, pension supplements, drug benefit progs, transportation, legal aid, income tax & health servs. The Ctr works closely with all orgs in the com that are devoted to the well being of sr adults. Est in 1975. Pres: Aaron Brotman; Chr of the Bd: Gordon Atlin; VPs: Dr Brian Hands, Frances Mandell, Belle Orson, H. Victor Rosenthal; Sec: David Langer; Treas: George Weinberger; Dirs: Barry Arbus, Norma Bain, Stephen Berger, Murray Betel, Harry Binder, Kitty Cohen, Yale Drazin, Ann Handelman, Max Handelman, Shirley Goldfarb, Stephen Kauffman, Barbara Kochberg, Betty Lebofsky, Cyril Magrill, David Phillips, Ira Pollock, Ethel Rosenberg, Myra Schiff, Esther Shiner, Joan Solway, Jeannette Stein; Co-Options: Helen Marr, Fran Olin, Gloria Strom, Dorothy Wiener; Exec Dir: Rhea Shulman. **15 Hove St, Downsview Ontario Canada M3H 4Y8.**

Beth David B'nai Israel, Beth Am Synagogue. Affiliated with United Syn of Am. Rabbi Albert Pappenheim; Cantor Efraim Sapir; Asst Rabbi & Youth Dir: Rabbi Philip S. Scheim; Pres: Irving Bornstein; Exec Dir: Bert Robins; Edu Dir: Saul Morganstein. **55 Yeomans Rd, Downsview Ontario Canada M3H 3J7 (416) 633–5500.**

Beth David B'nai Israel, Beth Am Synagogue, Library. 55 Yeomans Rd, Downsview Ontario Canada (416) 633–5500.

Beth Emeth Bais Yehuda Synagogue. Affiliated with United Syn of Am. Rabbi Joseph H. Kelman; Cantor Louis G. Danto; Asst Rabbi Barry Schneider; Pres: Fred Stoll; Exec Dir: Bernice Levine; Edu Dir: Saul Morganstein. **100 Elder St, Downsview Ontario Canada M3H 5G7 (416) 633–3838.**

Beth Emeth Bais Yehuda Synagogue, Library. 100 Elder St, Downsview Ontario Canada M3H 5G7 (416) 633–3838.

Beth Jacob V'Anshe Drildz Synagogue. Orthodox Cong. Rel Servs; Sisterhood; Brotherhood. F in 1904. In 1905 a bldg was purchased for use as a syn. This was the Russo Polish J Syn Bais Jakov. It attracted immigrants fr Poland. When the J population moved westward, it was time to seek other quarters for the Syn. Letters Patent were granted in 1919. Several weeks later, Beth Jacob Cong purchased land. In 1922 the new Syn opened its doors. With the changing of the neighborhood, the Syn once again moved to its present location. Rabbi Dr Moses J. Burak; Pres: R. Rosen; 1st VP: M.

Karoly; 2nd VP: J. Joseph; Treas: J. Rosenthal; Sec: B. Rubin; Brotherhood Pres: H. Vogel; Sisterhood Pres: Mrs J. Berlin. **147 Overbrook Pl, Downsview Ontario Canada (416) 638–5955.**

Canadian B'nai B'rith. 15 Hove St, Suite 200, Downsview Ontario Canada M3H 4Y8 (416) 633–6224.

Canadian Friends of Bar-Ilan University. 333 Wilson Ave, Suite 603, Downsview Ontario Canada M3H 1T2 (416) 635–1966, 5190.

Canadian Society for the Weizmann Institute of Science. 345 Wilson Ave, Suite 403, Downsview Ontario Canada M3H 5W1.

Israel Aliyah Center. 1110 Finch Ave W, Suite 700, Downsview Ontario Canada.

Israel Youth Program Centre. Com serv & drop-in ctr open to all J youth. Affiliated with the Youth & Hechalutz Dept of the Canadian Zionist Fed, Toronto & Montreal. To provide information & application to summer & long-term progs in Is for youth; to coord & participate in Is-oriented activities in Toronto. Promotion of summer youth progs in Is (kibbutz-ulpan & volunteer workers); information, application procedures, interviews, orientations; coord & information for Is working at summer camps in Ontario; programming with J stu groups, the J Com Ctr & other J orgs in Is-oriented activities; Sherut L'Am. 1 full-time employee; 1 part-time employee; 4 sclichim. First ctr opened in Montreal in Dec 1977; f in Toronto in Jan 1982 by Col Ben Ami Cohen. Facilities include drop-in ctr for progs, orientations & meetings. Dir: Stacey Greenman. **1000 Finch Ave W, Downsview Ontario Canada (416) 665–7733.**

Lubavitch Youth Organization. An outreach org that familiarizes J men & women & chil with J practices & philosophy. Affiliated with the Chabad Lubavitch Movement. To bring the light of Torah & J tradition to all corners of the world; to battle against assimilation, apathy & indifference to J living. Operation Helping Hand gives aid to Russian immigrants; on campus progs provide kosher foods; Org sponsors Fri night to Sun retreats, lectures, Shabbat servs & counseling, celebrations of holidays, seminars on Passover laws, Purim Party, Toys for Tots for chil in the hosp at Chanukah; helps with bldg of succas; distributes prayers bks for holidays; provides marriage & family counseling, Adult Edu Prog; helps est kosher kitchens in private homes; maintains Mitzvah Mobile which introduces J men to the wearing of Tefillin, distributes rel articles, serves as a traveling J library & audio visual ctr; maintains Succamobile; sponsors summer day camp, weekly TV prog, call in TV prog on Passover laws; sponsors youth conventions. F in 1955 by the Lubavitch Rebbe. Prints over 100,000 pieces of literature on J topics & holiday observances. Exec VP: Rabbi Z. Aaron Grossbaum; Chr: Dov Parshan. **44 Edinburgh Dr, Downsview Ontario Canada M3H 1B4 (416) 633–8020.**

National Council of Jewish Women of Canada. Voluntary serv org affiliated with the Intl Council of J Women. To further welfare in J & gen coms, locally, nationally & internationally; committed to human rights, Is & world J, the status of women, the environment & the quality of human life. Edu: teacher aids in public & parochial schs, special edu for the handicapped, the teaching of English as a second language, J festival workshops, audio visual teaching aids for public sch teachers, leadership training courses, volunteer servs training prog, jr K progs, activity leaders for enjoying your infant, toddler pre-sch progs, scholarships, stu aid; health servs: rehabilitation prog for heart attack patients & their families, hosp volunteers, mental health ctr volunteers, tay sachs screening clins, pre-natal progs, cancer clins, Canadian Natl Ins for the Blind Volunteers, testing for sight & hearing deficiencies; servs to srs: Drop in Ctr, day ctrs, volunteers in homes for the aged, kosher Meals-on-Wheels, Outreach Progs for Volunteers. Other servs include adult J edu courses; Day Care Ctr for J chil; Is Family Counseling Assn, Tel Aviv which is recognized by Sch of Social Work Tel Aviv Univ; servs to newly arrived J immigrants; J library volunteers; tutorial & recreational servs; chil abuse prevention progs; Women's Shelter for battered mothers. The Council co-sponsors servs in com camps, univ campuses & rel ctrs. F in 1897. As of May 1971, the Council has one governing body called the Natl Exec Council. NCJW is a mem of Canadian Commis for UNESCO, & Sub Commis on the Status of Women, Canadian Commis for UNESCO. Pres: Helen Marr; Hon Pres: Lucille Lorie; VPs: Evelyn Bernstein, Frances Bokser, Sharon Gray, Bunny Gurvey; Treas: Marcia Bernick; Adm Sec: Sheila Freeman; Rec Sec: Frances Olin; Exec Sec: Florence Greenberg. **1111 Finch Ave W, Suite 401, Downsview Ontario Canada M3J 2E5 (416) 633–1251.**

Pioneer Women – Na'amat. The training & edu of the Is woman & her family so that each can be best equipped to lead productive lives. For additional information, see – Pioneer Women Na'amat, New York City, NY. **272 Codsell Ave, Downsview Ontario Canada M3H 3X2 (416) 636–5425.**

Ulpanat Orot Girls' School – Nachman Sokol Torah Centre. J & gen studies HS which is fully accredited by the Ontario Ministry of Edu & has authority to issue diplomas for both grades 12 & 13. Affiliated with the Dept for Torah Edu & Culture in the Diaspora-Jerusalem. To combine intensive Torah edu with a quality gen study prog in an atmosphere of rel Zionism & identification with the State of Is. Full HS curricula in Ontario grades 9 to 13; full prog through grade 12 for all non-Ontario residents; day to day usage of spoken Heb. F in 1974 with stu in grades 10 & 11 in temporary quarters. A little more than a yr later, the sch moved to its present location. Out of town stu are accommodated in preselected homes. Each applicant is required to take an examination for the purpose of enabling the sch to assess her proficiency. Pres: Nachman Sokol; Chr of the Bd: Saul Koschitzky; Sec: Yitz Feldman; Treas: Aaron Frankel; Chr of the Mgmnt Cttee: Meyer Feldman; Chr of the Edu Cttee: Phil Schwartz; VPs: Henry Koschitzky, Jack Weinbaum, Kurt Rothschild; Exec Dir: Rabbi Dr David I. Aronson. **45 Canyon Ave, Downsview Ontario Canada M3H 3S4 (416) 638–5434.**

Yeshivat Bnei Akiva School Or Chaim – Israel & Golda Koschitzky Torah Centre. Yeshiva HS for boys which is fully accredited by the Ontario Ministry of Edu & has the authority to issue diplomas for both grades 12 & 13. Affiliated with the Dept for Torah Edu & Culture in the Diaspora-Jerusalem. To combine intensive Torah edu with a high quality gen study prog in an atmosphere of rel Zionism & identification with the State of Is. Four yr course of J studies: Talmud, Torah & Commentaries, Prophets, Mishna, J law, J Thought & Heb Literature; four yr course of gen academic studies: English, Mathematics, Biology, Chem, Physics, Language, Literature, Typing, Law, Am Hist, Canadian Hist, J Hist, & Physical Edu; Stu Council; yearbook; guidance servs; sports prog; dormitory accommodations including a resident dormitory supervisor & meals; provisions for scholarships & reduced fees. F in 1973, Or Chaim is the only Bnei Akiva HS in N Am. J studies are taught in Heb. The faculty has also been certified by the Ontario Ministry of Edu. Pres: Nachman Sokol; Chr of the Bd: Saul Koschitzky; Sec: Yitz Feldman; Treas: Aaron Frankel; Chr of the Mgmnt Cttee: Meyer Feldman; Chr of the Edu Cttee: Phil Schwartz; VPs: Henry Koschitzky, Jack Weinbaum, Kurt Rothschild; Exec Dir: Rabbi Dr David I. Aronson. **159 Almore Ave, Downsview Ontario Canada M3H 2H9 (416) 630–6772.**

Hamilton

Beth Jacob Synagogue. Affiliated with United Syn of Am. Rabbi Israel N. Silverman; Cantor David Bercovici; Pres: Gerald A. Swaye. **375 Aberdeen Ave, Hamilton Ontario Canada L8P 2R7 (416) 522–1351.**

Hamilton Jewish Federation. Includes United Jewish Welfare Fund. Organized 1934; merger 1971. Pres: Leslie Lasky; Exec Dir: Samuel Soifer. **57 Delaware Ave, Hamilton Ontario Canada L8M 1T6 (416) 528–8570.**

Temple Anshe Sholom. Affiliated with UAHC. 500 mems. Rabbi Bernard Baskin; Cantor Samuel Dov-Berman; Pres: Franklyn Shapiro; Sisterhood Pres: Gilda Gunn. **215 Cline Ave N, Hamilton Ontario Canada L85 4A1 (416) 528–0121.**

Kingston

Iyr Ha-Melech. Affiliated with UAHC. 15 mems. Pres: Danny Moore; Edu: Paul Manley. **842 Milford Dr, Kingston Ontario Canada K7P 1AB(613) 544–3088.**

Kitchener

Temple Shalom. Affiliated with UAHC. 27 mems. Pres: Mark L. Dorfman; Edu: Jennifer Shalinsky, Edward Goldfarb. **1284 Ottawa St S, Kitchener Ontario Canada N2E 1M1 (519) 743–0401.**

London

Congregation Beth Tefilah. Orthodox Cong. Daily Rel Servs; Talmud Torah; Sisterhood. F in 1966. London Ontario has a mikveh & eruv. Rabbi Yechezkel Zweig; Hon Life Pres: Isaac Moskowitz; Pres: Dr Stanley Sober; 1st VP: Dr Stanley Kochman; 2nd VP: Prof Morris Zaslow; Treas: Dr Meir Zamir; Rec Sec: Sam Sussman; Fin Sec: Tom Klinger; Gabbai Rishon: Morris Friedman; Gabbai Shaini: Dr Stanley Kochman; Hon Life Gabbai: Ralph Waldman; Trustees: Percy Bub, Lou East, David Fried, Jerry Goose, Israel Horowitz, Dr Harold Merskey, Morris Rozenson, Dr Marvin Sherebrin, Sam Siegal, Dr Alan Spires, Dr Gerald Wright. **1210 Adelaide St N, London Ontario Canada N5Y 4T6 (519) 433–7081.**

Congregation Or Shalom. Affiliated with United Syn of Am. Rabbi & Edu Dir: Howard S. Hoffman; Cantor Josef Freiman; Pres: Louis M. Kirshenbaum. **534 Huron St, London Ontario Canada N5Y 4J5 (519) 438–3081.**

London Jewish Community Centre. Social servs agy. To help J individuals in their capacity to function usefully in soc in intellectual, physical, edu

& cultural matters. Presch Group; babysitting servs; Sr Citizens Club; teen & chil groups; cultural progs for adults; J family progs; physical fitness progs. The Ctr serves as the meeting ground for all J individuals & groups; helps people function as mems of groups by providing organized group activities under supervision of resource people skilled with social, recreational, edu, athletic or cultural abilities. Est in the 1960's. Ctr Cttee Chr: Sandi Caplan; Exec Dir: Howard Borer. **532 Huron St, London Ontario Canada N5Y 4J5 (519) 433–2201.**

London Jewish Community Council. Co-ordinating body for the J com. To further the welfare of the J com; to plan for the philanthropic, social, cultural & edu advancement of the J com; to foster co-operation among orgs directed towards that goal. Ctr progs; com relations; edu; social servs; Vaad Hakashrut; Vaad Yeshivot; human rights; UJA. Pres: Herbert Perlmutter; 1st VP: Dr Jack Rosen; 2nd VP & Treas: Gloria Gilbert; Sec: Dr Bill Chodirker; Exec Mem at Large: Dr Hirsh Keidan; Exec Dir: Howard Borer. **532 Huron St, London Ontario Canada N5Y 4J5 (519) 433–2201.**

Mississauga

Solel Congregation. Affiliated with UAHC. 175 mems. Rabbi Lawrence A. Englander; Pres: Bernard Weitzman; Edu: Ann Bobker; Sisterhood Pres: Beverly Rothschild; Brotherhood Pres: Bernie Keyes. **2399 Folkway Dr, Mississauga Ontario Canada L5L 2M6 (416) 828–5915.**

Niagara Falls

Congregation B'nai Jacob. Conservative Cong. Rel Servs; Heb Sch; Men's Group; Sisterhood; Hadassah-Wizo; Youth Group. 40 families; 10 chil in the Heb Sch. The syn was constructed in 1937; com records date back to 1926. Rabbi Nathan Liberman; Pres & Pres Men's Group: Henry Muller; Pres Sisterhood: Beverley Blackstein. **5328 Ferry St, Niagara Falls Ontario Canada (416) 354–3934.**

Oakville

Beth El Congregation. Rabbi Aaron Horowitz; Pres: Solomon Chernia; Edu Dir: Thomas Beasley. **186 Morrison Rd, Oakville, Ontario Canada L6J 4J4 (416) 845–0837.**

Oshawa

Beth Zion Congregation of Oshawa. Affiliated with United Syn of Am. Rabbi Harvey Meirovich; Pres: Cyril Taylor. **144 King St E, Oshawa Ontario Canada L1H 1C2.**

Ottawa

Adath Shalom Congregation. Affiliated with United Syn of Am. Pres: Irwin M. Brondo. **PO Box 106, Postal Station B, Oshawa Ontario Canada K1P 6C3 (613) 225–7081.**

Agudath Israel Congregation. Conservative Syn affiliated with United Syn of Am. Rel Servs. Chartered in 1938. Rabbi Arnold Fine; Cantor David Aptowitzer. **1400 Coldrey Ave, Ottawa Ontario Canada K1Z 7P9 (613) 728–3501.**

Canada-Israel Committee – Ottawa Office. 170 Metcalfe St, Suite 400, Ottawa Ontario Canada K2P 1P3.

Center for the Study of Psychology & Judaism. 1747 Featherston Dr, Ottawa Ontario Canada K1H 6P4 (613) 731–9119.

Hillel Academy – Ottawa Talmud Torah Board. Com day sch for chil fr nursery level through eighth grade. To instill in the stu a love & an awareness of the J heritage & tradition, while being fluent in Heb language. Cirriculum includes gen & J studies; physical edu; daily french classes; Tutorial Prog in both Heb & gen studies is available at all grade levels. F by a group of individuals dedicated to furthering J edu in Ottawa around the 1940's. Dir of Edu: Rabbi Yaacov Kaploun; Prin Gen Studies: Robert H. Martin; Prin Talmud Torah Afternoon Heb Sch: Elizabeth Wolynetz. **453 Rideay St, Ottawa Ontario Canada K1N 5Z3 (613) 235–1841.**

Jewish Community Centre. 151 Chapel St, Ottawa Ontario Canada K1N 7Y2 (613) 232–7306.

Jewish Community Centre Library. 151 Chapel St, Ottawa Ontario Canada K1N 7Y2 (613) 232–7306.

Jewish Community Council of Ottawa. J Com Fed. Affiliated with Council of J Fed; Canadian J Cong. Central planning, fund-raising & co-ordinating agy for the J com of Ottawa. Acts as the rep & collective voice of com; identifies the rel, cultural, edu, soc & social welfare needs of the com & plans, encourages & conducts activities to satisfy those needs; conducts the annual UJA campaign; disburses proceeds of UJA through its planning, priorities & allocations process; authorizes other campaigns in com; adm Ottawa J Com Foun; co-ordinates activities of syns, orgs & other groups in com. 10,000 mems. 12 employees & 400 volunteers. F in 1934. Ottawa Jewish Bulletin & Review (bi–weekly). Pres:

Joseph Lieff; 1st VP: Dr Harvey Lithwick; 2nd VP: Gerald Berger; Treas: Charles Taylor; Sec: Lorry Greenberg; Exec VP: Hy Hochberg. **151 Chapel St, Ottawa Ontario Canada K1N 7Y2 (613) 232–7306.**

National Library of Canada, the Jacob M. Lowry Collection. 395 Wellington St, Ottawa Ontario Canada K1A ON4.

Ottawa Talmud Torah Afternoon School. To have the knowledge & ability to put into practice home observances & to participate in syn Servs; to dev a sense of identity & a feeling of kinship with world J & those in Eretz Yisrael. Edu K through 10th grade; special edu; Bar & Bat Mitzvah classes; Parent Assn. F in 1921 when the existing syn, which had previously operated a congregational sch, purchased an old public sch bldg for the purpose of amalgamated classes. The parent body is today, as it was then, rep of every syn in Ottawa, & of the com. Prin: Doris Bronstein; Dir of Edu: Richard Wagener; Sch Cttee Chr: Jonathan Fisher. **453 Rideau St, Ottawa Ontario Canada K1N 5Z3.**

Temple Israel. Reform Cong affiliated with UAHC. To promote J in all aspects of life by worship, rel edu, social action, welfare, social & com activities. Rel Servs; Rel Edu. 240 mems. Est in 1966 when four couples met to pursue their dream that there would be a liberal Reform cong in Canada's capital. In 1967 Temple Is Sch was started. Pub Temple Israel Bulletin (monthly). Pres: Elaine Singer; 1st VP: Stephen Harris; 2nd VP: Francine Altman; Treas: Eli Edelson; Sec: Brain Gold. **1301 Prince of Wales Dr, Ottawa Ontario Canada K2C 1N2 (613) 224–1802.**

Peterborough

Beth Israel Congregation. Affiliated with United Syn of Am. Rabbi Joseph Carmi; Pres: Phil Holland. **Weller St, Peterborough Ontario Canada (705) 745–7483.**

Saint Catharines

Temple Tikvah. Affiliated with UAHC. 39 mems. Pres: Arthur Friedman; Edu: Murray Diner. **83 Church St, PO Box 484, Saint Catharines Ontario Canada L2R 6Y9 (416) 682–4191.**

Saint Catherines

B'nai Israel. Affiliated with United Syn of Am. Rabbi A. Matts; Pres: Robert Slipacoff. **190 Church St, St Catherines Ontario Canada L2R 4C4 (416) 685–6767.**

Sarnia

Ahavas Isaac Synagogue. Affiliated with United Syn of Am. Rabbi Michael Engel; Pres: Robert Slipacoff. **202 Cobden St, Sarnia Ontario Canada.**

Thornhill

Temple Har Zion. Affiliated with UAHC. 300 mems. Rabbis: Michael S. Stroh, Daniel Gottlieb; Cantor Martin Steinhouse; Pres: Alan Dessau; Edu: Alan Bardikoff; Adm: Judi Cooper; Sisterhood Pres: Dvora Brown. **7360 Bayview Ave, Thornhill Ontario Canada L3T 2R7 (416) 889–2252.**

Toronto

Baycrest Terrace Reform Cong. Affiliated with UAHC. 60 mems. Pres: Victoria Lewis. **3560 Bathurst, Toronto Ontario Canada M6A 2E1 (416) 789–5131.**

Beth Sholom Synagogue. Affiliated with United Syn of Am. Rabbi Dr David Monson; Pres: Robert Rothman; Exec Dir: Sam Fox; Edu Dir: Cantor Samuel Frankel. **1445 Eglinton Ave W, Toronto Ontario Canada M6C 2E6 (416) 783–6103.**

Beth Torah Congregation. Affiliated with United Syn of Am. Rabbi Solomon Z. Domb; Pres: Irv Newman. **47 Glenbrook Ave, Toronto Ontario Canada M6B 2L7 (476) 782–3561.**

Beth Tzedec Congregation. Affiliated with United Syn of Am. To build an affirmative J; to bring the miracle of the Bible into daily life; to plant love of the J tradition in one's heart; to inspire respect for rel life in the com; to promote a rel fellowship among all its citizens. Daily Rel Servs; Jr Cong; Youth Group; library; Rel Sch; Brotherhood; Sisterhood; rel, social & cultural activities. Rel Sch: 450 stu; Primary Dept: 300 stu. Dedicated in 1955. Beth Tzedec Cong is a merger, effected in 1952, of two of the first & oldest congs in Toronto – Goel Tzedec & Beth Hamidrash Hagadol. In 1957 the Cong est a foun sch for the Primary Day Sch. Facilities include a sanctuary which seats 2,600 & rm for an additional 900 seats for the High Holy Days, a chapel which seats 325, a mus designated as the Canadian Branch of the J Mus. The Cong owns the Cecil Roth Collection & houses rare & priceless ritual articrafts. Rabbi J. Benjamin Friedberg; Assc Rabbi Robert Binder; Cantor Emeritus Joseph Cooper; Cantors: Paul H. Kowarsky, Morris Soberman; Pres: Paul Rothstein. **1700 Bathurst St, Toronto Ontario Canada M5P 3K3 (416) 781–3511.**

Beth Tzedec Congregation Library. For information on the Cong, see – Beth Tzedec Congregation, Toronto Ontario Canada. **1700 Bathurst St, Toronto Ontario Canada M5P 3K3 (416) 781–3511.**

Beth Tzedec Museum. To collect, preserve & exhibit original J artifacts of all times & places. The Cecil Roth Collection holds a large num of unique J artifacts, rare marriage contracts, Hanukkah lamps, Torah ornaments & Purim scrolls fr Italy, the Near & Far E, & Central Europe. Close to 1,000 items are card catalogued & researched. Exhibits concentrate on J holidays or other facets of the J life cycle. Special exhibits of J artists are arranged fr time to time. Est in 1964 by the Beth Tzedec Cong of Toronto. Chr: Ruth Krieger; Curator: S. Simchovitch. **1700 Bathurst St, Toronto Ontario Canada M5P 3K3 (416) 781–5658.**

Bialik Hebrew Day School. 12 Viewmount Ave, Toronto Ontario Canada M6C 1S6 (416) 783–3346.

Bialik Hebrew Day School, Library. 12 Viewmount Ave, Toronto Ontario Canada M6C 1S6 (416) 783–3346.

Board of Jewish Education. A central com agy for J edu affiliated with the Am Assn for J Edu; a dept of the United J Welfare Fund. To improve instruction in its affiliated schs by setting standards for teacher certification, coordinating the efforts of schs, developing meaningful progs & upgrading the professional quality of the ins & individuals. Recruits, evaluates & places qualified teachers; locates & assesses teacher shlichim fr Is; maintains a substitute teachers registry; maintains current & past records on all teachers in affiliated schs; provides pension & insurance information; acts as liaison between Fed of Heb Teachers & schs in salary negotiations; provides a consultation serv; gives seminars on methods for the teaching of Bible, Heb language, J hist & Is; sponsors teacher workshop on edu, methodology & tech; administers the Toronto J Teachers Seminary; supports Com Hebrew Academy (a day HS); provides subsidies to schs in the com; reviews tuition fee reductions; conducts Is study tours, weekend retreats with schs & youth groups, inter-schs music festivals; coords the local, regional & natl Bible contests; coords the UJA campaign in the schs & the UJA Walkathon; directs J Bk Mo activities including essay contests in Heb & English; maintains Media & Resource Ctr, Central Pedagogic Library, Information Bank, publicity & PR, guidance & counseling servs; administers scholarship awards; assures J content & programming in com agy; maintains contact with youth groups on & off campus; adminsters the Adult Edu Prog; help integration of Russian immigrant chil into J schs & orgs. 50 different sch units. F in 1949 as the Bureau of J Edu. In 1967 a reorganization took place & the Bd of J Edu was est as an arm of the United J Welfare Fund. Exec Dir: Rabbi Irwin E. Witty; Assc Dir: Harold R. Malitzky; Dir Media & Resource Ctr: Joseph Shoham; Dir of Sch Finances: Bernard Shoub; Sch Consultants: Dr Alexander Brown, Dr Shoshana Kurtz, Harvey Raben; CZF Shaliach Consultant: Aryeh Arad; Dir Emeritus: Dr Joseph Diamond; Chr: Irving Feldman; Chr Fiscal Cttee: Charles C. Zaionz; Chr Mgmnt & Academic Affairs: Suri Greenberg; Bd Mems: Ronald Appleby, Michael C. Benjamin, Sandra Brown, Donald Carr, Harold M. Chapman, Henrietta Chesnie, Philip Daniels, Harold Dessen, Robert B. Eisen, Madeline Epstein, Philip Epstein, Meyer Feldman, Sam Norman Filer, Sheila Freeman, John A. Geller, Ronald M. Heller, Aryeh Lebovic, Barnet Loftus, J. Sydney Midanik, Lewis J. E. Moses, Dr Lou Myers, David Rotenberg, Paul Rothstein, Samuel J. Sable, Les Scheininger, Murray Segal, Samuel Shainhouse, Ralph Shiff, Joseph J. Silver, Joseph Tanenbaum; Ex Officio: Rose Wolfe; Chr Emeritus: Stephen E. Berger, Melvyn Finkelstein, Herbert Solway, Harry Steiner. **22 Glen Park Ave, Toronto Ontario Canada M6B 2B9 (416) 781–4687.**

Canada-Israel Chamber of Commerce & Industry. First Canadian Pl, PO Box 31, 100 King St W, Toronto Ontario Canada M5X 1A9 (416) 362–7424.

Canada-Israel Cultural Foundation. 60 Bloor St W, Suite 1003, Toronto Ontario Canada M4W 3B8 (416) 921–2103.

Canadian Foundation for Jewish Culture. 150 Beverley St, Toronto Ontario Canada M5T 1Y6 (416) 869–3811.

Canadian Friends of Bar-Ilan University. 825 Eglinton Ave W, Suite 314, Toronto Ontario Canada M5N 1E7 (416) 783–8546.

Canadian Friends of the Hebrew University. 208 1 Yorkdale Rd, Toronto Ontario Canada M6A 3A1 (416) 789–2633.

Canadian Jewish Congress – Ontario Region. The official rep of J coms in Canada. Affiliated with the World J Congress. To dev the highest degree of peoplehood in the J of Canada by encouraging, carrying on & participating in activities of a natl, cultural & humanitarian nature. For additional information, see – Canadian Jewish Congress, Montreal Quebec Canada. **150 Beverley St, Toronto Ontario Canada M5T 1Y6.**

Canadian Technion Society. 2828 Bathurst St, Suite 502, Toronto Ontario Canada M6B 3A7.

Canadian Young Judaea Zionist Youth Movement. To promote Aliyah & Is; to bring J youth together & give them progs on J. Sponsors regular activities across the country; operates progs in 8 summer camps. F in 1917. The Judaen; The Yedion; The Young Judaean. Canadian Young Judaea is the largest Zionist youth movement in Canada. **Natl off: 788 Marlee Ave, Toronto Ontario Canada M6B 3K1 (416) 787–5350.**

The Canadian Zionist Federation – Central. To promote the Zionist ideal among the J population in Canada; assist in strengthening the J State & the enrichment of Canadian J life through J edu, Is & Zionist information, promotion of aliyah & activities among J youth in Canada. Aliyah, Edu, Culture, Information, Tourism, Youth & Hechalutz & Pub & Is Trade Depts – progs of major activities throughout Canada in these areas. Est in 1967. Chr: Lewis J.E. Moses. **788 Mariee Ave, Toronto Ontario Canada M6B 3K1 (416) 787–6171.**

Candian Jewish News. Periodical pub. **562 E Eglinton Ave, Suite 401, Toronto Ontario Canada M4P 1P1 (416) 481–6434.**

Habonim. 3101 Bathurst St, Suite 305, Toronto Ontario Canada.

Herut Women. 3417 Bathurst St, Toronto Ontario Canada.

Holy Blossom Religious School. 1950 Bathurst St, Toronto Ontario Canada M5P 3K9 (416) 781–9185.

Holy Blossom Religious School, Teachers' Reference Library. 1950 Bathurst St, Toronto Ontario Canada M5P 3K9 (416) 781–9185.

Holy Blossom Temple. Affiliated with UAHC. 2275 mems. Rabbis: Harvey J. Fields, Mark D. Shapiro, James Prosnit, Abraham Feinberg, W.G. Plaut; Cantor Benjamin Z. Maissner; Pres: Karl Bald; Edu: Steven Garten; Adm: Melville Olsberg; Sisterhood Pres: Diana Goodman; Brotherhood Pres: Joseph Silver. **1950 Bathurst St, Toronto Ontario Canada M5P 3K9 (416) 781–9185.**

Holy Blossom Temple Sisterhood Library. For information on the Temple, see – Holy Blossom Temple, Toronto Ontario Canada. **1950 Bathurst St, Toronto Ontario Canada M5P 3K9 (416) 781–9185.**

Israel Aliyah Center. 788 Marlee Ave, Toronto Ontario Canada M6B 3K1 (416) 781–4770.

Israel Government Tourist Office. 102 Bloor St W, Toronto Ontario Canada M5S 1M8 (416) 964–3784.

Jewish Information Service. Com information ctr; part of Toronto J Cong. Acts as a switchboard for the J com. Information & referral for J com; resources & servs including: progs for disabled, accessible facilities, J holidays & festivals, J Edu, volunteer opportunities; social serv agy; accomodation registry; recreation facilities; congs; J camps; employment. 2 employees; 90 volunteers. F 1973. Pub Jewish Community Directory Met Toronto, Jewish Singles Directory Met Toronto, Volunteer Opportunities Index, Volunteer News & Views. Facilities include off, outreach booth (kiosk). Served as consultant to a number of other cities setting up JIS, including NYC. Dir: Joel Verbin. **2953 Bathurst St, Suite 104, Toronto Ontario Canada M6B 3B2 (416) 789–7278.**

Jewish Public Library of Toronto. 22 Glen Park Ave, Toronto Ontario Canada M6B 2B9.

Jewish Standard. Periodical pub. **67 Mowat Ave, Suite 319, Toronto Ontario Canada M6K 3E3 (416) 363–3289.**

Joint Community Relations Committee. Cttee of Canadian Jewish Cong & B'nai B'rith. **150 Beverly St, Toronto Ontaria Canada (416) 869–3811.**

Labor Zionist Alliance. 14 Viewmount Ave, Toronto Ontario Canada M6B 1T3 (416) 787–0339.

Labor Zionist Movement of Canada. 3101 Bathurst St, Suite 305, Toronto Ontario Canada M6A 2A6 (416) 783–8440.

Maccabiah Lodge Number 3077, B'nai B'rith of Toronto. Dedicated to maintaining a sense of J identity among its mems in the Met Toronto area. Entertaining & informative social & philanthropic activities; sports oriented functions; fund raising events whose proceeds are disbursed among varying charities in both Canada & in Is. Maccabiah Lodge membership is predominantly young adult. Pres: Richard M. Ittleman; VPs: Michael Wolfe, Paul

Lockwood, Manny Brykman; Treas: Sheldon Buchalter; Fin Sec: Ron Reim. **B'nai B'rith, 164 Eglinton Ave E, Toronto Ontario Canada.**

National Joint Community Relations Committee. Cttee of Canadian Jewish Congress & B'nai B'rith in Canada. **150 Beverley St, Toronto Ontario Canada M5T 1Y6 (416) 869–3811.**

Palestine Economic Corporation of Canada, Ltd. 50 Wingold Ave, Toronto Ontario Canada.

Shaarei Shomayim Congregation. Orthodox Syn. To maintain & conduct a modern Orthodox Syn in keeping with the dictates of traditional Orthodox J; to provide, conduct, assc itself with or support schs for instruction in Heb, J rel studies, traditions, language, literature, hist of the J people & such other subjects that will minister to the rel, spiritual, edu & cultural needs of the J people; to maintain within the Syn, a ctr for the cultivation of J thought & action, & to foster & encourage the org of social, cultural & edu groups among the mems of the Cong & their chil. Rel Servs; Nursery & Jr Servs; Tefillin Club; Brotherhood; Cong Sch for child ranging in age fr 7 to 13; Boys Choir; chil library; Sisterhood; NCSY youth groups; Couples Club; Rabbi's Talmud Class; Heb classes; Bat Mitzvah class; Sing-A-Long; Adult Edu; teenage discussion group; arts & crafts for chil 12 to 14; scouts. Over 1,000 families. The forerunner of Shaarei Shomayim was an informal minyan held for 10 yrs in a private home. In 1928 the minyan, now called B'nai Jacob, was formally organized. In 1931, because of a conflict among the mems, part of the Cong withdrew & rented facilities in a house owned by the Brunswick Talmud Torah. The Cong, at first named the Hillcrest & later given its present name, remained at the Talmud Torah site until 1936 when it purchased land & began the construction of the syn. High Holiday Servs were held in the basement shell in 1936. On May 2, 1948 the cornerstone of the syn & Talmud Torah was unveiled. The sanctuary was ready for use by the High Holidays of 1948. The formal dedication took place on the weekend of Nov 25–27, 1949. As the J com moved northward, land was purchased farther N. Construction of the new syn, at its present site, began in Sept of 1964 & was completed in Sept of 1966. Servs continued at the old site until 1970 when the bldg was sold. Shaarei Shomayim is the largest Orthodox syn in Toronto. Rabbi Henry Hoschander; Cantor Harold Klein; Cantor Emeritus Nathan T. Adler; Dir of Youth: Amram Bendahan; Exec VP: Myer Dorn; Pres: Dr Marvin Gerstein; 1st VP: Dr Bernard Green; 2nd VP: Ben Stark; Hon Treas: Joseph Tanenbaum; Treas: Harold Spring; Sec: Martin Sable; Parnass: Chaim Weinberg; Gabbai: Samuel Verman; Brotherhood Pres: William Weissglas; Sisterhood Pres: Ruth Fruitman. **470 Glencairn Ave, Toronto Ontario Canada M5N 1V8 (416) 789–3213.**

Temple Sinai. Affiliated with UAHC. 1426 mems. Rabbis: Jordan Pearlson, Jeffrey B. Ableser; Cantor Severin Weingort; Pres: Heather Morris; Edu: Sandra F. Raben; Adm: Micki Brudner; Sisterhood Pres: Barbara Lewis; Brotherhood Pres: Alan Snider. **210 Wilson Ave, Toronto Ontario Canada M5M 3B1 (416) 487–4161.**

Toronto Hebrew Re-Establishment Service – Gmilath Chasodim Association. To aid worthy people to be & remain self supporting & self respecting citizens by aid of loans & such servs as the individual may require. Such loans & servs are rendered without interest or other charge. Makes interest free loans available to people who are in immediate need for whatever reason – immigrant help, dental, edu, relocation, furniture, family problems; counsels people in all ways of life. Est in 1924 by a few early J settlers in Canada. It started with a fund of $400 to help people in need on an interest free loan basis. The capital is now $370,000.00. During 58 yrs, the Assn has granted over 5 million dollars. The Assn processes about 400 applications each yr. The sec & exec dir are employed while the mems & dirs are volunteers. Pres: Sherman Hans; VP Loan Cttee Chr: Rose Czinner; Exec VP: Leon Neuschul; Treas & Co-Chr Capital Fund: Jack Kosoy; Investigation of Applicants: Lillie Herlick; V Chr Loan Cttee: Jack Schwartz; Co-Chr Capital Fund: Jack Zippan; Chr Nominating Cttee: Jonathan Miller; Nominating & Constitution Cttee Chr: Issie Fishman; Co-Chr Nominating Cttee: Brahm Seitz; Co-Chr Constitution Cttee: Yale Drazin; Co-Chr Membership Cttee: David Sefton, Dr Sheldon Sper; Chr Fin Cttee: George Weinberger; Hon Life Bd Mems: J.C. Oelbaum; Exec Dir: Victor Jacobson; Exec Sec: Jannet Bromberg; Bd of Dirs: Morris Adams, James Betesh, Dr George Bleier, Nathan Briks, Henry Bulmash, Joseph Cohen, Bernie Davis, William Eisenberg, Joseph Fleischmann, Wilfred Gordon, Nahemia Goldfield, J. Barney Goldhar, Samuel Kaiman, Nathan Kleinman, S. Lunenfeld, Mark A. Levy, Jacob Lipson, Louis L. Lockshin, Joseph Pifko, Leslie Reitman, Sam Rotman, Ernie Rubenstein, Lionel Sharpe, Sual Sigler, Max Wolfe. **3199 Bathurst St, Rm 205, Toronto Ontario Canada M6A 2B2 (416) 789–1844.**

Toronto Jewish Congress. Mem of CJF. Organized 1937. Pres: Wilfred Posluns; Exec VP: Irwin Gold. **150 Beverly St, Toronto Ontario Canada M5T 1Y6 (416) 977–3811.**

UAHC Canadian Council. Rel & edu org serving J congs throughout the US & Canada. To encourage & aid the org & dev of J congs; to promote J edu, & enrich & intensify J life; to foster other activities for the perpetuation & advancement of J. For additional information, see – UAHC – Union of American Hebrew Congregations, New York City, NY. Pres: Maurice A. Miller; Dir: Arthur Grant. **534 Lawrence Ave W, Suite 213, Toronto Ontario Canada M6A 1A2 (416) 787–9838.**

United Synagogue Day School. Affiliated with Solomon Schechter Day Schs Assn. **1700 Bathurst St, Toronto Ontario Canada M5P 3K3 (416) 781–5658.**

Women's Canadian ORT. Volunteer, charitable org affiliated with World ORT Union. Training schs; factory training & apprenticeship progs & Teacher Training Ins. 100,000 stu annually are enrolled worldwide in 75 schs. ORT is the world's largest non governmental vocational & technical training network. Natl Off Pres: Genya Intrator; VP: Harriet Morton; Exec Dir: Diane Uslaner. **3101 Bathurst St, Suite 404, Toronto Ontario Canada M6A 2A6 (416) 787–0339.**

Young Herut. 3417 Bathurst St, Toronto Ontario Canada.

Youth & Hechalutz Department (Israel Program Centre). 788 Marlee Ave, Toronto Ontario Canada M6B 3K1 (416) 783–4722.

Zionist Organization of Canada. 788 Marlee Ave, Toronto Ontario Canada M6B 3K1 (416) 781–3571.

Zionist Revisionist Organization of Canada. 3417 Bathurst St, Toronto Ontario Canada.

Willowdale

Beth Tikvah. Affiliated with United Syn of Am. Rabbi Robert Marcus; Cantor & Youth Dir: Mitchell Martin; Pres: Gershon Sone; Exec Dir: Stuart Razin. **3080 Bayview Ave, Willowdale Ontario Canada M2N 5L3 (416) 221–3433.**

Beth Tikvah Library. 3080 Bayview Ave, Willowdale Ontario Canada M2N 5L3.

Jewish Community Centre of Toronto. An affiliate of the Toronto J Congress, JWB & the United Way. To assure the qualitative survival of J life. Northern Branch: Camp Caravan – a travel camp for teens 12½ to 16; Counselor in Training Prog – for selected 15 yr olds; Fundale – a traditional day camp for chil ages 6 to 12 with special progs for 10 to 12 yr olds; Summer Fun – for chil ranging in age fr 4½ to 11; Out-In – a unique day camp for chil ages 11½ to 14½; Snoopy – a special camp for chil ages 3½ to 6; Sunshine – a camp for chil with special needs for ages 7 to 18; Racquet Camp – for boys & girls 10 to 14 yrs old interested in focusing on racquet sports; Arts Village – for chil 7 to 12 interested in specializing in cultural & artistic pursuits; other activities include – presch servs: for chil 3 mo to 5 yrs; chil activities: clubs, Shabbaton prog on Sat, weekday hobby groups, swim instruction, sports sch; pre teen activities: club groups, lounge progs, hobby groups, swim instruction; teen activities: clubs & hobby groups, BBYO, discussion series, dances, sports sch, leadership training prog; young adults: weekend socials, brunches, physical edu, athletic progs; adult activities: variety of progs for singles & formerly marrieds broken into age groups, physical edu; sr adults: social & physical edu activities; special groups: Friendship Club for retarded adults 16 to 45, Heb Club for the blind; Physical Edu Prog; Health Club; Koffler Ctr of Arts: Sch of Visual Arts with progs available for all ages in many visual art forms including Painting, Drawing, Ceramics & Stone Sculpture; Leah Posluns Theatre Sch: courses for chil & adults in all forms of acting, stage tech & other aspects of theatre production (responsible for all performing arts which take place under JCC sponsorship); Music Sch providing private & group lessons; Sch of Dance provides dance classes to persons of all ages; Public Affairs & Continuing Edu progs for young adults & adults; Koffler Gallery exhibiting outstanding works of sculpture, ceramics, painting & photography. NE Branch: Valley Tennis & Swim Ctr; activities for single parents & chil; teen age clubs & many special events throughout the yr. Bloor Branch: Nursery Sch; group servs; singles group; prog in dance; physical edu prog. Staff of 130. The JCC is an outgrowth of the J Girls Club, the YMHA & YWHA, & the J Boys Club which flourished during the 1920's & 1930's. After WWII it became increasingly difficult to operate the progs of these orgs in a variety of bldgs. It was decided that a new bldg was needed to house all activities. In Jul of 1948 the JCC Assn was est to raise funds for a ctr. The Bloor bldg was opened on Jan 1, 1953. As the movement of the J population indicated the necessity of a second bldg, the Northern bldg was constructed & was opened to the public on May 1, 1961. In 1977 The Leah Posluns Theatre & the Koffler Ctr of the Arts were added to the Northern bldg facility. At the same time, the physical edu facilities were expanded, In 1978 it was decided to reactivate the JCC name & each bldg was designated a branch of the JCC agy. In Jul of 1979 the NE Branch was added to the JCC. In Feb of 1980 the property of the Mayfair Valley Tennis Club was purchased by a group of businessmen. The JCC became the operator of this facility. Facilities include gymnasiums, indoor & outdoor tracks, tennis, squash, racquetball & handball cts, indoor & outdoor pools, sports fields, dance studios, playgrounds, classrooms & theaters. Chr of the Bd: Wilfred Posluns; Pres: Bernard S. Dales; VPs: Hersh Fogel, Bernard J. Kamin, Marvelle Koffler, Martin Mendelow, Fred Tittel; Treas: M. Diane Kettner; Asst Treas: Jack Hershoran; Sec: Kiva Barkin; Asst Sec: Sam Helfenbaum; Hon VPs: Harvey Blackstein, Louis Borsook, Senator David Croll, Theodore K. Draimin, Samuel Eckler, Madeleine Epstein, Bert Fine, Alex G. Fisher, Mrs Samuel Godfrey, Louis H. Posluns, R. Lou Ronson, Ellis I. Shapiro, H. Max Swartz, Alex Tobias, John Wahl; Exec Dir: Sid L. Brail; Asst Exec Dir & Dir Northern Branch: Paul Brownstein; Dir Bloor Branch: Irwin Soren; Dir Koffler Ctr of the Arts: Cindy Chazan; Dir Leah Posluns Theatre: Reva Stern-Tward; Dir NE Branch: Sheila Bellack; Business Adm: Eric H. Lakien. **N Branch, Leah Posluns Theatre & Koffler Ctr – 4588 Bathurst St, Willowdale Ontario Canada M2R 1W6 (416) 636–1880; Bloor Branch – 750 Spadina Ave, Toronto Ontario Canada M5S 2J2 (416) 924–6211; NE Branch – 1091 Finch Ave E, Willowdale Ontario Canada M2J 2X3 (416) 493–8866.**

Temple Emanu-El. Reform Cong affiliated with UAHC. To perpetuate & enhance the rel of our fathers; to uphold, teach & foster the essential principles, & moral & ethical values of J; to encourage & provide opportunities for divine worship, edu & servs as a Reform J cong & for the spread of enlightened rel sentiments; to work for fellowship with God; to promote a better understanding & relationship among all people of good will; & to advance the welfare of all those who may come under its influence. Daily Rel Servs; Choir; Brotherhood; Rel Sch; Heb Sch; Bar & Bat Mitzvah classes; youth & adult study progs; periodic Shabbat study progs; catering & banquet facilities for mems; library. 325 families. Est in 1958 by some mems of Holy Blossom Temple to dev a Reform cong in the NE sector of the city. In 1970 the Temple merged with Beth El Cong. The Temple maintains a Biblical Garden. Rabbi Arthur Bielfeld; Pres: Marvin Chapley; VP Rel Edu: Joan Goldfarb; VP Fundraising: Phil Rudolph; VP: Karen Sanders; VP House Chr: Sam Sarick; Treas: Morris Snow; Sec: Marshall Redhill; Adm Sec: Rhoda Goldstein. **120 Old Colony Rd, Willowdale Ontario Canada M2L 2K2 (416) 449–3880.**

United Synagogue Day School, Bayview Branch. Affiliated with Solomon Schechter Day Schs Assn. Prin: Dr Aaron Nussbaum; Chr: Dr Jack Pollock. **3080 Bayview Ave, Willowdale Ontario Canada (416) 225–1144.**

Windsor

Congregation Beth El. Affiliated with UAHC. 190 mems. Rabbi Jonathan V. Plaut; Cantor Sidney Resnick; Pres: James L. Cohen; Edu: Jonathan V. Plaut; Adm: Judy Hochberg; Sisterhood Pres: Sharon Hochberg, Marcey Katzman; Brotherhood Pres: Murray Joffe. **2525 Mark Ave, Windsor Ontario Canada N9E 2W2 (519) 969–2422.**

Jewish Community Council. Mem of CJF. Organized 1938. Pres: Lottie Bernholtz; Exec Dir: Joseph Eisenberg. **1641 Ouelette Ave, Windsor Ontario Canada N8X 1K9 (519) 254–7558.**

Windsor Jewish Community Council. 1641 Ouellette Ave, Windsor Ontario Canada N8X 1K9 (519) 254–7558.

QUEBEC

Chomedey

Congregation Shaar Shalom. Affiliated with United Syn of Am. Rabbi Perry Cohen; Cantor Syd Dworkin; Pres: David Jackson; Exec Dir: Stella Wasserman; Edu Dir: Frema Luther, Anita Nerwen. **4880 Notre Dame Blvd, Chomedey Quebec Canada H7W 1V4 (418) 688–8100.**

Cote St. Luc

The Nathan Dermer Library, Tifereth Beth David Jerusalem Synagogue. 6519 Baily Rd, Cote St Luc Quebec Canada (514) 484–3841.

Tifereth Beth David Jerusalem Synagogue. 6519 Baily Rd, Cote St Luc Quebec Canada (514) 484–3841.

Dollard des Ormeaux

Canadian Jewish Herald. Periodical pub. **17 Anselme Lavigne Blvd, Dollard des Ormeaux Quebec Canada H9A 1N3 (514) 684–7667.**

Congregation Beth Tikvah. To correlate traditional J with every endeavor of human existence. Rel Servs; Sun Sch; Heb afternoon classes; Nursery & K Prog; partner of the Heb Foun Day Sch; NCSY Youth Prog; Adult Edu; Drama Group; Sisterhood; Men's Club. 500 families; 300 chil in the Heb Sch; 325 stu in the Day Sch; 650 chil in the Youth Prog. F in 1962 with the org of an afternoon Heb sch in a private home. Later, a four rm cottage was purchased. By 1967 the syn became too small for the 100 families, the sch, & the youth & adult activities held there. In 1967 land was bought for a new larger syn. In 1968 High Holiday Servs were conducted in the new bldg. In the fall of 1970 the Heb Foun Sch became a full day sch. By 1973 the existing sch facilities became overcrowded & a new sch bldg was added. In 1975 a second story was added to the sch. With the continued growth of the J com, the syn & sch were once again overcrowded & so in 1978 proposals were made to build a new connecting sanctuary & sch which would house new classrooms, meeting rms & offs. Rabbi Dr Mordecai E. Zeitz; Pres: Bill Hurwitz; Chr of the Bd: Marty Goldenberg; VPs: Bryant Levy, Allan Richstone; Exec Trustees: Howie Cohen, Steve Favor, Lawrence Firestone, Herb Friedberg, Johnnie Posluns, Allan Rimer, Lou Orzech; Exec Dir of Youth: Roz Richstone; Parnass: Allan Margolese; Exec Sec: Sonny Vineberg; Treas: Tom Marer; Hon Parnass: David Levine; Pres Heb Foun Sch: Jack Dworkind; Sec: Brenda Held. **136 Westpark Blvd, Dollard des Ormeaux Quebec Canada H9A 2K2 (514) 683–5610.**

Temple Rodeph Shalom. Affiliated with UAHC. 86 mems. Rabbi Michael N. Stevens; Pres: Jack Charles; Sisterhood Pres: Sandra Fagen. **96 Fredmir Blvd, Dollard des Ormeaux Quebec Canada H9A 2R3 (514) 626–2173.**

Fairfax

Congregation Olam Tikvah. Affiliated with United Syn of Am. Rabbi Itzhaq M. Klirs; Pres: Irwin N. Jacobs; Edu Dir: Marcia Merlin; Exec Dir: Alvin Ungerleider. **3800 Glenbrook Rd, Fairfax VA 22031 (703) 978–3333.**

Hampstead

Adath Israel Congregation. Orthodox Cong. F in 1930. The first syn was in rented premises. The second syn was constructed in Outremont, Quebec in 1940. This syn still meets & functions. The third Adath Is syn was constructed in Hampstead, Quebec in 1981. The syn is noted for having the first congregational day sch in Canada. The day sch was f in 1940 & functioned as the Adath Israel Sch until 1966. Rabbi Michael Kramer; Rabbi Emeritus Charles Bender; Hazzan: Benjamin Hass; Hazzan Sheni: Nuchim Benjaminson; Pres: Morton J. Pearl; VPs: Hilliard Lippman, Dr Abraham Wexler, Sol

Zuckerman; Treas: Lowen Rosenthal; Sec: Gerald Feifer; Parnassim: Ralph Pinsky, Harry Cohen, Erwin Neumark; Hon Solicitors: Samuel E. Berger, Paul Nadler; Hon Notary: Robert Glazer. **223 Harrow Crescent, Hampstead Quebec Canada H3X 3X7 (514) 482–4252.**

Laval

Young Israel of Chomedey. To provide servs for the J com of Laval; to create an atmosphere of J warmth & companionship. Rel Servs; youth activities; Jr Cong; Youth Shabbat during which the youth conduct the Servs of the adult cong; week-end retreats; Adult Edu; social activities. F in 1958. Rabbi Dr Solomon J. Spiro; Cantor Moshe Ginz; Asst Cantor David Marmor; Pres: Mel Ostroff. **1025 Elizabeth Blvd, Laval Quebec Canada H7W 3J7 (514) 681–2571.**

Montreal

Allied Jewish Community Services. Mem of CJF. A merger of Fed of J Com Servs & Combined J Appeal. Organized 1965. Pres: Dr Harvey Sigman; Exec Dir: Emanuel Weiner. **5151 Cote St Catherine Rd, Montreal Quebec Canada H3W 1M6 (514) 735–3541.**

Bialik High School of the Jewish People's Schools & Peretz Schools. To educate the young generation toward an extensive knowledge of J culture, tradition & way of life; to effect a positive attitude towards J rel & ethical values, & the State of Is, & foster a sense of loyalty to Canada. Bialik HS; Secondary 1 to 5. 525 stu. Hon Pres: Joseph Berman, Harry I. Craimer, Dan Freedman, Daniel Kingstone, Leon Teitelbaum; Hon VPs: Mr & Mrs C. Balinsky, Jack Berliner, Bernard M. Bloomfield, Sam Chait, Cecil Pascal, Chaim Pripstein; Hon Mems of the Bd: Eli Kahn, Nathan Kalifon, Morris Kreisman, Beryl Pofelis, Bennie Sussman; Pres: Stanley Sternthal; Chr Exec Cttee: Freda Rashkovan; VPs: BenZion Dalfan, Eli Kobernick, Sol Polachek, Syd Shapiro, Philip Wiseman; Sec: Dr Bruce Costom; Treas: Mac Brotman; Prin Emeritus: Shlomo Wiseman, Jacob Zipper; Dir of Edu: Nachum Wilchesky; Exec Dir: Merle Frankel. **7946 Wavell Rd, Montreal Quebec Canada (514) 489–8291.**

Bnei Akiva of Montreal. 5497A Victoria Ave, Suite 103, Montreal Quebec Canada H3W 2R1 (514) 739–1119.

Brith Trumpeldor Betar of America. 5234 Clan Ranald Ave, Montreal Quebec Canada (514) 486–8926.

Camp B'nai B'rith, Inc. Overnight summer camp, day camp & sr citizen facility supported by B'nai B'rith Lodge & Women's Chapters, a constituent agy of the Allied J Com Servs of Montreal, & mem Quebec Camping Assn. To give financially & emotionally deprived chil a summer camping experience; to dev in the camper a pride & awareness of the State of Is & their own Jewishness. Overnight camp, library, Spinder Syn, counseling servs for recent immigrant chil & chil fr broken homes; day camp for chil ages 4 to 8½ yrs whose families summer in the area; intergenerational programming, Vatikim (Elders) prog, & mobile home sites for sr citizens at Camp B'nai B'rith in the Laurentians. 1,000 campers per summer; 300 sr citizens, 60 per session; 50 day campers at two sessions. Staff of 275–300 includes Jr & Sr counselors, specialists, supervisors, head counselors & camp dir. F in 1921 with a few tents; Sr Citizens prog f in 1977, with the day camp for chil of J families who spend their summers in the Laurentians est in 1979. There is a sliding fee scale policy. Campers pay fr full payment to no charge based on family finances. Full paying campers form a very small percentage of the camp population. On the camp grounds is Zentner Memorial Park with a granite sculpture depicting the six million Holocaust victims. Pres: Ronnie Wexelman; Camp Dir: Steve Forman; Chr Bd of Trustees: William Spinder; Chr Bd of Govs: Lou Finegold; VPs: Lou Backler, Syd Heitner, Freda Hirsh, Gerry Hirsh, Alan Maislin, Dr Michael Tenenbaum; Treas: Gerry Grudman; Secs: John J. Cohen, Joe Goldberg, Eddy Isenberg. **5151 Cote St Catherine Rd, Montreal Quebec Canada H3W 1M6 (514) 735–3669.**

Canada-Israel Committee – National Office. 1310 Greene Ave, Montreal Quebec Canada H3Z 2B2 (514) 934–0771.

Canada-Israel Securities Ltd, State of Israel Bonds. 1255 University St, Suite 1120, Montreal Quebec Canada (514) 878–1871.

Canadian Association for Labor Israel. Fund raising org. To help the Histadrut's social & welfare servs. Activities consist of: edu meetings, & confs with trade unions & people's orgs; the creation of Histadrut Trade Union Council, Friends of Amal & United Orgs for the Histadrut consisting of landsmanshaften, socs & ladies auxiliaries; the raising of funds for Histadrut ins. Est in 1923, this org was created as a movement to break the boycott against J labour participation in the bldg of Is as a co-operative state & as a J state in gen. This boycott was conducted by the bundist who then dominated the J trade unions. The Assn helped to build clins, hosps, trade schs, Hapoel, & youth cultural ctrs in Is. Pres: Bernard M. Bloomfield; VP: Bert Godfrey; Chr Budget Cttee: Ben Himel; Treas: Louis M. Bloomfield; Pres Canadian Friends of Amal: Harry Bloomfield; Chr Bd of Dirs Canadian Friends of Amal: Eugene Stearns; Sec: Abe Shurem; Exec Dir: Flora Naglie. **4770 Kent Ave, Montreal Quebec Canada H3W 1H2 (514) 735–1593.**

Canadian Friends of the Alliance Israelite Universelle. 5711 Edgemore Ave, Montreal Quebec Canada H4W 1V8 (514) 487–1243.

Canadian Friends of the Hebrew University. 1506 McGregor Ave, Montreal Quebec Canada H3G 1B9.

Canadian Jewish Congress. The official rep of J coms in Canada. Affiliated with the World J Congress. To dev the highest degree of peoplehood in the J of Canada by encouraging, carrying on & participating in activities of a natl, cultural & humanitarian nature. Canada-Is Prog: deals with matters relating to Is; coords the Is Action Prog. Canadian Cttee for Soviet J: responsible for the overall co-ordination of Soviet J activities in Canada; disseminates material & information; coords visits to Canada of Soviet activists; administers Adopt-a-Prisoner & Adopt-a-Family progs, & Contact USSR Campaign. Natl Cttee for J in Arab Lands: publicizes the plight of those J who still live in Arab countries; provides speakers, films, pamphlets, fact sheets, printed materials & displays for groups & orgs; maintains close contact with J coms throughout the world. Outreach Prog: promotes the interchange of opinion between the com & its leadership. Francophone Dept: informs the J com of the pol situation in Quebec; makes the J com known to French Canadians & sensitizes the Govt on the needs of Quebec's J citizens. Natl Rel Affairs Dept: sponsors intra-J progs, interfaith progs; in Ontario, the Orthodox Dept supervises & promotes the availability of all kosher products & facilitates their distribution across Canada. Natl Holocaust Remembrance Cttee: active in programming, commemoration & edu; coords memorial servs on Yom Hashoa (Holocaust Memorial Day); compiles, pub & distributes edu resource materials. Natl Youth Cttee: encourages J endeavours among young people; exposes young people to the opportunities for participation within Congress & obtains their views on the many issues the Congress deals with; provides grants to youth in smaller coms who wish to organize local progs; assists summer camps in programming. Natl Joint Com Relations Cttee: works to safeguard the status & rights of the J com; represents the interests of J before the federal & provincial govts. Natl Cttee of Yiddish: sponsors a wide range of Yiddish lectures & cultural progs; encourages the dev of Yiddish literature; resource ctr makes available teaching aids, records, bks & song bks in Yiddish. Edu Cttee: represents the interests of J edu before provincial govts & sch bds; supports J schs & adult edu progs; provides grants to Canadian authors; sponsors J Bk Mo, & J Music Mo; sponsors annual competitions for creative J literature. Natl Archives Prog: maintains collection of archival records & materials documenting the hist & achievements of the J com in Canada. Canadian J Historical Soc: promotes the study of J life in Canada. Audio-Visual Dept: collects & distributes films on a variety of subjects. United Restitution Org: assists individuals in making formal application to Germany for restitution & indemnification as well as aiding to secure material compensation for Nazi crimes. 6 regions across Canada. Est in 1919. Inter-Office Information, pub in English & French, reports on CJC activities across Canada; CJC Reports, a bi-weekly column, appears across Canada in the Anglo J press; Bulletin du Cercle Juif, pub four times a yr, features articles of interest for the French speaking com; CJC Handbook provides current information on definitive policies & continuing progs; Interim Reports keeps membership informed on ongoing progs & activities; The bulletin of J in Arab Lands Cttee, pub monthly, is mailed world wide. Pres: Prof Irwin Cotler; Hon Pres: Monroe Abbey; Chr of the Bd of Govs: Sol Kanee; Chr of the Natl Exec: Sam N. Filer; Assc Chr of the Natl Exec: Milton E. Harris; VP Alberta Region: S. Bruce Green; VP Atlantic Region: Ben Prossin; VP Manitoba/ Saskatchewan Region: Justice Guy Kroft; VP Ontario Region: Donald Carr; VP Pacific Region: Dr Moe Steinberg; VP Quebec Region: Dorothy Reitman; Treas: Edward B. Wolkove; Sec: Nachum Wilchesky; Hon Counsel: Norman May; Chr Alberta Region: Herb Leon; Chr Atlantic Region: Frank Medjuck; Chr Manitoba /Saskatchewan Region: Marjorie Blankstein; Chr Ontario Region: Mire Koschitzky; Chr Pacific Region: Irv Epstein; Chr Quebec Region: Frank Schlesinger; Exec VP: Alan Rose; Com Council Reps: Sol Shinder, Wilfred Posluns; Ad Personum: Morley Globerman; Natl Exec Dir: Stan Urman; Asst Natl Dir: William Stroll; Natl Dir Canadian Cttee for Soviet J: Martin Penn; Natl Communications Dir: Erol Araf; Comptroller: Murray Brass. **1590 Ave Docteur Penfield, Montreal Quebec Canada H3G 1C5 (514) 931–7531.**

Canadian Maccabiah Association. 1225 Hodge St, Montreal Quebec Canada (514) 748–7711, 487–4266.

Canadian ORT Organization. 5165 Sherbrooke St W, Suite 208, Montreal Quebec

Canada H4A 1T6 (514) 481–2787.

Canadian Sephardi Federation. 1310 Greene Ave, Montreal Quebec Canada H3Z 2B2 (514) 934–0804.

Canadian Society for the Weizmann Institute of Science. 5180 Queen Mary Rd, Suite 360, Montreal Quebec Canada.

Canadian Young Judaea. 5319 Decarie Blvd, Montreal Quebec Canada (514) 481–8910.

The Canadian Zionist Federation. To promote the Zionist ideal among the J population in Canada; to assist in strengthening the J State & the enrichment of Canadian J life through J edu, Is & Zionist information; to promote aliyah & activities among J youth in Canada. Aliyah, Edu, Culture, Information, Tourism, Youth & Hechalutz & Pub & Is Trade Depts – progs of major activities throughout Canada in these areas. Est in 1967. Pres: Judge Philip G. Givens; Hon Pres: Samuel Chait, Lawrence Freiman, Nathan Silver; Hon VPs: Clara Balinsky, Thomas O. Hecht; Deputy Pres: Ben Prossin, Max Schecter; Chr Exec Bd: Neri Bloomfield; V Chr Exec Bd: Samuel Shainhouse; Natl VPs: David Azrieli, Ben Milner, Abe Munk, Flora Naglie, Kurt Rothschild, Henri Simon, Mirial Small, Miriam Stern, Dr Sidney L. Wax; Exec VP: Dr Leon Kronitz; Treas: Solly Urman; Assc Treas: Morris Cohen, Samuel Druker; Sec: Maz Benaim; Assc Sec: Israel Nachshen, Edith Rothschild. **1310 Greene Ave, Montreal Quebec Canada H3Z 2B2 (514) 934–0804.**

Canpal-Canadian Israel Corp, Ltd. 1550 Maisonneuve Blvd W, Suite 1030, Montreal Quebec Canada H3G 1N2 (514) 935–1128.

Combined Jewish Organizations of Montreal. 4180 De Courtrai, Suite 218, Montreal Quebec Canada H3S 1C3 (514) 735–6577.

Friends of Pioneering Israel (Mapam). 600 Cote St Luc Rd, Montreal Quebec Canada.

Hadassah-Wizo Organization of Canada. To extend the material & moral support of the J women of Canada to the people of Is requiring such assistance; to support needy individuals in Hadassah-WIZO welfare ins in Is; to strengthen & foster J ideals & to encourage J & Heb culture; to cooperate with other orgs in the promotion of Canadian ideals of democracy. offers vocational & technical training for teenagers & young adults in chil & youth villages, in secondary schs & com cols; provides med assistance to the needy, sick & disabled at Asaf Harofe Hosp Rehabilitation Ctr for chil; supports 15 day care ctrs & K for J & Arab pre-schoolers fr culturally deprived homes or fr homes where parents face illness or must work; teaches Arab & J women various trades & skills at women's clubs, where legal advice & family counseling servs are provided; offers through youth clubs, located in disadvantaged neighborhoods, recreational facilities, tutoring & counseling; maintains com ctrs, sponsors Youth Aliyah Projs, & Chil Guidance Clin; provides scholarships, bursaries & dormitory facilities for needy stu at the Hebrew Univ; supports & assists the State of Is Bond Org; provides seminars, confs, leadership & edu. 17,000 mems & 1,500 male life assc across Canada. Est in 1917. Natl Offs Pres: Mirial Small; Exec VP: Lily Frank; Exec Adm: Mrs Simone Buchanan; Hon Pres: Mrs Chas Balinsky, Mrs A.J. Freiman, Mrs A. Raginsky, Mrs H. Singer, Mrs D.P. Gotlieb, Mrs Wm. Riven, Dr N. Cohen, Mrs Chas Eisenstat, Mrs H. Wisenthal, Mrs B.M. Bloomfield; VPs: Mrs H. Dubinsky, Mrs B. Liberman, Mrs D. Mandleman, Mrs D. Peters, Mrs M.J. Rosenberg, Mrs N. Torontow; Treas: Mrs A. Morris; Fin Sec: Mrs L.J. Kaplansky; Corsp Sec: Mrs I. Matlow; Rec Sec: Mrs L. Steinfeld; Gen Sec: Mrs A. Eichler, Mrs H. Fink, Mrs D. Frankenburg; Hon VPs: Mrs R. Cohen, Mrs N. Goodman, Mrs A.A. Keenberg, Mrs S. Rabinovitch, Mrs M. Rothberg, Mrs A. Waterman. **1310 Greene Ave, Montreal Quebec Canada H3Z 2B8 (514) 937–9431.**

Hashomer Hatzair. 5234 Clanranald Ave, Montreal Quebec Canada H3X 2S4.

Herut Women. 5234 Clanranald Ave, Montreal Quebec Canada H3X 2S4.

Herzl Family Practice Centre – Sir Mortimer B. Davis Jewish General Hospital. To serve the med needs of the J population. Med servs; social servs; psychological servs; nutritional servs. F in 1911 to serve the med needs of the J immigrant com. It was named after Theodore Herzl. In 1974, partly because of the advent of free med care, Herzl merged with the J Gen Hosp. Dir: Dr Michael Klein; Assc Dir for Adm: Hershey Dwoskin. **5750 Cote des Neiges, Montreal Quebec Canada H3T 1E2 (514) 739–6371.**

Israel Aliyah Center. 1310 Greene Ave, Montreal Quebec Canada (514) 934–0804, 931–1804.

Israel Bond Organization. 1255 University St, #1120, Montreal Quebec Canada H3B 3W7 (514)) 878–1871.

Jewish Colonisation Association of Canada. 5151 Cote St Catherine Rd, Montreal Quebec Canada H3W 1M6.

Jewish Family Services of the Baron de Hirsch Institute. A more satisfying personal & family life, & a healthier social & com fabric. Fin assistance; counseling; sch social servs; homemaker servs; legal aid; cemetery servs; family life edu. Est in 1863 as the Young Men's Hebrew Benevolent Soc. It was f on the ethical tradition of the mitzvah of charity. In 1890, with immigration increasing, a grant was received fr Baron Maurice de Hirsch to facilitate the work of this philanthropic soc. The soc was then renamed the Baron de Hirsch Ins. At the time, some of the principle activities were educating the poor chil & the est of a sheltering home for immigrants & orphans. Over the yrs, other servs were added. Ultimately, a Family Servs Dept was created as well as a Chil Welfare Serv. A Legal Aid Dept was created in 1922 to conduct a ct for J litigants. Pres: Avrum Orenstein; Chr Exec Cttee: Jacques Berkowitz; VPs: Charles Lusthaus, Lily Shatsky, Michael Worsoff; Sec: Monette Ulin; Treas: Sol Bultz; Exec Dir: Leon Ouaknine; Asst Exec Dir: Rabbi Steve M. Solomon. **5151 Cote St Catherine Rd, Montreal Quebec Canada H3W 1M6 (514) 731–3882.**

Jewish Hospital of Hope Centre. Fully accredited 132 bed hosp for the active treatment of the chronically ill. Provides med & paramed servs. F in 1942. Pres: Cecil A. Labow; 1st VP: Maurice Thomas; 2nd VP: Ben Chazonoff; Sec: Hyman Borts; Treas: Martin S. Labow; Gen Mgr: Melvin Simak. **7745 est rue Sherbrooke St E, Montreal Quebec Canada H1L1A3 (514) 352–3120.**

Jewish Immigrant Aid Services of Canada. 5151 Cote St Catherine Rd, Montreal Quebec Canada H3W 1M6 (514) 342–9351.

Jewish Labor Committee of Canada. 5165 Isabella Ave, Montreal Quebec Canada.

Jewish National Fund of Canada. Keren Kayemeth Le Israel, Inc. **1980 Sherbrooke St W, Suite 300, Montreal Quebec Canada H3H 2M7.**

Jewish People's Schools & Peretz Schools. To educate the young generation toward an extensive knowledge of J culture, tradition & way of life; to effect a positive attitude towards J rel & ethical values, & the State of Is, & foster a sense of loyalty to Canada. Six nurseries; Six K; two elementary schs grades 1-6. 120 chil in the nurseries; 170 chil in the K; 900 stu in the elementary grades. In 1911 the Nationale Radicale Shul was est to teach J, using Yiddish as the major language & the Heb language for the teaching of classical & traditional subjects. In 1914 a group broke away fr the sch & formed the J People's Sch with Heb as the main language although Yiddish & Yiddish literature would continue to be taught. In 1923 the Nationale Radicale Sch became known as the Yiddish Peretz Shulen. In 1971 the schs merged. The merger made possible the est of the Bialik HS. Hon Pres: Joseph Berman, Harry I. Craimer, Dan Freedman, Daniel Kingstone, Leon Teitelbaum; Hon VPs: Mr & Mrs C. Balinsky, Jack Berliner, Bernard M. Bloomfield, Sam Chait, Cecil Pascal, Chaim Pripstein; Hon Mems of the Bd: Eli Kahn, Nathan Kalifon, Morris Kreisman, Beryl Pofelis, Bennie Sussman; Pres: Stanley Sternthal; Chr Exec Cttee: Freda Rashkovan; VPs: Ben Zion Dalfan, Eli Kobernick, Sol Polachek, Syd Shapiro, Philip Wiseman; Sec: Dr Bruce Costom; Treas: Mac Brotman; Prin Emeritus: Shlomo Wiseman, Jacob Zipper; Dir of Edu: Nachum Wilchesky; Exec Dir: Merle Frankel. **5170 Van Horne Ave, Montreal Quebec Canada H3W 1J6 (514) 731–7741.**

Jewish Public Library of Montreal. Com library (constituent agy of Allied J Com Servs) affiliated with Canadian Library Assn, Am J Libraries, Quebec Library Assn. To provide public servs with an emphasis on J subjects to everyone. Reference ser; interlibrary loan serv; open stacks lending; recorded classical music concerts; film series; cultural prog in English, French, Yiddish, Heb (lectures, seminars, reviews); chil library; special chil prog; branch library in Chomedey-Laval, QB. Library contains 25% gen interest, 75% Judaica in 4 languages – English, French, Yiddish, Heb, including periodicals (hard copy & microforms), J vertical files (non-book materials), archives, rare bks, cassettes, records, special collection: J Canadiana. 5006 mems; 343 families; 2237 individuals; 1149 stu; Chil Library 1277 (presch to grade 8). 26 employees; 7 volunteers. F 1914 as J People's Univ & Library; later changed to J Public Library. Pub JPL News (quarterly bulletin), A Preliminary Guide to Jewish Canadiana (1981), Dreyfusiana – A Chapter From The History Of France (descriptive catalogue of an exhibition – Dec 1982), Canadian Jewish Periodcals (a revised listing, 1978), Holocaust, a bibliography (based on holdings of the library, 1979), The Early Jewish Presence In Canada by David Rome (1971), Recent Canadian Jewish Authors & La Langue Francaise by David Rome (1970), Procedures Manual of the Jewish Public Library of Montreal (1980). Facilities include reading rms, meeting rms, auditorium with a 500 seating capacity. Survived 68 years of financial ups & downs, five relocations, external & internal problems to emerge in the 1980's as a strong viable institution, successfully operating as a unique cultural entity. Exec Dir: Zipporah Dunsky-Shnay; Pres: Anna Gonshor; Chr, Exec 1st VP: Aaron Ain; VPs: Zave

Ettinger, Michael Rosenberg; Sec/Treas: Murray Yadin; Librarian Coord: Naomi Caruso; Head Cataloguer: Claire Stern; Reference Librarian: Ronald Finegold; Librarian Yiddish Dept: Zachary Baker; Library Coordinator: Naomi Caruso. **5151 Cote St Catherine Rd, Montreal Quebec Canada H3W 1M6 (514) 735–6535.**

Labor Zionist Movement of Canada. 4770 Kent Ave, Montreal Quebec Canada H3W 1H2 (514) 735–1593.

Maimonides Hospital & Home for the Aged. A McGill Univ affiliated teaching hosp. To serve, as in-dwelling patients, aged people who require nursing care that is difficult or impossible to obtain at home; to provide servs to people still capable of living at home but whose health status is such that its further deterioration would result in the need for institutional care. Med care; nursing care; physical therapy; occupational therapy; speech therapy; dental care; diet therapy; social servs; Day Hosp Prog; Home Care Prog; Meals-on-Wheels Prog. F in 1910. The Hosp maintains 387 beds. 99% of the patients are J. Kashrut is observed. There is a syn on the premises & a full time rabbi. Pres: Bernard Lang; VP: Joan Shuchat; Sec: Dorothy Sauras; Exec Dir: Louis J. Novick. **5795 Caldwell Ave, Montreal Quebec Canada H4W 1W3 (514) 488–2301.**

Mizrachi-Hapoel Hamizrachi Organization of Canada. 5497A Victoria Ave, Suite 101, Montreal Quebec Canada H3W 2R1 (514) 739–4748.

National Council of Jewish Women – Montreal Section. Voluntary serv org affiliated with the Natl Council of J Women. To further welfare in J & gen coms, locally, nationally & internationally; committed to human rights, Is & world J, the status of women, the environment, & the quality of human life. Edu: teacher aids in public & parochial schs, special edu for the handicapped, the teaching of English as a second language, J festival workshops, audio visual teaching aids for public sch teachers, leadership training courses, volunteer servs training prog, jr K progs, activity leaders for enjoying your infant, toddler presch progs, scholarships, stu aid; health servs: rehabilitation prog for heart attack patients & their families, hosp volunteers, mental health ctr volunteers, tay sachs screening clins, pre-natal progs, cancer clins, Canadian Natl Ins for the Blind Volunteers, testing for sight & hearing deficiencies; servs to srs: Drop in Ctr, day ctrs, volunteers in homes for the aged, kosher Meals-on-Wheels, outreach progs for volunteers. Other servs include Adult J Edu courses; Day Care Ctr for J chil; Is Family Counseling Assn, Tel Aviv which is recognized by Sch of Social Work, Tel Aviv Univ; servs to newly arrived J immigrants; J library volunteers; tutorial & recreational servs; chil abuse prevention progs; Women's Shelter for battered mothers. The Council co-sponsors servs in com camps, univ campuses & rel ctrs. Pres: Rosanne Beraznik. **5775 Victoria Ave, Montreal Quebec Canada H3W 2R4 (514) 733–7589.**

Pioneer Women – Na'amat. Women's labor Zionist org of Canada affiliated with Na'amat. Dedicated to the pursuit of social democracy in Is; to the achievement of equality for women both in Is & in Canada; to the promotion of J edu. Provides social servs to the underprivileged in Is; promotes J edu; lends support to J youth activities through Dror-Habonim; lends active support to allied campaigns for Is, Histadrut, Is Bonds, JNF, UIA, UJA; participates in com & serv orgs; supports cultural ins; formulates progs through Social Action Dept which dev awareness of Canadian issues; raises funds for the bldg & the operation of a network of social ins for Is working women, chil & mothers, including nurseries, day care ctrs & full care chil homes, vocational HS for girls, agricultural & academic boarding schs for teenagers, training courses for women, legal aid bureaus, progs to educate & integrate Arab & Druze women into the soc. F simultaneously with the Pioneer Women of the US. The Canadian org became autonomous in 1965. Since its inception, the Org has est 10 com ctrs & club houses in Is. Pres: Pearl Mekler; VP Adm: Florence Simon; VP Membership & Org: Rhona Blanshay; VP Na'amat Quota: Tillie Margolis; VP Prog: Raizel Spector; Treas: Erika Bloom; Sec: Layah Borod; Fin Sec: Freda Brass; Dues Sec: Etty Danzig; Exec Dir: Irene Welik. **4770 Kent Ave, Suite 304, Montreal Quebec Canada H3W 1H2 (514) 735–6253.**

Saidye Bronfman Centre. Dept of Fine Arts: prepares stu wishing to obtain the status of a professional artist, stu concentrating on art who wish to prepare for entrance to CEGEP, stu over 21 who wish to enter the Univ of Quebec after two yrs study at the Ctr, young stu wishing to dev their artistic ability; offers Drawing, Printmaking, Photography, Sculpture, Ceramics, Jewelry Making, Enamelling, Stained Glass, Chil & Teen Prog; offers Art Hist & Art Appreciation courses, Interior Design, Ikebana Japanese Flower Arrangement & a craft course to complement the prog, with diplomas & certificates issued after completing the required course work. Dept of Performing Arts: offers a Dance Prog & a Drama Prog. Other progs & facilities include McGill Univ off-campus courses; Harvey Golden Ins of J

Studies: offers adult courses on J Heritage, Heb & Yiddish; Dept of Continuing Edu; Saidye Bronfman Ctr Theatre: Yiddish drama theatre; mus. Stu who take courses at the Ctr in conjunction with Concordia Univ, receive credits applicable to the prog in which they are enrolled. Many of the rel courses are applicable to the Certificate in J Studies. Counseling servs available for those seeking help in the selection of courses. On request, courses can be arranged in the humanities, social sci, & the fine & performing arts for any group or org. Dir: James Dahan; Chr Bd of Mgmnt: Sam Shriar; Chr Public Affairs & Continuing Edu: Ethel Kesler; Chr Fine Arts: Robert Elman; Chr Performing Arts: Eric Poznansky; Production Mgr: Tim Babcock; Artistic Dir: Per Brask; Adm Asst: Gail Herscovitch; Dir Harvey Golden & Moe Levine Ins & Continuing Edu: Norma Joseph; Curator SBC Mus: Peter Thomas Krauz; Dir Sch of Fine Arts: Alina Michaely; Dir Sch of Performing Arts: Michael Springate; Dir Yiddish Drama Theatre: Dora Wasserman; Sec Harvey Golden Continuing Edu & Public Affairs: Ruth Benor; Sec Fine Arts: Helen Bloom; Sec Adm: Jodi Boretsky; Sec Performing Arts: Esther Fineberg; Sec SBC Mus: Maria Gould; Receptionist: Randy Kauffman; Sec to Dir: Marilyn Ornstein; Coord Continuing Edu: Ryna Pinsky; Sec PR: Marie Poirier. **5170 Cote St Catherine, Montreal Quebec Canada H3W 1M7 (514) 739–2301.**

Shaare Zedek Congregation. Conservative Cong affiliated with the United Syn of Am. To serve the spiritual, edu, cultural & social needs of the J residents of the com & to enhance the spiritual life of the com. Daily Rel Servs; classes; study groups; lectures; holiday progs; Panim el Panim – a home visiting prog; Youth Dept; Sisterhood; Men's Club. F in 1951 at a meeting attended by 16 J residents. In the early yrs, the Afternoon Heb Sch met in homes; Shabbat & Holiday Servs were held in the home of an exec mem of the Cong, & High Holy Day Servs were conducted in a social hall. The first bldg was completed in 1954 & it became the ctr of all activities. In 1955 the Cong entered into a cooperative agreement with the United Talmud Torahs of Montreal to have that ins conduct the elementary edu progs on the Cong's premises. A Heb Day Sch was later est in a different section of Montreal. In 1962 a new bldg, attached to the original one, was completed, at which time the original bldg became exclusively an edu ctr. Rabbi A. Bernard Leffell; Cantor Mendel Fogel; Pres: Hyman Brodkin; VPs: H. Laddie Schnaiberg, Seymour Levine, Arthur Greenberg; Treas: Charles Lazarus; Fin Sec: Harry Gore; Sec: Mrs Morris Steiger; Parnass: Louis Aronson; Pres Sisterhood: Mrs Hyman Lifshitz; Pres Men's Club: Issie Cohen. **5305 Rosedale Ave, Montreal Quebec Canada H4V 2H7 (514) 484–1122.**

Shaare Zion Congregation. Affiliated with the United Syn of Am. Rel Servs; Adult Edu; Sisterhood; Men's Club; youth activities; edu, cultural & social activities. The first & founding meeting was held in Sept 1925. A bldg was purchased, & in Nov the Syn was est & the Sisterhood was inaugurated. In 1926, after dedication, the Syn was chartered fr the Govt of the Province of Quebec, & in 1928 affiliated with the United Syn of Am. An Afternoon Heb Sch was est for chil ages 8–13 & a Sun Sch was introduced for chil ages 6–8. In 1928 the cemetery at Back River was consecrated. In 1929 Midrash classes were inaugurated. In 1931 Shaare Zion Hebrew Ins was est to accommodate chil living in the western area, & the Young People's Assembly was organized. In 1932 Bnai Is joined Shaare Zion Cong. In 1939 the syn bldg was destroyed by fire. In 1941 the first unit of the new syn was dedicated. In 1942 supplementary English readings & meditation were introduced at High Holy Day Servs. In 1945 construction of the sch bldg & syn began & in 1947 the syn was dedicated in tribute to the syns in Europe that were destroyed by the Nazis. In 1951 the Shaare Zion Library for Chil & Adults opened. In 1951 the Shaare Zion Academy Day Sch was inaugurated, construction was begun in 1954 & the bldg dedicated in 1957, with a 3-day-a-week Afternoon Heb Sch inaugurated in 1962. In 1969 the Academy was transferred & converted to Solomon Schechter Academy. In 1955 the Rabbi Dr Julius Berger Memorial Grove was est in Is by the Sisterhood & Men's Club in tribute to the Rabbi. In Mar a new cemetery was consecrated. Also in 1955 the Cong was honored by United Syn of Am with an award for outstanding achievement in the field of congregational day schs. Rabbi Maurice S. Cohen; Cantor Solomon Gisser; Exec Dir: Joseph Berlin. **5575 Cote St Luc Rd, Montreal Quebec Canada H3X 2C9 (514) 481–7727.**

Solomon Schechter Academy. Affiliated with Solomon Schechter Day Schs Assn. Prin: Rosa Finestone; Chr: H. Laddie Schnailberg. **5555 Cote St Luc Rd, Montreal Quebec Canada H3X 2C9 (514) 481–7719.**

Temple Emanu-El Beth Sholom. Affiliated with UAHC. 900 mems. Rabbis: Bernard Bloomstone, Harry J. Stern; Cantor Barry Abelson; Pres: Margery Miller; Edu: Joel Silver; Sisterhood Pres: Myra Cohen, Dorothy Frankel, Jane Isaacs; Brotherhood Pres: Norman Block. **4100 Sherbrooke St W, Montreal Quebec Canada H3Z 1A5 (514) 937–3575.**

United Jewish Relief Agencies of Canada. 1590 Docteur Penfield Ave, Montreal Quebec Canada H3G 1C5 (514) 931–7531.

United Jewish Teachers' Seminary. 5237 Clanranald Ave, Montreal Quebec Canada H3X 2S5 (514) 489–4401.

United Talmud Torahs of Montreal, Inc. Com J day sch system consisting of four elementary schs (nursery through grade 6) & two Herzliah HS (grade 7 through 11). To undertake, pursue, favor & aid edu conducive to the perpetuation of the Heb rel, ritual, language, festivals & customs; to aid those who desire to devote themselves to these studies; to assist them to attain these objectives. Gen & J studies taught in English, Heb & French; counseling prog; audio visual materials. A total of 2,000 stu. F in 1896. The schs have an Israeli exchange teachers prog. In 1973 the United Talmud Torahs of Montreal was awarded the prestigious Shazar Prize by the Pres of the State of Is as the outstanding J sch in Canada. Pres: Ted Lebovics; VP: Gershon Stern; Sec: Morton Kader; Treas: Stephen Bratt; VP & Chr of the Personnel Cttee: Seymour Sofer; VP & Co-Chr Elementary Edu Cttee: Dr Clyde Covit; Co-Chr Elementary Edu: Dr Henry Leighton; Co-Chr Herzliah HS Edu Cttee: Dr Ann Wechsler; Co-Chr Herzliah HS Edu Cttee: Dr Morton Lechter; Edu Dir: Rabbi Dr Jay Braverman; Exec Dir: Zave Ettinger; Coord Heb Studies Elementary Dept: Hanna Eliashiv; Coord Gen Studies Elementary Dept: Ala Gamulka. **4894 St Kevin Ave, Montreal Quebec Canada H3W 1P2 (514) 739–2291.**

YM-YWHA & NHS of Montreal. To dev progs & servs for the mems; to help assure that the J com in Montreal will survive as a creative, positive group & to ensure the enrichment of the lives of its individual mems; to promote a balance between pol, economic & cultural integration with the wider com on the one hand & the maintenance of the rich J culture, tradition & group experience on the other. Recreational activities for all ages; bellydancing; chinese kosher cooking; rollerskating; cultural activities & progs; Widow to Widow Prog; Cardiac Training Prog; Single Parent Prog; Russian Immigrant Prog; Educable Retarded Progs; Y Wooden Acres Country Camp. 15,000. The Y Assn was first conceived in 1908 & devoted itself initially to athletic & cultural pursuits. In 1910 the Y was chartered. In the following yrs, progs grew & membership rose. Fr 1914 to 1918 activities were reduced because of the war, & the Y held servs for J troops. In 1929 a new bldg was dedicated to the youth of Montreal. During the Great Depression, the Y placed 7,000 people in jobs. With the merging of the YM & the YWHA, & the rise of membership in a wide variety of progs, the bldg designed for 2,500 was serving 5,000. In May of 1948 the Davis Bldg was improved & expanded, & the Snowdon Bldg facility was begun. Fr 1950 on, the Y underwent several mergers & took on its present structure which includes six branches. Y branches: a new Davis Y (1966); Laval Y (1971); Ctr Communautaire Juif, & the Saidye Bronfman Ctr (1967); & the Y Wooden Acres Country Camp (1963). Pres: Philip Greenberg; Chr Bd of Trustees: Boris Levine; 1st VP: Marvin Corber; VPs: Mike Bacal, Edward M. Daniels, Gerald Guttman, Judy Litvack; Treas: Lionel Goldman; Sec: Naomi Deckelbaum, Victor Salem; PR Dir: Sherry Stein. **5500 Westbury Ave, Montreal Quebec Canada H3W 2W8 (514) 737–6551.**

Young Herut. 5234 Clanranald Ave, Montreal Quebec Canada H3X 2S4.

Zionist Revisionist Organization of Canada. 5234 Clanranald Ave, Montreal Quebec Canada H3X 2S4.

Mount Royal

Congregation Beth El. Affiliated with United Syn of Am. Rabbi Dr Allan N. Langner; Cantor Hyman Gisser; Pres: Lester Lazarus; Asst Rabbi: Rev W. Finer; Exec Dir: Ted Baker. **1000 Lucerne Rd, Mount Royal Quebec Canada H3R 2H9 (418) 738–4766.**

Westmount

Canadian Zionist Federation. 1310 Greene Ave, Westmount Quebec Canada H3Z 2B8 (514) 934–0804.

Congregation Shaar Hashomayim. Conservative Syn. Rel Servs; Jr Cong; Sisterhood; Men's Assn; library. 1,700 mems. In 1846 the Cong of English, Polish & German J was chartered. Ten yrs later, the Cong est Montreal's first Heb afternoon sch. As the Cong grew, the need to erect a permanent syn became apparent. On Jul 12, 1859 the cornerstone of the first Ashkenazic house of worship in Canada was laid. The bldg seated 150 men & 50 women. As the Cong again increased in num & the J com moved westward, newer premises were needed. On Oct 25, 1885 the cornerstone at the McGill Col Ave Syn was laid. The name Shaar Hashomayim was applied to the new syn. Again the Cong needed more spacious facilities, a new syn was built, & on Nov 10, 1921 the bldg was dedicated. There was rm for 1,500 people, a dozen sch rms for the Heb classes, a lecture hall seating 600, & a dome-capped salon for the Ladies Auxiliary. In 1967 Shaar Hashomayim was expanded to hold 2,000 in the sanctuary, a kitchen was built to serve up to 1,000, a library & mus were added, & a rose garden was planted. It is the largest syn in Montreal. It is one of the few Conservative congs to have separate seating. Rabbi Wilfred Shuchat; Asst Rabbi Robert D. Sutnick; Cantor Joseph Gross; Asst Cantor Herman Muller; Music Dir: Joseph Milo; Exec Dir: Morrie Klians; Dir Edu & Youth: Yecheil Glustein; Librarian & Curator: Terry Lightman; Hon Pres: Horace R. Cohen,. Dr Harry C. Ballon, Dr Charles Solomon, Monroe Abbey, William Victor, Nahum Gelber; Hon VPs: Hon Lazarus Phillips, Maxwell Cummings; Hon Parnass: Jack A. Shacter; Pres: Clarence Schneiderman; VPs: Gerald Brownstein, J. Stephen Lipper, Tamara Greenberg, Dr Abrasha Stilman, Dr Hyman Surchin; Treas: Henry Steinberg; Parnass: Dr William Cohen; Sec: David D. Cohen. **450 Kensington Ave, Westmount Quebec Canada H3Y 3A2 (514) 937–9471.**

Congregation Shaar Hashomayim, Shaar Hashomayim Library-Museum. For information on the Cong, see – Congregation Shaar Hashomayim, Westmount Quebec Canada. **450 Kensington Ave, Westmount Quebec Canada H3Y 3A2 (514) 937–9471.**

Hadassah-Wizo Organisation of Canada. 1310 Greene Ave, Westmount Quebec Canada H3Z 2B8 (514) 937–9431.

Israel Aliyah Center. 1310 Greene Ave, Westmount Quebec Canada H3Z 2B2 (514) 934–0804.

Sherut La'am. A year of service in Israel. **1310 Greene Ave, Westmount Quebec Canada H3Z 2B2 (514) 934–0804.**

Student Zionist Organisation. 1310 Greene Ave, Westmount Quebec Canada H3Z 2B2 (514) 934–0804.

United Israel Appeal of Canada, Inc. 1310 Greene Ave, Westmount Quebec Canada H3Z 2B2 (514) 932–1431.

Youth & Hechalutz Department (Israel Program Centre). 1310 Greene Ave, Westmount Quebec Canada H3Z 2B2 (514) 934–0804.

SASKATCHEWAN

Regina

Congregation Beth Jacob. 1640 Victoria Ave, Regina Saskatchewan Canada S4P 0P7 (306) 527-8643.

Saskatoon

Agudas Israel. 715 McKinnon Ave, Saskatoon Saskatchewan Canada S7H 2G2.

Agudas Israel Sisterhood, Jewish Community Library. 715 McKinnon Ave, Saskatoon Saskatchewan Canada S7H 2G2.

Jewish Community Centre, Congregation Agudas Israel. Conservative Cong affiliated with United Syn of Am. To est, maintain & conduct a syn, a sch& com ctr in the City of Saskatoon for the edu & instruction of the mems, their chil & particularly to educate & instruct them in the J rel, hist, tradition, & in the J & Heb language. Rel Servs; Heb Sch. In 1919 there were enough J in the city to warrant the bldg of a syn. The original Cong was organized as Orthodox. The mems came fr many parts of Eastern Europe. In 1958 a JCC was dedicated. This Ctr combined a syn, classrooms & a social hall, & served all the needs of the com. Since 1979 over 100 immigrants fr the Soviet Union have been integrated into the com with the help of the J Immigrant Aid Soc. Rabbi Saul Diament; Pres: Gladys R. Rose; 1st VP: Ben Goldstein; 2nd VP: June Avivi; Sec: David Singer; Treas: Pauline Laimon; Hon VPs: Senator Sidney L. Buckwold, Dr J. M. Goldenberg. **715 McKinnon Ave, Saskatoon Saskatchewan Canada S7H 2G2 (306) 343-7023.**

INDEX OF INSTITUTIONS

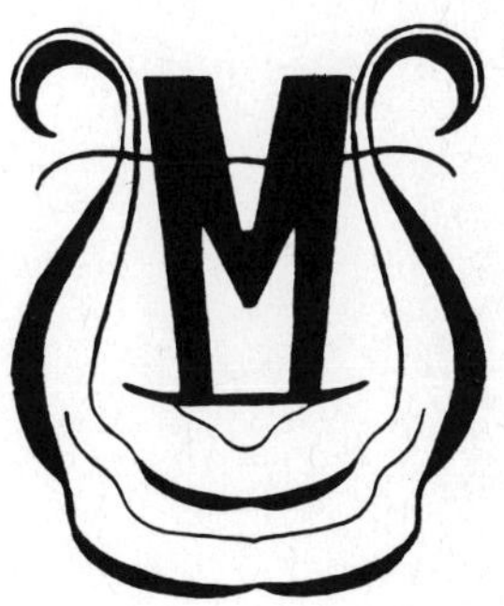

Index to Institutions